KW-481-362

## Samuel Johnson's Unpublished Revisions to the *Dictionary of the English Language*

This edition makes available for the first time the largest collection in existence of unpublished material by the great eighteenth-century writer and lexicographer Samuel Johnson. For the revised fourth edition (1773) of Johnson's *Dictionary of the English Language*, Johnson and his amanuensis annotated more than 120 interleaved folio pages of the first edition, but the printer for unknown reasons failed to include the corrections. These pages, including hundreds of authorial additions and changes to the text, are reproduced here in facsimile, along with a transcription, an extensive commentary and notes. This extraordinary archive offers a unique record of Johnson's methods of revision, his collaboration with his assistants, and the preparation of printer's copy in general. Johnson's deletion and editing of hundreds of new quotations, notes and definitions contributed by others sheds much new light on his intentions for his work and his attitudes towards language and literature.

Allen Reddick is Professor of English Literature at the University of Zürich and was formerly a Professor at Harvard University. Among his previous publications is *The Making of Johnson's Dictionary, 1746–1773* (Cambridge, 1990; revised edition, 1996). He has published on subjects including Samuel Johnson, Jonathan Swift, Thomas Hollis and eighteenth-century Italian painting.

# Samuel Johnson's Unpublished Revisions to the *Dictionary of the English Language*

A Facsimile Edition


Edited by

ALLEN REDDICK

With the collaboration of
Catherine Dille,
and assistance from
Regula Bisang and Antoinina Bevan Zlatar

CAMBRIDGE UNIVERSITY PRESS

CAMBRIDGE UNIVERSITY PRESS
Cambridge, New York, Melbourne, Madrid, Cape Town, Singapore, São Paulo

Cambridge University Press
The Edinburgh Building, Cambridge CB2 2RU, UK

Published in the United States of America by Cambridge University Press, New York

www.cambridge.org
Information on this title: www.cambridge.org/9780521844703



First published 2005

Printed in the United Kingdom at the University Press, Cambridge

*A catalogue record for this book is available from the British Library*

ISBN-13 987-0-521-84470-3 hardback
ISBN-10 0-521-84470-3 hardback

# Contents

# Acknowledgments

This project represents a true team effort stretching over several years. Of most importance has been the collaboration in many aspects of the project from Dr Catherine Dille. As one of the most talented Johnsonians of her generation, Catherine assisted me in conceptualizing the project and evaluating its worth. Her knowledge of Johnsonian and eighteenth-century contexts enabled her to analyse Johnson's intentions and his use of sources. Furthermore, she was responsible for finding and putting into place the software and typefaces and helped to develop the format of transcription; much of the dull but difficult work of transcribing was hers as well. Most of the sourcing was carried out by Catherine, involving countless trips to the British Library and the Bodleian; she also contributed to many other aspects of the project, including liaising with the reproductions department of the British Library and with the design team at Cambridge University Press. Much of the intelligence and elegance of the transcription is a result of her attention and design. I am greatly indebted to her, her exceptional abilities, and her willingness to embark on this grand project.

Regula Bisang worked tirelessly on all aspects of the transcription. Her eye for design and precision, together with her technical expertise in PageMaker, led to the format of drawn stylised lines, one of the most challenging aspects of the transcription. Time and time again, when faced with the complexities of representing the B material, Regula came up with effective solutions. Her skill with textual matters (learnt from her own research on the texts of *Hamlet*) averted many a mistake in this realm. Regula stepped in to assist me in countless ways.

Dr Antoinina Bevan Zlatar applied her expertise particularly to the footnotes, to making sense of the transcription and notes, and to my own commentary. Going far beyond conventional assistance, Antoinina proposed many points pertaining to Johnson's intentions that influenced my thinking throughout. Her ear for careful and accomplished prose style saved me from numerous errors and infelicities, as did her understanding of early modern English sources.

As my assistants at the University of Zürich, Regula Bisang and Antoinina Bevan Zlatar worked with a selflessness and devotion to this project that I have not encountered in over twenty years of professional life. Their support of me and this work, through difficult times, seeing the project through to the end, has been gratifying. I can never repay this debt.

A generous grant from the Schweizerische Nationalfonds zur Förderung der Wissenschaftlichen Forschung supported the employment of Dr Catherine Dille and Regula Bisang for a period of three years on The Zürich Johnson Project, of which the preparation of this volume was the principal part. It also generously financed the reproductions of the B materials contained in this volume and many other expenses incurred. We are all deeply grateful to this important organization and its valuable support of research.

The British Academy awarded me a Visiting Professorship at the University of Birmingham, which enabled me to work with Dr Anne McDermott on joint aspects of our projects. I gratefully acknowledge their assistance. I also offer my thanks to the School of English in Birmingham for accepting me so graciously. Anne's expertise on Johnson's *Dictionary* is unsurpassed, and I have benefited in countless ways from her knowledge and kindness through the years. As my host in 2002, she made my stay in Birmingham both profitable and enjoyable. I am grateful to her and to her husband John. Her own work on Johnson's methods of compiling the *Dictionary* and his use of sources has been particularly helpful to me. She brings out one's best collaborative instincts, and I look forward to contributing part of the material in this volume to her *Johnson's Dictionary Website*. I should also like to thank Dr Graham Nicholls, another crucial member of the Birmingham Johnson team, for sharing his time and expertise concerning Johnson's sources. His hospitality, and that of his wife June, are much appreciated.

Years ago, as my research assistant at Harvard, Scott Gordon undertook the first version of a transcription of the B materials. His care and diligence helped form the base upon which I have built, and I thank him once again, long after the fact.

I am grateful to the reproductions staffs of the British Library and the Beinecke Library, Yale University, for their superb assistance in the making of photographs and scans of the materials. Linda Bree, Maartje Scheltens and the design team at Cambridge University Press have been extraordinarily helpful in shaping this project and steering it through the Press. I am indebted to their imagination in the face of such a complex project and their care and attention in seeing it through.

My thanks go as well to Dr Peter Swaab, who reminded me that all of the characters in 'The Hunting of the Snark' have names beginning with the letter B.

Allen Reddick
Zürich, Switzerland

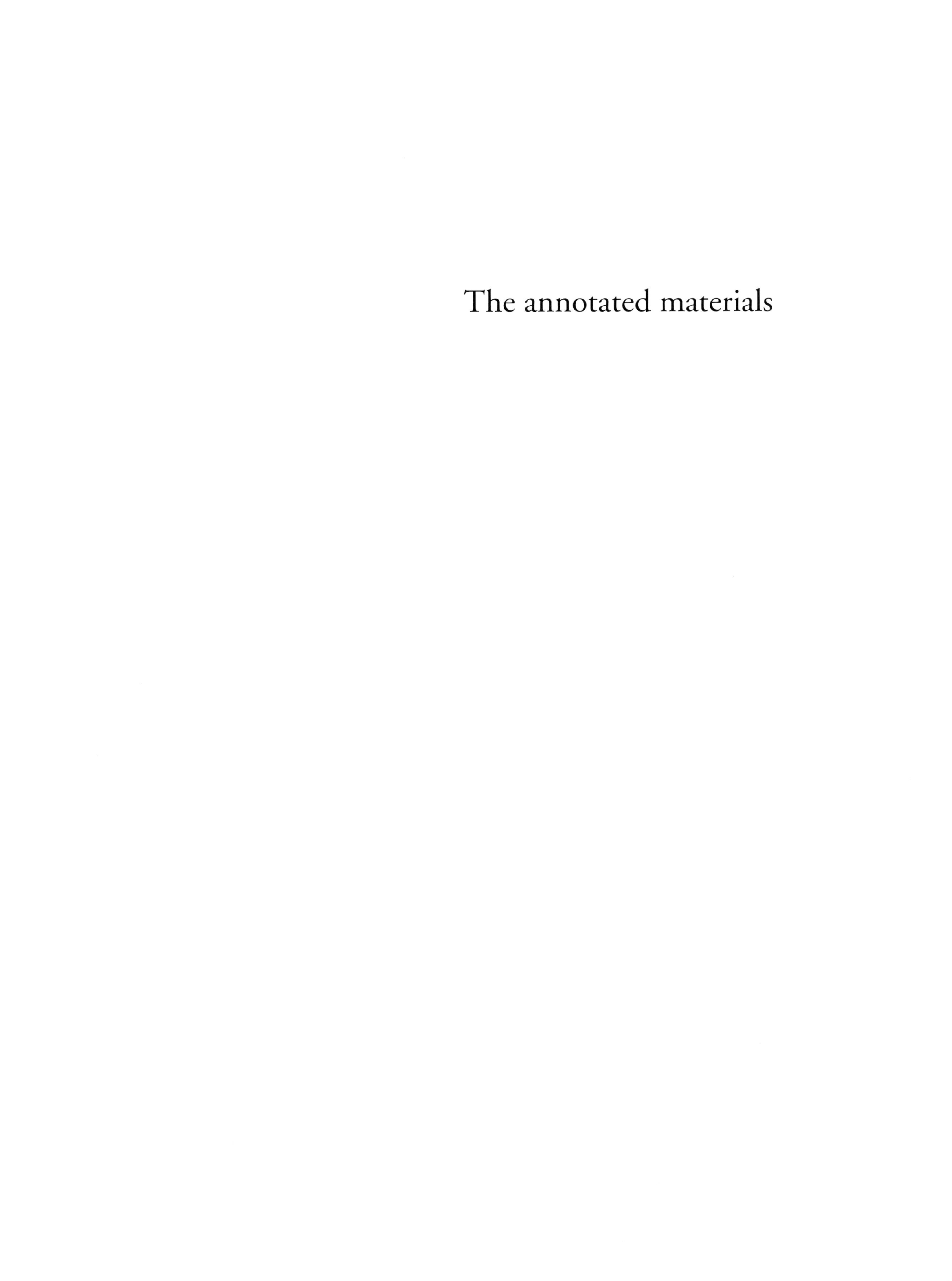

# The annotated materials

## Introduction

The aims of this volume are as follows:

(1) to reproduce in photographic facsimile 122 printed pages from the first edition of the *Dictionary* (with accompanying interleaves), covered in handwritten additions and corrections prepared by Johnson and an amanuensis as printer's copy for the revised fourth edition of the *Dictionary*, but never published;
(2) to provide the reader with a transcription that represents the changes graphically in an attempt to elucidate Johnson's intentions for the printer's copy;
(3) to reconstruct the history of Johnson's revision of the *Dictionary* and provide examples from the working papers (including illustrations and discussion of evidence from the Sneyd-Gimbel copy at Yale) which enable this history to be told;
(4) to provide an analysis of and commentary on some of Johnson's proposed changes that enable an understanding of his process of revision and intentions;
(5) to discuss Johnson's changes in the context of his comments on language and literature.

On 28 November 1754 Samuel Johnson wrote to his friend Thomas Warton at Oxford, 'I am glad of your hindrance in your Spenserian design, yet I would not have it delayed. Three hours a day stolen from sleep and amusement will produce it, let a servitour transcribe the quotations, and interleave them with references, to save time. This will shorten the work, and lessen the fatigue.' The precise nature of the 'design', never realized, to which Johnson refers remains uncertain (Warton observes on a later occasion that it involved 'publishing a volume of observations on the best of Spenser's works'; it could possibly also refer to a new edition of his *Observations on Spenser's Fairy Queen* published earlier that year).[1] It is also unclear precisely what he is recommending (should the amanuensis copy out on to blank leaves quotations from the printed text of Spenser, then write the references to the passages on extra leaves inserted between these leaves? This system would presumably give Warton sufficient space for his 'observations'). Whatever the case, the forthrightness with which Johnson recommends the use of interleaving and copying by an amanuensis in an adaptation or revision of an author's own work is striking, especially as the practice he describes seems to be similar to one he himself would later use in the one major revision of his *Dictionary*. For the preparation of printer's copy for the fourth edition, Johnson employed an amanuensis to copy proposed additions to the text on to interleaves facing first-edition pages of the *Dictionary*. These additions were then altered, screened and tailored by Johnson, then keyed into the desired place in the facing printed text, or simply deleted. Johnson apparently told Boswell that 'it was remarkable that when he revised & improved the last [fourth] edition of his Dict[iona]ry the Printer was never kept waiting'.[2] Certainly, it was the material he had his amanuenses gather, copy, gloss and annotate, that enabled him to proceed quickly and smoothly. His advice to Warton indicates his commitment to such a process of assistance from amanuenses copying on to interleaves and his determination to use this means, with such a large project, to 'shorten the work, and lessen the fatigue'.

To understand Johnson's process of revision, it is necessary to review the history of the original composition of the *Dictionary*.[3] In 1746–47, Johnson began the compilation of his *Dictionary* by establishing criteria for multiple definitions and word usage, and he proceeded to locate quotations illustrative of different words in printed works. He marked passages in literary, theological, humanistic and historical, as well as technical and other types of works, mainly written during the period between Sir Philip Sidney and Alexander Pope. These passages, marked in pencil usually with vertical lines indicating the beginning and end of the quotation, with the word illustrated underlined, and the first letter of the word written in the margin, would later be copied out by the amanuenses (at different times he had six in his employ) on to blank paper eventually cut into slips. The quotations would subsequently be organized and the passages copied into notebooks in the appropriate places in the wordlist. Eventually, in late 1749 or 1750, however, Johnson determined this procedure to be unworkable, for it left little room for accommodating the variety of usage he encountered. He had also mistakenly allowed the text to be copied on to both sides of the page in the notebooks, unsuitable for printer's copy. For these reasons, he abandoned the handwritten notebooks, recopying his material (in some cases clipping it out) into a more flexible form, allowing the selected quotations to determine his wordlist and definitions, eventually producing his printer's copy.

The abandoned manuscript in notebooks was not discarded, however, and was probably retained in Johnson's working materials for twenty years until he began his revision of the *Dictionary* for the fourth edition (the second and third editions had appeared in 1756 and 1765, respectively, each with very few authorial changes from the first edition).[4] It would appear that Johnson instructed one of the amanuenses still assisting him, probably the Scot William Macbean, to search through this material for the purpose of selecting quotations, originally gathered for the first edition, to be recycled under other head-words in the fourth edition. As with the original composition of the work, the revision centred around the incorporation of illustrative quotations. The reasons they used the manuscript rather than printed leaves probably involved the following factors: the manuscript versions of quotations were longer and fuller than the printed, edited and sometimes truncated versions; the manuscript notebooks provided blank spaces to copy out quotations and other material; and printed first-edition leaves may not have been available for use. (Fragments from these manuscript notebooks, some retaining portions of text from the early manuscript, are preserved among the slips in the

[1] *The Letters of Samuel Johnson*, ed. Bruce Redford (Princeton: Princeton University Press), vol. I, pp. 88–9.

[2] Boswell's *Note Book*, reproduced in *The R. B. Adam Library Relating to Dr. Samuel Johnson and His Era* (London, 1929), vol. II, between pp. 51 and 52.

[3] See Allen Reddick, *The Making of Johnson's Dictionary, 1746–1773* (Cambridge: Cambridge University Press, 1990, rev. ed. 1996), ch. 3, for a more detailed discussion.

[4] See Reddick, *Making*, ch. 5, for a more detailed discussion.

Sneyd-Gimbel materials at Yale.)[5] The amanuensis selected quotations for reuse (probably making selections himself, rather than as directed by Johnson), copied them on to clear portions of the notebooks, added in most cases a head-word, note on etymology or usage, and/or a definition, then clipped out the slip. These slips are preserved in the Sneyd-Gimbel copy. In the following stage, another amanuensis, probably V. J. Peyton, copied out the text verbatim from the slips on to blank leaves inserted between leaves of the first edition opposite the printed text to which the annotation belonged.[6] Next, Johnson reviewed this material, altered and deleted parts and excised entire proposed additions, added new material, and keyed in the prepared text to its precise location in the printed text. He also wrote numerous corrections and additions directly on the printed pages: rearranging material under entries, consolidating multiple entries, adding, altering, or deleting etymologies, notes on usage, and definitions, deleting or editing existing illustrative quotations, and correcting errors of various sorts. From an examination of the entire text of the fourth edition, it is clear that he altered this procedure slightly in other parts of the wordlist, and augmented the new additions with other illustrative quotations marked anew in printed books. However, it appears that he used interleaves prepared in this or a similar manner throughout the wordlist.

The material contained in this facsimile edition provides key evidence for reconstructing Johnson's procedures; furthermore, it offers hundreds of new Johnsonian readings for the *Dictionary*, never before published. It is necessary to account for its existence and the role it plays in the history of the revision.[7] The first-edition pages, comprising the wordlist of the *Dictionary* from the last page of the letter A through the letter B ('BYSTANDER'), are interleaved in the manner described above, with precise keys for the printer, alerting him to how and where the new material should be incorporated. If it is clear that these changes were intended to be made in the printed text, it remains uncertain why they were not in fact used. Most probably the materials were mislaid, in Johnson's workroom, at the printer's, or elsewhere. Their disappearance may coincide with Johnson's decision to augment the new recycled material with fresh quotations marked in other sources; when he returned his attention to the material, the pages may have been misplaced. Whatever the cause, it is clear that once the materials were unavailable, Johnson quickly turned to other sources to supply material for revising this part of the text. George Steevens, Johnson's collaborator on the revised edition of Shakespeare, which also appeared in 1773, had prepared and annotated his own interleaved text or partial text of the *Dictionary*, using third-edition leaves (1765). It is unknown whether Steevens intended his annotations and changes to be incorporated, or whether he was asked to prepare them by Johnson, but it is clear that when his own carefully prepared materials were no longer available, Johnson turned to Steevens's interleaved materials for this portion of the text. Johnson appears to have augmented Steevens's changes with a series of new quotations freshly gathered (almost exclusively through the use of Alexander Cruden's *Concordance to the Holy Scriptures* (first published 1737) and his 'Verbal Index' to *Paradise Lost* (first published 1741) and from the poems of Edward Young), and then submitted these sheets to the printer. The remainder of Steevens's annotated interleaved sheets (for letters A, C–Jailer) are bound together with the B materials in the British Library copy. His annotations and changes in these pages were not (except in a very few scattered instances) incorporated into the fourth edition. Johnson's B material owes its continued existence to the fact that it was never used as printer's copy, which would have been discarded thereafter. This material takes the place in the British Library copy of Steevens's annotated interleaved material for the letter B, which was used and discarded.

## The British Library copy: description and provenance (with the Sneyd-Gimbel copy)

The material presented in this volume, comprising the last page of 'A' and all of 'B' (sigs. 2N1–3U1), interleaved throughout, is bound within the first volume of a three-volume interleaved partial copy of the *Dictionary* in the British Library's collections (BL C.45.k.3).[8] The copy consists of printed leaves from the first and third editions, as described above. Johnson's and the amanuensis's handwriting (possibly that of V. J. Peyton) is limited to this first-edition portion, which was prepared by Johnson to be used as printer's copy for setting type for the fourth edition. The extensive annotations and alterations by George Steevens are limited to the third-edition portion. The only other hand in the copy is that of Charles Marsh, a later owner, who added an occasional note to the third-edition pages. The text of this partial copy stretches from entries A through JAILER (gatherings B–11R) with a few missing leaves: leaf 3U2, the last page of text for the letter B and the first page of text for C, and leaves 6E1, 6E2, and 6F1, constituting the last four pages of C and the first two of D. After almost every leaf with printed text, an interleaf is bound in; the interleaves in the section for the letter B and last page of A have the Strasbourg Lily watermark, and 'VI' or 'VJ' countermark, while the other interleaves have only an 'EVH' mark. One of the interleaves, between 2L2 and 2M1, is misbound and should precede 2N1, for its one annotation pertains to the first-edition text of page 2N$^{r}$; the handwritten material (relating to the entry AZURE) from this interleaf is reproduced in this volume. There are three worm holes in the top inside margin of these first-edition leaves, not found in the interleaves or the third-edition leaves. This would indicate, as would be expected, that the first-edition leaves were stored for some period of time in a batch apart from the third-edition sheets before being interleaved.

The printed sheets and interleaves are bound in three volumes as follows: volume I, A through the middle of BYSTANDER (B–3U1, followed by an interleaf); volume II, CABIN *n.s.* 4

[5] For a more detailed discussion of this and other aspects of the Sneyd-Gimbel materials, see the Appendix to this volume and Reddick, *Making*, Appendix A.

[6] It is known that William Macbean and V. J. Peyton worked on the revision of the *Dictionary*, and the handwriting on the slips in the Sneyd-Gimbel material appears to be that of William Macbean. Peyton's hand may be that on the interleaves, but a firm identification is not yet possible. At this stage, I have made only tentative identifications, refining and correcting some of the conclusions concerning the activities of these amanuenses in *The Making of Johnson's Dictionary*; subsequent analysis may confirm, contradict or revise these identifications.

[7] See Reddick, *Making*, ch. 5, for a more detailed discussion.

[8] See Reddick, *Making*, Appendix B and C, pp. 190–94.

through the middle of EAGLE, def. 1 (3X–7R1, preceded by an interleaf); and volume III, from the middle of EAGLE, def 1 through JAILER (7R2–11R2, followed by an interleaf). The materials were almost certainly unbound when they came into the possession of the British Museum, and divided into six or possibly seven sections or fascicles, each consisting of the complete or nearly complete pages for one or two letters, as the pattern of stamping of the accession date '13 JA 54' (13 January 1854) throughout the leaves makes clear. This date appears to have been stamped on the outside leaf of almost all the individual unbound fascicles. The stamping of the accession date on the interleaf now located between 2L2 and 2M1 is an indication that the British Museum binders misplaced it there, for when it arrived at the museum, it appears that the interleaf was on the outside of a fascicle, preceding 2N1 (which, on its recto, contains the beginning of text for the letter B). The present binding, probably the first, dates presumably from the late nineteenth or early twentieth century.

The provenance of this material is intertwined with that of the Sneyd-Gimbel materials (see Appendix for description). Both sets were apparently sold, unbound, with the rest of Johnson's library in 1785. The Sneyd-Gimbel materials, listed in the sale catalogue as Lot 644, and the materials now in the British Library, listed as Lot *649, were described respectively as '13, of Dr. Johnson's dictionary with MSS. notes' and 'Six of Dr Johnson's dictionary' (sold with 'a parcel of reviews and magazines'). Presumably the first description refers not to thirteen letters, for the Sneyd-Gimbel copy contains twelve, but to fascicles, one of the larger letters being broken up into two; similarly, the second description refers not to six letters (for the British Library copy consists of eight letters), but probably to six separate fascicles, each presumably sewn together. The purchaser of both sets was Charles Marsh (1735–1812), Fellow of the Society of Antiquaries. At the sale of his library on 7 February 1816, these sets, listed together as item 954 and described more accurately, though still incorrectly, as 'Johnson's Dictionary, Letters A. to L. N. & P. interleaved with MS. additions and Observations, and A. B. C. E. F. G. with additions by Johnson', were bought by Richard Heber. Auctioned in May and June of 1835 with the rest of Heber's library, the materials were offered in Part VII of *Bibliotheca Heberiana* as: '3581 Johnson's (S.) Dictionary, twelve parts, containing the Letters A to G, I, K, L, N, and P, with a great number of additions in the hand-writing of Dr. Johnson, chiefly consisting of quotations'. And '3582 – Third edition, the Letters A to H interleaved, with additions, some in the hand-writing of Dr. Johnson, 7 parts, – 1765' (probably counting as two parts the large section comprising entries for C and D).

The London bookseller Thomas Thorpe purchased both items and apparently immediately sold the set now in the British Library to John Hugh Smyth Pigott, of Brockley Hall in Somerset, in whose collection it remained until 1853, when it was bought for the British Museum at the sale of Smyth Pigott's library. Once the materials arrived at the museum, they were divided into six principal parts, divided fairly exactly by the alphabetical entries as follows: A, B, C–D, E, F, G–H. Thorpe probably sold the set now known as the Sneyd-Gimbel copy to Ralph Sneyd of Keele Hall, where it remained until it was sold by his descendant, Col. Ralph Sneyd, at Sotheby's in 1927, to Col. Richard Gimbel. The materials were not heard of again publicly before 1955, and they remained in the estate of Col. Gimbel until 1973, at which time they were given to Yale University.

## The printer's copy for the letter B

The new material copied on to the interleaves in the B material (2N1–3U1) consists of quotations, recycled from other entries in the first edition, illustrating both new and existing words in the wordlist; a few quotations gathered anew; completely new entries; notes on usage, especially Scottish and 'rural' words; new etymologies, notes on derivation, and definitions; and commentary on quotations.[9] Johnson's review and editing of these texts is frequently severe. He deletes many proposed additions entirely, including the great majority of definitions and notes on usage supplied by the amanuensis;[10] he alters quotations, frequently adds a new definition or some other clarification, then carefully marks the edited material for inclusion in the appropriate place in the text of the facing printed page. He normally adds a key beside the writing on the interleaf, usually a letter followed by a double-dagger, then he places the same key on the facing printed page in the spot where the material is to be inserted, usually accompanied by a line drawn to the spot. Johnson also makes frequent marginal additions and corrections to all parts of the text on the printed pages themselves; the amanuensis's hand is found only on the interleaves.

The British Library materials for the letter B also contain four slips, all with quotations written in the hand of the amanuensis, intended for inclusion in the fourth edition. Each slip was cut from an interleaf within the materials because the quotation had been written on the wrong interleaf. It was removed by Johnson or the amanuensis and glued to the margin of the printed sheet beside the entry to which it refers. The hole left in the interleaf after the slip was cut away has, in each case, been carefully patched in an apparent attempt to keep the printer's copy as neat as possible for the compositor. The slips, each keyed into the text by Johnson, are attached to the following pages: 2T$^{r}$ (two slips, illustrating BEAR *v.a.*, defs. 2 and 3, respectively); 2T$^{v}$ (BEAR *v.a.*, def. 29); and 2Z$^{v}$ (BEND *v.a.*, def 2). The annotations in the hand of the amanuensis are all in a light brown ink, while Johnson's are in a dark brown, nearly black ink. In one case, Johnson uses a purplish ink (2T2$^{r}$, under the entry To BEAR *v.n.* 4) also found in isolated cases in the Sneyd-Gimbel materials.

## George Steevens and Samuel Johnson

When Samuel Johnson began revising his great *Dictionary of the English Language* in 1771, he was at the same time engaged in revising his *Edition of the Works of William Shakespeare*, originally published in 1765. Both works would eventually appear in 1773,

[9] See Reddick, *Making*, Appendix B, pp. 190–91.

[10] Of approximately 309 proposed quotations and independent notes on words (i.e., those with separate Sneyd-Gimbel slips of their own), Johnson deletes 170 completely.

both assisted by the scholar George Steevens. Steevens provided the main impetus for the new edition of Shakespeare and performed the bulk of the work on the edition, including seeing it through the press. The extent of his involvement in the revision of the *Dictionary* has only recently been recognized; an examination of his work on both editions is crucial for understanding the nature and the very existence of the material contained in the British Library copy.[11]

George Steevens was a prodigious scholar, particularly of English Renaissance drama, and was recognized as such by his contemporaries. His collaboration on Johnson's *Shakespeare* commenced no later than 1765, when Steevens contributed some textual notes and other commentary to Johnson's edition. The cross-fertilization between the revised *Shakespeare* and the revised *Dictionary* has been documented by Arthur Sherbo and Carter Hailey, demonstrating the ways in which changes and additions in the revised *Dictionary* were probably prompted by Steevens's commentary in the edition of Shakespeare. Furthermore, Hailey has shown that a few of Steevens's annotations in the British Library copy, especially concerning Shakespeare, were adopted by Johnson in some form or may have inspired an alteration in the fourth edition. His handwritten annotations continued to have some effect on scattered changes made even in later editions of the *Dictionary*, and Steevens himself may have taken on an anonymous editorial role in editions published after Johnson's death. It is uncertain why only scattered suggestions from Steevens were incorporated. Some may have been passed on verbally between the men. It is known that Steevens and Johnson saw each other frequently at this time, and Steevens often visited Johnson's workroom.

In previous accounts of the British Library materials, it has been difficult to determine the relation of Steevens's annotations in the third-edition portion to Johnson's and the amanuensis's annotations in the first-edition portion covering the letter B. It now appears likely that Steevens undertook the annotating of the third-edition sheets to assist Johnson in his revision. Whether or not Steevens acted at Johnson's behest, once the material Johnson had prepared for the printer for the pages covering the letter B was lost or otherwise unavailable, he turned to Steevens's material and used his annotated interleaved third-edition sheets as the basis for the revision of the text for the letter B. Steevens's annotated pages are now absent from the materials precisely because they were used as printer's copy. Once Johnson's unused portion of first-edition annotated sheets were rediscovered, they were inserted among the materials in the place covering the letter B, vacated by the portion used by the printers for the fourth edition, Steevens's annotated third-edition sheets.

Many of the alterations that were made in the 1773 text for the letter B reflect the kinds of changes Steevens makes elsewhere on the interleaves (especially alterations of, and commentary on, Shakespearean texts), and a collation of the editions clearly reveals that this part of Johnson's fourth-edition text, uniquely, was set from third-edition sheets. The revision of the letter is anomalous in other ways as well. The section covering B is the only letter shorter in the revision than in the first edition (it is shortened by four pages). Compared to other letters in this part of the *Dictionary*, for the entries under B, fewer than half the number of new illustrative quotations are added. No quotations from the usual authors added to this part of the wordlist, such as Bacon, Spenser and Sir Thomas Browne, are incorporated. Yet if Johnson's B-material annotations and changes had been incorporated, the types and number of changes would be similar to those made to the other letters in this part of the *Dictionary*.

Unfortunately, there is no way to know with certainty why the B material prepared by Johnson and his amanuensis was not used by Johnson or the printer. It is important to understand that the full collaboration he allows from Steevens is probably accepted only in exigent circumstances, for it is only for the letter B section, with his own prepared material lost, that he incorporates Steevens's changes wholesale. Otherwise, Steevens's proposed changes in the third-edition British Library materials remain for the most part ignored.

[11] For a discussion of the relationship between Johnson and Steevens, see John Middendorf, 'Steevens and Johnson', in James Engell (ed.), *Johnson and His Age* (Cambridge, MA: Harvard University Press, 1984), pp. 125–35. For the relation between the two revised editions, see Arthur Sherbo, '1773: The Year of Revision', *Eighteenth-Century Studies* 7.1 (1973), pp. 18–39. For the valuable reassessment of Steevens's role in the revision of the *Dictionary*, to which my understanding of the British Library materials and the following paragraphs are much indebted, see Carter Hailey, '"This Instance Will Not Do": George Steevens, Shakespeare, and the Revision(s) of Johnson's *Dictionary*', *Studies in Bibliography* 54 (2001), pp. 243–64.

# Notes on selected changes and annotations

## Introduction

The annotations on the B material provide important clues about Johnson's method of revising, the extent of collaboration, and his attitudes towards his text. They also reveal something of the character of the amanuenses working with him. Johnson's editing and preparing of the transcribed material on the interleaves is particularly noteworthy. Because his preferences and indications to the printer are clearly marked, the manuscript material is unusually unambiguous in its record of his intentions and his relationship to the work of others involved in the project. He had presumably set one amanuensis, probably William Macbean, the task of selecting material from the first edition to be reused for other head-words. Yet Johnson severely truncated or deleted many of the quotations, definitions and notes eventually transcribed on the interleaves. The fact that so much transcribed material is rejected, and that much of it is atypical of Johnson's text and his desires for it, strongly suggests that the quotations were originally chosen, gathered and proposed by the amanuensis, and that all of the definitions and commentary he included were his own. This amanuensis writing on the Sneyd-Gimbel slips took the liberty of providing many notes on dialect, Scots usage, custom and history, as well as quotations and notes from Thomas Tusser's *Five Hundred Points of Husbandry* involving rural and antiquated words. Yet in *every case* the notes, as well as Tusser's verses, are excised by Johnson. It would appear that Johnson turned his amanuensis loose to gather material, presumably fully intending to take advantage of his linguistic and literary expertise, then severely curtailed and edited his proposed additions. Judging from the final result, it is hard to believe that Johnson encouraged this particular type of addition, though he must have at least given the amanuensis the freedom to make independent decisions on what would be proposed. Johnson's treatment of the text on the B material interleaves shows how he moves away from the collaborative, rejecting every single usage-note proposed by the amanuensis, and exhibits his firm control over the final form of the work.[12] It seems that the amanuenses were given more freedom in gathering and presenting material for inclusion in the text than has previously been thought; yet the evidence also demonstrates that they were allowed no say in the final copy. It is not overstating the case to conclude from the evidence in the B material that Johnson adopts a hostile attitude towards the amanuenses' material. The evidence presented in this unique source leads one to conclude, in fact, that Johnson's control of his final text is more strongly reserved to himself than could previously be demonstrated.

The evidence concerning Johnson's treatment of Scots and dialect usage is of considerable importance in that it supports the view that, at least in the revision of the *Dictionary*, Johnson tends to suppress linguistic difference within English, actively and repeatedly rejecting dialect or regional variations which pluralise the conception of the national and accepted language.[13] This has been a point of interest to linguists and critics of Johnson's attitude towards the 'national tongue' and its many variations, in particular Scots dialect. The astonishing fact that so many of Johnson's helpers on the *Dictionary* were themselves Scots (five) seems to open up the possibility that they were employed not only for their obvious skills, but also in an attempt to include a wide range of linguistic variation. Scottish writers and critics such as Robert Fergusson and Archibald Campbell savaged Johnson's *Dictionary*, in part for including so much Latinate English and excluding Scots usage.[14] The amanuensis, in the course of the revision, may well be trying to address criticisms of the *Dictionary* by proposing material from Scots dialect and quotations from Scottish authors. In October 1769 Johnson even insists that Boswell should 'complete a Dictionary of words peculiar to Scotland, of which [Boswell] shewed him a specimen . . . By collecting those of your country, you will do a useful thing towards the history of the language.'[15] Whether or not he thought of Boswell's efforts as related to his own lexicographic project, the revision of which would begin less than two years later, he demonstrates, at least, that he is aware of the importance of Scots dialect in its historical relation, if not its current relevance, to English.

[12] See the discussion of the amanuenses' attempts, and Johnson's treatment of the handwritten passages on the interleaves, within the context of collaboration, in my 'Revision and the Limits of Collaboration: Hands and Texts in Johnson's *Dictionary*', in Jack Lynch and Anne McDermott (eds.), *New Perspectives on Johnson's Dictionary* (Cambridge: Cambridge University Press, 2005); concerning usage-notes proposed by the amanuensis transcribed onto the interleaves, two cases might be borderline: Johnson accepts 'break fast' as an additional use of BREAK as well as a comment on Dryden's use of 'boisterous' under that entry. Otherwise, from the handwritten commentary (i.e., not quotations), he accepts very short definitions for twenty-seven different entries and three simple 'etymologies' (e.g., 'bonjour [French]').

[13] Janet Sorenson, *The Grammar of Empire in Eighteenth-Century British Writing* (Cambridge: Cambridge University Press, 2000), ch. 2, contains the most recent and in many ways most articulate expression of this view. For a different perspective, see Nicholas Hudson, 'Johnson's *Dictionary* and the Politics of "Standard English"', *Yearbook of English Studies* 28 (1998), pp. 77–93. See also James G. Basker, 'Scotticisms and the Problem of Cultural Identity in Eighteenth-Century Britain', *Eighteenth-Century Life* 15 (1991), pp. 81–95.

[14] Robert Fergusson, 'To Dr. Samuel Johnson: Food for a New Edition of his Dictionary', and 'To the Principal and Professors of the University of St. Andrews on their Superb Treat to Dr. Samuel Johnson', in *The Poems of Robert Fergusson*, vol. II, ed. Matthew P. McDiarmid (Edinburgh and London: Blackwood and Sons, 1956), pp. 204–06; Archibald Campbell, *Lexiphanes, a Dialogue* (London, 1767).

[15] James Boswell, *The Life of Samuel Johnson, LL.D.*, ed. G. B. Hill, rev. L. F. Powell, 6 vols. (Oxford: Clarendon Press, 1934–64), vol. II, pp. 91–92.

The two most likely amanuenses involved in this project were apparently capable in their own right. William Macbean later proposed to publish a supplement to Johnson's *Dictionary*, claiming to have collected a great deal of material to supply the 'deficiencies' of the work. The second amanuensis, whom I have tentatively identified as V. J. Peyton, was the author of works on the English language and apparently knew several modern languages.[16] The first amanuensis had clearly the more important responsibility of selecting quotations for reuse and contextualization. The next amanuensis had to be neat and careful, copying the text from the slips to the interleaves; he very rarely intentionally deviates from the handwritten material he copied. The occasional lapses put into relief the consistency with which he copied accurately; however, the slavishness with which he copies even obvious errors, or incoherent passages, suggests either a limited understanding or a simple dedication to copying verbatim.

Johnson's patterns of attention to certain aspects of his text and to the language itself are revealed in these materials. These patterns include: the expansion of the number of definitions under certain head-words, the consolidation of others, and the shifting of quotations to illustrate different definitions, usually in response to a reading or re-reading of the illustrative quotations, both existing and proposed; comments on usage, prompted by the quotations, especially 'not in use', 'antiquated', 'obsolete', 'elegant', 'proper' and 'a low word'; altering of definitions and notes in response to re-reading of existing quotations or incorporation of new; the editing and tightening of entries for concision and coherence, particularly through the deletion or abbreviation of quotations; the substitution of proper names for third-person pronouns, pointing a few quotations more directly towards theological and ideological connotations; and the active interest in accounting for phrasal or particle verbs.

Furthermore, Johnson's efforts illustrate the extent to which his *Dictionary* is an extended exercise in literary critical acumen, a glossary, in a sense, of the words in the works of writers in English. Johnson's attentions are engaged as much in literary as in philological expertise; the two overlap where Johnson attempts to delimit the words' semantic range. This is one reason Johnson is so exacting in his criticism of poetry (specifically the language of poetry) in the *Lives of the Poets* and elsewhere: at its basis runs a philological drive for attention to etymologically based, logically derived meaning, along with a commitment to meaning based on literary and other types of written usage. These impulses are sometimes contradictory. It is in this area that the B material reveals Johnson's critical and lexicographical processes most interestingly. The reading of new quotations – each considered for inclusion, altered slightly or radically, or simply deleted – the tailoring of those that survive to fit the existing text with new definitions or notes, and the revising of the existing text to accommodate the new passage, together provide, on page after page, the handwritten evidence for Johnson's literary and linguistic concerns and responses that embodies his *Dictionary*. Of the approximately 309 proposed new quotations and independent notes on the interleaves in the amanuensis's hand, 170 are completely excluded.[17] By any standard, this reflects stringent demands for inclusion, and with the nearly complete exclusion of proposed notes on usage and definitions, the treatment of the transcribed material provides a showcase for Johnson's attitudes towards language, literature and lexicography.

The notes that follow concerning selected changes do not attempt to address every noteworthy or interesting aspect of the materials, but rather they suggest patterns within the material and implications thereof.

[16] See Reddick, *Making*, pp. 62 and 211 n. 20.

[17] I have counted quotations from Tusser's *Notes* that are transcribed with quotations from Tusser's verse as one proposal. Notes on a word's use or derivation copied on a separate Sneyd-Gimbel slip I have counted as one. There are also eight quotations or notes written by Johnson on the interleaves and printed pages.

## Notes

BABION *n.s.*
This note is taken from the *Dictionnaire de Trévoux* and is translated either by Johnson or the amanuensis. The note reads as follows: 'BABIL, s.m. {. . .} Ménage veut qu'il vienne de *bambinare*, qui a été fait de *banbino* [sic], Italien, diminutif de *bambo*, lequel est dérivé du Syriaque *babion*, qui signifie *enfant*, d'où on a fait aussi *babiole* & *bimbelots*, signifiant des *poupées*.'

BABY *n.s.*
This note on Scottish usage ('Baby [Babee] In Scotland denotes a halfpenny, as alluding to the Head impressed on the Copper Coin') is the first of several examples in the BL materials. The addition is almost certainly supplied by the Scottish amanuensis William Macbean from his personal knowledge. Johnson deletes every example of material concerning Scottish usage proposed by the amanuenses. His reluctance to consider such material is a result of the fact that it is based on oral rather than written sources and that it involves dialect or regional variations, which Johnson tends to exclude. Other examples include BANDOG *n.s.*, To BELIEVE *v.n.*, To BETOKEN *v.a.*, To BLOW nails, BODLE *n.s.*, To BROADEN *v.a.*, and BUSINESS *n.s.*

BACCIVOROUS *adj.*
Johnson corrects this definition from a noun ('A devourer of berries') to an adjective ('Feeding on berries'). This obvious error in the first edition is corrected in the fourth to 'Devouring berries'.

BACHELORS *Button.*
In this instance, Johnson follows a procedure, which he repeats throughout the fourth edition, of shortening encyclopaedic passages from Phillip Miller's *Gardener's Dictionary* which serve as definitions for plants. The expansive passages (signed '*Millar*') in the first edition are often shortened drastically or deleted entirely. The deletions made room for additional material, especially new quotations, and also contributed to the general tendency towards conciseness of entries in the revised edition. The other instances of this kind of excision occur under BALM/BALM *Mint*, BALSAM *Apple*, BARBADOES *Cherry*, BARBERRY, BARLEY, BASIL, BASTARD *Cedar Tree*, BAY *Tree*, BEAD *Tree*, BEAN, BEAN *Caper*, BEAR'S-BREECH, BEAR'S-EAR (2), BEECH, BEST, BEET, BELFLOWER, BENJAMIN, BERRY-BEARING *Cedar*, BETONY, BINDWEED, BIRCH *Tree*, BIRDSEYE, BIRDSFOOT, BIRTHWORT, BISHOPSWEED, BITTERVETCH, BLACK-BRYONY, BLACKBERRIED *Heath*, BLADDER-NUT, BLESSED *Thistle*, BLOODFLOWER, BORAGE, BOTTLEFLOWER, BOX, BRAMBLE, BRASIL/BRAZIL (from Ephraim Chambers), BRYONY, BUCKSHORN PLANTAIN, BUCKTHORN, BUCKWHEAT, BUGLE, BUTCHER'S BROOM and BUTTERBUR.

BAIL *n.s.*
Johnson's addition to the quotation from John Cowell displays a careful reading of the passage for coherence, an attentiveness to the precision of legal language, and a familiarity with the circumstances described.

To BAIT *v.a.*
With his addition, 'to furnish with allurement of any kind', Johnson extends the definition ('To put meat upon a hook, in some place, to tempt fish or other animals') from the specific reference (fishing) to the figurative sense of setting a trap through enticement, necessitated by the three quotations already present under def. 1, two from Shakespeare, one from Gay.

BAIT *n.s.*
Again relying upon the word 'allurement' ('allurement, commonly to crimes or misery'), Johnson sharpens the definition ('A temptation; an enticement'), emphasizing ill consequences as well as intentions, as illustrated in almost all of the supporting quotations.

BALANCE *n.s.* 7
Johnson's changes to the definition accentuate the condition of the mind understood in the use of the word 'balance' in the Pope quotation which follows. The quotation is particularly illustrative, and the addition necessary, given that the quotation refers both to the 'balance' of emotions ('Love, hope, and joy' vs. 'Hate, fear, and grief') as well as to a balanced state of mind, exemplified by the parallelism of the lines. Johnson retains the definition 'equipoise' (defined as 'Equality of weight; equilibration; equality of force') and augments it with 'even state; equal[il]ity'.

BALDRICK *n.s.*
This represents a case in which the first amanuensis specifically offers his own expertise as a way of assisting in clarifying uncertainties and filling in missing information in the printed text. In the first edition of the *Dictionary*, under the entry BALDRICK *n.s.*, def. 1, Johnson had provided the following: 'A girdle. By some *Dictionaries* it is explained a *bracelet*; but I have not found it in that sense.' The annotation on the interleaf offers more confident (though partly incorrect) information on the word and its derivation: 'Baldrick, is very probably derived from the inventer or first wearer of this belt, who was called Balderic, baldric. It was worn by women as well as men across the breast.' The quotation from *The Faerie Queene* then follows. Johnson remained unimpressed with the entire proposed text, however, and struck through it. This is consistent with his general practice in the fourth edition of not adding new discursive pieces of information, particularly related to dialect or word derivation in English, and instead abbreviating existing notes under some entries. This is a patent indication that the amanuenses' efforts and interests were often contrary to Johnson's own sense of his work.

The annotation for BALDRICK is also the first of other instances in which the amanuensis quotes Spenser in passages which focus lingeringly on the female breast. In this passage, recycled from the entry To FORLYE *v.n.* in the first edition, the quotation mentions the baldrick's position 'Athwart her snowy breast', then details the condition of the breasts ('her dainty paps'), their comparison to 'young fruit in May/Now little gan to swell', and their appearance 'through her thin weed'. The amanuensis attempts to justify and in a way to gloss the quotation with the comment, 'It was worn by women as well as men across the breast.' Another instance occurs under BARK *n.s.*, 'Fair when her breast like a rich laden bark/With precious merchandize she forth doth lay' (from Spenser's *Amoretti*); this quotation, hardly illustrating the head-word, was recycled from either To DARK *v.a.* or MERCHANDISE *n.s.*

It is worth noting that two new quotations are offered for the entry BREAST itself, one from *Coriolanus* ('the breast of Hecuba/When she did suckle Hector lookd not lovelier/Than Hectors forehead when it spit forth blood/At Grecian swords contending'), the other from Prior's 'Alma: Or the Progress of the Mind' ('Round their lovely breast & head/Fresh flowers their mingled Odours shed'); each of them is explicitly admiring. The Shakespeare quotation is a favourite in the *Dictionary* (in the first edition under FOREHEAD *n.s.*, LOVELY *adj.*, To CONTEND *v.n.*, and To SUCKLE *v.a.*) and is in fact represented in the Sneyd-Gimbel material for B with two slips.

BALL *n.s.*
Johnson probably translated this passage (which provides the derivation of this word for the first edition) himself; no published English translation of William Baxter's Latin *Glossarium antiquitatum Britannicarum* (1719) existed. His explicit handwritten citation here suggests a special interest in the work. In other cases in the B material it seems more likely that the amanuensis carried out his own translation while recycling material from the first edition.

BANDOG *n.s.* See note on BABY *n.s.*

BANKRUPT *adj.*
In the printed fourth edition, Johnson's correction of the Italian form is incorporated and the following text added: 'It is said, that the money-changers of Italy had benches probably in the burse or exchange, and that when any became insolvent his *banco* was *rotto*, his bench was broke. It was once written *bankerout. Bankerout* is a verb.' This note is followed by two new lines from a quotation from *Love's Labour's Lost* already existing in the first edition on the same page, illustrating To BANQUET *v.a.*: 'Dainty bits/Make rich the ribs, but bankerout the wits. *Shakespeare.*' These notes are typical of the contributions of George Steevens, and it is most likely that he added the note on Italian usage in the materials he prepared that were used to revise the letter B. He probably took the quotation from the entry BANKEROUT in the adjacent column when preparing his annotations. It might be considered, however, that Johnson's knowledge of the correct Italian form 'bancorotto', rather than 'bancorupto', implies that he, too, might have been capable of adding the note on Italian money-changers; since he did not insert it in the B materials, however, it was probably added by Steevens.

BARBARITY *n.s.* See note on To BEFORTUNE *v.n.*

BARBARLIE *adv.*
This case is very interesting because it exhibits either Johnson or one of the amanuenses censuring the passage in question from Thomas Tusser. The indelicate lines are heavily inked out on the Sneyd-Gimbel slip making them completely indecipherable, the only case in both the Sneyd-Gimbel materials and the BL materials of such assiduous blacking-out. The complete quatrain reads as follows:

> If sheep or thy lamb, fal a wrigling with tail,
> go by and by search it, whiles help may preuaile:
> That barbarlie handled, I dare thee assure,
> cast dust in his arse, thou hast finisht the cure.

To BARK *v.a.*
This example demonstrates Johnson's careful process of adapting illustrative material for use in the printer's copy and the amanuensis's problems in adequately glossing the quoted material. The amanuensis has provided the following definition, copied from the Sneyd-Gimbel slip, to accompany the quotation from *Hamlet*: 'To cover with bark, to encase with bark; to encrust.' The definition is incorrect, however, as the ghost of Hamlet's father is not describing his being actually covered with bark, rather his being in a state of encrustation as if covered with bark. The amanuensis copying on to the slips badly misunderstood the passage he had found (probably under TETTER *n.s.*), a mistake presumably impossible for one familiar with the Ghost's speech. Johnson, attentive to the possibilities provided by the quotation, simply corrects the definition on the interleaf to the following: 'To cover as with bark.'

BARRIER *n.s.*
Johnson's note, 'It is used by Pope indifferently', referring accurately to Pope's use of the word with the accent on the first syllable in his first two quotations (from *Pope's Odyssey* and *Pope's Statius*) and the accent on the second syllable in the third (from *Pope's Essay on Man*), is an attempt to tighten the entry, clarifying in the fourth edition his observation concerning accent in the first. This example demonstrates the care with which Johnson reviews the evidence of usage presented by existing quotations and relates definitions and notes on usage to the quoted material.

BASILISK *n.s.*
In some copies of the first edition of the *Dictionary*, the page with this entry was printed without the *beta* at the beginning of the Greek word; it would appear that this is the case here (the inking from Johnson's pen is too thick to be sure), and that Johnson adds the missing letter for the compositor.

BAY *n.s.*
Although the final rearrangement of elements constituting this entry is not entirely clear, Johnson's efforts reveal an attempt to separate distinctions of the word beginning with the actual bark of the dog as distinct from a more figurative application to those pressured or endangered, or who apply pressure. The new quotation from *Titus Andronicus* (recycled, probably, from To UNCOUPLE *v.a.* in the first edition), literally invokes the baying of hunting dogs. The amanuensis writing on the Sneyd-Gimbel slip intends this association when he supplies the etymology, '2 abboi', before the quotation, drawing attention to the etymological note stating that '*abboi* [is] the barking of a dog at hand'. The quotations from Denham, Dryden's *Æneid* and *Virgil*, each intended to illustrate 'The state of any thing surrounded by enemies, and obliged to face them by an impossibility of escape', emphasize the use of the term applied to the victim of aggressive pursuit in battle. The use of 'bay' in the quotation from Swift refers

back to the aggressor and implies pressure, rather than the immediate threat implied in the hunting usage – thus the new sense 2: 'It is used of those that press another.'

In deleting the quotation from James Thomson's poetry illustrating BAY *n.s.* ('He stands at *bay*,/And puts his last weak refuge in despair.'), Johnson follows a pattern running throughout the fourth edition of deleting quotations from this author (for another example, see the quotation from 'Autumn' under BLOSSOM *n.s.*). Thomson is dropped more than any other author between the first and the fourth editions, probably because of his increased association with 'liberty' causes and what Johnson considered his strange poetic diction. In this case, one reason the quotation illustrating BAY is deleted may be the apparent vagueness or incoherence of 'put[ting] refuge in despair'. In the B materials, the amanuenses even propose two new Thomson quotations under To BLUSH and To BROADEN, but Johnson, predictably, crosses them out.

BE- See notes on To BEFORTUNE *v.n.* and To BETEEM *v.a.*

To BEAR *v.a.* and *v.n.*
The entries for To BEAR, both *v.a.* and *v.n.*, are significantly altered by Johnson.

The two slips attached to 2T^r provide an opportunity to observe a particular detail of the preparation of printer's copy. These slips bearing quotations from Pope and Sidney, as well as the slip with a quotation from *The Faerie Queene* originally attached to 2T^v (now detached, visible on the interleaf facing 2T^v), originally formed part of the interleaf between 2T and 2T2. These quotations, illustrations of transitive uses of the verb, had been mistakenly written down facing the entry for To BEAR *v.n.* on 2T2^r. Once the mistake was discovered, they were clipped from the interleaf and attached to the printed pages in relation to the appropriate entries for To BEAR *v.a.* The interleaf has been carefully patched. Johnson's insertion lines run from the printed page on to the slips (or *vice versa*) indicating clearly that the slips were glued in place before Johnson reviewed the material.

To BEAR *v.a.* 6
The brief passage from Dryden's 'Annus Mirabilis' ('Their Ensigns belgic lions bear') prompts Johnson to adapt the amanuensis's note ('In heraldry to bear any thing in a Coat') to add the very specific sense of the word as used in heraldry ('to carry in coat armour') to the thirty-eight other senses covering *v.a.* The other definitions are otherwise sufficient to cover the use of the word in the new quotations from Shakespeare (sense 23) and Spenser (29).

To BEAR *v.a.* 29 and 35
Johnson's efforts under To BEAR *v.a.* and *v.n.* exemplify his continuing interest in phrasal or particle verbs. In the Preface to the *Dictionary*, he specifically cites the importance of 'the combinations of verbs and particles'; the care he promised to take of this aspect of the language is evident in the changes he makes to these entries. Under def. 29, for example, he marks verb phrases to be italicized ('*born down*') and moves the two Swift quotations under the new definition for sense 35 ('To bear down. To overpower'). Initially, he reads the Dryden quotation ('Now with a noiseless gentle course . . . ') as belonging under sense 35 (as it contains the words '*bears* down'), but then he reconsiders, deeming the instance more appropriate to sense 29 ('To impel; to urge; to push'). In this case, he determines that the verb is independent of the 'particle' and not in a phrasal combination. For both Swift passages, the new definition ('To overpower') for *To bear down* is a much nearer gloss than the former 'To impel; to urge; to push', for To BEAR accompanied by the adverb 'down'.

To BEAR *v.n.* 12
Johnson adds the marginal comment, 'Bear up and board her Shakesp.', a citation from *The Tempest*, either after encountering the quotation under OUT *adv.* in the first edition ('When the butt is out we will drink water, not a drop before; bear up and board them') or possibly, and uncharacteristically, recalling it and adding it from memory. For a similar case, see Johnson's marginal note, 'The spiry fir, and shapely Box Pope.' on 3L2^v.

Johnson's changes to '*To bear up*' (senses 10–12) further reflect his intention to expand on his treatment of phrasal combinations. He divides the single sense in the first edition into three senses in the fourth, adding three new gradations of usage. The re-reading of the quotations from Broome and Atterbury (signalled by his addition of 'to endure without terrour, or dejection' to the definition) accurately reflects the psychological aspect of 'bearing up' under extreme misfortune, virtually absent from the existing definition 'To stand firm without falling'; neither the quotation from *The Winter's Tale* nor the quotation from Swift obviously illustrate 'Not to faint; not to sink'. The new definition 'To advance' accommodates the brief added Shakespeare quotation.

Cursive 'I' (2T2^v, 3L2^v and 3M^r)
The cursive 'I's written by Johnson at the top of 2T2^v, 3L2^v and 3M^r are nearly identical and appear to be unrelated to the printed text and not intended for the compositor. The most likely explanation is that Johnson is testing his pen nib and ink.

BEATITUDE *n.s.*
Identifying Mahomet as the subject of this quotation illustrates Johnson's attention to the review of quotations, his desire for clarity (especially in theological matters), and his knowledge of the source texts. Inserting the name of Mahomet allows Johnson to emphasize, by implication, the superior nature of the Christian faith. See similar examples, specifically citing Protestant valour, under To BEHEAD (Laud) and To BRAND (Luther).

BEAUTY *n.s.*
With his marginal annotation, 'it is used of whatever delights the eye or mind', Johnson aligns a particular aspect of beauty with its effects on the viewer (similar to the collective effect of beauty of def. 1). This change reflects a philosophical or aesthetic shift from the quality of beauty inherent in a thing or person to ascertaining beauty according to its effect on the perceiver. The alteration effects a more complex reading of the two illustrating quotations from Dryden and Addison.

BEAVOIR *n.s.* (interleaf facing 2U^v)
In this instance, the amanuensis copying on to the Sneyd-Gimbel slip attempts to make sense of a difficult passage in reusing a quotation from the first edition. The passage in Fairfax's translation

of Tasso, and as quoted under To VAIL *v.a.* in the first edition, reads as follows: 'The virgin 'gan her beavoir vale,/And thank'd him first, and thus began her tale.' The amanuensis appears to propose the meaning of 'face' for the word, in the sense here of 'veiling the face'; in fact, the word is associated with a visor or part of a helmet, and 'vale' or 'vail' means 'to doff or remove as a sign of respect or submission'. He then attempts to make clearer the obscure wording of the passage and the sequence of events described. In the process, and presumably unconsciously, he entered the citation as 'Spenser' rather than 'Fairfax', perhaps because the quotation resembles the archaizing quality of other Spenserian passages. The query symbol written on the Sneyd-Gimbel slip presumably signals his uncertainty over the meaning of the word and the accompanying quotation. From the pattern of cross-out strokes on the interleaf, it is likely that Johnson first crossed out the head-word and note on derivation and usage with horizontal strokes, then considered the quotation for inclusion, and only later crossed through it with vertical strokes.

BECAUSE *conjunct.*
Johnson's pointing hand, index or fist is not intended as an instruction to the printer or amanuensis. He uses it as a marginal sign in his books where he wishes to draw attention to a passage of particular religious significance for himself. In this case, Johnson points out Hammond's eloquent statement of the redemptive power of Christ's sacrifice and the requirement that a sinner reform in order to enjoy it. This reflects a prevalent concern for Johnson regarding the nature of sin, the fact of Christ's suffering, and the hope of redemption. In Johnson's marked copy of John Norris's *Meditations*, he draws the pointing hand in the margin next to a meditation on the passage of the soul after death and writes 'Father' just above it.

BEETLE *n.s.* and To BEETLE *v.n.*
Johnson's alterations on 2X$^v$ reflect a reconsideration of the derivation of these words. His alteration of the etymological note for To BEETLE, 'I know not the ground of this signification', reflects his thinking on the derivation of the noun to mean a mallet or hammer: 'This is probable corrupted from <u>beatle</u> of <u>beat</u>.' In the fourth edition, no etymological change is incorporated in either entry.

To BEFORTUNE *v.n.*
To the entry for the intransitive verb To BEFORTUNE, Johnson has added the note, 'elegant but not in use', illustrated by a quotation from Shakespeare's *Two Gentlemen of Verona.* He had previously demonstrated his interest in this particular kind of prefix formation in his note on the interleaf facing 2U2$^r$: '<u>Be</u> is an inseparable particle placed before verbs of which it seldom augments or changes the signification as to <u>bedeck</u>, and before nouns which it changes into verbs. As dew, to bedew.' This usage is virtually restricted to poetry and written use.

The epithet 'elegant' in Johnson's note may best be understood in relation to Johnson's critical insistence (voiced in the *Lives of the Poets* and elsewhere) that poets should follow logically derived semantic coherence to maintain propriety of sense and expression. His complaints against Gray and Thomson, among others, reflect this insistence, specifically his censure of what he considers incoherent, careless and unjustified semantic uses or poetical extensions. The term 'elegant' is central to Johnson's discussions of language and reflects the importance of precise, 'minute' gradations of meaning and expression ('pleasing by minuter beauties', as he defines 'elegant' in the *Dictionary*). In the 'Life of Gray', Johnson comments that Gray's 'epithet "buxom health" [in 'The Prospect of Eton College'] is not elegant; he seems not to understand the word'. Johnson's objection is based on his conviction that Gray's use of the word is not justified by rules or patterns of semantic derivation. Under BARBARITY *n.s.* 3, he adds to the definition ('Barbarism; impurity of speech') the marginal 'or inelegance [of speech]', equating inelegance in language with barbarism and the detrimental influence of other languages.

To BEGUILE *v.a.*
When Johnson alters the reference from the specific play (*Hamlet*) to the name of the author, he follows the general tendency in the fourth edition of shifting references from the work to the author.

To BEHEAD *v.a.*
Drawing attention to the subject of the passage ('Laud') and what was referred to by his followers as his martyrdom, Johnson reflects his political sympathies. He includes a disproportionate number of new quotations in the fourth edition from writers who were considered 'Laudians' and who were followers of Archbishop Laud's views and example. Laud supported the King against the Commons and enforced unity in the Church of England. His execution in 1645 was taken in succeeding generations as an example for nonjurors and others of conservative political and ecclesiastical views of the suffering necessary for those of faith in a just cause. See related examples under BEATITUDE (Mahomet) and To BRAND (Luther).

To BELIE *v.a.*
Johnson's careful rereading of the passage from Shakespeare's *Cymbeline* necessitates the addition of an expanded metaphorical sense of the word, 'To fill with lies'. His note, 'Not in use', emphasizes the unusual literary occurrence of the word in this sense.

BELIEF *n.s.* 3
When Johnson specifies 'the true faith' and incorporates the illustration from Blackmore from the interleaf ('A bold opposer of divine <u>belief</u>/Attempts religious fences to subvert/Strong in his rage, but destitute of art'), he takes the opportunity to alter the entry in such a way that he emphasizes the strength of the Christian faith under persecution.

To BELIEVE *v.n.*
This is one of several instances in which the amanuensis has apparently selected a new quotation from Tusser's *Husbandry* and along with it a note from the editor Daniel Hillman's annotations to the volume. (In these cases the quotation appears under no other word in the first edition and there exists no relevant Sneyd-Gimbel

slip.) In this instance, however, the amanuensis has included his own comment on Hillman's note, challenging his interpretation. Tusser's work was useful to the process of adding material to the *Dictionary* because of its use of dialect or 'rural' words, and Hillman's notes were crucial because they explained their meaning. Yet Johnson in nearly every case crosses out the Tusser quotations and notes on usage written on the interleaves. This case is also interesting in its final note on Scottish usage and the word's Germanic root. It appears that this passage was copied from a different manuscript source (though no Sneyd-Gimbel slip exists), since the note on Scottish usage has nothing to do with the somewhat garbled comments on the supposed Germanic origin, presumably supplied from another source. See also note on BABY *n.s.*

BELLGARDE *n.s.*
This quotation ('Upon her Eyelids many graces sat/Under the shadow of her even brows/Working bellguards and amorous retrait/And every one her with a grace endows') is almost certainly recycled from a quotation illustrating RETRAIT *n.s.* in the abandoned first-edition manuscript. The passage is identical to this in the first edition, but without the precise location of the passage ('F.Q. 2.3.25') as given on the interleaf. Presumably this information was provided in the manuscript version from which it was culled. The example displays the amanuensis's complete confusion: the word, defined accurately as 'A soft glance; a kind regard', is already in the wordlist as BELGARD *n.s.*, illustrated by this quotation; however, the amanuensis copying on to the Sneyd-Gimbel slip proposes 'pretty bower or retreat' as the meaning of the word, and it is copied in this form on to the interleaf. Johnson deletes the proposed material.

To BEND *v.a.* 2
The passage from Raleigh is of interest because it is an unusually full quotation, much longer than necessary, reflecting a conviction of religious 'certitude' as well as a distrust of 'the Act [or art] of education'. The passage was clipped from the interleaf, the interleaf carefully patched, and the slip glued to the relevant printed page. In this case, the way Johnson's pen-stroke and writing proceed from the printed page to the slip, it is clear that the slip was in place before the printed pages were annotated. In other words, this instance supplies further evidence that the amanuensis prepared the interleaved pages, copied passages and other material on to the interleaves, and then turned the materials over to Johnson for his annotations and alterations.

To BENUM *v.a.*
Johnson's moving of the South quotation ('It seizes upon the vitals, and *benums* the senses; and where there is no sense, there can be no pain') from def. 1 ('To make torpid; to take away the sensation and use of any part by cold, or by some obstruction') to def. 2 ('To stupify') reflects a subtle rereading of the quotation and a differentiation of meaning between the various passages. By associating the South quotation with the stupefaction of the senses, rather than the simple numbing of a part of the body, Johnson elicits the metaphorical qualities latent in South's prose concerning the effects of doubt and sin.

To BESIEGE *v.a.*
Both cases of proposed new material for this entry represent particular readings of a new quotation, and Johnson rejects both in favour of the more comprehensive definition already present in the text: 'To beleaguer; to lay siege to; to beset with armed forces; to endeavour to win a town or fortress, by surrounding it with an army, and forcing the defendants, either by violence or famine, to give admission'. In the process, he insists upon the military meaning of the word, enriching particularly the quotation from Pope: the hearses not only 'attend' and 'crowd' the gate, as the amanuensis had supposed, they lay siege to it, demanding the inhabitants give up their bodies. The preceding line in Pope's poem, 'On all the line a sudden vengeance waits', provides the violent prelude inviting the 'hearses' in the next.

To BESPEAK *v.a.*
Robert Dodsley's 'Agriculture', the first part of his *Public Virtue: A Poem. In Three Books*, was first published in 1753, yet quotations from the work were included in the first edition of the *Dictionary*, much of which was already being printed by the time the poem appeared. This source was probably used to extract quotations late in the process of compilation. Johnson seems to have turned to Dodsley's poem and marked only quotations that illustrate words beginning with the letter T (TEMPERANCE *n.s.* 1, THRESHER *n.s.*, TINKLE *v.n.* 1, and TWIRL. *v.a.*), attempting to fill up gaps in the text. All of these passages come from a 62-line portion of the poem, ll. 66–128, on pages 5–8. One of the amanuenses (the hand is different from that usually found on the slips) copied them directly out on to a piece of paper, one beneath the other, then cut them into slips. The passage illustrating To TWIRL, part of which is visible at the bottom of the Sneyd-Gimbel slip for THRESHER, occurs in the poem eight lines after the passage extracted for THRESHER. In this case, the slip used for THRESHER in the first edition appears to have been simply recycled by crossing out the word 'thresher' and underlining 'bespeak' in the passage.

To BETEEM *v.a.*, To BETHRAL *v.a.*, To BETIDE *v.n.*
Frequently for the entries comprising 'Be-' prefixed words, Johnson writes in the margin that the uses are 'obsolete' (To BETEEM), 'not in use' (To BETHRAL), or 'not in use' and 'somewhat antiquated' (To BETIDE), to cite a few examples on one page alone. He seems to be unusually interested in this type of 'be-' construction (see Johnson's note on 'Be-' on the interleaf facing 2U2r), while fully aware that it is almost entirely restricted to pre-1700 literary works. The comments on obsolescence, in light of his positive remarks on the use of 'Be-' as a prefix (see note on To BEFORTUNE above), may reflect a certain regret at the passing of this particular construction in active use.

To BETOKEN *v.a.* See note on BABY *n.s.*

BIG *adj.*
Johnson's marginal annotation in this case, '8. Loud sounding not exile; not slender', referring to the Shakespeare quotation on the interleaf, is more clearly understood with reference to the definition he provides for EXILE: 'Small; slender; not full; not powerful. Not in use, except in philosophical writings.'

BIGGIN *n.s.*
Johnson's commentary on Shakespeare's use of the word, 'It seems to mean in Shakespeare coarse cloath', reflects a more careful rereading of Shakespeare's lines and metaphor.

BLASPHEMOUS *adj.*
Noting that Sidney, as well as Milton, accents 'blasphemous' on the second syllable in the quotations that follow, Johnson displays a careful re-reading of the lines and also implies a line of influence in poetic practice between the two.

BLAST *n.s.*
Johnson's alterations to these entries (noun and verb) represent a vivid example of his efforts at making his entries coherent, particularly in the relation between definition and illustration and the delineation of multiple meanings. His addition of 'the power of the wind' to the definition 'A gust, or puff of wind' removes the random or occasional aspect of the definition, supplying instead the idea of a constant and destructive force. Understanding the aspect of power in the word 'blast' is necessary for a coherent reading of the two Shakespearean quotations, one from *Richard III*, the other from *King Lear*, which follow. The addition of '2 A particular wind' glosses the Dryden quotation not in terms of chance gusts, but of a determinate and identifiable wind, blowing with predictability and force. Inserting Dryden's lines written on the interleaf, 'If envious eyes their hurtful rays have cast,/More powerful verse shall free thee from their blast', to illustrate the existing definition, 'The stroke of a malignant planet; the infection of any thing pestilential', effects a witty, if hyperbolical, reading of Dryden's couplet.

To BLAST *v.a.*
Johnson's addition to To BLAST *v.a.*, def. 2, 'to wither before the time', accurately reflects the usage and binds together the quotations from the 'Book of Genesis' and Dryden. He reverses the order of senses 3 and 4 in order to maintain the continuum of definitions from the literal and graphic to the more metaphorical. In particular, the first three definitions pertain to a force that blights or plagues, especially plants or living and maturing things (particularly defs. 2 and the reordered 3). For the new def. 4 and the existing def. 5, the effect is more general and impersonal.

BLEMISH *n.s.*
Johnson's careful rearrangement of elements under this entry displays a substantial re-thinking of various aspects of the relation between definitions and quotations. The addition of the word 'disgrace' to def. 3 ('A soil; turpitude; taint; deformity') shifts the emphasis of this sense from an understanding of the word as an effect or mark upon oneself, to the effect pertaining to the observation or apprehension of a taint in relation to others, bringing it into the world of social control and perception. Presumably Johnson makes the change primarily to account for the quotation from Hooker, which pertains to others' perception of the Church and the Church's effects upon observers.

To BLOCK *v.a.*
Johnson's handwritten annotations to this entry, 'To obstruct . . . commonly with up emphatical', reflect his ongoing interest in phrasal or particle verbs and his careful reading of the illustrations beneath, as two of the four quotations employ the form 'block up'. 'To obstruct' also more accurately defines the use of the word in the Bacon quotation than either of the listed definitions.

BLOSSOM *n.s.*
For the deletion of Thomson quotations, see the note on BAY *n.s.*

To BLOSSOM *v.n.*
Two quotations from Richard Crashaw are proposed by the amanuensis for this entry, both probably recycled from the entry for NEW *adv.* in the first edition. The only other quotation from Crashaw in the B materials is proposed under BUD *n.s.* In all three cases, the passages are crossed out by Johnson. Each refers to light, and involves a metaphorical extension of the verb: light 'blossoming' or 'budding'. Johnson's deletion of these quotations probably results from his dislike of such poetical elaborations the transference of the literal to what he would consider a vague metaphorical sense.

To BLOT *v.a.*
Johnson's changes skilfully correct several anomalies in his text for this entry. Adding 'to soil; to sully' to the current def. 4 ('To disgrace; to disfigure') he more subtly and accurately reads the quotations from Dryden and Rowe in terms of dark discoloration of something white or clear, in association with the moral implications. In so doing, he retains the connection to the root sense of the word; yet to maintain his continuum of definitions, he reverses the order of the final two senses, bringing the graphic 'To darken' before the more metaphorical sense, 'To disgrace; to disfigure; to soil; to sully'.

To BLOW nails See note on BABY *n.s.*

To BLUSH *v.n.*
This re-arrangement of the quotations corrects a misreading of the two Shakespeare quotations as blushing to 'betray shame or confusion'. In the new arrangement, the blushing is read correctly to mean merely to display colour, without assigning further significance or meaning.

For the Thomson quotation on the interleaf, see note on BAY *n.s.*

BODLE *n.s.* See note on BABY *n.s.*

To BOLSTER *v.a.*?
The amanuensis presumably found the quotation from Shakespeare's *Henry VIII* in the following more or less comprehensible form under the first-edition entry for TYPE *n.s.*:

> 'Clean renouncing
> The faith they have in tennis, and tall stockings,
> Short bolster'd breeches, and those types of travel,
> And understanding again the honest men'. (1.3.29–32)

Re-copying a portion of the passage on to the interleaf to illustrate the verb 'BOLSTER' resulted in this version being incoherent as it stands: 'clean renouncing/Short bolsterd Breeches & those types of travel'. Such examples of incompetence are clear evidence that this material copied on to the interleaves was recycled in the first instance not by Johnson, but by the amanuensis. Johnson crosses out the quotation.

BOMBAST *n.s.*
Johnson's alterations to the first-edition text, particularly his speculative marginal note, suggest a dissatisfaction with the etymological note as it stands. This dissatisfaction is reflected in the entry for BUMBAST *n.s.*, 'falsely written for *bombast*; the etymology of which I am now very doubtful of'. In the B material, Johnson crosses out this note after the semi-colon. In the first edition, he derives BOMBAST from one of the names of Paracelsus, who was supposedly 'remarkable for sounding professions, and unintelligible language'; this note is replaced in the fourth edition with the following: 'A stuff of soft loose texture used formerly to swell the garment, and thence used to signify bulk or shew without solidity.' Under BUMBAST, the fourth-edition etymological note is changed to: 'falsely written for *bombast*; *bombast* and *bombazine* being mentioned, with great probability, by *Junius*, as coming from *boom*, a tree, and *sein*, silk; the silk or cotton of a tree. Mr. Steevens, with much more probability, deduces them all from *bombycinus*.' In fact, this is the correct derivation of the word. Furthermore, it demonstrates that Steevens's contributions, which in this case provide the correct information, were not yet known or available to Johnson at the point when he was preparing the B material, for he does not add the information to the entries at that time.

BORREL *n.s.*
The note on the interleaf reads: 'Borrel *n.s.* a poor rude illiterate person, who is of no other service to the public than to get children. So it is used in Chaucer. Unless you would derive it from poraille in the same author which signifies the low or poor people Jun.' This note is presumably an attempt to correct Johnson's printed note in the first edition, 'It is explained by *Junius* without etymology.' The amanuensis's note is an adaptation of the entry under 'BORELL MAN' in Edward Lye's 1743 edition of Junius's *Etymologicum Anglicanum*.

BOTED *adj.*
This would appear to be a case in which the amanuensis's misreading of the manuscript for the first-edition entry for JOURNEY *n.s.* led to confusion of words. The passage in *Henry IV, pt. 1* reads 'journey-bated', as does the passage as quoted (without hyphen) under JOURNEY. The amanuensis misreads 'bated' (lessened or weakened from the journey) as 'boted' (a general condition of having bots, or worms) and therefore misunderstands the passage. This instance reflects the zealousness of the first amanuensis, probably William Macbean, to discover and include new material, as well as his tendency, in certain cases, to misread and misunderstand quoted material.

BOX *n.s.*
Johnson adds this marginal comment, 'The spiry fir, and shapely Box Pope', either after encountering the quotation under SPIRY in the first edition ('Waste sandy valleys, once perplex'd with thorn,/The spiry firr, and shapely box adorn'), or possibly – and uncharacteristically – recalling it and adding it from memory. See the similar case, Johnson's marginal note 'Bear up and board her Shakesp.' under To BEAR *v.n.* 12.

BRACE *n.s.*, To BRAG *v.n.*, BRAGGART *adj.* and *n.s.*,

BRAGLESS *adj.*, BRAGLY *adv.*
On this page (3M^r) alone, Johnson notes in his annotations six different instances in which words are 'obsolete', used 'without propriety', or 'proper but little used'. Of these, three pertain to Shakespearean uses (BRACE *n.s.*, BRAGGART *n.s.*, BRAGLESS *adj.*). The marginal comment that 'Braggart', meaning 'A boaster', is 'obsolete' is of particular interest, since this use of the word is current today.

To BRAG *v.n.*
Johnson moves the following quotation from Sanderson's *Pax Ecclesiæ* from sense 1 to illustrate the new sense 4, '4 out is used without propriety': 'In *bragging* out some of their private tenets, as if they were the received established doctrine of the church of England.' This demonstrates again his evidently heightened interest in accounting for phrasal or particle verbs – and in this case, censuring incorrect formulations. Three of the four senses of To BRAG, including Johnson's addition, refer to particle extensions of verbs ('of' and 'on'), two of which ('on' and 'out') are censured as improper.

BRAKE *n.s.*
The new definition proposed by the amanuensis, 'Brake or fern' (gleaned from the quotation from Sir Thomas Browne) is adapted by Johnson who crosses out 'brake or' leaving 'fern', and remarks that 'it forms the original signification' of the word. This definition is indeed missing from the first-edition entry; its addition enables the presentation of a development of the senses of the word from the individual plant to the thicket made up of many plants. Today this derivation of 'brake as thicket' from 'brake as fern' is not accepted, however, though to Johnson it may have seemed self-evident. The amanuensis (probably William Macbean) wrote 'Brake, or fern Brachans Scottish' on the Sneyd-Gimbel slip bearing the Tusser quotation and editor's note, which has been crossed out. The predominance of the word 'brachan' or 'brachans' used by the Scots would presumably have enabled the amanuensis to supply this missing sense of the word for Johnson.

To BRAND *v.a.*
Johnson supplies the name 'Luther' to the existing quotation, thus creating a brief tableau of Protestant persecution. The passage is taken from Atterbury's 'An Answer to Some Considerations Upon the Spirit of Martin Luther' and the annotation suggests Johnson's familiarity with the text, despite the fact that he had selected this passage for the first edition nearly twenty-five years earlier. The examples under To BEHEAD (Laud) and BEATITUDE (Mahomet) are other instances in which he specifies the person's name in the quotation in order to stress Christian virtue, or Protestant will under persecution.

BRANDY-SHOP *n.s.*
This annotation is badly confused: not only is the author mistakenly given as 'Shop', but the passage makes no sense as written and is nothing like the original. Swift's *Directions to Servants* reads as follows: 'Remember how often you have been

stripped, and kicked out of Doors, your Wages all taken up beforehand, and spent in translated red-heeled Shoes, second-hand Toupees, and repaired Lace Ruffles, besides a swinging Debt to the Ale-wife and the Brandy-shop.' From wherever the Sneyd-Gimbel amanuensis recycled this passage, he wrote it on to the slip in this incoherent form. The amanuensis copying it on to the interleaf added further confusion by miscopying the attribution 'Shop' for 'Swift'. It is difficult to resist speculating on the reasons for the complete mishandling of this addition, considering the subject.

BRAWNY *adj.*
In this case, the amanuensis culling out materials to reuse in the fourth edition almost certainly found the quotation proposed for BRAWNY ('The sharp humour fretted the skin downward & in process of time became serpiginous and was covered with white brawny scales') under the entry SERPIGINOUS *adj.*, where it illustrates the head-word in a similar but not identical form: 'The skin behind her ear downwards became serpiginous, and was covered with white scales. Wiseman.' This version of the quotation lacks several words of the quotation proposed for 'brawny' on the interleaf, most importantly the word 'brawny' itself. In Wiseman's work, however, the passage reads 'branny', not 'brawny', and is even used to illustrate 'branny' in the first edition of the *Dictionary*. The source of the B-material quotation, therefore, could not be either the printed Wiseman text itself or the entry for BRANNY, both of which, clearly, read 'branny'. The quotation under SERPIGINOUS, the likely source, must have been longer in the manuscript form than in its printed form in the *Dictionary*, because it had to contain the additional words, in particular the word 'branny', easily misread in manuscript as 'brawny'. Johnson, not surprisingly, crosses out the quotation.

To BREATHE *v.a.*
The quotation from Prior contains a poetical figurative extension of verb usage (to 'breathe the song and touch the lire') of the kind often criticized by Johnson, particularly in its use by eighteenth-century poets. In this case, Johnson accepts the validity of the instance and provides a new definition, as none of the existing quotations involves vocality.

To BRIDLE *v.a.*
The source for the recycling of this quotation from Bacon's *Natural History* ('Both bodies are clammy and bridle the deflux of humours to the hurting' as it appears on the Sneyd-Gimbel slip) would appear to be CONGLUTINATION *n.s.*, as this is the only word under which a part of the passage is quoted in the first edition. However, the form of the quotation is significantly different under that entry: 'The cause is a temperate *conglutination*; for both bodies are clammy and viscous, and do bridle the deflux of humours to the hurts.' The most likely explanation for this discrepancy is that the quotation was much longer and fuller in the abandoned manuscript version where the amanuensis found it than it is in the printed text under CONGLUTINATION. It is also possible that the quotation had been copied out elsewhere in the first-edition manuscript under another entry yet was not printed in the first edition. This is only one example of many in which the quotation as recycled for the fourth edition appears to have been adapted from a longer version than that found in the printed first edition. The evidence is overwhelming that the handwritten version in the abandoned first-edition manuscript contained longer, unedited versions of the quoted texts.

To BRING *on v.a.*
Although it cannot be proven, it seems probable that this quotation and the other three quotations from Duncan Forbes added to the fourth edition (under ADHIBIT *v.a.*, COMMEMORATIVE *adj.*, and CONTRIBUTOR *n.s.*) were newly selected from a copy of Forbes's 'Letter to a Bishop' and *Some Thoughts Concerning Religion*, published together several times in the preceding years. None of the four quotations appears in the first edition, though *Some Thoughts Concerning Religion* is quoted several times there. Forbes was a prominent Scotsman as the President of the Court of Session, and 'P' before his name, an abbreviation for 'President', implies a certain familiarity. It seems likely that the amanuensis, probably William Macbean, made the decision to turn to his theological works to extract new quotations. The Sneyd-Gimbel slip for COMMAND *n.s.* reads as follows: '5 Command n.s. is in Scotl$^{d}$ applied to y$^{e}$ Decalogue The very tables in w$^{ch}$ ten commands were written were deposited in y$^{e}$ ark P. Forbes' (not included in the fourth edition).

To BROADEN *v.a.* See notes on BABY *n.s.* and BAY *n.s.*

To BUCKLE *v.a.*
Johnson's addition of 'to enclose' to def. '4. To confine' brilliantly captures the meaning of the usage in both Shakespeare quotations, the one proposed on the interleaf from *Troilus and Cressida* and the printed quotation from *As You Like It*. None of the existing definitions adequately provides the sense of spanning, surrounding with a barrier, and fencing in of something, required by these instances of 'buckle'. With the addition, the pressure of the 'waste' ('waist') in the slightly ridiculous reference to Priam's worth is felt as a result of buckling in his 'vast proportion', and the effect of grasping in the hand in the 'stretching of a span' that '*Buckles* in his sum of age' is elicited from the printed Shakespeare quotation.

BULLET *n.s.*
No eighteenth-century version of Swift's poem 'A Pastoral Dialogue' has been located with the variant reading 'Paddy': 'When at long bullets Paddy long did play/You sat and lous'd him all the sun shine day.' The usual reading is as follows: 'When you saw Tady at long-bullets play,/You sat and lows'd him all the Sun-shine Day.'

BUMBAST *n.s.* See note on BOMBAST *n.s.*

BURDEN *n.s.*
Johnson keys in the passage by Prior (recycled from the 1755 entry TWOFOLD *adj.*: 'Ews that erst brought forth but single lambs/Now drop'd their twofold burdens Prior') under BURDEN *n.s.*, def. 3: 'A birth: now obsolete'. Prior's poem dates only from 1718, and so Johnson's comment that the usage is obsolete can be read either as a censure of Prior or as an acknowledgement of the intentionally antiquated mode of the pastoral ode that Prior adopts.

To BURDEN *v.a.*
Johnson's changes to this entry are particularly interesting because in adding the new def. 2, 'To freight', he provides the entry with a movement from the more metaphorical connotation of the word ('To load; to incumber', illustrated by the quotation, 'Burden not

thyself above thy power' from Ecclesiasticus) to the literal, but particular, use ('To freight') connoting the loading of a ship or other vessel, illustrated by the new Dryden quotation, 'In burden'd Vessels first with speedy care/His plenteous stores do seasond timber send'. On the one hand, this alteration goes against his usual practice of beginning with the literal sense of the word and moving to the metaphorical, yet on the other, it illustrates Johnson's stated method of progressing in his definitions from the general to the particular use of a word.

BURDENOUS *adj.*
The amanuensis writing on to the Sneyd-Gimbel slip makes this entry ludicrous by transcribing the first line of the Spenser quotation not as 'She hath the bonds broke of eternal night' (followed by 'Her soul unbodied of the burdenous corpse'), but 'She hath the bones broke of eternal night.' The second amanuensis dutifully copied out the line with 'bones broke' on to the interleaf. The mistake is understandable in a case where the amanuensis is unfocused and paying no attention to the sense of the passages he is copying out. Since he is not supplying a definition or note on usage for the quotation, he may be working less attentively. The fact that both amanuenses copied out the same clear mistake, however, qualifies to some extent the impression of their competence, critical independence, and careful engagement in the work.

BUSINESS *n.s.* See note on BABY *n.s.*

To BUTT *v.a.*
The proposed material for this entry copied on to the interleaf and the Sneyd-Gimbel slip to which it relates contain clues to their histories in their texts. The slip is anomalous, physically and textually. It stretches to twice the width of most slips (presumably across a page of the abandoned notebook manuscript for the first edition) and appears to be two slips end to end. The one on the left pertains to the use of the word 'butt' as a verb ('To push, to run ag$^{st}$ w$^{th}$ any thing flat', followed by the quotation: 'If I join but w$^{th}$ y$^{e}$ words in construction & sense: as, but I will not, a butt of wine, y$^{e}$ ram will but, shoot at but, y$^{e}$ meaning of it will be ready to you Holder Sp.'). The portion of the slip on the right pertains to one use of the word as a noun: 'But a certain measure containing liquor' followed by 'w$^{n}$ y$^{e}$ but is out we will drink water' and the note, 'See also Holder under But boundary'. The amanuensis has evidently recycled the Holder quotation from the entry BUT *n.s.*, copied it on to one column of the notebook page, and then written in the next column the quotation from *The Tempest*, possibly from memory, as it is short and memorable and has no reference given, or perhaps he recycled it from the entry OUT *adv.* (def. 9). The note 'See also Holder under But boundary' is anomalous in these materials and unusual in the *Dictionary* itself. It confirms that the entry for BUT *n.s.* is the origin of the Holder quotation written on the slip. Clearly, the slip was intended to be cut into two, one slip for the '*v.a.*' sense, the other the noun. The fact that they are on the same slip caused problems for the second amanuensis copying on to the interleaf, for he dutifully copied the entire text seriatim and, in his confusion, copied the quotations in the wrong places in relation to the printed text. Perhaps as a result of the misplacement, and the anomalies of the entry (including the lack of a reference for the second quotation and the unusual note), Johnson deletes the entire text.

# Policy of citing sources

Locating the precise origin of illustrative quotations in Johnson's *Dictionary* is one of the great projects yet to be accomplished in Johnsonian scholarship. As a contribution, in part, to this project, this edition has attempted to provide the most evidence possible concerning the editions Johnson used when he originally selected (for the first edition of the *Dictionary*) the quotations that would later be copied on to the B material interleaves for recycling in the fourth edition (and in a very few cases, the editions used when selecting quotations anew for the fourth edition). A confident selection, however, has often remained elusive. Determining the editions from which Johnson selected his quotations is a complicated undertaking, especially as the quotations are often altered by Johnson before inclusion. Furthermore, there are often several likely possibilities, or the possibility (where there are single or very few citations) of 'hidden' sources including miscellanies, anthologies, or other works in which the author is quoted; each work must be located along a spectrum of certainty based upon available evidence. While some books are conclusively known to have been prepared by Johnson for the *Dictionary*, as is the case with the thirteen marked books that are extant, four of which are cited in the B material (Shakespeare, Bacon, Hale and South), other less certain, though probable, identifications have been possible through a study of internal evidence provided by the quotations themselves and works otherwise associated with or commented upon by Johnson.

The policy of this edition is to provide a source in the accompanying footnote for each proposed quotation on the interleaved pages. When it is known that Johnson used a particular edition, this has been cited (with reference to the list of editions). Where it is possible to narrow down the sources to a probable source, this has also been cited. In cases where it is not possible to identify with full confidence a specific early edition, modern editions have been referenced instead (as is the case with Swift, Dryden and Pope); in instances where no modern critical edition exists, I have turned to a contemporary edition that is possibly – even in some cases likely to have been – the edition Johnson used. In these cases, where there exist a large number of potential editions to choose among, I have generally chosen the edition closest to the 1755 publication date of the first edition, unless there was a compelling reason to do otherwise. A modern source is additionally provided for the Shakespeare and Bacon quotations (in square brackets in the footnotes) since the eighteenth-century editions are not readily accessible.

# Editions cited and works quoted

Books known to have been used by Johnson, and editions to which Johnson could have had access and which he may have used for his source of quotations, are divided into the following categories, signified by a system of asterisks: books known to have been marked for the 1755 *Dictionary* (***); probable source (**); and possible source (*). Where suitable modern editions exist for the last category, these modern editions have been cited without an asterisk. Where appropriate, a list in square brackets of the individual works quoted in the B material follows the publishing information for each edition.


[Allestree, Richard?], *The Causes of the Decay of Christian Piety* (London: J. H. for E. and R. Pawlet, 1704) *

Arbuthnot, John, *The History of John Bull*, ed. Alan W. Bower and Robert A. Erickson (Oxford: Clarendon Press, 1976) ['Lewis Baboon Turned Honest']

*Tables of Ancient Coins, Weights, and Measures* (London: J. Tonson, 1727) ['A Dissertation Concerning the Doses of Medicines given by Ancient Physicians'] **

Ascham, Roger, *The Schoolmaster* (1570), ed. Lawrence V. Ryan (Ithaca, NY: Cornell University Press, 1967) ['The Ready Way to the Latin Tongue'] *

Bacon, Francis, *The Works of Francis Bacon*, 4 vols. (London: A. Millar, 1740); vol. III marked for the *Dictionary.* ['Considerations Touching a War with Spain', *Essays Civil and Moral* ('XIII: Of Goodness and Goodness of Nature', 'IX: Of Vicissitude of Things'), 'An Historical Account of the Office of Alienations' (now attributed to William Lombarde, *Some few notes of the orders, proceedings, punishments, and privileges of the Lower House of Parliament, c.* 1584), *The History of the Reign of King Henry VII, Natural History, New Atlantis*, 'Physiological Remains'] ***

*The Works of Francis Bacon*, ed. James Spedding, R. L. Ellis, D. D. Heath, 14 vols. (London: Longman, 1857–74)

Bible, *The Holy Bible. Containing the Old and New Testaments . . . Authorized King James Version* (Cambridge: Cambridge University Press, 1990) [Isaiah, Jeremiah]

Blackmore, Richard, *Creation. A Philosophical Poem, Demonstrating the Existence and Providence of a God. In Seven Books*, 4th edn (London: printed for A. Bettesworth and J. Pemberton, 1718) *

Browne, Sir Thomas, *Pseudodoxia Epidemica*, ed. Robin Robbins, 2 vols. (Oxford: Clarendon Press, 1981)

Butler, Samuel, *Hudibras. In Three Parts. Written in the Time of the Late Wars. Corrected and Amended: with Additions* (London: D. Browne, J. Walthoe, J. Knapton [et al.], 1726); marked for the *Dictionary*, now lost ***

Camden, William, *Remains Concerning Britain,* ed. R. D. Dunn (Toronto: University of Toronto Press, 1984)

Carew, Richard, *The Survey of Cornwall. And an Epistle concerning the Excellencies of the English Tongue* (London: printed for Samuel Chapman, Daniel Browne and James Woodman, 1723) **

Charles I, King, *Eikon Basilike, The Portraiture of His Sacred Majesty in His Solitudes and Sufferings*, ed. Philip A. Knachel (Ithaca, NY: Cornell University Press, 1966)

Cowell, John, *The Interpreter: Or Booke Containing the Signification of Words* (London, 1607), edited in facsimile by R. C. Alston (Menston: The Scolar Press, 1972) *

Crashaw, Richard, *The Complete Poetry of Richard Crashaw*, ed. George W. Williams (New York: New York University Press, 1972) ['On the Frontispiece of Isaacson's Chronologie explained' ('Or Thus'), 'Sospetto d' Herode. Libro Primo', 'Upon the Death of the most desired Mr. Herrys']

Daniel, Samuel, *The Civil Wars*, ed. Laurence Michel (New Haven: Yale University Press, 1958)

Denham, John, *The Poetical Works of Sir John Denham*, ed. Theodore Howard Banks, Jr., 2nd edn (Hamden, CT: Archon Books, 1969) ['The Passion of Dido for Æneas']

Derham, William, *Physico-Theology: Or, a Demonstration of the Being and Attributes of GOD, from his Works of Creation*, 10th edn (London: W. Innys, 1742) *

*Dictionnaire Universel, François & Latin* [*Vulgairement appellé Dictionnaire de Trévoux*] . . . , nouvelle édition corrigée, 5 vols. (Paris: Nicolas Gosselin, 1732) *

Dillon, Wentworth, Earl of Roscommon, *An Essay on Translated Verse* (London, 1685), facsimile of 2nd edn (Menston: The Scolar Press, 1971) *

Dodsley, Robert, *Public Virtue: A Poem. In Three Books* (London: printed for R. and J. Dodsley, 1753) ['Agriculture'] **

Donne, John, *Poetical Works*, ed. Sir Herbert Grierson (London: Oxford University Press, 1933; repr. 1968) ['An Anatomie of the World. The First Anniversary', 'Elegy XI: The Bracelet, Upon the Loss of his Mistress' Chain, for which he made satisfaction', 'Loves Diet']

Dryden, John, *The Works of John Dryden*, 20 vols., gen. ed. H. T. Swedenberg, Jr. [et. al.] (Berkeley: University of California Press, 1956–2000) ['Annus Mirabilis', 'Astræa Redux', 'Ceyx and Alcyone, Out of the Tenth Book of Ovid's *Metamorphoses*', 'Cinyras and Myrrha, Out of the Tenth Book of Ovid's *Metamorphoses*', *Cleomenes*, 'The Cock and the Fox: Or, The Tale of the Nun's Priest, From Chaucer', *Dufresnoy's De Arte Graphica. The Art of Painting*, 'The First Book of Homer's *Ilias*', 'The Hind and the Panther: A Poem, In Three Parts', 'Preface to Sylvæ', *The Satires of Juvenal* ('Third', 'Sixth', 'Tenth'), 'Sigismonda and Guiscardo, from Boccace', *Virgil's Aeneis* (bks. VII, IX, XI), *Virgil's Georgics* (bk II), 'The Wife of Bath Her Tale']

Dryden, John, Jr., *The Satyrs of Decimus Junius Juvenalis: and of Aulus Persius Flaccus. Translated into English Verse by Mr. Dryden, And several other Eminent Hands* (London: printed for J. Tonson, 1735) ['Juvenal. The Fourteenth Satyr by Mr. John Dryden, Jun.'] *

Fairfax, Edward, tr. Torquato Tasso, *Godfrey of Bulloigne: or the Recovery of Jerusalem* (London: J. M. for Ric. Chiswell, Ric. Bentley, Tho. Sawbridge, and Geo. Wells, 1687) *

Forbes, Duncan, *Some Thoughts Concerning Religion, Natural and Revealed*, 'corrected' (Edinburgh: J. Cochran and Company, 1743) *

Gay, John, *Poetry and Prose*, ed. Vinton A. Dearing and Charles E. Beckwith, 2 vols. (Oxford: Clarendon Press, 1974) ['Trivia']

Glanvill, Joseph, *Scepsis Scientifica: Or, Confest Ignorance, the way to Science; In an Essay of The Vanity of Dogmatizing* (London: E. Cotes for Henry Eversden, 1665) **

Hale, Matthew, *The Primitive Origination of Mankind, Considered and Examined According to the Light of Nature* (London: William Gobid for William Shrowsbery, 1677); marked for the *Dictionary* ***

Hall, Joseph, *Works* (London: printed by T. Hodgkin for the proprietors, 1714) ['Epistles upon different Subjects'] *

Hayward, John, *The Life and Raigne of King Edward the Sixth*, ed. Barrett L. Beer (Kent, OH: Kent State University Press, 1993)

Herbert, George, *The Works of George Herbert*, ed. F. E. Hutchinson (Oxford: Clarendon Press, 1941) ['The Church-Porch']

Holder, William, *Elements of Speech: An Essay of Inquiry into The Natural Production of Letters* (London, 1669), edited in facsimile by R. C. Alston (Menston: The Scolar Press, 1967) **

Hooker, Richard, *Of the Laws of Ecclesiastical Polity*, vol. I, ed. Georges Edelen; vol. II, ed. W. Speed Hill (Cambridge, MA: Belknap Press of Harvard University Press, 1977)

Howell, James, *Dendrologia: Dodona's Grove, or The Vocall Forrest . . . with . . . Parables, reflecting on the Times. And England's Teares for the present Warres*, 2nd edn ([London]: 1644) ['England's Teares for the present Warres'] *

Jonson, Ben, *Ben Jonson* (*Works*), ed. C. H. Herford, Percy and Evelyn Simpson (Oxford: Clarendon Press, 1941; repr. and corrected 1970) [*Catiline*, 'Epigramme CXXIX: To Mime', 'The King's Entertainment at Welbeck']

Junius, Franciscus, *Etymologicum Anglicanum. Ex Autographo descripsit & accessionibus premultis auctum edidit Edwardus Lye* (Oxonij: 1743) **

Knolles, Richard, *The Turkish History from the Original of that Nation, to the Growth of the Ottoman Empire: with the Lives and Conquests of their Princes and Emperors*, 3 vols., 6th edn (London: printed for Tho. Basset, 1687) ['Solyman the Magnificent, Fourth Emperor of the Turks'] *

Locke, John, *An Essay Concerning Human Understanding*, ed. Peter H. Nidditch (Oxford: Clarendon Press, 1975)

Mayne, Jasper, *A late Printed Sermon Against False Prophets, Vindicated by Letter, from the causeless Aspersions of Mr. Francis Cheynell* ([Oxford?]: 1647) *

Mews, Peter, 'Ex-ale-tation' in Francis Beaumont and John Fletcher, *Poems. The golden remains of those so much admired dramatick poets, Francis Beaumont & John Fletcher gent* (London: W. Hope, 1660) **

Milton, John, *Complete Poems and Major Prose*, ed. Merritt Y. Hughes (Indianapolis: The Odyssey Press, 1957) [*Comus*, 'Lycidas', 'On the Morning of Christ's Nativity', *Paradise Lost, Paradise Regained, Samson Agonistes*]

More, Henry, *Divine Dialogues, Containing sundry Disquisitions & Instructions Concerning the Attributes of God and his Providence in the World*, 2nd edn (London: Joseph Downing, 1713) ['First Dialogue', 'Second Dialogue'] *

Moxon, Joseph, *Mechanick Exercises. Or the Doctrine of Handy-works*, 3rd edn (London: printed for Dan. Midwinter and Tho. Leigh, 1703) ['The Art of Joinery', 'Of Smithing in General']*

Peacham, Henry, *The Compleat Gentleman*, Third Impression . . . inlarged by [Thomas Blount] (London: E. Tyler for Richard Thrale, 1661) ['The Gentleman's Exercise'] *

Philips, John, *The Poems of John Philips*, ed. M. G. Lloyd Thomas (Oxford: Basil Blackwell, 1927) ['Bleinheim', 'Cyder']

Pope, Alexander, *The Poems of Alexander Pope*, gen. ed. John Butt, 11 vols. (London: Methuen, 1939–69) ['Astraea Redux', *The Dunciad*, 'Elegy to the Memory of an Unfortunate Lady', 'Epilogue to the Satires. Written in 1738. Dialogue I', 'Epistle III: To Lord Bathurst', 'The First Book of Statius his Thebais', *The Iliad*, 'Messiah. A Sacred Eclogue, In imitation of Virgil's Pollio', *The Odyssey*, 'Sandys's Ghost: Or a Proper New Ballad on the New Ovid's *Metamorphosis*']

Prior, Matthew, *The Literary Works of Matthew Prior*, ed. H. Bunker Wright and Monroe K. Spears, 2nd edn, 2 vols. (Oxford: Clarendon Press, 1971) ['Alma: or, the Progress of the Mind', 'Carmen Seculare, 1700. To the King', 'Second Hymn of Callimachus. To Apollo', 'Solomon on the Vanity of the World']

Raleigh, Sir Walter, *The Historie of the World. In Five Books . . . by Sir Walter Ralegh, Kt.*, 11th edn, 2 vols. (London: G. Conyers, J. J. and P. Knapton [et al.], 1736) *

Ray, John, *The Wisdom of God Manifested in the Works of the Creation. In Two Parts*, 11th edn, 'corrected' (London: printed for W. Innys, 1743) *

Rowe, Nicholas, *The Works of Nicholas Rowe, Esq.*, 2 vols. (London: H. Lintot, J. and R. Tonson and S. Draper, 1747) [*The Ambitious Step-Mother*] *

Sandys, George, *A Paraphrase Upon the Divine Poems* (London: J. M. for Abel Roper, 1676) ['A Paraphrase upon Job'] *

Shakespeare, William, *The Riverside Shakespeare: The Complete Works*, 2nd edn, ed. G. Blakemore Evans, J. J. M. Tobin [et al.] (Boston: Houghton Mifflin Company, 1997)

*The Works of Shakespear in eight volumes. The genuine text, collated with all the former editions, and then corrected and emended, is here settled; being restored from the blunders of the first editors, and the interpolations of the two last: with a comment and notes, critical and explanatory. By Mr. Pope and Mr. Warburton. [Edited by the latter.]* 8 vols. (J. and P. Knapton [et al.]: London, 1747); marked for the *Dictionary*. [*All's Well that Ends Well, Antony and Cleopatra, As You Like It, Coriolanus, Cymbeline, Hamlet,* 1 and 2 *Henry IV, Henry V,* 1, 2 and 3 *Henry VI, Henry VIII, Julius Caesar, King Lear, Love's Labour's Lost, Measure for Measure, Merry Wives of Windsor, Othello, Richard II, Richard III, The Taming of the Shrew, The Tempest, Timon of Athens, Titus Andronicus, Troilus and Cressida, Twelfth Night, The Winter's Tale*] ***

Sheffield, John, First Duke of Buckingham, *The Works of John Sheffield, Earl of Mulgrave, Marquis of Normanby, and Duke of Buckingham*, 3rd edn 'corrected', 2 vols. (London: T. Wotton [et al.], 1740) ['Some Account of the Revolution'] *

Sidney, Sir Philip, *The Countess of Pembroke's Arcadia (the New Arcadia)*, ed. Victor Skretkowicz (Oxford: Clarendon Press, 1987)

South, Robert, *Twelve Sermons Preached upon Several Occasions* (London: printed by J. H. for Thomas Bennet, 1692) ['Sermons XI', 'XII'] *

*Twelve Sermons Preached upon Several Occasions. The Second volume.* (London: printed by J. H. for Thomas Bennet, 1694); marked for the *Dictionary*. ['Sermons XX', 'XXI'] ***

Spenser, Edmund, *The Works of Edmund Spenser: A Variorum Edition*. ed. Edwin Greenlaw, Charles Grosvenor Osgood, Frederick Morgan Padelford and Ray Heffner (Baltimore: The Johns Hopkins University Press, 1949) [*Amoretti, The Faerie Queene*, 'Muiopotmos, or The Fate of the Butterflie', *The Shepheardes Calendar, A View of the Present State of Ireland*]

Swift, Jonathan, *The Poems of Jonathan Swift*, ed. Harold Williams, 2nd edn, 3 vols. (Oxford: Clarendon Press, 1958) ['The Legion Club', 'A Pastoral Dialogue', 'Some Free Thoughts Upon the Present State of Affairs', 'The Story of Baucis and Philemon']

*The Prose Works of Jonathan Swift*, ed. Herbert Davis, 14 vols. (Oxford: Basil Blackwell, 1939–68) [*Directions to Servants*, 'A Letter to the Shop-Keepers, Tradesmen, Farmers and Common-People of Ireland', 'Preface to *the Bishop of Sarum's Introduction*']

Taylor, Jeremy, *The Worthy Communicant: Or, a Discourse of the Nature, Effects, and Blessings consequent to the Worthy Receiving of the Lords Supper* (London: printed for Richard Wellington, 1701) *

Thomson, James, *The Seasons*, ed. James Sambrook (Oxford: Clarendon Press, 1981)

Tusser, Thomas, *Five Hundred Points of Husbandry: Directing What Corn, Grass, &c. is proper to be sown*, ed. [with notes] Daniel Hillman (London: printed for M. Cooper, 1744) **

Waller, Edmund, *The Works of Edmund Waller, Esq., in Verse and Prose. Published by Mr. Fenton* (London: printed for J. and R. Tonson and S. Draper, 1744) ['A Panegyric to my Lord Protector, of the present Greatness, and joint Interest, of his Highness and this Nation'] *

Walton, Izaak, *The Compleat Angler, 1653–1676*, ed. Jonquil Bevan (Oxford: Clarendon Press, 1983)

Whitgift, John, *The Works of John Whitgift, D. D.*, ed. John Ayre, 3 vols. (Cambridge: Cambridge University Press, 1851–53) ['The Defence of the Answer to the Admonition, against the reply of Thomas Cartwright']

Wiseman, Richard, *Eight Chirurgical Treatises, On these Following Heads . . .* 6th edn, 2 vols. (London: J. Walthoe [et al.], 1734) *

Woodward, John, *An Attempt Towards a Natural History of the Fossils of England; in A Catalogue of the English Fossils in the Collection of J. Woodward, M. D.,* 2 vols. (London: F. Fayram, J. Senex, J. Osborn and T. Longman, 1728–29) ***

*An Essay Toward a Natural History of the Earth: And Terrestrial Bodies, Especially Minerals: As Also of the Sea, Rivers, and Springs* (London: printed for Ric. Wilkin, 1695) **

Wotton, Henry, *Reliquiae Wottonianae: or, a Collection of Lives, Letters, Poems, with Characters of Sundry Personages*, 4th edn (London: B. Tooke and T. Sawbridge, 1685) ['The Life and Death of the Duke of Buckingham'] *

Photographic facsimile

a ⧧

Like panels round of marble clear
Where azur'd veins well mixt appear
Sidn. 1.



IL facing 2N[r] (misbound facing 2M[r])

3 Not level; unevenly.
I hap to step *awry*, where I see no path, and can discern but few steps afore me. *Brerewood on Languages.*

4. Not equally between two points.
Not tyrants fierce that unrepenting die,
Not Cynthia when her manteau's pinn'd *awry*,
Ere felt such rage. *Pope's Rape of the Lock.*

5. Not in a right state; perversely.
All *awry*, and which wried it to the most wry course of all, wit abused, rather to feign reason why it should be amiss, than how it should be amended. *Sidney, b. ii.*

Much of the soul they talk, but all *awry*,
And in themselves seek virtue, and to themselves
All glory arrogate, to God give none. *Paradise Regained.*

AXE. *n. s.* [eax, acse, Sax. *ascia*, Lat.] An instrument consisting of a metal head, with a sharp edge, fixed in a helve or handle, to cut with.

No metal can,
No, not the hangman's *axe*, bear half the keenness
Of thy sharp envy. *Shakesp. Merchant of Venice.*

There stood a forest on the mountain's brow,
Which overlook'd the shaded plains below;
No sounding *axe* presum'd these trees to bite,
Coeval with the world; a venerable sight. *Dryden's Fables.*

AXILLA. *n. s.* [*axilla*, Lat.] The cavity under the upper part of the arm, called the arm-pit. *Quincy.*

AXI'LLAR. } *adj.* [from *axilla*, Lat.] Belonging to the arm-
A'XILLARY. } pit.

In the same manner is the *axillary* artery distributed unto the hand; below the cubit, it divideth unto two parts.
*Brown's Vulgar Errours.*

A'XIOM. *n. s.* [*axioma*, Lat. ἀξίωμα, from ἀξιόω.]

1. A proposition evident at first sight, that cannot be made plainer by demonstration.
*Axioms*, or principles more general, are such as this, that the greater good is to be chosen before the lesser. *Hooker, l. i.*

2. An established principle to be granted without new proof.
The *axioms* of that law, whereby natural agents are guided, have their use in the moral. *Hooker, b. i.*
Their affirmations are unto us no *axioms*; we esteem thereof as things unsaid, and account them but in list of nothing.
*Brown's Vulgar Errours, b. i.*

A'XIS. *n. s.* [*axis*, Lat.] The line real or imaginary that passes through any thing, on which it may revolve.

But since they say our earth, from morn to morn,
On its own *axis* is oblig'd to turn;
That swift rotation must disperse in air
All things which on the rapid orb appear. *Blackmore.*

It might annually have compassed the sun, and yet never have once turned upon its *axis*. *Bentley's Sermons.*

On their own *axis* as the planets run,
And make at once their circle round the sun;
So two consistent motions act the soul,
And one regards itself, and one the whole.
*Pope's Essay on Man, epist. iii. l. 313.*

A'XLE. } *n. s.* [*axis*, Lat.] The pin which passes through
A'XLE-TREE. } the midst of the wheel, on which the circumvolutions of the wheel are performed. Axle tree is now generally used in prose.

Venerable Nestor
Should with a bond of air, strong as the *axle-tree*
On which heav'n rides, knit all the Grecians ears
To his experienc'd tongue. *Shakesp. Troilus and Cressida.*

The fly sate upon the *axle-tree* of the chariot-wheel, and said, what a dust do I raise? *Bacon's Essays.*

And the gilded car of day
His glowing *axle* doth allay
In the steep Atlantick stream. *Milton's Comus.*

He saw a greater sun appear,
Than his bright throne or burning *axle-tree* could bear.
*Milton's Christ's Nativity.*

AY. *adv.* [perhaps from *aio*, Lat.]

1. Yes; an *adverb* of answering affirmatively.
Return you thither?——
—*Ay*, madam, with the swiftest wing of speed.
*Shakesp. All's well that ends well.*
What say'st thou? Wilt thou be of our consort?
Say *ay*; and be the captain of us all.
*Shakesp. Two Gentlemen of Verona.*

2. It is a word by which the sense is enforced; even; yes, certainly; and more than that.
Remember it, and let it make thee crest-fall'n;
*Ay*, and allay this thy abortive pride. *Shakesp. Henry VI.*

AYE. *adv.* [apa, Saxon.] Always; to eternity; for ever. anciently they said for aye as now for ever.

And now in darksome dungeon, wretched thrall,
Remedyless for *aye* he doth him hold. *Fairy Queen, b. i.*

Either prepare to die,
Or on Diana's altar to protest,
For *aye*, austerity and single life.
*Shakespeare's Midsummer Night's Dream.*

The soul, though made in time, survives for *aye*;
And, though it hath beginning, sees no end.
*Sir John Davies.*

And hears the muses, in a ring,
*Aye* round about Jove's altar sing. *Milton's Il Penseroso.*

Th' astonish'd mariners *aye* ply the pump;
No stay, nor rest, till the wide breach is clos'd. *Philips.*

A'YGREEN. *n. s.* The same with *houseleek*; which see. *Dict.*

A'YRY. *n. s.* [See AIRY.] The nest of a bird of prey
I should discourse on the branches, the haggard, and then treat of their several *ayries*. *Walton's Angler.*

A'ZIMUTH. *n. s.* [Arab.]

1. The *azimuth* of the sun, or of a star, is an arch between the meridian of the place and any given vertical line.

2. *Magnetical azimuth*, is an arch of the horizon contained between the sun's *azimuth* circle and the magnetical meridian; or it is the apparent distance of the sun from the north or south point of the compass.

3. *Azimuth Compass*, is an instrument used at sea for finding the sun's magnetical *azimuth*.

4. *Azimuth Dial*, is a dial whose style or gnomon is at right angles to the plane of the horizon.

5. *Azimuths*, called also vertical circles, are great circles intersecting each other in the zenith and nadir, and cutting the horizon at right angles, in all the points thereof. *Chambers.*

AZU'RE. *adj.* [*azur*, Fr. *azurro*, Span. *lazur*, Arab. from *lazuli*, a blue stone.] Blue; faint blue.

The blue of the first order, though very faint and little, may be the colour of some substances; and the *azure* colour of the skies seems to be of this order. *Newton's Opticks.*

Thus replies
Minerva, graceful with her *azure* eyes. *Pope's Odyssey, b. i.*

The sea,
Far through his *azure* turbulent domain,
Your empire owns. *Thomson's Spring.*

Azured adj [from azure]
Blue; having the colour of azure. a f

# B.



B, The ſecond letter of the Engliſh alphabet, is pronounced as in moſt other European languages, by preſſing the whole length of the lips together, and forcing them open with a ſtrong breath. It has a near affinity with the other labial letters, and is confounded by the Germans with *P*, and by the Gaſcons with *V*; from which an epigrammatiſt remarks, that *bibere* and *vivere* are in Gaſcony the ſame. The Spaniards, in moſt words, uſe *B* or *V* indifferently.

BAA. *n. ſ.* [See the verb.] The cry of a ſheep.

To BAA. *v. n.* [*balo*, Lat.] To cry like a ſheep.

Or like a lamb, whoſe dam away is ſet,
He treble *baas* for help, but none can get. *Sidney.*

To BA'BBLE. *v. n.* [*babbelen*, Germ. *babiller*, Fr.]

1. To prattle like a child; to prate imperfectly.

My *babbling* praiſes I repeat no more,
But hear, rejoice, ſtand ſilent, and adore. *Prior.*

2. To talk idly, or irrationally.

John had conned over a catalogue of hard words; theſe he uſed to *babble* indifferently in all companies. *Arbuthn. J. Bull.*

Let the ſilent ſanctuary ſhow,
What from the *babbling* ſchools we may not know. *Prior.*

3. To talk thoughtleſsly; to tell ſecrets.

There is more danger in a reſerved and ſilent friend, than in a noiſy *babbling* enemy. *L'Eſtrange.*

4. To talk much.

The *babbling* echo mocks the hounds,
Replying ſhrilly to the well tun'd horns,
As if a double hunt were heard at once. *Shakeſp. Tit. Andr.*

And had I pow'r to give that knowledge birth,
In all the ſpeeches of the *babbling* earth. *Prior.*

The *babbling* echo had deſcry'd his face;
She, who in others words her ſilence breaks. *Addiſon's Ovid.*

BA'BBLE. *n. ſ.* [*babil*, Fr.] Idle talk; ſenſeleſs prattle.

This *babble* ſhall not henceforth trouble me;
Here is a coil with proteſtation! *Shakeſp. Two G. of Verona.*

Come, no more,
This is mere moral *babble*. *Milton.*

With volleys of eternal *babble*,
And clamour more unanſwerable. *Hudibras.*

The *babble*, impertinence, and folly, I have taken notice of in diſputes. *Glanville's Sceptis Scientifica.*

BA'BBLEMENT. *n. ſ.* [from *babble.*] Senſeleſs prate.

Deluded all this while with ragged notions and *babblements*, while they expected worthy and delightful knowledge. *Milton.*

BA'BBLER. *n. ſ.* [from *babble.*]

1. An idle talker; an irrational prattler.

We hold our time too precious to be ſpent
With ſuch a *babbler*. *Shakeſp. King John.*

Great *babblers*, or talkers, are not fit for truſt. *L'Eſtrange.*

The apoſtle of my text had no ſooner propoſed it to the greater maſters at Athens, but he himſelf was ridiculed as a *babbler*. *Rogers.*

2. A teller of ſecrets.

Utterers of ſecrets he from thence debarr'd;
*Babblers* of folly, and blazers of crime. *Fairy Queen, b.* ii.

BABE. *n. ſ.* [*baban*, Welch; *babbaerd*, Dutch.] An infant; a child of either ſex.

Thoſe that do teach your *babes*,
Do it with gentle means, and eaſy taſks;
He might have chid me ſo: for, in good faith,
I am a child to chiding. *Shakeſp. Othello.*

Nor ſhall Sebaſtian's formidable name
Be longer us'd, to lull the crying *babe*. *Dryden's Don Seb.*

The *babe* had all that infant care beguiles,
And early knew his mother in her ſmiles. *Dryden.*

BA'BERY. *n. ſ.* [from *babe.*] Finery to pleaſe a babe or child.

So have I ſeen trim books in velvet dight,
With golden leaves and painted *babery*
Of ſeely boys, pleaſe unacquainted ſight. *Sidney.*

BA'BISH. *adj.* [from *babe.*] Childiſh.

If he be baſhful, and will ſoon bluſh, they call him a *babiſh* and ill brought up thing. *Aſcham's Schoolmaſter.*

BABO'ON. *n. ſ.* [*babouin*, Fr. It is ſuppoſed by *Skinner* to be the augmentation of *babe*, and to import a *great babe.*] A monkey of the largeſt kind.

You had looked through the grate like a geminy of *baboons*. *Shakeſp. Merry Wives of Windſor.*

He caſt every human feature out of his countenance, and became a *baboon*. *Addiſon. Spect.* Nº 174.

BA'BY. *n. ſ.* [See BABE.]

1. A child; an infant.

The *baby* beats the nurſe, and quite athwart
Goes all decorum. *Shakeſp. Meaſure for Meaſure.*

The child muſt have ſugar plumbs, rather than make the poor *baby* cry. *Locke.*



He muſt marry, and propagate: the father cannot ſtay for the portion, nor the mother for *babies* to play with. *Locke.*

2. A ſmall image in imitation of a child, which girls play with.

The archduke ſaw that Perkin would prove a runnagate, and that it was the part of children to fall out about *babies*. *Bacon's Henry* VII.

Since no image can repreſent the great Creator, never think to honour him by your fooliſh puppets, and *babies* of dirt and clay. *Stillingfleet's Def. of Diſc. on Rom. Idolatry.*

BA'CCATED. *adj.* [*baccatus*, Lat.] Beſet with pearls; having many berries. *Dict.*

BACCHANA'LIAN. *n. ſ.* [from *bacchanalia*, Lat.] A riotous perſon; a drunkard.

BA'CCHANALS. *n. ſ.* [*bacchanalia*, Lat.] The drunken feaſts and revels of Bacchus, the god of wine.

Ha, my brave emperor, ſhall we dance now the Egyptian *bacchanals*, and celebrate our drink? *Shakeſp. Ant. and Cleop.*

What wild fury was there in the heathen *bacchanals*, which we have not ſeen equalled. *Decay of Piety.*

Both extremes were baniſhed from their walls,
Carthuſian faſts, and fulſome *bacchanals*. *Pope.*

B'ACCHUS BOLE. *n. ſ.* A flower not tall, but very full and broad-leaved; of a ſad light purple, and a proper white; having the three outmoſt leaves edged with a crimſon colour, bluiſh bottom, and dark purple. *Mortimer.*

BACCI'FEROUS. *adj.* [from *bacca*, a berry, and *fero*, to bear, Lat.] Berry-bearing.

*Bacciferous* trees are of four kinds.

1. Such as bear a caliculate or naked berry; the flower and calix both falling off together, and leaving the berry bare; as the ſaſſafras trees.

2. Such as have a naked monoſpermous fruit, that is, containing in it only one ſeed; as the arbutes.

3. Such as have but polyſpermous fruit, that is, containing two or more kernels or ſeeds within it; as the jaſminum, liguſtrum.

4. Such as have their fruit compoſed of many acini, or round ſoft balls ſet cloſe together like a bunch of grapes; as the uva marina. *Ray.*

BACCI'VOROUS. *adj.* [from *bacca*, a berry, and *voro*, to devour, Lat.] Devourer of berries. *Dict.*

BA'CHELOR. *n. ſ.* [This is a word of very uncertain etymology, it not being well known what was its original ſenſe. *Junius* derives it from βάκηλος, fooliſh; *Menage*, from *bas chevalier*, a knight of the loweſt rank; *Spelman*, from *baculus*, a ſtaff; *Cujas*, from *buccella*, an allowance of proviſion. The moſt probable derivation ſeems to be from *bacca laurus*, the berry of a laurel or bay; bachelors being young, are of good hopes, like laurels in the berry. In Latin, *baccalaureus.*]

1. A man unmarried.

Such ſeparation
Becomes a virtuous *bachelor* and a maid.
*Shakeſp. Midſummer Night's Dream.*

The haunting of thoſe diſſolute places, or reſort to courteſans, are no more puniſhed in married men than in *bachelors*. *Bacon's New Atlantis.*

A true painter naturally delights in the liberty which belongs to the *bachelor's* eſtate. *Dryden's Dufreſnoy.*

Let ſinful *bachelors* their woes deplore,
Full well they merit all they feel, and more. *Pope.*

2. A man who takes his firſt degrees at the univerſity in any profeſſion.

Being a boy, new *bachelor* of arts, I chanced to ſpeak againſt the pope. *Aſcham's Schoolmaſter.*

I appear before your honour, in behalf of Martinus Scriblerus, *bachelor* of phyſick. *Arbuthn. and Pope's Mart. Scriblerus.*

3. A knight of the loweſt order. This is a ſenſe now little uſed.

BA'CHELORS *Button.* [See CAMPION, of which it is a ſpecies.] All the ſorts of this plant are hardy; they grow above two foot, and produce their flower in June and July. *Millar.*

BA'CHELORSHIP. *n. ſ.* [from *bachelor.*] The condition of a bachelor.

Her mother, living yet, can teſtify,
She was the firſt fruit of my *bachelorſhip*. *Shakeſp. Hen.* VI.

BACK. *n. ſ.* [bac, bæc, Sax. *back*, Germ.]

1. The hinder part of the body, from the neck to the thighs.

As the voice goeth round, as well towards the *back* as towards the front of him that ſpeaketh, ſo likewiſe doth the echo: for you have many *back* echoes to the place where you ſtand. *Bacon's Nat. Hiſt.* Nº 247.

Part following enter, part remain without,
With envy hear their fellow's conqu'ring ſhout;
And mount on others *backs*, in hope to ſhare. *Dryden.*

2. The outer part of the hand when it is ſhut; oppoſed to the *palm*.

Methought love pitying me, when he ſaw this,
Gave me your hands, the *backs* and palms to kiſs. *Donne.*

3 3. The

Some imagining themselves possessed with a divine fury, far from being carried into the rage of Bachanalians, fall into toys which are only puerilities

Adject.
Jovial, extravagantly merry.

Some of his Odes are panegyrical; others moral; the rest jovial, or if I may so call them Bachainalian    Dryd.

As a poor pedlar he did wend
Bearing a truss of trifles at his back
As bells & babies & glasses in his Pack
Spens. Pas

Baby. [Babee]
In Scotland denotes a halfpenny; .. as alluding to the Head impressed on the Copper coin

Babion. Menage says this is a Syriac Word which Signifies a Child or puppet. From which bambo, bambino, bambinore. Ital. babil babilote fr. are derived    Trev.

Thinkest thou, mime, this is great or that they strive
Whose noise shall keep thy miming most alive
Whilst thou dost raise some play'r from the grave
Out dance the babion, or out boast the brave.
B. Johns.

Bachrach
Restor'd the fainting high and mighty
With brandy wine and Aquavitæ
And made them stoutly overcome
With bachrach hoccamor & Mum
Hud. 3.3

IL facing 2N[v]

blank page

3. The outward part of the body; that which requires cloaths; opposed to the *belly*.

Those who, by their ancestors, have been set free from a constant drudgery to their *backs* and their bellies, should bestow some time on their heads. *Locke.*

4. The rear; opposed to the *van*.

He might conclude, that Walter would be upon the king's *back*, as his majesty was upon his. *Clarendon, b.* viii.

5. The place behind.

Antheus, Sergestus grave, Cleanthus strong,
And at their *backs* a mighty Trojan throng. *Dryden.*

6. The part of any thing out of sight.

Trees set upon the *backs* of chimneys do ripen fruit sooner. *Bacon's Nat. Hist.* N° 856.

7. The thick part of any tool, opposed to the edge; as the *back* of a knife or sword; whence *backsword*, or sword with a *back*; ~~as~~

Bull dreaded not old Lewis either at *backsword*, single faulchion, or cudgel-play. *Arbuthnot's History of J. Bull.*

8. To turn the *back* on one, is to forsake him, or neglect him.

At the hour of death, all the friendships of the world shall bid him adieu, and the whole creation turn its *back* upon him. *South.*

9. To turn the *back*, is to go away; to be not within the reach of taking cognizance.

His *back* was no sooner turned, but they returned to their former rebellion. *Sir J. Davies on Ireland.*

BACK. *adv.* [from the noun.]

1. To the place from which one came.

*Back* you shall not to the house, unless
You undertake that with me. *Shakesp. Twelfth Night.*

He sent many to seek ~~the ship~~ Argo, threatening that if they brought not *back* Medea, they should suffer in her stead. *Raleigh's History of the World.*

But where they are, and why they came not *back*,
Is now the labour of my thoughts. *Milton.*
*Back* to thy native island might'st thou sail,
And leave half-heard the melancholy tale. *Pope's Odyssey.*

2. ~~Backwards~~ from the present station [to the former].

I've been surprised in an unguarded hour,
But must not now go *back*; the love that lay
Half smother'd in my breast, has broke through all
Its weak restraints. *Addison's Cato.*

3. Behind; not coming forward.

I thought to promote thee unto great honour; but lo the Lord hath kept thee *back* from honour. *Numb.* xxiv. 11.

~~Constrains the globe,~~ keeps *back* the hurtful weed. *Blackmore's Creation, b.* ii.

4. Toward things past.

I had always a curiosity to look *back* unto the ~~sorrows~~ [origin] of things, and to view in my mind the beginning and progress of a rising world. *Burnet's Theory of the Earth.*

5. Again; in return.

The lady's mad; yet if 'twere so,
She could not sway her house, command her followers,
Take and give *back* affairs, and their despatch,
With such a smooth, discreet, and stable bearing. *Shakesp. Twelfth Night.*

6. Again; a second time.

This Cæsar found, and that ungrateful age,
With losing him, went *back* to blood and rage. *Waller.*

The epistles being written from ladies forsaken by their lovers, many thoughts came *back* upon us in divers letters. *Dryd.*

To BACK. *v. a.* [from the noun *back*.]

1. To mount on the back of a horse.

That roan shall be my throne.
Well I will *back* him strait. ~~O Esperance!~~
~~Bid Butler lead him forth into the park.~~ *Shak. Henry* IV.

2. To break a horse; to train him to bear upon his back.

Direct us how to *back* the winged horse;
Favour his flight, and moderate his course. *Roscommon.*

3. To place upon the back.

As I slept, methought
Great Jupiter, upon his eagle *back'd*,
Appear'd to me. *Shakesp. Cymbeline.*

4. To maintain; to strengthen.

Belike, he means,
*Back'd* by the pow'r of Warwick, that false peer,
T' aspire unto the crown. *Shakesp. Henry* VI.

You are strait enough in the shoulders, you care not who sees your back: call you that *backing* of your friends? a plague upon such *backing!* give me them that will face me. *Sh. H.* VI.

These were seconded by certain demilaunces, and both *backed* with men at arms. *Sir J. Hayward.*

Did they not swear, in express words,
To prop and *back* the house of lords?
And after turn'd out the whole houseful. *Hudibras.*

A great malice, *backed* with a great interest, can have no advantage of a man, but from his expectations of something without himself. *South.*

How shall we treat this bold aspiring man?
Success still follows him, and *backs* his crimes. *Addis. Cato.*

5. To justify; to support.

The patrons of the ternary number of principles, and those that would have five elements, endeavour to *back* their experiments with a specious reason. *Boyle.*

We have I know not how many adages to *back* the reason of this moral. *L'Estrange.*

6. To second.

Factious, and fav'ring this or t'other side,
Their wagers *back* their wishes. *Dryden's Fables.*

To BA'CKBITE. *v. a.* [from *back* and *bite*.] To censure or reproach the absent.

Most untruly and maliciously do these evil tongues *backbite* and slander the sacred ashes ~~of that most just and honourable personage.~~ *Spenser's Ireland.*

I will use him well; ~~a friend i' th' court is better than a penny in purse.~~ Use his men well, ~~Davy,~~ for they are arrant knaves, and will *backbite*. *Shakesp. Henry* IV.

BA'CKBITER. *n. s.* [from *backbite*.] A privy calumniator; a censurer of the absent.

No body is bound to look upon his *backbiter*, or his underminer, his betrayer, or his oppressor, as his friend. *South.*

BA'CKBONE. *n. s.* [from *back* and *bone*.] The bone of the back.

The *backbone* should be divided into many vertebres for commodious bending, and not be one entire rigid bone. *Ray.*

BA'CKCARRY. Having on the back.

Manwood, in his forest laws, noteth it for one of the four circumstances, or cases, wherein a forester may arrest an offender against vert or venison in the forest, *viz.* stable-stand, dog-draw, *backcarry*, and bloody hand. *Cowel.*

BA'CKDOOR. *n. s.* [from *back* and *door*.] The door behind the house; privy passage.

The procession durst not return by the way it came; but, after the devotion of the monks, passed out at a *backdoor* of the convent. *Addison on Italy.*

Popery, which is so far shut out as not to re-enter openly, is stealing in by the *backdoor* of atheism. *Atterbury.*

BA'CKED. *adj.* [from *back*.] Having a back.

Lofty-neck'd,
Sharp headed, barrel belly'd, broadly *back'd*. *Dryd. Virgil.*

BA'CKFRIEND. *n. s.* [from *back* and *friend*.] A friend backwards; that is, an enemy in secret.

Set the restless importunities of talebearers and *backfriends* against fair words and professions. *L'Estrange.*

Far is our church from encroaching upon the civil power; as some who are *backfriends* to both, would maliciously insinuate. *South.*

BACKGA'MMON. *n. s.* [from *bach gammon*, Welch, a little battle.] A play or game at tables, with box and dice.

In what esteem are you with the vicar of the parish? can you play with him at *backgammon?* *Swift.*

BA'CKHOUSE. *n. s.* [from *back* and *house*.] The buildings behind the chief part of the house.

Their *backhouses*, of more necessary than cleanly service, as kitchens, stables, are climbed up unto by steps. *Carew's ~~Survey~~ of Cornwal.*

BA'CKPIECE. *n. s.* [from *back* and *piece*.] The piece of armour which covers the back.

The morning that he was to join battle, his armourer put on his *backpiece* before, and his breastplate behind. *Camden.*

BA'CKROOM. *n. s.* [from *back* and *room*.] A room behind; not in the front.

If you have a fair prospect backwards of gardens, it may be convenient to make *backrooms* the larger. *Mox. Mech. Exerc.*

BA'CKSIDE. *n. s.* [from *back* and *side*.]

1. The hinder part of any thing.

If the quicksilver were rubbed from the *backside* of the speculum, the glass would cause the same rings of colours, but more faint; the phænomena depends not upon the quicksilver, unless so far as it encreases the reflection of the *backside* of the glass. *Newton's Opticks.*

2. The hind part of an animal.

A poor ant carries a grain of corn, climbing up a wall with her head downwards and her *backside* upwards. *Addison.*

3. The yard or ground behind a house.

The wash of pastures, fields, commons, roads, streets, or *backsides*, are of great advantage to all sorts of land. *Mortimer.*

To BACKSLI'DE. *v. n.* [from *back* and *slide*.] To fall off; to apostatize: a word only used by divines.

Hast thou seen that which *backsliding* Israel hath done? She is gone up upon every high mountain, and under every green tree. *Jeremiah,* iii. 6.

BACKSLI'DER. *n. s.* [from *backslide*.] An apostate.

The *backslider* in heart shall be filled. *Prov.* xiv. 14.

BA'CKSTAFF. *n. s.* [from *back* and *staff*; because, in taking an observation, the observer's back is turned towards the sun.] An instrument useful in taking the sun's altitude at sea; invented by Captain Davies.

BA'CKSTAIRS. *n. s.* [from *back* and *stairs*.] The private stairs in the house.

I condemn the practice which hath lately crept into the court at the *backstairs*, that some pricked for sheriffs get out of the bill. *Bacon's Advice to Sir George Villiers.*

BACK-

Ba'ckstays. *n. ſ.* [from *back* and *ſtay.*] Ropes or ſtays which keep the maſts of a ſhip from pitching forward or overboard.

Ba'cksword. *n. ſ.* [from *back* and *ſword.*] A ſword with one ſharp edge.

Bull dreaded not old Lewis at *backſword.* *Arbuth. J. Bull.*

Ba'ckward. } *adv.* [from *back* and peaɲꝺ, Sax. that is, to-
Ba'ckwards. } wards the back.]

1. With the back forwards.

They went *backward*, and their faces were *backward.* *Gen.* ix.

2. Towards the back.

In leaping with weights, the arms are firſt caſt *backwards*, and then forwards, with ſo much the greater force; for the hands go *backward* before they take their riſe. *Bacon's Nat. H.*

3. On the back.

Then darting from her malignant eyes,
She caſt him *backward* as he ſtrove to riſe. *Dryden's Æneid.*

4. From the preſent ſtation to the place behind the back.

We might have met them dareful, beard to beard,
And beat them *backward* home. *Shakeſp. Macbeth.*

The monſtrous ſight
Struck them with horrour *backward*; but far worſe
Urg'd them behind. *Milton's Paradiſe Loſt, b.* vi.

5. Regreſſively.

Are not the rays of light, in paſſing by the edges and ſides of bodies, bent ſeveral times *backwards* and forwards with a motion like that of an eel? *Newton's Opticks.*

6. Towards ſomething paſt.

To prove the poſſibility of a thing, there is no argument to that which looks *backwards*; for what has been done or ſuffered, may certainly be done or ſuffered again. *South.*

7. Out of the progreſſive ſtate; reflex.

No, doubtleſs; for the mind can *backward* caſt
Upon herſelf, her underſtanding light. *Sir J. Davies.*

8. From a better to a worſe ſtate.

The work went *backward*; and the more he ſtrove
T' advance the ſuit, the farther from her love. *Dryden.*

9. Paſt; in time paſt.

They have ſpread one of the worſt languages in the world, if we look upon it ſome reigns *backwards.* *Locke.*

10. Perverſely; from the wrong end.

I never yet ſaw man,
But ſhe would ſpell him *backward*; if fair-fac'd,
She'd ſwear the gentleman ſhould be her ſiſter;
If black, why, nature, drawing of an antick,
Made a foul blot; if tall, a launce ill-headed.
*Shakeſp. Much ado about Nothing.*

Ba'ckward. *adj.*

1. Unwilling; averſe.

Cities laid waſte, they ſtorm'd the dens and caves;
For wiſer brutes are *backward* to be ſlaves. *Pope.*

We are ſtrangely *backward* to lay hold of this ſafe, this only method of cure. *Atterbury.*

Our mutability makes the friends of our nation *backward* to engage with us in alliances. *Addiſon. Freeholder.*

2. Heſitating.

All things are ready, if our minds be ſo;
Periſh the man, whoſe mind is *backward* now. *Shak. H. V.*

3. Sluggiſh; dilatory.

The mind is *backward* to undergo the fatigue of weighing every argument. *Watts's Improvement of the Mind.*

4. Dull; not quick or apprehenſive.

It often falls out, that the *backward* learner makes amends another way. *South.*

Ba'ckward. *n. ſ.* The things or ſtate behind or paſt.

What ſeeſt thou elſe
In the dark *backward* or abyſm of time? *Shakeſp. Tempeſt.*

Ba'ckwardly. *adv.* [from *backward.*]

1. Unwillingly; averſely; with the back forward.

Like Numid lions by the hunters chas'd,
Though they do fly, yet *backwardly* do go
With proud aſpect, diſdaining greater haſte. *Sidney.*

2. Perverſely.

I was the firſt man
That e'er receiv'd gift from him;
And does he think ſo *backwardly* of me,
That I'll requite it laſt? *Shakeſp. Timon.*

Ba'ckwardness. *n. ſ.* [from *backward.*] Dulneſs; unwillingneſs; ſluggiſhneſs.

The thing by which we are apt to excuſe our *backwardneſs* to good works, is the ill ſucceſs that hath been obſerved to attend well deſigned charities. *Atterbury.*

Ba'con. *n. ſ.* [probably from *baken*, that is, dried fleſh.]

1. The fleſh of a hog ſalted and dried.

High o'er the hearth a chine of *bacon* hung,
Good old Philemon ſeiz'd it with a prong,
Then cut a ſlice. *Dryden's Fables.*

2. To ſave the *bacon*, is a phraſe for preſerving one's ſelf from being unhurt; borrowed from the care of houſewives in the country, where they have ſeldom any other proviſion in the houſe than dried bacon, to ſecure it from the marching ſoldiers.

What frightens you thus? my good ſon! ſays the prieſt;
You murder'd, are ſorry, and have been confeſt.



O father! my ſorrow will ſcarce ſave my *bacon*;
For 'twas not that I murder'd, but that I was taken. *Prior.*

Baculo'metry. *n. ſ.* [from *baculus*, Lat. and μέτρον.] The art of meaſuring diſtances by one or more ſtaves. *Dict.*

BAD. *adj.* [*quaad*, Dutch; compar. *worſe*; ſuperl. *worſt.*]

1. Ill; not good: a general word uſed in regard to phyſical or moral faults, either of men or things.

Moſt men have politicks enough to make, through violence, the beſt ſcheme of government a *bad* one. *Pope.*

2. Vitious; corrupt.

Thou may'ſt repent,
And one *bad* act, with many deeds well done,
May'ſt cover. *Milton's Paradiſe Loſt, b.* xi. *l.* 256.

Thus will the latter, as the former, world
Still tend from *bad* to worſe. *Milton's Parad. Loſt, b.* xii.

Our unhappy fates
Mix thee amongſt the *bad*, or make thee run
Too near the paths, which virtue bids thee ſhun. *Prior.*

3. Unfortunate; unhappy.

The ſun his annual courſe obliquely made,
Good days contracted, and enlarg'd the *bad.* *Dryden.*

4. Hurtful; unwholeſome.

Reading was *bad* for his eyes, writing made his head ake. *Add.*

5. Sick.

Bad. } The preterite of *bid.*
Bade. }

And, for an earneſt of greater honour,
He *bad* me, from him, call thee Thane of Cawder. *Mach.*

Badge. *n. ſ.* [A word of uncertain etymology; derived by *Junius* from *bode* or *bade*, a meſſenger; and ſuppoſed to be corrupted from *badage*, the credential of a meſſenger: but taken by *Skinner* and *Minſhew* from *bagghe*, Dut. a jewel, or *bague*, a ring, Fr.]

1. A mark or cognizance worn to ſhew the relation of the wearer to any perſon or thing.

But on his breaſt a bloody croſs he bore,
The dear remembrance of his dying lord;
For whoſe ſweet ſake that glorious *badge* he wore. *Spenſer.*

The outward ſplendour of his office, is the *badge* and token of that glorious and ſacred character which he inwardly bears.
*Atterbury's Sermons.*

2. A token by which one is known.

A ſavage tygreſs on her helmet lies;
The famous *badge* Clarinda us'd to bear. *Fairfax, b.* ii.

3. The mark of any thing.

There appears much joy in him; even ſo much, that joy could not ſhew itſelf modeſt enough, without a *badge* of bitterneſs. *Shakeſp. Much ado about Nothing.*

Sweet mercy is nobility's true *badge.* *Shakeſ. Tit. Andron.*

Let him not bear the *badges* of a wreck,
Nor beg with a blue table on his back. *Dryden's Perſius.*

To Badge. *v. a.* [from the noun.] To mark as with a badge.

Your royal father's murder'd.——
—— Oh, by whom?——
Thoſe of his chamber, as it ſeem'd, had don't;
Their hands and faces were all *badg'd* with blood,
So were their daggers. *Shakeſp. Macbeth.*

Badger. *n. ſ.* [*bedour*, Fr.] An animal that earths in the ground, uſed to be hunted.

That a brock, or *badger*, hath legs of one ſide ſhorter than the other, is very generally received not only by theoriſts and unexperienced believers, but moſt who behold them daily.
*Brown's Vulgar Errours, b.* iii.

Badger legged. *adj.* [from *badger* and *legged.*] Having legs of an unequal length, as the badger is ſuppoſed to have.

His body crooked all over, big-bellied, *badger legged*, and his complexion ſwarthy. *L'Eſtrange.*

Ba'dger. *n. ſ.* [perhaps from the Latin *bajulus*, a carrier; but, by *Junius*, derived from the *badger*, a creature who ſtows up his proviſion.] One that buys corn and victuals in one place, and carries it unto another. *Cowel.*

Ba'dly. *adv.* [from *bad.*] In a bad manner; not well.

How goes the day with us? Oh tell me, Hubert.—
*Badly*, I fear. How fares your majeſty? *Shak. King John.*

Ba'dness. *n. ſ.* [from *bad.*] Want of good qualities, either natural or moral.

It was not your brother's evil diſpoſition made him ſeek his death; but a provoking merit, ſet awork by a reprovable *badneſs* in himſelf. *Shakeſp. King Lear.*

There is one convenience in this city, which makes ſome amends for the *badneſs* of the pavement. *Addiſon on Italy.*

I did not ſee how the *badneſs* of the weather could be the king's fault. *Addiſon. Freeholder.*

To Ba'ffle. *v. a.* [*beffier*, Fr.]

1. To elude.

They made a ſhift to think themſelves guiltleſs, in ſpite of all their ſins; to break the precept, and at the ſame time to *baffle* the curſe. *South.*

He hath deſerved to have the grace withdrawn, which he hath ſo long *baffled* and defied. *Atterbury.*

2. To confound; to defeat with ſome confuſion, as by perplexing or amuſing; to *baffle* is ſometimes leſs than to *conquer.*

Mezen-

Detractory

His forward Voice is to Speak well of his
friend: his backward Voice is to Spatter foul
Speeches and to detract Shak.

Baggagely adj. [Baggage]
Sorry, miserable, poor
No storing of pasture with baggagely tit
With ragged with aged & evil at hit.
Tuss. husb.

2 To allure; to entice ‡
If it be his estate that he drives at, he
will dazle his Eyes, and bait him in with the
luscious proposal of some gainful purchase
till the easy mans caught and hamper'd
South

Etruria lost,
He brings to Turnus' aid his *baffled* host. *Dryden's Æneid.*

When the mind has brought itself to close thinking, it may go on roundly. Every abstruse problem, every intricate question will not *baffle*, discourage, or break it. *Locke.*

3. To crush; to bring to nothing.

A foreign potentate trembles at a war with the English nation, ready to employ against him such revenues as shall *baffle* his designs upon their country. *Addison. Freeholder*, № 20.

BA'FFLE. *n. s.* [from the verb.] A defeat.

It is the skill of the disputant that keeps off a *baffle*. *South.*

The authors having missed of their aims, are fain to retreat with frustration and a *baffle*. *South.*

BA'FFLER. *n. s.* [from *baffle*.] He that puts to confusion, or defeats.

Experience, that great *baffler* of speculation, assures us the thing is too possible, and brings, in all ages, matter of fact to confute our suppositions. *Government of the Tongue*, § 2.

BAG. *n. s.* [belge, Sax. from whence perhaps by dropping, as is usual, the harsh consonant, came *bege*, *bage*, *bag*.]

1. A sack, or pouch, to put any thing in, as money, corn.

Cousin, away for England; haste before,
And, ere our coming, see thou shake the *bags*
Of hoarding abbots; their imprison'd angels
Set thou at liberty. *Shakesp. King John.*

What is it that opens thy mouth in praises? Is it that thy *bags* and thy barns are full? *South.*

Those waters were inclosed within the earth as in a *bag*. *Burnet's Theory of the Earth.*

Once, we confess, beneath the patriot's cloak,
From the crack'd *bag* the dropping guinea spoke. *Pope.*

2. That part of animals in which some particular juices are contained, as the poison of vipers.

The swelling poison of the several sects,
Which, wanting vent, the nation's health infects,
Shall burst its *bag*. *Dryden.*

Sing on, sing on, for I can ne'er be cloy'd;
So may thy cows their burden'd *bags* distend. *Dryden.*

3. An ornamental purse of silk tied to men's hair.

We saw a young fellow riding towards us full gallop, with a bob wig and black silken *bag* tied to it. *Addison. Spectator.*

4. A term used to signify different quantities of certain commodities; as a *bag* of pepper; a *bag* of hops.

To BAG. *v. a.* [from the noun.]

1. To put into a bag.

Accordingly he drain'd those marshy grounds,
And *bagg'd* them in a blue cloud. *Dryden's King Arthur.*

Hops ought not to be *bagged* up hot. *Mortimer's Husbandry.*

2. To load with a bag.

Like a bee *bagg'd* with his honey'd venom,
He brings it to your hive. *Dryden's Don Sebastian.*

To BAG. *v. n.* To swell like a full bag.

The skin seemed much contracted, yet it *bagged*, and had a porringer full of matter in it. *Wiseman's Surgery.*

Two kids that in the valley stray'd,
I found by chance, and to my fold convey'd:
They drain two *bagging* udders every day. *Dryden's Virgil.*

BA'GATELLE. *n. s.* [*bagatelle*, Fr.] A trifle; a thing of no importance.

Heaps of hair rings and cypher'd seals;
Rich trifles, serious *bagatelles*. *Prior.*

BA'GGAGE. *n. s.* [from *bag*, *bagage*, Fr.]

1. The furniture and utensils of an army.

The army was an hundred and seventy thousand footmen, and twelve thousand horsemen, beside the *baggage*. *Judith*, vii. 2.

Riches are the *baggage* of virtue; they cannot be spared, nor left behind, but they hinder the march. *Bacon.*

They were probably always in readiness, and carried among the *baggage* of the army. *Addison's Remarks on Italy.*

2. The goods that are to be carried away, as *bag* and *baggage*.

Dolabella designed, when his affairs grew desperate in Egypt, to pack up *bag* and *baggage*, and sail for Italy. *Arbuth. on Coins.*

3. A worthless woman; in French *bagasse*; so called, because such women follow camps.

A spark of indignation did rise in her, not to suffer such a *baggage* to win away any thing of hers. *Sidney.*

When this *baggage* meets with a man who has vanity to credit relations, she turns him to account. *Spectat.* № 205.

BA'GNIO. *n. s.* [*bagno*, Ital. a bath.] A house for bathing, sweating, and otherwise cleansing the body.

I have known two instances of malignant fevers produced by the hot air of a *bagnio*. *Arbuthnot on Air.*

BA'GPIPE. *n. s.* [from *bag* and *pipe*; the wind being received in a bag.] A musical instrument, consisting of a leathern bag, which blows up like a foot-ball, by means of a port vent or little tube fixed to it, and stopped by a valve; and three pipes or flutes, the first called the great pipe or drone, and the second the little one; which pass the wind out only at the bottom; the third has a reed, and is plaid on by compressing the bag under the arm, when full; and opening or stopping the holes, which are eight, with the fingers. The *bagpipe* takes in the compass of three octaves. *Chambers.*

No banners but shirts, with some bad *bagpipes* instead of drum and fife. *Sidney, b.* i.

He heard a *bagpipe*, and saw a general animated with the sound. *Addison. Freeholder*, № 27.

BAGPI'PER. *n. s.* [from *bagpipe*.] One that plays on a bagpipe.

Some that will evermore peep thro' their eyes,
And laugh, like parrots, at a *bagpiper*. *Shak. M. of Venice.*

BAGUETTE. *n. s.* [Fr. a term of architecture.] A little round moulding, less than an astragal; sometimes carved and enriched.

To BAIGNE. *v. a.* [*bagner*, Fr.] To drench; to soak: a word out of use.

The women forslow not to *baigne* them, unless they plead their heels, with a worse perfume than Jugurth found in the dungeon. *Carew's Survey of Cornwal.*

BAIL. *n. s.* [of this word the etymologists give many derivations; it seems to come from the French *bailler*, to put into the hand; to deliver up, as a man delivers himself up in surety.]

*Bail* is the freeing or setting at liberty one arrested or imprisoned upon action either civil or criminal, under security taken for his appearance. There is both common and special *bail*; *common bail* is in actions of small prejudice, or slight proof, called common, because any sureties in that case are taken: whereas, upon causes of greater weight, or apparent speciality, *special bail* or surety must be taken. There is a difference between *bail* and mainprise; for he that is mainprised, is at large, until the day of his appearance: but where a man is bailed, he is always accounted by the law to be in their ward and custody for the time, and they may, if they will, keep him in ward or in prison at that time, or otherwise at their will. *Cowel.*

Worry'd with debts, and past all hopes of *bail*,
The unpity'd wretch lies rotting in a jail. *Roscommon.*

And bribe with presents, or when presents fail,
They send their prostituted wives for *bail*. *Dryden.*

To BAIL. *v. a.* [from the noun.]

1. To give bail for another.

Let me be their bail—
They shall be ready at your highness' will,
To answer their suspicion——
Thou shalt not *bail* them. *Shakesp. Titus Andronicus.*

2. To admit to bail.

When they had *bailed* the twelve bishops, who were in the Tower, the house of commons, in great indignation, caused them immediately again to be recommitted to the Tower. *Clarendon.*

BA'ILABLE. *adj.* [from *bail*.] That may be set at liberty by bail or sureties.

BA'ILIFF. *n. s.* [a word of doubtful etymology in itself, but borrowed by us from *baillie*, Fr.]

1. A subordinate officer.

Lausanne is under the canton of Berne, and governed by a *bailiff* sent them every three years from the senate of Berne. *Addison on Italy.*

2. An officer whose business it is to execute arrests.

It many times happeneth, that, by the under-sheriffs and their *bailiffs*, the owner hath incurred the forfeiture, before he cometh to the knowledge of the process that runneth against him. *Bacon.*

A *bailiff*, by mistake, seized you for a debtor, and kept you the whole evening in a spunging-house. *Swift.*

Swift as a bard the *bailiff* leaves behind. *Pope.*

3. An under-steward of a manor.

BA'ILIWICK. *n. s.* [of *baillie*, Fr. and *ƿic*, Sax.] The place of the jurisdiction of a bailiff within his hundred, or the lord's franchise. It is that liberty which is exempted from the sheriff of the county, over which the lord of the liberty appointeth a bailiff. *Cowel.*

A proper officer is to walk up and down his *bailiwick*. *Spenser on Ireland.*

There issued writs to the sheriffs, to return the names of the several land-owners in their several *bailiwicks*. *Hale's Origin of Mankind.*

To BAIT. *v. a.* [baꞇan, Sax. *baitzen*, Germ.]

1. To put meat upon a hook, in some place, to tempt fish or other animals.

Oh, cunning enemy, that to catch a saint,
With saints dost *bait* thy hook! most dangerous
Is that temptation that doth goad us on
To sin in loving virtue. *Shakesp. Measure for Measure.*

Let's be revenged on him; let's appoint him a meeting, give him a show of comfort in his suit, and lead him on with a fine *baited* delay, till he hath pawned his horses to mine host of the garter. *Shakesp. Merry Wives of Windsor.*

Many sorts of fishes feed upon insects, as is well known to anglers, who *bait* their hooks with them. *Ray.*

How are the sex improv'd in am'rous arts!
What new-found snares they *bait* for human hearts! *Gay.*

2. To give meat to one's self, or horses, on the road.

What so strong,
But wanting rest, will also want of might?
The sun, that measures heaven all day long,
At night doth *bait* his steeds the ocean waves among. *F. Q.*

To BAIT. *v. a.* [from *battre*, Fr. to beat.] To attack with violence; to set dogs upon.

> Who seeming sorely chaffed at his band,
> As chained bear, whom cruel dogs do *bait*,
> With idle force did fain them to withstand. *Fairy Queen.*

> I will not yield
> To kiss the ground before young Malcolm's feet;
> And so be *baited* with the rabble's curse. *Shak. Macbeth.*

To BAIT. *v. n.* To stop at any place for refreshment; perhaps this word is more properly *bate*; to *abate* speed.

> But our desires, tyrannical extortion
> Doth force us there to set our chief delightfulness,
> Where but a *baiting* place is all our portion. *Sidney.*

> As one who on his journey *baits* at noon,
> Tho' bent on speed: so here the archangel paus'd. *Par. Lost.*

In all our journey from London to his house, we did not so much as *bait* at a whig inn. *Addison. Spectat.* N° 126.

To BAIT. *v. n.* [as an hawk.] To clap the wings; to make an offer of flying; to flutter.

> All plum'd like estridges, that with the wind
> *Baited* like eagles having lately bath'd;
> Glittering in golden coats like images. *Shakesp. Henry* IV.

> Hood my unman'd blood *baiting* in my cheeks
> With thy black mantle; till strange love, grown bold,
> Thinks true love acted simple modesty. *Shak. Rom. and Jul.*

> Another way I have to man my haggard,
> To make her come, and know her keepers call;
> That is, to watch her as we watch these kites,
> That *bait* and beat, and will not be obedient.
> *Shakesp. Taming of the Shrew.*

BAIT. *n. s.* [from the verb.]

1. Meat set to allure fish, or other animals, to a snare.

> The pleasant'st angling is to see the fish
> Cut with her golden oars the silver stream,
> And greedily devour the treacherous *bait*.
> *Shakesp. Much ado about Nothing.*

2. A temptation; an enticement.

> And that same glorious beauty's idle boast,
> Is but a *bait* such wretches to beguile. *Spens. sonnet* xli.

Taketh therewith the souls of men, as with certain *baits*. *Hooker, b.* v. § 35.

> Sweet words I grant, *baits* and allurements sweet
> But greatest hopes of greatest crosses meet. *Fairfax, b.* ii.

> Fruit, like that
> Which grew in paradise, the *bait* of Eve
> Us'd by the tempter. *Milton's Par. Lost, b.* x. *l.* 551.

> Secure from foolish pride's affected state,
> And specious flattery's more pernicious *bait*. *Roscommon.*

> Her head was bare,
> But for her native ornament of hair,
> Which in a simple knot was ty'd above:
> Sweet negligence! unheeded *bait* of love! *Dryden's Fab.*

> Grant that others could with equal glory,
> Look down on pleasures, and the *baits* of sense. *Add. Cato.*

3. A refreshment on a journey.

BAIZE. *n. s.* A kind of coarse open cloth stuff, having a long nap; sometimes frized on one side, and sometimes not frized, according to the uses it is intended for. This stuff is without wale, being wrought on a loom with two treddles, like flannel. *Chambers.*

To BAKE. *v. a.* participle passive, *baked*, or *baken*. [bæcan, Sax. *becken*, Germ. supposed by *Wachter* to come from *bec*, which, in the Phrygian language, signified *bread*.]

1. To heat any thing in a close place; generally in an oven.

He will take thereof, and warm himself; yea, he kindleth it, and *baketh* bread. *Isaiah*, xliv. 15.

The difference of prices of bread proceeded from their delicacy in bread, and perhaps something in their manner of *baking*. *Arbuthnot on Coins.*

2. To harden in the fire.

The work of the fire is a kind of *baking*; and whatsoever the fire *baketh*, time doth in some degree dissolve. *Bacon.*

3. To harden with heat.

> With vehement suns
> When dusty summer *bakes* the crumbling clods,
> How pleasant is't, beneath the twisted arch,
> To ply the sweet carouse! *Philips.*

> The sun with flaming arrows pierc'd the flood,
> And, darting to the bottom, *bak'd* the mud. *Dryden.*

To BAKE. *v. n.*

1. To do the work of baking.

I keep his house, and I wash, wring, brew, *bake*, scour, dress meat, and make the beds, and do all myself. *Shakesp. Merry Wives of Windsor.*

2. To be heated or baked.

> Fillet of a fenny snake,
> In the cauldron boil and *bake*. *Shakesp. Macbeth.*

BAKED *Meats.* Meats dressed by the oven.

There be some houses, wherein sweetmeats will relent, and *baked meats* will mould, more than others. *Bacon's Nat. Hist.*

BA'KEHOUSE. *n. s.* [from *bake* and *house*.] A place for baking bread.

I have marked a willingness in the Italian artizans, to distribute the kitchen, pantry, and *bakehouse*, under ground. *Wotton.*

BA'KEN. The *participle* from *to bake*.

There was a cake *baken* on the coals, and a cruse of water at his head. 1 *Kings*, xix. 6.

BA'KER. *n. s.* [from *to bake*.] He whose trade is to bake.

In life and health, every man must proceed upon trust, there being no knowing the intention of the cook or *baker*. *South.*

BA'LANCE. *n. s.* [*balance*, Fr. *bilanx*, Lat.]

1. One of the six simple powers in mechanicks, used principally for determining the difference of weight in heavy bodies. It is of several forms. *Chambers.*

2. A pair of scales.

A balance of power, either without or within a state, is best conceived by considering what the nature of a *balance* is. It supposes three things; first, the part which is held, together with the hand that holds it; and then the two scales, with whatever is weighed therein. *Swift.*

> For when on ground the burden'd *balance* lies,
> The empty part is lifted up the higher. *Sir John Davies.*

3. A metaphorical *balance*, or the mind employed in comparing one thing with another.

> I have in equal *balance* justly weighed,
> What wrong our arms may do, what wrongs we suffer:
> Griefs heavier than our offences. *Shakesp. Henry* IV.

4. The act of comparing two things, as by the *balance*.

Comfort arises not from others being miserable, but from this inference upon the *balance*, that we suffer only the lot of nature. *L'Estrange's Fables.*

Upon a fair *balance* of the advantages on either side, it will appear, that the rules of the gospel are more powerful means of conviction than such message. *Atterbury.*

5. The overplus of weight; that quantity by which, of two things weighed together, one exceeds the other.

Care being taken, that the exportation exceed in value the importation; and then the *balance* of trade must of necessity be returned in coin or bullion. *Bacon's Adv. to Sir G. Villiers.*

6. That which is wanting to make two parts of an account even; as, he stated the account with his correspondent, and paid the *balance*.

7. Equipoise; as *balance* of power. See the second sense.

> Love, hope, and joy, fair pleasure's smiling train,
> Hate, fear, and grief, the family of pain;
> These mixed with art, and to due bounds confin'd,
> Make and maintain the *balance* of the mind. *Pope.*

8. The beating part of a watch.

It is but supposing that all watches, whilst the *balance* beats, think; and it is sufficiently proved, that my watch thought all last night. *Locke.*

9. In astronomy. One of the twelve signs of the zodiack, commonly called *Libra*.

To BA'LANCE. *v. a.* [*balancer*, Fr.]

1. To weigh in a balance, either real or figurative; to compare by the balance.

If men would but *balance* the good and the evil of things, they would not venture soul and body for a little dirty interest. *L'Estrange's Fables.*

2. To regulate the weight in a balance.

> Heav'n that hath plac'd this island to give law,
> To *balance* Europe, and her states to awe. *Waller.*

3. To counterpoise; to weigh equal to.

The attraction of the glass is *balanced*, and rendered ineffectual by the contrary attraction of the liquor. *Newton's Opt.*

4. To regulate an account, by stating it on both sides.

Judging is, *balancing* an account, and determining on which side the odds lie. *Locke.*

5. To pay that which is wanting to make the two parts of an account equal.

> Give him leave
> To *balance* the account of Blenheim's day. *Prior.*

Though I am very well satisfied, that it is not in my power to *balance* accounts with my Maker, I am resolved, however, to turn all my endeavours that way. *Addison. Spectator.*

To BA'LANCE. *v. n.* To hesitate; to fluctuate between equal motives, as a balance plays when charged with equal weights.

Were the satisfaction of lust, and the joys of heaven, offered at any one's present possession, he would not *balance*, or err in the determination of his choice. *Locke.*

Since there is nothing that can offend, I see not why you should *balance* a moment about printing it. *Atterbury to Pope.*

BA'LANCER. *n. s.* [from *balance*.] The person that weighs any thing.

BA'LASS *Ruby. n. s.* [*balas*, Fr. supposed to be an Indian term.] A kind of ruby.

*Balass ruby* is of a crimson colour, with a cast of purple, and seems best to answer the description of the ancients. *Woodward on Fossils.*

To BALBU'CINATE. *v. n.* [from *balbutio*, Lat.] To stammer in speaking. *Dict.*

To BALBU'TIATE. *v. n.* The same with *balbucinate*. *Dict.*

BALCO'NY. *n. s.* [*balcon*, Fr. *balcone*, Ital.] A frame of iron, wood, or stone, before the window of a room.

Then

I

67

Ill news rides post while good news baits

· M. A. Agon 1537

IL facing 2O^v

A balk is what in some places is called a meer bank, being a narrow slyp of land between ground & ground Tuss. Notes

There horse being tide on a balk
Is ready with theefe for to walk
Tuss. Hus. for July

5 To balk the road, to turn out of it

b ‡ Espying the French ambassador with the Kings Coach ~~and others attending him~~, made them balk the beaten road, & teach post hackneys to leap hedges
Will. Buck.

Baldrick, is very probably derived from the inventer or first wearer of this belt, who was called Balderick, baldric. It was worn by women as well as men across the breast.

Knit with a golden baldric which forlay
Athwart her snowy breast, & did divide
Her dainty pases, which like young fruit in May
Now little gan to swell, and being tyd
Thro her thin weed, their places only signified
F. Q. 3. 29

Then pleaſure came, who, liking not the faſhion,
Began to make *balconies*, terraces,
Till ſhe had weaken'd all by alteration. *Herbert.*

When dirty waters from *balconies* drop,
And dext'rous damſels twirl the ſprinkling mop. *Gay.*

BALD. *adj.* [*bal*, Welch.]

1. Without hair.

Neither ſhall men make themſelves *bald* for them. *Jer.* xvi. 6.

I find it remarked by Marchetti, that the cauſe of baldneſs in men is the dryneſs of the brain, and its ſhrinking from the ſkull; he having obſerved, that in *bald* perſons, under the *bald* part, there was a vacuity between the ſkull and the brain. *Ray.*

He ſhould imitate Cæſar, who, becauſe his head was *bald*, covered that defect with laurels. *Addiſon. Spect.* N° 232.

2. Without natural covering.

Under an oak, whoſe boughs were moſs'd with age,
And high top *bald* with dry antiquity. *Shakeſp. As you like it.*

3. Without the uſual covering.

He is ſet at the upper end o' th' table; but they ſtand *bald* before him. *Shakeſp. Coriolanus.*

4. Unadorned; inelegant.

Hobbes, in the preface to his own *bald* tranſlation of the Ilias, begins the praiſe of Homer when he ſhould have ended it. *Dryden's Fables, Preface.*

And that, though labour'd, line muſt *bald* appear,
That brings ungrateful muſick to the ear. *Creech.*

5. Stripped; naked; without dignity; without value; bare.

What ſhould the people do with theſe *bald* tribunes?
On whom depending, their obedience fails
To th' greater bench. *Shakeſp. Coriolanus.*

6. *Bald* was uſed by the northern nations, to ſignify the ſame as *audax*, bold; and is ſtill in uſe. So *Baldwin*, and by inverſion *Winbald*, is *bold conqueror*; *Ethelbald*, *nobly bold*; *Eadbald*, *happily bold*; which are of the ſame import as *Thraſeas*, *Thraſymachus*, and *Thraſybulus*, &c. *Gibſon's Camden.*

BA'LDACHIN. *n. ſ.* [*baldachino*, Ital.] A piece of architecture, in form of a canopy, ſupported with columns, and ſerving as a covering to an altar. It properly ſignifies a rich ſilk, *du cange*, and was a canopy carried over the hoſt. *Build. Dict.*

BA'LDERDASH. *n. ſ.* [probably of bald, Sax. bold, and *daſh*, to mingle.] Any thing jumbled together without judgment; rude mixture; a confuſed diſcourſe.

To BA'LDERDASH. *v. a.* [from the noun.] To mix or adulterate any liquor.

BA'LDLY. *adv.* [from *bald.*] Nakedly; meanly; inelegantly.

BA'LDMONY. *n. ſ.* The ſame with GENTIAN, which ſee.

BA'LDNESS. *n. ſ.* [from *bald.*]

1. The want of hair.

2. The loſs of hair.

Which happen'd on the skin to light,
And there corrupting to a wound,
Spreads leproſy and *baldneſs* round. *Swift.*

3. Meanneſs of writing; inelegance.

BA'LDRICK. *n. ſ.* [of uncertain etymology.]

1. A girdle. By ſome *Dictionaries* it is explained a *bracelet*; but I have not found it in that ſenſe.

Athwart his breaſt a *baldrick* brave he ware,
That ſhin'd like twinkling ſtars, with ſtones moſt precious rare. *Fairy Queen*, *b.* i.

A radiant *baldrick*, o'er his ſhoulders ty'd,
Suſtain'd the ſword, that glitter'd at his ſide. *Pope.*

2. The zodiack.

That like the twins of Jove, they ſeem'd in ſight,
Which deck the *baldrick* of the heavens bright. *Spenſer.*

BALE. *n. ſ.* [*balle*, Fr.] A bundle or parcel of goods packed up for carriage.

One hired an aſs in the dog-days, to carry certain *bales* of goods to ſuch a town. *L'Eſtrange.*

It is part of the *bales* in which bohea tea was brought over from China. *Woodward on Foſſils.*

BALE. *n. ſ.* [bæl, Sax. *bale*, Dan. *bal*, *bol*, Icelandiſh.] Miſery; calamity.

She look'd about, and ſeeing one in mail,
Armed to point, ſought back to turn again;
For light ſhe hated as the deadly *bale*. *Fairy Queen*, *b.* i.

To BALE. *v. a.* A word uſed by the ſailors, who bid *bale* out the water; that is, *lave* it out, by way of diſtinction from pumping. *Skinner.*

To BALE. *v. n.* [*emballer*, Fr. *imballure*, Ital.] To make up into a bale.

BA'LEFUL. *adj.* [from *bale.*]

1. Full of miſery; full of grief; ſorrowful; ſad; woful.

Ah! luckleſs babe, born under cruel ſtar,
And in dead parents *baleful* aſhes bred. *Fairy Queen*, *b.* i.

But when I feel the bitter *baleful* ſmart,
Which her fair eyes unwares do work in me,
I think that I a new Pandora ſee. *Spenſer*, *ſonnet* xxiv.

Round he throws his *baleful* eyes,
That witneſs'd huge affliction and diſmay,
Mix'd with obdurate pride and ſtedfaſt hate. *Par. Loſt*, *b.* i.

2. Full of miſchief; deſtructive.

But when he ſaw his threat'ning was but vain,
He turn'd about, and ſearch'd his *baleful* books again. *F. Q.*

Boiling choler chokes,
By ſight of theſe, our *baleful* enemies. *Shakeſp. Henry* VI.

Unſeen, unfelt, the fiery ſerpent ſkims
Betwixt her linen and her naked limbs;
His *baleful* breath inſpiring, as he glides. *Dryden's Æneid.*

Happy Ierne, whoſe moſt wholeſome air
Poiſons envenom'd ſpiders, and forbids
The *baleful* toad, and vipers from her ſhore. *Philips.*

BA'LEFULLY. *adv.* [from *baleful.*] Sorrowfully; miſchievouſly.

BALK. *n. ſ.* [*balk*, Dut. and Germ.] A great beam, ſuch as is uſed in building; a rafter over an outhouſe or barn.

BALK. *n. ſ.* [derived by *Skinner* from *valicare*, Ital. to paſs over.] A ridge of land left unploughed between the furrows, or at the end of the field.

To BALK. *v. a.* [See the noun.]

1. To diſappoint; to fruſtrate.

Another thing in the grammar ſchools I ſee no uſe of, unleſs it be to *balk* young lads in the way to learning languages. *Locke.*

Every one has a deſire to keep up the vigour of his faculties, and not to *balk* his underſtanding by what is too hard for it. *Locke.*

But one may *balk* this good intent,
And take things otherwiſe than meant. *Prior.*

The prices muſt have been high; for a people ſo rich would not *balk* their fancy. *Arbuthnot on Coins.*

*Balk'd* of his prey, the yelling monſter flies,
And fills the city with his hideous cries. *Pope's Odyſſey.*

Is there a variance? enter but his door,
*Balk'd* are the courts, and conteſt is no more. *Pope.*

2. To miſs any thing.

By griſly Pluto he doth ſwear,
He rent his clothes, and tore his hair;
And as he runneth here and there,
An acorn cup he greeteth;
Which ſoon he taketh by the ſtalk,
About his head he lets it walk,
Nor doth he any creature *balk*,
But lays on all he meeteth. *Drayt. Nymphid.*

3. To omit, or refuſe any thing.

This was looked for at your hand, and this was *balkt*. *Shakeſp. Twelfth Night.*

4. To heap, as on a ridge. This, or ſomething like this, ſeems to be intended here.

Ten thouſand bold Scots, three and twenty knights,
*Balk'd* in their own blood, did Sir Walter ſee
On Holmedon's plains. *Shakeſp. Henry* IV.

BA'LKERS. *n. ſ.* [In fiſhery.] Men who ſtand on a cliff, or high place on the ſhore, and give a ſign to the men in the fiſhing-boats, which way the paſſage or ſhole of herrings is. *Cowel.*

The pilchards are purſued by a bigger fiſh, called a pluſher, who leapeth above water, and bewrayeth them to the *balker*. *Carew's Survey of Cornwal.*

BALL. *n. ſ.* [*bol*, Dan. *bol*, Dut.

*Bel*, diminutively *Belin*, the ſun, or Apollo of the Celtæ, was called by the ancient Gauls *Abellio*. Whatever was round, and in particular the head, was called by the ancients either *Bál*, or *Bel*, and likewiſe *Bél* and *Biil*. Among the modern Perſians, the head is called *Pole*; and the Flemings ſtill call the head *Bolle*. Πόλος is the head or poll, and πολεῖν, is to turn. Βῶλος likewiſe ſignifies a round ball, whence *bowl*, and *bell*, and *ball*, which the Welch term *bêl*. By the Scotch alſo the head is named *bhél*; whence the Engliſh *bill* is derived, ſignifying the beak of a bird. Figuratively, the Phrygians and Thurians, by βαλλην underſtood a king. Hence alſo, in the Syriack dialects, βαάλ, βηλ, and likewiſe Βῆλ, ſignifies lord, and by this name alſo the ſun; and, in ſome dialects, Ἢλ and Ἴλ, whence Ἴλος, and Ἥλιος, Φήλιος, and Βήλιος, and alſo in the Celtick diminutive way of expreſſion, Ἔλενος, Φέλενος, and Βέλενος, ſignified the ſun; and Ἑλένη, Φελένη, and Βελένη, the moon. Among the Teutonicks, *bol* and *heil* have the ſame meaning; whence the adjective *holig*, or *heilig*, is derived, and ſignifies divine or holy; and the aſpiration being changed into *ſ*, the Romans form their *Sol*. *Baxter.*

1. Any thing made in a round form.

The worms with many feet, which round themſelves into *balls* under logs of timber, but not in the timber. *Bacon.*

Nor arms they wear, nor ſwords and bucklers wield,
But whirl from leathern ſtrings huge *balls* of lead. *Dryden.*

Like a *ball* of ſnow tumbling down a hill, he gathered ſtrength as he paſſed. *Howel's Vocal Foreſt.*

Still unripen'd in the dewy mines,
Within the *ball* a trembling water ſhines,
That through the chryſtal darts. *Addiſon's Rem. on Italy.*

Such of thoſe corpuſcles as happened to combine into one maſs, formed the metallick and mineral *balls*, or nodules, which we find. *Woodward's Natural Hiſtory.*

2. A round thing to play with, either with the hand or foot, or a racket.

*Balls* to the ſtars, and thralls to fortune's reign,
Turn'd from themſelves, infected with their cage,
Where death is fear'd, and life is held with pain. *Sidney.*

Thoſe I have ſeen play at *ball*, grow extremely earneſt who ſhould have the *ball*. *Sidney.*

3. A

3. A ſmall round thing, with ſome particular mark, by which votes are given, or lots caſt.

Let lots decide it.
For ev'ry number'd captive put a *ball*
Into an urn; three only black be there,
The reſt, all white, are ſafe. *Dryden's Don Sebaſtian.*

Minos, the ſtrict inquiſitor, appears;
Round in his urn the blended *balls* he rowls;
Abſolves the juſt, and dooms the guilty ſouls. *Dryden.*

4. A globe; as, the *ball* of the earth.

Julius and Antony, thoſe lords of all,
Low at her feet preſent the conquer'd *ball.* *Granville.*

Ye gods, what juſtice rules the *ball?*
Freedom and arts together fall. *Pope.*

5. A globe borne as an enſign of ſovereignty.

Hear the tragedy of a young man, that by right ought to hold the *ball* of a kingdom; but, by fortune, is made himſelf a ball, toſſed from miſery to miſery, and from place to place. *Bacon's Henry* VII.

6. Any part of the body that approaches to roundneſs; as the lower and ſwelling part of the thumb, the apple of the eye.

Be ſubject to no ſight but mine; inviſible
To every eye *ball* elſe. *Shakeſp. Tempeſt.*

To make a ſtern countenance, let your brow bend ſo, that that it may almoſt touch the *ball* of the eye. *Peacham.*

7. The parchment ſpread over a hollow piece of wood, ſtuffed with hair or wool, which the printers dip in ink, to ſpread it on the letters.

BALL. *n. ſ.* [*bal*, Fr. from *ballare*, low Lat. from βαλλίζω, to dance.] An entertainment of dancing, at which the preparations are made at the expence of ſome particular perſon.

If golden ſconces hang not on the walls,
To light the coſtly ſuppers and the *balls.* *Dryden.*

He would make no extraordinary figure at a *ball*; but I can aſſure the ladies, for their conſolation, that he has writ better verſes on the ſex than any man. *Swift.*

BA'LLAD. *n. ſ.* [*balade*, Fr.] A ſong.

*Ballad* once ſignified a ſolemn and ſacred ſong, as well as trivial, when Solomon's Song was called the *ballad* of *ballads*; but now it is applied to nothing but trifling verſe. *Watts.*

An' I have not *ballads* made on you all, and ſung to filthy tunes, may a cup of ſack be my poiſon. *Shakeſp. Henry* IV.

Like the ſweet *ba'lad*, this amuſing lay
Too long detains the lover on his way. *Gay's Trivia.*

To BA'LLAD. *v. n.* [from the noun.] To make or ſing ballads.

Saucy lictors
Will catch at us like ſtrumpets, and ſcall'd rhimers
*Ballad* us out o' tune. *Shakeſp. Antony and Cleopatra.*

BA'LLAD-SINGER. *n. ſ.* [from *ballad* and *ſing*.] One whoſe employment it is to ſing ballads in the ſtreets.

No ſooner 'gan he raiſe his tuneful ſong,
But lads and laſſes round about him throng.
Not *ballad-ſinger*, plac'd above the crowd,
Sings with a note ſo ſhrilling, ſweet and loud. *Gay.*

BA'LLAST. *n. ſ.* [*ballaſte*, Dutch.]

1. Something put at the bottom of the ſhip to keep it ſteady to the center of gravity.

There muſt be ſome middle counſellors to keep things ſteady; for, without that *ballaſt*, the ſhip will roul too much. *Bacon's Eſſays.*

As for the ſtraight of it, this may be eaſily contrived, if there be ſome great weight at the bottom of the ſhip, being part of its *ballaſt*; which, by ſome cord within, may be looſened from it. *Wilkins's Mathematical Magick.*

As when empty barks or billows float,
With ſandy *ballaſt* ſailors trim the boat;
So bees bear gravel ſtones, whoſe poiſing weight
Steers through the whiſtling winds their ſteddy flight. *Dryd.*

2. That which is uſed to make any thing ſteady.

Why ſhould he ſink where nothing ſeem'd to preſs?
His lading little, and his *ballaſt* leſs. *Swift.*

To BA'LLAST. *v. a.* [from the noun.]

1. To put weight at the bottom of a ſhip, in order to keep her ſteady.

If this ark be ſo *ballaſted*, as to be of equal weight with the like magnitude of water, it will be moveable. *Wilkins's Mathematical Magick.*

2. To keep any thing ſteady.

Whilſt thus to *ballaſt* love, I thought,
And ſo more ſteddily t' have gone,
I ſaw, I had love's pinnace overfraught. *Donne.*

Now you have given me virtue for my guide,
And with true honour *ballaſted* my pride. *Dryden's Aureng.*

BALLE'TTE. *n. ſ.* [*ballette*, Fr.] A dance in which ſome hiſtory is repreſented.

BA'LLIARDS. *n. ſ.* [from *ball* and *yard*, or ſtick to puſh it with.] A play at which a ball is driven by the end of a ſtick; now corruptly called *billiards*.

With dice, with cards, with *balliards*, far unfit,
With ſhuttlecocks miſſeeming manly wit. *Hubberd's Tale.*

BA'LLISTER. See BALUSTRE.

BALLO'N. } *n. ſ.* [*ballon*, Fr.]
BALLO'ON. }

1. A large round ſhort-necked veſſel uſed in chymiſtry.

2. In architecture; a ball or globe placed on the top of a pillar.

3. In fireworks; a ball of paſteboard, ſtuffed with combuſtible matter, which, when fired, mounts to a conſiderable height in the air, and then burſts into bright ſparks of fire, reſembling ſtars.

BA'LLOT. *n. ſ.* [*ballote*, Fr.]

1. A little ball or ticket uſed in giving votes, being put privately into a box or urn.

2. The act of voting by ballot.

To BA'LLOT. *v. n.* [*balloter*, Fr.] To chooſe by ballot, that is, by putting little balls or tickets, with particular marks, privately in a box; by counting which it is known what is the reſult of the poll, without any diſcovery by whom each vote was given.

No competition arriving to a ſufficient number of balls, they fell to *ballot* ſome others. *Wotton.*

Giving their votes by *balloting*, they lie under no awe. *Swift.*

BALLOTA'TION. *n. ſ.* [from *ballot*.] The act of voting by ballot.

The election is intricate and curious, conſiſting of ten ſeveral *ballotations*. *Wotton.*

BALM. *n. ſ.* [*baume*, Fr. *balſamum*, Lat.]

1. The ſap or juice of a ſhrub, remarkably odoriferous.

*Balm* trickles through the bleeding veins
Of happy ſhrubs, in Idumean plains. *Dryden's Virgil.*

2. Any valuable or fragrant ointment.

Thy place is filled, thy ſceptre wrung from thee;
Thy *balm* waſh'd off wherewith thou waſt anointed. *Shakeſp. Henry* VI.

3. Any thing that ſooths or mitigates pain.

You were conducted to a gentle bath,
And *balms* apply'd to you. *Shakeſp. Macbeth.*

Your praiſe's argument, *balm* of your age;
Deareſt and beſt. *Shakeſp. King Lear.*

BALM. } *n. ſ.* [*meliſſa*, Lat.] The name of a plant.
BALM *Mint.* }

It is a verticillate plant, with a labiated flower, conſiſting of one leaf, whoſe upper lip is roundiſh, upright, and divided into two; but the under lip, into three parts: out of the flower-cup riſes the pointal, attended, as it were, with four embryos; theſe afterwards turn to ſo many ſeeds, which are roundiſh, and incloſed in the flower-cup; to theſe notes may be added, the flowers are produced from the wings of the leaves, but are not whorled round the ſtalks. The ſpecies are, 1. Garden *balm*. 2. Garden *balm*, with yellow variegated flowers. 3. Stinking Roman *balm*, with ſofter hairy leaves. The firſt of theſe ſorts is cultivated in gardens for medicinal and culinary uſe: it is propagated by parting the roots either in ſpring or autumn. When they are firſt planted, if the ſeaſon proves dry, you muſt carefully water them until they have taken root. *Millar.*

BALM *of Gilead.*

1. The juice drawn from the balſam tree, by making inciſions in its bark. Its colour is firſt white, ſoon after green; but when it comes to be old, it is of the colour of honey. The ſmell of it is agreeable, and very penetrating; the taſte of it bitter, ſharp and aſtringent. As little iſſues from the plant by inciſion, the *balm* ſold by the merchants, is made of the wood and green branches of the tree, diſtilled by fire, which is generally adulterated with turpentine. *Calmet.*

It ſeems moſt likely to me, that the zori of Gilead, which we render in our Engliſh bible by the word *balm*, was not the ſame with the balſam of Mecca, but only a better ſort of turpentine, then in uſe for the cure of wounds and other diſeaſes. *Prideaux's Connection.*

2. A plant remarkable for the ſtrong balſamick ſcent, which its leaves emit, upon being bruiſed; whence ſome have ſuppoſed, erroneouſly, that the *balm of Gilead* was taken from this plant. *Millar.*

To BALM. *v. a.* [from *balm*.]

1. To anoint with balm.

*Balm* his foul head with warm diſtilled waters,
And burn ſweet wood. *Shakeſp. Taming of the Shrew.*

2. To ſooth; to mitigate; to aſſuage.

Oppreſt nature ſleeps:
This reſt might yet have *balm'd* thy ſenſes,
Which ſtand in hard cure. *Shakeſp. King Lear.*

BA'LMY. *adj.* [from *balm*.]

1. Having the qualities of balm.

Soft on the flow'ry herb I found me laid,
In *balmy* ſweat; which with his beams the ſun
Soon dry'd. *Milton's Paradiſe Loſt, b.* viii.

2. Producing balm.

3. Soothing; ſoft; mild.

Come, Deſdemona, 'tis the ſoldier's life
To have their *balmy* ſlumbers wak'd with ſtrife. *Shak. Othello.*

Such viſions hourly paſs before my ſight,
Which from my eyes their *balmy* ſlumbers fright. *Dryden.*

4. Fragrant; odoriferous.

Thoſe rich perfumes which, from the happy ſhore,
The winds upon their *balmy* winds convey'd,
Whoſe guilty ſweetneſs firſt the world betray'd. *Dryden.*

a denomination given to a pyd horse

But no man sure e'ar left his house
And so dill'd Ball with thoughts so wild
To bring a midwife to his Spouse
Before he knew she was with Child
Prior

saucy lictors
Will catch at us like Strumpets & scald rhymers
Ballat us out of tune Shaks. Ant. & Cleo.

‡ a

Would I could share thy balmy even temper
And milkiness of blood Dryd

^ of which if any derivation could properly be sought, it may be derived from *bambino* Italian *a child*; to *bamboozle* will be to make like a child.



IL facing 2Pr

First Eurus to the rising morn is sent,
The regions of the *balmy* continent. *Dryden's Ovid.*

5. Mitigating; assuasive.

Oh *balmy* breath, that dost almost persuade
Justice to break her sword! *Shakesp. Othello.*

BA'LNEARY. *n. s.* [*balnearium*, Lat.] A bathing-room.

The *balnearies*, and bathing-places, he exposeth unto the summer setting. *Brown's Vulgar Errours, b. vi. c. 7.*

BALNEA'TION. *n. s.* [from *balneum*, Lat. a bath.] The act of bathing.

As the head may be disturbed by the skin, it may the same way be relieved, as is observable in *balneations*, and fomentations of that part. *Brown's Vulgar Errours, b. ii. c. 6.*

BA'LNEATORY. *adj.* [*balneatorius*, Lat.] Belonging to a bath or stove.

BA'LOTADE. *n. s.* The leap of an horse, so that when his fore-feet are in the air, he shews nothing but the shoes of his hinder-feet, without yerking out. A *balotade* differs from a capriole; for when a horse works at caprioles, he yerks out his hinder legs with all his force. *Farrier's Dict.*

BA'LSAM. *n. s.* [*balsamum*, Lat.] Ointment; unguent; an unctuous application thicker than oil, and softer than salve.

Christ's blood's our *balsam*; if that cure us here,
Him, when our judge, we shall not find severe. *Denham.*

BALSAM *Apple.* [*momordica*, Lat.] An annual Indian plant.

The flower consists of one leaf, is of the expanded bell-shaped kind, but so deeply cut, as to appear composed of five distinct leaves: the flowers are some male, or barren; others female, growing upon the top of the embryo, which is afterwards changed into a fruit, which is fleshy, and sometimes more or less tapering and hollow, and when ripe, usually bursts, and casts forth the seeds with an elasticity; which seeds are wrapped up in a membranous covering, and are, for the most part, indented on the edges. *Millar.*

BALSAM *Tree.*

This is a shrub which scarce grows taller than the pomegranate tree; it shoots out abundance of long slender branches, with a few small rounding leaves, always green; the wood of it is gummy, and of a reddish colour; the blossoms are like small stars, white, and very fragrant; whence spring out little pointed pods, inclosing a fruit like an almond, called carpobalsamum, as the wood is called xylobalsamum, and the juice opobalsamum; which see. This tree is cultivated in Arabia and Judea; but it is forbid to be sown or multiplied without the permission of the grand signior. *Calmet. Chambers.*

BALSA'MICAL. } *adj.* [from *balsam.*] Having the qualities of
BALSA'MICK. } balsam; unctuous; mitigating; soft; mild; oily.

If there be a wound in my leg, the vital energy of my soul thrusts out the *balsamical* humour of my blood to heal it. *Hale's Origin of Mankind.*

The aliment of such as have fresh wounds ought to be such as keeps the humours from putrefaction, and renders them oily and *balsamick*. *Arbuthnot on Diet.*

BA'LUSTER. *n. s.* [according to *du Cange*, from *balaustrium*, low Lat. a bathing place.] A small column or pilaster, from an inch and three quarters to four inches square or diameter. Their dimensions and forms are various; they are frequently adorned with mouldings; they are placed with rails on stairs, and in the fronts of galleries in churches.

This should first have been planched over, and railed about with *balusters*. *Carew's Survey of Cornwal.*

BA'LUSTRADE. *n. s.* [from *baluster.*] An assemblage of one or more rows of little turned pillars, called balusters, fixed upon a terras, or the top of a building, for separating one part from another.

BAM, BEAM, being initials in the name of any place, usually imply it to have been woody; from the Saxon beam, which we use in the same sense to this day. *Gibson's Camden.*

BA'MBOO. *n. s.* An Indian plant of the reed kind. It has several shoots, much larger than our ordinary reeds, which are knotty, and separated from space to space by joints. They are said by some, but by mistake, to contain sugar; the *bamboo* being much larger than the sugar-cane. The leaves grow out of each knot, and are prickly. They are four or five inches long, and an inch in breadth, somewhat pointed, and ribbed through the whole length with green and sharp fibres. Its flowers grow in ears, like those of wheat.

To BAMBO'OZLE. *v. a.* [a cant word not used in pure or in grave writings.] To deceive; to impose upon; to confound.

After Nick had *bamboozled* about the money, John called for counters. *Arbuthnot's John Bull.*

BAMBO'OZLER. *n. s.* [from *bamboozle.*] A tricking fellow; a cheat.

There are a set of fellows they call banterers and *bamboozlers*, that play such tricks. *Arbuthnot's John Bull.*

BAN. *n. s.* [*ban*, Teut. a publick proclamation, as of proscription, interdiction, excommunication, publick sale.]

1. Publick notice given of any thing, whereby any thing is publickly commanded or forbidden. This word we use especially in the publishing matrimonial contracts in the church, before marriage, to the end that if any man can say against the intention of the parties, either in respect of kindred or otherwise, they may take their exception in time. And, in the canon law, *banna sunt proclamationes sponsi & sponsæ in ecclesiis fieri soliti.* *Cowel.*

I bar it in the interest of my wife;
'Tis she is subcontracted to this lord,
And I her husband contradict your *bans*. *Shakesp. King Lear.*

Our *bans* thrice bid! and for our wedding-day
My kerchief bought! then press'd, then forc'd away! *Gay.*

2. A curse; excommunication.

Thou mixture rank of midnight weeds collected,
With Hecate's *ban* thrice blasted, thrice infected. *Hamlet.*

A great oversight it was of St. Peter, that he did not accurse Nero, whereby the pope might have got all; yet what need of such a *ban*, since friar Vincent could tell Atasalipa, that kingdoms were the pope's. *Raleigh's Essays.*

3. Interdiction.

Much more to taste it, under *ban* to touch. *Parad Lost.*

4. *Ban of the Empire*; a publick censure by which the privileges of any German prince are suspended.

He proceeded so far by treaty, that he was proferred to have the imperial *ban* taken off Altapinus, upon submission. *Howel.*

To BAN. *v. a.* [*bannen*, Dut. to curse.] To curse; to execrate.

Shall we think that it *baneth* the work which they leave behind them, or taketh away the use thereof? *Hooker, b. v.*

It is uncertain whether this word, in the foregoing sense, is to be deduced from *ban*, to curse, or *bane*, to poison.

In thy closet pent up, rue my shame,
And *ban* our enemies, both mine and thine. *Shakesp. H. VI.*

Before these Moors went a Numidian priest, bellowing out charms, and casting scrowls of paper on each side, wherein he cursed and *banned* the Christians. *Knolles's Hist. of the Turks.*

BANA'NA *Tree.* See PLANTAIN, of which it is a species.

BAND. *n. s.* [*bende*, Dut. band, Saxon.]

1. A tye; a bandage; that by which one thing is joined to another.

You shall find the *band*, that seems to tie their friendship together, will be the very strangler of their amity. *Shakesp. Antony and Cleopatra.*

2. A chain by which any animal is kept in restraint. This is now usually spelt, less properly, *bond.*

So wild a beast, so tame ytaught to be,
And buxom to his *bands*, is joy to see. *Hubberd's Tale.*

Since you deny him ent'rance, he demands
His wife, whom cruelly you hold in *bands*. *Dryd. Aurengz.*

3. Any means of union or connexion between persons.

Here's eight that must take hands,
To join in Hymen's *bands*. *Shakesp. As you like it.*

4. Something worn about the neck; a neckcloth. It is now restrained to a neckcloth of particular form worn by clergymen, lawyers, and students in colleges.

For his mind I do not care,
That's a toy that I could spare:
Let his title be but great,
His cloaths rich, and *band* sit neat. *Ben Johnson's Underwoods.*

He took his present lodging at the mansion-house of a taylor's widow, who washes and can clear-starch his *bands*. *Addison.*

5. Any thing bound round another.

In old statues of stone in cellars, the feet of them being bound with leaden *bands*, it appeared that the lead did swell. *Bacon.*

6. A company of persons joined together in any common design.

And, good my lord of Somerset, unite
Your troops of horsemen with his *bands* of foot. *Shakesp. Henry VI. p. i.*

We few, we happy few, we *band* of brothers. *Sh. H. V.*

The queen in white array before her *band*,
Saluting took her rival by the hand. *Dryden's Fables.*

On a sudden, methought this select *band* sprang forward, with a resolution to climb the ascent, and follow the call of that heavenly musick. *Tatler, N° 81.*

Strait the three *bands* prepare in arms to join,
Each *band* the number of the sacred Nine. *Pope.*

7. In architecture. Any flat low member or moulding, called also fascia, face, or plinth.

To BAND. *v. a.* [from *band.*]

1. To unite together into one body or troop.

The bishop, and the duke of Glo'ster's men,
Have fill'd their pockets full of pebble stones,
And *banding* themselves in contrary parts,
Do pelt at one another's pates. *Shakesp. Henry VI. p. i.*

Some of the boys *banded* themselves as for the major, and others for the king; who, after six days skirmishing, at last made a composition, and departed. *Carew's Survey of Cornwal.*

To live exempt
From heav'n's high jurisdiction, in new league
*Banded* against his throne. *Milton's Par. Lost, b. ii.*

2. To bind over with a band.

And by his mother stood an infant lover,
With wings unfledg'd, his eyes were *banded* over. *Dryden.*

BANDS *of a ſaddle*, are two pieces of iron nailed upon the bows of the ſaddle, to hold the bows in the right ſituation.

BA'NDAGE. *n. ſ.* [*bandage*, Fr.]

1. Something bound over another.

Zeal too had a place among the reſt, with a *bandage* over her eyes; though one would not have expected to have ſeen her repreſented in ſnow. *Addiſon. Freeholder*, Nº 27.

Cords were faſtened by hooks to my *bandages*, which the workmen had girt round my neck. *Gulliver's Travels.*

2. It is uſed, in ſurgery, for the fillet or roller wrapped over a wounded member; and, ſometimes, for the act or practice of applying *bandages*.

BANDBOX. *n. ſ.* [from *band* and *box*.] A ſlight box uſed for bands and other things of ſmall weight.

My friends are ſurprized to find two *bandboxes* among my books, till I let them ſee that they are lined with deep erudition. *Addiſon. Spectator*, Nº 85.

With empty *bandbox* ſhe delights to range,
And feigns a diſtant errand from the 'Change. *Gay's Trivia.*

BA'NDELET. *n. ſ.* [*bandelet*, Fr. In architecture.] Any little band, flat moulding, or fillet.

BA'NDIT. *n. ſ.* [*bandito*, Ital.] A man outlawed.

No ſavage fierce, *bandit*, or mountaineer,
Will dare to ſoil her virgin purity. *Milton's Poems.*

No *bandit* fierce, no tyrant mad with pride,
No cavern'd hermit, reſts ſelf ſatisfy'd. *Pope's Eſſay on Man.*

BANDITTO. *n. ſ.* in the plural *banditti*. [*bandito*, Ital.]

A Roman ſworder, and *banditto* ſlave,
Murder'd ſweet Tully. *Shakeſp. Henry* VI. *p.* ii.

BA'NDOG. *n. ſ.* [from *ban* or *band*, and *dog*. The original of this word is very doubtful. *Caius, de canibus Britannicis*, derives it from *band*, that is, *a dog chained up*. *Skinner* inclines to deduce it from *bana*, a *murderer*. May it not come from *ban a curſe*, as we ſay a *curſt cur*; or rather from *baund*, ſwelled or large, a *Daniſh* word; from whence, in ſome counties, they call a great nut a *ban-nut*.] A kind of large dog.

The time of night when Troy was ſet on fire,
The time when ſcreech-owls cry, and *bandogs* howl.
*Shakeſp. Henry* VI. *p.* ii.

Or privy, or pert, if any bin,
We have great *bandogs* will tear their ſkin. *Spenſ. Paſtorals.*

BA'NDOLEERS. *n. ſ.* [*bandouliers*, Fr.] Small wooden caſes covered with leather, each of them containing powder that is a ſufficient charge for a musket.

BA'NDROL. *n. ſ.* [*banderol*, Fr.] A little flag or ſtreamer; the little fringed ſilk flag that hangs on a trumpet.

BA'NDY. *n. ſ.* [from *bander*, Fr.] A club turned round at bottom for ſtriking a ball at play.

To BA'NDY. *v. a.* [probably from *bandy*, the inſtrument with which they ſtrike balls at play, which being crooked, is named from the term *bander un arc*, to ſtring or bend a bow.]

1. To beat to and fro, or from one to another.

They do cunningly, from one hand to another, *bandy* the ſervice like a tennis-ball. *Spenſer's Ireland.*

And like a ball *bandy'd* 'twixt pride and wit,
Rather than yield, both ſides the prize will quit. *Denham.*

What, from the tropicks, can the earth repel?
What vigorous arm, what repercuſſive blow,
*Bandies* the mighty globe ſtill to and fro? *Blackmore.*

2. To exchange; to give and take reciprocally.

Do you *bandy* looks with me, you raſcal? *Shakeſp. K. Lear.*

'Tis not in thee
To grudge my pleaſures, to cut off my train,
To *bandy* haſty words. *Shakeſp. King Lear.*

3. To agitate; to toſs about.

This hath been ſo *bandied* amongſt us, that one can hardly miſs books of this kind. *Locke.*

Ever ſince men have been united into governments, the endeavours after univerſal monarchy have been *bandied* among them. *Swift.*

Let not obvious and known truths, or ſome of the moſt plain and certain propoſitions, be *bandied* about in a diſputation.
*Watts's Improvement of the Mind.*

To BA'NDY. *v. n.* To contend, as at ſome game, in which each ſtrives to drive the ball his own way.

No ſimple man that ſees
This factious *bandying* of their favourites,
But that he doth preſage ſome ill event. *Shakeſp. Henry* VI.

A valiant ſon in law thou ſhalt enjoy:
One fit to *bandy* with thy lawleſs ſons,
To ruffle in the commonwealth. *Shakeſp. Tit. Andron.*

Could ſet up grandee againſt grandee,
To ſquander time away, and *bandy*,
Make lords and commoners lay ſieges
To one another's privileges. *Hudibras.*

After all the *bandying* attempts of reſolution, it is as much a queſtion as ever. *Glanville's Scepſis*, *c.* iv.

BA'NDYLEG. *n. ſ.* [from *bander*, Fr.] A crooked leg.

He tells aloud your greateſt failing,
Nor makes a ſcruple to expoſe
Your *bandyleg*, or crooked noſe. *Swift.*

BA'NDYLEGGED. *adj.* [from *bandyleg*.] Having crooked legs.

The Ethiopians had an one-eyed *bandylegged* prince; ſuch a perſon would have made but an odd figure. *Collier on Duelling.*

BANE. *n. ſ.* [bana, Sax. a murderer.]

1. Poiſon.

Begone, or elſe let me. 'Tis *bane* to draw
The ſame air with thee. *Ben Johnſon's Catiline.*

All good to me becomes
*Bane*; and in heav'n much worſe would be my ſtate.
*Milton's Par. Loſt*, *b.* ix. *l.* 122.

They, with ſpeed,
Their courſe through thickeſt conſtellations held,
Spreading their *bane*. *Milton's Par. Loſt*, *b.* x. *l.* 412.

Thus, am I doubly armed; my death and life,
My *bane* and antidote, are both before me:
This, in a moment, brings me to an end;
But that informs me I ſhall never die. *Addiſon's Cato.*

2. That which deſtroys; miſchief; ruin.

Inſolency muſt be repreſt, or it will be the *bane* of the Chriſtian religion. *Hooker*, *b.* ii. § 7.

I will not be afraid of death and *bane*,
Till Birnam foreſt come to Dunſinane. *Shakeſp. Macbeth.*

Suffices that to me ſtrength is my *bane*,
And proves the ſource of all my miſeries. *Milton's S. Agon.*

So entertain'd thoſe odorous ſweets the fiend,
Who came their *bane*. *Milton's Paradiſe Loſt*, *b.* iv. *l.* 167.

Who can omit the Gracchi, who declare
The Scipios' worth, thoſe thunderbolts of war,
The double *bane* of Carthage? *Dryden, Æneid* vi.

Falſe religion is, in its nature, the greateſt *bane* and deſtruction to government in the world. *South.*

To BANE. *v. a.* [from the noun.] To poiſon.

What if my houſe be troubled with a rat,
And I be pleas'd to give ten thouſand ducats
To have it *ban'd*. *Shakeſp. Merchant of Venice.*

BA'NEFUL. *adj.* [from *bane* and *full*.]

1. Poiſonous.

For voyaging to learn the direful art,
To taint with deadly drugs the barbed dart;
Obſervant of the gods, and ſternly juſt,
Ilus refus'd t' impart the *baneful* truſt. *Pope's Odyſſey*, *b.* i.

2. Deſtructive.

The ſilver eagle too is ſent before,
Which I do hope will prove to them as *baneful*,
As thou conceiv'ſt it to the commonwealth. *B. Johnſ. Catil.*

The nightly wolf is *baneful* to the fold,
Storms to the wheat, to buds the bitter cold. *Dryden's Virgil.*

BA'NEFULNESS. *n. ſ.* [from *baneful*.] Poiſonouſneſs; deſtructiveneſs.

B'ANEWORT. *n. ſ.* [from *bane* and *wort*.] A plant, the ſame with *deadly nightſhade*. See NIGHTSHADE.

To BANG. *v. a.* [*vengolen*, Dutch.]

1. To beat; to thump; to cudgel: a low and familiar word.

One receiving from them ſome affronts, met with them handſomely, and *banged* them to good purpoſe. *Howel's V. For.*

He having got ſome iron out of the earth, put it into his ſervants hands to fence with, and *bang* one another. *Locke.*

Formerly I was to be *banged*, becauſe I was too ſtrong, and now, becauſe I am too weak to reſiſt; I am to be brought down, when too rich, and oppreſſed, when too poor. *Arbuth. J. Bull.*

2. To handle roughly; to treat with violence in general.

The deſperate tempeſt hath ſo *bang'd* the Turks,
That their deſignment halts. *Shakeſp. Othello.*

You ſhould accoſt her with jeſts fire-new from the mint; you ſhould have *banged* the youth into dumbneſs.
*Shakeſp. Twelfth Night.*

BANG. *n. ſ.* [from the verb.] A blow; a thump; a ſtroke: a low word.

I am a bachelor.—That's to ſay, they are fools that marry; you'll bear me a *bang* for that. *Shakeſp. Julius Cæſar.*

With many a ſtiff twack, many a *bang*,
Hard crabtree and old iron rang. *Hudibras, cant.* ii.

I heard ſeveral *bangs* or buffets, as I thought, given to the eagle that held the ring of my box in his beak. *Gulliv. Travels.*

To BA'NISH. *v. a.* [*banir*, Fr. *banio*, low Lat. probably from *ban*, Teut. an outlawry, or proſcription.]

1. To condemn to leave his own country.

Oh, fare thee well!
Thoſe evils thou repeat'ſt upon thyſelf,
Have *baniſh'd* me from Scotland. *Shakeſp. Macbeth.*

2. To drive away.

It is for wicked men only to dread God, and to endeavour to *baniſh* the thoughts of him out of their minds. *Tillotſon.*

Succeſsleſs all her ſoft careſſes prove,
To *baniſh* from his breaſt his country's love. *Pope's Odyſſ.*

BA'NISHER. *n. ſ.* [from *baniſh*.] He that forces another from his own country.

In mere ſpite,
To be full quit of thoſe my *baniſhers*,
Stand I before thee here. *Shakeſp. Coriolanus.*

BA'NISHMENT. *n. ſ.* [*banniſſement*, Fr.]

1. The act of baniſhing another; as, he ſecured himſelf by the *baniſhment* of his enemies.

2. The

Bandog, may be a dog of bad Omen
the Schreech Owl which is reckond so being
Added
For in Scotland the Common people
observe that before a persons death happens
some dog and generally it is a Strange
dog comes at the dead of Night, & howles
three or four times at the door & goes
off quietly.



IL facing 2P<sup>v</sup>

Bannered Adj. [from banner] furnished with banners. c ǂ

With extended wings a banner'd host
Under spread ensigns marching might pass through
With Horse & Chariots Milton

a ǂ

Scots must have drink, they cannot live on keale
On haver bannocks or on haver jannocks
Beaum^t

~~They in grave and solemn wise unfolded
Matter which little purported, but words
Bank'd in right learned phrase~~
Rowe

b ǂ

Shoals
Of fish, that with their fins & shining scales
Glide under the green wave in sculls, that oft
Bank the mid sea Milt. P. L. B. 7. l. 400

~~Bankrupt Adj. divested of, stripped of all things.~~ d ǂ

d ǂ 2 ~~[illegible]~~ sometimes ǂ
Command a Mirrour hither straight
That I may see me what a face I have
Since it is bankrupt of his Majesty
Shaks.

2. The ſtate of being baniſhed; exile.

Now go we in content
To liberty, and not to *baniſhment.* *Shakeſp. As you like it.*

Round the wide world in *baniſhment* we roam,
Forc'd from our pleaſing fields and native home. *Dryden.*

BANK. *n. ſ.* [banc, Saxon.]

1. The earth riſing on each ſide of a water. We ſay, properly, the *ſhore* of the *ſea*, and the *banks* of a *river*, *brook*, or ſmall water.

Have you not made an univerſal ſhout,
That Tyber trembled underneath his *bank.* *Shak. Jul. Cæſ.*

Richmond, in Devonſhire, ſent out a boat
Unto the ſhore, to aſk thoſe on the *banks*,
If they were his aſſiſtants. *Shakeſp. Richard* III.

A brook whoſe ſtream ſo great, ſo good,
Was lov'd, was honour'd as a flood:
Whoſe *banks* the Muſes dwelt upon. *Craſhaw.*

'Tis happy when our ſtreams of knowledge flow,
To fill their *banks*, but not to overthrow. *Denham.*

O early loſt! what tears the river ſhed,
When the ſad pomp along his *banks* was led! *Pope.*

2. Any heap of earth piled up.

They beſieged him in Abel of Bethmaachah, and they caſt up a *bank* againſt the city; and it ſtood in the trench. *2 Samuel*, xx. 15.

3. [from *banc*, Fr. a bench.] A ſeat or bench of rowers.

Plac'd on your *banks*, the luſty Trojans ſweep
Neptune's ſmooth face, and cleave the yielding deep. *Waller.*

Mean time the king with gifts a veſſel ſtores,
Supplies the *banks* with twenty choſen oars. *Dryd. Homer.*

That *banks* of oars were not in the ſame plain, but raiſed above one another, is evident from deſcriptions of ancient ſhips. *Arbuthnot on Coins.*

4. A place where money is laid up to be called for occaſionally.

Let it be no *bank*, or common ſtock, but every man be maſter of his own money. Not that I altogether miſlike *banks*, but they will hardly be brooked in regard of certain ſuſpicions. *Bacon's Eſſays.*

This maſs of treaſure you ſhould now reduce;
But you your ſtore have hoarded in ſome *bank.* *Denham.*

Their pardons and indulgences, and giving men a ſhare in ſaints merits, out of the common *bank* and treaſury of the church, which the pope has the ſole cuſtody of. *South.*

5. The company of perſons concerned in managing a bank.

To BANK. *v. a.* [from the noun.]

1. To lay up money in a bank.

2. To incloſe with banks.

Amid the cliffs
And burning ſands, that *bank* the ſhrubby vales. *Thomſon.*

BA'NK-BILL. *n. ſ.* [from *bank* and *bill*] A note for money laid up in a bank, at the ſight of which the money is paid.

Let three hundred pounds be paid her out of my ready money, or *bank-bills.* *Swift's Laſt Will.*

BA'NKER. *n. ſ.* [from *bank.*] One that trafficks in money; one that keeps or manages a bank.

Whole droves of lenders croud the *banker's* doors,
To call in money. *Dryden's Spaniſh Friar.*

By powerful charms of gold and ſilver led,
The Lombard *bankers* and the change to waſte. *Dryden.*

BA'NKRUPCY. *n. ſ.* [from *bankrupt.*]

1. The ſtate of a man broken, or bankrupt.

2. The act of declaring one's ſelf bankrupt; as, he ſilenced the clamours of his creditors by a ſudden *bankrupcy.*

BA'NKRUPT. *adj.* [*banqueroute*, Fr. *bancorotto*, Ital.] In debt beyond the power of payment.

The king's grown *bankrupt*, like a broken man. *Shakeſp. Richard* III.

Sir, if you ſpend word for word with me,
I ſhall make your wit *bankrupt.* *Shak. Two Gent. of Verona.*

BA'NKRUPT. *n. ſ.* A man in debt beyond the power of payment.

Perkin gathered together a power, neither in number nor in hardineſs contemptible; but, in their fortunes, to be feared; being *bankrupts*, and many of them felons. *Bacon's Henry* VII.

It is with wicked men as with a *bankrupt*: when his creditors are loud and clamorous, and ſpeak big, he giveth them many good words. *Calamy.*

In vain at court the *bankrupt* pleads his cauſe;
His thankleſs country leaves him to her laws. *Pope.*

To BA'NKRUPT. *v. a.* To break; to diſable one from ſatisfying his creditors.

We caſt off the care of all future thrift, becauſe we are already *bankrupted.* *Hammond's Fundamentals.*

BA'NNER. *n. ſ.* [*banniere*, Fr. *banair*, Welch.]

1. A flag; a ſtandard; a military enſign.

From France there comes a power,
Who already have ſecret ſeize
In ſome of our beſt ports, and are at point
To ſhew their open *banner.* *Shakeſp. King Lear.*

All in a moment through the gloom were ſeen
Ten thouſand *banners* riſe into the air,
With orient colours waving. *Milton's Par. Loſt, b.* i.

He ſaid no more;
But left his ſiſter and his queen behind,
And wav'd his royal *banner* in the wind. *Dryden.*

Fir'd with ſuch motives, you do well to join
With Cato's foes, and follow Cæſar's *banners.* *Addiſon's Cato.*

2. A ſtreamer borne at the end of a lance, or elſewhere.

BA'NNERET. *n. ſ.* [from *banner.*] A knight made in the field, with the ceremony of cutting off the point of his ſtandard, and making it a banner. They are next to barons in dignity; and were anciently called by ſummons to parliament. *Blount.*

A gentleman told king Henry, that Sir Richard Croftes, made *banneret* at Stoke, was a wiſe man; the king anſwered, he doubted not that, but marvelled how a fool could know. *Cambden's Remains.*

BA'NNEROL, more properly BANDEROL. *n. ſ.* [from *banderole*, Fr.] A little flag or ſtreamer.

King Oſwald had a *bannerol* of gold and purple ſet over his tomb. *Camden's Remains.*

BA'NNIAN. *n. ſ.* A man's undreſs, or morning-gown; ſuch as is worn by the *Bannians* in the Eaſt Indies.

BA'NNOCK. *n. ſ.* A kind of oaten or peaſe meal cake, mixed with water, and baked upon an iron plate over the fire; uſed in the northern counties, and in Scotland.

BA'NQUET. *n. ſ.* [*banquet*, Fr. *banchetto*, Ital. *vanqueto*, Span.] A feaſt.

If a faſting day come, he hath on that day a *banquet* to make. *Hooker, b.* v. § 41.

In his commendations I am fed;
It is a *banquet* to me. *Shakeſp. Macbeth.*

You cannot have a perfect palace, except you have two ſeveral ſides; a ſide for the *banquet*, and a ſide for the houſhold; the one for feaſts and triumphs, and the other for dwelling. *Bacon's Eſſays.*

Shall the companions make a *banquet* of him? Shall they part him among the merchants? *Job*, xli. 6.

At that taſted fruit,
The ſun, as from Thyeſtean *banquet*, turn'd
His courſe intended. *Milton's Paradiſe Loſt, b.* x. *l.* 688.

That dares prefer the toils of Hercules
To dalliance, *banquets*, and ignoble eaſe. *Dryden's Juvenal.*

To BA'NQUET. *v. a.* [from the noun.] To treat any one with feaſts.

Welcome his friends,
Viſit his countrymen, and *banquet* them. *Shakeſp. Taming of the Shrew.*

They were *banqueted* by the way, and the nearer they approached, the more encreaſed the nobility. *Sir J. Hayward.*

To BA'NQUET. *v. n.* To feaſt; to fare daintily.

The mind ſhall *banquet*, tho' the body pine:
Fat paunches make lean pates, and dainty bits
Make rich the ribs, but banker out the wits. *Shakeſp. Love's Labour Loſt.*

So long as his innocence is his repaſt, he feaſts and *banquets* upon bread and water. *South.*

I purpos'd to unbend the evening hours,
And *banquet* private in the women's bow'rs. *Prior.*

BA'NQUETER. *n. ſ.* [from *banquet.*]

1. A feaſter; one that lives deliciouſly.

2. He that makes feaſts.

BA'NQUET-HOUSE. } *n. ſ.* [from *banquet* and *houſe.*] A
BA'NQUETING-HOUSE. } houſe where banquets are kept.

In a *banqueting-houſe*, among certain pleaſant trees, the table was ſet near to an excellent water-work. *Sidney.*

But at the walk's end behold, how rais'd on high
A *banquet-houſe* ſalutes the ſouthern ſky. *Dryden's Juvenal.*

BANQUE'TTE. *n. ſ.* [Fr. in fortification.] A ſmall bank at the foot of the parapet, for the ſoldiers to mount upon when they fire.

BA'NSTICLE. *n. ſ.* A ſmall fiſh, called alſo a ſtickleback.

To BA'NTER. *v. a.* [a barbarous word, without etymology, unleſs it be derived from *bâdiner*, Fr.] To play upon; to rally; to turn to ridicule; to ridicule.

The magiſtrate took it that he *bantered* him, and bad an officer take him into cuſtody. *L'Eſtrange.*

It is no new thing for innocent ſimplicity to be the ſubject of *bantering* drolls. *L'Eſtrange.*

Could Alcinous' gueſts withold
From ſcorn or rage? Shall we, cries one, permit
His leud romances, and his *bant'ring* wit? *Tate's Juvenal.*

BA'NTER. *n. ſ.* [from the verb.] Ridicule; raillery.

This humour, let it look never ſo ſilly, as it paſſes many times for frolick and *banter*, is one of the moſt pernicious ſnares in human life. *L'Eſtrange.*

Metaphyſicks are ſo neceſſary to a diſtinct conception, ſolid judgment, and juſt reaſoning on many ſubjects, that thoſe who ridicule it, will be ſuppoſed to make their wit and *banter* a refuge and excuſe for their own lazineſs. *Watts's Logick.*

BA'NTERER. *n. ſ.* [from *banter.*] One that banters; a droll.

What opinion have theſe religious *banterers* of the divine power? or what have they to ſay for this mockery and contempt? *L'Eſtrange.*

BA'NTLING. *n. ſ.* [if it has any etymology, it is perhaps corrup-

ted

ted from the old word *bairn*, *bairnling*, a little child.] A little child: a low word.

If the object of their love
Chance by Lucina's aid to prove,
They seldom let the *bantling* roar,
In basket, at a neighbour's door. *Prior.*

BA'PTISM. *n. s.* [*baptismus*, Lat. βαπτισμός.]

1. An external ablution of the body, with a certain form of words, which operates and denotes an internal ablution or washing of the soul from original sin. *Ayliffe's Parergon.*

*Baptism* is given by water, and that prescript form of words which the church of Christ doth use. *Hooker, b.* iv. § 1.

To his great *baptism* flock'd,
With awe, the regions round, and with them came
From Nazareth the son of Joseph deem'd,
Unmarkt, unknown. *Paradise Regained, b.* i. *l.* 21.

2. *Baptism* is often taken in Scripture for sufferings.

I have a *baptism* to be baptized with, and how am I straitened till it be accomplished? *Luke*, xii. 15.

BAPTI'SMAL. *adj.* [from *baptism.*] Of or pertaining to baptism.

When we undertake the *baptismal* vow, and enter on their new life, it would be apt to discourage us. *Hammond.*

BA'PTIST. *n. s.* [*baptiste*, Fr. βαπτιστής.] He that administers baptism.

Him the *Baptist* soon
Descry'd, divinely warn'd, and witness bore
As to his worthier—— *Parad. Regained, b.* i. *l.* 25.

BA'PTISTERY. *n. s.* [*baptisterium*, Lat.] The place where the sacrament of baptism is administred.

The great church, *baptistery*, and leaning tower, are well worth seeing. *Addison on Italy.*

To BAPTI'ZE. *v. a.* [*baptiser*, Fr. from βαπτίζω.] To christen; to administer the sacrament of baptism.

He to them shall leave in charge,
To teach all nations what of him they learn'd,
And his salvation; them who shall believe,
*Baptizing* in the profluent stream, the sign
Of washing them from guilt of sin, to life
Pure, and in mind prepar'd, if so befal,
For death, like that which the Redeemer dy'd.
*Milton's Paradise Lost.*

Let us reflect that we are christians; that we are called by the name of the Son of God, and *baptized* into an irreconcileable enmity with sin, the world, and the devil. *Rogers.*

BAPTI'ZER. *n. s.* [from *to baptize.*] One that christens; one that administers baptism.

BAR. *n s.* [*barre*, Fr.]

1. A piece of wood, iron, or other matter, laid cross a passage to hinder entrance.

And he made the middle *bar* to shoot through the boards from the one end to the other. *Exodus*, xxxvi. 33.

2. A bolt; a piece of iron or wood fastened to a door, and entering into the post or wall to hold it.

The fish-gate did the sons of Hassenaah build, who also laid the beams thereof, and set up the doors thereof, the locks thereof, and the *bars* thereof. *Nehem.* iii. 3.

3. Any obstacle which hinders or obstructs.

I brake up for it my decreed place, and set *bars* and doors, and said, hitherto shalt thou come, and no farther. *Job*, xxxviii. 10.

And had his heir surviv'd him in due course,
What limits, England, hadst thou found? what *bar*?
What world could have resisted? *Daniel's Civil War.*

Hard, thou know'st it, to exclude
Spiritual substance with corporeal *bar*. *Parad. Lost, b.* iv.

Must I new *bars* to my own joy create,
Refuse myself, what I had forc'd from fate? *Dryd. Aureng.*

Fatal accidents have set
A most unhappy *bar* between your friendship.
*Rowe's Ambitious Stepmother.*

4. A rock, or bank of sand, at the entrance of a harbour or river, which ships cannot sail over at low water.

5. Any thing used for prevention.

Lest examination should hinder and lett your proceedings, behold, for a *bar* against that impediment, one opinion newly added. *Hooker, Preface.*

Which Salique land the French unjustly gloze to be
The founder of this law, and female *bar*. *Shakesp. Hen.* V.

6. The place where causes of law are tried, or where criminals are judged; so called from the *bar* placed to hinder crouds from incommoding the court.

The great duke
Came to the *bar*, where, to his accusations,
He pleaded still not guilty. *Shakesp. Henry* VIII.

Some at the *bar* with subtlety defend,
Or on the bench the knotty laws untye. *Dryd. Juvenal.*

7. An inclosed place in a tavern or coffeehouse, where the housekeeper sits and receives reckonings.

I was under some apprehension that they would appeal to me; and therefore laid down my penny at the *bar*, and made the best of my way. *Addison. Spectator*, N° 403.

8. In law. A peremptory exception against a demand or plea brought by the defendant in an action, that destroys the action of the plaintiff for ever. It is divided into a *bar* to common intent, and a *bar* special: a *bar* to a common intent, is an ordinary or general *bar*, that disables the declaration or plea of the plaintiff: a *bar* special, is that which is more than ordinary, and falls out in the case in hand, upon some special circumstance of the fact. *Cowel.*

Bastardy is laid in *bar* of something that is principally commenced. *Ayliffe's Parergon.*

9. Any thing by which the compages or structure is held together.

I went down to the bottoms of the mountains: the earth, with her *bars*, was about me for ever. *Jonah*, ii. 6.

10. Any thing which is laid across another, as *bars* in heraldry.

11. *Bar of gold* or *silver*, is a lump or wedge from the mines, melted down into a sort of mould, and never wrought.

12. *Bars of a horse.* The upper part of the gums between the tusks and grinders, which bears no teeth, and to which the bit is applied, and, by its friction, the horse governed.

13. *Bars, in musick*, are strokes drawn perpendicularly across the lines of a piece of musick; used to regulate the beating or measure of musical time.

BAR SHOT. *n. s.* Two half bullets joined together by an iron bar; used in sea engagements for cutting down the masts and rigging.

To BAR. *v. a.* [from the noun.]

1. To fasten or shut any thing with a bolt, or bar.

My duty cannot suffer
T' obey in all your daughter's hard commands;
Though their injunction be to *bar* my doors,
And let this tyrannous night take hold upon you.
*Shakesp. King Lear.*

When you *bar* the window-shutters of your lady's bedchamber at nights, leave open the sashes to let in the air.
*Swift's Directions to the Chambermaid.*

2. To hinder; to obstruct.

When law can do no right,
Let it be lawful, that law *bar* no wrong. *Shakesp. K. Lear.*

3. To prevent.

The houses of the country were all scattered, and yet not so far off as that it *barred* mutual succour. *Sidney, b.* i.

Doth it not seem a thing very probable, that God doth purposely add, Do after my judgments; as giving thereby to understand, that his meaning in the former sentence was but to *bar* similitude in such things as were repugnant to his ordinances, laws, and statutes? *Hooker.*

4. To shut out from.

Hath he set bounds between their love and me?
I am their mother; who shall *bar* them from me?
*Shakesp. Richard III.*

Our hope of Italy not only lost,
But shut from ev'ry shore, and *barr'd* from ev'ry coast. *Dryd.*

5. To exclude from a claim.

God hath abridged it, by *barring* us from some things of themselves indifferent. *Hooker, b.* ii. § 4.

Give my voice on Richard's side,
To *bar* my master's heirs in true descent!
God knows I will not. *Shakesp. Richard* III.

His civil acts do bind and *bar* them all;
And as from Adam, all corruption take,
So, if the father's crime be capital,
In all the blood, law doth corruption make. *Sir J. Davies.*

It was thought sufficient not only to exclude them from that benefit, but to *bar* them from their money. *Clarendon.*

If he is qualified, why is he *barred* the profit, when he only performs the conditions? *Collier on Pride.*

6. To prohibit.

For though the law of arms doth *bar*
The use of venom'd shot in war. *Hudibras.*

What is a greater pedant than a mere man of the town? *Bar* him the playhouses, and you strike him dumb. *Addison.*

7. To except; to make an exception.

Well, we shall see your bearing.—
—Nay, but I *bar* to-night; you shall not gage me
By what we do to-night. *Shakesp. Merchant of Venice.*

8. In law. To hinder the process of a suit.

But buff and belt men never know these cares;
No time, nor trick of law, their action *bars*:
Their cause they to an easier issue put. *Dryden's Juvenal.*

From such delays as conduce to the finding out of truth, a criminal cause ought not to be *barred*. *Ayliffe's Parergon.*

If a bishop be a party to a suit, and excommunicates his adversary, such excommunication shall not disable or *bar* his adversary. *Ayliffe's Parergon.*

9. To *bar* a vein.

This is an operation performed upon the veins of the legs of a horse, and other parts, with intent to stop the malignant humours. It is done by opening the skin above it, disengaging it, and tying it both above and below, and striking between two ligatures.

Baptization n. s. [baptize]
The act of administring baptism
In maintenance of re-baptization
their Arguments are built upon this, that
heretics are not any part of the Church of
Christ    Hooker 3. 1.

a+

aa+

When these renowned noble peers of Greece
Through stubborn pride amongst themselves di
Forgetful of the famous golden fleece    Jar
Then Orpheus with his harp their strife did ~~bar~~
bar
Spenser.

a +

For your Claims fair Sis~~ter~~
I bar it in the interest of my wife
~~'Tis she is subcontracted to this lord~~
~~And I her Husband contradict your banns~~
Shaks.

IL facing 2P2v

Baralipton
(in logick) a Syllogism of two univer
sals a particular Affirmative
Apollo Stares & all Parnassus shakes
At the rude rumbling baralipton makes
Roscom.

† ~~turning to that place~~
He left his lofty Steed with golden fell
And goodly gorgeous barbes him found not there
F. Q. 2. 2. 11

Barbarlie Adv.
Like a barber, as when he cuts or
shaves close with Sheers
If Sheep or the lamb fell a wrigling with tail
Go by & by search it whils help may prevail
That barbarlie handled
Thou hast finished the Cure
Tuss. hus. for may

a †
Wouldst thou not rather chuse a small renown
To be the Mayor of some poor paltry town
Biggly to look & barbarously to speak
Dryd. Ju.

X Tho somewhat merrily, yet uncourteously
he railed upon England, objecting extreme
beggary & more barbarousness unto it
Ascham.

BARB. *n. ſ.* [*barba*, a beard, Lat.]

1. Any thing that grows in the place of the beard.

The barbel, ſo called by reaſon of his *barb* or wattels at his mouth, under his chaps. *Walton's Angler.*

2. The points that ſtand backward in an arrow, or fiſhing-hook, to hinder them from being extracted.

Nor leſs the Spartan fear'd, before he found
The ſhining *barb* appear above the wound. *Pope's Iliad.*

3. The armour for horſes.

Their horſes were naked, without any *barbs*; for albeit many brought *barbs*, few regarded to put them on. *Hayward.*

BARB. *n. ſ.* [contracted from *Barbary*.] A Barbary horſe.

Theſe horſes are brought from Barbary; they are commonly of a ſlender light ſize, and very lean and thin, uſually choſen for ſtallions. *Barbs*, as it is ſaid, may die, but never grow old; the vigour and mettle of *barbs* never ceaſe, but with their life. *Farrier's Dict.*

To BARB. *v. a.* [from the noun.]

1. To ſhave; to dreſs out the beard.

Shave the head, and tie the beard, and ſay it was the deſire of the penitent to be ſo *barbed* before his death. *Shakeſp. Meaſure for Meaſure.*

2. To furniſh horſes with armour.

A warriour train
That like a deluge pour'd upon the plain;
On *barbed* ſteeds they rode in proud array,
Thick as the college of the bees in May. *Dryden's Fables.*

3. To jag arrows with hooks.

The twanging bows
Send ſhowers of ſhafts, that on their *barbed* points
Alternate ruin bear. *Philips.*

BA'RBACAN. *n. ſ.* [*barbacane*, Fr. *barbacana*, Span.]

1. A fortification placed before the walls of a town.

Within the *barbacan* a porter ſate,
Day and night duly keeping watch and ward:
Nor wight, nor word mote paſs out of the gate,
But in good order, and with due regard. *Fairy Queen.*

2. A fortreſs at the end of a bridge.

3. An opening in the wall through which the guns are levelled.

BARBADOES *Cherry.* [*malphigia*, Lat.]

It has a ſmall quinquefid calix, of one leaf, having bifid ſegments; the flower conſiſts of five leaves, in form of a roſe, having ſeveral ſtamina collected in form of a tube; the ovary, in the bottom of the flower-cup, becomes a globular, fleſhy, ſoft fruit, in which is a ſingle capſule, containing three ſtony winged nuts. In the Weſt Indies, it riſes to be fifteen or ſixteen feet high, where it produces great quantities of a pleaſant tart fruit; propagated in gardens there, but in Europe it is a curioſity. *Millar.*

BA'RBA'DOES *Tar.* A bituminous ſubſtance, differing little from the petroleum floating on ſeveral ſprings in England and Scotland. *Woodward's Method of Foſſils.*

BARBA'RIAN. *n. ſ.* [*barbarus*, Lat. It ſeems to have ſignified at firſt only *foreign*, or a *foreigner*; but, in time, implied ſome degree of wildneſs or cruelty.]

1. A man uncivilized; untaught; a ſavage.

Proud Greece, all nations elſe *barbarians* held,
Boaſting, her learning all the world excell'd. *Denham.*

There were not different gods among the Greeks and *barbarians*. *Stillingfleet's Defence of Diſc. on Romiſh Idolatry.*

But with deſcending ſhow'rs of brimſtone fir'd,
The wild *barbarian* in the ſtorm expir'd. *Addiſon.*

2. A foreigner.

I would they were *barbarians*, as they are,
Though in Rome litter'd. *Shakeſp. Coriolanus.*

3. A brutal monſter; a man without pity: a term of reproach.

Thou fell *barbarian*!
What had he done? what could provoke thy madneſs
To aſſaſſinate ſo great, ſo brave a man! *A. Philips D. Mot.*

BARBA'RIAN. *adj.* Belonging to barbarians; ſavage.

Some felt the ſilent ſtroke of mould'ring age,
*Barbarian* blindneſs. *Pope's Epiſtles.*

BARBA'RICK. *adj.* [*barbaricus*, Lat.] Foreign; far-fetched.

The gorgeous Eaſt, with richeſt hand,
Show'rs on her kings *barbarick* pearl and gold. *Par. Loſt.*

The eaſtern front was glorious to behold,
With diamond flaming, and *barbarick* gold. *Pope.*

BA'RBARISM. *n. ſ.* [*barbariſmus*, Lat.]

1. A form of ſpeech contrary to the purity and exactneſs of any language.

The language is as near approaching to it, as our modern *barbariſm* will allow; which is all that can be expected from any now extant. *Dryden's Juvenal, Dedication.*

2. Ignorance of arts; want of learning.

I have for *barbariſm* ſpoke more
Than for that angel knowledge you can ſay.
*Shakeſp. Love's Labour Loſt.*

The genius of Raphael having ſucceeded to the times of *barbariſm* and ignorance, the knowledge of painting is now arrived to perfection. *Dryd. Dufreſnoy, Preface.*

3. Brutality; ſavageneſs of manners; incivility.

Moderation ought to be had in tempering and managing the Iriſh, to bring them from their delight of licentious *barbariſm* unto the love of goodneſs and civility. *Spenſer's State of Irel.*

Divers great monarchies have riſen from *barbariſm* to civility, and fallen again to ruin. *Sir J. Davies on Ireland.*

4. Cruelty; barbarity; unpitying hardneſs of heart.

They muſt per force have melted,
And *barbariſm* itſelf have pity'd him. *Shakeſp. Richard II.*

BARBA'RITY. *n. ſ.* [from *barbarous*.]

1. Savageneſs; incivility.

2. Cruelty; inhumanity.

And they did treat him with all the rudeneſs, reproach, and *barbarity* imaginable. *Clarendon, b.* viii.

3. Barbariſm; impurity of ſpeech.

Next Petrarch followed, and in him we ſee
What rhime improv'd in all its height, can be
At beſt a pleaſing ſound, and ſweet *barbarity*. *Dryden.*

Latin often expreſſes that in one word, which either the *barbarity* or narrowneſs of modern tongues cannot ſupply in more. *Dryden.*

Affected refinements, which ended by degrees in many *barbarities*, before the Goths had invaded Italy. *Swift.*

BA'RBAROUS. *adj.* [*barbare*, Fr. βάρβαρος.]

1. Stranger to civility; ſavage; uncivilized.

What need I ſay more to you? What ear is ſo *barbarous*, but hath heard of Amphialus? *Sidney.*

The doubtful damſel dare not yet commit
Her ſingle perſon to their *barbarous* truth. *Fairy Q. b.* i.

Thou art a Roman; be not *barbarous*. *Shakeſp. T. Andron.*

And he left governour, Philip, for his country a Phrygian, and for manners more *barbarous* than he that ſet him there. *2 Mac.* v. 22.

A *barbarous* country muſt be broken by war, before it be capable of government; and when ſubdued, if it be not well planted, it will eſtſoons return to barbariſm. *Davies on Ireland.*

2. Ignorant; unacquainted with arts.

They who reſtored painting in Germany, not having thoſe reliques of antiquity, retained that *barbarous* manner. *Dryden.*

3. Cruel; inhuman.

By their *barbarous* uſage, he died within a few days, to the grief of all that knew him. *Clarendon, b.* viii.

BA'RBAROUSLY. *adv.* [from *barbarous*.]

1. Ignorantly; without knowledge or arts.

2. In a manner contrary to the rules of ſpeech.

We *barbarouſly* call them bleſt,
Whilſt ſwelling coffers break their owner's reſt. *Stepney.*

3. Cruelly; inhumanly.

But yet you *barbarouſly* murder'd him. *Dryd. Span. Friar.*

She wiſhes it may proſper; but her mother uſed one of her nieces very *barbarouſly*. *Spectator*, Nº 483.

BA'RBAROUSNESS. *n. ſ.* [from *barbarous*.]

1. Incivility of manners.

Excellencies of muſick and poetry are grown to be little more, but the one fiddling, and the other rhiming; and are indeed very worthy of the ignorance of the friar, and the *barbarouſneſs* of the Goths. *Temple.*

2. Impurity of language.

It is alſo much degenerated and impaired, as touching the pureneſs of ſpeech; being overgrown with *barbarouſneſs*. *Brerewood on Languages.*

3. Cruelty.

The *barbarouſneſs* of the trial, and the perſuaſives of the clergy, prevailed to antiquate it. *Hale's Common Law of Engl.*

To BA'RBECUE. *v. a.* A term uſed in the Weſt-Indies for dreſſing a hog whole; which, being ſplit to the backbone, is laid flat upon a large gridiron, raiſed about two foot above a charcoal fire, with which it is ſurrounded.

Oldfield, with more than harpy throat endu'd,
Cries, ſend me, gods, a whole hog *barbecu'd*. *Pope.*

BA'RBECUE. *n. ſ.* A hog dreſt whole, in the Weſt Indian manner.

BA'RBED. *participial adj.* [from *to barb*.]

1. Furniſhed with armour.

His glittering armour he will command to ruſt,
His *barbed* ſteeds to ſtables. *Shakeſp. Richard II.*

2. Bearded; jagged with hooks or points.

If I conjecture right, no drizzling ſhow'r,
But rattling ſtorm of arrows *barb'd* with fire.
*Milton's Par. Loſt, b.* vi. *l.* 544.

BA'RBEL. *n. ſ.* [from *barb*.]

1. A kind of fiſh found in rivers, large and ſtrong, but coarſe.

The *barbel* is ſo called, by reaſon of the barb or wattels at his mouth, or under his chaps. *Walton's Angler.*

2. Knots of ſuperfluous fleſh growing up in the channels of the mouth of a horſe. *Farrier's Dict.*

BA'RBER. *n. ſ.* [from *to barb*.] A man who ſhaves the beard.

His chamber being ſtived with friends or ſuitors, he gave his legs, arms, and breaſts to his ſervants to dreſs; his head and face to his *barber*; his eyes to his letters, and his ears to petitioners. *Wotton.*

With thoſe thy boiſt'rous locks, no worthy match
For valour to aſſail ——
But by the *barber*'s razor beſt ſubdu'd. *Milton's Samſ. Agon.*

What system, Dick, has right averr'd
The cause, why woman has no beard?
In points like these we must agree;
Our *barber* knows as much as we. *Prior.*

To BA'RBER. *v. a.* [from the noun.] To dress out; to powder.

Our courteous Antony,
Whom ne'er the word of No, woman heard speak,
Being *barber'd* ten times o'er, goes to the feast.
*Shakesp. Antony and Cleopatra.*

BARBER-CHIRURGEON. *n. s.* A man who joins the practice of surgery to the barber's trade; such as were all surgeons formerly, but now it is used only for a low practiser of surgery.

He put himself into *barber-chirurgeons* hands, who, by unfit applications, rarified the tumour. *Wiseman's Surgery.*

BARBER-MONGER. *n. s.* A word of reproach in *Shakespeare*, which seems to signify a fop; a man decked out by his barber.

Draw, you rogue; for though it be night, the moonshines; I'll make a sop of the moonshine of you; you whoreson, cullionly, *barber-monger*, draw. *Shakesp. King Lear.*

BA'RBERRY. *n. s.* [*berberis*, Lat.] Pipperidge bush.

It is set with sharp prickles; the leaves are long, and serrated on the edges; the flowers consist of six leaves, which expand in form of a rose, and are of a yellow colour; the fruit is long, of an acid taste, and, for the most part, of a red colour, and grows in clusters; the bark of the tree is whitish. The species are, 1. The common *barberry*. 2. *Barberry* without stones. The first of these sorts is very common in England, and often planted for hedges. *Millar.*

*Barberry* is a plant that bears a fruit very useful in housewifery; that which beareth its fruit without stones is counted best. *Mortimer's Husbandry.*

BARD. *n. s.* [*bardd*, Welch.] A poet.

There is amongst the Irish a kind of people called *bards*, which are to them instead of poets; whose profession is to set forth the praises or dispraises of men in their poems or rhimes; the which are had in high regard and estimation among them. *Spenser on Ireland.*

And many *bards* that to the trembling chord,
Can tune their timely voices cunningly. *Fairy Queen, b.* i.

The *bard* who first adorn'd our native tongue,
Tun'd to his British lyre this ancient song,
Which Homer might without a blush rehearse. *Dryden.*

BARE. *adj.* [baɲe, Sax. *bar*, Dan.]

1. Naked; without covering.

The trees are *bare* and naked, which use both to cloath and house the kern. *Spenser on Ireland.*

Then stretch'd her arms t' embrace the body *bare*;
Her clasping hands inclose but empty air. *Dryden.*

In the old Roman statues, these two parts were always *bare*, and exposed to view, as much as our hands and face at present. *Addison's Travels.*

2. Uncovered in respect.

Though the lords used to be covered whilst the commons were *bare*, yet the commons would not be *bare* before the Scottish commissioners; and so none were covered. *Clarendon.*

3. Unadorned; plain; simple; without ornament.

Yet was their manners then but *bare* and plain;
For th' antique world excess and pride did hate. *Fairy Q.*

4. Detected; without concealment.

These false pretexts and varnish'd colours failing,
*Bare* in thy guilt, how foul must thou appear?
*Milton's Sampson Agonistes, l. 901.*

5. Poor; without plenty.

Were it for the glory of God, that the clergy should be left as *bare* as the apostles, when they had neither staff nor scrip; God would, I hope, endue them with the self-same affection. *Hooker, Preface.*

Even from a *bare* treasury, my success has been contrary to that of Mr. Cowley. *Dryden's Epistles, Dedication.*

6. Mere.

It was a *bare* petition of a state
To one whom they had punish'd. *Shakesp. Coriolanus.*

You have an exchequer of words, and no other treasure for your followers; for it appears, by their bare liveries, that they live by your *bare* words. *Shakesp. Two Gent. of Verona.*

Nor are men prevailed upon by *bare* words, only through a defect of knowledge; but carried, with these puffs of wind, contrary to knowledge. *South.*

7. Threadbare; much worn; as, *bare* liveries, in the last quotation from *Shakespeare*.

8. Not united with any thing else.

A desire to draw all things to the determination of *bare* and naked Scripture, hath caused much pains to be taken in abating the credit of man. *Hooker, b.* ii. § 7.

That which offendeth us, is the great disgrace which they offer unto our custom of *bare* reading the word of God. *Hooker.*

9. Sometimes it has *of* before the thing taken away.

Tempt not the brave and needy to despair;
For, tho' your violence should leave them *bare*
*Of* gold and silver, swords and darts remain. *Dryden's Juv.*

Making a law to reduce interest, will not raise the price of land; it will only leave the country *barer of* money. *Locke.*

To BARE. *v. a.* [from the adjective.] To strip; to make bare or naked.

The turtle on the *bared* branch,
Laments the wounds that death did launch. *Spenser.*

There is a fabulous narration, that an herb groweth in the likeness of a lamb, and feedeth upon the grass, in such sort as it will *bare* the grass round about. *Bacon's Natural History.*

Eriphyle here he found
*Baring* her breast, yet bleeding with the wound. *Dryden.*

He *bar'd* an ancient oak of all her boughs:
Then on a rising ground the trunks he plac'd. *Dryden.*

For virtue, when I point the pen,
*Bare* the mean heart that lurks beneath a star;
Can there be wanting to defend her cause,
Lights of the church, or guardians of the laws? *Pope.*

BARE, or BORE. The *preterite* of *to bear*. See To BEAR.

BA'REBONE. *n. s.* [from *bare* and *bone*.] Lean, so that the bones appear.

Here comes lean Jack, here comes *barebone*; how long is it ago, Jack, since thou sawest thy own knee? *Shakesp. Hen.* IV.

BAREFACED. *adj.* [from *bare* and *face*.]

1. With the face naked; not masked.

Your French crowns have no hair at all, and then you will play *barefaced*. *Shakesp. Midsummer's Night's Dream.*

2. Shameless; unreserved; without concealment; without disguise.

The animosities encreased, and the parties appeared *barefaced* against each other. *Clarendon, b.* viii.

It is most certain, that *barefaced* bawdry is the poorest pretence to wit imaginable. *Dryden.*

BAREFA'CEDLY. *adv.* [from *barefaced*.] Openly; shamefully; without disguise.

Though only some profligate wretches own it too *barefacedly*, yet, perhaps, we should hear more, did not fear tie people's tongues. *Locke.*

BAREFA'CEDNESS. *n. s.* [from *barefaced*.] Effrontery; assurance; audaciousness.

BA'REFOOT. *adj.* [from *bare* and *foot*.] Without shoes.

She must have a husband;
I must dance *barefoot* on her wedding day. *Shakesp.*

Going to find a *barefoot* brother out,
One of our order. *Shakesp. Romeo and Juliet.*

Ambitious love hath so in me offended,
That *barefoot* plod I the cold ground upon
With fainted vow. *Shakespeare.*

Envoys describe this holy man, with his Alcaydes about him, standing *barefoot*, bowing to the earth. *Addison.*

BAREFO'OTED. *adj.* Without shoes.

He himself, with a rope about his neck, *barefooted*, came to offer himself to the discretion of Leonatus. *Sidney, b.* ii.

BA'REGNAWN. *adj.* [from *bare* and *gnawn*.] Eaten bare.

Know my name is lost;
By treason's tooth *baregnawn* and cankerbit. *Shak. K Lear.*

BA'REHEADED. *adj.* [from *bare* and *head*.] Uncovered in respect.

He, *bareheaded*, lower than his proud steed's neck,
Bespoke them thus. *Shakesp. Richard* II.

Next, before the chariot, went two men *bareheaded*. *Bacon.*

The victor knight had laid his helm aside,
*Bareheaded*, popularly low he bow'd. *Dryden's Fables.*

BA'RELY. *adv.* [from *bare*.]

1. Nakedly.

2. Merely; only; without any thing more.

The external administration of his word is as well by reading *barely* the Scripture, as by explaining the same. *Hooker.*

The duke of Lancaster is dead;
And living too, for now his son is duke—
——*Barely* in title, not in revenue. *Shakesp. Richard* II.

He *barely* nam'd the street, promis'd the wine;
But his kind wife gave me the very sign. *Donne.*

Where the balance of trade *barely* pays for commodities with commodities, there money must be sent, or else the debts cannot be paid. *Locke.*

BA'RENESS. *n. s.* [from *bare*.]

1. Nakedness.

So you serve us,
Till we serve you; but when you have our roses,
You barely leave our thorns to prick ourselves,
And mock us with our *bareness*. *Shak. All's well that ends well.*

2. Leanness.

For their poverty, I know not where they had that; and for their *bareness*, they never learned that of me. *Shak. Hen.* IV.

3. Poverty.

Were it stript of its privileges, and made as like the primitive church for its *bareness* as its purity, it could legally want all such privileges. *South.*

4. Meanness of clothes.

BARGAIN. *n. s.* [*bargen*, Welch; *bargaigne*, Fr.]

1. A contract or agreement concerning the sale of something.

What is marriage but a very *bargain*? wherein is sought alliance, or portion or reputation, with some desire of issue; and not the faithful nuptial union of man and wife. *Bacon.*

+

a +

This Navy was the preparation of five years
It bare itself upon divine assistance
for it receiwed special blessing frome Pope
Sixtus
Bacon.

IL facing 2Q[v]

2^a † to cover with bark, ~~to encase with bark, to encrust.~~

A most instant tetter bark'd about
Most lazar like, with vile & loathsome crust
All my smooth body Shak.

Fair when her breast like a rich laden bark
With precious merchandize she forth doth lay.
Spenser

6 ‡

~~Barn~~^2 a kind of fish
Of round fish there are brit sprat
and barn. Carew Cornw.

Bark in Physic denotes the Jesuits or
peruvian bark, which see.

No more can be due to me,
Than at the *bargain* made was meant. *Donne.*

2. The thing bought or ſold.

Give me but my price for the other two, and you ſhall even have that into the *bargain.* *L'Eſtrange.*

He who is at the charge of a tutor at home, may give his ſon a more genteel carriage, with greater learning into the *bargain*, than any at ſchool can do. *Locke.*

3. Stipulation.

There was a difference between courteſies received from their maſter and the duke; for that the duke's might have ends of utility and *bargain*; whereas their maſter's could not. *Bacon's Henry VII.*

4. An unexpected reply, tending to obſcenity.

Where ſold he *bargains*, whipſtitch? *Dryden's Macflecknoe.*

As to *bargains*, few of them ſeem to be excellent, becauſe they all terminate in one ſingle point. *Swift.*

No maid at court is leſs aſham'd,
Howe'er for ſelling *bargains* fam'd. *Swift.*

5. An event; an upſhot: a low ſenſe.

I am ſorry for thy misfortune; however we muſt make the beſt of a bad *bargain*; thou art in jeopardy, that is certain. *Arbuthnot's Hiſtory of J. Bull.*

6. In law.

*Bargain* and ſale is a contract or agreement made for manours, lands, &c. alſo the transferring the property of them from the bargainer to the bargainee. *Cowel.*

To BA'RGAIN. *v. n.* [from the noun.] To make a contract for the ſale or purchaſe of any thing; often with *for.*

Henry is able to enrich his queen;
And not to ſeek a queen to make him rich.
So worthleſs peaſants *bargain for* their wives,
As market men for oxen, ſheep, or horſe. *Shakeſp. Hen.* VI.

For thoſe that are like to be in plenty, they may be *bargained for* upon the ground. *Bacon's Nat. Hiſt.* N° 675.

The thrifty ſtate will *bargain* ere they fight. *Dryden.*

It is poſſible the great duke may *bargain for* the republick of Lucca, by the help of his great treaſures. *Addiſon on Italy.*

BARGAINEE'. *n. ſ.* [from *bargain.*] He or ſhe that accepts a bargain.

BA'RGAINER. *n. ſ.* [from *bargain.*] The perſon who profers, or makes a bargain.

BARGE. *n. ſ.* [*bargie*, Dut. from *barga*, low Lat.]

1. A boat for pleaſure.

The *barge* ſhe ſat in, like a burniſh'd throne,
Burnt on the water. *Shakeſp. Antony and Cleopatra.*

It was conſulted, when I had taken my *barge*, and gone aſhore, that my ſhip ſhould have ſet ſail and left me there. *Raleigh's Eſſays.*

Plac'd in the gilded *barge*,
Proud with the burden of ſo ſweet a charge;
With painted oars the youths begin to ſweep
Neptune's ſmooth face. *Waller.*

2. A boat for burden.

BA'RGER. *n. ſ.* [from *barge.*] The manager of a barge.

Howſoever, many wafarers make themſelves glee, by putting the inhabitants in mind of this privilege; who again, eſpecially the women, like the Campellians in the north, and the London *bargers*, forſlow not to baigne them. *Carew's Survey of Cornwal.*

BARK. *n. ſ.* [*barck*, Dan.]

1. The rind or covering of a tree.

Trees laſt according to the ſtrength and quantity of their ſap and juice; being well munited by their *bark* againſt the injuries of the air. *Bacon's Nat. Hiſt.* N° 583.

Wand'ring in the dark,
Phyſicians for the tree have found the *bark.* *Dryden.*

2. A ſmall ſhip. [from *barca*, low Lat.]

Things, I ſay, being in this ſtate, it came to paſs, that the duke of Parma muſt have flown, if he would have come into England; for he could neither get *bark* nor mariner to put to ſea. *Bacon on the War with Spain.*

It was that fatal and perfidious *bark*,
Built in th' eclipſe, and rigg'd with curſes dark,
That ſunk ſo low that ſacred head of thine. *Milton.*

Who to a woman truſts his peace of mind,
Truſts a frail *bark* with a tempeſtuous wind. *Granville.*

To BARK. *v. n.* [beopcan, Saxon.]

1. To make the noiſe which a dog makes, when he threatens or purſues.

Sent before my time
Into this breathing world, ſcarce half made up,
And that ſo lamely and unfaſhionably,
That dogs *bark* at me. *Shakeſp. Richard* III.

Why do your dogs *bark* ſo? be there bears i'th' town? *Shakeſp. Merry Wives of Windſor.*

In vain the herdman calls him back again;
The dogs ſtand off afar, and *bark* in vain. *Cowley.*

2. To clamour at; to purſue with reproaches.

Vile is the vengeance on the aſhes cold,
And envy baſe, to *bark* at ſleeping fame. *Fairy Queen, b.* ii. *cant.* viii.

You dare patronage
The envious *barking* of your ſaucy tongue,
Againſt my lord the duke of Somerſet! *Shakeſp. Henry* VI.

To BARK. *v. a.* [from the noun.] To ſtrip trees of their bark.

The ſevereſt penalties ought to be put upon *barking* any tree that is not felled. *Temple.*

Theſe trees, after they are *barked*, and cut into ſhape, are tumbled down from the mountains into the ſtream. *Addiſon's Remarks on Italy.*

BARK-BARED. *adj.* [from *bark* and *bare.*] Stripped of the bark.

Excorticated and *bark-bared* trees may be preſerved, by nouriſhing up a ſhoot from the foot, or below the ſtripped place, cutting the body of the tree ſloping off a little above the ſhoot, and it will quickly heal, and be covered with bark. *Mortimer's Art of Husbandry.*

BA'RKER. *n. ſ.* [from *bark.*]

1. One that barks or clamours.

What hath he done more than a baſe cur? barked and made a noiſe? had a fool or two to ſpit in his mouth? But they are rather enemies of my fame than me, theſe *barkers.* *Ben Johnſon's Diſcovery.*

2. [from *bark* of trees.] One that is employed in ſtripping trees.

BA'RKY. *adj.* [from *bark.*] Conſiſting of bark; containing bark.

Ivy ſo enrings the *barky* fingers of the elm. *Shakeſp. Merry Wives of Windſor.*

BA'RLEY. *n. ſ.* [derived by *Junius* from בר]

It hath a thick ſpike; the calyx, huſk, awn, and flower, are like thoſe of wheat or rye, but the awns are rough; the ſeed is ſwelling in the middle, and, for the moſt part, ends in a ſharp point, to which the huſks are cloſely united. The ſpecies are, 1. Common long-eared *barley.* 2. Winter or ſquare *barley*, by ſome called *big.* 3. Sprat *barley*, or battledoor *barley.* All theſe ſorts of *barley* are ſown in the ſpring of the year, in a dry time. In ſome very dry light land, the *barley* is ſown early in March; but in ſtrong clayey ſoils it is not ſown till April. The ſquare *barley*, or *big*, is chiefly cultivated in the north of England, and in Scotland; and is hardier than the other ſorts. Where *barley* is ſown upon new broken up land, the uſual method is to plough up the land in March, and let it lie fallow until June; at which time it is ploughed again, and ſown with turneps, which are eaten by ſheep in winter, by whoſe dung the land is greatly improved; and then, in March following, the ground is ploughed again, and ſown with *barley.* *Millar.*

*Barley* is emollient, moiſtening, and expectorating; *barley* was choſen by Hippocrates as proper food in inflammatory diſtempers. *Arbuthnot on Aliments.*

BA'RLEYBRAKE. *n. ſ.* A kind of rural play.

By neighbours prais'd ſhe went abroad thereby,
At *barleybrake* her ſweet ſwift feet to try. *Sidney.*

BARLEY BROTH. *n. ſ.* [from *barley* and *broth.*] A low word, ſometimes uſed for ſtrong beer.

Can ſodden water,
A drench for ſurreyn'd jades, their *barley broth*,
Decoct their cold blood to ſuch valiant heat? *Shak. Hen.* V.

BARLEY CORN. *n. ſ.* [from *barley* and *corn.*] A grain of barley; the beginning of our meaſure of length; the third part of an inch.

A long, long journey, choak'd with brakes and thorns,
Ill meaſur'd by ten thouſand *barley corns.* *Tickell.*

BARLEY MOW. *n. ſ.* [from *barley* and *mow.*] The place where reaped barley is ſtowed up.

Whenever by yon *barley mow* I paſs,
Before my eyes will trip the tidy laſs. *Gay's Paſtorals.*

BARM. *n. ſ.* [*burm*, Welch; beopm, Sax.] Yeaſt; the ferment put into drink to make it work, and into bread, to lighten and ſwell it.

Are you not he
That ſometimes make the drink to bear no *barm*,
Miſlead light wand'rers, laughing at their harm? *Shakeſpear.*

You may try the force of imagination, upon ſtaying the working of beer when the *barm* is put into it. *Bacon's Nat. Hiſtory*, N° 992.

BA'RMY. *adj.* [from *barm.*] Containing barm.

Their jovial nights in frolicks and in play
They paſs, to drive the tedious hours away;
And their cold ſtomachs with crown'd goblets cheer,
Of windy cider, and of *barmy* bear. *Dryden's Virgil.*

BARN. *n. ſ.* [bepn, Sax.] A place or houſe for laying up any ſort of grain, hay, or ſtraw.

In vain the *barns* expect their promis'd load,
Nor *barns* at home, nor reeks are heap'd abroad. *Dryden.*

I took notice of the make of ſeveral *barns* here: after having laid a frame of wood, they place, at the four corners of it, four blocks, in ſuch a ſhape as neither mice nor vermin can creep up. *Addiſon on Italy.*

BA'RNACLE. *n. ſ.* [probably of beapn, Sax. a child, and aac, Sax. an oak.]

1. A

1. A bird like a goose, fabulously supposed to grow on trees.

Surely it is beyond even an atheist's credulity and impudence, to affirm that the first men might grow upon trees, as the story goes about *barnacles*; or perhaps might be the lice of some vast prodigious animals, whose species is now extinct. *Bentley's Sermons.*

And from the most refin'd of saints,
As naturally grow miscreants,
As *barnacles* turn solan geese
In th' islands of the Orcades. *Hudibras, p.* iii. *c.* ii.

2. An instrument made commonly of iron for the use of farriers, to hold a horse by the nose, to hinder him from struggling when any incision is made. *Farrier's Dict.*

BARO'METER. *n. s.* [from βάρος, weight, and μέτρον, measure.] A machine for measuring the weight of the atmosphere, and the variations in it, in order chiefly to determine the changes of the weather. It differs from the baroscope, which only shews that the air is heavier at one time than another, without specifying the difference. The *barometer* is founded upon the Torricellian experiment, so called from Torricelli the inventor of it, at Florence, in 1643; which is a glass tube filled with mercury, horizontally sealed at one end; the other open and immerged in a bason of stagnant mercury; so that, as the weight of the atmosphere diminishes, the mercury in the tube will descend, and, as it encreases, the mercury will ascend; the column of mercury suspended in the tube, being always equal to the weight of the incumbent atmosphere. Many attempts have been made to render the changes in the *barometer* more sensible, in order to measure the atmosphere more accurately; and hence arose a great number of *barometers*, of different structures. Dr. Halley observes, in the *Philosophical Transactions*, that in calm weather, when the air is inclined to rain, the mercury is commonly low; in serene good settled weather, high. On great winds, though unaccompanied with rain, the mercury is lowest of all, with regard to the point of the compass the wind blows on. The greatest heights of the mercury are on easterly and north-easterly winds, *cæteris paribus*. After great storms of wind, when the mercury has been low, it rises again very fast. In calm frosty weather, it stands high. The more northerly places find greater alterations than the more southern; and within the tropicks, and near them, there is little or no variation of the height of the mercury. The rising of the mercury forebodes fair weather after foul, and an easterly or north-easterly wind; its falling portends southerly or westerly winds, or both. In a storm, the mercury beginning to rise, is a pretty sure sign that it begins to abate. But there are frequently great changes in the air, without any perceptible alteration in the *barometer*. The alterations of the weight of the air, are generally allowed to be the cause of those in the *barometer*; but philosophers cannot easily determine whence those alterations rise in the atmosphere.

The measuring the heights of mountains, and finding the elevation of places above the level of the sea, hath been much promoted by barometrical experiments, founded upon that essential property of the air, its gravity or pressure. As the column of mercury in the *barometer* is counterpoised by a column of air of equal weight, so whatever causes make the air heavier or lighter, the pressure of it will be thereby encreased or lessened, and of consequence the mercury will rise or fall. Again, the air is condensed or expanded, in proportion to the weight or force that presses it. Hence it is, that the higher from the sea, in the midland countries, the mercury descends the lower; because the air becomes more rarified and lighter, and it falls lowest upon the tops of the highest mountains. *Harris.*

Gravity is another property of air, whereby it counterpoises a column of mercury from twenty-seven inches and one half to thirty and one half, the gravity of the atmosphere varying one tenth, which are its utmost limits; so that the exact specifick gravity of the air cannot be determined, when the *barometer* stands at thirty inches, with a moderate heat of the weather. *Arbuthnot on Air.*

BAROME'TRICAL. *adj.* [from *barometer*.] Relating to the barometer.

He is very accurate in making *barometrical* and thermometrical instruments. *Derham's Physico-Theology.*

BA'RON. *n. s.* [The etymology of this word is very uncertain. *Baro*, among the Romans, signified a brave warriour, or a brutal man; and, from the first of these significations, *Menage* derives *baron*, as a term of military dignity. Others suppose it originally to signify only a man; in which sense *baron*, or *varon*, is still used by the Spaniards; and, to confirm this conjecture, our law yet uses *baron* and *femme*, husband and wife. Others deduce it from *ber*, an old Gaulish word, signifying commander; others from the Hebrew בר, of the same import. Some think it a contraction of *par homme*, or *peer*, which seems least probable.]

1. A degree of nobility next to a viscount. It may be probably thought, that anciently, in England, all those were called *barons*, that had such signiories as we now call *court barons*. And it is said, that, after the conquest, all such came to the parliament, and sat as nobles in the upper house. But when, by experience, it appeared, that the parliament was too much crouded with such multitudes, it became a custom, that none should come, but such as the king, for their extraordinary wisdom or quality, thought good to call by writ; which writ ran *hac vice tantum*. After that, men, seeing that this state of nobility was but casual, and depending merely on the prince's pleasure, obtained of the king letters patent of this dignity to them and their heirs male: and these were called *barons* by letters patent, or by creation; whose posterity are now those *barons* that are called lords of the parliament; of which kind the king may create more at his pleasure. It is nevertheless thought, that there are yet *barons* by writ, as well as *barons* by letters patent, and that they may be discerned by their titles; the *barons* by writ being those, that to the title of lord have their own surnames annexed; whereas the *barons* by letters patent, are named by their baronies. These *barons* which were first by writ, may now justly also be called *barons* by prescription; for that they have continued *barons*, in themselves and their ancestors, beyond the memory of man. There are also *barons* by tenure, as the bishops of the land, who, by virtue of baronies annexed to their bishopricks, have always had place in the upper house of parliament, and are called lords spiritual.

2. *Baron* is an officer, as *barons* of the exchequer to the king: of these the principal is called lord chief *baron*, and the three others are his assistants, between the king and his subjects, in causes of justice, belonging to the exchequer.

3. There are also *barons* of the cinque ports; two to each of the seven towns, Hastings, Winchelsea, Rye, Rumney, Hithe, Dover, and Sandwich, that have places in the lower house of parliament. *Cowel.*

They that bear
The cloth of state above, are four *barons*
Of the cinque ports. *Shakesp. Henry* VIII.

4. *Baron* is used for the husband in relation to his wife. *Cowel.*

5. A *baron* of beef is when the two sirloins are not cut asunder, but joined together by the end of the backbone. *Dict.*

BA'RONAGE. *n. s.* [from *baron*.]

1. The body of barons and peers.

His charters of the liberties of England, and of the forest, were hardly, and with difficulty, gained by the *baronage* at Staines, *A. D.* 1215. *Hale's Common Law of England.*

2. The dignity of a baron.

3. The land which gives title to a baron.

BA'RONESS. *n. s.* [*baronessa*, Ital. *baronissa*, Lat.] A baron's lady.

BA'RONET. *n. s.* [of *baron* and *et*, diminutive termination.] The lowest degree of honour that is hereditary; it is below a baron and above a knight; and has the precedency of all other knights, except the knights of the garter. It was first founded by king James I. *A. D.* 1611. *Cowel.* But it appears by the following passage, that the term was in use before, though in another sense.

King Edward III. being bearded and crossed by the clergy, they being too strong for him, so as he could not order and reform things, was advised to direct out his writs to certain gentlemen of the best abilities, entitling them therein barons in the next parliament. By which means he had so many barons in his parliament, as were able to weigh down the clergy; which barons were not afterwards lords, but *baronets*, as sundry of them do yet retain the name. *Spenser on Ireland.*

BA'RONY. *n. s.* [*baronnie*, Fr. beorny, Sax.] That honour or lordship that gives title to a baron. Such are not only the fees of temporal barons, but of bishops also. *Cowel.*

BA'ROSCOPE. *n. s.* [βάρος and σκοπέω.] An instrument to shew the weight of the atmosphere. See BAROMETER.

If there was always a calm, the equilibrium could only be changed by the contents; where the winds are not variable, the alterations of the *baroscope* are very small. *Arbuth. on Air.*

BA'RRACAN. *n. s.* [*bouracan*, or *barracan*, Fr.] A strong thick kind of camelot.

BA'RRACK. *n. s.* [*barracca*, Span.]

1. Little cabins made by the Spanish fishermen on the sea shore; or little lodges for soldiers in a camp.

2. It is generally taken among us for buildings to lodge soldiers.

BA'RRATOR. *n. s.* [from *barat*, old Fr. from which is still retained *barateur*, a cheat.] A wrangler, and encourager of law suits.

Will it not reflect so much on thy character, Nic, to turn *barrator* in thy old days, a stirrer up of quarrels amongst thy neighbours. *Arbuthnot's History of J. Bull.*

BA'RRATRY. *n. s.* [from *barrator*.] The practice or crime of a barrator; foul practice in law.

'Tis arrant *barratry*, that bears
Point blank an action 'gainst our laws. *Hudibras.*

BA'RREL. *n. s.* [*baril*, Welch.]

1. A round wooden vessel to be stopped close.

It hath been observed by one of the ancients, that an empty *barrel* knocked upon with the finger, giveth a diapason to the sound of the like *barrel* full. *Bacon's Nat. History*, N° 186.

Trembling to approach
The little *barrel*, which he fears to broach. *Dryden's Persius.*

2. A particular measure in liquids. A *barrel* of wine is thirty one gallons and a half; of ale, thirty two gallons; of beer, thirty six gallons, and of beer vinegar, thirty four gallons.

3. In dry measure. A *barrel* of Essex butter contains one hundred and

blank page

IL facing 2Q2v

blank page

and six pounds; of Suffolk butter, two hundred and fifty six. A *barrel* of herrings should contain thirty two gallons wine measure, holding usually a thousand herrings.

Several colleges, instead of limiting their rents to a certain sum, prevailed with their tenants to pay the price of so many *barrels* of corn, as the market went. *Swift.*

4. Any thing hollow, as the *barrel* of a gun; that part which holds the shot.

Take the *barrel* of a long gun perfectly bored, set it upright with the breech upon the ground, and take a bullet exactly fit for it; then if you suck at the mouth of the *barrel* ever so gently, the bullet will come up so forcibly, that it will hazard the striking out your teeth. *Digby on Bodies.*

5. A cylinder; frequently that cylinder about which any thing is wound.

Your string and bow must be accommodated to your drill; if too weak, it will not carry about the *barrel.* *Moxon's Mechanical Exercises.*

6. *Barrel of the ear*, is a cavity behind the tympanum, covered with a fine membrane. *Dict.*

To BA'RREL. *v. a.* [from the noun.] To put any thing in a barrel for preservation.

I would have their beef beforehand *barrelled*, which may be used as it is needed. *Spenser on Ireland.*

*Barrel* up earth, and sow some seed in it, and put it in the bottom of a pond. *Bacon's Nat. Hist.* Nº 531.

BA'RREL-BELLIED. *adj.* [from *barrel* and *belly.*] Having a large belly.

Dauntless at empty noises; lofty neck'd,
Sharp headed, *barrel-belly'd*, broadly back'd. *Dryd. Virgil.*

BA'RREN. *adj.* [bane, Sax. naked; properly applied to trees or ground unfruitful.]

1. Without the quality of producing its kind; not prolifick; applied to animals.

They hail'd him father to a line of kings.
Upon my head they plac'd a fruitless crown,
And put a *barren* sceptre in my gripe,
No son of mine succeeding. *Shakesp. Macbeth.*

There shall not be male or female *barren* among you, or among your cattle. *Deuter.* vii. 14.

2. Unfruitful; not fertile; sterile.

The situation of this city is pleasant, but the water is naught, and the ground *barren.* 2 *Kings*, ii. 19.

Telemachus is far from exalting the nature of his country; he confesses it to be *barren.* *Pope's Odyssey, b. iv. notes.*

From his far excursion thro' the wilds
Of *barren* ether, faithful to his time,
They see the blazing wonder rise anew. *Thomson's Summer.*

3. Not copious; scanty.

Some schemes will appear *barren* of hints and matter, but prove to be fruitful. *Swift.*

4. Unmeaning; uninventive; dull.

There be of them that will make themselves laugh, to set on some quantity of *barren* spectators to laugh too. *Shakespeare.*

BA'RRENLY. *adv.* [from *barren.*] Unfruitfully.

BA'RRENNESS. *n. s.* [from *barren.*]

1. Want of offspring; want of the power of procreation.

I pray'd for children, and thought *barrenness*
In wedlock a reproach. *Milton's Agonistes, l.* 350.

No more be mention'd then of violence
Against ourselves; and wilful *barrenness*,
That cuts us off from hope. *Milton's Par. Lost, b.* x.

2. Unfruitfulness; sterility; infertility.

Within the self same hamlet, lands have divers degrees of value, through the diversity of their fertility or *barrenness.* *Bacon on Alienations.*

3. Want of invention; want of the power of producing any thing new.

The adventures of Ulysses are imitated in the Æneis; though the accidents are not the same, which would have argued him of a total *barrenness* of invention. *Dryden's Fables, Preface.*

4. Want of matter.

The importunity of our adversaries hath constrained us longer to dwell than the *barrenness* of so poor a cause could have seemed either to require or to admit. *Hooker, b.* v. § 22.

5. In theology: aridity; want of emotion or sensibility.

The greatest saints sometimes are fervent, and sometimes feel a *barrenness* of devotion. *Taylor's Guide to Devotion.*

BA'RRENWORT. *n. s.* [*epimedium*, Lat.] The name of a plant.

The stalks are divided into three branches, each sustaining three leaves, shaped like ivy; the calyx consists of four leaves; the flower, of four petals, hollow, and expanded in form of a cross; the pointal of the flower becomes a pod with one cell, having two valves, in which are contained round flat seeds. *Millar.*

BA'RRFUL. *adj.* [from *bar* and *full.*] Full of obstructions.

A *barrful* strife!
Whoe'er I woo, myself would be his wife. *Shak. Tw. Night.*

BARRICA'DE. *n. s.* [*barricade*, Fr.]

1. A fortification made in haste, of trees, earth, waggons, or any thing else, to keep off an attack.

2. Any stop; bar; obstruction.

BAR

There must be such a *barricade*, as would greatly annoy, or rather absolutely stop, the currents of the atmosphere. *Derham's Physico-Theology.*

To BARRICA'DE. *v. a.* [*barricader*, Fr.] To stop up a passage.

A new vulcano continually discharging that matter, which being till then *barricaded* up, and imprisoned in the bowels of the earth, was the occasion of very great and frequent calamities. *Woodward's Natural History.*

Now all the pavement sounds with trampling feet,
And the mixt hurry *barricades* the street,
Entangled here, the waggon's lengthen'd team. *Gay.*

BARRICA'DO. *n. s.* [*barricada*, Span.] A fortification; a bar; any thing fixed to hinder entrance.

The access of the town was only by a neck of land, between the sea on the one part, and the harbour water, or inner sea on the other; fortified clean over with a strong rampier and *barricado.* *Bacon's War with Spain.*

To BARRICADO. *v. a.* [from the noun.] To fortify; to bar; to stop up.

Fast we found, fast shut
The dismal gates, and *barricado'd* strong! *Paradise Lost.*

He had not time to *barricado* the doors; so that the enemy entered. *Clarendon, b.* viii.

The truth of causes we find so obliterated, that it seems almost *barricadoed* from any intellectual approach. *Harvey on Consumptions.*

BA'RRIER. *n. s.* [*barriere*, Fr. It is sometimes pronounced with the accent on the last syllable, but it is placed more properly on the first.]

1. A barricade; an entrenchment.

Safe in the love of heav'n an ocean flows
Around our realm, a *barrier* from the foes. *Pope's Odyssey.*

2. A fortification, or strong place, as on the frontiers of a country.

The queen is under the obligation of being guarantee of the Dutch having possession of the said *barrier*, and the revenues thereof, before a peace. *Swift.*

3. A stop; an obstruction.

If you value yourself as a man of learning, you are building a most unpassable *barrier* against all improvement. *Watts's Improvement of the Mind.*

4. A bar to mark the limits of any place.

For justs, and tourneys, and *barriers*, the glories of them are chiefly in the chariots, wherein the challengers make their entries. *Bacon's Essays.*

Pris'ners to the pillar bound,
At either *barrier* plac'd; nor, captives made,
Be freed, or arm'd anew. *Dryden's Fables.*

5. A boundary.

But wave whate'er to Cadmus may belong,
And fix, O muse, the *barrier* of thy song,
At Oedipus. *Pope's Statius.*

How instinct varies in the groveling swine,
Compar'd, half reas'ning elephant! with thine:
'Twixt that and reason, what a nice *barrier!*
For ever sep'rate, yet for ever near. *Pope's Essay on Man.*

BA'RRISTER. *n. s.* [from *bar.*] A person qualified to plead the causes of clients in the courts of justice, called an advocate or licentiate in other countries and courts. *Barristers*, now usually denominated counsellors at law, were formerly obliged to study eight years before they were passed, now only seven, and sometimes fewer. Outer *barristers* are pleaders without the bar, to distinguish them from inner *barristers*; such are the benchers, or those who have been readers, the council of the king, queen, and princes, who are admitted to plead within the bar. *Blount. Chambers.*

BA'RROW. *n. s.* [beꞃeꝑe, Sax. supposed by *Skinner* to come from *bear.*] Any kind of carriage moved by the hand, as a *handbarrow*; a frame of boards, with handles at each end, carried between two men; a *wheelbarrow*, that which one man pushes forward, by raising it upon one wheel.

Have I lived to be carried in a basket, like a *barrow* of butcher's offal, and to be thrown into the Thames? *Shakesp. Merry Wives of Windsor.*

No *barrow's* wheel
Shall mark thy stocking with a miry trace. *Gay's Trivia.*

BA'RROW. *n. s.* [bep̄g, Saxon.] A hog; whence *barrow* grease, or hog's lard.

BARROW, whether in the beginning or end of names of places, signifies a grove; from beaꞃpe, which the Saxons used in the same sense. *Gibson's Camden.*

BARROW is likewise used in Cornwal for a hillock, under which, in old times, bodies have been buried.

To BA'RTER. *v. n.* [*baratter*, Fr. to trick in traffick; from *barat*, craft, fraud.] To traffick by exchanging one commodity for another, in opposition to purchasing with money.

As if they scorn'd to trade and *barter*,
By giving or by taking quarter. *Hudibras, p.* iii. *c.* i.

A man has not every thing growing upon his soil, and therefore is willing to *barter* with his neighbour. *Collier.*

To BA'RTER. *v. a.*

1. To give any thing in exchange for something else.

For him was I exchang'd and ransom'd;
But with a baser man of arms by far,
Once, in contempt, they would have *barter'd* me.
*Shakesp. Henry* VI. *p.* i.

Then as thou wilt dispose the rest,
To those who, at the market rate,
Can *barter* honour for estate. *Prior.*

I see nothing left us, but to truck and *barter* our goods, like the wild Indians, with each other. *Swift.*

2. Sometimes it is used with the particle *away* before the thing given.

If they will *barter away* their time, methinks they should at least have some ease in exchange. *Decay of Piety.*

He also *bartered away* plums that would have rotted in a week, for nuts that would last good for his eating a whole year. *Locke.*

BA'RTER. *n. s.* [from the verb.] The act or practice of trafficking by exchange of commodities; sometimes the thing given in exchange.

From England they may be furnished with such things as they may want, and, in exchange or *barter*, send other things, with which they may abound. *Bacon's Advice to Villiers.*

He who corrupteth English with foreign words, is as wise as ladies that change plate for china; for which, I think, the laudable traffick of old cloaths is much the fairest *barter.* *Felton on the Classicks.*

BA'RTERER. *n. s.* [from *barter.*] He that trafficks by exchange of commodities.

BA'RTERY. *n. s.* [from *barter.*] Exchange of commodities.

It is a received opinion, that, in most ancient ages, there was only *bartery* or change of commodities amongst most nations. *Camden's Remains.*

BA'RTRAM. *n. s.* A plant; the same with *pellitory*; which see.

BA'RTON. *n. s.* The demesne lands of a manour; the manour-house itself; and sometimes the out-houses. *Blount.*

BASE. *adj.* [*bas*, Fr. *basso*, Ital. *baxo*, Span. *bassus*, low Latin; βάσις.]

1. Mean; vile; worthless.

The harvest white plumb is a *base* plumb, and the white date-plumb are no very good plumbs. *Bacon's Natural Hist.*

Pyreicus was only famous for counterfeiting all *base* things, as earthen pitchers, a scullery; whereupon he was surnamed Rupographus. *Peacham.*

2. Of mean spirit; disingenuous; illiberal; ungenerous; low; without dignity of sentiment.

Since the perfections are such in the party I love, as the feeling of them cannot come unto any unnoble heart; shall that heart, lifted up to such a height, be counted *base?* *Sidney.*

It is *base* in his adversaries thus to dwell upon the excesses of a passion. *Atterbury.*

I might be *base* enough to suspect, that you acted like some philosopher, who writ much better upon virtue than he practised it. *Swift.*

3. Of low station; of mean account; without dignity of rank; without honour.

If the lords and chief men degenerate, what shall be hoped of the peasants and *baser* people? *Spenser on Ireland.*

If that rebellion
Came like itself, in *base* and abject routs,
You reverend father, and these noble lords,
Had not been here. *Shakesp. Henry* IV. *p.* ii.

It could not else be, I should prove so *base*,
To sue and be denied such common grace. *Shak. Timon.*

And I will yet be more vile than this, and will be *base* in mine own sight. *2 Sam.* vi. 22.

Insurrections of *base* people are commonly more furious in their beginnings. *Bacon's Henry* VII.

He whose mind
Is virtuous, is alone of noble kind;
Though poor in fortune, of celestial race,
And he commits the crime who calls him *base.* *Dryden.*

4. Base-born; born out of wedlock, and by consequence of no honourable birth.

Why bastard? wherefore *base?*
When my dimensions are as well compact
As honest madam's issue. *Shakesp. King Lear.*

This young lord lost his life with his father in the field, and with them a *base* son. *Camden's Remains.*

5. Applied to metals: without value; it is used in this sense of all metal except gold and silver.

A guinea is pure gold, if it has nothing but gold in it, without any alloy or *baser* metal. *Watts's Logick.*

6. Applied to sounds, deep; grave. It is more frequently written *bass*, though the comparative *baser* seems to require *base.*

In pipes, the lower the note holes be, and the further from the mouth of the pipe, the more *base* sound they yield. *Bacon's Natural History, N° 178.*

BASE-BORN. *adj.* Born out of wedlock.

But see thy *base-born* child, thy babe of shame,
Who, left by thee, upon our parish came. *Gay.*

BASE-COURT. *n. s.* Lower court; not the chief court that leads to the house.

My lord, in the *base-court* he doth attend,
To speak with you. *Shakesp. Richard* II.

BASE-MINDED. *adj.* Mean spirited; worthless.

It signifieth, as it seemeth, no more than abject, *base-minded*, false hearted, coward, or nidget. *Camden's Remains.*

BASE-VIOL. *n. s.* [usually written *bass viol.*] An instrument which is used in concerts for the base sound.

At the very first grin he cast every human feature out of his countenance; at the second, he became the head of a *base-viol.* *Addison. Spectator,* N° 174.

BASE. *n. s.* [*bas*, Fr. *basis*, Lat.]

1. The bottom of any thing; commonly used for the lower part of a building, or column.

What if it tempt thee tow'rd the flood, my lord?
Or to the dreadful summit of the cliff,
That beetles o'er his *base* into the sea. *Shakesp. Hamlet.*

Firm Dorick pillars found your solid *base*;
The fair Corinthian crowns the higher space. *Dryden.*

Columns of polish'd marble firmly set
On golden *bases*, are his legs and feet. *Prior.*

2. The pedestal of a statue.

Men of weak abilities in great place, are like little statues set on great *bases*, made the less by their advancement. *Bacon.*

Mercury was patron of flocks, and the ancients placed a ram at the *base* of his images. *Broome's Notes on the Odyssey.*

3. That part of any ornament which hangs down, as housings.

Phalantus was all in white, having his *bases* and caparison embroidered. *Sidney.*

4. The broad part of any body; as the bottom of a cone.

5. Stockings, or perhaps the armour for the legs, from *bas*, Fr.

Nor shall it e'er be said that wight,
With gauntlet blue and *bases* white,
And round blunt truncheon by his side,
So great a man at arms defy'd. *Hudibras.*

6. The place from which racers or tilters run; the bottom of the field.

He said; to their appointed *base* they went;
With beating heart th' expecting sign receive,
And, starting all at once, the barrier leave. *Dryden's Virg.*

7. The string that gives a base sound.

At thy well sharpen'd thumb, from shore to shore,
The trebles squeak for fear, the *bases* roar. *Dryden's Mackf.*

8. An old rustick play; written by *Skinner*, bays.

He with two striplings (lads, more like to run
The country *base*, than to commit such slaughter)
Made good the passage. *Shakesp. Cymbeline.*

To BASE. *v. a.* [*baiser*, Fr.] To embase; to make less valuable by admixture of meaner metals.

I am doubtful whether men have sufficiently refined metals, which we cannot *base*; as, whether iron, brass, and tin be refined to the height? *Bacon's Natural History,* N° 849.

BA'SELY. *adv.* [from *base.*]

1. In a base manner; meanly; dishonourably.

The king is not himself, but *basely* led
By flatterers. *Shakesp. Richard* II.

A lieutenant *basely* gave it up, as soon as Essex in his passage demanded it. *Clarendon.*

With broken vows his fame he will not stain,
With conquest *basely* bought, and with inglorious gain. *Dryden.*

2. In bastardy.

These two Mitylene brethren, *basely* born, crept out of a small galliot unto the majesty of great kings. *Knolles's History of the Turks.*

BA'SENESS. *n. s.* [from *base.*]

1. Meanness; vileness; badness.

Such is the power of that sweet passion,
That it all sordid *baseness* doth expel. *Spens. Hymn on Love.*

When a man's folly must be spread open before the angels, and all his *baseness* ript up before those pure spirits, this will be a double hell. *South.*

Your soul's above the *baseness* of distrust:
Nothing but love could make you so unjust. *Dryd. Aureng.*

2. Vileness of metal.

We alleged the fraudulent obtaining and executing his patent, the *baseness* of his metal, and the prodigious sum to be coined. *Swift.*

3. Bastardy.

Why brand they us
With base? with *baseness?* bastardy? *Shakesp. King Lear.*

4. Deepness of sound.

The just and measured proportion of the air percussed towards the *baseness* or trebleness of tones, is one of the greatest secrets in the contemplation of sounds. *Bacon's Nat. History.*

To BASH. *v. n.* [probably from *base.*] To be ashamed; to be confounded with shame.

His countenance was bold, and *bashed* not
For Guyon's looks, but scornful eye-glance at him shot. *Fairy Queen, b.* ii. *c.* iv.

BASHA'W. *n. s.* [sometimes written *bassa.*] A title of honour and command among the Turks; the viceroy of a province; the general of an army.

The

3

Young broome or good pasture thy Ewes do
require
Warm Barth and in safety their lambs do
desire

Tuss. Husb. for Janry

Barth is commonly an inclosure or place
near the farm house well shelter'd where
the Ewes & lambs are brought in for warmth
note to Tuss.

Hence the common phrase he has a
warm berth for barth

oa ‡

~~Base in musie~~ The rough hoarse tones
in musicke opposed to the noble

the rolling sea resounding soft
In his big base them fitly answered
And on the rock the waves breaking aloft
A solemn mean unto them measured

Spens 2. 12

a ‡

The slacker strings are or the less
wound up the baser is the sound

Bacon.

i. it may come from abbaisser [illegible]

Fine basil desireth it may be her lot
To grow as a gelliflower trim in a pot
That ladies & gentils for whom ye do serve
May help her, as needeth, poor life to preserve.

Tuss. hus. for May

7 Base in music

the rolling Sea resounding soft
In his big base them fitly answered
And on the Rock the waves breaking aloft
A Solemn mean unto them measured

Spens. 2. 12

a‡ Thou hast talk'd
Of basilisks, of cannon, culverin
~~Of prisoners ransom & of soldiers slain~~

Shak.

IL facing 2R2r

The Turks made an expedition into Perſia; and becauſe of the ſtraits of the mountains, the *baſhaw* conſulted which way they ſhould get in. *Bacon's Apophthegms.*

BA'SHFUL. *adj.* [This word, with all thoſe of the ſame race, are of uncertain etymology. *Skinner* imagines them derived from *baſe*, or mean; *Minſhew*, from *verbaeſen*, Dut. to ſtrike with aſtoniſhment; *Junius*, from βάζειν, which he finds in *Heſychius* to ſignify ſhame. The conjecture of *Minſhew* ſeems moſt probable.]

1. Modeſt; ſhamefaced.

I never tempted her with word too large;
But, as a brother to his ſiſter, ſhew'd
*Baſhful* ſincerity, and comely love. *Shakeſp. M. ado about N.*

2. Sheepiſh; vitiouſly modeſt.

He looked with an almoſt *baſhful* kind of modeſty, as if he feared the eyes of man. *Sidney.*

Hence, *baſhful* cunning!
And prompt me plain and holy innocence. *Shakeſp. Tempeſt.*

Our authour, anxious for his fame to night,
And *baſhful* in his firſt attempt to write,
Lies cautiouſly obſcure. *Addiſon's Drummer, Prologue.*

BA'SHFULLY. *adv.* [from *baſhful.*] Timorouſly; modeſtly.

BA'SHFULNESS. *n. ſ.* [from *baſhful.*]

1. Modeſty, as ſhewn in outward appearance.

Philoclea a little muſed how to cut the thread even, with eyes, cheeks and lips, whereof each ſang their part, to make up the harmony of *baſhfulneſs.* *Sidney.*

Such looks, ſuch *baſhfulneſs* might well adorn
The cheeks of youths that are more nobly born. *Dryden.*

2. Vitious or ruſtick ſhame.

For fear had bequeathed his room to his kinſman *baſhfulneſs*, to teach him good manners. *Sidney, b.* i.

There are others who have not altogether ſo much of this fooliſh *baſhfulneſs*, and who aſk every one's opinion. *Dryden.*

BA'SIL. *n. ſ.* [*ocymum*, Lat.] The name of a plant.

This plant hath a labiated flower of one leaf, whoſe creſt is upright, roundiſh, notched, and larger than the beard, which is generally curled, or gently cut. Out of the flower cup riſes the pointal, attended by four embryos, that become ſo many ſeeds incloſed in a huſk, which was before the flower cup; the huſk is divided into two lips, the upper one growing upright, and is ſplit into two; but the under one is cut into ſeveral parts. The ſpecies are eight; 1. Common *baſil.* 2. Common *baſil*, with dark green leaves, and white flowers. 3. Leſſer *baſil*, with narrow ſerrated leaves. 4. The leaſt *baſil*, commonly called *buſh-baſil*, &c. Theſe annual plants are propagated from ſeeds in March, upon a moderate hot bed. In Auguſt they perfect their ſeeds. The firſt ſort is preſcribed in medicine; but the fourth is moſt eſteemed for its beauty and ſcent. *Millar.*

BA'SIL. *n. ſ.* The angle to which the edge of a joiner's tool is ground away.

BA'SIL. *n. ſ.* The ſkin of a ſheep tanned. *Dict.*

To BA'SIL. *v. a.* To grind the edge of a tool to an angle.

Theſe chiſſels are not ground to ſuch a baſil as the joiners chiſſels on one of the ſides, but are *baſiled* away on both the flat ſides; ſo that the edge lies between both the ſides in the middle of the tool. *Moxon's Mechanical Exerciſes.*

BASI'LICA. *n. ſ.* [βασιλική.] The middle vein of the arm ſo called, by way of pre-eminence. It is likewiſe attributed to many medicines for the ſame reaſon. *Quincy.*

BASI'LICAL. } *adj.* [from *baſilica.* See BASILICA.] Belonging
BASI'LICK. } to the baſilick vein.

Theſe aneuriſms following always upon bleeding the *baſilick* vein, muſt be aneuriſms of the humeral artery. *Sharp.*

BASI'LICK. *n. ſ.* [*baſilique*, Fr. βασιλική.] A large hall, having two ranges of pillars, and two iſles or wings, with galleries over them. Theſe *baſilicks* were firſt made for the palaces of princes, and afterwards converted into courts of juſtice, and laſtly into churches; whence a *baſilick* is generally taken for a magnificent church, as the *baſilick* of St. Peter at Rome.

BASI'LICON. *n. ſ.* [βασιλικὸν.] An ointment called alſo tetrapharmacon. *Quincy.*

I made inciſion into the cavity, and put a pledget of *baſilicon* over it. *Wiſeman's Surgery.*

BA'SILISK. *n. ſ.* [*baſiliſcus*, Lat. of βασιλίσκος, of βασιλεὺς, a king.]

1. A kind of ſerpent, called alſo a cockatrice, which is ſaid to drive away all others by his hiſſing, and to kill by looking.

Make me not ſighted like the *baſiliſk*;
I've look'd on thouſands who have ſped the better
By my regard, but kill'd none ſo. *Shakeſp. Winter's Tale.*

The *baſiliſk* was a ſerpent not above three palms long, and differenced from other ſerpents by advancing his head, and ſome white marks or coronary ſpots upon the crown. *Brown's Vulgar Errours.*

2. A ſpecies of cannon or ordnance.

There we imitate and practiſe to make ſwifter motions than any you have: and to make them ſtronger and more violent than yours are; exceeding your greateſt cannons and *baſiliſks.* *Bacon's New Atlantis.*

BA'SIN. *n. ſ.* [*baſun*, Fr. *bacile*, *bacino*, Ital. It is often written *baſon*, but not according to etymology.]

1. A ſmall veſſel to hold water for waſhing, or other uſes.

Let one attend him with a ſilver *baſin*,
Full of roſewater, and beſtrew'd with flowers.
*Shakeſp. Taming of the Shrew.*

We have little wells for infuſions, where the waters take the virtue quicker and better, than in veſſels and *baſins.* *Bacon.*

We behold a piece of ſilver in a *baſin*, when water is put upon it, which we could not diſcover before, as under the verge thereof. *Brown's Vulgar Errours.*

2. A ſmall pond.

On one ſide of the walk you ſee this hollow *baſin*, with its ſeveral little plantations lying conveniently under the eye of the beholder. *Spectator*, Nº 477.

3. A part of the ſea incloſed in rocks, with a narrow entrance.

The jutting land two ample bays divides;
The ſpacious *baſins* arching rocks incloſe,
A ſure defence from ev'ry ſtorm that blows. *Pope's Odyſſey.*

4. Any hollow place capacious of liquids.

If this rotation does the ſeas affect,
The rapid motion rather would eject
The ſtores, the low capacious caves contain,
And from its ample *baſin* caſt the main. *Blackmore's Creat.*

5. A dock for repairing and building ſhips.

6. In anatomy, a round cavity ſituated between the anterior ventricles of the brain.

7. A concave piece of metal by which glaſs grinders form their convex glaſſes.

8. A round ſhell or caſe of iron placed over a furnace, in which hatters mould the matter of a hat into form.

9. *Baſins of a balance*; the ſame with the ſcales; one to hold the weight, the other the thing to be weighed.

BA'SIS. *n. ſ.* [*baſis*, Lat.]

1. The foundation of any thing, as of a column or a building.

It muſt follow, that paradiſe, being raiſed to this height, muſt have the compaſs of the whole earth for a *baſis* and foundation. *Raleigh's Hiſtory of the World.*

Aſcend my chariot, guide the rapid wheels
That ſhake heav'n's *baſis.* *Milton's Paradiſe Loſt, b.* vi.

In altar-wiſe a ſtately pile they rear;
The *baſis* broad below, and top advanc'd in air. *Dryden.*

2. The loweſt of the three principal parts of a column, which are the *baſis*, *ſhaft*, and *capital.*

Upon our coming to the bottom, obſerving an Engliſh inſcription upon the *baſis*, we read it over ſeveral times. *Addiſon's Freeholder*, Nº 47.

3. That on which any thing is raiſed.

Such ſeems thy gentle height, made only proud
To be the *baſis* of that pompous load,
Than which a nobler weight no mountain bears. *Denham.*

4. The pedeſtal.

How many times ſhall Cæſar bleed in ſport,
That now on Pompey's *baſis* lies along
No worthier than the duſt? *Shakeſp. Julius Cæſar.*

5. The groundwork or firſt principle of any thing.

Build me thy fortune upon the *baſis* of valour.
*Shakeſp. Twelfth Night.*

The friendſhips of the world are oft
Confederacies in vice, or leagues of pleaſure;
Ours has ſevereſt virtue for its *baſis.* *Addiſon's Cato.*

To BASK. *v. a.* [*backeren*, Dut. *Skinner.*] To warm by laying out in the heat; uſed almoſt always of animals.

And ſtretched out all the chimney's length,
*Baſks* at the fire his hairy ſtrength. *Milton.*

He was *baſking* himſelf in the gleam of the ſun. *L'Eſtrange.*

'Tis all thy buſineſs, buſineſs how to ſhun,
To *baſk* thy naked body in the ſun. *Dryden's Perſius.*

To BASK. *v. n.* To lie in the warmth.

About him, and above, and round the wood,
The birds that haunt the borders of his flood;
That bath'd within, or *baſk'd* upon his ſide,
To tuneful ſongs their narrow throats apply'd. *Dryden.*

Unlock'd, in covers let her freely run,
To range thy courts, and *baſk* before the ſun. *Tickell.*

Some in the fields of pureſt æther play,
And *baſk* and whiten in the blaze of day. *Pope.*

BA'SKET. *n. ſ.* [*baſged*, Welch; *baſcauda*, Lat. *Barbara depictis venit baſcauda Britannis.* Martial.] A veſſel made of twigs, ruſhes, or ſplinters, or ſome other ſlender body interwoven.

Here is a *baſket*; he may creep in, and throw foul linen upon him, as if going to bucking. *Shak. Merry Wives of Windſ.*

Thus while I ſung, my ſorrows I deceiv'd,
And bending oſiers into *baſkets* weav'd. *Dryden.*

Poor Peg was forced to go hawking and peddling; now and then carrying a *baſket* of fiſh to the market. *Arbuth. J. Bull.*

BA'SKET-HILT. *n. ſ.* [from *baſket* and *hilt.*] A hilt of a weapon ſo made as to contain the whole hand, and defend it from being wounded.

His puiſſant ſword unto his ſide,
Near his undaunted heart, was ty'd:
With *baſket-hilt*, that would hold broth,
And ſerve for ſight and dinner both. *Hudibras, cant.* i.

Their

Their beef they often in their murrions ſtew'd,
And in their *baſket hilts* their bev'rage brew'd.
*King's Art of Cookery.*

BA'SKET-WOMAN. *n. ſ.* [from *baſket* and *woman.*] A woman that plies at markets with a baſket, ready to carry home any thing that is bought.

BASS. *adj.* [See BASE.] In muſick; grave; deep.

BASS-VIOL. See BASE-VIOL.

On the ſweep of the arch lies one of the Muſes, playing on a *baſs-viol.* *Dryden.*

BASS. *n. ſ.* [ſuppoſed by *Junius* to be derived, like *baſket*, from ſome Britiſh word ſignifying a *ruſh*; but perhaps more properly written *boſs*, from the French *boſſe.*] A mat uſed in churches.

Having woollen yarn, *baſs* mat, or ſuch like, to bind them withal. *Mortimer's Huſbandry.*

BASS-RELIEF. *n. ſ.* [from *bas*, and *relief*, raiſed work, Fr.] Sculpture, the figures of which do not ſtand out from the ground in their full proportion. *Felibien* diſtinguiſhes three kinds of *baſs-relief*; in the firſt, the front figures appear almoſt with the full relief; in the ſecond, they ſtand out no more than one half; and, in the third, much leſs, as in coins.

BA'SSA. See BASHAW.

BA'SSET. *n. ſ.* [*baſſet*, Fr.] A game at cards, invented at Venice.

Gameſters would no more blaſpheme; and lady Dabcheek's *baſſet* bank would be broke. *Dennis.*

*BASSO RELIEVO.* [Ital.] See BASS-RELIEF.

BASSO'N. } *n. ſ.* [*baſſon*, Fr.] A muſical inſtrument of the wind
BASSO'ON. } kind, blown with a reed, and furniſhed with eleven holes, which are ſtopped like other large flutes; its diameter at bottom is nine inches, and it ſerves for the baſs in concerts of hautboys, &c. *Trevoux.*

BA'SSOCK. *n. ſ.* The ſame with *baſs.*

BA'STARD. *n. ſ.* [*baſtardd*, Welch, of low birth; *baſtarde*, Fr.]

1. *Baſtard*, according to the civil and canon law, is a perſon born of a woman out of wedlock, or not married; ſo that, according to order of law, his father is not known. *Ayliffe.*

Him to the Lydian king Lycimnia bare,
And ſent her boaſted *baſtard* to the war. *Dryden.*

2. Any thing ſpurious or falſe.

It lies on you to ſpeak to th' people;
Not by your own inſtruction, but with words
But rooted in your tongue; *baſtards* and ſyllables
Of no allowance to your boſom's truth. *Shakeſp. Coriolanus.*

BA'STARD. *adj.* [from the noun.]

1. Begotten out of wedlock.

Peace is a very apoplexy, lethargy, inſenſible, a getter of more *baſtard* children than war's a deſtroyer of men. *Shakeſp. Coriolanus.*

2. Spurious; not genuine; ſuppoſititious; falſe; adulterate. In this ſenſe, any thing which bears ſome relation or reſemblance to another, is called ſpurious or *baſtard.*

You may partly hope that your father got you not, that you are not the Jew's daughter.—That were a kind of *baſtard* hope indeed. *Shakeſp. Merchant of Venice.*

Men who, under the diſguiſe of publick good, purſue their own deſigns of power, and ſuch *baſtard* honours as attend them. *Temple.*

BA'STARD *Cedar Tree.* [called *guazuma* in the Weſt Indies.]

The characters are; It hath a regular flower, conſiſting of five leaves, hollowed like a ſpoon at their baſe; but, at their tops, divided into two parts, like a fork. The flower cup conſiſts of three leaves, from whence ariſes the pointal, which afterwards becomes a roundiſh warted fruit, which has five cells, incloſing many ſeeds.

It grows plentifully in the low lands in Jamaica, where it riſes to the height of forty or fifty feet, and has a large trunk. The timber of this tree is cut into ſtaves, for caſes of all ſorts, and uſed for many other purpoſes. The fruit is eat by cattle, as it falls from the trees, and is eſteemed very good to fatten them; ſo that the planters often leave theſe trees ſtanding in their ſavannas, when they clear them from all other wood. *Millar.*

To BA'STARD. *v. a.* [from the noun.] To convict of being a baſtard; to ſtigmatize with baſtardy.

She lived to ſee her brother beheaded, and her two ſons depoſed from the crown, *baſtarded* in their blood, and cruelly murdered. *Bacon's Henry* VII.

To BA'STARDIZE. *v. a.* [from *baſtard.*]

1. To convict of being a baſtard.

2. To beget a baſtard.

I ſhould have been what I am, had the maidenlieſt ſtar in the firmament twinkled on my *baſtardizing.* *Shakeſp. King Lear.*

BA'STARDLY. *adv.* [from *baſtard.*] In the manner of a baſtard; ſpuriouſly.

Good ſeed degenerates, and oft obeys
The ſoil's diſeaſe, and into cockle ſtrays;
Let the mind's thoughts but be tranſplanted ſo
Into the body, and *baſtardly* they grow. *Donne.*

BA'STARDY. *n. ſ.* [from *baſtard.*] An unlawful ſtate of birth, which diſables the baſtard, both according to the laws of God and man, from ſucceeding to an inheritance. *Ayliffe's Parerg.*

Once ſhe ſlander'd me with *baſtardy*;
But whether I be true begot, or no,
That ſtill I lay upon my mother's head. *Shakeſp. K. John.*

In reſpect of the evil conſequents, the wife's adultery is worſe, as bringing *baſtardy* into a family. *Taylor's Holy Living.*

No more of *baſtardy* in heirs of crowns. *Pope's Epiſtles.*

To BASTE. *v. a.* participle paſſ. *baſted*, or *baſten.* [*baſtonner*, Fr. *Bazata*, in the Armorick dialect, ſignifies to ſtrike with a ſtick; from which perhaps *baſton* a ſtick, and all its derivatives, or collaterals, may be deduced.]

1. To beat with a ſtick.

Quoth ſhe, I grant it is in vain
For one's that *baſted* to feel pain,
Becauſe the pangs his bones endure,
Contribute nothing to the cure. *Hudibras.*

Tir'd with diſpute, and ſpeaking Latin,
As well as *baſting*, and bear baiting. *Hudibras.*

*Baſtings* heavy, dry, obtuſe,
Only dulneſs can produce;
While a little gentle jerking
Sets the ſpirits all aworking. *Swift.*

2. To drip butter, or any thing elſe, upon meat as it turns upon the ſpit.

Sir, I think the meat wants what I have, a *baſting.* *Shakeſp. Romeo and Juliet.*

3. To moiſten meat on the ſpit by falling upon it.

The fat of roaſted mutton falling on the birds, will ſerve to *baſte* them, and ſo ſave time and butter. *Swift's Directions to the Cook.*

4. To ſew ſlightly. [*baſter*, Fr. to ſtitch.]

BASTINA'DE. } *n. ſ.* [*baſtonnade*, Fr.]
BASTINA'DO. }

1. The act of beating with a cudgel; the blow given with a cudgel.

But this courteſy was worſe than a *baſtinado* to Zelmane; ſo that again, with rageful eyes, ſhe bad him defend himſelf. *Sidney, b.* ii.

And all thoſe harſh and rugged ſounds
Of *baſtinados*, cuts and wounds. *Hudibras.*

2. It is ſometimes taken for a Turkiſh puniſhment of beating an offender on the ſoals of his feet.

To BASTINA'DE. } *v. a.* [from the noun; *baſtonner*, Fr.] To
To BASTINA'DO. } beat; to give the baſtinado.

Nick ſeized the longer end of the cudgel, and with it began to *baſtinado* old Lewis, who had ſlunk into a corner, waiting the event of the ſquabble. *Arbuthnot's Hiſtory of J. Bull.*

BA'STION. *n. ſ.* [*baſtion*, Fr.] A huge maſs of earth, uſually faced with ſods, ſometimes with brick, rarely with ſtone, ſtanding out from a rampart, of which it is a principal part, and was anciently called a bulwark. *Harris.*

Toward: but how? ay there's the queſtion;
Fierce the aſſault, unarm'd the *baſtion.* *Prior.*

BAT. *n. ſ.* [*bat*, Sax. This word ſeems to have given riſe to a great number of words in many languages; as, *battre*, Fr. to beat; *baton*, *battle*, *beat*, *batty*, and others. It probably ſignified a weapon that did execution by its weight, in oppoſition to a ſharp edge; whence *whirlbat* and *brickbat.*] A heavy ſtick or club.

A handſome *bat* he held,
On which he leaned, as one far in eld. *Hubberd's Tale.*

They were fried in arm chairs, and their bones broken with *bats.* *Hakewell on Providence.*

BAT. *n. ſ.* [the etymology unknown.] An animal having the body of a mouſe, and the wings of a bird; not with feathers, but with a ſort of ſkin which is extended. It lays no eggs, but brings forth its young alive, and ſuckles them. It never grows tame, feeds upon flies, inſects, and fatty ſubſtances, ſuch as candles, oil, and cheeſe; and appears only in the ſummer evenings, when the weather is fine. *Calmet.*

When owls do cry,
On the *bat*'s back I do fly. *Shakeſp. Tempeſt.*

But then grew reaſon dark; that fair ſtar no more
Could the fair forms of good and truth diſcern;
*Bats* they became who eagles were before;
And this they got by their deſire to learn. *Sir J. Davies.*

Some animals are placed in the middle betwixt two kinds, as *bats*, which have ſomething of birds and beaſts. *Locke.*

Where ſwallows in the winter ſeaſon keep,
And how the drowſy *bat* and dormouſe ſleep. *Gay.*

BAT-FOWLING. *n. ſ.* [from *bat* and *fowl.*] A particular manner of birdcatching in the night time, while they are at rooſt upon perches, trees, or hedges. They light torches or ſtraw, and then beat the buſhes; upon which the birds flying to the flames, are caught either with nets, or otherwiſe.

You would lift the moon out of her ſphere, if ſhe would continue in it five weeks without changing.—We ſhould ſo, and then go a *bat-fowling.* *Shakeſp. Tempeſt.*

Bodies lighted at night by fire, muſt have a brighter luſtre given them than by day; as ſacking of cities, *bat-fowling*, &c. *Peacham on Drawing.*

BA'TABLE. *adj.* [from *bate.*] Diſputable.

blank page

IL facing 2R2$^v$

Love in her passions like a right make-bate
whisper'd to both Sides Arguments of Quarrel
Sidney

#

When baseness is exalted, do not bate
The place its honour for the persons sake
The Shrine is that which thou dost venerate
And not the beast that bears it on his back
Herbert T. of Saer. P

See with what outrage from the frosty
North
The early valiant Suede draws forth his
wings
In battailous array Phillips

make ready your stiff bats & Clubs
Shak.

a

Yet are the Men more loose than they
More kemb'd & bath'd & rub'd & trim'd
More sleek & soft & slacker limb'd
B. Johns.

*Batable* ground seems to be the ground heretofore in question, whether it belonged to England or Scotland, lying between both kingdoms. *Cowel.*

BATCH. *n. s.* [from *bake.*]

1. The quantity of bread baked at a time.

The joiner puts the boards into ovens after the *batch* is drawn, or lays them in a warm stable. *Mortimer's Husbandry.*

2. Any quantity of any thing made at once, so as to have the same qualities.

Except he were of the same meal and *batch.* *Ben. Johnson.*

BA'TCHELOR. See BACHELOR.

BATE. *n. s.* [perhaps contracted from *debate.*] Strife; contention; as a *make-bate.*

To BATE. *v. a.* [contracted from *abate.*]

1. To lessen any thing; to retrench.

Shall I bend low, and in a bondman's key,
With *bated* breath, and whisp'ring humbleness,
Say this? *Shakesp. Merchant of Venice.*

Nor envious at the sight will I forbear
My plenteous bowl, nor *bate* my plenteous cheer. *Dryden.*

2. To sink the price.

When the landholder's rent falls, he must either *bate* the labourer's wages, or not employ, or not pay him. *Locke.*

3. To lessen a demand.

*Bate* me some, and I will pay you some, and, as most debtors do, promise you infinitely. *Shakesp. Henry* IV.

4. To cut off; to take away.

*Bate* but the last, and 'tis what I would say. *Dryd. Sp. Friar.*

To BATE. *v. n.*

1. To grow less.

Bardolph, am not I fallen away vilely since this last election? Do I not *bate?* do I not dwindle? Why, my skin hangs about me like an old lady's loose gown. *Shak. Hen.* IV.

2. To remit; with *of* before the thing.

Abate thy speed, and I will *bate of* mine. *Dryden.*

BATE seems to have been once the preterite of *bite*, as *Shakespeare* uses *biting faulchion*; unless, in the following lines, it may be rather deduced from *beat.*

Yet there the steel staid not, but inly *bate*
Deep in his flesh, and open'd wide a red flood gate. *F. Queen.*

BA'TEFUL. *adj.* [from *bate* and *full.*] Contentious.

He knew her haunt, and haunted in the same,
And taught his sheep her sheep in food to thwart;
Which soon as it did *bateful* question frame,
He might on knees confess his guilty part. *Sidney.*

BA'TEMENT. *n. s.* [from *abatement.*] Diminution; a term only used among artificers.

To abate, is to waste a piece of stuff; instead of asking how much was cut off, carpenters ask what *batement* that piece of stuff had. *Moxon's Mechanical Exercises.*

BATH. *n. s.* [bað, Saxon.]

1. A *bath* is either hot or cold, either of art or nature. Artificial *baths* have been in great esteem with the ancients, especially in complaints to be relieved by revulsion, as inveterate headaches, by opening the pores of the feet, and also in cutaneous cases. But the modern practice has greatest recourse to the natural *baths*; most of which abound with a mineral sulphur, as appears from their turning silver and copper blackish. The cold *baths* are the most convenient springs, or reservatories, of cold water to wash in, which the ancients had in great esteem; and the present age can produce abundance of noble cures performed by them. *Quincy.*

Why may not the cold *bath*, into which they plunged themselves, have had some share in their cure? *Addison. Spectator.*

2. A state in which great outward heat is applied to the body, for the mitigation of pain, or any other purpose.

In the height of this *bath*, when I was more than half stewed in grease like a Dutch dish, to be thrown into the Thames. *Shakespeare's Merry Wives of Windsor.*

Sleep, the birth of each day's life, sore labour's *bath*,
Balm of hurt minds. *Shakesp. Macbeth.*

3. In chymistry, it generally signifies a vessel of water, in which another is placed that requires a softer heat than the naked fire. *Balneum Mariæ* is a mistake, for *balneum maris*, a sea or water *bath.* A sand heat is sometimes called *balneum siccum*, or *cinereum.* *Quincy.*

We see that the water of things distilled in water, which they call the *bath*, differeth not much from the water of things distilled by fire. *Bacon's Natural History*, N° 684.

4. A sort of Hebrew measure, containing the tenth part of an homer, or seven gallons and four pints, as a measure for things liquid; and three pecks and three pints, as a measure for things dry. *Calmet.*

Ten acres of vineyard shall yield one *bath*, and the seed of an homer shall yield an ephah. *Isaiah*, v. 10.

To BATHE. *v. a.* [baðian, Saxon.]

1. To wash in a bath.

Others, on silver lakes and rivers, *bath'd*
Their downy breast. *Milton's Paradise Lost, b.* x. *l.* 437.

Chancing to *bathe* himself in the river Cydnus, through the excessive coldness of these waters, he fell sick, near unto death, for three days. *South.*

2. To supple or soften by the outward application of warm liquours.

*Bathe* them and keep their bodies soluble the while by clysters, and lenitive boluses. *Wiseman's Surgery.*

I'll *bathe* your wounds in tears for my offence. *Dryden.*

3. To wash with any thing.

Phœnician Dido stood,
Fresh from her wound, her bosom *bath'd* in blood. *Dryden.*

Mars could in mutual blood the centaurs *bathe*,
And Jove himself give way to Cinthia's wrath. *Dryden.*

To BATHE. *v. n.* To be in the water, or in any thing resembling a bath.

Except they meant to *bathe* in reeking wounds,
I cannot tell. *Macbeth.*

The delighted spirit
To *bathe* in firy floods, or to reside
In thrilling regions of thick ribbed ice. *Sh. Meas. for Meas.*

The gallants dancing by the river side,
They *bathe* in summer, and in winter slide. *Waller.*

But *bathe*, and, in imperial robes array'd,
Pay due devotions. *Pope's Odyssey.*

BA'TING, or ABA'TING. *prep.* [from *bate*, or *abate.* This word, though a participle in itself, seems often used as a preposition.] Except.

The king, your brother, could not choose an advocate,
Whom I would sooner hear on any subject,
*Bating* that only one, his love, than you. *Rowe's R. Conv.*

If we consider children, we have little reason to think, that they bring many ideas with them, *bating*, perhaps, some faint ideas of hunger and thirst. *Locke.*

BA'TLET. *n. s.* [from *bat.*] A square piece of wood, with a handle, used in beating linen when taken out of the buck.

I remember the kissing of her *batlet*, and the cow's dugs that her pretty chopt hands had milked. *Shakesp. As you like it.*

BATO'ON. *n. s.* [*baston*, or *bâton*, Fr. formerly spelt *baston.*]

1. A staff or club.

We came close to the shore, and offered to land; but straightways we saw divers of the people with *bastons* in their hands, as it were, forbidding us to land. *Bacon's N. Atlantis.*

That does not make a man the worse,
Although his shoulders with *batoon*
Be claw'd and cudgell'd to some tune. *Hudibras.*

2. A truncheon or marshal's staff; a badge of military honour.

BA'TTAILLOUS. *adj.* [from *battaille*, Fr.] Having the appearance of a battle; warlike; with military appearance.

He started up, and did himself prepare
In sun bright arms and *battailous* array. *Fairfax, b.* i.

The French came foremost *battailous* and bold. *Fairf. b.* i.

A firy region, stretch'd
In *battailous* aspect, and nearer view
Bristled with upright beams innumerable
Of rigid spears, and helmets throng'd. *Paradise Lost, b.* vi.

BATTA'LIA. *n. s.* [*battaglia*, Ital.] The order of battle.

Next morning the king put his army into *battalia.* *Clarend.*

BATTA'LION. *n. s.* [*bataillon*, Fr.]

1. A division of an army; a troop; a body of forces. It is now confined to the infantry, and the number is uncertain, but generally from five to eight hundred men. Some regiments consist of one *battalion*, and others are divided into two, three, or more.

When sorrows come, they come not single spies,
But in *battalions.* *Shakesp. Hamlet.*

In this *battalion* there were two officers, called Thersites and Pandarus. *Tatler*, N° 56.

The pierc'd *battalions* disunited fall,
In heaps on heaps: one fate o'erwhelms them all. *Pope.*

2. An army. This sense is not now in use.

Six or seven thousand is their utmost power.
—Why, our *battalion* trebles that account. *Shakesp. Rich.* III.

To BA'TTEN. *v. a.* [a word of doubtful etymology.]

1. To fatten, or make fat; to feed plenteously.

We drove afield,
*Batt'ning* our flock with the fresh dews of night. *Milton.*

2. To fertilize.

The meadows here, with *batt'ning* ooze enrich'd,
Give spirit to the grass; three cubits high
The jointed herbage shoots. *Philips.*

To BA'TTEN. *v. n.* To grow fat; to live in indulgence.

Follow your function, go and *batten* on cold bits. *Sh. Coriol.*

Burnish'd and *batt'ning* on their food, to show
The diligence of careful herds below. *Dryden's H. and P.*

The lazy glutton safe at home will keep,
Indulge his sloth, and *batten* on his sleep. *Dryden.*

As at full length the pamper'd monarch lay,
*Batt'ning* in ease, and slumb'ring life away. *Garth.*

Tway mice, full blythe and amicable,
*Batten* beside erle Robert's table. *Prior.*

While paddling ducks the standing lake desire,
Or *batt'ning* hogs roll in the sinking mire. *Gay's Pastorals.*

BA'TTEN. *n. s.* A word used only by workmen.

A *batten* is a scantling of wooden stuff, two, three or four inches broad, seldom above one thick, and the length unlimited. *Moxon's Mechanical Exercises.*

To BA'TTER. *v. a.* [*battre*, to beat, Fr.]

1. To beat; to beat down; frequently uſed of walls thrown down by artillery, or of the violence of engines of war.

To appoint *battering* rams againſt the gates, to caſt a mount, and to build a fort. *Ezek.* xxi. 22.

These haughty words of hers
Have *batter'd* me like roaring cannon ſhot,
And made me almoſt yield upon my knees. *Shakeſp. H.* VI.

Britannia there, the fort in vain
Had *batter'd* been with golden rain:
Thunder itſelf had fail'd to paſs. *Waller.*

Be then, the naval ſtores, the nation's care,
New ſhips to build, and *batter'd* to repair. *Dryden.*

2. To wear with beating.

Crowds to the caſtle mounted up the ſtreet,
*Batt'ring* the pavement with their courſers feet. *Dryden.*

If you have a ſilver ſaucepan for the kitchen uſe, let me adviſe you to *batter* it well; this will ſhew conſtant good houſekeeping. *Swift's Directions to the Cook.*

3. Applied to perſons: to wear out with ſervice.

The *batter'd* veteran ſtrumpets here,
Pretend at leaſt to bring a modeſt ear. *Southern.*

I am a poor old *battered* fellow, and I would willingly end my days in peace. *Arbuthnot's Hiſtory of J. Bull.*

As the ſame dame, experienc'd in her trade,
By names of toaſts retails each *batter'd* jade. *Pope.*

To BA'TTER. *v. n.* A word uſed only by workmen.

The ſide of a wall, or any timber, that bulges from its bottom or foundation, is ſaid to *batter*. *Moxon's Mech. Exerciſes.*

BA'TTER. *n. ſ.* [from *to batter.*] A mixture of ſeveral ingredients beaten together with ſome liquour; ſo called from its being ſo much beaten.

One would have all things little, hence has try'd
Turkey poults freſh'd from th' egg in *batter* fry'd.
*King's Art of Cookery.*

BA'TTERER. *n. ſ.* [from *batter.*] He that batters.

BA'TTERY. *n. ſ.* [from *batter*, or *batterie*, Fr.]

1. The act of battering.

Strong wars they make, and cruel *battery* bend,
'Gainſt fort of reaſon, it to overthrow. *Fairy Queen, b.* ii.

Earthly minds, like mud walls, reſiſt the ſtrongeſt *batteries*. *Locke.*

2. The inſtruments with which a town is battered, placed in order for action.

Where is beſt place to make our *batt'ry* next?——
—— I think at the north gate. *Shakeſp. Henry* VI.

It plants this reaſoning and that argument, this conſequence and that diſtinction, like ſo many intellectual *batteries*, till at length it forces a way and paſſage into the obſtinate incloſed truth. *South.*

See, and revere th' artillery of heav'n,
Drawn by the gale, or by the tempeſt driv'n:
A dreadful fire the floating *batt'ries* make,
O'erturn the mountain, and the foreſt ſhake. *Blackmore.*

3. The frame, or raiſed work, upon which cannons are mounted.

4. In law, a violent ſtriking of any man. In treſpaſs for aſſault and *battery*, one may be found guilty of the aſſault, yet acquitted of the *battery*. There may therefore be aſſault without *battery*; but *battery* always implies an aſſault. *Chambers.*

Why does he ſuffer this rude knave now to knock him about the ſconce with a dirty ſhovel, and will not tell him of his action and *battery*? *Shakeſp. Hamlet.*

Sir, quo' the lawyer, not to flatter ye,
You have as good and fair a *battery*,
As heart can wiſh, and need not ſhame
The proudeſt man alive to claim. *Hudibras, p.* iii. *c.* iii.

BA'TTLE. *n. ſ.* [*bataille*, Fr.]

1. A fight; an encounter between oppoſite armies. We generally ſay a *battle* of many, and a *combat* of two.

The Engliſh army that divided was
Into two parts, is now conjoin'd in one;
And means to give you *battle* preſently. *Shakeſp. Henry* VI.

The *battle* done, and they within our power,
She'll never ſee his pardon. *Shakeſp. King Lear.*

The race is not to the ſwift, nor the *battle* to the ſtrong. *Eccleſ.* ix. 11.

So they joined *battle*, and the heathen being diſcomfited fled into the plain. 1 *Maccab.* iv. 14.

2. A body of forces, or diviſion of an army.

The king divided his army into three *battles*; whereof the vanguard only, well ſtrengthened with wings, came to fight. *Bacon's Henry* VII.

3. The main body, as diſtinct from the van and rear.

The earl of Angus led the avant-guard, himſelf followed with the *battle* a good diſtance behind, and after came the arrier. *Hayward.*

4. We ſay to join *battle*; to give *battle*.

To BA'TTLE. *v. n.* [*batailler*, Fr.] To join battle; to contend in fight.

'Tis ours by craft and by ſurprize to gain:
'Tis yours to meet in arms, and *battle* in the plain. *Prior.*

We daily receive accounts of ladies *battling* it on both ſides. *Addiſon. Freeholder*, N° 23.

I own, he hates an action baſe,
His virtues *batt'ling* with his place. *Swift.*

BA'TTLE-ARRAY. *n. ſ.* [See BATTLE and ARRAY.] Array, or order of battle.

Two parties of fine women, placed in the oppoſite ſide boxes, ſeemed drawn up in *battle-array* one againſt another. *Addiſon.*

BA'TTLE-AXE. *n. ſ.* A weapon uſed anciently, probably the ſame with a *bill*.

Certain tinners, as they were working, found ſpear heads, *battle-axes*, and ſwords of copper, wrapped in linen clouts. *Carew's Survey of Cornwal.*

BA'TTLEDOOR. *n. ſ.* [ſo called from *door*, taken for a flat board, and *battle*, or *ſtriking*.] An inſtrument with a handle and a flat blade, uſed in play to ſtrike a ball, or ſhuttlecock.

Play-things, which are above their ſkill, as tops, gigs, *battledoors*, and the like, which are to be uſed with labour, ſhould indeed be procured them. *Locke.*

BA'TTLEMENT. *n. ſ.* [generally ſuppoſed to be formed from *battle*, as the parts from whence a building is defended againſt aſſailants; perhaps only corrupted from *bâtiment*, Fr.] A wall raiſed round the top of a building, with embraſures, or interſtices, to look through, to annoy an enemy.

He fix'd his head upon our *battlements*. *Shak. Macbeth.*

Thou ſhalt make a *battlement* for thy roof, that thou bring not blood upon thine houſe, if any man fall from thence. *Deut.* xxii. 8.

Through this we paſs
Up to the higheſt *battlement*, from whence
The Trojans threw their darts. *Denham.*

Their ſtandard planted on the *battlement*,
Deſpair and death among the ſoldiers ſent. *Dryd. Aurengz.*

No, I ſhan't envy him, whoe'er he be,
That ſtands upon the *battlements* of ſtate;
I'd rather be ſecure than great. *Norris.*

The weighty mallet deals reſounding blows,
Till the proud *battlements* her tow'rs incloſe. *Gay's Trivia.*

BA'TTY. *adj.* [from *bat.*] Belonging to a bat.

Till o'er their brows death counterfeiting ſleep,
With leaden legs and *batty* wings doth creep.
*Shakeſp. Midſummer Night's Dream.*

BA'VAROY. *n. ſ.* A kind of cloke, or ſurtout.

Let the loop'd *bavaroy* the fop embrace,
Or his deep cloke be ſpatter'd o'er with lace. *Gay's Trivia.*

BA'UBEE. *n. ſ.* A word uſed in Scotland, and the northern counties, for a halfpenny.

Tho' in the draw'rs of my japan bureau,
To lady Gripeall I the Cæſars ſhow,
'Tis equal to her ladyſhip or me,
A copper Otho, or a Scotch *baubee*. *Bramſt. Man of Taſte.*

BA'VIN. *n. ſ.* [of uncertain derivation.] A ſtick like thoſe bound up in faggots; a piece of waſte wood.

He ambled up and down
With ſhallow jeſters and raſh *bavin* wits,
Soon kindled, and ſoon burnt. *Shakeſp. Henry* IV.

For moulded to the life in clouts,
Th' have pick'd from dunghills thereabouts,
He's mounted on a hazel *bavin*,
A crop'd malignant baker gave him. *Hudibras, p.* iii. *c.* iii.

The ſmaller truncheons make billet, *bavin*, and coals. *Mortimer's Art of Husbandry.*

To BAULK. See BALK.

BA'WBLE. *n. ſ.* [*Baubellum*, in barbarous Latin, ſignified a jewel, or any thing valuable, but not neceſſary. *Omnia baubella ſua dedit Othoni. Howden.* Probably from *beau*, Fr.] A gewgaw; a trifling piece of finery; a thing of more ſhow than uſe; a trifle. It is in general, whether applied to perſons or things, a term of contempt.

She haunts me in every place. I was on the ſea bank with ſome Venetians, and thither comes the *bawble*, and falls me thus about my neck. *Shakeſp. Othello.*

It is a paltry cap,
A cuſtard coffin, a *bawble*, a ſilken pie. *Shak. Tam. Shrew.*

If, in our conteſt, we do not interchange uſeful notions, we ſhall traffick toys and *bawbles*. *Government of the Tongue.*

This ſhall be writ to fright the fry away,
Who draw their little *bawbles*, when they play. *Dryden.*

A lady's watch needs neither figures nor wheels;
'Tis enough that 'tis loaded with *bawbles* and ſeals. *Prior.*

Our author then, to pleaſe you in your way,
Preſents you now a *bawble* of a play,
In gingling rhyme. *Granville.*

A prince, the moment he is crown'd,
Inherits every virtue round,
As emblems of the ſov'reign pow'r;
Like other *bawbles* of the Tow'r. *Swift.*

BA'WBLING. *adj.* [from *bawble.*] Trifling; contemptible: a word not now in uſe, except in converſation.

A *bawbling* veſſel was he captain of,
For ſhallow draught and bulk unprizable;
With which ſuch ſcathful grapple did he make,
With the moſt noble bottom of our fleet.
*Shakeſp. Twelfth Night.*

BA'W-

~~To beat. to pelt. to strike at.~~ ‡
The grecian phalanx moveless as a tower
On all sides batter'd yet resists his power
Pope

a ‡
If your work be too cold it will not feel the
weight of the hammer, as Smiths say,
when it will not batter under it Mox.

{Probably bavaroi from Bavaria, as a certain
kind of coach is called a Landau}

~~A body of men in genl~~ b ‡
From camp to camp
Fire ansrs fire & through their paly flames
Each battle sees the others umber'd face
Shak.

Battled adj. from Battle
Famous in battle
High battled Caesar will
Unstate his happiness be stag'd to th' Shew
Against a Sworder Shak. A & C.

a ǂ

The hunt is up, the Morn is bright & gray
The fields are fragrant & the Woods are green
Uncouple here and let us make a bay Shak.

BA'WCOCK. *n. ſ.* [perhaps from *beau*, or *baude*, and *cock*.] A familiar word, which ſeems to ſignify the ſame as *fine fellow*.

Why, how now, my *bawcock?* how doſt thou, chuck?
*Shakeſp. Twelfth Night.*

BAWD. *n. ſ.* [*baude*, old Fr.] A procurer, or procureſs; one that introduces men and women to each other, for the promotion of debauchery.

If your worſhip will take order for the drabs and the knaves, you need not to fear the *bawds*. *Shakeſp. Meaſure for Meaſ.*

This commodity,
This *bawd*, this broker, this all changing word,
Hath drawn him from his own determin'd aid. *Sh. K. John.*

Our author calls colouring *lena ſororis*, the *bawd* of her ſiſter deſign; ſhe dreſſes her up, ſhe paints her, ſhe procures for the deſign, and makes lovers for her. *Dryden's Dufreſnoy.*

To BAWD. *v. n.* [from the noun.] To procure; to provide gallants with ſtrumpets.

Leucippe is agent for the king's luſt, and *bawds*, at the ſame time, for the whole court. *Addiſon. Spectator*, Nº 266.

And in four months a batter'd harridan;
Now nothing's left, but wither'd, pale, and ſhrunk,
To *bawd* for others, and go ſhares with punk. *Swift.*

BA'WDILY. *adv.* [from *bawdy*.] Obſcenely.

BA'WDINESS. *n. ſ.* [from *bawdy*.] Obſceneneſs.

BA'WDRICK. *n. ſ.* [See BALDRICK.] A belt.

Freſh garlands too, the virgin's temples crown'd;
The youth's gilt ſwords wore at their thighs, with ſilver *bawdricks* bound. *Chapman's Iliad, b.* xviii.

BA'WDRY. *n. ſ.* [contracted from *bawdery*, the practice of a bawd.]

1. A wicked practice of procuring and bringing whores and rogues together. *Ayliffe's Parergon.*

Cheating and *bawdry* go together in the world. *L'Eſtrange.*

2. Obſcenity; unchaſte language.

Pr'ythee, ſay on; he's for a jig, or a tale of *bawdry*, or he ſleeps. *Shakeſp. Hamlet.*

I have no ſalt: no *bawdry* he doth mean:
For witty, in his language, is obſcene. *B. Johnſon.*

It is moſt certain, that barefaced *bawdery* is the pooreſt pretence to wit imaginable. *Dryden.*

BA'WDY. *adj.* [from *bawd*.] Obſcene; unchaſte; generally applied to language.

The *bawdy* wind that kiſſes all it meets,
Is huſh'd within the hollow mine of earth,
And will not hear't. *Shakeſp. Othello.*

Only they,
That come to hear a merry *bawdy* play,
Will be deceiv'd. *Shakeſp. Henry* VIII. *Prologue.*

Not one poor *bawdy* jeſt ſhall dare appear;
For now the batter'd veteran ſtrumpets here
Pretend at leaſt to bring a modeſt ear. *Southern.*

BA'WDY-HOUSE. *n. ſ.* A houſe where traffick is made by wickedneſs and debauchery.

Has the pope lately ſhut up the *bawdy-houſes*, or does he continue to lay a tax upon ſin? *Dennis.*

To BAWL. *v. n.* [*balo*, Lat.]

1. To hoot; to cry with great vehemence, whether for joy or pain. A word always uſed in contempt.

They *bawl* for freedom in their ſenſeleſs mood,
And ſtill revolt, when truth would ſet them free. *Par. Reg.*

To cry the cauſe up heretofore,
And *bawl* the biſhops out of door. *Hudibras.*

Through the thick ſhades th' eternal ſcribbler *bawls*,
And ſhakes the ſtatues on their pedeſtals. *Dryd. Juvenal.*

From his lov'd home no lucre him can draw;
The ſenate's mad decrees he never ſaw;
Nor heard at *bawling* bars corrupted law. *Dryden.*

Loud menaces were heard, and foul diſgrace,
And *bawling* infamy, in language baſe,
Till ſenſe was loſt in ſound, and ſilence fled the place.
*Dryden's Fables.*

So on the tuneful Margarita's tongue
The liſt'ning nymphs, and raviſh'd heroes hung;
But citts and fops the heav'n born muſick blame,
And *bawl*, and hiſs, and damn her into fame.
*Smith on J. Philips.*

I have a race of orderly elderly people, who can *bawl* when I am deaf, and tread ſoftly when I am only giddy and would ſleep. *Swift.*

2. To cry as a froward child.

A little child was *bawling*, and an old woman chiding it.
*L'Eſtrange's Fables.*

If they were never ſuffered to have what they cried for, they would never, with *bawling* and peeviſhneſs, contend for maſtery. *Locke.*

My huſband took him in, a dirty boy; it was the buſineſs of the ſervants to attend him, the rogue did *bawl* and make ſuch a noiſe. *Arbuthnot's Hiſtory of John Bull.*

To BAWL. *v. a.* To proclaim as a crier.

It grieved me, when I ſaw labours which had coſt ſo much, *bawled* about by common hawkers. *Swift.*

BA'WREL. *n. ſ.* A kind of hawk. *Dict.*

BA'WSIN. *n. ſ.* A badger. *Dict.*

BAY. *adj.* [*badius*, Lat.]

A *bay* horſe is what is inclining to a cheſnut; and this colour is various, either a light *bay* or a dark *bay*, according as it is leſs or more deep. There are alſo coloured horſes, that are called dappled *bays*. All *bay* horſes are commonly called brown by the common people.

All *bay* horſes have black manes, which diſtinguiſh them from the ſorrel, that have red or white manes.

There are light *bays* and gilded *bays*, which are ſomewhat of a yellowiſh colour. The cheſnut *bay* is that which comes neareſt to the colour of the cheſnut. *Farrier's Dict.*

I remember, my lord, you gave good words the other day of a *bay* courſer I rode on. 'Tis yours becauſe you liked it.
*Shakeſp. Timon.*

Poor Tom! proud of heart, to ride on a *bay* trotting horſe over four inch'd bridges. *Shakeſp. King Lear.*

His colour grey,
For beauty dappled, or the brighteſt *bay*. *Dryden's Virgil.*

BAY. *n. ſ.* [*baye*, Dutch.]

1. An opening into the land, where the water is ſhut in on all ſides, except at the entrance.

A reverend Syracuſan merchant,
Who put unluckily into this *bay*. *Shakeſp. Comedy of Err.*

We have alſo ſome works in the midſt of the ſea, and ſome *bays* upon the ſhore for ſome works, wherein is required the air and vapour of the ſea. *Bacon.*

Here in a royal bed the waters ſleep,
When tir'd at ſea, within this *bay* they creep. *Dryden.*

Some of you have already been driven to this *bay*.
*Dryden's Epiſtle to the Whigs.*

Hail, ſacred ſolitude! from this calm *bay*
I view the world's tempeſtuous ſea. *Roſcommon.*

2. A pond head raiſed to keep in ſtore of water for driving a mill.

BAY. *n. ſ.* [*abboi*, Fr. ſignifies the laſt extremity; as, *Innocence eſt aux abbois.* Boileau. *Innocence is in the utmoſt diſtreſs.* It is taken from *abboi*, the barking of a dog at hand, and thence ſignified the condition of a ſtag when the hounds were almoſt upon him.] The ſtate of any thing ſurrounded by enemies, and obliged to face them by an impoſſibility of eſcape.

This ſhip, for fifteen hours, ſate like a ſtag among hounds at the *bay*, and was ſieged and fought with, in turn, by fifteen great ſhips. *Bacon's War with Spain.*

Fair liberty purſu'd, and meant a prey
To lawleſs power, here turn'd, and ſtood at *bay*. *Denham.*

Nor flight was left, nor hopes to force his way;
Embolden'd by deſpair, he ſtood at *bay*;
Reſolv'd on death, he diſſipates his fears,
And bounds aloft againſt the pointed ſpears. *Dryden's Æneid.*

All, fir'd with noble emulation, ſtrive;
And, with a ſtorm of darts, to diſtance drive
The Trojan chief; who held at *bay*, from far
On his Vulcanian orb, ſuſtain'd the war. *Dryden's Virgil.*

We have now, for ten years together, turned the whole force and expence of the war, where the enemy was beſt able to hold us at a *bay*. *Swift.*

He ſtands at *bay*,
And puts his laſt weak refuge in deſpair. *Thomſon.*

BAY. *n. ſ.* In architecture, a term uſed to ſignify the magnitude of a building; as if a barn conſiſts of a floor and two heads, where they lay corn, they call it a barn of two *bays*. Theſe *bays* are from fourteen to twenty feet long, and floors, from ten to twelve broad, and uſually twenty feet long, which is the breadth of the barn. *Builder's Dict.*

If this law hold in Vienna ten years, I'll rent the faireſt houſe in it after threepence a *bay*. *Shakeſp. Meaſ. for Meaſ.*

There may be kept one thouſand buſhels in each *bay*, there being ſixteen *bays*, each eighteen foot long, about ſeventeen wide, or three hundred ſquare feet in each *bay*. *Mortimer.*

BAY *Tree.* [*laurus*, Lat.] This tree hath a flower of one leaf, ſhaped like a funnel, and divided into four or five ſegments. The male flowers, which are produced on ſeparate trees from the female, have eight ſtamina, which are branched into arms; the ovary of the female flowers becomes a berry, incloſing a ſingle ſeed within an horny ſhell, which is covered with a ſkin. The ſpecies are, 1. The common *bay* with male flowers. 2. The common fruit bearing *bay tree*. 3. The gold ſtriped *bay tree*, &c. The firſt and ſecond ſorts are old inhabitants of the Engliſh gardens; and as there are varieties obtained from the ſame ſeeds, they are promiſcuouſly cultivated, and are not to be diſtinguiſhed aſunder until they have produced flowers. Theſe plants are propagated either from ſeeds, or by laying down the tender branches, which will take root in one year's time. *Mill.*

I have ſeen the wicked in great power, and ſpreading himſelf like a green *bay tree*. *Pſalm* xxxvii 35.

BAY. *n. ſ.* A poetical name for an honorary crown or garland, beſtowed as a prize for any kind of victory or excellence.

Beneath his reign ſhall Euſden wear the *bays*. *Pope.*

To BAY. *v. n.* [*abboyer*, Fr.]

1. To bark as a dog at a thief, or at the game which he purſues.

And all the while ſhe ſtood upon the ground,
The wakeful dogs did never ceaſe to *bay*. *Fairy Queen, b.* i.

The

The hounds at nearer distance hoarsely *bay'd*;
The hunter close pursu'd the visionary maid;
She rent the heav'n with loud laments, imploring aid.
*Dryden's Fables.*

2. [from *bay*, an inclosed place.] To encompass about; to shut in.
We are at the stake,
And *bay'd* about with many enemies. *Shakesp. Julius Cæsar.*

To Bay. *v. a.* To follow with barking; to bark at.
I was with Hercules and Cadmus once,
When in the wood of Crete they *bay'd* the bear
With hounds of Sparta. *Shakesp. Midsum. Night's Dream.*
If he should do so,
He leaves his back unarm'd, the French and Welch
*Baying* him at the heels. *Shak. Henry IV.*

Bay *Salt.* Salt made of sea water, which receives its consistence from the heat of the sun, and is so called from its brown colour. The greatest quantities of this salt are made in France, on the coast of Bretagne, Saintonge, &c. from the middle of May to the end of August, by letting the sea water into square pits or basons, where its surface being struck and agitated by the rays of the sun, it thickens at first imperceptibly, and becomes covered over with a slight crust, which hardening by the continuance of the heat, is wholly converted into salt. The water in this condition is scalding hot, and the crystallization is perfected in eight, ten, or at most fifteen days. *Chamb.*

All eruptions of air, though small and slight, give sound, which we call crackling, puffing, spitting, &c. as in *bay salt* and bay leaves cast into the fire. *Bacon's Nat. History*, N° 123.

Bay *Window.* A window jutting outward, and therefore forming a kind of bay or hollow in the room.
It hath *bay windows* transparent as barricadoes.
*Shakesp. Twelfth Night.*

Bay *Yarn.* A denomination sometimes used promiscuously with woollen yarn. *Chambers.*

Ba'yard. *n. s.* [from *bay.*] A bay horse.

Ba'yonet. *n. s.* [*bayonette*, Fr.] A short sword or dagger fixed at the end of a musket, by which the foot hold off the horse.
One of the black spots is long and slender, and resembles a dagger or *bayonet*. *Woodward on Fossils.*

Bayze. See Baize.

*BDE'LLIUM. n. s.* [βδέλλιον; בדלח.] An aromatick gum brought from the Levant, used as a medicine and a perfume.
*Bdellium* is mentioned both by the ancient naturalists and in scripture; but it is doubtful whether any of these be the same with the modern kind. *Chambers.*
This *bdellium* is a tree of the bigness of an olive, whereof Arabia hath great plenty, which yieldeth a certain gum, sweet to smell to, but bitter in taste, called also *bdellium*. The Hebrews take the loadstone for *bdellium*. *Raleigh's History.*

To BE. *v. n.* [This word is so remarkably irregular, that it is necessary to set down many of its terminations.
Present. *I am, thou art, he is, we are,* &c.
eom, eart, is, aron, Sax.
Preter. *I was, thou wert, he was, we were,* &c.
pæs, pære, pas, pæron, Sax.
The conjunctive mood.
*I be, thou beest, he be, we be,* &c.
beo, bist, beo, beon, Sax.]

1. To have some certain state, condition, quality, or accident; as, the man *is* wise.
Seventy senators died
By their proscriptions, Cicero *being* one. *Shakesp. J. Cæsar.*
He hath to night *been* in unusual pleasure. *Macbeth.*
Be what thou hop'st to *be*, or what thou *art*,
Resign to death, it *is* not worth enjoying. *Shakesp. H. VI.*
Be but about
To say, she's a goodly lady, and
The justice of your hearts will add thereto,
'Tis pity she's not honest, honourable. *Shak. Winter's Tale.*
Let them shew the former things what they *be*, that we may consider them. *Isaiah*, xli. 22.
Therefore *be* sure,
Thou, when the bridegroom with his feastful friends
Passes to bliss at the mid hour of night,
Hast gain'd thy entrance, virgin wise and pure. *Par. Reg.*
Is it not easy to discern what such men would *be* at. *Stillingfl.*
To say a man has a clear idea of quantity, without knowing how great it *is*, *is* to say, he has the clear idea of the number of the sands, who knows not how many they *be*. *Locke.*

2. It is the auxiliary verb by which the verb passive is formed.
The wine of life *is* drawn, and the meer lees
*Is* left this vault to brag of. *Shakesp. Macbeth.*

3. To exist; to have existence.
The times have *been*,
That when the brains were out the man would die. *Macbeth.*
Here cease, ye pow'rs, and let your vengeance end,
Troy *is* no more, and can no more offend. *Dryden.*
All th' impossibilities, which poets
Count to extravagance of loose description,
Shall sooner *be*. *Rowe's Ambitious Stepmother.*
To *be* contents his natural desire;
He asks no angel's wing, nor seraph's fire. *Pope's Ess. on M.*

4. To have something by appointment or rule.
If all political power be derived only from Adam, and *be* to descend only to his successive heirs, by the ordinance of God, and divine institution, this is a right antecedent and paramount to all government. *Locke.*

BEACH. *n. s.* The shore; particularly that part that is dashed by the waves; the strand.
The fishermen, that walk upon the *beach*,
Appear like mice. *Shakesp. King Lear.*
Deep to the rocks of hell, the gather'd *beach*
They fasten'd, and the mole immense wrought on,
Over the foaming deep. *Milton's Par. Lost, b.* x. *l.* 299.
They find the washed amber further out upon the *beaches* and shores, where it has been longer exposed. *Woodward on Fossils.*

Be'ached. *adj.* [from *beach.*] Exposed to the waves.
Timon hath made his everlasting mansion
Upon the *beached* verge of the salt flood;
Which once a day, with his embossed froth,
The turbulent surge shall cover. *Shakesp. Timon.*

Be'achy. *adj.* [from *beach.*] Having beaches.
Other times, to see
The *beachy* girdle of the ocean
Too wide for Neptune's hips. *Shakesp. Henry IV.*

Be'acon. *n. s.* [beacon, Sax. from becn, a signal, and becnan, whence beckon, to make a signal.]

1. Something raised on an eminence, to be fired on the approach of an enemy, to alarm the country.
His blazing eyes, like two bright shining shields,
Did burn with wrath, and sparkled living fire;
As two broad *beacons* set in open fields,
Send forth their flames. *Fairy Queen, b.* i.
Modest doubt is called
The *beacon* of the wise. *Shakesp. Troilus and Cressida.*
The king seemed to account of the designs of Perkin as a may-game; yet had given order for the watching of *beacons* upon the coasts, and erecting more where they stood too thin. *Bacon's Henry VII.*
No flaming *beacons* cast their blaze afar,
The dreadful signal of invasive war. *Gay's Rural Sports*

2. Marks erected, or lights made in the night, to direct navigators in their courses, and warn them from rocks, shallows and sandbanks.

Bead. *n. s.* [beade, prayer, Saxon.]

1. Small globes or balls of glass or pearl, or other substance, strung upon a thread, and used by the Romanists to count their prayers; from whence the phrase to *tell beads*, or to be at one's *beads*, is to be at prayer.
That aged dame, the lady of the place,
Who all this while was busy at her *beads*. *Fairy Q. b.* i.
Thy voice I seem in every hymn to hear,
With ev'ry *bead* I drop too soft a tear. *Pope's El. to Abel.*

2. Little balls worn about the neck for ornament.
With scarfs and fans, and double change of brav'ry,
With amber bracelets, *beads*, and all such knav'ry.
*Shakesp. Taming of a Shrew.*

3. Any globular bodies.
Thy spirit within thee hath been so at war,
That *beads* of sweat have stood upon thy brow. *Sh. H. IV.*
Several yellow lumps of amber, almost like *beads*, with one side flat, had fastened themselves to the bottom. *Boyle.*

Bead *Tree.* [Azedarach.]
It hath pennated leaves like those of the ash; the flowers consist of five leaves, which expand in form of a rose; in the centre of the flower is a long fimbriated tube, containing the style; the fruit is roundish and fleshy, containing a hard furrowed nut, divided into five cells, each containing one oblong broadish seed. The outside pulp of the fruit in some countries is eaten; but the nut is, by religious persons, bored through, and strung as beads; whence it takes its name. It produces ripe fruits in Italy and Spain. *Millar.*

Be'adle. *n. s.* [bydel, Sax. a messenger; *bedeau*, Fr. *bedel*, Sp. *bedelle*, Dutch.]

1. A messenger or servitor belonging to a court. *Cowel.*

2. A petty officer in parishes, whose business it is to punish petty offenders.
A dog's obey'd in office.
Thou rascal *beadle*, hold thy bloody hand:
Why dost thou lash that whore? *Shakesp. King Lear.*
They ought to be taken care of in this condition, either by the *beadle* or the magistrate. *Spectator*, N° 130.
Their common loves, a lewd abandon'd pack,
The *beadle's* lash still flagrant on their back. *Prior.*

Be'adroll. *n. s.* [from *bead* and *roll.*] A catalogue of those who are to be mentioned at prayers.
The king, for the better credit of his espials abroad, did use to have them cursed by name amongst the *beadroll* of the king's enemies. *Bacon's Henry VII.*

Be'adsman. *n. s.* [from *bead* and *man.*] A man employed in praying, generally in praying for another.
An holy hospital,
In which seven *beadsmen*, that had vowed all
Their life to service of high heaven's king. *Fairy Queen, b.* i.

In

3

With Showers of Stones he drives them far away
The scattring dogs around at distance bay

To be out. at a loss to be puzzled.

This Youth was such a mercurial as could make his own part if at any time he chanced to be out Bac.

To be in with To Side with. to espouse any Cause

Those who pretended to be in with the principles upon which her Majesty proceeded, either absent themselves where the whole Cause depended, or Side directly with the enemy. Swift

Mine eyes
Seeing those beads of Sorrow Stand in thine
Began to Water. Shak.

ǂ

No *beaks* of Ships in naval triumph borne
Prior.

Names have been taken of civil honours, as King, Knight, partly for their Ancestors were such, or were kings of the *bean*, Christmass lords.
Cambden

To contain as a Cargo in a Ship
The mind of Man is too light & narrow a bottom to bear much certainty among the ruffling winds and tumultuary waves of passion humour & opinion and if the luggage be prized equally with the Jewels none will be cast out till all be lost and Shipwreck'd
Glanv. to Alb.

a ǂ

~~Root of a~~ A w well grown Stag whose Antlers rise ~~the Scent~~
High on his front, his *beams* invade the Skies
Dryd. Virg. Æ. 7. 667

IL facing 2T[r]

In thy danger,
Commend thy grievance to my holy prayer;
For I will be thy *beadſman*, Valentine. *Sh. T. Gentl. of Ver.*

BE'AGLE. *n. ſ.* [*bigle*, Fr.] A ſmall hound with which hares are hunted.

~~The reſt were various huntings.~~
The graceful goddeſs was array'd in green;
About her feet were little *beagles* ſeen,
That watch'd with upward eyes the motions of their queen. *Dryden's Fables.*

To plains with well bred *beagles* we repair;
And trace the mazes of the circling hare. *Pope.*

BEAK. *n. ſ.* [*bec*, Fr. *pig*, Welch.]

1. The bill or horny mouth of a bird.

His royal bird
Prunes the immortal wing, and cloys his *beak*,
As when his god is pleas'd. *Shakeſp. Cymbeline.*

He ſaw the ravens with their horny *beaks*
Food to Elijah bringing. *Milton's Par. Regained, b.* ii.

The magpye, lighting on the ſtock,
Stood chatt'ring with inceſſant din,
And with her *beak* gave many a knock. *Swift.*

2. A piece of braſs like a beak, fixed at the head of the ancient gallies, with which they pierced their enemies.

With boiling pitch another, near at hand,
From friendly Sweden brought, the ſeams inſtops;
Which, well laid o'er, the ſalt ſea waves withſtand,
And ſhakes them from the riſing *beak* in drops. *Dryden.*

3. A beak is a little ſhoe, at the toe about an inch long, turned up and faſtened in upon the forepart of the hoof. *Farrier's D.*

4. Any thing ending in a point like a beak; as the ſpout of a cup; a prominence of land.

Cuddenbeak, from a well advanced promontory, which entitled it *beak*, taketh a proſpect of the river. *Carew's Survey.*

BE'AKED. *adj.* [from *beak.*] Having a beak; having the form of a beak.

And queſtion'd every guſt of rugged winds,
That blows from off each *beaked* promontory. *Milton.*

BE'AKER. *n. ſ.* [from *beak.*] A cup with a ſpout in the form of a bird's beak.

And into pikes and muſqueteers
Stampt *beakers*, cups and porringers. *Hudibras, cant.* ii.

With dulcet bev'rage this the *beaker* crown'd,
Fair in the midſt, with gilded cups around. *Pope's Odyſſey.*

BEAL. *n. ſ.* [*bolla*, Ital.] A whelk or pimple.

To BEAL. *v. n.* [from the noun.] To ripen; to gather matter, or come to a head, as a ſore does.

BEAM. *n. ſ.* [beam, Sax. a tree; ſunnebeam, a ray of the ſun.]

1. The main piece of timber that ſupports the houſe.

A *beam* is the largeſt piece of wood in a building, which always lies croſs the building or the walls, ſerving to ſupport the principal rafters of the roof, and into which the feet of the principal rafters are framed. No building has leſs than two *beams*, one at each head. Into theſe, the girders of the garret floor are alſo framed; and if the building be of timber, the teazel-tenons of the poſts are framed. The proportions of *beams* in or near London, are fixed by act of parliament. A *beam* fifteen feet long, muſt be ſeven inches on each ſide its ſquare, and five on the other; if it be ſixteen feet long, one ſide muſt be eight inches, the other ſix; and ſo proportionable to their lengths. *Builder's Dict.*

The building of living creatures is like the building of a timber houſe; the walls and other parts have columns and *beams*, but the roof is tile, or lead, or ſtone. *Bacon's N. Hiſt.*

He heav'd, with more than human force, to move
A weighty ſtone, the labour of a team,
And rais'd from thence he reach'd the neighb'ring *beam*. *Dryd.*

2. Any large and long piece of timber: a *beam* muſt have more length than thickneſs, by which it is diſtinguiſhed from a block.

But Lycus, ſwifter,
Springs to the walls and leaves his foes behind,
And ſnatches at the *beam* he firſt can find. *Dryden's Æneid.*

3. That part of a balance, at the ends of which the ſcales are ſuſpended.

Poiſe the cauſe in juſtice' equal ſcales,
Whoſe *beam* ſtands ſure, whoſe rightful cauſe prevails.
*Shakeſp. Henry* VI. *p.* ii.

If the length of the ſides in the balance, and the weights at the ends be both equal, the *beam* will be in a horizontal ſituation: but if either the weights alone be equal, or the diſtances alone, the *beam* will accordingly decline. *Wilk. Mathem. Mag.*

4. The horn of a ſtag.

And taught the woods to echo to the ſtream
His dreadful challenge, and his claſhing *beam*. *Denham.*

5. The pole of a chariot; that piece of wood which runs between the horſes.

Juturna heard, and ſeiz'd with mortal fear,
Forc'd from the *beam* her brother's charioteer. *Dryden.*

6. Among weavers, a cylindrical piece of wood belonging to the loom, on which the web is gradually rolled as it is wove.

The ſtaff of his ſpear was like a weaver's *beam*. 1 *Chr.* xi. 23.

7. The ray of light emitted from ſome luminous body, or received by the eye.

~~Let them preſent me death upon the wheel,~~
~~Or~~ pile ten hills on the Tarpeian rock,
That the precipitation might downſtretch
Below the *beam* of ſight. *Shakeſp. Coriolanus.*

Pleaſing, yet cold, like Cynthia's ſilver *beam*. *Dryden.*

As heav'n's bleſt *beam* turns vinegar to ſour. *Pope.*

8 BEAM *of an anchor.* The ſtraight part or ſhank of an anchor, to which the hooks are faſtened.

9 BEAM *Compaſſes.* A wooden or braſs inſtrument, with ſliding ſockets, to carry ſeveral ſhifting points, in order to draw circles with very long radii; and uſeful in large projections, for drawing the furniture on wall dials. *Harris.*

To BEAM. *v. n.* [from the noun.] To emit rays or beams.

Each emanation of his fires
That *beams* on earth, each virtue he inſpires. *Pope.*

BEAM *Tree.* the ~~See~~ WILDSERVICE, ~~of which it is a ſpecies.~~

BE'AMY. *adj.* [from *beam.*]

1. Radiant; ſhining; emitting beams.

His double-biting axe, and *beamy* ſpear;
Each aſking a gigantick force to rear. *Dryden's Fables.*

All-ſeeing ſun!
Hide, hide in ſhameful night, thy *beamy* head. *Smith.*

2. Having horns or antlers.

Rouze from their deſert dens the briſtled rage
Of boars, and *beamy* ſtags in toils engage. *Dryden's Virgil.*

BEAN. *n. ſ.* [*faba*, Lat.]

It hath a papilionaceous flower, ſucceeded by a long pod, filled with large flat kidney-ſhaped ſeeds; the ſtalks are firm and hollow; the leaves grow by pairs, and are faſtened to a midrib. The ſpecies are, 1. The common garden *bean*. 2. The horſe *bean*. There are ſeveral varieties of the garden *beans*, ~~differing either in colour or ſize. The principal ſorts which are cultivated in England, are the Mazagan, the ſmall Liſbon, the Spaniſh, the Tokay, the Sandwich, and Windſor *bean*.~~ The Mazagan *bean* is brought from a ſettlement ~~of the Portugueſe on the coaſt~~ on Africa, ~~of the ſame name~~; and is by far the beſt ſort to plant for an early crop, ~~a great bearer, and alſo an excellent taſted *bean*.~~ The broad Spaniſh, Tokay, Sandwich, and Windſor *beans* are for the latter crops. *Millar.*

His allowance of oats and *beans* for his horſe was greater than his journey required. *Swift.*

BEAN *Caper.* [*fabago.*] an herb

~~The leaves of this plant are produced by pairs upon the ſame~~ ~~footſtalk, and the footſtalks grow oppoſite at the joints of the ſtalks; the cup of the flower conſiſts of five leaves; and the flowers have alſo five leaves, expanded like a roſe, with ſtamina ſurrounding the ſtyle, in the center of the flower cup. This ſtyle becomes a cylindrical fruit, five cornered, divided into five cells, each containing many flat ſeeds.~~ *Millar.*

BEAN *Treſſel.* An herb.

To BEAR. *v. a.* pret. *I bore*, or *bare*; part. paſſ. *bore*, or *born*. [beoran, beran, Sax. *bairan*, Gothick. It is ſounded as *bare*, as the *are* in *care* and *dare.*]

1. This is a word uſed with ſuch latitude, that it is not eaſily explained.

We ſay to *bear* a burden, to *bear* ſorrow or reproach, to *bear* a name, to *bear* a grudge, to *bear* fruit, or to *bear* children. The word *bear* is uſed in very different ſenſes. *Watts's Logick.*

2. To carry as a burden.

They *bear* him upon the ſhoulder; they carry him and ſet him in his place. *Iſaiah*, xlvi. 7.

And Solomon had threeſcore and ten thouſand that *bare* burdens. 1 *Kings*, v. 15.

As an eagle ſtirreth up her neſt, fluttereth over her young, ſpreadeth abroad her wings, taketh them, *beareth* them on her wings. *Deuteronomy*, xxxii. 11.

We ſee ſome, who, we think, have *born* leſs of the burden, rewarded above ourſelves. *Decay of Piety.*

Each sacred accent bears eternal weight
And each irrevocable word is fate.
Pope

3. To convey or carry.

My meſſage to the ghoſt of Priam *bear*;
Tell him a new Achilles ſent thee there. *Dryden's Æneid.*

A gueſt like him, a Trojan gueſt before,
In ſhew of friendſhip, ſought the Spartan ſhore,
And raviſh'd Helen from her huſband *bore*. *Dryd.*

The lad may prove well enough, if he oversoon think not too well of himself, and will bear away that he heareth of his Elders. Sidney

4. To carry as a mark of authority.

I do commit into your hand
Th' unſtained ſword that you have uſ'd to *bear*.
*Shakeſp.* ~~*Henry* IV. *p.* ii.~~

5. To carry as a mark of diſtinction.

He may not *bear* ſo fair and ſo noble an image of the divine glory, as the univerſe in its full ſyſtem. *Hale's Orig. of Mank.*

His pious brother, ſure the beſt
Who ever *bore* that name. *Dryden.*

The ſad ſpectators ſtiffen'd with their fears,
She ſees, and ſudden every limb ſhe ſmears;
Then each of ſavage beaſts the figure *bears*. *Garth.*

His ſupreme ſpirit or mind will *bear* its beſt reſemblance, when it repreſents the ſupreme infinite. *Cheyne's Phil. Prin.*

~~So we ſay, to *bear* arms in a coat.~~

6. To carry as in shew.
Look like the time; *bear* welcome in your eye,
Your hand, your tongue; look like the innocent flower,
But be the serpent under't. *Shakesp. King Lear.*

7. To carry as in trust.
He was a thief, and had the bag, and *bare* what was put therein. *John*, xii. 6.

8. To support; to keep from falling.
Under colour of rooting out popery, the most effectual means to *bear* up the state of religion may be removed, and so a way be made either for paganism, or for extreme barbarism to enter. *Hooker, b.* iv. § 1.
And Samson took hold of the two middle pillars, upon which the house stood, and on which it was *born* up. *Judges*, xvi. 29.
A religious hope does not only *bear* up the mind under her sufferings, but makes her rejoice in them. *Addison. Spectat.*
Some power invisible supports his soul,
And *bears* it up in all its wonted greatness. *Addison's Cato.*

9. To keep afloat.
The waters encreased, and *bare* up the ark, and it was lifted up above the earth. *Genesis*, vii. 17.

10. To support with proportionate strength.
Animals that use a great deal of labour and exercise, have their solid parts more elastick and strong; they can *bear*, and ought to have stronger food. *Arbuthnot on Aliments.*

11. To carry in the mind, as love, hate.
How did the open multitude reveal
The wond'rous love they *bear* him under hand! *Daniel's Civil War.*
They *bare* great faith and obedience to the kings. *Bacon.*
Darah, the eldest *bears* a generous mind,
But to implacable revenge inclin'd. *Dryden's Aurengz.*
The coward *bore* the man immortal spite. *Dryden's Ovid.*
As for this gentleman, who is fond of her, she *beareth* him an invincible hatred. *Swift.*
That inviolable love I *bear* to the land of my nativity, prevailed upon me to engage in so bold an attempt. *Swift.*

12. To endure, as pain, without sinking.
It was not an enemy that reproached me, then I could have *born* it. *Psalm* liv. 12.

13. To suffer; to undergo.
I have *born* chastisements, I will not offend any more. *Job*, xxxiv. 31.
That which was torn of beasts, I brought not unto thee, I I *bare* the loss of it; of my hand didst thou require it. *Genesis*, xxxi. 39.

14. To permit; to suffer without resentment.
Not the gods, nor angry Jove will *bear*
Thy lawless wand'ring walks in upper air. *Dryd. Æneid.*

15. To be capable of; to admit.
To reject all orders of the church which men have established, is to think worse of the laws of men in this respect, than either the judgment of wise men alloweth, or the law of God itself will *bear*. *Hooker, b.* iii.
Being the son of one earl of Pembroke, and younger brother to another, who liberally supplied his expence, beyond what his annuity from his father would *bear*. *Clarendon.*
Give his thought either the same turn, if our tongue will *bear* it, or, if not, vary but the dress. *Dryden.*
Do not charge your coins with more uses than they can *bear*. It is the method of such as love any science, to discover all others in it. *Addison on Medals.*
Had he not been eager to find mistakes, he would not have strained my words to such a sense as they will not *bear*. *Atterb.*
In all criminal cases, the most favourable interpretation should be put upon words that they possibly can *bear*. *Swift.*

16. To produce, as fruit.
There be some plants that *bear* no flower, and yet *bear* fruit: there be some that *bear* flowers, and no fruit: there be some that *bear* neither flowers nor fruit. *Bacon's Natural History.*
They wing'd their flight aloft; then stooping low,
Perch'd on the double tree that *bears* the golden bough. *Dryden's Æneid.*
Say, shepherd, say, in what glad soil appears
A wond'rous tree that sacred monarchs *bears*. *Pope's Past.*

17. To bring forth, as a child.
The queen that *bore* thee,
Oftner upon her knees than on her feet,
Died every day she liv'd. *Shakesp. Macbeth.*
Ye know that my wife *bare* two sons. *Genesis*, xliv. 27.
What could that have done?
What could the muse herself that Orpheus *bore*,
The muse herself, for her enchanting son? *Milton.*
The same Æneas, whom fair Venus *bore*
To fam'd Anchises on th' Idean shore. *Dryden's Æneid.*

18. To give birth to.
Here dwelt the man divine whom Samos *bore*,
But now self-banish'd from his native shore. *Dryden.*

19. To possess, as power or honour.
When vice prevails, and impious men *bear* sway,
The post of honour is a private station. *Addison's Cato.*

20. To gain; to win.
As it more concerns the Turk than Rhodes,
So may he with more facile question *bear* it;
For that it stands not in such warlike brace. *Shakesp. Othello.*
Because the Greek and Latin have ever *born* away the prerogative from all other tongues, they shall serve as touchstones to make our trials by. *Camden.*
Some think to *bear* it by speaking a great word, and being peremptory; and go on, and take by admittance that which they cannot make good. *Bacon.*

21. To maintain; to keep up.
He finds the pleasure and credit of *bearing* a part in the conversation, and of hearing his reasons approved. *Locke.*

22. To support any thing good or bad.
I was carried on to observe, how they did *bear* their fortunes, and principally, how they did employ their times. *Bacon's Holy War.*

23. To exhibit.
Ye Trojan flames, your testimony *bear*,
What I perform'd and what I suffer'd there. *Dryden.*

24. To be answerable for.
If I bring him not unto thee, let me *bear* the blame for ever. *Genesis*, xliii. 9.
O more than madmen! you yourselves shall *bear*
The guilt of blood and sacrilegious war. *Dryden.*

25. To supply.
What have you under your arm? Somewhat, that will *bear* your charges in your pilgrimage? *Dryden's Spanish Friar.*

26. To be the object of.
I'll be your father and your brother too;
Let me but *bear* your love, I'll bear your cares. *Shakesp. Henry IV. p.* ii.

27. To behave; to act in character.
Some good instruction give,
How I may *bear* me here. *Shakesp. Tempest.*
Hath he *born* himself penitent in prison? *Shakesp. Measure for Measure.*

28. To hold; to restrain.
Do you suppose the state of this realm to be now so feeble, that it cannot *bear* off a greater blow than this? *Hayward.*

29. To impel; to urge; to push.
The residue were so disordered as they could not conveniently fight or fly, and not only justled and *bore* down one another, but, in their confused tumbling back, brake a part of the avant-guard. *Sir J. Hayward.*
Contention, like a horse
Full of high feeding, madly hath broke loose,
And *bears* down all before him. *Shakesp. Henry IV. p.* ii.
Their broken oars, and floating planks, withstand
Their passage, while they labour to the land;
And ebbing tides *bear* back upon th' uncertain sand. *Dryden's Æneid.*
Now with a noiseless gentle course
It keeps within the middle bed;
Anon it lifts aloft the head,
And *bears* down all before it with impetuous force. *Dryden.*
Truth is *born* down, attestations neglected, the testimony of sober persons despised. *Swift.*
The hopes of enjoying the abbey lands would soon *bear* down all considerations, and been effectual incitement to their perversion. *Swift.*

30. To conduct; to manage.
My hope is
So to *bear* through, and out, the consulship,
As spite shall ne'er wound you, though it may me. *Ben. Johnson's Catiline.*

31. To press.
Cæsar doth *bear* me hard; but he loves Brutus. *Shakesp. Julius Cæsar.*
Though he *bear* me hard,
I yet must do him right. *Ben. Johnson's Catiline.*
These men *bear* hard upon the suspected party, pursue her close through all her windings. *Addison. Spectator*, N° 170.

32. To incite; to animate.
But confidence then *bore* thee on; secure
Either to meet no danger, or to find
Matter of glorious trial. *Milton's Par. Lost, b.* ii. *l.* 1175.

33. *To bear a body.* A colour is said to *bear a body* in painting, when it is capable of being ground so fine, and mixing with the oil so entirely, as to seem only a very thick oil of the same colour.

34. *To bear date.* To carry the mark of the time when any thing was written.

35. *To bear a price.* To have a certain value.

36. *To bear in hand.* To amuse with false pretences; to deceive.
Your daughter, whom she *bore in hand* to love
With such integrity, she did confess,
Was as a scorpion to her sight. *Shakesp. Cymbeline.*
He griev'd,
That so his sickness, age, and impotence,
Was falsely *born in hand*, sends out arrests
On Fortinbras. *Shakesp. Hamlet.*
He repaired to Bruges, desiring of the states of Bruges, to enter

To bear out

Be it thy course to busy giddy minds
With foreign quarrels that action hence borne out
May waste the memory of former days

~~In heraldry to bear any thing in a coat.~~

Their Ensigns belgic lions bear.
Dryd.

~~To contain to register, to record.~~

If I could find examples
Of thousands that had struck anointed kings
And flourish'd after, I'd not do't: But since
Nor brass nor stone nor parchment bears not one
Let villany itself forswear, Shak.

Yet so great was the puissance of his push
That from his saddle quite he did him bear
F. Q. 1. 335

To come up to, to Advance
When the but is out, we will drink water,
not a drop before, therefore bear up & board him
Shak.

v. a.
That proud Painim forward came so fierce
And full of wrath, that with his sharp head Spear
Through vainly crossed Shield he quite did pierce
And had his staggering Steed not shrunk for fear
Through Shield & body eke he should him bear

enter peaceably into their town, with a retinue fit for his eſtate; and *bearing* them *in hand*, that he was to communicate with them of divers matters of great importance, for their good. *Bacon's Henry VII.*

It is no wonder, that ſome would *bear* the world *in hand*, that the apoſtle's deſign and meaning is for preſbytery, though his words are for epiſcopacy. *South.*

37. *To bear off.* To carry away by force.

I will reſpect thee as a father, if
Thou *bear'ſt* my life *off* hence. *Shakeſp. Winter's Tale.*

The ſun views half the earth on either way,
And here brings on, and there *bears off* the day. *Creech.*

Give but the word, we'll ſnatch this damſel up,
And *bear* her *off*. *Addiſon's Cato.*

My ſoul grows deſperate.
I'll *bear* her *off*. *A. Philips's Diſtreſt Mother.*

38. *To bear out.* To ſupport; to maintain; to defend.

I hope your warrant will *bear out* the deed. *Shak. K. John.*

I can once or twice a quarter *bear out* a knave againſt an honeſt man. *Shakeſp. Henry IV. p. ii.*

Changes are never without danger, unleſs the prince be able to *bear out* his actions by power. *Sir J. Hayward.*

Quoth Sidrophel, I do not doubt
To find friends that will *bear* me *out*. *Hudibras.*

It is company only that can *bear* a man *out* in an ill thing. *South.*

I doubted whether that occaſion could *bear* me *out* in the confidence of giving your ladyſhip any further trouble. *Temple.*

To BEAR. *v. n.*

1. To ſuffer pain.

Stranger, ceaſe thy care;
Wiſe is the ſoul; but man is born to *bear*:
Jove weighs affairs of earth in dubious ſcales,
And the good ſuffers while the bad prevails. *Pope's Odyſſey.*

2. To be patient.

I cannot, cannot *bear*; 'tis paſt, 'tis done;
Periſh this impious, this deteſted ſon. *Dryden's Fables.*

3. To be fruitful or prolifick.

A fruit tree hath been blown up almoſt by the roots, and ſet up again, and the next year *bear* exceedingly. *Bacon.*

Betwixt two ſeaſon comes th' auſpicious air,
This age to bloſſom, and the next to *bear*. *Dryden.*

Melons on beds of ice are taught to *bear*,
And, ſtrangers to the ſun, yet ripen here. *Granville.*

4. To take effect; to ſucceed.

Having pawned a full ſuit of cloaths for a ſum of money, which, my operator aſſured me, was the laſt he ſhould want to bring all our matters to *bear*. *Guardian*, N° 166.

5. To act in character.

Inſtruct me
How I may formally in perſon *bear*,
Like a true friar. *Shakeſp. Meaſure for Meaſure.*

6. To tend; to be directed to any point.

The oily drops ſwimming on the ſpirit of wine, moved reſtleſly to and fro, ſometimes *bearing* up to one another, as if all were to unite into one body, and then falling off, and continuing to ſhift places. *Boyle.*

Never did men more joyfully obey,
Or ſooner underſtood the ſign to fly:
With ſuch alacrity they *bore* away.
Whoſe navy like a ſtiff-ſtretch'd cord did ſhew,
Till he *bore* in, and bent them into flight. *Dryden's Annus Mirab.* *Dryden.*

On this the hero fix'd an oak in ſight,
The mark to guide the mariners aright:
To *bear* with this, the ſeamen ſtretch their oars,
Then round the rock they ſteer, and ſeek the former ſhores. *Dryden's Æneid.*

In a convex mirrour, we view the figures and all other things, which *bear* out with more life and ſtrength than nature itſelf. *Dryden's Dufreſnoy.*

7. To act as an impellent, or as a reciprocal power; generally with the particles *upon* or *againſt*.

We were encounter'd by a mighty rock,
Which being violently *born upon*,
Our helpleſs ſhip was ſplitted in the midſt. *Shakeſpeare.*

Upon the tops of mountains, the air which *bears againſt* the reſtagnant quickſilver, is leſs preſſed. *Boyle.*

The ſides *bearing* one *againſt* the other, they could not lie ſo cloſe at the bottoms. *Burnet's Theory of the Earth.*

As a lion bounding in his way,
With force augmented *bears againſt* his prey,
Sideling to ſeize. *Dryden's Fables.*

Becauſe the operations to be performed by the teeth, require a conſiderable ſtrength in the inſtruments which move the lower jaw, nature hath provided this with ſtrong muſcles, to make it *bear* forcibly *againſt* the upper jaw. *Ray.*

The weight of the body doth *bear* moſt *upon* the knee-joints, in raiſing itſelf up, and moſt *upon* the muſcles of the thighs, in coming down. *Wilkins's Mathematical Magick.*

The waves of the ſea *bear* violently and rapidly *upon* ſome ſhores, the waters being pent up by the land. *Broome on the Odyſſey.*

8. To act upon.

Spinola, with his ſhot, did *bear upon* thoſe within, who appeared upon the walls. *Hayward.*

9. To be ſituated with reſpect to other places.

10. *To bear up.* To ſtand firm without falling.

So long as nature
Will *bear up* with this exerciſe, ſo long
I daily vow to uſe it. *Shakeſp. Winter's Tale.*

Perſons in diſtreſs may ſpeak of themſelves with dignity; it ſhews a greatneſs of ſoul, that they *bear up* againſt the ſtorms of fortune. *Broome's Notes on the Odyſſey.*

The conſciouſneſs of integrity, the ſenſe of a life ſpent in doing good, will enable a man to *bear up* under any change of circumſtances. *Atterbury.*

When our commanders and ſoldiers were raw and unexperienced, we loſt battles and towns; yet we *bore up* then, as the French do now; nor was there any thing deciſive in their ſucceſſes. *Swift.*

11. *To bear with.* To endure an unpleaſing thing.

They are content to *bear with* my abſence and folly. *Sidney.*

Though I muſt be content to *bear with* thoſe that ſay you are reverend grave men; yet they lie deadly, that tell you, you have good faces. *Shakeſp. Coriolanus.*

Look you lay home to him;
Tell him his pranks have been too broad to *bear with*. *Shakeſp. Hamlet.*

*Bear with* me then, if lawful what I aſk. *Paradiſe Loſt.*

BEAR. *n. ſ.* [bera, Saxon.]

1. A rough ſavage animal.

Every part of the body of theſe animals is covered with thick ſhaggy hair, of a dark brown colour, and their claws are hooked, which they uſe in climbing trees. They feed upon fruits, honey, bees, and fleſh. Some have falſely reported, that *bears* bring their young into the world ſhapeleſs, and that their dams lick them into form. The dams go no longer than thirty days, and generally produce five young ones. In the winter, they lie hid and aſleep, the male forty days, and the female four months; and ſo ſoundly for the firſt fourteen days, that blows will not wake them. In the ſleepy ſeaſon, they are ſaid to have no nouriſhment but from licking their feet; for it is certain they eat nothing, and, at the end of it, the males are very fat. This animal has naturally an hideous look, but when enraged it is terrible; and, as rough and ſtupid as it ſeems to be, it is capable of diſcipline; it leaps, dances, and plays a thouſand little tricks at the ſound of a trumpet. The fleſh of *bears* was much eſteemed by the ancients. They abound in Poland, Muſcovy, Lithuania, and the great foreſts in Germany; and alſo in the remote northern countries, where the ſpecies is white. *Calmet.*

Call hither to the ſtake my two brave *bears*,
Bid Saliſbury and Warwick come to me.—
—Are theſe thy *bears*? we'll bait thy *bears* to death,
And manacle the bearward in their chains. *Shak. Henry VI.*

Thou'dſt ſhun a *bear*;
But if thy flight lay tow'rd the roaring ſea,
Thou'dſt meet the *bear* i' th' mouth. *Shakeſp. King Lear.*

2. The name of two conſtellations, called the *greater* and *leſſer bear*; in the tail of the *leſſer bear*, is the pole ſtar.

E'en then when Troy was by the Greeks o'erthrown,
The *bear* oppos'd to bright Orion ſhone. *Creech.*

BEAR-BIND. *n. ſ.* A ſpecies of bindweed; which ſee.

BEAR-FLY. *n. ſ.* [from *bear* and *fly*.] An inſect.

There be of flies, caterpillars, canker-flies, and *bear-flies*. *Bacon's Natural Hiſtory.*

BEAR-GARDEN. *n. ſ.* [from *bear* and *garden*.]

1. A place in which bears are kept for ſport.

Hurrying me from the playhouſe, and the ſcenes there, to the *bear-garden*, to the apes, and aſſes, and tygers. *Stillingfl.*

I could not forbear going to a place of renown for the gallantry of Britons, namely to the *bear-garden*. *Spect.* N° 436.

2. Any place of tumult or miſrule.

BEAR-GARDEN. *adj.* A word uſed in familiar or low phraſe for *rude* or *turbulent*; as, a *bear-garden fellow*; that is, a man rude enough to be a proper frequenter of the bear-garden. *Bear-garden ſport*, is uſed for groſs inelegant entertainment.

BEAR'S-BREECH. *n. ſ.* [*acanthus*.] The name of a plant.

The leaves are like thoſe of the thiſtle; the flowers labiated; the under lip of the flower is divided into three ſegments, which, in the beginning, is curled up in the form of a tube; in the place of the under lip are produced the ſtamina, which ſupport the pointals; the cup of the flowers is compoſed of prickly leaves, the upper part of which is bent over, like an arch, and ſupplies the defect of the upper lip of the flower; the fruit is of an oval form, divided in the middle into two cells, each containing one ſmooth ſeed. The ſpecies are, 1. The ſmooth-leaved garden *bear's-breech*. 2. The prickly *bear's-breech*. 3. The middle *bear's-breech*, with ſhort ſpines, &c. The firſt is uſed in medicine, and is ſuppoſed to be the *mollis acanthus* of Virgil. The leaves of this plant are cut upon the capitals of the Corinthian pillars, and were formerly in great eſteem with the Romans. They are eaſily propagated by paring the roots in February or March, or by the ſeeds ſown at the ſame time. *Millar.*

BEAR'S-

BEAR'S-EAR, or *Auricula*. [*auricula ursi*, Lat.] The name of a plant.

It hath a perennial root; the leaves are thicker and smoother than those of the primrose; the cup of the flower is shorter, so that the tube appears naked; the flower is shaped like a funnel; the upper part is expanded, and divided into five segments; this is succeeded by a globular seed-vessel, containing many small seeds; every year it produces vast quantities of new flowers, differing in shape, size, or colour; and there is likewise a great variety in the leaves of these plants. They flower in April, and ripen their seeds in June. *Millar.*

BEAR'S-EAR, or *Sanicle*. [*cortusa*, Lat.]

This plant hath a perennial root; the leaves are roundish, rough, and crenated on the edges, like those of ground ivy; the cup of the flower is small, and divided into six parts; the flowers are shaped, like a funnel, cut at the top into many segments, and disposed in an umbel; the fruit is roundish, terminating in a point, and is closely fixt in the cup, in which are contained many small angular seeds. We have but one species of this plant, which is nearly allied to the *auricula ursi*; but the flowers are not quite so large and fair. It loses its leaves in winter, but puts out new ones early in the spring; and, in April, it produces flowers, which are sometimes succeeded by seed pods; but it is very rare that they perfect their seeds with us. *Millar.*

BEAR'S-FOOT. *n. s.* See HELLEBORE, of which it is a species.

BEAR'S-WORT. *n. s.* An herb.

BEARD. *n. s.* [beaꞃd, Saxon.]

1. The hair that grows on the lips and chin.

Ere on thy chin the springing *beard* began
To spread a doubtful down, and promise man. *Prior.*

2. *Beard* is used for the face; as, to do any thing to a man's *beard*, is to do it in defiance, or to his face.

Rail'd at their covenant, and jeer'd
Their rev'rend parsons to my *beard*. *Hudibras.*

3. *Beard* is used to mark age or virility; as, he has a long *beard*, means he is old.

This ancient ruffian, Sir, whose life I have spared at suit of his grey *beard*. *Shakesp. K. Lear.*

Some thin remains of chastity appear'd,
Ev'n under Jove, but Jove without a *beard*. *Dryden.*

Would it not be an insufferable thing, for a professor to have his authority, of forty years standing, confirmed by general tradition, and a reverend *beard*, overturned by an upstart novelist? *Locke.*

4. Sharp prickles growing upon the ears of corn.

The ploughman lost his sweat, and the green corn
Hath rotted ere its youth attain'd a *beard*.
*Shakesp. Midsummer Night's Dream.*

A certain farmer complained, that the *beards* of his corn cut the reapers and threshers fingers. *L'Estrange.*

5. A barb on an arrow.

6. The *beard* or chuck of a horse, is that part which bears the curb of the bridle. *Farrier's Dict.*

To BEARD. *v. a.* [from *beard*.]

1. To take or pluck by the beard, in contempt or anger.

No man so potent breathes upon the ground,
But I will *beard* him. *Shakesp. Henry* IV. *p.* i.

2. To oppose to the face; to set at open defiance.

He, whensoever he should swerve from duty, may be able to *beard* him. *Spenser's State of Ireland.*

The design of utterly extirpating monarchy and episcopacy, the presbyterians alone begun, continued, and would have ended, if they had not been *bearded* by that new party, with whom they could not agree about dividing the spoil. *Swift.*

BE'ARDED. *adj.* [from *beard*.]

1. Having a beard.

Think every *bearded* fellow, that's but yok'd,
May draw with you. *Shakesp. Othello.*

Old prophecies foretel our fall at hand,
When *bearded* men in floating castles land. *Dryden.*

2. Having sharp prickles, as corn.

As when a field
Of Ceres, ripe for harvest, waving bends
Her *bearded* grove of ears, which way the wind
Sways them. *Milton's Paradise Lost, b.* iv. *l.* 982.

The fierce virago
Flew o'er the fields, nor hurt the *bearded* grain. *Dryden.*

3. Barbed or jagged.

Thou shouldst have pull'd the secret from my breast,
Torn out the *bearded* steel to give me rest. *Dryd. Aurengz.*

BE'ARDLESS. *adj.* [from *beard*.]

1. Without a beard.

There are extant some coins of Cunobelin, king of Essex and Middlesex, with a *beardless* image, inscribed *Cunobelin*. *Cambden's Remains.*

2. Youthful.

And, as young striplings wheep the top for sport,
On the smooth pavement of an empty court,
The wooden engine flies and whirls about,
Admir'd with clamours of the *beardless* rout. *Dryden.*

BE'ARER. *n. s.* [from *to bear*.]

1. A carrier of any thing, who conveys any thing from one place or person to another.

He should the *bearers* put to sudden death,
Not shriving time allow'd. *Shakesp. Hamlet.*

Forgive the *bearer* of unhappy news;
Your alter'd father openly pursues
Your ruin. *Dryden's Aurengzebe.*

No gentleman sends a servant with a message, without endeavouring to put it into terms brought down to the capacity of the *bearer*. *Swift.*

2. One employed in carrying burthens.

And he set threescore and ten thousand of them to be *bearers* of burdens. *2 Chron.* ii. 18.

3. One who wears any thing.

O majesty!
When thou dost pinch thy *bearer*, thou dost sit
Like a rich armour worn in heat of day,
That scalds with safety. *Shakesp. Henry* IV. *p.* ii.

4. One who carries the body to the grave.

5. A tree that yields its produce.

This way of procuring autumnal roses, in some that are good *bearers*, will succeed. *Boyle.*

Reprune apricots and peaches, saving as much of the young likeliest shoots as are well placed; for the raw *bearers* commonly perish the new ones succeeding. *Evelyn's Kalendar.*

6. In architecture. A post or brick wall raised up between the ends of a piece of timber, to shorten its bearing; or to prevent its bearing with the whole weight at the ends only.

7. In heraldry. See SUPPORTER.

BE'ARHERD. *n. s.* [from *bear* and *herd*; as *shepherd*, from *sheep*.] A man that tends bears.

He that is more than a youth, is not for me; and he that is less than a man, I am not for him; therefore I will even take sixpence in earnest of the *bearherd*, and lead his apes into hell. *Shakesp. Much ado about Nothing.*

BE'ARING. *n. s.* [from *bear*.]

1. The site or place of any thing with respect to something else.

But of this frame, the *bearings* and the ties,
The strong connections, nice dependencies,
Gradations just, has thy pervading soul
Look'd through? or can a part contain the whole? *Pope.*

2. Gesture; mien; behaviour.

That is Claudio; I know him by his *bearing*.
*Shakesp. Much ado about Nothing.*

3. In architecture. *Bearing* of a piece of timber, with carpenters, is the space either between the two fixt extremes thereof, or between one extreme and a post, brick wall, &c. trimmed up between the ends, to shorten its *bearing*. *Builder's Dict.*

BE'ARWARD. *n. s.* [from *bear* and *ward*.] A keeper of bears.

We'll bait thy bears to death,
And manacle the *bearward* in their chains. *Shak. Henry* VI.

The bear is led after one manner, the multitude after another; the *bearward* leads but one brute, and the mountebank leads a thousand. *L'Estrange.*

BEAST. *n. s.* [*beste*, Fr. *bestia*, Lat.]

1. An animal distinguished from birds, insects, fishes, and man.

The man that once did fell the lion's skin,
While the *beast* liv'd, was kill'd with hunting him. *Shakesp.*

*Beasts* of chase are the buck, the doe, the fox, the martern, and the roe. *Beasts* of the forest are the hart, the hind, the hare, the boar, and the wolf. *Beasts* of warren are the hare and cony. *Cowel.*

2. An irrational animal, opposed to man; as man and *beast*.

I dare do all that may become a man;
Who dares do more, is none.——
——What *beast* was't then
That made you break this enterprize to me? *Macbeth.*

Medea's charms were there, Circean feasts,
With bowls that turn'd enamour'd youths to *beasts*. *Dryden.*

3. A brutal savage man, a man acting in any manner unworthy of a reasonable creature.

BE'ASTINGS. See BEESTINGS.

BE'ASTLINESS. *n. s.* [from *beastly*.] Brutality; practice of any kind contrary to the rules of humanity.

They held this land, and with their filthiness
Polluted this same gentle soil long time;
That their own mother loath'd their *beastliness*,
And 'gan abhor her brood's unkindly crime. *Fairy Queen.*

BE'ASTLY. *adj.* [from *beast*.]

1. Brutal; contrary to the nature and dignity of man. It is used commonly as a term of reproach.

Wouldst thou have thyself fall in the confusion of men, or remain a beast with beasts?—Ay—a *beastly* ambition. *Shakesp.*

You *beastly* knave, know you no reverence? *King Lear.*

With lewd, prophane, and *beastly* phrase,
To catch the world's loose laughter or vain gaze. *B. Johns.*

It is commonly charged upon the gentlemen of the army, that the *beastly* vice of drinking to excess, hath been lately, from their example, restored among us. *Swift.*

2. Having the nature or form of beasts.

Vain idols,
*Beastly* divinities, and droves of gods. *Prior.*

To

a If you should try your graving Tools
On the odious groupe of Fools
Draw the beasts as I describe them
From their features while I give them
Swift

b Beastlihead

Sick, sick, alas, a little lack of dead,
But I be relieved by your beastlihead
Spenser Kal.

IL facing 2T2[v]

a ‡

The walls of Bulloigne sore beaten and
shaken, and scarce maintainable he defended
~~the place against the Dauphin~~
Sr J. Hayw.d

To BEAT. *v. a.* preter. *beat*, part. paſſ. *beat*, or *beaten*. [*battre*, French.]

1. To ſtrike; to knock; to lay blows upon.

So fight I, not as one that *beateth* the air. 1 *Cor.* ix. 26.

He rav'd with all the madneſs of deſpair;
He roar'd, he *beat* his breaſt, he tore his hair. *Dryden.*

2. To puniſh with ſtripes or blows.

They've choſe a conſul that will from them take
Their liberties; make them of no more voice
Than dogs, that are as often *beat* for barking,
And therefore kept to do ſo. *Shakeſp. Coriolanus.*

Miſtreſs Ford, good heart, is *beaten* black and blue, that you cannot ſee a white ſpot about her. *Shakeſp. M. Wives of Windſ.*

There is but one fault for which children ſhould be *beaten*; and that is obſtinacy or rebellion. *Locke.*

3. To ſtrike an inſtrument of muſick.

Bid them come forth and hear,
Or at their chamber door I'll *beat* the drum,
Till it cry, ſleep to death. *Shakeſp. King Lear.*

4. To break to powder, or comminute by blows.

The people gathered manna, and ground it in mills, or *beat* it in a mortar, and baked it. *Numbers*, xi. 8.

They did *beat* the gold into thin plates, and cut it into wires, to work it. *Exodus*, xxxix. 3.

They ſave the laborious work of *beating* of hemp, by making the axletree of the main wheel of their corn mills longer than ordinary, and placing of pins in them, to raiſe large hammers like thoſe uſed for paper and fulling mills, with which they *beat* moſt of their hemp. *Mortimer's Husbandry.*

Neſtor, we ſee, furniſhed the gold, and he *beat* it into leaves, ſo that he had occaſion to make uſe of his anvil and hammer. *Broome's Notes on the Odyſſey.*

5. To ſtrike buſhes or ground, or make a motion to rouze game.

It is ſtrange how long ſome men will lie in wait to ſpeak, and how many other matters they will *beat* over to come near it. *Bacon's Eſſays.*

When from the cave thou riſeſt with the day,
To *beat* the woods, and rouze the bounding prey. *Prior.*

Together let us *beat* this ample field,
Try what the open, what the covert yield. *Pope.*

6. To threſh; to drive the corn out of the huſk.

She gleaned in the field, and *beat* out that ſhe had gleaned. *Ruth*, ii. 17.

7. To mix things by long and frequent agitation.

By long *beating* the white of an egg, you may bring it into white curds. *Boyle.*

8. To batter with engines of war.

And he *beat* down the tower of Penuel, and ſlew the men of the city. *Judges*, viii. 17.

9. To daſh, as water, or bruſh as wind.

Beyond this flood a frozen continent
Lies dark and wild; *beat* with perpetual ſtorms
Of whirlwind and dire hail. *Milt. Paradiſe Loſt, b.* ii.

With tempeſts *beat*, and to the winds a ſcorn. *Roſcommon.*

While winds and ſtorms his lofty forehead *beat*,
The common fate of all that's high or great. *Denham.*

As when a lion in the midnight hours,
*Beat* by rude blaſts, and wet with wintry ſhow'rs,
Deſcends terrific from the mountain's brow. *Pope.*

10. To tread a path.

While I this unexampled taſk eſſay,
Paſs awful gulfs, and *beat* my painful way,
Celeſtial Dove, divine aſſiſtance bring. *Blackmore.*

11. To make a path by marking it with tracks.

He that will know the truth of things, muſt leave the common and *beaten* track. *Locke.*

12. To conquer; to ſubdue; to vanquiſh.

If Hercules and Lichas play at dice,
Which is the better man? The greater throw
May turn by fortune from the weaker hand:
So is Alcides *beaten* by his page. *Shakeſp. Merchant of Venice.*

You ſouls of geeſe,
That bear the ſhapes of men, how have you run
From ſlaves that apes would *beat*? *Shakeſp. Coriolanus.*

Five times, Marcius,
I have fought with thee, ſo often haſt thou *beat* me. *Shakeſp.*

I have diſcern'd the foe ſecurely lie,
Too proud to fear a *beaten* enemy. *Dryden's Indian Emp.*

The common people of Lucca are firmly perſuaded, that one Lucqueſe can *beat* five Florentines. *Addiſon on Italy.*

Pyrrhus, king of Epirus, joining his ſhips to thoſe of the Syracuſans, *beat* the Carthaginians at ſea. *Arbuthnot on Coins.*

13. To harraſs; to over-labour.

It is no point of wiſdom for a man to *beat* his brains, and ſpend his ſpirits about things impoſſible. *Hakewell on Providence.*

And as in priſons mean rogues beat
Hemp, for the ſervice of the great;
So Whacum *beat* his dirty brains
T' advance his maſter's fame and gains. *Hudibras.*

I know not why any one ſhould waſte his time, and *beat* his head about the Latin grammar, who does not intend to be a critick. *Locke.*

14. To lay, or preſs, as ſtanding corn by hard weather.

Her own ſhall bleſs her;
Her foes ſhake, like a field of *beaten* corn,
And hang their heads with ſorrow. *Shakeſp. Henry* VIII.

15. To depreſs; to cruſh by repeated oppoſition; uſually with the particle *down*.

Albeit a pardon was proclaimed, touching any ſpeech tending to treaſon, yet could not the boldneſs be *beaten down* either with that ſeverity, or with this lenity be abated. *Hayward.*

Our warriours propagating the French language, at the ſame time they are *beating down* their power. *Addiſon. Spect.* N° 165.

Such an unlook'd for ſtorm of ills falls on me,
It *beats down* all my ſtrength. *Addiſon's Cato.*

16. To drive by violence.

Twice have I ſally'd, and was twice *beat* back. *Dryden.*

He that proceeds upon other principles in his inquiry, does at leaſt poſt himſelf in a party, which he will not quit, till he be *beaten* out. *Locke.*

He cannot *beat* it out of his head, but that it was a cardinal who picked his pocket. *Addiſon. Freeholder*, N° 44.

The younger part of mankind might be *beat* off from the belief of the moſt important points even of natural religion, by the impudent jeſts of a profane wit. *Watts's Impr. of the Mind.*

17. To move with fluttering agitation.

Thrice have I *beat* the wing, and rid with night
About the world. *Dryden's State of Innocence.*

18. *To beat down.* To endeavour by treaty to leſſen the price demanded.

Surveys rich moveables with curious eye,
*Beats down* the price, and threatens ſtill to buy. *Dryden.*

She perſuaded him to truſt the renegado with the money he had brought over for their ranſom; as not queſtioning but he would *beat down* the terms of it. *Addiſon. Spectat.* N° 199.

19. *To beat down.* To ſink or leſſen the value.

Uſury *beats down* the price of land; for the employment of money is chiefly either merchandizing or purchaſing; and uſury way-lays both. *Bacon's Eſſays*, N° 42.

20. *To beat up.* To attack ſuddenly; to alarm.

They lay in that quiet poſture, without making the leaſt impreſſion upon the enemy, by *beating up* his quarters, which might eaſily have been done. *Clarendon, b.* viii.

Will. fancies he ſhould never have been the man he is, had not he broke windows, knocked down conſtables, and *beat up* a lewd woman's quarters, when he was a young fellow. *Addiſ.*

21. *To beat the hoof.* To walk; to go on foot.

To BEAT. *v. n.*

1. To move in a pulſatory manner.

I would gladly underſtand the formation of a ſoul, and ſee it *beat* the firſt conſcious pulſe. *Collier on Thought.*

2. To daſh, as a flood or ſtorm.

This publick envy ſeemeth to *beat* chiefly upon miniſters. *Bacon's Eſſays*, N° 9.

Your brow, which does no fear of thunder know,
Sees rowling tempeſts vainly *beat* below. *Dryden.*

And one ſees many of the like hollow ſpaces worn in the bottoms of the rocks, as they are more or leſs able to reſiſt the impreſſions of the water that *beats* againſt them. *Addiſon.*

3. To knock at a door.

The men of the city beſet the houſe round about, and *beat* at the door, and ſpake to the maſter of the houſe. *Judg.* xix. 22.

4. To move with frequent repetitions of the ſame act or ſtroke.

No pulſe ſhall keep
His nat'ral progreſs, but ſurceaſe to *beat*. *Sh. Rom. and Jul.*

My temp'rate pulſe does regularly *beat*;
Feel, and be ſatisfy'd. *Dryden's Perſius, Sat.* iii.

A man's heart *beats*, and the blood circulates, which it is not in his power, by any thought or volition, to ſtop. *Locke.*

5. To throb; to be in agitation, as a ſore ſwelling.

A turn or two I'll walk,
To ſtill my *beating* mind. *Shakeſp. Tempeſt.*

6. To fluctuate; to be in agitation.

The tempeſt in my mind
Doth from my ſenſes take all feeling elſe,
Save what *beats* there. *Shakeſp. King Lear.*

7. To try different ways; to ſearch.

I am always *beating* about in my thoughts for ſomething that may turn to the benefit of my dear countrymen. *Addiſon. Guard.*

To find an honeſt man, I *beat* about,
And love him, court him, praiſe him in or out. *Pope.*

8. To act upon with violence.

The ſun *beat* upon the head of Jonah, that he fainted, and wiſhed in himſelf to die. *Jonah*, iv. 48.

9. To ſpeak frequently; to repeat; to enforce by repetition.

We are drawn on into a larger ſpeech, by reaſon of their ſo great earneſtneſs, who *beat* more and more upon theſe laſt alleged words. *Hooker, b.* ii. § 4.

How frequently and fervently doth the ſcripture *beat* upon this cauſe? *Hakewell on Providence.*

10. *To beat up*; as, to *beat up* for ſoldiers. The word *up* ſeems redundant.

BEAT. *part. paſſive.* [from the verb.]

Like a rich veſſel *beat* by ſtorms to ſhore,
'Twere madneſs ſhould I venture out once more. *Dryden.*

BEAT. *n. ſ.* [from the verb.]

1. Stroke.

2. Manner of ſtriking.

Albeit the baſe and treble ſtrings of a viol be turned to an uniſon; yet the former will ſtill make a bigger or broader ſound than the latter, as making a broader *beat* upon the air. *Grew's Coſmologia Sacra, b.* ii. *c.* 2.

With a careleſs *beat*,
Struck out the mute creation at a heat. *Dryd. Hind and P.*

3. Manner of being ſtruck; as, the *beat* of the pulſe, or a drum.

BE'ATEN. *particip. adj.* [from *to beat.*]

What makes you, Sir, ſo late abroad,
Without a guide, and this no *beaten* road? *Dryd. W. of Bath.*

BE'ATER. *n. ſ.* [from *beat.*]

1. An inſtrument with which any thing is comminuted or mingled.

Beat all your mortar with a *beater* three or four times over, before you uſe it; for thereby you incorporate the ſand and lime well together. *Moxon's Mechanical Exerciſes.*

2. A perſon much given to blows.

The beſt ſchoolmaſter of our time, was the greateſt *beater.* *Aſcham's Schoolmaſter.*

BEATI'FICAL. } *adj.* [*beatificus*, low Lat. from *beatus*, happy.]
BEATI'FICK. } That which has the power of making happy, or compleating fruition; bliſsful. It is uſed only of heavenly fruition after death.

Admiring the riches of heav'n's pavement
Than ought divine or holy elſe, enjoy'd
In viſion *beatifick.* *Milton's Par. Loſt, b.* i. *l.* 684.

It is alſo their felicity to have no faith; for, enjoying the *beatifical* viſion in the fruition of the object of faith, they have received the full evacuation of it. *Brown's Vulgar Errours, b.* i.

We may contemplate upon the greatneſs and ſtrangeneſs of the *beatifick* viſion; how a created eye ſhould be ſo fortified, as to bear all thoſe glories, that ſtream from the fountain of uncreated light. *South.*

BEATI'FICALLY. *adv.* [from *beatifical.*] In ſuch a manner as to compleat happineſs.

*Beatifically* to behold the face of God in the fulneſs of wiſdom, righteouſneſs and peace, is bleſſedneſs no way incident unto the creatures beneath man. *Hakewell on Providence.*

BEATIFICA'TION. *n. ſ.* [from *beatifick.*] A term in the Romiſh church, diſtinguiſhed from canonization. *Beatification* is an acknowledgment made by the pope, that the perſon beatified is in heaven, and therefore may be reverenced as bleſſed; but is not a conceſſion of the honours due to ſaints, which are conferred by canonization.

To BEA'TIFY. *v. a.* [*beatifico*, Lat.]

1. To make happy; to bleſs with the completion of celeſtial enjoyment.

I wiſh I had the wings of an angel, to have aſcended into paradiſe, and to have beheld the forms of thoſe *beatified* ſpirits, from which I might have copied my archangel. *Dryden.*

The uſe of ſpiritual conference is unimaginable and unſpeakable, eſpecially if free and unreſtrained, bearing an image of that converſation which is among angels and *beatified* ſaints. *Hammond's Fundamentals.*

We ſhall know him to be the fulleſt good, the neareſt to us, and the moſt certain; and, conſequently, the moſt *beatifying* of all others. *Brown's Coſmologia Sacra, b.* iii. *c.* 4.

2. To ſettle the character of any perſon by a publick acknowledgment that he is received in heaven, though he is not inveſted with the dignity of a ſaint.

Over againſt this church ſtands a large hoſpital, erected by a ſhoemaker, who has been *beatified*, though never ſainted. *Addiſon on Italy.*

BE'ATING. *n. ſ.* [from *beat.*] Correction; puniſhment by blows.

Playwright, convict of publick wrongs to men,
Takes private *beatings*, and begins again. *Ben. Johnſon.*

BEA'TITUDE. *n. ſ.* [*beatitudo*, Lat.]

1. Bleſſedneſs; felicity; happineſs: commonly uſed of the joys of heaven.

The end of that government, and of all man's aims, is agreed to be *beatitude*, that is, his being completely well. *Digby.*

This is the image and little repreſentation of heaven; it is *beatitude* in picture. *Taylor's Holy Living.*

He ſet out the felicity of his heaven, by the delights of ſenſe; ſlightly paſſing over the accompliſhment of the ſoul, and the *beatitude* of that part which earth and viſibilities too weakly affect. *Brown's Vulgar Errours, b.* i. *c.* 2.

2. A declaration of bleſſedneſs made by our Saviour to particular virtues.

BEAU. *n. ſ.* [*beau*, Fr. It is ſounded like *bo*, and has often the French plural *beaux.*] A man of dreſs; a man whoſe great care is to deck his perſon.

What, will not *beaux* attempt to pleaſe the fair? *Dryden.*

The water nymphs are too unkind
To Vill'roy; are the land nymphs ſo?
And fly they all, at once combin'd
To ſhame a general, and a *beau*? *Prior.*

BEA

You will become the delight of nine ladies in ten, and the envy of ninety-nine *beaux* in a hundred. *Swift's Direct. to Footm.*

BE'AVER. *n. ſ.* [*bievre*, Fr.]

1. An animal, otherwiſe named the *caſtor*, amphibious, and remarkable for his art in building his habitation; of which many wonderful accounts are delivered by travellers. His ſkin is very valuable on account of the fur.

The *beaver* being hunted, biteth off his ſtones, knowing that for them only his life is ſought. *Hakewell on Providence.*

They placed this invention upon the *beaver*, for the ſagacity and wiſdom of that animal; indeed from its artifice in building. *Brown's Vulgar Errours, c.* 4.

2. A hat of the beſt kind; ſo called from being made of the fur of beaver.

You ſee a ſmart rhetorician turning his hat, moulding it into different cocks, examining the lining and the button during his harangue: A deaf man would think he was cheapening a *beaver*, when he is talking of the fate of a nation. *Addiſon. Sp.*

The broker here his ſpacious *beaver* wears,
Upon his brow ſit jealouſies and cares. *Gay's Trivia.*

3. The part of a helmet that covers the face. [*baviere*, Fr.]

His dreadful hideous head
Cloſe couched on the *beaver*, ſeem'd to throw,
From flaming mouth, bright ſparkles firy red. *Fairy Queen.*

Big Mars ſeems bankrupt in their beggar'd hoſt,
And faintly through a ruſty *beaver* peeps. *Shakeſp. H. V.*

He was ſlain upon a courſe at tilt, the ſplinters of the ſtaff going in at his *beaver.* *Bacon's Eſſays,* Nº 36.

BE'AVERED. *adj.* [from *beaver.*] Covered with a beaver; wearing a beaver.

His *beaver'd* brow a birchen garland bears,
Dropping with infant's blood, and mother's tears:
All fleſh is humbled. *Pope's Dunciad.*

BEAU'ISH. *adj.* [from *beau.*] Befitting a beau; foppiſh.

BEAU'TEOUS. *adj.* [from *beauty.*] Fair; elegant in form; pleaſing to the ſight; beautiful. This word is chiefly poetical.

I can, Petrucio, help thee to a wife,
With wealth enough, and young, and *beauteous.* *Shakeſp. Taming of the Shrew.*

Alas! not hoping to ſubdue,
I only to the flight aſpir'd;
To keep the *beauteous* foe in view,
Was all the glory I deſir'd. *Prior.*

BEAU'TEOUSLY. *adv.* [from *beauteous.*] In a beauteous manner; in a manner pleaſing to the ſight; beautifully.

Look upon pleaſures not upon that ſide that is next the ſun, or where they look *beauteouſly*; that is, as they come towards you to be enjoyed. *Taylor's Holy Living.*

BEAU'TEOUSNESS. *n. ſ.* [from *beauteous.*] The ſtate or quality of being beauteous; beauty.

From leſs virtue, and leſs *beauteouſneſs*,
The gentiles fram'd them gods and goddeſſes. *Donne.*

BEAU'TIFUL. *adj.* [from *beauty* and *full.*] Fair; having the qualities that conſtitute beauty, or give delight.

He ſtole away and took by ſtrong hand all the *beautiful* women in his time. *Raleigh's Hiſt. of the World.*

The principal and moſt important parts of painting, is to know what is moſt *beautiful* in nature, and moſt proper for that art; that which is the moſt *beautiful*, is the moſt noble ſubject: ſo, in poetry, tragedy is more *beautiful* than comedy, becauſe the perſons are greater whom the poet inſtructs, and conſequently the inſtructions of more benefit to mankind. *Dryden's Dufreſnoy, Preface.*

*Beautiful* looks are rul'd by fickle minds,
And ſummer ſeas are turn'd by ſudden winds. *Prior.*

BEAU'TIFULLY. *adv.* [from *beautiful.*] In a beautiful manner.

No longer ſhall the boddice aptly lac'd,
From thy full boſom to thy ſlender waiſt,
That air and harmony of ſhape expreſs,
Fine by degrees, and *beautifully* leſs. *Prior.*

BEAU'TIFULNESS. *n. ſ.* [from *beautiful.*] The quality of being beautiful; beauty; excellence of form.

To BEAU'TIFY. *v. a.* [from *beauty.*] To adorn; to embelliſh; to deck; to grace; to add beauty to.

Never was ſorrow more ſweetly ſet forth, their faces ſeeming rather to *beautify* their ſorrow, than their ſorrow to cloud the beauty of their faces. *Hayward on Edward* VI.

Sufficeth not that we are brought to Rome,
To *beautify* thy triumphs and return,
Captive to thee and to thy Roman yoke. *Shakeſp. T. Andron.*

Theſe were not created to *beautify* the earth alone, but for the uſe of man and beaſt. *Raleigh's Hiſtory of the World.*

How all conſpire to grace
Th' extended earth, and *beautify* her face. *Blackmore's Creat.*

There is charity and juſtice; and the one ſerves to heighten and *beautify* the other. *Atterbury.*

To BEAU'TIFY. *v. n.* To grow beautiful; to advance in beauty.

It muſt be a proſpect pleaſing to God himſelf, to ſee his creation for ever *beautifying* in his eyes, and drawing nearer to him, by greater degrees of reſemblance. *Addiſon. Spectator.*

BEAU'TY. *n. ſ.* [*beauté*, Fr.]

1. That

~~Beavoir n.s. (beau & voir) fr. face~~
~~visage. not in use~~

She then her beavoir slid veil
But first she thank'd him & then 'gan her tale
Spens.

Pleasing. harmonious. delightful to the ear
In Sidney we find a transition of the common
attributes of the Eyes & Ears.

a ǂ He might hear her sing this Song with a
Voice no less beautiful to his Ears, than her
goodness was full of harmony to his Eyes
Sidney

c ǂ Can I without the detestable Stain of Ungratefulness abstain from loving him, who far exceeds
the beautifulness of his Shape with the beautifulness of his mind, is content so to abase himself as
to become Dametas's Servant for my Sake
Sidney

a ǂ Then are the public duties of religion best ordered, when the militant Church doth resemble by
sensible means that hidden dignity and glory
wherewith the Church triumphant in heaven is
beautified
Hooker 5.5.

Nor is't too hard to beautify each month
with files of party colour'd fruits that please
The tongue & view at once
Philips

a ‡ Be is an inseparable particle placed before verbs of which it seldom augments or changes the signification as to ~~bedeck~~ bedeck, and before nouns which it changes into verbs. as dew, to bedew.

1. That aſſemblage of graces, or proportion of parts, which pleaſes the eye.

*Beauty* conſiſts of a certain compoſition of colour and figure, cauſing delight in the beholder. *Locke.*

Your *beauty* was the cauſe of that effect,
Your *beauty*, that did haunt me in my ſleep.—
—If I thought that, I tell thee, homicide,
Theſe nails ſhould rend that *beauty* from my cheeks.
*Shakeſp. Richard* III.

*Beauty* is beſt in a body that hath rather dignity of preſence than *beauty* of aſpect. The beautiful prove accompliſhed, but not of great ſpirit, and ſtudy for the moſt part rather behaviour than virtue. *Bacon.*

The beſt part of *beauty* is that which a picture cannot expreſs. *Bacon's Ornament. Ration.* N° 64.

Of the *beauty* of the eye I ſhall ſay little, leaving that to poets and orators; that it is a very pleaſant and lovely object to behold, if we conſider the figure, colours, ſplendour of it, is the leaſt I can ſay. *Ray on Creation.*

He view'd their twining branches with delight,
And prais'd the *beauty* of the pleaſing ſight. *Pope.*

2. A particular grace, feature, or ornament.

The ancient pieces are beautiful, becauſe they reſemble the *beauties* of nature; and nature will ever be beautiful, which reſembles thoſe *beauties* of antiquity. *Dryden's Dufreſnoy.*

Wherever you place a patch, you deſtroy a *beauty*. *Addiſon.*

3. Any thing more eminently excellent than the reſt of that with which it is united.

This gave me an occaſion of looking backward on ſome *beauties* of my author in his former books. *Dryd. Fab. Pref.*

With incredible pains have I endeavoured to copy the ſeveral *beauties* of the ancient and modern hiſtorians. *Arbuthnot.*

4. A beautiful perſon.

Remember that Pellean conquerour,
A youth, how all the *beauties* of the eaſt
He ſlightly view'd, and ſlightly overpaſs'd. *Paradiſe Loſt.*

What can thy ends, malicious *beauty*, be?
Can he, who kill'd thy brother, live for thee? *Dryden.*

To Beau'ty. *v. a.* [from the noun.] To adorn; to beautify; to embelliſh.

The harlot's cheek, *beautied* with plaſt'ring art,
Is not more ugly to the thing that helps it,
Than is my deed to your moſt painted word. *Shak. Hamlet.*

Beauty-spot. *n. ſ.* [from *beauty* and *ſpot.*] A ſpot placed to direct the eye to ſomething elſe, or to heighten ſome beauty; a foil; a patch.

The filthineſs of ſwine makes them the *beauty-ſpot* of the animal creation. *Grew's Coſmologia Sacra, b.* iii. *c.* 2. § 49.

Becafi'co. *n. ſ.* [*becafigo*, Span.] A bird like a nightingale, feeding on figs and grapes; a fig-pecker. *Pineda.*

The robin-redbreaſt, till of late, had reſt,
And children ſacred held a martin's neſt;
Till *becaficos* ſold ſo dev'liſh dear,
To one that was, or would have been, a peer. *Pope.*

To Beca'lm. *v. a.* [from *calm.*]

1. To ſtill the elements.

The moon ſhone clear on the *becalmed* flood. *Dryden.*

2. To keep a ſhip from motion.

A man *becalmed* at ſea, out of ſight of land, in a fair day, may look on the ſun, or ſea, or ſhip, a whole hour, and perceive no motion. *Locke.*

3. To quiet the mind.

Soft whiſp'ring airs, and the lark's mattin ſong,
Then woo to muſing, and *becalm* the mind
Perplex'd with irkſome thoughts. *Philips.*

Baniſh his ſorrows, and *becalm* his ſoul
With eaſy dreams. *Addiſon's Cato.*

4. To *becalm* and to *calm* differ in this, that *to calm* is to ſtop motion, and *to becalm* is to with-hold from motion.

Beca'me. The preterite of *become*; which ſee.

Beca'use. *conjunct.* [from *by* and *cauſe.*]

1. For this reaſon that; on this account that; for this cauſe that.

How great ſoever the ſins of any perſon are, Chriſt died for him, *becauſe* he died for all; and he died for thoſe ſins, *becauſe* he died for all ſins; only he muſt reform. *Hammond's Fundam.*

Men do not ſo generally agree in the ſenſe of theſe as of the other, *becauſe* the intereſts, and luſts, and paſſions of men, are more concerned in the one than the other. *Tillotſ. Preface.*

2. It has, in ſome ſort, the force of a *prepoſition*; but, becauſe it is compounded of a noun, has *of* after it.

Infancy demands aliment, ſuch as lengthens fibres without breaking, *becauſe of* the ſtate of accretion. *Arbuth. on Aliments.*

To Becha'nce. *v. n.* [from *be* and *chance.*] To befal; to happen to: a word proper, but now in little uſe.

My ſons, God knows what has *bechanced* them.
*Shakeſp. Henry* VI. *p.* ii.

All happineſs *bechance* to thee at Milan.
*Shakeſp. Two Gentlemen of Verona.*

Be'chicks. *n. ſ.* [βηχικα, of βὴξ, a cough.] Medicines proper for relieving coughs. *Dict.*

To BECK. *v. a.* [beacn, Sax. *bec*, Fr. head.] To make a ſign with the head.

B E C

Bell, book, and candle, ſhall not drive me back,
When gold and ſilver *beck* me to come on. *Shakeſ. K. John.*

Oh, this falſe ſoul of Egypt, this gay charm,
Whoſe eye *beck'd* forth my wars, and called them home.
*Shakeſp. Antony and Cleopatra.*

Beck. *n. ſ.* [from the verb.]

1. A ſign with the head; a nod.

Haſte thee, nymph, and bring with thee
Quips, and cranks, and wanton wiles,
Nods, and *becks*, and wreathed ſmiles. *Milton.*

2. A nod of command.

Neither the luſty kind ſhewed any roughneſs, nor the eaſier any idleneſs; but ſtill like a well obeyed maſter, whoſe *beck* is enough for diſcipline. *Sidney, b.* ii.

Then forthwith to him takes a choſen band
Of ſpirits, likeſt to himſelf in guile,
To be at hand, and at his *beck* appear. *Milton's Par. Reg.*

The menial fair, that round her wait,
At Helen's *beck* prepare the room of ſtate. *Pope's Odyſſ. b.* iii.

To Be'ckon. *v. a.* [from *beck*, or beacn, Sax. a ſign.] To make a ſign to.

With her two crooked hands ſhe ſigns did make,
And *beckon'd* him. *Fairy Queen, b.* ii. *cant.* iv. *ſtanz.* 13.

It *beckons* you to go away with it,
As if it ſome impartment did deſire
To you alone. *Shakeſp. Hamlet.*

With this his diſtant friends he *beckons* near,
Provokes their duty, and prevents their fear. *Dryden.*

To Be'ckon. *v. n.* To make a ſign.

Alexander *beckoned* with the hand, and would have made his defence unto the people. *Acts*, xix. 33.

When he had raiſed my thoughts by thoſe tranſporting airs, he *beckoned* to me, and, by the waving of his hand, directed me to approach. *Addiſon. Spectator*, N° 159.

Sudden you mount! you *beckon* from the ſkies,
Clouds interpoſe, waves roar, and winds ariſe. *Pope.*

To Becli'p. *v. a.* [of be clyppan, Sax.] To embrace. *Dict.*

To Beco'me. *v. a.* pret. *I became*; comp. pret. *I have become.* [from *by* and *come.*]

1. To enter into ſome ſtate or condition, by a change from ſome other.

The Lord God breathed into his noſtrils the breath of life, and man *became* a living ſoul. *Gen.* ii. 7.

And unto the Jews I *became* a Jew, that I might gain the Jews. 1 *Cor.* ix. 20.

A ſmaller pear, grafted upon a ſtock that beareth a greater pear, will *become* great. *Bacon's Natural Hiſtory*, N° 453.

My voice thou oft haſt heard, and haſt not fear'd,
But ſtill rejoic'd; how is it now *become*
So dreadful to thee? *Milton's Paradiſe Loſt, b.* x. *l.* 120.

So the leaſt faults, if mix'd with faireſt dead,
Of future ill *become* the fatal ſeed. *Prior.*

2. *To become of.* To be the fate of; to be the end of; to be the final condition of. It is obſervable, that this word is never, or very ſeldom, uſed but with the interrogative *what.*

*What* is then *become of* ſo huge a multitude, as would have overſpread a great part of the continent? *Raleigh's Eſſays.*

Perplex'd with thoughts, *what* would *become*
*Of* me, and all mankind. *Milton's Par. Loſt, b.* xii. *l.* 275.

The firſt hints of the circulation of the blood were taken from a common perſon's wondering *what became of* all the blood which iſſued out of the heart. *Graunt's Bills of Mortality.*

*What* will *become of* me then? for when he is free, he will infallibly accuſe me. *Dryden's Spaniſh Friar.*

*What became of* this thoughtful buſy creature, when removed from this world, has amazed the vulgar, and puzzled the wiſe. *Rogers's Sermons.*

3. In the following paſſage, the phraſe, *where is he become*, is uſed for *what is become of him.*

I cannot joy, until I be reſolved
*Where* our right valiant father *is become.* *Shakeſp. Hen.* VI.

To Beco'me. *v. a.* [from *be* or *by*, and cpemen, Sax. to pleaſe.]

1. Applied to perſons; to appear in a manner ſuitable to ſomething.

If I *become* not a cart as well as another man, a plague on my bringing up. *Shakeſp. Henry* IV. *p.* i.

Why would I be a queen? becauſe my face
Would wear the title with a better grace;
If I *became* it not, yet it would be
Part of your duty, then, to flatter me. *Dryd. Conq. of Gran.*

2. Applied to things; to be ſuitable to the perſon; to befit; to be congruous to the appearance, or character, or circumſtances, in ſuch a manner as to add grace; to be graceful.

She to her ſire made humble reverence,
And bowed low, that her right well *became*,
And added grace unto her excellence. *Fairy Queen, b.* i.

I would I had ſome flowers of the ſpring that might
*Become* your time of day; and your's, and your's,
That wear upon your virgin branches yet
Your maidenheads growing. *Shakeſp. Winter's Tale.*

Yet be ſad, good brothers;
For, to ſpeak truth, it very well *becomes* you. *Sh. Henry* IV.

Your

Your diſhonour
Mangles true judgment, and bereaves the ſtate
Of that integrity, which ſhould *become* it. *Shakeſp. Coriol.*

Wicherly was of my opinion, or, rather, I of his: for it *becomes* me ſo to ſpeak of ſo excellent a poet. *Dryd. Dufr. Pref.*

He utterly rejected their fables concerning their gods, as not *becoming* good men, much leſs thoſe which were worſhipped for gods. *Stillingfl. Def. of Diſc. on Rom. Idolatry.*

BECO'MING. *particip. adj.* [from *become.*] That which pleaſes by an elegant propriety; graceful. It is ſometimes uſed with the particle *of*; but generally without any government of the following words.

Of thee, kind boy, I aſk no red and white
To make up my delight,
No odd *becoming* graces,
Black eyes, or little know not what, in faces. *Suckling.*

Their diſcourſes are ſuch as belong to their age, their calling, and their breeding; ſuch as are *becoming of* them, and *of* them only. *Dryd. Fables, Preface.*

Yet ſome *becoming* boldneſs I may uſe;
I've well deſerv'd, nor will he now refuſe. *Dryd. Aurengz.*

Make their pupils repeat the action, that they may correct what is conſtrained in it, till it be perfected into an habitual and *becoming* eaſineſs. *Locke.*

BECO'MING. *n. ſ.* [from *become.*] Behaviour: a word not now in uſe.

Sir, forgive me,
Since my *becomings* kill me, when they do not
Eye well to you. *Shakeſp. Antony and Cleopatra.*

BECO'MINGLY. *adv.* [from *becoming.*] After a becoming or proper manner.

BECO'MINGNESS. *n. ſ.* [from *becoming.* See To BECOME.] Decency; elegant congruity; propriety.

Nor is the majeſty of the divine government greater in its extent, than the *becomingneſs* hereof is in its manner and form. *Grew's Coſmologia Sacra, b.* iii. *c.* 1.

BED. *n. ſ.* [beð, Sax.]

1. Something made to ſleep on.

Lying not erect, but hollow, which is in the making of the *bed*; or with the legs gathered up, which is in the poſture of the body, is the more wholſome. *Bacon's Nat. Hiſt.* Nº 738.

Rigour now is gone to *bed*,
And advice with ſcrupulous head. *Milton.*

Thoſe houſes then were caves, or homely ſheds,
With twining oziers fenc'd, and moſs their *beds.* *Dryden.*

2. Lodging; the convenience of a place to ſleep in.

On my knees I beg,
That you'll vouchſafe me, raiment, *bed,* and food. *Shakeſp. King Lear.*

3. Marriage.

George, the eldeſt ſon of this ſecond *bed,* was, after the death of his father, by the ſingular care and affection of his mother, well brought up. *Clarendon.*

4. Bank of earth raiſed in a garden.

Herbs will be tenderer and fairer, if you take them out of *beds,* when they are newly come up, and remove them into pots, with better earth. *Bacon's Nat. Hiſt.* Nº 459.

5. The channel of a river, or any hollow.

So high as heav'd the tumid hills, ſo low
Down ſunk a hollow bottom, broad, and deep,
Capacious *bed* of waters. *Milt. Par. Loſt, b.* vii. *l.* 288.

The great magazine for all kinds of treaſure is ſuppoſed to be the *bed* of the Tiber. We may be ſure, when the Romans lay under the apprehenſions of ſeeing their city ſacked by a barbarous enemy, that they would take care to beſtow ſuch of their riches that way, as could beſt bear the water. *Addiſon.*

6. The place where any thing is generated, or repoſited.

See hoary Albula's infected tide
O'er the warm *bed* of ſmoaking ſulphur glide. *Addiſon.*

7. A layer; a ſtratum; a body ſpread over another.

I ſee no reaſon, but the ſurface of the land ſhould be as regular as that of the water, in the firſt production of it; and the ſtrata, or *beds* within, lie as even. *Burnet's Theory.*

8. *To bring to* BED. To deliver of a child. It is often uſed with the particle *of*; as, *ſhe was brought to* bed of *a daughter.*

Ten months after Florimel happen'd to wed,
And was *brought* in a laudable manner *to bed.* *Prior.*

9. *To make the* BED. To put the bed in order after it has been uſed.

I keep his houſe, and I waſh, wring, brew, bake, ſcour, dreſs meat, and *make the beds,* and do all myſelf. *Shakeſp. Merry Wives of Windſor.*

BED *of a Mortar.* [with gunners.] A ſolid piece of oak hollowed in the middle, to receive the breech and half the trunnions. *Dict.*

BED *of a great gun.* That thick plank which lies immediately under the piece, being, as it were, the body of the carriage. *Dict.*

To BED. *v. a.* [from the noun.]

1. To go to bed with.

They have married me:
I'll to the Tuſcan wars, and never *bed* her. *Shakeſp. All's well that ends well.*

2. To be placed in bed.

She was publickly contracted, ſtated as a bride, and ſolemnly *bedded*; and, after ſhe was laid, Maximilian's ambaſſadour put his leg, ſtript naked to the knee, between the eſpouſal ſheets. *Bacon's Henry* VII.

3. To be made partaker of the bed.

There was a doubt ripped up, whether Arthur was *bedded* with his lady. *Bacon's Henry* VII.

4. To ſow, or plant in earth.

Lay the turf with the graſs-ſide downward, upon which lay ſome of your beſt mould to *bed* your quick in, and lay your quick upon it. *Mortimer's Husbandry.*

5. To lay in a place of reſt, or ſecurity.

Let coarſe bold hands, from ſlimy neſt,
The *bedded* fiſh in banks outwreſt. *Donne.*

A ſnake *bedded* himſelf under the threſhold of a country-houſe. *L'Eſtrange's Fables.*

6. To lay in order; in ſtrata.

And as the ſleeping ſoldiers in th' alarm,
Your *bedded* hairs, like life in excrements,
Start up, and ſtand on end. *Shakeſp. Hamlet.*

To BED. *v. n.* To cohabit.

If he be married, and *bed* with his wife, and afterwards relapſe, he may poſſibly fancy that ſhe infected him. *Wiſeman's Surgery.*

To BEDA'BBLE. *v. a.* [from *dabble.*] To wet; to beſprinkle. It is generally applied to perſons, in a ſenſe including inconvenience.

Never ſo weary, never ſo in woe,
*Bedabbled* with the dew, and torn with briars,
I can no further crawl, no further go. *Shakeſp. Midſummer Night's Dream.*

To BEDA'GGLE. *v. a.* [from *daggle.*] To bemire; to ſoil cloaths, by letting them reach the dirt in walking.

To BEDA'SH. *v. a.* [from *daſh.*] To bemire by throwing dirt; to beſpatter; to wet with throwing water.

When thy warlike father, like a child,
Told the ſad ſtory of my father's death,
That all the ſtanders by had wet their cheeks,
Like trees *bedaſh'd* with rain. *Shakeſp. Richard* III.

To BEDA'WB. *v. a.* [from *dawb.*] To dawb over; to beſmear; to ſoil, with ſpreading any viſcous body over it.

A piteous coarſe, a bloody piteous coarſe,
Pale, pale as aſhes, all *bedawb'd* in blood,
All in gore blood. *Shakeſp. Romeo and Juliet.*

To BEDA'ZZLE. *v. a.* [from *dazzle.*] To make the ſight dim by too much luſtre.

My miſtaken eyes,
That have been ſo *bedazzled* by the ſun,
That every thing I look on ſeemeth green. *Shakeſp. Taming of the Shrew.*

BEDCHA'MBER. *n. ſ.* [from *bed* and *chamber.*] The chamber appropriated to reſt.

They were brought to the king, abiding then in his *bedchamber.* *Hayward.*

He was now one of the *bedchamber* to the prince. *Clarendon.*

BEDCLO'ATHS. *n. ſ.* [from *bed* and *cloaths.* It has no *ſingular.*] Coverlets ſpread over a bed.

For he will be ſwine drunk, and, in his ſleep, he does little harm, ſave to his *bedcloaths* about him. *Shakeſp. All's well that ends well.*

BE'DDER. } *n. ſ.* [from *bed.*] The nether-ſtone of an oil-mill. *Dict.*
BEDE'TTER. }

BE'DDING. *n. ſ.* [from *bed.*] The materials of a bed; a bed.

There be no inns where meet *bedding* may be had; ſo that his mantle ſerves him then for a bed. *Spenſer's Ireland.*

Firſt, with aſſiduous care from winter keep,
Well fother'd in the ſtalls, thy tender ſheep;
Then ſpread with ſtraw the *bedding* of thy fold,
With fern beneath, to fend the bitter cold. *Dryd. Georg.*

Arcite return'd, and, as in honour ty'd,
His foe with *bedding,* and with food ſupply'd. *Dryden.*

To BEDE'CK. *v. a.* [from *deck.*] To deck; to adorn; to grace.

Thou ſham'ſt thy ſhape, thy love, thy wit,
And uſeſt none in that true uſe indeed,
Which ſhould *bedeck* thy ſhape, thy love, thy wit. *Shakeſp. Romeo and Juliet.*

Female it ſeems,
That ſo *bedeck'd,* ornate, and gay,
Comes this way. *Milton's Samſ. Agoniſtes, l.* 710.

With ornamental drops *bedeck'd* I ſtood,
And writ my victory with my enemy's blood. *Norris.*

Now Ceres, in her prime,
Smiles fertile, and with ruddieſt freight *bedeckt.* *Philips.*

BE'DEHOUSE. *n. ſ.* [from bede, Sax. a prayer, and *houſe.*] An hoſpital or almshouſe, where the poor people prayed for their founders and benefactors.

BEDE'TTER. See BEDDER.

To BEDE'W. *v. a.* [from *dew.*] To moiſten gently, as with the fall of dew.

*Bedew* her paſture's graſs with faithful Engliſh blood. *Shakeſp. Richard* II.

Let

for what is become of him, or where is he
I cannot say untill I be resolv'd
Where our right valiant father is become
Shak. H. 6. p. 3<sup>d</sup>

a ‡
How becomingly does Philopolis exercise
his Office, like a long practis'd Moderator
More. D. D.

c ‡
Fearing to be seen within a bed
Colewarts he conceal'd his wily head
There sculk'd
Dryd.

Gladsome they quaff yet not exceed the bounds
Of healthy temp'rance nor encroach on Night
Season of rest, but well bedew'd repair
Each to his home with unsupplanted feet

Philips

O ‡

His venerable Age. bedew'd with tears.

Pope Ulyss.

Up starts the bedlam
And reverence made accosted thus the Queen

Dryd.

p ‡

The Venom was insinuated into the whole
mass, and the World was little better than a com
:mon fold of phrentics and bedlams

Woodw.



IL facing 2X[r]

Let all the tears that should *bedew* my herse,
Be drops of balm to sanctify thy head. *Shakesp. Hen.* IV.

The countess received a letter from him, whereunto all the while she was writing her answer, she *bedewed* the paper with her tears. *Wotton.*

What slender youth, *bedew'd* with liquid odours,
Courts thee on roses, in some pleasant cave? *Milton.*

Balm from a silver box distill'd around,
Shall all *bedew* the roots, and scent the sacred ground. *Dryd.*

He said: and falling tears his face *bedew*. *Dryd. Æneid.*

BE'DFELLOW. *n. s.* [from *bed* and *fellow.*] One that lies in the same bed.

He loves your people,
But tie him not to be their *bedfellow*. *Shakesp. Coriolanus.*

Misery acquaints a man with strange *bedfellows*.
*Shakesp. Tempest.*

And how doth my cousin, your *bedfellow*?
And your fairest daughter, and mine? *Shakesp. Henry* IV.

Why doth the crown lie there upon his pillow,
Being so troublesom a *bedfellow*? *Shakesp. Henry* IV.

A man would as soon choose him for his *bedfellow* as his playfellow. *L'Estrange.*

What charming *bedfellows*, and companions for life, men choose out of such women? *Addison. Guardian*, N° 120.

To BEDI'GHT. *v. a.* [from *dight.*] To adorn; to dress; to set off.

A maiden fine *bedight* he hapt to love;
The maiden fine *bedight* his love retains,
And for the village he forsakes the plains. *Gay.*

To BEDI'M. *v. a.* [from *dim.*] To make dim; to obscure; to cloud; to darken.

I have *bedimm'd*
The noontide sun, call'd forth the mutinous winds,
And 'twixt the green sea and the azur'd vault
Set roaring war. *Shakesp. Tempest.*

To BEDI'ZEN. *v. a.* [from *dizen.*] To dress out.

BE'DLAM. *n. s.* [corrupted from *Bethlehem*, the name of a religious house in London, converted afterwards into an hospital for the mad and lunatick.]

1. A madhouse; a place appointed for the cure of lunacy.
2. A madman; a lunatick.

Let's follow the old earl, and get the *bedlam*
To lead him where he would; his roguish madness
Allows itself to any thing. *Shakesp. King Lear.*

BE'DLAM. *adj.* [from the noun.] Belonging to a madhouse; fit for a madhouse.

The country gives me proof and precedent
Of *bedlam* beggars, who, with roaring voices,
Strike in their numb'd and mortify'd bare arms,
Pins, wooden pricks. *Shakesp. King Lear.*

BE'DLAMITE. *n. s.* [from *bedlam.*] An inhabitant of Bedlam; a madman.

If wild ambition in thy bosom reign,
Alas! thou boast'st thy sober sense in vain;
In these poor *bedlamites* thyself survey. *Lewis's Miscel.*

BE'DMAKER. *n. s.* [from *bed* and *make.*] A person in the universities, whose office it is to make the beds, and clean the chambers.

I was deeply in love with my *bedmaker*, upon which I was rusticated for ever. *Spectator*, N° 598.

BE'DMATE. *n. s.* [from *bed* and *mate.*] A bedfellow; one that partakes of the same bed.

Had I so good occasion to lie long
As you, prince Paris, nought but heav'nly business
Should rob my *bedmate* of my company. *Shak. Tr. and Cress.*

BE'DMOULDING. } *n. s.* [from *bed* and *mould.*] A term
BE'DDING MOULDING. } used by workmen, to signify those members in the cornice, which are placed below the coronet. *Builder's Dict.*

BE'DPOST. *n. s.* [from *bed* and *post.*] The post at the corner of the bed, which supports the canopy.

I came the next day prepared, and placed her in a clear light, her head leaning to a *bedpost*, another standing behind, holding it steady. *Wiseman's Surgery.*

BE'DPRESSER. *n. s.* [from *bed* and *press.*] A heavy lazy fellow.

This sanguine coward, this *bedpresser*, this horseback-breaker, this huge hill of flesh. *Shakesp. Henry IV. p.* i.

To BEDRA'GGLE. *v. a.* [from *be* and *draggle.*] To soil the cloaths, by suffering them, in walking, to reach the dirt.

Poor Patty Blount, no more be seen
*Bedraggled* in my walks so green. *Swift.*

To BEDRE'NCH. *v. a.* [from *be* and *drench.*] To drench; to soak; to saturate with moisture.

Far off from the mind of Bolingbroke
It is, such crimson tempest should *bedrench*
The fresh green lap of fair king Richard's land.
*Shakesp. King Richard* III.

BE'DRID. *adj.* [from *bed* and *ride.*] Confined to the bed by age or sickness.

Norway, uncle of young Fortinbras,
Who, impotent and *bedrid*, scarcely hears
Of this his nephew's purpose. *Shakesp. Hamlet.*

Lies he not *bedrid*? and, again, does nothing,
But what he did being childish. *Shakesp. Winter's Tale.*

Now, as a myriad
Of ants durst th' emperor's lov'd snake invade;
The crawling galleys, seagulls, finny chips,
Might brave our pinnaces, our *bedrid* ships. *Donne.*

Hanging old men, who were *bedrid*, because they would not discover where their money was. *Clarendon, b.* viii.

Infirm persons, when they come to be so weak as to be fixed to their beds, hold out many years; some have lain *bedrid* twenty years. *Ray.*

BE'DRITE. *n. s.* [from *bed* and *rite.*] The privilege of the marriage bed.

Whose vows are, that no *bedrite* shall be paid
Till Hymen's torch be lighted. *Shakesp. Tempest.*

To BEDRO'P. *v. a.* [from *be* and *drop.*] To besprinkle; to mark with spots or drops; to speckle.

Not so thick swarm'd once the soil
*Bedrop'd* with blood of Gorgon. *Milt. Par. Lost, b.* x. *l.* 527.

Our plenteous streams a various race supply;
The silver eel in shining volumes roll'd,
The yellow carp, in scales *bedrop'd* with gold. *Pope's W. For.*

BE'DSTEAD. *n. s.* [from *bed* and *stead.*] The frame on which the bed is placed.

Chimnies with scorn rejecting smoak;
Stools, tables, chairs, and *bedsteads* broke. *Swift.*

BE'DSTRAW. *n. s.* [from *bed* and *straw.*] The straw laid under a bed to make it soft.

Fleas breed principally of straw or mats, where there hath been a little moisture; or the chamber or *bedstraw* kept close, and not aired. *Bacon's Nat. Hist.* N° 696.

BEDSWE'RVER. *n. s.* [from *bed* and *swerve.*] One that is false to the bed; one that ranges or swerves from one bed to another.

She's a *bedswerver*, even as bad as those,
That vulgars give bold'st titles to. *Shakesp. Winter's Tale.*

BE'DTIME. *n. s.* [from *bed* and *time.*] The hour of rest; sleeping time.

What masks, what dances shall we have,
To wear away this long age of three hours,
Between our after-supper and *bedtime*?
*Shakesp. Midsummer Night's Dream.*

After evening repasts, till *bedtime*, their thoughts will be best taken up in the easy grounds of religion. *Milt. on Education.*

The scouring drunkard, if he does not fight
Before his *bedtime*, takes no rest that night. *Dryden's Juv.*

To BEDU'NG. *v. a.* [from *be* and *dung.*] To cover, or manure with dung.

To BEDU'ST. *v. a.* [from *be* and *dust.*] To sprinkle with dust.

BE'DWARD. *adv.* [from *bed* and *ward.*] Toward bed.

In heart
As merry, as when our nuptial day was done,
And tapers burnt to *bedward*. *Shakesp. Coriolanus.*

To BEDWA'RF. *v. a.* [from *be* and *dwarf.*] To make little, to hinder in growth; to stunt.

'Tis shrinking, not close weaving, that hath thus
In mind and body both *bedwarfed* us. *Donne.*

BE'DWORK. *n. s.* [from *bed* and *work.*] Work done in bed; work performed without toil of the hands.

The still and mental parts,
That do contrive how many hands shall strike,
When fulness call them on, and know, by measure
Of their observant toil, the enemy's weight;
Why this hath not a finger's dignity,
They call this *bedwork*, mapp'ry, closet war.
*Shakesp. Troilus and Cressida.*

BEE. *n. s.* [beo, Saxon.]

1. The animal that makes honey, remarkable for its industry and art.

So work the honey *bees*,
Creatures that, by a ruling nature, teach
The art of order to a peopled kingdom. *Shakesp. Hen.* V.

From the Moorish camp,
There has been heard a distant humming noise,
Like *bees* disturb'd, and arming in their hives. *Dryden.*

A company of poor insects, whereof some are *bees*, delighted with flowers, and their sweetness; others beetles, delighted with other viands. *Locke.*

2. An industrious and careful person. This signification is only used in familiar language.

BEE-EATER. *n. s.* [from *bee* and *eat.*] A bird that feeds upon bees.

BEE-FLOWER. *n. s.* [from *bee* and *flower.*] A species of foolstones; which see. It grows upon dry places, and flowers in April. *Millar.*

BEE-GARDEN. *n. s.* [from *bee* and *garden.*] A place to set hives of bees in.

A convenient and necessary place ought to be made choice of, for your apiary, or *bee-garden*. *Mortimer's Husbandry.*

BEE-HIVE. *n. s.* [from *bee* and *hive.*] The case, or box, in which bees are kept.

BEE-MASTER. *n. s.* [from *bee* and *master.*] One that keeps bees.

They that are *bee-masters*, and have not care enough of them, must not expect to reap any considerable advantage by them. *Mortimer's Husbandry.*

BEECH. *n. s.* [bece, or boc, Saxon.]

This tree hath leaves somewhat resembling those of the hornbeam; the male flowers grow together in a round bunch, at remote distances from the fruit, which consists of two triangular nuts, inclosed in a rough hairy rind, divided into four parts. There is but one species of this tree at present known, except two varieties, with striped leaves. It will grow to a considerable stature, though the soil be stony and barren; as also, upon the declivities of mountains. The shade of this tree is very injurious to most sorts of plants, which grow near it, but is generally believed to be very salubrious to human bodies. The timber is of great use to turners and joiners. The mast is very good to fatten swine and deer; and affords a sweet oil, and has supported some families with bread. *Millar.*

Black was the forest, thick with *beech* it stood. *Dryden.*

Nor is that sprightly wildness in their notes,
Which, clear and vigorous, warbles from the *beech*.
*Thomson's Spring.*

BE'ECHEN. *adj.* [bucene, Sax.] Consisting of the wood of the beech; belonging to the beech.

With diligence he'll serve us when we dine,
And in plain *beechen* vessels fill our wine. *Dryden's Juv.*

BEEF. *n. s.* [*bœuf*, French.]

1. The flesh of black cattle prepared for food.

What say you to a piece of *beef* and mustard?
*Shakesp. Taming of the Shrew.*

The fat of roasted *beef* falling on the birds, will baste them. *Swift.*

2. An ox, bull, or cow, considered as fit for food. In this sense it has the plural *beeves*; the singular is seldom found.

A pound of man's flesh
Is not so estimable or profitable,
As flesh of muttons, *beeves*, or goats. *Shakesp. M. of Ven.*

Alcinoüs slew twelve sheep, eight white-tooth'd swine,
Two crook-haunch'd *beeves*. *Chapman's Odyssey.*

There was not any captain, but had credit for more victuals than we spent there; and yet they had of me fifty *beeves* among them. *Sir Walter Raleigh's Apology.*

On hides of *beeves*, before the palace gate,
Sad spoils of luxury! the suitors sate. *Pope's Odyssey.*

BEEF. *adj.* [from the substantive.] Consisting of the flesh of black cattle.

If you are employed in marketing, do not accept of a treat of a *beef* stake, and a pot of ale, from the butcher. *Swift.*

BEEF-EATER. *n. s.* [from *beef* and *eat*, because the commons is beef when on waiting.] A yeoman of the guard.

BE'EMOL. *n. s.* This word I have found only in the example, and know nothing of the etymology, unless it be a corruption of *bymodule*, from *by* and *modulus*, a note; that is, a note out of the regular order.

There be intervenient in the rise of eight, in tones, two *beemols*, or half notes; so as, if you divide the tones equally, the eight is but seven whole and equal notes. *Bacon's Nat. Hist.*

BEEN. [beon, Saxon.] The *participle preterite* of To BE; which see.

BEER. *n. s.* [*bir*, Welch.] Liquour made of malt and hops. It is distinguished from ale, either by being older or smaller.

Here's a pot of good double *beer*, neighbour; drink.
*Shakesp. Henry VI. p. ii.*

It were good to try clarifying with almonds in new *beer*.
*Bacon's Natural History*, N° 768.

Flow, Welsted! flow, like thine inspirer, *beer*;
Tho' stale, not ripe; tho' thin, yet never clear;
So sweetly mawkish, and so smoothly dull;
Heady, not strong; and foaming, tho' not full. *Pope.*

BE'ESTINGS. See BIESTINGS.

BEET. *n. s.* [*beta*, Lat.] The name of a plant.

It hath a thick, fleshy root; the flowers have no visible leaves, but many stamina, or threads, collected into a globe; the cup of the flower is divided into five segments; the seeds are covered with an hard outer coat, and grow two or three together in a bunch. The species are: 1. The common white *beet*. 2. The common green *beet*. 3. The common red *beet*. 4. The turnep-rooted red *beet*. 5. The great red *beet*. 6. The yellow *beet*. 7. The Swiss or Chard *beet*. The two first mentioned are preserved in gardens, for the use of their leaves in pot herbs. The other sorts are propagated for their roots, which are boiled as parsneps. The red *beet* is most commonly cultivated and used in garnishing dishes. The Swiss beet is by some much esteemed. *Millar.*

BE'ETLE. *n. s.* [bytel, Saxon.]

1. An insect distinguished by having hard cases or sheaths, under which he folds his wings.

They are as shards, and he their *beetle*. *Sh. Ant. and Cleop.*

The poor *beetle*, that we tread upon,
In corporal suff'rance finds a pang as great,
As when a giant dies. *Shakesp. Measure for Measure.*

Others come in place, sharp of sight, and too provident for that which concerned their own interest; but as blind as *beetles* in foreseeing this great and common danger.
*Knolles's History of the Turks.*

A grott there was with hoary moss o'ergrown,
The clasping ivies up the ruins creep,
And there the bat and drowsy *beetle* sleep. *Garth.*

The butterflies and *beetles* are such numerous tribes, that I believe, in our own native country alone, the species of each kind may amount to one hundred and fifty, or more. *Ray.*

2. A heavy mallet, or wooden hammer, with which wedges are driven.

If I do, fillip me with a three-man *beetle*. *Shakesp. Henry* IV.

When, by the help of wedges and *beetles*, an image is cleft out of the trunk of some well grown tree; yet, after all the skill of artificers to set forth such a divine block, it cannot, one moment, secure itself from being eaten by worms, or defiled by birds, or cut in pieces by axes. *Stillingfleet.*

To BE'ETLE. *v. n.* [from the noun.] To jut out; to hang over.

What if it tempt you tow'rd the flood, my lord?
Or to the dreadful summit of the cliff,
That *beetles* o'er his base into the sea. *Shakesp. Hamlet.*

Or where the hawk,
High in the *beetling* cliff, his airy builds. *Thomson's Spring.*

BEETLEBRO'WED. *adj.* [from *beetle* and *brow*.] Having prominent brows.

BEETLEHE'ADED. *adj.* [from *beetle* and *head*.] Loggerheaded; wooden headed; having a head stupid, like the head of a wooden beetle.

A whoreson, *beetleheaded*, flap-ear'd knave.
*Shakesp Taming of the Shrew.*

BE'ETLESTOCK. *n. s.* [from *beetle* and *stock*.] The handle of a beetle.

To crouch, to please, to be a *beetlestock*
Of thy great master. *Shakespeare.*

BE'ETRAVE. } See BEET.
BE'ET RADISH. }

BEEVES. *n. s.* [The *plural* of *beef*.] Black cattle; oxen.

One way, a band select from forage drives
A herd of *beeves*, fair oxen, and fair kine,
From a fat meadow ground. *Milton's Paradise Lost, b.* xi.

Others make good the paucity of their breed with the length and duration of their days; whereof there want not examples in animals uniparous: first, in bisulcous or cloven-hoofed, as camels and *beeves*; whereof there is above a million annually slain in England. *Brown's Vulgar Errours, b.* vi. *c.* 6.

*Beeves*, at his touch, at once to jelly turn,
And the huge boar is shrunk into an urn. *Pope's Dunciad.*

To BEFA'LL. *v. n.* [from *fall*. It *befell*, it *hath befallen*.]

1. To happen to: used generally of ill.

Let me know
The worst that may *befall* me in this case.
*Shakesp. Midsummer Night's Dream.*

Other doubt possesses me, lest harm
*Befall* thee, sever'd from me. *Milton's Parad Lost, b.* ix.

This venerable person, who probably heard our Saviour's prophecy of the destruction of Jerusalem, drew his congregation out of those unparalleled calamities, which *befell* his countrymen. *Addison on the Christian Religion.*

This disgrace has *befallen* them, not because they deserved it, but because the people love new faces. *Addison's Freeholder.*

2. To happen to, as good.

Bion asked an envious man, that was very sad, what harm had befallen unto him, or what good had *befallen* unto another man? *Bacon's Apophthegms.*

No man can certainly conclude God's love or hatred to any person, from what *befalls* him in this world. *Tillotson.*

3. To happen; to come to pass.

But since th' affairs of men are still uncertain,
Let's reason with the worst that may *befall*. *Shak. J. Cæsar.*

I have reveal'd
This discord which *befell*, and was in heav'n
Among th' angelick pow'rs. *Milton's Parad. Lost, b* vi.

4. It is used sometimes with *to* before the person to whom any thing happens.

Some great mischief hath *befall'n*
*To* that meek man. *Milton's Paradise Lost, b.* xi.

5. *To befall of.* To become of; to be the state or condition of: a phrase little used.

Do me the favour to dilate at full,
What hath *befall'n of* them, and thee, till now.
*Shakespeare's Comedy of Errours.*

To BEFI'T. *v. a.* [from *be* and *fit*.] To suit; to be suitable to; to become.

Blind is his love, and best *befits* the dark.
*Shakesp. Romeo and Juliet.*

Out of my sight, thou serpent!—That name best
*Befits* thee, with him leagu'd; thyself as false. *Parad. Lost.*

I will bring you where she sits,
Clad in splendour, as *befits*
Her deity. *Milton.*

Thou, what *befits* the new lord mayor,
Art anxiously inquisitive to know. *Dryden.*

To

. 1 Dover-court Beetle I suppose signifies a very large Beetle, alluding to the rood of Dover, which was very large & remarkable in our Authors time; or from the proverb yet in use, a Dover-court, all speakers & no hearers, signifying a great noise, which a great Beetle may be supposed to make     Tuss. no

. A Dover court be

‡ 6 To come by descent, ~~not~~ a accidence

. The empire of Almaigne were not unlike to befal to Spain, if it should break     Bacon.

a ǂ

The palm tree alone giveth unto Man what=
=soever his Life beggeth at natures hand

Ral.

To BEFO'OL. *v. a.* [from *be* and *fool.*] To infatuate; to fool; to deprive of understanding; to lead into errour.

Men *befool* themselves infinitely, when, by venting a few sighs, they will needs persuade themselves that they have repented. *South.*

Jeroboam thought policy the best piety, though in nothing more *befooled*; the nature of sin being not only to defile, but to infatuate. *South.*

BEFO'RE. *prep.* [biforan, Sax.]

1. Farther onward in place.

Their common practice was to look no further *before* them than the next line; whence it will follow, that they can drive to no certain point. *Dryden.*

2. In the front of; not behind.

Who shall go
*Before* them in a cloud, and pillar of fire:
By day a cloud, by night a pillar of fire,
To guide them in their journey, and remove
Behind them, while th' obdurate king pursues. *Par. Lost.*

3. In the presence of; noting authority or conquest.

Great queen of gathering clouds,
See, we fall *before* thee!
Prostrate we adore thee! *Dryden's Albion.*

The Alps and Pyreneans sink *before* him. *Addison's Cato.*

4. In the presence of; noting respect.

We see that blushing, and the casting down of the eyes both, are more when we come *before* many. *Bacon.*

They represent our poet betwixt a farmer and a courtier, when he drest himself in his best habit, to appear *before* his patron. *Dryden's Virgil, Dedication.*

5. In sight of.

*Before* the eyes of both our armies here,
Let us not wrangle. *Shakesp. Julius Cæsar.*

6. Under the cognizance of; noting jurisdiction.

If a suit be begun *before* an archdeacon, the ordinary may license the suit to an higher court. *Ayliffe's Parergon.*

7. In the power of; noting the right of choice.

Give us this evening; thou hast morn and night,
And all the year *before* thee, for delight. *Dryden.*

He hath put us in the hands of our own counsel. Life and death, prosperity and destruction, are *before* us. *Tillotson.*

8. By the impulse of something behind.

Her part, poor soul! seeming as burdened
With lesser weight, but not with lesser woe,
Was carried with more speed *before* the wind. *Sh. Com. of Err.*

Hurried by fate, he cries, and born *before*
A furious wind, we leave the faithful shore. *Dryden.*

9. Preceding in time.

Particular advantages it has before all the books which have appeared *before* it in this kind. *Dryden's Dufresnoy.*

10. In preference to.

We should but presume to determine which should be the fittest, till we see he hath chosen some one, which one we may then boldly say to be the fittest, because he hath taken it *before* the rest. *Hooker, b.* iii.

We think poverty to be infinitely desirable *before* the torments of covetousness. *Taylor's Holy Living.*

11. Prior to; nearer to any thing; as, the eldest son is *before* the younger in succession.

12. Superiour to; as, he is *before* his competitors both in right and power.

BEFORE. *adv.*

1. Sooner than; earlier in time.

Heav'nly born,
*Before* the hills appear'd, or fountain flow'd,
Thou with eternal wisdom didst converse. *Par. Lost, b.* vii.

*Before* two months their orb with light adorn,
If heav'n allow me life, I will return. *Dryden's Fables.*

2. In time past.

Such a plenteous crop they bore
Of purest and well winnow'd grain,
As Britain never knew *before.* *Dryden.*

3. In some time lately past.

I shall resume somewhat which hath been *before* said, touching the question beforegoing. *Hale's Origin of Mankind.*

4. Previously to; in order to.

*Before* this elaborate treatise can become of use to my country, two points are necessary. *Swift.*

5. To this time; hitherto.

The peaceful cities of th' Ausonian shore,
Lull'd in their ease, and undisturb'd *before,*
Are all on fire. *Dryden's Æneid.*

6. Already.

You tell me, mother, what I knew *before,*
The Phrygian fleet is landed on the shore. *Dryden's Æneid.*

7. Farther onward in place.

Thou'rt so far *before,*
The swiftest wing of recompence is slow
To overtake. *Shakespeare.*

BEFO'REHAND. *adv.* [from *before* and *hand.*]

1. In a state of anticipation, or preoccupation; sometimes with the particle *with.*

Quoth Hudibras, I am *beforehand*
In that already, *with* your command. *Hudibras.*

Your soul has been *beforehand with* your body,
And drunk so deep a draught of promis'd bliss,
She slumbers o'er the cup. *Dryden's Don Sebastian.*

I have not room for many reflections; the last cited author has been *beforehand with* me, in its proper moral. *Addison.*

2. Previously; by way of preparation, or preliminary.

His profession is to deliver precepts necessary to eloquent speech; yet so, that they which receive them, may be taught *beforehand* the skill of speaking. *Hooker, b.* i.

It would be resisted by such as had *beforehand* resisted the general proofs of the gospel. *Atterbury.*

When the lawyers brought extravagant bills, Sir Roger used to bargain *beforehand,* to cut off a quarter of a yard in any part of the bill. *Arbuthnot's History of J. Bull.*

3. In a state of accumulation, or so as that more has been received than expended.

Stranger's house is at this time rich, and much *beforehand*; for it hath laid up revenue these thirty-seven years. *Bacon.*

4. At first; before any thing is done.

What is a man's contending with insuperable difficulties, but the rolling of Sisyphus's stone up the hill, which is *beforehand* to return upon him again? *L'Estrange's Fables.*

BEFO'RETIME. *adv.* [from *before* and *time.*] Formerly; of old time.

*Beforetime* in Israel, when a man went to enquire of God, thus he spake. 1 *Sam.* ix. 9.

To BEFO'RTUNE. *v. n.* [from *be* and *fortune.*] To happen to; to betide.

I give consent to go along with you;
Recking as little what betideth me,
As much I wish all good *befortune* you.
*Shakesp. Two Gentlemen of Verona.*

To BEFO'UL. *v. a.* [from *be* and *foul.*] To make foul; to soil; to dirt.

To BEFRI'END. *v. a.* [from *be* and *friend.*] To favour; to be kind to; to countenance; to shew friendship to; to benefit.

If it will please Cæsar
To be so good to Cæsar, as to hear me,
I shall beseech him to *befriend* himself. *Shakesp. J. Cæsar.*

Now if your plots be ripe, you are *befriended*
With opportunity. *Denham's Sophy.*

See them embarked,
And tell me if the winds and seas *befriend* them. *Addison.*

Be thou the first true merit to *befriend*;
His praise is lost, who stays till all commend. *Pope.*

Brother-servants must always *befriend* one another. *Swift.*

To BEFRI'NGE. *v. a.* [from *be* and *fringe.*] To decorate, as with fringes.

When I flatter, let my dirty leaves
Cloath spice, line trunks, or, flutt'ring in a rowe,
*Befringe* the rails of Bedlam and Soho. *Pope.*

To BEG. *v. n.* [*beggeren,* Germ.] To live upon alms; to live by asking relief of others.

I cannot dig; to *beg* I am ashamed. *Luke,* xvi. 3.

To BEG. *v. a.*

1. To ask; to seek by petition.

He went to Pilate, and *begged* the body. *Matth.* xxvii. 58.

2. To take any thing for granted, without evidence or proof.

We have not *begged* any principles or suppositions, for the proof of this; but taking that common ground, which both Moses and all antiquity present. *Burnet's Theory of the Earth.*

To BEGE'T. *v. a.* I *begot,* or *begat*; I have *begotten,* or *begot.* [begettan, Saxon; to obtain. See To GET.]

1. To generate; to procreate; to become the father of children.

But first come the hours, which were *begot*
In Jove's sweet paradise, of day and night,
Which do the seasons of the year allot. *Spenser's Epithal.*

I talk of dreams,
Which are the children of an idle brain,
*Begot* of nothing but vain phantasy. *Shakesp. Romeo and Jul.*

Who hath *begotten* me these, seeing I have lost my children, and am desolate. *Isaiah,* xlix. 21.

'Twas he the noble Claudian race *begat.* *Dryden's Æneid.*

Love is *begot* by fancy, bred
By ignorance, by expectation fed. *Granville.*

2. To produce, as effects.

If to have done the thing you gave in charge,
*Beget* you happiness, be happy then;
For it is done. *Shakesp. Richard* II.

My whole intention was to *beget,* in the minds of men, magnificent sentiments of God and his works. *Cheyne's Phil. Prin.*

3. To produce, as accidents.

Is it a time for story, when each minute
*Begets* a thousand dangers? *Denham's Sophy.*

4. It is sometimes used with *on,* or *upon,* before the mother.

*Begot upon*
His mother Martha by his father John. *Spectator.*

BEGE'TTER. *n. s.* [from *beget.*] He that procreates, or begets; the father.

For

For what their prowess gain'd, the law declares
Is to themselves alone, and to their heirs:
No share of that goes back to the *begetter*,
But if the son fights well, and plunders better. *Dryden.*

Men continue the race of mankind, commonly without the intention, and often against the consent and will of the *begetter*. *Locke.*

**Be'ggar.** *n. s.* [from *beg*. It is more properly written *begger*; but the common orthography is retained, because the derivatives all preserve the *a*.]

1. One who lives upon alms; one who has nothing but what is given him.

He raiseth up the poor out of the dust, and lifteth up the *beggar* from the dunghill, to set them among princes. *1 Samuel*, ii. 8.

We see the whole equipage of a *beggar* so drawn by Homer, as even to retain a nobleness and dignity. *Broome on the Odyssey.*

2. One who supplicates for any thing; a petitioner; for which, *beggar* is a harsh and contemptuous term.

What subjects will precarious kings regard?
A *beggar* speaks too softly to be heard. *Dryd. Conq. of Gran.*

3. One who assumes what he does not prove.

These shameful *beggars* of principles, who give this precarious account of the original of things, assume to themselves to be men of reason. *Tillotson.*

To **Be'ggar.** *v. a.* [from the noun.]

1. To reduce to beggary; to impoverish.

Whose heavy hand hath bow'd you to the grave,
And *beggar'd* your's for ever. *Shakesp. Macbeth.*

They shall spoil the clothiers wool, and *beggar* the present spinners. *Graunt's Bills of Mortality.*

If the miser durst his farthings spare,
With heav'n, for twopence, cheaply wipes his score,
Lifts up his eyes, and hastes to *beggar* more. *Gay's Trivia.*

2. To deprive.

Necessity, of matter *beggar'd*,
Will nothing stick our persons to arraign
In ear and ear. *Shakesp. Hamlet.*

3. To exhaust.

For her person,
It *beggar'd* all description; she did lie
In her pavilion, cloth of gold, of tissue,
O'er-picturing Venus. *Shakesp. Antony and Cleopatra.*

**Be'ggarliness.** *n. s.* [from *beggarly*.] The state of being beggarly; meanness; poverty.

**Be'ggarly.** *adj.* [from *beggar*.] Mean; poor; indigent; in the condition of a beggar: used both of persons and things.

I ever will, though he do shake me off
To *beggarly* divorcement, love him dearly. *Shakesp. Othello.*

Who, that beheld such a bankrupt *beggarly* fellow as Cromwell entering the parliament house, with a thread bare torn cloak, and a greasy hat, could have suspected, that he should, by the murder of one king, and the banishment of another, ascend the throne? *South.*

The next town has the reputation of being extremely poor and *beggarly*. *Addison on Italy.*

Corusodes, by extreme parsimony, saved thirty-four pounds out of a *beggarly* fellowship. *Swift.*

**Be'ggarly.** *adv.* [from *beggar*.] Meanly; despicably; indigently.

Touching God himself, hath he revealed, that it is his delight to dwell *beggarly*? and that he taketh no pleasure to be worshipped, saving only in poor cottages? *Hooker, b.* v.

**Be'ggary.** *n. s.* [from *beggar*.] Indigence; poverty in the utmost degree.

On he brought me into so bare a house, that it was the picture of miserable happiness and rich *beggary*. *Sidney, b.* ii.

While I am a beggar, I will rail,
And say there is no sin, but to be rich:
And being rich, my virtue then shall be,
To say there is no vice, but *beggary*. *Shakesp. King John.*

We must become not only poor for the present, but reduced, by further mortgages, to a state of *beggary* for endless years to come. *Swift.*

To **Begi'n.** *v. n.* I *began*, or *begun*; I have *begun*. [beginnan, Sax. from *be*, or *by to*, and ginnan, gaan, or gan, to go.]

1. To enter upon something new: applied to persons.

*Begin* every day to repent; not that thou shouldst at all defer it; but all that is past ought to seem little to thee, seeing it is so in itself. *Begin* the next day with the same zeal, fear, and humility, as if thou hadst never *begun* before. *Taylor.*

I'll sing of heroes and of kings;
*Begin* my muse. *Cowley.*

2. To commence any action or state; to do the first act, or first part of an act; to make the first step from not doing to doing.

They *began* at the ancient men which were before the house. *Ezekiel*, ix. 6.

Of these no more you hear him speak;
He now *begins* upon the Greek:
These rang'd and show'd, shall, in their turns,
Remain obscure as in their urns. *Prior.*

*Beginning* from the rural gods, his hand
Was lib'ral to the pow'rs of high command. *Dryden's Fab.*

Rapt into future times, the bard *begun*,
A virgin shall conceive. *Pope's Messiah.*

3. To enter upon existence; as, the world *began*; the practice *began*.

4. To have its original.

And thus the hard and stubborn race of man,
From animated rock and flint *began*. *Blackmore.*

From Nimrod first the savage chase *began*;
A mighty hunter, and his game was man. *Pope.*

5. To take rise.

Judgment must *begin* at the house of God. *1 Pet.* iv. 17.

The song *begun* from Jove. *Dryden.*

All *began*,
All ends in love of God, and love of man. *Pope.*

6. To come into act.

Now and then a sigh he stole,
And tears *began* to flow. *Dryden.*

To **Begin.** *v. a.*

1. To do the first act of any thing; to pass from not doing to doing, by the first act.

Ye nymphs of Solyma, *begin* the song. *Pope's Messiah.*

They have been awaked, by these awful scenes, to *begin* religion; and, afterwards, their virtue has improved itself into more refined principles, by divine grace. *Watts.*

2. To trace from any thing as the first ground.

The apostle *begins* our knowledge in the creatures, which leads us to the knowledge of God. *Locke.*

3. *To begin with.* To enter upon; to fall to work upon.

A lesson which requires so much time to learn, had need be early *begun with*. *Government of the Tongue.*

**Begi'nner.** *n. s.* [from *begin*.]

1. He that gives the first cause, or original, to any thing.

Thus heaping crime on crime, and grief on grief,
To loss of love adjoining loss of friend,
I meant to purge both with a third mischief,
And, in my woe's *beginner*, it to end. *Fairy Queen, b.* ii.

Socrates maketh Ignatius, the bishop of Antioch in Syria, the first *beginner* thereof, even under the apostles themselves. *Hook.*

2. An unexperienced attempter; one in his rudiments; a young practitioner.

Palladius, behaving himself nothing like a *beginner*, brought the honour to the Iberian side. *Sidney, b.* i.

They are, to *beginners*, an easy and familiar introduction; a mighty augmentation of all virtue and knowledge in such as are entered before. *Hooker, b.* v. §. 37.

I have taken a list of several hundred words in a sermon of a new *beginner*, which not one hearer could possibly understand. *Swift.*

**Begi'nning.** *n. s.* [from *begin*.]

1. The first original or cause.

Wherever we place the *beginning* of motion, whether from the head or the heart, the body moves and acts by a consent of all its parts. *Swift.*

2. The entrance into act, or being.

Also in the day of your gladness, and in your solemn days, and in the *beginnings* of your months, you shall blow the trumpets over your burnt offering. *Numbers*, x. 10.

Youth, what man's age is like to be, doth show;
We may our end by our *beginning* know. *Denham.*

3. The state in which any thing first is.

By viewing nature, nature's handmaid, art
Makes mighty things from small *beginnings* grow:
Thus fishes first to shipping did impart,
Their tail the rudder, and their head the prow. *Dryden.*

4. The rudiments, or first grounds or materials.

The understanding is passive; and whether or not it will have these *beginnings*, and materials of knowledge, is not in its own power. *Locke.*

5. The first part of any thing.

The causes and designs of an action, are the *beginning*; the effects of these causes, and the difficulties that are met with in the execution of these designs, are the middle; and the unravelling and resolution of these difficulties, are the end. *Pope on Epick Poetry.*

To **Begi'rd.** *v. a.* I *begirt*, or *begirded*; I have *begirt*. [from *be* and *gird*.]

1. To bind with a girdle.

Or should she confident,
As sitting queen ador'd on beauty's throne,
Descend, with all her winning charms *begirt*,
T' enamour. *Milton's Paradise Lost, b.* ii. *l.* 213.

2. To surround; to encircle; to encompass.

*Begird* th' almighty throne,
Beseeching, or besieging. *Milton's Paradise Lost, b.* v. *l.* 868.

At home surrounded by a servile croud,
Prompt to abuse, and in detraction loud:
Abroad *begirt* with men, and swords, and spears;
His very state acknowledging his fears. *Prior.*

3. To shut in with a siege; to beleaguer; to block up.

It was so closely *begirt* before the king's march into the west, that the council humbly desired his majesty, that he would relieve it. *Clarendon, b.* viii.

To

††

He that does the first part of ~~He who leads the way, he who first treads~~ any thing
~~of a thing~~
You full little think that you must be the
beginner of the Discourse yourself. More

~~Begging n. s. (beg-in. Infan infant) first~~
~~Beattes~~

IL facing 2X2$^{v}$

Begone in composition, as Woebegone, depress'd with woe

A man so spiritless
So dull, so dead in look, so woebegone
Drew Priams Curtain in the dead of Night
And would have told him all his Troy was burn'd
But Priam found the fire, ere he his Tongue
Shak. H. 4. 2.

Begone Oppress'd
Fancred be sure his life's Joy set at Nought
So woebegone was he with pains of love
Fairf. 1. 9.

Of before the thing beguiled of
Other mens insatiable desire of revenge, wholly beguiled church & state of the benefit of all my retractions & concessions
K. Charles.

To BEGI'RT. *v. a.* [This is, I think, only a corruption of *begird*; perhaps by the printer.] To begird. See BEGIRD.

And, Lentulus, *begirt* you Pompey's house,
To seize his sons alive; for they are they
Must make our peace with him. *Ben. Johnson's Catiline.*

BE'GLERBEG. *n. s.* [Turkish.] The chief governour of a province among the Turks.

To BEGNA'W. *v. a.* [from *be* and *gnaw.*] To bite; to eat away; to corrode; to nibble.

His horse is stark spoiled with the staggers, *begnawn* with the bots, waid in the back, and shoulder shotten. *Shakesp. Taming of the Shrew.*

The worm of conscience still *begnaw* thy soul. *Shakesp. Richard III.*

BEGO'NE. *interject.* [only a coalition of the words *be gone.*] Go away; hence; haste away.

*Begone!* the goddess cries, with stern disdain;
*Begone!* nor dare the hallow'd stream to stain.
She fled, for ever banish'd from the train. *Addison.*

BEGO'T. } *The participle passive* of the verb *beget.*
BEGO'TTEN. }

Remember that thou wast *begot* of them. *Ecclus,* vii. 28.

The first he met, Antiphates the brave,
But base *begotten* on a Theban slave. *Dryden's Æneid.*

To BEGRE'ASE. *v. a.* [from *be* and *grease.*] To soil or dawb with unctuous or fat matter.

To BEGRI'ME. *v. a.* [from *be* and *grime.* See GRIME and GRIM.] To soil with dirt deep impressed; to soil in such a manner that the natural hue cannot easily be recovered.

Her name, that was as fresh
As Dian's visage, is now *begrim'd*, and black
As my own face. *Shakesp. Othello.*

To BEGUI'LE. *v. a.* [from *be* and *guile.*]

1. To impose upon; to delude; to cheat.

This I say, lest any man should *beguile* you with enticing words. *Coloss.* ii. 4.

The serpent me *beguil'd*, and I did eat! *Milton's Paradise Lost, b. x.*

Whosoever sees a man, who would have *beguiled*, and imposed upon him, by making him believe a lie, he may truly say, that is the man who would have ruined me. *South.*

2. To deceive; to evade.

Is wretchedness depriv'd that benefit,
To end itself by death? 'Twas yet some comfort,
When misery could *beguile* the tyrant's rage,
And frustrate his proud will. *Shakesp. King Lear.*

3. To deceive pleasingly; to amuse.

With these sometimes she doth her time *beguile*;
These do by fits her phantasy possess. *Sir J. Davies.*

Sweet leave me here a while;
My spirits grow dull, and fain I would *beguile*
The tedious day with sleep. *Hamlet.*

BEGU'N. The *participle passive* of *begin.*

But thou bright morning star, thou rising sun,
Which in these latter times hast brought to light
Those mysteries, that, since the world *begun*,
Lay hid in darkness and eternal night. *Sir J. Davies.*

BEHA'LF. *n. s.* [This word *Skinner* derives from *half*, and interprets it, *for my half*; as, *for my part.* It seems to me rather corrupted from *behoof*, profit; the pronunciation degenerating easily to *behafe*; which, in imitation of other words so founded, was written, by those who knew not the etymology, *behalf.*]

1. Favour; cause.

He was in confidence with those who designed the destruction of Strafford; against whom he had contracted some prejudice, in the *behalf* of his nation. *Clarendon, b.* viii.

Were but my heart as naked to thy view,
Marcus would see it bleed in his *behalf.* *Addison's Cato.*

Never was any nation blessed with more frequent interpositions of divine providence in its *behalf.* *Atterbury.*

2. Vindication; support.

He might, in his presence, defy all Arcadian knights, in the *behalf* of his mistress's beauty. *Sidney.*

Lest the fiend,
Or in *behalf* of man, or to invade
Vacant possession, some new trouble raise. *Paradise Lost.*

Others believe, that, by the two Fortunes, were meant prosperity or affliction; and produce, in their *behalf*, an ancient monument. *Addison's Remarks on Italy.*

To BEHA'VE. *v. a.* [from *be* and *have.*]

1. To carry; to conduct: used almost always with the reciprocal pronoun.

We *behaved* not *ourselves* disorderly among you. *Thessal.* iii. 7.

Manifest signs came from heaven, unto those that *behaved themselves* manfully. 2 *Macc.* ii. 21.

To their wills wedded, to their errours slaves,
No man, like them, they think, *himself behaves.* *Denham.*

We so live, and so act, as if we were secure of the final issue and event of things, however we may *behave ourselves.* *Atterbury.*

2. It seems formerly to have had the sense of, to govern; to subdue; to discipline: but this is not now used.

But who his limbs with labours, and his mind
*Behaves* with cares, cannot so easy miss. *Fairy Queen, b.* ii.

With such sober and unnoted passion,
He did *behave* his anger ere 'twas spent,
As if he had but prov'd an argument. *Shakesp. Timon.*

To BEHAVE. *v. n.* To act; to conduct one's self. It is taken either in a good or a bad sense; as, he *behaved* well or ill.

BEHA'VIOUR. *n. s.* [from *behave.*]

1. Manner of behaving one's self, whether good or bad; manners.

Mopsa, curious in any thing but her own good *behaviour*, followed Zelmane. *Sidney.*

2. External appearance.

And he changed his *behaviour* before them, and feigned himself mad in their hands. 1 *Sam.* xxi. 13.

3. Gesture; manner of action, adapted to particular occasions.

Well witnessing the most submissive *behaviour*, that a thralled heart could express. *Sidney.*

When we make profession of our faith, we stand; when we acknowledge our sins, or seek unto God for favour, we fall down; because the gesture of constancy becometh us best in the one, in the other the *behaviour* of humility. *Hooker, b.* v.

One man sees how much another man is a fool, when he dedicates his *behaviour* to love. *Shakesp. Much ado about Noth.*

4. Elegance of manners; gracefulness.

He marked, in Dora's dancing, good grace and handsome *behaviour.* *Sidney, b.* i.

The beautiful prove accomplished, but not of great spirit; and study, for the most part, rather *behaviour* than virtue. *Bacon's Ornam. Rational.* № 63.

He who adviseth the philosopher, altogether devoted to the Muses, sometimes to offer sacrifice to the altars of the Graces, thought knowledge imperfect without *behaviour.* *Wotton.*

5. Conduct; general practice; course of life.

To him, who hath a prospect of the state that attends men after this life, depending on their *behaviour* here, the measures of good and evil are changed. *Locke.*

6. *To be upon one's behaviour.* A familiar phrase, noting such a state as requires great caution; a state in which a failure in behaviour will have bad consequences.

Tyrants themselves *are upon their behaviour* to a superiour power. *L'Estrange's Fables.*

To BEHE'AD. *v. a.* [from *be* and *head.*] To deprive of the head; to kill by cutting off the head.

See a reverend Syracusan merchant
*Beheaded* publickly. *Shakesp. Romeo and Juliet.*

His *beheading* he underwent with all christian magnanimity. *Clarendon, b.* vii.

On each side they fly,
By chains connext, and, with destructive sweep,
*Behead* whole troops at once. *Philips.*

Mary, queen of the Scots, was *beheaded* in the reign of queen Elizabeth. *Addison on Italy.*

BEHE'LD. *particip. passive*, from *behold*; which see.

All hail! ye virgin daughters of the main!
Ye streams, beyond my hopes *beheld* again! *Pope's Odyssey.*

BE'HEMOTH. *n. s. Behemoth*, in Hebrew, signifies beasts in general, particularly the larger kind, fit for service. But Job speaks of an animal, which he calls *behemoth*, and describes its particular properties at large, in *chap.* xl. 15. *Bochart* has taken much care to make it appear to be the *hippopotamus*, or river-horse. *Sanctius* thinks it is an ox. The Fathers suppose the devil to be meant by it. But we agree with the generality of interpreters, in their opinion, that it is the elephant. *Calmet.*

Behold now *behemoth*, which I made with thee; he eateth grass as an ox. *Job*, xl. 15.

Behold! in plaited mail
*Behemoth* rears his head. *Thomson's Summer, l.* 695.

BE'HEN. } *n. s.* Valerian roots. Also a fruit resembling the tamarisk, from which perfumers extract an oil. *Dict.*
BEN. }

BEHE'ST. *n. s.* [from *be* and *hest*; hæs, Saxon.] Command; precept; mandate.

Her tender youth had obediently lived under her parents *behests*, without framing, out of her own will, the forechoosing of any thing. *Sidney, b.* ii.

Such joy he had their stubborn hearts to quell,
And sturdy courage tame with dreadful awe,
That his *behest* they fear'd as proud tyrant's law. *Fairy Q.*

I, messenger from everlasting Jove,
In his great name thus his *behest* do tell. *Fairfax, b.* i. *st.* 17.

To visit oft those happy tribes,
On high *behests* his angels to and fro
Pass'd frequent. *Milton's Paradise Lost, b.* vi. *l.* 153.

Reign thou in hell, thy kingdom; let me serve
In heav'n God ever blest, and his divine
*Behests* obey, worthiest to be obey'd! *Paradise Lost, b.* vi.

To BEHI'GHT. *v. a.* pret. *behot*, part. *behight.* [from hatan, to promise, Sax.]

1. To promise.

Sir Guyon, mindful of his vow yplight,
Up roſe from drowſy couch, and him addreſt,
Unto the journey which he had *behight*.
*Fairy Queen*, b. ii. cant. ii.

2. To entruſt; to commit.
That moſt glorious houſe that gliſt'reth bright,
Whereof the keys are to thy hand *behight*
By wiſe Fidelia. *Fairy Queen*, b. i. *cant.* x. *ſtanz.* 50.

3. Perhaps to call; to name; *hight* being often put, in old authors, for *named*, or *was named*.

BEHI'ND. *prep.* [hindan, Saxon.]

1. At the back of another.
Acomates haſted with two hundred harquebuſiers, which he had cauſed his horſemen to take *behind* them upon their horſes. *Knolles's Hiſtory of the Turks.*

2. On the back part; not before.
She came in the preſs *behind*, and touched. *Mark*, v. 27.

3. Towards the back.
The Benjamites looked *behind* them. *Judges*, xx. 40.

4. Following another.
Her huſband went with her, weeping *behind* her. 2*Sam.* iii. 16.

5. Remaining after the departure of ſomething elſe.
He left *behind* him, myſelf, and a ſiſter, both born in one hour. *Shakeſp. Twelfth Night.*
Piety and virtue are not only delightful for the preſent, but they leave peace and contentment *behind* them. *Tillotſon.*

6. Remaining after the death of thoſe to whom it belonged.
What he gave me to publiſh, was but a ſmall part of what he left *behind* him. *Pope's Letters.*

7. At a diſtance from ſomething going before.
Such is the ſwiftneſs of your mind,
That, like the earth's, it leaves our ſenſe *behind*. *Dryden.*

8. Inferiour to another; having the poſteriour place with regard to excellence.
After the overthrow of this firſt houſe of God, a ſecond was erected; but with ſo great odds, that they wept, which beheld how much this latter came *behind* it. *Hooker*, b. 5. § 1.

9. On the other ſide of ſomething.
From light retir'd, *behind* his daughter's bed,
He, for approaching ſleep, compos'd his head. *Dryden.*

BEHI'ND. *adv.*

1. Out of ſight; not yet produced to view; remaining.
We cannot be ſure, that we have all the particulars before us; and that there is no evidence *behind*, and yet unſeen, which may caſt the probability on the other ſide. *Locke.*

2. Moſt of the former ſenſes may become *adverbial*, by ſuppreſſing the *accuſative caſe*; as, I left my money *behind*, or *behind me.*

BEHI'NDHAND. *adv.* [from *behind* and *hand.*]

1. In a ſtate in which rents or profits, or any advantage, is anticipated; ſo that leſs is to be received, or more performed, than the natural or juſt proportion.
Your trade would ſuffer, if your being *behindhand* has made the natural uſe ſo high, that your tradeſman cannot live upon his labour. *Locke.*

2. Not upon equal terms, with regard to forwardneſs. In this ſenſe, it is followed by *with.*
Conſider, whether it is not better to be half a year *behindhand with* the faſhionable part of the world, than to ſtrain beyond his circumſtances. *Spectator*, N° 488.

3. *Shakeſpeare* uſes it as an *adjective*, but licentiouſly, for backward; tardy.
And theſe thy offices,
So rarely kind, are as interpreters
Of my *behindhand* ſlackneſs. *Shakeſp. Winter's Tale.*

To BEHO'LD. *v. a.* pret. *I beheld, I have beheld*, or *beholden.* [behealban, Saxon.] To view; to ſee; to look upon.
Son of man, *behold* with thine eyes, and hear with thine ears. *Ezek.* xl. 4.
When ſome young Theſſalians, on horſeback, were *beheld* afar off, while their horſes watered, while their heads were depreſſed, they were conceived by the ſpectator to be one animal. *Brown's Vulgar Errours*, b. i. c. 4.
Man looks aloft, and, with erected eyes,
*Beholds* his own hereditary ſkies. *Dryden.*
At this, the former tale again he told,
With thund'ring tone, and dreadful to *behold*. *Dryden's Fab.*

BEHO'LD. *interject.* [from the verb.] See; lo: a word by which attention is excited, or admiration noted.
*Behold!* I am with thee, and will keep thee. *Gen.* xxviii. 15.
When out of hope, *behold* her! not far off,
Such as I ſaw her in my dream, adorn'd
With what all earth or heaven could beſtow,
To make her amiable. *Milton's Paradiſe Loſt*, b. viii. l. 481.

BEHO'LDEN. *particip. adj.* [gehouden, Dutch; that is, held in obligation. It is very corruptly written *beholding.*] Obliged; bound in gratitude; with the particle *to.*
Horns, which ſuch as you are fain to be *beholden to* your wives for. *Shakeſp. As you like it.*
Little are we *beholden to* your love,
And little looked for at your helping hands. *Shakeſp. R.* III.
I found you next; in reſpect of bond both of near alliance, and particularly of communication in ſtudies: wherein I muſt acknowledge myſelf *beholden to* you. *Bacon's Eſſays.*
I think myſelf mightily *beholden to* you for the reprehenſion you then gave us. *Addiſon. Guardian*, N° 109.
We, who ſee men under the awe of juſtice, cannot conceive, what ſavage creatures they would be without it; and how much *beholden* we are *to* that wiſe contrivance. *Atterbury.*

BEHO'LDER. *n. ſ.* [from *behold.*] Spectator; he that looks upon any thing.
Was this the face,
That, like the ſun, did make *beholders* wink? *Shakeſp. R.* II.
Theſe beaſts among
*Beholders* rude, and ſhallow to diſcern
Half what in thee is fair, one man except,
Who ſees thee? *Milton's Paradiſe Loſt*, b. ix. l. 543.
Things of wonder give no leſs delight
To the wiſe Maker's, than *beholder's* ſight. *Denham.*
The juſtling chiefs in rude encounters join,
Each fair *beholder* trembling for her knight. *Granville.*
The charitable foundations in the church of Rome, exceed all the demands of charity, and raiſe envy, rather than compaſſion, in the breaſts of *beholders*. *Atterbury.*

BEHO'LDING. *adj.* [corrupted from *beholden.*] Obliged. See BEHOLDEN.
Becauſe I would not be *beholding* to fortune for any part of the victory, I deſcended. *Sidney*, b. ii.

BEHO'LDING. *n. ſ.* Obligation.
Love to virtue, and not to any particular *beholdings*, hath expreſſed this my teſtimony. *Carew's Survey of Cornwal.*

BEHO'LDINGNESS. *n. ſ.* [from *beholding*, miſtaken for *beholden.*] The ſtate of being obliged.
The king invited us to his court, ſo as I muſt acknowledge a *beholdingneſs* unto him. *Sidney*, b. ii.
In this my debt I ſeem'd loth to confeſs,
In that I ſhunn'd *beholdingneſs*. *Donne.*

BEHO'OF. *n. ſ.* [from *behoove.*] That which behooves; that which is advantageous; profit; advantage.
Her majeſty may alter any thing of thoſe laws, that may be more both for her own *behoof*, and for the good of the people. *Spenſer on Ireland.*
No mean recompence it brings
To your *behoof*: if I that region loſt,
All uſurpation thence expell'd, reduce
To her original darkneſs, and your ſway. *Milton.*
Wer't thou ſome ſtar, which, from the ruin'd roof
Of ſhak'd Olympus, by miſchance didſt fall;
Which careful Jove, in nature's true *behoof*,
Took up, and in fit place did reinſtate. *Milton.*
Becauſe it was for the *behoof* of the animal, that, upon any ſudden accident, it might be awakened, there were no ſhuts or ſtopples made for the ears. *Ray on the Creation.*
It would be of no *behoof*, for the ſettling of government, unleſs there were a way taught, how to know the perſon to whom belonged this power and dominion. *Locke.*

To BEHO'OVE. *v. n.* [behoꝼan, Saxon; *it is a duty.*] To be fit; to be meet; either with reſpect to duty, neceſſity, or convenience. It is uſed only imperſonally with *it.*
For better examination of their quality, *it behooveth* the very foundation and root, the higheſt wellſpring and fountain of them, to be diſcovered. *Hooker*, b. i. § 1.
He did ſo prudently temper his paſſions, as that none of them made him wanting in the offices of life, which *it behooved*, or became him to perform. *Atterbury.*
But ſhould you lure the monarch of the brook,
*Behooves* you then to ply your fineſt art. *Thomſon's Spring.*

BEHO'OVEFUL. *adj.* [from *behoof.*] Uſeful; profitable; advantageous. This word is ſomewhat antiquated.
It is very *behooveful* in this country of Ireland, where there are waſte deſerts full of graſs, that the ſame ſhould be eaten down. *Spenſer on Ireland.*
Laws are many times full of imperfections; and that which is ſuppoſed *behooveful* unto men, proveth oftentimes moſt pernicious. *Hooker*, b. iv. §. 14.
Madam, we have culled ſuch neceſſaries
As are *behooveful* for our ſtate tomorrow. *Sh. Rom. and Jul.*
It may be moſt *behooveful* for princes, in matters of grace, to tranſact the ſame publickly: ſo it is as requiſite, in matters of judgment, puniſhment, and cenſure, that the ſame be tranſacted privately. *Clarendon.*

BEHO'OVEFULLY. *adv.* [from *behooveful.*] Profitably; uſefully.
Tell us of more weighty diſlikes than theſe, and that may more *behoovefully* import the reformation. *Spenſer on Ireland.*

BEHO'T. [*preterite*, as it ſeems, of *behight*, to promiſe.]
With ſharp intended ſting ſo rude him ſmote,
That to the earth him drove as ſtriken dead,
Ne living wight would have him life *behot*. *Fairy Q.* b. i.

To BEHO'WL. *v. a.* [from *be* and *howl.*]

1. To howl at.
Now the hungry lion roars,
And the wolf *behowls* the moon. *Shakeſp. Midſum. N. Dr.*

2. Perhaps, to howl over, or lament clamorouſly.

BE'ING. *particip.* [from *be.*]

Thoſe,

~~3. To call; to give out~~ c ǂ
aread old father, why of late
Didst thou behight me born of English blood
Whom all a fairys son doen nominate
2.2.1.10. 64

o ǂ
No untruth can possibly avail the patron and defender long, for things most truly are like:
:wise most behoovefully spoken Hooker

IL facing 2Y[v]

~~To surround, to encompass, to set round~~

He rears no limbs about him sound
With Sores and Sicknesses beleaguer'd round
Dryd.

IL facing 2Y2[r]

Thoſe, who have their hope in another life, look upon themſelves as *being* on their paſſage through this. *Atterbury.*

Be'ing. *n. ſ.* [from *be.*]

1. Exiſtence; oppoſed to nonentity.

Of him all things have both received their firſt *being*, and their continuance to be that which they are. *Hooker, b. v.*

Yet is not God the author of her ill,
Though author of her *being*, and being there. *Davies.*

There is none but he,
Whoſe *being* I do fear: and under him
My genius is rebuked. *Shakeſp. Macbeth.*

Thee, Father, firſt they ſung, omnipotent,
Immutable, immortal, infinite,
Eternal king! Thee, author of all *being*,
Fountain of light! *Milton's Par. Loſt, b.* iii. *l.* 374.

Merciful and gracious, thou gaveſt us *being*, raiſing us from nothing to be an excellent creation. *Taylor's Guide to Devotion.*

Conſider every thing as not yet in *being*; then examine, if it muſt needs have been at all, or what other ways it might have been. *Bentley.*

2. A particular ſtate or condition.

Thoſe happy ſpirits, which ordain'd by fate
For future *being*, and new bodies wait. *Dryden's Æneid.*

Heav'n from all creatures hides the book of fate;
From brutes what men, from men what ſpirits know;
Or who could ſuffer *being* here below? *Pope's Eſſay on Man.*

3. The perſon exiſting.

Ah, fair, yet falſe; ah, *being* form'd to cheat,
By ſeeming kindneſs, mixt with deep deceit. *Dryden.*

It is folly to ſeek the approbation of any *being*, beſides the ſupreme; becauſe no other *being* can make a right judgment of us, and becauſe we can procure no conſiderable advantage from the approbation of any other *being*. *Addiſon. Spectator.*

As now your own, our *beings* were of old,
And once inclos'd in woman's beauteous mold. *Pope.*

Be'ing. *conjunct.* [from *be.*] Since. *Dict.*

Be it so. A phraſe of anticipation, *ſuppoſe it be ſo*; or of permiſſion, *let it be ſo.*

My gracious duke,
*Be't ſo* ſhe will not here, before your grace,
Conſent to marry with Demetrius;
I beg the ancient privilege of Athens. *Sh. Midſ. N. Dream.*

To Bela'bour. *v. a.* [from *be* and *labour.*] To beat; to thump: a word in low ſpeech.

What ſeveral madneſſes in men appear:
Oreſtes runs from fancy'd furies here;
Ajax *belabours* there an harmleſs ox,
And thinks that Agamemnon feels the knocks. *Dryden, jun.*

He ſees virago Nell *belabour*,
With his own ſtaff, his peaceful neighbour. *Swift.*

To Bela'ce. *v. a.* [Sea term.] To faſten; as to *belace* a rope. *D.*

Be'lamie. *n. ſ.* [*bel amie*, Fr.] A friend; an intimate. This word is out of uſe.

Wiſe Socrates
Pour'd out his life, and laſt philoſophy,
To the fair Critias, his deareſt *belamie*. *Fairy Q. b.* ii. *c.* vii.

Be'lamour. *n. ſ.* [*bel amour*, Fr.] Gallant; conſort; paramour: obſolete.

Lo, lo, how brave ſhe decks her bounteous bow'r,
With ſilken curtains, and gold coverlets,
Therein to ſhrowd her ſumptuous *belamour*. *Fairy Q. b.* ii.

Bela'ted. *adj.* [from *be* and *late.*] Benighted; out of doors late at night.

Fairy elves,
Whoſe midnight revels, by a foreſt ſide,
Or fountain, ſome *belated* peaſant ſees,
Or dreams he ſees. *Milton's Paradiſe Loſt, b.* i. *l.* 781.

Or near Fleetditch's oozy brinks,
*Belated*, ſeems on watch to lie. *Swift.*

To Bela'y. *v. a.* [from *be* and *lay*; as, to *waylay*, to lie in wait, to lay wait for.]

1. To block up; to ſtop the paſſage.

The ſpeedy horſe all paſſages *belay*,
And ſpur their ſmoaking ſteeds to croſs their way. *Dryden.*

2. To place in ambuſh.

'Gainſt ſuch ſtrong caſtles needeth greater might,
Than thoſe ſmall forces ye were wont *belay*. *Spenſ. ſonn.* xiv.

To Belay *a rope.* [Sea term.] To ſplice; to mend a rope, by laying one end over another.

To Belch. *v. n.* [bealcan, Saxon.]

1. To eject the wind from the ſtomach; to eruct.

The waters boil, and, *belching* from below,
Black ſands as from a forceful engine throw. *Dryden's Virg.*

The ſymptoms are, a ſour ſmell in their fæces, *belchings*, and diſtenſions of the bowels. *Arbuthnot on Aliments.*

2. To iſſue out by eructation.

A triple pile of plumes his creſt adorn'd,
On which with *belching* flames Chimæra burn'd. *Dryden.*

To Belch. *v. a.* To throw out from the ſtomach; to eject from any hollow place. It is a word implying coarſeneſs; hatefulneſs; or horrour.

They are all but ſtomachs, and we all but food;
They eat us hungerly, and, when they're full,
They'll *belch* us. *Shakeſpeare.*

The bitterneſs of it I now *belch* from my heart. *Sh. Cymbel.*

Immediate in a flame,
But ſoon obſcur'd with ſmoke, all heav'n appear'd,
From thoſe deep-throated engines *belch'd. Parad. Loſt, b.* vi.

The gates that now
Stood open wide, *belching* outrageous flame
Far into chaos, ſince the fiend paſs'd through. *Parad. Loſt.*

Rough as their ſavage lords who rang'd the wood,
And, fat with acorns, *belch'd* their windy food. *Dryden.*

There *belcht* the mingl'd ſtreams of wine and blood,
And human fleſh, his indigeſted food. *Pope's Odyſſey, b.* ix.

When I an am'rous kiſs deſign'd,
I *belch'd* an hurricane of wind. *Swift.*

Belch. *n. ſ.* [from the verb.]

1. The act of eructation.

2. A cant term for malt liquour.

A ſudden reformation would follow, among all ſorts of people; porters would no longer be drunk with *belch*. *Dennis.*

Belda'm. *n. ſ.* [*belle dame*, which, in old French, ſignified probably an old woman, as *belle age*, old age.]

1. An old woman; generally a term of contempt, marking the laſt degree of old age, with all its faults and miſeries.

Then ſing of ſecret things that came to paſs,
When *beldam* nature in her cradle was. *Milton.*

2. A hag.

Why, how now, Hecat, you look angerly?—
—Have I not reaſon, *beldams*, as you are?
Saucy and overbold? *Shakeſp. Macbeth.*

The reſty ſieve wagg'd ne'er the more;
I wept for woe, the teſty *beldam* ſwore. *Dryden.*

To Bele'aguer. *v. a.* [*beleggeren*, Dutch.] To beſiege; to block up a place; to lie before a town.

Their buſineſs, which they carry on, is the general concernment of the Trojan camp, then *beleaguer'd* by Turnus and the Latins. *Dryden's Dufreſnoy, Preface.*

Againſt *beleaguer'd* heav'n the giants move:
Hills pil'd on hills, on mountains mountains lie,
To make their mad approaches to the ſky. *Dryden. Ovid.*

Bele'agurer. *n. ſ.* [from *beleaguer.*] One that beſieges a place.

Belemni'tes. *n. ſ.* [from βέλος, a dart or arrow, becauſe of its reſemblance to the point of an arrow.] Arrowhead, or fingerſtone, of a whitiſh and ſometimes a gold colour.

Belflo'wer. *n. ſ.* [from *bell* and *flower*, becauſe of the ſhape of its flower; in Latin *campanula.*] A plant.

The flower conſiſts of one leaf, ſhaped like a bell, and, before it is blown, is of a pentagonal figure; and, when fully opened, cut into five ſegments at the top. The ſeed veſſel is divided into three cells, each having a hole at the bottom, by which the ſeed is emitted. There is a vaſt number of the ſpecies of this plant. 1. The talleſt pyramidal *belflower.* 2. The blue peach-leaved *belflower.* 3. The white peach-leaved *belflower.* 4. Garden *belflower*, with oblong leaves and flowers; commonly called *Canterbury bells.* 5. Canary *belflower*, with orrach leaves and a tuberoſe root. 6. Blue *belflower*, with edible roots, commonly called *rampions.* 7. Venus looking glaſs *belflower*, &c. The firſt ſort is commonly cultivated to adorn chimnies, halls, &c. in ſummer. It produces ſometimes twelve branches, four or five feet high, with large beautiful flowers, almoſt the whole length of the ſtalks. The peach-leaved *belflowers* are very hardy, and may be planted in open beds or borders, where they will flower very ſtrong. The *Canterbury bells* are biennial. The *Canary belflower* is one of the moſt beautiful plants of the greenhouſe, yielding its flowers in December, January, and February. The *rampion* is propagated for its root, which was formerly in greater eſteem in England than at preſent. The ſorts of *Venus looking-glaſs* are annual plants. *Millar.*

Belfo'under. *n. ſ.* [from *bell* and *found.*] He whoſe trade it is to found or caſt bells.

Thoſe that make recorders know this, and likewiſe *belfounders*, in fitting the tune of their bells. *Bacon's Natural Hiſt.*

Be'lfry. *n. ſ.* [*Beffroy*, in French, is a tower; which was perhaps the true word, till thoſe, who knew not its original, corrupted it to *belfry*, becauſe bells were in it.] The place where the bells are rung.

Fetch the leathern bucket that hangs in the *belfry*; that is curiouſly painted before, and will make a figure. *Gay's What d'ye call it.*

Belga'rd. *n. ſ.* [*belle egard*, Fr.] A ſoft glance; a kind regard: an old word, now wholly diſuſed.

Upon her eyelids many graces ſat,
Under the ſhadow of her even brows,
Working *belgards*, and amorous retreats. *Fairy Q. b.* ii. *c.* iii.

To Beli'e. *v. a.* [from *be* and *lie.*]

1. To counterfeit; to feign; to mimick.

Which durſt, with horſes hoofs that beat the ground,
And martial braſs, *belie* the thunder's ſound. *Dryden.*

The ſhape of man, and imitated beaſt
The walk, the words, the geſture could ſupply,
The habit mimick, and the mien *belie*. *Dryden's Fables.*

3 2. To

2. To give the lie to; to charge with falſehood.

Sure there is none but fears a future ſtate;
And when the moſt obdurate ſwear they do not,
Their trembling hearts *belie* their boaſtful tongues. *Dryden.*

Paint, patches, jewels laid aſide,
At night aſtronomers agree,
The evening has the day *belied*,
And Phyllis is ſome forty-three. *Prior.*

3. To calumniate; to raiſe falſe reports of any man.

'Tis ſlander, whoſe breath
Rides on the poſting winds, and doth *belie*
All corners of the world. *Shakeſp. Cymbeline.*

Thou doſt *belie* him, Piercy, thou *belieſt* him;
He never did encounter with Glendower. *Shakeſp. Hen.* IV.

4. To give a falſe repreſentation of any thing.

Uncle, for heav'n's ſake, comfortable words.—
—Should I do ſo, I ſhould *belie* my thoughts. *Shakeſp. R.* II.

Tuſcan Valerus by force o'ercame,
And not *belied* his mighty father's name. *Dryden's Æneid.*

In the diſpute whate'er I ſaid,
My heart was by my tongue *belied*;
And in my looks you might have read,
How much I argu'd on your ſide. *Prior.*

BELI'EF. *n. ſ.* [from *believe.*]

1. Credit given to ſomething which we know not of ourſelves, on account of the authority by which it is delivered.

Thoſe comforts that ſhall never ceaſe,
Future in hope, but preſent in *belief.* *Wotton.*

Faith is a firm *belief* of the whole word of God, of his goſpel, commands, threats, and promiſes. *Wake's Prep. for Death.*

2. The theological virtue of faith, or firm confidence of the truths of religion.

No man can attain *belief* by the bare contemplation of heaven and earth; for that they neither are ſufficient to give us as much as the leaſt ſpark of light concerning the very principal myſteries of our faith. *Hooker, b.* [illegible] §. 22.

3. Religion; the body of tenets held by the profeſſors of faith.

In the heat of general perſecution, whereunto chriſtian *belief* was ſubject upon the firſt promulgation, it much confirmed the weaker minds, when relation was made how God had been glorified through the ſufferings of martyrs. *Hooker, b.* v.

4. Perſuaſion; opinion.

He can, I know, but doubt to think he will;
Yet hope would fain ſubſcribe, and tempts *belief.* *Milton.*

All treaties are grounded upon the *belief*, that ſtates will be found in their honour and obſervance of treaties. *Temple.*

5. The thing believed; the object of belief.

Superſtitious prophecies are not only the *belief* of fools, but the talk ſometimes of wiſe men. *Bacon.*

6. Creed; a form containing the articles of faith.

BELI'EVABLE. *adj.* [from *believe.*] Credible; that which may be credited or believed.

To BELI'EVE. *v. a.* [ᵹelyƿan, Saxon.]

1. To credit upon the authority of another, or from ſome other reaſon than our perſonal knowledge.

A propoſition, which they are perſuaded, but do not know to be true, it is not ſeeing, but *believing*. *Locke.*

Ten thouſand things there are, which we *believe* merely upon the authority or credit of thoſe who have ſpoken or written of them. *Watts's Logick.*

2. To put confidence in the veracity of any one.

The people may hear when I ſpeak with thee, and *believe* thee for ever. *Exodus,* xix. 9.

To BELIEVE. *v. n.*

1. To have a firm perſuaſion of any thing.

They may *believe* that the Lord God of their fathers, the God of Abraham, the God of Iſaac, and the God of Jacob, hath appeared unto thee. *Geneſis,* xlv.

2. To exerciſe the theological virtue of faith.

Now God be prais'd, that, to *believing* ſouls,
Gives light in darkneſs, comfort in deſpair. *Shakeſp. H.* VI.

For with the heart man *believeth* unto righteouſneſs, and with the mouth confeſſion is made unto ſalvation. *Romans,* x. 10.

3. With the particle *in*; to hold as an object of faith.

*Believe in* the Lord your God, ſo ſhall you be eſtabliſhed. *2 Chron.* xx. 20.

4. With the particle *upon*; to truſt; to place full confidence in; to reſt upon with faith.

To them gave he power to become the ſons of God, even to them that *believe on* his name. *John,* i. 12.

5. *I believe*, is ſometimes uſed as a way of ſlightly noting ſome want of certainty or exactneſs.

Though they are, *I believe*, as high as moſt ſteeples in England, yet a perſon, in his drink, fell down, without any other hurt than the breaking of an arm. *Addiſon on Italy.*

BELI'EVER. *n. ſ.* [from *believe.*]

1. He that believes, or gives credit.

Diſcipline began to enter into conflict with churches, which, in extremity, had been *believers* of it. *Hooker, Pref.*

2. A profeſſour of chriſtianity.

Infidels themſelves did diſcern in matters of life, when *believers* did well, when otherwiſe. *Hooker, b.* 2. §. 2.

If he which writeth, do that which is forcible, how ſhould he which readeth, be thought to do that, which, in itſelf, is of no force to work belief, and to ſave *believers*? *Hooker, b.* v.

Myſteries held by us have no power, pomp, or wealth, but have been maintained by the univerſal body of true *believers*, from the days of the apoſtles, and will be to the reſurrection; neither will the gates of hell prevail againſt them. *Swift.*

BELI'EVINGLY. *adv.* [from *to believe.*] After a believing manner.

BELI'KE. *adv.* [from *like*, as *by likelihood.*]

1. Probably; likely; perhaps.

There came out of the ſame woods a horrible foul bear, which fearing, *belike*, while the lion was preſent, came furiouſly towards the place where I was. *Sidney.*

*Belike* fortune was afraid to lay her treaſures, where they ſhould be ſtained with ſo many perfections. *Sidney.*

Lord Angelo, *belike*, thinking me remiſs in my office, awakens me with this unwonted putting on. *Shakeſp. M. for Meaſ.*

Joſephus affirmeth, that one of them remained even in his time; meaning, *belike*, ſome ruin or foundation thereof. *Raleigh's Hiſtory of the World.*

2. It is ſometimes uſed in a ſenſe of irony; as, *we are to ſuppoſe.*

We think, *belike*, that he will accept what the meaneſt of them would diſdain. *Hooker, b.* viii. § 15.

God appointed the ſea to one of them, and the land to the other, becauſe they were ſo great, that the ſea could not hold them both; for elſe, *belike*, if the ſea had been large enough, we might have gone a fiſhing for elephants. *Brerew. on Languages.*

BELI'VE. *adv.* [bılıve, Sax. probably from bı and lıfe, in the ſenſe of vivacity; ſpeed; quickneſs.] Speedily; quickly: a word out of uſe.

By that ſame way the direful dames do drive
Their mournful chariot, fill'd with ruſty blood,
And down to Pluto's houſe are come *belive.* *Fairy Q. b.* i.

BELL. *n. ſ.* [bel, Saxon; ſuppoſed, by *Skinner*, to come from *pelvis*, Lat. a baſin. See BALL.]

1. A veſſel, or hollow body of caſt metal, formed to make a noiſe by the act of a clapper, hammer, or ſome other inſtrument ſtriking againſt it. *Bells* are always in the towers of churches, to call the congregation together.

Your flock, aſſembled by the *bell*,
Encircled you, to hear, with rev'rence. *Shakeſp. Henry* IV.

Get thee gone, and dig my grave thyſelf,
And bid the merry *bells* ring to thy ear,
That thou art crowned, not that I am dead. *Shakeſp. H.* IV.

Four *bells* admit twenty four changes in ringing, and five *bells* one hundred and twenty. *Holder's Elements of Speech.*

He has no one neceſſary attention to any thing, but the *bell*, which calls to prayers twice a day. *Addiſon. Spect.* Nº 264.

2. It is uſed for any thing in the form of a *bell*, as the cups of flowers.

Where the bee ſucks, there ſuck I,
In a cowſlip's *bell* I lie. *Shakeſp. Tempeſt.*

The humming bees that hunt the golden dew,
In ſummer's heat on tops of lilies feed,
And creep within their *bells* to ſuck the balmy ſeed. *Dryden.*

3. A ſmall hollow globe of metal perforated, and containing in it a ſolid ball; which, when it is ſhaken by bounding againſt the ſides, gives a ſound.

As the ox hath his yoke, the horſe his curb, and the faulcon his *bells*, ſo hath man his deſire. *Shakeſp. As you like it.*

4. *To bear the bell.* To be the firſt, from the wether, that carries a *bell* among the ſheep, or the firſt horſe of a drove that has *bells* on his collar.

5. The Italians have carried away the *bell* from all other nations, as may appear both by their books and works. *Hakewell on Providence.*

*To ſhake the bells.* A phraſe, in *Shakeſpeare*, taken from the *bells* of a hawk.

Neither the king, nor he that loves him beſt,
The proudeſt he that holds up Lancaſter,
Dares ſtir a wing, if Warwick *ſhakes his bells.* *Shakeſp. H.* VI.

To BELL. *v. n.* [from the noun.] To grow in buds or flowers, in the form of a bell.

Hops, in the beginning of Auguſt, *bell*, and are ſometimes ripe. *Mortimer's Huſbandry.*

BELL-FASHIONED. *adj.* [from *bell* and *faſhion.*] Having the form of a bell.

The thorn apple riſes with a ſtrong round ſtalk, having large *bell-faſhioned* flowers at the joints. *Mortimer's Art of Huſbandry.*

BELLE. *n. ſ.* [*beau, belle*, Fr.] A young lady.

What motive could compel
A well-bred lord t' aſſault a gentle *belle*;
O ſay, what ſtranger cauſe yet unexplor'd,
Could make a gentle *belle* reject a lord? *Pope's R. of the Lock.*

BELLES LETTRES. *n. ſ.* [Fr.] Polite literature. It has no *ſingular*.

The exactneſs of the other, is to admit of ſomething like diſcourſe, eſpecially in what regards the *belles lettres.* *Tatler.*

BE'LLIBONE. *n. ſ.* [from *bellus*, beautiful, and *bonus*, good, Lat. *belle & bonne*, Fr.] A woman excelling both in beauty and goodneſs. A word now out of uſe.

o ‡

~~Venerious [illegible], a [illegible] chief~~
A bold Opposer of divine Belief
Attempts religious fences to subvert
Strong in his rage, but destitute of Art
Blackm. Crea.

Now stub up the bushes, the grass to be fine,
Least neighbour do dailie so hack them believe
That neither thy bushes nor pasture can thrive
Tusser. Husb. for Janry.

Tussers Annotator takes believe to signify in the night, which, adds he, is more put in for rhymes sake that the Neighbour should be Supposed to work in the Night [This is contra: dictory for the Original says daily hack

In Scotland it signifies soon, immediatly, as when will you come, belive from believen Germ

Bellgards (belle & garde Fr.)
pretty bower or retreat

Upon her Eyelids many graces sat
Under the Shadow of her even brows:
Working bellguards and amorous retrait
And every one her with a grace endows
F. Q. 2. 3. 25

q ‡

As he had an inventive brain so there never lived any man that believed better of it and of himself
Raleigh

To bellow. v. a. To utter a thing with loud Noise

A Numidian Priest bellowing out certain Super:stitions charms, cast divers scrowls of paper on each side the way, wherein he cursed & ban'd the Christians

Knolles

2 +

~~Not any fowl, but~~ my folk and people are grown half wild in many places; they would not worry one another so in that wolvish belluine manner else; ~~they would not prompt to themselves into such a mixt mongrel war~~ Howel Eng. tea

Pan may be proud, that ever he begot
Such a *bellibone*,
And Syrinx rejoice, that ever was her lot
To bear such a one. *Spenser's Pastorals.*

Belli'gerous. *adj.* [*belliger*, Lat.] Waging war. *Dict.*

Be'lling. *n. s.* A hunting term, spoken of a roe, when she makes a noise in rutting time. *Dict.*

Belli'potent. *adj.* [*bellipotens*, Lat.] Puissant; mighty in war. *Dict.*

To Be'llow. *v. n.* [bellan, Saxon.]

1. To make a noise as a bull.

Jupiter became a bull, and *bellow'd*; the green Neptune
A ram, and bleated. *Shakesp. Winter's Tale.*

What bull dares *bellow*, or what sheep dares bleat
Within the lion's den? *Dryden's Spanish Friar.*

But now, the husband of a herd must be
Thy mate, and *bellowing* sons thy progeny. *Dryden.*

2. To make any violent outcry.

He fasten'd on my neck, and *bellow'd* out,
As he'd burst heav'n. *Shakesp. King Lear.*

3. To vociferate; to clamour. In this sense, it is a word of contempt.

The dull fat captain, with a hound's deep throat,
Would *bellow* out a laugh in a base note. *Dryd. Pers. sat.* v.

This gentleman is accustomed to roar and *bellow* so terribly loud, that he frightens us. *Tatler*, No 54.

4. To roar as the sea in a storm; or as the wind; to make any continued noise, that may cause terrour.

Till, at the last, he heard a dreadful sound,
Which through the wood loud *bellowing* did rebound.
*Fairy Queen, b.* i. *cant.* 7. *stanz.* 7.

The rising rivers float the nether ground;
And rocks the *bellowing* voice of boiling seas rebound. *Dryd.*

Be'llows. *n. s.* [bılᵹ, Sax. perhaps it is corrupted from *bellies*, the wind being contained in the hollow, or *belly*. It has no *singular*; for we usually say *a pair of bellows*; but *Dryden* has used *bellows* as a *singular*.]

1. The instrument used to blow the fire.

Since sighs into my inward furnace turned,
For *bellows* serve to kindle more the fire. *Sidney.*

One, with great *bellows*, gather'd filling air,
And, with forc'd wind, the fuel did inflame. *Fairy Q. b.* ii.

The smith prepares his hammer for the stroke,
While the lung'd *bellows* hissing fire provoke. *Dryden's Juv.*

The lungs, as *bellows*, supply a force of breath; and the *aspera arteria* is as the nose of *bellows*, to collect and convey the breath. *Holder's Elements of Speech.*

2. In the following passage, it is *singular*.

Thou neither, like a *bellows*, swell'st thy face,
As if thou wert to blow the burning mass
Of melting ore. *Dryden's Persius, sat.* v.

Be'lluine. *adj.* [*belluinus*, Lat.] Beastly; belonging to a beast; savage; brutal.

If human actions were not to be judged, men would have no advantage over beasts. At this rate, the animal and *belluine* life would be the best. *Atterbury's Preface to his Sermons.*

BE'LLY. *n. s.* [*balg*, Dutch; *bol*, *bola*, Welch.]

1. That part of the human body which reaches from the breast to the thighs, containing the bowels.

The body's members
Rebell'd against the *belly*; thus accus'd it;—
That only like a gulf it did remain,
Still cupboarding the viand, never bearing
Like labour with the rest. *Shakesp. Coriolanus.*

2. In beasts, it is used, in general, for that part of the body next the ground.

And the Lord said unto the serpent, upon thy *belly* shalt thou go, and dust shalt thou eat all the days of thy life. *Gen.* iii. 14.

3. The womb; in this sense, it is commonly used ludicrously or familiarly.

I shall answer that better, than you can the getting up of the negro's *belly*: the Moor is with child by you.
*Shakesp. Merchant of Venice.*

The secret is grown too big for the pretence, like Mrs. Primly's big *belly*. *Congreve's Way of the World.*

4. That part of man which requires food, in opposition to the *back*, or that which demands cloaths.

They were content with a licentious and idle life, wherein they might fill their *bellies* by spoil, rather than by labour.
*Sir J. Hayward.*

Whose god is their *belly*. *Phil.* iii. 19.

He that sows his grain upon marble, will have many a hungry *belly* before harvest. *Arbuthnot's History of J. Bull.*

5. The part of any thing that swells out into a larger capacity.

Fortune sometimes turneth the handle of the bottle, which is easy to be taken hold of; and, after, the *belly*, which is hard to grasp. *Bacon's Ornament. Ration.*

An Irish harp hath the concave, or *belly*, not along the strings, but at the end of the strings. *Bacon's Nat. History*, No 146.

6. Any place in which something is inclosed.

Out of the *belly* of hell cried I, and thou heardst my voice.
*Jonah*, ii. 2.

To Be'lly. *v. n.* [from the noun.] To swell into a larger capacity; to hang out; to bulge out.

Thus by degrees day wastes, signs cease to rise,
For *bellying* earth, still rising up, denies
Their light a passage, and confines our eyes.
*Creech's Manilius.*

The pow'r appeas'd, with winds suffic'd the sail,
The *bellying* canvas strutted with the gale. *Dryden's Fables.*

Loud ratt'ling shakes the mountains and the plain,
Heav'n *bellies* downwards, and descends in rain. *Dryden.*

'Midst these disports, forget they not to drench
Themselves with *bellying* goblets. *Philips.*

Be'llyache. *n. s.* [from *belly* and *ache*.] The colick; or pain in the bowels.

Be'llybound. *adj.* [from *belly* and *bound*.] Diseased, so as to be costive, and shrunk in the belly.

Be'lly-fretting. *n. s.* [from *belly* and *fret*.]

1. [With farriers.] The chafing of a horse's belly with the foregirt.

2. A great pain in a horse's belly, caused by worms. *Dict.*

Be'llyful. *n. s.* [from *belly* and *full*.] As much food as fills the belly, or satisfies the appetite.

Be'llygod. *n. s.* [from *belly* and *god*.] A glutton; one who makes a god of his belly.

What infinite waste they made this way, the only story of Apicius, a famous *bellygod*, may suffice to shew.
*Hakewell on Providence.*

Be'lly-pinched. *adj.* [from *belly* and *pinch*.] Starved.

This night, wherein the cubdrawn bear would couch,
The lion, and the *belly-pinched* wolf,
Keep their furr dry; unbonnetted he runs. *Shakesp. K. Lear.*

Be'llyroll. *n. s.* [from *belly* and *roll*.] A roll so called, as it seems, from entering into the hollows.

They have two small harrows that they clap on each side of the ridge, and so they harrow right up and down, and roll it with a *bellyroll*, that goes between the ridges, when they have sown it. *Mortimer's Husbandry.*

Be'lly-timber. *n. s.* [from *belly* and *timber*.] Food; materials to support the belly.

Where *belly-timber*, above ground
Or under, was not to be found. *Hudibras, cant.* i.

The strength of every other member
Is founded on your *belly-timber*. *Prior.*

Be'lly-worm. *n. s.* [from *belly* and *worm*.] A worm that breeds in the belly.

Be'lman. *n. s.* [from *bell* and *man*.] He whose business it is to proclaim any thing in towns, and to gain attention by ringing his bell.

It was the owl that shriek'd, the fatal *belman*
Which gives the stern'st good night. *Shakesp. Macbeth.*

Where Titian's glowing paint the canvas warm'd,
Now hangs the *belman*'s song, and pasted here
The colour'd prints of Overton appear. *Gay's Trivia.*

The *belman* of each parish, as he goes his circuit, cries out every night, Past twelve o' clock. *Swift.*

Be'lmetal. *n. s.* [from *bell* and *metal*.] The metal of which bells are made; being a mixture of five parts copper with one of pewter.

*Belmetal* has copper one thousand pounds, tin from three hundred to two hundred pounds, brass one hundred and fifty pounds. *Bacon's Physical Remains.*

Colours which arise on *belmetal*, when melted and poured on the ground, in open air, like the colours of water bubbles, are changed by viewing them at divers obliquities. *Newton's Opt.*

To Belo'ck. *v. a.* [from *be* and *lock*.] To fasten, as with a lock.

This is the hand, with which a vow'd contract
Was fast *belock'd* in thine. *Shakesp. Measure for Measure.*

Be'lomancy. *n. s.* [from βέλος and μαντεία.]

*Belomancy*, or divination by arrows, hath been in request with Scythians, Alans, Germans, with the Africans and Turks of Algier. *Brown's Vulgar Errours, b.* v. *c.* 22.

To Belo'ng. *v. n.* [*belangen*, Dutch.]

1. To be the property of.

To light on a part of a field *belonging* to Boaz. *Ruth*, ii. 3.

2. To be the province or business of.

There is no need of any such redress;
Or if there were, it not *belongs* to you. *Shakesp. Hen.* IV.

The declaration of these latent philosophers *belongs* to another paper. *Boyle.*

To Jove the care of heav'n and earth *belongs*. *Dryd. Virg.*

3. To adhere, or be appendent to.

He went into a desart *belonging* to Bethsaida. *Luke*, ix. 10.

4. To have relation to.

To whom *belongest* thou? whence art thou? 1 *Sam.* xxx. 13.

5. To be the quality or attribute of.

The faculties *belonging* to the supreme spirit, are unlimited and boundless, fitted and designed for infinite objects.
*Cheyne's Philosophical Principles.*

6. To be referred to.

He careth for things that *belong* to the Lord. 1 *Cor.* vii. 32.

Belo'ved. *participle.* [from *belove*, derived of *love*. It is observable,

servable, that, though the *participle* be of very frequent use, the *verb* is seldom or never admitted; as we say, you are much *beloved* by me, but not, I *belove* you.] Loved; dear.

I think, it is not meet,
Mark Anthony, so well *belov'd* of Cæsar,
Should outlive Cæsar. *Shakesp. Julius Cæsar.*

In likeness of a dove
The spirit descended, while the father's voice
From heav'n pronounc'd him his *beloved* son.
*Milton's Paradise Regained, b. i. l.* 32.

BELO'W. *prep.* [from *be* and *low*.]

1. Under in place; not so high.

He'll beat Aufidius' head *below* his knee,
And tread upon his neck. *Shakesp. Macbeth.*

2. Inferiour in dignity.

The noble Venetians think themselves equal at least to the electors of the empire, and but one degree *below* kings. *Addison on Italy.*

3. Inferiour in excellence.

His Idylliums of Theocritus are as much *below* his Manilius, as the fields are below the stars. *Felton on the Classicks.*

4. Unworthy of; unbefitting.

'Tis much *below* me on his throne to sit;
But when I do, you shall petition it. *Dryden's Indian Emp.*

BELO'W. *adv.*

1. In the lower place; in the place nearest the center.

To men standing *below* on the ground, those that be on the top of Paul's, seem much less than they are, and cannot be known; but, to men above, those *below* seem nothing so much lessened, and may be known. *Bacon's Nat. History,* N° 205.

The upper regions of the air perceive the collection of the matter of the tempests and winds before the air here *below*; and therefore the obscuring of the smaller stars, is a sign of tempest following. *Bacon's Natural History,* N° 818.

His sultry heat infects the sky;
The ground *below* is parch'd, the heav'ns above us fry. *Dryd.*

This said, he led them up the mountain's brow,
And shews them all the shining fields *below*. *Dryden.*

2. On earth; in opposition to *heaven.*

And let no tears from erring pity flow,
For one that's bless'd above, immortaliz'd *below*.
*Smith, To the Memory of J. Philips.*

The fairest child of Jove,
*Below* for ever sought, and bless'd above. *Prior.*

3. In hell; in the regions of the dead; opposed to *heaven* and *earth.*

The gladsome ghosts in circling troops attend,
Delight to hover near; and long to know
What bus'ness brought him to the realms *below*. *Dryd. Æn.*

When suff'ring saints aloft in beams shall glow,
And prosp'rous traitors gnash their teeth *below*. *Tickell.*

To BELO'WT. *v. a.* [from *be* and *lowt*, a word of contempt.] To treat with opprobrious language; to call names.

Sieur Gaulard, when he heard a gentleman report, that, at a supper, they had not only good cheer, but also savoury epigrams, and fine anagrams, returning home, rated and *belowted* his cook, as an ignorant scullion, that never dressed him either epigrams or anagrams. *Camden's Remains.*

BELSWA'GGER. *n. s.* A cant word for a whoremaster.

You are a charitable *belswagger*; my wife cried out fire, and you called out for engines. *Dryden's Spanish Friar.*

BELT. *n. s.* [belt, Sax. *baltheus*, Lat.] A girdle; a cincture in which a sword, or some weapon, is commonly hung.

He cannot buckle his distemper'd cause
Within the *belt* of rule. *Shakesp. Macbeth.*

Ajax slew himself with the sword given him by Hector, and Hector was dragged about the walls of Troy by the *belt* given him by Ajax. *South.*

Then snatch'd the shining *belt*, with gold inlaid;
The *belt* Eurytion's artful hands had made. *Dryden's Æneid.*

BELWE'THER. *n. s.* [from *bell* and *wether*.] A sheep which leads the flock with a bell on his neck.

The fox will serve my sheep to gather,
And drive to follow after their *belwether*. *Spens. Hub. Tale.*

To offer to get your living by the copulation of cattle; to be a bawd to a *belwether*. *Shakesp. As you like it.*

The flock of sheep, and *belwether*, thinking to break into another's pasture, and being to pass over another bridge, justled till both fell into the ditch. *Howel's England's Tears.*

To BELY'. See BELIE.

To BEMA'D. *v. a.* [from *be* and *mad*.] To make mad; to turn the brain.

Making just report
Of how unnatural and *bemadding* sorrow,
The king hath cause to plain. *Shakesp. King Lear.*

To BEMI'RE. *v. a.* [from *be* and *mire*.] To drag, or incumber in the mire; to soil by passing through dirty places.

Away they rode in homely sort,
Their journey long, their money short,
The loving couple well *bemir'd*;
The horse and both the riders tir'd. *Swift.*

To BEMO'AN. *v. a.* [from *to moan*.] To lament; to bewail; to express sorrow for.

He falls, he fills the house with heavy groans,
Implores their pity, and his pain *bemoans*. *Dryden's Æneid.*

The gods themselves the ruin'd seats *bemoan*,
And blame the mischiefs that themselves have done.
*Addison's Remarks on Italy.*

BEMO'ANER. *n. s.* [from the verb.] A lamenter; the person that laments.

To BEMO'IL. *v. a.* [*be* and *moil*, from *mouiller*, Fr.] To bedraggle; to bemire; to encumber with dirt and mire.

Thou shouldst have heard in how miry a place, how she was *bemoiled*, how he left her with the horse upon her. *Shakesp.*

To BEMO'NSTER. *v. a.* [from *be* and *monster*.] To make monstrous.

Thou chang'd, and self-converted thing! for shame,
*Bemonster* not thy feature. *Shakesp. King Lear.*

BEMU'SED. *adj.* [from *to muse*.] Overcome with musing; dreaming: a word of contempt.

Is there a parson much *bemus'd* in beer,
A maudlin poetess, a rhiming peer? *Pope's Epistles.*

BEN. See BEHEN.

BENCH. *n. s.* [benc, Sax. *banc*, Fr.]

1. A seat, distinguished from a *stool* by its greater length.

The seats and *benches* shone of ivory,
An hundred nymphs sat side by side about. *Spens. Vis. of Bellay.*

All Rome is pleas'd, when Statius will rehearse,
And longing crouds expect the promis'd verse;
His lofty numbers, with so great a gust,
They hear, and swallow with such eager lust:
But while the common suffrage crown'd his cause,
And broke the *benches* with their loud applause,
His muse had starv'd, had not a piece unread,
And by a player bought, supply'd her bread. *Dryd. Juvenal.*

2. A seat of justice; the seat where judges sit.

A son set your decrees at naught:
To pluck down justice from your awful *bench*;
To trip the course of law, and blunt the sword
That guards the peace and safety of your person.
*Shakesp. Henry IV. p. ii.*

Cyriac, whose grandsire on the royal *bench*
Of British Themis, with no mean applause,
Pronounc'd, and in his volumes taught our laws,
Which others at their bar so often wrench. *Milton.*

3. The persons sitting on a *bench*; as, the whole *bench* voted the same.

Fools to popular praise aspire,
Of publick speeches, which worse fools admire;
While, from both *benches*, with redoubl'd sounds,
Th' applause of lords and commoners abounds. *Dryd. Virg.*

To BENCH. *v. a.* [from the noun.]

1. To furnish with benches.

'Twas *bench'd* with turf, and, goodly to be seen,
The thick young grass arose in fresher green. *Dryden's Fab.*

2. To seat upon a bench.

His cupbearer, whom I from meaner form
Have *bench'd*, and rear'd to worship. *Shakesp. Winter's Tale.*

BE'NCHER. *n. s.* [from *bench*.] Those gentlemen of the inns of court are called *benchers*, who have been readers; they being admitted to plead within the bar, are also called inner barristers. The *benchers*, being the seniors of the house, are intrusted with its government and direction, and out of them is a treasurer yearly chosen. *Blount. Chambers.*

I was taking a walk in the gardens of Lincoln's-Inn, a favour that is indulged me by several *benchers*, who are grown old with me. *Tatler,* N° 100.

To BEND. *v. a.* pret. *bended*, or *bent*; part. pass. *bended*, or *bent*. [benban, Saxon; *bander*, Fr. as *Skinner* thinks, from *pandare*, Lat.]

1. To make crooked; to crook; to inflect.

The rainbow compasseth the heaven with a glorious circle, and the hands of the Most High hath *bended* it. *Ecclus,* xliii. 12.

They *bend* their bows, they whirl their slings around:
Heaps of spent arrows fall, and strew the ground;
And helms, and shields, and rattling arms resound. *Dryden's Fab.*

2. To direct to a certain point.

Octavius, and Mark Anthony,
Came down upon us with a mighty power,
*Bending* their expedition tow'rd Philippi. *Shakesp. J. Cæsar.*

Why dost thou *bend* thy eyes upon the earth,
And start so often, when thou sitt'st alone. *Shakesp.*

Your gracious eyes upon this labour *bend*. *Fairfax, b.* i.

To that sweet region was our voyage *bent*,
When winds, and ev'ry warring element,
Disturb'd our course. *Dryden's Virgil.*

Then, with a rushing sound, th' assembly *bend*
Diverse their steps: the rival rout ascend
The royal dome. *Pope's Odyssey, b.* ii. *l.* 295.

3. To apply.

Men will not *bend* their wits to examine, whether things, wherewith they have been accustomed, be good or evil. *Hooker.*

He is within, with two right reverend fathers,
Divinely *bent* to meditation. *Shakesp. Richard* III.

When

2 ‡
[Tran. Iconick]

Bemock v. a to mock at; to scorn to deride.

~~Of whom~~ your Swords ~~are temper'd~~ [The elements] may as well
Wound the loud winds, or with bemockt at Stabs
Kill the still closing waters Shak

p ‡

~~Still the place below in opposition to above~~

But with the upside down to show
Its inclination for below. Swift

[N]ever any man whose mind the Art of
[edu]cation hath not bencted; whose eyes a
[...]ish superstition hath not afterwards blincted
[who]se apprehensions are Sober, but hath found
[...]irresistible Necessity One true God
Sir W. Ral.

o ‡

~~Bemire v. to debase mentally~~

Base minded Wretches are your thoughts so
deeply bemired in the trade of Ordinary
Worldlings, as for respect of ~~gain~~ some paultry
wool ~~may yield you~~, to let ~~so much~~ time pass
without knowing perfectly her estate
Sidney.



IL facing 2Z[v]

To enervate

The posture of flattery
Thinkst thou the fiery fever will go out
With titles blown from Adulation?
Will it give place to flexure & low bends?
Shak.

To yield to ~~Submit~~
So when a lion shakes his dreadful Mane
And angry grows: if he that first took pain
To tame his Youth, approach the haughty beast
He bends to him but frights away the rest
Waller

~~In all the~~ light and influence ~~that~~ the heavens bestow upon this lower world, tho the lower world cannot equal the benefaction yet with grateful return, it reflects those rays that it cannot recompence
South.

I will engage to find him above an hundred beneficed Clergymen who have not so much among them all to maintain themselves and their families
Swift

When he fell into the gout, he was no longer able to *bend* his mind or thoughts to any publick business. *Temple.*

4. To put any thing in order for use; a metaphor taken from bending the bow.

I'm settled, and *bend* up
Each corporal agent to this terrible feat. *Shakesp. King Lear.*

As a fowler was *bending* his net, a blackbird asked him what he was doing. *L'Estrange, fab.* xcvi.

5. To incline.

But when to mischief mortals *bend* their will,
How soon they find fit instruments of ill? *Pope's R. of the L.*

6. To subdue; to make submissive; as, war and famine will *bend* our enemies.

7. *To bend the brow.* To knit the brow; to frown.

Some have been seen to bite their pen, scratch their head, *bend their brows*, bite their lips, beat the board, and tear their paper. *Camden's Remains.*

To Bend. *v. n.*

1. To be incurvated.

2. To lean or jut over.

There is a cliff, whose high and *bending* head
Looks fearfully on the confined deep. *Shakesp.*

Earth seems
Far stretch'd around, to meet the *bending* sphere. *Thomson.*

3. To resolve, to determine.

Not so, for once, indulg'd they sweep the main,
Deaf to the call, or, hearing, hear in vain;
But, *bent* on mischief, bear the waves before. *Dryd. Fables.*

While good, and anxious for his friend,
He's still severely *bent* against himself;
Renouncing sleep, and rest, and food, and ease. *Addis. Cato.*

A state of slavery, which they are *bent* upon with so much eagerness and obstinacy. *Addison. Freeholder.*

He is every where *bent* on instruction, and avoids all manner of digressions. *Addison's Essay on the Georgicks.*

4. To be submissive; to bow.

The sons of them that afflicted thee, shall come *bending* unto thee. *Isaiah*, lx. 14.

Bend. *n. s.* [from *to bend.*]

1. Flexure; incurvation.

'Tis true, this god did shake;
His coward lips did from their colour fly;
And that same eye, whose *bend* doth awe the world,
Did lose its lustre. *Shakesp. Julius Cæsar.*

2. The crooked timbers which make the ribs or sides of a ship. *Skinner.*

3. With heralds. One of the eight honourable ordinaries, containing a fifth when uncharged; but when charged, a third part of the escutcheon. It is made by two lines, drawn thwartways from the dexter chief to the sinister base point. *Harris.*

Be'ndable. *adj.* [from *bend.*] That may be incurvated; that may be inclined.

Be'nder. *n. s.* [from *to bend.*]

1. The person who bends.

2. The instrument with which any thing is bent.

These bows, being somewhat like the long bows in use amongst us, were bent only by a man's immediate strength, without the help of any *bender*, or rack, that are used to others. *Wilkins's Mathematical Magick.*

Be'ndwith. *n. s.* An herb. *Dict.*

Bene'aped. *adj.* [from *neap.*] A ship is said to be *beneaped*, when the water does not flow high enough to bring her off the ground, over a bar, or out of a dock. *Dict.*

Bene'ath. *prep.* [beneoþ, Sax. beneden, Dutch.]

1. Under; lower in place.

Their woolly fleeces, as the rites requir'd,
He laid *beneath* him, and to rest retir'd. *Dryden, Æn.* vii.

Ages to come might Ormond's picture know;
And palms for thee *beneath* his laurels grow. *Prior.*

2. Under, as overborn or overwhelmed by some pressure.

Our country sinks *beneath* the yoke;
It weeps, it bleeds, and each new day a gash
Is added to her wounds. *Shakesp. Macbeth.*

And oft on rocks their tender wings they tear,
And sink *beneath* the burdens which they bear. *Dryden's Virg.*

3. Lower in rank, excellence, or dignity.

We have reason then to be persuaded, that there are far more species of creatures above us, than there are *beneath.* *Locke.*

4. Unworthy of; unbeseeming; not equal to.

He will do nothing that is *beneath* his high station, nor omit doing any thing which becomes it. *Atterbury.*

Bene'ath. *adv.*

1. In a lower place; under.

I destroyed the Amorite before them; I destroyed his fruits from above, and his roots from *beneath.* *Amos*, ii. 9.

The earth which you take from *beneath*, will be barren and unfruitful. *Mortimer's Art of Husbandry.*

2. Below, as opposed to *heaven.*

Any thing that is in heaven above, or that is in the earth *beneath.* *Exodus*, xx. 4.

Be'nedict. *adj.* [*benedictus*, Lat.] Having mild and salubrious qualities: an old physical term.

It is not a small thing won in physick, if you can make rhubarb, and other medicines that are *benedict*, as strong purgers as those that are not without some malignity. *Bacon's N. Hist.*

Benedi'ction. *n. s.* [*benedictio*, Lat.]

1. Blessing; a decretory pronunciation of happiness.

A sov'reign shame so bows him; his unkindness,
That stript her from his *benediction*, turn'd her
To foreign casualties, gave her dear rights
To his doghearted daughters. *Shakesp. King Lear.*

From him will raise
A mighty nation; and upon him show'r
His *benediction* so, that, in his seed,
All nations shall be blest. *Milton's Par. Lost, b.* xii. *l.* 125.

2. The advantage conferred by blessing.

Prosperity is the blessing of the Old Testament; adversity is the blessing of the New; which carrieth the greater *benediction*, and the clearer revelation of God's favour. *Bacon's Essays.*

3. Acknowledgments for blessings received; thanks.

Could he less expect
Than glory and *benediction*, that is, thanks? *Parad. Reg.*

Such ingenious and industrious persons are delighted in searching out natural rarities; reflecting upon the Creator of them his due praises and *benedictions.* *Ray on the Creation.*

4. The form of instituting an abbot.

What consecration is to a bishop, that *benediction* is to an abbot; but in a different way: for a bishop is not properly such, till consecration; but an abbot, being elected and confirmed, is properly such before *benediction.* *Ayliffe's Parergon.*

Benefa'ction. *n. s.* [from *benefacio*, Lat.]

1. The act of conferring a benefit.

2. The benefit conferred; which is the more usual sense.

One part of the *benefactions*, was the expression of a generous and grateful mind. *Atterbury.*

Benefa'ctor. *n. s.* [from *benefacio*, Lat.] He that confers a benefit; frequently he that contributes to some publick charity.

Then swell with pride, and must be titled gods,
Great *benefactors* of mankind, deliverers,
Worshipp'd with temple, priest, and sacrifice.
*Milton's Paradise Regained, b.* iii. *l* 82.

From that preface he took his hint, though he had the baseness not to acknowledge his *benefactor.* *Dryden's Fables, Pref.*

I cannot but look upon the writer as my *benefactor*, if he conveys to me an improvement of my understanding. *Addison. Freeholder*, N° 40.

Whoever makes ill returns to his *benefactor*, must needs be a common enemy to mankind. *Swift's Gulliver's Travels.*

Benefa'ctress. *n. s.* [from *benefactor.*] A woman who confers a benefit.

Be'nefice. *n. s.* [from *beneficium*, Lat.] Advantage conferred on another. This word is generally taken for all ecclesiastical livings, be they dignities or others. *Cowel.*

And of the priest eftsoons 'gan to enquire,
How to a *benefice* he might aspire. *Spenser's Hubb. Tale.*

Much to himself he thought, but little spoke,
And, undepriv'd, his *benefice* forsook. *Dryden's Fables.*

Be'neficed. *adj.* [from *benefice.*] Possessed of a benefice, or church preferment.

The usual rate between the *beneficed* man and the religious person, was one moiety of the benefice. *Ayliffe's Parergon.*

Bene'ficence. *n. s.* [from *beneficent.*] The practice of doing good; active goodness.

You could not extend your *beneficence* to so many persons; yet you have lost as few days as that excellent emperour. *Dryden's Juvenal, Dedicat.*

Love and charity extends our *beneficence* to the miseries of our brethren. *Rogers.*

Bene'ficent. *adj.* [from *beneficus*, *beneficentior*, Lat.] Kind; doing good. It differs from *benign*, as the act from the disposition; *beneficence* being kindness, or *benignity*, exerted in action.

Such a creature could not have his origination from any less than the most wise and *beneficent* being, the great God. *Hale's Origin of Mankind.*

But Phœbus, thou, to man *beneficent*,
Delight'st in building cities. *Prior.*

Benefi'cial. *adj.* [from *beneficium*, Lat.]

1. Advantageous; conferring benefits; profitable; useful; with *to* before the person benefited.

Not that any thing is made to be *beneficial to* him, but all things for him, to shew beneficence and grace in them. *Hooker, l.* i. § 8.

This supposition grants the opinion to conduce to order in the world, and consequently to be very *beneficial to* mankind. *Tillotson, sermon* i.

The war, which would have been most *beneficial to* us, and destructive to the enemy, was neglected. *Swift.*

Are the present revolutions in circular orbs, more *beneficial* than the other would be? *Bentley's Sermons.*

2. Helpful; medicinal.

In the first access of such a disease, any deobstruent, without much acrimony, is *beneficial.* *Arbuthnot on Diet.*

Benefi'cial. *n. s.* An old word for a benefice.

For

For that the groundwork is, and end of all,
How to obtain a *beneficial*. *Spenſer's Hubberd's Tale.*

BENEFI'CIALLY. *adv.* [from *beneficial.*] Advantageouſly; profitably; helpfully.

BENEFI'CIALNESS. *n. ſ.* [from *beneficial.*] Uſefulneſs; profit; helpfulneſs.

Though the knowledge of theſe objects be commendable for their contentation and curioſity, yet they do not commend their knowledge to us, upon the account of their uſefulneſs and *beneficialneſs*. *Hale's Origin of Mankind.*

BENEFI'CIARY. *adj.* [from *benefice.*] Holding ſomething in ſubordination to another; having a dependent and ſecondary poſſeſſion, without ſovereign power.

The duke of Parma was tempted by no leſs promiſe, than to be made a feudatory, or *beneficiary* king of England, under the ſeignory in chief of the pope. *Bacon's War with Spain.*

BENEFI'CIARY. *n. ſ.* He that is in poſſeſſion of a benefice.

A benefice is either ſaid to be a benefice with the cure of ſouls, or otherwiſe. In the firſt caſe, if it be annexed to another benefice, the *beneficiary* is obliged to ſerve the pariſh church in his own proper perſon. *Ayliffe's Parergon.*

BE'NEFIT. *n. ſ.* [*beneficium*, Lat.]

1. A kindneſs; a favour conferred; an act of love.

When noble *benefits* ſhall prove
Not well diſpos'd, the mind grown once corrupt,
They turn to vicious forms. *Shakeſp. Henry* VIII.

Bleſs the Lord, O my ſoul, and forget not all his *benefits*. *Pſalm* ciii. 2.

As many as offer'd life,
Neglect not, and the *benefit* embrace
By faith, not void of works. *Paradiſe Loſt, b.* xii. *l.* 426.

2. Advantage; profit; uſe.

The creature abateth his ſtrength for the *benefit* of ſuch as put their truſt in thee. *Wiſdom*, xvi. 24.

3. In law.

*Benefit of clergy* is an ancient liberty of the church, when a prieſt, or one within orders, is arraigned of felony before a ſecular judge, he may pray his *clergy*; that is, pray to be delivered to his ordinary, to purge himſelf of the offence objected to him: and this might be done in caſe of murder. The ancient law, in this point of *clergy*, is much altered; for clerks are no more delivered to their ordinaries to be purged, but now every man, though not within orders, is put to read at the bar, being found guilty, and convicted of ſuch felony as this *benefit* is granted for; and ſo burnt in the hand, and ſet free for the firſt time, if the ordinary's commiſſioner, or deputy, ſtanding by, do ſay, *Legit ut clericus*; or, otherwiſe, ſuffereth death for his tranſgreſſion. *Cowel.*

To BE'NEFIT. *v. a.* [from the noun.] To do good to; to advantage.

What courſe I mean to hold,
Shall nothing *benefit* your knowledge. *Shakeſp. Wint. Tale.*

He was ſo far from *benefiting* trade, that he did it a great injury, and brought Rome in danger of a famine. *Arbuthnot.*

To BE'NEFIT. *v. n.* To gain advantage.

To tell you therefore what I have *benefited* herein, among old renowned authors, I ſhall ſpare. *Milton on Education.*

BENE'MPT. *adj.* [See NEMPT.] Appointed; marked out; an obſolete word.

Much greater gifts for Guerdon thou ſhalt gain,
Than kid or coſſet, which I thee *benempt*;
Then up, I ſay. *Spenſer's Paſtorals.*

To BENE'T. *v. a.* [from *net.*] To enſnare; to ſurround as with toils.

Being thus *benetted* round with villains,
Ere I could mark the prologue, to my bane,
They had begun the play. *Shakeſp. Hamlet.*

BENE'VOLENCE. *n. ſ.* [*benevolentia*, Lat.]

1. Diſpoſition to do good; kindneſs; charity; good will.

Graſp the whole worlds of reaſon, life, and ſenſe,
In one cloſe ſyſtem of *benevolence*. *Pope's Eſſay on Man.*

2. The good done; the charity given.

3. A kind of tax.

This tax, called a *benevolence*, was deviſed by Edward IV. for which he ſuſtained much envy. It was aboliſhed by Richard III. *Bacon's Henry* VII.

BENE'VOLENT. *adj.* [*benevolens, benevolentia*, Lat.] Kind; having good will, or kind inclinations.

Thou good old man, *benevolent* as wiſe. *Pope's Odyſſey.*

Nature all
Is blooming and *benevolent* like thee. *Thomſon.*

BENE'VOLENTNESS. *n. ſ.* The ſame with *benevolence*.

BENGA'L. *n. ſ.* [from *Bengal* in the Eaſt Indies.] A ſort of thin ſlight ſtuff, made of ſilk and hair, for womens apparel.

BE'NJAMIN. *n. ſ.* [*Benzoin.*] The name of a tree.

From a calyx, which conſiſts of four leaves, are produced three ſmall flowers, which have an oblong tube; the upper part, which is expanded, is divided into eight ſegments; between which are ſeveral ſhort threads, and, in the middle of the tube, is the ovarium, which becomes a fruit. It was brought from Virginia into England, and is propagated by laying down the tender branches in the ſpring of the year. *Millar.*

BE'NJAMIN. *n. ſ.* A gum. See BENZOIN.

To BENI'GHT. *v. a.* [from *night.*]

1. To involve in darkneſs; to embarraſs by want of light; to bring on night.

He that has light within his own breaſt,
May ſit i' th' centre, and enjoy bright day;
But he that hides a dark ſoul, and foul thoughts,
*Benighted* walks under the mid-day ſun;
Himſelf is his own dungeon. *Milton.*

Thoſe bright ſtars that did adorn our hemiſphere, as thoſe dark ſhades that did *benight* it, vaniſh. *Boyle.*

But what ſo long in vain, and yet unknown
By poor mankind's *benighted* wit, is ſought,
Shall in this age to Britain firſt be ſhown. *Dryd. Ann. Mir.*

A ſtorm begins, the raging waves run high,
The clouds look heavy, and *benight* the ſky. *Garth's Ovid.*

The miſerable race of men, that live
*Benighted* half the year, benumm'd with froſts
Under the polar Bear. *Philips.*

2. To ſurpriſe with the coming on of night.

Being *benighted*, the ſight of a candle I ſaw a good way off, directed me to a young ſhepherd's houſe. *Sidney, b.* i.

Or ſome *benighted* angel, in his way,
Might eaſe his wings; and, ſeeing heav'n appear
In its beſt work of mercy, think it there. *Dryden.*

BENI'GN. *adj.* [*benignus*, Lat. It is pronounced without the *g*, as if written *benine*; but the *g* is preſerved in *benignity.*]

1. Kind; generous; liberal; actually good. See BENEFICENT.

This turn hath made amends! Thou haſt fulfill'd
Thy words, Creator bounteous and *benign!*
Giver of all things fair. *Milton's Parad. Loſt, b.* viii. *l.* 492.

So ſhall the world go on,
To good malignant, to bad men *benign*. *Par. Loſt, b.* xii.

We owe more to heav'n than to the ſword,
The wiſh'd return of ſo *benign* a lord. *Waller.*

What heaven beſtows upon the earth, in kind influences and *benign* aſpects, is paid it back again in ſacrifice and adoration. *South.*

They who delight in the ſuffering of inferiour creatures, will not be very compaſſionate or *benign*. *Locke.*

Diff'rent are thy names,
As thy kind hand has founded many cities,
Or dealt *benign* thy various gifts to men. *Prior.*

2. Wholeſome; not malignant.

Theſe ſalts are of a *benign* mild nature, in healthy perſons; but, in others, retain their original qualities, which they diſcover in cachexies. *Arbuthnot on Aliments.*

BENIGN *Diſeaſe*, is when all the uſual ſymptoms appear in the ſmall pox, or any acute diſeaſe, favourably, and without any irregularities, or unexpected changes. *Quincy.*

BENI'GNESS. *n. ſ.* [from *benign.*] The ſame with *benignity*.

BENI'GNITY. *n. ſ.* [from *benign.*]

1. Gracioufneſs; goodneſs; actual kindneſs.

He which uſeth the benefit of any ſpecial *benignity*, may enjoy it with good conſcience. *Hooker, b.* v. § 9.

The king was deſirous to eſtabliſh peace rather by *benignity* than blood. *Hayward.*

It is true, that his mercy will forgive offenders, or his *benignity* co-operate to their converſions. *Brown's Vulgar Errours.*

Although he enjoys the good that is done him, he is unconcerned to value the *benignity* of him that does it. *South.*

2. Salubrity; wholeſome quality; friendlineſs to vital nature.

Bones receive a quicker agglutination in ſanguine than in cholerick bodies, by reaſon of the *benignity* of the ſerum, which ſendeth out better matter for a callus. *Wiſeman's Surgery.*

BENI'GNLY. *adv.* [from *benign.*] Favourably; kindly; graciouſly.

'Tis amazement more than love,
Which her radiant eyes do move;
If leſs ſplendour wait on thine,
Yet they ſo *benignly* ſhine,
I would turn my dazled ſight
To behold their milder light. *Waller.*

Oh truly good, and truly great!
For glorious as he roſe, *benignly* ſo he ſet. *Prior.*

BE'NISON. *n. ſ.* [*benir*, to bleſs; *beniſſons*, Fr.] Bleſſing; benediction.

We have no ſuch daughter; nor ſhall ever ſee
That face of hers again; therefore, begone
Without our grace, our love, our *beniſon*. *Shakeſp. K. Lear.*

Unmuffle, ye fair ſtars, and thou, fair moon,
That wont'ſt to love the traveller's *beniſon*. *Milton.*

BE'NNET. *n. ſ.* An herb; the ſame with *avens*, which ſee.

BENT. *n. ſ.* [from the verb *to bend.*]

1. The ſtate of being bent; a ſtate of flexure; curvity.

Strike gently, and hold your rod at a *bent* a little while. *Walton's Angler.*

2. Degree of flexure.

There are divers ſubtle inquiries concerning the ſtrength required to the bending of bows, the force they have in the diſcharge, according to the ſeveral *bents*; and the ſtrength required to be in the ſtring of them. *Wilkins's Mathematical Magick.*

3. De-

Made duskish or black

If virtue no benighted beauty lack
Your Son in law is far more fair than black
Shak.

Your grace and those your nobles here present, be pleased benignly to bow your ears to hear the tragedy of a Young Man
Bacon

O

The benefited Subject Should render some small portion of his gain as well towards the Maintenance of his own commodity as for the Supporting of the kings expence
Bacon

Improperly used by Denham for left as a token.
Viewing the Trojan reliques she unsheath'd
Æneas' Sword, not for that use bequeath'd
Denh.

Came he to sing a ravens note
Whose dismal tune bereft my Vital powers
Shak

The right for which I love are bereft me
Shak. Othello

Alcinous Orchard various apples bears
Unlike are bergamots & pounder pears
Dryd. V. Geo.

3. Declivity.

A mountain stood,
Threat'ning from high, and overlook'd the wood:
Beneath the lowring brow, and on a *bent*,
The temple stood of Mars armipotent. *Dryd. Pal. and Arc.*

4. Utmost power, as of a bent bow.

Then let thy love be younger than thyself,
Or thy affection cannot hold the *bent*. *Shakesp. Tw. Night.*

We both obey,
And here give up ourselves, in the full *bent*,
To lay our service freely at your feet. *Shakesp. Hamlet.*

5. Application of the mind; strain of the mental powers.

The understanding should be brought to the knotty parts of knowledge, that try the strength of thought, and a full *bent* of the mind, by insensible degrees. *Locke.*

6. Inclination; disposition towards something.

O who does know the *bent* of womens fantasy!
*Fairy Queen, b. i. cant. iv. stanz. 24.*

To your own *bents* dispose you; you'll be found,
Be you beneath the sky. *Shakesp. Winter's Tale.*

He knew the strong *bent* of the country towards the house of York. *Bacon's Henry* VII.

Soon inclin'd t' admit delight,
The *bent* of nature! *Milton's Par. Lost, b.* xi. *l.* 597.

The golden age was first; when man, yet new,
No rule but uncorrupted reason knew;
And, with a native *bent*, did good pursue. *Dryden. Ovid.*

Let there be the same propensity and *bent* of will to religion, and there will be the same sedulity and indefatigable industry. *South.*

'Tis odds but the scale turns at last on nature's side, and the evidence of one or two senses gives way to the united *bent* and tendency of all the five. *Atterbury.*

7. Determination; fixed purpose.

Their unbelief we may not impute unto insufficiency in the mean which is used, but to the wilful *bent* of their obstinate hearts against it. *Hooker, b.* v. § 22.

Yet we saw them forced to give way to the *bent*, and current humour of the people, in favour of their ancient and lawful government. *Temple.*

8. Turn of the temper, or disposition; shape, or fashion, superinduced by art.

Not a courtier,
Although they wear their faces to the *bent*
Of the king's look, but hath a heart that is
Glad at the thing they scoul at. *Shakesp. Cymbeline.*

Two of them hath the very *bent* of honour.
*Shakesp. Much ado about Nothing.*

Then thy streight rule set virtue in my sight,
The crooked line reforming by the right;
My reason took the *bent* of thy command,
Was form'd and polish'd by thy skilful hand. *Dryden's Pers.*

9. Tendency; flexion; particular direction.

The exercising the understanding, in the several ways of reasoning, teacheth the mind suppleness, to apply itself more dexterously to *bents* and turns of the matter, in all its researches. *Locke.*

10. A stalk of grass, called *bent-grass*.

His spear, a *bent* both stiff and strong,
And well near of two inches long;
The pile was of a horse-fly's tongue,
Whose sharpness naught reversed. *Drayt. Nymphid.*

Then the flowers of the vines, it is a little dust, like the dust of a *bent*, which grows upon the cluster, in the first coming forth. *Bacon's Essays.*

June is drawn in a mantle of dark grass-green, upon his head a garland of *bents*, kingcups, and maidenhair. *Peacham on Drawing.*

BE'NTING *Time.* [from *bent.*] The time when pigeons feed on bents before peas are ripe.

Bare *benting times*, and moulting months, may come,
When, lagging late, they cannot reach their home.
*Dryden's Hind and Panther.*

To BENU'M. *v. a.* [benumen, Saxon.]

1. To make torpid; to take away the sensation and use of any part by cold, or by some obstruction.

So stings a snake that to the fire is brought,
Which harmless lay with cold *benumm'd* before.
*Fairfax, b.* ii. *stanz.* 85.

The winds blow moist and keen, which bids us seek
Some better shroud, some better warmth, to cherish
Our limbs *benumm'd*. *Milton's Paradise Lost, b.* x. *l.* 1069.

My sinews slacken, and an icy stiffness
*Benums* my blood. *Denham's Sophy.*

It seizes upon the vitals, and *benums* the senses; and where there is no sense, there can be no pain. *South.*

Will they be the less dangerous, when warmth shall bring them to themselves, because they were once frozen and *benummed* with cold? *L'Estrange, fab.* ix.

2. To stupify.

These accents were her last: the creeping death
*Benumm'd* her senses first, then stopp'd her breath. *Dryden.*

BENZO'IN. *n. s.* A medicinal kind of resin imported from the East Indies, and vulgarly called *benjamin*. It is procured by making an incision in a tree, whose leaves resemble those of the lemon tree. It is of a yellowish colour, an agreeable scent, it melts easily, and is of three sorts. The first, which is esteemed the best, comes from Siam, and is called *amygdaloides*, being interspersed with white spots, resembling broken almonds. The second is black, and very odoriferous; it drops from young trees, and comes from Sumatra. The third is also black, but less odoriferous, and is found in Java and Sumatra. *Trevoux. Chambers.*

The liquor we have distilled from *benzoin*, is subject to frequent vicissitudes of fluidity and firmness. *Boyle.*

BENZOIN *Tree.* See BENJAMIN *Tree.*

To BEPA'INT. *v. a.* [from *paint.*] To cover with paint.

Thou know'st, the mask of night is on my face,
Else would a maiden blush *bepaint* my cheek.
*Shakesp. Romeo and Juliet.*

To BEPI'NCH. *v. a.* [from *pinch.*] To mark with pinches.

In their sides, arms, shoulders, all *bepincht*,
Ran thick the weals, red with blood, ready to start out.
*Chapman's Iliad.*

To BEPI'SS. *v. a.* [from *piss.*] To wet with urine.

One caused, at a feast, a bagpipe to be played, which made the knight *bepiss* himself, to the great diversion of all then present, as well as confusion of himself. *Derham's Physico-Theol.*

To BEQUE'ATH. *v. a.* [cpiþ, Sax. a will.] To leave by will to another.

She had never been disinherited of that goodly portion, which nature had so liberally *bequeathed* to her. *Sidney.*

Let's choose executors, and talk of wills;
And yet not so—for what can we *bequeath*,
Save our deposed bodies to the ground? *Shakesp. Richard* II.

My father *bequeath'd* me by will but a poor thousand crowns.
*Shakesp. As you like it.*

Methinks this age seems resolved to *bequeath* posterity somewhat to remember it. *Glanville's Scepsis, c.* 21.

For you, whom best I love and value most,
But to your service I *bequeath* my ghost. *Dryden's Fables.*

BEQUE'ATHMENT. *n. s.* [from *bequeath.*] A legacy. *Dict.*

BEQU'EST. *n. s.* [from *bequeath.*] Something left by will; a legacy.

He claimed the crown to himself, pretending an adoption, or *bequest*, of the kingdom unto him by the Confessor.
*Hale's Common Law of England.*

To BERA'TTLE. *v. a.* [from *rattle.*] To rattle off; to make a noise at in contempt.

These are now the fashion, and so *berattle* the common stage, so they call them, that many, wearing rapiers, are afraid of goosequills, and dare scarce come thither. *Shakesp. Hamlet.*

BE'RBERRY. *n. s.* [*berberis*, sometimes written *barberry*, which see] A berry of a sharp taste, used for pickles.

Some never ripen to be sweet, as tamarinds, *berberries*, crabs, sloes, &c. *Bacon's Natural History*, N° 644.

To BEREA'VE. *v. n.* preter. *I bereaved*, or *bereft*. [bereoꝑian, Saxon.]

1. To strip of; to deprive of. It has generally the particle *of* before the thing taken away.

Madam, you have *bereft* me *of* all words,
Only my blood speaks to you in my veins. *Shakesp. M. of V.*

That when thou com'st to kneel at Henry's feet,
Thou may'st *bereave* him *of* his wits with wonder.
*Shakesp. Henry* VI. *p.* i.

There was never a prince *bereaved of* his dependences by his council, except there hath been either an overgreatness in one counsellor. *Bacon's Essays.*

The sacred priests with ready knives *bereave*
The beasts *of* life. *Dryden's Æneid.*

To deprive us of metals, is to make us mere savages; it is to *bereave* us *of* all arts and sciences, *of* history and letters, nay *of* revealed religion too, that inestimable favour of heaven.
*Bentley's Sermons.*

2. Sometimes it is used without *of*.

*Bereave* me not,
Whereon I live! thy gentle looks, thy aid,
Thy counsel, in this uttermost distress. *Parad. Lost, b.* x.

3. To take away from.

All your interest in those territories
Is utterly *bereft* you, all is lost. *Shakesp. Henry* VI. *p.* ii.

BERE'AVEMENT. *n. s.* [from *bereave.*] Deprivation. *Dict.*

BERE'FT. *part. pass.* of *bereave.*

The chief of either side, *bereft* of life,
Or yielded to the foe, concludes the strife. *Dryden's Fab.*

BERG. See BURROW.

BE'RGAMOT. *n. s.* [*bergamotte*, Fr.]

1. A sort of pear, commonly called *burgamot*. See PEAR.

2. A sort of essence, or perfume, drawn from a fruit produced by ingrafting a lemon tree on a bergamot pear stock.

3. A sort of snuff, which is only clean tobacco, with a little of the essence rubbed into it.

BE'RGMASTER. *n. s.* [from beꞃᵹ, Sax. and *master.*] The bailiff, or chief officer, among the Derbyshire miners.

BE'RGMOTE. *n. s.* [of beꞃᵹ, a mountain, and moꞇe, a meeting, Saxon.] A court held upon a hill for deciding controversies among the Derbyshire miners. *Blount.*

To BERHY'ME. *v. a.* [from *rhyme.*] To celebrate in rhyme, or verses: a word of contempt.

Now is he for the numbers that Petrarch flow'd in: Laura to his lady was but a kitchen wench; marry, she had a better love to *berhyme* her. *Shakesp. Romeo and Juliet.*

I sought no homage from the race that write;
I kept, like Asian monarchs, from their sight:
Poems I heeded, now *berhymed* so long,
No more than thou, great George! a birthday song. *Pope.*

BERLI'N. *n. s.* [from *Berlin*, the city where they were first made.] A coach of a particular form.

Beware of Latin authors all!
Nor think your verses sterling,
Though with a golden pen you scrawl,
And scribble in a *berlin.* *Swift.*

BERME. *n. s.* [Fr. In fortification.] A space of ground three, four, or five feet wide, left without between the foot of the rampart and the side of the mote, to prevent the earth from falling down into the mote; and sometimes it is palisadoed. *Harris.*

To BERO'B. *v. a.* [from *rob.*] To rob; to plunder; to wrong any, by taking away something from him by stealth or violence.

She said, ah dearest lord! what evil star
On you hath frown'd, and pour'd his influence bad,
That of yourself you thus *berobbed* are. *Fairy Queen, b.* viii.

BE'RRY. *n. s.* [beꞃıᵹ, Sax. from beꞃan, to bear.] Any small fruit, with many seeds or small stones.

She smote the ground, the which straight forth did yield
A fruitful olive tree, with *berries* spread,
That all the gods admir'd. *Spens. Muiopotmos.*

The strawberry grows underneath the nettle,
And wholesome *berries* thrive and ripen best,
Neighbour'd by fruit of basest quality. *Shakesp. Henry* V.

To BE'RRY. *v. n.* [from the noun.] To bear berries.

BE'RRY-BEARING *Cedar.* [*cedrus baccifera.*]

The leaves are squamose, somewhat like those of the cypress. The katkins, or male flowers, are produced at remote distances from the fruit on the same tree. The fruit is a berry, inclosing three hard seeds in each. The species are, 1. The yellow *berry-bearing cedar.* 2. The Phœnician *cedar.* These trees are propagated by sowing their berries, which are brought from the Streights, in boxes of light sandy earth; but they are at present very rare, and only to be found in some curious old collections. The wood is of great use in the Levant, is large timber, and may be thought the shittim-wood mentioned in the Scripture, of which many of the ornaments to the famous temple of Solomon were made. It is accounted excellent for carving, and esteemed equal almost to any sort of timber for its durableness. *Millar.*

BE'RRY-BEARING *Orach.* See MULBERRY BLIGHT.

BERT, is the same with our *bright*; in the Latin, *illustris* and *clarus.* So *Ecbert, eternally famous*, or *bright*; *Sigbert, famous conquerour.* And she who was termed by the Germans *Bertha*, was by the Greeks called *Eudoxia*, as is observed by *Lintprandus.* Of the same sort were these, *Phædrus, Epiphanius, Photius, Lampridius, Fulgentius, Illustrius.* *Gibson's Camden.*

BERTH. *n. s.* [with sailors.] See BIRTH.

BE'RTRAM. *n. s.* [*pyrethrum*, Lat.] A sort of herb, called also *bastard pellitory.*

BE'RYL. *n. s.* [*beryllus*, Lat.] A kind of precious stone.

May thy billows roul ashore
The *beryl* and the golden ore. *Milton.*

The *beryl* of our lapidaries is only a fine sort of cornelian, of a more deep bright red, sometimes with a cast of yellow, and more transparent than the common cornelian. *Woodward's Method of Fossils.*

To BESCRE'EN. *v. a.* [from *screen.*] To cover with a screen; to shelter; to conceal.

What man art thou, that thus *bescreen'd* in night,
So stumblest on my counsel? *Shakesp. Romeo and Juliet.*

To BESE'ECH. *v. a.* pret. I *besought*, I have *besought.* [from recan, Sax. *versoeken*, Dutch.]

1. To entreat; to supplicate; to implore; sometimes before a person.

I *beseech* you, Sir, pardon me; it is only a letter from my brother, that I have not all over-read. *Shakesp. King Lear.*

I *beseech* thee for my son Onesimus, whom I have begotten in my bonds. *Philemon*, 10.

I, in the anguish of my heart, *beseech* you
To quit the dreadful purpose of your soul. *Addison's Cato.*

2. To beg; to ask; before a thing.

But Eve fell humble, and *besought*
His peace, and thus proceeded in her plaint. *Par. Lost, b.* x.

Before I come to them, I *beseech* your patience, whilst I speak something to ourselves here present. *Sprat.*

To BESE'EM. *v. n.* [*beziemen*, Dutch.] To become; to be fit; to be decent for.

What form of speech, or behaviour, *beseemeth* us in our prayers to Almighty God? *Hooker, b.* v. § 34.

This oversight
*Beseems* thee not, in whom such virtues spring. *Fairfax, b.* iv. *stanz.* 58.

Verona's ancient citizens
Cast by their brave *beseeming* ornaments. *Shakesp. Romeo and Juliet.*

What thoughts he had, *beseems* not me to say;
Though some surmise he went to fast and pray. *Dryden.*

BESE'EN. *particip.* [from *besie. Skinner.* This word I have only found in *Spenser.*] Adapted; adjusted; becoming.

Forth came that ancient lord and aged queen,
Armed in antique robes down to the ground,
And sad habiliments, right well *beseen.* *Fairy Queen, b.* i.

To BESE'T. *v. a.* pret. I *beset*; I have *beset.* [beꞅıꞇꞇan, Sax.]

1. To besiege; to hem in; to inclose, as with a siege.

Follow him that's fled;
The thicket is *beset*, he cannot 'scape. *Shakes. T. G. of Ver.*

Now, Cæsar, let thy troops *beset* our gates,
And barr each avenue———
Cato shall open to himself a passage. *Addison's Cato.*

I know thou look'st on me, as on a wretch
*Beset* with ills, and cover'd with misfortunes. *Addis. Cato.*

2. To embarrass; to perplex; to entangle without any means of escape.

Now, daughter Sylvia, you are hard *beset.* *Shakesp. Two Gentlemen of Verona.*

Thus Adam, sore *beset*, reply'd. *Milton's Par. Lost, b.* x.

Sure, or I read her visage much amiss,
Or grief *besets* her hard. *Rowe's Jane Shore.*

We be in this world *beset* with sundry uneasinesses, distracted with different desires. *Locke.*

3. To waylay; to surround.

Draw forth thy weapon; we're *beset* with thieves;
Rescue thy mistress. *Shakesp. Taming of the Shrew.*

The only righteous in a world perverse,
And therefore hated, therefore so *beset*
With foes, for daring single to be just. *Paradise Lost, b.* xi.

True fortitude I take to be the quiet possession of a man's self, and an undisturbed doing his duty, whatever evil *besets*, or danger lies in his way. *Locke.*

4. To fall upon; to harrass.

But they him spying, both with greedy force
At once upon him ran, and him *beset*
With strokes of mortal steel. *Fairy Queen, b.* ii. *cant.* ii.

To BESHRE'W. *v. a.* [The original of this word is somewhat obscure; as it evidently implies *to wish ill*, some derive it from *beschryen*, Germ. to enchant. *Topsel*, in his *Book of Animals*, deduces it from the *shrew mouse*, an animal, says he, so poisonous, that its bite is a severe curse. A *shrew* likewise signifies a scolding woman; but its origin is not known.]

1. To wish a curse to.

Nay, quoth the cock; but I *beshrew* us both,
If I believe a saint upon his oath. *Dryden's Fables.*

2. To happen ill to.

*Beshrew* thee, cousin, which didst lead me forth
Of that sweet way I was in to despair. *Shakesp. Richard* II.

Now much *beshrew* my manners, and my pride,
If Hermia meant to say Lysander lied. *Shakesp.*

BESI'DE. }
BESI'DES. } *prep.* [from *be* and *side.*]

1. At the side of another; near.

*Beside* the hearse a fruitful palmtree grows,
Ennobled since by this great funeral. *Fairfax, b.* iii. *st.* 72.

He caused me to sit down *beside* him. *Bacon's N. Atlantis.*

At his right hand, Victory
Sat eagle-wing'd: *beside* him hung his bow. *Par. Lost, b.* vi.

Fair Lavinia fled the fire
Before the gods, and stood *beside* her sire. *Dryden's Æneid.*

Fair is the kingcup that in meadow blows;
Fair is the daisy that *beside* her grows. *Gay's Pastorals.*

Now under hanging mountains,
*Beside* the falls of fountains,
Unheard, unknown,
He makes his moan. *Pope's St. Cæcilia.*

2. Over and above.

Doubtless, in man there is a nature found,
*Beside* the senses, and above them far. *Sir J. Davies.*

In brutes, *besides* the exercise of sensitive perception and imagination, there are lodged instincts antecedent to their imaginative faculty. *Hale's Origin of Mankind.*

We may be sure there were great numbers of wise and learned men, *beside* those whose names are in the christian records, who took care to examine our Saviour's history. *Addison on the Christian Religion.*

Precepts of morality, *besides* the natural corruption of our tempers, are abstracted from ideas of sense. *Addison's Essay on the Georgicks.*

3. Not according to, though not contrary; as we say, some things are *beside* nature, some are *contrary* to nature.

The Stoicks did hold a necessary connexion of causes; but they believed, that God doth act *præter* & *contra naturam*, *besides*

blank page

~~To attend, to crowd~~

Frequent hearses shall besiege your gates l ‡

Pop.

~~To invest. To block up with a fleet~~

Your much lov'd fleet shall with a wide Command
Besiege the petty Monarchs of the Land k ‡

Dryd.

Here too the Thresher brandishing his flail
Bespeaks a Master.

Dodsly's Agricult.

*fides* and against nature. *Bramhall against Hobbes.*

To say a thing is a chance, as it relates to second causes, signifies no more, than that there are some events *beside* the knowledge, purpose, expectation, and power of second causes. *South.*

Providence often disposes of things by a method *beside*, and above the discoveries of man's reason. *South.*

It is *beside* my present business to enlarge upon this speculation. *Locke.*

4. Out of; in a state of deviating from.

You are too wilful blame,
And, since your coming here, have done
Enough to put him quite *besides* his patience. *Shakesp. H.* IV.

Of vagabonds we say,
That they are ne'er *beside* their way. *Hudibras, cant.* i.

These may serve as landmarks, to shew what lies in the direct way of truth, or is quite *besides* it. *Locke.*

5. Before a reciprocal pronoun, out of; as, *beside himself*; out of the order of rational beings; out of his wits.

They be carried *besides themselves*, to whom the dignity of publick prayer doth not discover somewhat more fitness in men of gravity, than in children. *Hooker, b.* ii. § 31.

Only be patient, till we have appeas'd
The multitude, *beside themselves* with fear. *Shakesp. J. Cæs.*

Festus said with a loud voice, Paul, thou art *beside thyself*: much learning doth make thee mad. *Acts*, xxvi. 24.

BESIDE. } *adv.*
BESIDES. }

1. More than that; over and above.

If Cassio do remain,
He hath a daily beauty in his life,
That makes me ugly; and, *besides*, the Moor
May unfold me to him; there stand I in peril. *Othello.*

*Besides*, you know not, while you here attend,
Th' unworthy fate of your unhappy friend. *Dryden's Æn.*

That man that doth not know those things, which are of necessity for him to know, is but an ignorant man, whatever he may know *besides*. *Tillotson, serm.* i.

Some wondered, that the Turk never attacks this treasury. But, *besides*, that he has attempted it formerly with no success, it is certain the Venetians keep too watchful an eye. *Addison's Remarks on Italy.*

2. Not in this number; beyond this class; not included here.

And the men said unto Lot, hast thou here any *besides*? *Genesis*, xix. 12.

Outlaws and robbers, who break with all the world *besides*, must keep faith among themselves. *Locke.*

All that we feel of it begins and ends
In the small circle of our foes or friends;
To all *beside* as much an empty shade,
An Eugene living, as a Cæsar dead. *Pope's Essay on Man.*

And dead, as living, 'tis our author's pride
Still to charm those who charm the world *beside*. *Pope.*

BESI'DERY. *n. s.* A species of pear, which see.

To BESI'EGE. *v. a.* [from *siege.*] To beleaguer; to lay siege to; to beset with armed forces; to endeavour to win a town or fortress, by surrounding it with an army, and forcing the defendants, either by violence or famine, to give admission.

And he shall *besiege* thee in all thy gates, until thy high and fenced walls come down. *Deut.* xxviii. 52.

The queen, with all the northern earls and lords,
Intend here to *besiege* you in your castle. *Shakesp. Henry* VI.

BESI'EGER. *n. s.* [from *besiege.*] One employed in a siege.

There is hardly a town taken, in the common forms, where the *besiegers* have not the worse of the bargain. *Swift.*

To BESLU'BBER. *v. a.* [from *slubber.*] To dawb; to smear.

He persuaded us to tickle our noses with speargrass, and make them bleed; and then *beslubber* our garments with it, and swear it was the blood of true men. *Shakesp. Henry* IV.

To BESME'AR. *v. a.* [from *smear.*]

1. To bedawb; to overspread with something that sticks on.

He lay as in a dream of deep delight,
*Besmear'd* with precious balm, whose virtuous might
Did heal his wounds. *Fairy Queen, b.* i. *cant.* ii.

That face of his I do remember well;
Yet when I saw it last, it was *besmear'd*
As black as Vulcan. *Shakesp. Twelfth Night.*

First Moloch! horrid king! *besmear'd* with blood
Of human sacrifice, and parents tears. *Paradise Lost, b.* i.

Her fainting hand let fall the sword, *besmear'd*
With blood. *Sir J. Denham.*

Her gushing blood the pavement all *besmear'd*. *Dryden.*

2. To soil; to foul.

My honour would not let ingratitude
So much *besmear* it. *Shakesp. Merchant of Venice.*

To BESMI'RCH. *v. a.* To soil; to discolour.

Perhaps he loves you now,
And now no soil of cautel doth *besmirch*
The virtue of his will. *Shakesp. Hamlet.*

Our gayness, and our gilt, are all *besmirch'd*
With rainy marching in the painful field. *Shakesp. Henry* V.

To BESMO'KE. *v. a.* [from *smoke.*]

1. To foul with smoke.

2. To harden or dry in smoke.

To BESMU'T. *v. a.* [from *smut.*] To blacken with smoke or soot.

BE'SOM. *n. s.* [besm, besma, Saxon.] An instrument to sweep with.

Bacon commended an old man that sold *besoms*: a proud young fellow came to him for a *besom* upon trust; the old man said, borrow of thy back and belly, they will never ask thee again; I shall dun thee every day. *Bacon's Apophthegms.*

I will sweep it with the *besom* of destruction, saith the Lord of hosts. *Isaiah*, xiv. 22.

To BESO'RT. *v. a.* [from *sort.*] To suit; to fit; to become.

Such men as may *besort* your age,
And know themselves and you. *Shakesp. King Lear.*

BESO'RT. *n. s.* [from the verb.] Company; attendance; train.

I crave fit disposition for my wife,
With such accommodation and *besort*,
As levels with her breeding. *Shakesp. Othello.*

To BESO'T. *v. a.* [from *sot.*]

1. To infatuate; to stupify; to dull; to take away the senses.

Swinish gluttony
Ne'er looks to heav'n amidst his gorgeous feast,
But, with *besotted* base ingratitude,
Crams and blasphemes his feeder. *Milton.*

Or fools *besotted* with their crimes,
That know not how to shift betimes. *Hudibras, p.* iii. *c.* ii.

He is *besotted*, and has lost his reason; and what then can there be for religion to take hold of him by. *South.*

2. To make to doat.

Paris, you speak
Like one *besotted* on your sweet delights. *Shakesp. Troilus and Cressida.*

Trust not thy beauty; but restore the prize,
Which he, *besotted* on that face and eyes,
Would rend from us. *Dryden's Fables.*

BESO'UGHT. [*part. passive* of *beseech*; which see.]

Hasten to appease
Th' incensed Father, and th' incensed Son,
While pardon may be found, in time *besought*. *Milt. Paradise Lost, b.* v. *l.* 848.

To BESPA'NGLE. *v. a.* [from *spangle.*] To adorn with spangles; to besprinkle with something shining.

Not Berenice's locks first rose so bright,
The heav'ns *bespangling* with dishevell'd light. *Pope.*

To BESPA'TTER. *v. a.* [from *spatter.*] To soil by throwing filth; to spot or sprinkle with dirt or water.

Those who will not take vice into their bosoms, shall yet have it *bespatter* their faces. *Government of the Tongue*, § 5.

His weapons are the same which women and children use; a pin to scratch, and a squirt to *bespatter*. *Swift, lett.* lxix.

Fair Britain, in the monarch blest,
Whom never faction could *bespatter*. *Swift.*

To BESPA'WL. *v. a.* [from *spawl.*] To dawb with spittle.

To BESPE'AK. *v. a.* I *bespoke*, or *bespake*; I have *bespoke*, or *bespoken*. [from *speak.*]

1. To order, or entreat any thing beforehand, or against a future time.

If you will marry, make your loves to me;
My lady is *bespoke*. *Shakesp. King Lear.*

Here is the cap your worship did *bespeak*. *Shakesp. Taming of the Shrew.*

When Baboon came to Strutt's estate, his tradesmen waited upon him, to *bespeak* his custom. *Arbuthnot's Hist. of J. Bull.*

A heavy writer was to be encouraged, and accordingly many thousand copies were *bespoke*. *Swift.*

2. To make way by a previous apology.

My preface looks as if I were afraid of my reader, by so tedious a *bespeaking* of him. *Dryden.*

3. To forebode; to tell something beforehand.

Thy started fears *bespoke* dangers, and formed ominous prognosticks, in order to scare the allies. *Swift, Examin.* N° 45.

4. To speak to; to address. This sense is chiefly poetical.

With hearty words her knight she 'gan to chear,
And, in her modest manner, thus *bespake*,
Dear knight. *Fairy Queen, b.* i. *cant.* i. *stanz.* 8.

At length with indignation thus he broke
His awful silence, and the powers *bespoke*. *Dryden.*

Then staring on her with a ghastly look,
And hollow voice, he thus the queen *bespoke*. *Dryden.*

5. To betoken; to shew.

When the abbot of St. Martin was born, he had so little of the figure of a man, that it *bespoke* him rather a monster. *Locke.*

He has dispatch'd me hence,
With orders that *bespeak* a mind compos'd. *Addison's Cato.*

BESPE'AKER. *n. s.* [from *bespeak.*] He that bespeaks any thing.

They mean not with love to the *bespeaker* of the work, but delight in the work itself. *Wotton's Architecture.*

To BESPE'CKLE. *v. a.* [from *speckle.*] To mark with speckles, or spots.

To BESPE'W. *v. a.* [from *spew.*] To dawb with spew or vomit.

To BESPI'CE. *v. a.* [from *spice.*] To season with spices.

Thou might'st *bespice* a cup
To give mine enemy a lasting wink. *Shakesp. Winter's Tale.*

To

To Bespi't. *v. a.* I *bespat*, or *bespit*; I have *bespit*, or *bespitten.* [from *spit.*] To dawb with spittle.

Bespo'ke. [*irreg. particip.* from *bespeak*; which see.]

To Bespo't. *v. a.* [from *spot.*] To mark with spots.

Mildew rests on the wheat, *bespotting* the stalks with a different colour from the natural. *Mortimer's Husbandry.*

To Bespre'ad. *v. a.* [from *spread.*] To spread over; to cover over.

His nuptial bed,
With curious needles wrought, and painted flowers *bespread.* *Dryden.*

The globe is equally *bespread*; so that no place wants proper inhabitants. *Derham's Physico-Theology.*

To Besprí'nkle. *v. a.* [from *sprinkle.*] To sprinkle over; to scatter over.

He indeed imitating the father poet, whose life he had also written, hath *besprinkled* his work with many fabulosities. *Brown's Vulgar Errours, b. i. c. 8.*

A purple flood
Flows from the trunk, that welters in the blood:
The bed *besprinkles*, and bedews the ground. *Dryden.*

To Bespu'tter. *v. a.* [from *sputter.*] To sputter over something; to dawb any thing by sputtering, or throwing out spittle upon it.

Best. *adj.* the *superlative* from *good.* [beꞇ, beꞇepa, beꞅꞇ, good, better, best, Saxon.]

1. Most good; that which has good qualities in the highest degree.

And he will take your fields, even the *best* of them, and give them to his servants. *1 Samuel*, viii. 14.

When the *best* things are not possible, the best may be made of those that are. *Hooker, b.* v. § 9.

When he is *best*, he is a little more than a man; and when he is worst, he is a little better than a beast. *Shakesp. M. of Ven.*

I think it a good argument to say, the infinitely wise God hath made it so: and therefore it is *best.* But it is too much confidence of our own wisdom, to say, I think it *best*, and therefore God hath made it so. *Locke.*

An evil intention perverts the *best* actions, and makes them sins. *Addison. Spectator*, N° 213.

2. *The best.* The utmost power; the strongest endeavour; the most; the highest perfection.

I profess not talking: only this,
Let each man do his *best.* *Shakesp. Henry* IV. *p.* i.
The duke did his *best* to come down. *Bacon's War with Sp.*
He does this to the *best* of his power. *Locke.*
My friend, said he, our sport is at the *best.* *Addis. Ovid.*

3. *To make the best.* To carry to its greatest perfection; to improve to the utmost.

Let there be freedom to carry their commodities where they may *make the best* of them, except there be some special cause of caution. *Bacon.*

His father left him an hundred drachmas; Alnaschar, in order to *make the best* of it, laid it out in glasses. *Addison. Spect.*

We set sail, and *made the best* of our way, till we were forced, by contrary winds, into St. Remo. *Addison on Italy.*

Best. *adv.* [from *well.*] In the highest degree of goodness.

He shall dwell in that place where he shall choose in one of thy gates, where it liketh him *best.* *Deut.* xxiii. 16.

Best is sometimes used in composition.

These latter *best-be-trust-spies* had some of them further instructions, to draw off the best friends and servants of Perkin, by making remonstrances to them, how weakly his enterprize and hopes were built. *Bacon's Henry* VII.

By this law of loving even our enemies, the christian religion discovers itself to be the most generous and *bestnatured* institution that ever was in the world. *Tillotson, sermon* v.

To Besta'in. *v. a.* [from *stain.*] To mark with stains; to spot.

We will not line his thin *bestained* cloke
With our pure honours. *Shakesp. King John.*

To Beste'ad. *v. a.* I *bested*; I have *bested.* [from *stead.*]

1. To profit.

Hence vain deluding joys,
The brood of folly, without father bred,
How little you *bestead*,
Or fill the fixed mind with all your toys. *Milton.*

2. To treat; to accommodate.

And they shall pass through it hardly *bestead*, and hungry. *Isaiah*, viii. 21.

Be'stial. *adj.* [from *beast.*]

1. Belonging to a beast, or to the class of beasts.

His wild disorder'd walk, his haggard eyes,
Did all the *bestial* citizens surprize. *Dryden's Hind and P.*

2. Having the qualities of beasts; brutal; below the dignity of reason or humanity; carnal.

I have lost the immortal part of myself, and what remains is *bestial.* *Shakesp. Othello.*

Moreover, urge his hateful luxury,
And *bestial* appetite, in change of lust. *Shakesp. Rich.* III.
For those, the race of Israel oft forsook
Their living strength, and, unfrequented, left
His righteous altar, bowing lowly down
To *bestial* gods. *Milton's Paradise Lost, b.* i. *l.* 435.

The things promised are not gross and carnal, such as may court and gratify the most *bestial* part of us. *Decay of Piety.*

Bestia'lity. *n. s.* [from *bestial.*] The quality of beasts; degeneracy from human nature.

What can be a greater absurdity, than to affirm *bestiality* to be the essence of humanity, and darkness the center of light? *Arbuthnot and Pope's Mart. Scribl.*

Be'stially. *adv.* [from *bestial.*] Brutally; in a manner below humanity.

To Besti'ck. *v. a.* preter. I *bestuck*, I have *bestuck.* [from *stick.*] To stick over with any thing; to mark any thing by infixing points or spots here and there.

Truth shall retire,
*Bestuck* with sland'rous darts; and works of faith
Rarely be found. *Milt. Par. Lost, b.* xii. *l.* 536.

To Besti'r. *v. a.* [from *stir.*]

1. To put into vigorous action. It is seldom used otherwise than with the reciprocal pronoun.

As when men wont to watch
On duty, sleeping found by whom they dread,
Rouze and *bestir themselves* ere well awake. *Milton.*
*Bestirs her* then, and from each tender stalk
Whatever earth, all-bearing mother, yields,
She gathers. *Par. Lost, b.* v.

But, as a dog that turns the spit,
*Bestirs himself*, and plies his feet
To climb the wheel, but all in vain,
His own weight brings him down again. *Hudibras, p.* ii. *c.* iii.

What aileth them, that they must needs *bestir themselves* to get in air, to maintain the creature's life? *Ray on Creation.*

2. It is used by *Shakespeare* with a common word.

I am scarce in breath, my lord.—No marvel you have so *bestirred* your valour, you cowardly rascal! *Shakesp. King Lear.*

To BESTO'W. *v. a.* [*besteden*, Dutch.]

1. To give; to confer upon.

All men would willingly have yielded him praise; but his nature was such as to *bestow* it upon himself, before any could give it. *Sidney.*

All the dedicate things of the house of the Lord did they *bestow* upon Baalim. 2 *Chron.* xxiv. 7.

Sir Julius Cæsar had, in his office, the disposition of the six clarks places; which he had *bestowed* to such persons as he thought fit. *Clarendon.*

2. To give as charity.

Our Saviour doth plainly witness, that there should not be as much as a cup of cold water *bestowed* for his sake, without reward. *Hooker, b.* ii. § 8.

And though he was unsatisfied in getting,
Which was a sin; yet in *bestowing*, madam,
He was most princely. *Shakesp. Henry* VIII.

Spain to your gift alone her Indies owes;
For what the pow'rful takes not, he *bestows.* *Dryden.*

You always exceed expectations: as if yours was not your own, but to *bestow* on wanting merit. *Dryden's Fables, Ded.*

3. To give in marriage.

Good rev'rend father, make my person yours;
And tell me how you would *bestow* yourself. *Shakesp.*

I could have *bestowed* her upon a fine gentleman, who extremely admired her. *Tatler*, N° 75.

4. To give as a present.

Pure oil and incense on the fire they throw,
And fat of victims which his friends *bestow.* *Dryden.*

5. To apply.

The sea was not the duke of Marlborough's element; otherwise the whole force of the war would infallibly have been *bestowed* there. *Swift.*

6. To lay out upon.

And thou shalt *bestow* that money for whatsoever thy soul lusteth after, for oxen, for sheep, or for wine. *Deut.* xiv. 26.

7. To lay up; to stow; to place.

And when he came to the tower, he took them from their hand, and *bestowed* them in the house. 2 *Kings*, v. 24.

Besto'wer. *n. s.* [from *bestow.*] Giver; he that confers any thing; disposer.

They all agree in making one supreme God; and that there are several beings that are to be worshipped under him; some as the *bestowers* of thrones, but subordinate to the Supreme. *Stillingfl.*

Bestra'ught. *particip.* [Of this *participle* I have not found the *verb*; by analogy we may derive it from *bestract*; perhaps it is corrupted from *distraught.*] Distracted; mad; out of one's senses; out of one's wits.

Ask Marian, the fat alewife, if she knew me not. What!
I am not *bestraught.* *Shakesp. Tam. the Shrew.*

To Bestre'w. *v. a.* particip. pass. *bestrewed*, or *bestrown.* [from *strew.*] To sprinkle over.

So thick *bestrown*,
Abject and lost lay these, covering the flood. *Par. Lost, b.* i.

To Bestri'de. *v. a.* I *bestrid*; I have *bestrid*, or *bestridden.* [from *stride.*]

1. To stride over any thing; to have any thing between one's legs.

Why

you with the rest,
Causeless have laid disgraces on my head
And with your best endeavours have stirred up
my liefest liege to be mine enemy

Bestadde for bestead [Stay]
the pret of bestay
To hinder, to prevent, to indispose,
to disorder, not as Spens. Glos. would
have it Ordered, disposed.

What e foul evil hath thee so bestad?
Whilom thou wast peregal to the best,
And wont to make the shepherds glad
With piping & dancing did pass the rest
Mischief mought to that mischance befall
That so hath reft us of our merriment
But reeds me with pain doth thee apall

To apply one's thoughts or mind to any thing
That other on his friends his thoughts bestows
The covetous worldling in his anxious mind
Thinks only on the wealth he left behind
To dispose; to arrange in Order Dryd.

a ~~Through the Hall there walk'd~~
A jolly yeoman, ~~Marshal of the same~~
Whose name was Appetite, he did bestow
Both guests & meats, whenever in they came
~~And knew them how to Order without blame~~
Spens

Having with before the thing bestowed
Sour eyed disdain & discord shall bestow
The union of their bed with weed so loathly
That you shall hate it Shak.

We hear our bloody Cousins are bestowed
b In England & in Ireland not confessing
Their cruel parricide filling their hearers
With strange invention Shak

c In fenced towrs bestowed is their grain
Before thou camst this kingdom to invade Fairf
If I had had time to have made new liverys
I would have bestowed the thousand I borrowed
But it is no matter. Shak.

This Arm had aided yours this hand bestrown
Our floors with blood, and push'd the Slaughter on
~~Nor had the Sire been separate from the Son.~~
Pop. Odyss.

IL facing 3A2v

4

7

6 ‡

Thy on his shield like Iron Sledges bet
T. 2. 2.2. 22

6 ‡

To fall out; to happen
Whatever fortune good or bad betide
No time shall find me wanting to my truth
Dryd.

Betight pret past [illegible]
Say it out Diggon whatever it hight
For nought but well mought him betight
He is so meek wise merciable
And with his Word his work is convenable
Spens. Pa.

To indicate
All these things are fleshy & plump & have
great eyes, all which betoken moisture
retaind and not drawn out Bacon

Betoken v. s.
is retaind in Scotland the same
with token

Why, man, he doth *bestride* the narrow world
Like a colossus. *Shakesp. Julius Cæsar.*
Make him *bestride* the ocean, and mankind
Ask his consent, to use the sea and wind. *Waller.*

2. To step over.

That I see thee here,
Thou noble thing! more dances my rapt heart,
Than when I first my wedded mistress saw
*Bestride* my threshold. *Shakesp. Coriolanus.*

3. It is often used of riding.

He *bestrides* the lazy pacing clouds,
And sails upon the bosom of the air. *Shakesp. Rom. and Jul.*
That horse, that thou so often hast *bestrid:*
~~That horse, that I so carefully have dress'd.~~ *Shakesp. R. II.*
Venetians do not more uncouthly ride,
Than did their lubber state mankind *bestride.* *Dryden.*
The bounding steed you pompously *bestride,*
Shares with his lord the pleasure and the pride. *Pope.*

4. It is used sometimes of a man standing over something which he defends.

He *bestrid*
An o'erpress'd Roman, and i' th' consul's view
Slew three opposers: ~~Tarquin's self he met,~~
~~And struck him on his knee.~~ *Shakesp. Coriolanus.*

Let us rather
Hold fast the mortal sword; and, like good men,
*Bestride* our downfaln birthdom: *Shakesp. Macbeth.*

If thou see me down in the battle, and *bestride* me, so; 'tis a point of friendship. *Shakesp. Henry* IV. *p.* i.

He doth *bestride* a bleeding land,
Gasping for life, ~~under great Bolingbroke.~~ *Shak. Henry* IV.

To BESTU'D. *v. a.* [from *stud.*] To adorn with studs, or shining prominences.

Th' unsought diamonds
Would so emblaze the forehead of the deep,
And so *bestud* with stars, that they below
Would grow inur'd to light. *Milton.*

BET. *n. s.* [pebbian, to wager; pet, a wager, Sax. from which the etymologists derive *bet.* I should rather imagine it to come from betan, to mend, encrease, or *better,* as a *bet* encreases the original wager.] A wager; something laid to be won upon certain conditions.

The hoary fool, who many days
Has struggl'd with continu'd sorrow,
Renews his hope, and blindly lays
The desp'rate *bet* upon tomorrow. *Prior.*

His pride was in piquette,
Newmarket fame, and judgment at a *bet:* *Pope.*

To BET. *v. a.* [from the noun.] To wager; to stake at a wager.

He drew a good bow: and dead? John of Gaunt loved him well, and *betted* much upon his head. *Shakesp. Henry* IV. *p.* ii.

He flies the court for want of clothes,
Cries out 'gainst cocking, since he cannot *bet.* *B. Johnson.*

The god, unhappily engag'd,
Complain'd, and sigh'd, and cry'd, and fretted,
Lost ev'ry earthly thing he *betted.* *Prior.*

BET. The old preterite of *beat.*

He staid for a better hour, till the hammer had wrought and *bet* the party more pliant. *Bacon's Henry* VII.

To BETA'KE. *v. a.* preter. I *betook;* part. pass. *betaken.* [from *take.*]

1. To take; to seize: an obsolete sense.

Then to his hands that writ he did *betake,*
Which he disclosing read. *Fairy Queen, b.* i. *c.* xii. *st.* 25.

2. To have recourse to; with the reciprocal pronoun.

The adverse party *betaking itself* to such practices as men embrace, when they behold things brought to desperate extremities. *Hooker, b.* iv. § 14.

~~Thou tyrant!~~
Do not repent these things; for they are heavier
Than all thy woes can stir: therefore *betake thee*
To nothing but despair. *Shakesp. Winter's Tale.*

The rest, in imitation, to like arms
*Betook them,* and the neighb'ring hills up tore.
*Milton's ~~Paradise Lost, b.* vi. *l.* 663.~~*

3. To apply; with the reciprocal pronoun.

With ease such fond chimeras we pursue,
As fancy frames for fancy to subdue:
But when *ourselves* to action we *betake,*
It shuns the mint, like gold that chymists make. *Dryden.*

As my observations have been the light whereby I have hitherto steer'd my course, so I here *betake myself* to them again. *Woodward's Natural History.*

4. To move; to remove.

Soft she withdrew; and, like a wood nymph light,
Oread or Dryad, or of Delia's train,
*Betook her* to the groves. *Milton's Paradise Lost, b.* ix. *l.* 389.

They both *betook them* several ways;
Both to destroy. *Milton's Paradise Lost, b.* x. *l.* 610.

To BETE'EM. *v. a.* [from *teem.*] To bring forth; to bestow; to give.

So would I, said th' enchanter, glad and fain
*Beteem* to you his sword, you to defend;
But that this weapon's pow'r I well have kend,
To be contrary to the work that ye intend. *Fairy Q. b.* ii.

Belike for want of rain; which I could well
*Beteem* them from the tempest of mine eyes.
*Shakesp. ~~Midsummer Night's Dream.~~*

To BETHI'NK. *v. a.* I *bethought;* I have *bethought.* [from *think.*] To recal to reflection; to bring back to consideration, or recollection. It is generally used with the reciprocal pronoun, and *of* before the subject of thought.

They were sooner in danger than they could almost *bethink themselves of* change. *Sidney, b.* ii.

I have *bethought me of* another fault. *Shak. Meas. for M.*

I, better *bethinking myself,* and misliking his determination, gave him this order. *Raleigh's Essays.*

He himself,
Insatiable of glory, had lost all:
Yet *of* another plea *bethought him* soon. *Parad. Regained.*

The nets were laid, yet the birds could never *bethink themselves,* till hamper'd, and past recovery. *L'Estrange.*

Cherippus, then in time *yourself bethink,*
And what your rags will yield by auction sink. *Dryden.*

A little consideration may allay his heat, and make him *bethink himself,* whether this attempt be worth the venture. *Locke.*

BE'THLEHEM. *n. s.* [See BEDLAM.] An hospital for lunaticks.

BE'THLEHEMITE. *n. s.* [See BEDLAMITE.] A lunatick; an inhabitant of a madhouse.

BETHO'UGHT. *particip.* [from *bethink;* which see.]

To BETHRA'L. *v. a.* [from *thrall.*] To enslave; to conquer; to bring into subjection.

Ne let that wicked woman 'scape away,
For she it is that did my lord *bethral.* *Shakesp. King John.*

To BETHU'MP. *v. a.* [from *thump.*] To beat; to lay blows upon: a ludicrous word.

I was never so *bethumpt* with words,
Since first I call'd my brother's father dad. *Shak. King John.*

To BETI'DE. *v. n.* pret. *It betided,* or *betid;* part. pass. *betid.* [from ꞇiꝺ, Sax. See TIDE.]

1. To happen to; to befal; to bechance; whether good or bad.

Said he then to the Palmer, reverend sire,
What great misfortune hath *betid* this knight? *Fairy Queen.*

But say, if our deliverer up to heav'n
Must reascend, what will *betide* the few,
His faithful, left among th' unfaithful herd,
The enemies of truth? *Milton's Paradise Lost, b.* xii. *l.* 480.

2. Sometimes it has *to.*

Neither know I,
What is *betid to* Cloten; but remain
Perplext in all. *Shakesp. Cymbeline.*

3. To come to pass; to fall out; to happen.

She, when her turn was come her tale to tell,
Told of a strange adventure that *betided,*
Betwixt the fox and th' ape by him misguided. *Spens. Hubb.*

In winter's tedious nights, sit by the fire
With good old folks, and let them tell thee tales
Of woful ages, long ago *betid.* *Shakesp. Richard* II.

Let me hear from thee by letters,
Of thy success in love; and what news else
*Betideth* here in absence of thy friend. *Sh. Two Gent. of Ver.*

4. To become.

If he were dead, what would *betide* of thee? *Sh. Rich.* III.

BETI'ME. } *adv.* [from *by* and *time;* that is, by the proper
BETI'MES. } time.]

1. Seasonably; early.

Send succours, lords, and stop the rage *betime.*
*Shakesp. ~~Henry* VI. *p.* ii.~~*

To measure life, learn thou *betimes,* and know
Toward solid good what leads the nearest way. *Par. Reg.*

2. Soon; before long time has passed.

Whiles they are weak, *betimes* with them contend;
For when they once to perfect strength do grow,
Strong wars they make. *Fairy Queen, b.* ii. *c.* iv. *st.* 34.

He tires *betimes,* that spurs too fast *betimes.* *Sh. Rich.* II.

There be some have an over early ripeness in their years, which fadeth *betimes:* these are first, such as have brittle wits, the edge whereof is soon turned. *Bacon's Essays.*

Remember thy Creator in the days of thy youth; that is, enter upon a religious course *betimes.* *Tillotson, sermon* i.

Short is the date, alas! of modern rhymes;
And 'tis but just to let them live *betimes.* *Pope's Essay on Crit.*

3. Early in the day.

He that drinks all night, and is hanged *betimes* in the morning, may sleep the sounder next day. *Sh. Measure for Measure.*

They rose *betimes* in the morning, ~~and offered sacrifice.~~
1 *Macc.* iv. 52.

BE'TLE. ~~BE'TRE.~~ *n. s.* An Indian plant, called water pepper. *Dict.*

To BETO'KEN. *v. a.* [from *token.*]

1. To signify; to mark; to represent.

We know not wherefore churches should be the worse, if, at this

this time, when they are delivered into God's own possession, ceremonies fit to *betoken* such intents, and to accompany such actions, be usual. *Hooker, b. v. § 12.*

2. To foreshew; to presignify.

The kindling azure, and the mountain's brow,
Illum'd with fluid gold, his near approach
*Betoken* glad. *Thomson's Summer, l. 80.*

Be'tony. *n. s.* [*betonica*, Lat.] A plant.

The leaves are green, rough, and crenated on the edges: the flowers are disposed in a spike; the upper crest of the flower is advanced, and divided into two segments; the beard, or lower part of the flower, is divided into three, and the middle segment is bifid; each flower is, for the most part, succeeded by four naked seeds. The species are, 1. Common or wood *betony*. 2. *Betony*, with a white flower. 3. Greater Danish *betony*. The first is very common in woods and shady places, and is greatly esteemed as a vulnerary herb. *Millar.*

Beto'ok. [*irreg. pret.* from *betake*; which see.]

To Beto'ss. *v. a.* [from *toss.*] To disturb; to agitate; to put into violent motion.

What said my man, when my *betossed* soul
Did not attend him as we rode? *Shakesp. Romeo and Juliet.*

To BETRA'Y. *v. a.* [*trahir*, Fr.]

1. To give into the hands of enemies by treachery, or breach of trust.

If ye be come to *betray* me to mine enemies, seeing there is no wrong in mine hands, the God of our fathers look thereon, and rebuke it. *1 Chron.* xii. 17.

Jesus said unto them, the Son of man shall be *betrayed* into the hands of men. *Matt.* xvii. 22.

For fear is nothing else but a *betraying* of the succours which reason offereth. *Wisdom*, xvii. 12.

He was not to be won, either by promise or reward, to *betray* the city. *Knolles's History of the Turks.*

2. To discover that which has been entrusted to secrecy.

3. To make known something that were better concealed.

Be swift to hear, but be cautious of your tongue, lest you *betray* your ignorance. *Watts's Improvement of the Mind.*

4. To make liable to fall into something inconvenient.

His abilities created in him great confidence; and this was like enough to *betray* him to great errours, and many enemies. *King Charles.*

The bright genius is ready to be so forward, as often *betrays* itself into great errours in judgment. *Watts.*

5. To show; to discover; in a neutral sense.

The Veian and the Gabian tow'rs shall fall,
And one promiscuous ruin cover all;
Nor, after length of years, a stone *betray*
The place where once the very ruins lay. *Addison on Italy.*

Betra'yer. *n. s.* [from *betray.*] He that betrays; a traitor.

The wise man doth so say of fear, that it is a *betrayer* of the forces of reasonable understanding. *Hooker, b. v. § 3.*

You cast down your courage through fear, the *betrayer* of all succours which reason can afford. *Sir J. Hayward.*

They are only a few *betrayers* of their country; they are to purchase coin, perhaps, at half price, and vend it among us to the ruin of the publick. *Swift.*

To Betri'm. *v. a.* [from *trim.*] To deck; to dress; to grace; to adorn; to embellish; to beautify; to decorate.

Thy banks with pionied and tulip'd brims,
Which spungy April at thy hest *betrims*,
To make cold nymphs chaste crowns. *Shakesp. Tempest.*

To Betro'th. *v. a.* [from *troth*; *betrowen*, Dutch.]

1. To contract to any one, in order to marriage; to affiance.

He, in the first flower of my freshest age,
*Betrothed* me unto the only heir
Of a most mighty king, most rich and sage. *Fairy Q. b.* i.

To her, my lord,
Was I *betrothed*, ere I Hermia saw. *Shakesp. Midsum. N. Dr.*

By soul's publick promise she
Was sold then, and *betroth'd* to Victory. *Cowley's Davideis.*

2. To unite any one to another by promise of marriage.

And what man is there that hath *betrothed* a wife, and hath not taken her? let him go and return unto his house. *Deut.* xx. 7.

3. To nominate to a bishoprick, in order to consecration.

If any person be consecrated a bishop to that church, whereunto he was not before *betrothed*, he shall not receive the habit of consecration, as not being canonically promoted. *Ayliffe.*

To Betru'st. *v. a.* [from *trust.*] To entrust; to put into the power of another, in confidence of fidelity.

*Betrust* him with all the good, which our own capacity will allow us, or his sufficiency encourage us to hope for, either in this life, or that to come. *Grew's Cosmologia Sacra, b.* iii. *c.* 5.

Whatsoever you would *betrust* to your memory, let it be disposed in a proper method. *Watts's Improvement of the Mind.*

Be'tter. *adj.* The *comparative* of *good.* [bet, *good*, betera, *better*, Sax.] Having good qualities in a greater degree than something else. See Good.

He has a horse *better* than the Neapolitan's; a *better* bad habit of frowning than the count Palatine. *Shakesp. Merchant of Venice.*

I have seen *better* faces in my time,
Than stand on any shoulders that I see
Before me at this instant. *Shakesp. King Lear.*

Having a desire to depart, and be with Christ; which is far *better*. *Phil.* i. 23.

*The* Better.

1. The superiority; the advantage; with the particle *of* before him, or that, over which the advantage is gained.

The Corinthians that morning, as the days before, had *the better*. *Sidney, b.* ii.

The voyage of Drake and Hawkins was unfortunate; yet, in such sort, as doth not break our prescription, to have had *the better of* the Spaniards. *Bacon's War with Spain.*

Dionysius, his countryman, in an epistle to Pompey, after an express comparison, affords him *the better of* Thucydides. *Brown's Vulgar Errours, b.* i. *c.* 8.

You think fit
To get *the better of* me, and you shall;
Since you will have it so—I will be yours. *Southerne.*

The gentleman had always so much *the better of* the satyrist, that the persons touched did not know where to fix their resentment. *Prior, Preface to his Poems.*

2. Improvement; as, *for the better*, so as to improve it.

If I have altered him any where *for the better*, I must at the same time acknowledge, that I could have done nothing without him. *Dryden's Fab. Preface.*

Be'tter. *adv.* [comparative of *well.*] Well, in a greater degree.

Then it was *better* with me than now. *Hos.* vii.

*Better* a mechanick rule were stretched or broken, than a great beauty were omitted. *Dryd. Virg. Dedication.*

The *better* to understand the extent of our knowledge, one thing is to be observed. *Locke.*

He that would know the idea of infinity, cannot do *better*, than by considering to what infinity is attributed. *Locke.*

To Be'tter. *v. a.* [from the noun.]

1. To improve; to meliorate.

The very cause of his taking upon him our nature, was to *better* the quality, and to advance the condition thereof. *Hooker, b.* viii. § 54.

He is furnished with my opinion, which is *bettered* with his own learning. *Shakesp. Merchant of Venice.*

Heir to all his lands and goods,
Which I have *better'd*, rather than decreas'd.
*Shakesp. Taming of the Shrew.*

But Jonathan, to whom both hearts were known,
With well-tim'd zeal, and with an artful care,
Restor'd, and *better'd* soon, the nice affair. *Cowley's David.*

The church of England, the purest and best reformed church in the world; so well reformed, that it will be found easier to alter than to *better* its constitution. *South.*

The Romans took pains to hew out a passage for these lakes, to discharge themselves, for the *bettering* of the air. *Addison.*

2. To surpass; to exceed.

The works of nature do always aim at that which cannot be *bettered*. *Hooker, b.* i. § 5.

He hath born himself beyond the promise of his age; he hath, indeed, better *bettered* expectation, than you must expect of me to tell you. *Shakesp. Much ado about Nothing.*

What you do
Still *betters* what is done; when you speak sweet,
I'd have you do it ever. *Shakesp. Winter's Tale.*

3. To advance.

The king thought his honour would suffer, during a treaty, to *better* a party. *Bacon's Henry* VII.

Be'tter. *n. s.* [from the adjective.] Superiour in goodness.

Their *betters* would be hardly found, if they did not live among men, but in a wilderness by themselves. *Hooker, b.* i.

The courtesy of nations allows you my *better*, in that you are the first-born. *Shakesp. As you like it.*

That ye thus hospitably live,
Is mighty grateful to your *betters*,
And makes e'en gods themselves your debtors. *Prior.*

I have some gold and silver by me, and shall be able to make a shift, when many of my *betters* are starving. *Swift.*

Be'ttor. *n. s.* [from *to bet.*] One that lays betts or wagers.

I observed a stranger among them, of a genteeler behaviour than ordinary; but notwithstanding he was a very fair *bettor*, nobody would take him up. *Addison. Spectator*, No 126.

Be'tty. *n. s.* [probably a cant word, without etymology.] An instrument to break open doors.

Record the stratagems, the arduous exploits, and the nocturnal scalades of needy heroes, describing the powerful *betty*, or the artful picklock. *Arbuthnot's History of J. Bull.*

Betwe'en. *prep.* [betpeonan, betpinan, Saxon; from the original word tpa, *two.*]

1. In the intermediate space.

What modes
Of smell the headlong lioness *between*,
And hound sagacious on the tainted green? *Pope.*

2. From

~~To lead in a way by any means~~ a

The emission of the loose & Adventitious
Moisture doth betray the radical Moisture
and carrieth it for Company Bac.

To catch with a Snare or trap b
With gins betray the fitchat & the Moldiwarp
Walton Ang.

These ingenious exercises betrayed in
him an extraordinary quickness of
wit and learning Peacham

~~To seize with as infection; to taint~~ c
Stinks which the Nostrils strait abhor are
not the most pernicious but such Airs as
have some similitude with mans body, and
insinuate themselves & betray the Spirits
Bac.

Stet

Unlucky bettors will lose on both sides
Shefiel Buck.

IL facing 3B$^{v}$

p ‡

To bewonder v. a. | from wonder. |

To amaze, astonish.

We stood bewondered, another while delighted with the rare bravery ~~thereof, till seeing such streams of blood as threatned a drowning life, we galloped toward them to part them~~ Sidney b. 2.



o ‡

~~To guard against in order to avoid a thing~~

Vapours fired do shew the Mariner

From what point of his Compass to beware

Impetuous winds Milt.

IL facing 3B2[r]

2. From one to another; noting intercourse.

He should think himself unhappy, if things should go so *between* them, as he should not be able to acquit himself of ingratitude towards them both. *Bacon's Henry* VII.

3. Belonging to two in partnership.

I ask, whether Castor and Pollux, with only one soul *between* them, which thinks and perceives in one what the other is never conscious of, are not two distinct persons? *Locke.*

4. Bearing relation to two.

If there be any discord or suits *between* them and any of the family, they are compounded and appeased. *Bacon's Atlantis.*

Friendship requires, that it be *between* two at least; and there can be no friendship where there are not two friends. *South.*

5. In separation, or distinction of one from the other.

Their natural constitutions put so wide a difference *between* some men, that art would never master. *Locke.*

Children quickly distinguish *between* what is required of them, and what not. *Locke.*

6. *Between* is properly used of two, and *among* of more; but perhaps this accuracy is not always preserved.

BETWI'XT. *prep.* [betƿyx, Saxon. It has the same signification with *between*, and is indifferently used for it.]

1. In the midst of two:

Hard by, a cottage chimney smokes,
From *betwixt* two aged oaks. *Milton.*

Methinks, like two black storms on either hand,
Our Spanish army and your Indians stand;
This only place *betwixt* the clouds is clear. *Dryd. Ind. Emp.*

If contradicting interests could be mixt,
Nature herself has cast a bar *betwixt*. *Dryden's Aurengzebe.*

2. From one to another.

Five years since there was some speech of marriage
*Betwixt* myself and her. *Shakesp. Measure for Measure.*

BE'VEL. } *n. s.* In masonry and joinery, a kind of square, one
BE'VIL. } leg of which is frequently crooked, according to the sweep of an arch or vault. It is moveable on a point or centre, and so may be set to any angle. An angle that is not square, is called a *bevil angle*, whether it be more obtuse, or more acute, than a right angle. *Builder's Dict.*

Their houses are very ill built, their walls *bevil*, without one right angle in any apartment. *Swift's Gulliver's Travels.*

To BE'VEL. *v. a.* [from the noun.] To cut to a bevel angle.

These rabbets are ground square; but the rabbets on the groundsel are *bevelled* downwards, that rain may the freelier fall off. *Moxon's Mechanical Exercises.*

BE'VER. See BEAVER.

BE'VERAGE. *n. s.* [from *bevere*, to drink, Ital.]

1. Drink; liquour to be drank in general.

I am his cupbearer;
If from me he have wholesome *beverage*,
Account me not your servant. *Shakesp. Winter's Tale.*

Grains, pulses, and all sorts of fruits, either bread or *beverage*, may be made almost of all. *Brown's Vulgar Errours, b.* iii.

A pleasant *beverage* he prepar'd before,
Of wine and honey mix'd. *Dryden's Fables.*

The coarse lean gravel on the mountain sides,
Scarce dewy *bev'rage* for the bees provides. *Dryden's Virgil.*

2. *Beverage*, or water cyder, is made by putting the mure into a fat, adding water, as you desire it stronger or smaller. The water should stand forty eight hours on it, before you press it; when it is pressed, tun it up immediately. *Mortimer's Husb.*

3. A treat upon wearing a new suit of cloaths.

4. A treat at first coming into a prison, called also *garnish*.

BE'VY. *n. s.* [*beva*, Ital.]

1. A flock of birds.

2. A company; an assembly.

And in the midst thereof, upon the floor,
A lovely *bevy* of fair ladies sat,
Courted of many a jolly paramour. *Fairy Queen, b.* ii. *c.* ix.

They on the plain
Long had not walk'd, when, from the tents, behold
A *bevy* of fair women. *Milton's Paradise Lost, b.* xi. *l.* 582.

Nor rode the nymph alone,
Around a *bevy* of bright damsels shone. *Pope's Odyssey.*

To BEWA'IL. *v. a.* [from *wail.*] To bemoan; to lament; to express sorrow for.

In this city he
Hath widow'd and unchilded many a one,
Which to this hour *bewail* the injury. *Shakesp. Coriolanus.*

Thy ambition,
Thou scarlet sin, robb'd this *bewailing* land
Of noble Buckingham, my father in law. *Shakesp. H.* VIII.

Yet wiser Ennius gave command to all
His friends, not to *bewail* his funeral. *Sir J. Denham.*

I cannot but *bewail*, as in their first principles, the miseries and calamities of our children. *Addison. Spectator*, N° 127.

To BEWA'RE. *v. n.* [from *be* and *ware*, or *wary*; that is, cautious: thus, in an old treatise, I have found, *be ye ware*. See WARY. ȝeƿarian, Saxon; *warer*, Danish.]

1. To regard with caution; to be suspicious of danger from: generally the particle *of* goes before the thing which excites caution.

You must *beware of* drawing or painting clouds, winds, and thunder, towards the bottom of your piece. *Dryden's Dufres.*

Every one ought to be very careful to *beware* what he admits for a principle. *Locke.*

Warn'd by the sylph, oh, pious maid, *beware!*
This to disclose is all thy guardian can;
*Beware of* all, but most *beware of* man. *Pope's Rape of the L.*

2. It is observable, that it is only used in such forms of speech as admit the word *be*: thus we say, *he may beware, let him beware; he will beware*; but not, *he did beware*, or *he has been ware*.

To BEWE'EP. *v. a.* [from *weep.*] To weep over or upon; to bedew with tears.

Old fond eyes,
*Beweep* this cause again; I'll pluck ye out,
And cast you, with the waters that you lose,
To temper clay. *Shakesp. King Lear.*

Larded all with sweet flowers,
Which *bewept* to the grave did go,
With true love showers. *Shakesp. Hamlet.*

To BEWE'T. *v. a.* [from *wet.*] To wet; to moisten; to bedew; to water.

His napkin, with his true tears all *bewet*,
Can do no service on her sorrowful cheeks.
*Shakesp. Titus Andronicus.*

To BEWI'LDER. *v. a.* [from *wild.*] To lose in pathless places; to confound for want of a plain road; to perplex; to entangle; to puzzle.

We parted thus; I homeward sped my way,
*Bewilder'd* in the wood till dawn of day. *Dryden's Fables.*

We no solution of our question find;
Your words *bewilder*, not direct the mind. *Blackmore.*

Our understanding traces 'em in vain,
Lost and *bewilder'd* in the fruitless search. *Addison's Cato.*

It is good sometimes to lose and *bewilder* ourselves in such studies. *Watts's Improvement of the Mind.*

To BEWI'TCH. *v. a.* [from *witch.*]

1. To injure by witchcraft, or fascination, or charms.

Look how I am *bewitch'd*; behold, mine arm
Is like a blasted sapling wither'd up. *Shakesp. Richard* III.

I have forsworn his company hourly this twenty year, and yet I am *bewitched* with the rogue's company. If the rascal has not given me medicines to make me love him, I'll be hang'd. *Shakesp. Henry* IV.

My flocks are free from love, yet look so thin;
What magick has *bewitch'd* the woolly dams,
And what ill eyes beheld the tender lambs? *Dryden's Virgil.*

2. To charm; to please to such a degree, as to take away the power of resistance.

Doth even beauty beautify,
And most *bewitch* the wretched eye. *Sidney, b.* ii.

The charms of poetry our souls *bewitch*;
The curse of writing is an endless itch. *Dryden's Juvenal.*

I do not know, by the character that is given of her works, whether it is not for the benefit of mankind that they were lost; they were filled with such *bewitching* tenderness and rapture, that it might have been dangerous to have given them a reading. *Addison. Spectator*, N° 223.

BEWI'TCHERY. *n. s.* [from *bewitch.*] Fascination; charm; resistless prevalence.

There is a certain *bewitchery*, or fascination in words, which makes them operate with a force beyond what we can give an account of. *South.*

BEWI'TCHMENT. *n. s.* [from *bewitch.*] Fascination; power of charming.

I will counterfeit the *bewitchment* of some popular man, and give it bountifully to the desirers. *Shakesp. Coriolanus.*

To BEWRA'Y. *v. a.* [ƿregan, beƿregan, Saxon.]

1. To betray; to discover perfidiously.

Fair feeling words he wisely 'gan display,
And, for her humour fitting purpose, fain
To tempt the cause itself for to *bewray*. *Fairy Queen, b.* i.

2. To shew; to make visible: this word is now little in use.

She saw a pretty blush in Philodea's cheeks *bewray* a modest discontentment. *Sidney.*

Men do sometimes *bewray* that by deeds, which to confess they are hardly drawn. *Hooker, b.* i. § 7.

Next look on him that seems for counsel fit,
Whose silver locks *bewray* his store of days. *Fairfax, b.* iii.

BEWRA'YER. *n. s.* [from *bewray.*] Betrayer; discoverer; divulger.

When a friend is turned into an enemy, and a *bewrayer* of secrets, the world is just enough to accuse the perfidiousness of the friend. *Addison. Spectator*, N° 225.

BEYO'ND. *prep.* [beȝeond, beȝeondan, Saxon.]

1. Before; at a distance not yet reached.

What's fame? a fancy'd life in others breath,
A thing *beyond* us, ev'n before our death
Just what you hear, you have. *Pope's Essay on Man.*

2. On the farther side of.

Neither is it *beyond* the sea, that thou shouldst say, who shall go over the sea for us, and bring it unto us. *Deut.* xxx. 13.

Now

Now we are on land, we are but between death and life; for we are *beyond* the old world and the new. *Bacon's New Atlantis.*

We cannot think men *beyond* ſea will part with their money for nothing. *Locke.*

3. Farther onward than.

He that ſees a dark and ſhady grove,
Stays not, but looks *beyond* it on the ſky. *Herbert.*

4. Paſt; out of the reach of.

*Beyond* the infinite and boundleſs reach
Of mercy, if thou did'ſt this deed of death,
Art thou damn'd, Hubert. *Shakeſp. King John.*

Yet theſe declare
Thy goodneſs *beyond* thought, and pow'r divine.
*Milton's Paradiſe Loſt, b. v. l. 158.*

The juſt, wiſe, and good God, neither does, nor can require of man any thing that is impoſſible, or naturally *beyond* his power to do. *South.*

Conſider the ſituation of our earth; it is placed ſo conveniently, that plants flouriſh, and animals live; this is matter of fact, and *beyond* all diſpute. *Bentley's Sermons.*

5. Above; exceeding to a greater degree than.

Timotheus was a man both in power, riches, parentage, goodneſs, and love of his people, *beyond* any of the great men of my country. *Sidney.*

One thing, in this enormous accident, is, I muſt confeſs, to me *beyond* all wonder. *Wotton.*

To his expences, *beyond* his income, add debauchery, idleneſs, and quarrels amongſt his ſervants, whereby his manufactures are diſturbed, and his buſineſs neglected. *Locke.*

As far as they carry conviction to any man's underſtanding, my labours may be of uſe: *beyond* the evidence it carries with it, I adviſe him not to follow any man's interpretation. *Locke.*

6. Above in excellence.

His ſatires are incomparably *beyond* Juvenal's; if to laugh and rally, is to be preferred to railing and declaiming. *Dryden.*

7. Remote from; not within the ſphere of.

With equal mind, what happens, let us bear;
Nor joy, nor grieve too much for things *beyond* our care.
*Dryden's Fables.*

8. *To go beyond*, is to deceive; to circumvent.

She made earneſt benefit of his jeſt, forcing him to do her ſuch ſervices, as were both cumberſome and coſtly; while he ſtill thought he *went beyond* her, becauſe his heart did not commit the idolatry. *Sidney.*

That no man *go beyond*, and defraud his brother in any matter. *1 Theſſ.* iv. 6.

BE'ZEL. } *n. ſ.* That part of a ring in which the ſtone is
BE'ZIL. } fixed.

BE'ZOAR. *n. ſ.* [from *pa*, againſt, and *zahar*, poiſon, Perſick.] A medicinal ſtone, formerly in high eſteem as an antidote, and brought from the Eaſt Indies, where it is ſaid to be found in the dung of an animal of the goat kind, called *pazan*; the ſtone being formed in its belly, and growing to the ſize of an acorn, and ſometimes to that of a pigeon's egg. Were the real virtues of this ſtone anſwereable to its reputed ones, it were doubtleſs a panacea. Indeed its rarity, and the peculiar manner of its formation, which is now ſuppoſed to be fabulous, have perhaps contributed as much to its reputation as its intrinſick worth. At preſent, it begins to be diſcarded in the practice of medicine, as of no efficacy at all. There are alſo ſome occidental *bezoars* brought from Peru, which are reckoned inferiour to the oriental. The name of this ſtone is alſo applied to ſeveral chymical compoſitions, deſigned for antidotes, or counter-poiſons; as mineral, ſolar, and jovial *bezoars*. *Savary. Chambers.*

BEZOA'RDICK. *adj.* [from *bezoar.*] Medicines compounded with *bezoar*.

The *bezoardicks* are neceſſary to promote ſweat, and drive forth the putrefied particles. *Floyer on the Humours.*

BIA'NGULATED. } *adj.* [from *binus* and *angulus*, Lat.] Having
BIA'NGULOUS. } corners or angles. *Dict.*

BI'AS. *n. ſ.* [*biais*, Fr. ſaid to come from *bihay*, an old Gauliſh word, ſignifying *croſs*, or *thwart.*]

1. The weight lodged on one ſide of a bowl, which turns it from the ſtrait line.

Madam, we'll play at bowls——
——'Twill make me think the world is full of rubs,
And that my fortune runs againſt the *bias*. *Shakeſp. R.* II.

2. Any thing which turns a man to a particular courſe; or gives the direction to his meaſures.

You have been miſtook:
But nature to her *bias* drew in that. *Shakeſp. Twelfth Night.*

This is that boaſted *bias* of thy mind,
By which one way to dulneſs 'tis inclin'd. *Dryden's Mackfl.*

Morality influences mens lives, and gives a *bias* to all their actions. *Locke.*

Wit and humour, that expoſe vice and folly, furniſh uſeful diverſions. Raillery, under ſuch regulations, unbends the mind from ſeverer contemplations, without throwing it off from its proper *bias*. *Addiſon's Freeholder*, Nº 45.

Thus nature gives us, let it check our pride,
The virtue neareſt to our vice ally'd;
Reaſon the *bias* turns to good or ill. *Pope's Eſſay on Man.*

3. Propenſion; inclination.

As for the religion of our poet, he ſeems to have ſome little *bias* towards the opinions of Wickliff. *Dryd. Fab. Preface.*

To BI'AS. *v. a.* [from the noun.] To incline to ſome ſide; to balance one way; to prejudice.

Were I in no more danger to be miſled by ignorance, than I am to be *biaſſed* by intereſt, I might give a very perfect account. *Locke.*

A deſire leaning to either ſide, *biaſſes* the judgment ſtrangely; by indifference for every thing but truth, you will be excited to examine. *Watts's Improvement of the Mind.*

BI'AS. *adv.* It ſeems to be uſed *adverbially* in the following paſſage, conformably to the French, *mettre une choſe de biais*, to give any thing a wrong interpretation.

Every action that hath gone before,
Whereof we have record, trial did draw
*Bias* and thwart, not anſwering the aim.
*Shakeſp. Troilus and Creſſida.*

BIB. *n. ſ.* A ſmall piece of linen put upon the breaſts of children, over their cloaths.

I would fain know, why it ſhould not be as noble a taſk, to write upon a *bib* and hanging-ſleeves, as on the *bulla* and *prætexta*. *Addiſon on ancient Medals.*

To BIB. *v. n.* [*bibo*, Lat.] To tipple; to ſip; to drink frequently.

He playeth with *bibbing* mother Meroë, as though ſhe was ſo named, becauſe ſhe would drink mere wine without water. *Camden.*

To appeaſe a froward child, they gave him drink as often as he cried; ſo that he was conſtantly *bibbing*, and drank more in twenty four hours than I did. *Locke.*

BIBA'CIOUS. *adj.* [*bibax*, Lat.] Much addicted to drinking. *D.*

BIBA'CITY. *n. ſ.* [*bibacitas*, Lat.] The quality of drinking much.

BI'BBER. *n. ſ.* [from *to bib.*] A tippler; a man that drinks often.

BI'BLE. *n. ſ.* [from βιβλίον, a book; called, by way of excellence, *The Book.*] The ſacred volume in which are contained the revelations of God.

If we paſs from the apoſtolic to the next ages of the church, the primitive chriſtians looked on their *bibles* as their moſt important treaſure. *Government of the Tongue*, § 3.

We muſt take heed how we accuſtom ourſelves to a ſlight and irreverent uſe of the name of God, and of the phraſes and expreſſions of the holy *bible*, which ought not to be applied upon every ſlight occaſion. *Tillotſon, ſermon iv.*

In queſtions of natural religion, we ſhould confirm and improve, or connect our reaſonings, by the divine aſſiſtance of the *bible*. *Watts's Logick.*

BIBLIO'GRAPHER. *n. ſ.* [from βιβλὸς, and γράφω, to write.] A writer of books; a tranſcriber. *Dict.*

BIBLIOTHE'CAL. *adj.* [from *bibliotheca*, Lat.] Belonging to a library. *Dict.*

BI'BULOUS. *adj.* [*bibulus*, Lat.] That which has the quality of drinking moiſture; ſpungy.

Strow'd *bibulous* above, I ſee the ſands,
The pebbly gravel next, and guttur'd rocks. *Thomſon.*

BICA'PSULAR. *adj.* [*bicapſularis*, Lat.] A plant whoſe ſeed veſſel is divided into two parts.

BICE. *n. ſ.* The name of a colour uſed in painting. It is either green or blue.

Take green *bice*, and order it as you do your blue *bice*, you may diaper upon it with the water of deep green. *Peacham.*

BICI'PITAL. } *adj.* [*biceps*, *bicipitis*, Lat.]
BICI'PITOUS. }

1. Having two heads.

While men believe *bicipitous* conformation in any ſpecies, they admit a gemination of principal parts. *Brown's Vulg. Err.*

2. It is applied to one of the muſcles of the arm.

A piece of fleſh is exchanged from the *bicipital* muſcle of either party's arm. *Brown's Vulgar Errours, b.* ii. *c.* 3.

To BI'CKER. *v. n.* [*bicre*, Welſh, a conteſt.]

1. To ſkirmiſh; to fight without a ſet battle; to fight off and on.

They fell to ſuch a *bickering*, that he got a halting, and loſt his picture. *Sidney.*

In thy face
I ſee thy fury; if I longer ſtay,
We ſhall begin our ancient *bickerings*. *Shakeſp. Henry* VI.

2. To quiver; to play backward and forward.

And from about him fierce effuſion rowl'd
Of ſmoke, and *bickering* flame, and ſparkles dire.
*Milton's Paradiſe Loſt, b. vi. l. 671.*

An icy gale, oft ſhifting o'er the pool,
Breathes a blue film, and, in its mid career,
Arreſts the *bickering* ſtream. *Thomſon's Winter, l. 730.*

BI'CKERER. *n. ſ.* [from the verb.] A ſkirmiſher.

BI'CKERN. *n. ſ.* [apparently corrupted from *beakiron.*] An iron ending in a point.

blank page

2 a †

He durst not bide
~~brute~~ rabblement whose like he never saw
But got his ready Steed & fast away
gan ride
F.Q. 1. 65

X 5 a ——

9 †

In threats the foremost, but the lag in fight
When didst thou thrust amidst the mingled press
Content to bid the war aloof in peace
Dryd. Il

A blackſmith's anvil is ſometimes made with a pike, or *bickern*, or beakiron, at one end. *Moxon's Mechan. Exerciſes.*

BICO'RNE. }
BICO'RNOUS. } *adj.* [*bicornis*, Lat.] Having two horns.

We ſhould be too critical, to queſtion the letter Y, or *bicornous* element of Pythagoras; that is, the making of the horns equal. *Brown's Vulgar Errours, b.* v. *c.* 19.

BICO'RPORAL. *adj.* [*bicorpor*, Lat.] Having two bodies.

To BID. *v. a.* pret. I *bid*, *bad*, *bade*, I have *bid*, or *bidden*. [biðan, Saxon.]

1. To deſire; to aſk; to call; to invite.

I am *bid* forth to ſupper, Jeſſica;
There are my keys. *Shakeſp. Merchant of Venice.*

Go ye into the highways, and, as many as you ſhall find, *bid* to the marriage. *Matt.* xxii. 9.

We ought, when we are *bidden* to great feaſts and meetings, to be prepared beforehand. *Hakewell on Providence.*

2. To command; to order; before things or perſons.

Saint Withold footed thrice the wold,
He met the nightmare, and her name told,
*Bid* her alight, and her troth plight. *Shakeſp. King Lear.*

He chid the ſiſters,
When firſt they put the name of king upon me,
And *bade* them ſpeak to him. *Shakeſp. Macbeth.*

Haſte to the houſe of ſleep, and *bid* the god,
Who rules the nightly viſions with a nod,
Prepare a dream. *Dryden's Fables.*

Curſe on the tongue that *bids* this general joy.
Can they be friends of Antony, who revel
When Antony's in danger? *Dryd. All for Love.*

Thames heard the numbers, as he flow'd along,
And *bade* his willows learn the moving ſong. *Pope.*

Acquire a government over your ideas, that they may come when they are called, and depart when they are *bidden*. *Watts's Logick.*

3. To offer; to propoſe; as, to *bid* a price.

Come, and be true.—
—Thou *bidſt* me to my loſs: for true to thee,
Were to prove falſe. *Shakeſp. Cymbeline.*

When a man is reſolute to keep his ſins while he lives, and yet unwilling to relinquiſh all hope, he will embrace that profeſſion, which *bids* faireſt to the reconciling thoſe ſo diſtant intereſts. *Decay of Piety.*

As when the goddeſſes came down of old,
With gifts, their young Dardanian judge they try'd,
And each *bade* high to win him to their ſide. *Granville.*

To give intereſt a ſhare in friendſhip, is to ſell it by inch of candle; he that *bids* moſt ſhall have it: and when it is mercenary, there is no depending on it. *Collier on Friendſhip.*

4. To proclaim; to offer; or to make known by ſome publick voice.

Our bans thrice *bid!* and for our wedding day
My kerchief bought! then preſs'd, then forc'd away.
*Gay's What d'ye call it.*

5. To pronounce; to declare.

You are retir'd,
As if you were a feaſted one, and not
The hoſteſs of the meeting; pray you, *bid*
Theſe unknown friends to's welcome. *Shakeſp. Wint. Tale.*

Divers of them, as we paſſed by them, put their arms a little abroad; which is their geſture, when they *bid* any welcome. *Bacon's New Atlantis.*

How, Didius, ſhall a Roman, ſore repuls'd,
Greet your arrival to this diſtant iſle?
How *bid* you welcome to theſe ſhatter'd legions? *A. Philips.*

6. To denounce.

Thyſelf and Oxford, with five thouſand men,
Shall croſs the ſeas, and *bid* falſe Edward battle.
*Shakeſp. Henry VI. p. iii.*

One *bid* war to all that durſt ſupply
The place of thoſe her cruelty made die. *Waller.*

The captive cannibal, oppreſt with chains,
Yet braves his foes, reviles, provokes, diſdains;
Of nature fierce, untameable, and proud,
He *bids* defiance to the gaping croud,
And ſpent at laſt, and ſpeechleſs as he lies,
With fiery glances mocks their rage, and dies. *Granville.*

7. To pray. See BEAD.

If there come any unto you, and bring not this doctrine, receive him not into your houſe, neither *bid* him God ſpeed. *2 John*, 10.

When they deſired him to tarry longer with them, he conſented not, but *bade* them farewel. *Acts*, xviii. 21.

By ſome haycock, or ſome ſhady thorn,
He *bids* his beads both even ſong and morn. *Dryd. W. of B.*

BI'DALE. *n. ſ.* [from *bid* and *ale*.] An invitation of friends to drink at a poor man's houſe, and there to contribute charity. *Dict.*

BI'DDEN. *part. paſſ.* [from *to bid*.]

1. Invited.

There were two of our company *bidden* to a feaſt of the family. *Bacon.*

Madam, the *bidden* gueſts are come. *A. Philips.*

2. Commanded.

'Tis theſe that early taint the female ſoul,
Inſtruct the eyes of young coquettes to roll,
Teach infants cheeks a *bidden* bluſh to know,
And little hearts to flutter at a beau. *Pope's R. of the Lock.*

BI'DDER. *n. ſ.* [from *to bid*.] One who offers or propoſes a price.

He looked upon ſeveral dreſſes which hung there, and expoſed to the purchaſe of the beſt *bidder*. *Addiſon. Spectator.*

BI'DDING. *n. ſ.* [from *bid*.] Command; order.

How, ſay'ſt thou, that Macduff denies his perſon
At our great *bidding*? *Shakeſp. Macbeth.*

At his ſecond *bidding*, darkneſs fled,
Light ſhone, and order from diſorder ſprung.
*Milton's Parad. Loſt, b.* iii. *l.* 712.

To BIDE. *v. a.* [biðan, Sax.] To endure; to ſuffer.

Poor naked wretches, whereſoe'er you are,
That *bide* the pelting of this pitileſs ſtorm. *Shakeſp. K. Lear.*

The wary Dutch this gathering ſtorm foreſaw,
And durſt not *bide* it on the Engliſh coaſt. *Dryd. Ann. Mir.*

To BIDE. *v. n.*

1. To dwell; to live; to inhabit.

All knees to thee ſhall bow, of them that *bide*
In heav'n, or earth, or under earth in hell. *Par. Loſt, b.* iii.

2. To remain in a place.

Safe in a ditch he *bides*,
With twenty trenched gaſhes on his head;
The leaſt a death to nature. *Shakeſp. Macbeth.*

3. To continue in a ſtate.

And they alſo, if they *bide* not ſtill in unbelief, ſhall be graffed in. *Romans*, xi. 23.

4. It has probably all the ſignifications of the word *abide*; which ſee: but it being grown ſomewhat obſolete, the examples of its various meanings are not eaſily found.

BIDE'NTAL. *adj.* [*bidens*, Lat.] Having two teeth.

Ill management of forks is not to be helped, when they are only *bidental*. *Swift.*

BI'DING. *n. ſ.* [from *bide*.] Reſidence; habitation.

At Antwerp has my conſtant *biding* been. *Rowe's J. Sh.*

BIE'NNIAL. *adj.* [*biennis*, Lat.] Of the continuance of two years.

Then why ſhould ſome be very long lived, others only annual or *biennial*? *Ray on the Creation.*

BIER. *n. ſ.* [from *to bear*, as *feretrum*, in Latin, from *fero*.] A carriage, or frame of wood, on which the dead are carried to the grave.

And now the prey of fowls he lies,
Nor wail'd of friends, nor laid on groaning *bier*. *Fairy Q.*

They bore him barefaced on the *bier*,
And on his grave remains many a tear. *Shakeſp. Hamlet.*

He muſt not float upon his wat'ry *bier*,
Unwept. *Milton.*

Griefs always green, a houſhold ſtill in tears:
Sad pomps, a threſhold throng'd with daily *biers*,
And liveries of black. *Dryden's Juvenal, ſat.* x.

Make as if you hanged yourſelf, they will convey your body out of priſon in a *bier*. *Arbuthnot's J. Bull.*

BI'ESTINGS. *n. ſ.* [byꞅꞇınᵹ, Saxon.] The firſt milk given by a cow after calving, which is very thick.

And twice beſides, her *bieſtings* never fail
To ſtore the dairy with a brimming pale. *Dryden's Virgil.*

BIFA'RIOUS. *adj.* [*bifarius*, Lat.] Twofold; what may be underſtood two ways. *Dict.*

BI'FEROUS. *adj.* [*biferens*, Lat.] Bearing fruit twice a year.

BI'FID. }
BI'FIDATED. } *adj.* [*bifidus*, Lat. a botanical term.] Divided in two; ſplit in two; opening with a cleft.

BIFO'LD. *adj.* [from *binus*, Lat. and *fold*.] Twofold; double.

If beauty have a ſoul, this is not ſhe;
If ſouls guide vows, if vows are ſanctimony;
If ſanctimony be the gods delight;
If there be rule in unity itſelf,
This is not ſhe; O madneſs of diſcourſe!
That cauſe ſets up with and againſt thyſelf!
*Bifold* authority. *Shakeſp. Troilus and Creſſida.*

BIFO'RMED. *adj.* [*biformis*, Lat.] Compounded of two forms, or bodies.

BIFU'RCATED. *adj.* [from *binus*, two, and *furca*, a fork, Lat.] Shooting out, by a diviſion, into two heads.

A ſmall white piece, *bifurcated*, or branching into two, and finely reticulated all over. *Woodward on Foſſils.*

BIFURCA'TION. *n. ſ.* [from *binus* and *furca*, Lat.] Diviſion into two; opening into two parts.

The firſt catachreſtical and far derived ſimilitude, it holds with man; that is, in a *bifurcation*, or diviſion of the root into two parts. *Brown's Vulgar Errours, b.* ii. *c.* 6.

BIG. *adj.* [This word is of uncertain, or unknown etymology; *Junius* derives it from βαγαῖος; *Skinner*, from *bug*, which, in *Daniſh*, ſignifies the belly.]

1. Great in bulk; large.

Both in addition and diviſion, either of ſpace or duration, when the idea under conſideration becomes very *big*, or very ſmall;

ſmall, its preciſe bulk becomes very obſcure and confuſed. *Locke.*

A troubled ocean, to a man who ſails in it, is, I think, the *biggeſt* object that he can ſee in motion. *Spectator*, Nº 489.

Then commerce brought into the publick walk
The buſy merchant, the *big* warehouſe built. *Thomſon.*

2. Teeming; pregnant; great with young; with the particle *with*.

A bear *big with* young hath ſeldom been ſeen. *Bacon.*

Lately on yonder ſwelling buſh,
*Big with* many a common roſe,
This early bud began to bluſh. *Waller.*

3. Sometimes with *of*; but rarely.

His gentle lady,
*Big of* this gentleman, our theam, deceas'd
As he was born. *Shakeſp. Cymbeline.*

4. Full of ſomething; and deſirous, or about, to give it vent.

The great, th' important day,
*Big with* the fate of Cato and of Rome. *Addiſon's Cato.*

Now *big with* knowledge of approaching woes,
The prince of augurs, Halithreſes, roſe. *Pope's Odyſſey.*

5. Diſtended; ſwoln; ready to burſt; uſed often of the effects of paſſion, as grief, rage.

Thy heart is *big*; get thee apart, and weep. *Shakeſp. Julius Cæſar.*

6. Great in air and mien; proud; ſwelling; tumid; haughty; ſurly.

How elſe, ſaid he, but with a good bold face,
And with *big* words, and with a ſtately pace. *Hub. Tale.*

To the meaner man, or unknown in the court, ſeem ſomewhat ſolemn, coy, *big*, and dangerous of look, talk, and anſwer. *Aſcham's Schoolmaſter.*

If you had but looked *big*, and ſpit at him, he'd have run. *Shakeſp. Winter's Tale.*

Or does the man i' th' moon look *big*,
Or wear a huger perriwig,
Than our own native lunaticks. *Hudibras, p.* ii. *cant.* iii.

Of governments that once made ſuch a noiſe, and looked ſo *big* in the eyes of mankind, as being founded upon the deepeſt counſels, and the ſtrongeſt force; nothing remains of them but a name. *South.*

In his moſt proſperous ſeaſon, he fell under the reproach of being a man of *big* looks, and of a mean and abject ſpirit. *Clarendon.*

Thou thyſelf, thus inſolent in ſtate,
Art but perhaps ſome country magiſtrate,
Whoſe power extends no farther than to ſpeak
*Big* on the bench, and ſcanty weights to break. *Dryden.*

To grant *big* Thraſo valour, Phormio ſenſe,
Should indignation give, at leaſt offence. *Garth.*

7. Great in ſpirit; lofty; brave.

What art thou? have not I
An arm as big as thine? a heart as *big*?
Thy words, I grant, are *bigger*: for I wear not
My dagger in my mouth. *Shakeſp. Cymbeline.*

BI'GAMIST. *n. ſ.* [*bigamus*, low Lat.] One that has committed bigamy. See BIGAMY.

By the papal canons, a clergyman, that has a wife, cannot have an eccleſiaſtical benefice; much leſs can a *bigamiſt* have ſuch a benefice, according to that law. *Ayliffe's Parergon.*

BI'GAMY. *n. ſ.* [*bigamia*, low Latin.]

1. The crime of having two wives at once.

A beauty-waining and diſtreſſed widow
Seduc'd the pitch and height of all his thoughts,
To baſe declenſion, and loath'd *bigamy*. *Shakeſp. Richard* III.

Randal determined to commence a ſuit againſt Martin, for *bigamy* and inceſt. *Arbuthnot and Pope's Martinus Scriblerus.*

2. In the canon law. The marriage of a ſecond wife, or of a widow, or a woman already debauched; which, in the church of Rome, were conſidered as bringing a man under ſome incapacities for eccleſiaſtical offices.

BIGBE'LLIED. *adj.* [from *big* and *belly*.] Pregnant; with child; great with young.

When we have laught to ſee the ſails conceive,
And grow *bigbellied* with the wanton wind. *Shakeſp. Midſummer Night's Dream.*

Children, and *bigbellied* women require antidotes ſomewhat more grateful to the palate. *Harvey on the Plague.*

So many well ſhaped innocent virgins are blocked up, and waddling up and down like *bigbellied* women. *Addiſon. Spect.*

We purſued our march, to the terrour of the market people, and the miſcarriage of half a dozen *bigbellied* women. *Addiſon's Freeholder.*

BI'GGIN. *n. ſ.* [*beguin*, Fr.] A child's cap.

Sleep now!
Yet not ſo ſound, and half ſo deeply ſweet,
As he, whoſe brow with homely *biggin* bound,
Snores out the watch of night. *Shakeſp. Henry* IV. *p.* ii.

BIGHT. *n. ſ.* It is explained by *Skinner*, the circumference of a coil of rope.

BI'GLY. *adv.* [from *big*.] Tumidly; haughtily; with a bluſtering manner.

Would'ſt thou not rather chooſe a ſmall renown,
To be the may'r of ſome poor paltry town;
*Bigly* to look, and barb'rouſly to ſpeak;
To pound falſe weights, and ſcanty meaſures break? *Dryden's Juvenal, ſat.* x.

BI'GNESS. *n. ſ.* [from *big*.]

1. Bulk; greatneſs of quantity.

If panicum be laid below, and about the bottom of a root, it will cauſe the root to grow to an exceſſive *bigneſs*. *Bacon.*

People were ſurpriſed at the *bigneſs*, and uncouth deformity of the camel. *L'Eſtrange's Fables.*

The brain of man, in reſpect of his body, is much larger than in any other animal's; exceeding in *bigneſs* three oxens brains. *Ray on the Creation.*

2. Size; whether greater or ſmaller.

Several ſorts of rays make vibrations of ſeveral *bigneſſes*, which, according to their *bigneſſes*, excite ſenſations of ſeveral colours; and the air, according to their *bigneſſes*, excites ſenſations of ſeveral ſounds. *Newton's Opticks.*

BI'GOT. *n. ſ.* [The etymology of this word is unknown; but it is ſuppoſed, by *Camden* and others, to take its riſe from ſome occaſional phraſe.] A man devoted to a certain party; prejudiced in favour of certain opinions; a blind zealot. It is uſed often with *to* before the object of zeal; as, a *bigot to* the Carteſian tenets.

Religious ſpite, and pious ſpleen bred firſt
This quarrel, which ſo long the *bigots* nurſt. *Tate. Juvenal.*

In philoſophy and religion, the *bigots* of all parties are generally the moſt poſitive. *Watts's Improvement of the Mind.*

BI'GOTED. *adj.* [from *bigot*.] Blindly prepoſſeſſed in favour of ſomething; irrationally zealous; with *to*.

*Bigotted to* this idol, we diſclaim
Reſt, health, and eaſe, for nothing but a name. *Garth.*

Preſbyterian merit, during the reign of that weak, *bigotted*, and ill adviſed prince, will eaſily be computed. *Swift.*

BI'GOTRY. *n ſ.* [from *bigot*.]

1. Blind zeal; prejudice; unreaſonable warmth in favour of party or opinions; with the particle *to*.

Were it not for a *bigotry to* our own tenets, we could hardly imagine, that ſo many abſurd, wicked, and bloody principles, ſhould pretend to ſupport themſelves by the goſpel. *Watts.*

2. The practice or tenet of a bigot.

Our ſilence makes our adverſaries think we perſiſt in thoſe *bigotries*, which all good and ſenſible men deſpiſe. *Pope.*

BI'GSWOLN. *adj.* [from *big* and *ſwoln*.] Turgid; ready to burſt.

Might my *bigſwoln* heart
Vent all its griefs, and give a looſe to ſorrow. *Addiſ. Cato.*

BI'G-UDDERED. *adj.* [from *big*, and *udder*.] Having large udders; having dugs ſwelled with milk.

Now driv'n before him, through the arching rock,
Came, tumbling heaps on heaps, th' unnumber'd flock,
*Big-udder'd* ews, and goats of female kind. *Pope's Odyſſey.*

BI'LANDER. *n. ſ.* [*belandre*, Fr.] A ſmall veſſel of about eighty tons burden, uſed for the carriage of goods. It is a kind of hoy, manageable by four or five men, and has maſts and ſails after the manner of a hoy. They are uſed chiefly in Holland, as being particularly fit for the canals. *Savary. Trevoux.*

Like *bilanders* to creep
Along the coaſt, and land in view to keep. *Dryden.*

BI'LBERRY. *n. ſ.* [from bılıg, Sax. a bladder, and *berry*; according to *Skinner*.] The ſame with *whortleberry*; which ſee.

Cricket, to Windſor chimneys ſhalt thou leap;
There pinch the maids as blue as *bilberries*. *Shakeſp. Merry Wives of Windſor.*

BI'LBO. *n. ſ.* [corrupted from *Bilboa*, where the beſt weapons are made.] A rapier; a ſword.

To be compaſſed like a good *bilbo*, in the circumference of a peck, hilt to point, heel to head. *Shakeſp. M. W. of Windſor.*

BI'LBOES. *n. ſ.* A ſort of ſtocks, or wooden ſheckles for the feet, uſed for puniſhing offenders at ſea.

Methought I lay,
Worſe than the mutines, in the *bilboes*. *Shakeſp. Hamlet.*

BILE. *n. ſ.* [*bilis*, Lat.] A thick, yellow, bitter liquour, ſeparated in the liver, collected in the gall-bladder, and diſcharged into the lower end of the duodenum, or beginning of the jejunum, by the common duct. Its uſe is to ſheathe or blunt the acids of the chyle; becauſe they, being entangled with its ſulphurs, thicken it ſo, that it cannot be ſufficiently diluted by the ſuccus pancreaticus, to enter the lacteal veſſels. *Quincy.*

In its progreſſion, ſoon the labour'd chyle
Receives the confluent rills of bitter *bile*;
Which, by the liver ſever'd from the blood,
And ſtriving through the gall-pipe, here unload
Their yellow ſtreams. *Blackmore.*

BILE. *n. ſ.* [bıle, Sax. perhaps from *bilis*, Lat. This is generally ſpelt *boil*; but, I think, leſs properly.] A ſore angry ſwelling.

But yet thou art my fleſh, my blood, my daughter;
Or, rather, a diſeaſe that's in my fleſh;
Thou art a *bile* in my corrupted blood. *Shakeſp. King Lear.*

Thoſe *biles* did run—ſay ſo—did not the general run? were not that a botchy ſore? *Shakeſp. Troilus and Creſſida.*

A furun-

~~With regard to the Voice~~

His big manly Voice
Turning again towards childish treble pipes
And Whistles in his sound Shak.

Bigg n. s.
In the northern counties of England it signi:
fies a Species of barley.
It might save abundance of labour in our
Northern parts, where they reap their barley
Oats and bigg. Tuss. Notes

a. A kind of hook; an offensive weapon
That beastly rabble that came down
From all the garrets in the town
And stall & shopboards in vast swarms
with new chalk'd *bills* & rusty arms
Hudib.

Billed Adj. fr. Bill
having a Bill or Beak
c A christian boy in Constantinople had
like to have been stoned for gagging in
a waggishness a long *billed* fowl.

. The Centurions and their charges
distinctly billeted, already in the enter.
tainment to be on foot at an hours warning
Shaks. Cor.

IL facing 3C2r

A furunculus is a painful tubercle, with a broad basis, arising in a cone. It is generally called a *bile*, and, in it its state, is accompanied with inflammation, pulsation, and tension. *Wiseman's Surgery.*

BILGE *in a ship.* The compass or breadth of the ship's bottom. *Skinner.*

To BILGE. *v. n.* [from the noun.] To spring a leak; to let in water, by striking upon a rock: a sea term. *Skinner.*

BI'LIARY. *adj.* [from *bilis*, Lat.] Belonging to the bile.

Voracious animals, and such as do not chew, have a great quantity of gall; and some of them have the *biliary* duct inserted into the pylorus. *Arbuthnot on Aliments.*

BI'LINGSGATE. *n. s.* [A cant word, borrowed from *Bilingsgate* in London, a place where there is always a croud of low people, and frequent brawls and foul language.] Ribaldry; foul language.

There stript, fair rhet'rick languish'd on the ground,
And shameful *bilingsgate* her robes adorn. *Dunciad, b.* iv.

BILI'NGUOUS. *adj.* [*bilinguis*, Lat.] Having, or speaking two tongues.

BI'LIOUS. *adj.* [from *bilis*, Lat.] Consisting of bile; partaking of bile.

Why *bilious* juice a golden light puts on,
And floods of chyle in silver currents run. *Garth.*

When the taste of the mouth is bitter, it is a sign of redundance of a *bilious* alkali. *Arbuthnot on Aliments.*

To BILK. *v. a.* [derived by Mr. *Lye* from the Gothick, *bilaican.*] To cheat; to defraud, by running in debt, and avoiding payment.

*Bilk'd* stationers for yeomen stood prepar'd. *Dryden.*

What comedy, what farce can more delight,
Than grinning hunger, and the pleasing sight
Of your *bilk'd* hopes? *Dryden's Juvenal, sat.* v.

BILL. *n. s.* [bile, Sax. See BALL.] The beak of a fowl.

Their *bills* were thwarted crossways at the end, and, with these, they would cut an apple in two at one snap. *Carew's Survey of Cornwal.*

It may be tried, whether birds may not be made to have greater or longer *bills*, or greater and longer talons. *Bacon's Natural History, N° 757.*

In his *bill*
An olive leaf he brings, pacifick sign! *Paradise Lost, b.* xi.

No crowing cock does there his wings display,
Nor with his horny *bill* provoke the day. *Dryden's Fables.*

BILL. *n. s.* [bille, Sax. *bipile*, a two edged axe.]

A kind of hatchet with a hooked point, used in country work, as a *hedging bill*; so called from its resemblance in form to the beak of a bird of prey.

Standing troops are servants armed, who use the lance and sword, as other servants do the sickle, or the *bill*, at the command of those who entertain them. *Temple.*

1. A kind of weapon anciently carried by the foot; a battle axe.

Yea distaff women manage rusty *bills*;
Against thy seat both young and old rebel. *Shakesp. R.* II.

BILL. *n. s.* [*billet*, French.]

A written paper of any kind.

He does receive
Particular addition from the *bill*
That writes them all alike. *Shakesp. Macbeth.*

An account of money.

Ordinary expence ought to be limited by a man's estate, and ordered to the best, that the *bills* may be less than the estimation abroad. *Bacon's Essays.*

A law presented to the parliament, not yet made an act.

No new laws can be made, nor old laws abrogated or altered, but by parliament; where *bills* are prepared, and presented to the two houses. *Bacon's Advice to Villiers.*

How now, for mitigation of this *bill*,
Urg'd by the commons? Doth his majesty
Incline to it, or no? *Shakesp. Henry* V.

An act of parliament.

There will be no way left for me to tell you, that I remember you, and that I love you; but that one, which needs no open warrant, or secret conveyance; which no *bills* can preclude, or no kings prevent. *Atterbury to Pope.*

A physician's prescription.

Like him that took the doctor's *bill*,
And swallow'd it instead o' th' pill. *Hudibras, p.* i. *cant.* ii.

The medicine was prepar'd according to the *bill*. *L'Estrange, fab.* 183.

Let them, but under your superiours, kill,
When doctors first have sign'd the bloody *bill*. *Dryden.*

An advertisement.

And in despair, their empty pit to fill,
Set up some foreign monster in a *bill*. *Dryden.*

In law.

1. An obligation, but without condition or forfeiture for nonpayment. 2. A declaration in writing, that expresseth either the grief and the wrong, that the complainant hath suffered by the party complained of; or else some fault, that the party complained of, hath committed against some law. This *bill* is sometimes offered to justices errants in the general assizes; but most to the lord chancellor. It containeth the fact complained of, the damages thereby suffered, and petition of process against the defendant for redress. *Cowel.*

The fourth thing very maturely to be consulted by the jury, is, what influence their finding the *bill* may have upon the kingdom. *Swift.*

8. *A bill of mortality.* An account of the numbers that have died in any district.

Most who took in the weekly *bills of mortality*, made little other use of them, than to look at the foot, how the burials encreased or decreased. *Graunt's Bills of Mortality.*

So liv'd our sires, ere doctors learn'd to kill,
And multiply'd with theirs the weekly *bill*. *Dryden.*

9. *A bill of fare.* An account of the season of provisions, or of the dishes at a feast.

It may seem somewhat difficult to make out the *bills of fare* for some of the forementioned suppers. *Arbuthnot on Coins.*

10. *A bill of exchange.* A note ordering the payment of a sum of money in one place, to some person assigned by the drawer or remitter, in consideration of the value paid to him in another place.

The comfortable sentences are our *bills of exchange*, upon the credit of which we lay our cares down, and receive provisions. *Taylor's Rule of living holy.*

All that a *bill of exchange* can do, is to direct to whom money is due, or taken up upon credit, in a foreign country, shall be paid. *Locke.*

To BILL. *v. n.* [from *bill*, a beak.] To caress, as doves by joining bills; to be fond.

Doves, they say, will *bill*, after their pecking, and their murmuring. *Ben Johnson's Catiline.*

Still amorous, and fond, and *billing*,
Like Philip and Mary on a shilling. *Hudibras, p.* iii. *c.* i.

They *bill*, they tread; Alcyone compress'd,
Seven days sits brooding on her floating nest. *Dryden.*

He that bears th' artillery of jove,
The strong pounc'd eagle, and the *billing* dove. *Dryden.*

To BILL. *v. a.* [from *bill*, a writing.] To publish by an advertisement: a cant word.

His masterpiece was a composition that he *billed* about under the name of a sovereign antidote. *L'Estrange.*

BI'LLET. *n. s.* [*billet*, French.]

1. A small paper; a note.

When he found this little *billet*, in which was only written, *Remember Cæsar*, he was exceedingly confounded. *Clarendon.*

2. A ticket directing soldiers at what house to lodge.

3. *Billet doux*, or a soft *billet*; a love letter.

'Twas then, Belinda! if report say true,
Thy eyes first open'd on a *billet doux*. *Pope's Rape of the L.*

Bawds and pimps will be carrying about *billet doux*. *Arbuthnot and Pope's Martinus Scriblerus.*

4. A small log of wood for the chimney.

Let us then calculate, when the bulk of a faggot or *billet*, is dilated and rarified to the degree of fire, how vast a place it must take up. *Digby on Bodies.*

Their *billet* at the fire was found. *Prior.*

To BI'LLET. *v. a.* [from the noun.]

1. To direct a soldier by a ticket, or note, where he is to lodge.

Retire thee; go where thou art *billeted*:
Away, I say. *Shakesp. Othello.*

2. To quarter soldiers.

They remembered him of charging the kingdom, by *billeting* soldiers. *Raleigh's History of the World.*

The counties throughout the kingdom were so incensed, and their affections poisoned, that they refused to suffer the soldiers to be *billeted* upon them. *Clarendon.*

BI'LLIARDS. *n. s. without a singular.* [*billard*, Fr. of which that language has no etymology; and therefore they probably derived from England both the play and the name; which is corrupted from *balyards*; yards or sticks with which a ball is driven along a table. Thus *Spenser*:

*Balyards* much unfit,
And shuttlecocks misseeming manly wit. *Hubb. Tale.*]

A game at which a ball is forced against another on a table.

Let it alone; let's to *billiards*. *Shakesp. Antony and Cleop.*

Even nose and cheek, withal,
Smooth as is the *billiard* ball. *Ben. Johnson's Underwoods.*

Some are forced to bound or fly upwards, almost like ivory balls meeting on a *billiard* table. *Boyle.*

When the ball obeys the stroke of a *billiard* stick, it is not any action of the ball, but bare passion. *Locke.*

BI'LLOW. *n. s.* [*bilge*, Germ. *bolg*, Dan. probably of the same original with *bilg*, Sax. a bladder.] A wave swoln, and hollow.

From whence the river Dee, as silver cleen,
His tumbling *billows* roll with gentle rore. *Fairy Queen, b.* i.

*Billows* sink by degrees, even when the wind is down that first stirred them. *Wotton.*

Chasing Nereus with his trident throws
The *billows* from the bottom. *Sir J. Denham.*

But when loud *billows* lash the sounding shore,
The hoarse rough verse should like the torrent roar. *Pope.*

To

To Bi'llow. *v. n.* [from the noun.] To swell, or roll, as a wave.

> The *billowing* snow, and violence of the show'r,
> That from the hills disperse their dreadful store,
> And o'er the vales collected ruin pour. *Prior.*

Bi'llowy. *adj.* [from *billow.*] Swelling; turgid; wavy.

> And whitening down the mossy-tinctur'd stream,
> Descends the *billowy* foam. *Thomson's Spring, l.* 380.

Bin. *n. s.* [binne, Sax.] A place where bread, or corn, or wine, is reposited.

The most convenient way of picking hops, is into a long square frame of wood, called a *bin.* *Mortimer's Husbandry.*

> As when from rooting in a *bin,*
> All pouder'd o'er from tail to chin,
> A lively maggot sallies out,
> You know him by his hazel snout. *Swift.*

Bi'nary. *adj.* [from *binus,* Lat.] Two; dual; double.

Bi'nary *Arithmetick.* A method of computation proposed by Mr. Leibnitz, in which, in lieu of the ten figures in the common arithmetick, and the progression from ten to ten, he has only two figures, and uses the simple progression from two to two. This method appears to be the same with that used Chinese four thousand years ago. *Chambers.*

To BIND. *v. a.* pret. *I bound*; particip. pass. *bound,* or *bounden.* [bindan, Saxon.]

1. To confine with bonds; to enchain.

Wilt thou play with him as with a bird? or wilt thou *bind* him for thy maidens? *Job,* xli. 5.

2. To gird; to enwrap; to involve.

Who hath *bound* the waters in a garment. *Prov.* xxx. 4.

3. To fasten to any thing.

Thou shalt *bind* this line of scarlet thread in the window, which thou didst let us down by. *Joshua,* ii. 18.

Keep my commandments, and live: and my law, as the apple of thine eye. *Bind* them upon thy fingers, write them upon the table of thine heart. *Prov.* vii. 3, 4.

4. To fasten together.

Gather ye together first the tares, and *bind* them in bundles, to burn them. *Matt.* xiii. 20.

5. To cover a wound with dressings and bandages.

When he saw him, he had compassion on him, and went to him, and *bound* up his wounds. *Luke,* x. 34.

Having filled up the bared cranium with our dressings, we *bound* up the wound. *Wiseman's Surgery.*

6. To compel; to constrain.

Those canons, or imperial constitutions, which have not been received here, do not *bind.* *Hale's Common Law of Engl.*

7. To oblige by stipulation, or oath.

If a man vow a vow, or swear an oath to *bind* his soul with a bond, he shall not break his word. *Numbers,* xxx. 2.

Swear by the solemn oath, that *binds* the gods. *Pope.*

8. To oblige by duty or law.

> Though I am *bound* to every act of duty,
> I am not *bound* to that, all slaves are free to. *Shakesp. Othello.*

Duties expresly required in the plain language of Scripture, ought to *bind* our consciences more than those which are but dubiously inferred. *Watts's Improvement of the Mind.*

9. To oblige by kindness.

10. To confine; to hinder.

> Now I'm cabin'd, cribb'd, confin'd, *bound* in
> To saucy doubts and fears. *Shakesp. Macbeth.*

You will sooner, by imagination, *bind* a bird from singing, than from eating or flying. *Bacon's Natural Hist.* N° 989.

Though passion be the most obvious and general, yet it is not the only cause that *binds* up the understanding, and confines it, for the time, to one object, from which it will not be taken off. *Locke.*

> In such a dismal place,
> Where joy ne'er enters, which the sun ne'er cheers,
> *Bound* in with darkness, overspread with damps. *Dryden.*

11. To hinder the flux of the bowels; to make costive.

Rhubarb hath manifestly in it parts of contrary operations; parts that purge, and parts that *bind* the body. *Bacon.*

The whey of milk doth loose, the milk doth *bind.* *Herbert.*

12. To restrain.

The more we are *bound* up to an exact narration, we want more life, and fire, to animate and inform the story. *Felton.*

13. *To bind a book.* To put it in a cover.

> Was ever book, containing such vile matter,
> So fairly *bound?* *Shakesp. Romeo and Juliet.*
> Those who could never read the grammar,
> When my dear volumes touch the hammer,
> May think books best, as richest *bound.* *Prior.*

14. *To bind to.* To oblige to serve some one.

> If still thou do'st retain
> The same ill habits, the same follies too,
> Still thou art *bound to* vice, and still a slave. *Dryden's Pers.*

15. *To bind to.* To contract with any body.

Art thou *bound to* a wife? seek not to be loosed. 1 *Cor.* vii.

16. *To bind over.* To oblige to make appearance.

Sir Roger was staggered with the reports concerning this woman, and would have *bound her over* to the country sessions. *Addison. Spectator,* N° 117.

To Bind. *v. n.*

1. To contract the parts together; to grow stiff and hard.

If the land rise full of clots, and if it is a *binding* land, you must make it fine by harrowing of it. *Mortimer's Husbandry.*

2. To make costive.

3. To be obligatory.

The promises and bargains for truck, between a Swiss and an Indian, in the woods of America, are *binding* to them, though they are perfectly in a state of nature, in reference to one another. *Locke.*

Bind. *n. s.* A species of hops.

The two best sorts are the white and the grey *bind*; the latter is a large square hop, and more hardy. *Mortimer.*

Bi'nder. *n. s.* [from *to bind.*]

1. A man whose trade it is to bind books.

2. A man that binds sheaves.

> Three *binders* stood, and took the handfuls reapt
> From boys that gather'd quickly up. *Chapman's Iliads.*

A man, with a *binder,* may reap an acre of wheat in a day, if it stand well. *Mortimer's Husbandry.*

3. A fillet; a shred cut to bind with.

Upon that I laid a double cloth, of such length and breadth as might serve to encompass the fractured member; which I cut from each end to the middle, into three *binders.* *Wiseman.*

Bi'nding. *n. s.* [from *bind.*] A bandage.

This beloved young woman began to take off the *binding* of his eyes. *Tatler,* N° 55.

Bi'ndweed. *n. s.* [*convolvulus,* Lat.] The name of a plant.

It hath, for the most part, trailing stalks; the leaves grow alternately on the branches; the flower consists of one leaf, shaped like a bell, whose mouth is widely expanded; the ovary becomes a roundish membraneous fruit, wrapped up within the flower cup; and is generally divided into three cells, each containing one angular seed. The species are thirty six. 1. The common white great *bindweed,* vulgarly called *bearbind.* 2. Lesser field *bindweed,* with a rose coloured flower, vulgarly called *gravelbind.* 3. Common sea *bindweed,* with round leaves. 4. Great American *bindweed,* with spacious yellow sweet scented flowers, commonly called *Spanish arbour vine,* or *Spanish woodbine.* 5. White and yellow Spanish potatoes. 6. Red Spanish potatoes. 7. The jalap, &c. The first of these species is a very troublesome weed in gardens; and the second sort is still a worse weed than the former. The third sort is found upon gravelly or sandy shores, where the salt water overflows: this is a strong purge, and, as such, is often used in medicine. The fourth sort is common in the hot parts of America, and is planted to cover arbours and seats: one of these plants will grow to the length of sixty or an hundred feet, and produce great quantities of side branches, and large fragrant yellow flowers, succeeded by three large angular seeds. The two kinds of potatoes are much cultivated in the West Indies, for food; and, from the roots, a drink is made, called *mobby,* stronger or weaker: it is a sprightly liquour, but not subject to fly into the head; nor will it keep beyond four or five days. These roots have been brought from America, and are cultivated in Spain and Portugal; but, in general, they are not so well liked as the common potato, being too sweet and luscious. The jalap, whose root has been long used in medicine, is a native of the province of Halapa, about two days journey from La Vera Cruz. *Millar.*

*Bindweed* is of two sorts, the larger and the smaller; the first sort flowers in September, and the last in June and July. *Mortimer's Husbandry.*

Bi'nocle. *n. s.* [from *binus* and *oculus.*] A kind of dioptrick telescope, fitted so with two tubes joining together in one, as that a distant object may be seen with both eyes together. *Harris.*

Bino'cular. *adj.* [from *binus* and *oculus,* Lat.] Having two eyes.

Most animals are *binocular,* spiders, for the most part, octonocular, and some senocular. *Derham's Physico-Theology.*

Bino'mial *Root.* [in algebra.] A root composed of only two parts or members, connected with the signs *plus* or *minus.* *Harris.*

Bino'minous. *adj.* [from *binus* and *nomen,* Lat.] Having two names.

Bio'grapher. *n. s.* [βίος and γράφω.] A writer of lives; a relator not of the history of nations, but of the actions of particular persons.

Our Grubstreet *biographers* watch for the death of a great man, like so many undertakers, on purpose to make a penny of him. *Addison. Freeholder,* N° 35.

Bio'graphy. *n. s.* [βίος and γράφω.]

In writing the lives of men, which is called *biography,* some authors place every thing in the precise order of time when it occurred. *Watts's Logick.*

Bi'ovac. } *n. s.* [Fr. from *wey wach,* a double guard, Germ. in war.] A guard at night performed by the whole army; which, either at a siege, or lying before an enemy, every evening draws out from its tents or huts, and continues all night in arms before its lines or camp, to prevent any surprise. *To raise the biovac,* is to return the army to their tents at break of day. *Trevoux. Harris.*

16 To bind over
in law to give bail for appearance
by entring into recognizance
So tho my ankle she has quitted
My heart continues still committed
And like a bail'd & main priz'd lover
Altho at large I am bound over
Hudib.

e
f

6
17 To confine, to circumscribe as in bounds
The ministry is not now bound to any
one tribe, now none is secluded from
that function of any degree
Whitgift

2

7
18 To unite, to tie together as with cement
They were now like sand without lime
ill bound together, & at a gaze, looking
strange one upon another, not knowing
who was faithful to their side
Bacon. H. 7

1

IL facing 3C2v

IL facing 3D$^{r}$

**Bi'parous.** *adj.* [from *binus* and *pario*, Lat.] Bringing forth two at a birth.

**Bi'partite.** *adj.* [from *binus* and *partior*, Lat.] Having two correſpondent parts; divided into two.

**Biparti'tion.** *n. ſ.* [from *bipartite.*] The act of dividing into two; or of making two correſpondent parts.

**Bi'ped.** *n. ſ.* [*bipes*, Lat.] An animal with two feet.

No ſerpent, or fiſhes oviparous, have any ſtones at all; neither *biped* nor quadruped oviparous, have any exteriourly. *Brown's Vulgar Errours, b.* iii. *c.* 4.

**Bi'pedal.** *adj.* [*bipedalis*, Lat.] Two feet in length; or having two feet.

**Bipe'nnated.** *adj.* [from *binus* and *penna*, Lat.] Having two wings.

All *bipennated* inſects have poiſes joined to the body. *Derham's Phyſico-Theology.*

**Bipe'talous.** *adj.* [of *bis*, Lat. and πέταλον.] A flower conſiſting of two leaves. *Dict.*

**Bi'quadrate.** } *n. ſ.* [in algebra.] The fourth power, ariſing
**Biquadra'tick.** } from the multiplication of a ſquare number, or quantity by itſelf. *Harris.*

**BIRCH** *Tree.* [bipc, Sax. *betula*, Lat.]

The leaves are like thoſe of the poplar; the ſhoots are very ſlender and weak; the katkins are produced at remote diſtances from the fruits, on the ſame tree; the fruit becomes a little ſquamoſe cone; the ſeeds are winged, and the tree caſts its outer rind every year. This tree is propagated by ſuckers, which may be tranſplanted either in October or February; it delights in a poor ſoil. The timber of this tree is uſed to make chairs, &c. It is alſo planted for hop-poles, hoops, &c. and it is often uſed to make brooms. *Millar.*

**Bi'rchen.** *adj.* [from *birch.*] Made of birch.

His beaver'd brow a *birchen* garland bears. *Dunciad, b.* iv.

**BIRD.** *n. ſ.* [bipð, or bpið, a chicken, Saxon.] A general term for the feathered kind; a fowl. In common talk, *fowl* is uſed for the larger, and *bird* for the ſmaller kind of feathered animals.

The poor wren,
The moſt diminutive of *birds*, will fight,
Her young ones in her neſt, againſt the owl. *Macbeth.*

Sh' had all the regal makings of a queen;
As holy oil, Edward confeſſor's crown,
The rod and *bird* of peace, and all ſuch emblems,
Laid nobly on her. *Shakeſp. Henry* VIII.

The *bird* of Jove, ſtoop'd from his airy tour,
Two *birds* of gayeſt plume before him drove.
*Milton's Paradiſe Loſt, b.* xi. *l.* 186.

Hence men and beaſts the breath of life obtain,
And *birds* of air, and monſters of the main. *Dryden's Æn.*

There are ſome *birds* that are inhabitants of the water, whoſe blood is cold as fiſhes, and their fleſh is ſo like in taſte, that the ſcrupulous are allowed them on fiſh days. *Locke.*

Some ſquire perhaps you take delight to rack,
Who viſits with a gun, preſents with *birds*. *Pope.*

**To Bird.** *v. n.* [from the noun.] To catch birds.

I do invite you tomorrow morning to my houſe, to breakfaſt; after, we'll a *birding* together. *Shakeſp. M. W. of Windſ.*

**Bi'rdbolt.** *n. ſ.* [from *bird* and *bolt*, or *arrow.*] A ſmall ſhot, or arrow, to be ſhot at birds.

To be generous, guiltleſs, and of free diſpoſition, is to take thoſe things for *birdbolts*, that you deem cannon bullets. *Shakeſp. Twelfth Night.*

**Bi'rdcage.** *n. ſ.* [from *bird* and *cage.* See Cage.]

*Birdcages* taught him the pulley, and tops the centrifugal force. *Arbuthnot and Pope's Martinus Scriblerus.*

**Bi'rdcatcher.** *n. ſ.* [from *bird* and *catch.*] One that makes it his employment to take birds.

A poor lark entered into a miſerable expoſtulation with a *birdcatcher*, that had taken her in his net. *L'Eſtrange.*

**Bi'rder.** *n. ſ.* [from *bird.*] A birdcatcher.

**Bi'rding piece.** *n. ſ.* [from *bird* and *piece.*] A fowling piece; a gun to ſhoot birds with.

I'll creep up into the chimney.—There they always uſe to diſcharge their *birding pieces*; creep into the kill hole. *Shakeſp. Merry Wives of Windſor.*

**Bi'rdlime.** *n. ſ.* [from *bird* and *lime.*] A glutinous ſubſtance, which is ſpread upon twigs, by which the birds that light upon them are entangled.

*Birdlime* is made of the bark of holly, boiled for ten or twelve hours; and when the green coat is ſeparated from the other, they cover it up for a fortnight, in a moiſt place, and pound it into a tough paſte, that no fibres of the wood be left; then it is waſhed in a running ſtream, till no motes appear, and put up to ferment for four or five days, and ſcummed as often as any thing ariſes, and then laid up for uſe; at which time they incorporate with it a third part of nut oil, over the fire. The *birdlime* brought from Damaſcus is ſuppoſed to be made of ſebeſtens, the kernels being frequently found in it; but this will not endure the froſt or wet. That brought from Spain is of an ill ſmell; but the bark of our lantone, or wayfaring ſhrub, will make very good *birdlime*. *Chambers.*

Holly is of ſo viſcous a juice, as they make *birdlime* of the bark of it. *Bacon's Natural Hiſtory*, Nº 592.

With ſtores of gather'd glue, contrive
To ſtop the vents and crannies of their hive;
Not *birdlime*, or Idean pitch, produce
A more tenacious maſs of clammy juice. *Dryden's Virgil.*

I'm enſnar'd;
Heav'ns *birdlime* wraps me round, and glues my wings.
*Dryden's King Arthur.*

The woodpecker, and other birds of this kind, becauſe they prey upon flies which they catch with their tongue, have a couple of bags filled with a viſcous humour, as if it were a natural *birdlime*, or liquid glue. *Grew's Coſmologia Sacra, b.* i. *c.* 5.

**Bi'rdman.** *n. ſ.* [from *bird* and *man.*] A birdcatcher; a fowler.

As a fowler was bending his net, a blackbird aſked him what he was doing; why, ſays he, I am laying the foundations of a city; and ſo the *birdman* drew out of ſight. *L'Eſtrange.*

**Bi'rdseye.** *n. ſ.* [*Adonis*, Lat.] The name of a plant.

The leaves are like fennel or chamomile; the flowers conſiſt of many leaves, which are expanded in form of a roſe; the ſeeds are collected into oblong heads. The ſpecies are, 1. The common red *birds eye*. 2. The long leaved yellow *birds eye*, &c. The firſt ſort is ſown in open borders, as an annual flower plant. The yellow ſort is uncommon in England. *Millar.*

**Bi'rdsfoot.** [*ornithopodium*, Lat.] The name of a plant.

It has a papilionaceous flower; the ovary, which riſes out of the flower cup, afterwards becomes a pod, ſometimes diſtinguiſhed into bells by tranſverſe partitions, full of ſeeds, for the moſt part roundiſh; the leaves grow by threes, but have two wings, or little leaves, at the origin of their foot ſtalks. The ſpecies are, 1. The talleſt hairy *birdsfoot* trefoil, with a glomerated flower. 2. Upright hoary *birdsfoot* trefoil, &c. The firſt of theſe plants is, by ſome, ſuppoſed to be the *cytiſus* of Virgil; it dies to the ground with us every winter, and riſes again the ſucceeding ſpring; and, when the roots are ſtrong, the ſhoots will riſe to four or five feet high, and produce flowers in great plenty; if it be cut while young, the cows are very fond of it, but horſes will not eat it, unleſs they are very hungry. *Millar.*

**Bi'rdsnest.** *n. ſ.* An herb. *Dict.*

**Bi'rdstongue.** *n. ſ.* An herb. *Dict.*

**Bi'rgander.** *n. ſ.* A fowl of the gooſe kind. *Dict.*

**Birt.** *n. ſ.* A fiſh; the ſame with the *turbot*; which ſee.

**BIRTH.** *n. ſ.* [beoph, Sax.]

1. The act of coming into life.

But thou art fair, and, at thy *birth*, dear boy,
Nature and fortune join'd to make thee great. *Shakeſp. K. J.*

In Spain, our ſprings like old mens children be,
Decay'd and wither'd from their infancy;
No kindly ſhowers fall on our barren earth,
To hatch the ſeaſons in a timely *birth*. *Dryden.*

2. Extraction; lineage.

Moſt virtuous virgin, born of heav'nly *birth*. *Fairy Q.*

All truth I ſhall relate: nor firſt can I
Myſelf to be of Grecian *birth* deny. *Sir J. Denham.*

3. Rank which is inherited by deſcent.

He doth object, I am too great of *birth*.
*Shakeſp. Merry Wives of Windſor.*

Be juſt in all you ſay, and all you do;
Whatever be your *birth*, you're ſure to be
A peer of the firſt magnitude to me. *Dryden's Juvenal.*

4. The condition, or circumſtances, in which any man is born.

High in his chariot then Haleſus came,
A foe by *birth* to Troy's unhappy name. *Dryden's Virgil.*

5. Thing born; production.

The people fear me; for they do obſerve
Unfather'd heirs and loathly *births* of nature. *Shakeſp. H.* IV.

That poets are far rarer *births* than kings,
Your nobleſt father prov'd. *Ben. Johnſon's Epigrams.*

Who of themſelves
Abhor to join: and, by imprudence mix'd,
Produce prodigious *births*, of body, or mind.
*Milton's Paradiſe Loſt, b.* xi. *l.* 687.

She, for this many thouſand years,
Seems to have practis'd with much care,
To frame the race of woman fair;
Yet never could a perfect *birth*
Produce before, to grace the earth. *Waller.*

His eldeſt *birth*
Flies, mark'd by heav'n, a fugitive o'er earth. *Prior.*

The vallies ſmile, and, with their flow'ry face,
And wealthy *births*, confeſs the flood's embrace. *Blackmore.*

Others hatch their eggs, and tend the *birth*, till it is able to ſhift for itſelf. *Addiſon. Spectator*, Nº 120.

6. The act of bringing forth.

That fair Syrian ſhepherdeſs,
Who after years of barrenneſs,
The highly favour'd Joſeph bore
To him that ſerv'd for her before;

And at her next *birth*, much like thee,
Through pangs fled to felicity. *Milton.*

7. The ſeamen call a due or proper diſtance between ſhips lying at an anchor, or under ſail, a *birth*. Alſo the proper place aboard for a meſs to put their cheſts, &c. is called the *birth* of that meſs. Alſo a convenient place to moor a ſhip in, is called a *birth*. *Harris.*

Bi'rthday. *n. ſ.* [from *birth* and *day*.]

1. The day on which any one is born.

Orient light,
Exhaling firſt from darkneſs, they beheld
*Birthday* of heaven and earth. *Milton's Paradiſe Loſt, b.* vii.

2. The day of the year in which any one was born, annually obſerved.

This is my *birthday*; as this very day
Was Caſſius born. *Shakeſp. Julius Cæſar.*

They tell me, 'tis my *birthday*, and I'll keep it
With double pomp of ſadneſs:
'Tis what the day deſerves, which gave me breath. *Dryden.*

Your country dames,
Whoſe cloaths returning *birthday* claims. *Prior.*

Bi'rthdom. *n. ſ.* [This is erroneouſly, I think, printed in *Shakeſpeare, birthdoom.* It is derived from *birth* and *dom.* See Dom; as *kingdom, dukedom.*] Privilege of birth.

Let us rather
Hold faſt the mortal ſword; and, like good men,
Beſtride our downfaln *birthdom*. *Shakeſp. Macbeth.*

Bi'rthnight. *n. ſ.* [from *birth* and *night*.]

1. The night in which any one is born.

Th' angelick ſong in Bethlehem field,
On thy *birthnight*, that ſung the Saviour born. *Par. Regain.*

2. The night annually kept in memory of any one's birth.

A youth more glitt'ring than a *birthnight* beau. *Pope.*

Bi'rthplace. *n. ſ.* [from *birth* and *place*.] Place where any one is born.

My *birthplace* have I and my lovers left;
This enemy's town I'll enter. *Shakeſp. Coriolanus.*

A degree of ſtupidity beyond even what we have been ever charged with, upon the ſcore of our *birthplace* and climate. *Swift's Addreſs to Parliament.*

Bi'rthright. *n. ſ.* [from *birth* and *right*.] The rights and privileges to which a man is born; the right of the firſt born.

Thy blood and virtue
Contend for empire in thee, and thy goodneſs
Shares with thy *birthright*. *Shakeſp. All's well that ends well.*

And haſt been found
By merit, more than *birthright*, Son of God.
*Milton's Parad. Loſt, b.* iii. *l.* 308.

I lov'd her firſt, I cannot quit the claim,
But will preſerve the *birthright* of my paſſion. *Otway's Orph.*

While no baſeneſs in this breaſt I find,
I have not loſt the *birthright* of my mind. *Dryden's Aurengz.*

To ſay, that liberty and property are the *birthright* of the Engliſh nation, but that if a prince invades them by illegal methods, we muſt upon no pretence reſiſt, is to confound governments. *Addiſon's Whig Examiner.*

Birthstra'ngled. *adj.* [from *birth* and *ſtrangle*.] Strangled or ſuffocated in being born.

Finger of *birthſtrangl'd* babe,
Ditch deliver'd by a drab. *Shakeſp. Macbeth.*

Bi'rthwort. *n. ſ.* [from *birth* and *wort*; I ſuppoſe from a quality of haſtening delivery. *Ariſtolochia*, Lat.] The name of a plant.

The ſtalks are flexible; the leaves are placed alternately on the branches; the flowers conſiſt of one leaf, are of an anomalous figure, hollowed like a pipe, and ſhaped like a tongue, generally hooked; the flower cup turns to a membraneous, oval ſhaped fruit, divided into five cells, and full of flat ſeeds. The ſpecies are, 1. The round rooted *birthwort*. 2. The climbing *birthwort*. 3. Spaniſh *birthwort*, &c. The firſt and ſecond are ſometimes uſed in medicine, and are eaſily propagated by parting their roots. *Millar.*

*BI'SCOTIN. n. ſ.* [French.] A confection made of flour, ſugar, marmalade, eggs, &c.

Bi'scuit. *n. ſ.* [from *bis*, twice, Lat. and *cuit*, baked, Fr.]

1. A kind of hard dry bread, made to be carried to ſea; it is baked for long voyages four times.

The *biſcuit* alſo in the ſhips, eſpecially in the Spaniſh gallies, was grown hoary, and unwholeſome. *Knolles's Hiſtory of the Turks.*

Many have been cured by abſtinence from drink, eating dry *biſcuit*, which creates no thirſt, and ſtrong frictions four or five times a day. *Arbuthnot on Diet.*

2. A compoſition of fine flour, almonds, and ſugar, made by the confectioners.

To Bise'ct. *v. a.* [from *binus* and *ſeco*, to cut, Lat.] To divide into two parts.

The rational horizon *biſecteth* the globe into two equal parts. *Brown's Vulgar Errours, b.* vi. *c.* 5.

Bise'ction. *n. ſ.* [from the verb.] A geometrical term, ſignifying the diviſion of any quantity into two equal parts.

BI'SHOP. *n. ſ.* [from *epiſcopus*, Lat. the Saxons formed biſcop, which was afterwards ſoftened into *biſhop*.] One of the head order of the clergy.

A *biſhop* is an overſeer, or ſuperintendant, of religious matters in the chriſtian church. *Ayliffe's Parergon.*

You ſhall find him well accompany'd
With reverend fathers, and well learned *biſhops*.
*Shakeſp. Richard III.*

Their zealous ſuperſtition thinks, or pretends, they cannot do God a greater ſervice, than to deſtroy the primitive, apoſtolical, and anciently univerſal government of the church by *biſhops*. *K. Charles.*

In caſe a *biſhop* ſhould commit treaſon and felony, and forfeit his eſtate, with his life, the lands of his biſhoprick remain ſtill in the church. *South.*

On the word *biſhop*, in French *evêque*, I would obſerve, that there is no natural connexion between the ſacred office and the letters or ſound; for *evêque*, and *biſhop*, ſignify the ſame office, though there is not one letter alike in them. *Watts's Logick.*

Bi'shop. *n. ſ.* A cant word for a mixture of wine, oranges, and ſugar.

Fine oranges,
Well roaſted, with ſugar and wine in a cup,
They'll make a ſweet *biſhop*, when gentle folks ſup. *Swift.*

To Bi'shop. *v. a.* [from the noun.] To confirm; to admit ſolemnly into the church.

They are prophane, imperfect, oh! too bad,
Except confirm'd and *biſhoped* by thee. *Donne.*

Bi'shoprick. *n. ſ.* [biſcoprice, Saxon.] The dioceſe of a biſhop; the diſtrict over which the juriſdiction of a biſhop extends.

It will be fit, that, by the king's ſupreme power in cauſes eccleſiaſtical, they be ſubordinate under ſome biſhop, and *biſhoprick*, of this realm. *Bacon's Advice to Villiers.*

A virtuous woman ſhould reject marriage, as a good man does a *biſhoprick*; but I would adviſe neither to perſiſt in refuſing. *Addiſon. Spectator,* Nº 89.

Thoſe paſtors had epiſcopal ordination, poſſeſſed preferments in the church, and were ſometimes promoted to *biſhopricks* themſelves. *Swift on the Sentiments of a Church of E. man.*

Bi'shopsweed. [*Ammi*, Lat.] The name of a plant.

This is an umbelliferous weed, with ſmall ſtriated ſeeds; the petals of the flowers are unequal, and ſhaped like a heart. The ſeeds of the greater *biſhopsweed* are uſed in medicine, and ſhould be ſown in an open ſituation, early in the ſpring. *Mill.*

Bisk. *n. ſ.* [*biſque*, Fr.] Soup; broth made by boiling ſeveral ſorts of fleſh.

A prince, who in a foreſt rides aſtray,
And, weary, to ſome cottage finds the way,
Talks of no pyramids, or fowl, or *bisks* of fiſh,
But hungry ſups his cream ſerv'd up in earthen diſh.
*King's Art of Cookery.*

Bi'sket. See Biscuit.

Bi'smuth. *n. ſ.* The ſame as *marcaſite*; it properly ſignifies a hard, white, brittle, mineral ſubſtance, of a metalline nature, found at Miſnia; though ſuppoſed to be only a recrementitious matter thrown off in the formation of tin, as unfit to enter its compoſition. There are ſome, however, who eſteem it a metal *ſui generis*; though it uſually contains ſome ſilver. There is an artificial *biſmuth* made, for the ſhops, of tin. *Quincy.*

Bi'ssextile. *n. ſ.* [from *bis*, and *ſextilis*, Lat.] Leap year; the year in which the day, ariſing from ſix odd hours in each year, is intercalated.

The year of the ſun conſiſteth of three hundred and ſixty five days and ſix hours, wanting eleven minutes; which ſix hours omitted, will, in time, deprave the compute; and this was the occaſion of *biſſextile*, or leap year. *Brown's Vulgar Errours, b.* iv. *c.* 12.

Towards the latter end of February is the *biſſextile* or intercalar day; called *biſſextile*, becauſe the ſixth of the calends of March is twice repeated. *Holder on Time.*

Bi'sson. *adj.* [derived by *Skinner* from *by* and *ſin*.] Blind.

But who, oh! who hath ſeen the mobled queen,
Run barefoot up and down, threat'ning the flames
With *biſſon* rheum. *Shakeſp. Hamlet.*

What harm can your *biſſon* conſpectuities glean out of this character. *Shakeſp. Coriolanus.*

*BI'STRE. n. ſ.* [French.] A colour made of chimney ſoot boiled, and then diluted with water; uſed by painters in waſhing their deſigns. *Trevoux.*

Bi'stort. *n. ſ.* [*biſtorta*, Lat.] The name of a plant called alſo *ſnakeweed*; which ſee.

Bi'stoury. *n. ſ.* [*biſtouri*, Fr.] A ſurgeon's inſtrument uſed in making inciſions, of which there are three ſorts; the blade of the firſt turns like that of a lancet; but the ſtraight *biſtoury* has the blade fixed in the handle; the crooked *biſtoury* is ſhaped like a half moon, having the edge on the inſide. *Chambers.*

Bisu'lcous. *adj.* [*biſulcus*. Lat.] Clovenfooted.

For the ſwine, although multiparous, yet being *biſulcous*, and only clovenhoofed, are farrowed with open eyes, as other *biſulcous* animals. *Brown's Vulgar Errours, b.* iii. *c.* 26.

Bit. *n. ſ.* [bitol, Saxon.] Signifies the whole machine of all the iron

blank page

a ‡

5 Bit the extremity of any thing that fastens
perhaps for bite
The gimlet hath a worm at the end of
its bit    Mox. Mech. Exer.

6 ‡ Bit the preterite of bite
The Sharp Steel arriving forcibly
On his broad Shield bit not but glancing fell
On his Horse Neck
F. Q. 2. 5. 4.

Not for that Silly old morality
These as these links were knit our loves should be
Mourn I that I thy Sevenfold chain have lost
Nor for the lucks sake but the bitter cost
Donne

iron appurtenances of a bridle, as the bit-mouth, the branches, the curb, the sevil holes, the tranchefil, and the cross chains; but sometimes it is used to signify only the bit-mouth in particular. *Farrier's Dict.*

They light from their horses, pulling off their *bits*, that they might something refresh their mouths upon the grass. *Sidney.*

We have strict statutes, and most biting laws,
The needful *bits* and curbs of headstrong steeds.
*Shakesp. Measure for Measure.*

He hath the *bit* fast between his teeth, and away he runs. *Stillingfleet.*

Unus'd to the restraint
Of curbs and *bits*, and fleeter than the winds. *Addis. Cato.*

Bit. *n. s.* [from *bite.*]

1. As much meat as is put into the mouth at once.

How many prodigal *bits* have slaves and peasants
This night englutted? *Shakesp. Timon of Athens.*

Follow your function, go and batten on cold *bits*. *Shakesp.*

The mice found it troublesome to be still climbing the oak for every *bit* they put in their bellies. *L'Estrange.*

By this the boiling kettle had prepar'd,
And to the table sent the smoaking lard,
A sav'ry *bit*, that serv'd to relish wine. *Dryden's Fables.*

John was the darling; he had all the good *bits*, was crammed with good pullet, chicken, and capon. *Arbuthnot's J. Bull.*

2. A small piece of any thing.

Then clap four slices of pilaster on't,
That, lac'd with *bits* of rustick, makes a front. *Pope.*

He bought at thousands, what with better wit
You purchase as you want, and *bit* by *bit*. *Pope's Epistles.*

His majesty has power to grant a patent for stamping round *bits* of copper, to every subject he hath. *Swift.*

3. A Spanish West Indian silver coin, valued at sevenpence halfpenny.

4. *A bit the better or worse.* In the smallest degree.

There are few that know all the tricks of these lawyers; for aught I can see, your case is not a *bit* clearer than it was seven years ago. *Arbuthnot's History of J. Bull.*

To Bit. *v. a.* [from the noun.] To put the bridle upon a horse.

Bitch. *n. s.* [bicce, Saxon.]

1. The female of the canine kind; as the wolf, the dog, the fox, the otter.

And at his feet a *bitch* wolf suck did yield
To two young babes. *Spens. Vision of Bellay.*

I have been credibly informed, that a *bitch* will nurse, play with, and be fond of young foxes, as much as, and in place of her puppies. *Locke.*

2. A name of reproach for a woman.

John had not run a madding so long, had it not been for an extravagant *bitch* of a wife. *Arbuthnot's History of J. Bull.*

To BITE. *v. a.* pret. I *bit*; part. pass. I have *bit*, or *bitten*. [bitan, Saxon.]

1. To crush, or pierce with the teeth.

My very enemy's dog,
Though he had *bit* me, should have stood that night
Against my fire. *Shakesp. King Lear.*

Such smiling rogues as these,
Like rats, oft *bite* the holy cords in twain,
Too intricate t' unloose. *Shakesp. King Lear.*

These are the youths that thunder at a playhouse, and fight for *bitten* apples. *Shakesp. Henry VIII.*

He falls; his arms upon his body sound,
And with his bloody teeth he *bites* the ground. *Dryden.*

There was lately a young gentleman *bit* to the bone, who has now indeed recovered. *Tatler*, N° 62.

Their foul mouths have not opened their lips without a falsity; though they have showed their teeth as if they would *bite* off my nose. *Arbuthnot and Pope's Martinus Scriblerus.*

2. To give pain by cold.

Here feel we the icy phang,
And churlish chiding of the winter's wind;
Which when it *bites* and blows upon my body,
Ev'n till I shrink with cold, I smile. *Shakesp. As you like it.*

Full fifty years harness'd in rugged steel,
I have endur'd the *biting* winter's blast,
And the severer heats of parching summer.
*Rowe's Ambitious Stepmother.*

3. To hurt or pain with reproach.

Each poet with a diff'rent talent writes;
One praises, one instructs, another *bites*. *Roscommon.*

4. To cut; to wound.

I've seen the day, with my good *biting* faulchion,
I would have made them skip. *Shakesp. King Lear.*

5. To make the mouth smart with an acrid taste.

It may be the first water will have more of the scent, as more fragrant; and the second more of the taste, as more bitter, or *biting*. *Bacon's Natural History*, N° 21.

6. To cheat; to trick; to defraud: a low phrase.

Asleep and naked as an Indian lay,
An honest factor stole a gem away:
He pledg'd it to the knight; the knight had wit,
So kept the diamond, and the rogue was *bit*. *Pope.*

If you had allowed half the fine gentlemen to have conversed with you, they would have been strangely *bit*, while they thought only to fall in love with a fair lady. *Pope's Letters.*

Bite. *n. s.* [from the verb.]

1. The seizure of any thing by the teeth.

Does he think he can endure the everlasting burnings, or arm himself against the *bites* of the never dying worm? *South.*

Nor dogdays parching heat, that splits the rocks,
Are half so harmful as the greedy flocks;
Their venom'd *bite*, and scars indented on the stocks.
*Dryden's Virgil's Georgicks, b.* ii. *l.* 522.

2. The act of a fish that takes the bait.

I have known a very good fisher angle diligently four or six hours for a river carp, and not have a *bite*. *Walton's Angler.*

3. A cheat; a trick; a fraud; in low and vulgar language.

Let a man be ne'er so wise,
He may be caught with sober lies;
For take it in its proper light,
'Tis just what coxcombs call a *bite*. *Swift.*

4. A sharper; one who commits frauds.

Bi'ter. *n. s.* [from *bite.*]

1. He that bites.

Great barkers are no *biters*. *Camden's Remains.*

2. A fish apt to take the bait.

He is so bold, that he will invade one of his own kind, and you may therefore easily believe him to be a bold *biter*. *Walton.*

3. A tricker; a deceiver.

A *biter* is one who tells you a thing, you have no reason to disbelieve in itself, and perhaps has given you, before he bit you, no reason to disbelieve it for his saying it; and, if you give him credit, laughs in your face, and triumphs that he has deceived you. He is one who thinks you a fool, because you do not think him a knave. *Spectator*, N° 504.

Bi'ttacle. *n. s.* A frame of timber in the steerage of a ship, where the compass is placed. *Dict.*

Bi'tten. *particip. pass.* [from *to bite*; which see.]

BI'TTER. *adj.* [biꞇeꞃ, Saxon.]

1. Having a hot, acrid, biting taste, like wormwood.

*Bitter* things are apt rather to kill than engender putrefaction. *Bacon's Nat. Hist.* N° 696.

Though a man in a fever should, from sugar, have a *bitter* taste, which, at another time, produces a sweet one; yet the idea of *bitter* in that man's mind, would be as clear and distinct from the idea of sweet, as if he had tasted only gall. *Locke.*

2. Sharp; cruel; severe.

Friends now fast sworn,
Unseparable, shall within this hour,
On a dissension of a doit, break out
To *bitterest* enmity. *Shakesp. Coriolanus.*

Husbands, love your wives, and be not *bitter* against them. *Coloss.* iii. 19.

The word of God, instead of a *bitter*, teaches us a charitable zeal. *Sprat.*

3. Calamitous; miserable.

Noble friends and fellows, whom to leave
Is only *bitter* to him, only dying;
Go with me, like good angels, to my end. *Shakesp. H.* VIII.

A dire induction am I witness to;
And will to France, hoping, the consequence
Will prove as *bitter*, black, and tragical. *Shakesp. Rich.* III.

Tell him, that if I bear my *bitter* fate,
'Tis to behold his vengeance for my son. *Dryden's Æneid.*

4. Painful; inclement.

And shun the *bitter* consequence: for know,
The day thou eat'st thereof, my sole command
Transgrest, inevitably thou shalt die. *Paradise Lost, b.* viii.

The fowl the borders fly,
And shun the *bitter* blast, and wheel about the sky. *Dryden.*

5. Sharp; reproachful; satirical.

Go with me,
And, in the breath of *bitter* words, let's smother
My damned son. *Shakesp. Richard* III.

6. Mournful; afflicted.

Wherefore is light given unto him that is in misery, and life unto the *bitter* in soul? *Job*, iii. 20.

7. In any manner, unpleasing or hurtful.

*Bitter* is an equivocal word; there is *bitter* wormwood, there are *bitter* words, there are *bitter* enemies, and a *bitter* cold morning. *Watts's Logick.*

Bi'ttergourd. *n. s.* [*colocynthis*, Lat.] The name of a plant. It is, in all respects, like the gourd, excepting the leaves of the plant being deeply jagged, and the fruit being excessively bitter, and not eatable. There are several varieties of this plant, which are very common in divers parts of the East and West Indies. *Millar.*

Bi'tterly. *adv.* [from *bitter.*]

1. With a bitter taste.

2. In a bitter manner; sorrowfully; calamitously.

I so lively acted with my tears,
That my poor mistress, moved therewithal,
Wept *bitterly*. *Shakesp. Two Gentlemen of Verona.*

Bitterly

*Bitterly* haſt thou paid, and ſtill art paying
That rigid ſcore. *Milton's Agoniſtes, l. 432.*

3. Sharply; ſeverely.

His behaviour is not to cenſure *bitterly* the errours of their zeal. *Sprat.*

Bi'ttern. *n. ſ.* [*butour*, Fr.] A bird with long legs, and a long bill, which feeds upon fiſh; remarkable for the noiſe which he makes, uſually called *bumping*. See Bittour.

The poor fiſh have enemies enough, beſides ſuch unnatural fiſhermen as otters, the cormorant, and the *bittern*. *Walton.*

So that ſcarce

The *bittern* knows his time, with bill ingulpht,
To ſhake the ſounding marſh. *Thomſon's Spring.*

Bi'ttern. *n. ſ.* [from *bitter.*] A very bitter liquour, which drains off in making of common ſalt, and uſed in the preparation of Epſom ſalt. *Quincy.*

Bi'tterness. *n. ſ.* [from *bitter.*]

1. A bitter taſte.

The idea of whiteneſs, or *bitterneſs*, is in the mind, exactly anſwering that power which is in any body to produce it there. *Locke.*

2. Malice; grudge; hatred; implacability.

The *bitterneſs* and animoſity between the chief commanders was ſuch, that a great part of the army was marched. *Clarend.*

3. Sharpneſs; ſeverity of temper.

His ſorrows have ſo overwhelm'd his wits,
Shall we be thus afflicted in his wreaks,
His fits, his frenzy, and his *bitterneſs?* *Shakeſp. Tit. Andr.*

Pierpoint and Crew appeared now to have contracted more *bitterneſs* and ſourneſs than formerly, and were more reſerved towards the king's commiſſioners. *Clarendon, b.* viii.

4. Satire; piquancy; keenneſs of reproach.

Some think their wits have been aſleep, except they dart out ſomewhat piquant, and to the quick: men ought to find the difference between ſaltneſs and *bitterneſs*. *Bacon, Eſſay* 33.

5. Sorrow; vexation; affliction.

There appears much joy in him, even ſo much, that joy could not ſhew itſelf modeſt enough, without a badge of *bitterneſs*. *Shakeſp. Much ado about Nothing.*

They ſhall mourn for him, as one mourneth for his only ſon, and ſhall be in *bitterneſs* for him, as one that is in *bitterneſs* for his firſtborn. *Zech.* xii. 10.

Moſt purſue the pleaſures, as they call them, of their natures, which begin in ſin, are carried on with danger, and end in *bitterneſs*. *Wake's Preparation for Death.*

I oft, in *bitterneſs* of ſoul, deplor'd
My abſent daughter, and my dearer lord. *Pope's Odyſſey.*

Bi'ttersweet. *n. ſ.* [from *bitter* and *ſweet.*] The name of an apple, which has a compound taſte of ſweet and bitter.

It is but a *bitterſweet* at beſt, and the fine colours of the ſerpent do by no means make amends for the ſmart and poiſon of his ſting. *South.*

When I expreſs the taſte of an apple, which we call the *bitterſweet*, none can miſtake what I mean. *Watts's Logick.*

Bi'ttervetch. *n. ſ.* [*orobus*, Lat.]

This plant hath a papilionaceous flower, out of whoſe empalement riſes the pointal, wrapt up in the membrane, which becomes a round pod, full of oval ſhaped ſeeds; two leaves, joined together, grow upon a rib that terminates in a point. *Millar.*

Bi'ttour. *n. ſ.* [*butour*, Fr.] The name of a bird, commonly called the *bittern*; [See Bittern.] but perhaps as properly *bittour*.

Then to the waters brink ſhe laid her head;
And, as a *bittour* bumps within a reed,
To thee alone, O lake, ſhe ſaid, I tell. *Dryden's W. of Bath.*

Bitu'me. *n. ſ.* [from *bitumen.*] Bitumen. See BITUMEN.

Mix with theſe
Idæan pitch, quick ſulphur, ſilver's ſpume,
Sea onion, hellebore, and black *bitume*. *May's Virgil.*

BITU'MEN. *n. ſ.* [Lat.] A fat unctuous matter dug out of the earth, or ſcummed off lakes, as the Aſphaltis in Judæa, of various kinds; ſome ſo hard as to be uſed for coals; others ſo glutinous as to ſerve for mortar. *Savary.*

It is reported, that *bitumen* mingled with lime, and put under water, will make, as it were, an artificial rock, the ſubſtance becometh ſo hard. *Bacon's Nat. Hiſtory*, N° 783.

The fabrick ſeem'd a work of riſing ground,
With ſulphur and *bitumen* caſt between. *Dryden's Fables.*

*Bitumen* is a body that readily takes fire, yields an oil, and is ſoluble in water. *Woodward's Method of Foſſils.*

Bitu'minous. *adj.* [from *bitumen.*] Having the nature and qualities of bitumen; compounded of bitumen.

Naphtha, which was the *bituminous* mortar uſed in the walls of Babylon, grows to an entire and very hard matter, like a ſtone. *Bacon's Phyſical Remains.*

The fruitage fair to ſight, like that which grew
Near that *bituminous* lake, where Sodom flam'd.
*Milton's Par. Loſt, b. x. l. 562.*

Biva'lve. *adj.* [from *binus* and *valvæ*, Lat.] Having two valves or ſhutters; a term uſed of thoſe fiſh that have two ſhells, as oyſters; and of thoſe plants whoſe ſeed pods open their whole length, to diſcharge their ſeeds, as peas.

In the cavity lies looſe the ſhell of ſome ſort of *bivalve*, larger than could be introduced in at either of theſe holes. *Woodward on Foſſils.*

Biva'lvular. *adj.* [from *bivalve.*] Having two valves. *Dict.*

Bi'xwort. *n. ſ.* An herb. *Dict.*

Bi'zantine. *n. ſ.* [more properly ſpelt *byzantine*; from *Byzantium.*] A great piece of gold valued at fifteen pound, which the king offereth upon high feſtival days; it is yet called a *bizantine*, which anciently was apiece of gold coined by the emperours of Conſtantinople. *Camden's Remains.*

To BLAB. *v. a.* [*blabberen*, Dutch.]

1. To tell what ought to be kept ſecret; it uſually implies rather thoughtleſſneſs than treachery; but may be uſed in either ſenſe.

The gaudy, *blabbing*, and remorſeful day,
Is crept into the boſom of the ſea. *Shakeſp. Henry* VI.

Thy dues be done, and none left out,
Ere the *blabbing* eaſtern ſcout
The nice morn on the Indian ſteep,
From her cabin'd loophole peep. *Milton.*

Nature has made man's breaſt no windores,
To publiſh what he does within doors;
Nor what dark ſecrets there inhabit,
Unleſs his own raſh folly *blab* it. *Hudibras, p.* ii. *c.* ii.

Sorrow nor joy can be diſguis'd by art,
Our foreheads *blab* the ſecrets of our heart. *Dryden's Juv.*

It is unlawful to give any kind of religious worſhip to a creature; but the very *indices* of the fathers cannot eſcape the *index expurgatorius*, for *blabbing* ſo great a truth. *Stillingfleet.*

Nor whiſper to the tattling reeds
The blackeſt of all female deeds;
Nor *blab* it on the lonely rocks,
Where echo ſits, and liſt'ning mocks. *Swift.*

2. To tell; in a good ſenſe.

That delightful engine of her thoughts,
That *blabb'd* them with ſuch pleaſing eloquence,
Is torn from forth that pretty hollow cage.
*Shakeſp. Titus Andronicus.*

To Blab. *v. n.* To tattle; to tell tales.

Your mute I'll be;
When my tongue *blabs*, then let mine eyes not ſee.
*Shakeſp. Twelfth Night.*

Blab. *n. ſ.* [from the verb.] A teltale; a thoughtleſs babbler; a treacherous betrayer of ſecrets.

The ſecret man heareth many confeſſions; for who will open himſelf to a *blab*, or babbler? *Bacon, Eſſay* 6.

To have reveal'd
Secrets of man, the ſecrets of a friend,
Contempt and ſcorn of all, to be excluded
All friendſhip, and avoided as a *blab*. *Milton's Agoniſtes.*

Whoever ſhews me a very inquiſitive body, I'll ſhew him a *blab*, and one that ſhall make privacy as publick as a proclamation. *L'Eſtrange.*

I ſhould have certainly gone about ſhewing my letters, under the charge of ſecrecy, to every *blab* of my acquaintance. *Swift's Letters.*

Bla'bber. *n. ſ.* [from *blab.*] A tattler; a teltale.

To Bla'bber. *v. n.* To whiſtle to a horſe. *Skinner.*

Bla'bberlipped. *Skinner.* See Blobberlipped.

BLACK. *adj.* [blac, Saxon.]

1. Of the colour of night.

In the twilight in the evening, in the *black* and dark night. *Prov.* vii. 9.

By Ariſtotle it ſeems to be implied, in theſe problems which enquire why the ſun makes man *black*, and not the fire, why it whitens wax, yet blacks the ſkin. *Brown's Vulgar Errours.*

2. Dark.

The heaven was *black* with clouds and wind, and there was a great rain. *1 Kings*, xviii. 45.

3. Cloudy of countenance; ſullen.

She hath abated me of half my train;
Look'd *black* upon me. *Shakeſp. King Lear.*

4. Horrible; wicked; atrocious.

Either my country never muſt be freed,
Or I conſenting to ſo *black* a deed. *Dryden's Indian Emp.*

5. Diſmal; mournful.

A dire induction am I witneſs to;
And will to France, hoping, the conſequence,
Will prove as bitter, *black*, and tragical. *Shakeſp. Rich.* III.

6. *Black and blue.* The colour of a bruiſe; a ſtripe.

Miſtreſs Ford, good heart, is beaten *black and blue*, that you cannot ſee a white ſpot about her. *Merry Wives of Windſor.*

And, wing'd with ſpeed and fury, flew
To reſcue knight from *black and blue*. *Hudibras, cant.* ii.

Black-browed. *adj.* [from *black* and *brow.*] Having black eyebrows; gloomy; diſmal; threatening.

Come, gentle night; come, loving, *black-brow'd* night,
Give me my Romeo. *Shakeſp. Romeo and Juliet.*

Thus when a *black-brow'd* guſt begins to riſe,
White foam at firſt on the curl'd ocean fries,
Then roars the main, the billows mount the ſkies.
*Dryden, Æneid* vii. *l.* 736.

What black magician conjures up this Fiend
To stop devoted charitable deeds
Shak. R. 3.

IL facing 3E[r]

BLACK-BRYONY. *n. s.* [*tamnus*, Lat.] The name of a plant.

It is male and female in different plants; the flowers of the male plant consist of one leaf, and are bell shaped; but these are barren; the embryos are produced on the female plants, which become oval berries, including roundish seeds. These plants have no clasper, as the white bryony hath. The species are, 1. The common *black-bryony*. 2. *Black bryony* of Crete, with a trifid leaf, *&c.* The first is rarely cultivated in gardens, but grows wild under hedges, and is gathered for medicinal use. It may be easily propagated by sowing the seeds, soon after they are ripe, under the shelter of bushes; where, in the spring, the plants will come up, and spread their branches over the bushes. *Millar.*

BLACK-CATTLE. Oxen; bulls; and cows.

The other part of the grazier's business is what we call *black-cattle*, producing hides, tallow, and beef, for exportation. *Swift.*

BLACK-EARTH. *n. s.* It is every where obvious on the surface of the ground, and what we call mould. *Woodw. on Fossils.*

BLACK-GUARD. *adj.* [from *black* and *guard.*] A cant word amongst the vulgar; by which is implied a dirty fellow; of the meanest kind.

Let a *black-guard* boy be always about the house, to send on your errands, and go to market for you on rainy days. *Swift.*

BLACK-LEAD. *n. s.* [from *black* and *lead.*] A mineral found in the lead-mines, much used for pencils; it is not fusible, or not without a very great heat.

You must first get your *black-lead* sharpened finely, and put fast into quills, for your rude and first draught. *Peacham.*

BLACK-MAIL. *n. s.* A certain rate of money, corn, cattle, or other consideration, paid to men allied with robbers, to be by them protected from the danger of such as usually rob or steal. *Cowel.*

BLACK-PUDDING. *n. s.* [from *black* and *pudding.*] A kind of food made of blood and grain.

Through they were lin'd with many a piece
Of ammunition bread and cheese,
And fat *black-puddings*, proper food
For warriours that delight in blood. *Hudibras, p. i. cant.* i.

BLACK-ROD. *n. s.* [from *black* and *rod.*] The usher belonging to the order of the garter; so called from the *black rod* he carries in his hand. He is of the king's chamber, and likewise usher of the parliament. *Cowel.*

BLACK. *n. s.* [from the adjective.]

1. A black colour.

*Black* is the badge of hell,
The hue of dungeons, and the scowl of night.
*Shakesp. Love's Labour Lost.*

For the production of *black*, the corpuscles must be less than any of those which exhibit colours. *Newton's Opticks.*

2. Mourning.

Rise, wretched widow, rise; nor, undeplor'd,
Permit my ghost to pass the Stygian ford:
But rise, prepar'd in *black*, to mourn thy perish'd lord.
*Dryden's Fables.*

3. A blackamoor.
4. That part of the eye which is black.

It suffices that it be in every part of the air, which is as big as the *black* or sight of the eye. *Digby.*

To BLACK. *v. a.* [from the noun.] To make black; to blacken.

*Blacking* over the paper with ink, not only the ink would be quickly dried up, but the paper, that I could not burn before, would be quickly set on fire. *Boyle on Colours.*

Then in his fury *black'd* the raven o'er,
And bid him prate in his white plumes no more.
*Addison's Ovid's Metamorph. b. ii.*

BLA'CKAMOOR. *n. s.* [from *black* and *Moor.*] A man by nature of a black complexion; a negro.

They are no more afraid of a *blackamoor*, or a lion, than of a nurse, or a cat. *Locke on Education,* § 115.

BLA'CKBERRIED *Heath.* [*empetrum*, Lat.] The name of a plant.

It hath leaves like those of the heath; the flowers are male and female, which grow in different parts of the same plant; the male flowers have no petals; the female are succeeded by blackberries, in each of which are contained three or four hard seeds. This little shrub grows wild upon the mountains in Staffordshire, Devonshire, and Yorkshire. *Millar.*

BLA'CKBERRY *Bush. n. s.* A species of bramble; which see.

BLA'CKBERRY. *n. s.* The fruit of the blackberry bush.

The policy of these crafty sneering rascals, that stale old mouse-eaten cheese Nestor, and that same dogfox Ulysses, is not proved worth a *blackberry*. *Shakesp. Troilus and Cressida.*

Then sad he sung the children in the wood;
How *blackberries* they pluck'd in desarts wild,
And fearless at the glittering fauchion smil'd. *Gay's Past.*

BLA'CKBIRD. *n. s.* [from *black* and *bird.*] The name of a bird.

Of singing birds, they have linnets, goldfinches, *blackbirds*, thrushes, and divers others. *Carew's Survey of Cornwal.*

A schoolboy ran unto't, and thought
The crib was down, the *blackbird* caught. *Swift.*

To BLA'CKEN. *v. a.* [from *black.*]

1. To make of a black colour.

Vol. I.

Bless'd by aspiring winds, he finds the strand
*Blacken'd* by crouds. *Prior.*
While the long fun'rals *blacken* all the way. *Pope.*

2. To darken.

That little cloud that appear'd at first to Elijah's servant, no bigger than a man's hand, but presently after grew, and spread, and *blackened* the face of the whole heaven. *South.*

3. To defame; or make infamous.

Let us *blacken* him what we can, said that miscreant Harrison, of the blessed king, upon the wording and drawing up his charge against his approaching trial. *South.*

The morals *blacken'd*, when the writings 'scape
The libell'd person, and the pictur'd shape. *Pope.*

To BLA'CKEN. *v. n.* To grow black.

The hollow sound
Sung in the leaves, the forest shook around,
Air *blacken'd*, roll'd the thunder, groan'd the ground. *Dryden.*

BLA'CKISH. *adj.* [from *black.*] Somewhat black.

Part of it all the year continues in the form of a *blackish* oil. *Boyle.*

BLA'CKMOOR. *n. s.* [from *black* and *Moor.*] A negro.

The land of Chus makes no part of Africa; nor is it the habitation of *blackmoors*; but the country of Arabia, especially the happy and stony. *Brown's Vulgar Errours, b.* vi. *c.* 11.

More to west
The realm of Bacchus to the *blackmoor* sea. *Par. Reg. b.* iv.

BLA'CKNESS. *n. s.* [from *black.*]

1. Black colour.

*Blackness* is only a disposition to absorb, or stifle, without reflection, most of the rays of every sort that fall on the bodies. *Locke's Elements of Natural Philosophy, c.* ii.

There would emerge one or more very black spots, and, within those, other spots of an intenser *blackness*. *Newt. Opt.*

His tongue, his prating tongue, had chang'd him quite,
To sooty *blackness* from the purest white. *Addison's Ovid.*

2. Darkness.

His faults in him seem as the spots of heav'n,
More fiery by night's *blackness*. *Shakesp. Ant. and Cleopatra.*

BLA'CKSMITH. *n. s.* [from *black* and *smith.*] A smith that works in iron; so called from being very smutty.

The *blacksmith* may forge what he pleases. *Howel's E. Tears.*

Shut up thy doors with bars and bolts; it will be impossible for the *blacksmith* to make them so fast, but a cat and a whoremaster will find a way through them. *Spectator,* Nº 205.

BLA'CKTAIL. *n. s.* [from *black* and *tail.*] A fish; a kind of perch, by some called *ruffs*, or *popes*. See POPE. *Dict.*

BLA'CKTHORN. *n. s.* [from *black* and *thorn.*] The same with the sloe. See PLUM, of which it is a species.

BLA'DDER. *n. s.* [blædre, Saxon; *blader*, Dutch.]

1. That vessel in the body which contains the urine.

The *bladder* should be made of a membranous substance, and extremely dilatable for receiving and containing the urine, till an opportunity of emptying it. *Ray on the Creation.*

2. It is often filled with wind, to which allusions are frequently made.

That huge great body which the giant bore,
Was vanquish'd quite, and of that monstrous mass
Was nothing left, but like an empty *bladder* was. *Fairy Q.*

A *bladder* but moderately filled with air, and strongly tied, being held near the fire, grew exceeding turgid and hard; but afterwards being brought nearer to the fire, it suddenly broke, with so loud a noise as made us for a while after almost deaf. *Boyle.*

3. It is usual for those that learn to swim, to support themselves with blown bladders.

I have ventur'd,
Like little wanton boys, that swim on *bladders*,
These many summers, in a sea of glory;
But far beyond my depth: my highblown pride
At length broke under me. *Shakesp. Henry* VIII.

4. A blister; a pustule.

BLA'DDER-NUT. *n. s.* [*staphylodendron*, Lat.] A plant.

The flower consists of several leaves, which are placed circularly, and expand in form of a rose; out of whose many headed flower cup rises the pointal, which becomes a membranaceous fruit, somewhat like the inflated bladder of fishes, and divided into two or three cells, containing seeds in form of a scull. The species are, 1. The common wild *bladder-nut*. 2. Three leaved Virginian *bladder-nut*. 3. *Bladder-nut*, with single shining leaves. 4. *Bladder-nut*, with narrow bay leaves. 5. Three leaved American *bladder-nut*, with cut leaves. The first of these trees is found wild in the woods and other shady places, in the northern parts of England. The second sort is a native of America, but is so hardy as to endure the severest cold of our climate in the open air. Both these kinds are propagated, by sowing their seeds early in the spring. They will commonly grow in England to the height of twelve or fourteen feet. *Mill.*

BLA'DDER-SENA. *n. s.* [*colutea*, Lat.] The name of a plant.

It hath a papilionaceous flower, succeeded by pods, resembling the inflated bladder of fishes, in which are contained several kidney shaped seeds. The species are five. These shrubs grow to the height of eight or ten feet; and, among flowering trees,

trees, the oddness of their flowers and pods will make a pretty variety. *Millar.*

BLADE. *n. s.* [blæb, bleb, Sax. *bled*, Fr.] The spire of grass before it grows to seed; the green shoots of corn which rise from the seed. This seems to me the primitive signification of the word *blade*; from which, I believe, the *blade* of a sword was first named, because of its similitude in shape; and, from the *blade* of a sword, that of other weapons or tools.

There is hardly found a plant that yieldeth a red juice in the *blade* or ear, except it be the tree that beareth *sanguis draconis.* *Bacon.*

He sends to his feeding flocks betimes, t' invade
The rising bulk of the luxuriant *blade.* *Dryden's Georg.*

If we were able to dive into her secret recesses, we should find that the smallest *blade* of grass, or most contemptible weed, has its particular use. *Swift on the Faculties of the Mind.*

Hung on every spray, on every *blade*
Of grass, the myriad dewdrops twinkle round. *Thomson.*

BLADE. *n. s.* [*blatte*, Germ. *blad*, Dutch.]
The sharp or striking part of a weapon or instrument, distinct from the handle. It is usually taken for a weapon, and so called probably from the likeness of a sword *blade* to a *blade* of grass.

He fought all round about, his thirsty *blade*
To bathe in blood of faithless enemy. *Fairy Queen, b.* i.

She knew the virtue of her *blade*, nor would
Pollute her sabre with ignoble blood. *Dryden's Hind and P.*

Be his this sword, whose *blade* of brass displays
A ruddy gleam; whose hilt a silver blaze. *Pope.*

3. A brisk man, either fierce or gay, called so in contempt. So we say *mettle* for *courage.*

You'll find yourself mistaken, Sir, if you'll take upon you to judge of these *blades* by their garbs, looks, and outward appearance. *L'Estrange.*

Then turning about to the hangman, he said,
Dispatch me, I pri'thee, this troublesome *blade.* *Prior.*

BLADE *of the Shoulder.* } *n. s.* The bone called by anatomists the
BLA'DEBONE. } scapula, or scapular bone.

He fell most furiously on the broiled relicks of a shoulder of mutton, commonly called a *bladebone.* *Pope.*

To BLADE. *v. a.* [from the noun.] To furnish, or fit with a blade.

BLA'DED. *adj.* [from *blade.*] Having blades or spires.

Her silver visage in the wat'ry glass,
Decking with liquid pearl the *bladed* grass.
*Shakesp. Midsummer Night's Dream.*

As where the lightning runs along the ground,
Nor *bladed* grass, nor bearded corn succeeds,
But scales of scurf and putrefaction breeds. *Dryden.*

BLAIN. *n. s.* [blegene, Sax. *bleyne*, Dutch.] A pustule; a botch; a blister.

Itches, *blains*,
Sow all th' Athenian bosoms, and the crop
Be general leprosy. *Shakesp. Timon.*

Botches and *blains* must all his flesh imboss,
And all his people. *Milton's Par. Lost, b.* xii. *l.* 180.

Whene'er I hear a rival nam'd,
I feel my body all inflam'd;
Which breaking out in boils and *blains*,
With yellow filth my linen stains. *Swift.*

BLA'MABLE. *adj.* [from *blame.*] Culpable; faulty.

Virtue is placed between two extremes, which are on both sides equally *blamable.* *Dryden's Dufresnoy.*

BLA'MABLENESS. *n. s.* [from *blamable.*] Fault; the state of being liable to blame.

BLA'MABLY. *adv.* [from *blamable.*] Culpably; in a manner liable to censure.

A process may be carried on against a person, that is maliciously or *blamably* absent, even to a definitive sentence. *Ayliffe.*

To BLAME. *v. a.* [*blâmer*, Fr.]

1. To censure; to charge with a fault: it generally implies a slight censure.

Our pow'r
Shall do a court'sy to our wrath, which men
May *blame*, but not controul. *Shakesp. King Lear.*

Porphyrius, you too far did tempt your fate;
'Tis true, your duty to me it became;
But praising that, I must your conduct *blame.*
*Dryden's Tyrannick Love.*

Each finding, like a friend,
Something to *blame*, and something to commend. *Pope.*

2. To *blame* has usually the particle *for* before the fault.

The reader must not *blame* me *for* making use here, all along of the word sentiment. *Locke.*

3. Sometimes, but rarely, *of.*

Tomoreus he *blam'd of* inconsiderate rashness, for that he would busy himself in matters not belonging to his vocation.
*Knolles's History of the Turks.*

BLAME. *n. s.* [from the verb.]

1. Fault; imputation of a fault.

In arms, the praise of success is shared amongst many; yet the *blame* of misadventures is charged upon one.
*Sir J. Hayward.*

They lay the *blame* on the poor little ones, sometimes passionately enough, to divert it from themselves. *Locke.*

2. Crime; that which produces or deserves censure.

Who would not judge us to be discharged of all *blame*, which are confest to have no great fault, even by their very word and testimony, in whose eyes no fault of ours hath ever hitherto been accustomed to seem small. *Hooker, b.* v. § 27.

I unspeak mine own detraction; here abjure
The taints and *blames* I laid upon myself,
For strangers to my nature. *Shakesp. Macbeth.*

3. Hurt.

Therewith upon his crest,
With rigour so outrageous he smit,
That a large share it hew'd out of the rest,
And glancing down his shield, from *blame* him fairly blest.
*Fairy Queen, b.* i. *cant.* ii. *stanz.* 18.

4. There is a peculiar structure of this word, in which it is not very evident whether it be a *noun* or a verb; but I conceive it to be the *noun. To blame*, in French, *à tort.*

You were *to blame*, I must be plain with you,
To part so slightly with your wife's first gift.
*Shakesp. Merchant of Venice.*

I do not ask whether they were mistaken; but, on supposition they were not, whether they were *to blame* in the manner. *Stillingfleet.*

Now we should hold them much *to blame*,
If they went back before they came. *Prior.*

BLA'MEFUL. *adj.* [from *blame* and *full.*] Criminal; guilty; meriting blame.

Is not the causer of these timeless deaths,
As *blameful* as the executioner? *Shakesp. Richard* III.

Bluntwitted lord, ignoble in demeanour,
If ever lady wrong'd her lord so much,
Thy mother took into her *blameful* bed
Some stern untutor'd churl. *Shakesp. Henry* VI. *p.* ii.

BLA'MELESS. *adj.* [from *blame.*]

1. Guiltless; innocent; exempt from censure or blame.

She found out the righteous, and preserved him *blameless* unto God. *Wisdom*, x. 5.

The flames ascend on either altar clear,
While thus the *blameless* maid address'd her pray'r. *Dryden.*

Such a lessening of our coin will deprive great numbers of *blameless* men, of a fifth part of their estates. *Locke.*

2. Sometimes it is used with *of.*

We will be *blameless of* this thine oath. *Joshua*, ii. 17.

BLA'MELESLY. *adv.* [from *blameless.*] Innocently; without crime.

It is the wilful opposing explicit articles, and not the not believing them when not revealed, or not with that conviction, against which he cannot *blamelesly*, without pertinacy, hold out, that will bring danger of ruin on any. *Hammond's Fundamentals.*

BLA'MELESNESS. *n. s.* [from *blameless.*] Innocence; exemption from censure.

Having resolved, with him in Homer, that all is chargeable on Jupiter and fate, they infer, with him, the *blamelesness* of the inferiour agent. *Hammond's Fundamentals.*

BLA'MER. *n. s.* [from *blame.*] One that blames or finds fault; a censurer.

In me you've hallowed a pagan muse,
And denizon'd a stranger, who, mistaught
By *blamers* of the times they marr'd, hath sought
Virtues in corners. *Donne.*

BLAMEWO'RTHY. *adj.* [from *blame* and *worthy.*] Culpable; blameable; worthy of blame or censure.

Although the same should be *blameworthy*, yet this age hath reasonably well forborn to incur the danger of any such blame. *Hooker, b.* v. § 12.

To BLANCH. *v. a.* [*blanchir*, Fr.]

1. To whiten; to change from some other colour to white.

You can behold such sights,
And keep the natural ruby of your cheeks,
When mine is *blanch'd* with fear. *Shakesp. Macbeth.*

A way of whiting wax cheaply may be of use; and we have set down the practice of tradesmen who *blanch* it. *Boyle.*

And sin's black dye seems *blanch'd* by age to virtue.
*Dryden's Spanish Friar.*

2. To strip or peel such things as have husks.

Their suppers may be bisket, raisins of the sun, and a few *blanched* almonds. *Wiseman's Surgery.*

3. To obliterate; to wash out; to balk; to pass over.

The judges thought it dangerous to admit ifs and ands, to qualify treason; whereby every one might express his malice, and *blanch* his danger. *Bacon's Henry* VII.

You are not transported in an action that warms the blood and is appearing holy, to *blanch*, or take for admitted, the point of lawfulness. *Bacon's Holy War.*

To BLANCH. *v. n.* To evade; to shift; to speak soft.

*Optimi consiliarii mortui*; books will speak plain, when counsellors *blanch.* *Bacon.*

BLA'NCHER. *n. s.* [from *blanch.*] A whitener. *Dict.*

BLAND. *adj.* [*blandus*, Lat.] Soft; mild; gentle.

In

9 †

~~2 Irregularity, confusion, cause of blame~~

~~A jolly yeoman Marshall of the hall~~
~~Whose name was Appetite~~ he did bestow
Both guests and meals whenever in they came
And knew them how to Order without blame

Spens

~~2 A natural instrument of defence~~

8 †

He who made
This knowing beast hath arm'd him with a blade
He feeds on lofty hills nor lives by prey

Sandys Job.

p †

Blameworthiness n s {from blameworthy}
State of deserving blame

There is no cause to blame the Prince for sometimes hearing them, the blameworthiness is, that to hear them, he rather goes to Solitariness, than makes them come to Company

Sidney

-p†

IL facing 3E$^{v}$

blank page

In her face excuse
Came prologue; and apology too prompt;
Which, with *bland* words at will, she thus address'd.
*Milton's Par. Lost, b.* ix. *l.* 855.

An even calm
Perpetual reign'd, save what the zephyrs *bland*
Breath'd o'er the blue expanse. *Thomson's Spring.*

To BLA'NDISH. *v. a.* [*blandior*, Lat.] To smooth; to soften. I have met with this word in no other passage.

Must'ring all her wiles,
With *blandish'd* parleys, feminine assaults,
Tongue-batteries, she surceas'd not day nor night,
To storm me over-watch'd, and weary'd out.
*Milton's Agonistes, l.* 402.

BLA'NDISHMENT. *n. s.* [from *blandish*; *blanditiæ*, Lat.]

1. Act of fondness; expression of tenderness by gesture.

The little babe up in his arms he hent;
Who, with sweet pleasure and bold *blandishment*,
'Gan smile. *Fairy Queen, b.* ii. *c.* ii. *stanz.* 1.

Each bird and beast, behold
Approaching two and two; these cow'ring low
With *blandishment*. *Milt. Paradise Lost, b.* viii. *l.* 351.

2. Soft words; kind speeches.

He was both well and fair spoken, and would use strange sweetness and *blandishment* of words, where he desired to effect or persuade any thing that he took to heart. *Bacon's H.* VII.

3. Kind treatment; caress.

Him Dido now with *blandishment* detains;
But I suspect the town where Juno reigns. *Dryden's Virgil.*

In order to bring those infidels within the wide circle of whiggish community, neither *blandishments* nor promises are omitted. *Swift's Examiner*, N° 47.

BLANK. *adj.* [*blanc*, Fr. derived by *Menage* from *Albianus*, thus: *Albianus, albianicus, bianicus, biancus, bianco, blanicus, blancus, blanc*; by others, from *blanc*, which, in Danish, signifies *shining*; in conformity to which, the Germans have *blancker*, to *shine*; the Saxons, blæcan; and the English, *bleach*, to *whiten.*]

1. White.

To the *blank* moon
Her office they prescrib'd: to th' other five
Their planetary motions. *Parad. Lost, b.* x. *l.* 656.

2. ~~Without~~ writing; unwritten; empty of all marks.

Our substitutes at home shall have *blank* charters,
Whereto, when they know that men are rich,
They shall subscribe them for large sums of gold.
*Shakesp.* ~~*Richard* II.~~

Upon the debtor side, I find innumerable articles; but, upon the creditor side, little more than *blank* paper. *Addison. Spectat.*

3. Confused; crushed; dispirited; subdued; depressed.

There without such boast, or sign of joy,
Solicitous and *blank*, he thus began. *Par. Regained, b.* ii.

Adam soon as he heard
The fatal trespass done by Eve, amaz'd,
Astonied stood, and *blank*, while horrour chill
Ran through his veins, and all his joints relax'd.
*Milton's* ~~*Paradise Lost, b.* ix. *l.* 888.~~

But now no face divine contentment wears;
'Tis all *blank* sadness, or continual fears. *Pope.*

4. Without rhime; where the rhime is *blanched*, or missed.

The lady shall say her mind freely, or the *blank* verse shall halt for it. *Shakesp. Hamlet.*

Long have your ears been fill'd with tragick parts;
Blood and *blank* verse have harden'd all your hearts.
*Addison's* ~~*Drummer, Prologue.*~~

Our *blank* verse, where there is no rhime to support the expression, is extremely difficult to such as are not masters in the tongue. *Addison's Remarks on Italy.*

BLANK. *n. s.* [from the adjective.]

1. A void space.

I cannot write a paper full as I used to do; and yet I will not forgive a *blank* of half an inch from you. *Swift.*

2. A lot, by which nothing is gained; which has no prize marked upon it.

If you have heard your general talk of Rome,
And of his friends there, it is lots to *blanks*
My name hath touch'd your ears. *Shakesp. Coriolanus.*

In fortune's lottery lies
A heap of *blanks*, like this, for one small prize. *Dryden.*

The world the coward will despise,
When life's a *blank*, who pulls not for a prize. *Dryden.*

3. A paper from which the writing is effaced.

She has left him
The *blank* of what he was;
I tell thee, eunuch, she has quite unmann'd him. *Dryden.*

4. A paper unwritten; any thing without marks or characters.

For him, I think not on him; for his thoughts,
Would they were *blanks*, rather than fill'd with me.
*Shakesp.* ~~*Twelfth Night.*~~

Omission to do what is necessary,
Seals a commission to a *blank* of danger. *Shakesp. Tr. and Cr.*

For the book of knowledge fair,
Presented with an universal *blank*
Of nature's works, to me expung'd and ras'd. *Par. Lost.*

A life so spent is one great *blank*, which, though not blotted with sin, is yet without any characters of grace or virtue.
*Rogers*, ~~*Serm.* xiii.~~

5. The point to which an arrow is directed; so called, because, to be more visible, it was marked with white.

Slander,
Whose whisper o'er the world's diameter,
As level as the cannon to his *blank*,
Transports its poison'd shot. *Shakesp. Hamlet.*

6. Aim; shot.

The harlot king
Is quite beyond my aim; out of the *blank*
And level of my brain. *Shakesp. Winter's Tale.*

I have spoken for you all my best,
And stood within the *blank* of his displeasure,
For my free speech. *Shakesp. Othello.*

7. Object to which any thing is directed.

See better, Lear, and let me still remain
The true *blank* of thine eye. *Shakesp. King Lear.*

To BLANK. *v. a.* [from *blank*; *blanchir*, Fr.]

1. To damp; to confuse; to dispirit.

Each opposite, that *blanks* the face of joy,
Meet what I would have well, and it destroy. *Shakesp. Haml.*

Dagon must stoop, and shall ere long receive
Such a discomfit, as shall quite despoil him
Of all these boasted trophies won on me,
And with confusion *blank* his worshippers. *Milton's Agonist.*

If the atheist, when he dies, should find that his soul remains, how will this man be amazed and *blanked?* *Tillotson.*

2. To efface; to annul.

All former purposes were *blanked*, the governour at a bay, and all that charge lost and cancelled. *Spenser on Ireland.*

BLA'NKET. *n. s.* [*blanchette*, Fr.]

1. An woollen cover, soft, and loosely woven, spread commonly upon a bed, over the linen sheet, for the procurement of warmth.

Nor heav'n peep through the *blanket* of the dark,
To cry, hold! hold! *Shakesp. King Lear.*

The abilities of man must fall short on one side or other, like too scanty a *blanket* when you are abed; if you pull it upon your shoulders, you leave your feet bare; if you thrust it down upon your feet, your shoulders are uncovered. *Temple.*

Himself among the storied chiefs he spies,
As from the *blanket* high in air he flies. *Pope's Dunciad.*

2. A kind of pear, sometimes written *blanquet*. See PEAR.

To BLA'NKET. *v. a.* [from the noun.]

1. To cover with a blanket.

My face I'll grime with filth;
*Blanket* my loins; tie all my hair in knots. *Sh. King Lear.*

2. To toss in a blanket, by way of penalty or contempt.

Ah, oh! he cry'd, what street, what lane, but knows
Our purgings, pumpings, *blanketings*, and blows? *Pope.*

BLA'NKLY. *adv.* [from *blank*.] In a blank manner; with whiteness; with paleness; with confusion.

To BLARE. *v. n.* [*blaren*, Dutch.] To bellow; to roar. *Skinn.*

To BLASPHE'ME. *v. a.* [*blasphemo*, low Lat.]

1. To speak in terms of impious irreverence of God.

2. To speak evil of.

The truest issue of thy throne,
By his own interdiction stands accurs'd,
And does *blaspheme* his breed. *Shakes. Macbeth.*

Those who from our labours heap their board,
*Blaspheme* their feeder, and forget their lord. *Pope's Odyssey.*

To BLASPHE'ME. *v. n.* To speak blasphemy.

Liver of *blaspheming* Jew,
Gall of goat, and slips of yew. *Shakesp. Macbeth.*

I punished them oft in every synagogue, and compelled them to *blaspheme*. *Acts*, xxvi. 11.

BLASPHE'MER. *n. s.* [from *blaspheme*.] A wretch that speaks of God in impious and irreverent terms.

Who was before a *blasphemer*, and a persecutor, and injurious. 1 *Tim.* i. 13.

Even that *blasphemer* himself would inwardly reverence him, as he in his heart really despises him for his cowardly base silence. *South.*

Deny the curst *blasphemer*'s tongue to rage,
And turn God's fury from an impious age. *Tickell.*

Should each *blasphemer* quite escape the rod,
Because the insult's not to man, but God. *Pope.*

BLA'SPHEMOUS. *adj.* [from *blaspheme*. It is usually spoken with the accent on the first syllable, but used by *Milton*, with it on the second.] Impiously irreverent with regard to God.

O man, take heed how thou the gods do move,
To cause full wrath, which thou canst not resist;
*Blasphemous* words the speaker vain do prove. *Sidney, b.* ii.

And dar'st thou to the Son of God propound,
To worship thee accurst; now more accurst
For this attempt, bolder than that on Eve,
And more *blasphemous?* *Milton's Paradise Regained, b.* iii.

A man can hardly pass the streets, without having his ears grated with such horrid and *blasphemous* oaths and curses. *Tillot.*

That any thing that wears the name of a christian, or but of man,

man, ſhould venture to own ſuch a villainous, impudent, and *blaſphemous* aſſertion in the face of the world, as this! *South.*

BLASPHEMOUSLY. *adv.* [from *blaſpheme.*] Impiouſly; with wicked irreverence.

Where is the right uſe of his reaſon, while he would *blaſphemouſly* ſet up to controul the commands of the Almighty? *Swift.*

BLA'SPHEMY. *n. ſ.* [from *blaſpheme.*]

*Blaſphemy*, ſtrictly and properly, is an offering of ſome indignity, or injury, unto God himſelf, either by words or writing. *Ayliffe's Parergon.*

But that my heart's on future miſchief ſet,
I would ſpeak *blaſphemy*, ere bid you fly;
But fly you muſt. *Shakeſp. Henry VI. p.* ii.

Intrinſick goodneſs conſiſts in accordance, and ſin in contrariety, to the ſecret will of God; or elſe God could not be defined good, ſo far as his thoughts and ſecrets, but only ſuperficially good, as far as he is pleaſed to reveal himſelf, which is perfect *blaſphemy* to imagine. *Hammond's Fundamentals.*

BLAST. *n. ſ.* [from blæſt, Saxon; *blaſen*, Germ. to blow.]

1. A guſt, or puff of wind.

They that ſtand high, have many *blaſts* to ſhake them;
And, if they fall, they daſh themſelves to pieces.
*Shakeſp. Richard III.*

Welcome, then,
Thou unſubſtantial air, that I embrace;
The wretch that thou haſt blown unto the worſt,
Owes nothing to thy *blaſts*. *Shakeſp. King Lear.*

Perhaps thy fortune doth controul the winds,
Doth looſe or bind their *blaſts* in ſecret cave. *Fairfax, b.* i.

Three ſhips were hurry'd by the ſouthern *blaſt*,
And on the ſecret ſhelves with fury caſt. *Dryden's Æneid.*

2. The ſound made by blowing any inſtrument of wind muſick.

In peace there's nothing ſo becomes a man,
As modeſt ſtilneſs and humility;
But when the *blaſt* of war blows in our ears,
Then imitate the action of the tyger. *Shakeſp. Henry V.*

He blew his trumpet—the angelick *blaſt*
Fill'd all the regions. *Milt. Par. Loſt, b.* xi. *l.* 76.

The Veline fountains, and ſulphureous Nar,
Shake at the baleful *blaſt*, the ſignal of the war. *Dryden's Æn.*

Whether there be two different goddeſſes called Fame, or one goddeſs ſounding two different trumpets, it is certain, villainy has as good a title to a blaſt from the proper trumpet, as virtue has from the former. *Swift.*

3. The ſtroke of a malignant planet; the infection of any thing peſtilential.

By the *blaſt* of God they periſh. *Job*, iv. 9.

To BLAST. *v. a.* [from the noun.]

1. To ſtrike with ſome ſudden plague or calamity.

You nimble lightnings, dart your blinding flames
Into her ſcornful eyes! infect her beauty,
You fenſuck'd fogs, drawn by the powerful ſun,
To fall and *blaſt* her pride. *Shakeſp. King Lear.*

Oh! Portius, is there not ſome choſen curſe,
Some hidden thunder in the ſtore of heaven,
Red with uncommon wrath, to *blaſt* the man,
Who owes his greatneſs to his country's ruin. *Addiſon. Cato.*

2. To make to wither.

Upon this *blaſted* heath you ſtop our way. *Macbeth.*

And behold ſeven thin ears, and *blaſted* with the eaſtwind ſprung up after them. *Gen.* xli. 6.

She that like lightning ſhin'd, while her face laſted,
The oak now reſembles, which lightning had *blaſted*. *Waller.*

To his green years your cenſures you would ſuit,
Not *blaſt* that bloſſom, but expect the fruit. *Dryden.*

Agony unmix'd, inceſſant gall
Corroding every thought, and *blaſting* all
Love's paradiſe. *Thomſon's Spring, l.* 1075.

4. To injure; to invalidate.

He ſhews himſelf either very weak, if he will take my word, when he thinks I deſerve no credit; or very malicious, if he knows I deſerve credit, and yet goes about to *blaſt* it.
*Stillingfleet's Defence of Diſcourſes on Romiſh Idolatry.*

3. To cut off; to hinder from coming to maturity.

This commerce, Jeſhophat king of Juda endeavoured to renew; but his enterprize was *blaſted* by the deſtruction of veſſels in the harbour. *Arbuthnot on Coins.*

5. To confound; to ſtrike with terrour.

Trumpeters,
With brazen din, *blaſt* you the city's ears;
Make mingle with your ratt'ling tabourines.
*Shakeſp. Antony and Cleopatra.*

BLA'STMENT. *n. ſ.* [from *blaſt.*] Blaſt; ſudden ſtroke of infection.

In the morn, and liquid dew of youth,
Contagious *blaſtments* are moſt imminent. *Shakeſp. Hamlet.*

BLA'TANT. *adj.* [*blatttant*, Fr.] Bellowing as a calf.

You learn'd this language from the *blatant* beaſt. *Dryden.*

To BLA'TTER. *v. n.* [from *blatero*, Lat.] To roar; to make a ſenſeleſs noiſe. It is a word not now uſed.

She rode at peace, through his only pains and excellent endurance, however envy liſt to *blatter* againſt him. *Spenſ. Irel.*

BLATTERA'TION. *n. ſ.* [*blateratio*, Lat.] Noiſe; ſenſeleſs roar.

BLAY. *n. ſ.* A ſmall white river fiſh; called alſo a *bleak*, which ſee.

BLAZE. *n. ſ.* [blaſe, a torch, Saxon.]

1. A flame; the light of the flame: *blaze* implies more the light than the heat.

They are in a moſt warlike preparation, and hope to come upon them in the heat of their diviſion.—The main *blaze* of it is paſt; but a ſmall thing would make it flame again.
*Shakeſp. Coriolanus.*

Thy throne is darkneſs in th' abyſs of light,
A *blaze* of glory that forbids the ſight. *Dryden's Hind and P.*

What groans of men ſhall fill the martial field!
How fierce a *blaze* his flaming pile ſhall yield!
What fun'ral pomp ſhall floating Tiber ſee! *Dryden's Æn.*

2. Publication; wide diffuſion of report.

For what is glory but the *blaze* of fame;
The people's praiſe, if always praiſe unmixt?
*Milton's Paradiſe Loſt, b.* iii. *l.* 47.

3. *Blaze* is a white mark upon a horſe, deſcending from the forehead almoſt to the noſe. *Farrier's Dict.*

To BLAZE. *v. n.* [from the noun.]

1. To flame; to ſhew the light of the flame.

Thus you may long live an happy inſtrument for your king and country; you ſhall not be a meteor, or a *blazing* ſtar, but *ſtella fixa*; happy here, and more happy hereafter.
*Bacon's Advice to Villiers.*

The third fair morn now *blaz'd* upon the main,
Then gloſſy ſmooth lay all the liquid plain. *Pope's Odyſſey.*

2. To be conſpicuous.

To BLAZE. *v. a.*

1. To publiſh; to make known; to ſpread far and wide.

The noiſe of this fight, and iſſue thereof, being *blazed* by the country people to ſome noblemen thereabouts, they came thither. *Sidney, b.* ii.

My words, in hopes to *blaze* a ſtedfaſt mind,
This marble choſe, as of like temper known. *Sidney.*

Thou ſhalt live, till we can find a time
To *blaze* your marriage, reconcile your friends,
Beg pardon of thy prince, and call thee back.
*Shakeſp. Romeo and Juliet.*

When beggars die, there are no comets ſeen;
The heav'ns themſelves *blaze* forth the death of princes.
*Shakeſp. Julius Cæſar.*

But he went out, and began to publiſh it much, and to *blaze* abroad the matter. *Mark*, i. 45.

Such muſick worthieſt were to *blaze*
The peerleſs height of her immortal praiſe,
Whoſe luſtre leads us. *Milton.*

Far beyond
The ſons of Anak, famous now and *blaz'd*,
Fearleſs of danger, like a petty god
I walk'd about. *Milton's Agoniſtes, l.* 527.

Whoſe follies, *blaz'd* about, to all are known,
And are a ſecret to himſelf alone. *Granville.*

But, mortals, know, 'tis ſtill our greateſt pride
To *blaze* thoſe virtues, which the good would hide. *Pope.*

2. To blazon; to give an account of enſigns armorial in proper terms. This is not now uſed.

This, in ancient times, was called a fierce; and you ſhould then have *blazed* it thus: he bears a fierce, ſable, between two fierces, or. *Peacham on Drawing.*

3. To inflame; to fire. This is not a proper uſe.

Pall'd thy *blazed* youth
Becomes aſſuag'd, and doth beg the alms
Of palſied eld. *Shakeſp. Meaſure for Meaſure.*

BLA'ZER. *n. ſ.* [from *blaze.*] One that ſpreads reports.

Utterers of ſecrets he from thence debarr'd,
Babblers of folly, and *blazers* of crime;
His larum-bell might loud and wide be heard,
When cauſe requir'd, but never out of time;
Early and late it rung, at evening and at prime. *Fairy Queen.*

To BLA'ZON. *v. a.* [*blaſonner*, Fr.]

1. To explain, in proper terms, the figures on enſigns armorial.

King Edward gave to them the coat of arms, which I am not herald enough to *blazon* into Engliſh. *Addiſon. Guardian.*

2. To deck; to embelliſh; to adorn.

Then *blazons* in dread ſmiles her hideous form;
So lightning gilds the unrelenting ſtorm. *Garth's Diſpenſat.*

3. To diſplay; to ſet to ſhow.

O thou goddeſs,
Thou divine nature! how thyſelf thou *blazon'ſt*
In theſe two princely boys! they are as gentle
As zephyrs blowing below the violet,
Not wagging his ſweet head. *Shakeſp. Cymbeline.*

4. To celebrate; to ſet out.

One that excels the quirk of *blazoning* pens,
And, in terreſtrial veſture of creation,
Does bear all excellency. *Shakeſp. Othello.*

5. To blaze about; to make publick.

What's

6 ‡

If matter of fact breaks out & blazes with too great an evidence to be denied; Why still there are other lenitives that friendship will apply.
South

‡

If envious eyes their hurtful rays have cast,
More powerful Verse shall free thee from their blast
Dryd.

IL facing 3E2v

c I

2 To stain with blood
His shining helmet he gan soon unlace
And left his headless body bleeding all the place.
T. L. 2. 8. 52

2

2. Siker, thou's but a lazy loorde
And rekes much of thy swinke
That with fond terms & witless words
To bleer mine eyes dost think
Spenser

IL facing 3F[r]

What's this but libelling against the senate,
And *blazoning* our injustice every where? *Shakesp. Tit. Andr.*

BLA'ZON. *n. s.* [from the verb.]

1. The art of drawing or explaining coats of arms.

Proceed unto beasts that are given in arms, and teach me what I ought to observe in their *blazon*. *Peacham.*

2. Show; divulgation; publication.

But this eternal *blazon* must not be
To ears of flesh and blood. *Shakesp. Hamlet.*

3. Celebration; proclamation of some quality.

I am a gentleman.—I'll be sworn thou art;
Thy tongue, thy face, thy limbs, action, and spirit,
Do give thee five-fold *blazon*. *Shakesp. Twelfth Night.*

Men con over their pedigrees, and obtrude the *blazon* of their exploits upon the company. *Collier on Pride.*

BLA'ZONRY. *n. s.* [from *blazon*.] The art of blazoning.

Give me certain rules as to the principles of *blazonry*. *Peacham on Drawing.*

To BLEACH. *v. a.* [*bleechen*, Germ.] To whiten; commonly to whiten by exposure to the open air.

When turtles tread, and rooks and daws;
And maidens *bleach* their summer smocks.
*Shakesp. Love's Labour Lost.*

Should I not seek
The clemency of some more temp'rate clime,
To purge my gloom; and, by the sun refin'd,
Bask in his beams, and *bleach* me in the wind? *Dryden.*

For there are various penances enjoin'd,
And some are hung to *bleach* upon the wind;
Some plung'd in waters. *Dryden's Æneid.*

To BLEACH. *v. n.* To grow white; to grow white in the open air.

The white sheet *bleaching* in the open field. *Sh. W. Tale.*

On every nerve
The deadly winter seizes; shuts up sense;
Lays him along the snows, a stiffen'd corse,
Stretch'd out, and *bleaching* in the northern blast. *Thomson.*

BLEAK. *adj.* [blac, blæc, Saxon.]

1. Pale.
2. Cold; chill.

Intreat the north
To make his *bleak* winds kiss my parched lips,
And comfort me with cold. *Shakesp. King John.*

The goddess that in rural shrine
Dwell'st here with Pan, or Sylvan, by blest song
Forbidding every *bleak* unkindly fog
To touch the prosperous growth of this tall wood. *Milton.*

Her desolation presents us with nothing but *bleak* and barren prospects. *Addison. Spectator*, N° 477.

Say, will ye bless the *bleak* Atlantick shore,
Or bid the furious Gaul be rude no more. *Pope.*

BLEAK. *n. s.* [from his white or *bleak* colour.] A small river fish.

The *bleak*, or freshwater sprat, is ever in motion, and therefore called by some the river swallow. His back is of a pleasant, sad sea water green; his belly white and shining like the mountain snow. *Bleaks* are excellent meat, and in best season in August. *Walton's Angler.*

BLE'AKNESS. *n. s.* [from *bleak*.] Coldness; chilness.

The inhabitants of Nova Zembla go naked, without complaining of the *bleakness* of the air in which they are born; as the armies of the northern nations keep the field all winter. *Addison. Guardian*, N° 102.

BLE'AKY. *adj.* [from *bleak*.] Bleak; cold; chill.

On shrubs they browze, and, on the *bleaky* top
Of rugged hills, the thorny bramble crop. *Dryden.*

BLEAR. *adj.* [*blaer*, a blister, Dutch.]

1. Dim with rheum or water; sore with rheum.

It is an ancient tradition, that *blear* eyes affect sound eyes. *Bacon's Natural History*, N° 923.

It is no more in the power of calumny to blast the dignity of an honest man, than of the *blear* eyed owl to cast scandal on the sun. *L'Estrange.*

His *blear* eyes ran in gutters to his chin;
His beard was stubble, and his cheeks were thin. *Dryden.*

When thou shalt see the *blear* ey'd fathers teach
Their sons this harsh and mouldy sort of speech. *Dryden.*

2. Dim; obscure in general; or that which makes dimness.

Thus I hurl
My dazling spells into the spungy air,
Of power to cheat the eye with *blear* illusion,
And give it false presentments. *Milton.*

To BLEAR. *v. a.* [from the adjective.]

1. To make the eyes watry, or sore with rheum.

All tongues speak of him, and the *bleared* sights
Are spectacled to see him. *Shakesp. Coriolanus.*

The Dardanian wives,
With *bleared* visages, come forth to view
Th' issue of th' exploit. *Shakesp. Merchant of Venice.*

When I was young, I, like a lazy fool,
Would *blear* my eyes with oil, to stay from school;
Averse to pains. *Dryden's Persius, sat.* iii.

2. To dim the eyes.

This may stand for a pretty superficial argument, to *blear* our eyes, and lull us asleep in security. *Raleigh's Essays.*

BLE'AREDNESS. *n. s.* [from *bleared*.] The state of being bleared, or dimmed with rheum.

The defluxion falling upon the edges of the eyelids, makes a *blearedness*. *Wiseman's Surgery.*

To BLEAT. *v. n.* [blætan, Sax.] To cry as a sheep.

We were as twinn'd lambs, that did frisk i' th' sun,
And *bleat* the one at th' other. *Shakesp. Winter's Tale.*

You may as well use question with the wolf,
Why he hath made the ewe *bleat* for the lamb.
*Shakesp. Merchant of Venice.*

While on sweet grass her *bleating* charge does lie,
Our happy lover feeds upon her eye. *Roscommon.*

What bull dares bellow, or what sheep dares *bleat*
Within the lion's den? *Dryden's Spanish Friar.*

BLEAT. *n. s.* [from the verb.] The cry of a sheep or lamb.

Set in my ship, mine ear reach'd, where we rod,
The bellowing of oxen, and the *bleat*
Of fleecy sheep. *Chapman's Odyssey, b.* xii.

The rivers and their hills around,
With lowings, and with dying *bleats* resound. *Dryden.*

BLEB. *n. s.* [*blaen*, to swell, Germ.] A blister. *Skinner.*

BLED. *particip.* [from *to bleed*.]

To BLEED. *v. n.* pret. I *bled*; I have *bled*. [bleban, Saxon.]

1. To lose blood; to run with blood.

I *bleed* inwardly for my lord. *Shakesp. Timon.*

*Bleed, bleed*, poor country!
Great tyranny, lay thou thy basis sure;
For goodness dare not check thee! *Shakesp. Macbeth.*

Many, upon the seeing of others *bleed*, or strangled, or tortured, themselves are ready to faint, as if they *bled*. *Bacon's Nat. History*, N° 795.

2. To die a violent death.

The lamb thy riot dooms to *bleed* today;
Had he thy reason, would he skip and play? *Pope.*

3. To drop, as blood. It is applied to any thing that drops from some body, as blood from an animal.

For me the balm shall *bleed*, and amber flow,
The coral redden, and the ruby glow. *Pope's Windf. Forest.*

To BLEED. *v. a.* To let blood; to take blood from.

That from a patriot of distinguish'd note,
Have *bled*, and purg'd me to a simple vote. *Pope.*

BLEIT. } *adj.* Bashful. It is used in Scotland, and the border-
BLATE. } ing counties.

To BLE'MISH. *v. a.* [from *blame*, *Junius*; from *blême*, white, Fr. *Skinner*.]

1. To mark with any deformity.

Likelier that my outward face might have been disguised, than that the face of so excellent a mind could have been thus *blemished*. *Sidney.*

2. To defame; to tarnish, with respect to reputation.

Not that my verse would *blemish* all the fair;
But yet if some be bad, 'tis wisdom to beware. *Dryden.*

Those, who, by concerted defamations, endeavour to *blemish* his character, incur the complicated guilt of slander and perjury. *Addison. Freeholder.*

BLE'MISH. *n. s.* [from the verb.]

1. A mark of deformity; a scar; a diminution of beauty.

As he hath caused a *blemish* in a man, so shall it be done to him again. *Lev.* xxiv. 20.

Open it such a distance off from the eyelid, that you divide not that; for, in so doing, you will leave a remediless *blemish*. *Wiseman's Surgery.*

2. Reproach; disgrace; imputation.

Live thou, and to thy mother dead attest,
That clear she died from *blemish* criminal. *Fairy Queen, b.* ii.

That you have been earnest, should be no *blemish* or discredit at all unto you. *Hooker, Preface.*

And if we shall neglect to propagate these blessed dispositions, what others can undertake it, without some *blemish* to us? some reflection on our negligence? *Sprat.*

None more industriously publish the *blemishes* of an extraordinary reputation, than such as lie open to the same censures; raising applause to themselves, for resembling a person of an exalted reputation, though in the blamable parts of his character. *Addison. Spectator*, N° 256.

3. A soil; turpitude; taint; deformity.

First shall virtue be vice, and beauty be counted a *blemish*,
Ere that I leave with song of praise her praise to solemnize. *Sidney, b.* i.

Is conformity with Rome a *blemish* unto the church of England, and unto churches abroad an ornament? *Hooker, b.* iv. § 6.

Not a hair perish'd:
On their sustaining garments not a *blemish*,
But fresher than before. *Shakesp. Tempest.*

Evadne's husband 'tis a fault
To love, a *blemish* to my thought. *Waller's M. Trag.*

That your duty may no *blemish* take,
I will myself your father's captive make. *Dryd. Indian Emp.*

Such a mirth as this is capable of making a beauty, as well as a *blemish*, the ſubject of deriſion. *Addiſon. Spect.* Nº 291.

To Blench. *v. n.* To ſhrink; to ſtart back; to fly off.

I'll obſerve his looks;
I'll tent him to the quick; if he but *blench*,
I know my courſe. *Shakeſp. Hamlet.*

Patience herſelf, what goddeſs ere ſhe be,
Doth leſſer *blench* at ſufferance than I do. *Shakeſp. Tr. and Cr.*

Hold you ever to our ſpecial drift;
Though ſometimes you do *blench* from this to that,
As cauſe doth miniſter. *Shakep. Merry Wives of Windſor.*

To Blench. *v. a.* To hinder; to obſtruct.

The rebels beſieged them, winning the even ground on the top, by carrying up great truſſes of hay before them, to *blench* the defendants ſight, and dead their ſhot. *Carew's Survey.*

To BLEND. *v. a.* preter. I *blended*; anciently, *blent*. [blenban, Saxon.]

1. To mingle together.

'Tis beauty truly *blent*, whoſe red and white
Nature's own ſweet and cunning hand hath laid on. *Shakeſp. Twelfth Night.*

The miſtion taught by the ancients is too ſlight or groſs; for bodies, mixed according to their hypotheſis, would not appear ſuch to the acute eyes of a lynx, who would diſcern the elements, if they were no otherwiſe mingled, than but *blended*, but not united. *Boyle.*

He had his calmer influence, and his mien
Did love and majeſty together *blend*. *Dryden.*

The grave, where even the great find reſt,
And *blended* lie th' oppreſſor and th' oppreſs'd. *Pope.*

2. To confound.

The moon ſhould wander from her beaten way, the times and ſeaſons of the year *blend* themſelves by diſordered and confuſed mixture. *Hooker, b.* i. § 3.

3. To pollute; to ſpoil; to corrupt. This ſignification was anciently much in uſe, but is now wholly obſolete.

Which when he ſaw, he burnt with jealous fire;
The eye of reaſon was with rage *yblent*. *Fairy Queen, b.* ii.

Regard of worldly muck doth foully *blend*,
And low abaſe the high heroick ſpirit. *Fairy Queen, b.* ii.

The whilſt thy kingdom from thy head is rent,
And thy throne royal with diſhonour *blent*. *Spenſ. Hubb.*

Ble'nder. *n. ſ.* [from *to blend*.] The perſon that mingles.

Blent. The obſolete *participle* of *blend*. See Blend.

To BLESS. *v. a.* [bleꞅꞅian, Saxon.]

1. To make happy; to proſper.

The quality of mercy is not ſtrain'd;
It droppeth as the gentle rain of heaven
Upon the place beneath. It is twice *bleſs'd*;
It *bleſſeth* him that gives, and him that takes. *Merch. of Ven.*

Had I but died an hour before this chance,
I had liv'd a *bleſſed* time: for, from this inſtant,
There's nothing. *Shakeſp. Macbeth.*

This kingdom enjoyed the greateſt calm, and the fulleſt meaſure of felicity, that any people, in any age for ſo long time together, have been *bleſſed* with. *Clarendon.*

Happy this iſle, which ſuch a hero *bleſt*;
What virtue dwells not in his loyal breaſt? *Waller.*

In vain with folding arms the youth aſſay'd
To ſtop her flight, and ſtrain the flying ſhade;
But ſhe return'd no more, to *bleſs* his longing eyes. *Dryden.*

O hoſpitable Jove! we thus invoke,
*Bleſs* to both nations this auſpicious hour. *Dryden's Æn.*

2. To wiſh happineſs to another; to pronounce a bleſſing upon him.

And this is the bleſſing wherewith Moſes the man of God *bleſſed* the children of Iſrael, before his death. *Deut.* xxxiii. 1.

3. To praiſe; to glorify for benefits received; to celebrate.

Unto us there is one only guide of all agents natural, and he both the creator and worker of all in all, alone to be *bleſſed*, adored, and honoured by all for ever. *Hooker, b.* i. § 3.

But *bleſs'd* be that great pow'r, that hath us bleſs'd
With longer life than earth and heav'n can have. *Davies.*

4. It ſeems, in one place of *Spenſer*, to ſignify the ſame as *to wave*; *to brandiſh*; *to flouriſh*.

Whom when the prince to battle new addreſt,
And threat'ning high his dreadful ſtroke did ſee,
His ſparkling blade about his head he *bleſt*,
And ſmote off quite his right leg by the knee. *Fairy Q. b.* i.

Ble'ssed. *particip. adj.* [from *to bleſs*.] Happy; enjoying heavenly felicity.

Ble'ssed *Thiſtle*. [cnicus, Lat.] The name of a plant.

The characters are; It hath floſculous flowers; conſiſting of many florets, which are multifid, and ſtand upon the embryo; theſe florets are incloſed in a ſcaly cup, ſurrounded with leaves. The ſpecies are; 1. The *bleſſed thiſtle*. 2. The yellow diſtaff *thiſtle*. The *bleſſed thiſtle* is cultivated in gardens for the herb, which is dried and preſerved for medicinal uſes; but of late years it hath been leſs uſed than formerly. *Millar.*

Ble'ssedly. *adv.* [from *bleſſed*.] Happily.

This accident of Clitophon's taking had ſo *bleſſedly* procured their meeting. *Sidney, b.* i.



Ble'ssedness. *n. ſ.* [from *bleſſed*.]

1. Happineſs; felicity.

Many times have I, leaning to yonder palm, admired the *bleſſedneſs* of it, that it could bear love without the ſenſe of pain. *Sidney.*

His overthrow heap'd happineſs upon him;
For then, and not till then, he felt himſelf,
And found the *bleſſedneſs* of being little. *Shakeſp. Hen.* VIII.

2. Sanctity.

Earthlier happy is the roſe diſtill'd,
Than that, which, withering on the virgin thorn,
Grows, lives, and dies in ſingle *bleſſedneſs*. *Shakeſp. Midſummer Night's Dream.*

3. Heavenly felicity.

It is ſuch an one, as, being begun in grace, paſſes into glory, *bleſſedneſs*, and immortality. *South.*

4. Divine favour.

Ble'sser. *n. ſ.* [from *bleſs*.] He that bleſſes, or gives a bleſſing; he that makes any thing proſper.

When thou receiveſt praiſe, take it indifferently, and return it to God, as the giver of the gift, or the *bleſſer* of the action. *Taylor's Holy Living.*

Ble'ssing. *n. ſ.* [from *bleſs*.]

1. Benediction; a prayer by which happineſs is implored for any one.

2. A declaration by which happineſs is promiſed in a prophetick and authoritative manner.

The perſon that is called, kneeleth down before the chair, and the father layeth his hand upon his head, or her head, and giveth the *bleſſing*. *Bacon's New Atlantis.*

3. Any of the means of happineſs; a gift; an advantage; a benefit.

Nor are his *bleſſings* to his banks confin'd,
But free, and common, as the ſea and wind. *Denham.*

Political jealouſy is very reaſonable in perſons perſuaded of the excellency of their conſtitution, who believe that they derive from it the moſt valuable *bleſſings* of ſociety. *Addiſon.*

A juſt and wiſe magiſtrate is a *bleſſing* as extenſive as the community to which he belongs: a *bleſſing* which includes all other *bleſſings* whatſoever, that relate to this life. *Atterbury.*

4. Divine favour.

My pretty couſin,
*Bleſſing* upon you! *Shakeſp. Macbeth.*

I had moſt need of *bleſſing*, and amen,
Stuck in my throat. *Shakeſp. Macbeth.*

Honour thy father and mother, both in word and deed, that a *bleſſing* may come upon thee from them. *Ecclus*, iii. 8.

He ſhall receive the *bleſſing* from the Lord. *Pſalm* xxix. 5.

5. The Hebrews, under this name, often underſtand the preſents which friends make to one another; in all probability, becauſe they are generally attended with *bleſſings* and compliments both from thoſe who give, and thoſe who receive. *Calmet.*

And Jacob ſaid, receive my preſent at my hand; take, I pray thee, my *bleſſing* that is brought to thee. *Gen.* xxxiii. 10.

Blest. *particip. adj.* [from *bleſs*.]

Peace to thy gentle ſhade, and endleſs reſt!
*Bleſt* in thy genius, in thy love too *bleſt*! *Pope.*

Blew. The *preterite* from *blow*; which ſee.

The reſt fled into a ſtrong tower, where, ſeeing no remedy, they deſperately *blew* up themſelves, with a great part of the caſtle, with gunpowder. *Knolles's Hiſtory of the Turks.*

Bleyme. *n. ſ.* An inflammation in the foot of a horſe, proceeding from bruiſed blood, between the ſole and the bone. *Farrier's Dict.*

Blight. *n. ſ.* [The etymology unknown.]

1. Mildew; according to *Skinner*; but it ſeems taken by moſt writers, in a general ſenſe, for any cauſe of the failure of fruits.

I complained to the oldeſt and beſt gardeners, who often fell into the ſame misfortune, and eſteemed it ſome *blight* of the ſpring. *Temple.*

2. Any thing nipping, or blaſting.

When you come to the proof once, the firſt *blight* of froſt ſhall moſt infallibly ſtrip you of all your glory. *L'Eſtrange.*

To Blight. *v. a.* [from the noun.]

1. To corrupt with mildew.

This vapour bears up along with it any noxious mineral ſteams; it then blaſts vegetables, *blights* corn and fruit, and is ſometimes injurious even to men. *Woodward's Natural Hiſt.*

2. In general, to blaſt; to hinder from fertility.

My country neighbours do not find it impoſſible to think of a lame horſe they have, or their *blighted* corn, till they have run over in their minds all beings. *Locke.*

But leſt harſh care the lover's peace deſtroy,
And roughly *blight* the tender buds of joy,
Let reaſon teach. *Lyttleton.*

BLIND. *adj.* [blind, Saxon.]

1. Without ſight; deprived of the ſenſe of ſeeing; dark.

The *blind* man that governs his ſteps by feeling, in defect of eyes, receives advertiſement of remote things through a ſtaff. *Digby on the Soul.*

Thoſe

5 Blesse, Cisley, good Mistress, that Bishop doth ban
For burning the Milk of her Cheese to the Pan

Tusser husb. for Apr.

When the Bishop passed by in former times, every one ran out to partake of his blessing, and those who left their milk upon the fire might find it burnt to the pan when they came back, & perhaps ban or curse the Bishop as the Occasion of it: Hence it is likely it grew into a Custom to curse the Bishop when any such disaster happened; for which our Author would have the Mistress bless anglice (or rather ironice) correct her Servant both for her negligence & unmannerliness. Tuss notes.

IL facing 3F[v]

blank page

Thoſe other two equall'd with me in fate,
So were I equall'd with them in renown!
*Blind* Thamyris, and *blind* Mæonides;
And Tireſias, and Phineus, prophets old. *Par. Loſt, b.* iii.

2. Intellectually dark; unable to judge; ignorant; with *to* before that which is unſeen.

All authors *to* their own defects are *blind*;
Hadſt thou, but Janus like, a face behind,
To ſee the people, what ſplay-mouths they make;
To mark their fingers, pointed at thy back. *Dryden's Perſ.*

3. Sometimes *of*.

*Blind of* the future, and by rage miſled,
He pulls his crimes upon his people's head. *Dryden's Fab.*

4. Unſeen; out of the publick view; private; generally with ſome tendency to ſome contempt or cenſure.

To grievous and ſcandalous inconveniencies they make themſelves ſubject, with whom any *blind* or ſecret corner is judged a fit houſe of common prayer. *Hooker, b.* v. § 25.

5. Not eaſily diſcernible; hard to find; dark; obſcure; unſeen.

There be alſo *blind* fires under ſtone, which flame not out; but oil being poured upon them, they flame out. *Bacon.*

Where elſe
Shall I inform my unacquainted feet
In the *blind* mazes of this tangl'd wood? *Milton.*

How have we wander'd a long diſmal night,
Led through *blind* paths by each deluding light. *Roſcommon.*

Part creeping underground, their journey *blind*,
And climbing from below, their fellows meet. *Dryden.*

So mariners miſtake the promis'd guſt,
And, with full ſails, on the *blind* rocks are loſt. *Dryden.*

A poſtern door, yet unobſerv'd and free,
Join'd by the length of a *blind* gallery,
To the king's cloſet bed. *Dryden's Æneid.*

6. *Blind Veſſels.* [with chymiſts.] Such as have no opening but on one ſide.

To Blind. *v. a.* [from the noun.]

1. To make blind; to deprive of ſight.

You nimble lightnings, dart your *blinding* flames
Into her ſcornful eyes! *Shakeſp. King Lear.*

Of whoſe hand have I received any bribe to *blind* mine eyes therewith? and I will reſtore it. 1 *Sam.* xii. 3.

A blind guide is certainly a great miſchief; but a guide that *blinds* thoſe whom he ſhould lead, is undoubtedly a much greater. *South.*

2. To darken; to obſcure to the eye.

So whirl the ſeas, ſuch darkneſs *blinds* the ſky,
That the black night receives a deeper dye. *Dryden's Fab.*

3. To obſcure to the underſtanding.

The ſtate of the controverſy between us he endeavoured, with all his art, to *blind* and confound. *Stillingfleet.*

Blind. *n. ſ.*

1. Something to hinder the ſight.

Hardly any thing in our converſation is pure and genuine; civility caſts a *blind* over the duty, under ſome cuſtomary words. *L'Eſtrange.*

2. Something to miſlead the eye, or the underſtanding.

Theſe diſcourſes ſet an oppoſition between his commands and decrees; making the one a *blind* for the execution of the other. *Decay of Piety.*

To Bli'ndfold. *v. a.* [from *blind* and *fold.*] To hinder from ſeeing, by blinding the eyes.

When they had *blindfolded* him, they ſtruck him on the face. *Luke*, xxii. 64.

Bli'ndfold. *adj.* [from the verb.] Having the eyes covered.

And oft himſelf he chanc'd to hurt unwares,
Whilſt reaſon, blent through paſſion, nought deſcried,
But, as a *blindfold* bull, at random fares,
And where he hits, nought knows, and where he hurts,
nought cares. *Fairy Queen, b.* ii. *c.* iv. *ſtanz.* 7.

Who *blindfold* walks upon a river's brim,
When he ſhould ſee, has he deſerv'd to ſwim? *Dryden.*

When lots are ſhuffled together, or a man *blindfold* caſts a dye, what reaſon can he have to preſume, that he ſhall draw a white ſtone rather than a black? *South.*

They will look into the ſtate of the nation with their own eyes, and be no longer led *blindfold* by a male legiſlature. *Addiſon. Freeholder*, N° 32.

Bli'ndly. *adv.* [from *blind.*]

1. Without ſight.

2. Implicitely; without examination.

The old king, after a long debate,
By his imperious miſtreſs *blindly* led,
Has given Cydaria to Orbellan's bed. *Dryd. Indian Emp.*

How ready zeal for intereſt and party, is to charge atheiſm on thoſe, who will not, without examining, ſubmit, and *blindly* ſwallow their nonſenſe. *Locke.*

3. Without judgment or direction.

How ſeas, and earth, and air, and active flame,
Fell through the mighty void; and, in their fall,
Were *blindly* gather'd in this goodly ball. *Dryden's Silenus.*

Bli'ndman's buff. *n. ſ.* A play in which ſome one is to have his eyes covered, and hunt out the reſt of the company.

Diſguis'd in all the maſk of night,
We left our champion on his flight:
At *blindman's buff* to grope his way,
In equal fear of night and day. *Hudibras, p.* iii. *c.* ii.

He imagines I ſhut my eyes again; but ſurely he fancies I play at *blindman's buff* with him; for he thinks I never have my eyes open. *Stillingfleet's Defence of Diſc. on Romiſh Idolatry.*

Bli'ndness. *n. ſ.* [from *blind.*]

1. Want of ſight.

Nor can we call it choice, when what we chuſe,
Folly and *blindneſs* only could refuſe. *Denham.*

2. Ignorance; intellectual darkneſs.

All the reſt as born of ſavage brood,
But with baſe thoughts are into *blindneſs* led,
And kept from looking on the lightſome day. *Spenſer.*

Whenſoever we would proceed beyond thoſe ſimple ideas, we fall preſently into darkneſs and difficulties, and can diſcover nothing farther but our own *blindneſs* and ignorance. *Locke.*

Bli'ndside. *n. ſ.* [from *blind* and *ſide.*] Weakneſs; foible; weak part.

He is too great a lover of himſelf; but this is one of his *blindſides*; and the beſt of men, I fear, are not without them. *Swift's Wonderful Wonder of Wonders.*

Bli'ndworm. *n. ſ.* [from *blind* and *worm.*] A ſmall viper, the leaſt of our Engliſh ſerpents, but venemous.

You ſpotted ſnakes, with double tongue,
Thorny hedgehogs, be not ſeen;
Newts and *blindworms*, do no wrong;
Come not near our fairy queen. *Shakeſp. Mid. N. Dr.*

The greater ſlow worm, called alſo the *blindworm*, is commonly thought to be blind, becauſe of the littleneſs of his eyes. *Grew's Muſæum.*

To BLINK. *v. n.* [*blincken*, Daniſh.]

1. To wink, or twinkle with the eyes.

So politick, as if one eye
Upon the other were a ſpy;
That to trepan the one to think
The other blind, both ſtrove to *blink*. *Hudibras, p.* iii. *c.* ii.

2. To ſee obſcurely.

What's here! the portrait of a *blinking* idiot. *Shakeſp. Merchant of Venice.*

Sweet and lovely well,
Shew me thy chink, to *blink* through with mine eyne. *Shakeſp. Midſummer Night's Dream.*

His figure ſuch as might his ſoul proclaim;
One eye was *blinking*, and one leg was lame. *Pope's Iliad.*

Bli'nkard. *n. ſ.* [from *blink.*]

1. One that has bad eyes.

2. Something twinkling.

In ſome parts we ſee many glorious and eminent ſtars, in others few of any remarkable greatneſs, and, in ſome, none but *blinkards*, and obſcure ones. *Hakewell on Providence.*

BLISS. *n. ſ.* [bliꝑꝑe, Sax. from bliðaꝑian, to rejoice.]

1. The higheſt degree of happineſs; bleſſedneſs; felicity; generally uſed of the happineſs of bleſſed ſouls.

A mighty Saviour hath witneſſed of himſelf, I am the way; the way that leadeth us from miſery into *bliſs*. *Hooker, b.* i.

Dim ſadneſs did not ſpare
That time celeſtial viſages; yet, mix'd
With pity, violated not their *bliſs*. *Par. Loſt, b.* x. *l.* 25.

With me
All my redeem'd may dwell, in joy and *bliſs*. *Par. Loſt, b.* xi.

2. Felicity in general.

Condition, circumſtance is not the thing;
*Bliſs* is the ſame in ſubject or in king. *Pope.*

Bli'ssful. *adj.* [from *bliſs* and *full.*] Full of joy; happy in the higheſt degree.

Yet ſwimming in that ſea of *bliſsful* joy,
He nought forgot. *Fairy Queen, b.* i. *c.* i. *ſtan.* 41.

The two ſaddeſt ingredients in hell, are deprivation of the *bliſsful* viſion, and confuſion of face. *Hammond.*

Reaping immortal fruits of joy and love,
Uninterrupted joy, unrival'd love,
In *bliſsful* ſolitude. *Milton's Paradiſe Loſt, b.* iii. *l.* 69.

Firſt in the fields I try the ſilvan ſtrains,
Nor bluſh to ſport in Windſor's *bliſsful* plains. *Pope.*

Bli'ssfully. *adv.* [from *bliſsful.*] Happily.

Bli'ssfulness. *n. ſ.* [from *bliſsful.*] Happineſs; fulneſs of joy.

To Bli'ssom. *v. n.* To caterwaul; to be luſtful. *Dict.*

BLI'STER. *n. ſ.* [*bluyſter*, Dutch.]

1. A puſtule formed by raiſing the cuticle from the cutis, and filled with ſerous blood.

In this ſtate ſhe gallops, night by night,
O'er ladies lips, who ſtrait on kiſſes dream,
Which oft the angry mob with *bliſters* plagues,
Becauſe their breaths with ſweetmeats tainted are. *Shakeſp. Romeo and Juliet.*

I found a great *bliſter* drawn by the garlick, but had it cut, which run a good deal of water, but filled again by next night. *Temple.*

2. Any ſwelling made by the ſeparation of a film or ſkin from the other parts.

Upon

Upon the leaves there riseth a tumour like a *blister*. *Bacon.*

To BLI'STER. *v. n.* [from the noun.] To rise in blisters.

If I prove honeymouth, let my tongue *blister*,
And never to my red look'd anger be
The trumpet any more. *Shakesp. Winter's Tale.*

Embrace thy knees with loathing hands,
Which *blister* when they touch thee. *Dryden's Don Sebast.*

To BLI'STER. *v. a.*

1. To raise blisters by some hurt, as a burn, or rubbing.

Look, here comes one, a gentlewoman of mine,
Who falling in the flames of her own youth,
Hath *blister'd* her report. *Shakesp. Measure for Measure.*

2. To raise blisters with a medical intention.

I *blistered* the legs and thighs; but was too late, he died howling. *Wiseman's Surgery.*

BLITHE. *adj.* [blıðe, Saxon.] Gay; airy; merry; joyous; sprightly; mirthful.

We have always one eye fixed upon the countenance of our enemies; and, according to the *blithe* or heavy aspect thereof, our other eye sheweth some other suitable token either of dislike or approbation. *Hooker, b.* iv. § 9.

Then sigh not so, but let them go,
And be you *blithe* and bonny. *Shakesp. M. ado about Noth.*

For that fair female troop thou saw'st, that seem'd
Of goddesses, so *blithe*, so smooth, so gay;
Yet empty of all good. *Milton's Paradise Lost, b.* xi.

To whom the wily adder, *blithe* and glad:
Empress! the way is ready, and not long. *Par. Lost, b.* ix.

And the milkmaid singeth *blithe*,
And the mower whets his scythe. *Milton.*

Should he return, that troop so *blithe* and bold,
Precipitant in fear, would wing their flight. *Pope.*

BLI'THLY. *adv.* [from *blithe.*] In a blithe manner.

BLI'THNESS. } *n. s.* [from *blithe.*] The quality of being
BLI'THSOMNESS. } blithe.

BLI'THSOME. *adj.* [from *blithe.*] Gay; cheerful.

Frosty blasts deface
The *blithsome* year: trees of their shrivell'd fruits
Are widow'd. *Philips.*

To BLOAT. *v. a.* [probably from *blow.*] To swell, or make turgid with wind.

His rude essays
Encourage him, and *bloat* him up with praise,
That he may get more bulk before he dies. *Dryden.*

The strutting petticoat smooths all distinctions, levels the mother with the daughter. I cannot but be troubled to see so many well-shaped innocent virgins *bloated* up, and waddling up and down like bigbellied women. *Addison. Spectator.*

To BLOAT. *v. n.* To grow turgid.

If a person of a firm constitution begins to *bloat*, from being warm grows cold, his fibres grow weak. *Arbuthnot.*

BLO'ATEDNESS. *n. s.* [from *bloat.*] Turgidness; swelling; tumour.

Lassitude, laziness, *bloatedness*, and scorbutical spots, are symptoms of weak fibres. *Arbuthnot on Aliments.*

BLO'BBER. *n. s.* [from *blob.*] A word used in some counties for a bubble.

There swimmeth also in the sea a round slimy substance, called a *blobber*, reputed noisome to the fish. *Carew.*

BLO'BBERLIP. *n. s.* [from *blob*, or *blobber*, and *lip.*] A thick lip.

They make a wit of their insipid friend,
His *blobberlips* and beetlebrows commend. *Dryden's Juvenal.*

BLO'BLIPPED. } *adj.* Having swelled or thick lips.
BLO'BBERLIPPED. }

A *bloblipped* shell, which seemeth to be a kind of mussel. *Grew's Museum.*

His person deformed to the highest degree; flat nosed, and *blobberlipped.* *L'Estrange.*

BLOCK. *n. s.* [*block*, Dutch; *bloc*, Fr.]

1. A heavy piece of timber, rather thick than long.

2. A mass of matter.

Homer's apotheosis consists of a groupe of figures, cut in the same *block* of marble, and rising one above another. *Addison.*

3. A massy body.

Small causes are sufficient to make a man uneasy, when great ones are not in the way: for want of a *block*, he will stumble at a straw. *Swift's Thoughts on various Subjects.*

4. A rude piece of timber; in contempt.

When, by the help of wedges and beetles, an image is cleft out of the trunk of some tree, yet, after all the skill of artificers to set forth such a divine *block*, it cannot one moment secure itself from being eaten by worms. *Stillingfleet.*

5. The piece of wood on which hats are formed.

He wears his faith but as the fashion of his hat; it ever changes with the next *block*. *Shakesp. Much ado about Nothing.*

6. The wood on which criminals are beheaded.

Some guard these traitors to the *block* of death,
Treason's true bed, and yielder up of breath. *Shakesp. H.IV.*

At the instant of his death, having a long beard, after his head was upon the *block*, he gently drew his beard aside, and said, this hath not offended the king. *Bacon's Apophthegms.*

I'll drag him thence,
Even from the holy altar to the *block*. *Dryden's W. of B.*

7. An obstruction; a stop.

Can he ever dream, that the suffering for righteousness sake is our felicity, when he sees us run so from it, that no crime is *block* enough in our way, to stop our flight? *Decay of Piety.*

8. A sea term for a pully.

9. A blockhead; a fellow remarkable for stupidity.

The country is a desert, where the good
Gain'd, inhabite not; born's not understood;
There men become beasts, and prone to all evils;
In cities, *blocks.* *Donne.*

What tongueless *blocks* were they, would they not speak? *Shakesp. Richard III.*

To BLOCK. *v. a.* [*bloquer*, Fr.] To shut up; to inclose, so as to hinder egress.

The states about them should neither by encrease of dominion, nor by *blocking* of trade, have it in their power to hurt or annoy. *Bacon's War with Spain.*

Recommend it to the governour of Abingdon, to send some troops to *block* it up, from infesting the great road. *Clarendon.*

They *block* the castle kept by Bertram;
But now they cry, down with the palace, fire it. *Dryden.*

The abbot raises an army, and *blocks* up the town on the side that faces his dominions. *Addison on Italy.*

BLOCK-HOUSE. *n. s.* [from *block* and *house.*] A fortress built to obstruct or block up a pass.

His entrance is guarded with *block-houses*, and that on the town's side fortified with ordnance. *Carew's Survey of Cornw.*

Rochester water reacheth far within the land, and is under the protection of some *block-houses.* *Raleigh's Essays.*

BLOCK-TIN. *n. s.* [from *block* and *tin.*] So the tradesmen call that which is most pure or unmixed, and as yet unwrought. *Boyle.*

BLOCKA'DE. *n. s.* [from *block.*] A siege carried on by shutting up the place.

The enemy was necessitated wholly to abandon the *blockade* of Olivenza. *Tatler*, N° 51.

Round the goddess roll
Broad hats and hoods, and caps, a sable shoal;
Thick, and more thick, the black *blockade* extends. *Pope.*

To BLOCKA'DE. *v. a.* [from the noun.] To shut up.

Huge bales of British cloth *blockade* the door,
A hundred oxen at your levee roar. *Pope.*

BLO'CKHEAD. *n. s.* [from *block* and *head.*] A stupid fellow; a dolt; a man without parts.

Your wit will not so soon out as another man's will; it is strongly wedged up in a *blockhead.* *Shakesp. Coriolanus.*

We idly sit like stupid *blockheads*,
Our hands committed to our pockets. *Hudibras, p.* iii. *c.* ii.

A *blockhead* rubs his thoughtless skull,
And thanks his stars he was not born a fool. *Pope.*

BLO'CKHEADED. *adj.* [from *blockhead.*] Stupid; dull.

Says a *blockheaded* boy, these are villainous creatures. *L'Estrange's Fables.*

BLO'CKISH. *adj.* [from *block.*] Stupid; dull.

Make a lott'ry,
And, by decree, let *blockish* Ajax draw
The sort to fight with Hector. *Shakesp. Troilus and Cress.*

BLO'CKISHLY. *adv.* [from *blockish.*] In a stupid manner.

BLO'CKISHNESS. *n. s.* [from *blockish.*] Stupidity.

BLO'MARY. *n. s.* The first forge in the iron mills, through which the metal passes, after it has been first melted from the mine. *Dict.*

BLO'NKET. *n. s.* [I suppose for *blanket.*]

Our *blonket* livery's been all too sad
For thilke same season, when all is yclad
With pleasance. *Spenser's Pastorals.*

BLOOD. *n. s.* [blod, Saxon.]

1. The red liquour that circulates in the bodies of animals.

But flesh with the life thereof, which is the *blood* thereof, shall you not eat. *Gen.* ix. 4.

2. Child; progeny.

We'll no more meet, no more see one another:
But yet thou art my flesh, my *blood*, my daughter. *Shakesp. King Lear.*

3. Family; kindred.

As many and as well born *bloods* as those,
Stand in his face, to contradict his claim. *Shakesp. K. John.*

O! what an happiness is it to find
A friend of our own *blood*, a brother kind. *Waller.*

According to the common law of England, in administration, the whole *blood* ought to be preferred to the half *blood*. *Ayliffe's Parergon.*

4. Descent; lineage.

Epithets of flattery, deserved by few of them; and not running in a *blood*, like the perpetual gentleness of the Ormond family. *Dryden's Fab. Dedication.*

5. Blood royal; royal lineage.

They will almost
Give us a prince o' th' *blood*, a son of Priam,
In change of him. *Shakesp. Troilus and Cressida.*

6. Birth; high extraction.

I am a gentleman of *blood* and breeding. *Shakesp. K. Lear.*

7. Mur-

Fill out the black bole of blithe to the song
And let them be merrie all harvest time long
Tuss. husb. for Aug.<sup></sup>

IL facing 3F2v

blank page

7. Murder; violent death.

It will have blood; they say, *blood* will have blood. *Shakesp. Macbeth.*

The voice of thy brother's *blood* crieth unto me from the ground. *Gen.* iv. 10.

8. Life.

When wicked men have slain a righteous person in his own house, upon his bed, shall I not therefore now require his *blood* at your hand? 2 *Sam.* iv. 11.

9. *For blood.* Though his blood or life was at stake: a low phrase.

A crow lay battering upon a muscle, and could not, *for his blood*, break the shell to come at the fish. *L'Estrange.*

10. The carnal part of man.

Flesh and *blood* hath not revealed it unto thee, but my father which is in heaven. *Matt.* xvi. 17.

11. Temper of mind; state of the passions.

Will you, great sir, that glory blot,
In cold *blood*, which you gain'd in hot? *Hudibras.*

12. Hot spark; man of fire.

The news put divers young *bloods* into such a fury, as the English ambassadors were not, without peril, to be outraged. *Bacon's Henry* VII.

13. The juice of any thing.

He washed his garments in wine, and his cloaths in the *blood* of grapes. *Gen.* xlix. 11.

To BLOOD. *v. a.* [from the noun.]

1. To stain with blood.

When the faculties intellectual are in vigour, not drenched, or, as it were, *blooded* by the affections. *Bacon's Apophth.*

Then all approach the slain with vast surprise,
And, scarce secure, reach out their spears afar,
And *blood* their points, to prove their partnership in war. *Dryden's Fables.*

He was *blooded* up to his elbows by a couple of Moors, whom he had been butchering with his own imperial hands. *Addison.*

2. To enter; to enure to blood, as a hound.

Fairer than fairest, let none ever say,
That ye were *blooded* in a yielded prey. *Spenser, sonn.* xx.

3. To blood, is sometimes to let blood medically.

4. To heat; to exasperate.

By this means, matters grew more exasperate; the auxiliary forces of French and English were much *blooded* one against another. *Bacon's Henry* VII.

BLOOD-BOLTERED. *adj.* [from *blood* and *bolter.*] Blood-sprinkled.

The *blood-bolter'd* Banquo smiles upon me. *Macbeth.*

BLOOD-HOT. *adj.* [from *blood* and *hot.*] Hot in the same degree with blood.

A good piece of bread first to be eaten, will gain time to warm the beer *blood-hot*, which then he may drink safely. *Locke.*

To BLOOD-LET. *v. a.* [from *blood* and *let.*] To bleed; to open a vein medicinally.

The chyle is not perfectly assimilated into blood, by its circulation through the lungs, as is known by experiments of *blood-letting*. *Arbuthnot on Aliments.*

BLOOD-LETTER. *n. s.* [from *blood-let.*] A phlebotomist; one that takes away blood medically.

This mischief happening to aneurisms, proceedeth from the ignorance of the *blood-letter*, who, not considering the errour committed in letting blood, binds up the arm carelessly. *Wiseman's Surgery.*

BLOOD-STONE. *n. s.* [from *blood* and *stone.*] The name of a stone.

There is a stone, which they call the *blood-stone*, which, worn, is thought to be good for them that bleed at the nose; which, no doubt, is by astriction, and cooling of the spirits. *Bacon.*

The *blood-stone* is green, spotted with a bright blood-red. *Woodward on Fossils.*

BLOOD-THIRSTY. *adj.* [from *blood* and *thirst.*] Desirous to shed blood.

And high advancing his *blood-thirsty* blade,
Struck one of those deformed heads. *Fairy Queen, b.* i.

The image of God the *blood-thirsty* have not; for God is charity and mercy itself. *Raleigh's History.*

BLOOD-VESSEL. *n. s.* [from *blood* and *vessel.*] A vessel appropriated by nature to the conveyance of the blood.

The skins of the forehead were extremely tough and thick, and had not in them any *blood-vessel*, that we were able to discover. *Addison. Spectator,* № 275.

BLO'ODFLOWER. *n. s.* [*hæmanthus*, Lat.] A plant.

This plant was originally brought from the Cape of Good Hope, and has been many years preserved in the curious gardens in Holland, where they now have many sorts, but in England it is still very rare. *Millar.*

BLOODGUI'LTINESS. *n. s.* [from *blood* and *guilty.*] Murder; the crime of shedding blood.

And were there rightful cause of difference,
Yet were't not better, fair it to accord,
Than with *bloodguiltiness* to heap offence,
And mortal vengeance join to crime abhorr'd. *Fairy Q. b.* ii.

BLO'ODHOUND. *n. s.* [from *blood* and *hound.*] A hound that follows by the scent, and seizes with great fierceness.

Hear this, hear this, thou tribune of the people:
Thou zealous, publick *bloodhound*, hear, and melt. *Dryden.*

Where are these rav'ning *bloodhounds*, that pursue
In a full cry, gaping to swallow me? *Southerne's Inn. Adult.*

A *bloodhound* will follow the tract of the person he pursues, and all hounds the particular game they have in chace. *Arbuthnot on Aliments.*

And though the villain 'scape a while, he feels
Slow vengeance, like a *bloodhound*, at his heels. *Swift.*

BLO'ODILY. *adv.* [from *bloody.*] With disposition to shed blood; cruelly.

I told the pursuivant,
As too triumphing, how mine enemies,
To day at Pomfret, *bloodily* were butcher'd. *Shakesp. R.* III.

This day, the poet, *bloodily* inclin'd,
Has made me die, full sore against my mind. *Dryden.*

BLO'ODINESS. *n. s.* [from *bloody.*] The state of being bloody.

It will manifest itself by its *bloodiness*; yet sometimes the scull is so thin as not to admit of any. *Sharp's Surgery.*

BLO'ODLESS. *adj.* [from *blood.*]

1. Without blood; dead.

He cheer'd my sorrows, and, for sums of gold,
The *bloodless* carcase of my Hector sold. *Dryden's Æneid.*

2. Without slaughter.

War brings ruin where it should amend;
But beauty, with a *bloodless* conquest, finds
A welcome sov'reignty in rudest minds. *Waller.*

BLO'ODSHED. *n. s.* [from *blood* and *shed.*]

1. The crime of blood, or murder.

Full many mischiefs follow cruel wrath;
Abhorred *bloodshed*, and tumultuous strife,
Unmanly murder, and unthrifty scath. *Fairy Queen, b.* i.

All murders past do stand excus'd in this;
And this so sole, and so unmatchable,
Shall prove a deadly *bloodshed* but a jest,
Exampled by this heinous spectacle. *Shakesp. King John.*

A man, under the transports of a vehement rage, passes a different judgment upon murder and *bloodshed*, from what he does when his revenge is over. *South.*

2. Slaughter.

So by him Cæsar got the victory,
Through great *bloodshed*, and many a sad assay. *Fairy Q. b.* ii.

Of wars and *bloodshed*, and of dire events,
I could with greater certainty foretel. *Dryden's Tyran. Love.*

BLO'ODSHEDDER. *n. s.* [from *bloodshed.*] Murderer.

He that taketh away his neighbour's living, slayeth him: and he that defraudeth the labourer of his hire, is a *bloodshedder*. *Ecclus*, xxxiv. 22.

BLO'ODSHOT. } *adj.* [from *blood* and *shot.*] Filled with
BLOODSHO'TTEN. } blood bursting from its proper vessels.

And that the winds their bellowing throats would try,
When redd'ning clouds reflect his *bloodshot* eye. *Garth.*

BLO'ODSUCKER. *n. s.* [from *blood* and *suck.*]

1. A leech; a fly; any thing that sucks blood.

2. A cruel man; a murderer.

God keep the prince from all the pack of you;
A knot you are of damned *bloodsuckers*. *Shakesp. Rich.* III.

The nobility cried out upon him, that he was a *bloodsucker*, a murderer, and a parricide. *Hayward.*

BLO'ODY. *adj.* [from *blood.*]

1. Stained with blood.

2. Cruel; murderous; applied either to men or facts.

By continual martial exercises, without blood, she made them perfect in that *bloody* art. *Sidney, b.* ii.

False of heart, light of ear, *bloody* of hand. *Shakesp. K. Lear.*

I grant him *bloody*,
Luxurious, avaricious, false, deceitful. *Shakesp. Macbeth.*

Thou *bloodier* villain,
Than terms can give thee out. *Shakesp. Macbeth.*

Alas! why gnaw you so your nether lip?
Some *bloody* passion shakes your very frame;
These are portents: but yet I hope, I hope,
They do not point on me. *Shakesp. Othello.*

The *bloody* fact
Will be aveng'd; and th' other's faith approv'd
Lose no reward; though here thou see him die,
Rolling in dust and gore. *Milton's Paradise Lost, b.* xi. *l.* 457.

The *bloodiest* vengeance which she could pursue,
Would be a trifle to my loss of you. *Dryden's Indian Emp.*

Proud Nimrod first the *bloody* chace began,
A mighty hunter, and his prey was man. *Pope's W. Forest.*

BLOODY-FLUX. See FLUX.

Cold, by retarding the motion of the blood, and suppressing perspiration, produces giddiness, sleepiness, pains in the bowels, looseness, *bloody-fluxes*. *Arbuthnot on Air.*

BLOODY-MINDED. *adj.* [from *bloody* and *mind.*] Cruel; inclined to bloodshed.

I think you'll make me mad: truth has been at my tongue's end this half hour, and I have not the power to bring it out, for fear of this *bloody-minded* colonel. *Dryden's Spanish Friar.*

BLOOM. *n. s.* [*blum*, Germ. *bloem*, Dutch.]

1. A blossom; the flower which precedes the fruit.

How nature paints her colours, how the bee
Sits on the *bloom*, extracting liquid ſweet. *Par. Loſt, b.* v.

A medlar tree was planted by;
The ſpreading branches made a goodly ſhow,
And full of opening *blooms* was ev'ry bough. *Dryden.*

Haſte to yonder woodbine bow'rs;
The turf with rural dainties ſhall be crown'd,
While opening *blooms* diffuſe their ſweets around. *Pope.*

2. The ſtate of immaturity; the ſtate of any thing improving, and ripening to higher perfection.

Were I no queen, did you my beauty weigh,
My youth in *bloom*, your age in its decay. *Dryden's Aurengz.*

3. The blue colour upon plums and grapes newly gathered.
4. [In the iron works.] A piece of iron wrought into a maſs, two feet ſquare.

To BLOOM. *v. n.* [from the noun.]

1. To bring or yield bloſſoms.

The rod of Aaron for the houſe of Levi was budded, and brought forth buds, and *bloomed* bloſſoms, and yielded almonds. *Numb.* xvii. 8.

It is a common experience, that if you do not pull off ſome bloſſoms the firſt time a tree *bloometh*, it will bloſſom itſelf to death. *Bacon's Natural Hiſt.* N° 449.

2. To produce, as bloſſoms.

Rites and cuſtoms, now ſuperſtitious, when the ſtrength of virtuous, devout, or charitable affection *bloomed* them, no man could juſtly have condemned as evil. *Hooker, b.* v. § 3.

3. To be in a ſtate of youth and improvement.

Beauty, frail flow'r, that ev'ry ſeaſon fears,
*Blooms* in thy colours for a thouſand years. *Pope's Epiſtles.*

O greatly bleſs'd with every *blooming* grace!
With equal ſteps the paths of glory trace. *Pope's Odyſſ. b.* i.

BLO'OMY. *adj.* [from *bloom.*] Full of blooms; flowery.

O nightingale! that on yon *bloomy* ſpray
Warbleſt at eve, when all the woods are ſtill. *Milton.*

Departing ſpring could only ſtay to ſhed
Her *bloomy* beauties on the genial bed,
But left the manly ſummer in her ſtead. *Dryden.*

Hear how the birds, on ev'ry *bloomy* ſpray,
With joyous muſick wake the dawning day. *Pope.*

BLORE. *n. ſ.* [from *blow.*] Act of blowing; blaſt.

Out ruſht, with an unmeaſur'd roar,
Thoſe two winds, tumbling clouds in heaps; uſhers to either's *blore.* *Chapman's Iliads.*

BLO'SSOM. *n. ſ.* [blorme, Sax.] The flower that grows on any plant, previous to the ſeed or fruit. We generally call thoſe flowers *bloſſoms*, which are not much regarded in themſelves, but as a token of ſome following production.

Cold news for me:
Thus are my *bloſſoms* blaſted in the bud,
And caterpillars eat my leaves away. *Shakeſp. Henry* IV.

Merrily, merrily ſhall I live now,
Under the *bloſſom* that hangs on the bough. *Shakeſp. Tempeſt.*

The pulling off many of the *bloſſoms* of a fruit tree, doth make the fruit fairer. *Bacon's Natural Hiſtory*, N° 449.

To his green years your cenſure you would ſuit,
Not blaſt the *bloſſom*, but expect the fruit. *Dryden.*

Sweeter than ſpring.
Thou ſole ſurviving *bloſſom* from the root,
That nouriſh'd up my fortune. *Thomſon's Autumn.*

To BLO'SSOM. *v. n.* [from the noun.] To put forth bloſſoms.

This is the ſtate of man: to day he puts forth
The tender leaves of hope; tomorrow *bloſſoms*,
And bears his bluſhing honours thick upon him. *Sh. H.* VIII.

Although the figtree ſhall not *bloſſom*, neither ſhall fruit be in the vines, yet I will rejoice in the Lord. *Habb.* iii. 17.

The want of rain at *bloſſoming* time, often occaſions the dropping off of the bloſſoms, for want of ſap. *Mortimer.*

To BLOT. *v. a.* [from *blottir*, Fr. to hide.]

1. To obliterate; to make writing inviſible, by covering it with ink.

You that are king,
Have caus'd him, by new act of parliament,
To *blot* out me, and put his own ſon in. *Shakeſp. Henry* VI.

Ev'n copious Dryden wanted, or forgot,
The laſt and greateſt art, the art to *blot.* *Pope.*

A man of the moſt underſtanding will find it impoſſible to make the beſt uſe of it, while he writes in conſtraint, perpetually ſoftening, correcting, or *blotting* out expreſſions. *Swift.*

2. To efface; to eraſe.

O Bertran, oh! no more my foe, but brother:
One act like this *blots* out a thouſand crimes. *Dryden.*

Theſe ſimple ideas, offered to the mind, the underſtanding can no more refuſe, nor alter, nor *blot* out, than a mirrour can refuſe, alter, or obliterate, the images which the objects produce. *Locke.*

3. To make black ſpots on a paper; to blur.

Heads overfull of matter, be like pens over full of ink, which will ſooner *blot*, than make any fair letter at all. *Aſcham's Schoolmaſter.*

O ſweet Portia!
Here are a few of the unpleaſant'ſt words
That ever *blotted* paper. *Shakeſp. Merchant of Venice.*

4. To diſgrace; to diſfigure.

Unknit that threat'ning unkind brow;
It *blots* thy beauty, as froſt bites the meads,
Confounds thy fame. *Shakeſp. Taming of the Shrew.*

My guilt thy growing virtues did defame;
My blackneſs *blotted* thy unblemiſh'd name. *Dryden's Æn.*

For mercy's ſake, reſtrain thy hand,
Blot not thy innocence with guiltleſs blood. *Rowe.*

5. To darken.

He ſung how earth *blots* the moon's gilded wane,
Whilſt fooliſh men beat ſounding braſs in vain. *Cowley.*

BLOT. *n. ſ.* [from the verb.]

1. An obliteration of ſomething written.

Let flames on your unlucky papers prey,
Your wars, your loves, your praiſes, be forgot,
And make of all an univerſal *blot.* *Dryden's Juven. ſat.* vii.

2. A blur; a ſpot upon paper.
3. A ſpot in reputation; a ſtain; a diſgrace; a reproach.

Make known,
It is no vicious *blot*, murder, or foulneſs,
That hath depriv'd me. *Shakeſp. King Lear.*

A lie is a foul *blot* in a man; yet it is continually in the mouth of the untaught. *Ecclus*, xx. 24.

A diſappointed hope, a *blot* of honour, a ſtrain of conſcience, an unfortunate love, will ſerve the turn. *Temple.*

4. [At backgammon.] When a ſingle man lies open to be taken up; whence to hit a *blot.*

He is too great a maſter of his art, to make a *blot* which may ſo eaſily be hit. *Dryden's Dedication, Æneid.*

BLOTCH. *n. ſ.* [from *blot.*] A ſpot or puſtule upon the ſkin.

Spots and *blotches*, of ſeveral colours and figures, ſtraggling over the body; ſome are red, others yellow, livid, or black. *Harvey on Conſumptions.*

To BLOTE. *v. a.* To ſmoke, or dry by the ſmoke; as *bloted* herrings, or red herrings.

BLOW. *n. ſ.* [*blowe*, Dutch.]

1. A ſtroke.

A moſt poor man, made tame to fortune's *blows*,
Who, by the art of known and feeling ſorrows,
Am pregnant to good pity. *Shakeſp. King Lear.*

A woman's tongue,
That gives not half ſo great a *blow* to th' ear,
As will a cheſnut. *Shakeſp. Taming of the Shrew.*

Words of great contempt, commonly finding a return of equal ſcorn, *blows* were faſtened upon the moſt pragmatical of the crew. *Clarendon.*

2. The fatal ſtroke; the ſtroke of death.

Aſſuage your thirſt of blood, and ſtrike the *blow.* *Dryd.*

3. A ſingle action; a ſudden event.

Every year they gain a victory, and a town; but if they are once defeated, they loſe a province at a *blow.* *Dryden.*

4. The act of a fly, by which ſhe lodges eggs in fleſh.

I much fear, leſt with the *blows* of flies,
His braſs inflicted wounds are fill'd. *Chapman's Iliads.*

To BLOW. *v. n.* pret. *blew*; particip. paſſ. *blown.* [blapan, Sax.]

1. To move with a current of air.

At his ſight the mountains are ſhaken, and at his will the ſouth wind *bloweth.* *Ecclus*, xliii. 16.

Fruits, for long keeping, gather before they are full ripe, and in a dry day, towards noon, and when the wind *bloweth* not ſouth; and when the moon is in decreaſe. *Bacon's Nat. Hiſt.*

By the fragrant winds that *blow*
O'er th' Elyſian flow'rs. *Pope's St. Cæcilia.*

2. This word is uſed ſometimes imperſonally with *it.*

*It blew* a terrible tempeſt at ſea once, and there was one ſeaman praying. *L'Eſtrange.*

If *it blows* a happy gale, we muſt ſet up all our ſails, though it ſometimes happens, that our natural heat is more powerful than our care and correctneſs. *Dryden's Dufreſnoy.*

3. To pant; to puff; to be breathleſs.

Here's Mrs. Page at the door, ſweating and *blowing*, and looking wildly. *Shakeſp. Merry Wives of Windſor.*

Each aking nerve refuſe the lance to throw,
And each ſpent courſer at the chariot *blow.* *Pope's Iliad.*

4. To breathe.

Says the ſatyr, if you have gotten a trick of *blowing* hot and cold out of the ſame mouth, I've e'en done with ye. *L'Eſtrange.*

5. To ſound by being blown.

Nor with leſs dread the loud
Ethereal trumpet from on high 'gan *blow.* *Par. Loſt, b.* vi.

There let the prating organ *blow*,
To the full-voic'd quire below. *Milton.*

6. To ſound, or play muſically by wind.

When ye *blow* an alarm, then the camps that lie on the eaſt parts ſhall go forward. *Numb.* x. 5.

7. *To blow over.* To paſs away without effect.

Storms, though they *blow over* divers times, yet may fall at laſt. *Bacon's Eſſays*, N° 16.

When the ſtorm is *blown over*,
How bleſt is the ſwain,
Who begins to diſcover
An end of his pain. *Granville.*

Corruption like a general flood
Shall deluge all; and av'rice creeping on
Spread like a low-born mist & blot the Sun
Pope

Crashaw transfers it to the effulgence
of light
He saw heavens blossom with a New born light
On which as on a glorious Stranger gaz'd
The golden eyes of night whose beams made
bright
The way to bethlem and as boldly blaz'd
Nor ask'd leave of the Sun by day as Night
Crashaw

I've seen the Mornings lovely ray
Hover o'er the new born day;
With rosy wings so richly bright
As if he scorn'd to think of Night
When a ruddy storm whose scoule
Made heavens radiant face look foul
Call'd for an untimely Night
To blot the newly blossom'd light
Crashaw

~~To spread or publish with a view to betray~~
Tis a man betray'd lost & blown by such Agents
as he employs in his greatest & nearest concerns
The cause of it is from this that he misplaced
his confidence & took hypocrisy for fidelity
South

To promulgate to publish

Th' apostles could not be confin'd
To these or those but severally design'd
Their large Commission round the World to blow
Dryd.

6 To blow nails: a proverbial expression
for poor Comfort, akin to that in Scotland
He blows a cold coal
Our love is not so great Hortensio
But we may blow our nails together
And fast it fairly out Shak
When icicles hang down from wall
And Dick the Shepherd blows his Nail. Idem.

IL facing 3G[v]

Blue n. s. The Sky
Throw out our Eyes for brave Othello
Ev'n till we make the main & th'aerial blue
An indistinct regard   Shak.



IL facing 3G2r

But thoſe clouds being now happily *blown over*, and our ſun clearly ſhining out again, I have recovered the relapſe. *Denham.*

8. *To blow up.* To fly into the air by the force of gunpowder.

On the next day, ſome of the enemy's magazines *blew up*; and it is thought they were deſtroyed on purpoſe by ſome of their men. *Tatler*, N° 59.

To Blow. *v. a.*

1. To drive by the force of the wind.

Though you unty the winds,
Though bladed corn be lodg'd, and trees *blown* down,
Though caſtles topple on their warders heads. *Macbeth.*

Fair daughter, *blow* away thoſe miſts and clouds,
And let thy eyes ſhine forth in their full luſtre. *Denham.*

Theſe primitive heirs of the chriſtian church, could not ſo eaſily *blow* off the doctrine of paſſive obedience. *South.*

2. To inflame with wind.

I have created the ſmith that *bloweth* the coals in the fire. *Iſaiah*, liv. 16.

3. To ſwell; to puff into ſize.

No *blown* ambition doth our arms incite,
But love, dear love, and our ag'd father's right. *King Lear.*

4. To form by blowing them into ſhape.

Spherical bubbles, that boys ſometimes *blow* with water, to which ſoap hath given a tenacity. *Boyle.*

5. To ſound an inſtrument of wind muſick.

Where the bright ſeraphim, in burning row,
Their loud uplifted angel trumpets *blow*. *Milton.*

6. To warm with the breath.

When iſicles hang by the wall,
And Dick the ſhepherd *blows* his nail,
And Tom bears logs into the hall,
And milk comes frozen home in pail. *Shak. L. Lab. Loſt.*

7. To ſpread by report.

But never was there man of his degree,
So much eſteem'd, ſo well belov'd as he:
So gentle of condition was he known,
That through the court his courteſy was *blown*. *Dryden.*

8. *To blow out.* To extinguiſh by wind or the breath.

Your breath firſt kindled the dead coal of war,
And brought in matter, that ſhould feed this fire:
And now 'tis far too huge to be *blown out*,
With that ſame weak wind which enkindled it. *Sh. K. John.*

Moon, ſlip behind ſome cloud, ſome tempeſt, riſe,
And *blow out* all the ſtars that light the ſkies. *Dryden.*

9. *To blow up.* To raiſe or ſwell with breath.

A plague of ſighing and grief! it *blows* a man *up* like a bladder. *Shakeſp. Henry* IV. *p.* i.

*Blown up* with the conceit of his merit, he did not think he had received good meaſure from the king. *Bacon's Hen.* VII.

Before we had exhauſted the receiver, the bladder appeared as full as if *blown up* with a quill. *Boyle.*

It was my breath that *blew* this tempeſt *up*,
Upon your ſtubborn uſage of the pope. *Shakeſp. K. John.*

His preſence ſoon *blows up* the unkindly fight,
And his loud guns ſpeak thick like angry men. *Dryden.*

An empty bladder gravitates no more than when *blown up*, but ſomewhat leſs; yet deſcends more eaſily, becauſe with leſs reſiſtance. *Grew's Coſmologia Sacra, b.* ii. *c.* 6.

When the mind finds herſelf very much inflamed with devotion, ſhe is too much inclined to think that it is *blown up* with ſomething divine within herſelf. *Addiſ. Spect.* N° 201.

10. *To blow up.* To deſtroy with gunpowder; to raiſe into the air.

The captains hoping, by a mine, to gain the city, approached with ſoldiers ready to enter upon *blowing up* of the mine. *Knolles's Hiſtory of the Turks.*

Their chief *blown up* in air, not waves, expir'd,
To which his pride preſum'd to give the law. *Dryden.*

Not far from the ſaid well, *blowing up* a rock, he formerly obſerved ſome of theſe. *Woodward on Foſſils.*

11. To infect with the eggs of flies.

I would no more endure
This wooden ſlavery, than I would ſuffer
The fleſh-fly *blow* my mouth. *Shakeſp. Tempeſt.*

Rather at Nilus' mud
Lay me ſtark naked, and let the water flies
*Blow* me into abhorring. *Shakeſp. Antony and Cleopatra.*

12. *To blow upon.* To make ſtale.

I am wonderfully pleaſed, when I meet with any paſſage in an old Greek or Latin author, that is not *blown upon*, and which I have never met with in any quotation. *Addiſon.*

He will whiſper an intrigue that is not yet *blown upon* by common fame. *Addiſon. Spectator*, N° 105.

To Blow. *v. n.* [blopan, Saxon.] To bloom; to bloſſom.

We loſe the prime to mark how ſpring
Our tended plants, how *blows* the citron grove,
What drops the myrrh, and what the balmy reed.
*Milton's Paradiſe Loſt, b.* v. *l.* 22.

This royal fair
Shall, when the bloſſom of her beauty's *blown*,
See her great brother on the Britiſh throne. *Waller.*

Fair is the kingcup that in meadow *blows*,
Fair is the daiſy that beſide her grows. *Gay's Paſtorals.*



For thee Idume's ſpicy foreſts *blow*,
And ſeeds of gold in Ophir's mountains glow. *Pope.*

Blo'wer. *n. ſ.* [from *blow.*] A melter of tin.

Add his care and coſt in buying wood, and in fetching the ſame to the blowing-houſe, together with the *blowers*, two or three months extreme and encreaſing labour. *Carew's Survey.*

Blown. The *participle paſſive* of *blow*.

All the ſparks of virtue, which nature had kindled in them, were ſo *blown* to give forth their uttermoſt heat, that juſtly it may be affirmed, they inflamed the affections of all that knew them. *Sidney, b.* ii.

The trumpets ſleep, while cheerful horns are *blown*,
And arms employ'd on birds and beaſts alone. *Pope.*

Blo'wpoint. *n. ſ.* A child's play.

Shortly boys ſhall not play
At ſpancounter or *blowpoint*, but ſhall pay
Toll to ſome courtier. *Donne.*

Blowth. *n. ſ.* [from *blow*.] Bloom, or bloſſom.

Ambition and covetouſneſs being but green, and newly grown up, the ſeeds and effects were as yet but potential, and in the *blowth* and bud. *Raleigh's Hiſtory of the World.*

Blowze. *n. ſ.* A ruddy fat-faced wench.

Blo'wzy. *adj.* [from *blowze.*] Sun burnt; high coloured.

BLU'BBER. *n. ſ.* [See Blob.] The part of a whale that contains the oil.

To Blu'bber. *v. n.* [from the noun.] To weep in ſuch a manner as to ſwell the cheeks.

Even ſo lies ſhe,
*Blubb'ring* and weeping, weeping and *blubb'ring*.
*Shakeſp. Romeo and Juliet.*

A thief came to a boy that was *blubbering* by the ſide of a well, and aſked what he cried for. *L'Eſtrange.*

Soon as Glumdalclitch miſs'd her pleaſing care,
She wept, ſhe *blubber'd*, and ſhe tore her hair. *Swift.*

To Blu'bber. *v. a.* To ſwell the cheeks with weeping.

Fair ſtreams repreſent unto me my *blubbered* face; let tears procure your ſtay. *Sidney.*

The wild wood gods arrived in the place,
There find the virgin doleful, deſolate,
With ruffled raiment, and fair *blubber'd* face,
As her outrageous foe had left her late. *Fairy Queen, b.* i.

Tir'd with the ſearch, not finding what ſhe ſeeks,
With cruel blows ſhe pounds her *blubber'd* cheeks. *Dryden.*

Blu'bbered. *particip. adj.* [from *to blubber.*] Swelled; big; applied commonly to the lip.

Thou ſing with him, thou booby! never pipe
Was ſo profan'd, to touch that *blubber'd* lip. *Dryden.*

Blu'dgeon. *n. ſ.* A ſhort ſtick, with one end loaded, uſed as an offenſive weapon.

BLUE. *adj.* [blæp, Sax. *bleu*, Fr.] One of the ſeven original colours.

There's gold, and here,
My *blueſt* veins to kiſs; a hand that kings
Have lipt. *Shakeſp. Antony and Cleopatra.*

Where fires thou find'ſt unrak'd, and hearths unſwept,
There pinch the maids as *blue* as bilberry.
*Shakeſp. Merry Wives of Windſor.*

O coward conſcience! how doſt thou afflict me?
The lights burn *blue*—Is it not dead midnight?
Cold fearful drops ſtand on my trembling fleſh.
*Shakeſp. Richard* III.

Why does one climate, and one ſoil endue
The bluſhing poppy with a crimſon hue;
Yet leave the lily pale, and tinge the violet *blue?* *Prior.*

There was ſcarce any other colour ſenſible, beſides red and *blue*; only the *blues*, and principally the ſecond *blue*, inclined a little to green. *Newton's Opticks.*

Bluebo'ttle. *n. ſ.* [from *blue* and *bottle.*]

1. A flower of the bell ſhape; a ſpecies of *bottleflower*; which ſee.

If you put *bluebottles*, or other blue flowers, into an ant-hill, they will be ſtained with red; becauſe the ants thruſt their ſtings, and inſtil into them their ſtinging liquour. *Ray.*

2. A fly with a large blue belly.

Say, ſire of inſects, mighty Sol,
A fly upon the chariot-pole
Cries out, what *bluebottle* alive
Did ever with ſuch fury drive? *Prior.*

Blue-eyed. *adj.* [from *blue* and *eye.*] Having blue eyes.

Riſe then, fair *blue-ey'd* maid, riſe and diſcover
Thy ſilver brow, and meet thy golden lover. *Craſhaw.*

Nor to the temple was ſhe gone, to move,
With prayers, the *blue-ey'd* progeny of Jove. *Dryden.*

Blueha'ired. *adj.* [from *blue* and *hair.*] Having blue hair.

This place,
The greateſt and the beſt of all the main,
He quarters to his *bluehair'd* deities. *Milton's Par. Regain.*

Blu'ely. *adv.* [from *blue.*] With a blue colour.

This 'ſquire he drop'd his pen full ſoon,
While as the light burnt *bluely*. *Swift.*

Blu'eness. *n. ſ.* [from *blue.*] The quality of being blue.

In a moment our liquour may be deprived of its *blueneſs*, and reſtored to it again, by the affuſion of a few drops of liquours. *Boyle on Colours.*

Bluff. *adj.* Big; ſurly; bluſtering.

Like thoſe whom ſtature did to crowns prefer,
Black-brow'd and *bluff*, like Homer's Jupiter. *Dryden.*

Blu'ish. *adj.* [from *blue.*] Blue in a ſmall degree.

Side ſleeves and ſkirts, round underborne, with a *bluiſh* tinſel. *Shakeſp. Much ado about Nothing.*

At laſt, as far as I could caſt my eyes
Upon the ſea, ſomewhat, methought, did riſe
Like *bluiſh* miſts. *Dryden's Indian Emperour.*

Here, in full light, the ruſſet plains extend,
There wrapt in clouds the *bluiſh* hills aſcend. *Pope.*

Blu'ishness. *n. ſ.* [from *blue.*] A ſmall degree of blue colour.

I could make, with crude copper, a ſolution without the *bluiſhneſs*, that is wont to accompany its vulgar ſolutions. *Boyle.*

To BLU'NDER. *v. n.* [*blunderen*, Dutch; perhaps from *blind.*]

1. To miſtake groſsly; to err very widely; to miſtake ſtupidly. It is a word implying contempt.

It is one thing to forget matter of fact, and another to *blunder* upon the reaſon of it. *L'Eſtrange.*

The grandees and giants in knowledge, who laughed at all beſides themſelves, as barbarous and inſignificant, yet *blundered*, and ſtumbled, about their grand and principal concern. *South.*

2. To flounder; to ſtumble.

He who now to ſenſe, now nonſenſe leaning,
Means not, but *blunders* round about a meaning. *Pope.*

To Blunder. *v. a.* To mix fooliſhly or blindly.

He ſeems to underſtand no difference between titles of reſpect and acts of worſhip; between expreſſions of eſteem and devotion; between religious and civil worſhip: for he *blunders* and confounds all theſe together; and whatever proves one, he thinks, proves all the reſt. *Stillingfleet.*

Blu'nder. *n. ſ.* [from the verb.] A groſs or ſhameful miſtake.

It was the advice of Schomberg to an hiſtorian, that he ſhould avoid being particular in the drawing up of an army, and other circumſtances in the day of battle; for that he had obſerved notorious *blunders* and abſurdities committed by writers not converſant in the art of war. *Addiſon. Freeholder.*

It is our own ignorance that makes us charge thoſe works of the Almighty, as defects or *blunders*, as ill-contrived or ill-made. *Derham's Phyſico-Theology.*

Blu'nderbuss. *n. ſ.* [from *blunder.*] A gun that is charged with many bullets, ſo that, without any exact aim, there is a chance of hitting the mark.

There are *blunderbuſſes* in every loop-hole, that go off of their own accord, at the ſqueaking of a fiddle. *Dryden.*

Blu'nderer. *n. ſ.* [from *blunder.*] A man apt to commit blunders; a blockhead.

Another ſort of judges will decide in favour of an authour, or will pronounce him a mere *blunderer*, according to the company they have kept. *Watts's Improvement of the Mind.*

Blu'nderhead. *n. ſ.* [from *blunder* and *head.*] A ſtupid fellow.

At the rate of this thick-ſkulled *blunderhead*, every plowjobber ſhall take upon him to read upon divinity. *L'Eſtrange.*

BLUNT. *adj.* [etymology uncertain.]

1. Dull on the edge or point; not ſharp.

If the iron be *blunt*, and he do not whet the edge, then muſt he put to more ſtrength. *Eccleſ.* x. 10.

Thanks to that beauty, which can give an edge to the *blunteſt* ſwords. *Sidney, b.* i.

2. Dull in underſtanding; not quick.

Valentine being gone, I'll quickly croſs,
By ſome ſly trick, *blunt* Thurio's dull proceeding.
*Shakeſp. Two Gentlemen of Verona.*

Whitehead, a grave divine, was of a *blunt* ſtoical nature; one day the queen happened to ſay, I like thee the better, becauſe thou liveſt unmarried. He anſwered; Madam, I like you the worſe. *Bacon's Apophthegms.*

3. Rough; not delicate; not civil.

The mayor of the town came to ſeize them in a *blunt* manner, alleging a warrant to ſtop them. *Wotton.*

'Tis not enough your counſel ſtill be true;
*Blunt* truths more miſchief than nice falſehoods do. *Pope.*

4. Abrupt; not elegant.

To uſe too many circumſtances, ere one come to the matter, is weariſome; to uſe none at all, is *blunt*. *Bacon.*

5. Hard to penetrate. This uſe is improper.

I find my heart hardened and *blunt* to new impreſſions; it will ſcarce receive or retain affections of yeſterday. *Pope, Lett.* lxxxiii. *to Swift.*

To Blunt. *v. a.* [from the noun.]

1. To dull the edge or point.

So ſicken waining moons too near the ſun,
And *blunt* their creſcents on the edge of day. *Dryden.*

Earthly limbs, and groſs allay,
*Blunt* not the beams of heav'n, and edge of day. *Dryden.*

He had ſuch things to urge againſt our marriage,
As, now declar'd, would *blunt* my ſword in battle,
And daſtardize my courage. *Dryden's Don Sebaſtian.*

2. To repreſs, or weaken any appetite, deſire, or power of the mind.

*Blunt* not his love;
Nor looſe the good advantage of his grace,
By ſeeming cold. *Shakeſp. Henry* IV. *p.* 2.

Blu'ntly. *adv.* [from *blunt.*]

1. In a blunt manner; without ſharpneſs.

2. Coarſely; plainly; roughly.

I can keep honeſt counſels, marr a curious tale in telling it, and deliver a plain meſſage *bluntly*. *Shakeſp. King Lear.*

A man of honeſt blood,
Who to his wife, before the time aſſign'd
For childbirth came, thus *bluntly* ſpoke his mind. *Dryden.*

Blu'ntness. *n. ſ.* [from *blunt.*]

1. Want of edge or point; dulneſs; obtuſeneſs; want of ſharpneſs.

The crafty boy, that had full oft eſſay'd
To pierce my ſtubborn and reſiſting breaſt,
But ſtill the *bluntneſs* of his darts betray'd. *Suckling.*

2. Coarſeneſs; roughneſs of manners; rude ſincerity.

His ſilence grew wit, his *bluntneſs* integrity, his beaſtly ignorance, virtuous ſimplicity. *Sidney, b.* i.

Manage diſputes with civility; whence ſome readers will be aſſiſted to diſcern a difference betwixt *bluntneſs* of ſpeech and ſtrength of reaſon. *Boyle.*

Falſe friends, his deadlieſt foes, could find no way,
But ſhows of honeſt *bluntneſs* to betray. *Dryd. H. and Pan.*

Blu'ntwitted. *adj.* [from *blunt* and *wit.*] Dull; ſtupid.

*Bluntwitted* lord, ignoble in demeanour. *Shakeſp. H.* VI.

BLUR. *n. ſ.* [*borra*, Span. a blot. *Skinn.*] A blot; a ſtain; a ſpot.

Man, once fallen, was nothing but a great *blur*; a total univerſal pollution. *South.*

To Blur. *v. a.* [from the noun.]

1. To blot; to efface; to obſcure.

Such an act,
That *blurs* the grace and bluſh of modeſty,
Calls virtue hypocrite. *Shakeſp. King Lear.*

Long is it ſince I ſaw him;
But time hath nothing *blurr'd* thoſe lines of favour,
Which then he wore. *Shakeſp. Cymbeline.*

Concerning innate principles, I deſire theſe men to ſay, whether they can, or cannot, by education and cuſtom, be *blurred* and blotted out. *Locke.*

2. To blot; to ſtain.

Sarcaſms may eclipſe thine own,
But cannot *blur* my loſt renown. *Hudibras, p.* i. *cant.* iii.

To Blurt. *v. a.* [without etymology.] To ſpeak inadvertently; to let fly without thinking.

Others caſt out bloody and deadly ſpeeches at random, and cannot hold, but *blurt* out thoſe words, which afterwards they are forced to eat. *Hakewell on Providence.*

They had ſome belief of a Deity, which they, upon ſurprizal, thus *blurt* out. *Government of the Tongue,*

To BLUSH. *v. n.* [*bloſen*, Dutch.]

1. To betray ſhame or confuſion, by a red colour in the cheek.

I have mark'd
A thouſand *bluſhing* apparitions
To ſtart into her face; a thouſand innocent ſhames,
In angel whiteneſs, bear away theſe bluſhes.
*Shakeſp. Much ado about Nothing.*

Pale and bloodleſs,
Being all deſcended to the lab'ring heart,
Which with the heart there cools, and ne'er returneth
To *bluſh* and beautify the cheek again. *Shakeſp. Henry* VI.

I will go waſh:
And when my face is fair, you ſhall perceive
Whether I *bluſh*, or no. *Shakeſp. Cymbeline.*

All theſe things are graceful in a friend's mouth, which are *bluſhing* in a man's own. *Bacon, Eſſay* 28.

Shame cauſeth *bluſhing*; *bluſhing* is the reſort of the blood to the face; although *bluſhing* will be ſeen in the whole breaſt, yet that is but in paſſage to the face. *Bacon's Nat. Hiſtory.*

*Bluſh* then, but *bluſh* for your deſtructive ſilence,
That tears your ſoul. *Smith's Phædr. and Hippolitus.*

2. To carry a red colour, or any ſoft and bright colour.

To day he puts forth
The tender leaves of hope; tomorrow bloſſoms,
And bears his *bluſhing* honours thick upon him. *Sh. H.* VI.

Along thoſe *bluſhing* borders, bright with dew. *Thomſon.*

3. It has *at* before the cauſe of ſhame.

He whin'd, and roar'd away your victory,
That pages *bluſh'd at* him; and men of heart
Look'd wond'ring at each other. *Shakeſp. Coriolanus.*

You have not yet loſt all your natural modeſty, but *bluſh at* your vices. *Calamy's Sermons.*

Blush. *n. ſ.* [from the verb.]

1. The colour in the cheeks, raiſed by ſhame or confuſion.

The virgin's wiſh, without her fears, impart,
Excuſe the *bluſh*, and pour out all the heart. *Pope.*

2. A red or purple colour.

But here the roſes *bluſh* ſo rare,
Here the mornings ſmile ſo fair,
As if neither cloud, nor wind,
But would be courteous, would be kind. *Craſhaw.*

3. Sudden

Brutal, roughly insolent
They say the world is warre than it wont
All for her Shepherds is beastly & bloont
Others saine but how truly I note
All for they holden shame of their cote
Spens. past.

To blush according to Thomson
To exhibit, shew.
Her lips blush deeper sweets
Spring 690

IL facing 3G2[v]

4 a cast or tinge of Colour ~~particularly red~~

A loose earth of a pale flesh colour, that is white with a blush of red

Wood^d fofs.

4 To accost: to address

Him the prince with gentle court did board

Sir knight mought I of you this courtsy read

To weet why on your shield so goodly scord

Bear ye the picture of that ladys head

F. Q. 2. 9. 2.

3 v. a with of

Do not smile at me, that I boast her of

For thou shalt find she will outstrip all praise

Shak.

3. Sudden appearance; a ſignification that ſeems barbarous, yet uſed by good writers.

All purely identical propoſitions, obviouſly and at firſt *bluſh*, appear to contain no certain inſtruction in them. *Locke.*

BLU'SHY. *adj.* [from *bluſh*.] Having the colour of a bluſh.

Bloſſoms of trees, that are white, are commonly inodorate; thoſe of apples, crabs, and peaches, are *bluſhy*, and ſmell ſweet. *Bacon's Natural Hiſt.* Nº 507.

Stratonica entering, moved a *bluſhy* colour in his face; but, deſerting him, he relapſed into the ſame paleneſs and languour. *Harvey on Conſumptions.*

To BLU'STER. *v. n.* [ſuppoſed from *blaſt*.]

1. To roar as a ſtorm; to be violent and loud.

Earth his uncouth mother was,
And *bluſt'ring* Æolus his boaſted ſire. *Spenſer.*

So now he ſtorms with many a ſturdy ſtoure;
So now his *bluſt'ring* blaſt each coaſt doth ſcour. *Spenſer.*

2. To bully; to puff; to ſwagger; to be tumultuous.

My heart's too big to bear this, ſays a *bluſtering* fellow; I'll deſtroy myſelf. Sir, ſays the gentleman, here's a dagger at your ſervice; ſo the humour went off. *L'Eſtrange.*

Either he muſt ſink to a downright confeſſion, or elſe he muſt huff and *bluſter*, till perhaps he raiſe a counter-ſtorm. *Government of the Tongue.*

Virgil had the majeſty of a lawful prince, and Statius only the *bluſtering* of a tyrant. *Dryden's Spaniſh Friar, Dedication.*

There let him reign the jailor of the wind;
With hoarſe commands his breathing ſubjects call,
And boaſt and *bluſter* in his empty hall. *Dryden's Æneid.*

BLU'STER. *n. ſ.* [from the verb.]

1. Roar; noiſe; tumult.

The ſkies look grimly,
And threaten preſent *bluſters*. *Shakeſp. Twelfth Night.*

To the winds they ſet
Their corners; when with *bluſter* to confound
Sea, air, and ſhore. *Milton's Paradiſe Loſt, b. x. l.* 665.

So, by the brazen trumpet's *bluſter*,
Troops of all tongues and nations muſter. *Swift.*

2. Boaſt; boiſterouſneſs; turbulence; fury.

Spare thy Athenian cradle, and thoſe kin,
Which in the *bluſter* of thy wrath muſt fall
With thoſe that have offended. *Shakeſp. Timon.*

A coward makes a great deal more *bluſter* than a man of honour. *L'Eſtrange.*

BLU'STERER. *n. ſ.* [from *bluſter*.] A ſwaggerer; a bully; a tumultuous noiſy fellow.

BLU'STROUS. *adj.* [from *bluſter*.] Tumultuous; noiſy.

The ancient heroes were illuſtrious
For being benign, and not *bluſtrous*. *Hudibras, p.* i. *c.* iii.

BMI. *n. ſ.* A note in muſick.

Gamut I am, the ground of all accord,
*Bmi*, Bianca, take him for thy lord. *Shakeſp. Tam. Shrew.*

BO. *interj.* A word of terrour; from *Bo*, an old northern captain, of ſuch fame, that his name was uſed to terrify the enemy. *Temple.*

BOAR. *n. ſ.* [ban, Saxon; *beer*, Dutch.] The male ſwine.

To fly the *boar*, before the *boar* purſues,
Were to incenſe the *boar* to follow us. *Shakeſp. Rich.* III.

She ſped the *boar* away;
His eyeballs glare with fire, ſuffus'd with blood;
His neck ſhoots up a thickeſt thorny wood;
His briſtled back a trench impal'd appears. *Dryden's Fables.*

BO'AR-SPEAR. *n. ſ.* [from *boar* and *ſpear*.] A ſpear uſed in hunting the boar.

And in her hand a ſharp *boar-ſpear* ſhe held,
And at her back a bow and quiver gay,
Stuff'd with ſteel-headed darts. *Fairy Queen, b.* i. *c.* iii.

Echion threw the firſt, but miſs'd his mark,
And ſtruck his *boar-ſpear* on a maple bark. *Dryden's Ovid.*

BOARD. *n. ſ.* [*baurd*, Goth. bꞃæd, Saxon.]

1. A piece of wood of more length and breadth than thickneſs.

With the ſaw they have ſundred trees in *boards* and planks. *Raleigh's Eſſays.*

Every houſe has a *board* over the door, whereon is written the number, ſex, and quality of the perſons living in it. *Temple.*

Go now, go truſt the wind's uncertain breath,
Remov'd four fingers from approaching death;
Or ſeven at moſt, when thickeſt is the *board*. *Dryden's Juv.*

2. A table. [from *burdd*, Welch.]

Soon after which, three hundred lords he ſlew,
Of Britiſh blood, all ſitting at his *board*. *Fairy Queen, b.* ii.

In bed he ſlept not, for my urging it;
At *board* he fed not, for my urging it. *Shakeſp. Com. of Err.*

I'll follow thee in fun'ral flames; when dead,
My ghoſt ſhall thee attend at *board* and bed. *Sir J. Denham.*

Cleopatra made Antony a ſupper, which was ſumptuous and royal; howbeit there was no extraordinary ſervice upon the *board*. *Hakewell on Providence.*

May ev'ry god his friendly aid afford;
Pan guard thy flock, and Ceres bleſs thy *board*. *Prior.*

3. Entertainment; food.

4. A table at which a council or court is held.



Both better acquainted with affairs, than any other who ſat then at that *board*. *Clarendon.*

5. An aſſembly ſeated at a table; a court of juriſdiction.

I wiſh the king would be pleaſed ſometimes to be preſent at that *board*; it adds a majeſty to it. *Bacon's Advice to Villiers.*

6. The deck or floor of a ſhip; *on board* ſignifies in a ſhip.

Now *board* to *board* the rival veſſels row,
The billows lave the ſkies, and ocean groans below. *Dryd.*

Our captain thought his ſhip in ſo great danger, that he confeſſed himſelf to a capuchin, who was *on board*. *Addiſon.*

He ordered his men to arm long poles with ſharp hooks, wherewith they took hold of the tackling, which held the mainyard to the maſt of their enemy's ſhip; then, rowing their own ſhip, they cut the tackling, and brought the mainyard by the *board*. *Arbuthnot on Coins.*

To BOARD. *v. a.* [from the noun.]

1. To enter a ſhip by force; the ſame as to ſtorm, uſed of a city.

I *boarded* the king's ſhip: now on the beak,
Now in the waſte, the deck, in every cabin,
I flam'd amazement. *Shakeſp. Tempeſt.*

Yet not inclin'd the Engliſh ſhip to *board*,
More on his guns relies than on his ſword,
From whence a fatal volley we receiv'd;
It miſs'd the duke; but his great heart it griev'd. *Waller.*

Arm, arm, ſhe cry'd, and let our Tyrians *board*
With our's his fleet, and carry fire and ſword. *Denham.*

2. To attack, or make the firſt attempt upon a man; *aborder quelqu'un*, Fr.

Whom thus at gaze, the Palmer 'gan to *board*
With goodly reaſon, and thus fair beſpake. *Fairy Q. b.* ii.

Away, I do beſeech you, both away;
I'll *board* him preſently. *Shakeſp. Hamlet.*

Sure unleſs he knew ſome ſtrain in me, that I knew not myſelf, he would never have *boarded* me in this fury. *Shakeſpeare.*

They learn what aſſociates and correſpondents they had, and how far every one is engaged, and what new ones they meant afterwards to try or *board*. *Bacon's Henry* VII.

3. To lay or pave with boards.

Having thus *boarded* the whole room, the edges of ſome boards lie higher than the next board; therefore they peruſe the whole floor; and, where they find any irregularities, plane them off. *Moxon's Mechanical Exerciſes.*

To BOARD. *v. n.* To live in a houſe, where a certain rate is paid for eating.

That we might not part,
As we at firſt did *board* with thee,
Now thou wouldſt taſte our miſery. *Herbert.*

We are ſeveral of us, gentlemen and ladies, who *board* in the ſame houſe; and, after dinner, one of our company ſtands up, and reads your paper to us all. *Spectator*, Nº 961.

To BOARD. *v. a.* To place as a boarder in another's houſe.

BO'ARD-WAGES. *n. ſ.* [from *board* and *wages*.] Wages allowed to ſervants to keep themſelves in victuals.

What more than madneſs reigns,
When one ſhort ſitting many hundreds drains,
And not enough is left him, to ſupply
*Board-wages*, or a footman's livery? *Dryden's Juv. ſat.* i.

BO'ARDER. *n. ſ.* [from *board*.] A tabler; one that eats with another at a ſettled rate.

BO'ARDING-SCHOOL. *n. ſ.* [from *board* and *ſchool*.] A ſchool where the ſcholars live with the teacher.

A blockhead, with melodious voice,
In *boarding-ſchools* can have his choice. *Swift.*

BO'ARISH. *adj.* [from *boar*.] Swiniſh; brutal; cruel.

I would not ſee thy cruel nails
Pluck out his poor old eyes; nor thy fierce ſiſter,
In his anointed fleſh ſtick *boariſh* phangs. *Shakeſp. K. Lear.*

To BOAST. *v. n.* [*boſt*, Welch.]

1. To brag; to diſplay one's own worth, or actions, in great words; to talk oſtentatiouſly; with *of*.

For I know the forwardneſs of your mind, for which I *boaſt of* you to them of Macedonia. *2 Cor.* ix. 2.

2. Sometimes it is uſed with *in*.

Some ſurgeons I have met, carrying bones about in their pockets, *boaſting in* that which was their ſhame. *Wiſeman.*

3. To exalt one's ſelf.

Thus with your mouth you have *boaſted* againſt me, and multiplied your words againſt me. *Ezek.* xxxv. 13.

To BOAST. *v. a.*

1. To brag of; to diſplay with oſtentatious language.

For if I have *boaſted* any thing to him of you, I am not aſhamed. *2 Cor.* vii. 14.

If they vouchſafed to give god the praiſe of his goodneſs; yet they did it only, in order to *boaſt* the intereſt they had in him. *Atterbury.*

2. To magnify; to exalt.

They that truſt in their wealth, and *boaſt* themſelves in the multitude of their riches. *Pſalm* xlix. 6.

Confounded be all them that ſerve graven images, that *boaſt* themſelves *of* idols. *Pſalm* xcvii. 7.

BOAST. *n. ſ.* [from the verb.]

1. A cauſe of boaſting; an occaſion of pride; the thing boaſted.

Not Tyro, nor Mycene, match her name,
Nor great Alcmena, the proud *boasts* of fame. *Pope's Odyss.*

2. An expression of ostentation; a proud speech.

Thou that makest thy *boast* of the law, through breaking the law dishonourest thou God? *Rom.* ii. 23.

The world is more apt to find fault than to commend; the *boast* will probably be censured, when the great action that occasioned it, is forgotten. *Spectator*, Nº 255.

Bo'aster. *n. s.* [from *boast.*] A bragger; a man that vaunts any thing ostentatiously.

Complaints the more candid and judicious of the chymists themselves are wont to make of those *boasters*, that confidently pretend, that they have extracted the salt or sulphur of quicksilver, when they have disguised it by additaments, wherewith it resembles the concretes. *Boyle.*

No more delays, vain *boaster!* but begin;
I prophesy beforehand I shall win:
I'll teach you how to brag another time. *Dryden's Virgil.*

He the proud *boasters* sent, with stern assault,
Down to the realms of night. *Philips.*

Bo'astful. *adj.* [from *boast* and *full.*] Ostentatious; inclined to brag.

*Boastful*, and rough, your first son is a 'squire;
The next a tradesman, meek, and much a liar. *Pope.*

Bo'astingly. *adv.* [from *boasting.*] Ostentatiously.

We look on it as a pitch of impiety, *boastingly* to avow our sins; and it deserves to be considered, whether this kind of confessing them, have not some affinity with it. *Decay of Piety.*

BOAT. *n. s.* [bat, Saxon.]

1. A vessel to pass the water in. It is usually distinguished from other vessels, by being smaller and uncovered, and commonly moved by rowing.

I do not think that any one nation, the Syrian excepted, to whom the knowledge of the ark came, did find out at once the device of either ship or *boat*, in which they durst venture themselves upon the seas. *Raleigh's Essays.*

An effeminate scoundrel multitude!
Whose utmost daring is to cross the Nile,
In painted *boats*, to fright the crocodile. *Tate. Juv. sat.* xv.

2. A ship of a small size; as, a *passage boat, pacquet boat, advice boat, fly boat.*

Boa'tion. *n. s.* [from *boare*, Lat.] Roar; noise; loud sound.

In Messina insurrection, the guns were heard from thence as far as Augusta and Syracuse, about an hundred Italian miles. These distances being, in a short time, in loud *boations*. *Derham's Physico-Theology.*

Bo'atman. } *n. s.* [from *boat* and *man.*] He that manages a
Bo'atsman. } boat.

*Boatsmen* through the crystal water show,
To wond'ring passengers, the walls below. *Dryden.*

That booby Phaon only was unkind,
An ill-bred *boatman*, rough as waves and wind. *Prior.*

Bo'atswain. *n. s.* [from *boat* and *swain.*] An officer on board a ship, who has charge of all her rigging, ropes, cables, anchors, sails, flags, colours, pendants, &c. He also takes care of the long-boat and its furniture, and steers her either by himself or his mate. He calls out the several gangs and companies to the execution of their watches, works, and spells; and he is also a kind of provost marshal, seizes, and punishes all offenders, that are sentenced by the captain, or court martial of the whole fleet. *Harris.*

Sometimes the meanest *boatswain* may help to preserve the ship from sinking. *Howel's Pre-eminence of Parliament.*

To BOB. *v. a.* [of uncertain etymology; *Skinner* deduces it from *bobo*, foolish, Span.]

1. To cut. *Junius.*

2. To beat; to drub; to bang.

Those bastard Britons, whom our fathers
Have in their own land beaten, *bobb'd*, and thump'd.
*Shakesp. Richard III.*

3. To cheat; to gain by fraud.

I have *bobbed* his brain more than he has beat my bones.
*Shakesp. Troilus and Cressida.*

Live, Roderigo!
He calls me to a restitution large,
Of gold and jewels, that I *bobb'd* from him,
As gifts to Desdemona. *Shakesp. Othello.*

Here we have been worrying one another, who should have the booty, till this cursed fox has *bobbed* us both on't. *L'Estr.*

To Bob. *v. n.* To play backward and forward; to play loosely against any thing.

And sometimes lurk I in a gossip's bowl,
In very likeness of a roasted crab;
And when she drinks, against her lips I *bob*,
And on her wither'd dewlap pour the ale. *Midsum. N. Dr.*

They comb, and then they order ev'ry hair;
A birthday jewel *bobbing* at their ear. *Dryd. Persius, sat.* i.

You may tell her,
I'm rich in jewels, rings, and *bobbing* pearls,
Pluck'd from Moors ears. *Dryden's Spanish Friar.*

Bob. *n. s.* [from the verb neuter.]

1. Something that hangs so as to play loosely; generally an ornament at the ear; a pendant; an ear-ring.

The gaudy gossip, when she's set agog,
In jewels drest, and at each ear a *bob*. *Dryd. Juv. sat.* vi.

2. The word repeated at the end of a stanza.

To bed, to bed, will be the *bob* of the song. *L'Estrange.*

3. A blow.

I am sharply taunted, yea, sometimes with pinches, nips, and *bobs*. *Ascham's Schoolmaster.*

Bo'bbin. *n. s.* [*bobine*, Fr. from *bombyx*, Lat.] A small pin of wood, with a notch, to wind the thread about, when women weave lace.

The things you follow, and make songs on now, should be sent to knit, or sit down to *bobbins*, or bone-lace. *Tatler.*

Bo'bbinwork. *n. s.* [from *bobbin* and *work.*] Work woven with bobbins.

Not netted nor woven with warp and woof, but after the manner of *bobbinwork*. *Grew's Musæum.*

Bo'bcherry. *n. s.* [from *bob* and *cherry.*] A play among children, in which the cherry is hung so as to bob against the mouth.

*Bobcherry* teaches at once two noble virtues, patience and constancy; the first, in adhering to the pursuit of one end; the latter, in bearing a disappointment. *Arb. and Pop. M. Scr.*

Bo'btail. [from *bob*, in the sense of *cut.*] Cut tail; short tail.

Avaunt, you curs!
Be thy mouth or black or white,
Or *bobtail* like, or trundle tail,
Tom will make him weep and wail. *Shakesp. King Lear.*

Bo'btailed. *adj.* [from *bobtail.*] Having a tail cut, or short.

There was a *bobtailed* cur cried in a gazette, and one that found him, brought him home to his master. *L'Estrange.*

B'obwig. *n. s.* [from *bob* and *wig.*] A short wig.

A young fellow riding towards us full gallop, with a *bobwig* and a black silken bag tied to it, stopt short at the coach, to ask us how far the judges were behind. *Spectator*, Nº 129.

Bo'casine. *n. s.* A sort of linen cloth; a fine buckram. *Dict.*

Bo'ckelet. } *n. s.* A kind of long-winged hawk. *Dict.*
Bo'ckeret. }

To BODE. *v. a.* [bodian, Sax.] To portend; to be the omen of. It is used in a sense of either good or bad.

This *bodes* some strange eruption to our state. *Hamlet.*

By this design, you have opposed their false policy, with true and great wisdom; what they *boded* would be a mischief to us, you are providing, shall be one of our principal strengths. *Sprat's Sermons.*

It happen'd once, a *boding* prodigy!
A swarm of bees that cut the liquid sky,
Upon the topmost branch in clouds alight. *Dryden's Æneid.*

If firy red his glowing globe descends,
High winds and furious tempests he portends:
But if his cheeks are swoln with livid blue,
He *bodes* wet weather by his watry hue. *Dryden's Georg.*

To Bode. *v. n.* To be an omen; to foreshew.

Sir, give me leave to say, whatever now
The omen prove, it *boded* well to you. *Dryden's Aurengz.*

Bo'dement. *n. s.* [from *bode.*] Portent; omen; prognostick.

This foolish, dreaming, superstitious girl
Makes all these *bodements*. *Shakesp. Troilus and Cressida.*

Macbeth shall never vanquisht be, until
Great Birnam wood to Dunsinane's high hill
Shall come against him.——
——That will never be:
Sweet *bodements*, good. *Shakesp. Macbeth.*

To Bodge. *v. n.* [a word in *Shakespeare*, which is perhaps corrupted from *boggle.*] To boggle; to stop; to fail.

With this we charg'd again; but out! alas,
We *bodg'd* again; as I have seen a swan,
With bootless labour, swim against the tide. *Shakesp. H.* VI.

Bo'dice. *n. s.* [from *bodies.*] Stays; a waistcoat quilted with whalebone, worn by women.

Her *bodice* halfway she unlac'd,
About his arms she slily cast
The silken band, and held him fast. *Prior.*

This consideration should keep ignorant nurses and *bodice* makers from meddling. *Locke on Education*, § 11.

Bo'diless. *adj.* [from *body.*] Incorporeal; without a body.

Which *bodiless* and immaterial are,
And can be only lodg'd within our minds. *Davies.*

This is the very coinage of your brain,
This *bodiless* creation ecstasy
Is very cunning in. *Shakesp. Hamlet.*

These are but shadows,
Phantoms *bodiless* and vain,
Empty visions of the brain. *Swift.*

Bo'dily. *adj.* [from *body.*]

1. Corporeal; containing body.

What resemblance could wood or stone bear to a spirit void of all sensible qualities, and *bodily* dimensions? *South.*

2. Relating to the body, not the mind.

Of such as resorted to our Saviour Christ, being present on earth, there came not any unto him with better success, for the benefit of their souls everlasting happiness, than they whose *bodily* necessities gave occasion of seeking relief. *Hooker, b.* v.

Virtue

Impervious with a teachers Air
Boastful he claims a right to wisdoms Chair
Blackm.

O earth bear witness
And crown what I profess with kind event
If I speak true; if hollowly invert
What best ye boded me to Mischief
Shak. Temp.

+

Bodied Adj. (body) Having a body ~~an outward~~ corporeal form
I wish you would assume some constant figure
wherein I might say I grappled with a bodied
Adversary. Dr. Maine

'Bodle n. s.

It's a small Scotish coin of copper as big as a doit, three of which make a babee or halfpenny It is otherwise called twa pennies [daa pheign Erse] This coin is now wore out to make way for the English Copper, as the Scottish Silver and gold Coins have before done for the Sterling money of England.

Boddle is a weed like the may weed, but bears a large yellow flower:. Tis hardy and will grow again, unless the roots are clean pull'd up. The Seed is also very Spreading
Tuss. Notes

The brake & the cockle be noisome too much
Yet like unto boddle no weed there is Such
Tuss. husb. for May

v. n. To dilute as boiling water
Air in Ovens tho it doth boil & dilate itself and is repercussed, yet it is without Noise Bacon

Virtue atones for *bodily* defects; beauty is nothing worth, without a mind. *L'Eſtrange.*

As clearneſs of the *bodily* eye doth diſpoſe it for a quicker ſight, ſo doth freedom from luſt and paſſion, diſpoſe us for the moſt perfect acts of reaſon. *Tillotſon.*

I would not have children much beaten for their faults, becauſe I would not have them think *bodily* pain the greateſt puniſhment. *Locke on Education,* § 115.

3. Real; actual.

Whatever hath been thought on in this ſtate,
That could be brought to *bodily* act, ere Rome
Had circumvention? *Shakeſp. Coriolanus.*

Bo'DILY. *adv.* Corporeally; united with matter.

It is his human nature, in which the godhead dwells *bodily*, that is advanced to theſe honours, and to this empire. *Watts.*

Bo'DKIN. *n. ſ.* [*boddiken*, or ſmall body, *Skinner.*]

1. An inſtrument with a ſmall blade and ſharp point, uſed to bore holes.

Each of them had *bodkins* in their hands, wherewith continually they pricked him. *Sidney's Arcadia.*

2. An inſtrument to draw a thread or ribbond through a loop.

Or plung'd in lakes of bitter waſhes lie,
Or wedg'd whole ages in a *bodkin*'s eye. *Pope's R. of the L.*

3. An inſtrument to dreſs the hair.

You took conſtant care
The *bodkin*, comb, and eſſence to prepare:
For this your locks in paper-durance bound. *Pope.*

BO'DY. *n. ſ.* [bodiᵹ, Saxon; it originally ſignified the height or ſtature of a man.]

1. The material ſubſtance of an animal, oppoſed to the immaterial ſoul.

All the valiant men aroſe, and ~~went all night, and~~ took the *body* of Saul, and the *bodies* of his ſons, from the wall. 1 *Sam.* xxxi. 12.

Take no thought for your life, what ye ſhall eat, or what ye ſhall drink; nor yet for your *body*, what ye ſhall put on. *Matt.* vi. 25.

By cuſtom, ~~practice,~~ and patience, all difficulties and hardſhips, whether of *body* or of fortune, are made eaſy ~~to us.~~ *L'Eſtrange.*

2. Matter; oppoſed to ſpirit.

3. A perſon; a human being; whence *ſomebody*, and *nobody*.

Surely, a wiſe *body*'s part it were not, to put out his fire, becauſe his fooliſh neighbour, from whom he borrowed wherewith to kindle it, might ſay, were it not for me, thou wouldſt freeze. *Hooker, b.* iv. § 9.

A deflowred maid!
And by an eminent *body*, that enforc'd
The law againſt it! *Shakeſp. Meaſure for Meaſure.*

'Tis a paſſing ſhame,
That I, unworthy *body* as I am,
Should cenſure thus on lovely gentlemen. *Sh. Two G. of Ver.*

No *body* ſeeth me; what need I to fear? the Moſt High will not remember my ſins. *Ecclus,* xxiii. 18.

All civility and reaſon obliged every *body* to ſubmit. *Clarend.*

Good may be drawn out of evil, and a *body*'s life may be ſaved, without having any obligation to his preſerver. *L'Eſtr.*

4. Reality; oppoſed to repreſentation.

A ſhadow of things to come; but the *body* is of Chriſt. *Coloſſ.*

5. A collective maſs; a joint power.

There is in the knowledge both of God and man this certainty, that life and death have divided between them the whole *body* of mankind. *Hooker, b.* v. § 49.

There were ſo many diſaffected perſons of the nobility, that there might a *body* ſtart up for the king. *Clarendon, b.* viii.

When ~~theſe~~ pigmies pretend to form themſelves into a *body*, it is time ~~[illegible]~~ men of figure, to look about us. *Addiſon.* ~~*Guardian,* N° 108.~~

6. The main army; the battle; diſtinct from the wings, van and rear.

The van of the king's army was led by the general and Wilmot; in the *body* was the king and the prince; and the rear conſiſted of one thouſand foot, commanded under colonel Thelwell. *Clarendon, b.* viii.

7. A corporation; a number of men united by ſome common tye.

I ſhall now mention a particular, wherein your whole *body* will be certainly againſt me, and the laity, almoſt to a man, on my ſide. *Swift.*

Nothing was more common, than to hear that reverend *body* charged with what is inconſiſtent, deſpiſed for their poverty, and hated for their riches. *Swift.*

8. The outward condition.

I verily, as abſent in *body*, have judged. 1 *Cor.* v. 3.

9. The main part; the bulk; as, the *body*, or hull, of a ſhip; the *body* of a coach; the *body* of a church; the *body*, or trunk, of a man; the *body*, or trunk, of a tree.

Thence ſent rich merchandizes by boat to Babylon, from whence, by the *body* of Euphrates, as far as it bended weſtward, and, afterward, by a branch thereof. *Raleigh's Hiſtory.*

This city has navigable rivers, that run up into the *body* of Italy, by which they might ſupply many countries with fiſh. *Addiſon's Remarks on Italy.*

10. A ſubſtance.

Even a metalline *body*, and therefore much more a vegetable or animal, may, by fire, be turned into water. *Boyle.*

11. [In geometry.] Any ſolid figure.

12. A pandect; a general collection; as, a *body* of the civil law; a *body* of divinity.

13. Strength; as, wine of a good *body*.

BODY-CLOATHS. *n. ſ.* [from *body* and *cloaths.*] Cloathing for horſes that are dieted.

~~However it be, I am informed,~~ that ſeveral aſſes are kept in *body-cloaths*, and ſweated every morning upon the heath. *Addiſon.* ~~*Spectator,* N° [illegible]~~

To Bo'DY. *v. a.* [from the noun.] To produce in ſome form.

As imagination *bodies* forth
The forms of things unknown, the poet's pen
Turns them to ſhape. *Shakeſp. Midſummer Night's Dream.*

BOG. *n. ſ.* [*bog*, ſoft, Iriſh.] A mariſh; a moraſs; a ground too ſoft to bear the weight of the body.

Through fire and through flame, through ford and whirlpool, o'er *bog* and quagmire. *Shakeſp. King Lear.*

A gulf profound! as that Serbonian *bog*,
Betwixt Damiata and Mount Caſius old. *Par. Loſt, b.* ii.

He walks upon *bogs* and whirlpools; wheresoever he treads, he ſinks. *South.*

Learn from ſo great a wit, a land of *bogs*
With ditches fenc'd, a heaven fat with fogs. *Dryden.*

He is drawn, by a ſort of *ignis fatuus*, into *bogs* and mire, almoſt every day of his life. *Watts's Improvement of the Mind.*

BOG-TROTTER. *n. ſ.* [from *bog* and *trot.*] One that lives in a boggy country.

To BO'GGLE. *v. n.* [from *bogil*, Dutch, a ſpectre; a bugbear; a phantom.]

1. To ſtart; to fly back; to fear to come forward.

You *boggle* ſhrewdly; every feather ſtarts you. *Shakeſp. All's well that ends well.*

We ſtart and *boggle* at every unuſual appearance, and cannot endure the ſight of the bugbear. *Glanville's Scepſis, c.* 16.

Nature, that rude, and in her firſt eſſay,
Stood *boggling* at the roughneſs of the way;
Us'd to the road, unknowing to return,
Goes boldly on, and loves the path when worn. *Dryden.*

2. To heſitate; to be in doubt.

And never *boggle* to reſtore
The members you deliver o'er,
Upon demand. *Hudibras, p.* iii. *c.* i.

The well-ſhaped changeling is a man that has a rational ſoul, ſay ~~you~~. Make the ears a little longer, and more pointed, and the noſe a little flatter than ordinary, and then you begin to *boggle*. *Locke.*

3. To play faſt and looſe; to diſſemble.

When ſummoned to his laſt end, it was no time for him to *boggle* with the world. *Howel's Vocal Foreſt.*

Bo'GGLER. *n. ſ.* [from *boggle.*] A doubter; a timorous man.

You have been a *boggler* ever. *Shakeſp. Ant. and Cleop.*

Bo'GGY. *adj.* [from *bog.*] Marſhy; ſwampy.

Their country was very narrow, low, and *boggy*, and, by great induſtry and expences, defended from the ſea. *Arbuthnot.*

Bo'GHOUSE. *n. ſ.* [from *bog* and *houſe.*] A houſe of office.

BOHE'A. *n. ſ.* [an Indian word.] A ſpecies of tea, of higher colour, and more aſtringent taſte, than green tea.

Coarſe pewter, appearing to conſiſt chiefly of lead, is part of the bales in which *bohea* tea was brought from China. *Woodw.*

~~As ſome frail cup of China's faireſt mold,~~
~~The tumults of the boiling *bohea* braves,~~
~~And holds ſecure the coffee's ſable waves.~~ ~~*Tickell.*~~

She went from op'ra, park, aſſembly, play,
To morning walks, and pray'rs three hours a day;
To part her time 'twixt reading and *bohea*,
To muſe, and ſpill her ſolitary tea. *Pope.*

To BOIL. *v. n.* [*bouiller*, Fr. *bullio*, Lat.]

1. To be agitated by heat; to fluctuate with heat.

He ſaw there *boil* the firy whirlpools. *Chapman's Odyſſey.*

Suppoſe the earth removed, and placed nearer to the ſun, in the orbit of Mercury, there the whole ocean would *boil* with extremity of heat. *Bentley.*

2. To be hot; to be fervent, or effervescent.

That ſtrength with which my *boiling* youth was fraught,
When in the vale of Balaſor I fought. *Dryden's Aurengzebe.*

Well I knew,
What perils youthful ardour would purſue,
That *boiling* blood would carry thee too far. *Dryden's Æn.*

3. To move with an agitation like that of boiling water.

Then headlong ſhoots beneath the daſhing tide,
The trembling fins the *boiling* waves divide. *Gay.*

In the dubious point, where, with the pool,
Is mixt the trembling ſtream, or where it *boils*
Around the ſtone. *Thomſon's Spring.*

4. To be in hot liquour, in order to be made tender by the heat.

Fillet of a fenny ſnake,
In the cauldron *boil* and bake. *Shakeſp. Macbeth.*

5. To cook by boiling.

If you live in a rich family, roaſting and *boiling* are below the

the dignity of your office, and which it becomes you to be ignorant of. *Swift's Directions to the Cook.*

6. *To boil over.* To run over the veſſel with heat.

A few ſoft words and a kiſs, and the good man melts; ſee how nature works and *boils over* in him. *Congreve's Old Batchel.*

This hollow was a vaſt cauldron, filled with melted matter, which, as it *boiled over* in any part, ran down the ſides of the mountain. *Addiſon on Italy.*

To Boil. *v. a.* To heat, by putting into boiling water; to ſeeth.

To try whether ſeeds be old or new, the ſenſe cannot inform; but if you *boil* them in water, the new ſeeds will ſprout ſooner. *Bacon's Natural Hiſtory.*

In eggs *boiled* and roaſted, into which the water entereth not at all, there is ſcarce any difference to be diſcerned. *Bacon.*

Boil. *n. ſ.* See Bile.

Bo'ilary. *n. ſ.* [from *to boil.*] A place at the ſalt-works where the ſalt is boiled.

Bo'iler. *n. ſ.* [from *boil.*]

1. The perſon that boils any thing.

That ~~ſuch~~ alterations of terreſtrial matter are not impoſſible, ſeems evident from that notable practice of the *boilers* of ſaltpetre. *Boyle.*

2. The veſſel in which any thing is boiled.

This coffee-room is much frequented; and there are generally ſeveral pots and *boilers* before the fire. *Woodward.*

BOISTEROUS. *adj.* [*byſter*, furious, ~~Dutch.~~]

1. Violent; loud; roaring; ſtormy.

By a divine inſtinct, men's minds miſtruſt
Enſuing danger; as by proof we ſee
The waters ſwell before a *boiſterous* ſtorm. *Shakeſp. R. III.*

As when loud winds a well-grown oak would rend
Up by the roots, this way and that they bend
His reeling trunk, and with a *boiſt'rous* ſound
Scatter his leaves, and ſtrew them on the ground. *Waller.*

2. Turbulent; tumultuous; furious.

~~Spirit of peace,~~
Wherefore do you ſo ill tranſlate yourſelf
Out of the ſpeech of peace, that bears ſuch grace,
Into the harſh and *boiſt'rous* tongue of war? *Shakeſp. H. IV.*

His ſweetneſs won a more regard
Unto his place, than all the *boiſt'rous* moods
That ignorant greatneſs practiſeth. *Ben. Johnſon's Catiline.*

God, into the hands of their deliverer,
Puts invincible might,
To quell the mighty of the earth, th' oppreſſor,
The brute and *boiſt'rous* force of violent men. *Milton.*

~~Still muſt I beg thee not to name Sempronius~~
Lucia; I like not that loud *boiſterous* man. *Addiſon's Cato.*

3. Unwieldy.

His *boiſterous* club, ſo buried in the ground,
He could not rearen up again ſo light,
But that the knight him at avantage found. *Fairy Q. b.* i.

4. It is uſed by *Woodward* of heat.

When the ſun hath gained a greater ſtrength, the heat becomes too powerful and *boiſterous* for them. *Natural Hiſtory.*

Bo'isterously. *adv.* [from *boiſterous.*] Violently; tumultuouſly.

A ſceptre ſnatch'd, with an unruly hand,
Muſt be as *boiſterouſly* maintain'd, as gain'd. *Sh. King John.*

Thoſe are all remains of the univerſal deluge, when the water of the ocean, being *boiſterouſly* turned out upon the earth, bore along with it all moveable bodies. *Woodward's N. Hiſt.*

Another faculty of the intellect comes *boiſterouſly* in, and wakes me from ſo pleaſing a dream. *Swift's Letters.*

Bo'isterousness. *n. ſ.* [from *boiſterous.*] The ſtate or quality of being boiſterous; tumultuouſneſs; turbulence.

Bo'lary. *adj.* [from *bole.*] Partaking of the nature of bole, or clay.

A weak and inanimate kind of loadſtone, with a few magnetical lines, but chiefly conſiſting of a *bolary* and clammy ſubſtance. *Brown's Vulgar Errours, b.* ii. *c.* 3.

BOLD. *adj.* [balð, Saxon.]

1. Daring; brave; ſtout; courageous; magnanimous; fearleſs; intrepid.

The wicked flee when no man purſueth; but the righteous are *bold* as a lion. *Prov.* xxviii. 1.

I have ſeen the councils of a noble country grow *bold*, or timorous, according to the fits of his good or ill health that managed them. *Temple.*

2. Executed with ſpirit, and without mean caution.

Theſe, nervous, *bold*; thoſe, languid and remiſs. *Raſcom.*

The cathedral church is a very *bold* work, and a maſterpiece in Gothick architecture. *Addiſon on Italy.*

3. Confident; not ſcrupulous; not timorous.

We were *bold* in our God to ſpeak unto you the goſpel of God with much contention. 1 *Theſſ.* ii. 2.

I can be *bold* to ſay, that this age is adorned with ſome men of that judgment, that they could open new and undiſcovered ways to knowledge. *Locke.*

4. Impudent; rude.

In thy proſperity he will be as thyſelf, and will be *bold* over thy ſervants. If thou be brought low, he will be againſt thee. *Ecclus,* vi. 11.

5. Licentious; ſuch as ſhew great liberty of fiction.

Which no *bold* tales of Gods or monſters ſwell,
But human paſſions, ſuch as with us dwell. *Waller.*

6. Standing out to the view; ſtriking to the eye.

Catechreſes and hyperboles are to be uſed judiciouſly, and placed in poetry, as heightenings and ſhadows are in painting, to make the figures *bolder*, and cauſe it to ſtand off to ſight. *Dryden's State of Innocence, Preface.*

7. Open; ſmooth; even; level: a ſailor's term.

Her dominions lie ſcattered, and have *bold* acceſſible coaſts. *Howel's Vocal Foreſt.*

8. *To make bold.* To take freedoms: a phraſe not grammatical, though common. *To be bold* is better; as, *I was bold to ſpeak.*

I have *made bold* to ſend to your wife;
My ſuit is, that ſhe will to Deſdemona
Procure me ſome acceſs. *Shakeſp. Othello.*

*Making* ſo *bold*,
My fears forgetting manners, ~~to unſeal~~
~~Their grand commiſſion.~~ *Shakeſp. Hamlet.*

And were y' as good as George a Green,
I ſhall *make bold* to turn agen. *Hudibras, p.* ii. *c.* ii.

I durſt not *make* thus *bold* with Ovid, leſt ſome future Milbourn ſhould ariſe. *Dryden's Fables, Preface.*

Some men have the fortune to be eſteemed wits, only for *making bold* to ſcoff at theſe things, which the greateſt part of mankind reverence. *Tillotſon.*

To Bo'lden. *v. a.* [from *bold.*] To make bold; to give confidence.

Quick inventers, and fair ready ſpeakers, being *boldened* with their preſent abilities, to ſay more, and perchance better too, at the ſudden, for that preſent, than any other can do, uſe leſs help of diligence and ſtudy. *Aſcham's Schoolmaſter.*

I am much too vent'rous,
In tempting of your patience; but am *bolden'd*
Under your promis'd pardon. *Shakeſp. Henry* VIII.

Bo'ldface. *n. ſ.* [from *bold* and *face.*] Impudence; ſaucineſs; a term of reproach and repreheníion.

How now, *boldface!* cries an old ~~trot~~; ſirrah, we eat our own hens, ~~I'd have you to know,~~ and what you eat, you ſteal. *L'Eſtrange.*

Bo'ldfaced. *adj.* [from *bold* and *face.*] Impudent.

I have ſeen thoſe fillieſt of creatures; and, ſeeing their rare works, I have ſeen enough to confute all the *boldfaced* atheiſts of this age. *Bramhall againſt Hobbes.*

Bo'ldly. *adv.* [from *bold.*]

1. In a bold manner; with courage; with ſpirit.

Thus we may *boldly* ſpeak, being ſtrengthened with the example of ſo reverend a prelate. *Hooker, b.* v. § 19.

I ſpeak to ſubjects, and a ſubject ſpeaks,
Stirr'd up by heav'n thus *boldly* for his king. *Shakeſp. R.* III.

2. It may perhaps be ſometimes uſed in a bad ſenſe, for *impudently.*

Bo'ldness. *n. ſ.* [from *bold.*]

1. Courage; bravery; intrepidity; ſpirit; fortitude; magnanimity; daringneſs.

Her horſe ſhe rid ſo, as might ſhew a fearful *boldneſs*, daring to do that, which ſhe knew not how to do. *Sidney, b.* ii.

2. Exemption from caution, and ſcrupulous nicety.

The *boldneſs* of the figures is to be hidden, ſometimes by the addreſs of the poet, that they may work their effect upon the mind. *Dryden's State of Innocence, Preface.*

3. Freedom; liberty.

Great is my *boldneſs* of ſpeech toward you; great is my glorying in you. 2 *Cor.* vii. 4.

4. Confident truſt in God.

Our fear excludeth not that *boldneſs* which becometh ſaints. *Hooker, b.* v. § 47.

We have *boldneſs* and acceſs with confidence, by the faith of him. *Epheſ.* iii. 12.

Having therefore *boldneſs* to enter into the holieſt by the blood of Jeſus. *Heb.* x. 19.

5. Aſſurance; freedom from ~~baſhfulneſs~~

Wonderful is the caſe of *boldneſs* in civil buſineſs; what firſt? *Boldneſs.* What ſecond, and third? *Boldneſs.* And yet *boldneſs* is a child of ignorance and baſeneſs, far inferiour to other parts. *Bacon's Eſſays,* N° 12.

Sure if the guilt were theirs, they could not charge thee
With ſuch a gallant *boldneſs:* if 'twere thine,
Thou couldſt not hear't with ſuch a ſilent ſcorn. *Denham.*

His diſtance, though it does not inſtruct him to think wiſer than other princes, yet it helps him to ſpeak with more *boldneſs* what he thinks. *Temple.*

*Boldneſs* is the power to ſpeak or do what we intend, before others, without fear or diſorder. *Locke.*

6. Impudence.

That moderation, which uſeth to ſuppreſs *boldneſs*, and to make them conquer that ſuffer. *Hooker, Dedication.*

BOLE. *n. ſ.*

1. The body or trunk of a tree.

All fell upon the high-hair'd oaks, and down their curled brows
Fell buſtling to the earth; and up went all the *boles* and boughs. *Chapman's Iliads.*

^ perhaps borrowed from the north term
Juist le brave not well understood.

~~v. a rolls to~~ a ‡

There is that hand bolden'd to blood & war
That must the sword in wondrous actions weild
Daniel c. w.

b ‡

5 Dryden uses it for rough, tough, unweildy
The leathern outside boistrous as it was
Gave way and bent beneath her strict embrace
Dryd. Boc.

IL facing 3H2v

Resembling a bolt applied to thunder

Was this a face
To stand against the deep dread bolted thunder
In the most terrible & nimble stroke
Of quick cross lightning Shak. L.

Short bolsterd Breeches & those types of travel
clean renouncing
Shak

Forth popp'd the Sprite so thin
And from the keyhole bolted out
All upright as a pien Swift



Pease bolt with thy pease he will have
his houshold to and his hog
Tuss Husb.

Pease bolt is pease in the haum or Straw
Tuss Notes

× Hence the proverb a Fools bolt is soon shot.

4 We must bind our passions in Chains & double
our guards least like mad folks they break their
locks & bolts & do all the mischief they can
Tayl. Comt.

IL facing 3I^r

But when the ſmoother *bole* from knots is free,
We make a deep inciſion in the tree. *Dryden's Virgil, Georg.*
View well this tree, the queen of all the grove;
How vaſt her *bole*, how wide her arms are ſpread;
How high above the reſt ſhe ſhoots her head! *Dryden.*

2. A kind of earth.
*Bole Armeniack* is an aſtringent earth, which takes its name from Armenia, the country from which we have it. *Woodward.*

3. A meaſure of corn, containing ſix buſhels.
Of good barley put eight *boles*, that is, about ſix Engliſh quarters, in a ſtone trough. *Mortimer.*

BO'LIS. *n. ſ.* [Lat.]
*Bolis* is a great firy ball, ſwiftly hurried through the air, and generally drawing a tail after it. Ariſtotle calls it *capra*. There have often been immenſe balls of this kind. *Muſchenbroeck.*

BOLL. *n. ſ.* A round ſtalk or ſtem; as, a *boll* of flax.

To BOLL. *v. n.* [from the noun.] To riſe in a ſtalk.
And the flax and the barley was ſmitten: for the barley was in the ear, and the flax was *bolled*. *Exodus*, ix. 31.

BO'LSTER. *n. ſ.* [bolſtre, Sax. *bolſter*, Dutch.]

1. Something laid on the bed, to raiſe and ſupport the head; commonly a bag filled with down or feathers.
Perhaps ſome cold bank is her *bolſter* now,
Or 'gainſt the rugged bark of ſome broad elm,
Leans her unpillow'd head. *Milton.*
This arm ſhall be a *bolſter* for thy head;
I'll fetch clean ſtraw to make a ſoldier's bed. *Gay.*

2. A pad, or quilt, to hinder any preſſure, or fill up any vacuity.
Up goes her hand, and off ſhe ſlips
The *bolſters* that ſupply her hips. *Swift.*

3. A pad, or compreſs, to be laid on a wound.
The bandage is the girt, which hath a *bolſter* in the middle, and the ends tacked firmly together. *Wiſeman's Surgery.*

4. In horſemanſhip.
The *bolſters* of a ſaddle are thoſe parts raiſed upon the bows, to hold the rider's thigh. *Farrier's Dict.*

To BO'LSTER. *v. a.* [from the noun.]

1. To ſupport the head with a bolſter.

2. To afford a bed to.
Mortal eyes do ſee them *bolſter*,
More than their own. *Shakeſp. Othello.*

3. To hold wounds together with a compreſs.
The practice of *bolſtering* the cheeks forward, does little ſervice to the wound, and is very uneaſy to the patient. *Sharp.*

4. To ſupport; to hold up; to maintain. This is now an expreſſion ſomewhat coarſe and obſolete.
We may be made wiſer by the publick perſuaſions grafted in men's minds, ſo they be uſed to further the truth, not to *bolſter* errour. *Hooker, b.* iii. § 4.
The lawyer ſets his tongue to ſale for the *bolſtering* out of unjuſt cauſes. *Hakewell on Providence.*
It was the way of many to *bolſter* up their crazy, doating conſciences with confidences. *South.*

BOLT. *n. ſ.* [*boult*, Dutch; βολὶς.]

1. An arrow; a dart ſhot from a croſsbow.
Yet mark'd I where the *bolt* of Cupid fell;
It fell upon a little weſtern flower;
Before milk white, now purple with love's wound.
*Shakeſp. Midſummer Night's Dream.*
The blunted *bolt* againſt the nymph he dreſt;
But, with the ſharp, transfix'd Apollo's breaſt. *Dryden.*

2. Lightning; a thunderbolt.
Sing'd with the flames, and with the *bolts* transfix'd,
With native earth your blood the monſters mix'd. *Dryden.*

3. *Bolt upright*; that is, upright as an arrow.
Bruſh-iron, native or from the mine, conſiſteth of long ſtriæ, about the thickneſs of a ſmall knitting needle, *bolt upright*, like the briſtles of a ſtiff bruſh. *Grew's Muſæum.*
As I ſtood *bolt upright* upon one end, one of the ladies burſt out. *Addiſon. Spectator*, N° 90.

4. The bar of a door, ſo called from being ſtrait like an arrow; we now ſay, *ſhoot the bolt*, when we ſpeak of faſtening or opening a door.
'Tis not in thee, to oppoſe the *bolt*
Againſt my coming in. *Shakeſp. King Lear.*

5. An iron to faſten the legs of a priſoner.
Away with him to priſon; lay *bolts* enough upon him.
*Shakeſp. Meaſure for Meaſure.*

6. A ſpot or ſtain. ~~See BLOOD-BOLTERED.~~
That ſupernal judge, that ſtirs good thoughts
In my breaſt, of ſtrong authority,
To look into the *bolts* and ſtains of right. *Shakeſp. K. John.*

To BOLT. *v. a.* [from the noun.]

1. To ſhut or faſten with a bolt.
The *bolted* gates flew open at the blaſt;
The ſtorm ruſh'd in, and Arcite ſtood aghaſt. *Dryden.*

2. To blurt out, or throw out precipitantly.
I hate when vice can *bolt* her arguments,
And virtue has no tongue to check her pride. *Milton.*

3. To faſten, as a bolt or pin; to pin; to keep together.
That I could reach the axel, where the pins are,
Which *bolt* this frame; that I might pull them out. *B. Johnſ.*

4. To fetter; to ſhackle.
It is great
To do that thing that ends all other deeds,
Which ſhackles accidents, and *bolts* up change.
*Shakeſp. ~~Antony and Cleopatra.~~*

5. To ſift; or ſeparate the parts of any thing with a ſieve. [*bluter*, Fr.]
~~Saying~~, he now had *boulted* all the flour,
And that it was a groom of baſe degree,
Which of my love was partner. *Fairy Queen, b.* ii. *c.* 4.
In the *bolting* and ſifting of fourteen years of power and favour, all that came out could not be pure meal. *Wotton.*
I cannot *bolt* this matter to the bran,
As Bradwardin and holy Auſtin can. *Dryden's Fables.*

6. To examine by ſifting; to try out; to lay open.
It would be well *bolted* out, whether great refractions may not be made upon reflections, as well as upon direct beams.
*Bacon's Natural Hiſtory*, N° 762.
The judge, ~~or~~ jury, ~~or~~ parties, ~~or the~~ council, or attornies, propounding occaſional queſtions, beats and *bolts* out the truth much better than when the witneſs delivers only a formal ſeries.
~~*Hale's Hiſtory of the Common Law.*~~
Time and nature will *bolt* out the truth of things, through all diſguiſes. *L'Eſtrange.*

7. To purify; to purge.
The fanned ſnow
That's *bolted* by the northern blaſt twice o'er. *Winter's Tale.*

To BOLT. *v. n.* To ſpring out with ſpeed and ſuddenneſs; to ſtart out with the quickneſs of an arrow.
This Puck ſeems but a dreaming dolt,
Still walking like a ragged colt,
And oft out of a buſh doth *bolt*,
Of purpoſe to deceive us. *Drayton's Nymphid.*
They erected a fort, and ~~from thence they~~ *bolted* like beaſts of the foreſt, ſometimes into the foreſt, ſometimes into the woods and faſtneſſes, and ſometimes back again to their den.
*Bacon's ~~War with Spain.~~*
As the houſe was all in a flame, out *bolts* a mouſe from the ruins, to ſave herſelf. *L'Eſtrange.*
I have reflected on thoſe men, who, from time to time, have ſhot themſelves into the world. I have ſeen many ſucceſſions of them; ſome *bolting* out upon the ſtage with vaſt applauſe, and others hiſſed off. *Dryden.*
The birds to foreign ſeats repair'd,
And beaſts, that *bolted* out, and ſaw the foreſt bar'd. *Dryd.*

BOLT-ROPE. *n. ſ.* [from *bolt* and *rope*.] The rope on which the ſail of a ſhip is ſewed and faſtened. *Sea Dict.*

BO'LTER. *n. ſ.* [from the verb.] A ſieve to ſeparate meal from bran or huſks; or to ſeparate finer from coarſer parts.
Theſe hakes, and divers others of the fore-cited, are taken with threads, and ſome of them with the *bolter*, which is a ſpiller of a bigger ſize. *Carew's Survey of Cornwal.*
Dowlas, filthy dowlas: I have given them away to bakers wives, and they have made *bolters* of them. *Shakeſp. Henry* IV.
With a good ſtrong chopping-knife mince the two capons, bones and all, as ſmall as ordinary minced meat; put them into a large neat *bolter*. *Bacon's Natural Hiſt.* N° 46.
When ſuperciliouſly he ſifts
Through coarſeſt *bolter* others gifts. *Hudibras*, p. i. c. iii.

BO'LTHEAD. *n. ſ.* A long ſtrait-necked glaſs veſſel, for chymical diſtillations, called alſo a *matraſs*, or *receiver*.
This ~~ſpirit abounds in~~ ſalt, which may be ſeparted, by putting the liquour into a *bolthead*, with a long and narrow neck.
~~*Boyle's Sceptical Chymiſtry.*~~

BO'LTING-HOUSE. *n. ſ.* [from *bolt* and *houſe*.] The place where meal is ſifted.
The jade is returned as white, and as powdered, as if ſhe had been at work in a *bolting-houſe*. *Dennis's Letters.*

BO'LTSPRIT. } *n. ſ.* A maſt running out at the head of a ſhip,
BO'WSPRIT. } not ſtanding upright, but aſlope. The but-end of it is generally ſet againſt the foot of the foremaſt; ſo that they are a ſtay to one another. The length without board is ſufficient to let its ſails hang clear of all incumbrances. If the *boltſprit* fail in bad weather, the foremaſt cannot hold long after. *Bowſprit* is perhaps the right ſpelling. *Sea Dictionary.*
Sometimes I'd divide,
And burn in many places; on the topmaſt,
The yards, and *boltſprit*, would I flame diſtinctly. *Sh. Temp.*

BO'LUS. *n. ſ.* [βῶλος.] A form of medicine, in which the ingredients are made up into a ſoft maſs, larger than pills, to be ſwallowed at once.
Keep their bodies ſoluble the while by clyſters, lenitive *boluſes* of caſſia and manna, with ſyrup of violets. *Wiſeman.*
By poets we are well aſſur'd,
That love, alas! can ne'er be cur'd;
A complicated heap of ills,
Deſpiſing *boluſes* and pills. *Swift.*

BOMB. *n. ſ.* [*bombus*, Lat.]

1. A loud noiſe.
There was an upper chamber, which being thought weak, was ſupported by a pillar of iron, of the bigneſs of one's arm in the midſt; which, if you had ſtruck, would make a little flat

noise in the room, but a great *bomb* in the chamber beneath. *Bacon's Natural Hist.* Nº 151.

2. A hollow iron ball, or shell, filled with gunpowder, and furnished with a vent for a fusee, or wooden tube, filled with combustible matter; to be thrown out from a mortar, which had its name from the noise it makes. The fusee, being set on fire, burns slowly till it reach the gunpowder, which goes off at once, bursting the shell to pieces with incredible violence; whence the use of *bombs* in besieging towns. The largest are about eighteen inches in diameter. By whom they were invented, is not known, and the time is uncertain, some fixing it to 1588, and others to 1495. *Chambers.*

The loud cannon missive iron pours,
And in the slaught'ring *bomb* Gradivus roars. *Rowe.*

To BOMB. *v. a.* [from the noun.] To fall upon with bombs; to bombard.

Our king thus trembles at Namur,
Whilst Villeroy, who ne'er afraid is,
To Bruxelles marches on secure,
To *bomb* the monks, and scare the ladies. *Prior.*

BOMB-CHEST. *n. s.* [from *bomb* and *chest*.] A kind of chest filled usually with bombs, and sometimes only with gunpowder, placed under ground, to tear and blow it up in the air, with those who stand on it. They are now much disused. *Chambers.*

BOMB-KETCH. } *n. s.* A kind of ship, strongly built, to bear
BOMB-VESSEL. } the shock of a mortar, when bombs are to be fired into a town.

Nor could an ordinary fleet, with *bomb-vessels*, hope to succeed against a place that has in its arsenal gallies and men of war. *Addison on Italy.*

BO'MBARD. *n. s.* [*bombardus*, Lat.] A great gun; a cannon: it is a word now obsolete.

They planted in divers places twelve great *bombards*, wherewith they threw huge stones into the air, which, falling down into the city, might break down the houses. *Knolles's History.*

To BOMBA'RD. *v. a.* [from the noun.] To attack with bombs.

A medal is struck on the English failing in their attempts on Dunkirk, when they endeavoured to blow up a fort, and *bombard* the town. *Addison on ancient Medals.*

BOMBARDI'ER. *n. s.* [from *bombard*.] The engineer whose employment it is to shoot bombs.

The *bombardier* tosses his balls sometimes into the midst of a city, with a design to fill all around him with terrour and combustion. *Tatler*, Nº 88.

BOMBA'RDMENT. *n. s.* [from *bombard*.] An attack made upon any city, by throwing bombs into it.

Genoa is not yet secure from a *bombardment*, though it is not so exposed as formerly. *Addison on Italy.*

BO'MBASIN. *n. s.* [*bombasin*, Fr.. from *bombycinus*, silken, Lat.] A slight silken stuff, for mourning.

BO'MBAST. *n. s.* [This word seems to be derived from *Bombastius*, one of the names of Paracelsus; a man remarkable for sounding professions, and unintelligible language.] Fustian; big words, without meaning.

Not pedants motley tongue, soldiers *bombast*,
Mountebanks drug-tongue, nor the terms of law,
Are strong enough preparatives to draw
Me to hear this. *Donne.*

Are all the flights of heroick poetry to be concluded *bombast*, unnatural, and mere madness, because they are not affected with their excellencies? *Dryden's State of Innocence, Preface.*

BO'MBAST. *adj.* [from the substantive.] High sounding; of big sound without meaning.

He, as loving his own pride and purpose,
Evades them with a *bombast* circumstance,
Horribly stuff'd with epithets of war. *Shakesp. Othello.*

BOMBILA'TION. *n. s.* [from *bombus*, Lat.] Sound; noise; report.

How to abate the vigour, or silence the *bombilation* of guns, a way is said to be by borax and butter, mixt in a due proportion, which will almost take off the report, and also the force of the charge. *Brown's Vulgar Errours, b.* ii. *c.* 5.

BOMBY'CINOUS. *adj.* [*bombycinus*, Lat.] Silken; made of silk. *D.*

BONA ROBA. *n. s.* [Ital. a fine gown.] A whore.

We knew where the bona robas were. *Shakesp. Henry* IV.

BONA'SUS. *n. s.* [Lat.] A kind of buffalo, or wild bull.

BONCHRE'TIEN. *n. s.* [French.] A species of pear, so called, probably, from the name of a gardener. See PEAR.

BOND. *n. s.* [bond, Sax. bound; it is written indifferently, in many of its senses, *bond*, or *band*. See BAND.]

1. Cords, or chains, with which any one is bound.

There left me, and my man, both bound together;
Till, gnawing with my teeth my *bonds* asunder,
I gain'd my freedom. *Shakesp. Comedy of Errours.*

2. Ligament that holds any thing together.

Let any one send his contemplation to the extremities of the universe, and see, what conceivable hoops, what *bond* he can imagine to hold this mass of matter in so close a pressure together. *Locke.*

3. Union; connexion.

Observe, in working up the walls, that no side of the house, nor any part of the walls, be wrought up three feet above the other, before the next adjoining wall be wrought up to it, so that they may be all joined together, and make good *bond*. *Mortimer's Husbandry.*

4. Chains; imprisonment; captivity.

Whom I perceived to have nothing laid to his charge, worthy of death, or of *bonds*. *Acts*, xxiii. 29.

5. Cement of union; cause of union; link of connexion.

Wedding is great Juno's crown;
O blessed *bond* of board and bed! *Shakesp. As you like it.*

Love cools, brothers divide, and the *bond* is cracked 'twixt son and father. *Shakesp. King Lear.*

6. A writing of obligation to pay a sum, or perform a contract.

Go with me to a notary, seal me there
Your single *bond*. *Shakesp. Merchant of Venice.*

What if I ne'er consent to make you mine;
My father's promise ties me not to time;
And *bonds* without a date, they say are void. *Dryden.*

7. Obligation; law by which any man is obliged.

Unhappy that I am! I cannot heave
My heart into my mouth: I love your majesty
According to my *bond*, no more nor less. *Shakesp. K. Lear.*

Take which you please, it dissolves the *bonds* of government and obedience. *Locke.*

BOND. *adj.* [from *bind*, perhaps for *bound*; from zebonden, Saxon.] Captive; in a servile state.

Whether we be Jews or Gentiles, whether we be *bond* or free. 1 *Cor.* xii. 13.

BO'NDAGE. *n. s.* [from *bond*.] Captivity; imprisonment; state of restraint.

You only have overthrown me, and in my *bondage* consists my glory. *Sidney, b.* ii.

Say, gentle princess, would you not suppose
Your *bondage* happy, to be made a queen?—
—To be a queen in *bondage*, is more vile
Than is a slave in base servility. *Shakesp. Henry* VI. *p.* i.

Our cage
We make a choir, as doth the prison'd bird,
And sing our *bondage* freely. *Shakesp. Cymbeline.*

He must resolve by no means to be enslaved, and brought under the *bondage* of observing oaths, which ought to vanish, when they stand in competition with eating or drinking, or taking money. *South.*

The king, when he design'd you for my guard,
Resolv'd he would not make my *bondage* hard. *Dryden.*

If she has a struggle for honour, she is in a *bondage* to love; which gives the story its turn that way. *Pope; notes on Iliad.*

BO'NDMAID. *n. s.* [from *bond*, captive, and *maid*.] A woman slave.

Good sister, wrong me not, nor wrong yourself,
To make a *bondmaid* and a slave of me. *Shakesp. T. Shrew.*

BO'NDMAN. *n. s.* [from *bond* and *man*.] A man slave.

Amongst the Romans, in making of a *bondman* free, was it not wondered wherefore so great ado should be made; the master to present his slave in some court, to take him by the hand, and not only to say, in the hearing of the publick magistrate, I will that this man become free; but, after those solemn words uttered, to strike him on the cheek, to turn him round, the hair of his head to be shaved off, the magistrate to touch him thrice with a rod; in the end, a cap and a white garment given him. *Hooker, b.* iv. § 1.

O freedom! first delight of human kind;
Not that which *bondmen* from their masters find. *Dryden.*

BONDSE'RVANT. *n. s.* [from *bond* and *servant*.] A slave; a servant without the liberty of quitting his master.

And if thy brother, that dwelleth by thee, be waxen poor, and be sold unto thee; thou shalt not compel him to serve as a *bondservant*. *Lev.* xxv. 39.

BONDSE'RVICE. *n. s.* [from *bond* and *service*.] The condition of a bondservant; slavery.

Upon those did Solomon levy a tribute of *bondservice*. 1 *Kings*, ix. 21.

BO'NDSLAVE. *n. s.* [from *bond* and *slave*.] A man in slavery; a slave.

Love enjoined such diligence, that no apprentice, no, no *bondslave*, could ever be, by fear, more ready at all commandments, than that young princess was. *Sidney, b.* ii.

All her ornaments are taken away; of a freewoman she is become a *bondslave*. 1 *Mac.* ii. 11.

Commonly the *bondslave* is fed by his lord, but here the lord was fed by his *bondslave*. *Sir J. Davies on Ireland.*

BO'NDSMAN. *n. s.* [from *bond* and *man*.]

1. A slave.

Carnal greedy people, without such a precept, would have no mercy upon their poor *bondsmen* and beasts. *Derh. Ph. Theol.*

2. A person bound, or giving security for another.

BO'NDSWOMAN. *n. s.* [from *bond* and *woman*.] A woman slave.

My lords, the senators
Are sold for slaves, and their wives for *bondswomen*. *Ben. Johnson's Catiline.*

BONE.

a ‡

ombilious Adj. [Bombilo Latin]

~~to buzz like a bee, or bombylius a fly~~

making a humming noise

he whame or burrel fly is vexatious to
rses in Summer, not by stinging them, but
y by their bombilious noise, or tickling
sticking their nits or eggs in the hair
... Derh. Ph. Th.

O. I

Bonjour [French] ~~a complimental salutation~~ Good day

An it please your majesty
To hunt the panther & the hart with me,
With horn & hound, we'll give your grace bonjour
Shak

BONE. *n. ſ.* [ban, Saxon.]

1. The ſolid parts of the body of an animal are made up of hard fibres, tied one to another by ſmall tranſverſe fibres, as thoſe of the muſcles. In a fœtus they are porous, ſoft, and eaſily diſcerned. As their pores fill with a ſubſtance of their own nature, ſo they increaſe, harden, and grow cloſe to one another. They are all ſpongy, and full of little cells, or are of a conſiderable firm thickneſs, with a large cavity, except the teeth; and where they are articulated, they are covered with a thin and ſtrong membrane, called the perioſteum. Each bone is much bigger at its extremity than in the middle, that the articulations might be firm, and the *bones* not eaſily put out of joint. But, becauſe the middle of the *bone* ſhould be ſtrong, to ſuſtain its alloted weight, and reſiſt accidents, the fibres are there more cloſely compacted together, ſupporting one another; and the *bone* is made hollow, and conſequently not ſo eaſily broken, as it muſt have been, had it been ſolid and ſmaller. *Quincy.*

Thy *bones* are marrowleſs, thy blood is cold. *Macbeth.*

There was lately a young gentleman bit to the *bone*. *Tatler.*

2. A fragment of meat; a bone with as much fleſh as adheres to it.

Like Æſop's hounds, contending for the *bone*,
Each pleaded right, and would be lord alone. *Dryden.*

3. *To be upon the bones.* To attack.

Puſs had a month's mind *to be upon the bones* of him, but was not willing to pick a quarrel. *L'Eſtrange.*

4. *To make no bones.* To make no ſcruple; a metaphor, taken from a dog, who readily ſwallows meat that has no bones.

5. BONES. A ſort of bobbins, made of trotter bones, for weaving bonelace.

6. BONES. Dice.

But then my ſtudy was to cog the dice,
And dext'rouſly to throw the lucky ſice:
To ſhun ames ace that ſwept my ſtakes away;
And watch the box, for fear they ſhould convey
Falſe *bones*, and put upon me in the play. *Dryden's Perſ.*

To BONE. *v. a.* [from the noun.] To take out the bones from the fleſh.

BO'NELACE. *n. ſ.* [from *bone* and *lace*; the bobbins with which lace is woven being frequently made of bones.] Flaxen lace, ſuch as women wear on their linen.

The things you follow, and make ſongs on now, ſhould be ſent to knit, or ſit down to bobbins or *bonelace*. *Tatler.*

We deſtroy the ſymmetry of the human figure, and fooliſhly contrive to call off the eye from great and real beauties, to childiſh gewgaw ribbands and *bonelace*. *Spectator*, Nº 99.

BO'NELESS. *adj.* [from *bone*.] Without bones.

I would, while it was ſmiling in my face,
Have pluckt my nipple from his *boneleſs* gums,
And daſht the brains out. *Shakeſp. King Lear.*

To BO'NESET. *v. n.* [from *bone* and *ſet*.] To reſtore a bone out of joint to its place; or join a bone broken to the other part.

A fractured leg ſet in the country by one pretending to *boneſetting*. *Wiſeman's Surgery.*

BO'NESETTER. *n. ſ.* [from *boneſet*.] A chirurgeon; one who particularly profeſſes the art of reſtoring broken or luxated bones.

At preſent my deſire is only to have a good *boneſetter*. *Denham's Sophy.*

BO'NFIRE. *n. ſ.* [from *bon*, good, Fr. and *fire*.] A fire made for ſome publick cauſe of triumph or exultation.

Ring ye the bells to make it wear away,
And *bonfires* make all day. *Spenſer's Epithalamium.*

How came ſo many *bonfires* to be made in queen Mary's days? Why, ſhe had abuſed and deceived her people. *South.*

Full ſoon by *bonfire*, and by bell,
We learnt our liege was paſſing well. *Gay.*

BO'NGRACE. *n. ſ.* [*bonne grace*, Fr.] A forehead-cloth, or covering for the forehead. *Skinner.*

I have ſeen her beſet all over with emeralds and pearls, ranged in rows about her cawl, her peruke, her *bongrace*, and chaplet. *Hakewell on Providence.*

BO'NNET. *n. ſ.* [*bonet*, Fr.] A covering for the head; a hat; a cap.

Go to them with this *bonnet* in thy hand,
And thus far having ſtretch'd it, here be with them,
Thy knee buſſing the ſtones; for, in ſuch buſineſs,
Action is eloquence. *Shakeſp. Coriolanus.*

They had not probably the ceremony of veiling the *bonnet* in their ſalutations; for, in medals, they ſtill have it on their heads. *Addiſon on ancient Medals.*

BO'NNET. [In fortification.] A kind of little ravelin, without any ditch, having a parapet three feet high, anciently placed before the points of the ſaliant angles of the glacis; being paliſadoed round: of late alſo uſed before the angles of baſtions, and the points of ravelins.

BO'NNET *à preſtre*, or prieſt's cap, is an outwork, having at the head three ſaliant angles, and two inwards. It differs from the double tenaille, becauſe its ſides, inſtead of being parallel, grow narrow at the gorge, and open wider at the front.

BO'NNETS. [In the ſea language.] Small ſails ſet on the courſes





on the mizzen, mainſail, and foreſail of a ſhip, when theſe are too narrow or ſhallow to cloath the maſt, or in order to make more way in calm weather. *Chambers.*

BO'NNILY. *adv.* [from *bonny*.] Gayly; handſomely; plumply.

BO'NNINESS. *n. ſ.* [from *bonny*.] Gayety; handſomeneſs; plumpneſs.

BO'NNY. *adj.* [from *bon*, *bonne*, Fr. It is a word now almoſt confined to the Scottiſh dialect.]

1. Handſome; beautiful.

Match to match I have encounter'd him,
And made a prey for carrion kites and crows,
Ev'n of the *bonny* beaſt he lov'd ſo well. *Shakeſp. Henry VI.*

Thus wail'd the louts in melancholy ſtrain,
Till *bonny* Suſan ſped acroſs the plain. *Gay's Paſtorals.*

2. Gay; merry; frolickſome; cheerful; blithe.

Then ſigh not ſo, but let them go,
And be you blithe and *bonny*. *Shakeſp. Much ado about N.*

3. It ſeems to be generally uſed in converſation for *plump*.

BONNY-CLABBER. *n. ſ.* A word uſed in ſome counties for ſour buttermilk.

We ſcorn, for want of talk, to jabber,
Of parties o'er our *bonny-clabber*;
Nor are we ſtudious to enquire,
Who votes for manours, who for hire. *Swift.*

BO'NUM MAGNUM. *n. ſ.* See PLUM; of which it is a ſpecies.

BO'NY. *adj.* [from *bone*.]

1. Conſiſting of bones.

At the end of this hole is a membrane, faſtened to a round *bony* limb, and ſtretched like the head of a drum; and therefore, by anatomiſts, called *tympanum*. *Ray on the Creation.*

2. Full of bones.

BO'OBY. *n. ſ.* [a word of no certain etymology; *Henſhaw* thinks it a corruption of *bull-beef* ridiculouſly; *Skinner* imagines it to be derived from *bobo*, fooliſh, Span. *Junius* finds *bowbard* to be an old Scottiſh word for a *coward*, a *contemptible fellow*; from which he naturally deduces *booby*; but the original of *bowbard* is not known.] A dull, heavy, ſtupid fellow; a lubber.

But one exception to this fact we find,
That *booby* Phaon only was unkind,
An ill-bred boatman, rough as waves and wind. *Prior.*

Young maſter next muſt riſe to fill him wine,
And ſtarve himſelf to ſee the *booby* dine. *King.*

BOOK. *n. ſ.* [boc, Sax. ſuppoſed from *boc*, a beech; becauſe they wrote on beechen boards, as *liber* in Latin, from the rind of a tree.]

1. A volume in which we read or write.

See a *book* of prayer in his hand;
True ornaments to know a holy man. *Shakeſp. Richard III.*

Receive the ſentence of the law for ſins,
Such as by God's *book* are adjudg'd to death. *Shakeſp. Henry IV.*

But in the coffin that had the *books*, they were found as freſh as if they had been but newly written; being written on parchment, and covered over with watch candles of wax. *Bacon.*

*Books* are a ſort of dumb teachers; they cannot anſwer ſudden queſtions, or explain preſent doubts: this is properly the work of a living inſtructor. *Watts.*

2. A particular part of a work.

The firſt *book* we divide into ſections; whereof the firſt is theſe chapters paſt. *Burnet's Theory of the Earth.*

3. The regiſter in which a trader keeps an account of his debts.

This life
Is nobler than attending for a check;
Prouder, than ruſtling in unpaid for ſilk:
Such gain the cap of him that makes them fine,
Yet keeps his *book* uncroſs'd. *Shakeſp. Cymbeline.*

4. *In books.* In kind remembrance.

I was ſo much *in his books*, that, at his deceaſe, he left me the lamp by which he uſed to write his lucubrations. *Addiſon.*

5. *Without book.* By memory; by repetition; without reading.

Sermons read they abhor in the church; but ſermons *without book*, ſermons which ſpend their life in their birth, and may have publick audience but once. *Hooker*, b. v. § 21.

To BOOK. *v. a.* [from the noun.] To regiſter in a book.

I beſeech your grace, let it be *booked* with the reſt of this day's deeds; or I will have it in a particular ballad elſe, with mine own picture on the top of it. *Shakeſp. Henry IV. p.* ii.

He made wilful murder high treaſon; he cauſed the marchers to *book* their men, for whom they ſhould make anſwer. *Davies on Ireland.*

BOOK-KEEPING. *n. ſ.* [from *book* and *keep*.] The art of keeping accounts, or recording the tranſactions of a man's affairs, in ſuch a manner, that at any time he may thereby know the true ſtate of the whole, or any part, of his affairs, with clearneſs and expedition. *Harris.*

BO'OKBINDER. *n. ſ.* [from *book* and *bind*.] A man whoſe profeſſion it is to bind books.

BO'OKFUL. *adj.* [from *book* and *full*.] Full of notions gleaned from books; crouded with undigeſted knowledge.

The

The *bookful* blockhead, ignorantly read,
With loads of learned lumber in his head,
With his own tongue still edifies his ears,
And always list'ning to himself appears. *Pope's Ess. on Crit.*

BO'OKISH. *adj.* [from *book*.] Given to books; acquainted only with books. It is generally used contemptuously.

I'll make him yield the crown,
Whose *bookish* rule hath pull'd fair England down.
*Shakesp. Henry VI. p. ii.*

I'm not *bookish*, yet I can read waiting gentlewoman in the 'scape. *Shakesp. Winter's Tale.*

Xantippe follows the example of her namesake; being married to a *bookish* man, who has no knowledge of the world. *Spectator*, Nº 482.

BO'OKISHNESS. *n. s.* [from *bookish*.] Much application to books; over-studiousness.

BOOKLE'ARNED. *adj.* [from *book* and *learned*.] Versed in books, or literature: a term implying some slight contempt.

Whate'er these *booklearn'd* blockheads say,
Solon's the veri'st fool in all the play. *Dryden's Persius.*

He will quote passages out of Plato and Pindar, at his own table, to some *booklearned* companion, without blushing. *Swift.*

BOOKLE'ARNING. *n. s.* [from *book* and *learning*.] Skill in literature; acquaintance with books; a term of some contempt.

They might talk of *booklearning* what they would; but, for his part, he never saw more unfeaty fellows than great clerks. *Sidney.*

Neither does it so much require *booklearning* and scholarship, as good natural sense, to distinguish true and false, and to discern what is well proved, and what is not. *Burnet's Th. Earth.*

BO'OKMAN. *n. s.* [from *book* and *man*.] A man whose profession is the study of books.

This civil war of wits were much better us'd
On Navarre and his *bookmen*; for here 'tis abus'd.
*Shakesp. Love's Labour Lost.*

BO'OKMATE. *n. s.* [from *book* and *mate*.] Schoolfellow.

This Armado is a Spaniard that keeps here in court,
A phantasm, a monarch, and one that makes sport
To the prince and his *bookmates*. *Shakesp. Love's Labour Lost.*

BO'OKSELLER. *n. s.* [from *book* and *sell*.] He whose profession it is to sell books.

He went to the *bookseller*, and told him in anger, he had sold a book in which there was false divinity.
*Walton's Life of Bishop Saunderson.*

BO'OKWORM. *n. s.* [from *book* and *worm*.]

1. A worm or mite that eats holes in books, chiefly when damp.

My lion, like a moth or *bookworm*, feeds upon nothing but paper, and I shall beg of them to diet him with wholesome and substantial food. *Guardian*, Nº 114.

2. A student too closely given to books; a reader without judgment.

Among those venerable galleries and solitary scenes of the university, I wanted but a black gown, and a salary, to be as mere a *bookworm* as any there. *Pope's Letters.*

BO'OLY. *n. s.* [an Irish term.]

All the Tartarians, and the people about the Caspian sea, which are naturally Scythians, live in herds; being the very same that the Irish *boolies* are, driving their cattle continually with them, and feeding only on their milk and white meats. *Spenser's Ireland.*

BOOM. *n. s.* [from *boom*, a tree, Dutch.]

1. [In sea language.] A long pole used to spread out the clue of the studding sail; and sometimes the clues of the mainsail and foresail are boomed out.

2. A pole with bushes or baskets, set up as a mark to shew the sailors how to steer in the channel, when a country is overflown. *Sea Dict.*

3. A bar of wood laid cross a harbour, to keep off the enemy.

As his heroick worth struck envy dumb,
Who took the Dutchman, and who cut the *boom*. *Dryden.*

To BOOM. *v. n.* [from the noun. A sea term.] To rush with violence; as a ship is said to come *booming*, when she makes all the sail she can.

Forsook by thee, in vain I sought thy aid,
When *booming* billows clos'd above my head. *Pope's Odyss.*

BOON. *n. s.* [from bene, Sax. a petition.] A gift; a grant; a benefaction; a present.

Vouchsafe me for my meed but one fair look:
A smaller *boon* than this I cannot beg,
And less than this, I'm sure, you cannot give.
*Shakesp. Two Gentlemen of Verona.*

That courtier, who obtained a *boon* of the emperour, that he might every morning whisper him in the ear, and say nothing, asked no unprofitable suit for himself. *Bacon.*

The blust'ring fool has satisfy'd his will;
His *boon* is giv'n; his knight has gain'd the day,
But lost the prize. *Dryden's Fables.*

What rhetorick didst thou use,
To gain this mighty *boon*? she pities me! *Addison's Cato.*

BOON. *adj.* [*bon*, Fr.] Gay; merry; as, a *boon* companion.

Satiate at length,
And heighten'd as with wine, jocund and *boon*,
Thus to herself she pleasingly began. *Parad. Lost*, b. ix.

I know the infirmity of our family; we are apt to play the *boon companion*, and throw our money away in our cups.
*Arbuthnot's Hist. of J. Bull.*

BOOR. *n. s.* [*beer*, Dutch; ȝebure, Sax.] A ploughman; a country fellow; a lout; a clown.

The bare sense of a calamity is called grumbling; and if a man does but make a face upon the *boor*, he is presently a malecontent. *L'Estrange.*

He may live as well as a *boor* of Holland, whose cares of growing still richer waste his life. *Temple.*

To one well-born, th' affront is worse and more,
When he's abus'd and baffl'd by a *boor*. *Dryden.*

BO'ORISH. *adj.* [from *boor*.] Clownish; rustick; untaught; uncivilized.

Therefore, you clown, abandon, which is in the vulgar, leave the society, which, in the *boorish*, is, company of this female. *Shakesp. As you like it.*

BO'ORISHLY. *adv.* [from *boorish*.] In a boorish manner; after a clownish manner.

BO'ORISHNESS. *n. s.* [from *boorish*.] Clownishness; rusticity; coarseness of manners.

BOOSE. *n. s.* [boȝiȝ, Sax.] A stall for a cow or an ox.

To BOOT. *v. a.* [*baten*, to profit, Dutch; bot, in Saxon, is recompence, repentance, or fine paid by way of expiation; botan is, to repent, or to compensate; as,

He iſ piſ ꝥ biꞇ and boꞇe,
And beꞇ bıꝩoꞃen bome.]

1. To profit; to advantage.

It shall not *boot* them, who derogate from reading, to excuse it, when they see no other remedy; as if their intent were only to deny, that aliens and strangers from the family of God are won, or that belief doth use to be wrought at the first in them, without sermons. *Hooker*, b. v. § 22.

For what I have, I need not to repeat;
And what I want, it *boots* not to complain. *Shakesp. R. II.*

If we shun
The purpos'd end, or here lie fixed all,
What *boots* it us these wars to have begun. *Fairfax*, b. i.

What *boots* the regal circle on his head,
That long behind he trails his pompous robe? *Pope.*

2. To enrich; to benefit.

And I will *boot* thee with what gift beside,
That modesty can beg. *Shakesp. Ant. and Cleopatra.*

BOOT. *n. s.* [from the verb.]

1. Profit; gain; advantage.

My gravity,
Wherein, let no man hear me, I take pride,
Could I, with *boot*, change for an idle plume,
Which the air beats for vain. *Shakesp. Measure for Meas.*

2. *To boot.* With advantage; over and above.

Canst thou, O partial sleep, give thy repose
To the wet seaboy, in an hour so rude:
And, in the calmest and the stillest night,
With all appliances, and means *to boot*,
Deny it to a king? *Shakesp. Henry IV. p. ii.*

Man is God's image; but a poor man is
Christ's stamp *to boot*: both images regard. *Herbert.*

He might have his mind and manners formed, and he be instructed *to boot* in several sciences. *Locke.*

3. It seems, in the following lines, used for *booty*, or plunder.

Others, like soldiers, armed in their stings,
Make *boot* upon the summer's velvet buds. *Shakesp. Henry V.*

BOOT. *n. s.* [*bottas*, Armorick; *botes*, a shoe, Welch; *botte*, French.]

1. A covering for the leg, used by horsemen.

That my leg is too long—
—No; that it is too little.—
—I'll wear a *boot*, to make it somewhat rounder.
*Shakesp. Two Gentlemen of Verona.*

Shew'd him his room, where he must lodge that night,
Pull'd off his *boots*, and took away the light. *Milton.*

Bishop Wilkins says, he does not question, but it will be as usual for a man to call for his wings, when he is going a journey, as it is now to call for his *boots*. *Addison. Guardian.*

2. A kind of rack for the leg, formerly used in Scotland for torturing criminals.

BOOT *of a Coach.* The space between the coachman and the coach.

To BOOT. *v. a.* [from the noun.] To put on boots.

*Boot*, *boot*, Master Shallow; I know the young king is sick for me: let us take any man's horses. *Shakesp. Henry IV. p. ii.*

BOOT-HOSE. *n. s.* [from *boot* and *hose*.] Stockings to serve for boots; spatterdashes.

His lacquey with a linen stock on one leg, and a *boot-hose* on the other, gartered with a red and blue list.
*Shakesp. Taming of the Shrew.*

BOOT-TREE. *n. s.* [from *boot* and *tree*.] Two pieces of wood, shaped like a leg, to be driven into boots, for stretching and widening them.

BO'OTCATCHER. *n. s.* [from *boot* and *catch*.] The person whose business at an inn is to pull off the boots of passengers.

The

If in a Coach one Side of the boot be down & the other up, and if a beggar beg on the Close Side, you will think that he were on the open Side

Bac.

She people that thus live'd in those
grow thereby the more barbarous & practising
what villanies they will against private men
by stealing their goods or murdering them
Spens

3 v. a
~~To confine, to keep within bounds~~

, I fear your disposition
That Nature which contemns its Origin
Cannot be border'd certain in itself
~~She that herself will sliver & disbranch~~
From her material sap perforce must wither
And come to deadly use Shak.

v. a
2 To peirce thro' by struggling
Consider
What riots seen, what bustling crowds I bor'd
How oft I cross'd where carts & coaches roar'd
Gay

IL facing 3Kr

The oftler and the *bootcatcher* ought to partake. *Swift.*

Bo'oted. *adj.* [from *boot.*] In boots; in a horfeman's habit.

A *booted* judge fhall fit to try his caufe,
Not by the ftatute, but by martial laws. *Dryden's Juvenal.*

Booth. *n. f.* [*boed*, Dutch; *bwth*, Welch.] A houfe built of boards, or boughs, to be ufed for a fhort time.

The clothiers found means to have all the queft made of the northern men, fuch as had their *booths* ftanding in the fair. *Camden's Remains.*

Much mifchief will be done at Bartholomew fair, by the fall of a *booth.* *Swift's Predictions.*

Bo'otless. *adj.* [from *boot.*]

1. Ufelefs; unprofitable; unavailing; without advantage.

When thofe accurfed meffengers of hell
Came to their wicked man, and 'gan tell
Their *bootlefs* pains, and ill fucceeding night. *Fairy Q. b.* i.

God did not fuffer him, being defirous of the light of wifdom, with *bootlefs* expence of travel, to wander in darknefs. *Hooker, b.* i. *p.* 36.

*Bootlefs* fpeed,
When cowardice purfues, and valour flies. *Shakefpeare.*

Let him alone;
I'll follow him no more with *bootlefs* pray'rs:
He feeks my life. *Shakefp. Merchant of Venice.*

2. Without fuccefs; perhaps without booty; *Shakefpeare* having, in another place, ufed the word *boot* for *booty.*

Thrice from the banks of Wye,
And fandy bottom'd Severn, have I fent
Him *bootlefs* home, and weatherbeaten back. *Shakefp. H.* IV.

Bo'oty. *n. f.* [*buyt*, Dutch; *butin*, Fr.]

1. Plunder; pillage; fpoils gained from the enemy.

One way a band felect from forage drives
A herd of beeves, fair oxen, and fair kine,
Their *booty.* *Milton's Paradife Loft, b.* xi. *l.* 650.

His confcience is the hue and cry that purfues him; and when he reckons that he has gotten a *booty*, he has only caught a Tartar. *L'Eftrange.*

For, fhould you to extortion be inclin'd,
Your cruel guilt will little *booty* find. *Dryden's Juv. fat.* viii.

2. Things gotten by robbery.

If I had a mind to be honeft, I fee, fortune would not fuffer me; fhe drops *booties* in my mouth. *Shakefp. Winter's Tale.*

3. *To play booty.* To play difhoneftly, with an intent to lofe. The French ufe, *Je fuis botte*, when they mean to fay, *I will not go.*

We underftand what we ought to do; but when we deliberate, we *play booty* againft ourfelves; our confciences direct us one way, our corruptions hurry us another. *L'Eftrange.*

I have fet this argument in the beft light, that the ladies may not think I *write booty.* *Dryden.*

Bope'ep. *n. f.* [from *bo* and *peep.*] To look out, and draw back as if frighted, or with the purpofe to fright fome other.

Then they for fudden joy did weep,
And I for forrow fung,
That fuch a king fhould play *bopeep*,
And go the fools among. *Shakefp. King Lear.*

That ferve inftead of peaceful barriers,
To part th' engagements of their warriours,
Where both from fide to fide may fkip,
And only encounter at *bopeep.* *Hudibras, p.* iii. *c.* iii.

There the devil plays at *bopeep*, puts out his horns to do mifchief, then fhrinks them back for fafety. *Dryden's Span. Friar.*

*BORA'CHIO. n. f.* [*borracho*, Span.] A drunkard.

How you ftink of wine! D' ye think my niece will ever endure fuch a *borachio!* you're an abfolute *borachio.* *Congreve's Way of the World.*

Bo'rable. *adj.* [from *bore.*] That may be bored.

Bo'rage. *n. f.* [from *borago*, Lat.] A plant.

The leaves are broad and rough; the flowers confift of one leaf; are of a wheel fhape, and divided into five fegments, almoft to the bottom, which end in fharp points, like a ftar; the apices, in the middle of the flower, are fharp-pointed, and adhere together; the feeds are rough, and appear like a viper's head. This plant is often ufed in the kitchen, and for a cool tankard in the fummer time; and the flowers are ufed in medicinal cordials. *Millar.*

*BO'RAMEZ. n. f.* The Scythian lamb, generally known by the name of *Agnus Scythicus.*

Much wonder is made of the *boramez*, that ftrange plantanimal, or vegetable lamb of Tartary, which wolves delight to feed on; which hath the fhape of a lamb, affordeth a bloody juice upon breaking, and liveth while the plants be confumed about it. *Brown's Vulgar Errours, b.* iii. *c.* 27.

*BO'RAX. n. f.* [*borax*, low Latin.] An artificial falt, prepared from fal armoniac, nitre, calcined tartar, fea falt, and alum, diffolved in wine. It is principally ufed to folder metals, and fometimes an uterine ingredient in medicine. *Quincy.*

Bo'rdel. *n. f.* [*bordeel*, Teut. *bordel*, Armorick.] A brothel; a bawdyhoufe.

Making even his own houfe a ftews, a *bordel*, and a fchool of lewdnefs, to inftil vice into the unwary years of his poor children. *South.*





BO'RDER. *n. f.* [*bord*, Germ. *bord*, Fr.]

1. The outer part or edge of any thing.

They have, of Paris work, looking-glaffes, bordered with broad *borders* of cryftal, and great counterfeit precious ftones. *Bacon's Natural Hift.* N° 960.

The light muft ftrike on the middle, and extend its greateft clearnefs on the principal figures; diminifhing by degrees, as it comes nearer and nearer to the *borders.* *Dryden's Dufrefnoy.*

2. The march or edge of a country; the confine.

If a prince keep his refidence on the *border* of his dominions, the remote parts will rebel; but if he make the centre his feat, he fhall eafily keep them in obedience. *Spenfer.*

3. The outer part of a garment, generally adorned with needlework, or ornaments.

4. A bank raifed round a garden, and fet with flowers; a narrow rank of herbs or flowers.

Thereto arriving, round about doth fly
From bed to bed, from one to other *border*,
And takes furvey, with curious bufy eye,
Of every flower and herb there fet in order. *Spenfer's Muiop.*

All with a *border* of rich fruit trees crown'd,
Whofe loaded branches hide the lofty mound:
Such various ways the fpacious alleys lead,
My doubtful mufe knows not what path to tread. *Waller.*

To Bo'rder. *v. n.* [from the noun.]

1. To confine upon; to touch fomething elfe at the fide or edge.

It *bordereth* upon the province of Croatia, which, in time paft, was continual wars with the Turks garrifons. *Knolles's Hiftory of the Turks.*

Virtue and Honour had their temples *bordering* on each other, and are fometimes both on the fame coin. *Addifon.*

2. To approach nearly to.

All wit, which *borders* upon profanenefs, and makes bold with thofe things to which the greateft reverence is due, deferves to be branded with folly. *Tillotfon.*

To Bo'rder. *v. a.*

1. To adorn with a border of ornaments.

2. To reach; to touch; to confine upon.

Sheba and Raamah are thofe parts of Arabia, which *border* the fea called the Perfian gulf. *Raleigh's Hiftory.*

Bo'rderer. *n. f.* [from *border.*] He that dwells on the borders, extreme parts, or confines.

They of thofe marches, gracious fovereign!
Shall be a wall fufficient to defend
Our inland from the pilfering *borderers.* *Shakefp. Henry* V.

An ordinary horfe will carry two facks of fand; and, of fuch, the *borderers* on the fea do beftow fixty, at leaft in every acre; but moft hufbands double that number. *Carew's Survey.*

The eafieft to be drawn
To our fociety, and to aid the war:
The rather for their feat, being next *bord'rers*
On Italy; and that they abound with horfe. *B. Johnf. Catil.*

The king of Scots in perfon, with Perkin in his company, entered with a great army, though it chiefly confifted of *borderers*, being raifed fomewhat fuddenly. *Bacon's Henry* VII.

Volga's ftream
Sends oppofite, in fhaggy armour clad,
Her *borderers*; on mutual flaughter bent,
They rend their countries. *Philips.*

To Bo'rdrage. *v. n.* [from *border.*] To plunder the borders.

Long time in peace his realm eftablifhed,
Yet oft annoy'd with fundry *bordragings*
Of neighbour Scots, and foreign fcatterlings. *Fairy Q. b.* ii.

To BORE. *v. a.* [boꞃian, Sax.] To pierce in a hole.

I'll believe as foon,
This whole earth may be *bor'd*; and that the moon
May through the centre creep. *Shakep. Midfum. Night's Dr.*

Mulberries will be fairer, if you *bore* the trunk of the tree through, and thruft, into the places *bored*, wedges of fome hot trees. *Bacon's Natural Hift.* N° 456.

Take the barrel of a long gun, perfectly *bored*, and fet it upright, and take a bullet exactly fit for it; and then if you fuck at the mouth of the barrel never fo gently, the bullet will come up fo forcibly, that it will hazard the ftriking out your teeth. *Digby on Bodies.*

But Capys, and the graver fort, thought fit
The Greeks fufpected prefent to commit
To feas or flames; at leaft, to fearch and *bore*
The fides, and what that fpace contains t'explore. *Denham.*

Thofe diminutive caterpillars are able, by degrees, to pierce or *bore* their way into a tree, with very fmall holes; which, after they are fully entered, grow together. *Ray.*

Confider, reader, what fatigues I've known,
What riots feen, what buftling crouds I *bor'd*,
How oft I crofs'd where carts and coaches roar'd. *Gay.*

To Bore. *v. n.*

1. To make a hole.

A man may make an inftrument to *bore* a hole an inch wide, or half an inch, and fo lefs; not to *bore* a hole of a foot. *Wilkins's Mathematical Magick.*

2. To pufh forward towards a certain point.

Thoſe milk paps,
That through the window lawn *bore* at men's eyes,
Are not within the leaf of pity writ. *Shakeſp. Timon.*

Nor ſouthward to the raining regions run;
But *boring* to the weſt, and hov'ring there,
With gaping mouths they draw prolifick air. *Dryden.*

To BORE. *v. n.* [with farriers.] Is when a horſe carries his noſe near the ground. *Dict.*

BORE. *n. ſ.* [from the verb.]

1. The hole made by boring.

Into hollow engines long and round,
Thick ramm'd, at th' other *bore* with touch of fire
Dilated, and infuriate. *Milton's Paradiſe Loſt, b.* vi.

We took a cylindrical pipe of glaſs, whoſe *bore* was about a quarter of an inch in diameter. *Boyle.*

2. The inſtrument with which a hole is bored.

So ſhall that hole be fit for the file, or ſquare *bore*, if the curioſity of your propoſed work cannot allow it to paſs without filing. *Moxon's Mechanical Exerciſes.*

3. The ſize of any hole.

Our careful monarch ſtands in perſon by,
This new-caſt cannon's firmneſs to explore;
The ſtrength of big-corn'd powder loves to try,
And ball and cartridge ſorts for every *bore*. *Dryden.*

It will beſt appear in the *bores* of wind inſtruments; therefore cauſe pipes to be made with a ſingle, double, and ſo on, to a ſextuple *bore*; and mark what tone every one giveth. *Bacon.*

BORE. The *preterite* of *bear*.

The father *bore* it with undaunted ſoul,
Like one who durſt his deſtiny controul;
Yet with becoming grief he *bore* his part,
Reſign'd his ſon, but not reſign'd his heart. *Dryden.*

'Twas my fate
To kill my father, and pollute his bed,
By marrying her who *bore* me. *Dryden and Lee's OEdipus.*

BO'REAL. *adj.* [*borealis*, Lat.] Northern.

Crete's ample fields diminiſh to our eye;
Before the *boreal* blaſts the veſſels fly. *Pope's Odyſſey.*

*BO'REAS. n. ſ.* [Lat.] The north wind.

*Boreas*, and Cærias, and Argeſtas loud,
And Thraſcias, rend the woods, and ſeas up-turn.
*Milton's Paradiſe Loſt, b.* x. *l.* 699.

BO'REE. *n. ſ.* A kind of dance.

Dick could neatly dance a jig,
But Tom was beſt at *borees*. *Swift.*

BO'RER. *n. ſ.* [from *bore.*] A piercer; an inſtrument to make holes with.

The maſter-bricklayer muſt try all the foundations, with a *borer*, ſuch as well-diggers uſe, to try what ground they have. *Moxon's Mechanical Exerciſes.*

BORN. The *participle paſſive* of *bear*.

Their charge was always *born* by the queen, and duly paid out of the exchequer. *Bacon.*

The great men were enabled to oppreſs their inferiours; and their followers were *born* out and countenanced in wicked actions. *Sir John Davies on Ireland.*

Upon ſome occaſions, Clodius may be bold and inſolent, *born* away by his paſſion. *Swift.*

To be BORN. *v. n. paſſ.* [derived from the word to *bear*, in the ſenſe of *bringing forth*; as, my mother *bore* me twenty years ago; or, I was *born* twenty years ago.]

1. To come into life.

When we are *born*, we cry, that we are come
To this great ſtage of fools. *Shakeſp. King Lear.*

Nor nature's law with fruitleſs ſorrow mourn,
But die, O mortal man! for thou waſt *born*. *Prior.*

All that are *born* into the world, are ſurrounded with bodies, that perpetually and diverſly affect them. *Locke.*

2. It is uſually ſpoken with regard to circumſtances; as, he was *born* a prince; he was *born* to empire; he was *born* for greatneſs; that is, formed at the birth.

The ſtranger that dwelleth with you, ſhall be unto you as one *born* among you, and thou ſhalt love him as thyſelf. *Levit.* xix. 34.

Yet man is *born* unto trouble, as the ſparks fly upward. *Job*, v. 7.

A friend loveth at all times, and a brother is *born* for adverſity. *Prov.* xvii. 17.

The new *born* babe by nurſes overlaid. *Dryden.*

Either of you knights may well deſerve
A princeſs *born*; and ſuch is ſhe you ſerve. *Dryden's Fab.*

Two riſing creſts his royal head adorn;
*Born* from a god, himſelf to godhead *born*. *Dryden's Æn.*

Both muſt alike from heav'n derive their light;
Theſe *born* to judge, as well as thoſe to write. *Pope.*

For all mankind alike require their grace;
All *born* to want; a miſerable race! *Pope's Odyſſey.*

I was *born* to a good eſtate, although it now turneth to little account. *Swift's Story of an injured Lady.*

Their lands are let to lords, who never deſigned to be tenants, naturally murmur at the payment of rents, as a ſubſerviency they were not *born* to. *Swift.*

3. It has uſually the particle *of* before the mother.

Be bloody, bold, and reſolute, laugh to ſcorn
The pow'r of man; for none *of* woman *born*
Shall harm Macbeth. *Shakeſp. Macbeth.*

I being *born of* my father's firſt wife, and ſhe *of* his third, ſhe converſes with me rather like a daughter than a ſiſter. *Tatler.*

BO'ROUGH. *n. ſ.* [bophoe, Saxon.]

1. It ſignified anciently a ſurety, or a man bound for others.

A *borough*, as I here uſe it, and as the old laws ſtill uſe, is not a borough town, that is, a franchiſed town; but a main pledge of an hundred free perſons, therefore called a free *borough*, or, as you ſay, *franeplegium*. For *borth*, in old Saxon, ſignifieth a pledge or ſurety; and yet it is ſo uſed with us in ſome ſpeeches, as Chaucer faith, *St. John to Borch*; that is, for aſſurance and warranty. *Spenſer's Ireland.*

2. A town with a corporation.

BO'ROUGH *Engliſh*, is a cuſtomary deſcent of lands or tenements, whereby, in all places where this cuſtom holds, lands and tenements deſcend to the youngeſt ſon; or, if the owner have no iſſue, to his youngeſt brother. *Cowel.*

BO'RREL. *n. ſ.* [it is explained by *Junius* without etymology.] A mean fellow.

Siker thou ſpeak'ſt like a lewd lorrel,
Of heaven, to deemen ſo:
Howbe I am but rude and *borrel*,
Yet nearer ways I know. *Spenſer's Paſt.*

To BO'RROW. *v. a.* [*borgen*, Dutch; bopgian, Saxon.]

1. To take ſomething from another upon credit.

He *borrowed* a box of the ear of the Engliſhman, and ſwore he would pay him again when he was able. *Shakeſp. Merchant of Venice.*

We have *borrowed* money for the king's tribute, and that upon our lands and vineyards. *Neh.* v. 4.

2. To aſk of another the uſe of ſomething for a time.

Then he ſaid, go, *borrow* thee veſſels abroad of all thy neighbours. 2 *Kings*, iv. 3.

Where darkneſs and ſurprize made conqueſt cheap!
Where virtue *borrowed* the arms of chance,
And ſtruck a random blow! *Dryden's Span. Friar.*

3. To take ſomething of another.

A *borrow'd* title haſt thou bought too dear;
Why didſt thou tell me that thou wert a king? *Sh. H.* IV.

They may *borrow* ſomething of inſtruction even from their paſt guilt. *Decay of Piety.*

I was engaged in the tranſlation of Virgil, from whom I have *borrowed* only two months. *Dryden's Dufreſn.*

Theſe verbal ſigns they ſometimes *borrow* from others, and ſometimes make themſelves; as one may obſerve among the new names children give to things. *Locke.*

Some perſons of bright parts have narrow remembrance; for having riches of their own, they are not ſolicitous to *borrow*. *Watts's Improvement of the Mind.*

4. To uſe as one's own, though not belonging to one.

Unkind and cruel, to deceive your ſon
In *borrow'd* ſhapes, and his embrace to ſhun. *Dryden's Æn.*

BO'RROW. *n. ſ.* [from the verb.] The thing borrowed.

Yet of your royal preſence I'll adventure
The *borrow* of a week. *Shakeſp. Winter's Tale.*

BO'RROWER. *n. ſ.* [from *borrow.*]

1. He that borrows; he that takes money upon truſt.

His talk is of nothing but of his poverty, for fear belike leſt I ſhould have proved a young *borrower*. *Sidney, b.* ii.

Neither a *borrower* nor a lender be;
For loan oft loſes both itſelf and friend,
And borrowing dulls the edge of huſbandry. *Hamlet.*

Go not, my horſe, the better;
I muſt become a *borrower* of the night
For a dark hour or twain. *Shakeſp. Macbeth.*

But you invert the cov'nants of her truſt,
And harſhly deal, like an ill *borrower*,
With that which you receiv'd on other terms. *Milton.*

2. He that takes what is another's, and uſes it as his own.

Some ſay, that I am a great *borrower*; however, none of my creditors have challenged me for it. *Pope.*

BO'SCAGE. *n. ſ.* [*boſcage*, Fr.] Wood, or woodlands; repreſentation of woods.

We bent our courſe thither, where we ſaw the appearance of land; and, the next day, we might plainly diſcern that it was a land flat to our ſight, and full of *boſcage*, which made it ſhew the more dark. *Bacon's N. Atlantis.*

Chearful paintings in feaſting and banqueting rooms; graver ſtories in galleries; landſkips and *boſcage*, and ſuch wild works, in open terraces, or ſummer-houſes. *Wotton.*

BO'SKY. *adj.* [*boſque*, Fr.] Woody.

And with each end of thy blue bow do'ſt crown
My *boſky* acres, and my unſhrub'd down. *Shakeſp. Tempeſt.*

I know each land, and every alley green,
Dingle, or buſhy dell, of this wild wood,
And every *boſky* bourn from ſide to ſide. *Milton.*

BO'SOM. *n. ſ.* [boſme, boſom, Saxon.]

1. The embrace of the arms holding any thing to the breaſt.

2. The breaſt; the heart.

Our

Borrel n. s. a poor rude illiterate person, who is of no other Service to the public than to get Chil:dren. So it is used in Chaucer. Unless you would derive it from poraille in the same Author which Signifies the low or poor people  Jun

Siker thou speakst like a lewd lorell
Of heaven to deemen so
How be I am but rude & borrell
Yet nearer ways I know   Spens.

~~Boss~~ 47 ~~[illegible]~~ a small sea fish
Of round fish there are smelts
~~ruller couper~~ and Boss. Carew

Boted adj. troubled with the bots, a kind of
Worm in horses

So are the horses of the enemy
In general boted & brought low
The better part of ours are full of rest
Shak.

IL facing 3K2r

Our good old friend,
Lay comforts to your *bosom*; and bestow
Your needful counsel to our businesses. *Shakesp. King Lear.*

3. An inclosure.

Unto laws thus made and received by a whole church, they which live within the *bosom* of that church, must not think it a matter indifferent, either to yield, or not to yield, obedience. *Hooker, b.* ii.

4. The folds of the dress that cover the breast.

Put now thy hand into thy *bosom*; and he put his hand into his *bosom*: and when he took it out, behold his hand was leprous as snow. *Exodus*, iv. 6.

5. The tender affections; kindness; favour.

Whose age has charms in it, whose title more,
To pluck the common *bosoms* on his side. *Shakesp. K. Lear.*

To whom the great Creator thus reply'd:
O Son, in whom my soul hath chief delight;
Son of my *bosom*, Son who art alone
My word, my wisdom, and effectual might. *Par. Lost, b.* iii.

6. Inclination; desire.

If you can pace your wisdom
In that good path that I could wish it go,
You shall have your *bosom* on this wretch.
*Shakesp. Measure for Measure.*

Bosom, in composition, implies intimacy; confidence; a fondness.

No more that thane of Cawder shall deceive
Our *bosom-int'rest*; go, pronounce his death. *Macbeth.*

This Antonio,
Being the *bosom-lover* of my lord,
Must needs be like my lord. *Shakesp. Merchant of Venice.*

Those domestick traitors, *bosom-thieves*,
Whom custom hath call'd wives; the readiest helps
To betray the heady husbands, rob the easy.
*Ben. Johnson's Catiline.*

He sent for his *bosom-friends*, with whom he most confidently consulted, and shewed the paper to them; the contents whereof he could not conceive. *Clarendon.*

The fourth privilege of friendship is that which is here specified in the text, a communication of secrets. A *bosom-secret*, and a *bosom-friend*, are usually put together. *South.*

She who was a *bosom-friend* of her royal mistress, he calls an insolent woman, the worst of her sex. *Addison's Whig Exam.*

To Bo'som. *v. a.* [from the noun.]

1. To inclose in the bosom.

*Bosom* up my counsel;
You'll find it wholesome. *Shakesp. Henry* VIII.

I do not think my sister so to seek,
Or so unprincipl'd in virtue's book,
And the sweet peace that *bosoms* goodness ever. *Milton.*

2. To conceal in privacy.

The groves, the fountains, and the flow'rs,
That open now their choicest *bosom'd* smells,
Reserv'd for night, and kept for thee in store. *Par. Lost, b.* v.

Towers and battlements it sees,
*Bosom'd* high in tufted trees,
Where perhaps some beauty lies,
The cynosure of neighbouring eyes. *Milton.*

To happy convents, *bosom'd* deep in vines,
Where slumber abbots, purple as their wines. *Pope.*

Bo'son. *n. s.* [corrupted from *boatswain.*]

The barks upon the billows ride,
The master will not stay;
The merry *boson* from his side
His whistle takes, to check and chide
The ling'ring lad's delay. *Dryden's Albion.*

Boss. *n. s.* [*bosse*, Fr.]

1. A stud; an ornament raised above the rest of the work; a shining prominence.

What signifies beauty, strength, youth, fortune, embroidered furniture, or gaudy *bosses*? *L'Estrange.*

This ivory was intended for the *bosses* of a bridle, was laid up for a prince, and a woman of Caria or Mæonia dyed it.
*Pope's Notes on Iliad.*

2. The part rising in the midst of any thing.

He runneth upon him, even on his neck, upon the thick *bosses* of his bucklers. *Job*, xv. 26.

3. A thick body of any kind.

A *boss* made of wood, with an iron hook, to hang on the laths, or on a ladder, in which the labourer puts the mortar at the britches of the tiles. *Moxon's Mechanical Exercises.*

If a close appulse be made by the lips, then is framed M; if by the *boss* of the tongue to the palate, near the throat, then K.
*Holder's Elements of Speech.*

Bo'ssage. *n. s.* [in architecture.]

1. Any stone that has a projecture, and is laid in a place in a building, to be afterwards carved.

2. Rustick work, which consists of stones, which seem to advance beyond the naked of a building, by reason of indentures or channels left in the joinings: these are chiefly in the corners of edifices, and called rustick quoins. *Builder's Dict.*

Bo'svel. *n. s.* A species of *crowfoot*; which see.

Bota'nical. } *adj.* [from βοτάνη, an herb.] Relating to herbs;
Bota'nick. } skilled in herbs.

Some *botanical* criticks tell us, the poets have not rightly followed the traditions of antiquity, in metamorphosing the sisters of Phaeton into poplars. *Addison on Italy.*

Bo'tanist. *n. s.* [from *botany.*] One skilled in plants; one who studies the various species of plants.

The uliginous lacteous matter, taken notice of by that diligent *botanist*, was only a collection of corals. *Woodward.*

Then spring the living herbs, beyond the power
Of *botanist* to number up their tribes. *Thomson's Spring.*

Botano'logy. *n. s.* [βοτανολογία.] A discourse upon plants. *D.*

BO'TANY. *n. s.* [from βοτάνη, an herb.] The science of plants; that part of natural history which relates to vegetables.

BOTA'RGO. *n. s.* [*botarga*, Span.] A relishing sort of food, made of the roes of the mullet fish; much used on the coasts of the Mediterranean, as an incentive to drink. *Chambers.*

BOTCH. *n. s.* [*bozza*, pronounced *botza*, Ital.]

1. A swelling, or eruptive discoloration of the skin.

Time, which rots all, and makes *botches* pox,
And, plodding on, must make a calf an ox,
Hath made a lawyer. *Donne.*

*Botches* and blains must all his flesh imboss,
And all his people. *Milton's Paradise Lost, b.* xii. *l.* 180.

It proves far more incommodious, which, if it were propelled in boils, *botches*, or ulcers, as in the scurvy, would rather conduce to health. *Harvey on Consumptions.*

2. A part in any work ill finished, so as to appear worse than the rest.

With him,
To leave no rubs or *botches* in the work,
Fleance, his son, must embrace the fate. *Shakesp. Macbeth.*

3. An adscititious, adventitious part clumsily added.

If both those words are not notorious *botches*, I am much deceived; though the French translator thinks otherways.
*Dryden's Dedication, Æneid.*

A comma ne'er could claim
A place in any British name;
Yet, making here a perfect *botch*,
Thrusts your poor vowel from his notch. *Swift.*

To Botch. *v. a.* [from the noun.]

1. To mend or patch cloaths clumsily.

Their coats, from *botching* newly brought, are torn. *Dryden.*

2. To mend any thing awkwardly.

To *botch* up what th' had torn and rent,
Religion and the government. *Hudibras, p.* iii. *c.* ii.

3. To put together unsuitably, or unskilfully; to make up of unsuitable pieces.

Go with me to my house,
And hear thou there, how many fruitless pranks
This ruffian hath *botch'd* up, that thou thereby
May smile at this. *Shakesp. Twelfth Night.*

Her speech is nothing,
Yet the unshaped use of it doth move
The hearers to collection; they aim at it,
And *botch* the words up fit to their own thoughts. *Hamlet.*

For treason *botch'd* in rhyme will be thy bane;
Rhime is the rock on which thou art to wreck. *Dryden.*

4. To mark with botches.

Young Hylas, *botch'd* with stains too foul to name,
In cradle here renews his youthful frame. *Garth's Dispens.*

Bo'tcher. *n. s.* [from *botch.*] A mender of old cloaths; the same to a taylor as a cobler to a shoemaker.

He was a *botcher*'s prentice in Paris, from whence he was whipt for getting the sheriff's fool with child.
*Shakesp. All's well that ends well.*

*Botchers* left old cloaths in the lurch,
And fell to turn and patch the church. *Hudibras, c.* ii.

Bo'tchy. *adj.* [from *botch.*] Marked with botches.

And those boils did run—say so—Did not the general run?
Were not that a *botchy* sore? *Shakesp. Troilus and Cress.*

Bote. *n. s.* [bote, Sax. a word now out of use.]

1. A compensation or amends for a man slain, which is bound to another. *Cowel.*

2. It was used for any payment.

Both. *adj.* [batu, batþa, Sax.] The two; as well the one as the other. *Et l'un & l'autre*, Fr. It is used only of two.

And the next day, *both* morning and afternoon, he was kept by our party. *Sidney, b.* ii.

Moses and the prophets, Christ and his apostles, were in their times all preachers of God's truth; some by word, some by writing; some by *both*. *Hooker, b.* v. § 19.

Which of them shall I take?
*Both*? one? or neither? neither can be enjoy'd,
If *both* remain alive. *Shakesp. King Lear.*

Two lovers cannot share a single bed;
As therefore *both* are equal in degree,
The lot of *both* he left to destiny. *Dryden's Fables.*

A Venus and a Helen have been seen,
*Both* perjur'd wives, the goddess and the queen. *Granville.*

Both. *conj.* [from the adjective.] As well: it has the conjunction *and* to correspond with it.

*Both* the boy was worthy to be prais'd,
*And* Stimichon has often made me long,
To hear, like him, ſo ſoft, ſo ſweet a ſong. *Dryden's Paſt.*

Bo'TRYOID. *adj.* [βοτρυοειδὴς.] Having the form of a bunch of grapes.

The outſide is thick ſet with *botryoid* efflorescencies, or ſmall knobs, yellow, bluiſh, and purple; all of a ſhining metallick hue. *Woodward of Foſſils.*

Bots. *n. ſ.* [*without a ſingular.*] A ſpecies of ſmall worms in the entrails of horſes; anſwering, perhaps, to the *aſcarides* in human bodies.

Peaſe and beans are as dank here as a dog, and that is the next way to give poor jades the *bots:* this houſe is turned upſide down ſince Robin the oſtler died. *Shakeſp. Henry* IV. *p.* i.

BO'TTLE. *n. ſ.* [*bouteille*, Fr.]

1. A ſmall veſſel of glaſs, or other matter, with a narrow mouth, to put liquour in.

The ſhepherd's homely curds,
His cold thin drink out of his leather *bottle*,
Is far beyond a prince's delicates. *Shakeſp. Henry* VI. *p.* iii.

Many have a manner, after other men's ſpeech, to ſhake their heads. A great officer would ſay, it was as men ſhake a *bottle*, to ſee if there was any wit in their heads, or no. *Bacon.*

Then if thy ale in glaſs thou wouldſt confine,
Let thy clean *bottle* be entirely dry. *King's Molly of Mount.*

He threw into the enemy's ſhips earthen *bottles* filled with ſerpents, which put the crew in diſorder, and made them fly. *Arbuthnot on Coins.*

2. A quantity of wine uſually put into a bottle; a quart.

Sir, you ſhall ſtay, and take t'other *bottle*. *Spect.* N° 462.

3. A quantity of hay or graſs bundled up.

Methinks I have a great deſire to a *bottle* of hay; good hay, ſweet hay, hath no fellow. *Shakeſp. Midſum. Night's Dream.*

But I ſhould wither in one day, and paſs
To a lock of hay, that am a *bottle* of graſs. *Donne.*

To Bo'TTLE. *v. a.* [from the noun.] To incloſe in bottles.

You may have it a moſt excellent cyder royal, to drink or to *bottle*. *Mortimer's Husbandry.*

When a hogſhead of wine is to be *bottled* off, waſh your bottles immediately before you begin; but be ſure not to drain them. *Swift's Directions to the Butler.*

Bo'TTLE is often compounded with other words; as, *bottle-friend*, a drinking friend; *bottle-companion.*

Sam, who is a very good *bottle-companion*, has been the diverſion of his friends. *Addiſon. Spect.* N° 89.

Bo'TTLEFLOWER. *n. ſ.* [*cyanus*, Lat.] A plant.

~~It hath a ſquamoſe hairy calyx; the diſk of the flower is almoſt plain, but the outer florets, round the borders, are large, tubulous, and deeply cut in; theſe outer florets are always barren; but the inner florets have a ſingle naked ſeed ſucceeding each.~~ The ſpecies are, ~~1. The greater broad leaved *blue bottle*, commonly~~ called *globe-flower*. ~~2. The greater narrow leaved *blue bottle*, or *globe flower*. 3. The purple *ſweet ſultan*.~~ 4. *Corn-bottle*, with a white flower. The firſt and ſecond ſorts are abiding plants, which increaſe greatly by their creeping roots. The *ſweet ſultans* will begin to flower, and continue till the froſt prevents them. The *corn-bottles* were alſo annuals, which, for the diverſity of their flowers, were propagated in gardens; but ~~of late years they are almoſt excluded.~~ *Millar.*

Bo'TTLESCREW. *n. ſ.* [from *bottle* and *ſcrew.*] A ſcrew to pull out the cork.

A good butler always breaks off the point of his *bottleſcrew* in two days, by trying which is hardeſt, the point of the ſcrew, or the neck of the bottle. *Swift.*

BO'TTOM. *n. ſ.* [botm, Saxon; *bodem*, Germ.]

1. The loweſt part of any thing.
2. The ground under the water.

Shallow brooks that flow'd ſo clear,
The *bottom* did the top appear. *Dryden.*

3. The foundation; the ground-work.

On this ſuppoſition my reaſonings proceed, and cannot be affected by objections which are far from being built on the ſame *bottom*. *Atterbury.*

4. A dale; a valley; a low ground.

In the purlieus ſtands a ſheep-cote,
Weſt of this place; down in the neighbour *bottom*. *Shakeſp. As you like it.*

On both the ſhores of that fruitful *bottom*, which I have before mentioned, are ſtill to be ſeen the marks of ancient edifices. *Addiſon on Italy.*

Equal convexity could never be ſeen: the inhabitants of ſuch an earth could have only the proſpect of a little circular plane, which would appear to have an acclivity on all ſides; ſo that every man would fancy himſelf the loweſt, and that he always dwelt and moved in a *bottom*. *Bentley.*

5. The part moſt remote from the view; the deepeſt part.

His propoſals and arguments ſhould with freedom be examined to the *bottom*, that, if there be any miſtake in them, no body may be miſled by his reputation. *Locke.*

6. Bound; limit.

But there's no *bottom*, none,
In my voluptuouſneſs. *Shakeſp. Macbeth.*

7. The utmoſt extent or profundity of any man's capacity, whether deep or ſhallow.

As I return, I will fetch off theſe juſtices: I do ſee the *bottom* of Juſtice Shallow: how ſubject we old men are to the vice of lying! *Shakeſp Henry* IV. *p.* ii.

8. The laſt reſort; the remoteſt cauſe; firſt motion.

He wrote many things which are not publiſhed in his name; and was at the *bottom* of many excellent counſels, in which he did not appear. *Addiſon.*

9. A ſhip; a veſſel for navigation.

A bawbling veſſel was he captain of,
With which, ſuch ſcathful grapple did he make
With the moſt noble *bottom* of our fleet. *Shakeſp. T. Night.*

My ventures are not in one *bottom* truſted;
Nor to one place. *Shakeſp. Merchant of Venice.*

We have memory, not of one ſhip that ever returned, and but of thirteen perſons only, at ſeveral times, that choſe to return in our *bottoms*. *Bacon's New Atlantis.*

He's a fooliſh ſeaman,
That when his ſhip is ſinking, will not
Unlade his hopes into another *bottom*. *Denham's Sophy.*

He puts to ſea upon his own *bottom*; holds the ſtern himſelf; and now, if ever, we may expect new diſcoveries. *Norris.*

He ſpreads his canvas, with his pole he ſteers,
The freights of flitting ghoſts in his thin *bottom* bears. *Dryd.*

10. A chance; an adventure; or ſecurity.

He began to ſay, that himſelf and the prince were too much to venture in one *bottom*. *Clarendon, b.* viii.

We are embarked with them on the ſame *bottom*, and muſt be partakers of their happineſs or miſery. *Spect.* N° 273.

11. A ball of thread wound up together.

This whole argument will be like *bottoms* of thread, cloſe wound up. *Bacon's War with Spain.*

The ſilkworms finiſh their *bottoms* in about fifteen days. *Mortimer's Husbandry.*

Each Chriſtmas they accounts did clear,
And wound their *bottom* round the year. *Prior.*

12. BOTTOM *of a lane.* The loweſt end.
13. BOTTOM *of beer.* The grounds, or dregs.

To Bo'TTOM. *v. a.* [from the noun.]

1. To build upon; to fix upon as a ſupport.

They may have ſomething of obſcurity, as being *bottomed* upon, and fetched from the true nature of the things. *Hale.*

Pride has a very ſtrong foundation in the mind; it is *bottomed* upon ſelf-love. *Collier on Pride.*

The grounds upon which we *bottom* our reaſoning, are but a part; ſomething is left out, which ſhould go into the reckoning. *Locke.*

Every action is ſuppoſed to be *bottomed* upon ſome principle. *Atterbury.*

2. To wind upon ſomething; to twiſt thread round ſomething.

Therefore, as you unwind your love for him,
Leſt it ſhould ravel, and be good to none,
You muſt provide to *bottom* it on me. *Shakeſp. T. G. of Ver.*

To Bo'TTOM. *v. n.* To reſt upon as its ſupport.

Find out upon what foundation any propoſition, advanced, *bottoms*; and obſerve the intermediate ideas, by which it is joined to that foundation upon which it is erected. *Locke.*

Bo'TTOMED. *adj.* [from *bottom.*] Having a bottom; it is uſually compounded.

There being prepared a number of *flat-bottomed* boats, to tranſport the land-forces, under the wing and protection of the great navy. *Bacon's War with Spain.*

Bo'TTOMLESS. *adj.* [from *bottom.*] Without a bottom; fathomleſs.

Wickedneſs may well be compared to a *bottomleſs* pit, into which it is eaſier to keep one's ſelf from falling, than, being fallen, to give one's ſelf any ſtay from falling infinitely. *Sidney.*

Is not my ſorrow deep, having no bottom?
Then be my paſſions *bottomleſs* with them. *Shakeſp. T. Andr.*

Him the Almighty pow'r
Hurl'd headlong, flaming from th' etherial ſky,
To *bottomleſs* perdition. *Milton's Par. Loſt, b.* i. *l.* 47.

Bo'TTOMRY. *n. ſ.* [in navigation and commerce.] The act of borrowing money on a ſhip's bottom; that is, by engaging the veſſel for the repayment of it, ſo as that, if the ſhip miſcarry, the lender loſes the money advanced; but, if it arrives ſafe at the end of the voyage, he is to repay the money lent, with a certain premium or intereſt agreed on; and this on pain of forfeiting the ſhip. *Harris.*

*BOUCHET*. *n. ſ.* [French.] A ſort of pear. *Dict.*

Boud. *n. ſ.* An inſect which breeds in malt; called alſo a *weevil.* *Dict.*

To Bouge. *v. n.* [*bouge*, Fr.] To ſwell out.

Bough. *n. ſ.* [boᵹ, Saxon; the *gh* is mute.] An arm or large ſhoot of a tree, bigger than a branch, yet not always diſtinguiſhed from it.

He ſaw a vine-labourer, that, finding a *bough* broken, took a branch of the ſame *bough*, and tied it about the place broken. *Sidney, b.* ii.

Their lord and patron loud did him proclaim,
And at his feet their laurel *boughs* did throw. *Fairy Q. b.* i.

From

The Caledonian Oak begirt with Lions of
his own Stem: The Lillies and the Roses red
and white did bougeon round about him

Howel



IL facing 3K2v

Bough, a gibbet or gallows

Perhaps it might be on the bough of the nearest tree they came to that was strong enough for the purpose

Some who have not deserved Judgment of death tho otherwise perhaps offending have been for their goods sake caught up and carried straight to the bough a thing indeed very piti ful & horrible   Spens. Irel.

He bar'd an ancient Oak of all her boughs
Then on a rising ground the trunk he plac'd
Which with the spoils of his dead foe he grac'd
Dry. Æ.

From the *bough*
She gave him of that fair enticing fruit. *Parad. Loſt, b.* ix.

As the dove's flight did guide Æneas, now
May thine conduct me to the golden *bough*. *Denham.*

Under ſome fav'rite myrtle's ſhady *boughs*,
They ſpeak their paſſions in repeated vows. *Roſcommon.*

See how, on every *bough*, the birds expreſs,
In their ſweet notes, their happineſs. *Dryden's Indian Emp.*

'Twas all her joy the rip'ning fruits to tend,
And ſee the *boughs* with happy burdens bend. *Pope.*

BOUGHT. preter. of *to buy*; ~~which see~~.

BOUGHT. *n. ſ.* [from *to bow*.]

1. A twiſt; a link; a knot.

His huge long tail wound up in hundred folds,
Whoſe wreathed *boughts* whenever he unfolds,
And thick entangled knots adown does ſlack. *Fairy Q. b.* i.

Immortal verſe,
Such as the meeting ſoul may pierce
In notes, with many a winding *bought*
Of linked ſweetneſs, long drawn out. *Milton.*

2. A flexure.

The flexure of the joints is not the ſame in elephants as in other quadrupeds, but nearer unto thoſe of a man; the *bought* of the fore-legs not directly backward, but laterally, and ſomewhat inward. *Brown's Vulgar Errours, b.* iii. *c.* i.

BOUILLON. *n. ſ.* [French.] Broth; ſoup; any thing made to be ſupped: a term uſed in cookery.

BO'ULDER *Walls.* [in architecture.] Walls built of round flints or pebbles, laid in a ſtrong mortar; uſed where the ſea has a beach caſt up, or where there are plenty of flints. *Builder's Dict.*

To BOULT. *v. a.* See To BOLT.

To BOUNCE. *v. n.* [a word formed, ſays *Skinner*, from the ſound.]

1. To fall or fly againſt any thing with great force, ſo as to rebound.

The fright awaken'd Arcite with a ſtart,
Againſt his boſom *bounc'd* his heaving heart. *Dryden.*

Juſt as I was putting out my light, another *bounces* as hard as he can knock. *Swift's Bickerſtaff detected.*

2. To ſpring; to make a ſudden leap.

High nonſenſe is like beer in a bottle, which has, in reality, no ſtrength and ſpirit, but frets, and flies, and *bounces*, and imitates the paſſions of a much nobler liquour. *Add. Whig Exam.*

Rous'd by the noiſe,
And muſical clatter,
They *bounce* from their neſt,
No longer will tarry. *Swift.*

Out *bounc'd* the maſtiff of the triple head;
Away the hare with double ſwiftneſs fled. *Swift.*

3. To boaſt; to bully: a ſenſe uſed only in familiar ſpeech.

4. To be bold, or ſtrong.

Forſooth the *bouncing* Amazon,
Your buſkin'd miſtreſs, and your warriour love,
To Theſeus muſt be wedded. *Shakeſp. Midſum. Night's Dr.*

BOUNCE. *n. ſ.* [from the verb.]

1. A ſtrong ſudden blow.

The *bounce* burſt ope the door; the ſcornful fair
Relentleſs look'd, and ſaw him beat his quiv'ring feet in air. *Dryden.*

2 A leap; a start.

~~2.~~ 3. A ſudden crack or noiſe. as by a quick disruption

What cannoneer begot this luſty blood?
He ſpeaks plain cannon fire, and ſmoke, and *bounce*;
He gives the baſtinado with his tongue. *Shakeſp. K. John.*

Two hazel-nuts I threw into the flame,
And to each nut I gave a ſweetheart's name;
This with the loudeſt *bounce* me ſore amaz'd,
That in a flame of brighteſt colour blaz'd. *Gay.*

~~3.~~ 4. A boaſt; a threat; in low language.

BO'UNCER. *n. ſ.* [from *bounce*.] A boaſter; a bully; an empty threatner.

BOUND. *n. ſ.* [from *bind*.]

1. A limit; a boundary; that by which any thing is terminated.

Illimitable ocean! without *bound*;
Without dimenſion; where length, breadth, and height,
And time, and place, are loſt. *Paradiſe Loſt, b.* ii. *l.* 892.

Thoſe vaſt Scythian regions were ſeparated by the common natural *bounds*, of rivers, ~~lakes~~, mountains, woods, or marſhes. *Temple.*

Indus and Ganges, our wide empire's *bounds*,
Swell their dy'd currents with their natives wounds. *Dryden.*

Through all th' infernal *bounds*,
Which flaming Phlegethon ſurrounds,
Sad Orpheus ſought his conſort loſt. *Pope's St. Cæcilia.*

2. A limit by which any excurſion is reſtrained.

Hath he ſet *bounds* between their love and me?
I am their mother, who ſhall bar me from them. *Rich.* III.

Stronger and fiercer by reſtraint he roars,
And knows no *bound*, but makes his pow'r his ſhores. *Denh.*

Any *bounds* made with body, even adamantine walls, are far from putting a ſtop to the mind, in its farther progreſs in ſpace. *Locke.*

3. [from *to bound, v. n.*] A leap; a jump; a ſpring.

Do but note a wild and wanton herd,
Or race of youthful and unhandled colts,
Fetching mad *bounds*, bellowing, and neighing loud. *Shakeſp. Merchant of Venice.*

The horſes ſtarted with a ſudden *bound*,
And flung the reins and chariot to the ground. *Addiſ. Ovid.*

Dext'rous he 'ſcapes the coach with nimble *bounds*,
Whilſt ev'ry honeſt tongue ſtop thief reſounds. *Gay.*

4. A rebound; the leap of ſomething flying back by the force of the blow.

Theſe inward diſguſts are but the firſt *bound* of this ball of contention. *Decay of Piety.*

To BOUND. *v. a.* [from the noun.]

1. To limit; to terminate.

A lofty tow'r, and ſtrong on every ſide,
With treble walls, which Phlegethon ſurrounds,
Whoſe firy flood the burning empire *bounds*. *Dryden's Æn.*

2. To reſtrain; to confine.

Take but degree away, untune that ſtring,
The *bounded* waters
Would lift their boſoms higher than the ſhores,
And make a ſop of all this ſolid globe. *Shakeſp. Tr. and Cr.*

To BOUND. *v. n.* [*bondir*, Fr.]

1. To jump; to ſpring; to move forward by leaps.

My mother's blood
Runs on the dexter cheek, and this ſiniſter
*Bounds* in my ſire's. *Shakeſp. Troilus and Creſſida.*

Torriſmond appear'd,
Gave me his hand, and led me lightly o'er,
Leaping and *bounding* on the billows heads. *Dryden.*

Before his lord the ready ſpaniel *bounds*,
Panting with hope, he tries the furrow'd grounds. *Pope.*

When ſudden through the woods a *bounding* ſtag
Ruſh'd headlong down, and plung'd amidſt the river. *Rowe.*

Warbling to the vary'd ſtrain, advance
Two ſprightly youths, to form the *bounding* dance. *Pope.*

2. To rebound; to fly back by repercuſſion.

Mark then a *bounding* valour in our Engliſh;
That being dead, like to the bullets grazing,
Breaks out into a ſecond courſe of miſchief. *Shakeſp. H.* V.

To BOUND. *v. a.* To make to bound.

If I might buffet for my love, or *bound* my horſe for her favours, I would lay on like a butcher, and ſit like a jackanapes, never off. *Shakeſp. Henry* V.

If love, ambitious, ſought a match of birth,
Whoſe veins *bound* richer blood than lady Blanch. *Rich.* III.

BOUND. *participle paſſive* of *bind*.

Nay, ſaid Pamela, none ſhall take that office from myſelf, being ſo much *bound* as I am for my education. *Sidney, b.* ii.

This is Antonio,
To whom I am ſo infinitely *bound*.—
—You ſhould in all ſenſe be much *bound* to him;
For, as I hear, he was much *bound* for you. *Merch. of Ven.*

The gentleman is learn'd, a moſt rare ſpeaker,
To nature none more *bound*. *Shakeſp. Henry* VIII.

The biſhops of Hungary, being wonderfully rich, were *bound* to keep great numbers of horſemen, which they uſed to bring into the field. *Knolles's Hiſtory of the Turks.*

They ſummoned the governour to deliver it to them, or elſe they would not leave one ſtone upon another. To which the governour made no other reply, than that he was not *bound* to repair it; but, however, he would, by God's help, keep the ground afterwards. *Clarendon, b.* viii.

BOUND. *adj.* [a word of doubtful etymology.] Deſtined; intending to come to any place.

His be that care, whom moſt it doth concern,
Said he; but whither with ſuch haſty flight
Art thou now *bound*? for well might I diſcern
Great cauſe, that carries thee ſo ſwift and light. *Fairy Q. b.* ii.

To be *bound* for a port one deſires extremely, and ſail to it, with a fair gale, is very pleaſant. *Temple.*

Willing we ſought your ſhores, and hither *bound*,
The port ſo long deſir'd, at length we found. *Dryden.*

BO'UNDARY. *n. ſ.* [from *bound*.] Limit; bound.

He ſuffers the confluence and clamours of the people to paſs all *boundaries* of laws, and reverence to his authority. *K. Charles.*

Senſation and reflection are the *boundaries* of our thoughts; beyond which the mind, whatever efforts it would make, is not able to advance. *Locke.*

Great part of our ſins conſiſt in the irregularities attending the ordinary purſuits of life; ſo that our reformation muſt appear, by purſuing them within the *boundaries* of duty. *Rogers.*

BO'UNDEN. *participle paſſive* of *bind*. bound is used in all the senses of bind, bounden perhaps only for obliged; required by law, or duty.

Hereafter, in a better world than this,
I ſhall deſire more love and knowledge of you.—
—I reſt much *bounden* to you: fare you well. *Shakeſp.*

We alſo moſt humbly beſought him to accept of us as his true ſervants, by as juſt a right as ever men on earth were *bounden*. *Bacon's New Atlantis.*

To be careful for a proviſion of all neceſſaries for ourſelves, and thoſe who depend on us, is a *bounden* duty. *Rogers.*

Bo'UNDING-STONE. } *n. ſ.* A ſtone to play with.
BOUND-STONE. }

I am paſt a boy;
A ſceptre's but a play-thing, and a globe
A bigger *bounding-ſtone.* *Dryden's Don Sebaſtian.*

Bo'UNDLESSNESS. *n. ſ.* [from *boundleſs.*] Exemption from limits.

God has corrected the *boundleſsneſs* of his voluptuous deſires, by ſtinting his capacities. *South.*

Bo'UNDLESS. *adj.* [from *bound.*] Unlimited; unconfined; immeaſurable; illimitable.

Beyond the infinite and *boundleſs* reach
Of mercy, if thou didſt this deed of death,
Art thou damn'd, Hubert. *Shakeſp. King John.*

Heav'n has of right all victory deſign'd;
Whence *boundleſs* power dwells in a will confin'd. *Dryden.*

Man ſeems as *boundleſs* in his deſires, as God is in his being; and therefore nothing but God himſelf can ſatisfy him. *South.*

Though we make duration *boundleſs* as it is, we cannot extend it beyond all being. God fills eternity, and it is hard to find a reaſon, why any one ſhould doubt that he fills immenſity. *Locke.*

Some guide the courſe of wand'ring orbs on high,
Or roll the planets through the *boundleſs* ſky. *Pope.*

Bo'UNTEOUS. *adj.* [from *bounty.*] Liberal; kind; generous; munificent; beneficent: a word uſed chiefly in poetry for *bountiful.*

Every one,
According to the gift, which *bounteous* nature
Hath in him inclos'd. *Shakeſp. Macbeth.*

Her ſoul abhorring avarice,
*Bounteous*; but almoſt *bounteous* to a vice. *Dryden.*

Bo'UNTEOUSLY. *adv.* [from *bounteous.*] Liberally; generouſly; largely.

He *bounteouſly* beſtow'd unenvy'd good
On me. *Dryden's State of Innocence.*

Bo'UNTEOUSNESS. *n. ſ.* [from *bounteous.*] Munificence; liberality; kindneſs.

He filleth all things living with *bounteouſneſs.* *Pſalms.*

Bo'UNTIFUL. *adj.* [from *bounty* and *full.*]

1. Liberal; generous; munificent.

As *bountiful* as mines of India. *Shakeſp. Henry* IV. *p.* i.

If you will be rich, you muſt live frugal; if you will be popular, you muſt be *bountiful.* *Taylor's Rule of living holy.*

I am obliged to return my thanks to many, who, without conſidering the man, have been *bountiful* to the poet. *Dryden.*

God, the *bountiful* authour of our being. *Locke.*

2. It has *of* before the thing given, and *to* before the perſon receiving.

Our king ſpares nothing, to give them the ſhare of that felicity, *of* which he is ſo *bountiful to* his kingdom. *Dryden's Dufr.*

Bo'UNTIFULLY. *adv.* [from *bountiful.*] Liberally; in a bountiful manner; largely.

And now thy alms is giv'n,
And thy poor ſtarv'ling *bountifully* fed. *Donne.*

It is affirmed, that it never raineth in Egypt; the river *bountifully* requiting it in its inundation. *Brown's Vulgar Errours.*

Bo'UNTIFULNESS. *n. ſ.* [from *bountiful.*] The quality of being bountiful; generoſity.

Enriched to all *bountifulneſs.* *2 Cor.* ix. 11.

Bo'UNTIHEAD. } *n. ſ.* [from *bounty* and *head*, or *hood.* See
Bo'UNTIHEDE. } HOOD.] Goodneſs; virtue. It is now
Bo'UNTIHOOD. } wholly out of uſe.

This goodly frame of temperance,
Formerly grounded, and faſt ſettled
On firm foundation of true *bountihead.* *Fairy Q. b.* ii.

How ſhall frail pen, with fear diſparaged,
Conceive ſuch ſovereign glory, and great *bountihood*? *F. Q.*

BO'UNTY. *n. ſ.* [*bonté*, Fr.]

1. Generoſity; liberality; munificence.

We do not ſo far magnify her exceeding *bounty*, as to affirm, that ſhe bringeth into the world the ſons of men, adorned with gorgeous attire. *Hooker, b.* iii. § 4.

If you knew to whom you ſhew this honour,
I know you would be prouder of the work,
Than cuſtomary *bounty* can enforce you. *Shakeſp.*

Such moderation with thy *bounty* join,
That thou may'ſt nothing give, that is not thine. *Denham.*

Thoſe godlike men, to wanting virtue kind,
*Bounty* well plac'd preferr'd, and well deſign'd,
To all their titles. *Dryden's Juv. ſat.* v.

2. It ſeems diſtinguiſhed from charity, as a *preſent* from an *alms*; being uſed, when perſons, not abſolutely neceſſitous, receive gifts; or when gifts are given by great perſons.

Tell a miſer of *bounty* to a friend, or mercy to the poor, and he will not underſtand it. *South.*

Her majeſty did not ſee this aſſembly ſo proper to excite charity and compaſſion; though I queſtion not but her royal *bounty* will extend itſelf to them. *Addiſon. Guardian,* Nº 105.

To Bo'URGEON. *v. n.* [*bourgeonner*, Fr.] To ſprout; to ſhoot into branches; to put forth buds.

Long may the dew of heaven diſtil upon them, to make them *bourgeon*, and propagate among themſelves. *Howel.*

O that I had the fruitful heads of Hydra,
That one might *bourgeon* where another fell!
Still would I give thee work! *Dryden's Don Sebaſtian.*

BOURN. *n. ſ.* [*borne*, Fr.]

1. A bound; a limit.

*Bourn*, bound of land, tilth, vineyard, none. *Sh. Tempeſt.*

That undiſcover'd country, from whoſe *bourn*
No traveller e'er returns. *Shakeſp. Hamlet.*

Falſe,
As dice are to be wiſh'd, by one that fixes
No *bourn* 'twixt his and mine. *Shakeſp. Winter's Tale.*

I know each lane, and every alley green,
And every boſky *bourn* from ſide to ſide. *Milton.*

2. [from buꞃn, Saxon.] A brook; a torrent: whence many towns, ſeated near brooks, have names ending in *bourn.* It is not now uſed in either ſenſe; though the ſecond continues in the Scottiſh dialect.

Ne ſwelling Neptune, ne loud thund'ring Jove,
Can change my cheer, or make me ever mourn;
My little boat can ſafely paſs this perilous *bourn.* *Fairy Q.*

To BOUSE. *v. n.* [*buyſen*, Dut.] To drink laviſhly; to tope.

As he rode, he ſomewhat ſtill did eat,
And in his hand did bear a *bouſing* can,
Of which he ſipt. *Fairy Queen, b.* iii. *c.* iv.

Bo'USY. *adj.* [from *bouſe.*] Drunken.

The gueſts upon the day appointed came,
Each *bouſy* farmer, with his ſimp'ring dame. *King.*

With a long legend of romantick things,
Which in his cups the *bouſy* poet ſings. *Dryden's Juv. ſat.* x.

BOUT. *n. ſ.* [*botta*, Ital.] A turn; as much of an action as is performed at one time, without interruption; a ſingle part of any action carried on by ſucceſſive intervals.

The play began: Pas durſt not Coſma chace;
But did intend next *bout* with her to meet. *Sidney.*

Ladies, that have your feet
Unplagu'd with corns, we'll have a *bout.* *Shakeſp.*

When in your motion you are hot,
As make your *bouts* more violent to that end,
He calls for drink. *Shakeſp. Hamlet.*

If he chance to 'ſcape this diſmal *bout*,
The former legatees are blotted out. *Dryden's Juv. ſat.* xii.

A weaſel ſeized a bat; the bat begged for life: ſays the weaſel, I give no quarter to birds: ſays the bat, I am a mouſe; look on my body: ſo ſhe got off for that *bout.* *L'Eſtrange.*

We'll ſee when 'tis enough,
Or if it wants the nice concluding *bout.* *King.*

*BOUTEFEU. n. ſ.* [French.] An incendiary; one who kindles feuds and diſcontents.

Animated by a baſe fellow, called John à Chamber, a very *boutefeu*, who bore much ſway among the vulgar, they entered into open rebellion. *Bacon's Henry* VII.

Nor could ever any order be obtained impartially to puniſh the known *boutefeus*, and open incendiaries. *King Charles.*

Beſides the herd of *boutefeus*,
We ſet on work without the houſe. *Hudibras.*

Bo'UTISALE. *n. ſ.* [I ſuppoſe from *booty*, or *booty*, and *ſale.*] A ſale at a cheap rate; as booty or plunder is commonly ſold.

To ſpeak nothing of the great *boutiſale* of colleges and chantries. *Sir J. Hayward.*

*BOUTS RIMEZ.* [French.] The laſt words or rhimes of a number of verſes given to be filled up.

To BOW. *v. a.* [buꝫen, Saxon.]

1. To bend, or inflect.

A threepence *bow'd*, would hire me,
Old as I am, to queen it. *Shakeſp. Henry* VIII.

Orpheus, with his lute, made trees,
And the mountain tops, that freeze,
*Bow* themſelves when he did ſing. *Shakeſp. Henry* VIII.

Some *bow* the vines, which bury'd in the plain,
Their tops in diſtant arches riſe again. *Dryden's Virgil.*

The mind has not been made obedient to diſcipline, when at firſt it was moſt tender, and moſt eaſy to be *bowed.* *Locke.*

2. To bend the body in token of reſpect or ſubmiſſion.

They came to meet him, and *bowed* themſelves to the ground before him. *2 Kings*, ii. 15.

Is it to *bow* down his head as a bulruſh, and to ſpread ſackcloth and aſhes under him? wilt thou call this a faſt, and an acceptable day to the Lord? *Iſaiah*, lviii. 5.

3. To bend, or incline, in condeſcenſion.

Let it not grieve thee to *bow* down thine ear to the poor, and give him a friendly anſwer. *Ecclus*, iv. 8.

4. To depreſs; to cruſh.

Are you ſo goſpell'd,
To pray for this good man, and for his iſſue,
Whoſe heavy hand hath *bow'd* you to the grave,
And beggar'd yours for ever. *Shakeſp. Macbeth.*

Now waſting years my former ſtrength confound,
And added woes may *bow* me to the ground. *Pope.*

To Bow. *v. n.*

1. To bend; to ſuffer flexure.

2. To make a reverence.

~~To turn as a ballance, to weigh down~~

the fair Soul herself weigh'd
between lothness & Obedience at which end
the beam Should bow Shak.

To incline, to dispose
She that Should all parts to reunion bow
She that had all magnetic force alone
To draw and fasten sundred parts in one
Donne

IL facing 3L[v]

b ǂ

~~to~~ Bent. ~~[illegible]~~

Children like tender Osiers take the bow
And as they first are fashion'd always grow
Dryd jun.r Juv. 14

Now my task is smoothly done a ǂ ~~[illegible]~~
I can fly, or I can run
Quickly to the green earths end
Where the bow'd Welkin slow doth bend
Milt

Rather let my head
Stoop to the block, than these knees *bow* to any,
Save to the God of heav'n, and to my king. *Shakesp. H.* VI.

This is the great idol to which the world *bows*; to this we pay our devoutest homage. *Decay of Piety.*

Admir'd, ador'd by all the circling crowd,
For wheresoe'er she turn'd her face, they *bow'd*. *Dryden.*

3. To stoop.

The people *bowed* down upon their knees, to drink water. *Judges*, vii. 6.

4. To sink under pressure.

They stoop, they *bow* down together; they could not deliver the burden. *Isaiah*, xlvi. 2.

Bow. *n. s.* [from the verb. It is pronounced, like the verb, as *now*, *bow*.] An act of reverence or submission, by bending the body.

Some clergy too she wou'd allow,
Nor quarrel'd at their awkward *bow*. *Swift.*

Bow. *n. s.* [pronounced as *grow*, *no*, *lo*, without any regard to the *w*.]

1. An instrument of war, made by holding wood or metal bent with a string, which, by its spring, shoots arrows with great force.

Take, I pray thee, thy weapons, thy quiver and thy *bow*, and go out to the field, and take me some venison. *Gen.* xxvii. 3.

The white faith of hist'ry cannot show,
That e'er the musket yet could beat the *bow*.
*Alleyne's Henry* VII.

Twining woody haunts, or the tough yew
To *bows* strong-straining. *Thomson's Autumn.*

2. A rainbow.

I do set my *bow* in the cloud, and it shall be for a token of a covenant between me and the earth. *Gen.* ix. 13.

3. The instrument with which string-instruments are struck.

Their instruments were various in their kind;
Some for the *bow*, and some for breathing wind:
The sawtry, pipe, and hautboy's noisy band,
And the soft lute trembling beneath the touching hand.
*Dryden's Fables.*

4. The doubling of a string in a slip-knot.

Make a knot, and let the second knot be with a *bow*.
*Wiseman's Surgery.*

5. A yoke.

As the ox hath his *bow*, Sir, the horse his curb, and the faulcon his bells, so man hath his desire. *Shakesp. As you like it.*

6. Bow *of a saddle*. The *bows of a saddle* are two pieces of wood laid archwise, to receive the upper part of a horse's back, to give the saddle its due form, and to keep it tight. *Farrier's D.*

7. Bow *of a ship*. That part of her which begins at the loof, and compassing ends of the stern, and ends at the sternmost parts of the forecastle. If a ship hath a broad bow, they call it a *bold bow*; if a narrow thin bow, they say she hath a *lean bow*. The piece of ordnance that lies in this place, is called the *bowpiece*; and the anchors that hang here, are called her *great* and *little bowers*.

8. Bow is also a mathematical instrument, made of wood, formerly used by seamen in taking the sun's altitude.

9. Bow is likewise a beam of wood or brass, with three long screws, that direct a lath of wood or steel to any arch; used commonly to draw draughts of ships, projections of the sphere, or wherever it is requisite to draw long arches. *Harris.*

Bow-bearer. *n. s.* [from *bow* and *bear*.] An under-officer of the forest. *Cowel.*

Bow-bent. *adj.* [from *bow* and *bent*.] Crooked.

A sibyl old, *bow-bent* with crooked age,
That far events full wisely could presage. *Milton.*

Bow-hand. *n. s.* [from *bow* and *hand*.] The hand that draws the bow.

Surely he shoots wide on the *bow-hand*, and very far from the mark. *Spenser's Ireland.*

Bow-legged. *adj.* [from *bow* and *leg*.] Having crooked legs.

Bow-shot. *n. s.* [from *bow* and *shot*.] The space which an arrow may pass in its flight from the bow.

Though he were not then a *bow-shot* off, and made haste; yet, by that time he was come, the thing was no longer to be seen. *Boyle's Spring of the Air.*

To Bo'wel. *v. a.* [from the noun.] To pierce the bowels.

But to the *bowell'd* cavern darting deep
The mineral kinds confess thy mighty power. *Thomson.*

BO'WELS. *n. s.* [*boyaux*, Fr.]

1. Intestines; the vessels and organs within the body.

He smote him therewith in the fifth rib, and shed out his *bowels*. 2 *Sam.* xx. 10.

2. The inner parts of any thing.

Had we no quarrel else to Rome, but that
Thou art thence banish'd, we would muster all
From twelve to seventy; and pouring war
Into the *bowels* of ungrateful Rome,
Like a bold flood appear. *Shakesp. Coriolanus.*

His soldiers spying his undaunted spirit,
A Talbot! Talbot! cried out amain,
And rush'd into the *bowels* of the battle. *Shakesp. Henry* VI.

As he saw drops of water distilling from the rock, by following the veins, he has made himself two or three fountains in the *bowels* of the mountain. *Addison on Italy.*

BOW

3. Tenderness; compassion.

He had no other consideration of money, than for the support of his lustre; and whilst he could do that, he cared not for money; having no *bowels* in the point of running in debt, or borrowing all he could. *Clarendon.*

4. This word seldom has a *singular*, except in writers of anatomy.

Bo'wer. *n. s.* [from *bough* or *branch*, or from the verb *to bow* or *bend*.]

1. An arbour; a sheltered place covered with green trees, twined and bent.

But, O sad virgin, that thy power
Might raise Musæus from his *bower*. *Milton.*

To Gods appealing, when I reach their *bow'rs*
With loud complaints, they answer me in show'rs. *Waller.*

Refresh'd, they wait them to the *bow'r* of state,
Where, circl'd with his peers, Atrides sat. *Pope.*

2. It seems to signify, in *Spenser*, a blow; a stroke: *bourrer*, Fr. to fall upon.

His rawbone arms, whose mighty brawned *bowers*
Were wont to rive steel plates, and helmets hew,
Were clean consum'd, and all his vital powers
Decay'd. *Spenser's Fairy Queen, b.* i. *cant.* viii. *stanz.* 41.

Bo'wer. *n. s.* [from the *bow* of a ship.] Anchors so called. See Bow.

To Bo'wer. *v. a.* [from the noun.] To embower; to inclose.

Thou didst *bower* the spirit,
In mortal paradise of such sweet flesh. *Shakesp.*

Bo'wery. *adj.* [from *bower*.] Full of bowers.

Landskips how gay the *bow'ry* grotto yields,
Which thought creates, and lavish fancy builds. *Tickell.*

~~Snatch'd through the verdant maze, the hurried eye~~
~~Distracted wanders: now~~ the *bowery* walk
Of covert close, where scarce a speck of day
Falls on the lengthen'd gloom, ~~protracted sweeps.~~ *Thomson.*

To Bowge. See To Bouge.

BOWL. *n. s.* [*buelin*, Welch; which signifies, according to *Junius*, any thing made of horn, as drinking cups anciently were. It is pronounced *bole*.]

1. A vessel to hold liquids, rather wide than deep; distinguished from a cup, which is rather deep than wide.

Give me a *bowl* of wine;
I have not that alacrity of spirit,
Nor cheer of mind, that I was wont to have. *Richard* III.

If a piece of iron be fastened on the side of a *bowl* of water, a loadstone, in a boat of cork, will presently make into it. *Brown's Vulgar Errours, b.* ii. *c.* iii.

The sacred priests, with ready knives, bereave
The beasts of life, and in full *bowls* receive
The streaming blood. *Dryden's Æneid.*

While the bright Sein, t' exalt the soul,
With sparkling plenty crowns the *bowl*,
And wit and social mirth inspires. *Fenton to Lord Gower.*

2. The hollow part of any thing.

If you are allowed a large silver spoon for the kitchen, let half the *bowl* of it be worn out with continual scraping. *Swift's Directions to the Cook.*

3. A basin, or fountain.

But the main matter is so to convey the water, as it never stay either in the *bowl* or in the cistern. *Bacon's Essays.*

BOWL. *n. s.* [*boule*, Fr. It is pronounced as *cow*, *howl*.] A round mass, which may be rolled along the ground.

Like to a *bowl* upon a subtle ground,
I've tumbl'd past the throw. *Shakesp. Coriolanus.*

How finely dost thou times and seasons spin!
And make a twist checker'd with night and day!
Which, as it lengthens, winds, and winds us in,
As *bowls* go on, but turning all the way. *Herbert.*

Like him, who would lodge a *bowl* upon a precipice, either my praise falls back, or stays not on the top, but rowls over. *Dryden's Juvenal, Dedication.*

Men may make a game at *bowls* in the summer, and a game at whisk in the winter. *Dennis's Letters.*

Though that piece of wood, which is now a *bowl*, may be made square, yet, if roundness be taken away, it is no longer a *bowl*. *Watts's Logick.*

To Bowl. *v. a.* [from the noun.]

1. To play at bowls.

2. To throw bowls at any thing.

Alas! I had rather be set quick i' th' earth,
And *bowl'd* to death with turnips. *Merry W. of Windsor.*

Bo'wlder-stones. *n. s.* Lumps or fragments of stones or marble, broke from the adjacent cliffs, rounded by being tumbled to and again by the action of the water; whence their name. *Woodward on Fossils.*

Bo'wler. *n. s.* [from *bowl*.] He that plays at bowls.

Bo'wline. } *n. s.* [sea term.] A rope fastened to the middle
Bo'wling. } part of the outside of a sail; it is fastened in three or four parts of the sail, called the *bowling bridle*. The use of the *bowling* is to make the sails stand sharp or close to a wind. *Harr.*

Bo'wling-

Bo'wling-green. *n. ſ.* [from *bowl* and *green.*] A level piece of ground, kept ſmooth for bowlers.

A bowl equally poiſed, and thrown upon a plain *bowling-green*, will run neceſſarily in a direct line. *Bentley.*

Bo'wman. *n. ſ.* [from *bow* and *man.*] An archer; he that ſhoots with a bow.

The whole city ſhall flee, for the noiſe of the horſemen and *bowmen.* *Jerem.* iv. 29.

Bo'wsprit. *n. ſ.* [from the *bow* of the ſhip.] This word is generally ſpelt *boltſprit*; which ſee.

To Bo'wssen. *v. a.* [probably of the ſame original with *bowſe*, but found in no other paſſage.] To drench; to ſoak.

The water fell into a cloſe walled plot; upon this wall was the frantick perſon ſet, and from thence tumbled headlong into the pond; where a ſtrong fellow toſſed him up and down, until the patient, by foregoing his ſtrength, had ſomewhat forgot his fury: but if there appeared ſmall amendment, he was *bowſſened* again and again, while there remained in him any hope of life, for recovery. *Carew's Survey of Cornwal.*

Bo'wstring. *n. ſ.* [from *bow* and *ſtring.*] The ſtring by which the bow is kept bent.

He hath twice or thrice cut Cupid's *bowſtring*, and the little hangman dare not ſhoot at him. *Shakeſp. Much ado about Noth.*

Sound will be conveyed to the ear, by ſtriking upon a *bowſtring*, if the horn of the bow be held to the ear. *Bacon.*

Bo'wyer. *n. ſ.* [from *bow.*]

1. An archer; one that uſes the bow.

Call for vengeance from the *bowyer* king. *Dryden.*

2. One whoſe trade is to make bows.

BOX. *n. ſ.* [box, Saxon; *buxus*, Lat.] A tree.

The characters are; The leaves are pennated, and evergreen; it hath male flowers, that are produced at remote diſtances from the fruit, on the ſame tree; the fruit is ſhaped like a porridge-pot inverted, and is divided into three cells, containing two ſeeds in each, which, when ripe, are caſt forth by the elaſticity of the veſſels. ~~The ſpecies are; 1. The box-tree. 2. The narrow-leaved box-tree. 3. Striped box. 4. The golden edged box-tree. 5. The dwarf box. 6. The dwarf ſtriped box. 7. The ſilver edged box. On Boxhill, near Darking in Surrey, were formerly many large trees of this kind; but, of late years, their number is pretty much decreaſed; yet ſome remain of a conſiderable bigneſs.~~ The wood is very uſeful ~~for engravers and mathematical inſtrument-makers~~; being ſo hard, cloſe, and ponderous, as to ſink in water. *Millar.*

~~*Box*, there are two ſorts of it; the dwarf box, and a taller ſort, that grows to a conſiderable height.~~ The dwarf *box* is very good for borders, and is eaſily kept in order, with one clipping in the year. It will ~~increaſe of ſlips ſet in March, or about Bartholomew-tide, and may be raiſed of layers and ſuckers, and will~~ proſper on the declivity of cold, dry, barren, chalky hills, where nothing elſe will grow. *Mortimer.*

Box. *n. ſ.* [box, Sax. *buſte*, Germ.]

1. A caſe made of wood, or other matter, to hold any thing. It is diſtinguiſhed from *cheſt*, as the *leſs* from the *greater*. It is ſuppoſed to have its name from the *box* wood.

A perfect magnet, though but in an ivory *box*, will, through the *box*, ſend forth his embracing virtue to a beloved needle. *Sidney, b.* ii.

About his ſhelves
A beggarly account of empty *boxes*. *Shakeſp. Rom. and Jul.*

This head is to open a moſt wide voracious mouth, which ſhall take in letters and papers. There will be under it a *box*, of which the key will be kept in my cuſtody, to receive ſuch papers as are dropped into it. *Addiſon. Guard.* N° 98.

This caſket India's glowing gems unlocks,
And all Arabia breathes from yonder *box*. *Pope.*

2. The caſe of the mariners compaſs.

3. The cheſt into which money given is put.

So many more, ſo every one was uſed,
That to give largely to the *box* refuſed. *Spenſer.*

4. The ſeats in the playhouſe, where the ladies are placed.

'Tis left to you, the *boxes* and the pit
Are ſovereign judges of this ſort of wit. *Dryden.*

She glares in balls, front *boxes*, and the ring,
A vain, unquiet, glittering, wretched thing. *Pope.*

To Box. *v. a.* [from the noun.] To incloſe in a box.

*Box'd* in a chair, the beau impatient ſits,
While ſpouts run clatt'ring o'er the roof by fits. *Swift.*

BOX. *n. ſ.* [*bock*, a cheek, Welch.] A blow on the head given with the hand.

For the *box* o' th' ear that the prince gave you, he gave it like a rude prince. *Shakeſp. Henry* IV.

If one ſhould take my hand perforce, and give another a *box* on the ear with it, the law puniſheth the other. *Bramhall* ~~*againſt Hobbes.*~~

There may happen concuſſions of the brain from a *box* on the ear. *Wiſeman's Surgery.*

Olphis, the fiſherman, received a *box* on the ear from Theſtylis. *Addiſon. Spectator*, N° 233.

To Box. *v. n.* [from the noun.] To fight with the fiſt.

The aſs very fairly looked on, till they had *boxed* themſelves a-weary, and then left them fairly in the lurch. *L'Eſtrange.*

A leopard is like a cat; he *boxes* with his forefeet, as a cat doth her kitlins. *Grew.*

The fighting with a man's ſhadow conſiſts in brandiſhing two ſticks, loaden with plugs of lead; this gives a man all the pleaſure of *boxing*, without the blows. *Spectat.* N° 115.

He hath had ſix duels, and four and twenty *boxing* matches, in defence of his majeſty's title. *Spectator*, N° 629.

To Box. *v. a.* To ſtrike with the fiſt.

Bo'xen. *adj.* [from *box.*]

1. Made of box.

The young gentlemen learned, before all other things, to deſign upon tablets of *boxen* wood. *Dryden's Dufreſnoy.*

As lads and laſſes ſtood around,
To hear my *boxen* hautboy ſound. *Gay's Paſtorals.*

2. Reſembling box.

Her faded cheeks are chang'd to *boxen* hue,
And in her eyes the tears are ever new. *Dryden.*

Bo'xer. *n. ſ.* [from *box.*] A man who fights with his fiſt.

BOY. *n. ſ.* [*bub*, Germ. the etymology is not agreed on.]

1. A male child; not a girl.

2. One in the ſtate of adoleſcence; older than an infant, yet not arrived at puberty or manhood.

Speak thou, *boy*;
Perhaps thy childiſhneſs will move him more
Than can our reaſons. *Shakeſp. Coriolanus.*

Sometimes forgotten things, long caſt behind,
Ruſh forward in the brain, and come to mind:
The nurſe's legends are for truths receiv'd,
And the man dreams but what the *boy* believ'd. *Dryden.*

3. A word of contempt for young men, as noting their immaturity.

Men of worth and parts will not eaſily admit the familiarity of *boys*, who yet need the care of a tutor. *Locke.*

The pale *boy*-ſenator yet tingling ſtands,
~~And holds his breeches cloſe with both his hands.~~ *Pope.*

To Boy. *v. n.* [from the noun.] To act apiſhly, or like a boy.

Anthony
Shall be brought drunken forth, and I ſhall ſee
Some ſqueaking Cleopatra *boy* my greatneſs,
I' th' poſture of a whore. *Shakeſp. Antony and Cleopatra.*

Bo'yhood. *n. ſ.* [from *boy.*] The ſtate of a boy; the part of life in which we are boys.

If you ſhould look at him, in his *boyhood*, through the magnifying end of a perſpective, and, in his manhood, through the other, it would be impoſſible to ſpy any difference; the ſame air, the ſame ſtrut. *Swift.*

Bo'yish. *adj.* [from *boy.*]

1. Belonging to a boy.

I ran it through, e'en from my *boyiſh* days,
To th' very moment that he bade me tell it. *Shakeſp. Othello.*

2. Childiſh; trifling.

This unheard ſauicneſs, and *boyiſh* troops,
The king doth ſmile at, and is well prepar'd
To whip this dwarfiſh war, theſe pigmy arms. *Sh. K. John.*

Young men take up ſome Engliſh poet for their model, and imitate him, without knowing wherein he is defective, where he is *boyiſh* and trifling. *Dryden.*

Bo'yishly. *adv.* [from *boyiſh.*] Childiſhly; triflingly.

Bo'yishness. *n. ſ.* [from *boyiſh.*] Childiſhneſs; triviſhneſs.

Bo'yism. *n. ſ.* [from *boy.*] Puerility; childiſhneſs.

He had complained he was farther off, by being ſo near, and a thouſand ſuch *boyiſms*, which Chaucer rejected as below the ſubject. *Dryden's Fab. Preface.*

Bp. An abbreviation of biſhop.

BRA'BBLE. *n. ſ.* [~~*brabbelen*, Dutch.~~] A clamorous conteſt; a ſquabble; a broil.

Here in the ſtreets, deſperate in ſhame and ſtate,
In private *brabble* did we apprehend him. *Shakeſp. T. Night.*

To Bra'bble. *v. n.* [~~from the noun.~~] To clamour; to conteſt noiſily.

Bra'bbler. *n. ſ.* [from *brabble.*] A clamorous, quarrelſome, noiſy fellow.

To BRACE. *v. a.* [*embraſſer*, Fr.]

1. To bind; to tie cloſe with bandages.

The women of China, by *bracing* and binding them from their infancy, have very little feet. *Locke.*

2. To intend; to make tenſe; to ſtrain up.

The tympanum is not capable of tenſion that way, in ſuch a manner as a drum is *braced*. *Holder's Elements of Speech.*

The diminution of the force of the preſſure of the external air, in *bracing* the fibres, muſt create a debility in muſcular motion. *Arbuthnot on Air.*

Brace. *n. ſ.* [from the verb.]

1. Cincture; bandage.

2. That which holds any thing tight.

The little bones of the ear-drum do the ſame office in ſtraining and relaxing it, as the *braces* of the war drum do in that. *Derham's Phyſico-Theology.*

3. Brace. [in architecture.] Is a piece of timber framed in with bevil joints, uſed to keep the building from ſwerving either way. *Builder's Dict.*

4. Braces. [a ſea term.] Ropes belonging to all the yards, except

2

The breasts, Sire
Then Shook from out his pile the Seeds of fire
And Snapt his Box: ~~He stroak'd his belly down~~
~~Rosy and reverend~~ Pope



IL facing 3L2v

3 Brag n. s. a game at cards

Bragg adv boastingly

Seest how bragg yon bullock bears
So Smirk So Smooth his pricked ears
His horns been as brade as rainbow bent
His dewlap as lithe as lass of Kent
See how he venteth into the wind
Weenist of love is not his mind
Spenser

Unto the bush her eye did sudden glance
In which vain Braggadocio was mewed
And saw it Stir F. Q. 2. 3. 34

If this poor brach of Venice whom I cherish
For his quick hunting, Stand the putting on
I'll have our Mich. Cassio on the hip
Shak. Oth.

The Salt Medway that trickling Streams
Adown the dales of Kent
Till with the elder Brother Thames
His brackish waves be meynt
Spens. Pa.

cept the mizen. They have a pendant feized to the yard-arm, two *braces* to each yard; and, at the end of the pendant, a block is feized, through which the rope called the *brace* is reeved. The *braces* ferve to fquare and traverfe the yards. *Sea Dict.*

5. BRACES *of a coach.* Thick ftraps of leather on which it hangs.

6. Harnefs.

7. BRACE. [in printing.] A crooked line inclofing a paffage, which ought to be taken together, and not feparately; as in a triplet.

> Charge Venus to command her fon,
> Wherever elfe fhe lets him rove,
> To fhun my houfe, and field, and grove;
> Peace cannot dwell with hate or love. *Prior.*

8. Warlike preparation; from *bracing* the armour; as we fay, *girded* for the battle.

> As it more concerns the Turk than Rhodes,
> So may he with more facile queftion bear it;
> For that it ftands not in fuch warlike *brace*,
> But altogether lacks th' abilities
> That Rhodes is drefs'd in. *Shakefp. Othello.*

9. Tenfion; tightnefs.

The moft frequent caufe of deafnefs is the laxnefs of the tympanum, when it has loft its *brace* or tenfion. *Holder.*

BRACE. *n. f.* [of uncertain etymology.]

1. A pair; a couple. It is not *braces*, but *brace*, in the *plural.*

> Down from a hill the beafts that reign in woods,
> Firft hunter then, purfu'd a gentle *brace*,
> Goodlieft of all the foreft, hart and hind. *Par. Loft, b.* xi.
> Ten *brace* and more of greyhounds, fnowy fair,
> And tall as ftags, ran loofe, and cours'd around his chair. *Dryden's Fables.*

2. It is ufed generally in converfation as a fportfman's word.

He is faid, this fummer, to have fhot with his own hands fifty *brace* of pheafants. *Addifon. Freeholder*, № 36.

3. It is applied to men in contempt.

> But you, my *brace* of lords, were I fo minded,
> I here could pluck his highnefs' frown upon you. *Sh. Tempeft.*

BRA'CELET. *n. f.* [*bracelet*, Fr.]

1. An ornament for the arms.

Both his hands were cut off, being known to have worn *bracelets* of gold about his wrifts. *Sir J. Hayward.*

> Tie about our tawny wrifts
> *Bracelets* of the fairy twifts. *Ben. Johnfon's Fairy Prince.*

A very ingenious lady ufed to wear, in rings and *bracelets*, ftore of thofe gems. *Boyle.*

2. A piece of defenfive armour for the arm.

BRA'CER. *n. f.* [from *brace.*] A cincture; a bandage.

When they affect the belly, they may be reftrained by a *bracer*, without much trouble. *Wifeman's Surgery.*

BRACH. *n. f.* [*braque*, Fr.] A bitch hound.

Truth's a dog muft to kennel; he muft be whipped out; when the lady *brach* may ftand by the fire, and ftink. *Shakefp.*

BRA'CHIAL. *adj.* [from *brachium*, an arm, Lat.] Belonging to the arm.

BRACHY'GRAPHY. *n. f.* [βραχὺς, fhort, and γράφω, to write.] The art or practice of writing in a fhort compafs.

All the certainty of thofe high pretenders, bating what they have of the firft principles, and the word of God, may be circumfcribed by as fmall a circle as the creed, when *brachygraphy* had confined it within the compafs of a penny. *Glanville.*

BRACK. *n. f.* [from *break.*] A breach; a broken part.

The place was but weak, and the *bracks* fair; but the defendants, by refolution, fupplied all the defects. *Hayward.*

Let them compare my work with what is taught in the fchools, and if they find in theirs many *bracks* and fhort ends, which cannot be fpun into an even piece, and, in mine, a fair coherence throughout, I fhall promife myfelf an acquiefcence. *Digby on the Soul, Dedicat.*

BRA'CKET. *n. f.* A piece of wood fixed for the fupport of fomething.

Let your fhelves be laid upon *brackets*, being about two feet wide, and edged with a fmall lath. *Mortimer.*

BRA'CKISH. *adj.* [*brack*, Dutch.] Salt; fomewhat falt: it is ufed particularly of the water of the fea.

Pits upon the fea fhore turn into frefh water, by percolation of the falt through the fand: but it is farther noted, after a time, the water in fuch pits will become *brackifh* again. *Bacon.*

> When I had gain'd the brow and top,
> A lake of *brackifh* waters on the ground,
> Was all I found. *Herbert.*

> The wife contriver, on his end intent,
> Mix'd them with falt, and feafon'd all the fea.
> What other caufe could this effect produce?
> The *brackifh* tincture through the main diffufe? *Blackmore.*

BRA'CKISHNESS. *n. f.* [from *brackifh.*] Saltnefs.

All the artificial ftrainings, hitherto difcovered, leave a *brackifhnefs* in falt water, that makes it unfit for animal ufes. *Cheyne's Philofophical Principles.*

BRAD, being an initial, fignifies *broad, fpacious*, from the Saxon bʀab, and the Gothick *braid.* *Gibfon's Camden.*

BRA

BRAD. *n. f.* A fort of nail to floor rooms with. They are about the fize of a tenpenny nail, but have not their heads made with a fhoulder over their fhank, as other nails, but are made pretty thick towards the upper end, that the very top may be driven into, and buried in the board they nail down; fo that the tops of thefe *brads* will not catch the thrums of the mops, when the floor is wafhing. *Moxon's Mechanical Exercifes.*

To BRAG. *v. n.* [*braggeren*, Dutch.]

1. To boaft; to difplay oftentatioufly; to tell boaftful ftories.

> Thou coward! art thou *bragging* to the ftars?
> Telling the bufhes that thou look'ft for wars,
> And wilt not come? *Shakefp. Midfum. Night's Dream.*

Mark me, with what violence fhe firft loved the Moor, but for *bragging*, and telling her fantaftical lies. *Shakefp. Othello.*

In *bragging* out fome of their private tenets, as if they were the received eftablifhed doctrine of the church of England. *Sanderfon's Pax Ecclefiæ.*

The rebels were grown fo ftrong there, that they intended then, as they already *bragged*, to come over, and make this the feat of war. *Clarendon.*

Mrs. Bull's condition was looked upon as defperate by all the men of art; but there were thofe that *bragged* they had an infallible ointment. *Arbuthnot's Hift. of J. Bull.*

2. It has *of* before the thing boafted.

Knowledge being the only thing *whereof* we poor old men can *brag*, we cannot make it known but by utterance. *Sidney.*

> Verona *brags of* him,
> To be a virtuous and well govern'd youth. *Shakefp.*

> Ev'ry bufy little fcribbler now,
> Swells with the praifes which he gives himfelf,
> And taking fanctuary in the croud,
> *Brags of* his impudence, and fcorns to mend. *Rofcommon.*

3. *On* is ufed, but improperly.

> Yet lo! in me what authors have to *brag on*,
> Reduc'd at laft to hifs in my own dragon. *Pope's Dunciad.*

BRAG. *n. f.* [from the verb.]

1. A boaft; a proud expreffion.

> A kind of conqueft
> Cæfar made here; but made not here his *brag*
> Of came, and faw, and overcame. *Shakefp. Cymbeline.*

It was fuch a new thing for the Spaniards to receive fo little hurt, upon dealing with the Englifh, as Avellaneda made great *brags* of it, for no greater matter than the waiting upon the Englifh afar off. *Bacon's War with Spain.*

2. The thing boafted.

> Beauty is nature's *brag*, and muft be fhewn
> In courts, at feafts, and high folemnities,
> Where moft may wonder. *Milton.*

BRAGGADO'CIO. *n. f.* [from *brag.*] A puffing, fwelling, boafting fellow.

The world abounds in terrible fanfarons, in the mafque of men of honour; but thefe *braggadocios* are eafy to be detected. *L'Eftrange.*

By the plot, you may guefs much of the characters of the perfons; a *braggadocio* captain, a parafite, and a lady of pleafure. *Dryden.*

BRA'GGART. *adj.* [from *brag.*] Boaftful; vainly oftentatious.

> Shall I, none's flave, of high-born or rais'd men
> Fear frowns; and my miftrefs, truth, betray thee
> To th' huffing, *braggart*, puft nobility? *Donne.*

BRA'GGART. *n. f.* [from *brag.*] A boafter.

> Who knows himfelf a *braggart*,
> Let him fear this; for it will come to pafs,
> That every *braggart* fhall be found an afs. *Shakefp. All's well that ends well.*

BRA'GGER. *n. f.* [from *brag.*] A boafter; an oftentatious fellow.

Such as have had opportunity to found thefe *braggers* thoroughly, by having fometimes endured the penance of their fottifh company, have found them, in converfe, empty and infipid. *South.*

BRA'GLESS. *adj.* [from *brag.*] Without a boaft; without oftentation.

> The bruit is, Hector's flain, and by Achilles.——
> ——If it is fo, *braglefs* let it be,
> Great Hector was as good a man as he. *Shak. Tr. and Creff.*

BRA'GLY. *adv.* [from *brag.*] Finely; fo as it may be bragged.

> Seeft not thilk hawthorn ftud,
> How *bragly* it begins to bud,
> And utter his tender head?
> Flora new calleth forth each flower,
> And bids make ready Maia's bower. *Spenfer's Paft.*

To BRAID. *v. a.* [bʀæban, Saxon.] To weave together.

> Clofe the ferpent fly,
> Infinuating, wove with gordian twine
> His *braided* train, and of his fatal guile
> Gave proof unheeded. *Milton's Par. Loft, b.* iv. *l.* 347.

Ofier wands, lying loofely, may each of them be eafily diffociated from the reft; but when *braided* into a bafket, they cohere ftrongly. *Boyle.*

> A ribband did the *braided* treffes bind,
> The reft was loofe, and wanton'd in the wind. *Dryden.*

Since

Since in *braided* gold her foot is bound,
And a long trailing manteau ſweeps the ground,
Her ſhoe diſdains the ſtreet. *Gay's Trivia.*

BRAID. *n. ſ.* [from the verb.] A texture; a knot, or complication of ſomething woven together.

Liſten where thou art ſitting,
Under the gloſſy, cool, tranſlucent wave,
In twiſted *braids* of lillies knitting
The looſe train of thy amber-dropping hair. *Milton.*

No longer ſhall thy comely traces break
In flowing ringlets on thy ſnowy neck,
Or ſit behind thy head, an ample round,
In graceful *braids*, with various ribbon bound. *Prior.*

BRAID. *adj.* [To *brede*, in *Chaucer*, is to *deceive*.] An old word, which ſeems to ſignify *deceitful*.

Since Frenchmen are ſo *braid*,
Marry 'em that will. I'll live and die a maid.
*Shakeſp. All's well that ends well.*

BRAILS. *n. ſ.* [Sea term.] Small ropes reeved through blocks, which are ſeized on either ſide the ties, a little off upon the yard; ſo that they come down before the ſails of a ſhip, and are faſtened at the ſkirt of the ſail to the crengles. Their uſe is, when the ſail is furled acroſs, to hale up its bunt, that it may the more readily be taken up or let fall. *Harris.*

BRAIN. *n. ſ.* [bꞃæȝen, Sax. *breyne*, Dutch.]

1. That collection of veſſels and organs in the head, from which ſenſe and motion ariſe.

The *brain* is divided into *cerebrum* and *cerebellum*. *Cerebrum* is that part of the *brain*, which poſſeſſes all the upper and forepart of the *cranium*, being ſeparated from the *cerebellum* by the ſecond proceſs of the *dura mater*, under which the *cerebellum* is ſituated. The ſubſtance of the *brain* is diſtinguiſhed into outer and inner; the former is called *corticalis*, *cinerea*, or *glanduloſa*; the latter, *medullaris*, *alba*, or *nervea*. *Cheſelden.*

If I be ſerved ſuch another trick, I'll have my *brains* ta'en out, and buttered, and give them to a dog for a new year's gift. *Shakeſp. Merry Wives of Windſor.*

That man proportionably hath the largeſt *brain*, I did, I confeſs, ſomewhat doubt, and conceived it might have failed in birds, eſpecially ſuch as having little bodies, have yet large cranies, and ſeem to contain much *brain*, as ſnipes and woodcocks; but, upon trial, I find it very true. *Brown's Vulgar Errours.*

2. That part in which the underſtanding is placed; therefore taken for the underſtanding.

The force they are under is a real force, and that of their fate but an imaginary conceived one; the one but in their *brains*, the other on their ſhoulders. *Hammond's Fundamentals.*

A man is firſt a geometrician in his *brain*, before he be ſuch in his hand. *Hale's Origin of Mankind.*

3. Sometimes the affections.

My ſon Edgar! had he a hand to write this, a heart and *brain* to breed it in? *Shakeſp. King Lear.*

To BRAIN. *v. a.* [from the noun.] To daſh out the brains; to kill by beating out the brains.

Why, as I told thee, 'tis a cuſtom with him i' th' afternoon to ſleep; there thou may'ſt *brain* him. *Shakeſp. Tempeſt.*

Outlaws of nature,
Fit to be ſhot and *brain'd*, without a proceſs,
To ſtop infection; that's their proper death. *Dryden.*

Next ſeiz'd two wretches more, and headlong caſt,
*Brain'd* on the rock, his ſecond dire repaſt. *Pope's Odyſſey.*

BRA'INISH. *adj.* [from *brain*.] Hotheaded; furious; as, *cerebroſus* in Latin.

In his lawleſs fit,
Behind the arras hearing ſomething ſtir,
He whips his rapier out, and cries, a rat!
And, in his *brainiſh* apprehenſion, kills
The unſeen good old man. *Shakeſp. Hamlet.*

BRA'INLESS. *adj.* [from *brain*.] Silly; thoughtleſs; witleſs.

Some *brainleſs* men have, by great travel and labour, brought to paſs, that the church is now aſhamed of nothing more than of ſaints. *Hooker, b.* v. § 20.

If the dull *brainleſs* Ajax come ſafe off,
We'll dreſs him up in voices. *Shakeſp. Troilus and Creſſida.*

The *brainleſs* ſtripling, who, expell'd the town,
Damn'd the ſtiff college, and pedantick gown,
Aw'd by thy name, is dumb. *Tickell.*

BRA'INPAN. *n. ſ.* [from *brain* and *pan*.] The ſkull containing the brains.

With thoſe huge bellows in his hands, he blows
New fire into my head: my *brainpan* glows. *Dryden.*

BRA'INSICK. *adj.* [from *brain* and *ſick*.] Diſeaſed in the underſtanding; addleheaded; giddy; thoughtleſs.

Nor once deject the courage of our minds,
Becauſe Caſſandra's mad; her *brainſick* raptures
Cannot diſtaſte the goodneſs of a quarrel. *Troilus and Creſſ.*

They were *brainſick* men, who could neither endure the government of their king, nor yet thankfully receive the authours of their deliverance. *Knolles's Hiſtory of the Turks.*

BRA'INSICKLY. *adv.* [from *brainſick*.] Weakly; headily.

Why, worthy thane,
You do unbend your noble ſtrength to think
So *brainſickly* of things. *Shakeſp. Macbeth.*

BRA'INSICKNESS. *n. ſ.* [from *brainſick*.] Indiſcretion; giddineſs.

BRAIT. *n. ſ.* A term uſed by jewellers for a rough diamond. *D.*

BRAKE. The *preterite* of *break*.

He thought it ſufficient to correct the multitude with ſharp words, and *brake* out into this cholerick ſpeech. *Knolles's Hiſt.*

BRAKE. *n. ſ.* [of uncertain etymology.] A thicket of brambles, or of thorns.

A dog of this town uſed daily to fetch meat, and to carry the ſame unto a blind maſtiff, that lay in a *brake* without the town. *Carew's Survey of Cornwal.*

If I'm traduc'd by tongues, which neither know
My faculties nor perſon; let me ſay,
'Tis but the fate of place, and the rough *brake*
That virtue muſt go through. *Shakeſp. Henry* VIII.

In every buſh and *brake*, where hap may find
The ſerpent ſleeping. *Milton's Par. Loſt, b.* ix. *l.* 160.

Full little thought of him the gentle knight,
Who, flying death, had there conceal'd his flight;
In *brakes* and brambles hid, and ſhunning mortal ſight.
*Dryden's Fables.*

BRAKE. *n. ſ.*

1. An inſtrument for dreſſing hemp or flax.
2. The handle of a ſhip's pump.
3. A baker's kneading trough.
4. A ſharp bit or ſnaffle for horſes. *Dict.*

BRA'KY. *adj.* [from *brake*.] Thorny; prickly; rough.

Redeem arts from their rough and *braky* ſeats, where they lie hid and overgrown with thorns, to a pure, open light, where they may take the eye, and may be taken by the hand.
*Ben. Johnſon's Diſcovery.*

BRA'MBLE. *n. ſ.* [bꞃemlaꞅ, Sax. *rubus*, Lat.]

1. This plant hath a flower conſiſting of five leaves, which are placed circularly, and expand in form of a roſe; the flower-cup is divided into five parts, containing many ſtamina, or chives, in the boſom of the flower; in the centre of which riſes the pointal, which afterwards becomes the fruit, conſiſting of many protuberances, and full of juice. The ſpecies are; 1. The common *bramble*, or blackberry buſh. 2. The dewberry buſh, or leſſer *bramble*. 3. The common greater *bramble* buſh, with white fruit. 4. The greater *bramble* buſh, with a beautiful ſtriped leaf. 5. The raſpberry buſh, or hindberry. 6. The raſpberry buſh, with white fruit. 7. The raſpberry buſh, with late red fruit. 8. The raſpberry buſh, without thorns. 9. The Virginian raſpberry buſh, with black fruit. The firſt and ſecond ſorts are very common in hedges, and upon dry banks, in moſt parts of England, and are rarely cultivated in gardens. The third ſort was found by Mr. Jacob Bobart in a hedge, not far from Oxford. The fourth ſort is a variety of the common *bramble*, differing therefrom only in having ſtriped leaves. The raſpberry buſh is alſo very common in divers woods, in the northern counties of England; but is cultivated in all curious gardens, for the ſake of its fruit. All theſe plants are eaſily propagated by ſuckers, which they ſend from the roots in great plenty. The beſt time to take them off, and tranſplant them, is in October. *Millar.*

2. It is taken, in popular language, for any rough prickly ſhrub.

The buſh my bed, the *bramble* was my bow'r,
The woods can witneſs many a woful ſtore. *Spenſer's Paſt.*

There is a man haunts the foreſt, that abuſes our young plants with carving Roſalind on their barks; hangs odes upon hawthorns, and elegies on *brambles*; all, forſooth, deifying the name of Roſalind. *Shakeſp. As you like it.*

Content with food, which nature freely bred,
On wildings and on ſtrawberries they fed:
Cornels and *bramble* berries gave the reſt,
And falling acorns furniſh'd out a feaſt. *Dryden's Ovid.*

Thy younglings, Cuddy, are but juſt awake,
No thruſtles ſhrill the *bramble* buſh forſake. *Gay's Paſt.*

BRA'MBLING. *n. ſ.* A bird, called alſo a *mountain chaffinch*. *Dict.*

BRAN. *n. ſ.* [*brenna*, Ital.] The huſks of corn ground; the refuſe of the ſieve.

From me do back receive the flow'r of all,
And leave me but the *bran*. *Shakeſp. Coriolanus.*

The citizens were driven to great diſtreſs for want of victuals; bread they made of the coarſeſt *bran*, moulded in cloaths; for otherwiſe it would not cleave together. *Hayward.*

In the ſifting of fourteen years of power and favour, all that came out, could not be pure meal, but muſt have, among it, a certain mixture of padar and *bran*, in this lower age of human fragility. *Wotton.*

I cannot bolt this matter to the *bran*,
As Bradwardin and holy Auſtin can. *Dryden's Fables.*

Then water him, and, drinking what he can,
Encourage him to thirſt again with *bran*. *Dryden's Virgil.*

BRANCH. *n. ſ.* [*branche*, Fr.]

1. The ſhoot of a tree from one of the main boughs. See BOUGH.

Why grow the *branches*, when the root is gone?
Why wither not the leaves that want their ſap? *Shakeſp.*

2. Any member or part of the whole; any diſtinct article; any ſection or ſubdiviſion.

Your

a✗ 1 ~~Brake or~~ fern this forms the original signification

This is notoriously discoverable in some differencies of brake or fern Bro. V. E.

The brake & the Cockle be noisome too much
Yet like unto boddle no weed there is such
Tuss. Hus. for May

With the reciprocal pronoun
To distribute it self
The many pairs of Nerves distributing and
branching themselves to all parts of the body
are wonderfull to behold

Brandy-Shop n. s. Brandy & Shop.
A public place where brandy is drank
and sold
A swinging Score to the brandy Shop
Shop.

Your oaths are paſt, and now ſubſcribe your names,
That his own hand may ſtrike his honour down,
That violates the ſmalleſt *branch* herein.
*Shakeſp. Love's Labour Loſt.*

The belief of this was of ſpecial importance, to confirm our hopes of another life, on which ſo many *branches* of chriſtian piety does immediately depend. *Hammond's Fundamentals.*

In the ſeveral *branches* of juſtice and charity, comprehended in thoſe general rules, of loving our neighbour as ourſelves, and of doing to others as we would have them do to us, there is nothing but what is moſt fit and reaſonable. *Tillotſon.*

This precept will oblige us to perform our duty, according to the nature of the various *branches* of it. *Rogers.*

3. Any part that ſhoots out from the reſt.

And ſix *branches* ſhall come out of the ſides of it; three *branches* of the candleſtick out of the one ſide, and three *branches* of the candleſtick out of the other ſide. *Exod.* xxv. 32.

His blood, which diſperſeth itſelf by the *branches* of veins, may be reſembled to waters carried by brooks. *Raleigh's Hiſt.*

4. A ſmaller river running into, or proceeding from a larger.

If, from a main river, any *branch* be ſeparated and divided, then, where that *branch* doth firſt bound itſelf with new banks, there is that part of the river where the *branch* forſaketh the main ſtream, called the head of the river. *Raleigh's Hiſtory.*

5. Any part of a family deſcending in a collateral line.

His father, a younger *branch* of the ancient ſtock planted in Somerſetſhire, took to wife the widow. *Carew's Survey.*

6. The offspring; the deſcendant.

Great Anthony! Spain's well-beſeeming pride,
Thou mighty *branch* of emperours and kings! *Craſhaw.*

7. The antlers or ſhoots of a ſtag's horn.

8. The *branches* of a bridle are two pieces of bended iron, that bear the bit-mouth, the chains, and the curb, in the interval between the one and the other. *Farrier's Dict.*

9. [In architecture.] The arches of Gothick vaults; which arches tranſverſing from one angle to another, diagonal ways, form a croſs between the other arches, which make the ſides of the ſquare, of which the arches are diagonals. *Harris.*

To Branch. *v. n.* [from the noun.]

1. To ſpread in branches.

They were trained together in their childhoods, and there rooted betwixt them ſuch an affection, which cannot chooſe but *branch* now. *Shakeſp. Winter's Tale.*

The cauſe of ſcattering the boughs, is the haſty breaking forth of the ſap; and therefore thoſe trees riſe not in a body of any height, but *branch* near the ground. The cauſe of the Pyramis, is the keeping in of the ſap, long before it *branch*, and the ſpending of it, when it beginneth to *branch* by equal degrees. *Bacon's Natural Hiſt.* N° 588.

Plant it round with ſhade
Of laurel, ever-green, and *branching* plain. *Milt. Agoniſtes.*

Straight as a line in beauteous order ſtood,
Of oaks unſhorn a venerable wood;
Freſh was the graſs beneath, and ev'ry tree
At diſtance planted, in a due degree,
Their *branching* arms in air, with equal ſpace,
Stretch'd to their neighbours with a long embrace. *Dryden.*

One ſees her thighs transform'd, another views
Her arms ſhot out, and *branching* into boughs. *Addiſon, Ovid.*

2. To ſpread into ſeparate and diſtinct parts and ſubdiviſions.

The Alps at the one end, and the long range of Appenines that paſſes through the body of it, *branch* out, on all ſides, into ſeveral different diviſions. *Addiſon on Italy.*

If we would weigh, and keep in our minds, what it is we are conſidering, that would beſt inſtruct us when we ſhould, or ſhould not, *branch* into farther diſtinctions. *Locke.*

3. To ſpeak diffuſively, or with the diſtinction of the parts of a diſcourſe.

I have known a woman *branch* out into a long diſſertation upon the edging of a petticoat. *Spectator*, N° 247.

4. To have horns ſhooting out into antlers.

The ſwift ſtag from under ground
Bore up his *branching* head. *Milton's Par. Loſt, b.* vii. *l.* 470.

To Branch. *v. a.*

1. To divide as into branches.

The ſpirit of things animate are all continued within themſelves, and are *branched* in canals, as blood is; and the ſpirits have not only branches, but certain cells or ſeats, where the principal ſpirits do reſide. *Bacon's Natural Hiſt.*

2. To adorn with needlework, repreſenting flowers and ſprigs.

In robe of lily white ſhe was array'd,
That from her ſhoulder to her heel down raught,
The train whereof looſe far behind her ſtray'd,
*Branch'd* with gold and pearl, moſt richly wrought.
*Spenſer's Fairy Queen, b.* ii. *cant.* 9.

Bra'ncher. *n. ſ.* [from *branch.*]

1. One that ſhoots out into branches.

If their child be not ſuch a ſpeedy ſpreader and *brancher*, like the vine, yet he may yield, with a little longer expectation, as uſeful and more ſober fruit than the other. *Wotton.*

2. In falconry, a young hawk. [*branchier*, Fr.]

I enlarge my diſcourſe to the obſervation of the eires, the *brancher*, and the two ſorts of lentners. *Walton's Angler.*



Bra'nchiness. *n. ſ.* [from *branchy.*] Fulneſs of branches.

Bra'nchless. *adj.* [from *branch.*]

1. Without ſhoots or boughs.

2. Without any valuable product; naked.

If I loſe mine honour,
I loſe myſelf; better I were not yours,
Than yours ſo *branchleſs*. *Shakeſp. Antony and Cleopatra.*

Bra'nchy. *adj.* [from *branch.*] Full of branches; ſpreading.

Trees on trees o'erthrown,
Fall crackling round him, and the foreſts groan;
Sudden full twenty on the plain are ſtrow'd,
And lopp'd, and lighten'd of their *branchy* load. *Pope.*

What carriage can bear away all the various, rude, and unwieldy loppings of a *branchy* tree at once? *Watts.*

BRAND. *n. ſ.* [bꞃanð, Saxon.]

1. A ſtick lighted, or fit to be lighted in the fire.

Have I caught thee?
He that parts us ſhall bring a *brand* from heav'n,
And fire us hence. *Shakeſp. King Lear.*

Take it, ſhe ſaid, and when your needs require,
This little *brand* will ſerve to light your fire. *Dryden's Fab.*

If, with double diligence they labour to retrieve the hours they have loſt, they ſhall be ſaved; though this is a ſervice of great difficulty, and like a *brand* plucked out of the fire. *Rogers.*

2. A ſword, in old language. [*brandar*, Runick.]

They looking back, all the eaſtern ſide beheld
Of paradiſe, ſo late their happy ſeat!
Wav'd over by that flaming *brand*; the gate
With dreadful faces throng'd, and firy arms.
*Milton's Paradiſe Loſt, b.* xii. *l.* 643.

3. A thunderbolt.

The fire omnipotent prepares the *brand*,
By Vulcan wrought, and arms his potent hand;
Then flaming hurls it. *Granville.*

4. A mark made by burning a criminal with a hot iron, to note him as infamous.

Clerks convict ſhould be burned in the hand, both becauſe they might taſte of ſome corporal puniſhment, and that they might carry a *brand* of infamy. *Bacon's Hen.* VII.

The rules of good and evil are inverted, and a *brand* of infamy paſſes for a badge of honour. *L'Eſtrange.*

Where did his wit on learning fix a *brand*,
And rail at arts he did not underſtand? *Dryden's Macfleckno.*

To Brand. *v. a.* [*branden*, Dutch.] To mark with a brand, or note of infamy.

Have I liv'd thus long a wife, a true one,
Never yet *branded* with ſuſpicion? *Shakeſp. Henry* VIII.

The king was after *branded*, by Perkin's proclamation, for an execrable breaker of the rights of holy church. *Bacon.*

*Brand* not their actions with ſo foul a name;
Pity, at leaſt, what we are forc'd to blame. *Dryden.*

Ha! dare not for thy life, I charge thee, dare not
To *brand* the ſpotleſs virtue of my prince. *Rowe.*

Our Punick faith
Is infamous, and *branded* to a proverb. *Addiſon's Cato.*

The ſpreader of the pardons anſwered him an eaſier way, by *branding* him with hereſy. *Atterbury.*

Bra'ndgoose. *n. ſ.* A kind of wild fowl, leſs than a common gooſe, having its breaſt and wings of a dark colour. *Dict.*

To Bra'ndish. *v. a.* [from *brand*, a ſword.]

1. To wave, or ſhake, or flouriſh, as a weapon.

Brave Macbeth,
Diſdaining fortune, with his *brandiſh'd* ſteel,
Like valour's minion, carved out his paſſage. *Shakeſp.*

He ſaid, and *brandiſhing* at once his blade,
With eager pace purſu'd the flaming ſhade. *Dryden.*

Let me march their leader, not their prince;
And, at the head of your renown'd Cydonians,
*Brandiſh* this fam'd ſword. *Smith's Phædr. and Hippol.*

2. To play with; to flouriſh.

He, who ſhall employ all the force of his reaſon, only in *brandiſhing* of ſyllogiſms, will diſcover very little. *Locke.*

Bra'ndling. *n. ſ.* The name for a particular worm.

The dew-worm, which ſome alſo call the lob-worm, and the *brandling*, are the chief. *Walton's Angler.*

Bra'ndy. *n. ſ.* [contracted from *brandewine*, or *burnt wine.*] A ſtrong liquour diſtilled from wine.

If he travels the country, and lodgeth at inns, every dram of *brandy* extraordinary that you drink, raiſeth his character.
*Swift's Directions to the Footman.*

Bra'ndy-wine. The ſame with *brandy.*

It has been a common ſaying, A hair of the ſame dog; and thought, that *brandy-wine* is a common relief to ſuch. *Wiſeman.*

BRA'NGLE. *n. ſ.* [uncertainly derived.] Squabble; wrangle.

The payment of tythes in this kingdom, is ſubject to many frauds, *brangles*, and other difficulties, not only from papiſts and diſſenters, but even from thoſe who profeſs themſelves proteſtants. *Swift.*

To Bra'ngle. *v. n.* [from the noun.] To wrangle; to ſquabble.

When polite converſing ſhall be improved, company will be no no longer peſtered with dull ſtory-tellers, nor *brangling* diſputers. *Swift's Introduct. to genteel Converſation.*

BRA'NGLEMENT. *n. ſ.* [from *brangle.*] The ſame with *brangle.*

BRANK. *n. ſ.* Buckwheat, or *brank*, is a grain very uſeful and advantageous in dry barren lands. *Mortimer.*

BRA'NNY. *adj.* [from *bran.*] Having the appearance of bran.

It became ſerpiginous, and was, when I ſaw it, covered with white *branny* ſcales. *Wiſeman.*

BRA'SIER. *n. ſ.* [from *braſs.*]

1. A manufacturer that works in braſs.

There is a fellow ſomewhat near the door, he ſhould be a *braſier* by his face. *Shakeſp. Henry* VIII.

*Braſiers* that turn andirons, pots, kettles, &c. have their lathe made different from the common turners lathe. *Moxon.*

2. A pan to hold coals. [probably from *embraſer*, Fr.]

It is thought they had no chimneys, but were warmed with coals on *braſiers.* *Arbuthnot on Coins.*

BRASI'L. } *n. ſ.* An American wood, commonly ſuppoſed to have
BRAZI'L. } been thus denominated, becauſe firſt brought from Braſil: though Huet ſhews it had been known by that name, many years before the diſcovery of that country; and the beſt ſort comes from Fernambuc. The tree ordinarily grows in dry barren rocky places, is very thick and large, uſually crooked and knotty; its flowers, which are of a beautiful red, exhale an agreeable ſmell, which ſtrengthens the brain. The bark is ſo thick, that when the trunk is peeled, which might before be equal in circumference to the body of a man, it is reduced to that of his leg. The wood is heavy, and ſo dry, that it ſcarce raiſes any ſmoke. It is uſed by turners, and takes a good poliſh; but chiefly in dying, though it gives but a ſpurious red. *Chamb.*

BRASS. *n. ſ.* [bꞃaꞅ, Sax. *pres*, Welch.]

1. A yellow metal, made by mixing copper with lapis calaminaris. It is uſed, in popular language, for any kind of metal in which copper has a part.

*Braſs* is made of copper and calaminaris. *Bacon.*

Men's evil manners live in *braſs*, their virtues
We write in water. *Shakeſp. Henry* VIII.

Let others mold the running maſs
Of metals, and inform the breathing *braſs.* *Dryden.*

2. Impudence.

BRA'SSINESS. *n. ſ.* [from *braſſy.*] An appearance like braſs; ſome quality of braſs.

BRA'SSY. *adj.* [from *braſs.*]

1. Partaking of braſs.

The part in which they lie, is near black, with ſome ſparks of a *braſſy* pyrites in it. *Woodward.*

2. Hard as braſs.

Loſſes,
Enough to preſs a royal merchant down,
And pluck commiſeration of his ſtate
From *braſſy* boſoms, and rough hearts of flint. *Shakeſp.*

3. Impudent.

BRAST. *particip. adj.* [from *burſt.*] Burſt; broken.

There creature never paſt,
That back returned without heavenly grace,
But dreadful furies which their chains have *braſt*,
And damned ſprights ſent forth to make ill men agaſt.
*Fairy Queen, b.* v. *c.* v. *ſtanz.* 31.

BRAT. *n. ſ.* [Its etymology is uncertain; bꞃatt, in Saxon, ſignifies a blanket; from which, perhaps, the modern ſignification may have come.]

1. A child, ſo called in contempt.

He leads them like a thing
Made by ſome other deity than nature,
That ſhapes man better; and they follow him,
Againſt us *brats*, with no leſs confidence,
Than boys purſuing ſummer butterflies. *Shakeſp. Coriolanus.*

This *brat* is none of mine:
Hence with it, and, together with the dame,
Commit them to the fire. *Shakeſp. Winter's Tale.*

The friends, that got the *brats*, were poiſon'd too;
In this ſad caſe what could our vermin do? *Roſcommon.*

Jupiter ſummoned all the birds and beaſts before him, with their *brats* and little ones, to ſee which of them had the prettieſt children. *L'Eſtrange.*

I ſhall live to ſee the inviſible lady, to whom I was obliged, and whom I never beheld, ſince ſhe was a *brat* in hanging-ſleeves. *Swift.*

I give command to kill or ſave,
Can grant ten thouſand pounds a year,
And make a beggar's *brat* a peer. *Swift.*

2. The progeny; the offspring.

The two late conſpiracies were the *brats* and offspring of two contrary factions. *South.*

BRAVA'DO. *n. ſ.* [from *bravada*, Span.] A boaſt; a brag.

Spain, to make good the *bravado*,
Names it the invincible armado. *Anonymous.*

BRAVE. *adj.* [*brave*, Fr.]

1. Courageous; daring; bold; generous; high-ſpirited.

An Egyptian ſoothſayer made Antonius believe, that his genius, which otherways was *brave* and confident, was, in the preſence of Octavius Cæſar, poor and cowardly. *Bacon.*

From armed foes to bring a royal prize,
Shows your *brave* heart victorious as your eyes. *Waller.*

2. Gallant; having a noble mien; lofty; graceful.

I'll prove the prettier fellow of the two,
And wear my dagger with a *braver* grace. *Shakeſp.*

3. Magnificent; grand.

Rings put upon his fingers,
And *brave* attendants near him, when he wakes;
Would not the beggar then forget himſelf? *Shakeſp.*

But whoſoe'er it was nature deſign'd
Firſt a *brave* place, and then as *brave* a mind. *Denham.*

4. Excellent; noble: it is an indeterminate word, uſed to expreſs the ſuperabundance of any valuable quality in men or things.

Let not old age diſgrace my high deſire,
O heavenly ſoul, in human ſhape contain'd;
Old wood inflam'd doth yield the *braveſt* fire,
When younger doth in ſmoke his virtue ſpend. *Sidney.*

If there be iron-ore, and mills, iron is a *brave* commodity where wood aboundeth. *Bacon.*

If a ſtateſman has not this ſcience, he muſt be ſubject to a *braver* man than himſelf, whoſe province it is to direct all his actions to this end. *Digby on the Soul, Dedication.*

BRAVE. *n. ſ.* [*brave*, Fr.]

1. A hector; a man daring beyond decency or diſcretion.

Hot *braves*, like thee, may fight, but know not well
To manage this, the laſt great ſtake. *Dryden.*

Morat's too inſolent, too much a *brave*,
His courage to his envy is a ſlave. *Dryden's Aurengz.*

2. A boaſt; a challenge; a defiance.

There end thy *brave*, and turn thy face in peace;
We grant thou canſt outſcold us. *Shakeſp. King John.*

To BRAVE. *v. a.* [from the noun.]

1. To defy; to challenge; to ſet at defiance.

He upbraids Iago, that he made him
*Brave* me upon the watch. *Shakeſp. Othello.*

My nobles leave me, and my ſtate is *brav'd*,
Ev'n at my gates, with ranks of foreign powers. *Shakeſp.*

The ills of love, not thoſe of fate I fear;
Theſe I can *brave*, but thoſe I cannot bear. *Dryden.*

Like a rock unmov'd, a rock that *braves*
The raging tempeſt, and the riſing waves. *Dryden's Æneid.*

2. To carry a boaſting appearance of.

Both particular perſons and factions are apt enough to flatter themſelves, or, at leaſt, to *brave* that which they believe not. *Bacon's Eſſays*, Nº 16.

BRA'VELY. *adv.* [from *brave.*] In a brave manner; courageouſly; gallantly; ſplendidly.

Martin Swart, with his Germans, performed *bravely.* *Bacon.*

No fire, nor foe, nor fate, nor night,
The Trojan hero did affright,
Who *bravely* twice renew'd the fight. *Denham.*

Your valour *bravely* did th' aſſault ſuſtain,
And fill'd the moats and ditches with the ſlain. *Dryden.*

BRA'VERY. *n. ſ.* [from *brave.*]

1. Courage; magnanimity; generoſity; gallantry.

Certainly it denotes no great *bravery* of mind, to do that out of a deſire of fame, which we could not be prompted to by a generous paſſion for the glory of him that made us. *Spectator*, Nº 255.

Juba, to all the *bravery* of a hero,
Adds ſofteſt love, and more than female ſweetneſs. *Addiſon.*

2. Splendour; magnificence.

Where all the *bravery* that eye may ſee,
And all the happineſs that heart deſire,
Is to be found. *Spenſer's Hubberd's Tale.*

3. Show; oſtentation.

Let princes chooſe miniſters more ſenſible of duty than of riſing, and ſuch as love buſineſs rather upon conſcience than upon *bravery.* *Bacon's Eſſays*, Nº 37.

4. Bravado; boaſt.

Never could man, with more unmanlike *bravery*, uſe his tongue to her diſgrace, which lately had ſung ſonnets of her praiſes. *Sidney's Arcadia.*

For a *bravery* upon this occaſion of power, they crowned their new king in the cathedral church of Dublin. *Bacon.*

There are thoſe that make it a point of *bravery*, to bid defiance to the oracles of divine revelation. *L'Eſtrange.*

BRA'VO. *n. ſ.* [*bravo*, Ital.] A man who murders for hire.

For boldneſs, like the *bravoes* and banditti, is ſeldom employed, but upon deſperate ſervices. *Government of the Tongue.*

No *bravoes* here profeſs the bloody trade,
Nor is the church the murd'rer's refuge made. *Gay's Trivia.*

To BRAWL. *v. n.* [*brouiller*, or *brauler*, Fr.]

1. To quarrel noiſily and indecently.

She troubled was, alas! that it might be,
With tedious *brawlings* of her parents dear. *Sidney.*

Here comes a man of comfort, whoſe advice
Hath often ſtill'd my *brawling* diſcontent. *Shakeſp.*

How now, Sir John! what, are you *brawling* here?
Does this become your place, your time, your buſineſs?
*Shakeſp. Henry* IV. *p.* ii.

Their

Brast ~~part of burst~~ v n.

This fer burst in Stilrechired in Scotland
No gate So Strong, no lock So firm & fast
But with that piercing Noise flew Open
quite or brast
F.Q. 1. 8. 4

1 Bravery
We Stood beewndered another while delighted with the rare bravery thereof till seeing Streams of blood we gallop'd towards them to part them
Sidney

a/b The Lord will take away the bravery of your tinkling Ornaments    Isaiah

5 Beauty, Splendour, delightful Charms
How are the glories of the Field Spun, and by what pencil are they limn'd in their unaffected bravery    Glanv. Seeps

IL facing 3M2v

3 ~~This~~ This is his hand
His foot mercurial, his martial thighs
The Brawns of Hercules
Shak

~~The flesh of any other~~ Animal

A Mortress made with the Brawn of Capons, stampt, strain'd and mingled with like quantity of Almond butter is excellent to nourish the weak
Bac.

The Sharp humour fretted the Skin downward & in process of time became serpiginous and was covered with white brawny Scales
Wisem.

A gentle kind, whose sides with cruel Steel
Through lanced, her bleeding life does rain:
While the sad pang approaching she does feel
Brays out her latest breath & ope her eyes doth Seal
F.Q. 2.1.39

Their batt'ring cannon charged to the mouths,
Till their ſoul-fearing clamours have *brawl'd* down
The flinty ribs of this contemptuous city. *Shakeſp. K. John.*

In council ſhe gives licence to her tongue
Loquacious, *brawling*, ever in the wrong. *Dryden's Fables.*

Leave all noiſy conteſts, all immodeſt clamours, *brawling* language, and eſpecially all perſonal ſcandal and ſcurrility to the meaneſt part of the vulgar world. *Watts.*

2. To ſpeak loud and indecently.

His diviſions, as the times do *brawl*,
Are in three heads; one pow'r againſt the French,
And one againſt Glendower. *Shakeſp. Henry* IV. *p.* ii.

3. To make a noiſe.

As he lay along
Under an oak, whoſe antique root peeps out
Upon the brook that *brawls* along this wood. *Shakeſp.*

BRAWL. *n. ſ.* [from the verb.] Quarrel; noiſe; ſcurrility.

He findeth, that controverſies thereby are made but *brawls*; and therefore wiſheth, that, in ſome lawful aſſembly of churches, all theſe ſtrifes may be decided. *Hooker, Preface.*

Never ſince that middle ſummer's ſpring
Met we on hill, in dale, foreſt, or mead,
But with thy *brawls* thou haſt diſturb'd our ſport.
*Shakeſp. Midſummer Night's Dream.*

That bonum is an animal,
Made good with ſtout polemick *brawl*. *Hudibras.*

BRA'WLER. *n. ſ.* [from *brawl.*] A wrangler; a quarrelſome, noiſy fellow.

An advocate may incur the cenſure of the court, for being a *brawler* in court, on purpoſe to lengthen out the cauſe. *Ayliffe.*

BRAWN. *n. ſ.* [of uncertain etymology.]

1. The fleſhy or muſculous part of the body.

The *brawn* of the arm muſt appear full, ſhadowed on one ſide, then ſhew the wriſt-bone thereof. *Peacham.*

But moſt their looks on the black monarch bend,
His riſing muſcles and his *brawn* commend;
His double biting ax, and beamy ſpear,
Each aſking a gigantick force to rear. *Dryden's Fables.*

2. The arm, ſo called from its being muſculous.

I'll hide my ſilver beard in a gold beaver,
And in my vantbrace put this wither'd *brawn*. *Shakeſp.*

I had purpoſe
Once more to hew thy target from thy *brawn*. *Shakeſp.*

3. Bulk; muſcular ſtrength.

Thy boiſt'rous hands are then of uſe, when I,
With this directing head, thoſe hands apply;
*Brawn* without brain is thine. *Dryden's Fables.*

4. The fleſh of a boar.

The beſt age for the boar is from two years to five years old, at which time it is beſt to geld him, or ſell him for *brawn*. *Mortimer.*

5. A boar.

BRA'WNER. *n. ſ.* [from *brawn.*] A boar killed for the table.

At Chriſtmas time be careful of your fame,
See the old tenant's table be the ſame;
Then if you would ſend up the *brawner* head,
Sweet roſemary and bays around it ſpread. *King.*

BRA'WNINESS. *n. ſ.* [from *brawny.*] Strength; hardneſs.

This *brawnineſs* and inſenſibility of mind, is the beſt armour we can have againſt the common evils and accidents of life. *Locke.*

BRA'WNY. *adj.* [from *brawn.*] Muſculous; fleſhy; bulky; of great muſcles and ſtrength.

The *brawny* fool, who did his vigour boaſt,
In that preſuming confidence was loſt. *Dryden's Juven.*

The native energy
Turns all into the ſubſtance of the tree,
Starves and deſtroys the fruit, is only made
For *brawny* bulk, and for a barren ſhade. *Dryden's Virgil.*

To BRAY. *v. a.* [bꞃacan, Sax. *braier*, Fr.] To pound; or grind ſmall.

I'll burſt him; I will *bray*
His bones as in a mortar. *Chapman's Iliads.*

Except you would *bray* chriſtendom in a mortar, and mould it into a new paſte, there is no poſſibility of a holy war. *Bacon.*

To BRAY. *v. n.* [*broire*, Fr. *barrio*, Lat.]

1. To make a noiſe as an aſs.

Laugh, and they
Return it louder than an aſs can *bray*. *Dryden's Juvenal.*

2. To make an offenſive or diſagreeable noiſe.

What, ſhall our feaſt be kept with ſlaughter'd men?
Shall *braying* trumpets, and loud churliſh drums,
Clamours of hell, be meaſures to our pomp? *Shakeſp.*

Arms on armour claſhing, *bray'd*
Horrible diſcord. *Milton's Paradiſe Loſt, b.* vi. *l.* 209.

'Agad if he ſhould hear the lion roar, he'd cudgel him into an aſs, and to his primitive *braying*. *Congreve's Old Batchelor.*

BRAY. *n. ſ.* [from the verb.] Noiſe; ſound.

Boiſt'rous untun'd drums,
And harſh reſounding trumpets dreadful *bray*. *Shakeſp.*

BRA'YER. *n. ſ.* [from *bray.*]

1. One that brays like an aſs.

Hold! cry'd the queen; a cat-call each ſhall win;
Equal your merits, equal is your din!
But that this well-diſputed game may end,
Sound forth, my *brayers!* and the welkin rend. *Pope.*

2. [With printers; from *to bray*, or *beat.*] An inſtrument to temper the ink.

To BRAZE. *v. a.* [from *braſs.*]

1. To ſolder with braſs.

If the nut be not to be caſt in braſs, but only hath a worm *brazed* into it, this niceneſs is not ſo abſolutely neceſſary, becauſe that worm is firſt turned up, and bowed into the grooves of the ſpindle, and you may try that before it is *brazed* in the nut. *Moxon's Mechanical Exerciſes.*

2. To harden to impudence.

I have ſo often bluſhed to acknowledge him, that now I am *brazed* to it. *Shakeſp. King Lear.*

If damned cuſtom hath not *braz'd* it ſo,
That it is proof and bulwark againſt ſenſe. *Shakeſp. Hamlet.*

BRA'ZEN. *adj.* [from *braſs.*]

1. Made of braſs.

Get alſo a ſmall pair of *brazen* compaſſes, and a fine ruler, for taking the diſtance. *Peacham.*

A bough his *brazen* helmet did ſuſtain;
His heavier arms lay ſcatter'd on the plain. *Dryden's Æn.*

2. Proceeding from braſs: a poetical uſe.

Trumpeters
With *brazen* din blaſt you the city's ear,
Make mingle with your rattling tabourines. *Shakeſp.*

3. Impudent.

To BRA'ZEN. *v. n.* To be impudent; to bully.

When I uſed to reprimand him for his tricks, he would talk ſaucily, lye, and *brazen* it out, as if he had done nothing amiſs. *Arbuthnot's Hiſt. of J. Bull.*

BRA'ZENFACE. *n. ſ.* [from *brazen* and *face.*] An impudent wretch.

You do, if you ſuſpect me in any diſhoneſty.——Well ſaid, *brazenface*; hold it out. *Shakeſp. Merry Wives of Windſ.*

BRA'ZENFACED. *adj.* [from *brazenface.*] Impudent; ſhameleſs.

What a *brazenfaced* varlet art thou, to deny thou knoweſt me? Is it two days ago, ſince I tript up thy heels, and beat thee before the king? *Shakeſp. King Lear.*

Quick-witted, *brazenfac'd*, with fluent tongues,
Patient of labours, and diſſembling wrongs. *Dryden.*

BRA'ZENNESS. *n. ſ.* [from *brazen.*]

1. Appearing like braſs.

2. Impudence.

BRA'ZIER. *n. ſ.* See BRASIER.

The halfpence and farthings in England, if you ſhould ſell them to the *brazier*, you would not loſe above a penny in a ſhilling. *Swift's Draper's Letters.*

BREACH. *n. ſ.* [from *break*; *breche*, Fr.]

1. The act of breaking any thing.

This tempeſt
Daſhing the garment of this peace, aboded
The ſudden *breach* on't. *Shakeſp. Henry* VIII.

2. The ſtate of being broken.

O you kind gods!
Cure this great *breach* in his abuſed nature. *Shakeſp.*

3. A gap in a fortification made by a battery.

The wall was blown up in two places; by which *breach* the Turks ſeeking to have entered, made bloody fight. *Knolles.*

Till mad with rage upon the *breach* he fir'd,
Slew fiends and foes, and in the ſmoke retir'd. *Dryden.*

4. The violation of a law or contract.

That oath would ſure contain them greatly, or the *breach* of it bring them to ſhorter vengeance. *Spenſer's Ireland.*

What are thoſe *breaches* of the law of nature and nations, which do forfeit all right in a nation to govern? *Bacon.*

*Breach* of duty towards our neighbours, ſtill involves in it a *breach* of duty towards God. *South.*

The laws of the goſpel are the only ſtanding rules of morality; and the penalties affixed by God to the *breach* of thoſe laws, the only guards that can effectually reſtrain men within the true bounds of decency and virtue. *Rogers.*

5. The opening in a coaſt.

But th' heedful boatman ſtrongly forth did ſtretch
His brawny arms, and all his body ſtrain,
That th' utmoſt ſandy *breach* they ſhortly fetch,
While the dread danger does behind remain. *Fairy Queen.*

6. Difference; quarrel; ſeparation of kindneſs.

It would have been long before the jealouſies and *breaches* between the armies, would have been compoſed. *Clarendon.*

7. Infraction; injury.

This *breach* upon his kingly power was without a precedent. *Clarendon.*

BREAD. *n. ſ.* [bꞃeoꝺ, Saxon.]

1. Food made of ground corn.

Mankind have found the means to make them into *bread*, which is the lighteſt and propereſt aliment for human bodies. *Arbuthnot on Aliments.*

*Bread* that decaying man with ſtrength ſupplies,
And gen'rous wine, which thoughtful ſorrow flies. *Pope.*

2. Food in general, such as nature requires; to *get bread*, implies, to get sufficient for support without luxury.

In the sweat of thy face shalt thou eat *bread*. *Gen.* iii. 19.

If these pretenders were not supported by the simplicity of the inquisitive fools, the trade would not find them *bread*. *L'Estrange.*

This dowager on whom my tale I found,
A simple sober life in patience led,
And had but just enough to buy her *bread*. *Dryden.*

When I submit to such indignities,
Make me a citizen, a senator of Rome;
To sell my country, with my voice, for *bread*. *Philips.*

I neither have been bred a scholar, a soldier, nor to any kind of business; this creates uneasiness in my mind, fearing I shall in time want *bread*. *Spectator*, N° 203.

3. Support of life at large.

God is pleased to try our patience by the ingratitude of those, who, having eaten of our *bread*, have lift up themselves against us. *King Charles.*

But sometimes virtue starves, while vice is fed;
What then? Is the reward of virtue *bread*? *Pope.*

BREAD-CHIPPER. *n. s.* [from *bread* and *chip*.] One that chips bread; a baker's servant.

No abuse, Hal, on my honour; no abuse.——Not to dispraise me, and call me pantler, and *bread-chipper*, and I know not what? *Shakesp. Henry* IV. *p.* ii.

BREAD-CORN. *n. s.* [from *bread* and *corn*.] Corn of which bread is made.

There was not one drop of beer in the town; the bread, and *bread-corn*, sufficed not for six days. *Hayward.*

When it is ripe, they gather it, and, bruising it among *bread-corn*, they put it up into a vessel, and keep it as food for their slaves. *Broome's Notes on the Odyssey, b.* viii.

BREAD-ROOM. *n. s.* [In a ship.] A part of the hold separated by a bulk-head from the rest, where the bread and bisket for the men are kept. *Sea Dict.*

BREADTH. *n. s.* [from bpab, broad, Saxon.] The measure of any plain superficies from side to side.

There is in Ticinum, in Italy, a church that hath windows only from above: it is in length an hundred feet, in *breadth* twenty, and in height near fifty; having a door in the midst. *Bacon's Nat. Hist.* N° 794.

The river Ganges, according unto later relations, if not in length, yet in *breadth* and depth, may be granted to excel it. *Brown's Vulgar Errours, b.* vi. *c.* 7.

Then all approach the slain with vast surprize,
Admire on what a *breadth* of earth he lies. *Dryden.*

In our Gothick cathedrals, the narrowness of the arch makes it rise in height; the lowness opens it in *breadth*. *Addison.*

To BREAK. *v. a.* pret. I *broke*, or *brake*; part. pass. *broke*, or *broken*. [bpecan, Saxon.]

1. To part by violence.

When I *brake* the five loaves among five thousand, how many baskets of fragments took ye up? *Mark*, viii. 19.

Let us *break* their bands asunder, and cast away their cords from us. *Psalm* ii. 3.

See, said the sire, how soon 'tis done;
Then took and *broke* them one by one:
So strong you'll be in friendship ty'd;
So quickly *broke*, if you divide. *Swift.*

2. To burst, or open by force.

Moses tells us, that the fountains of the earth were *broke* open, or clove asunder. *Burnet's Theory.*

3. To pierce; to divide, as light divides darkness.

By a dim winking lamp, which feebly *broke*
The gloomy vapours, he lay stretch'd along. *Dryden.*

4. To destroy by violence.

This is the fabrick, which, when God *breaketh* down, none can build up again. *Burnet's Theory.*

5. To overcome; to surmount.

Into my hand he forc'd the tempting gold,
While I with modest struggling *broke* his hold. *Gay.*

6. To batter; to make breaches or gaps in.

I'd give bay Curtal, and his furniture,
My mouth no more were *broken* than these boys,
And writ as little beard. *Shakesp. All's well that ends well.*

7. To crush or destroy the strength of the body.

O father abbot!
An old man, *broken* with the storms of state,
Is come to lay his weary bones among ye;
Give him a little earth for charity. *Shakesp. Henry* VIII.

The breaking of that parliament
*Broke* him; as that dishonest victory
At Chæronea, fatal to liberty,
Kill'd with report that old man eloquent. *Milton.*

Have not some of his vices weakened his body, and *broke* his health? have not others dissipated his estate, and reduced him to want? *Tillotson.*

8. To sink or appal the spirit.

I'll brave her to her face;
I'll give my anger its free course against her:
Thou shalt see, Phœnix, how I'll *break* her pride. *Philips.*

9. To subdue.

Why, then, thou can'st not *break* her to the lute.—
—Why, no; for she hath broke the lute to me.
*Shakesp. Taming the Shrew.*

Behold young Juba, the Numidian prince,
With how much care he forms himself to glory,
And *breaks* the fierceness of his native temper. *Addison's Cato.*

10. To crush; to disable; to incapacitate.

The defeat of that day at Cropredy was much greater than it then appeared to be; and it even *broke* the heart of his army. *Clarendon.*

Your hopes without are vanish'd into smoke;
Your captains taken, and your armies *broke*. *Dryden.*

11. To weaken the mind.

Opprest nature sleeps:
This rest might yet have balm'd thy *broken* senses,
Which, if conveniency will not allow,
Stand in hard cure. *Shakesp. King Lear.*

If any dabler in poetry dares venture upon the experiment, he will only *break* his brains. *Felton on the Classicks.*

12. To tame; to train to obedience.

What boots it to *break* a colt, and to let him streight run loose at random? *Spenser's State of Ireland.*

So fed before he's *broke*, he'll bear
Too great a stomach patiently to feel
The lashing whip, or chew the curbing steel. *May's Virgil.*

That hot-mouth'd beast that bears against the curb,
Hard to be *broken* even by lawful kings. *Dryden.*

No sports but what belong to war they know,
To *break* the stubborn colt, to bend the bow. *Dryden.*

Virtues like these,
Make human nature shine, reform the soul,
And *break* our fierce barbarians into men. *Addison's Cato.*

13. To make bankrupt.

For this few know themselves: for merchants *broke*,
View their estate with discontent and pain. *Davies.*

The king's grown bankrupt, like a *broken* man. *Shakesp.*

With arts like these, rich Matho, when he speaks,
Attracts all fees, and little lawyers *breaks*. *Dryden.*

A command or call to be liberal, all of a sudden impoverishes the rich, *breaks* the merchant, and shuts up every private man's exchequer. *South.*

14. To crack or open the skin, so as that the blood comes.

She could have run and waddled all about; even the day before she *broke* her brow; and then my husband took up the child. *Shakesp. Romeo and Juliet.*

Weak soul! and blindly to destruction led:
She break her heart! she'll sooner *break* your head. *Dryden.*

15. To violate a contract or promise.

Lovers *break* not hours,
Unless it be to come before their time. *Shakesp. T. G. of Ver.*

Pardon this fault, and, by my soul I swear,
I never more will *break* an oath with thee. *Shakesp.*

Did not our worthies of the house,
Before they *broke* the peace, *break* vows? *Hudibras.*

16. To infringe a law.

Unhappy man! to *break* the pious laws
Of nature, pleading in his children's cause. *Dryden.*

17. To intercept; to hinder the effect of.

*Break* their talk, mistress, quickly; my kinsman shall speak for himself. *Shakesp. Merry Wives of Windsor.*

Spirit of wine, mingled with common water, yet so as if the first fall be *broken*, by means of a sop, or otherwise, it stayeth above. *Bacon's Physical Remains.*

Think not my sense of virtue is so small;
I'll rather leap down first, and *break* your fall. *Dryden.*

As one condemn'd to leap a precipice,
Who sees before his eyes the depth below,
Stops short, and looks about for some kind shrub,
To *break* his dreadful fall. *Dryden's Spanish Friar.*

She held my hand, the destin'd blow to *break*,
Then from her rosy lips began to speak. *Dryden.*

18. To interrupt.

Some solitary cloister will I choose,
Coarse my attire, and short shall be my sleep,
*Broke* by the melancholy midnight bell. *Dryden's Sp. Friar.*

The father was so moved, that he could only command his voice, *broke* with sighs and sobbings, so far as to bid her proceed. *Addison. Spectator*, N° 164.

The poor shade shiv'ring stands, and must not *break*
His painful silence, till the mortal speak. *Tickell.*

Sometimes in *broken* words he sigh'd his care,
Look'd pale, and tumbled when he view'd the fair. *Gay.*

19. To separate company.

Did not Paul and Barnabas dispute with that vehemence, that they were forced to *break* company? *Atterbury.*

20. To dissolve any union.

It is great folly, as well as injustice, to *break* off so noble a relation. *Collier of Friendship.*

21. To reform; with *of*.

The French were not quite *broken of* it, until some time after they became christians. *Grew's Cosmologia Sacra, b.* iii. *c.* 6.

22. To

Where mice and rats devour'd poetic bread
And with heroic Verse luxuriously were fed
Dry. Juv.

IL facing 3N[v]

—†

26 breakfast
A thousand men have broke their fasts to day,
That ne'er shall dine, unless thou yield the Crown
Shak.

34. To break up
He brake up his Court and retired himself
his wife and children into a forrest thereby,
Wherein he hath built two fine lodges
Sidney

To break the Ice, a proverbial expression
for to open a way.
Thus I have broke the ice to invention for
the lively representation of floods & rivers —
necessary for painters and poets. Peacham

To break forth
To declare to quit allegiance
The Earl of Desmond before his breaking forth
into rebellion, conveyed secretly all his lands
to Feoffees in trust Spenser

To discompose — to interrupt Sleep
Lull'd with the sweet Nepenthe of a Court
There where no fathers brothers friendships
Once break their rest or stir them from their grace
place
Pope

IL facing 3N2r

22. To open something new; to propound something by an overture.

When any new thing shall be propounded, no counsellor should suddenly deliver any positive opinion, but only hear it, and, at the most, but to *break* it, at first, that it may be the better understood at the next meeting. *Bacon.*

I, who much desir'd to know
Of whence she was, yet fearful how to *break*
My mind, adventur'd humbly thus to speak. *Dryden's Fab.*

23. *To break the back.* To strain or dislocate the vertebræ with too heavy burdens.

I'd rather crack my sinews, *break my back*,
Than you should such dishonour undergo. *Shakesp. Tempest.*

24. *To break the back.* To disable one's fortune.

O, many
Have *broke their backs*, with laying manors on 'em,
For this great journey. *Shakesp. Henry* VIII.

25. *To break a deer.* To cut it up at table.

26. *To break fast.* To eat the first time in the day.

27. *To break ground.* To plow.

When the price of corn falleth, men generally give over surplus tillage, and *break no more ground* than will serve to supply their own turn. *Carew's Survey of Cornwal.*

The husbandman must first *break the land*, before it be made capable of good seed. *Sir J. Davies on Ireland.*

28. *To break ground.* To open trenches.

29. *To break the heart.* To destroy with grief.

Good my lord, enter here.——
—Will't *break my heart?*——
I'd rather *break mine own.* *Shakesp. King Lear.*

Should not all relations bear a part?
It were enough to *break a single heart.* *Dryden.*

30. *To break a jest.* To utter a jest unexpected.

31. *To break the neck.* To lux, or put out the neck joints.

I had as lief thou didst *break his neck*, as his fingers. *Shakesp.*

32. *To break off.* To put a sudden stop.

33. *To break off.* To preclude by some obstacle suddenly interposed.

To check the starts and sallies of the soul,
And *break off* all its commerce with the tongue. *Addison.*

34. *To break up.* To dissolve; to put a sudden end to.

Who cannot rest till he good fellows find;
He *breaks up* house, turns out of doors his mind. *Herbert.*

He threatened, that the tradesmen would beat out his teeth, if he did not retire immediately, and *break up* the meeting. *Arbuthnot's History of J. Bull.*

35. *To break up.* To open; to lay open.

The shells being thus lodged amongst this mineral matter, when this comes now to be *broke up*, it exhibits impressions of the shells. *Woodward on Fossils.*

36. *To break up.* To separate or disband.

After taking the strong city of Belgrade, Solyman returning to Constantinople, *broke up* his army, and there lay still the whole year following. *Knolles's History of the Turks.*

37. *To break upon the wheel.* To punish by stretching a criminal upon the wheel, and breaking his bones with bats.

38. *To break wind.* To give vent to wind in the body.

To Break. *v. n.*

1. To part in two.

Give sorrow words, the grief that does not speak,
Whispers the o'erfraught heart, and bids it *break.* *Shakesp.*

2. To burst.

The clouds are still above; and, while I speak,
A second deluge o'er our heads may *break.* *Dryden.*

The Roman camp
Hangs o'er us black and threatning, like a storm
Just *breaking* on our heads. *Dryden's All for Love.*

3. To burst by dashing, as waves on a rock.

He could compare the confusion of a multitude to that tumult in the Icarian sea, dashing and *breaking* among its crowd of islands. *Pope's Essay on Homer.*

At last a falling billow stops his breath,
*Breaks* o'er his head, and whelms him underneath. *Dryden.*

4. To break as a swelling; to open, and discharge matter.

Some hidden abscess in the mesentery, *breaking* some few days after, was discovered to be an aposteme. *Harvey.*

Ask one who hath subdued his natural rage, how he likes the change, and undoubtedly he will tell you, that it is no less happy than the ease of a *broken* imposthume, after the painful gathering and filling of it. *Decay of Piety.*

5. To open as the morning.

The day *breaks* not, it is my heart,
Because that I and you must part.
Stay, or else my joys will die,
And perish in their infancy. *Donne.*

When a man thinks of any thing in the darkness of the night, whatever deep impressions it may make in his mind, they are apt to vanish as soon as the day *breaks* about him. *Addison. Spectator*, N° 465.

6. To burst forth; to exclaim.

Every man,
After the hideous storm that follow'd, was
A thing inspir'd; and, not consulting, *broke*
Into a general prophecy. *Shakesp. Henry* VIII.

7. To become bankrupt.

I did mean, indeed, to pay you with this; which, if, like an ill venture, it come unluckily home, I *break*, and you, my gentle creditors, lose. *Shakesp. Henry* IV. *p.* ii. *Epilogue.*

He that puts all upon adventures, doth oftentimes *break*, and come to poverty. *Bacon's Essays*, N° 35.

Cutler saw tenants *break*, and houses fall,
For very want he could not build a wall. *Pope.*

8. To decline in health and strength.

Yet thus, methinks, I hear them speak;
See how the dean begins to *break*:
Poor gentleman! he droops apace. *Swift.*

9. To issue out with vehemence.

Whose wounds, yet fresh, with bloody hands he strook,
While from his breast the dreadful accents *broke.* *Pope.*

10. To make way with some kind of suddenness, impetuosity, or violence.

Calamities may be nearest at hand, and readiest to *break* in suddenly upon us, which we, in regard of times or circumstances, may imagine to be farthest off. *Hooker, b.* v. § 41.

The three mighty men *broke* through the host of the Philistines. 2 *Sam.* xxiii. 16.

They came into Judah, and *brake* into it. 2 *Chron.* xxi. 17.

Or who shut up the sea within doors, when it *brake* forth, as if it had issued out of the womb? *Job*, xxxviii. 8.

This, this is he; softly awhile,
Let us not *break* in upon him. *Milton's Agonistes, l.* 115.

He resolved, that Balfour should use his utmost endeavour to *break* through with his whole body of horse. *Clarendon, b.* viii.

When the channel of a river is overcharged with water, more than it can deliver, it necessarily *breaks* over the banks, to make itself room. *Hale's Origin of Mankind.*

Sometimes his anger *breaks* through all disguises,
And spares not gods nor men. *Denham's Sophy.*

Till through those clouds the sun of knowledge *brake*,
And Europe from her lethargy did wake. *Denham.*

Oh! could'st thou *break* through fate's severe decree,
A new Marcellus shall arise in thee. *Dryden's Æneid.*

At length I've acted my severest part;
I feel the woman *breaking* in upon me,
And melt about my heart, my tears will flow. *Addison's Cato.*

How does the lustre of our father's actions,
Through the dark cloud of ills that cover him,
*Break* out, and burn with more triumphant blaze! *Addison.*

And yet, methinks, a beam of light *breaks* in,
On my departing soul. *Addison's Cato.*

There are not wanting some, who, struck with the usefulness of these charities, *break* through all the difficulties and obstructions that now lie in the way towards advancing them. *Atterbury.*

Almighty pow'r, by whose most wise command,
Helpless, forlorn, uncertain here I stand;
Take this faint glimmering of thyself away,
Or *break* into my soul with perfect day! *Arbuthnot.*

Heav'n its sparkling portals wide display,
And *break* upon thee in a flood of day! *Pope's Messiah.*

I must pay her the last duty of friendship wherever she is, though I *break* through the whole plan of life which I have formed in my mind. *Swift's Letters.*

11. To come to an explanation.

But perceiving this great alteration in his friend, he thought fit to *break* with him thereof. *Sidney, b.* i.

Stay with me awhile;
I am to *break* with thee of some affairs,
That touch me near. *Shakesp. Two Gentlemen of Verona.*

*Break* with them, gentle love,
About the drawing as many of their husbands
Into the plot, as can; if not, to rid 'em,
That'll be the easier practice. *B. Johnson's Catiline.*

12. To fall out; to be friends no longer.

Be not afraid to *break*
With murd'rers, and traitors, for the saving
A life so near and necessary to you,
As is your country's. *B. Johnson's Catiline.*

To *break* upon the score of danger or expence, is to be mean and narrow-spirited. *Collier on Friendship.*

Sighing, he says, we must certainly *break*,
And my cruel unkindness compels him to speak. *Prior.*

13. *To break from.* To separate from with some vehemence.

How didst thou scorn life's meaner charms,
Thou who cou'dst *break from* Laura's arms? *Roscommon.*

Thus radiant *from* the circling crowd he *broke*;
And thus with manly modesty he spoke. *Dryden's Virgil.*

This custom makes bigots and scepticks; and those that *break from* it, are in danger of heresy. *Locke.*

14. *To break in.* To enter unexpectedly, without proper preparation.

The doctor is a pedant, that, with a deep voice, and a magisterial air, *breaks in* upon conversation, and drives down all before him. *Addison on Italy.*

15. To

15. *To break.* To diſcard.

When I ſee a great officer *broke*, a change made in the court, or the miniſtry, and this under the moſt gracious princeſs that ever reigned. *Swift.*

16. *To break looſe.* To eſcape from captivity.

Who would not, finding way, *break looſe* from hell,
And boldly venture to whatever place,
Fartheſt from pain? *Milton's Par. Loſt, b.* iv. *l.* 889.

17. *To break looſe.* To ſhake off reſtraint.

If we deal falſely in covenant with God, and *break looſe* from all our engagements to him, we releaſe God from all the promiſes he has made to us. *Tillotſon.*

18. *To break off.* To deſiſt ſuddenly.

Do not peremptorily *break off*, in any buſineſs, in a fit of anger; but howſoever you ſhew bitterneſs, do not act any thing that is not revocable. *Bacon.*

Pius Quintus, at the very time when that memorable victory was won by the Chriſtians at Lepanto, being then hearing of cauſes in conſiſtory, *broke off* ſuddenly, and ſaid to thoſe about him, it is now more time we ſhould give thanks to God. *Bacon.*

When you begin to conſider, whether you may ſafely take one draught more, let that be accounted a ſign late enough to *break off.* *Taylor's Rule of living holy.*

19. *To break off from.* To part from with violence.

I muſt *from* this enchanting queen *break off.* *Shakeſp.*

20. *To break out.* To diſcover itſelf in ſudden effects.

Let not one ſpark of filthy luſtful fire
*Break out*, that may her ſacred peace moleſt. *Spenſer.*

They ſmother and keep down the flame of the miſchief, ſo as it may not *break out* in their time of government; what comes afterwards, they care not. *Spenſer's Ireland.*

Such a deal of wonder is *broken out* within this hour, that ballad-makers cannot be able to expreſs it. *Shakeſp.*

As fire *breaks out* of flint by percuſſion, ſo wiſdom and truth iſſueth out of the agitation of argument. *Howel.*

Fully ripe, his ſwelling fate *breaks out*,
And hurries him to mighty miſchiefs on. *Dryden.*

All turn'd their ſides, and to each other ſpoke;
I ſaw their words *break out* in fire and ſmoke. *Dryden.*

Like a ball of fire, the further thrown,
Still with a greater blaze ſhe ſhone,
And her bright ſoul *broke out* on ev'ry ſide. *Dryden.*

There can be no greater labour, than to be always diſſembling; there being ſo many ways by which a ſmothered truth is apt to blaze, and *break out.* *South.*

They are men of concealed fire, that doth not *break out* in the ordinary circumſtances of life. *Addiſon on the War.*

A violent fever *broke out* in the place, which ſwept away great multitudes. *Addiſon. Spectator*, N° 164.

21. *To break out.* To have eruptions from the body, as puſtules or ſores.

22. *To break out.* To become diſſolute.

He *broke* not *out* into his great exceſſes, while he was reſtrained by the counſels and authority of Seneca. *Dryden.*

23. *To break up.* To ceaſe; to intermit.

It is credibly affirmed, that, upon that very day, when the river firſt riſeth, great plagues in Cairo uſe ſuddenly to *break up.* *Bacon's Natural Hiſt.* N° 743.

24. *To break up.* To diſſolve itſelf.

Theſe, and the like conceits, when men have cleared their underſtanding, by the light of experience, will ſcatter and *break up*, like miſt. *Bacon's Nat. Hiſt.* N° 124.

The ſpeedy depredation of air upon watery moiſture, and verſion of the ſame into air, appeareth in nothing more viſible, than the ſudden diſcharge or vaniſhing of a little cloud of breath, or vapour, from glaſs, or any poliſhed body; for the miſtineſs ſcattereth, and *breaketh up* ſuddenly. *Bacon.*

But, ere he came near it, the pillar and croſs of light *brake up*, and caſt itſelf abroad, as it were, into a firmament of many ſtars. *Bacon's New Atlantis.*

What we obtain by converſation, is oftentimes loſt again, as ſoon as the company *breaks up*, or, at leaſt, when the day vaniſhes. *Watts.*

25. *To break up.* To begin holidays; to be diſmiſſed from buſineſs.

Our army is diſpers'd already:
Like youthful ſteers unyok'd, they took their courſe
Eaſt, weſt, north, ſouth: or, like a ſchool *broke up*,
Each hurries tow'rds his home and ſporting-place. *Shakeſp.*

26. *To break with.* To part friendſhip with any.

There is a ſlave whom we have put in priſon,
Reports, the Volſcians, with two ſeveral powers,
Are entered in the Roman territories.—
—Go ſee this rumourer whipt. It cannot be,
The Volſcians dare *break with* us. *Shakeſp. Coriolanus.*

Can there be any thing of friendſhip in ſnares, hooks, and trapans? Whoſoever *breaks with* his friend upon ſuch terms, has enough to warrant him in ſo doing, both before God and and man. *South.*

Invent ſome apt pretence,
To *break with* Bertran. *Dryden's Spaniſh Friar.*

27. It is to be obſerved of this extenſive and perplexed *verb*, that, in all its ſignifications, whether *active* or *neutral*, it has ſome reference to its primitive meaning, by implying either detriment, ſuddenneſs, or violence.

BREAK. *n. ſ.* [from the verb.]

1. State of being broken; opening.

From the *break* of day until noon, the roaring of the cannon never ceaſed. *Knolles's Hiſt. of the Turks.*

For now, and ſince firſt *break* of day, the fiend,
Mere ſerpent in appearance, forth was come. *Parad. Loſt.*

They muſt be drawn from far, and without *breaks*, to avoid the multiplicity of lines. *Dryden's Dufreſnoy.*

The ſight of it would be quite loſt, did it not ſometimes diſcover itſelf through the *breaks* and openings of the woods that grow about it. *Addiſon.*

2. A pauſe; an interruption.

3. A line drawn, noting that the ſenſe is ſuſpended.

All modern traſh is
Set forth with num'rous *breaks* and daſhes. *Swift.*

BRE'AKER. *n. ſ.* [from *break.*]

1. He that breaks any thing.

Cardinal, I'll be no *breaker* of the law. *Shakeſp. H. IV.*

If the churches were not employed to be places to hear God's law, there would be need of them, to be priſons for the *breakers* of the laws of men. *South.*

2. A wave broken by rocks or ſandbanks.

To BRE'AKFAST. *v. n.* [from *break* and *faſt.*] To eat the firſt meal in the day.

As ſoon as Phœbus' rays inſpect us,
Firſt, Sir, I read, and then I *breakfaſt.* *Prior.*

BRE'AKFAST. *n. ſ.* [from the verb.]

1. The firſt meal in the day.

The duke was at *breakfaſt*, the laſt of his repaſts in this world. *Wotton.*

2. The thing eaten at the firſt meal.

Hope is a good *breakfaſt*, but it is a bad ſupper. *Bacon.*

A good piece of bread would be often the beſt *breakfaſt* for my young maſter. *Locke.*

3. A meal, or food in general.

Had I been ſeized by a hungry lion,
I would have been a *breakfaſt* to the beaſt. *Shakeſp.*

I lay me down to gaſp my lateſt breath,
The wolves will get a *breakfaſt* by my death,
Yet ſcarce enough their hunger to ſupply. *Dryden.*

BRE'AKNECK. *n. ſ.* [from *break* and *neck.*] A fall in which the neck is broken; a ſteep place endangering the neck.

I muſt
Forſake the court; to do't or no, is certain
To me a *breakneck.* *Shakeſp. Winter's Tale.*

BRE'AKPROMISE. *n. ſ.* [from *break* and *promiſe.*] One that makes a practice of breaking his promiſe.

I will think you the moſt atheiſtical *breakpromiſe*, and the moſt hollow lover. *Shakeſp. As you like it.*

BRE'AKVOW. *n. ſ.* [from *break* and *vow.*] He that practiſes the breach of vows.

That daily *breakvow*, he that wins of all,
Of kings, of beggars, old men, young men, maids.
*Shakeſp. King John.*

BREAM. *n. ſ.* [*brame*, Fr.] The name of a fiſh.

The *bream* being at full growth, is a large fiſh; he will breed both in rivers and ponds, but loves beſt to live in ponds. He is, by *Geſner*, taken to be more elegant than wholſome. He is long in growing, but breeds exceedingly in a water that pleaſes him, and, in many ponds, ſo faſt as to overſtock them, and ſtarve the other fiſh. He is very broad, with a forked tail, and his ſcales ſet in excellent order. He hath large eyes, and a narrow ſucking mouth, two ſets of teeth, and a lozing bone, to help his grinders. The male is obſerved to have two large melts, and the female two large bags of eggs or ſpawn. *Walton's Angler.*

A broad *bream*, to pleaſe ſome curious taſte,
While yet alive in boiling water caſt,
Vex'd with unwonted heat, boils, flings about. *Waller.*

BREAST. *n. ſ.* [bꞃeoꞅꞇ, Saxon.]

1. The middle part of the human body, between the neck and the belly.

2. The dugs or teats of women which contain the milk.

The ſubſtance of the breaſts is compoſed of a great number of glands, of an oval figure, which lie in a great quantity of fat. Their excretory ducts, as they approach the nipple, join and unite together, till at laſt they form ſeven, eight, or more, ſmall pipes, called *tubuli lactiferi*, which have ſeveral croſs canals, by which they communicate with one another, that if any of them be ſtopped, the milk, which was brought to it, might not ſtagnate, but paſs through by the other pipes, which all terminate in the extremity of the nipple. They have arteries and veins from the ſubclavian and intercoſtal. They have nerves from the vertebral pairs, and from the ſixth pair of the brain. Their uſe is to ſeparate the milk for the nouriſhment of the fœtus. The tubes, which compoſe the glands of the *breaſt* in maids, like a ſphincter muſcle, contract ſo cloſely, that no part of the blood can enter them; but when the womb grows big with

2 the breast of Hecuba
When she did suckle Hector lookd not lovelier
Than Hectors forehead when it spit forth blood
At Grecian Swords contending
Shak.

‡

Round their lovely breast & head
Fresh flowers their mingled Odours shed
Prior



IL facing 3N2v

[3] ~~& any efflux, any visible emanation~~
Holding the electrick unto the light, Many particles thereof will be discharged from it, which motion is perform'd by the breath of the effluvium issuing with agility: ~~For as the electric cooleth the projection of the atoms ceaseth.~~
Bro. V. E.

[2] The breast of Hecuba
When she did suckle Hector look'd not lovelier
Shak

Breasted [breast] b
Having a breast heart or disposition of any kind
Since you to nonregardance cast my faith
And that I partly know the instrument
That screws me from my true place in your favour
Live you the marble-breasted tyrant still
Shak.

3 To nightly trance or breathed spell
Inspires the pale ey'd priest from the prophetic cell
Milton

4 One v.a strange draught prescribed by Hippocrates for a short breathed man was half a gallon of hydromel with a little vinegar, to be taken at once. This seems to be prescribed as well for exercise as medicine
Arbuth.

~~5 a~~ c 7 To utter vocally
The captives as their tyrant shall require
That they should breath the song & touch the lire
Shall say can Jacob's servile race rejoice
Untun'd the music & disus'd the voice
Prior

Breathful Adj. [breath] d
Odorous strong scented
~~Embathed balm & cheerful galingale~~
Fresh costmary & breathful camomil
~~Dull poppy and drink-quickning~~
Spens.

Breath in Shakespear is transfer'd to suffrage or vote
Were he to stand for consul, never would he
Appear in the market place, nor on him put
The napless vesture of humility
Nor shewing as the manner is his wounds
To th' people, beg their stinking breaths
Shak. Cor.

with a fœtus, and compreſſes the deſcending trunk of the great artery, the blood flows in a greater quantity, and with a greater force, through the arteries of the *breaſts*, and forces a paſſage into their glands, which, being at firſt narrow, admits only of a thin water; but growing wider by degrees, as the womb grows bigger, the glands receive a thick ſerum, and, after birth, they run with a thick milk; becauſe that blood, which before did flow to the fœtus, and, for three or four days afterwards, by the uterus, beginning then to ſtop, does more dilate the mamillary glands. *Quincy.*

They pluck the fatherleſs from the *breaſt*. *Job*, xxiv. 9.

3. The part of a beaſt that is under the neck, between the fore-legs.

4. The heart; the conſcience; the diſpoſition of the mind.

Needleſs was written law, where none oppreſt;
The law of man was written in his *breaſt*. *Dryden's Ovid.*

5. The paſſions; the regard.

Margarita firſt poſſeſs'd,
If I remember well, my *breaſt*. *Cowley.*

To Breast. *v. a.* [from the noun.] To meet in front; to oppoſe breaſt to breaſt.

The threaden ſails
Draw the huge bottoms through the furrow'd ſea,
*Breaſting* the lofty ſurge. *Shakeſp. Henry* V.

Bre'astbone. *n. ſ.* [from *breaſt* and *bone.*] The bone of the breaſt; the ſternum.

The belly ſhall be eminent by ſhadowing the flank, and under the *breaſtbone*. *Peacham.*

Bre'astcasket. *n. ſ.* [from *breaſt* and *caſket.*] With mariners. The largeſt and longeſt caſkets, which are a ſort of ſtrings placed in the middle of the yard.

Bre'astfast. *n. ſ.* [from *breaſt* and *faſt.*] In a ſhip. A rope faſtened to ſome part of her forward on, to hold her head to a warp, or the like. *Harris.*

Bre'asthigh. *adj.* [from *breaſt* and *high.*] Up to the breaſt.

The river itſelf gave way unto her, ſo that ſhe was ſtraight *breaſthigh*. *Sidney.*

Lay madam Partlet baſking in the ſun,
*Breaſthigh* in ſand. *Dryden's Fables.*

Bre'asthooks. *n. ſ.* [from *breaſt* and *hook.*] With ſhipwrights. The compaſſing timbers before, that help to ſtrengthen the ſtem, and all the forepart of the ſhip. *Harris.*

Bre'astknot. *n. ſ.* [from *breaſt* and *knot.*] A knot or bunch of ribbands worn by women on the breaſt.

Our ladies have ſtill faces, and our men hearts, why may we not hope for the ſame atchievements from the influence of this *breaſtknot*? *Addiſon. Freeholder*, Nº 11.

Bre'astplate. *n. ſ.* [from *breaſt* and *plate.*] Armour for the breaſt.

What ſtronger *breaſtplate* than a heart untainted?
Thrice is he arm'd, that hath his quarrel juſt. *Shakeſp.*

'Gainſt ſhield, helm, *breaſtplate*, and, inſtead of thoſe,
Five ſharp ſmooth ſtones from the next brook he choſe. *Cowley.*

This venerable champion will come into the field, armed only with a pocket-piſtol, before his old ruſty *breaſtplate* could be ſcoured, and his cracked headpiece mended. *Swift.*

Bre'astplough. *n. ſ.* [from *breaſt* and *plough.*] A plough uſed for paring turf, driven by the breaſt.

The *breaſtplough*, which a man ſhoves before him. *Mortim.*

Bre'astropes. *n. ſ.* [from *breaſt* and *rope.*] In a ſhip. Thoſe ropes which faſten the yards to the parrels, and, with the parrels, hold the yards faſt to the maſt. *Harris.*

Bre'astwork. *n. ſ.* [from *breaſt* and *work.*] Works thrown up as high as the breaſt of the defendants; the ſame with *parapet*.

Sir John Aſtley caſt up *breaſtworks*, and made a redoubt for the defence of his men. *Clarendon, b.* viii.

Breath. *n. ſ.* [bꞃaᵹ, Saxon.]

1. The air drawn in and ejected out of the body by living animals.

Whither are they vaniſh'd?
Into the air: and what ſeem'd corporal
Melted, as *breath* into the wind. *Shakeſp. King Lear.*

2. Life.

No man has more contempt than I of *breath*;
But whence haſt thou the pow'r to give me death? *Dryden.*

3. The ſtate or power of breathing freely; oppoſed to the condition in which a man is breathleſs and ſpent.

At other times, he caſts to ſue the chace
Of ſwift wild beaſts, or run on foot a race,
T' enlarge his *breath*, large breath in arms moſt needful,
Or elſe, by wreſtling, to wax ſtrong and heedful. *Spenſer.*

What is your difference? ſpeak.—
—I am ſcarce in *breath*, my lord. *Shakeſp. King Lear.*

Spaniard, take *breath*; ſome reſpite I'll afford;
My cauſe is more advantage than your ſword. *Dryden.*

Our ſwords ſo wholly did the fates employ,
That they, at length, grew weary to deſtroy;
Refus'd the work we brought, and out of *breath*,
Made ſorrow and deſpair attend for death. *Dryden's Aureng.*

4. Reſpiration; the power of breathing.

Reſt, that gives all men life, gave him his death,
And too much breathing put him out of *breath*. *Milton.*

5. Reſpite; pauſe; relaxation.

Give me ſome *breath*; ſome little pauſe, dear lord,
Before I poſitively ſpeak. *Shakeſp. Richard* III.

6. Breeze; moving air.

Vent all thy paſſion, and I'll ſtand its ſhock,
Calm and unruffled as a ſummer's ſea,
When not a *breath* of wind flies o'er its ſurface. *Addiſ. Cato.*

7. A ſingle act; an inſtant.

You menace me, and court me in a *breath*,
Your Cupid looks as dreadfully as death. *Dryden.*

Bre'athable. *adj.* [from *breath.*] That may be breathed; as, *breathable* air.

To Breathe. *v. n.* [from *breath.*]

1. To draw in and throw out the air by the lungs.

Safe return'd, the race of glory paſt,
New to his friends embrace, had *breath'd* his laſt. *Pope.*

2. To live.

Let him *breathe*, between the heav'ns and earth,
A private man in Athens. *Shakeſp. Antony and Cleopatra.*

3. To take breath; to reſt.

He preſently followed the victory ſo hot upon the Scots, that he ſuffered them not to *breathe*, or gather themſelves together again. *Spenſer's State of Ireland.*

Three times they *breath'd*, and three times did they drink,
Upon agreement. *Shakeſp. Henry* IV. *p.* i.

When France had *breath'd*, after inteſtine broils,
And peace and conqueſt crown'd her foreign toils. *Roſcomm.*

4. To paſs by breathing.

Shall I not then be ſtifled in the vault;
To whoſe foul mouth no healthſome air *breathes* in,
And there be ſtrangl'd ere my Romeo comes? *Shakeſp.*

To Breathe. *v. a.*

1. To inſpire, or inhale into one's own body, and eject or expire out of it.

They wiſh to live,
Their pains and poverty deſire to bear,
To view the light of heav'n, and *breathe* the vital air. *Dryd.*

They here began to *breathe* a moſt delicious kind of æther, and ſaw all the fields about them covered with a kind of purple light. *Tatler*, Nº 81.

2. To inject by breathing.

He *breathed* into us the breath of life, a vital active ſpirit; whoſe motions, he expects, ſhould own the dignity of its original. *Decay of Piety.*

I would be young, be handſome, be belov'd,
Could I but *breathe* myſelf into Adraſtus. *Dryden.*

3. To expire; to eject by breathing.

She is called, by ancient authours, the tenth muſe; and, by Plutarch, is compared to Caius, the ſon of Vulcan, who *breathed* out nothing but flame. *Spectator*, Nº 223.

4. To exerciſe; to keep in breath.

Thy greyhounds are as ſwift as *breathed* ſtags. *Shakeſp.*

5. To inſpire; to move or actuate by breath.

The artful youth proceed to form the quire;
They *breathe* the flute, or ſtrike the vocal wire. *Prior.*

6. To exhale; to ſend out as breath.

His altar *breathes*
Ambroſial odours, and ambroſial flow'rs. *Milton's Par. Loſt.*

8. To utter privately.

I have tow'rd heaven *breath'd* a ſecret vow,
To live in prayer and contemplation. *Shakeſp. Mer. of Ven.*

9. To give air or vent to.

The ready cure to cool the raging pain,
Is underneath the foot to *breathe* a vein. *Dryden's Virgil.*

Bre'ather. *n. ſ.* [from *breathe.*]

1. One that breathes, or lives.

She ſhows a body rather than a life,
A ſtatue than a *breather*. *Shakeſp. Antony and Cleopatra.*

I will chide no *breather* in the world but myſelf. *Shakeſp.*

2. One that utters any thing.

No particular ſcandal once can touch,
But it confounds the *breather*. *Shakeſp. Meaſ. for Meaſure.*

3. Inſpirer; one that animates or infuſes by inſpiration.

The *breather* of all life does now expire:
His milder father ſummons him away. *Norris.*

Bre'athing. *n. ſ.* [from *breathe.*]

1. Aſpiration; ſecret prayer.

While to high heav'n his pious *breathings* turn'd,
Weeping he hop'd, and ſacrificing mourn'd. *Prior.*

2. Breathing place; vent.

The warmth diſtends the chinks, and makes
New *breathings*, whence new nouriſhment ſhe takes. *Dryd.*

Bre'athless. *adj.* [from *breath.*]

1. Out of breath; ſpent with labour.

Well knew
The prince, with patience and ſufferance ſly,
So haſty heat ſoon cooled to ſubdue;
Tho' when he *breathleſs* wax, that battle 'gan renew. *Fairy Q.*

I remember when the fight was done,
When I was dry with rage, and extreme toil,

*Breathless*, and faint, leaning upon my sword,
Came there a certain lord. *Shakesp. Henry* IV. *p.* i.

Many so strained themselves in their race, that they fell down *breathless* and dead. *Hayward.*

*Breathless* and tir'd, is all my fury spent,
Or does my glutted spleen at length relent? *Dryden's Æn.*

2. Dead.

Kneeling before this ruin of sweet life,
And breathing to this *breathless* excellence,
The incense of a vow, a holy vow. *Shakesp. King John.*

Yielding to the sentence, *breathless* thou
And pale shalt lie, as what thou buriest now. *Prior.*

BRED. *particip. pass.* [from *to breed.*]

Their malice was *bred* in them, and their cogitation would never be changed. *Wisdom*, xii. 10.

BREDE. *n. s.* See BRAID.

In a curious *brede* of needle-work, one colour falls away by such just degrees, and another rises so insensibly, that we see the variety, without being able to distinguish the total vanishing of the one, from the first appearance of the other. *Addison.*

BREECH. *n. s.* [supposed from bɲæcan, Sax.]

1. The lower part of the body; the back part.

When the king's pardon was offered by a herauld, a lewd boy turned towards him his naked *breech*, and used words suitable to that gesture. *Hayward.*

The storks devour snakes and other serpents; which when they begin to creep out at their *breeches*, they will presently clap them close to a wall, to keep them in. *Grew's Musæum.*

2. Breeches.

~~Ah! that thy father had been so resolv'd!—~~
—~~That~~ you might still have worn the petticoat,
And ne'er have stoln the *breech* from Lancaster. *Shakespeare.*

3. The hinder part of a piece of ordnance.

So cannons, when they mount vast pitches,
Are tumbl'd back upon their *breeches.* *Anonym.*

To BREECH. *v. a.* [from the noun.]

1. To put into breeches.

2. To fit any thing with a breech; as, to *breech* a gun.

BRE'ECHES. *n. s.* [bɲæc, Sax. from *bracca*, an old Gaulish word; so that *Skinner* imagines the name of the part covered with *breeches*, to be derived from that of the garment. In this sense it has no *singular.*]

1. The garment worn by men over the lower part of the body.

Petrachio is coming in a new hat and an old jerkin, and a pair of old *breeches*, thrice turned. *Shakesp. Taming the Shrew.*

Rough satires, sly remarks, ill-natur'd speeches,
Are always aim'd at poets that wear *breeches.* *Prior.*

Give him a single coat to make, he'd do't;
A vest, or *breeches*, singly; but the brute
Cou'd ne'er contrive all three to make a suit.
*King's Art of Cookery.*

2. To wear the *breeches*, is, to usurp the authority of the husbands.

The wife of Xanthus was proud and domineering, as if her fortune, and her extraction, had entitled her to the *breeches.* *L'Estrange.*

To BREED. *v. a.* preter. I *bred*, I have *bred.* [bɲæban, Sax.]

1. To procreate; to generate; to produce more of the species.

None fiercer in Numidia *bred*,
With Carthage were in triumph led. *Roscommon.*

2. To occasion; to cause; to produce.

Thereat he roared for exceeding pain,
That, to have heard, great horrour would have *bred.* *F. Q.*

Our own hearts we know, but we are not certain what hope the rites and orders of our church have *bred* in the hearts of others. *Hooker, b.* iv.

What hurt ill company, and overmuch liberty, *breedeth* in youth! *Ascham's Schoolmaster.*

Intemperance and lust *breed* infirmities and diseases, which, being propagated, spoil the strain of a nation. *Tillotson.*

3. To contrive; to hatch; to plot.

My son Edgar! had he a hand to write this! a heart and brain to *breed* it in! *Shakesp. King Lear.*

4. To produce from one's self.

Children would *breed* their teeth with much less danger. *Locke on Education.*

5. To give birth to; to be the native place.

Mr. Harding, and the worthiest divine christendom hath *bred* for the space of some hundreds of years, were brought up together in the same university. *Hooker.*

Hail, foreign wonder!
Whom, certain, these rough shades did never *breed.* *Milton.*

6. To educate; to qualify by education.

Whoe'er thou art, whose forward years are bent
On state-affairs to guide the government;
Hear first what Socrates of old has said
To the lov'd youth, whom he at Athens *bred.* *Dryden.*

To *breed* up the son to common sense,
Is evermore the parent's least expence. *Dryden's Juvenal.*

And left the pillagers, to rapine *bred*,
Without controul, to strip and spoil the dead. *Dryden.*

His farm may not remove his children too far from him, or the trade he *breeds* them up in. *Locke.*

7. To bring up; to take care of from infancy.

*Bred* up in grief, can pleasure be our theme?
Our endless anguish, does not nature claim?
Reason and sorrow are to us the same. *Prior.*

Ah, wretched me! by fates averse decreed
To bring thee forth with pain, with care to *breed.* *Dryden.*

To BREED. *v. n.*

1. To bring young.

Lucina, it seems, was *breeding*, and she did nothing but entertain the company with a discourse upon the difficulty of reckoning to a day. *Spectator*, N° 431.

2. To encrease by new production.

But could youth last, and love still *breed*,
Had joys no date, and age no need;
Then these delights my mind might move
To live with thee, and be thy love. *Raleigh.*

3. To be produced; to have birth.

Where they most *breed* and haunt, I have observ'd,
The air is delicate. *Shakesp. King Lear.*

There is a worm that *breedeth* in old snow, and dieth soon after it cometh out of the snow. *Bacon's Nat. Hist.* N° 696.

The caterpillar is one of the most general of worms, and *breedeth* of dew and leaves. *Bacon.*

It hath been the general tradition and belief, that maggots and flies *breed* in putrefied carcases. *Bentley.*

4. To raise a breed.

In the choice of swine, choose such to *breed* of as are of long large bodies. *Mortimer.*

BREED. *n. s.* [from the verb.]

1. A cast; a kind; a subdivision of species.

I bring you witnesses,
Twice fifteen thousand hearts of England's *breed.* *Shakesp.*

The horses were young and handsome, and of the best *breed* in the north. *Shakesp. Henry* VIII.

Walled towns, stored arsenals, and ordnance; all this is but a sheep in a lion's skin, except the *breed* and disposition of the people be stout and warlike. *Bacon's Essays*, N° 30.

Infectious streams of crowding sins began,
And through the spurious *breed* and guilty nation ran. *Roscommon.*

Rode fair Ascanius on a firy steed,
Queen Dido's gift, and of the Tyrian *breed.* *Dryden.*

A cousin of his last wife's was proposed; but John would have no more of the *breed.* *Arbuthnot's Hist. of J. Bull.*

2. Progeny; offspring.

If thou wilt lend this money, lend it not
As to thy friend; for when did friendship take
A *breed* of barren metal of his friend? *Shakesp. Mer. of Ven.*

3. A number produced at once; a hatch.

She lays them in the sand, where they lie till they are hatched; sometimes above an hundred at a *breed.* *Grew's Musæum.*

BRE'EDBATE. *n. s.* [from *breed* and *bate.*] One that breeds quarrels; an incendiary.

An honest, willing, kind fellow, as ever servant shall come in house withal; and, I warrant you, no teltale, nor no *breedbate.* *Shakesp. Merry Wives of Windsor.*

BRE'EDER. *n. s.* [from *breed.*]

1. That which produces any thing.

Time is the nurse and *breeder* of all good. *Shakesp.*

2. The person which brings up another.

Time was, when Italy and Rome have been the best *breeders* and bringers up of the worthiest men. *Ascham's Schoolmaster.*

3. A female that is prolifick.

Get thee to a nunnery; why wouldst thou be a *breeder* of sinners? *Shakesp. Hamlet.*

Here is the babe, as loathsome as a toad,
Amongst the fairest *breeders* of our time. *Shakesp. Tit. Andr.*

Let there be an hundred persons in London, and as many in the country, we say, that if there be sixty of them *breeders* in London, there are more than sixty in the country. *Graunt.*

Yet if a friend a night or two should need her,
He'd recommend her as a special *breeder.* *Pope.*

4. One that takes care to raise a breed.

The *breeders* of English cattle turned much to dairy, or else kept their cattle to six or seven years old. *Temple.*

BRE'EDING. *n. s.* [from *breed.*]

1. Education; instruction; qualifications.

She had her *breeding* at my father's charge,
A poor physician's daughter. *Shakesp. All's well that ends well.*

I am a gentleman of blood and *breeding.* *Shakesp. K. Lear.*

I hope to see it a piece of none of the meanest *breeding*, to be acquainted with the laws of nature. *Glanville's Scepsis, Pref.*

2. Manners; knowledge of ceremony.

As men of *breeding*, sometimes men of wit,
T' avoid great errours, must the less commit. *Pope.*

The Graces from the court did next provide
*Breeding*, and wit, and air, and decent pride. *Swift.*

3. Nurture; care to bring up from the infant state.

Why was my *breeding* order'd and prescrib'd,
As of a person separate to God,
Design'd for great exploits. *Milton's Agonistes, l.* 30.

BREESE. *n. s.* [bɲioɲa, Saxon.] A stinging fly; the gadfly.

The

blank page

Faint, weary, sore, embroiled.
grieved, brent
With heat, toil, wounds, Arms, smart & fire
F.Q. 1.11.28

2. Shortness of breath
Sure he meant brevity
in breath short winded
Shak.

2. Winds that tempests brew
When through Arabian groves they take their flight
Made wanton with rich Odours, lose their spite
Dryd

The learned write, the inſect *breeſe*
Is but the mongrel prince of bees. *Hudibras.*
A fierce loud buzzing *breeſe*, their ſtings draw blood,
And drive the cattle gadding through the wood;
Seiz'd with unuſual pains, they loudly cry;
Tanagrus haſtens thence, and leaves his channels dry. *Dryd.*

BREEZE. *n. ſ.* [*brezza*, Ital.] A gentle gale; a ſoft wind.

We find, that theſe hotteſt regions of the world, ſeated under the equinoctial line, or near it, are ſo refreſhed with a daily gale of eaſterly wind, which the Spaniards call *breeze*, that doth ever more blow ſtrongeſt in the heat of the day. *Raleigh.*

From land a gentle *breeze* aroſe by night,
Serenely ſhone the ſtars, the moon was light,
And the ſea trembled with her ſilver light. } *Dryden.*

Gradual ſinks the *breeze*
Into a perfect calm: that not a breath
Is heard to quiver through the cloſing wood. *Thomſon.*

BRE'EZY. *adj.* [from *breeze.*] Fanned with gales.

The ſeer, while zephyrs curl the ſwelling deep,
Baſks on the *breezy* ſhore, in grateful ſleep,
His oozy limbs. *Pope's Odyſſey, b.* iii. *l.* 545.

BRE'HON. *n. ſ.* An Iriſh word.

In the caſe of murder, the *brehon*, that is, their judge, will compound between the murderer and the party murdered, which proſecute the action, that the malefactor ſhall give unto them, or to the child or wife of him that is ſlain, a recompence, which they call an eriach. *Spenſer's State of Ireland.*

BREME. *adj.* [from bꞃemman, Sax. to rage or fume.] Cruel; ſharp; ſevere.

And when the ſhining ſun laugheth once,
You deemen the ſpring come at once:
But eft, when you count, you freed from fear,
Comes the *breme* winter, with chamfred brows,
Full of wrinkles, and froſty furrows. *Spenſer's Paſtorals.*

BRENT. *adj.* [from bꞃennan, Sax. to burn.] Burnt.

What flames, quoth he, when I thee preſent ſee
In danger rather to be drent than *brent?* *Fairy Queen, b.* ii.

BREST. *n. ſ.* [In architecture.] That member of a column, called alſo the *torus*, or *tore*.

BREST *Summers.* The pieces in the outward parts of any timber building, and in the middle floors, into which the girders are framed. *Harris.*

BRET. *n. ſ.* A fiſh of the turbut kind, called alſo *burt* or *brut*. *Dict.*

BRE'THREN. *n. ſ.* [The *plural* of *brother*.] See BROTHER.

All theſe ſects are *brethren* to each other in faction, ignorance, iniquity, perverſeneſs, pride. *Swift.*

*BREVE.* *n. ſ.* [In muſick.] A note or character of time, equivalent to two meaſures or minims. *Harris.*

BRE'VIARY. *n. ſ.* [*breviaire*, Fr. *breviarium*, Lat.]

1. An abridgment; an epitome; a compendium.

Creſconius, an African biſhop, has given us an abridgment, or *breviary* thereof. *Ayliffe's Parergon.*

2. The book containing the daily ſervice of the church of Rome.

BRE'VIAT. *n. ſ.* [from *brevis*, *brevio*, Lat.] A ſhort compendium.

It is obvious for the ſhalloweſt diſcourſer to infer, that the whole counſel of God, as far as it is incumbent for man to know, is compriſed in that one *breviat* of evangelical truth. *Decay of Piety.*

BRE'VIATURE. *n. ſ.* [from *brevio*, Lat.] An abbreviation.

BREVI'ER. *n. ſ.* A particular ſize of letter uſed in printing; ſo called, probably, from being originally uſed in printing a *breviary*; as,

Nor love thy life, nor hate, but what thou liv'ſt,
Live well, how long or ſhort, permit to heav'n. *Milton.*

BRE'VITY. *n. ſ.* [*brevitas*, Lat.] Conciſeneſs; ſhortneſs; contraction into few words.

Virgil, ſtudying *brevity*, and having the command of his own language, could bring thoſe words into a narrow compaſs, which a tranſlator cannot render without circumlocutions. *Dryden.*

To BREW. *v. a.* [*brouwen*, Dutch; *brawen*, German; bꞃupan, Saxon.]

1. To make liquours by mixing ſeveral ingredients.

We have drinks alſo *brewed* with ſeveral herbs, and roots, and ſpices. *Bacon.*

Mercy guard me!
Hence with thy *brew'd* enchantments, foul deceiver. *Milton.*

2. To prepare by mixing things together.

Here's neither ruſh nor ſhrub to bear off any weather at all, and another ſtorm *brewing*. *Shakeſp. Tempeſt.*

Take away theſe chalices; go, *brew* me a pottle of ſack finely. *Shakeſp. Merry Wives of Windſor.*

Or *brew* fierce tempeſts on the watry main,
Or o'er the globe diſtil the kindly rain. *Pope's R. of the L.*

3. To contrive; to plot.

I found it to be the moſt malicious and frantick ſurmiſe, and the moſt contrary to his nature, that, I think, had ever been *brewed* from the beginning of the world, howſoever countenanced by a libellous pamphlet of a fugitive phyſician, even in print. *Wotton.*

To BREW. *v. n.* To perform the office of a brewer.

I keep his houſe, and waſh, wring, *brew*, bake, ſcour, dreſs meat, and make the beds, and do all myſelf. *Shakeſp.*

BREW. *n. ſ.* [from the verb.] Manner of brewing; or thing brewed.

Trial would be made of the like *brew* with potato roots, or burr roots, or the pith of artichokes, which are nouriſhing meats. *Bacon's Natural Hiſtory*, N° 47.

BRE'WAGE. *n. ſ.* [from *brew.*] Mixture of various things.

Go, brew me a pottle of ſack finely.
———With eggs, Sir?———
—Simple of itſelf: I'll no pullet-ſperm in my *brewage*.
*Shakeſp. Merry Wives of Windſor.*

BRE'WER. *n. ſ.* [from *brew.*] A man whoſe profeſſion it is to make beer.

When *brewers* marr their malt with water. *Sh. King Lear.*

Men every day eat and drink, though I think no man can demonſtrate out of Euclid or Apollonius, that his baker, or *brewer*, or cook, has not conveyed poiſon into his meat or drink. *Tillotſon.*

BRE'WHOUSE. *n. ſ.* [from *brew* and *houſe.*] A houſe appropriated to brewing.

In our *brewhouſes*, bakehouſes, and kitchens, are made divers drinks, breads, and meats. *Bacon's New Atlantis.*

BRE'WING. *n. ſ.* [from *brew.*] Quantity of liquour brewed.

A *brewing* of new beer, ſet by old beer, maketh it work again. *Bacon's Natural Hiſtory*, N° 314.

BRE'WIS. *n. ſ.* A piece of bread ſoaked in boiling fat pottage, made of ſalted meat.

BRI'AR. *n. ſ.* See BRIER.

BRIBE. *n. ſ.* [*Bribe*, in French, originally ſignifies a piece of bread, and is applied to any piece taken from the reſt; it is therefore likely, that a *bribe* originally ſignified, among us, a ſhare of any thing unjuſtly got.] A reward given to pervert the judgment, or corrupt the conduct.

You have condemn'd and noted Lucius Pella,
For taking *bribes* here of the Sardians. *Shakeſp. Julius Cæſar.*

Nor leſs may Jupiter to gold aſcribe,
When he turn'd himſelf into a *bribe*. *Waller.*

If a man be covetous, profits or *bribes* may put him to the teſt. *L'Eſtrange.*

There's joy when to wild will you laws preſcribe,
When you bid fortune carry back her *bribe*. *Dryden.*

To BRIBE. *v. a.* [from the noun.] To gain by bribes; to give bribes, rewards, or hire, to bad purpoſes. It is ſeldom, and not properly, uſed in a good ſenſe.

How pow'rful are chaſte vows! the wind and tide
You *brib'd* to combat on the Engliſh ſide. *Dryden.*

BRI'BER. *n. ſ.* [from *bribe.*] One that pays for corrupt practices.

Affection is ſtill a *briber* of the judgment; and it is hard for a man to admit a reaſon againſt the thing he loves; or to confeſs the force of an argument againſt an intereſt. *South.*

BRI'BERY. *n. ſ.* [from *bribe.*] The crime of taking rewards for bad practices.

There was a law made by the Romans, againſt the *bribery* and extortion of the governours of provinces: before, ſays Cicero, the governours did bribe ~~and extort as much as was ſufficient~~ for themſelves; but now they bribe ~~and extort~~ as ~~much as may be enough no~~t only for themſelves, but for judges, ~~jurors, and magiſtrates~~. *Bacon.*

No *bribery* of courts, or cabals of factions, or advantages of fortune, can remove him from the ſolid foundations of honour and fidelity. *Dryden's Aurengz. Preface.*

BRICK. *n. ſ.* [*brick*, Dutch; *brique*, Fr. according to *Menage*, from *imbrex*, Lat. whence *brica*.]

1. A maſs of burnt clay, ſquared for the uſe of builders.

For whatſoever doth ſo alter a body, as it returneth not again to that it was, may be called *alteratio major*; as coals made of wood, or *bricks* of earth. *Bacon's Natural Hiſtory.*

They generally gain enough by the rubbiſh and *bricks*, which the preſent architects value much beyond thoſe of a modern make, to defray the charges of their ſearch. *Addiſon.*

But ſpread, my ſons, your glory thin or thick,
On paſſive paper, or on ſolid *brick*. *Pope's Dunciad.*

2. A loaf ſhaped like a brick.

To BRICK. *v. a.* [from the noun.] To lay with bricks.

The ſexton comes to know where he is to be laid, and whether his grave is to be plain or *bricked*. *Swift.*

BRI'CKBAT. *n. ſ.* [from *brick* and *bat.*] A piece of brick.

Earthen bottles, filled with hot water, do provoke in bed a ſweat more daintily than *brickbats* hot. *Bacon's Natural Hiſt.*

BRI'CKCLAY. *n. ſ.* [from *brick* and *clay.*] Clay uſed for making brick.

I have obſerved it only in pits wrought for tile and *brickclay*. *Woodward on Foſſils.*

BRI'CKDUST. *n. ſ.* [from *brick* and *duſt.*] Duſt made by pounding bricks.

This ingenious authour, being thus ſharp ſet, got together a convenient quantity of *brickduſt*, and diſpoſed of it into ſeveral papers. *Spectator*, N° 283.

BRI'CKEARTH. *n. ſ.* [from *brick* and *earth.*] Earth uſed in making bricks.

They grow very well both on the hazelly *brickearths*, and on gravel. *Mortimer.*

BRICK-KILN. *n.ſ.* [from *brick* and *kiln.*] A kiln; a place to burn bricks.

Like the Iſraelites in the *brick-kilns*, they multiplied the more for their oppreſſion. *Decay of Piety.*

BRI'CKLAYER. *n.ſ.* [from *brick* and *lay.*] A man whoſe trade it is to build with bricks; a brick-maſon.

The elder of them, being put to nurſe,
And ignorant of his birth and parentage,
Became a *bricklayer*, when he came to age. *Shakeſp. H. VI.*

If you had liv'd, Sir,
Time enough to have been interpreter
To Babel's *bricklayers*, ſure the tow'r had ſtood. *Donne.*

BRI'CKMAKER. *n.ſ.* [from *brick* and *make.*] One whoſe trade it is to make bricks.

They are common in clay-pits; but the *brickmakers* pick them out of the clay. *Woodward on Foſſils.*

BRI'DAL. *adj.* [from *bride.*] Belonging to a wedding; nuptial; connubial.

Our wedding chear to a ſad fun'ral feaſt,
Our ſolemn hymns to ſullen dirges change,
Our *bridal* flowers ſerve for a buried corſe. *Shakeſp.*
Come, I will bring thee to thy *bridal* chamber. *Shakeſp.*

The amorous bird of night
Sung ſpouſal, and bid haſte the ev'ning ſtar,
On his hill-top to light the *bridal* lamp. *Parad. Loſt, b.* viii.

Your ill-meaning politician lords,
Under pretence of *bridal* friends and gueſts,
Appointed to await me thirty ſpies. *Milton's Agoniſt. l.* 1195.

When to my arms thou brought'ſt thy virgin love,
Fair angels ſung our *bridal* hymn above. *Dryden.*

With all the pomp of woe, and ſorrow's pride!
Oh, early loſt! oh, fitter to be led
In chearful ſplendour to the *bridal* bed! *Walſh.*

For her the ſpouſe prepares the *bridal* ring,
For her white virgins hymenæals ſing. *Pope's Eloiſa to Abel.*

BRI'DAL. *n.ſ.* The nuptial feſtival.

Nay, we muſt think, men are not gods;
Nor of them look for ſuch obſervance always,
As fits the *bridal.* *Shakeſp. Othello.*

Sweet day, ſo cool, ſo calm, ſo bright,
The *bridal* of the earth and ſky,
Sweet dews ſhall weep thy fall to-night;
For thou muſt die. *Herbert.*

In death's dark bow'rs our *bridals* we will keep,
And his cold hand
Shall draw the curtain when we go to ſleep. *Dryden.*

BRIDE. *n.ſ.* [bꞃyꝺ, Saxon; *brudur*, in Runick, ſignifies a beautiful woman.] A woman new married.

Help me mine own love's praiſes to reſound,
Ne let the fame of any be envy'd;
So Orpheus did for his own *bride.* *Spenſer's Epithalamium.*

The day approach'd, when fortune ſhould decide
Th' important enterprize, and give the *bride.* *Dryden's Fab.*

Theſe are tributes due from pious *brides*,
From a chaſte matron, and a virtuous wife. *Smith's Phædr.*

BRI'DEBED. *n.ſ.* [from *bride* and *bed.*] Marriage-bed.

Now until the break of day,
Through this houſe each fairy ſtray;
To the beſt *bridebed* will we,
Which by us ſhall bleſſed be. *Shakeſp. Midſum. Night's Dr.*

Would David's ſon, religious, juſt, and brave,
To the firſt *bridebed* of the world receive
A foreigner, a heathen, and a ſlave? *Prior.*

BRI'DECAKE. *n.ſ.* [from *bride* and *cake.*] A cake diſtributed to the gueſts at the wedding.

With the phant'ſies of hey-troll,
Troll about the bridal bowl,
And divide the broad *bridecake*
Round about the bride's ſtake. *Ben. Johnſon's Underwoods.*

The writer, reſolved to try his fortune, faſted all day, and, that he might be ſure of dreaming upon ſomething at night, procured an handſome ſlice of *bridecake*, which he placed very conveniently under his pillow. *Spectator*, Nº 597.

BRI'DEGROOM. *n.ſ.* [from *bride* and *groom.*] A new married man.

As are thoſe dulcet ſounds in break of day,
That creep into the dreaming *bridegroom's* ear,
And ſummon him to marriage. *Shakeſp. Merch. of Venice.*

Why, happy *bridegroom!*
Why doſt thou ſteal ſo ſoon away to bed? *Dryden.*

BRI'DEMEN. }
BRI'DEMAIDS. } *n.ſ.* The attendants on the bride and bridegroom.

BRI'DESTAKE. *n.ſ.* [from *bride* and *ſtake.*] It ſeems to be a poſt ſet in the ground, to dance round, like a maypole.

And divide the broad bridecake,
Round about the *brideſtake.* *Ben. Johnſon's Underwoods.*

BRIDEWELL. *n.ſ.* [The palace built by St. *Bride's*, or *Bridget's well*, was turned into a workhouſe.] A houſe of correction.

He would contribute more to reformation than all the workhouſes and *Bridewells* in Europe. *Spectator*, Nº 157.

BRIDGE. *n.ſ.* [bꞃic, Saxon.]

1. A building raiſed over water for the convenience of paſſage.

What need the *bridge* much broader than the flood?
*Shakeſp. Much ado about Nothing.*
And proud Araxes, whom no *bridge* could bind. *Dryden.*

2. The upper part of the noſe.

The raiſing gently the *bridge* of the noſe, doth prevent the deformity of a ſaddle noſe. *Bacon's Natural Hiſtory*, Nº 28.

3. The ſupporter of the ſtrings in ſtringed inſtruments of muſick.

To BRIDGE. *v.a.* [from the noun.] To raiſe a bridge over any place.

Came to the ſea; and over Helleſpont
*Bridging* his way, Europe with Aſia join'd. *Par. Loſt, b.* x.

BRI'DLE. *n.ſ.* [*bride*, Fr.]

1. The headſtall and reins by which a horſe is reſtrained and governed.

Creeping and crying, till they ſeiz'd at laſt
His courſer's *bridle*, and his feet embrac'd. *Dryden's Fables.*

2. A reſtraint; a curb; a check.

The king reſolved to put that place, which ſome men fancied to be a *bridle* upon the city, into the hands of ſuch a man as he might rely upon. *Clarendon.*

A bright genius often betrays itſelf into many errours, without a continual *bridle* on the tongue. *Watts.*

To BRI'DLE. *v.a.* [from the noun.]

1. To reſtrain, or guide by a bridle.

I *bridle* in my ſtruggling muſe with pain,
That longs to launch into a bolder ſtrain. *Addiſon.*

2. To put a bridle on any thing.

The queen of beauty ſtop'd her *bridled* doves;
Approv'd the little labour of the Loves. *Prior.*

3. To reſtrain; to govern.

The diſpoſition of theſe things is committed to them, whom law may at all times *bridle*, and ſuperiour power controul. *Hooker, b.* v. § 9.

With a ſtrong, and yet a gentle hand,
You *bridle* faction, and our hearts command. *Waller.*

To BRI'DLE. *v.n.* To hold up the head.

BRI'DLEHAND. *n.ſ.* [from *bridle* and *hand.*] The hand which holds the bridle in riding.

In the turning, one might perceive the *bridlehand* ſomething gently ſtir; but, indeed, ſo gently, as it did rather diſtil virtue than uſe violence. *Sidney, b.* ii.

The heat of ſummer put his blood into a ferment, which affected his *bridlehand* with great pain. *Wiſeman's Surgery.*

BRIEF. *adj.* [*brevis*, Lat. *brief*, Fr.]

1. Short; conciſe. It is now ſeldom uſed but of words.

A play there is, my lord, ſome ten words long,
Which is as *brief* as I have known a play;
But by ten words, my lord, it is too long,
Which makes it tedious. *Shakeſp. Midſum. Night's Dream.*

I will be mild and gentle in my words.—
—And *brief*, good mother, for I am in haſte. *Shakeſp. R.* III.

I muſt begin with rudiments of art,
To teach you gamut in a *briefer* ſort,
More pleaſant, pithy, and effectual. *Shakeſp. Tam. Shrew.*
They nothing doubt prevailing, and to make it *brief* wars.
*Shakeſp. Coriolanus.*

The *brief* ſtile is that which expreſſeth much in little.
*Ben. Johnſon's Diſcovery.*

If I had quoted more words, I had quoted more profaneneſs; and therefore Mr. Congreve has reaſon to thank me for being *brief.* *Collier's View of the Stage.*

2. Contracted; narrow.

The ſhrine of Venus, or ſtraight pight Minerva,
Poſtures beyond *brief* nature. *Shakeſp. Cymbeline.*

BRIEF. *n.ſ.* [*brief*, Dutch, a letter.]

1. A writing of any kind.

There is a *brief*, how many ſports are ripe:
Make choice of which your highneſs will ſee firſt. *Shakeſp.*

The apoſtolical letters are of a twofold kind and difference, *viz.* ſome are called *briefs*, becauſe they are compriſed in a ſhort and compendious way of writing. *Ayliffe's Parergon.*

2. A ſhort extract, or epitome.

But how you muſt begin this enterprize,
I will your highneſs thus in *brief* adviſe. *Fairy Queen, b.* ii.

I doubt not but I ſhall make it plain, as far as a ſum or *brief* can make a cauſe plain. *Bacon's Holy War.*

The *brief* of this tranſaction is, theſe ſprings that ariſe here, are impregnated with vitriol. *Woodward on Foſſils.*

3. In law.

A writ whereby a man is ſummoned to anſwer to any action; or it is any precept of the king in writing, iſſuing out of any court, whereby he commands any thing to be done. *Cowel.*

4. The writing given the pleaders, containing the caſe.

The *brief* with weighty crimes was charg'd,
On which the pleader much enlarg'd. *Swift.*

5. Letters patent, giving licence to a charitable collection for any publick or private loſs.

6. [In muſick.] A meaſure of quantity, which contains two ſtrokes down in beating time, and as many up. *Harris.*

BRI'EFLY. *adv.* [from *brief.*] Conciſely; in few words.

u ǂ
7 Down with the nose
Down with it flat, take the bridge quite away
Shak. T.A.

ǂ

Bridaltee } n.s. ~~Bridal~~
Bridalty } Wodelig

At Quintin he
In honour of this bridaltee
Hath challeng'd either wide Countee
B. Johns. Underw.

v. a
To restrain the flux of humour
Both bodies are clammy and bridle the
Deflux to the hurting without penning them
in too much
Bac.

IL facing 3O2v

6 To excite, to rub up, in allusion to polishing.

This faith must be not only living, but lively, it must be brightend and stirred up & put into a posture by a particular exercise of the several Virtues requisite to a due performance of this duty South

I will speak in that manner which the subject requires; that is, probably, and moderately, and *briefly*. *Bacon.*

The modest queen a while, with downcast eyes,
Ponder'd the speech; then *briefly* thus replies. *Dryden.*

BRI'EFNESS. *n. s.* [from *brief.*] Conciseness; shortness.

They excel in grandity and gravity, in smoothness and propriety, in quickness and *briefness*. *Camden's Remains.*

BRIER. *n. s.* [bpæn, Sax.] A plant.

The sweet and the wild sorts are both species of the *rose*; which see.

What subtle hole is this,
Whose mouth is cover'd with rude growing *briers?* *Shakesp.*

Then thrice under a *brier* doth creep,
Which at both ends was rooted deep,
And over it three times doth leap;
Her magick much availing. *Drayton's Nymphid.*

BRI'ERY. *adj.* [from *brier.*] Rough; thorny; full of briers.

BRIG, and possibly also BRIX, is derived from the Saxon bpicg, a bridge; which, to this day, in the northern counties, is called a *brigg*, and not a *bridge*. *Gibson's Camden.*

BRIGA'DE. *n. s.* [*brigade*, Fr. It is now generally pronounced with the accent on the last syllable.] A division of forces; a body of men, consisting of several squadrons of horse, or battalions of foot.

Or fronted *brigades* form. *Paradise Lost, b.* ii.

Here the Bavarian duke his *brigades* leads,
Gallant in arms, and gaudy to behold. *Philips.*

BRIGA'DE *Major.* An officer appointed by the brigadier to assist him in the management and ordering of his brigade; and he there acts as as a major general does in an army. *Harris.*

BRIGADI'ER *General.* An officer who commands a brigade of horse or foot in an army; next in order below a major general.

BRI'GAND. *n. s.* [*brigand*, Fr.] A robber; one that belongs to a band of robbers.

There might be a rout of such barbarous theevish *brigands* in some rocks; but it was a degeneration from the nature of man, a political creature. *Bramhal against Hobbes.*

BRI'GANDINE. } *n. s.* [from *brigand.*]
BRI'GANTINE. }

1. A light vessel; such as has been formerly used by corsairs or pirates.

Like as a a warlike *brigandine*, apply'd
To fight, lays forth her threatful pikes afore
The engines, which in them sad death do hide. *Spenser.*

Scarce five years are past,
Since in your *brigantine* you sail'd to see
The Adriatick wedded. *Otway's Venice Preserved.*

The consul obliged him to deliver up his fleet, and restore the ships, reserving only to himself two *brigantines*. *Arbuthnot.*

2. A coat of mail.

Then put on all thy gorgeous arms, thy helmet
And *brigandine* of brass, thy broad habergeon,
Vantbrass, and greves. *Milton's Agonistes, l.* 1119.

BRIGHT. *adj.* [beopr, Saxon.]

1. Shining; glittering; full of light.

Through a cloud
Drawn round about thee like a radiant shrine,
Dark, with excessive *bright*, thy skirts appear. *Par. L. b.* iii.

Then shook the sacred shrine, and sudden light
Sprung through the vaulted roof, and made the temple *bright*. *Dryden.*

2. Clear; evident.

He must not proceed too swiftly, that he may with more ease, with *brighter* evidence, and with surer success, draw the learner on. *Watts's Improvement of the Mind.*

3. Illustrious; as, a *bright* reign, a *bright* action.

4. Witty; acute; subtle; as a *bright* genius.

To BRI'GHTEN. *v. a.* [from *bright.*]

1. To make bright; to make to shine.

The purple morning rising with the year,
Salutes the spring, as her celestial eyes
Adorn the world, and *brighten* all the skies. *Dryden.*

2. To make luminous by light from without.

An ecstasy, that mothers only feel,
Plays round my heart, and *brightens* up my sorrow,
Like gleams of sunshine in a louring sky. *Philips's D. Moth.*

3. To make gay, or alert.

Hope elevates, and joy
*Brightens* his crest. *Milton's Paradise Lost, b.* ix. *l.* 634.

4. To make illustrious.

The present queen would *brighten* her character, if she would exert her authority to instil virtues into her people. *Swift.*

Yet time ennobles, or degrades each line;
It *brighten'd* Craggs's, and may darken thine. *Pope.*

5. To make acute, or witty.

To BRI'GHTEN. *v. n.* To grow bright; to clear up; as, *the sky brightens.*

BRI'GHTLY. *adv.* [from *bright.*] Splendidly; with lustre.

Safely I slept, till *brightly* dawning shone
The morn conspicuous on her golden throne. *Pope.*

BRI'GHTNESS. *n. s.* [from *bright.*]

1. Lustre; splendour; glitter.

The blazing *brightness* of her beauty's beam,
And glorious light of her sun-shining face,
To tell, were as to strive against the stream. *Fairy Q. b.* i.

A sword, by long lying still, will contract a rust, which shall deface its *brightness*. *South.*

Vex'd with the present moment's heavy gloom,
Why seek we *brightness* from the years to come? *Prior.*

2. Acuteness.

The *brightness* of his parts, the solidity of his judgment, and the candour and generosity of his temper, distinguished him in an age of great politeness. *Prior.*

BRI'LLIANCY. *n. s.* [from *brilliant.*] Lustre; splendour.

BRILLIANT. *adj.* [*brillant*, Fr.] Shining; sparkling; splendid; full of lustre.

So have I seen in larder dark
Of veal a lucid loin,
Replete with many a *brilliant* spark,
As wise philosophers remark,
At once both stink and shine. *Dorset.*

BRI'LLIANT. *n. s.* A diamond of the finest cut, formed into angles, so as to refract the light, and shine more.

In deference to his virtues, I forbear
To shew you what the rest in orders were;
This *brilliant* is so spotless and so bright,
He needs not foil, but shines by his own proper light. *Dryd.*

BRI'LLIANTNESS. *n. s.* [from *brilliant.*] Splendour; lustre.

BRILLS. *n. s.* The hair on the eyelids of a horse. *Dict.*

BRIM. *n. s.* [*brim*, Icelandish.]

1. The edge of any thing.

His hat being in the form of a turban, daintily made, the locks of his hair came down about the *brims* of it. *Bacon.*

2. The upper edge of any vessel.

To make the coming hours o'erflow with joy,
And pleasure down the *brim*. *Shakesp. All's well that ends well.*

How my head in ointment swims!
How my cup o'erlooks her *brims!* *Crashaw.*

So when with crackling flames a cauldron fries,
The bubbling waters from the bottom rise,
Above the *brims* they force their firy way. *Dryden's Æn.*

Thus in a bason drop a shilling,
Then fill the vessel to the *brim*,
You shall observe, as you are filling,
The pond'rous metal seems to swim. *Swift.*

3. The top of any liquour.

The feet of the priests that bare the ark, were dipped in the *brim* of the water. *Josh.* iii. 15.

4. The bank of a fountain.

It told me it was Cynthia's own,
Within whose cheerful *brims*
That curious nymph had oft been known
To bathe her snowy limbs. *Drayton.*

To BRIM. *v. a.* [from the noun.] To fill to the top.

May thy *brimmed* waves, for this,
Their full tribute never miss,
From a thousand rills. *Milton.*

This said, a double wreath Evander twin'd;
And poplars black and white his temples bind:
Then *brims* his ample bowl; with like design
The rest invoke the gods, with sprinkled wine. *Dryden.*

To BRIM. *v. n.* To be full to the brim.

Now horrid frays
Commence, the *brimming* glasses now are hurl'd
With dire intent. *Philips.*

BRI'MFUL. *adj.* [from *brim* and *full.*] Full to the top; overcharged.

Measure my case, how by thy beauty's filling,
With seed of woes my heart *brimful* is charg'd. *Sidney, b.* i.

We have try'd the utmost of our friends;
Our legions are *brimful*, our cause is ripe. *Shakesp. J. Cæs.*

Her *brimful* eyes, that ready stood,
And only wanted will to weep a flood,
Releas'd their watry store. *Dryden's Fables.*

The good old king at parting wrung my hand,
His eyes *brimful* of tears; then sighing, cry'd,
Prithee, be careful of my son. *Addison's Cato.*

BRI'MFULNESS. *n. s.* [from *brimful.*] Fulness to the top.

The Scot, on his unfurnish'd kingdom,
Came pouring like a tide into a breach,
With ample and *brimfulness* of his force. *Shakesp. Hen.* V.

BRI'MMER. *n. s.* [from *brim.*] A bowl full to the top.

When healths go round, and kindly *brimmers* flow,
Till the fresh garlands on their foreheads glow. *Dryden.*

BRI'MMING. *adj.* [from *brim.*] Full to the brim.

And twice besides her beestings never fail,
To store the dairy with a *brimming* pail. *Dryden.*

BRI'MSTONE. *n. s.* [corrupted from *brin* or *brenstone*, that is, firy stone.] Sulphur. See SULPHUR.

From his infernal furnace forth he threw
Huge flames, that dimmed all the heaven's light,
Enroll'd in duskish smoke and *brimstone* blue. *Fairy Q. b.* i.

This vapour is generally supposed to be sulphureous, though I can see no reason for such a supposition: I put a whole bundle of of lighted *brimſtone* matches to the ſmoke, they all went out in an inſtant. *Addiſon on Italy.*

BRI'MSTONY. *adj.* [from *brimſtone.*] Full of brimſtone; containing ſulphur; ſulphureous.

BRI'NDED. *adj.* [*brin*, Fr. a branch.] Streaked; tabby; marked with branches.

Thrice the *brinded* cat hath mew'd. *Shakeſp. Macbeth.*
She tam'd the *brinded* lioneſs,
And ſpotted mountain pard. *Milton.*
My *brinded* heifer to the ſtake I lay;
Two thriving calves ſhe ſuckles twice a day. *Dryden.*

BRI'NDLE. *n. ſ.* [from *brinded.*] The ſtate of being brinded.
A natural *brindle.* *Clariſſa.*

BRI'NDLED. *adj.* [from *brindle.*] Brinded; ſtreaked.
The boar, my ſiſters! aim the fatal dart,
And ſtrike the *brindled* monſter to the heart. *Addiſon's Ovid.*

BRINE. *n. ſ.*

1. Water impregnated with ſalt.

The encreaſing of the weight of water, will encreaſe its power of bearing; as we ſee *brine*, when it is ſalt enough, will bear an egg. *Bacon's Nat. Hiſtory*, Nº 790.

Diſſolve the ſheeps dung in water, and add to it as much ſalt as will make it a ſtrong *brine*, in this liquour, to ſteep your corn. *Mortimer.*

2. The ſea.

All, but mariners,
Plung'd in the foaming *brine*, did quit the veſſel,
Then all afire with me. *Shakeſp. Tempeſt.*
The air was calm, and, on the level *brine*,
Sleek Panope, with all her ſiſters, play'd. *Milton.*
As when two adverſe winds
Engage with horrid ſhock, the ruffled *brine*
Roars ſtormy. *Philips:*

3. Tears.

What a deal of *brine*
Hath waſh'd thy ſallow cheeks for Roſaline! *Shakeſp.*

BRI'NEPIT. *n. ſ.* [from *brine* and *pit.*] Pit of ſalt water.
Then I lov'd thee,
And ſhew'd thee all the qualities o' th' iſle,
The freſh ſprings, *brinepits*, barren place, and fertile. *Shakeſp. Tempeſt.*

To BRING. *v. a.* [bꞃingan, Sax. preter. I *brought*; part. paſſ. *brought*; bꞃohꞇ, Sax.]

1. To fetch from another place; diſtinguiſhed from to *carry*, or convey, to another place.

I was the chief that rais'd him to the crown,
And I'll be chief to *bring* him down again. *Shakeſp. H. VI.*

And as ſhe was going to fetch it, he called to her, and ſaid, *Bring* me, I pray thee, a morſel of bread in thy hand. *1 Kings*, xvii. 11.

A regiſtry of lands may furniſh eaſy ſecurities of money, that ſhall be *brought* over by ſtrangers. *Temple.*

2. To convey in one's own hand; not to ſend by another.

And if my wiſh'd alliance pleaſe your king,
Tell him he ſhould not ſend the peace, but *bring.* *Dryden.*

3. To produce; to procure.

There is nothing will *bring* you more honour, and more eaſe, than to do what right in juſtice you may. *Bacon.*

4. To cauſe to come.

He proteſts he loves you,
And needs no other ſuitor, but his liking
To *bring* you in again. *Shakeſp. Othello.*

There is but one God, who made heaven and earth, and ſea and winds; but the folly and madneſs of mankind *brought* in the images of gods. *Stillingfleet.*

The fountains of the great deep being broke open, ſo as a general deſtruction and devaſtation was *brought* upon the earth, and all things in it. *Burnet's Theory.*

*Bring* back gently their wandering minds, by going before them in the train they ſhould purſue, without any rebuke. *Locke.*

The great queſtion, which, in all ages, has diſturbed mankind, and *brought* on them thoſe miſchiefs. *Locke.*

5. To introduce.

Since he could not have a ſeat among them himſelf, he would *bring* in one, who had more merit. *Tatler*, Nº 81.

6. To reduce; to recal.

Nathan's fable had ſo good an effect, as to *bring* the man after God's own heart to a right ſenſe of his guilt. *Spect.* Nº 83.

7. To attract; to draw along.

In diſtillation, the water aſcends difficultly, and *brings* over with it ſome part of the oil of vitriol. *Newton's Opticks.*

8. To put into any particular ſtate or circumſtances, to make liable to any thing.

Having got the way of reaſoning, which that ſtudy neceſſarily *brings* the mind to, they might be able to transfer it to other parts of knowledge, as they ſhall have occaſion. *Locke.*

The queſtion for *bringing* the king to juſtice was immediately put, and carried without any oppoſition, that I can find. *Swift's Presbyterian Plea.*

9. To conduct.

A due conſideration of the vanities of the world, will naturally *bring* us to the contempt of it; and the contempt of the world will as certainly *bring* us home to ourſelves. *L'Eſtrange.*

The underſtanding ſhould be *brought* to the difficult and knotty parts of knowledge, by inſenſible degrees. *Locke.*

10. To recal; to ſummons.

But thoſe, and more than I to mind can *bring*,
Menalcas has not yet forgot to ſing. *Dryden.*

11. To induce; to prevail upon.

The nature of the things, contained in thoſe words, would not ſuffer him to think otherwiſe, how, or whenſoever, he is *brought* to reflect on them. *Locke.*

It ſeems ſo prepoſterous a thing to men, to make themſelves unhappy in order to happineſs, that they do not eaſily *bring* themſelves to it. *Locke.*

Profitable employments would be no leſs a diverſion than any of the idle ſports in faſhion, if men could but be *brought* to delight in them. *Locke.*

12. *To bring about.* [See ABOUT.] To bring to paſs; to effect.

This he conceives not hard to *bring about*,
If all of you would join to help him out. *Dryden's Ind. Emp.*

This turn of mind ~~threw off the oppoſitions of envy and competition; it~~ enabled him to gain the moſt vain and impracticable into his deſigns, and to *bring about* ſeveral great events, for the advantage of the publick. *Addiſon's Freeholder.*

13. *To bring forth.* To give birth to; to produce.

The good queen,
For ſhe is good, hath *brought* you *forth* a daughter:
Here 'tis; commends it to your bleſſing. *Shakeſp.*
More wonderful
Than that which, by creation, firſt *brought forth*
Light out of darkneſs! *Paradiſe Loſt*, *b.* xii. *l.* 472:
Bewail thy falſehood, and the pious works
It hath *brought forth*, to make thee memorable
Among illuſtrious women, faithful wives. *Milton's Agoniſt.*
~~Bellona leads thee to thy lover's hand,~~
Another queen *brings forth* another brand,
To burn with foreign fires her native land! *Dryden, Æneid* vii. *l* 444.

Idleneſs and luxury *bring forth* poverty and want; and this tempts men to injuſtice; and that cauſeth enmity and animoſity. *Tillotſon.*

The value of land is raiſed, when it is fitted to *bring forth* a greater quantity of any valuable product. *Locke.*

14. *To bring forth.* To bring to light.

The thing that is hid, *bringeth* he *forth* to light. *Job*, xxviii. 11.

15. *To bring in.* To reduce.

Send over into that realm ſuch a ſtrong power of men, as ſhould perforce *bring in* all that rebellious rout, and looſe people. *Spenſer on Ireland.*

16. *To bring in.* To afford gain.

The ſole meaſure of all his courteſies is, what return they will make him, and what revenue they will *bring* him *in.* *South.*

Trade *brought* us *in* plenty and riches. *Locke.*

17. *To bring in.* To introduce.

Entertain no long diſcourſe with any; but, if you can, *bring in* ſomething to ſeaſon it with religion. *Taylor.*

The fruitfulneſs of Italy and the like, are not *brought in* by force, but naturally riſe out of the argument. *Addiſon.*

Quotations are beſt *brought in*, to confirm ſome opinion controverted. *Swift.*

18. *To bring off.* To clear; to procure to be acquitted; to cauſe to eſcape.

I truſted to my head, that has betrayed me; and I found fault with my legs, that would otherwiſe have *brought* me *off.* *L'Eſtrange.*

Set a kite upon the bench, and it is forty to one he'll *bring off* a crow at the bar. *L'Eſtrange.*

The beſt way to avoid this imputation, and to *bring off* the credit of our underſtanding, is to be truly religious. *Tillotſon.*

19. *To bring on.* To engage in action.

If there be any that would reign, and take up all the time, let him find means to take them off, and *bring* others *on.* *Bacon, Eſſay* 36.

20. *To bring over.* To convert; to draw to a new party.

This liberty ſhould be made uſe of upon few occaſions, of ſmall importance, and only with a view of *bringing over* his own ſide, another time, to ſomething of greater and more publick moment. *Swift on the Sentiments of a Ch. of Engl. man.*

The proteſtant clergy will find it, perhaps, no difficult matter to *bring* great numbers *over* to the church. *Swift.*

21. *To bring out.* To exhibit; to ſhew.

If I make not this cheat *bring out* another, and the ſhearers prove ſheep, let me be unrolled. *Shakeſp. Winter's Tale.*

Which he could *bring out*, where he had,
And what he bought them for, and paid. *Hudibras.*
Theſe ſhake his ſoul, and, as they boldly preſs,
*Bring out* his crimes, and force him to confeſs. *Dryden.*

Another way made uſe of, to find the weight of the denarii, was by the weight of Greek coins; but thoſe experiments *bring out* the denarius heavier. *Arbuthnot.*

22. *To bring under.* To ſubdue; to repreſs.

That ſharp courſe which you have ſet down, for the *bringing* under

To bring. In the following passage the dis:tinction now a days made betwixt bringing from a place and carrying to another is not regarded. Bring is used in both.

he who brought me hither
Will bring me hence, no other guide I seek
Parad. reg. 1

To bring to with the reciprocal pronoun
To induce to prevail on
The real or supposed unpleasantness of the Actions Seems so preposterous a thing to make them:selves unhappy in order to happiness, that they do not easily bring themselves to it
Locke

To bring low
To reduce to subject, to take from a former State into another more depressed, to degrade to dispirit.

How comes it then to pass that having been once so low brought & thoroughly subjected, they afterwards lifted up themselves so strongly again
Spenser Irl.

To bring to death, to execute publickly
The Earl of Desmond was by false sub:ornation of K. Edw. 4th's Queen brought to his death at most unjustly tho a good subject
Spenser

To bring on v. a.
To induce as an efficient cause
Men corrupted themselves so monstruously, that the Deity brought on a flood which destroyed the whole earth
P. Forbes

To import in a Mercantile Sense
As for any Merchandise you have brought You shall have your return in Merchandise gold or silver
Bacon

Let him be testimonied in his own bringings forth, and he shall appear a Scholar, a States man and a Soldier
Shak.

To give Opinion or Verdict
He sent letters to the Council, wherein he acknowledged himself much favoured by them in that they had brought his cause fineable
Hayw

To brine v. a. [from the Noun]
To Season, to Salt.
This custom of picking out of the Sheaves all smutty Corn may be saved where the Seed was well brined; for that takes off all the poor thin corn which produces the smutty ears

To bring acquainted
Now we being brought known unto her, the time that we spent in curing some wounds After once we were acquainted she con:tinually haunted us
Sidney

IL facing 3P2r

*under* of thoſe rebels of Ulſter, and preparing a way for their perpetual reformation. *Spenſer's Ireland.*

To ſay, that the more capable, or the better deſerver, hath ſuch right to govern, as he may compulſorily *bring under* the leſs worthy, is idle. *Bacon's Holy War.*

23. *To bring up.* To educate; to inſtruct; to form.

The well *bringing up* of the people, ſerves as a moſt ſure bond to hold them. *Sidney, b.* i.

He that takes upon him the charge of *bringing up* young men, eſpecially young gentlemen, ſhould have ſomething more in him than Latin. *Locke.*

They frequently converſed with this lovely virgin, who had been *brought up* by her father in the ſame courſe of knowledge. *Addiſon. Guardian*, Nº 167.

24. *To bring up.* To bring into practice.

Several obliging deferences, condeſcenſions, and ſubmiſſions, with many outward forms and ceremonies, were firſt of all *brought up* among the politer part of mankind, who lived in courts and cities. *Spectator*, Nº 119.

25. *To bring up.* To cauſe to advance.

*Bring up* your army; but, I think, you'll find,
They've not prepar'd for us. *Shakeſp. Coriolanus.*

BRI'NGER. *n. ſ.* [from *bring.*] The perſon that brings any thing.

Yet the firſt *bringer* of unwelcome news
Hath but a loſing office: and his tongue
Sounds ever after as a ſullen bell,
Remember'd tolling a dead friend. *Shakeſp. Henry* IV. *p.* ii.
Beſt you ſee ſafe the *bringer*
Out of the hoſt: I muſt attend mine office. *Shakeſp.*

BRI'NGER UP. Instructor; educator.

Italy and Rome have been breeders and *bringers up* of the worthieſt men. *Aſcham's Schoolmaſter.*

BRI'NISH. *adj.* [from *brine.*] Having the taſte of brine; ſalt.

Nero would be tainted with remorſe
To hear and ſee her plaints, her *briniſh* tears. *Shakeſp.*
For now I ſtand, as one upon a rock,
Environ'd with a wilderneſs of ſea,
Who marks the waxing tide grow wave by wave;
Expecting ever when ſome envious ſurge
Will, in his *briniſh* bowels, ſwallow him. *Shakeſp. T. Andr.*

BRI'NISHNESS. *n. ſ.* [from *briniſh.*] Saltneſs; tendency to ſaltneſs.

BRINK. *n. ſ.* [*brink*, Daniſh.] The edge of any place, as of a precipice or a river.

Th' amazed flames ſtand gather'd in a heap,
And from the precipice's *brink* retire,
Afraid to venture on ſo large a leap. *Dryden's Ann. Mirab.*

We ſtand therefore on the *brinks* and confines of thoſe ſtates at the day of doom. *Atterbury.*

So have I ſeen, from Severn's *brink*,
A flock of geeſe jump down together;
Swim where the bird of Jove wou'd ſink,
And, ſwimming, never wet a feather. *Swift.*

BRI'NY. *adj.* [from *brine.*] Salt.

He, who firſt the paſſage try'd,
In harden'd oak his heart did hide;
Or his, at leaſt, in hollow wood,
Who tempted firſt the *briny* flood. *Dryden.*
Then, *briny* ſeas, and taſteful ſprings, farewel,
Where fountain nymphs, confus'd with Nereïds, dwell.
*Addiſon's Remarks on Italy.*

A muriatick or *briny* taſte ſeems to be produced by a mixture of an acid and alkaline ſalt; for ſpirit of ſalt, and ſalt of tartar, mixed, produce a ſalt like ſea ſalt. *Arbuthnot on Aliments.*

BRI'ONY. See BRYONY.

BRISK. *adj.* [*bruſque*, Fr.]

1. Lively; vivacious; gay; ſprightly; applied to men.

Pr'ythee, die, and ſet me free,
Or elſe be
Kind and *briſk*, and gay like me. *Sir J. Denham.*

A creeping young fellow, that had committed matrimony with a *briſk* gameſome laſs, was ſo altered in a few days, that he was liker a ſceleton than a living man. *L'Eſtrange.*

Why ſhou'd all honour then be ta'en
From lower parts, to load the brain:
When other limbs we plainly ſee,
Each in his way, as *briſk* as he? *Prior.*

2. Powerful; ſpirituous.

Our nature here is not unlike our wine;
Some ſorts, when old, continue *briſk* and fine. *Denham.*
Under ground, the rude Riphæan race
Mimick *briſk* cyder, with the brake's product wild,
Sloes pounded, hips, and ſervis' harſheſt juice. *Philips.*

It muſt needs be ſome exteriour cauſe, and the *briſk* acting of ſome objects without me, whoſe efficacy I cannot reſiſt. *Locke.*

3. Vivid; bright.

Objects appeared much darker, becauſe my inſtrument was overcharged; had it magnified thirty or twenty five times, it would have made the object appear more *briſk* and pleaſant. *Newton's Opticks.*

To BRISK UP. *v. n.* To come up briſkly.

BRI'SKET. *n. ſ.* [*brichet*, Fr.] The breaſt of an animal.



See that none of the wool be wanting, that their gums be red, teeth white and even, and the *briſket* ſkin red. *Mortimer.*

BRI'SKLY. *adv.* [from *briſk.*] Actively; vigorouſly.

We have ſeen the air in the bladder ſuddenly expand itſelf ſo much, and ſo *briſkly*, that it manifeſtly lifted up ſome light bodies that leaned upon it. *Boyle.*

I could plainly perceive the creature to ſuck in many of the moſt minute animalcula, that were ſwimming *briſkly* about in the water. *Ray on the Creation.*

BRI'SKNESS. *n. ſ.* [from *briſk.*]

1. Livelineſs; vigour; quickneſs.

Some remains of corruption, though they do not conquer and extinguiſh, yet will ſlacken and allay the vigour and *briſkneſs* of the renewed principle. *South.*

2. Gayety.

But the moſt diſtinguiſhing part of his character ſeems to me, to be his *briſkneſs*, his jollity, and his good humour. *Dryd.*

BRI'STLE. *n. ſ.* [bꞃiꞅꞇl, Sax.] The ſtiff hair of ſwine.

I will not open my lips ſo wide as a *briſtle* may enter. *Shakeſp.*

~~He is covered with hair, and not, as the~~ boar, with *briſtles*, ~~which~~ probably ſpends more upon the ſame matter which, in other creatures, makes the horns; for *briſtles* ſeem to be nothing elſe but a horn ſplit into a multitude of little ones. *Grew.*

Two boars whom love to battle draws,
With riſing *briſtles*, and with frothy jaws,
Their adverſe breaſts with tuſks oblique they wound. *Dryd.*

To BRI'STLE. *v. a.* [from the noun.] To erect in briſtles.

Now for the bare-pickt bone of majeſty,
Doth dogged war *briſtle* his angry creſt,
And ſnarleth in the gentle eyes of peace. *Shakeſp. K. John.*
Which makes him plume himſelf, and *briſtle* up
The creſt of youth againſt your dignity. *Shakeſp. H.* IV.

To BRI'STLE. *v. n.* To ſtand erect as briſtles.

Be it ounce, or cat, or bear,
Pard, or boar with *briſtled* hair,
In thy eye that ſhall appear,
When thou wak'ſt, it is thy dear. *Shakeſp. Midſum. N. Dr.*
Stood Theodore ſurpriz'd in deadly fright,
With chatt'ring teeth, and *briſtling* hair upright;
Yet arm'd with inborn worth. *Dryden's Fables.*
Thy hair ſo *briſtles* with unmanly fears,
As fields of corn that riſe in bearded ears. *Dryden's Perſius.*

*To* BRISTLE *a thread.* To fix a briſtle to it.

BRI'STLY. *adj.* [from *briſtle.*] Thick ſet with briſtles.

The leaves of the black mulberry are ſomewhat *briſtly*, which may help to preſerve the dew. *Bacon's Natural Hiſt.*

If the eye were ſo acute as to rival the fineſt microſcope, the ſight of our own ſelves would affright us; the ſmootheſt ſkin would be beſet all over with ~~rugged ſcales and~~ *briſtly* hairs. *Bentley.*

Thus maſtful beech the *briſtly* cheſnut bears,
And the wild aſh is white with bloomy pears. *Dryden's Virg.*
The careful maſter of the ſwine,
Forth haſted he to tend his *briſtly* care. *Pope's Odyſſ. b.* xiv.

BRI'STOL STONE. A kind of ſoft diamond found in a rock near the city of Briſtol.

Of this kind of cryſtal are the better and larger ſort of *Briſtol ſtones*, and the Kerry ſtones of Ireland. *Woodward.*

BRIT. *n. ſ.* The name of a fiſh.

The pilchards were wont to purſue the *brit*, upon which they feed, into the havens. *Carew's Survey of Cornwal.*

To BRITE. } *v. n.* Barley, wheat, or hops, are ſaid to *brite*,
To BRIGHT. } when they grow over-ripe. *Dict.*

BRITTLE. *adj.* [bꞃiꞇꞇan, Saxon.] Fragile; apt to break; not tough.

The wood of vines is very durable; though no tree hath the twigs, while they are green, ſo *brittle*, yet the wood dried is extremely tough. *Bacon's Natural Hiſt.* Nº 622.

From earth all came, to earth muſt all return,
Frail as the cord, and *brittle* as the urn. *Prior.*
Of airy pomp, and fleeting joys,
What does the buſy world conclude at beſt,
But *brittle* goods, that break like glaſs? *Granville.*

If the ſtone is *brittle*, it will often crumble, and paſs in the form of gravel. *Arbuthnot on Diet.*

BRI'TTLENESS. *n. ſ.* [from *brittle.*] Aptneſs to break; fragility.

A wit quick without brightneſs, ſharp without *brittleneſs*. *Aſcham's Schoolmaſter.*

Artificers, in the tempering of ſteel, by holding it but a minute or two longer or leſſer in the flame, give it very differing tempers, as to *brittleneſs* or toughneſs. *Boyle.*

BRIZE. *n. ſ.* The gadfly.

A *brize*, a ſcorned little creature,
Through his fair hide his angry ſting did threaten. *Spenſer.*

BROACH. *n. ſ.* [*broche*, Fr.]

1. A ſpit.

He was taken into ſervice in his court, to a baſe office in his kitchen; ſo that he turned a *broach*, that had worn a crown. *Bacon's Henry* VII.

Whoſe offered entrails ſhall his crime reproach,
And drip their fatneſs from the hazle *broach*. *Dryden's Virgil.*

2. A

2. A muſical inſtrument, the ſounds of which are made by turning round a handle. *Dict.*

3. [With hunters.] A ſtart of the head of a young ſtag, growing ſharp like the end of a ſpit. *Dict.*

To BROACH. *v. a.* [from the noun.]

1. To ſpit; to pierce as with a ſpit.

As by a low but loving likelihood,
Were now the general of our gracious empreſs,
As in good time he may, from Ireland coming,
Bringing rebellion *broached* on his ſword. *Shakeſp. Henry* V.

He felled men as one would mow hay, and ſometimes *broached* a great number of them upon his pike, as one would carry little birds ſpitted upon a ſtick. *Hakewell on Providence.*

2. To pierce a veſſel in order to draw the liquour; to tap.

3. To open any ſtore.

I will notably provide, that you ſhall want neither weapons, victuals, nor aid; I will open the old armouries, I will *broach* my ſtore, and bring forth my ſtores. *Knolles's Hiſtory.*

4. To give out, or utter any thing.

This errour, that Piſon was Ganges, was firſt *broached* by Joſephus. *Raleigh.*

Thoſe who were the chief inſtruments of raiſing the noiſe, made uſe of thoſe very opinions themſelves had *broached*, for arguments to prove, that the change of miniſters was dangerous. *Swift's Examiner*, N° 45.

5. To let out any thing.

And now the field of death, the liſts,
Were enter'd by antagoniſts,
And blood was ready to be *broach'd*,
When Hudibras in haſte approach'd. *Hudibras, cant.* ii.

BRO'ACHER. *n. ſ.* [from *broach.*]

1. A ſpit.

The youth approach'd the fire, and, as it burn'd,
On five ſharp *broachers* rank'd, the roaſt they turn'd;
Theſe morſels ſtay'd their ſtomachs. *Dryden.*

2. An opener, or utterer of any thing; the firſt authour.

There is much pride and vanity in the affectation of being the firſt *broacher* of an heretical opinion. *L'Eſtrange.*

Numerous parties denominate themſelves, not from the grand Authour and Finiſher of our faith, but from the firſt *broacher* of their idolized opinions. *Decay of Piety.*

This opinion is commonly, but falſely, aſcribed to Ariſtotle, not as its firſt *broacher*, but as its ableſt patron. *Cheyne.*

BROAD. *adj.* [bɲad, Saxon.]

1. Wide; extended in breadth; diſtinguiſhed from length.

The weeds that his *broad* ſpreading leaves did ſhelter,
Are pull'd up root and all by Bolingbroke. *Shakeſp. R.* II.

The top may be juſtly ſaid to grow *broader*, as the bottom narrower. *Temple.*

Of all your knowledge this vain fruit you have,
To walk with eyes *broad* open to your grave. *Dryden.*

So lofty was the pile, a Parthian bow,
With vigour drawn, muſt ſend the ſhaft below,
The bottom was full twenty fathom *broad. Dryden's Fables.*

He launch'd the firy bolt from pole to pole,
*Broad* burſt the lightnings, deep the thunders roll. *Pope.*

As cloath'd in cloudy ſtorm,
Weak, wan, and *broad*, he ſkirts the ſouthern ſky. *Thomſon.*

2. Large.

To keep him at a diſtance from falſehood and cunning, which has always a *broad* mixture of falſehood; this is the fitteſt preparation of a child for wiſdom. *Locke.*

3. Clear; open.

In mean time he, with cunning to conceal
All thought of this from others, himſelf bore
In *broad* houſe, with the wooers us before. *Chapman's Odyſſ.*

It no longer ſeeks the ſhelter of night and darkneſs, but appears in the *broadeſt* light. *Decay of Piety.*

If children were left alone in the dark, they would be no more afraid than in *broad* ſunſhine. *Locke.*

4. Groſs; coarſe.

The reeve and the miller are diſtinguiſhed from each other, as much as the lady prioreſs and the *broad* ſpeaking gap-toothed wife of Bath. *Dryden's Fables, Pref.*

Love made him doubt his *broad* barbarian ſound;
By love, his want of words and wit he found. *Dryden.*

If open vice be what you drive at,
A name ſo *broad* will ne'er connive at. *Dryden's Albion.*

The *broadeſt* mirth unfeeling folly wears,
Leſs pleaſing far than virtue's very tears. *Pope.*

Room for my lord! three jockeys in his train;
Six huntſmen with a ſhout precede his chair;
He grins, and looks *broad* nonſenſe with a ſtare. *Pope.*

5. Obſcene; fulſom; tending to obſcenity.

As chaſte and modeſt as he is eſteemed, it cannot be denied, but in ſome places he is *broad* and fulſome. *Dryden's Juv. Ded.*

Though, now arraign'd, he read with ſome delight;
Becauſe he ſeems to chew the cud again,
When his *broad* comment makes the text too plain. *Dryden.*

6. Bold; not delicate; not reſerved.

Who can ſpeak *broader* than he that has no houſe to put his head in? Such may rail againſt great buildings. *Shakeſp.*

From *broad* words, and 'cauſe he fail'd
His preſence at the tyrant's feaſt, I hear,
Macduff lives in diſgrace. *Shakeſp. Macbeth.*

BROAD *as long.* Equal upon the whole.

The mobile are ſtill for levelling; that is to ſay, for advancing themſelves: for it is as *broad as long*, whether they riſe to others, or bring others down to them. *L'Eſtrange.*

BROAD-CLOTH. *n. ſ.* [from *broad* and *cloth.*] A fine kind of cloath.

Thus, a wiſe taylor is not pinching;
But turns at ev'ry ſeam an inch in:
Or elſe, be ſure, your *broad-cloth* breeches
Will ne'er be ſmooth, nor hold their ſtitches. *Swift.*

BROAD-EYED. *adj.* [from *broad* and *eye.*] Having a wide ſurvey.

In deſpite of *broad-ey'd* watchful day,
I would into thy boſom pour my thoughts:
But, ah! I will not. *Shakeſp. King John.*

BROAD-LEAVED. *adj.* [from *broad* and *leaf.*] Having broad leaves.

Narrow and *broad-leaved* cyprus-graſs of the ſame ſort. *Woodward on Foſſils.*

To BRO'ADEN. *v. n.* [from *broad.*] To grow broad. I know not whether this word occurs, but in the following paſſage.

Low walks the ſun, and *broadens* by degrees,
Juſt o'er the verge of day. *Thomſon's Summer, l.* 1605.

BRO'ADLY. *adv.* [from *broad.*] In a broad manner.

BRO'ADNESS. *n. ſ.* [from *broad.*]

1. Breadth; extent from ſide to ſide.

2. Coarſeneſs; fulſomneſs.

I have uſed the cleaneſt metaphor I could find, to palliate the *broadneſs* of the meaning. *Dryden.*

BRO'ADSHOULDERED. *adj.* [from *broad* and *ſhoulder.*] Having a large ſpace between the ſhoulders.

Big-bon'd, and large of limbs, with ſinews ſtrong,
*Broadſhouldered*, and his arms were round and long. *Dryden.*

I am a tall, *broadſhouldered*, impudent, black fellow; and, as I thought, every way qualified for a rich widow. *Spectator.*

BRO'ADSIDE. *n. ſ.* [from *broad* and *ſide.*]

1. The ſide of a ſhip, diſtinct from the head or ſtern.

From vaſter hopes than this he ſeem'd to fall,
That durſt attempt the Britiſh admiral:
From her *broadſides* a ruder flame is thrown,
Than from the firy chariot of the ſun. *Waller.*

2. The volly of ſhot fired at once from the ſide of a ſhip.

3. [In printing.] A ſheet of paper containing one large page.

BRO'ADSWORD. *n. ſ.* [from *broad* and *ſword.*] A cutting ſword, with a broad blade.

He, in fighting a duel, was run through the thigh with a *broadſword*. *Wiſeman.*

BRO'ADWISE. *adv.* [from *broad* and *wiſe.*] According to the direction of the breadth.

If one ſhould, with his hand, thruſt a piece of iron *broadwiſe* againſt the flat cieling of his chamber, the iron would not fall as long as the force of the hand perſeveres to preſs againſt it. *Boyle.*

BROCA'DE. *n. ſ.* [*brocado*, Span.] A ſilken ſtuff, variegated with colours of gold or ſilver.

I have the conveniency of buying and importing rich *brocades*. *Spectator*, N° 288.

Or ſtain her honour, or her new *brocade*,
Forget her pray'rs, or miſs a maſquerade. *Pope.*

BROCA'DED. *adj.* [from *brocade.*]

1. Dreſt in brocade.

2. Woven in the manner of a brocade.

Should you the rich *brocaded* ſuit unfold,
Where riſing flow'rs grow ſtiff with froſted gold. *Gay.*

BRO'CAGE. *n. ſ.* [from *broke.*]

1. The gain gotten by promoting bargains.

Yet ſure his honeſty
Got him ſmall gains, but ſhameleſs flattery,
And filthy *brocage*, and unſeemly ſhifts,
And borrow baſe, and ſome good ladies gifts. *Spenſer.*

2. The hire given for any unlawful office.

As for the politick and wholeſome laws, they were interpreted to be but *brocage* of an uſurer, thereby to woo and win the hearts of the people. *Bacon's Henry* VII.

3. The trade of dealing in old things.

Poor poet ape, that would be thought our chief,
Whoſe works are e'en the frippery of wit,
From *brocage* is become ſo bold a thief,
As we, the rob'd, leave rage, and pity it. *Ben. Johnſon.*

So much as the quantity of money is leſſened, ſo much muſt the ſhare of every one that has a right to this money be the leſs, whether he be landholder, for his goods, or labourer, for his hire, or merchant, for his *brocage*. *Locke.*

BRO'CCOLI. *n. ſ.* [Ital.] See CABBAGE; of which it is a ſpecies.

Content with little, I can piddle here,
On *broccoli* and mutton round the year;
But ancient friends, tho' poor or out of play,
That touch my bell, I cannot turn away. *Pope.*

To BROCHE. See To BROACH.

Broad Sealn. s [broad & Seal]
Patent to which the great Seal of Britain is appended
You will wonder how such an Ordinary fellow, as this Mr Wood could have got his Majestys broad Seal. Swift

To broaden v. a. [from broad]
To make any thing Spacious & wide.
'Tis used in Scotland and perhaps in no other place to be found but in the following passage unless he be mistook it for browden'd which in the Scotish dialect denotes lowring frightful, alluding to knitting the brows
Whence glaring oft with many a broaden'd Orb
He frights the Nations Thoms. Aut. 780

Broad fronted [broad & front]
Having a Spacious large forehead
broad fronted Cæsar
When thou wast here above the ground. I was a Morsel for a Monarch. Shak A & Cl.

‡ Diffused Spread every way
Fame is no plant that grows on Mortal Soil
Nor in the glistering foil
Set off to th' world, nor in broad rumour lies
Milt

~~Bronchial~~
~~A scaly fish with a forked tail.~~
The head, and one of the bronchial fins, ~~& the body with the scales & tail~~, appear ~~all~~ very fair
Woodw.

To broid v. n. [broder fr.]
To be in any winding figure as embroidery
Over the Chairs a State of Ivy; which is curiously wrought with Silver & Silk of divers Colours, broiding or binding in the Ivy; ever the Work of Some of the Daughters
Bac. n. atl.

So Geoffry of Boullion, at one draught of his bow, ſhooting againſt David's tower in Jeruſalem, *broched* three feetleſs birds. *Camden's Remains.*

Brock. *n. ſ.* [bɲoc, Saxon.] A badger.

Bro'cket. *n. ſ.* A red deer, two years old.

Brogue. *n. ſ.* [*brog*, Iriſh.]

1. A kind of ſhoe.

I thought he ſlept; and put
My clouted *brogues* from off my feet, whoſe rudeneſs
Anſwer'd my ſteps too loud. *Shakeſp. Cymbeline.*

Sometimes it is given out, that we muſt either take three halfpence, or eat our *brogues.* *Swift.*

2. A cant word for a corrupt dialect, or manner of pronunciation.

To BRO'IDER. *v. a.* [*brodir*, Fr.] To adorn with figures of needle-work.

A robe and a *broidered* coat, and a girdle. *Exodus*, xxviii. 4.

Infant Albion lay
In mantles *broider'd* o'er with gorgeous pride. *Tickell.*

Bro'idery. *n. ſ.* [from *broider.*] Embroidery; flower-work; additional ornaments wrought upon cloath.

The golden *broidery* tender Milkah wove,
The breaſt to Kenna ſacred, and to love,
Lie rent and mangled. *Tickell.*

BROIL. *n. ſ.* [*brouiller*, Fr.] A tumult; a quarrel.

Say to the king thy knowledge of the *broil*,
As thou didſt leave it. *Shakeſp. Macbeth.*

He has ſent the ſword both of civil *broils*, and publick war, amongſt us. *Wake.*

Rude were their revels, and obſcene their joys,
The *broils* of drunkards, and the luſt of boys. *Granville.*

To BROIL. *v. a.* [*bruler*, Fr.] To dreſs or cook by laying on the coals, or before the fire.

Some ſtrip the ſkin, ſome portion out the ſpoil,
Some on the fire the reeking entrails *broil.* *Dryden's Æneid.*

To Broil. *v. n.* To be in the heat.

Where have you been *broiling?*—
——Among the croud i' th' abbey, where a finger
Could not be wedg'd in more. *Shakeſp. Henry* VIII.

Long ere now all the planets and comets had been *broiling* in the ſun, had the world laſted from all eternity. *Cheyne.*

To BROKE. *v. n.* [of uncertain etymology. *Skinner* ſeems inclined to derive it from *to break*, because *broken* men turn factors or *brokers. Caſaubon*, from πράττειν. *Skinner* thinks, again, that it may be contracted from *procurer*. Mr. *Lye* more probably deduces it from bɲuccan, Sax. to be buſy.] To tranſact buſineſs for others, or by others. It is uſed generally in reproach.

He does, indeed,
And *brokes* with all that can, in ſuch a ſuit,
Corrupt the tender honour of a maid. *Shakeſp.*

The gains of bargains are of a more doubtful nature, when men ſhould wait upon other's neceſſity; *broke* by ſervants and inſtruments to draw them on. *Bacon.*

Bro'king. *particip. adj.* In the broker's hands.

Redeem from *broking* pawn the blemiſh'd crown,
Wipe off the duſt that hides our ſceptre's gilt. *Shakeſp.*

Bro'ken. [*particip. paſſ.* of *break.*]

Preſerve men's wits from being *broken* with the very bent of ſo long attention. *Hooker.*

Bro'ken meat. Fragments; meat that has been cut.

Get three or four chairwomen to attend you conſtantly in the kitchen, whom you pay at ſmall charges; only with the *broken meat*, a few coals, and all the cinders. *Swift.*

Bro'kenhearted. *adj.* [from *broken* and *heart.*] Having the ſpirits cruſhed by grief or fear.

He hath ſent me to bind up the *brokenhearted.* *Iſa.* lxi. 1.

Bro'kenly. *adv.* [from *broken.*] Without any regular ſeries.

Sir Richard Hopkins hath done ſomewhat of this kind, but *brokenly* and glancingly; intending chiefly a diſcourſe of his own voyage. *Hakewell on Providence.*

Bro'ker. *n. ſ.* [from *to broke.*]

1. A factor; one that does buſineſs for another; one that makes bargains for another.

*Brokers*, who, having no ſtock of their own, ſet up and trade with that of other men; buying here, and ſelling there, and commonly abuſing both ſides, to make out a little paultry gain. *Temple.*

Some South-ſea *broker*, from the city,
Will purchaſe me, the more's the pity;
Lay all my fine plantations waſte,
To fit them to his vulgar taſte. *Swift.*

2. One who deals in old houſhold goods.

3. A pimp; a match-maker.

A goodly *broker!*
Dare you preſume to harbour wanton lines?
To whiſper and conſpire againſt my youth? *Shakeſp.*

In chuſing for yourſelf, you ſhew'd your judgment;
Which being ſhallow, you ſhall give me leave
To play the *broker* in mine own behalf. *Shakeſp. Henry* VI.

Bro'kerage. *n. ſ.* [from *broker.*] The pay or reward of a broker. See Brocage.

Bro'nchocele. *n. ſ.* [βρογχοκήλη.] A tumour of that part of the aſpera arteria, called the *bronchus.* *Quincy.*

Bro'nchial. } *adj.* [βρόγχος.] Belonging to the throat.
Bro'nchick. }

Inflammation of the lungs may happen either in the *bronchial* or pulmonary veſſels, and may ſoon be communicated from one to the other, when the inflammation affects both the lobes. *Arbuthnot on Diet.*

Broncho'tomy. *n. ſ.* [βρόγχος and τέμνω.] That operation which opens the windpipe by inciſion, to prevent ſuffocation in a quinſey. *Quincy.*

The operation of *bronchotomy* is an inciſion made into the aſpera arteria, to make way for the air into the lungs, when reſpiration is obſtructed by any tumour compreſſing the larynx. *Sharp's Surgery.*

Brond. *n. ſ.* See Brand.

Fooliſh old man, ſaid then, the pagan wroth,
That weeneſt words or charms may force withſtond;
Soon ſhalt thou ſee, and then believe for troth,
That I can carve with this enchanted *brond.* *Fairy Q. b.* ii.

Bronto'logy. *n. ſ.* [βροντὴ and λογία.] A diſſertation upon thunder. *Dict.*

Bronze. *n. ſ.* [*bronze*, Fr.]

1. Braſs.

Imbrown'd with native *bronze*, lo! Henley ſtands,
Tuning his voice, and balancing his hands. *Pope's Dunc.*

2. A medal.

I view with anger and diſdain,
How little gives thee joy or pain;
A print, a *bronze*, a flower, a root,
A ſhell, a butterfly can do't. *Prior.*

BROOCH. *n. ſ.* [*broke*, Dutch.]

1. A jewel; an ornament of jewels.

Ay, marry, our chains and our jewels.—
Your *brooches*, pearls, and owches. *Shakeſp. Henry* IV. *p.* ii.

Richly ſuited, but unſeaſonable; juſt like the *brooch* and the toothpick, which we wear not now. *Shakeſp.*

I know him well; he is the *brooch*, indeed,
And gem of all the nation. *Shakeſp. Hamlet.*

2. [With painters.] A painting all of one colour. *Dict.*

To Brooch. *v. a.* [from the noun.] To adorn with jewels.

Not th' imperious ſhew
Of the full-fortun'd Cæſar, ever ſhall
Be *brooch'd* with me. *Shakeſp. Antony and Cleopatra.*

To BROOD. *v. n.* [bɲædan, Saxon.]

1. To ſit on eggs; to hatch them.

Thou from the firſt
Waſt preſent, and, with mighty wings outſpread,
Dove-like ſat'ſt *brooding* on the vaſt abyſs,
And mad'ſt it pregnant. *Milton's Par. Loſt, b.* i. *l.* 21.

Here nature ſpreads her fruitful ſweetneſs round,
Breathes on the air, and *broods* upon the ground. *Dryden.*

2. To cover chickens under the wing.

Exalted hence, and drunk with ſecret joy,
Their young ſucceſſion all their cares employ;
They breed, they *brood*, inſtruct and educate,
And make proviſion for the future ſtate. *Dryden's Virgil.*

Find out ſome uncouth cell,
Where *brooding* darkneſs ſpreads his jealous wings,
And the night raven ſings. *Milton.*

3. To watch, or conſider any thing anxiouſly.

Defraud their clients, and, to lucre ſold,
Sit *brooding* on unprofitable gold,
Who dare not give. *Dryden's Æneid.*

As rejoicing miſers
*Brood* o'er their precious ſtores of ſecret gold. *Smith's Phædr.*

4. To mature any thing by care.

It was the opinion of Clinias, as if there were ever amongſt nations a *brooding* of a war, and that there is no ſure league but impuiſſance to do hurt. *Bacon's War with Spain.*

To Brood. *v. a.* To cheriſh by care; to hatch.

Of crouds afraid, yet anxious when alone,
You'll ſit and *brood* your ſorrows on a throne. *Dryden.*

Brood. *n. ſ.* [from the verb.]

1. Offspring; progeny.

The heavenly father keep his *brood*
From foul infection of ſo great a vice. *Fairfax, b.* i.

With terrours, and with clamours compaſs'd round,
Of mine own *brood*, that on my bowels feed. *Par. L. b.* ii.

Or any other of that heav'nly *brood*,
Let down in cloudy throne to do the world ſome good. *Milton.*

Ælian diſcourſes of ſtorks, and their affection toward their *brood*, whom they inſtruct to fly. *Brown's Vulgar Errours.*

2. Generation.

Have you forgotten Libya's burning waſtes,
Its barren rocks, parch'd earth, and hills of ſand,
Its tainted air, and all its *broods* of poiſon? *Addiſon's Cato.*

3. A hatch; the number hatched at once.

I was wonderfully pleaſed to ſee the different workings of inſtinct in a hen followed by a *brood* of ducks. *Spect.* N° 121.

4. Something brought forth; a production.

Such things become the hatch and *brood* of time. *Shakesp.*

5. The act of covering the eggs.

Something's in his soul,
O'er which his melancholy sits on *brood*;
And I doubt the hatch and the disclose
Will be some danger. *Shakesp. Hamlet.*

BRO'ODY. *adj.* [from *brood.*] In a state of sitting on the eggs; inclined to sit.

The common hen, all the while she is *broody*, sits, and leads her chickens, and uses a voice which we call clocking. *Ray.*

BROOK. *n. s.* [bꞃoc, or bꞃoca, Saxon.] A running water, less than a river; a rivulet.

A substitute shines brightly as a king,
Until a king be by; and then his state
Empties itself, as doth an inland *brook*
Into the main of waters. *Shakesp. Merchant of Venice.*

Or many grateful altars I would rear,
Of grassy turf; and pile up every stone,
Of lustre, from the *brook*; in memory,
Of monument to ages. *Milton's Par. Lost, b.* xi. *l.* 325.

And to Cephisus' *brook* their way pursue:
The stream was troubled, but the ford they knew. *Dryden.*

Springs make little rivulets; those united, make *brooks*; and those coming together, make rivers, which empty themselves into the sea. *Locke.*

To BROOK. *v. a.* [bꞃucan, Sax.] To bear; to endure; to support.

Even they, which *brook* it worst, that men should tell them of their duties, when they are told the same by a law, think very well and reasonably of it. *Hooker, b.* i.

A thousand more mischances than this one,
Have learn'd me to *brook* this patiently. *Shakesp. T. G. of Ver.*

How use doth breed a habit in a man!
This shadowy desart, unfrequented woods,
I better *brook* than flourishing peopl'd towns. *Shakesp.*

Heav'n, the seat of bliss,
*Brooks* not the works of violence, and war. *Par. Lost, b.* vi.

Most men can much rather *brook* their being reputed knaves, than for their honesty be accounted fools. *South.*

Restraint thou wilt not *brook*; but think it hard,
Your prudence is not trusted as your guard. *Dryden.*

To BROOK. *v. n.* To endure; to be content.

He, in these wars, had flatly refused his aid; because he could not *brook*, that the worthy prince Plangus was, by his chosen Tiridates, preferred before him. *Sidney's Arcadia.*

BRO'OKLIME. *n. s.* [*becabunga*, Lat.] A sort of water speedwell; very common in ditches.

BROOM. *n. s.* [bꞃom, Saxon.]

1. This tree hath a papilionaceous flower, whose pointal, which rises from the flower-cup, afterward becomes a short, roundish, swelling pod, containing, for the most part, one kidney-shaped seed in each. *Millar.*

Ev'n humble *broom*, and osiers, have their use,
And shade for sheep, and food for flocks, produce. *Dryden.*

2. A besom; so called from the matter of which it is made.

~~Not a mouse~~
~~Shall disturb this hallow'd house;~~
I am sent with *broom* before,
To sweep the dust behind the door. *Sh. Midsum. Night's Dr.*

If they came into the best apartment, to set any thing in order, they were saluted with a *broom*. *Arbuthnot's John Bull.*

BRO'OMLAND. *n. s.* [*broom* and *land.*] Land that bears broom.

I have known sheep cured of the rot, when they have not been far gone with it, only by being put into *broomlands*. *Mortimer's Husbandry.*

BRO'OMSTAFF. *n. s.* [from *broom* and *staff.*] The staff to which the *broom* is bound; the handle of a besom.

They fell on; I made good my place; at length they came to the *broomstaff* with me; I defied 'em still. *Shakesp. H.* VIII.

From the age,
That children tread this worldly stage,
*Broomstaff*, or poker, they bestride,
And round the parlour love to ride. *Prior.*

Sir Roger pointed at something behind the door, which I found to be an old *broomstaff*. *Spectator,* N° 117.

BRO'OMY. *adj.* [from *broom.*] Full of broom.

If it grow mossy or *broomy*, which these lands are inclined to, then break it up again, and order it as you did before, laying of it down again from the wheat-stubble. *Mortimer.*

The youth with *broomy* stumps began to trace
The kennel edge, where wheels had worn the place. *Swift.*

BROTH. *n. s.* [bꞃoð, Sax.] Liquour in which flesh is boiled.

You may make the *broth* for two days, and take the one half every day. *Bacon's Physical Remains.*

Instead of light desserts, and luscious froth,
Our authour treats to-night with Spartan *broth*. *Southerne.*

If a nurse, after being sucked dry, eats *broth*, the infant will suck the *broth* almost unaltered. *Arbuthnot on Aliments.*

BRO'THEL. } *n. s.* [*bordel*, Fr.] A house of lewd enter-
BRO'THELHOUSE. } tainment; a bawdyhouse.

Perchance
I saw him enter such a house of sale,
Videlicet, a *brothel*. *Shakesp. Hamlet.*

Then courts of kings were held in high renown,
Ere made the common *brothels* of the town:
There, virgins honourable vows receiv'd,
But chaste as maids in monasteries liv'd. *Dryden's. W. of B.*

From its old ruins *brothelhouses* rise,
Scenes of lewd loves, and of polluted joys. *Dryden's Mackfl.*

The libertine retires to the stews, and to the *brothel*. *Rogers.*

BRO'THER. *n. s.* [bꞃoðeꞃ, bꞃoðoꞃ, Saxon.] Plural, *brothers*, or *brethren.*

1. One born of the same father and mother.

Be sad, good *brothers*;
Sorrow so royally in you appears,
That I will deeply put the fashion on. *Shakesp. Hen.* IV.

Whilst kin their kin, *brother* the *brother* foils,
Like ensigns all, against like ensigns bend. *Daniel.*

T' whom Michael! thus, he also mov'd, reply'd:
These two are *brethren*, Adam, and to come
Out of thy loins. *Milton's Paradise Lost, b.* xi. *l.* 454.

Comparing two men, in reference to one common parent, it is very easy to form the ideas of *brothers*. *Locke.*

2. Any one closely united.

We few, we happy few, we band of *brothers*;
For he, to day that sheds his blood with me,
Shall be my *brother*. *Shakesp. Henry* V.

3. Any one resembling another in manner, form, or profession.

He also that is slothful in his work, is *brother* to him that is a great waster. *Prov.* xviii. 9.

4. *Brother* is used, in theological language, for man in general.

BRO'THERHOOD. *n. s.* [from *brother* and *hood.*]

1. The state or quality of being a brother.

This deep disgrace of *brotherhood*
Touches me deeper than you can imagine. *Shakesp. R.* II.

Finds *brotherhood* in thee no sharper spur? *Shakesp. R.* II.

So it be a right to govern, whether you call it supreme fatherhood, or supreme *brotherhood*, will be all one, provided we know who has it. *Locke.*

2. An association of men for any purpose; a fraternity.

There was a fraternity of men at arms, called the *brotherhood* of St. George, ~~erected by parliament, consisting of thirteen the most noble and worthy persons.~~ *Davies on Ireland.*

3. A class of men of the same kind.

He was sometimes so engaged among the wheels, that not above half the poet appeared; at other times, he became as conspicuous as any of the *brotherhood*. *Addison. Guardian.*

BRO'THERLY. *adj.* [from *brother.*] Natural; such as becomes or beseems a brother.

He was a priest, and looked for a priest's reward; which was our *brotherly* love, and the good of our souls and bodies. *Bacon.*

Though more our money than our cause,
Their *brotherly* assistance draws. *Denham.*

They would not go before the laws, but follow them; obeying their superiours, and embracing one another in *brotherly* piety and concord. *Addison's Freeholder,* N° 33.

BRO'THERLY. *adv.* After the manner of a brother; with kindness and affection.

I speak but *brotherly* of him; but should I anatomize him to thee as he is, I must blush and weep, and thou look pale and wonder. *Shakesp. As you like it.*

BROUGHT. [*participle passive* of *bring.*]

The Turks, possessed with a needless fear, forsook the walls, and could not, by any persuasions or threats of the captains, be *brought* on again to the assault. *Knolles's History.*

The instances *brought* by our authour are but slender proofs. *Locke.*

BROW. *n. s.* [bꞃopa, Saxon.]

1. The arch of hair over the eye.

'Tis now the hour which all to rest allow,
And sleep sits heavy upon every *brow*. *Dryden's Ind. Emp.*

2. The forehead.

She could have run, and waddled about;
For even the day before she broke her *brow*. *Shakesp.*

So we some antique hero's strength,
Learn by his launce's weight and length;
As these vast beams express the beast,
Whose shady *brows* alive they drest. *Waller.*

3. The general air of the countenance.

Then call them to our presence, face to face,
And frowning *brow* to *brow*. *Shakesp. Richard* II.

Though all things foul would bear the *brows* of grace,
Yet grace must look still so. *Shakesp. Macbeth.*

4. The edge of any high place.

The earl, nothing dismayed, came forwards that day unto a little village, called Stoke, and there encamped that night, upon the *brow* or hanging of a hill. *Bacon's Henry* VII.

On the *brow* of the hill beyond that city, they were somewhat perplexed by espying the French embassador, with the king's coach, and others, attending him. *Wotton.*

Them with fire, and hostile arms,
Fearless assault; and, to the *brow* of heav'n
Pursuing, drive them out from God and bliss. *Par. L. b.* vi.

To BROW. *v. a.* [from the noun.] To bound; to limit; to be at the edge of.

Tending

a ‡

‡ With these I went a brother of the war
Nor idle stood with unassisting hands
When Savage beasts and Mens more Savage bands
Their virtuous toil subdued: yet these I sway'd Dryd.

b ‡

4 ‡ A Member of some particular Order who lives under certain rules

~~In either of these Ships~~ there should be a mission of the fellows or brethren of Solomons house ~~to give us knowledge of the Sciences Manufactures and inventions of all the World~~

Bac. N. Atl.

, 1 brush Scythe, I take to be an Old Scythe
to cut up weeds as nettles hemlock &c Tuss. no
A brush Sith & grass Sith with rests to Stand
Tuss. thus.

Tending my flocks hard by i' th' hilly crofts,
That *brow* this bottom glad. *Milton.*

To Bro'wbeat. *v. a.* [from *brow* and *beat.*] To depreſs with ſevere brows, and ſtern or lofty looks.

It is not for a magiſtrate to frown upon, and *browbeat* thoſe who are hearty and exact in their miniſtry; and, with a grave, inſignificant nod, to call a reſolved zeal, want of prudence. *South.*

What man will voluntarily expoſe himſelf to the imperious *browbeatings* and ſcorns of great men? *L'Eſtrange.*

Count Tariff endeavoured to *browbeat* the plaintiff, while he was ſpeaking; but though he was not ſo imprudent as the count, he was every whit as ſturdy. *Addiſon.*

I will not be *browbeaten* by the ſupercilious looks of my adverſaries, who now ſtand cheek by jowl by your worſhip. *Arbuthnot and Pope's Mart. Scriblerus.*

Bro'wbound. *adj.* [from *brow* and *bound.*] Crowned; having the head encircled with a diadem.

In that day's feats,
He prov'd the beſt man i' th' field, and, for his meed,
Was *browbound* with the oak. *Shakeſp. Coriolanus.*

Bro'wsick. *adj.* [from *brow* and *ſick.*] Dejected; hanging the head.

But yet a gracious influence from you,
May alter nature in our *browſick* crew. *Suckling.*

BROWN. *adj.* [bꞃun, Saxon.] The name of a colour, compounded of black and any other colour.

*Brown*, in High Dutch, is called *braun*; in the Netherlands, *bruyn*; in French, *coleur brune*; in Italian, *bruno*; in Greek, ὀρφνινα αἴθοψ, from the colour of the Ethiopians; for αἴθω is to burn, and ὤψ, a face; for that blackneſs or ſwarthineſs in their faces, is procured through heat. In Latin it is called *fuſcus*, *quaſi* φῶς σκιᾶται, that is, from darkening or overſhadowing the light; or of φώσκειν, which is to burn or ſcorch. *Peacham.*

I like the new tire within excellently, if the hair were a little *browner.* *Shakeſp. Much ado about Nothing.*

From whence high Ithaca overlooks the floods,
*Brown* with o'ercharging ſhades and pendent woods. *Pope.*

Long untravell'd heaths,
With deſolation *brown*, he wanders waſte. *Thomſon.*

Bro'wnbill. *n. ſ.* [from *brown* and *bill.*] The ancient weapon of the Engliſh foot; why it is called *brown*, I have not diſcovered; but we now ſay *brown musket* from it.

And *brownbills*, levied in the city,
Made bills to paſs the grand committee. *Hudibras.*

Bro'wnish. *adj.* [from *brown.*] Somewhat brown.

A *browniſh* grey iron-ſtone, lying in thin ſtrata, is poor, but runs freely. *Woodward on Foſſils.*

Bro'wnness. *n. ſ.* [from *brown.*] A brown colour.

She would confeſs the contention in her own mind, between that lovely, indeed moſt lovely, *brownneſs* of Muſidorus's face, and this colour of mine. *Sidney, b.* ii.

Bro'wnstudy. *n. ſ.* [from *brown* and *ſtudy.*] Gloomy meditations; ſtudy in which we direct our thoughts to no certain point.

They live retired, and then they doze away their time in drowſineſs and *brownſtudies*; or, if briſk and active, they lay themſelves out wholly in making common places. *Norris.*

To BROWSE. *v. a.* [*brouſer*, Fr.] To eat branches, or ſhrubs.

And being down, is trod in the durt
Of cattle, and *brouſed*, and ſorely hurt. *Spenſer's Paſtorals.*

Thy palate then did deign
The roughest berry on the rudeſt hedge:
Yea, like the ſtag, when ſnow the paſture ſheets,
The barks of trees thou *browſedſt.* *Shakeſp. Ant. and Cleop.*

To Browse. *v. n.* To feed: it is uſed with the particle *on.*

They have ſcared away two of my beſt ſheep; if any where I have them, 'tis by the ſea-ſide, *browſing on* ivy. *Shakeſp.*

A goat, hard preſſed, took ſanctuary in a vineyard; ſo ſoon as he thought the danger over, he fell preſently a *browſing upon* the leaves. *L'Eſtrange.*

Could eat the tender plant, and, by degrees,
*Browſe on* the ſhrubs, and crop the budding trees. *Blackm.*

The Greeks were the deſcendants of ſavages, ignorant of agriculture, and *browſing on* herbage, like cattle. *Arbuthnot.*

Browse. *n. ſ.* [from the verb.] Branches, or ſhrubs, fit for the food of goats, or other animals.

The greedy lioneſs the wolf purſues,
The wolf the kid, the wanton kid the *browſe.* *Dryden.*

On that cloud-piercing hill,
Plinlimmon, from afar the traveller kens,
Aſtoniſh'd, how the goats their ſhrubby *browſe*
Gnaw pendent. *Philips.*

To BRUISE. *v. a.* [*briſer*, Fr.] To cruſh or mangle with the heavy blow of ſomething not edged or pointed; to cruſh by any weight; to beat into groſs powder; to beat together coarſely.

Fellows in arms, and my moſt loving friends,
*Bruis'd* underneath the yoke of tyranny. *Shakeſp. R.* III.

And fix far deeper in his head their ſtings,
Than temporal death ſhall *bruiſe* the victor's heel,
Or theirs whom he redeems. *Par. Loſt, b.* xii *l.* 433.

B R U

As in old chaos heav'n with earth confus'd,
And ſtars with rocks together cruſh'd and *bruis'd.* *Waller.*

They beat their breaſts with many a *bruiſing* blow,
Till they turn'd livid, and corrupt the ſnow. *Dryden's Fab.*

Bruise. *n. ſ.* [from the verb.] A hurt with ſomething blunt and heavy.

One arm'd with metal, th' other with wood,
This fit for *bruiſe*, and that for blood. *Hudibras.*

I ſince have labour'd
To bind the *bruiſes* of a civil war,
And ſtop the iſſues of their waſting blood. *Dryden.*

Bru'isewort. *n. ſ.* An herb; the ſame with Comfrey; which ſee.

BRUIT. *n. ſ.* [*bruit*, Fr.] Rumour; noiſe; report.

Wherewith a *bruit* ran from one to the other, that the king was ſlain. *Sidney, b.* ii.

Upon ſome *bruits* he apprehended a fear, which moved him to ſend to Sir William Herbert to remain his friend. *Hayw.*

I am not
One that rejoices in the common wreck,
As common *bruit* doth put it. *Shakeſp. Timon.*

To Bruit. *v. a.* [from the noun.] To report; to noiſe abroad; to rumour. Neither the verb nor the noun are now much in uſe.

His death,
Being *bruited* once, took fire and heat away
From the beſt temper'd courage in his troops. *Shak. Hen.* V.

It was *bruited*, that I meant nothing leſs than to go to Guiana. *Raleigh's Eſſays.*

Bru'mal. *adj.* [*brumalis*, Lat.] Belonging to the winter.

About the *brumal* ſolſtice, it hath been obſerved, even unto a proverb, that the ſea is calm, and the winds do ceaſe, till the young ones are excluded, and forſake their neſts. *Brown's Vulgar Errours, b.* iii. *c.* 10.

Brun, Bran, Brown, Bourn, Burn, are all derived from the Sax. boꞃn, bouꞃn, bꞃunna, buꞃna; all ſignifying a river or brook. *Gibſon's Camden.*

Brune'tt. *n. ſ.* [*brunette*, Fr.] A woman with a brown complexion.

Your fair women therefore thought of this faſhion, to inſult the olives and the *brunettes.* *Addiſon. Guardian*, N° 109.

Bru'nion. *n. ſ.* [*brugnon*, Fr.] A ſort of fruit between a plum and a peach. *Trevoux.*

Brunt. *n. ſ.* [*brunſt*, Dutch.]

1. Shock; violence.

Erona choſe rather to bide the *brunt* of war, than venture him. *Sidney, b.* ii.

God, who caus'd a fountain, at thy pray'r,
From the dry ground to ſpring, thy thirſt t' allay
After the *brunt* of battle. *Milton's Agoniſtes, l.* 581.

Faithful miniſters are to ſtand and endure the *brunt*: a common ſoldier may fly, when it is the duty of him that holds the ſtandard to die upon the place. *South.*

2. Blow; ſtroke.

A wicked ambuſh, which lay hidden long
In the cloſe covert of her guileful eyen,
Thence breaking forth, did thick about me throng,
Too feeble I t' abide the *brunt* ſo ſtrong. *Spenſer's Sonnets.*

The friendly rug preſerv'd the ground,
And headlong knight, from bruiſe or wound,
Like featherbed betwixt a wall,
An heavy *brunt* of cannon-ball. *Hudibras.*

BRUSH. *n. ſ.* [*broſſe*, Fr. from *bruſcus*, Lat.]

1. An inſtrument to clean any thing, by rubbing off the dirt or ſoil. It is generally made of briſtles ſet in wood.

2. It is uſed for the larger and ſtronger pencils uſed by painters.

Whence comes all this rage of wit? this arming all the pencils and *bruſhes* of the town againſt me? *Stillingfleet.*

With a ſmall *bruſh* you muſt ſmear the glue well upon the joint of each piece. *Moxon's Mechanical Exerciſes.*

3. A rude aſſault; a ſhock; rough treatment; which, by the ſame metaphor, we call a *ſcouring.*

Let grow thy ſinews till their knots be ſtrong,
And tempt not yet the *bruſhes* of the war. *Shakeſp.*

It could not be poſſible, that, upon ſo little a *bruſh* as Waller had ſuſtained, he could not be able to follow and diſturb the king. *Clarendon, b.* viii.

Elſe when we put it to the puſh,
They had not giv'n us ſuch a *bruſh.* *Hudibras.*

To Brush. *v. a.* [from the noun.]

1. To ſweep or rub with a bruſh.

If he be not in love with ſome woman, there is no believing old ſigns; he *bruſhes* his hat o' morning; what ſhould that bode? *Shakeſp. Much ado about Nothing.*

2. To ſtrike with quickneſs, as in bruſhing.

The wrathful beaſt about him turned light,
And him ſo rudely paſſing by, did *bruſh*
With his long tail, that horſe and man to ground did ruſh. *Spenſer's Fairy Queen, b.* i. *cant.* ii. *ſtanz.* 16.

Has Somnus *bruſh'd* thy eyelids with his rod? *Dryden.*

His ſon Cupavo *bruſh'd* the briny flood,
~~Upon his ſtern a brawny [illegible] flood.~~ *Dryden's Æneid.*

2 High

High o'er the billows flew the maſſy load,
And near the ſhip came thund'ring on the flood,
It almoſt *bruſh'd* the helm. *Pope's Odyſſey, b.* ix.

3. To paint with a bruſh.

You have commiſſioned me to paint your ſhop, and I have done my beſt to *bruſh* you up like your neighbours. *Pope.*

4. To carry away, by an act like that of bruſhing.

And from the boughs *bruſh* off the evil dew,
And heal the harms of thwarting thunder blew. *Milton.*

The receptacle of waters, into which the mouths of all rivers muſt empty themſelves, ought to have ſo ſpacious a ſurface, that as much water may be continually *bruſhed* off by the winds, and exhaled by the ſun, as, beſides what falls again, is brought into it by all the rivers. *Bentley.*

5. To move as the bruſh.

A thouſand nights have *bruſh'd* their balmy wings
Over theſe eyes. *Dryden's Don Sebaſtian.*

To Brush. *v. n.*

1. To move with haſte: a ludicrous word, applied to men.

Nor wept his fate, nor caſt a pitying eye,
Nor took him down, but *bruſh'd* regardleſs by. *Dryden.*

The French had gather'd all their force,
And William met them in their way;
Yet off they *bruſh'd*, both foot and horſe. *Prior.*

2. To fly over; to ſkim lightly.

Nor love is always of a vicious kind,
But oft to virtuous acts inflames the mind,
Awakes the ſleepy vigour of the ſoul,
And, *bruſhing* o'er, adds motion to the pool. *Dryden's Fab.*

Bru'sher. *n. ſ.* [from *bruſh.*] He that uſes a bruſh.

Sir Henry Wotton uſed to ſay, that criticks were like *bruſhers* of noblemens cloaths. *Bacon's Apophthegms.*

Bru'shwood. *n. ſ.* [from *bruſh* and *wood.* I know not whether it may not be corrupted from *browſewood.*] Rough, low, cloſe, ſhrubby thickets; ſmall wood fit for fire.

It ſmokes, and then with trembling breath ſhe blows,
Till in a cheerful blaze the flames aroſe.
With *bruſhwood*, and with chips, ſhe ſtrengthens theſe,
And adds at laſt the boughs of rotten trees. *Dryden's Fab.*

Bru'shy. *adj.* [from *bruſh.*] Rough or ſhaggy, like a bruſh.

I ſuſpected, that it might have proceeded from ſome ſmall unheeded drop of blood, wiped off by the *bruſhy* ſubſtance of the nerve, from the knife wherewith it was cut. *Boyle.*

To Bru'stle. *v. n.* [bꞃaȝtlan, Saxon.] To crackle; to make a ſmall noiſe. *Skinner.*

Bru'tal. *adj.* [*brutal*, Fr. from *brute.*]

1. That which belongs to a brute; that which we have in common with brutes.

There is no oppoſing *brutal* force to the ſtratagems of human reaſon. *L'Eſtrange.*

2. Savage; cruel; inhuman.

The *brutal* bus'neſs of the war
Is manag'd by thy dreadful ſervants' care. *Dryden.*

Bruta'lity. *n. ſ.* [*brutalité*, Fr.] Savageneſs; churliſhneſs; inhumanity.

Courage, in an ill-bred man, has the air, and eſcapes not the opinion of *brutality.* *Locke.*

To Brut'alize. *v. n.* [*brutaliſer*, Fr.] To grow brutal or ſavage.

Upon being carried to the Cape of Good Hope, he mixed, in a kind of tranſport, with his countrymen, *brutalized* with them in their habit and manners, and would never again return to his foreign acquaintance. *Addiſon's Freeholder.*

To Bruta'lize. *v. a.* To make brutal or ſavage.

Bru'tally. *adv.* [from *brutal.*] Churliſhly; inhumanly; cruelly.

Mrs. Bull aimed a knife at John, though John threw a bottle at her head, very *brutally* indeed. *Arbuthnot.*

BRUTE. *adj.* [*brutus*, Lat.]

1. Senſeleſs; unconſcious.

Nor yet are we ſo low and baſe as their atheiſm would depreſs us; not walking ſtatues of clay, not the ſons of *brute* earth, whoſe final inheritance is death and corruption. *Bentl.*

2. Savage; irrational; ferine.

Even *brute* animals make uſe of this artificial way of making divers motions, to have ſeveral ſignifications to call, warn, chide, cheriſh, threaten. *Holder's Elements of Speech.*

In the promulgation of the Moſaick law, if ſo much as a *brute* beaſt touched the mountain, it was to be ſtruck through with a dart. *South.*

3. Beſtial; in common with beaſts.

Then to ſubdue, and quell, through all the earth,
*Brute* violence, and proud tyrannick pow'r. *Par. Regained.*

4. Rough; ferocious; uncivilized.

The *brute* philoſopher, who ne'er has prov'd
The joy of loving, or of being lov'd, *Pope.*

Brute. *n. ſ.* [from the adjective.] A brute creature; a creature without reaſon; a ſavage.

What may this mean? Language of man pronounc'd
By tongue of *brute*, and human ſenſe expreſs'd? *Par. Loſt.*
To judgment he proceeded, on th' accurs'd
Serpent, tho' *brute*; unable to transfer
The guilt on him, who made him inſtrument
Of miſchief. *Milton's Paradiſe Loſt, b.* x. *l.* 165.

*Brutes* may be conſidered as either, aerial, terreſtrial, aquatick, or amphibious. I call thoſe aerial, which have wings, wherewith they can ſupport themſelves in the air; terreſtrial are thoſe, whoſe only place of reſt is upon the earth; aquatick are thoſe, whoſe conſtant abode is upon the water. *Locke.*

To thoſe three preſent impulſes, of ſenſe, memory, and inſtinct, moſt, if not all, the ſagacities of *brutes* may be reduced. *Hale's Origin of Mankind.*

Heav'n from all creatures hides the book of fate;
All but the page preſcrib'd, this preſent ſtate;
From *brutes* what men, from men what ſpirits know;
Or who could ſuffer being here below? *Pope's Eſſ. on Man.*

To Brute. *v. a.* [written ill for *bruit.*] To report.

This, once *bruted* through the army, filled them all with heavineſs. *Knolles's Hiſtory of the Turks.*

Bru'teness. *n. ſ.* [from *brute.*] Brutality; a word not now uſed.

Thou dotard vile,
That with thy *bruteneſs* ſhend'ſt thy comely age. *Fairy Q.*

To Bru'tify. *v. a.* [from *brute.*] To make a man a brute.

O thou falacious woman! am I then *brutified?* Ay; feel it here; I ſprout, I bud, I bloſſom, I am ripe horn mad. *Congreve's Old Batchelor.*

Bru'tish. *adj.* [from *brute.*]

1. Beſtial; reſembling a beaſt.

Oſiris, Iſis, Orus, and their train,
With monſtrous ſhapes and ſorceries abus'd
Fanatick Egypt, and her prieſts, to ſeek
Their wand'ring gods diſguis'd in *brutiſh* forms. *Par. Loſt.*

2. Having the qualities of a brute; rough; ſavage; ferocious.

Brutes, and *brutiſh* men, are commonly more able to bear pain, than others. *Grew's Coſmologia Sacra, b.* ii. *c.* 6.

3. Groſs; carnal.

For thou thyſelf haſt been a libertine,
As ſenſual as the *brutiſh* ſting itſelf. *Shakeſp. As you like it.*

After he has ſlept himſelf into ſome uſe of himſelf, by much ado he ſtaggers to his table again, and there acts over the ſame *brutiſh* ſcene. *South.*

4. Ignorant; untaught; uncivilized.

They were not ſo *brutiſh*, that they could be ignorant to call upon the name of God. *Hooker, b.* v. § 35.

Bru'tishly. *adv.* [from *brutiſh.*] In the manner of a brute; of a ſavage and unnatural man.

I am not ſo diffident of myſelf, as *brutiſhly* to ſubmit to any man's dictates. *K. Charles.*

For a man to found a confident practice upon a diſputable principle, is *brutiſhly* to outrun his reaſon. *South.*

Bru'tishness. *n. ſ.* [from *brutiſh.*] Brutality; ſavageneſs; inſenſibility.

All other courage, beſides that, is not true valour, but *brutiſhneſs.* *Sprat.*

Bry'ony. *n. ſ.* [*bryonia*, Lat.] A plant.

It has a climbing ſtalk, with ſpines; the leaves are like thoſe of the vine; the flowers conſiſt of one leaf, which is expanded at the top, and divided into five parts, and, in the female plants, ſucceeded by round berries, growing on footſtalks; the flowers of the male plants have five apices in each, but are barren. The ſpecies are, 1. The common white *bryony.* 2. Smooth African *bryony*, with deep cut leaves, and yellow flowers, &c. The firſt ſort grows upon dry banks, under hedges, in many parts of England; but may be cultivated in a garden for uſe, by ſowing the berries in the ſpring of the year, in a dry poor ſoil. The roots of this plant have been formerly cut into a human ſhape, and carried about the country, and ſhewn as mandrakes. *Mill.*

Bub. *n. ſ.* [a cant word.] Strong malt liquour.

Or if it be his fate to meet
With folks who have more wealth than wit,
He loves cheap port, and double *bub*,
And ſettles in the humdrum club. *Prior.*

BUBBLE. *n. ſ.* [*bobbel*, Dutch.]

1. A ſmall bladder of water; a film of water filled with wind.

*Bubbles* are in the form of a hemiſphere; air within, and a little ſkin of water without: and it ſeemeth ſomewhat ſtrange, that the air ſhould riſe ſo ſwiftly, while it is in the water, and, when it cometh to the top, ſhould be ſtayed by ſo weak a cover as that of the *bubble* is. *Bacon's Natural Hiſtory*, Nº 24.

The colours of *bubbles*, with which children play, are various, and change their ſituation variouſly, without any reſpect to confine or ſhadow. *Newton's Opticks.*

2. Any thing which wants ſolidity and firmneſs; any thing that is more ſpecious than real.

The earl of Lincoln was induced to participate, not lightly upon the ſtrength of the proceedings there, which was but a *bubble*, but upon letters from the lady Margaret. *Bacon.*

Then a ſoldier,
Seeking the *bubble*, reputation,
Even in the cannon's mouth. *Shakeſp. As you like it.*

War, he ſung, is toil and trouble,
Honour but an empty *bubble*,
Fighting ſtill, and ſtill deſtroying. *Dryden.*

a

The human body hath preference above
the most perfect brutal nature. J. Hale

The Goddess with disdain bestows
Mast & acorns brutal food
Pope

5 To buckle v. a
To comprize, to measure the compass of any thing alluding to a belt buckled round ones waste.

Will you with counters sum
The vast proportion of his infinite
And buckle in a waste most fathomless
With spans & Inches so diminutive
As fears & reasons? Shak

Bubukle n. s. for bubo or Carbuncle.
a word of Shakespears making, if not a mistake for buboil.

His face is all Bubukles & whelks & knobs
and flames of fire Shak.

To buck v. n. To be washed in strong lye
Throw foul linnen upon him as if it were going to bucking Shak

3. A cheat; a falſe ſhow.

The nation then too late will find,
Directors promiſes but wind,
South-ſea at beſt a mighty *bubble*. *Swift.*

4. The perſon cheated.

Ceaſe, deareſt mother, ceaſe to chide;
Gany's a cheat, and I'm a *bubble*;
Yet why this great exceſs of trouble. *Prior.*

He has been my *bubble* theſe twenty years, and, to my certain knowledge, underſtands no more of his own affairs, than a child in ſwaddling clothes. *Arbuthnot's Hiſt. of J. Bull.*

To BU'BBLE. *v. n.* [from the noun.] To riſe in bubbles.

Alas! a crimſon river of warm blood,
Like to a *bubbling* fountain ſtirr'd with wind,
Doth riſe and fall. *Shakeſp. Titus Andronicus.*

Adder's fork, and blindworm's ſting,
Lizard's leg, and owlet's wing:
For a charm of pow'rful trouble,
Like a hellbroth boil and *bubble*. *Shakeſp. Macbeth.*

Still *bubble* on, and pour forth blood and tears. *Dryden.*

2. To run with a gentle noiſe.

For thee the *bubbling* ſprings appear'd to mourn,
And whiſpering pines made vows for thy return. *Dryden.*

The ſame ſpring ſuffers at ſome times a very manifeſt remiſſion of its heat: at others, as manifeſt an increaſe of it; yea, ſometimes to that exceſs, as to make it boil and *bubble* with extreme heat. *Woodward's Nat. Hiſt.*

Not *bubbling* fountains to the thirſty ſwain,
Not ſhow'rs to larks, or ſunſhine to the bee,
Are half ſo charming as thy ſight to me. *Pope.*

To BU'BBLE. *v. a.* To cheat: a cant word.

He tells me, with great paſſion, that ſhe has *bubbled* him out of his youth; and that ſhe has drilled him on to five and fifty. *Addiſon. Spectator*, Nº 89.

Charles Mather could not *bubble* a young beau better with a toy. *Arbuthnot's Hiſt. of J. Bull.*

BU'BBLER. *n. ſ.* [from *bubble*.] A cheat.

What words can ſuffice to expreſs, how infinitely I eſteem you, above all the great ones in this part of the world; above all the Jews, jobbers, and *bubblers*. *Digby to Pope.*

BU'BBY. *n. ſ.* A woman's breaſt.

Foh! ſay they, to ſee a handſome, briſk, genteel, young fellow, ſo much governed by a doating old woman; why don't you go and ſuck the *bubby*? *Arbuthnot's John Bull.*

BU'BO. *n. ſ.* [Lat. from βουϐὼν, the groin.] That part of the groin from the bending of the thigh to the ſcrotum: and therefore all tumours in that part are called *buboes*. *Quincy.*

I ſuppurated it after the manner of a *bubo*, opened it, and endeavoured deterſion. *Wiſeman's Surgery.*

BUBONOCE'LE. *n. ſ.* [Lat. from βουϐὼν, the groin, and κήλη, a rupture.] A particular kind of rupture, when the inteſtines break down into the groin. *Quincy.*

When the inteſtine, or omentum, falls through the rings of the abdominal muſcles into the groin, it is called *hernia inguinalis*, or, if into the ſcrotum, *ſcrotalis*: theſe two, though the firſt only is properly ſo called, are known by the name of *bubonocele*. *Sharp's Surgery.*

BUCANI'ERS. *n. ſ.* A cant word for the privateers, or pirates, of America.

BUCCELLA'TION. *n. ſ.* [*buccella*, a mouthful, Lat.] In ſome chymical authours, ſignifies a dividing into large pieces. *Harris.*

BUCK. *n. ſ.* [*bauche*, Germ. ſuds, or lye.]

1. The liquour in which cloaths are waſhed.

*Buck?* I would I could waſh myſelf of the *buck*: I warrant you, buck, and of the ſeaſon too it ſhall appear. *Shakeſp.*

2. The cloaths waſhed in the liquour.

Of late, not able to travel with her furred pack, ſhe waſhes *bucks* here at home. *Shakeſp. Henry* VI. *p.* ii.

BUCK. *n. ſ.* [*bwch*, Welch; *bock*, Dutch; *bouc*, Fr.] The male of the fallow deer; the male of rabbets, and other animals.

*Bucks*, goats, and the like, are ſaid to be tripping or ſaliant, that is, going or leaping. *Peacham.*

To BUCK. *v. a.* [from the noun.] To waſh clothes.

Here is a baſket; he may creep in here, and throw foul linen upon him, as if it were going to *bucking*. *Shakeſp.*

To BUCK. *v. n.* [from the noun.] To copulate as bucks and does.

The chief time of ſetting traps, is in their *bucking* time. *Mortimer.*

BU'CKBASKET. *n. ſ.* The baſket in which cloaths are carried to the waſh.

They conveyed me into a *buckbasket*; rammed me in with foul ſhirts, foul ſtockings, and greaſy napkins. *Shakeſp.*

BU'CKBEAN. *n. ſ.* [*bocksboonen*, Dutch.] A plant; a ſort of *trefoil*.

The bitter nauſeous plants, as centaury, *buckbane*, gentian, of which tea may be made, or wines by infuſion. *Floyer.*

BU'CKET. *n. ſ.* [*baquet*, Fr.]

1. The veſſel in which water is drawn out of a well.

Now is this golden crown like a deep well,
That owes two *buckets*, filling one another;
The emptier ever dancing in the air,
The other down unſeen, and full of water. *Shakeſp. R.* II.

Is the ſea ever likely to be evaporated by the ſun, or to be emptied with *buckets*? *Bentley.*

2. The veſſels in which water is carried, particularly to quench a fire.

Now ſtreets grow throng'd, and, buſy as by day,
Some run for *buckets* to the hallow'd quire;
Some cut the pipes, and ſome the engines play;
And ſome, more bold, mount ladders to the fire. *Dryden.*

The porringers, that in a row
Hung high, and made a glitt'ring ſhow,
To a leſs noble ſubſtance chang'd,
Were now but leathern *buckets* rang'd. *Swift.*

BU'CKLE. *n. ſ.* [*bwccl*, Welch, and the ſame in the Armorick; *boucle*, Fr.]

1. A link of metal, with a tongue or catch made to faſten one thing to another.

Fair lined ſlippers for the cold,
With *buckles* of the pureſt gold. *Shakeſp.*

The chlamys was a ſort of ſhort cloak tied with a *buckle*, commonly to the right ſhoulder. *Arbuthnot on Coins.*

Three ſeal-rings; which after, melted down,
Form'd a vaſt *buckle* for his widow's gown. *Pope.*

2. The ſtate of the hair criſped and curled, by being kept long in the ſame ſtate.

The greateſt beau was dreſſed in a flaxen periwig; the wearer of it goes in his own hair at home, and lets his wig lie in *buckle* for a whole half year. *Spectator*, Nº 129.

That live-long wig, which Gorgon' ſelf might own,
Eternal *buckle* takes in Parian ſtone. *Pope.*

To BU'CKLE. *v. a.* [from the noun.]

1. To faſten with a buckle.

Like ſaphire, pearl, in rich embroidery,
*Buckled* below fair knighthood's bending knee. *Shakeſp.*

France, whoſe armour conſcience *buckl'd* on,
Whom zeal and charity brought to the field. *Shakeſp.*

Thus, ever, when I *buckle* on my helmet,
Thy fears afflict thee. *Philips.*

When you carry your maſter's riding-coat, wrap your own in it, and *buckle* them up cloſe with a ſtrap. *Swift.*

2. To prepare to do any thing: the metaphor is taken from *buckling* on the armour.

The Saracen, this hearing, roſe amain,
And catching up in haſte his three ſquare ſhield,
And ſhining helmet, ſoon him *buckled* to the field. *Fairy Q.*

3. To join in battle.

The Lord Gray, captain of the men at arms, was forbidden to charge, until the foot of the avantguard were *buckled* with them in front. *Hayward.*

4. To confine.

How brief the life of man
Runs his erring pilgrimage!
That the ſtretching of a ſpan
*Buckles* in his ſum of age. *Shakeſp. As you like it.*

To BU'CKLE. *v. n.* [*bucken*, Germ.]

1. To bend; to bow.

As the wretch, whoſe fever-weaken'd joints,
Like ſtrengthleſs hinges, *buckle* under life,
Impatient of his fit, breaks like a fire
Out of his keeper's arms. *Shakeſp. Henry* IV. *p.* ii.

Now a covetous old crafty knave,
At dead of night, ſhall raiſe his ſon, and cry,
Turn out, you rogue! how like a beaſt you lie;
Go *buckle* to the law. *Dryden.*

2. *To buckle to.* To apply to; to attend. See *active*, ſecond ſenſe.

This is to be done in children, by trying them, when they are by lazineſs unbent, or by avocation bent another way, and endeavouring to make them *buckle to* the thing propoſed. *Locke.*

3. *To buckle with.* To engage with; to encounter.

For ſingle combat, thou ſhalt *buckle with* me. *Shakeſp.*

Yet thou, they ſay, for marriage doſt provide;
Is this an age to *buckle with* a bride? *Dryden's Juv. ſat.* vi.

BU'CKLER. *n. ſ.* [*bwccled*, Welch; *bouclier*, Fr.] A ſhield; a defenſive weapon buckled on the arm.

He took my arms, and, while I forc'd my way,
Through troops of foes, which did our paſſage ſtay;
My *buckler* o'er my aged father caſt,
Still fighting, ſtill defending as I paſt. *Dryden's Aurengzebe.*

This medal compliments the emperour in the ſame ſenſe as the old Romans did their dictator Fabius, when they called him the *buckler* of Rome. *Addiſon on ancient Medals.*

To BU'CKLER. *v. a.* [from the noun.] To ſupport; to defend.

Fear not, ſweet wench, they ſhall not touch thee, Kate;
I'll *buckler* thee againſt a million. *Shakeſp. Tam. the Shrew.*

Can Oxford, that did ever fence the right,
Now *buckler* falſhood with a pedigree? *Shakeſp. Henry* VI.

BU'CKLER-THORN. *n. ſ.* *Chriſt's-thorn.*

BU'CKMAST. *n. ſ.* The fruit or maſt of the beech tree.

BU'CKRAM. *n. ſ.* [*bougran*, Fr.] A ſort of ſtrong linen cloth, ſtiffened with gum, uſed by taylors and ſtaymakers.

I have peppered two of them; two, I am ſure, I have paid, two rogues in *buckram* ſuits. *Shakeſp. Henry* IV.

BU'CKRAMS. *n. ſ.* The ſame with *wild garlick*. See GARLICK.

**Bu'ckshorn Plantain.** *n. ſ.* [*coronopus*, Lat. from the form of the leaf.] A plant.

It agrees in flower and fruit with the plantain; but its leaves are deeply cut in on the edges; whereas the leaves of the plantain are either entire, or but ſlightly indented. The ſpecies are four; 1. Garden *buckshorn plantain*, or hartſhorn, *&c.* The firſt ſpecies, though entitled a garden plant, yet is found wild upon moſt commons, and barren heaths; where, from the poorneſs of the ſoil, it appears to be very different from the garden kind, as being little more than a fourth part ſo large. This ſpecies was formerly cultivated in gardens as a ſalad herb, but, at preſent, is little regarded, and wholly diſuſed. *Miller.*

**Bu'ckthorn.** *n. ſ.* [*rhamnus*, Lat. ſuppoſed to be ſo called from bucc, Sax. the belly.]

It hath a funnel-ſhaped flower, conſiſting of one leaf, divided toward the top into four or five ſegments; out of the flower-cup riſes the pointal, which becomes a ſoft roundiſh berry, very full of juice, incloſing four hard ſeeds. The ſpecies are, Common purging *buckthorn*. 2. Leſſer purging *buckthorn*. 3. *Buckthorn*, with long ſpines, and a white bark of Montpelier. The firſt of theſe trees is very common in hedges; the berries of which are uſed in medicine, particularly for making a ſyrup, which was formerly in great uſe; though, of late, other ſorts of berries have either been mixed with thoſe of the *buckthorn*, or wholly ſubſtituted in their place; which mixture hath ſpoiled the ſyrup, and rendered it leſs eſteemed. The *buckthorn* berries may be diſtinguiſhed whether they are right or not, by opening them, and obſerving the number of ſeeds in each; for theſe have commonly four. The ſecond ſort is leſs common in England. Both theſe ſorts may be propagated, by laying down their tender branches in autumn. The firſt ſort will grow to the height of eighteen or twenty feet; the ſecond ſort ſeldom riſes above eight feet high. They may alſo be propagated by ſeeds. *Miller.*

**Bu'ckwheat.** *n. ſ.* [*buckweitz*, Germ. *fagopyrum*, Lat.]

The flowers grow in a ſpike, or branched from the wings of the leaves; the cup of the flower is divided into five parts, and reſembles the petals of a flower; the ſeeds are black, and three cornered. The ſpecies are, 1. Common upright *buckwheat*. 2. Common creeping *buckwheat*. The firſt is cultivated in England, and is a great improvement to dry barren lands. The ſecond grows wild, and is ſeldom cultivated. *Miller.*

**Buco'lick.** *adj.* [βουκολικα, from βουκόλος, a cowherd.] Paſtoral.

**BUD.** *n. ſ.* [*bouton*, Fr.] The firſt ſhoot of a plant; a gem.

Be as thou waſt wont to be;
See as thou waſt wont to ſee:
Dian's *bud* o'er Cupid's flower
Hath ſuch force and bleſſed power. *Shakeſp. Midſ. N. Dr.*

Writers ſay, as the moſt forward *bud*
Is eaten by the canker ere it blow,
Even ſo by love the young and tender wit
Is turn'd to folly, blaſting in the *bud*,
Loſing his verdure even in the prime. *Shakeſp. T. G. of Ver.*

When you the flow'rs for Chloe twine,
Why do you to her garland join,
The meaneſt *bud* that falls from mine? *Prior.*

Inſects wound the tender *buds*, with a long hollow trunk, and depoſit an egg in the hole, with a ſharp corroding liquour, that cauſeth a ſwelling in the leaf, and cloſeth the orifice. *Bentley.*

To **Bud.** *v. n.* [from the noun.]

1. To put forth young ſhoots, or gems.

*Bud* forth as a roſe growing by the brook of the field. *Ecclus*, xxxix. 13.

There the fruit, that was to be gathered from ſuch a conflux, quickly *budded* out. *Clarendon, b.* ii.

Heav'n gave him all at once, then ſnatch'd away,
Ere mortals all his beauties could ſurvey;
Juſt like the flow'r that *buds* and withers in a day. *Dryd.*

Tho' lab'ring yokes on their own necks they fear'd,
And felt for *budding* horns on their ſmooth foreheads rear'd. *Dryden's Silenus.*

2. To be in the bloom, or growing.

Young *budding* virgin, fair and freſh and ſweet,
Whither away, or where is thy abode? *Shakeſp.*

To **Bud.** *v. a.* To inoculate; to graff by inſerting a bud into the rind of another tree.

Of apricocks, the largeſt maſculine is much improved by *budding* upon a peach ſtock. *Temple.*

To **BUDGE.** *v. n.* [*bouger*, Fr.] To ſtir; to move off the place: a low word.

All your priſoners
In the lime grove, which weatherfends your cell,
They cannot *budge* till your releaſe. *Shakeſp. Tempeſt.*

The mouſe ne'er ſhun'd the cat, as they did *budge*
From raſcals worſe than they. *Shakeſp. Coriolanus.*

I thought th' hadſt ſcorn'd to *budge*
For fear. *Hudibras, cant.* ii.

**Budge.** *adj.* [of uncertain etymology.] Surly; ſtiff; formal.

O fooliſhneſs of men! that lend their ears
To thoſe *budge* doctors of the ſtoicks. *Milton.*

**Budge.** *n. ſ.* The dreſſed ſkin or fur of lambs. *Dict.*

**Bu'dger.** *n. ſ.* [from the verb.] One that moves or ſtirs from his place.

Let the firſt *budger* die the other's ſlave,
And the gods doom him after. *Shakeſp. Coriolanus.*

**Bu'dget.** *n. ſ.* [*bogette*, Fr.]

1. A bag, ſuch as may be eaſily carried.

If tinkers may have leave to live,
And bear the ſowſkin *budget*;
Then my account I well may give,
And in the ſtocks avouch it. *Shakeſp. Winter's Tale.*

Sir Robert Clifford, in whoſe boſom, or *budget*, moſt of Perkin's ſecrets were laid up, was come into England. *Bacon.*

His *budget* with corruptions cramm'd,
The contributions of the damn'd. *Swift.*

2. It is uſed for a ſtore, or ſtock.

It was nature, in fine, that brought off the cat, when the fox's whole *budget* of inventions failed him. *L'Eſtrange.*

**Buff.** *n. ſ.* [from *buffalo*.]

1. A ſort of leather prepared from the ſkin of the buffalo; uſed for waiſt belts, pouches, *&c.*

A ropy chain of rheums, a viſage rough,
Deform'd, unſeatur'd, and a ſkin of *buff*. *Dryden's Juvenal.*

2. The ſkins of elks and oxen dreſſed in oil, and prepared after the ſame manner as that of the buffalo.

3. A military coat made of thick leather, ſo that a blow cannot eaſily pierce it.

A fiend, a fury, pitileſs and rough,
A wolf, nay worſe, a fellow all in *buff*. *Shakeſp.*

To **BUFF.** *v. a.* [*buffe*, Fr.] To ſtrike: it is a word not in uſe.

There was a ſhock,
To have *buff'd* out the blood
From ought but a block. *Ben. Johnſon's Underwoods.*

**BU'FFALO.** *n. ſ.* [Ital.] A kind of wild ox.

Become th' unworthy browſe
Of *buffaloes*, ſalt goats, and hungry cows. *Dryden's Virgil.*

**Bu'ffet.** *n. ſ.* [*buffetto*, Ital.] A blow with the fiſt; a box on the ear.

O, I could divide myſelf, and go to *buffets*, for moving ſuch a diſh of ſkimmed milk with ſo honourable an action. *Shakeſp.*

A man that fortune's *buffets* and rewards
Haſt ta'en with equal thanks. *Shakeſp. Hamlet.*

Go, baffl'd coward, leſt I run upon thee,
And with one *buffet* lay thy ſtructure low. *Milton's Agoniſt.*

Round his hollow temples, and his ears,
His buckler beats; the ſon of Neptune, ſtunn'd
With theſe repeated *buffets*, quits the ground. *Dryden.*

**Buffe't.** *n. ſ* [*buffette*, Fr.] A kind of cupboard; or ſet of ſhelves, where plate is ſet out to ſhew, in a room of entertainment.

The rich *buffet* well-colour'd ſerpents grace,
And gaping Triton's ſpew to waſh your face. *Pope.*

To **Bu'ffet.** *v. n.* [from the noun.] To ſtrike with the hand; to box; to beat.

Why, woman, your huſband is in his old lunes again; he ſo *buffets* himſelf on the forehead, crying, peer out, peer out! that any madneſs I ever yet beheld, ſeemed but tameneſs. *Shakeſp.*

Our ears are cudgell'd; not a word of his
But *buffets* better than a fiſt of France. *Shakeſp. K. John.*

The torrent roar'd, and we did *buffet* it
With luſty ſinews; throwing it aſide. *Shakeſp. Jul. Cæſar.*

Inſtantly I plung'd into the ſea,
And, *buffeting* the billows to her reſcue,
Redeem'd her life with half the loſs of mine. *Otway.*

To **Bu'ffet.** *v. n.* To play a boxing-match.

If I might *buffet* for my love, I could lay on like a butcher. *Shakeſp. Henry* V.

**Bu'ffeter.** *n. ſ.* [from *buffet*.] A boxer; one that buffets.

**Bu'ffle.** *n. ſ.* [*beuffle*, Fr.] The ſame with *buffalo*; a wild ox.

To **Bu'ffle.** *v. n.* [from the noun.] To puzzle; to be at a loſs.

This was the utter ruin of that poor, angry, *buffling*, well-meaning mortal, Piſtorides, who lies equally under the contempt of both parties. *Swift.*

**Bu'ffleheaded.** *adj.* [from *buffle* and *head*.] A man with a large head, like a buffalo; dull; ſtupid; fooliſh.

**BUFFO'ON.** *n. ſ.* [*buffon*, Fr.]

1. A man whoſe profeſſion is to make ſport, by low jeſts and antick poſtures; a jackpudding.

No prince would think himſelf greatly honoured, to have his proclamation canvaſſed on a publick ſtage, and become the ſport of *buffoons*. *Watts.*

2. A man that practiſes indecent raillery.

It is the nature of drolls and *buffoons*, to be inſolent to thoſe that will bear it, and ſlaviſh to others. *L'Eſtrange.*

The bold *buffoon*, whene'er they trade the green,
Their motion mimicks, but with geſt obſcene. *Garth.*

**Buffo'onery.** *n. ſ.* [from *buffoon*.]

1. The practice or art of a buffoon.

Courage, in an ill-bred man, has the air, and eſcapes not the opinion of brutality; learning becomes pedantry, and wit *buffoonery*. *Lock on Education.*

2. Low jeſts; ridiculous pranks; ſcurrile mirth. *Dryden* places the accent, improperly, on the firſt ſyllable.

Where publick miniſters encourage *buffoonery*, it is no wonder

2

Applied to light
Let truth be
Ne'er so far distant, yet chronology
will have a perspicil to find her out
Discern the dawn of her eternal day
As when the rosy Morn buds into day
Crashaw

3 To build to compose, to frame any intellectual piece
Who would not sing for Lycidas he knew
Himself to sing & build the lofty rhyme
Milton

What hinder'd? Did fear of envy, distrust of want? Alas what bugs are these to fright men from heaven
Bp. Hall to Sutton

~~2. The materials for building~~
Oak Cedar and Chesnut are the best builders and some for piers
Bacon

1 Builded part. pass. of build
Antony
Let not the piece of Virtue which is set
As the cement of our love,
To keep it builded be the ram to batter
The fortress of it
Shak

IL facing 3R2[r]

der if buffoons fet up for publick minifters. *L'Eftrange.*
And whilft it lafts, let *buffoonery* fucceed,
To make us laugh; for never was more need. *Dryden.*

BUG. *n. f.* A ftinking infect bred in old houfhold ftuff. In the following paffage, wings are erroneoufly afcribed to it.
Yet let me flap this *bug* with gilded wings,
This painted child of dirt, which ftinks and ftings. *Pope.*

BUG. } *n. f.* [It is derived by fome from *big*, by others from
BU'GBEAR. } *pug*; *bug*, in Welch, has the fame meaning.] A frightful object; a walking fpectre, imagined to be feen; generally now ufed for a falfe terrour to frighten babes.
Each trembling leaf and whiftling wind they hear,
As ghaftly *bug* their hair on end does rear,
Yet both do ftrive their fearfulnefs to feign. *Fairy Q. b.* ii.
Sir, fpare your threats;
The *bug* which you would fright me with, I feek. *Shakefp.*
Haft not flept to-night? would he not, naughty man, let it fleep? a *bugbear* take him. *Shakefp. Troilus and Creffida.*
We have a horrour for uncouth monfters; but, upon cuftom and experience, all thefe *bugs* grow familiar and eafy to us. *L'Eftrange.*
Such *bugbear* thoughts, once got into the tender minds of children, fink deep, fo as not eafily, if ever, to be got out again. *Locke.*
To the world, no *bugbear* is fo great,
As want of figure, and a fmall eftate. *Pope.*

BU'GGINESS. *n. f.* [from *buggy.*] Being infected with bugs.

BU'GGY. *adj.* [from *bug.*] Abounding with bugs.

BU'GLE. } *n. f.* [from bugen, Sax. to bend, *Skinner*; from
BU'GLEHORN. } *bucula*, Lat. a heifer, *Junius*; from *bugle*, the bonafus. *Lye.*] A hunting horn.
Then took that fquire an horny *bugle* fmall,
Which hung adown his fide in twifted gold,
And taffels gay. *Fairy Queen, b.* i. *c.* viii. *ftanz.* 3.
That I will have a recheate winded in my forehead, or hang my *bugle* in an invifible baldrick, all women fhall pardon me. *Shakefp. Much ado about Nothing.*
He gave his *buglehorn* a blaft,
That through the woodland echo'd far and wide. *Tickell.*

BU'GLE. *n. f.* A fhining bead of black glafs.
*Bugle* bracelets, necklace amber,
Perfume for a lady's chamber. *Shakefp. Winter's Tale.*
'Tis not your inky brows, your black filk hair,
Your *bugle* eyeballs, nor your cheek of cream,
That can entame my fpirits to your worfhip. *Shakefp.*

BU'GLE. *n. f.* [from *bugula*, Lat.] A plant.
It hath a flower confifting of one leaf, divided into three parts; out of the flower-cup arifes the pointal, fixed like a nail, attended by four embryos, which become fo many oblong feeds, fhut up in a husk; the flowers are placed in whorles round the ftalk. The fpecies are, 1. Common *bugle*. 2. The greateft *bugle* of the Alps. 3. Hairy eaftern *bugle*, with an inverted blue flower, fpotted with white. 4. Eaftern *bugle*, with a purplifh violet coloured flower, &c. The firft and fecond forts grow wild in moift woods and meadows, and continue in flower from May to September. The *bugle* is greatly efteemed as a vulnerary herb, and is ufed both externally and internally. They are very hardy plants, and propagate greatly by their trailing ftalks. *Miller.*

BU'GLE. *n. f.* A fort of wild ox. *Philips's World of Words.*

BU'GLOSS. [from *bugloffum*, Lat.] The herb ox-tongue.
The flowers are fmall and tubulous, divided at the top into five obtufe fegments, and are expanded in a round form; the feeds are like the head of a viper. They may be cultivated by fowing their feeds in the fpring; its flowers are ufed in medicinal cordials. *Miller.*

To BUILD. *v. a.* preter. I *built*, I have *built*. [*bilden*, Dutch.]

1. To raife from the ground; to make a fabrick, or an edifice.
Thus faith the Lord, thou fhalt not *build* me an houfe to dwell in. *Hooker, b.* ii. § 6.
When ufurers tell their gold in the field,
And whores and bawds do churches *build*. *Shakefp.*
When the head-drefs was *built* up in a couple of cones and fpires, which ftood fo exceffively high on the fide of the head, that a woman, who was but a pigmy without her head-drefs, appeared like a coloffus upon putting it on. *Spectator*, N° 98.
To *build*, to plant, whatever you intend,
To rear the column, or the arch to bend. *Pope.*

2. To raife any thing on a fupport or foundation.
Love *built* on beauty, foon as beauty, dies;
Choofe this face, chang'd by no deformities. *Donne.*
I would endeavour to deftroy thofe curious, but groundlefs ftructures, that men have *built* up of opinions alone. *Boyle.*

To BUILD. *v. n.* To depend on; to reft on.
By a man's authority, we here underftand the force which his word hath for the affurance of another's mind, that *buildeth* upon it. *Hooker.*
Some *build* rather upon the abufing of others, and putting tricks upon them, than upon foundnefs of their own proceedings. *Bacon's Effays*, N° 23.
Even thofe who had not tafted of your favours, yet *built* fo much on the fame of your beneficence, that they bemoaned the lofs of their expectations. *Dryden's Fables, Dedication.*
This is certainly a much furer way, than to *build* on the interpretations of an authour, who does not confider how the ancients ufed to think. *Addifon on ancient Medals.*

BUI'LDER. *n. f.* [from *build.*] He that builds; an architect.
But fore-accounting oft makes *builders* mifs;
They found, they felt, they had no leafe of blifs. *Sidney.*
When they, which had feen the beauty of the firft temple built by Solomon, beheld how far it excelled the fecond, which had not *builders* of like abilities, the tears of their grieved eyes the prophets endeavoured, with comforts, to wipe away. *Hooker, b.* v. § 14.
Mark'd out for fuch an ufe, as if 'twere meant
T' invite the *builder*, and his choice prevent. *Denham.*
Her wings with lengthen'd honour let her fpread,
And, by her greatnefs, fhew her *builder's* fame. *Prior.*

BUI'LDING. *n. f.* [from *build.*] A fabrick; an edifice.
Thy fumptuous *buildings*, and thy wife's attire,
Have coft a mafs of publick treafury. *Shakefp. Henry* VI.
View not this fpire by meafure giv'n
To *buildings* rais'd by common hands:
That fabrick rifes high as heav'n,
Whofe bafis on devotion ftands. *Prior.*
Among the great variety of ancient coins which I faw at Rome, I could not but take particular notice of fuch as relate to any of the *buildings* or ftatues that are ftill extant. *Addifon.*

BUILT. *n. f.* [from *build.*] The form; the ftructure.
As is the *built*, fo different is the fight;
Their mounting fhot is on our fails defign'd;
Deep in their hulls our deadly bullets light,
And through the yielding planks a paffage find. *Dryden.*
There is hardly any country, which has fo little fhipping as Ireland; the reafon muft be, the fcarcity of timber proper for this *built*. *Temple.*

BULB. *n. f.* [*bulbus*, Lat.] A round body, or root.
Take up your early autumnal tulips, and *bulbs*, if you will remove them. *Evelyn's Kalend.*
If we confider the *bulb*, or ball of the eye, the exteriour membrane, or coat thereof, is made thick, tough, or ftrong, that it is a very hard matter to make a rupture in it. *Ray.*

BULBA'CEOUS. *adj.* [*bulbaceus*, Lat.] The fame with *bulbous*. *D.*

BU'LBOUS. *adj.* [from *bulb.*] Containing bulbs; confifting of bulbs.
There are of roots, *bulbous* roots, fibrous roots, and hirfute roots. And I take it, in the *bulbous*, the fap hafteneth moft to the air and fun. *Bacon's Nat. Hiftory*, N° 616.
Set up your traps for vermin, efpecially amongft your *bulbous* roots. *Evelyn's Kalendar.*
There leaves, after they are fwelled out, like a *bulbous* root, to make the bottle, bend inward, or come again clofe to the ftalk. *Ray on the Creation.*
The beginning of the internal jugulars have a *bulbous* cavity. *Ray on the Creation.*

To BULGE. *v. n.* [It was originally written *bilge*; *bilge* was the lower part of the fhip, where it fwelled out; from bilg, Sax. a bladder.]

1. To take in water; to founder.
Thrice round the fhip was toft,
Then *bulg'd* at once, and in the deep was loft. *Dryden.*

2. To jut out.
The fide, or part of the fide of a wall, or any timber that *bulges* from its bottom or foundation, is faid to batter, or hang over the foundation. *Moxon's Mechanical Exercifes.*

BU'LIMY. *n. f.* [βουλιμία, from βοῦς, an ox, and λιμός, hunger.] An enormous appetite, attended with fainting, and coldnefs of the extremities. *Dict.*

BULK. *n. f.* [*bulcke*, Dutch, the breaft, or largeft part of a man.]

1. Magnitude; fize; quantity.
Againft thefe forces there were prepared near one hundred fhips; not fo great of *bulk* indeed, but of a more nimble motion, and more ferviceable. *Bacon's War with Spain.*
The Spaniards and Portuguefe have fhips of great *bulk*, but fitter for the merchant than the man of war; for burden than for battle. *Raleigh's Effays.*
Though an animal arrives at its full growth, at a certain age, perhaps it never comes to its full *bulk* till the laft period of life. *Arbuthnot on Aliments.*

2. Greatnefs; largenefs.
Things, or objects, cannot enter into the mind, as they fubfift in themfelves, and, by their own natural *bulk*, pafs into the apprehenfion; but they are taken in by their ideas. *South.*

3. The grofs; the majority.
Thofe very points, in which thefe wife men difagreed from the *bulk* of the people, are points in which they agreed with the received doctrines of our nature. *Addifon. Freeholder*, N° 51.
Change in property, through the *bulk* of a nation, makes flow marches, and its due power always attends it. *Swift.*
The *bulk* of the debt muft be leffened gradually. *Swift.*

4. Main fabrick.
He rais'd a figh, fo piteous and profound,
That it did feem to fhatter all his *bulk*,
And end his being. *Shakefp. King Lear*

5. The

5. The main part of a ship's cargo; as, to *break bulk*, is to open the cargo.

BULK. *n. ſ.* [from *bielcke*, Dan. a beam.] A part of a building jutting out.

Here ſtand behind this *bulk*. Straight will he come:
Wear thy good rapier bare, and put it home. *Shakeſp. Othello.*

The keeper coming up, found Jack with no life in him; he took down the body, and laid it on a *bulk*, and brought out the rope to the company. *Arbuthnot's Hiſtory of John Bull.*

BU'LKHEAD. *n. ſ.* A partition made acroſs a ſhip, with boards, whereby one part is divided from another. *Harris.*

BU'LKINESS. *n. ſ.* [from *bulky.*] Greatneſs of ſtature, or ſize.

Wheat, or any other grain, cannot ſerve inſtead of money, becauſe of its *bulkineſs*, and too quick change of its quantity. *Locke.*

BU'LKY. *adj.* [from *bulk.*] Of great ſize or ſtature.

Latreus, the *bulkieſt* of the double race,
Whom the ſpoil'd arms of ſlain Haleſus grace. *Dryden.*

Huge Telephus, a formidable page,
Cries vengeance; and Oreſtes' *bulky* rage,
Unſatisfy'd with margins cloſely writ,
Foams o'er the covers. *Dryden's Juvenal, ſat.* i.

The manner of ſea engagements, which was to bore and ſink the enemy's ſhips with the roſtra, gave *bulky* and high ſhips a great advantage. *Arbuthnot on Coins.*

BULL. *n. ſ.* [*bulle*, Dutch.]

1. The male of black cattle; the male to a cow.

A proper gentlewoman, Sir, and a kinſwoman of my maſter's.—Even ſuch kin as the pariſh heifers are to the town *bull.* *Shakeſp. Henry IV. p.* ii.

*Bulls* are more criſp upon the forehead than cows. *Bacon.*

Beſt age to go to *bull*, or calve, we hold,
Begins at four, and ends at ten years old. *May's Virgil.*

The nobler herds,
Where round the lordly *bull*, in rural eaſe,
They ruminating lie. *Thomſon's Summer, l.* 920.

2. In the ſcriptural ſenſe, an enemy powerful, fierce, and violent.

Many *bulls* have compaſſed me: ſtrong *bulls* of Baſhan have beſet me round. *Pſalm* xxii. 12.

3. One of the twelve ſigns of the zodiack.

At laſt from Aries rolls the bounteous ſun,
And the bright *Bull* receives him. *Thomſon's Spring.*

4. A letter publiſhed by the pope.

A *bull* is letters called apoſtolick by the canoniſts, ſtrengthened with a leaden ſeal, and containing in them the decrees and commandments of the pope or biſhop of Rome. *Ayliffe.*

There was another ſort of ornament wore by the young nobility, called *bullæ*; round, or of the figure of a heart, hung about their necks like diamond croſſes. Thoſe *bullæ* came afterwards to be hung to the diplomas of the emperours and popes, from whence they had the name of *bulls.* *Arbuthnot.*

It was not till after a freſh *bull* of Leo's had declared how inflexible the court of Rome was in the point of abuſes. *Atterb.*

5. A blunder; a contradiction.

I confeſs it is what the Engliſh call a *bull*, in the expreſſion, though the ſenſe be manifeſt enough. *Pope's Letters.*

BULL, in compoſition, generally notes the large ſize of any thing, as *bull-head*, *bulruſh*, *bull-trout*; and is therefore only an incluſive particle, without much reference to its original ſignification.

BULL-BAITING. *n. ſ.* [from *bull* and *bait.*] The ſport of baiting bulls with dogs.

What am I the wiſer for knowing that Trajan was in the fifth year of his tribuneſhip, when he entertained the people with a horſe-race or *bull-baiting?* *Addiſon on ancient Medals.*

BULL-BEEF. *n. ſ.* [from *bull* and *beef.*] Coarſe beef; the fleſh of bulls.

They want their porridge and their fat *bull-beeves.* *Shakeſp.*

BULL-BEGGAR. *n. ſ.* [This word probably came from the inſolence of thoſe who begged, or raiſed money by the pope's bull.] Something terrible; ſomething to fright children with.

Theſe fulminations from the Vatican were turned into ridicule; and, as they were called *bull-beggars*, they were uſed as words of ſcorn and contempt. *Ayliffe's Parergon.*

BULL-CALF. *n. ſ.* [from *bull* and *calf.*] A he-calf; uſed for a ſtupid fellow: a term of reproach.

And, Falſtaff, you carried your guts away as nimbly, and roared for mercy, and ſtill ran and roared, as ever I heard *bull-calf.* *Shakeſp. Henry* IV.

BULL-DOG. *n. ſ.* [from *bull* and *dog.*] A dog of a particular form, remarkable for his courage. He is uſed in baiting the bull; and this ſpecies is ſo peculiar to Britain, that they are ſaid to degenerate when they are carried to other countries.

All the harmleſs part of him is no more than that of a *bull-dog*; they are tame no longer than they are not offended. *Addiſon. Spectator*, N° 438.

BULL-FINCH. *n. ſ.* A ſmall bird, that has neither ſong nor whiſtle of its own, yet is very apt to learn, if taught by the mouth. *Philips's World of Words.*

The blackbird whiſtles from the thorny brake,
The mellow *bull-finch* anſwers from the groves. *Thomſon.*

BULL-FLY. } *n. ſ.* An Inſect. *Philips's World of Words.*
BULL-BEE. }

BULL-HEAD. *n. ſ.* [from *bull* and *head.*]

1. A ſtupid fellow; a blockhead.

2. The name of a fiſh.

The miller's thumb, or *bull-head*, is a fiſh of no pleaſing ſhape; it has a head big and flat, much greater than ſuitable to its body; a mouth very wide, and uſually gaping; he is without teeth, but his lips are very rough, much like a file; he hath two fins near to his gills, which are roundiſh or creſted; two fins under his belly, two on the back, one below the vent, and the fin of his tail is round. Nature hath painted the body of this fiſh with whitiſh, blackiſh, browniſh ſpots. They are uſually full of ſpawn all the ſummer, which ſwells their vents in the form of a dug. The *bull-head* begins to ſpawn in April; in winter we know no more what becomes of them than of eels or ſwallows. *Walton's Angler.*

3. A little black water vermin. *Philips's World of Words.*

BULL-TROUT. *n. ſ.* A kind of trout.

There is, in Northumberland, a trout called a *bull-trout*, of a much greater length and bigneſs than any in theſe ſouthern parts. *Walton's Angler.*

BULL-WEED. *n ſ.* The ſame with *knapweed*; which ſee.

BULL-WORT, or BISHOPS-WEED. *n. ſ.* [*ammi*, Lat.] An umbelliferous plant with ſmall ſtriated ſeeds; the petals of the flowers are unequal, and ſhaped like a heart. Its ſeeds are uſed in medicine. *Miller.*

BU'LLACE. *n. ſ.* A wild four plum. See PLUM.

In October, and the beginning of November, come ſervices, medlars, *bullaces*; roſes cut or removed, to come late; holyoaks, and ſuch like. *Bacon's Eſſays*, N° 47.

BU'LLET. *n. ſ.* [*boulet*, Fr.] A round ball of metal, uſually ſhot out of guns.

As when the deviliſh ironengine wrought
In deepeſt hell, and fram'd by furies ſkill,
With windy nitre and quick ſulphur fraught,
And ramm'd with *bullet* round, ordain'd to kill. *Fairy Q. b.* i.

Giaffer, their leader, deſperately fighting amongſt the foremoſt of the janizaries, was at once ſhot with two *bullets*, and ſlain. *Knolles's Hiſtory of the Turks.*

And as the built, ſo different is the fight;
Their mounting ſhot is on our ſails deſign'd:
Deep in their hulls our deadly *bullets* light,
And through the yielding planks a paſſage find. *Dryden.*

BU'LLION. *n. ſ.* [*billon*, Fr.] Gold or ſilver in the lump; unwrought; uncoined.

The balance of trade muſt of neceſſity be returned in coin or *bullion.* *Bacon's Advice to Villiers.*

A ſecond multitude,
With wond'rous art, found out the maſſy ore,
Severing each kind, and ſcumm'd the *bullion* droſs. *Milton's Paradiſe Loſt.*

*Bullion* is ſilver, whoſe workmanſhip has no value. And thus foreign coin hath no value here for its ſtamp, and our coin is *bullion* in foreign dominions. *Locke.*

In every veſſel there is ſtowage for immenſe treaſures, when the cargo is pure *bullion.* *Addiſon on the State of the War.*

BULLI'TION. *n. ſ.* [from *bullio*, Lat.] The act or ſtate of boiling.

There is to be obſerved in theſe diſſolutions, which will not eaſily incorporate, what the effects are, as the *bullition*; the precipitation to the bottom; the ejaculation towards the top; the ſuſpenſion in the midſt; and the like. *Bacon's Phyſical Rem.*

BU'LLOCK. *n. ſ.* [from *bull.*] A young bull.

Why, that's ſpoken like an honeſt drover: ſo they ſell *bullocks.* *Shakeſp. Much ado about Nothing.*

Some drive the herds; here the fierce *bullock* ſcorns
Th' appointed way, and runs with threat'ning horns. *Cowley.*

Until the tranſportation of cattle into England was prohibited, the quickeſt trade of ready money here was driven by the ſale of young *bullocks.* *Temple.*

BU'LLY. *n. ſ.* [*Skinner* derives this word from *burly*, as a corruption in the pronunciation; which is very probably right: or from *bulky*, or *bull-eyed*; which are leſs probable. May it not come from *bull*, the pope's letter, implying the inſolence of thoſe who came inveſted with authority from the papal court?] A noiſy, bluſtering, quarrelling fellow: it is generally taken for a man that has only the apperance of courage.

Mine hoſt of the garter.—What ſays my *bully* rock? Speak ſcholarly and wiſely. *Shakeſp. Merry Wives of Windſor.*

All on a ſudden the doors flew open, and in comes a crew of roaring *bullies*, with their wenches, their dogs, and their bottles. *L'Eſtrange's Fables.*

'Tis ſo ridic'lous, but ſo true withal,
A *bully* cannot ſleep without a brawl. *Dryden's Juv. ſat.* iii.

A ſcolding hero is, at the worſt, a more tolerable character than a *bully* in petticoats. *Addiſon's Freeholder*, N° 38.

The little man is a *bully* in his nature, but, when he grows cholerick, I confine him till his wrath is over. *Addiſon. Spect.*

To BU'LLY. *v. a.* [from the noun.] To overbear with noiſe or menaces.

Prentices, pariſh clerks, and hectors meet,
He that is drunk, or *bully'd*, pays the treat. *King's Cookery.*

To BU'LLY. *v. n.* To be noiſy and quarrelſome.

BU'LRUSH. *n. ſ.* [from *bull* and *ruſh.*] A large ruſh, ſuch as grows

6 Enormity
That they are Sins of no Small bulk,
none can doubt that observes Heresy is
rank'd with, Idolatry Witchcraft & Hatred
D. Piety

‡ 2.[2] play at bowls called long bullets.
When at long bullets Paddy long did play
You sat and lous'd him all the Sun Shine day
Swift

v.m.
He began to leave off his roaring & bullying
about the streets, he put on a serious air
Arb. J. Bull

That a Bittern maketh that mugient noise, or bumping, by putting its bill into a reed, or as Aldrovandus conceives, by putting the same in water or mud, and after a while retaining the Air, by suddenly excluding it again, is not easily made out

Bro. V. E. 3. 26.



IL facing 3S[r]

grows in rivers, without knots; though *Dryden* has given it the epithet *knotty*, confounding it, probably, with the reed.

To make fine cages for the nightingale,
And baskets of *bulrushes*, was my wont. *Spenser.*

All my praises are as but a *bulrush* cast upon a stream; they are born up by the strength of the current. *Dryden.*

The edges were with bending osiers crown'd;
The *knotty bulrush* next in order stood,
And all within of reeds a trembling wood. *Dryden's Fables.*

BU'LWARK. *n. s.* [*bolwercke*, Dutch; probably only from its strength and largeness.]

1. A fortification; a citadel.

But him the squire made quickly to retreat,
Encountering fierce with single sword in hand,
And 'twixt him and his lord did like a *bulwark* stand.
*Spenser's Fairy Queen, b.* i. *cant.* viii. *stanz.* 12.

Who oft repair
Their earthen *bulwarks* 'gainst the ocean flood. *Fairfax, b.* i.

Taking away needless *bulwarks*, divers were demolished upon the sea coasts. *Hayward.*

We have *bulwarks* round us;
Within our walls are troops enur'd to toil. *Addison's Cato.*

Our naval strength is a general *bulwark* to the ~~British~~ nation.
*Addison's* ~~*Freeholder*, N° 42.~~

2. A security.

Some making the wars their *bulwark*, that have before gored the gentle bosom of peace with pillage and robbery. *Shakesp.*

To BU'LWARK. *v. a.* [from the noun.] To fortify; to strengthen with bulwarks.

And yet no *bulwark'd* town, or distant coast,
Preserves the beauteous youth from being seen. *Addison.*

BUM. *n. s.* [*bomme*, Dutch.]

1. The buttocks; the part on which we sit.

The wisest aunt telling the saddest tale,
Sometime for threefoot stool mistaketh me,
Then slip I from her *bum*, down topples she. *Shakesp.*

~~This said,~~ he gently rais'd the knight,
And set him on his *bum* upright. *Hudibras.*

From dusty shops neglected authours come,
Martyrs of pies, and relicks of the *bum*. *Dryden's Mackfl.*

The learned Sydenham does not doubt,
But profound thought will bring the gout;
And that with *bum* on couch we lie,
Because our reason's soar'd too high. *W—n.*

2. It is used, in composition, for any thing mean or low, as *bumbailiff*.

BUMBA'ILIFF. *n. s.* [from *bum* and *bailiff*.] A bailiff of the meanest kind; one that is employed in arrests.

Go, Sir Andrew, scout me for him at the corner of the orchard, like a *bumbailiff*. *Shakesp. Twelfth Night.*

BU'MBARD. *n. s.* [wrong written for *bombard*; which see.] A great gun; a great barrel.

Yond same black cloud, yond huge one looks
Like a foul *bumbard*, that would shed his liquour.
*Shakesp.* ~~*Tempest.*~~

BU'MBAST. *n. s.* [falsely written for *bombast*; ~~the etymology of which I am now very doubtful of~~; *bombast* and *bombasine* ~~being~~ mentioned, with great probability, by *Junius*, as coming from *boom*, a tree, and *sein*, silk; the silk or cotton of a tree.]

1. A cloth made by sewing one stuff upon another; patchwork.

The usual *bumbast* of black bits sewed into ermine, our English women are made to think very fine. *Grew.*

2. Linen stuffed with cotton; stuffing.

We have received your letters full of love,
And, in our maiden council, rated them
As courtship, pleasant jest, and courtesy,
As *bumbast*, and as lining to the time. *Shakesp.*

BUMP. *n. s.* [perhaps from *bum*, as being prominent.] A swelling; a protuberance.

It had upon its brow a *bump* as big as a young cockrel's stone; a perilous knock, and it cried bitterly. *Shakesp. Rom. and Jul.*

Not though his teeth are beaten out, his eyes
Hang by a string, in *bumps* his forehead rise. *Dryden's Juv.*

To BUMP. *v. a.* [from *bombus*, Lat.] To make a loud noise, or bomb. [See BOMB.] It is applied, I think, only to the bittern.

Then to the water's brink she laid her head,
And as a bittour *bumps* within a reed,
To thee alone, O lake, she said——— *Dryden.*

BU'MPER. *n. s.* [from *bump*.] A cup filled till the liquour swells over the brims.

Places his delight
All day in plying *bumpers*, and at night
Reels to the bawds. *Dryden's Juv. sat.* viii.

BU'MPKIN. *n. s.* [This word is of uncertain etymology; *Henshaw* derives it from *pumpkin*, a kind of worthless gourd, or melon. This seems harsh. *Bump* is used amongst us for a knob, or lump; may not *bumpkin* be much the same with *clodpate*, *loggerhead*, *block*, and *blockhead*.] An awkward heavy rustick; a country lout.

The poor *bumpkin*, that had never seen nor heard of such delights before, blessed herself at the change of her condition. *L'Estrange's Fables.*

A heavy *bumpkin*, taught with daily care,
Can never dance three steps with a becoming air. *Dryden.*

In his white cloak the magistrate appears,
The country *bumpkin* the same liv'ry wears. *Dryden.*

It was a favour to admit them to breeding; they might be ignorant *bumpkins* and clowns, if they pleased. *Locke.*

BU'MPKINLY. *adj.* [from *bumpkin*.] Having the manners or appearance of a clown; clownish.

He is a simple, blundering, and yet conceited fellow, who, aiming at description, and the rustick wonderful, gives an air of *bumpkinly* romance to all he tells. *Clarissa.*

BUNCH. *n. s.* [*buncker*, Danish, the crags of the mountains.]

1. A hard lump; a knob.

They will carry their treasures upon the *bunches* of camels, to a people that shall not profit them. *Josh.* xxx. 6.

He felt the ground, which he had wont to find even and soft, to be grown hard with little round balls or *bunches*, like hard boiled eggs. *Boyle.*

2. A cluster; many of the same kind growing together.

Vines, with clust'ring *bunches* growing. *Shakesp. Tempest.*

Titian said, that he knew no better rule for the distribution of the lights and shadows, than his observations drawn from a *bunch* of grapes. *Dryden's Dufresnoy.*

For thee, large *bunches* load the bending vine,
And the last blessings of the year are thine. *Dryden.*

3. A number of things tied together.

And on his arms a *bunch* of keys he bore. *Fairy Q. b.* i.

All? I know not what ye call all; but if I fought not with fifty of them, I am a *bunch* of radish. *Shakesp. Henry* IV. *p.* i.

Ancient Janus, with his double face,
And *bunch* of keys, the porter of the place. *Dryden.*

The mother's *bunch* of keys, or any thing they cannot hurt themselves with, serves to divert little children. *Locke.*

4. Any thing bound into a knot.

Upon the top of all his lofty crest,
A *bunch* of hairs discolour'd diversly,
With sprinkled pearl and gold full richly drest. *Fairy Q. b.* i.

To BUNCH. *v. n.* [from the noun.] To swell out in a bunch; to grow out in protuberances.

It has the resemblance of a large champignon before it is opened, *bunching* out into a large round knob at one end. *Woodward on Fossils.*

BUNCHBA'CKED. *adj.* [from *bunch* and *back*.] Having bunches on the back.

The day shall come, that thou shalt wish for me,
To help thee curse this pois'nous *bunchback'd* toad. *Shakesp.*

BU'NCHINESS. *n. s.* [from *bunchy*.] The quality of being bunchy, or growing in bunches.

BU'NCHY. *adj.* [from *bunch*.] Growing into bunches; knotty.

He is more especially distinguished from other birds, by his *bunchy* tail, and the shortness of his legs. *Grew's Musæum.*

BU'NDLE. *n. s.* [byndle, Sax. from bynd.]

1. A number of things bound together.

As to the *bundles* of petitions in parliament, they were, for the most part, petitions of private persons. *Hale's Law of Engl.*

Try, lads, can you this *bundle* break;
Then bids the youngest of the six
Take up a well-bound heap of sticks. *Swift.*

In the north, they bind them up in small *bundles*, and make small ricks of them. *Mortimer's Husbandry.*

2. A roll; any thing rolled up cylindrically.

She carried a great *bundle* of Flanders lace under her arm; but finding herself overloaden, she dropped the good man, and brought away the *bundle*. *Spectator*, N° 499.

To BU'NDLE. *v. a.* [from the noun.] To tie in a bundle; to tie together; with *up*.

We ~~ought to~~ put things together, ~~as well~~ as we can, ~~doctrinæ causâ~~; but, after all, several things will not be *bundled up* together, under our terms and ways of speaking. *Locke.*

See how the double nation lies,
Like a rich coat with skirts of frize;
As if a man, in making posies,
Should *bundle* thistles *up* with roses. *Swift.*

BUNG. *n. s.* [*bing*, Welch.] A stopple for a barrel.

After three nights are expired, the next morning pull out the *bung* stick, or plug. *Mortimer.*

To BUNG. *v. a.* [from the noun.] To stop; to close up.

BU'NGHOLE. *n. s.* [from *bung* and *hole*.] The hole at which the barrel is filled, and which is afterward stopped up.

Why may not imagination trace the noble dust of Alexander, till he find it stopping a *bunghole*. *Shakesp.*

To BU'NGLE. *v. n.* [See BUNGLER.] To perform clumsily.

When men want light,
They make but *bungling* work. *Dryden's Spanish Friar.*

Letters to me are not seldom opened, and then sealed in a *bungling* manner before they come to my hands. *Swift to Pope.*

To BU'NGLE. *v. a.* To botch; to manage clumsily; to conduct awkwardly.

Other devils, that suggest by-treasons
Do botch and *bungle* up damnation,
With patches, colours, and with forms being fetcht
From glist'ring semblances of piety. *Shakesp. Henry* V.

They make lame miſchief, though they mean it well:
Their int'reſt is not finely drawn, and hid,
But ſeams are coarſely *bungled* up, and ſeen. *Dryden's D. Seb.*

BU'NGLE. *n. ſ.* [from the verb.] A botch; an awkwardneſs; an inaccuracy; a clumſy performance.

Errours and *bungles* are committed, when the matter is inapt or contumacious. *Ray on the Creation.*

BU'NGLER. *n. ſ.* [*bwngler*, Welch; *q. bôn y glêr*, i. e. the laſt or loweſt of the profeſſion. *Davies.*] A bad workman; a clumſy performer; a man without ſkill.

Painters, at the firſt, were ſuch *bunglers*, and ſo rude, that, when they drew a cow or a hog, they were fain to write over the head what it was; otherwiſe the beholder knew not what to make of it. *Peacham on Drawing.*

Hard features every *bungler* can command;
To draw true beauty ſhews a maſter's hand. *Dryden.*

A *bungler* thus, who ſcarce the nail can hit,
With driving wrong will make the pannel ſplit. *Swift.*

BU'NGLINGLY. *adv.* [from *bungling*.] Clumſily; awkwardly.

To denominate them monſters, they muſt have had ſome ſyſtem of parts, compounded of ſolids and fluids, that executed, though but *bunglingly*, their peculiar functions. *Bentley.*

BUNN. *n. ſ.* [*bunelo*, Span.] A kind of ſweet bread.

Thy ſongs are ſweeter to mine ear,
Than to the thirſty cattle rivers clear;
Or winter porridge to the lab'ring youth,
Or *bunns* and ſugar to the damſel's tooth. *Gay's Paſtorals.*

BUNT. *n. ſ.* [corrupted, as *Skinner* thinks, from *bent*.] A ſwelling part; an increaſing cavity.

The Wear is a frith, reaching ſlopewiſe through the ooze, from the land to low water mark, and having in it a *bunt* or cod, with an eye-hook, where the fiſh entering, upon the coming back with the ebb, are ſtopped from iſſuing out again, forſaken by the water, and left dry on the ooze. *Carew.*

To BUNT. *v. n.* [from the noun.] To ſwell out, as the ſail *bunts* out.

BU'NTER. *n. ſ.* A cant word for a woman who picks up rags about the ſtreet; and uſed, by way of contempt, for any low vulgar woman.

BU'NTING. *n. ſ.* The name of a bird.

Then my dial goes not true; I took this lark for a *bunting*. *Shakeſp. All's well that ends well.*

BUOY. *n. ſ.* [*bouë*, or *boye*, Fr. *boya*, Span.] A piece of cork or wood floating on the water, tied to a weight at the bottom.

The fiſhermen, that walk upon the beach,
Appear like mice; and yond tall anchoring bark
Diminiſh'd to her cock; her cock a *buoy*,
Almoſt too ſmall for ſight. *Shakeſp. King Lear.*

Like *buoys*, that never ſink into the flood,
On learning's ſurface we but lie and nod. *Pope's Dunciad.*

To BUOY. *v. a.* [from the noun. The *u* is mute in both.] To keep afloat; to bear up by ſpecifick lightneſs.

All art is uſed to ſink epiſcopacy, and launch preſbytery in England; which was lately *buoyed* up in Scotland, by the like artifice of a covenant. *K. Charles.*

The water which riſes out of the abyſs, for the ſupply of ſprings and rivers, would not have ſtopped at the ſurface of the earth, but marched directly up into the atmoſphere, wherever there was heat enough in the air to continue its aſcent, and *buoy* it up. *Woodward's Nat. Hiſt.*

To BUOY. *v. n.* To float.

Riſing merit will *buoy* up at laſt. *Pope's Eſſay on Crit.*

BUO'YANCY. *n. ſ.* [from *buoyant*.] The quality of floating.

All the winged tribes owe their flight and *buoyancy* to it. *Derham's Phyſico-Theology.*

BUO'YANT. *adj.* [from *buoy*.] Floating; light; that which will not ſink.

I ſwom with the tide, and the water under me was *buoyant*. *Dryden.*

His once ſo vivid nerves,
So full of *buoyant* ſpirit, now no more
Inſpire the courſe. *Thomſon's Autumn, l.* 455.

BUR, BOUR, BOR, come from the Sax. bun, an inner-chamber, or place of ſhade and retirement. *Gibſon's Camden.*

BUR. *n. ſ.* [*bourre*, Fr. is *down*; the *bur* being filled with a ſoft *tomentum*, or down.] A rough head of a plant, which ſticks to the hair or cloaths.

Nothing teems,
But hateful docks, rough thiſtles, keckſies, *burs*,
Loſing both beauty and utility. *Shakeſp. Henry* V.

Hang off, thou cat, thou *bur*; vile thing, let looſe;
Or I will ſhake thee from me like a ſerpent. *Shakeſp.*

Dependents and ſuitors are always the *burs*, and ſometimes the briers of favourites. *Wotton.*

Whither betake her
From the chill dew, amongſt rude *burs* and thiſtles. *Milton.*

And where the vales with violets once were crown'd,
Now knotty *burs* and thorns diſgrace the ground. *Dryden.*

A fellow ſtuck like a *bur*, that there was no ſhaking him off. *Arbuthnot's Hiſt. of J. Bull.*

BU'RBOT. *n. ſ.* A fiſh full of prickles. *Dict.*

BU'RDELAIS. *n. ſ.* A ſort of grape. See VINE.

BU'RDEN. *n. ſ.* [byrðen, Sax. and therefore properly written *burthen*. It is ſuppoſed to come from *burdo*, Lat. a male, as *onus* from ὄνος, an aſs.]

1. A load; ſomething to be carried.

Camels have their provender
Only for bearing *burdens*, and ſore blows
For ſinking under them. *Shakeſp. Coriolanus.*

It is of uſe in lading of ſhips, and may help to ſhew what *burden* in the ſeveral kinds they will bear. *Bacon's Phyſ. Rem.*

2. Something grievous or weariſome.

Couldſt thou ſupport
That *burden*, heavier than the earth to bear? *Par. Loſt, b.* x.

None of the things they are to learn, ſhould ever be made a *burden* to them, or impoſed on them as a taſk. *Locke.*

Deaf, giddy, helpleſs, left alone,
To all my friends a *burden* grown. *Swift.*

3. A birth: now obſolete.

Thou hadſt a wife once, called Æmilia,
That bore thee at a *burden* two fair ſons. *Shakeſp.*

4. The verſe repeated in a ſong.

At ev'ry cloſe ſhe made, th' attending throng
Reply'd, and bore the *burden* of the ſong. *Dryden's Fab.*

5. The quantity that a ſhip will carry; or the capacity of a ſhip.

To BU'RDEN. *v. a.* [from the noun.] To load; to incumber.

*Burden* not thyſelf above thy power. *Ecclus*, xiii. 2.

I mean not that other men be eaſed, and you *burdened*. *Cor.* viii. 13.

BU'RDENER. *n. ſ.* [from *burden*.] A loader; an oppreſſour.

BU'RDENOUS. *adj.* [from *burden*.]

1. Grievous; oppreſſive; weariſome.

Make no jeſt of that which hath ſo earneſtly pierced me through, nor let that be light to thee, which to me is ſo *burdenous*. *Sidney, b.* i.

2. Uſeleſs.

To what can I be uſeful, wherein ſerve,
But to ſit idle on the houſhold hearth,
A *burd'nous* drone; to viſitants a gaze. *Milton's Agoniſtes.*

BU'RDENSOME. *adj.* [from *burden*.] Grievous; troubleſome to be born.

His leiſure told him, that his time was come,
And lack of load made his life *burdenſome*. *Milton.*

Could I but live till *burdenſome* they prove,
My life would be immortal as my love. *Dryden's Ind. Emp.*

Aſſiſtances always attending us, upon the eaſy condition of our prayers, and by which the moſt *burdenſome* duty will become light and eaſy. *Rogers.*

BU'RDENSOMENESS. *n. ſ.* [from *burdenſome*.] Weight; heavineſs; uneaſineſs to be born.

BU'RDOCK. *n. ſ.* See DOCK.

BUREAU'. *n. ſ.* [*bureau*, Fr.] A cheſt of drawers. It is pronounced as if it were ſpelt *buro*.

For not the deſk with ſilver nails,
Nor *bureau* of expence,
Nor ſtandiſh well japan'd, avails
To writing of good ſenſe. *Swift.*

BURG. *n. ſ.* See BURROW.

BU'RGAGE. *n. ſ.* [from *burg*, or *burrow*.] A tenure proper to cities and towns, whereby men of cities or burrows hold their lands or tenements of the king, or other lord, for a certain yearly rent. *Cowel.*

The groſs of the borough is ſurveyed together in the beginning of the county; but there are ſome other particular *burgages* thereof, mentioned under the titles of particular mens poſſeſſions. *Hale's Origin of Mankind.*

BU'RGAMOT. *n. ſ.* [*bergamotte*, Fr.] A ſpecies of pear.

BU'RGANET. } *n. ſ.* [from *bourginote*, Fr.] A kind of helmet.
BU'RGONET. }

Upon his head his gliſtering *burganet*,
The which was wrought by wonderous device,
And curiouſly engraven, he did fit. *Spenſer's Muiopotmos.*

This day I'll wear aloft my *burgonet*,
Ev'n to affright thee with the view thereof. *Shakeſp. H.* VI.

The demy Atlas of this earth, the arm
And *burgonet* of man. *Shakeſp. Antony and Cleopatra.*

I was page to a footman, carrying after him his pike and *burganet*. *Hakewell on Providence.*

BURGEO'IS. *n. ſ.* [*bourgeois*, Fr.]

1. A citizen; a burgeſs.

It is a republick itſelf, under the protection of the eight ancient cantons. There are in it an hundred *burgeois*, and about a thouſand ſouls. *Addiſon on Italy.*

2. A type of a particular ſort, probably ſo called from him who firſt uſed it; as,

Laugh where we muſt, be candid where we can,
But vindicate the ways of God to man. *Pope.*

BU'RGESS. *n. ſ.* [*bourgeois*, Fr.]

1. A citizen; a freeman of a city, or corporate town.

2. A repreſentative of a town corporate.

The whole caſe was diſperſed by the knights of ſhires, and *burgeſſes* of towns, through all the veins of the land. *Wotton.*

BURGH. *n. ſ.* [See BURROW.] A corporate town or burrow.

Many towns in Cornwal, when they were firſt allowed to ſend

2

~~Burdened Adj. (from burden)~~
~~Carrying a burden or freight~~

c ‡ In burden'd Vessels first with speedy care
His plenteous Stores do season'd timber send
Dry. A. M.

b ‡ Ewes that erst brought forth but single lambs
Now drop'd their twofold burdens Prior.

3. She hath the bones broke of eternal Night
Her Soul unbodied of the burdenous corpse
Spens.

3 Weighty unwieldy.
To what a cumbersome unwieldiness
And burdenous Corpulence my love had grown
But what I did to make it less
Give it a Diet made it feed upon
That which love worst endures, Discretion
Donne

The Burial must be by the smallness of the proportion, as fifty to one, which will be but Sixpence gain in fifty shillings; or it must be holpen by somewhat which may fix the Silver, never to be restored or vapor'd away when incorporated into such a Mass of gold Bacon

To kill
The mareweed doth burn & the thistle doth fret
The fitches pull downward both rie and the Wheat
Tuss. husb. May

Mayweed is like Camomile, but a filthy stinking weed & burns, that is kills all the Corn near it. Tuss. notes

She spited with great Courtesy that one that did nothing should be able to resist her, burned away with Choler any Notions that might grow out of her sweet Disposition. Sidney.

5 To shine as fire
The Knights with their bright burning blades
Broke their rude troops & Orders did confound
Hewing and slashing F. Q. 2. 9. 15

ſend burgeſſes to the parliament, bore another proportion to London than now; for ſeveral of theſe *burghs* ſend two burgeſſes, whereas London itſelf ſends but four. *Graunt.*

BU'RGHER. *n. ſ.* [from *burgh.*] One who has a right to certain privileges in this or that place. *Locke.*

It irks me, the poor dappled fools,
Being native *burghers* of this deſart city,
Should in their own confines, with forked heads,
Have their round haunches gor'd. *Shakeſp. As you like it.*

After the multitude of the common people was diſmiſſed, and the chief of the *burghers* ſent for, the imperious letter was read before the knights of the order, and the better ſort of citizens. *Knolles's Hiſtory of the Turks.*

BU'RGHERSHIP. *n. ſ.* [from *burgher.*] The privilege of a burgher.

BU'RGHMASTER. See BURGOMASTER.

BU'RGLAR. *n. ſ.* [See BURGLARY.] The crime of houſebreaking.

BURGLARY. *n. ſ.* [from *burg*, a houſe, and *larron*, a thief.] In the natural ſignification of the word, is nothing but the robbing of a houſe: but as it is a term of art, our common lawyers reſtrain it to robbing a houſe by night, or breaking in with an intent to rob, or do ſome other felony. The like offence committed by day, they call houſe-robbing, by a peculiar name. *Cowel.*

What ſay you, father? *Burglary* is but a venial ſin among ſoldiers. *Dryden's Spaniſh Friar.*

BU'RGOMASTER. *n. ſ.* [from *burg* and *maſter.*] One employed in the government of a city.

They chuſe their councils and *burgomaſters* out of the burgeois, as in the other governments of Switzerland. *Addiſon.*

BURH, is a tower; and from that, a defence or protection; ſo *Cwenburh* is a woman ready to aſſiſt; *Cuthbur*, eminent for aſſiſtance. *Gibſon's Camden.*

BU'RIAL. *n. ſ.* [from *to bury.*]

1. The act of burying; ſepulture; interment.

Nor would we deign him *burial* of his men. *Shakeſp.*

See my wealthy Andrew dock'd in ſand,
Vailing her high top lower than her ribs,
To kiſs her *burial.* *Shakeſp. Merchant of Venice.*

Your body I ſought, and had I found
Deſign'd for *burial* in your native ground. *Dryden's Æneid.*

2. The act of placing any thing under earth or water.

We have great lakes, both ſalt and freſh; we uſe them for *burials* of ſome natural bodies: for we find a difference of things buried in earth, and things buried in water. *Bacon.*

3. The church ſervice for funerals.

The office of the church is performed by the pariſh prieſt, at the time of his interment, if not prohibited unto perſons excommunicated, and laying violent hands on themſelves, by a rubrick of the *burial* ſervice. *Ayliffe's Parergon.*

BU'RIER. *n. ſ.* [from *bury.*] He that buries; he that performs the act of interment.

Let one ſpirit of the firſtborn Cain
Reign in all boſoms, that, each heart being ſet
On bloody courſes, the rude ſcene may end,
And darkneſs be the *burier* of the dead. *Shakeſp. Henry* IV.

BU'RINE. *n. ſ.* [French.] A graving tool; a graver.

Wit is like the graver's *burine* upon copper, or the corrodings of aquafortis, which engrave and indent the characters, that they can never be defaced. *Government of the Tongue.*

BU'RLACE. *n. ſ.* [corruptly written for *burdelais.*] A ſort of grape. See VINE.

To BURL. *v. a.* To dreſs cloth as fullers do. *Dict.*

BURLESQUE. *adj.* [Fr. from *burlare*, Ital. to jeſt.] Jocular; tending to raiſe laughter, by unnatural or unſuitable language or images.

Homer, in his character of Vulcan and Therſites, in his ſtory of Mars and Venus, in his behaviour of Irus, and in other paſſages, has been obſerved to have lapſed into the *burleſque* character, and to have departed from that ſerious air, which ſeems eſſential to the magnificence of an epick poem. *Addiſon. Spectator, Nº 279.*

BURLE'SQUE. *n. ſ.* Ludicrous language, or ideas; ridicule.

When a man lays out a twelvemonth on the ſpots in the ſun, however noble his ſpeculations may be, they are very apt to fall into *burleſque.* *Addiſon on ancient Medals.*

To BURLE'SQUE. *v. a.* [from the adjective.] To turn to ridicule.

Would Homer apply the epithet divine to a modern ſwineherd? if not, it is an evidence, that Eumeus was a man of conſequence; otherwiſe Homer would *burleſque* his own poetry. *Broome's Notes on the Odyſſey.*

BU'RLINESS. *n. ſ.* [from *burly.*] Bulk; bluſter.

BU'RLY. *adj.* [*Junius* has no etymology; *Skinner* imagines it to come from *boorlike*, clowniſh.] Great of ſtature; great of ſize; bulky; tumid.

Steel, if thou turn thine edge, or cut not out the *burly* boned clown in chines of beef, ere thou ſleep in thy ſheath, I beſeech Jove on my knees, thou may'ſt be turned into hobnails. *Shakeſp. Henry* VI. *p.* ii.

It was the orator's own *burly* way of nonſenſe. *Cowley.*

Away with all your Carthaginian ſtate,
Let vanquiſh'd Hannibal without doors wait,
Too *burly* and too big to paſs my narrow gate. } *Dryden.*

Her huſband, it ſeems, being a very *burly* man, ſhe thought it would be leſs trouble for her to bring away little Cupid. *Addiſon. Spectator, Nº 499.*

To BURN. *v. a.* [bernan, Saxon.]

1. To conſume with fire.

That where ſhe fed his amorous deſires
With ſoft complaints, and felt his hotteſt fires,
There other flames might waſte his earthly part,
And *burn* his limbs, where love had *burn'd* his heart. *Dryden.*

O that I could but weep, to vent my paſſion!
But this dry ſorrow *burns* up all my tears. *Dryden's Sp. Fr.*

A fleſhy excreſcence, becoming exceeding hard, is ſuppoſed to demand extirpation, by *burning* away the induration, or amputating. *Sharp's Surgery.*

2. To wound or hurt with fire or heat.

Hand for hand, foot for foot, *burning* for *burning*, wound for wound, ſtripe for ſtripe. *Exodus*, xxi. 25.

To BURN. *v. n.*

1. To be on fire; to be kindled.

The barge ſhe ſat in, like a burniſh'd throne,
*Burnt* on the water. *Shakeſp. Antony and Cleopatra.*

O coward conſcience! how doſt thou afflict me?
The light *burns* blue — Is it not dead midnight?
Cold trembling drops ſtand on my trembling fleſh. *Shakeſp.*

Oh! prince, oh! wherefore *burn* your eyes? and why
Is your ſweet temper turn'd to fury? *Rowe's Royal Convert.*

2. To be inflamed with paſſion.

When I *burnt* in deſire to queſtion them further, they made themſelves air, into which they vaniſhed. *Shakeſp. Macbeth.*

Tranio, I *burn*, I pine, I periſh Tranio,
If I atchieve not this young modeſt girl. *Shakeſp.*

3. To act as fire.

Theſe things ſting him
So venomouſly, that *burning* ſhame detains him
From his Cordelia. *Shakeſp. King Lear.*

In Raleigh mark their every glory mix'd;
Raleigh, the ſcourge of Spain! whoſe breaſt with all
The ſage, the patriot, and the hero *burn'd.* *Thomſon.*

4. To be hot

I had a glimpſe of him; but he ſhot by me
Like a young hound upon a *burning* ſcent. *Dryden's Sp. Fr.*

BURN. *n. ſ.* [from the verb.] A hurt cauſed by fire.

We ſee the phlegm of vitriol is a very effectual remedy againſt *burns.* *Boyle.*

BU'RNER. *n. ſ.* [from *burn.*] A perſon that burns any thing.

BU'RNET. *n. ſ.* [*pimpinella*, Lat.] The name of a plant.

The common *burnet* is found wild in great plenty upon dry chalky hills; yet is often cultivated in gardens for medicinal uſes. *Millar.*

The even mead that erſt brought ſweetly forth
The freckled cowſlip, *burnet*, and green clover. *Shakeſp.*

BU'RNING. *n. ſ.* [from *burn.*] Fire; flame; ſtate of inflammation.

The mind ſurely, of itſelf, can feel none of the *burnings* of a fever. *South.*

In liquid *burnings*, or on dry to dwell,
Is all the ſad variety of hell. *Dryden's State of Innocence.*

BU'RNING-GLASS. *n. ſ.* [from *burning* and *glaſs.*] A glaſs which collects the rays of the ſun into a narrow compaſs, and ſo increaſes their force.

The appetite of her eye did ſeem to ſcorch me up like a *burning-glaſs.* *Shakeſp. Merry Wives of Windſor.*

Love is of the nature of a *burning-glaſs*, which, kept ſtill in one place, fireth; changed often, it doth nothing. *Suckling.*

O diadem, thou centre of ambition,
Where all its different lines are reconciled,
As if thou wert the *burning-glaſs* of glory. *Dryden and Lee.*

To BU'RNISH. *v. a.* [*burnir*, Fr.] To poliſh; to give a gloſs to.

The barge ſhe ſat in, like a *burniſh'd* throne,
Burnt on the water. *Shakeſp. Antony and Cleopatra.*

Miſlike me not for my complexion,
The ſhadow'd livery of the *burniſh'd* ſun,
To whom I am a neighbour, and near bred. *Shakeſp.*

Make a plate of them, and *burniſh* it as they do iron. *Bacon.*

The frame of *burniſh'd* ſteel, that caſt a glare
From far, and ſeem'd to thaw the freezing air. *Dryden.*

To BU'RNISH. *v. n.* To grow bright or gloſſy.

I've ſeen a ſnake in human form,
All ſtain'd with infamy and vice,
Leap from the dunghill in a trice,
*Burniſh*, and make a gawdy ſhow,
Become a gen'ral, peer, and beau. *Swift.*

To BU'RNISH. *v. n.* [of uncertain etymology.] To grow; to ſpread out.

This they could do, while Saturn fill'd the throne,
Ere Juno *burniſh'd*, or young Jove was grown. *Dryden's Juv. ſat.* xiii.

To ſhoot, and ſpread, and *burniſh* into man. *Dryden.*

Mrs.

Mrs. Primly's great belly; ſhe may lace it down before, but it *burniſhes* on her lips. *Congreve's Way of the World.*

BU'RNISHER. *n. ſ.* [from *burniſh.*]

1. The perſon that burniſhes or poliſhes.
2. The tool with which bookbinders give a gloſs to the leaves of books; it is commonly a dog's tooth ſet in a ſtick.

BURNT. [*particip. paſſ.* of *burn.*]

I find it very difficult to know,
Who, to refreſh th' attendants to a grave,
*Burnt* claret firſt, or Naples biſket gave. *King's Cookery.*

BURR. *n. ſ.* [See BUR.] The lobe or lap of the ear. *Dict.*

BURR *Pump.* [In a ſhip.] A pump by the ſide of a ſhip, into which a ſtaff ſeven or eight foot long is put; having a burr or knob of wood at the end, which is drawn up by a rope faſtened to the middle of it, called alſo a *bilge pump.* *Harris.*

BU'RRAS *Pipe.* [With ſurgeons.] An inſtrument or veſſel uſed to keep corroding powders in, as vitriol, precipitate. *Harris.*

BU'RREL. *n. ſ.* A ſort of pear, otherwiſe called the *red butter pear,* from its ſmooth, delicious, and ſoft pulp, which is ripe in the end of September. *Phillips's World of Words.*

BU'RREL *Fly.* [from *bourreler,* Fr. to execute; to torture.] An inſect, called alſo *oxfly, gadbee,* or *breeze.* *Dict.*

BU'RREL *Shot.* [from *bourreler,* to execute, Fr. and *ſhot.*] In gunnery. Small bullets, nails, ſtones, pieces of old iron, *&c.* put into caſes, to be diſcharged out of the ordnance; a ſort of caſe-ſhot. *Harris.*

BU'RROCK. *n. ſ.* A ſmall wear or dam, where wheels are laid in a river for catching of fiſh. *Phillips's World of Words.*

BU'RROW, BERG, BURG, BURGH. *n. ſ.* [derived from the Saxon bunᵹ, bẏnᵹ, a city, tower, or caſtle. *Gibſon's Camden.*]

1. A corporate town, that is not a city, but ſuch as ſends burgeſſes to the parliament. All places that, in former days, were called *borough,* were ſuch as were fenced or fortified. *Cowel.*

King of England ſhalt thou be proclaim'd
In ev'ry *burrow,* as we paſs along. *Shakeſp. Henry* VI. *p.* iii.

Poſſeſſion of land was the original right of election among the commons; and *burrows* were entitled to ſit, as they were poſſeſſed of certain tracts. *Temple.*

2. The holes made in the ground by conies.

When they ſhall ſee his creſt up again, and the man in blood, they will out of their *burrows,* like conies after rain, and revel all with him. *Shakeſp. Coriolanus.*

To BU'RROW. *v. n.* [from the noun.] To make holes in the ground; to mine, as conies or rabbits.

Some ſtrew ſand among their corn, which, they ſay, prevents mice and rats *burrowing* in it; becauſe of its falling into their ears. *Mortimer.*

Little ſinuſes would often form, and *burrow* underneath. *Sharp's Surgery.*

BU'RSAR. *n. ſ.* [*burſarius,* Lat.]

1. The treaſurer of a college.
2. Students ſent as exhibitioners to the univerſities in Scotland by each preſbytery, from whom they have a ſmall yearly allowance for four years.

BURSE. *n. ſ.* [*bourſe,* Fr. *burſa,* Lat. a purſe; or from *byrſa,* Lat. the exchange of Carthage.] An exchange where merchants meet, and ſhops are kept; ſo called, becauſe the ſign of the purſe was anciently ſet over ſuch a place; whence the Exchange in the Strand was termed Britain's Burſe by James I. *Phillips.*

To BURST. *v. n.* I *burſt*; I have *burſt,* or *burſten.* [bunſtan, Saxon.]

1. To break, or fly open.

So ſhall thy barns be filled with plenty, and thy preſſes ſhall *burſt* out with new wine. *Prov.* iii. 10.

2. To fly aſunder.

Yet am I thankful; if my heart were great,
'Twould *burſt* at this. *Shakeſp. All's well that ends well.*

3. To break away; to ſpring.

You *burſt,* ah cruel! from my arms,
And ſwiftly ſhoot along the mall,
Or ſoftly glide by the canal. *Pope.*

4. To come ſuddenly.

A reſolved villain,
Whoſe bowels ſuddenly *burſt* out; the king
Yet ſpeaks, and, peradventure, may recover. *Shakeſp.*
If the worlds
In worlds incloſ'd, ſhou'd on his ſenſes *burſt,*
He wou'd abhorrent turn. *Thomſon's Summer, l.* 310.

5. To come by violence.

Well didſt thou, Richard, to ſuppreſs thy voice;
For had the paſſions of thy heart *burſt* out,
I fear, we ſhould have ſeen decypher'd there
More ranc'rous ſpight. *Shakeſp. Henry* VI. *p.* i.

Where is the notable paſſage over the river Euphrates, *burſting* out by the vallies of the mountain Antitaurus; from whence the plains of Meſopotamia, then part of the Perſian kingdom, begin to open themſelves. *Knolles's Hiſtory of the Turks.*

Young ſpring protrudes the *burſting* gems. *Thomſon.*

6. To begin an action violently.

She *burſt* into tears, and wrung her hands. *Arbuthnot.*

To BURST. *v. a.* To break ſuddenly; to make a quick and violent diſruption.

My breaſt I'll *burſt* with ſtraining of my courage,
And from my ſhoulders crack my arms aſunder,
But I will chaſtiſe this high-minded ſtrumpet. *Shakeſp.*
He faſten'd on my neck, and bellow'd out,
As if he would *burſt* heav'n. *Shakeſp. King Lear.*

Moſes ſaith alſo, the fountains of the great abyſs were *burſt* aſunder, to make the deluge; and what means this abyſs, and the burſting of it, if reſtrained to Judea? what appearance is there of this diſruption there? *Burnet's Theory.*

If the juices of an animal body were, ſo as by the mixture of the oppoſites, to cauſe an ebullition, they would *burſt* the veſſels. *Arbuthnot on Aliments.*

BURST. *n. ſ.* [from the verb.] A ſudden diſruption; a ſudden and violent action of any kind.

Since I was man,
Such ſheets of fire, ſuch *burſt* of horrid thunder,
Such groans of roaring wind and rain, I never
Remember to have heard. *Shakeſp. King Lear.*
Down they came, and drew
The whole roof after them, with *burſt* of thunder,
Upon the heads of all. *Milton's Agoniſtes, l.* 1650.
Impriſon'd fire, in the cloſe dungeons pent,
Roar to get looſe, and ſtruggle for a vent,
Eating their way, and undermining all,
Till with a mighty *burſt* whole mountains fall. *Addiſon.*

BURST. } *participial adj.* [from *burſt.*] Diſeaſed with a hernia, or rupture.
BU'RSTEN. }

BU'RSTENESS. *n. ſ.* [from *burſt.*] A rupture, or hernia.

BU'RSTWORT. *n. ſ.* [from *burſt* and *wort*; *herniaria,* Lat.] An herb good againſt ruptures. *Dict.*

BURT. *n. ſ.* A flat fiſh of the turbot kind.

To BU'RTHEN. *v. a.* } See BURDEN.
BU'RTHEN. *n. ſ.* }

Sacred to ridicule his whole life long,
And the ſad *burthen* of ſome merry ſong. *Pope.*

BU'RTON. *n. ſ.* [In a ſhip.] A ſmall tackle to be faſtened any where at pleaſure, conſiſting of two ſingle pullies, for hoiſting ſmall things in or out. *Phillips's World of Words.*

BU'RY. } *n. ſ.* [from bunᵹ, Sax.] A dwelling-place; a termination ſtill added to the names of ſeveral places; as, *Aldermanbury,* St. *Edmund's bury.* *Phillips's World of Words.*
BE'RY. }

BU'RY. *n. ſ.* [corrupted from *borough.*]

It is his nature to dig himſelf *buries,* as the coney doth; which he doth with very great celerity. *Grew.*

To BURY. *v. a.* [bẏnᵹean, Saxon.]

1. To inter; to put into a grave.

When he lies along,
After your way his tale pronounc'd, ſhall *bury*
His reaſons with his body. *Shakeſp. Coriolanus.*

2. To inter, with the rites and ceremonies of ſepulture.

Slave, thou haſt ſlain me!
If ever thou wilt thrive, *bury* my body. *Shakeſp. King Lear.*
If you have kindneſs left, there ſee me laid;
To *bury* decently the injur'd maid,
Is all the favour. *Waller.*

3. To conceal; to hide.

This is the way to make the city flat,
And *bury* all, which yet diſtinctly ranges,
In heaps and piles of ruin. *Shakeſp. Coriolanus.*

4. To place one thing within another.

A tearing groan did break
The name of Antony; it was divided
Between her heart and lips; ſhe render'd life,
Thy name ſo *bury'd* in her. *Shakeſp. Antony and Cleopatra.*

BU'RYING-PLACE. *n. ſ.* A place appointed for the ſepulture of dead bodies.

The place was formerly a church-yard, and has ſtill ſeveral marks in it of graves and *burying-places.* *Spectator,* Nº 110.

BUSH. *n. ſ.* [*bois,* Fr.]

1. A thick ſhrub.

Eft through the thick they heard one rudely ruſh,
With noiſe whereof, he, from his lofty ſteed,
Down fell to ground, and crept into a *buſh,*
To hide his coward head from dying dread. *Fairy Q. b.* ii.

The poller, and exactor of fees, juſtifies the reſemblance of the courts of juſtice to the *buſh,* whereunto while the ſheep flies for defence from the weather, he is ſure to loſe part of the fleece. *Bacon's Eſſays,* Nº [illegible]

Her heart was that ſtrange *buſh,* whoſe ſacred fire,
Religion did not conſume, but inſpire
Such piety, ſo chaſte uſe of God's day,
That what we turn to feaſt, ſhe turn'd to pray. *Donne.*
With ſuch a care,
As roſes from their ſtalks we tear,
When we would ſtill prefer them new,
And freſh as on the *buſh* they grew. *Waller.*
The ſacred ground
Shall weeds and pois'nous plants refuſe to bear;
Each common *buſh* ſhall Syrian roſes wear. *Dryden's Virg.*

2. A bough of a tree fixed up at a door, to ſhew that liquours are ſold there.

If

choose skilfully Saltfish not burnt at the Stone
Buy such as be good or else let it alone

Tuss. Husb.

By burnt to the Stone I understand as is dried on the beach in too hot weather, whereby it loses its whiteness & is apt to have a rank Smell Tuss. No.

Burranet n. s. a Sea bird
Amongst the first Sort we reckon —
Pents, Means, Smurrs Creysers and Burranets

Carew.

If in the must of wine or wort of beer, while it worketh before it be tunn'd, the burrage stay a small time, & be chang'd with fresh, it is a Sovereign drink for — Melancholy

Bac.

67

The wheame or burrel fly is vexatious to horses in Summer, not by stinging them, but only by their bombylous noise or tickling them in sticking their nits or eggs on the hair

Derh. ph. Theo.

In 1578 was that famous lammas day which buried the reputation of Don John of Austria

Bac. Spain

— 1 State of being busy

~~10 A fantastic unnecessary intermedling,~~
in the same sense with busy body & is Still
retaind in Scotland

He with no more civility, tho with much more
<u>busyness</u> than those under fellows had shewd
began in a captious manner to put interrogatories
unto him Sidney

If it be true, that good wine needs no *buſh*, 'tis true that a good play needs no epilogue. *Shakeſp. As you like it.*

To Bush. *v. n.* [from the noun.] To grow thick.

The roſes *buſhing* round
About her glow'd; half ſtooping to ſupport
Each flow'r of tender ſtalk. *Milton's Par. Loſt, b.* ix.

A guſhing fountain broke
Around it, and above, for ever green,
The *buſhing* alders form'd a ſhady ſcene. *Pope's Odyſſey.*

Bu'shel. *n. ſ.* [*boiſſeau*, Fr. *buſſellus*, low Lat.]

1. A meaſure containing eight gallons; a ſtrike.

His reaſons are as two grains of wheat hid in two *buſhels* of chaff; you ſhall ſeek all day ere you find them; and when you have them, they are not worth the ſearch. *Shakeſp.*

2. It is uſed, in common language, indefinitely for a large quantity.

The worthies of antiquity bought the rareſt pictures with *buſhels* of gold, without counting the weight or the number of pieces. *Dryden's Dufreſnoy.*

3. *Buſhels of a cart-wheel.* Irons within the hole of the nave, to preſerve it from wearing. [from *bouche*, Fr. a mouth.] *Dict.*

Bu'shiness. *n. ſ.* [from *buſhy*.] The quality of being buſhy.

Bu'shment. *n. ſ.* [from *buſh*.] A thicket; a cluſter of buſhes.

Princes thought how they might diſcharge the earth of woods, briars, *buſhments*, and waters, to make it more habitable and fertile. *Raleigh's Hiſtory of the World.*

Bu'shy. *adj.* [from *buſh*.]

1. Thick; full of ſmall branches, not high.

The gentle ſhepherd ſat beſide a ſpring,
All in the ſhadow of a *buſhy* brier. *Spenſer's Paſtorals.*

Generally the cutting away of boughs and ſuckers at the root and body, doth make trees grow high; and, contrariwiſe, the polling and cutting of the top, make them ſpread and grow *buſhy*. *Bacon's Nat. Hiſtory*, N° 424.

2. Thick like a buſh.

Statues of this god, with a thick *buſhy* beard, are ſtill many of them extant in Rome. *Addiſon on Italy.*

3. Full of buſhes.

The kids with pleaſure browſe the *buſhy* plain;
The ſhow'rs are grateful to the ſwelling grain. *Dryden.*

Bu'siless. *adj.* [from *buſy*.] At leiſure; without buſineſs; unemployed.

Theſe ſweet thoughts do even refreſh my labour,
Moſt *buſileſs* when I do it. *Shakeſp.*

Bu'sily. *adv.* [from *buſy*.] With an air of importance; with an air of hurry; actively; importunately.

Or if too *buſily* they will enquire
Into a victory, which we diſdain,
Then let them know, the Belgians did retire,
Before the patron ſaint of injur'd Spain. *Dryden.*

Bu'siness. *n. ſ.* [from *buſy*.]

1. Employment; multiplicity of affairs.

Muſt *buſineſs* thee from hence remove?
Oh! that's the worſt diſeaſe of love. *Donne.*

2. An affair. In this ſenſe it has the *plural.*

Beſtow
Your needful counſel to our *buſineſſes*,
Which crave the inſtant uſe. *Shakeſp. King Lear.*

3. The ſubject of buſineſs; the affair or object that engages the care.

You are ſo much the *buſineſs* of our ſouls, that while you are in ſight, we can neither look nor think on any elſe; there are no eyes for other beauties. *Dryden.*

The great *buſineſs* of the ſenſes, being to take notice of what hurts or advantages the body. *Locke.*

4. Serious engagement, in oppoſition to trivial tranſactions.

I never knew one, who made it his *buſineſs* to laſh the faults of other writers, that was not guilty of greater himſelf. *Addiſ.*

He had *buſineſs* enough upon his hands, and was only a poet by accident. *Prior's Preface.*

When diverſion is made the *buſineſs* and ſtudy of life, though the actions choſen be in themſelves innocent, the exceſs will render them criminal. *Rogers.*

5. Right of action.

What *buſineſs* has a tortoiſe among the clouds? *L'Eſtrange.*

6. A point; a matter of queſtion; ſomething to be examined or conſidered.

Fitneſs to govern, is a perplexed *buſineſs*; ſome men, ſome nations, excel in the one ability, ſome in the other. *Bacon.*

7. Something to be tranſacted.

They were far from the Zidonians, and had no *buſineſs* with any one. *Judges*, xviii. 7.

8. Something required to be done.

To thoſe people that dwell under or near the equator, this ſpring would be moſt peſtilent; as for thoſe countries that are nearer the poles, in which number are our own, and the moſt conſiderable nations of the world, a perpetual ſpring will not do their *buſineſs*; they muſt have longer days, a nearer approach of the ſun. *Bentley.*

9. *To do one's buſineſs.* To kill, deſtroy, or ruin him.

Busk. *n. ſ.* [*buſque*, Fr.] A piece of ſteel or whalebone, worn by women to ſtrengthen their ſtays.

Off with that happy *buſk*, which I envy,
That ſtill can be, and ſtill can ſtand ſo nigh. *Donne.*

Bu'skin. *n. ſ.* [*broſeken*, Dutch.]

1. A kind of half boot; a ſhoe which comes to the midleg.

The foot was dreſſed in a ſhort pair of crimſon velvet *buſkins*; in ſome places open, to ſhew the fairneſs of the ſkin. *Sidney.*

Sometimes Diana he her takes to be,
But miſſeth bow, and ſhafts, and *buskins* to her knee.
*Spenſer's Fairy Queen, b.* i. *cant.* vi. *ſtanz.* 16.

There is a kind of ruſticity in all thoſe pompous verſes; ſomewhat of a holiday ſhepherd ſtrutting in his country *buſkins*. *Dryden.*

2. A kind of high ſhoe wore by the ancient actors of tragedy, to raiſe their ſtature.

Great Fletcher never treads in *buskins* here,
Nor greater Johnſon dares in ſocks appear. *Dryden.*
In her beſt light the comick Muſe appears,
When ſhe, with borrow'd pride the *buskin* wears. *Smith.*

Bu'skined. *adj.* [from *buskin*.] Dreſſed in buſkins.

Or what, though rare, of later age,
Ennobl'd hath the *buskin'd* ſtage? *Milton.*
Here, arm'd with ſilver bows, in early dawn,
Her *buskin'd* virgins trac'd the dewy lawn. *Pope.*

Bu'sky. *adj.* [written more properly by *Milton*, *bosky*. See Bosky.] Woody; ſhaded with woods; overgrown with trees.

How bloodily the ſun begins to peer
Above yon *busky* hill! *Shakeſp. Henry* IV. *p.* i.

BUSS. *n. ſ.* [*bus*, the mouth, Iriſh; *baiſer*, Fr.]

1. A kiſs; a ſalute with the lips.

Thou doſt give me flattering *buſſes*.—By my troth, I kiſs thee with a moſt conſtant heart. *Shakeſp. Henry* IV. *p.* ii.

Some ſquire perhaps you take delight to rack,
Who viſits with a gun, preſents with birds,
Then gives a ſmacking *buſs*. *Pope.*

2. A boat for fiſhing. [*buſſe*, German.]

If the king would enter towards building ſuch a number of boats and *buſſes*, as each company could eaſily manage, it would be an encouragement both of honour and advantage. *Temple.*

To Buss. *v. a.* [from the noun.] To kiſs; to ſalute with the lips.

Yonder walls, that partly front your town,
Yond towers, whoſe wanton tops do *buſs* the clouds,
Muſt kiſs their feet. *Shakeſp. Troilus and Creſſida.*

Go to them with this bonnet in thy hand,
Thy knee *buſſing* the ſtones; for, in ſuch buſineſs,
Action is eloquence. *Shakeſp. Coriolanus.*

Bust. *n. ſ.* [*buſto*, Ital.] A ſtatue repreſenting a man to his breaſt.

Agrippa, or Caligula, is a common coin, but a very extraordinary *buſt*; and a Tiberius, a rare coin, but a common *buſt*. *Addiſon on Italy.*

Ambition ſigh'd: ſhe found it vain to truſt
The faithleſs column, and the crumbling *buſt*. *Pope.*

Bu'stard. *n. ſ.* [*biſtarde*, Fr.] A wild turkey.

His ſacrifices were phenicopters, peacocks, *buſtards*, turkeys, pheaſants; and all theſe were daily offered. *Hakewell.*

To Bu'stle. *v. n.* [of uncertain etymology; perhaps from *buſy*.] To be buſy; to ſtir; to be active.

Come, *buſtle*, *buſtle*—capariſon my horſe. *Shakeſp. R.* III.

God take king Edward to his mercy,
And leave the world for me to *buſtle* in. *Shakeſp. Rich.* III.

Sir Henry Vane was a buſy and *buſtling* man, who had credit enough to do his buſineſs in all places. *Clarendon, b.* ii.

A poor abject worm,
That crawl'd awhile upon a *buſtling* world,
And now am trampled to my duſt again. *Southerne's Oroonoko.*
Ye ſov'reign lords, who ſit like gods in ſtate,
Awing the world, and *buſtling* to be great! *Granville.*

Bu'stle. *n. ſ.* [from the verb.] A tumult; a hurry; a combuſtion.

Wiſdom's ſelf
Oft ſeeks to ſweet retired ſolitude;
She plumes her feathers, and lets grow her wings,
That, in the various *buſtle* of reſort,
Were all too ruffl'd. *Milton.*

This is the creature that pretends to knowledge, and that makes ſuch a noiſe and *buſtle* for opinions. *Glanville's Sceptis.*

Such a doctrine made a ſtrange *buſtle* and diſturbance in the world, which then ſat warm and eaſy in a free enjoyment of their luſts. *South.*

If the Count had given them a pot of ale after it, all would have been well, without any of this *buſtle*. *Spectator*, N° 481.

Bu'stler. *n. ſ.* [from *buſtle*.] An active ſtirring man.

BU'SY. *adj.* [byrgian, Sax. It is pronounced as *biſſy*.]

1. Employed with earneſtneſs.

My miſtreſs ſends you word, that ſhe is *buſy*, and cannot come. *Shakeſp. Taming the Shr.*

The chriſtians, ſometimes valiantly receiving the enemy, and ſometimes charging them again, repulſed the proud enemy, ſtill *buſy* with them. *Knolles's Hiſtory of the Turks.*

2. Buſtling; active; meddling.

The next thing which ſhe waking looks upon,
On meddling monkey, or on *buſy* ape,
She ſhall purſue it with the ſoul of love. *Shakeſp.*

This *buſy* pow'r is working day and night;
For when the outward ſenſes reſt do take,
A thouſand dreams, fantaſtical and light,
With flutt'ring wings, do keep her ſtill awake. *Davies.*

The coming ſpring would firſt appear,
And all this place with roſes ſtrow,
If *buſy* feet would let them grow. *Waller.*

All written ſince that time, ſeem to have little more than events we are glad to know, or the controverſy of opinions, wherein the *buſy* world has been ſo much employed. *Temple.*

Religious motives and inſtincts are ſo *buſy* in the heart of every reaſonable creature, that no man would hope to govern a ſociety, without regard to thoſe principles. *Addiſon. Freeholder.*

To BU'SY. *v. a.* [from the noun.] To employ; to engage; to make or keep buſy.

He in great paſſion all this while did dwell,
More *buſying* his quick eyes her face to view,
Than his dull ears to hear what ſhe did tell. *Fairy Queen, b.* i.

The pleaſure which I took at my friend's pleaſure herein, idly *buſied* me thus to expreſs the ſame. *Carew's Survey.*

My Harry,
Be it thy courſe to *buſy* giddy minds
With foreign quarrels. *Shakeſp. Henry* IV. *p.* ii.

While they were *buſied* to lay the foundations, their buildings were overthrown by an earthquake, and many thouſands of the Jews were overwhelmed. *Raleigh's Hiſtory.*

The points which *buſied* the devotion of the firſt ages, and the curioſity of the later. *Decay of Piety.*

The ideas it is *buſied* about, ſhould be natural and congenial ones, which it had in itſelf. *Locke.*

The learning and diſputes of the ſchools have been much *buſied* about genus and ſpecies. *Locke.*

For the reſt, it muſt be owned, he does not *buſy* himſelf, by entering deep into any party, but rather ſpends his time in acts of hoſpitality. *Swift.*

BU'SYBODY. *n. ſ.* [from *buſy* and *body.*] A vain, meddling, fantaſtical perſon.

Going from houſe to houſe, tatlers and *buſybodies*, are the canker and ruſt of idleneſs; as idleneſs is the ruſt of time. *Taylor's Holy Living.*

*Buſybodies* and intermeddlers are a dangerous ſort of people to have to do withal. *L'Eſtrange.*

She is well acquainted with all the favourite ſervants, *buſybodies*, dependants, and poor relations of all perſons of condition in the whole town. *Spectator,* Nº 437.

BUT. *conjunct.* [bute, butan, Saxon.]

1. Except.

An emiſſion of immateriate virtues we are a little doubtful to propound, it is ſo prodigious: *but* that it is ſo conſtantly avouched by many. *Bacon.*

Who can it be, ye gods! *but* perjur'd Lycon?
Who can inſpire ſuch ſtorms of rage, *but* Lycon?
Where has my ſword left one ſo black, *but* Lycon?
*Smith's Phædra and Hippolitus.*

Your poem hath been printed, and we have no objection *but* the obſcurity of ſeveral paſſages, by our ignorance in facts and perſons. *Swift.*

2. Yet; nevertheleſs. It ſometimes only enforces *yet.*

Then let him ſpeak, and any that ſhall ſtand without, ſhall hear his voice plainly; *but* yet made extreme ſharp and exile, like the voice of puppets: and yet the articulate ſounds of the words will not be confounded. *Bacon's Nat. Hiſt.* Nº 155.

Our wants are many, and grievous to be born, *but* quite of another kind. *Swift.*

3. The particle which introduces the minor of a ſyllogiſm; now.

If there be a liberty and poſſibility for a man to kill himſelf today, then it is not abſolutely neceſſary that he ſhall live till tomorrow; *but* there is ſuch a liberty, therefore no ſuch neceſſity. *Bramhall againſt Hobbes.*

God will one time or another make a difference between the good and the evil. *But* there is little or no difference made in this world: therefore there muſt be another world, wherein this difference ſhall be made. *Watts's Logick, Introduct.*

4. Only; nothing more than.

If my offence be of mortal kind,
That not my ſervice, paſt or preſent ſorrows,
Can ranſom me into his love again;
*But* to know ſo, muſt be my benefit. *Shakeſp. Othello.*

And *but* infirmity,
Which waits upon worn times, hath ſomething ſeiz'd
His wiſh'd ability, he had himſelf
The lands and waters meaſur'd. *Shakeſp. Winter's Tale.*

What nymph ſoe'er his voice *but* hears,
Will be my rival, though ſhe have *but* ears. *Ben. Johnſon.*

No, Aurengzebe, you merit all my heart,
And I'm too noble *but* to give a part. *Dryden.*

Did *but* men conſider the true notion of God, he would appear to be full of goodneſs. *Tillotſon.*

If we do *but* put virtue and vice in equal circumſtances, the advantages of eaſe and pleaſure will be found to be on the ſide of religion. *Tillotſon.*

The miſchiefs or harms that come by play, inadvertency, or ignorance, are not at all, or *but* very gently, to be taken notice of. *Locke on Education.*

If a reader examines Horace's art of poetry, he will find *but* very few precepts in it, which he may not meet with in Ariſtotle. *Addiſon. Spectator.*

Prepar'd I ſtand: he was *but* born to try
The lot of man, to ſuffer and to die. *Pope's Odyſſey.*

5. Than.

The full moon was no ſooner up, and ſhining in all its brightneſs, *but* he privately opened the gate of paradiſe. *Guardian,* Nº 167.

6. But that; without this conſequence that.

Froſts that conſtrain the ground,
Do ſeldom their uſurping power withdraw,
*But* raging floods purſue their haſty hand. *Dryden.*

7. Otherwiſe than that.

It cannot be *but* nature hath ſome director, of infinite power, to guide her in all her ways. *Hooker, b.* i. § 3.

Who ſhall believe,
*But* you miſuſe the reverence of your place? *Shakeſp.*

8. Not otherwiſe than.

A genius ſo elevated and unconfined as Mr. Cowley's, was *but* neceſſary to make Pindar ſpeak Engliſh. *Dryden.*

9. By any other means than.

Out of that will I cauſe thoſe of Cyprus to mutiny: whoſe qualification ſhall come into no true taſte again, *but* by tranſplanting of Caſſio. *Shakeſp. Othello.*

10. If it were not for this; if this were not.

Believe me, I had rather have loſt my purſe
Full of cruzades. And *but* my noble Moor
Is true of mind, and made of no ſuch baſeneſs,
As jealous creatures are, it were enough
To put him to ill-thinking. *Shakeſp. Othello.*

I here do give thee that with all my heart,
Which, *but* thou haſt already, with all my heart
I would keep from thee. *Shakeſp. Othello.*

11. However; howbeit.

I do not doubt but I have been to blame;
*But*, to purſue the end for which I came,
Unite your ſubjects firſt, then let us go,
And pour their common rage upon the foe. *Dryden.*

12. It is uſed after *no doubt*, *no queſtion*, and ſuch words, and ſignifies the ſame with *that*. It ſometimes is joined with *that*.

They made no account, *but that* the navy ſhould be abſolutely maſter of the ſeas. *Bacon's War with Spain.*

I fancied to myſelf a kind of eaſe in the change of the paroxyſm; never ſuſpecting *but that* the humour would have waſted itſelf. *Dryden.*

There is no queſtion *but* the king of Spain will reform moſt of the abuſes. *Addiſon on Italy.*

13. That. This ſeems no proper ſenſe in this place.

It is not therefore impoſſible, *but* I may alter the complexion of my play, to reſtore myſelf into the good graces of my fair critics. *Dryden's Aurengzebe, Preface.*

14. Otherwiſe than.

I ſhould ſin
To think *but* nobly of my grandmother. *Shakeſp. Tempeſt.*

15. Even; not longer ago than.

Beroe *but* now I left; whom, pin'd with pain,
Her age and anguiſh from theſe rites detain. *Dryden.*

It is evident, in the inſtance I gave *but* now, the conſciouſneſs went along. *Locke.*

16. A particle by which the meaning of the foregoing ſentence is bounded or reſtrained.

Thus fights Ulyſſes, thus his fame extends,
A formidable man, *but* to his friends. *Dryden.*

17. An objective particle; yet it may be objected.

*But* yet, madam——
I do not like *but* yet; it does allay
The good precedence; fie upon *but* yet!
*But* yet is as a jaylour, to bring forth
Some monſtrous malefactor. *Shakeſp. Antony and Cleopatra.*

Muſt the heart then have been formed and conſtituted, before the blood was in being? *But* here again, the ſubſtance of the heart itſelf is moſt certainly made and nouriſhed by the blood, which is conveyed to it by the coronary arteries. *Bentl.*

18. But for; without; had not this been.

Raſh man! forbear, *but* for ſome unbelief,
My joy had been as fatal as my grief. *Waller.*

Her head was bare,
*But* for her native ornament of hair,
Which in a ſimple knot was ty'd above. *Dryden's Fables.*

When the fair boy receiv'd the gift of right,
And, *but* for miſchief, you had dy'd for ſpight. *Dryden.*

BUT. *n. ſ.* [*bout*, French.] A boundary.

*But*, if I aſk you what I mean by that word, you will anſwer, I mean this or that thing, you cannot tell which; but if I join it with the words in conſtruction and ſenſe, as, but I will not, a

2, To push, to run against with any thing flat

, It, join but with the words in construction and, sense, as but I will not, a but of wine, the ram will but, shoot at but; the meaning of it will be ready to you  Holder Sp.

But a certain Measure containing Liquor
When the Butt is out we will drink water
, See also Holder under But, boundary

, Fortunes displeasure is but, Sluttish, if it
, smell so strongly as thou speakst of, I will
hence forth eat no fish of Fortunes buttering

, Shak

Any thing that Strikes in to another abuts or is
is directed in Some kind of Angle into it

The fen and quamire so marish by kind
And are to be drained
Which yearly undrained & Suffred uncut
Annoieth the Meadows that thereon do butt

Tuss. Husb. for May.

Fortunes displeasure is but Sluttish, if it
Smell So Strongly as thou speakst of: I will
henceforth eat no fish of fortunes buttering

Shak.



Prisage now called butlerage is a Custom
whereby the Prince challenges out of every
Bark loaden with wine containing less than
forty tuns two tons of Wine at his price

Cowel

a but of wine, *but* and boundary, the ram will but, shoot at but, the meaning of it will be as ready to you as any other word. *Holder's Elements of Speech.*

BUT. *n. s.* [In sea language.] The end of any plank which joins to another on the outside of a ship, under water. *Harris.*

BUT-END. *n. s.* [from *but* and *end.*] The blunt end of any thing; the end upon which it rests.

The reserve of foot galled their foot with several vollies, and then fell on them with the *but-ends* of their muskets. *Clarendon.*

Thy weapon was a good one when I wielded it, but the *but-end* remains in my hands. *Arbuthnot's John Bull.*

Some of the soldiers accordingly pushed them forwards with the *but-ends* of their pikes, into my reach. *Gulliver's Travels.*

BU'TCHER. *n. s.* [*boucher*, Fr.]

1. One that kills animals to sell their flesh.

The shepherd and the *butcher* both may look upon one sheep with pleasing conceits. *Sidney.*

Hence he learnt the *butcher's* guile,
How to cut your throat, and smile;
Like a *butcher* doom'd for life,
In his mouth to wear his knife. *Swift.*

2. One that is delighted with blood.

Honour and renown are bestowed on conquerours, who, for the most part, are but the great *butchers* of mankind. *Locke.*

To BU'TCHER. *v. a.* [from the noun.] To kill; to murder.

In suff'ring thus thy brother to be slaughter'd,
Thou shewest the naked pathway to thy life,
Teaching stern murder how to *butcher* thee. *Shakesp. R.* II.

Uncharitably with me have you dealt,
And shamefully by you my hopes are *butcher'd.* *Shakesp.*

The poison and the dagger are at hand to *butcher* a hero, when the poet wants brains to save him. *Dryden's Don Sebast.*

BUTCHERS-BROOM, or Kneeholly. *n. s.* [*ruscus*, Lat.] The flower-cup consists of one leaf, cut into several divisions, out of which is produced a globular bell-shaped flower, consisting also of one leaf, in the center of which rises the pointal, which afterwards becomes a soft roundish fruit, in which are inclosed one or two hard seeds. It is very common in the woods, in divers parts of England, and is rarely cultivated in gardens. The roots are sometimes used in medicine, and the green shoots are cut and bound into bundles, and sold to the butchers, who use it as besoms to sweep their blocks; from whence it had the name of butchers broom.

BU'TCHERLINESS. *n. s.* [from *butcherly.*] In a butcherly manner.

BU'TCHERLY. *adj.* [from *butcher.*] Cruel; bloody; barbarous.

There is a way, which, brought into schools, would take away this *butcherly* fear in making of Latin. *Ascham's Schoolm.*

What stratagems, how fell, how *butcherly*,
This deadly quarrel daily doth beget! *Shakesp. Henry* VI.

BU'TCHERY. *n. s.* [from *butcher.*]

1. The trade of a butcher.

Yet this man, so ignorant in modern *butchery*, has cut up half an hundred heroes, and quartered five or six miserable lovers, in every tragedy he has written. *Pope.*

2. Murder; cruelty; slaughter.

If thou delight to view thy heinous deeds,
Behold this pattern of thy *butcheries.* *Shakesp. Rich.* III.

The *butchery*, and the breach of hospitality, is represented in this fable under the mask of friendship. *L'Estrange.*

Can he a son to soft remorse incite,
Whom goals, and blood, and *butchery* delight? *Dryden.*

3. The place where blood is shed.

This is no place, this house is but a *butchery*;
Abhor it, fear it, do not enter it. *Shakesp. As you like it.*

BU'TLER. *n. s.* [*bouteiller*, Fr. *boteler*, or *botiller*, old English, from *bottle*; he that is employed in the care of bottling liquours.] A servant in a family employed in furnishing the table.

*Butlers* forget to bring up their beer time enough. *Swift.*

BU'TLERAGE. *n. s.* [from *butler.*] The duty upon wines imported, claimed by the king's butler.

Those ordinary finances are casual or uncertain, as be the escheats, the customs, *butlerage*, and impost. *Bacon.*

BU'TLERSHIP. *n. s.* [from *butler.*] The office of a butler.

BU'TMENT. *n. s.* [*aboutement*, Fr.] That part of the arch which joins it to the upright pier.

The supporters or *butments* of the said arch cannot suffer so much violence, as in the precedent flat posture. *Wotton.*

BUTT. *n. s.* [*but*, Fr.]

1. The place on which the mark to be shot at is placed.

He calls on Bacchus, and propounds the prize;
The groom his fellow groom at *butts* defies,
And bends his bow, and levels with his eyes. *Dryd.*

2. The point at which the endeavour is directed.

Be not afraid though you do see me weapon'd;
Here is my journey's end; here is my *butt*,
The very sea-mark of my journey's end. *Shakesp. Othello.*

3. The object of aim; the thing against which any attack is directed.

The papists were the most common-place, and the *butt* against whom all the arrows were directed. *Clarendon.*

4. A man upon whom the company break their jests.

I played a sentence or two at my *butt*, which I thought very smart, when my ill genius suggested to him such a reply as got all the laughter on his side. *Spectator*, Nº 175.

5. A stroke given in fencing.

If disputes arise
Among the champions for the prize;
To prove who gave the fairer *butt*,
John shews the chalk on Robert's coat. *Prior.*

BUTT. *n. s.* [butt, Saxon.] A vessel; a barrel containing one hundred and twenty six gallons of wine; a butt contains one hundred and eight gallons of beer; and from fifteen to twenty two hundred weight, is a butt of currans.

I escaped upon a *butt* of sack, which the sailors heaved overboard. *Shakesp. Tempest.*

To BUTT. *v. a.* [*botten*, Dutch.] To strike with the head.

Come, leave your tears: a brief farewel: the beast
With many heads *butts* me away. *Shakesp. Coriolanus.*

Nor wars are seen,
Unless, upon the green,
Two harmless lambs are *butting* one the other. *Wotton.*

A snow-white steer, before thy altar led,
*Butts* with his threat'ning brows, and bellowing stands. *Dryden's Æneid.*

A ram will *butt* with his head, though he be brought up tame, and never saw that manner of fighting. *Ray on the Cr.*

BU'TTER. *n. s.* [butteɲe, Sax. *butyrum*, Lat.]

1. An unctuous substance made by agitating the cream of milk, till the oil separates from the whey.

And he took *butter* and milk, and the calf which he had dressed, and set before them. *Gen.* xviii. 8.

2. *Butter of antimony.* A chymical preparation, made by uniting the acid spirits of sublimate corrosive with regulus of antimony. It is a great caustick. *Harris.*

3. *Butter of tin*, is made with tin and sublimate corrosive. This preparation continually emits fumes. *Harris.*

To BU'TTER. *v. a.* [from the noun.]

1. To smear, or oil with butter.

'Twas her brother, that, in pure kindness to his horse, *buttered* his hay. *Shakesp. King Lear.*

Words *butter* no parsnips. *L'Estrange.*

2. To encrease the stakes every throw, or every game: a cant term among gamesters.

It is a fine simile in one of Mr. Congreve's prologues, which compares a writer to a *buttering* gamester, that stakes all his winning upon one cast; so that if he loses the last throw, he is sure to be undone. *Addison. Freeholder*, Nº 40.

BU'TTERBUMP. *n. s.* A fowl; the same with *bittourn.*

BU'TTERBUR. *n. s.* [*petasites*, Lat.]

It is a plant with a flosculous flower, consisting of many florets, divided into many parts, sitting on the embryo, and continued in a cylindrical empalement, divided also into many parts; the embryo becomes afterwards a seed furnished with down, and the flowers appear before the leaves. It is used in medicine, and grows wild in great plenty by the sides of ditches. *Millar.*

BU'TTERFLOWER. *n. s.* A yellow flower, with which the fields abound in the month of May.

Let weeds, instead of *butterflow'rs*, appear,
And meads, instead of daisies, hemlock bear. *Gay.*

BU'TTERFLY. *n. s.* [buttepflege, Saxon.] A beautiful insect, so named because it first appears at the beginning of the season for butter.

Eftsoons that damsel, by her heav'nly might,
She turned into a winged *butterfly*,
In the wide air to make her wand'ring flight. *Spenser.*

Tell old tales, and laugh
At gilded *butterflies*; and hear poor rogues
Talk of court news. *Shakesp. King Lear.*

And so befel, that as he cast his eye
Among the colworts on a *butterfly*,
He saw false Reynard. *Dryden's Fables.*

That which seems to be a powder upon the wings of a *butterfly*, is an innumerable company of extreme small feathers, not to be discerned without a microscope. *Grew.*

BU'TTERIS. *n. s.* An instrument of steel set in a wooden handle, used in paring the foot, or cutting the hoof of a horse. *Farr. D.*

BU'TTERMILK. *n. s.* [from *butter* and *milk.*] The whey that is separated from the cream when butter is made.

A young man, who was fallen into an ulcerous consumption, devoted himself to *buttermilk*, by which sole diet he recovered. *Harvey on Consumptions.*

The scurvy of mariners is cured by acids; as ripe fruits, lemons, oranges, *buttermilk*; and alkaline spirits hurt them. *Arbuthnot on Diet.*

BU'TTERPRINT. *n. s.* [from *butter* and *print.*] A piece of carved wood, used to mark butter.

A *butterprint*, in which were engraven figures of all sorts and sizes, applied to the lump of butter, left on it the figure. *Locke.*

BU'TTERTOOTH. *n. s.* [from *butter* and *tooth.*] The great broad foreteeth.

BU'TTERWOMAN. *n. s.* [from *butter* and *woman.*] A woman that sells butter.

Tongue,

Tongue, I muſt put you into a *butterwoman's* mouth, and buy myſelf another of Bajazet's mute, if you prattle me into theſe perils. *Shakeſp. All's well that ends well.*

BU'TTERWORT. *n. ſ.* A plant; the ſame with *ſanicle.*

BU'TTERY. *adj.* [from *butter.*] Having the appearance or qualities of butter.

Nothing more convertible into hot cholerick humours, than its *buttery* parts. *Harvey on Conſumptions.*

The beſt oils, thickened by cold, have a white colour; and milk itſelf has its whiteneſs from the caſeous fibres, and its *buttery* oil. *Floyer on the Humours.*

BU'TTERY. *n. ſ.* [from *butter*; or, according to *Skinner,* from *bouter,* Fr. to place or lay up.] The room where proviſions are laid up.

Go, ſirrah, take them to the *buttery,*
And give them friendly welcome every one. *Shakeſp.*

All that need a cool and freſh temper, as cellars, pantries, and *butteries,* to the north. *Wotton.*

My guts ne'er ſuffer'd from a college-cook,
My name ne'er enter'd in a *buttery* book.
*Brampſton's Man of Taſte.*

BU'TTOCK. *n. ſ.* [ſuppoſed, by *Skinner,* to come from *aboutir,* Fr. inſerted by *Junius* without etymology.] The rump; the part near the tail.

It is like a barber's chair that fits all the *buttocks.* *Shakeſp.*

Such as were not able to ſtay themſelves, ſhould be holden up by others of more ſtrength, riding behind them upon the *buttocks* of the horſe. *Knolles's Hiſtory of the Turks.*

The tail of a fox was never made for the *buttocks* of an ape.
*L'Eſtrange's Fables.*

BU'TTON. *n. ſ.* [*bottwn,* Welch; *bouton,* Fr.]

1. A catch, or ſmall ball, by which the dreſs of man is faſtened.

Pray you, undo this *button.* *Shakeſp. King Lear.*

I mention thoſe ornaments, becauſe of the ſimplicity of the ſhape, want of ornaments, *buttons,* loops, gold and ſilver lace, they muſt have been cheaper than ours. *Arbuthnot on Coins.*

2. Any knob or ball faſtened to a ſmaller body.

We faſtened to the upper marble certain wires, and a *button.* *Boyle.*

Fair from its humble bed I rear'd this flow'r,
Suckled and chear'd, with air, and ſun and ſhow'r;
Soft on the paper ruff its leaves I ſpread,
Bright with the gilded *button* tipt its head. *Pope's Dunciad.*

3. The bud of a plant.

The canker galls the infants of the ſpring,
Too oft before their *buttons* be diſclos'd. *Shakeſp. Hamlet.*

BU'TTON. *n. ſ.* The ſea urchin, which is a kind of crabfiſh that has prickles inſtead of feet. *Ainſworth.*

To BU'TTON. *v. a.* [from the noun.]

1. To dreſs; to cloath.

One whoſe hard heart is *button'd* up with ſteel. *Shakeſp.*

He gave his legs, arm, and breaſt, to his ordinary ſervant, to *button* and dreſs him. *Wotton.*

2. To faſten with buttons.

BU'TTONHOLE. *n. ſ.* [from *button* and *hole.*] The loop in which the button of the cloaths is caught.

Let me take you a *buttonhole* lower. *Shakeſp. Love's Lab. L.*

I'll pleaſe the maids of honour, if I can:
Without black velvet breeches, what is man?
I will my ſkill in *buttonholes* diſplay,
And brag, how oft I ſhift me ev'ry day. *Bramſt. M. of Taſte.*

BU'TTRESS. *n. ſ.* [from *aboutir,* Fr.]

1. A prop; a wall built to ſupport another wall.

No jutting frize,
*Buttreſs,* nor coigne of vantage, but this bird,
Hath made his pendant bed, and procreant cradle. *Shakeſp.*

Fruit trees, ſet upon a wall againſt the ſun, between elbows or *buttreſſes* of ſtone, ripen more than upon a plain wall. *Bacon.*

But we inhabit a weak city here,
Which *buttreſſes* and props but ſcarcely bear. *Dryden's Juv.*

2. A prop; a ſupport.

It will concern us to examine the force of this plea, which our adverſaries are ſtill ſetting up againſt us, as the ground pillar and *buttreſs* of the good old cauſe of nonconformity. *South.*

To BU'TTRESS. *v. a.* [from the noun.] To prop; to ſupport.

BU'TWINK. *n. ſ.* The name of a bird. *Dict.*

BUTYRA'CEOUS. *adj.* [*butyrum,* Lat. butter.] Having the qualities of butter.

Chyle has the ſame principles as milk; a viſcidity from the caſeous parts, and an oilineſs from the *butyraceous* parts.
*Floyer on the Humours.*

BU'TYROUS. *adj.* [*butyrum,* Lat.] Having the properties of butter.

Its oily red part is from the *butyrous* parts of chyle. *Floyer.*

BU'XOM. *adj.* [bucſum, Sax. from bugan, to bend. It originally ſignified *obedient,* as *John de Trevisa,* a clergyman, tells his patron, that he is *obedient and* buxom *to all his commands.* In an old form of marriage uſed before the Reformation, the bride promiſed to be *obedient and* buxom *in bed and at board*; from which expreſſion, not well underſtood, its preſent meaning ſeems to be derived.]

1. Obedient; obſequious.

He did tread down, and diſgrace all the Engliſh, and ſet up and countenance the Iriſh; thinking thereby to make them more tractable and *buxom* to his government. *Spenſer's Ireland.*

He, with broad ſails,
Winnow'd the *buxom* air. *Milton.*

2. Gay; lively; briſk.

I'm born
Again a freſh child of the *buxom* morn,
Heir of the ſun's firſt beams. *Craſhaw.*

Zephyr, with Aurora playing,
As he met her once a maying,
Fill'd her with thee, a daughter fair,
So *buxom,* blithe, and debonnair. *Milton.*

Sturdy ſwains,
In clean array, for ruſtick dance prepare,
Mixt with the *buxom* damſels, hand in hand,
They friſk and bound. *Philips.*

3. Wanton; jolly.

Almighty Jove deſcends, and pours
Into his *buxom* bride his fruitful ſhow'rs. *Dryden's Virgil.*

She feign'd the rites of Bacchus! cry'd aloud,
And to the *buxom* god the virgin vow'd. *Dryden's Æneid.*

BU'XOMLY. *adv.* [from *buxom.*] Wantonly; amorouſly.

BU'XOMNESS. *n. ſ.* [from *buxom.*] Wantonneſs; amorouſneſs.

To BUY. *v. a.* preter. I *bought*; I have *bought.* [bicgean, Sax.]

1. To purchaſe; to acquire by paying a price; to obtain for money, or ſomething equivalent; to gain by ſale, not gift or theft.

They muſt *buy* up no corn growing within twelve miles of Geneva, that ſo the filling of their magazines may not prejudice their market. *Addiſon on Italy.*

2. To procure ſome advantage by ſomething that deſerves it, or at ſome price.

I have *bought*
Golden opinions from all ſorts of people. *Shakeſp. Macbeth.*

Pent to linger
But with a grain a day, I would not *buy*
Their mercy at the price of one fair word. *Shakeſp. Coriol.*

Pleaſure with praiſe, and danger they would *buy,*
And with a foe that would not only fly. *Denham.*

3. To manage by money.

You, and all the kings of chriſtendom,
Are led ſo groſsly by this meddling prieſt,
Dreading the curſe that money may *buy* out. *Shakeſp. K. J.*

What pitiful things are power, rhetorick, or riches, when they would terrify, diſſuade, or *buy* off conſcience? *South.*

To BUY. *v. n.* To treat about a purchaſe.

I will *buy* with you, ſell with you, talk with you, walk with you, and ſo following. *Shakeſp. Merchant of Venice.*

BU'YER. *n. ſ.* [from *to buy.*] He that buys; a purchaſer.

When a piece of art is ſet before us, let the firſt caution be, not to aſk who made it, leſt the fame of the authour do captivate the fancy of the *buyer.* *Wotton's Architecture.*

To BUZZ. *v. n.* [*bizzen,* Teut. to growl. *Junius.*]

1. To hum; to make a noiſe like bees, flies, or waſps.

And all the chamber filled was with flies,
Which *buzzed* all about, and made ſuch ſound,
That they encumber'd all men's ears and eyes,
Like many ſwarms of bees aſſembled round. *Fairy Q. b.* ii.

There be more waſps, that *buzz* about his noſe,
Will make this ſting the ſooner. *Shakeſp. Henry* VIII.

Herewith aroſe a *buzzing* noiſe among them, as if it had been the ruſtling ſound of the ſea afar off. *Hayward.*

For ſtill the flowers ready ſtand,
One *buzzes* round about,
One lights, one taſtes, gets in, gets out. *Suckling.*

What though no bees around your cradle flew,
Nor on your lips diſtill'd their golden dew;
Yet have we oft' diſcover'd, in their ſtead,
A ſwarm of drones that *buzz'd* about your head. *Pope.*

We join, like flies and waſps, in *buzzing* about wit. *Swift.*

2. To whiſper; to prate.

There is ſuch confuſion in my pow'rs,
As after ſome oration fairly ſpoke
By a beloved prince, there doth appear
Among the *buzzing* multitude. *Shakeſp. Merch. of Venice.*

To BUZZ. *v. a.* To whiſper; to ſpread ſecretly.

Where doth the world thruſt forth a vanity,
That is not quickly *buzz'd* into his ears? *Shakeſp. Rich.* II.

I will *buzz* abroad ſuch prophecies,
That Edward ſhall be fearful of his life. *Shakeſp. Hen.* VI.

Did you not hear
A *buzzing* of a ſeparation
Between the king and Catherine? *Shakeſp. Henry* VIII.

They might *buzz* and whiſper it one to another, and, tacitely withdrawing from the preſence of the apoſtles, they then lift their voices, and noiſe it about the city. *Bentley.*

BUZZ. *n. ſ.* [from the verb.] A hum; a whiſper; a talk.

The hive of a city or kingdom, is in beſt condition, when there is leaſt noiſe or *buzz* in it. *Bacon's Apophthegms.*

Where I found the whole outward room in a *buzz* of politicks. *Addiſon. Spectator,* Nº 403.

c ✝
When ~~the~~ the world was buxome fresh & Young
Her Sons were undebauch'd & therefore Strong
Dryd. Juv.

, To procure

his possessions
Altho' by confiscation they are ours
We do instate & widow you with all
To buy you a better husband
, Shak: M. M.

To buy of
And, I bought the field of Hanameel
Jer. 32.9

6 ✝
Buttrice is A kind of cutting instrument with which the hoofs of horses are pared
, A buttrice & pincers, & hammer & nail
Tuss. husb.

blank page

IL facing 3U[r]

B Y

BU'ZZARD. *n. s.* [*busard*, Fr.]

1. A degenerate or mean species of hawk.

More pity that the eagle should be maul'd,
While kites and *buzzards* prey at liberty. *Shakesp. R.* III.

The noble *buzzard* ever pleas'd me best;
Of small renown, 'tis true: for, not to lie,
We call him but a hawk by courtesy. *Dryden's Hind and P.*

2. A blockhead; a dunce.

Those blind *buzzards*, who, in late years, of wilful maliciousness, would neither learn themselves, nor could teach others any thing at all. *Ascham's Schoolmaster.*

BU'ZZER. *n. s.* [from *buzz*.] A secret whisperer.

Her brother is in secret come from France,
And wants not *buzzers* to infect his ear
With pestilent speeches of his father's death. *Shak. Hamlet.*

BY. *prep.* [bi, biᵹ, Saxon.]

1. It notes the agent.

The Moor is with child *by* you, Launcelot. *Shak. Hen.* VI.

The grammar of a language is sometimes to be carefully studied *by* a grown man. *Locke.*

2. It notes the instrument, and is always used after a verb neuter, where *with* would be put after an active; as, he was killed *with* a sword; he died *by* a sword.

But *by* Pelides' arms when Hector fell,
He chose Æneas, and he chose as well. *Dryden, Æn.* vi.

3. It notes the cause of any event.

This fight had the more weight with him, as *by* good luck not above two of that venerable body were fallen asleep. *Addison, Freeholder.*

4. It notes the means by which any thing is performed.

You must think, if we give you any thing, we hope to gain *by* you. *Shakesp. Coriolanus.*

Happier! had it suffic'd him to have known
Good *by* itself, and evil not at all. *Parad. Lost, b.* xi. *l.* 89.

The heart knows that *by* itself, which nothing in the world besides can give it any knowledge of. *South.*

We obtain the knowledge of a multitude of propositions *by* sensation and reflection. *Watts's Logick.*

5. It shews the manner of an action.

I have not patience; she consumes the time
In idle talk, and owns her false belief:
Seize her *by* force, and bear her hence unheard. *Dryden's Don Sebastian.*

*By* chance, within a neighbouring brook,
He saw his branching horns, and alter'd look. *Addison.*

6. It has a signification, noting the method in which any successive action is performed, with regard to time or quantity.

The best for you, is to re-examine the cause, and to try it even point *by* point, argument *by* argument, with all the exactness you can. *Hooker, Preface.*

We are not to stay all together, but to come by him where he stands, *by* ones, *by* twos, and *by* threes. *Shakesp. Coriolanus.*

He calleth them forth *by* one, and *by* one, by the name, as he pleaseth, though seldom the order be inverted. *Bacon.*

The captains were obliged to break that piece of ordnance, and so *by* pieces to carry it away, that the enemy should not get so great a spoil. *Knolles's History of the Turks.*

Common prudence would direct me to take them all out, and examine them one *by* one. *Boyle.*

Others will soon take pattern and encouragement by your building; and so house *by* house, street *by* street, there will at last be finished a magnificent city. *Sprat.*

Explor'd her, limb *by* limb, and fear'd to find
So rude a gripe had left a livid mark behind. *Dryden's Fab.*

Thus year *by* year they pass, and day *by* day,
Till once, 'twas on the morn of chearful May,
The young Æmilia——— *Dryden's Fab.*

I'll gaze for ever on thy god like father,
Transplanting one *by* one into my life,
His bright perfections, till I shine like him. *Addison's Cato.*

Let the blows be *by* pauses laid on. *Locke.*

7. It notes the quantity had at one time.

Bullion will sell *by* the ounce for six shillings and fivepence unclipped money. *Locke.*

What we take daily *by* pounds, is at least of as much importance as of what we take seldom, and only *by* grains and spoonfuls. *Arbuthnot on Aliments, Preface.*

The North, *by* myriads, pours her mighty sons;
Great nurse of Goths, of Alans, and of Huns. *Pope.*

8. At, or in; noting place.

We see the great effects of battles *by* sea; the battle of Actium decided the empire of the world. *Bacon's Essays.*

Arms, and the man, I sing, who, forc'd *by* fate,
Expell'd, and exil'd, left the Trojan shore;
Long labours both *by* sea and land he bore. *Dryden's Æn.*

I would have fought *by* land, where I was stronger:
You hinder'd it; yet, when I fought at sea,
Forsook me fighting. *Dryden's All for Love.*

9. According to; noting permission.

It is lawful, both *by* the laws of nature and nations, and *by* the law divine, which is the perfection of the other two. *Bacon's Holy War.*

10. According to; noting proof.

The present, or like, system of the world cannot possibly have been eternal, *by* the first proposition; and, without God, it could not naturally, nor fortuitously, emerge out of a chaos, *by* the third proposition. *Bentley.*

The faculty, or desire, being infinite, *by* the preceding proposition, may contain, or receive both these. *Cheyne.*

11. After; according to; noting imitation or conformity.

The gospel gives us such laws, as every man, that understands himself, would chuse to live *by*. *Tillotson.*

In the divisions I have made, I have endeavoured, the best I could, to govern myself *by* the diversity of matter. *Locke.*

This ship, by good luck, fell into their hands at last, and served as a model to build others *by*. *Arbuthnot on Coins.*

12. From; noting judgment or token.

Thus, *by* the musick, we may know,
When noble wits a hunting go,
Through groves that on Parnassus grow. *Waller.*

*By* what he has done, before the war in which he was engaged, we may expect what he will do after a peace. *Dryden.*

The son of Hercules he justly seems,
*By* his broad shoulders and gigantick limbs. *Dryden.*

Who's that stranger? *By* his warlike port,
His fierce demeanour, and erected look,
He's of no vulgar note. *Dryden's All for Love.*

Judge the event
*By* what has pass'd. *Dryden's Spanish Friar.*

The punishment is not to be measured *by* the greatness or smallness of the matter, but *by* the opposition it carries, and stands in, to that respect and submission that is due to the father. *Locke*

*By* your description of the town, I imagine it to lie under some great enchantment. *Pope's Letters.*

*By* what I have always heard and read, I take the strength of a nation— *Swift.*

13. It notes the sum of the difference between two things compared.

Meantime she stands provided of a Laius,
More young and vigorous too *by* twenty springs. *Dryden.*

Her brother Rivers,
Ere this, lies shorter *by* the head at Pomfret. *Rowe's Jane Shore.*

By giving the denomination to less quantities of silver *by* one twentieth, you take from them their due. *Locke.*

14. It notes co-operation, or cohabitation.

*By* her he had two children at one birth. *Shakesp. Hen.* VI.

15. For; noting continuance of time. This sense is not now in use.

Ferdinand and Isabella recovered the kingdom of Granada from the Moors; having been in possession thereof *by* the space of seven hundred years. *Bacon's Henry* VII.

16. As soon as; not later than; noting time.

*By* this, the sons of Constantine which fled,
Ambrise and Uther, did ripe years attain. *Fairy Q. b.* ii.

Hector, *by* the fifth hour of the sun,
Will, with a trumpet, 'twixt our tents and Troy,
Tomorrow morning call some knight to arms. *Shakesp. Troilus and Cressida.*

He err'd not; for, *by* this, the heav'nly bands
Down from a sky of jasper lighted now
In paradise. *Milton's Paradise Lost, b.* x. *l.* 208.

These have their course to finish round the earth
*By* morrow ev'ning. *Paradise Lost, b.* iv. *l.* 662.

The angelick guards ascended, mute and sad
For man: for, of his state *by* this they knew. *Par. L. b.* x.

*By* that time a siege is carried on two or three days, I am altogether lost and bewildered in it. *Addison. Spect.* N° 165.

*By* this time, the very foundation was removed. *Swift.*

*By* the beginning of the fourth century from the building of Rome, the tribunes proceeded so far as to accuse and fine the consuls. *Swift.*

17. Beside; noting passage.

Many beautiful places standing along the sea-shore, make the town appear much longer than it is, to those that sail *by* it. *Addison on Italy.*

18. Beside; near to; in presence; noting proximity of place.

So thou may'st say, the king lies *by* a beggar, if a beggar dwell near him; or the church stands *by* thy tabour, if thy tabour stand *by* the church. *Shakesp. Twelfth Night.*

Here he comes himself;
If he be worth any man's good voice,
That good man sit down *by* him. *Ben. Johnson's Catiline.*

A spacious plain, whereon
Were tents of various hue: *by* some, were herds
Of cattle grazing. *Milton's Paradise Lost, b.* xi. *l.* 557.

Stay *by* me; thou art resolute and faithful;
I have employment worthy of thy arm. *Dryden's D. Sebast.*

19. Before *himself*, *herself*, or *themselves*, it notes the absence of all others.

Sitting in some place, *by himself*, let him translate into English his former lesson. *Ascham's Schoolmaster*

Solyman resolved to assault the breach, after he had, *by himself*

*ſelf*, in a melancholy mood, walked up and down in his tent.
*Knolles's Hiſt. of the Turks.*

I know not whether he will annex his diſcourſe to his appendix, or publiſh it *by itſelf*, or at all. *Boyle's Spring of the Air.*

He will imagine, that the king, and his miniſters, ſat down, and made them *by themſelves*, and then ſent them to their allies, to ſign. *Swift.*

More pleas'd to keep it, till their friends could come,
Then eat the ſweeteſt *by themſelves* at home. *Pope.*

20. It is the ſolemn form of ſwearing.

His godhead I invoke, *by* him I ſwear. *Dryden's Fab.*

21. At hand.

He kept then ſome of the ſpirit *by* him, to verify what he believes. *Boyle.*

The merchant is not forced to keep ſo much money *by* him, as in other places, where they have not ſuch a ſupply. *Locke.*

22. It is uſed in forms of adjuring, or obteſting.

Which, O! avert *by* yon etherial light,
Which I have loſt for this eternal night;
Or if, by dearer ties, you may be won,
*By* your dead ſire, and *by* your living ſon. *Dryden's Æn.*
Now *by* your joys on earth, your hopes in heav'n,
O ſpare this great, this good, this aged king! *Dryden.*
O, cruel youth!
*By* all the pain that wrings my tortur'd ſoul!
*By* all the dear deceitful hopes you gave me,
O, ceaſe! at leaſt, once more delude my ſorrows.
*Smith's Phædrus and Hippolita.*

23. It ſignifies ſpecification and particularity.

Upbraiding heav'n, from whence his lineage came,
And cruel calls the gods, and cruel thee, *by* name. *Dryden.*

24. By proxy of; noting ſubſtitution.

The gods were ſaid to feaſt with Ethiopians; that is, they were preſent with them *by* their ſtatues. *Broome, notes on Odyſſ.*

25. In the ſame direction with.

They are alſo ſtriated, or furrowed, *by* the length, and the ſides curiouſly punched, or pricked. *Grew.*

BY. *adv.*

1. Near; at a ſmall diſtance.

And in it lies, the god of ſleep;
And, ſnorting *by*,
We may deſcry
The monſters of the deep. *Dryden's Albion.*

2. Beſide; paſſing.

I did hear
The galloping of horſe. Who was't came *by?*
*Shakeſp. Macbeth.*

3. In preſence.

The ſame words in my lady Philoclea's mouth, as from one woman to another, ſo as there was no other body *by*, might have had a better grace. *Sidney.*

I'll not be *by*, the while, my lieges, farewel:
What will become hereof, there's none can tell.
*Shakeſp. Richard* III.
There while I ſing, if gentle youth be *by*,
That tunes my lute, and winds the ſtrings ſo high. *Waller.*
Pris'ners and witneſſes were waiting *by*;
Theſe had been taught to ſwear, and thoſe to die.
*Roſcommon.*

You have put a principle into him, which will influence his actions, when you are not *by*. *Locke.*

BY AND BY. In a ſhort time.

He overtook Amphialus, who had been ſtaid here, and *by and by* called him to fight with him. *Sidney.*

The noble knight alighted *by and by*,
From lofty ſteed, and bad the lady ſtay,
To ſee what end of fight ſhould him befall that day.
*Spenſer's Fairy Queen, b.* i. *cant.* viii. *ſtanz.* 2.
In the temple, *by and by*, with us,
Theſe couples ſhall eternally be knit.
*Shakeſp. Midſummer's Night's Dream.*
O how this ſpring of love reſembleth
Th' uncertain glory of an April day;
Which now ſhews all the beauty of the ſun,
And *by and by* a cloud takes all away.
*Shakeſp. Two Gentlemen of Verona.*
Now a ſenſible man, *by and by* a fool, and preſently a beaſt.
*Shakeſp. Othello.*



BY. *n. ſ.* [from the prepoſition.] Something not the direct and immediate object of regard.

In this inſtance, there is, upon the *by*, to be noted, the percolation of the verjuice through the wood. *Bacon's Natural Hiſtory, N° 50.*

This wolf was forced to make bold, ever and anon, with a ſheep in private, by the *by*. *L'Eſtrange.*

Hence we may underſtand, to add that upon the *by*, that it is not neceſſary. *Boyle.*

So, while my lov'd revenge is full and high,
I'll give you back your kingdom by the *by*.
*Dryden's Conqueſt of Granada.*

BY, in compoſition, implies ſomething out of the direct way; and, conſequently, ſome obſcurity, as a *by-road*; ſomething irregular, as a *by-end*; or ſomething collateral, as a *by-concernment*; or private, as a *by-law*. This compoſition is uſed at pleaſure, and will be underſtood by the examples following.

BY-COFFEEHOUSE. *n. ſ.* A coffeehouſe in an obſcure place.

I afterwards entered a *by-coffeehouſe*, that ſtood at the upper end of a narrow lane, where I met with a nonjuror.
*Addiſon. Spectator, N° 403.*

BY-CONCERNMENT. *n. ſ.* An affair which is not the main buneſs.

Our plays, beſides the main deſign, have under-plots, or *by-concernments*, or leſs conſiderable perſons and intrigues, which are carried on with the motion of the main plot.
*Dryden on Dramatick Poeſy.*

BY-DEPENDENCE. *n. ſ.* An appendage; ſomething accidentally depending on another.

Theſe,
And your three motives to the battle, with
I know not how much more, ſhould be demanded;
And all the other *by-dependences*,
From chance to chance. *Shakeſp. Cymbeline.*

BY-DESIGN. *n. ſ.* An incidental purpoſe.

And if ſhe miſs the mouſe-trap lines,
They'll ſerve for other *by-deſigns*,
And make an artiſt underſtand,
To copy out her ſeal or hand;
Or find void places in the paper,
To ſteal in ſomething to entrap her. *Hudibras, p.* iii. *c.* iii.

BY-END. *n. ſ.* Private intereſt; ſecret advantage.

All people that worſhip for fear, profit, or ſome other *by-end*, fall within the intendement of this fable. *L'Eſtrange.*

BY-GONE. *adj.* [a Scotch word.] Paſt.

Tell him, you're ſure
All in Bohemia's well: this ſatisfaction
The *by-gone* day proclaim'd. *Shakeſp. Winter's Tale.*

As we have a conceit of motion coming, as well as *bygone*; ſo have we of time, which dependeth thereupon.
*Grew's Coſmologia Sacra, b.* ii. *c.* iii.

BY-INTEREST. *n. ſ.* Intereſt diſtinct from that of the publick.

Various factions and parties, all aiming at *by-intereſt*, without any ſincere regard to the publick good. *Atterbury.*

BY-LAW. *n. ſ.*

*By-laws* are orders made in court-leets, or court-barons, by common aſſent, for the good of thoſe that make them, farther than the publick law binds. *Cowel.*

There was alſo a law, to reſtrain the *by-laws* and ordinances of corporations. *Bacon's Henry* VII.

In the beginning of this record is inſerted the charter of inſtitution; to which are added two *by-laws*, as a comment upon the general law. *Addiſon. Spectator, N°* 608.

BY-MATTER. *n. ſ.* Something incidental.

I knew one, that, when he wrote a letter, he would put that which was moſt material into the poſtſcript, as if it had been a *by-matter*. *Bacon's Eſſays, N°* 23.

BY-NAME. *n. ſ.* A nickname; name of reproach, or accidental appellation.

Robert, eldeſt ſon to the Conquerour, uſed ſhort hoſe, and thereupon was *by-named* Court-hoſe, and ſhewed firſt the uſe of them to the Engliſh. *Camden's Remains.*

BY-PAST. *adj.* Paſt; a term of the Scotch dialect.

Wars, peſtilences, and diſeaſes, have not been fewer for theſe three hundred years *by-paſt*, than ever they have been ſince we have had records. *Cheyne's Philoſophical Principles.*

BY-PATH. *n. ſ.* A private or obſcure path.

Heav'n knows, my ſon,
By what *by-paths*, and indirect crooked ways,
I got this crown. *Shakeſp. Henry* IV. *p.* ii.

BY-RESPECT. *n. ſ.* Private end or view.

It may be, that ſome, upon *by-reſpects*, find ſomewhat friendly uſage in uſance, at ſome of their hands.
*Carew's Survey of Cornwal.*

The archbiſhops and biſhops, next under the king, have the government of the church: be not you the mean to prefer any to thoſe places, for any *by-reſpects*, but only for their learning, gravity, and worth. *Bacon's Advice to Villiers.*

Auguſtus, who was not altogether ſo good as he was wiſe, had ſome *by-reſpects* in the enacting of this law; for to do any thing for nothing, was not his maxim.
*Dryden's Juvenal, Dedication.*

BY-ROAD. *n. ſ.* An obſcure unfrequented path.

Through ſlipp'ry *by-roads*, dark and deep,
They often climb, and often creep. *Swift.*

BY-ROOM. *n. ſ.* A private room within another.

I pr'ythee, do thou ſtand in ſome *by-room*, while I queſtion my puny drawer to what end he gave the ſugar.
*Shakeſp. Henry* IV. *p.* i.

BY-SPEECH. *n. ſ.* An incidental or caſual ſpeech, not directly relating to the point.

When they come to allege what word and what law they meant, their common ordinary practice is to quote *by-ſpeeches* in ſome hiſtorical narration or other, and to uſe them as if they were written in moſt exact form of law. *Hooker, b.* iii. § 4.

BY-STANDER. *n. ſ.* A looker one; one unconcerned.

She

# Transcription

## Rationale and explanation of the transcription

The purpose behind this transcription has been to provide clarity of representation with brief explanation and occasional analysis of Johnson's efforts. Explanations of certain changes are to be found in the transcription itself and in the footnotes. Analysis has, for the most part, been reserved for the prefatory notes, which should be seen not as exhaustive, but suggestive of larger issues of significance reflected in these materials. In the pursuit of clarity, I have included in the transcription as much of the printed text from the first-edition printed pages as seemed necessary for identification and understanding of the relevant change. While many of the proposed alterations could be understood simply by consulting the transcription alone, it is assumed that the reader will alternate between the facsimile page and the transcription.

All material handwritten by Johnson, whether on the interleaves or the printed pages, is reproduced in bold within angle brackets. All annotations on the printed pages are in Johnson's distinctive hand. Most of the material written on the interleaves is in the hand of the amanuensis, possibly V. J. Peyton. All cross-out strokes are Johnson's unless otherwise indicated. All ink marks made directly on these pages are transcribed, even those not intended for the compositor, such as Johnson's cursive 'I' at the top of three separate pages and his tic-tac-toe doodle on another. Exceptions to this rule are the frequent cases of inking from the facing interleaf page. In those cases where the inking was likely to cause confusion for the compositor, or is likely to confuse the reader of this volume, I have provided an explanatory note. Johnson's smear-outs of his own handwriting present a particular challenge for the transcriber. In order to erase his handwritten additions, Johnson frequently smears out (probably with his thumb or the heal of his hand, or perhaps with a cloth) a sentence, phrase, word, letter, mark of punctuation, or caret while the ink is still wet. Occasionally, he smears his writing, intentionally or otherwise, then indicates (with the instruction 'Stet' or some other means) that the writing should stand. In other cases, the writing is smeared accidentally. In each of these cases, I have represented the smear-outs with a range of shading, explaining in an editorial note what was intended. Curly brackets or braces are employed for every editorial comment within the transcription itself. Such editorial commentary has been kept to a minimum on the transcription of the interleaves.

The usual format for footnotes begins with the identification of the author and the source of a quotation. In each instance, the source is either a copy of a book that Johnson used to mark quotations for use in the original compilation of the *Dictionary*, an edition he is likely to have used, or may have used, in selecting quotations for the first edition, or a modern scholarly edition. Throughout I have made use of obvious short titles directing the reader to the appropriate work in the list of editions and works preceding the facsimile reproductions. Where the source provided is a marked book (Shakespeare, Bacon, Matthew Hale, or Robert South), it is indicated in the note with an asterisk (*) preceding the short title. In the cases of Shakespeare and Bacon, the first citation for each refers to the marked book: *The Works of Shakespear*, in eight volumes, edited by William Warburton and published in 1747, and *The Works of Francis Bacon*, in four volumes, published in 1740, respectively. The second citation, in square brackets, refers to the *Riverside* edition of Shakespeare, and the fourteen-volume edition of Bacon's works published by James Spedding in the nineteenth century, respectively. Some footnotes then specify any special circumstances or aspects pertinent to the citation and its transmission.

The next element in the footnotes records the existence of a slip from the Sneyd-Gimbel copy (noted as 'S-G') carrying the same manuscript text as the passage copied onto the interleaf. Any discrepancies between the two versions of the text, or any special aspects of the Sneyd-Gimbel slip are recorded within parenthesis following 'S-G'. Finally, occurrences of the passage in the first edition are recorded with the notation '*1755*', followed by the head-words under which the quotation appears verbatim or in some variant form. When the head-word is unqualified by any adjective, then the passage as quoted under that word in the first edition entry is identical or nearly identical to the version of the quotation written on the interleaf, or is longer and incorporates the entire quotation on the interleaf. The designation 'slightly shorter' means that the passage cited in the first edition lacks two to four of the words in the version in the B materials. 'Shorter' signifies that at least four words are lacking. 'Much shorter' means that the quotation in the first edition derives from the same passage in a printed source, but lacks a significant portion of the quotation on the interleaf. Similarly, 'slightly different', 'different" and 'very different' record the extent to which the printed first-edition version varies from the interleaf version, where the source of the passage is the same, the length similar, but the quotation contains different words and phrases. That there is a considerable amount of personal judgement involved in these categories is clear, yet I have done my best to apply the categories systematically.

The importance of these designations lies in the fact that they may be helpful in determining the immediate source for the quotation that was recycled for use in the fourth edition. As I have discussed earlier, the passages were, for the most part, recycled from the first edition through the use of the abandoned pre-first-edition manuscript. Those quotations which appear in a version 'shorter' or 'much shorter', or 'different' and 'very different', are less likely to have been the source of the recycled quotation for the amanuensis; however, since we cannot know for certain what form the quotation took in the manuscript version, the length of the quotation and its variation from the form on the interleaf is not conclusive evidence.

For most of the proposed quotations on the interleaves, slips from the Sneyd-Gimbel copy exist, indicating that these slips were the medium through which the amanuensis recycled the quotation and other material for the fourth edition. Some few quotations, especially from Thomas Tusser's *Husbandry*, appear to have been selected anew rather than recycled. In those cases in which a Sneyd-Gimbel slip is absent, but the quotation appears under another entry or other entires in the first edition, it is probable that the slip was once extant but is now lost. It follows that the passage was probably recycled from one of the first-edition entries.

## Conventions and abbreviations

As a rule, the transcription follows two different strategies for annotated first-edition pages and for interleaves, respectively. The transcription of the printed first-edition pages bearing Johnson's manuscript revisions aims to render the chronology of the process of revision by placing the original printed version, crossed out, in front of Johnson's revision, the latter always in bold and within angle brackets. (Exceptions to this rule are discussed below.) The transcription of the interleaves, conversely, aims to reproduce graphically the spatial layout of the manuscript page. In cases in which Johnson or the amanuensis altered letters or numbers by writing over them, whether on the printed page or the interleaf, the chronology of the process of revision is rendered by placing the original version, crossed out, in front of the revised version. In cases where Johnson intends something to be inserted in a line of text on the printed page, the word or other element is transcribed in bold within angle brackets in the place it is to be inserted. (Exceptions involving marginal annotations are discussed below.)

In the transcription, I have represented all additions and changes made by Johnson and his amanuensis. In some cases, this has been effected through the use of stylized conventions. A special problem in transcribing the revisions made on the first-edition pages is posed in those cases where Johnson draws lines and inserts marginal numbers to indicate that portions of the first-edition printed text are to be transposed. To enable the reader to understand Johnson's changes, I have represented these annotations graphically, to the extent possible, through the use of stylized lines (with accompanying explanation). In order to accomplish this, it was necessary to indent the text transcribed so as to create an artificial margin that would allow for the reproduction of Johnson's drawn lines and numbers. In these cases, I adopted the conventions used for the transcription of the interleaves so as to reproduce as clearly as possible the spatial layout on the printed page. Any additional revisions made by Johnson in the portions of text to be transposed are transcribed following the usual conventions employed for the annotated printed pages.

Similarly, for the sake of visual and conceptual clarity, some of Johnson's marginal symbols or words on the printed page have been transcribed in imitation of their spatial arrangement. These symbols or words are represented on the appropriate line inside the print margin of the transcription, requiring a false margin for that line of text. A frequent example is Johnson's delete sign, the large cursive 'd'. Where necessary, a note has been provided explaining Johnson's strategy. In a few cases, I have also transcribed annotations Johnson made within the text according to spatial arrangement, rather than placing the original version first, crossed out, followed by Johnson's change (see, for example, BAY *adj.*). These rare exceptions are made in cases dictated by visual and conceptual clarity.

For the annotations on the printed page, spatial economy demanded that the layout for the transcription of the printed page always begin at the top of the column and record seriatim portions of the text with changes, without attempting to imitate the spacing of the printed text. Exceptions to this procedure are the columns and the line breaks of the printed text, which have been faithfully respected. Ellipses are employed to designate omitted portions of the text. A space between lines of text designates a larger gap in the printed text, usually involving at least one entry. For the transcription of the handwritten annotations on the interleaf, however, an attempt has been made to imitate the spatial arrangement of the text.

Smear-outs have been recorded as follows:

| | |
|---|---|
| [light grey box] | where a word in print is crossed out with a pen stroke, but the cross-out stroke is smeared out so as to indicate that the word should be retained, the word is represented against a light grey background. |
| [dark grey box] | (a) where a hand-written word, letter, or other inked mark (other than a cross-out stroke) is intentionally smeared out indicating that it is to be deleted, the mark is displayed against a dark grey background. (b) where a hand-written word or letter is accidentally smeared, it is also displayed against a dark grey background. In these cases, Johnson may have rewritten the word or letter so as to indicate that it is to stand. |

Further conventions:

| | |
|---|---|
| [bracket lines] | represents the lines Johnson draws to indicate transposition of portions of text. |
| [scooping line] | represents the scooping line Johnson draws to raise the attribution to the line above. He often shortens quotations and attributions in an attempt to save a line of type. |
| ‡ | represents the 'double-dagger' printer's sign or reference mark, which Johnson draws as two short parallel horizontal lines dissected by a verticle. |
| {???} | represents an indecipherable word, letter, or letters; the estimated number of letters is indicated by question marks within curly brackets. |
| word{?} | represents illegible handwritten words or letters, nevertheless deducible with probability from the context; the word or letters are given followed by a question mark within curly brackets. |
| ♦ | highlights changes in the B material that are discussed in the 'Notes on selected changes' at the beginning of the volume. |

The abbreviations used in the transcription are as follows:

aman. = amanuensis
def. = definition
del. = deletes
IL = interleaf
ital. = italicises
J. = Johnson
p., pp. = page, pages
q., qs. = quotation, quotations

{AZU′RE. *adj.*}
**<a ‡>**
Like pomels round of marble clear
Where azur'd veins wellmixt appear
Sidn. ~~2.~~[1] {J. crosses out.}

**13 JA 54**
{BL accession number in red ink.}

[1] Sidney, *Arcadia*, bk II, p. 192. S-G. Q. added in *1773*.

{IL facing 2N[r]. Misbound between 2L2 and 2M.}

## AXL

{AWRY′. *adv.*}
3. {…}
I **<‸may may>** hap to step *awry*, where I see no path, and can discern but few steps afore me. *Brerewood on Languages.*
{Smearing of 'may' inserted above line prompts J. to write 'may' in margin.}
4. {…}
~~Not tyrants fierce that unrepenting die,~~
Not Cynthia when her manteau's pinn'd *awry*,
Ere felt such rage. *Pope's Rape of the Lock.*

*AXI′LLA. n.s.* {…} The cavity under the upper part of the arm<;>~~called~~ the arm-pit. *Quincy.*
{J. alters comma to semi-colon.}
AXI′LLAR. } adj. {…}
A′XILLARY. }
~~In the same manner is~~ the *axillary* artery **<‸is>** distributed unto the hand; below the cubit, it divideth unto two parts. *Brown's Vulgar Errours.*

A′XIS. *n.s.* {…}
On their own *axis* as the planets run,
And make at once their circle round the sun;
So two consistent motions act the soul,
And one regards itself, and one the whole.
*Pope~~'s Essay on Man, epist.~~* ~~iii.~~ ~~*l.* 313.~~
A′XLE. } *n.s.* {…} The pin which passes through
A′XLE-TREE. } the midst of the wheel, on which the circumvolutions of the wheel are performed. **<Axle here is now scarcely used in poetry.>**

## AZU

AY. *adv.* {…}
1. {…}
What say'st thou? Wilt thou be of our consort?
Say *ay*; and be the captain of us all.
*Shakesp.* ~~*Two Gentlemen of Verona.*~~

AYE. *adv.*{…} Always; to eternity; for ever. **<anciently they said for aye as now for ever.>**
And now in darksome dungeon, wretched thrall,
Remedyless for *aye* he doth him hold. *Fairy Queen, b.* i.
{J. ital. 'for'.}
Either prepare to die,
Or on Diana's altar to protest,
For *aye*, austerity and single life. {J. ital. 'for'.}
*Shakespeare's* ~~*Midsummer Night's Dream.*~~
The soul, though made in time, survives for *aye*;
And, though it hath beginning, sees no end.
~~*Sir John*~~ *Davies.*

A′YGREEN. *n.s.* The same with *houseleek*; ~~which see.~~ *Dict.*
{J. removes italics for '*houseleek*'.}
A′YRY. *n.s.* [See AIRY.] **<The nest of a bird of prey>**

**<Azured adj. [from azure]**
**Blue; having the colour of azure. a ‡>**

**13 JA 54**
{BL accession number in red ink.}

{sig. 2N[r]}

**BAB**

To BA´BBLE. *v.n.* {...}
{Vertical lines inking from facing IL.}
2. To <u>talk</u> idly, or irrationally.
<2> {...} *Arbuthn. J. Bull.*
<1> {...} *Prior.*
{J. reverses order of Prior and Arbuthnot qs., presumably to establish chronological sequence.}

BA´BBLEMENT. *n.s.* {...} Senseless prate. <^**not in use.**>

BA´BBLER. *n.s.* {...}
1. {...}
The apostle ~~of my text~~ had no sooner proposed <^>~~it~~ to the ~~greater~~ masters at Athens, but he himself was ridiculed as a *babbler.* *Rogers.*
{No material for caret to key in as replacement for pronoun 'it'.}

BABE. *n.s.* [*baban*, Welch; *babbaerd*, Dutch.<^**<u>bambo</u>, <u>bambino</u>, Italian**>]

BA´BY. *n.s.* {...}

**BAC**

2. {...}
~~The archduke saw that Perkin would prove a runnagate; and that~~ it was the part of the children to fall out about *babies.* *Bacon's Henry* VII.
Since no image can represent the great Creator, never think to honour him by your foolish puppets, and *babies* of dirt and clay. *Stillingfleet's ~~Def. of Disc. on Rom. Idolatry.~~*

BA´CCHANALS. *n.s.* {...} ~~The~~ drunken feasts ~~and~~ <**like the**> revels of Bacchus, the god of wine.

B´ACCHUS BOLE. *n.s.* A flower ~~not tall, but~~ very full and broad-leaved; of a sad light purple, and a ~~proper~~ white; having the three outmost leaves edged with a crimson colour, bluish bottom, and dark purple. *Mortimer.*

BACCI´VOROUS. *adj.* {...}♦
<F{?}>
~~A devourer of berries.~~ <**Feeding on berries**> *Dict.*
{The letter J. writes above line appears to be 'F', perhaps first letter of 'Feeding', but might be 'd' for 'delete'.}

BA´CHELORS *Button.* ~~[See~~ CAMPION, of ~~which it is~~ a species.~~]~~
<3> <2> <1>
~~All the sorts of this plant are hardy; they grow above two foot, and produce their flower in June and July.~~ *Millar.*
{J. reorders def. to read 'a species of CAMPION'.}♦

{sig. 2N^v}

{BA´BY. *n.s.*}
As a poor pedlar he did wend
Bearing a truss of trifles at his back
As bells & babies & glasses in his Pack
Spens. Pas[1]

{BA´BY. *n.s.*}♦
Baby. [Babee]
In Scotland denotes a halfpenny, as
alluding to the Head impressed on the Copper
Coin[2]

{BABION. new}♦
Babion. Menage says this is a Syriac
Word which signifies a child or puppet. From
which bambo, bambino, bambinore. Ital. babil.
babilote fr. are derived Trev.[3]
Thinkst thou, mime, this is great or that they strive
Whose noise shall keep thy miming most alive
Whilst thou dost raise some play'r from the grave
Outdance the <u>babion</u>, or outboast the brave.
B. Johns.[4]

{BACCHANA´LIAN. *n.s.*}
Some imagining themselves possessed with a
divine fury, far from being carried into the
rage of <u>Bachanalians</u>, fall into toys which
are only puerilities[5]

{BACCHANA´LIAN.}
Adject.
Jovial, extravagantly merry.
Some of his Odes are panegyrical; others
moral; the rest jovial, or if I may so call
them Bacchanalian Dryd.[6]

{BACHRACH. new}
Bachrach
Restor'd the fainting high and mighty
With brandy wine and Aquavitæ
And made them stoutly overcome
With <u>bachrach</u> hoccamor & Mum
Hud. 3.3[7]
{Proposed entry for 'BACHRACH' neither crossed out nor keyed in.}

1 Spenser, *Shepheardes Calendar* (*Works* VII), 'May', ll. 238-240. S-G. *1755* PEDLER *n.s.*, TRUSS *n.s.*
2 S-G.
3 *Dictionnaire Universel François & Latin (Dictionnaire de Trévoux)* [translation aman.?], vol. I, col. 777. S-G.
4 Ben Jonson, 'Epigramme CXXIX: To Mime' (*Works* VIII), ll. 9-12. S-G. *1755* To MIME *v.n.*
5 Dryden, *Dufresnoy's Art of Painting* (*Works* XX), p. 124. *1755* PUERILITY *n.s.* (shorter)
6 Dryden, 'Preface to Sylvæ' (*Works* III), p. 16. S-G. *1755* JOVIAL *adj.* (slightly shorter)
7 Samuel Butler, *Hudibras*, pt III, canto III, ll. 297-300. S-G. *1755* HOCK/HOCKAMORE *n.s.*

{IL facing 2N^v}

{blank page}

{IL facing 2N2$^{r}$}

## BAC

{BACK. *n.s.*}

7. The thick part of any tool, opposed to the edge; as the *back* of a knife or a sword; whence *backsword*, or sword with a *back*; ~~as,~~

8. To turn the *back* on one, is to forsake him, or neglect him.
{J. ital. entire phrase.}

9. To turn the *back*, is to go away; {...}
{J. ital. entire phrase.}

BACK. *adv.* {...}

1. {...}

He sent many to seek ~~the ship~~ Argo, threatening that if they brought not *back* Medea, they should suffer in her stead.
*Raleigh's History of the World.*

2. ~~Backward;~~ from the present station~~,~~<**to the former.**>

3. {...}

~~Constrains the glebe,~~ keep~~s~~ *back* the hurtful weed.
*Blackmore's Creation, b.* ii.

4. {...}

I had always a curiosity to look *back* unto the ~~sorrows~~ <**origin**> of things, and to view in my mind the beginning and progress of a rising world. *Burnet's Theory of the Earth.*

To BACK. *v.a.* {...}

1. {...}

That roan shall be my throne.
Well I will *back* him strait. ~~O Esperance!~~
~~Bid Butler lead him forth into the park.~~ *Shak. Henry* IV.

## BAC

To BA´CKBITE. *v.a.* {...}

Most untruly and maliciously do these evil tongues *backbite* and slander the sacred ashes ~~of that most just and honourable personage.~~ *Spenser's Ireland.*

I will use him well; ~~a friend i' th' court is better than a penny in purse.~~ Use his men well, ~~Davy,~~ for they are arrant knaves, and will *backbite*. *Shakesp. Henry* IV.

BA´CKHOUSE. *n.s.* {...}

Their *backhouses*, of more necessary than cleanly service, as kitchens, stables, are climbed up unto by steps.
*Carew~~'s Survey~~ of Cornwal.*

{sig. 2N2$^{r}$}

## BAC

BA´CKWARD. } *adv.* {…}
BA´CKWARDS.

1. {…}
They went *backward*, and their faces were *backward*. *Gen.* ix.
{J. removes italics from second instance of '*backward*'.}

3. {…}
Then darting <^**rage**> from her malignant eyes,
She cast him *backward* as he strove to rise. *Dryden's Æneid.*

7. Out of the progressive state; reflex<**ly**>.

9. {…}
~~They~~ <**The French**> have spread <^**over Europe**> one of the worst languages in the world,
if we look upon it some reigns *backwards.* *Locke.*

BA´CKWARD. *adj.*
1. Unwilling; averse.
{…} *Pope.* <~~2~~ **4**>
{…} *Atterbury.* <**3**>
{…} *Addison. Freeholder.* <**2**>
~~2. Hesitating.~~
All things are ready, if our minds be so; <**1**>
Perish the man, whose mind is *backward* now. *Shak. H.* V.
<**2**>~~3~~. Sluggish; dilatory.<~~**hesita**~~>

<**3**>~~4~~. Dull; not quick or apprehensive.
{J. consolidates entry for BACKWARD *adj.* under one head-word with three senses: Shakespeare q. (from sense 2) is moved to first place under def. 1, Addison q. to second, Atterbury q. to third, and Pope q. to last place, presumably to establish chronological sequence. J. deletes def. 2 and renumbers subsequent senses. J. prob. first intended to place Shakespeare q. under new def. 2, adding 'hesitating' to def., then reconsidered and crossed out the word.}

BA´CKWARD. *n.s.* The things or state behind or past/<**; not in use.**>

BA´CKWARDLY. *adv.* {…}
1./Unwillingly; aversely;\with the back forward./
{J. moves third phrase to first place.}

## BAF

{Vertical lines inking from facing IL.}

BACULO´METRY. *n.s.* {…} The art of measuring distances by ~~one or more~~ staves. *Dict.* <***d***>

~~BADGER. *n.s.*~~ <**2**> {…} An animal that earthes in the ground, used to be hunted.
{…} *Brown's Vulgar Errours, b.* iii.
BADGER LEGGED. *adj.* {…} Having legs <**2**> of an unequal length, as the badger is <^> supposed to <^**falsely**> have.<^>
{No material for last caret to key in.}
{…} *L'Estrange.*
BA´DGER. *n.s.* {…} <**1**> One that buys corn and victuals in one place, <**1**> and carries it unto another. *Cowel.*
{J. consolidates entry for BADGER *n.s.* under one head-word with two senses and reorders the senses. Although it is not completely certain, he apparently intends second entry for BADGER *n.s.* to become first sense and first entry to become second sense. Entry for BADGER LEGGED. *adj.* to follow.}

To BA´FFLE. *v.a.* {…}
1. To elude. <**to make ineffectual by some expedient.**>

{sig. 2N2v}

{BA´CKWARD. new}
Detractory.
His forward voice is to speak well of his ~
friend: his backward Voice is to spatter foul
Speeches and to detract Shak.[1]

[1] Shakespeare, *Tempest* (**Works* I), 2.2, p. 45 [2.2.90-92]. S-G. *1755* To SPATTER *v.a.*

{IL facing 2N2v}

Baggagely adj. [Baggage]
Sorry, miserable, poor
No storing of pasture with baggagely tit
With ragged with aged & evil at hit.
Tuss. husb.[1]

[1] Thomas Tusser, *Husbandry*, 'September', p. 114. S-G. *1755* TIT *n.s.*
[2] 'cha' superimposed on 'po', altering 'purpose' to 'purchase'.
[3] Robert South, 'Sermon XII' (*Twelve Sermons* 1692), p. 610. *1755* GAINFUL *adj.*, LUSCIOUS *adj.* (shorter)

{To BAIT. *v.a.* 2}
<2> To allure; to entice <‡>
If it be his estate that he drives at, he
will dazle his Eyes, and bait him in with the
luscious proposal of some gainful ~~purpo~~chase[2]
till the easy mans caught and hamper'd
South[3]

{IL facing 2O^r}

## BAG

BA'FFLER. *n.s.* {...}

Experience, that great *baffler* of speculation, ~~assures us the thing is too possible, and~~ brings, in all ages, matter of fact to confute our suppositions. *Government of the Tongue*, § 2.

BAG. *n.s.* {...}

1. A sack, or pouch, to put any thing in, as money, corn. **<a bag implies something more capacious than a purse.>**

2. That part of animals in which some particular juices are contained, as the poison of vipers. **<the milk of cows>**

{J.'s addition prompted by second Dryden q. following.}

{...} *Dryden.*

Sing on, sing on, for I can ne'er be cloy'd;
So may thy cows their burden'd *bags* distend. *Dryden.*

BA'GGAGE. *n.s.* {...}

1. {...}

~~They~~ **<Movable Rostra>** were probably always in readiness, and carried among the *baggage* of the army. *Addison's Remarks on Italy.*

<✝> 3. A worthless woman; in French *bagaste*; so called, because such women follow camps.

{Purpose of mark unclear; may be a cross or dagger.}

## BAI

BAIL. *n.s.* {...}♦

{...} There is a difference between *bail* and mainprise; for he that is mainprised, is at large, until the day of his appearance: but where a man is bailed, he is always accounted by the law to be in the~~ir~~ ward and custody for the time **<^of those who are his sureties.>**: and they may, if they will, keep him in ward or in prison at that time, or otherwise at their will. *Cowel.*

To BAIL. *v.a.* {...}

2. {...}

When they had *bailed* the twelve bishops, who were in the Tower, the house of commons, in great indignation, caused them ~~immediately~~ again to be recommitted to the Tower. <~~d~~ **Qu**> *Clarendon.*/

{J. apparently queries quotation; intention uncertain.}

BA'ILIFF. *n.s.* {...}

1. {...}

Lausanne is under the canton of Berne, and governed by a *bailiff* sent them every three years from ~~the senate of~~ Berne. *Addison ~~on Italy~~.*

BA'ILIWICK. *n.s.* {...}

~~There issued writs to~~ the sheriffs, ~~to~~ return<^**ed**> the names of the several land-owners in their several *bailiwicks.* *Hale~~'s Origin of Mankind.~~*

To BAIT. *v.a.* {...}♦

1. To put meat upon a hook, in some place, to tempt fish or other animals. **<to furnish with allurement of any kind>**

{J.'s addition prompted by figurative uses of word in *Merry Wives of Windsor* and Gay qs. under def. 1.}

Let's be revenged on him; let's appoint him a meeting, give him a show of comfort in his suit, and lead him on with a sure *baited* delay, till he hath pawned his horses to mine host of the garter. *Shakesp. Merry Wives of Windsor.*

How are the sex improv'd in am'rous arts!
What new-found snares they *bait* for human hearts! *Gay.*

<——— **a ‡**>

{J. keys in def. 2 and South q. for To BAIT *v.a.* from IL; the matching key on IL is not lettered.}

~~2~~<**3**>. To give meat to one's self, or horses, on the road.

{sig. 2O^r}

<4>~~To BAIT. *v.a.*~~ [from *battre*, Fr. to beat.] To attack with violence; to set dogs upon.
{J. consolidates entry for To BAIT. *v.a.* under one head-word with four senses but retains the alternate etymology in sense 4.}

To BAIT. *v.n.* <^**1**> To stop at any place for refreshment; perhaps this word is more properly *bate*; to *abate* speed.
{...} *Par. Lost.*
<**b** ‡ ——— >
{J. keys in Milton q. from IL.}
~~To BAIT. *v. n.* [*as an hawk.*]~~ <2 [**Battre French**]> To clap the wings; to make an offer of flying; to flutter.
{J. consolidates entry for To BAIT. *v.n.* under one head-word with two senses.}
{...}

Another way I have to man my haggard,
To make her come, and know her keepers call;
That is, to watch her as we watch these kites,
That *bait* and beat, and will not be obedient.
*Shakesp.* ~~*Taming of the Shrew.*~~

BAIT. *n.s.* {...}♦
2. A temptation; an enticement. <~~**generally**~~^ **allurement, commonly to crimes or misery**>
{...}
~~T~~<**He t**>aketh therewith the souls of men, as with certain *baits*.
*Hooker, b.* v. § 35.

To BAKE. *v.a.* {...}
2. To harden ~~in~~ <**by action of**> the fire.

To BAKE. *v.n.*
1. {...}
I keep his house, and I wash, wring, brew, *bake,* scour, dress meat, and make the beds, and do all myself.
*Shakesp.* ~~*Merry Wives of Windsor.*~~



BA′LANCE. *n.s.* {...}♦
5. {...}
Care being taken, that the exportation exceed in value the importation; ~~and~~ then the *balance* of trade must of necessity be returned in coin or bullion. *Bacon's Adv. to Sir G. Villiers.*

7. Equipoise; ~~as *balance* of power. See the second sense.~~ <**even state; equalility.**>

Love, hope, and joy, fair pleasure's smiling train,
Hate, fear, and grief, the family of pain;
These mixed with art, and to due bounds confin'd,
Make and maintain the balance of the mind. Pope.

{J. re-reads and reinterprets use of word in Pope q. following; writes 'equalility' for 'equality'.}

To BA′LANCE. *v.a.* [~~*b*~~<*b*>*alancer*, Fr.]

3. {...} {Inking is accidental.}

To BA′LANCE. *v.n.* To hesitate; to fluctuate between equal motives, as a balance plays when charged with equal weights. <^ **this use of the word is French**>

To BALBU′TIATE. *v.n.* ~~The same with *balbucinate*.~~ <**To stammer**>
*Dict.*

{sig. 2O[v]}

{To BAIT. *v.n.* 1.}
<**b** ‡>
Evil news rides post while good news baits
Milt. Agon 1537[1]

[1] Milton, *Samson Agonistes*, l. 1538 (Milton reads 'rides post'). S-G. *1755* NEWS *n.s.* (with 'rides fast' for 'rides post')

{IL facing 2O[v]}

{BA´LDRICK. *n.s.*}♦
Baldrick, is very probably derived from the inventer or first wearer of this belt, who was called Balderick, baldric. It was worn by women as well as men across the breast.
Knit with a golden <u>baldric</u> which forlay
Athwart her snowy breast, & did divide
Her dainty paps, which like young fruit in May
Now little gan to swell, and being ty'd
Thro her thin weed, their places only signified
F.Q. 3. 29[1]

{BALK. *n.s.*}
A balk is what in Some places is called a mier bank, being a narrow slip of land between ground & ground Tuss. Notes

<a ‡>
There horse being tide on a <u>balk</u>
Is ready with theese for to walk
Tuss. Hus. for July[2]

{To BALK *v.a.*}
5 To balk the road; to turn out of it
<b ‡> Espying the French Ambassador with the Kings Coach ~~and others attending him,~~ made them <u>balk</u> the beaten road, & teach post hackneys to leap hedges
Wott. Buck.[3]

1 Spenser, *Faerie Queene* (*Works* II), bk II, canto III, st. xxix, ll. 5-9. S-G. *1755* To FORLYE *v.n.* (q. only)
2 Thomas Tusser, *Husbandry*, 'July', p. 88. S-G (note and q.).
3 Henry Wotton,'The Life and Death of the Duke of Buckingham', p. 213. S-G. *1755* POSTHACKNEY *n.s.*

{IL facing 2O2r}

**BAL** **BAL**

BALD. *adj.* {…}
{Inking from facing IL.}

BA´LDACHIN. *n.s.* {…}
It properly signifies a rich silk, ~~*du cange*,~~ and was a canopy carried over the host. <**<u>Du Cange</u>.**> *Build. Dict.*
{J. strikes out '*du cange*', incorrectly incorporated into def. in *1755*, and changes attribution to '*Du Cange*', i.e. one of the dictionaries of Charles Dufresne Du Cange. Presumably intends '*Build. Dict.*' to be deleted.}

BA´LDMONY. *n.s.* ~~The same with~~ <u>GENTIAN</u>/ ~~which see.~~ <**an herb**>
{J. underlines 'GENTIAN' either to italicize or to indicate lower case; J.'s instructions to printer unclear.}

To BALE. *v.a.* <^**[from bailler French]**> A word used by the sailors, who bid *bale* out the water; that is, *lave* it out, by way of distinction from pumping. *Skinner.*
To BALE. *v.n.* [*emb*<a>*ller*, Fr. *imballure*, Ital.] To make up into a bale.
BA´LEFUL. *adj.* {…}
2. Full of mischief; destructive. <**this is better <u>baneful</u>**>

BALK. *n.s.* {…}
A ridge of land left unploughed between the furrows, or at the <‡ **a**> end of the field.
{J. keys in Tusser q. from IL.}
To BALK. *v.a.* {…}
2. {…}
By grisly Pluto he doth swear,
He rent his clothes, and tore his hair;
And as he runneth here and there,
An acorn cup he greeteth;
Which soon he taketh by the stalk,
About his head he lets it walk,
Nor doth he any creature *balk*,
But lays on all he meeteth. *Drayt. Nymphid.*
<——— **b** ‡>
{J. keys in Wotton q. from IL.}

4. To heap, as on a ridge. This, or something like this, seems to be intended here. <, **unless ~~their~~{?}reading be mistaken**>

BALL. *n.s.* [*bol*, Dan. *bol.* Dut.] <— — — —>
*Bel*, diminutively *Belin*, the sun, or Apollo of the Celtæ, was called by the ancient Gauls *Abellio*. {. . .} Among the Teutonicks, *bol* and *beil* have the same meaning; whence the adjective *bolig*, or *beilig*, is derived, and signifies divine or holy; and the aspiration being changed into *s*, the Romans form their *Sol*. <]> *Baxter.* <**<u>Gloss. Brit.</u>**>
{J. indicates that the quotation should begin immediately after the etymology; he specifies which of Baxter's works is quoted.}♦

{sig. 2O2r}

## BAL

BA´LLAST. *n.s.* {…}
1. {…}

There must be some middle counsellors to keep things steady; for, without that *ballast*, the ship will roul ~~too much~~.
*Bacon's ~~Essays~~.*

~~As for the ascent of it, this may be easily contrived, if there be~~ some great weight at the bottom of the ship, being part of its *ballast*; ~~which,~~ by some cord within, may be loosened from it. *Wilkins's Mathematical Magick.*

To BA´LLAST. *v.a.*
1. {…}

If this ark be so *ballasted*, as to be of equal weight with the like magnitude of water, it will be moveable.
*Wilkins's ~~Mathematical Magick~~.*

BA´LLIARDS. *n.s.* [from *ball* and *yard*, ~~or~~ <**the**> stick to push it with.]

## BAL

BALM.
BALM *Mint.* } *n.s.* {…} ~~The name of a plant.~~

~~It is~~ a verticillate plant, with a labiated flower {…} the flowers are produced from the wings of the leaves, but are not whorled round the stalks. ~~The species are, 1. Garden *balm*.~~ 2. Garden *balm*, with yellow variegated flowers. 3. Stinking Roman *balm*, with softer hairy leaves. The first of these sorts is cultivated in gardens for medicinal and culinary use: it is propagated by parting the roots either in spring or autumn. When they are first planted, if the season proves dry, you must ~~carefully water them until they have taken root.~~ *Millar.*

BALM *of Gilead*. {…}
2. A plant remarkable for the strong balsamick scent, which its leaves emit, upon being bruised; whence some ~~have~~ supposed, erroneously, that the *balm of Gilead* was taken from this plant.
*Millar.*

To BALM. *v.a.* {…}
1. To anoint with balm. <**or something balsamick**>

2. {…}

Opprest nature sleeps:
This rest might yet have *balm'd* thy senses,
~~Which stand in hard cure.~~ *Shakesp. King Lear.*

BA´LMY. *adj.* {…}
1. Having the qualities of balm. <**moist**{?}**and** ~~**oily**~~{?} **soft**>
3. {…}

*Dryden.*
<————‡ **a**>

{J. keys in Dryden q. from IL.}

{sig. 2O2ᵛ}

{BALL. *n.s.*}
a denomination given to a pyd horse

But no man sure e'er left his house
And saddl'd Ball with thoughts so wild
To bring a midwife to his Spouse
Before he knew she was with child
Prior[1]

{To BA´LLAD. *v.n.*}
Saucy lictors
Will catch at us like Strumpets & scald rhymers
Ballad us out of tune
Shaks. Ant. & Cleo.[2]

{BA´LMY *adj.* 3.}
<‡ **a**>
Would I could share thy balmy even temper
And milkiness of blood Dryd[3]

1 Matthew Prior, 'Alma: Or, the Progress of the Mind' (*Works* I), canto I, ll. 152-155. S-G. *1755* To SADDLE *v.a.*
2 Shakespeare, *Antony and Cleopatra* (**Works* VII), 5.5, p. 220 [5.2.214-16]. S-G. *1755* already under To BALLAD *v.n.*; To CATCH *v.a.* 12, SCALD *adj.*, LICTOR *n.s.* (shorter)
3 Dryden, *Cleomenes* (*Works* XVI), 1.1.113-114. S-G. *1755* MILKINESS *n.s.*

{IL facing 2O2ᵛ}

{To BAMBO´OZLE. *v.a.*}

**<‸of which if any derivation could properly be sought, it may be deduced from bambo Italian a child, so bamboozle will be to treat like a child.>**[1]

[1] IL entirely in J.'s hand.

{IL facing 2P[r]}

## BAN

BA´LOTADE. *n.s.* The leap of an horse, so that when his fore-feet are in the air, he shews ~~nothing but~~ the shoes of his hinder-feet, without yerking out. A *balotade* differs from a capriole; for when a horse ~~works at~~ caprioles, he yerks out his hinder legs with all his force. *Farrier's Dict.*

BALSAM *Apple.* {...}

~~The flower consists of one leaf, is of the expanded bell-shaped~~ kind, but so deeply cut, as to appear composed of five distinct leaves: the flowers are some male, or barren; others female, growing upon the top of the embryo, which is afterwards changed into a fruit, which is fleshy, and sometimes more or less tapering and hollow, and, when ripe, usually bursts, and casts forth the seeds with an elasticity; which seeds are wrapped up in a membranous ~~covering, and are, for the most part, indented on the edges.~~ *Millar.*

BALSAM *Tree.* **<The plant that produces balm>**

~~This is~~ a shrub which scarce grows taller than the pomegranate tree; {...} whence spring out little pointed pods, inclosing a fruit like an almond, called carpobalsamum, as the wood is called xylobalsamum, and the juice opobalsamum; ~~which see.~~ {...} *Calmet. Chambers.*

BALSA´MICAL. } *adj.* {...}
BALSA´MICK. }

If there be a wound ~~in my leg,~~ the vital energy of my soul thrusts out the *balsamical* humour of my blood to heal it. *Hale's ~~Origin of Mankind.~~*

BA´MBOO. *n.s.* An Indian plant of the reed kind. {...} ~~Its flowers grow in ears, like those of wheat.~~

To BAMBO´OZLE. *v.a.* [a cant word not used in pure or in grave writings<‸>.]

{J. keys in new etymological note from IL.}

BAN. *n.s.* {...}

1. {...}

## BAN

I bar it in the interest of my wife;
~~'Tis she is subcontracted to this lord,~~
And I her husband contradict your *bans.* *Shakesp. King Lear.*
Our *bans* thrice bid! and for our wedding-day <3>
To draw her neck into the *bans.* *Hudibras.* <2>
2. A curse; excommunication. <5>
My kerchief bought! then press'd, then forc'd away! *Gay.* <4>
In th' interim, spare for no trepans <1>
Thou mixture rank of midnight weeds collected,
With Hecate's *ban* thrice blasted, thrice infected. *Hamlet.*

{J. re-establishes the correct order of the lines of quoted text, severely misarranged in *1755*: 1 and 2 complete the couplet from *Hudibras*, 3 and 4 complete the next couplet from Gay, all under def. 1; *Hamlet* q. is only illustration for def. 2.}

To BAN. *v.a.* {...} to curse; to execrate.

Shall we think that it *baneth* the work which they leave behind them, or taketh away the use thereof. *Hooker. b.* v. <2>

It is uncertain whether this word, in the ~~foregoing sense~~ **<following passage>**, is to be deduced from *ban*, to curse, or *bane*, to poison. <1>

{J. reverses order of texts for clarity.}

BANA´NA *Tree.* ~~See PLANTAIN; of which it is~~ a species **<of a Plantain>**.

BAND. *n.s.* {...}

6. {...}

And, good my lord of Somerset, unite
Your troops of horsemen with his *bands* of foot.
*Shakesp. ~~Henry VI p. i.~~*

{...}

~~On a sudden, methought~~ this select *band* sprang forward, with a resolution to climb the ascent, and follow the call of that heavenly musick. *Tatler,* N° 81.

{sig. 2P[r]}

BA´NDIT. *n.s.* [*bandit*<‸t>*o*, Ital.] A man outlawed.**<by a ~~ban~~ or proclamation.>**

No savage fierce, *bandit*, or mountaineer,
<2> Will dare to soil her virgin purity. *Milton's Poems.*
No *bandit* fierce, no tyrant mad with pride,
No cavern'd hermit, rests self satisfy'd. *Pope's Essay on Man.*
BANDITTO. *n.s.* in the plural *banditti.* ~~[*bandito*, Ital.]~~
<1> A Roman sworder, and *banditto* slave,
Murder'd sweet Tully. *Shakesp. Henry* VI. *p.*ii.

{J. consolidates entries; BANDIT/BANDITTO. *n.s.* forms the new headword; J. appears to have originally crossed out 'BANDITTO', then reconsidered, smearing out his stroke. Note on plural and Shakespeare q. to precede other qs.}

To BA´NDY. *v.a.* {...}
3. {...}

Let not obvious and known truths, or ~~some of the most~~ plain and certain propositions, be *bandied* about in a disputation.
*Watt~~'s Improvement of the Mind.~~*



BANE. *n.s.* [bana, Sax. a murderer<‸~~;~~**in Runick a cause of destruction**]>
2. {...}

Who can omit the Gracchi, who declare
The Scipios' worth, those thunderbolts of war, <2>
The double *bane* of Carthage? *Dryden, Æneid* vi.
False religion is, in its nature, the greatest *bane* and destruction to government in the world. *South.* <1>

{J. reverses order to maintain chronological sequence.}

BA´NEFUL. *adj.* {...}
1. {...}

~~For~~ **<We>** voyaging to learn the direful art,
To taint with deadly drugs the barbed dart;
Observant of the gods, and sternly just,
Ilus refus'd t' impart the *baneful* trust. *Pope's Odyssey, b.*i.

B´ANEWORT. *n.s.* {...} A plant, the same with *deadly nightshade*. ~~See NIGHTSHADE.~~

{Vertical lines inking from facing IL.}

{BA′NDOG. *n.s.*}♦

Bandog, may be a dog of bad omen
the Schreich Owl which is reckond so being
added

For in Scotland the Common people
observe that before a persons death hap̄ens
some dog and generally it is a strange
dog comes at the dead of night, & howles
three or four times at the door & goes
off quietly.[1]

[1] S-G. Horizontal bar over letter 'p' indicates repetition of letter.

{To BANK. *v.a.*}
They in grave and solemn wise unfolded
Matter which little purported, but words
Bank'd in right learned phrase
Rowe[1]

**<b ‡>**
————Shoals
Of fish, that with their fins & shining scales
Glide under the green wave in sculls that oft
Bank the mid sea
Milt. P.L. B. 7. l. 400[2]

~~Bankrupt Adj divested of, Stript of a thing.~~[3]
**<d ‡> <2 It has sometimes of>**
Command a Mirrour hither straight **<d ‡>**
That I may see me what a face I have
Since it is bankrupt of his Majesty
Shaks.[4]

Bannered Adj. <**[from banner]**> **<c ‡>**
**<Furnished with banners.>**
With extended wings a bannerd host
Under spread ensigns marching might pass through
With Horse & chariots Milton[5]

{BA´NNOCK. *n.s.*}
**<a ‡>**
Scots must have drink, they cannot live on keale
Or haverbannocks or on haverjunnocks
Beaumt.[6]

[1] Nicholas Rowe, *The Ambitious Step-Mother* (*Works* I), 1.1, p. 14 (Rowe reads 'Rank'd' for 'Bank'd'). S-G. *1755* To PURPORT *v.a.* (with 'Rank'd'; aman. probably misread first-edition ms. as 'Bank'd')
[2] Milton, *Paradise Lost*, bk VII, ll. 401-404. S-G. *1755* SCULL *n.s.*, FRY *n.s.*, To SHINE *v.n.* (shorter) and To GLIDE *v.n.* (shorter)
[3] J. crosses out etymological note and adds '2 It has sometimes of'.
[4] Shakespeare, *Richard II* (*Works* IV), 4.3, p. 73 [4.1.265-67]. S-G (def. and q.). Both S-G and marked book read 'That it may shew me what a face I have'.
[5] Milton, *Paradise Lost*, bk II, ll. 885-87. S-G.
[6] Peter Mews, 'Ex-ale-tation', sig. M7v; other passages of poem also quoted under ALEBERRY *n.s.* (*1773*) and SYLLABUB *n.s.* (*1755* and *1773*). S-G.

{IL facing 2P2r}

BANK. *n.s.* {...}
2. {...}

They besieged him in Abel of Bethmaachah, and they cast up a *bank* against the city; and it stood in the trench.

2 *Samuel*, ~~xx. 15.~~

4. {...}

Let it be no *bank*, or common stock, but every man be master of his own money. Not that I ~~altogether~~ mislike *banks*, but they will hardly be brooked in regard of certain suspicions.

*Bacon~~'s Essays~~.*

To BANK. *v.a.* {...}
<2> +<2>. To lay up money in a bank.
<1> <~~2>2~~<1>. To inclose with banks. <**to fill as with a bank**>

<**b** ‡> Amid the cliffs
And burning sands, that *bank* the shrubby vales. *Thomson.*

{J. keys in Milton q. from IL at first place under new def. 1; J.'s augmentation of def. apparently a gloss of word in new Milton q.}

BA´NKRUPCY. *n.s.* {...}
2. The act of declaring one's self bankrupt; as, he ~~silenced~~ <**raised**> the clamours of his creditors by a sudden *bankrupcy*.
<^1>BA´NKRUPT. *adj.* [{...} *bancor~~up~~*<**ot**>*to*, Ital.]<^> In debt beyond the power of payment.♦

The king's grown *bankrupt*, like a broken man.

*Shakesp.* ~~*Richard* III.~~

{...} *Shak. Two Gent. of Verona.*
<**d** ‡——— > {J. keys in Shakespeare q. from IL.}

BA´NKRUPT. *n.s.* {...}

It is with wicked men <^~~**and**~~{?} **conscience**> as with a *bankrupt:* when his creditors are loud and clamorous, and speak big, he giveth them many good words. *Calamy.*

To BA´NKRUPT. *v.a.* {...}

We cast off the care of all future th~~irst~~<**rift**>, because we are already *bankrupted*. *Hammond's Fundamentals.*

BA´NNER. *n.s.* {...}
2. A streamer borne at the end of a lance, or elsewhere.
<——— **c** ‡>
{J. keys in new entry for BANNERED *adj.* from IL.}
BA´NNOCK. *n.s.* {...}
< **a** ‡>
{J. keys in Beaumont q. from IL.}

To BA´NQUET. *v.a.* {...}

Welcome his friends,
Visit his countrymen, and *banquet* them.

*Shakesp.* ~~*Taming of the Shrew.*~~

To BA´NQUET. *v.n.* {...}

The mind shall *banquet*, tho' the body pine;
Fat paunches make lean pates, and dainty bits
Make rich the ribs, but banker<‿>out the wits.

{J. indicates 'bankerout' one word.} *Shakesp.* ~~*Love's Labour Lost.*~~

BA´NQUET-HOUSE. }
BA´NQUETING-HOUSE. } *n.s.* {...} A house where ~~banquets~~ <**feasts**> are kept.

{sig. 2P2r}

<**a** ‡———> {J. keys in entry for BAPTIZATION. *n.s.* with Hooker q. from IL.}

To BAPTI´ZE. *v.a.* {...}

He to them shall leave in charge,
To teach all nations what of him they learn'd,
And his salvation; them who shall believe,
*Baptizing* in the profluent stream, the sign
Of washing them from guilt of sin, to life
Pure, and in mind prepar'd, if so befal,
For death, like that which the Redeemer dy'd.

*Milton's ~~Paradise Lost.~~*

BAR. *n.s.* {...}

3. {...}

I brake up for it my decreed place, and set *bars* and doors, and said, hitherto shalt thou come, and no farther.

*Job*, ~~xxxviii. 10~~.

{...}

Fatal accidents have set
A most unhappy *bar* between your friendship.

*Rowe's ~~Ambitious Stepmother.~~*

BAR

To BAR. *v.a.* {...}

1. {...}

My duty cannot suffer
T' obey in all your daughter's hard commands;
Though their injunction be to *bar* my doors,
And let this tyrannous night take hold upon you.

*Shakesp. ~~King Lear.~~*

When you *bar* the window-shutters of your lady's bedchamber at nights, leave open the sashes to let in the air.

*Swift's ~~Directions to the Chambermaid~~*.

3. To prevent.

{...} *Sidney, b.* i.

<**2**> Doth it not seem a thing very probable, that God doth purposely add, Do after my judgments; as giving thereby to understand, that his meaning in the former sentence was but to *bar* similitude in such things as were repugnant to his ordinances, laws, and statutes? *Hooker.*

4. To shut out from.

Hath he set bounds between their love and me?
I am their mother; who shall *bar* them from me?

*Shakesp. ~~Richard III~~.*

Our hope of Italy not only lost,
But shut from ev'ry shore, and *barr'd* from ev'ry coast. *Dryd.*

<**1**> 5. To exclude from a claim**, <or right.>**

6. To prohibit.

<——— **aa** ‡>

{J. keys in Spenser q. from IL.}

~~For though~~ the law of arms doth *bar*
The use of venom'd shot in war. *Hudibras.*

{...} *Addison.*

7. To except; to make an exception.

{J. moves Hooker q. to first place under def. 7.}

<——— **a** ‡>

{J. keys in Shakespeare q. from IL.}

Baptization n.s. [baptize]
The act of administring baptism
In maintenance of re-baptization
their Arguments are built upon this, that
heretics are not any part of the Church of
Christ Hooker 3.1.[1]

<a ‡>

{To BAR. *v.a.* 6.}

**<aa ‡>**

When these renouned noble peers of Greece
Through stubborn pride among themselves did
Forgetful of the famous golden fleece Jar
Then Orpheus with his harp their strife did ~~bar~~[2]
Spenser.[3] **<bar>**

{To BAR. *v.a.* 7.}

**<a ‡>** For your claim fair sis~~ter~~
I bar it in the interest of my wife
~~'Tis she is subcontracted to this lord~~
~~And I her Husband contradict your ban~~~~ns~~.
Shaks.[4]

1 Richard Hooker, *Ecclesiastical Polity*, vol. I, bk III, ch. i, p. 200. *1755* REBAPTIZATION *n.s.*

2 Word written off edge of IL onto printed page 2Q$^r$; J. crosses out 'bar' and rewrites word on IL where compositor can read it.

3 Spenser, *Amoretti* (*Works* VIII), 'Sonnet XLIIII', ll. 1-4. S-G. *1755* To JAR *v.n.* 4

4 Shakespeare, *King Lear* (**Works* VI), 5.6, p. 134 [5.3.84-87]. J. crosses out 'ter' of 'sister' and 'ns' of 'banns', which aman. copied off edge of IL onto printed page 2Q$^r$. S-G. *1755* SUBCONTRACTED *part. adj.* (slightly shorter), BAN *n.s.* 1 (shorter), To CONTRADICT *v.a.* (much shorter)

{IL facing 2P2$^v$}

Baralypton
/in logick/ a Syllogism of two univer
sals a particular affirmative
AppollApollo stares & all Parnassus shakes
At the rude rumbling baralypton makes
Roscom.[1]

{BARB. *n.s.* 3.}
<a ‡> ~~turning to that place~~
He left his loft steed with golden fell
And goodly gorgeous <u>barbes</u> him found not there
F.Q. ~~3~~2.2.11[2]

Barbarlie Adv.♦
Like a Barber, as when he cuts or
Shaves close with Sheers
If sheep or the lamb fall a wrigling with tail
Go by & by search it whils help may prevail
That barbarlie handled
Thou hast finishd the Cure
Tuss. hus. for May[3]

{BA′RBAROUSLY. *adv.* 2.}
<a+>
Wouldst thou not rather chuse a small renown
To be the Mayor of some poor paltry town
Biggly to look & barbarously to speak
Dryd. Ju.[4]

{BA′RBAROUSNESS. *n.s.* 1.}
<X> Tho somewhat merrily, yet uncourteously he railed upon England, objecting extreme beggary & more barbarousness unto it
Ascham.[5]

[1] Wentworth Dillon, Earl of Roscommon, *An Essay on Translated Verse*, p. 5. Aman. writes 'Appoll', smears it out, and writes 'Apollo', superimposing letter 'A' on 'll'. *1755* To RUMBLE *v.n.* (with 'baralipton' instead of 'baralypton')

[2] Spenser, *Faerie Queene* (*Works* II), bk II, canto II, st. xi, ll. 5-7. Aman. superimposes '2' on '3'. S-G. *1755* BARB *n.s.*

[3] Thomas Tusser, *Husbandry*, 'May', p. 55. S-G (slip appears to have been clipped from ms. text; slip lacks head-word and note on usage; end of third line and beginning of fourth line heavily crossed out rendering illegible this part of text: 'I dare thee assure,/cast dust in his arse,'; q. on IL therefore incomplete. *1755* To WRIGGLE *v.n.* (q. only through 'prevail')

[4] Dryden,'The Tenth Satyr of Juvenal' (*Works* IV), ll. 162-4. S-G. *1755* BIGLY *adv.*, MAYOR *n.s.* (shorter), and To POUND *v.a.* 1 (different)

[5] Roger Ascham, 'The Ready Way to the Latin Tongue', p. 150. *1755* UNCOURTEOUSLY, *adv.*

{IL facing 2Q$^{r}$}

BARB. *n.s.* {...}
3. The armour for horses.
**<a ‡——————>**
{J. keys in Spenser q. from IL.}

BARBADOES *Cherry.* {...} **<A plant>**
It has a small quinquefid calix, of one leaf having bifid segments; the flower consists of five leaves, in form of a rose, having several stamina collected in form of a tube; the ovary, in the bottom of the flower-cup, becomes a globular, fleshy, ~~soft fruit; in which is a single capsule, containing three stony winged nuts.~~ In the West Indies, it rises to be fifteen or sixteen feet high, where it produces great quantities of a pleasant tart fruit; ~~propagated in gardens there,~~ but in Europe it is a curiosity. *Millar.*



BARBA´RITY. *n.s.* {...}♦
3. Barbarism; impurity <^**or inelegance**> of speech.
{...}
Affected refinements, ~~which~~ ended by degrees in many *bar-* **<*d*>** *barities*, before the Goths had invaded Italy. *Swift.*
{J. writes marginal deletion sign, referring to 'which'.}
BA´RBAROUS. *adj.* [*barbare*, Fr. <^; **barbarus Latin;**> βαρβαρος.]
1. {...}
~~And~~ ~~h~~<**H**>e left governour, Philip, for his country a Phrygian, and for manners more *barbarous* than he that set him there.
2 *Macc.* v. 22.

BA´RBAROUSLY. *adv.* {...}
2. In a manner contrary to the rules of speech.
<——————————— **a +**>
{J. keys in Dryden q. from IL.}

3. Cruelly; inhumanly.
{...}
She wishes ~~it~~ <**she**> may prosper; but her mother used one of her nieces very *barbarously.* *Spectator*, N° 483.
BA´RBAROUSNESS. *n.s.* {...}
1. Incivility of manners.

{J. keys in Ascham q. from IL.}

2. Impurity of language.
It is ~~also much~~ degenerated and impaired, as touching the pureness of speech; being overgrown with *barbarousness.*
*Brerewood* ~~*on Languages*~~.

To BA´RBECUE. *v.a.* A term used in the West-Indies for dressing a hog whole; which, being split to the backbone, is laid flat upon a large gridiron, raised about two foot above a charcoal fire, ~~with which it is surrounded~~. <***d***>
{J. writes marginal deletion sign.}

BA´RBED. *participial adj.* {...}
2. {...}

If I conjecture right, no drizzling show'r,
But rattling storm of arrows *barb'*d with fire.
*Milton's* ~~*Par. Lost, b. vi. l. 544*~~.

BA´RBER. *n.s.* {...}
His chamber being stived with friends or suitors, ~~he~~ <**Villiers**> gave his legs, arms, and breasts to his servants to dress; his head and face to his *barber*; his eyes to his letters, and his ears to petitioners. *Wotton.*
{Crossed-out letters along outside edge of right margin part of text from IL facing 2P2v copied off edge of page.}

{sig. 2Qr}

To BA´RBER. *v.a.* {…}

Our courteous Antony,
Whom ne'er the word of No, woman heard speak,
Being *barber'd* ten times o'er, goes to the feast.
*Shakesp.* ~~*Antony and Cleopatra*~~.

BA´RBERRY. *n.s.* {…} Pipperidge bush.

~~It is set with sharp prickles, the leaves are long, and serrat-~~ ed on the edges; the flowers consist of six leaves, which expand in form of a rose, and are of a yellow colour; the fruit is long, of an acid taste, and, for the most part, of a red colour, and grows in clusters; the bark of the tree is whitish. The species are, 1. The common *barberry*. 2. *Barberry* without stones. The first of these sorts is very common in England, ~~and often planted for hedges.~~ ~~*Millar.*~~

BARD. *n.s.* {…}

There is amongst the Irish a kind of people called *bards*, which are to them instead of poets; whose profession is to set forth the praises or dispraises of men in their poems or rhimes; the which are had in high regard and estimation ~~among them~~. *Spenser* ~~*on Ireland*~~.

BARE. *adj.* {…}

1. {…}

In the old Roman statues, the~~se two parts~~ **<neck and arms>** were always *bare*, and exposed to view, as much as our hands and face ~~at present~~. <u>*Addison*</u>~~*'s Travels*~~.

4. {…}

These false pretexts and varnish'd colours failing,
*Bare* in thy guilt, how foul must thou appear?
*Milton*~~*'s Sampson Agonistes, l. 901*~~.

6. Mere.

{…} *Shakesp. Coriolanus.*

<2> You have an exchequer of words, and no other treasure for your followers; for it appears, by their <u>bare</u> liveries, that they live by your <u>*bare*</u> words. *Shakesp. Two Gent. of Verona.*

{J. ital. 'bare' and removes italics from '*bare*'.}

<1> Nor are men prevailed upon by *bare* words, only through a defect of knowledge; but carried, with these puffs of wind, contrary to knowledge. *South.*

7. Threadbare; much worn; ~~as, *bare* liveries, in the last quotation from *Shakespeare.*~~

{J. moves Shakespeare q. to first place under def. 7, thus rendering note unnecessary.}

BARE, or BORE. The *preterite* of *to bear*. See To BEAR.

**<a †>**

{J. keys in Bacon q. from IL}

BAREFACED. *adj.* {…}

2. Shameless; unreserved; <‸**being**> without concealment; without disguise.

BA`REHE<´>ADED. *adj.* {…} {J. moves stress mark.}

{Inking on Shakespeare q. from facing IL.}

BA´RENESS. *n.s.* {…}

1. {…}

So you serve us,
Till we serve you; but when you have our roses,
You barely leave our thorns to prick ourselves,
And mock us with our *bareness*. *Shak.* ~~*All's well that ends well*~~.

{sig. 2Q[v]}

{BARE, or BORE. The *preterite* of *to bear*.}

<a †>

This navy was the preparation of five years
It bare itself upon divine assistance
for it received special blessing frome Pope
Sixtus Bacon.[1]

[1] Bacon, 'Considerations Touching a War with Spain' (**Works* III), p. 523 [XIV, p. 486]. S-G ('from' mistakenly copied 'frome' on IL). *1755* REDUCEMENT *n.s.* (very different)

{IL facing sig. 2Qv}

{To BARK. *v.a.* 2.}♦

<a +> <as>
<2> To cover ^ with bark, ~~to encase with bark; to encrust.~~ {J. crosses out.}

A most instant tetter bark'd about
Most lazar like, with vile & loathsome Crust
All my smooth body Shak.[3]

{BARK. *n.s.*}
Fair when her breast like a rich laden bark
With precious merchandize she forth doth lay.
Spenser.[1]

{BARN. *n.s.* 2.} <b ‡>
~~Barn n.s.~~ <2> a kind of fish
Of round fish there are brit sprat
and barn. Carew Cornw.[4]

{BARK. *n.s.*}
Bark in Physic denotes the Jesuits or
peruvian bark, which See.[2]

[1] Spenser, *Amoretti* (*Works* VIII), 'Sonnet LXXXI', ll. 5-6. S-G. *1755* To DARK *v.a.*, MERCHANDISE *n.s.*
[2] S-G.
[3] Shakespeare, *Hamlet* (**Works* VIII), 1.10, p. 148 [1.5.71-73]. S-G (with 'v.a. To bark/from y^e noun/' at top). *1755* TETTER *n.s.*
[4] Richard Carew, *Survey of Cornwall,* bk I, [30]. S-G. *1755* SMELT *n.s.*, SPRAT *n.s.*, SCAD *n.s.* (different)

{IL facing 2Q2^r}

{BA´RGAIN. *n.s.*}
3. Stipulation. **<equivalent>**

There was a difference between courtesies received from their master and the duke; for that the duke's might have ends of utility and *bargain*; whereas their master's could not.

*Bacon*~~*'s Henry VII*~~.

5. {...}

I am sorry for thy misfortune; however we must make the best of a bad *bargain*/ ~~thou art in jeopardy, that is certain.~~

*Arbuthnot*~~*'s History of J. Bull.*~~

BARGE. *n.s.* {...}
1. A boat for pleasure/<**, or convenience**>
{...}

It was consulted, when I had taken my *barge*, and gone a-shore, that my ship should have ~~set sail and~~ left me there.

*Raleigh*~~*'s Essays*~~.

BA´RGER. *n.s.* {...}

~~Howsoever, many wafarers make themselves glee, by put-ting~~ the inhabitants ~~in mind of this privilege; who again,~~ especially the women, like the ~~Campellians in the north, and the~~ London *bargers*, forslow not to baigne them.

*Carew*~~*'s Survey of Cornwal.*~~

{J. crosses out 'like the', then smears out stroke to retain coherence.}

BARK. *n.s.* {...}
2. {...}

Things, ~~I say,~~ being in this state, it came to pass, that the duke of Parma must have flown, if he would have come into England; for he could neither get *bark* nor mariner to put to sea. *Bacon on the War with Spain.*

To BARK. *v.n.* {...}
1. {...}

**<I was>** Sent before my time
Into this breathing world, scarce half made up,
And that so lamely and unfashionably,
That dogs *bark* at me. *Shakesp. Richard* III.

Why do your dogs *bark* so? ~~be there bears i' th' town?~~
*Shakesp*~~*. Merry Wives of Windsor.*~~

2. {...}

You dare patronage
The envious *barking* of ~~your~~ **<that>** saucy tongue,
Against my lord the duke of Somerset! *Shakesp. Henry* VI.

To BARK. *v.a.* {...} <‸ ‸**1**>To strip trees of their bark.

{...}

These trees, after they are *barked*, and cut into shape, are tumbled ~~down~~ from the mountains into the stream.

*Addison*~~*'s Remarks on Italy.*~~
<⌐**a** ‡>

{J. keys in def. 2 and Shakespeare q. from IL; extraneous mark before '**a** ‡'.}

BA<´>RK-BARED. *adj.* {...}

Excorticated and *bark-bared* trees {...}, and be covered with bark.

*Mortimer*~~*'s Art of Husbandry.*~~

BA´RKER. *n.s.* {...}
1. {...}

What hath he done more than a base cur? barked and made a noise? had a fool or two to spit in his mouth? But they are rather enemies of my fame than me, these *barkers*.

~~*Ben.*~~ *Johnson*~~*'s Discovery.*~~

BA´RLEY. *n.s.* {. . .}

It hath a thick spike {...} 3. Sprat *barley*, or battledoor *barley*. ~~All these sorts of *barley* are sown in the spring of the year, in a dry time.~~ In some very dry light land, the *barley* is sown early in March; but in strong clayey soils it is not sown till April. The square *barley*, or *big*, is chiefly cultivated in the north of England, and in Scotland; and is hardier than the other sorts. Where *barley* is sown upon new broken up land, the usual method is to plough up the land in March, and let it lie fallow until June; at which time it is ploughed again, and sown with turneps, which are eaten by sheep in winter, by whose dung the land is ~~greatly improved; and then, in March following, the ground is ploughed again, and sown with *barley.*~~ *Millar.*

BARM. *n.s.* {...}

You may try the force of imagination, upon staying the working of beer when the *barm* is put into it.

*Bacon*~~*'s Nat. History,* Nº 992.~~

BARN. *n.s.* {...} <‸ ‸**1**> A place or house for laying up any sort of grain, hay, or straw, ~~*&c.*~~ <**b** ‡>

{J. keys in Carew q. from IL.}

BARO′METER. *n.s.* {...}
A machine for measuring the weight of the atmosphere, {...}

which is a glass tube filled with mercury, ~~horizontally~~ <**hermetically**> sealed at one end; {...} in order to measure the atmosphere more accurately; ~~and hence arose a great number of *barometers*, of different structures. Dr.~~ Halley observes, ~~in the *Philosophical Transactions*,~~ that in calm weather, when the air is inclined to rain, the mercury is commonly low; in serene good settled weather, high. {...}

But there are frequently great changes in the air, without any perceptible alteration in the *barometer*. ~~The alterations of the weight of the air, are generally allowed to be the cause of those in the *barometer*; but philosophers cannot easily determine whence those alterations rise in the atmosphere.~~ {...} *Harris.*

Gravity is another property of air, {...} so that the exact specifick gravity of the air cannot be determined<.> ~~when~~ the *barometer* stands <^ **sometimes**> at thirty inches, with a moderate heat of the weather. *Arbuthnot on Air.*



BA′RONAGE. *n.s.* {...}
1. {...}

His charters of the liberties of England, and of the forest, were hardly, and with difficulty, gained by ~~his~~ <**the**> *baronage* at Staines, *A.D.* 1215. *Hale's Common Law of England.*

BA′RONET. *n.s.* {...}

It was first founded by king James I. *A.D.* 1611. *Cowel.* ~~But~~ ~~i~~<**I**>t appears by the following passage, that the term was in use before, though in another sense.

BA′RRATOR. *n.s.* {...}

Will it not reflect ~~as much~~ on thy character, Nic, to turn *barrator* in thy old days, a stirrer up of quarrels amongst thy neighbours. *Arbuthnot's History of J. Bull.*

{sig. 2Q2v}

{blank page}

{IL facing 2Q2v}

{blank page}

{IL facing 2R[r]}

## BAR

BA´RRENNESS. *n.s.* {...}

2. {...}

Within the self same hamlet, lands have divers degrees of value, through the diversity of their fertility or *barrenness.*

*Bacon ~~on Alienations~~.*

3. ~~Want of invention;~~ want of the power of producing any thing new.

BA´RREN WORT. *n.s.* {...}

The stalks are divided into three branches, {...}
in which are ~~contained~~ round flat seeds.

*Millar.*/

## BAR

To BARRICA´DE. *v.a.* {...}

A new vulcano ~~continually~~ discharg~~ing~~**<es>** that matter, which being till then *barricaded* up, and imprisoned in ~~the bowels of~~ the earth, was the occasion of ~~very great and~~ frequent calamities. *Woodward~~'s Natural History~~.*

To BARRICA´DO. *v.a.* {...}

The truth of causes we find ~~so obliterated, that it seems~~ almost *barricadoed* from any intellectual approach.

*Harvey on Consumptions.*

BA´RRIER. *n.s.* [*barriere*, Fr. It is sometimes pronounced with the accent on the last syllable, but it is placed more properly on the first<‸>.] **<‸it is used by Pope indifferently>**♦

{J.'s note refers to Pope's inconsistent accenting of word in the qs. below.}

1. A ~~barricade;~~ **<security;>** an entrenchment.

Safe in the love of heav'n an ocean flows
Around our realm, a *barrier* from the foes. Pope's *Odyssey.*

3. {...}

If you value yourself as a man of learning, you are building a most unpassable *barrier* against all improvement.

*Watts~~'s Improvement of the Mind~~.*

4. {...}

**<Let p>**~~P~~ris'ners to the pillar bound,
At either *barrier* plac'd; nor, captives made,
Be freed, or arm'd anew. *Dryden's Fables.*

5. {...}

But wave whate'er to Cadmus may belong,
And fix, O muse, the *barrier* of thy song,
At Oedipus. *Pope's Statius.*

How instinct varies in the groveling swine,
Compar'd, half reas'ning elephant! with thine:
'Twixt that and reason, what a nice *barrier!*
For ever sep'rate, yet for ever near. *Pope's Essay on Man.*

BA´RROW. *n.s.* {...}

**<1>** Any kind of carriage moved by the hand, as a *hand-barrow;* a frame of boards, with handles at each end, carried between two men; a *wheelbarrow*, that which one man pushes forward, by raising it upon one wheel.

Have I lived to be carried in a basket, like a *barrow* of butcher's offal, and to be thrown into the Thames?

*Shakesp. ~~Merry Wives of Windsor~~.*

**<2>** ~~BA´RROW.~~ *n.s.* [beꞃᵹ, Saxon.] {...}

**<3>** BARROW, whether in the beginning or end of names of places, signifies a grove; from beaꞃƿe, which the Saxons used in the same sense. *Gibson's Camden.*

**<4>** BARROW is likewise used in Cornwal for a hillock, under which, in old times, bodies have been buried.

{J. consolidates four separate entries for BARROW *n.s.* under one headword with four senses.}

{sig. 2R[r]}

{To BA´RTER. *v.a.*}
1. {...}
For him was I exchang'd and ransom'd;
But with a baser man of arms by far,
Once, in contempt, they would have *barter'd* me.
*Shakesp.* ~~*Henry* VI. *p.* i.~~

BA´RTER. *n.s.* {...}
He who corrupteth English with foreign words, is as wise as ladies that change plate for china; for which, I think, the laudable traffick of old cloaths is much the fairest *barter.*
*Felton* ~~*on the Classicks*.~~

BASE. *adj.* {...}
6. {...}
In pipes, the lower the note holes be, and the further from the mouth of the pipe, the more *base* sound they yield.
*Bacon's* ~~*Natural History*, N° 178.~~

**<a ‡——————>**
{J. keys in Bacon q. from IL.}



BASE. *n.s.* {...}
6. The place from which racers or tilters run; the bottom of the field.
{...} *Dryden's Virg.*
<—————————————— **oa ‡**>
<7>
{J. keys in new def. 7 and Spenser q. from IL.}
~~7~~<8>. The string that gives a base sound.
{...} *Dryden' s Mackfl.*
<~~——┼┼┼—— 9~~>
{J. draws line to key in new sense 9, then crosses out line and number.}
~~8~~<9>. An old rustick play; {...}

To BASE. *v.a.* [*bas*~~i~~<s>*er*, Fr.] {'s' superimposed on 'i'.} {...}

BA´SELY. *adv.* {...}
1. {...}
With broken vows his fame he will not stain,
With conquest *basely* bought, ~~and with~~ inglorious gain.
*Dryden.*
2. {...}
These two Mitylene brethren, *basely* born, crept out of a small galliot unto the majesty of great kings.
*Knolles*~~'s *History of the Turks*.~~

To BASH. *v.n.* {...}
His countenance was bold, and *bash*~~'~~<e>*d* not
For Guyon's looks, but scornful eye-glance at him shot.
*Fairy Queen, b.* ii. *c.* iv.
{J. changes 'bash'd' to 'bashed'.}

{BARTH. new}
Young broome or good pasture thy Ewes do
require
Warm barth and in safety their lambs do
desire
Tuss. Husb. for Janry
Barth is commonly an inclosure or place
near the farm house well shelterd where
the Ewes & lambs are brought in for warmth
Note to Tuss.
Hence the common phrase he has a
warm birth for barth[1]

{BASE. *n.s.* 7.}
**<oa ‡>**
<7> ~~base in music~~ **<The rough hoarse sound in musick opposed to the noble>**
The rolling sea resounding soft
In his big base them fitly answered
And on the rock the waves breaking aloft
A solemn mean unto them measured
Spens 2.12[2]

{BASE. *adj.* 6.}
**<a ‡>**
The slacker strings are or the less
wound up the baser is the sound
Bacon.[3]

[1] Thomas Tusser, *Husbandry*, 'January', pp. 7-8. Verses not keyed in, possibly an oversight. S-G (all on one slip).
[2] Spenser, *Faerie Queene* (*Works* II), bk II, canto XII, st. xxxiii, ll. 1-4. S-G. *1755* MEAN *n.s.* 2
[3] Bacon, *Natural History* (**Works* III), cent. II, § 179, p. 43 [II, cent. II, §179, p. 408]. S-G. *1755* START *n.s.* 5

{IL facing 2Rv}

{BA'SHFUL. *adj.* 2.}
<‸**it may come from <u>abbaisser</u> French**>[3]

{BA'SIL. *n.s.*}
Fine basil desireth it may be her lot
To grow as a gelliflower trim in a pot
That ladies & gentils for whom ye do serve
May help her, as needeth, poor life to preserve.
Tuss. hus. for May[1]

{BASE. *n.s.* 7.}
7 Base in music
the rolling sea resounding soft
In his big <u>base</u> them fitly answered
And on the Rock the waves breaking aloft
A solemn mean unto them measured
Spens. 2. 12[4]

{BA'SILISK. *n.s.* 2.}
<**a** ‡> Thou hast talk'd
Of basilisks, of cannon, culverin
~~Of prisoners ransom & of soldiers slain~~
Shak.[2]

[1] Thomas Tusser, *Husbandry*, 'May', p. 66. *1755* GENTILE *n.s.*
[2] Shakespeare, *1 Henry IV* (**Works* IV), 2.6, p. 129 [2.3.50-54]. S-G (with '2' at top). *1755* FORTINS *n.s.* (much shorter), RETIRE *n.s.* (much shorter)
[3] J. writes note for insertion under BASHFUL on facing printed page 2R2$^r$.
[4] Aman. writes def. and q. on IL facing wrong p.; he then crosses both out and apparently recopies def. and q. onto IL facing 2R$^v$.

{IL facing 2R2$^r$}

BA´SHFUL. *adj.* [This word, {…} The conjecture of *Minshew* seems most probable.<^>]
{J. keys in note on derivation from IL.}
2. Sheepish; viciously modest/<; **timorous.**>

BA´SIL. *n.s.* {…}
~~This plant hath a labiated flower of one leaf, whose crest is~~ upright, roundish, notched, and larger than the beard, which is generally curled, or gently cut. Out of the flower cup rises the pointal, attended by four embryos, that become so many seeds inclosed in a husk, which was before the flower cup; the husk is divided into two lips, the upper one growing upright, and is split into two; but the under one is cut into several parts. The species are eight; 1. Common *basil.* 2. Common *basil,* with dark green leaves, and white flowers. 3. Lesser *basil,* with narrow serrated leaves. 4. The least *basil,* commonly called *bush-basil, &c.* These annual plants are propagated from seeds in March, upon a moderate hot bed. In August they perfect their seeds. The first sort is prescribed in medi~~cine; but the fourth is most esteemed for its beauty and scent.~~
*Millar.*

BA´SIL. *n.s.* The angle to which the edge of a joiner's tool is ground away.
BA´SIL. *n.s.*<^**[perhaps from the city Basil]**>The skin of a sheep tanned. *Dict.*
{J. apparently intends to reverse order of entries.}

BA´SILISK. *n.s.* [*basiliscus,* Lat. of [?]<*β*>*ασιλισκος,* of *βασιλευς,* a king.]
{J. corrects or adds Greek beta.}♦
1. {…}
The *basilisk* was a serpent not above three palms long, and differenced from other serpents by advancing his head, and some white marks or coronary spots upon the crown.
*Brown's ~~Vulgar Errours.~~*
2. A species of cannon or ordnance.
< ++
**a**——————> {J. keys in Shakespeare q. from IL.}
~~There~~ we ~~imitate and practise to~~ make swifter motions than any you have: and to make them stronger and more violent than yours are; exceeding your greatest cannons and *basilisks.*
*Bacon's New Atlantis.*/

BA´SIN. *n.s.* {…}

BAS

1. {…}
Let one attend him with a silver *basin,*
Full of rosewater, and bestrew'd with flowers.
*Shakesp. ~~Taming of the Shrew.~~*

7. A concave piece of metal by which glass grinders form their convex glasses. **<Dict>**
8. A round shell or case of iron placed over a furnace, in which hatters mould the matter of a hat into form. **<Dict>**
{J. indicates definitions are borrowed from another reference source, in this case Chambers's *Cyclopædia,* as are definitions 5 (probably) and 6; Chambers has 'BASON'.}

BA´SIS. *n.s.* {…}
2. {…}
Upon our coming to the bottom, observing an English inscription upon the *basis,* we read it over several times.
*Addison~~'s Freeholder, Nº 47~~.*

5. {…}
Build me thy fortune upon the *basis* of valour.
*Shakesp. ~~Twelfth Night.~~*

BASS-RELIEF. *n.s.* {...}
<**In s**>Sculpture, the figures of which do not stand out from the ground in their full proportion. {...}
{J. begins to alter definition to read 'In sculpture', but changes his mind and smears out the alteration.}

BA'SSET. *n.s.* {...}
~~Gamesters would no more blaspheme, and lady~~ Dabcheek's *basset* bank would be broke. *Dennis.*

BASSO'N. } *n.s.* {...} A musical instrument of the wind
BASSO'ON. } kind, blown with a reed, and furnished with eleven holes, which are stopped like other large flutes; its diameter at bottom is nine inches, and it serves for the bass in concerts of hautboys, ~~*&c.*~~ *Trevoux.*

BA'STARD. *adj.* {...}
1. {...}
Peace is a very apoplexy, lethargy, insensible, a getter of more *bastard* children than war's a destroyer of men.
*Shakesp.*~~*Coriolanus.*~~

BA'STARD *Cedar Tree.* [called *guazuma* in the West Indies.]
The characters are; It hath a regular flower, consisting of five leaves, hollowed like a spoon at their base; but, at their tops, divided into two parts, like a fork. The flower cup consists of three leaves, from whence arises the pointal, which afterwards becomes a roundish warted fruit, which has five cells, inclosing many seeds.
It grows plentifully in the low lands in Jamaica, where it rises to the height of forty or fifty feet, and has a large trunk. The timber of this tree is cut into staves, for cases of all sorts, and used for many other purposes. The fruit is eat by cattle, as it falls from the trees, and is esteemed very good to fatten them; so that the planters often leave these trees standing in their savannas, when they clear them from all other wood.
*Millar.*



To BASTE. *v.a.* {...}
2. {...}
Sir, I think the meat wants what I have, a *basting.*
*Shakesp.* ~~*Romeo and Juliet.*~~
3. {...}
The fat of roasted mutton falling on the birds, will serve to *baste* them, and so save time and butter.
*Swift*~~*'s Directions to the Cook.*~~

BASTINA'DE. } *n.s.* {...}
BASTINA'DO. }
1. {...}
~~But~~ this courtesy was worse than a *bastinado* to Zelmane; so that ~~again~~, with rageful eyes, she bad him defend himself.
*Sidney, b.* ii./

BA'STION. *n.s.* {...} <╫>
To<||>ward: but how? ay there's the question;
Fierce the assault, unarm'd the *bastion.* *Prior.*
{J. adds a space between 'To' and 'ward'.}

BAT. *n.s.* {...} An animal having the body of a mouse<,> and the wings of a bird;<^**fitted for flight**> not with feathers, but with a sort of skin which is extended. {...} *Calmet.*
{...}
But then grew reason dark; that ~~fair star~~ <**she**> no more
Could the fair forms of good and truth discern;
*Bats* they became who eagles were before;
And this they got by their desire to learn. *Sir J. Davies.*

BAT-FOWLING. *n.s.* {...}
Bodies lighted at night by fire, must have a brighter lustre given them than by day; as sacking of cities, *bat-fowling,* ~~*&c.*~~ <***d***>
*Peacham on Drawing.*

{sig. 2R2[v]}

{blank page}

{IL facing 2R2[v]}

{BATE. *n.s.*}
Love in her passions like a right make bate
whisper'd to both sides arguments of Quarrel
Sidney[1]

{To BATE. *v.a.* 1.}

<ǂ>

When baseness is exalted, do not bate
The place its honour for the persons sake.
The shrine is that which thou dost venerate
And not the beast that bears it on his back.
Herbert T. of Sacr. P[2]

{To BATHE. *v.a.* 1.}

<**a** ‡>

Yet are the men more loose than they
More kemb'd & bath'd & rub'd & trim'd
More sleek & soft & slacker limb'd
B. Johns.[3]

{BA'TTAILLOUS. *adj.*}
See with what outrage from the frosty north
The early valiant Suede draws forth his wings
In battaillous array Phillips[4]

{BAT *n.s.*}
Make ready your stiff bats & Clubs
Shak.[5]

[1] Sidney, *Arcadia*, bk II, pp. 207-8. S-G. *1755* MAKEBATE *n.s.*
[2] George Herbert, *The Temple*, 'The Church-Porch', ll. 265-8, p. 17. S-G. *1755* To VENERATE *v.a.*
[3] Ben Jonson, *Catiline* (*Works* I), Act 1, ll. 560-62. S-G (with 'v.a. 1' at top). *1755* To TRIM *v.a.*, SLEEK *n.s.*, To KEMB *v.a.*(shorter)
[4] John Philips, 'Bleinheim', ll. 405-407. S-G. *1755* OUTRAGE *n.s.* (spelt 'battailous')
[5] Shakespeare, *Coriolanus* (**Works* VI), 1.2, p. 436 [1.1.161]. S-G. *1755* RAT *n.s.*, READY *adj.*

{IL facing 2S^r}

## BAT

To BATE. *v.a.* {...}
1. {...}

*Shakesp. Merchant of Venice.*

<ǂ————— >
{J. keys in Herbert q. from IL.}

BATE seems to have been once the preterite of *bite*, as *Shakespeare* uses *biting faulchion*; unless, in the following lines, it may be rather deduced from *beat*. <∧**but** ~~**I rather derive from**~~ **bite**>

To BATHE. *v.a.* {...}
1. {...}

*Milton's Paradise Lost, b.* x. *l.* 437.

< **a** ‡ ————— >
{J. keys in Jonson q. from IL.}

## BAT

To BATHE. *v.n.* {...}
~~Except~~ they meant to *bathe* in reeking wounds,
~~I cannot tell.~~ ~~*Macbeth.*~~ <**Shakesp.**>
The delighted spirit
~~To~~ <**Must**> *bathe* in firy floods, or to reside
In thrilling regions of thick ribbed ice. *Sh. Meas. for Meas.*

{sig. 2S^r}

To BA´TTER. *v.a.* {...}
1. {...}
{...} *Dryden.*
<‡ ———————— >
{J. keys in Pope q. from IL.}

To BA´TTER. *v.n.* {...}
<**1**> The side of a wall, or any timber, that bulges from its bottom or foundation, is said to *batter.* *Moxon's Mech. Exercises.*
<**a** ‡ ————————> {J. keys in Moxon q. from IL.}
BA´TTER. *n.s.* {...}
One would have all things little, hence has try'd
Turkey poults fresh'd from th' egg in *batter* fry'd.
*King's ~~Art of Cookery.~~*

BA´TTLE. *n.s.* {...}
3. {...}
~~The earl of~~ Angus led the avant-guard, himself followed with the *battle* a good distance behind, and after came the arrier.
*Hayward.*/
~~4.~~<^ **4 An army drawn up b** ‡>We say to join *battle*; to give *battle.*
{J. keys in Shakespeare q. from IL.}

BA´TTLE-AXE. *n.s.* {...}
~~Certain~~ tinners, ~~as they were~~ working, found spear heads, *battle-axes*, and swords of copper, wrapped in linen clouts.
*Carew~~'s Survey of Cornwal~~.*
BA´TTLEDOOR. *n.s.* {...}
Play-things, which are above their skill, as tops, gigs, *battle-doors*, and the like, which are to be used with labour, should ~~indeed~~ be procured ~~them~~. <**for children**> *Locke.*
BA´TTLEMENT. *n.s.* {...}
~~Thou shalt~~ make a *battlement* for thy roof, that thou bring not blood upon thine house, if any man fall from thence.
*Deut.* xxii. 8./
{...}
The weighty mallet deals resounding blows,
Till the proud *battlements* her tow'rs inclose. *Gay's Trivia.*
B´ATTY. *adj.* {...}
Till o'er their brows death counterfeiting sleep,
With leaden legs and *batty* wings doth creep.
*Shakesp. ~~Midsummer Night's Dream.~~*
BA´VAROY. *n.s.* <^~~**probably bavarois**~~> A kind of cloke, or surtout.

BA´WBLING. *adj.* {...}
A *bawbling* vessel was he captain of,
For shallow draught and bulk unpriz~~ed~~<**able**>;
With which such scathful grapple did he make,
With the most noble bottom of our fleet.
*Shakesp. Twelfth Night.*

{To BA'TTER. *v.a.* 1.}
~~To beat, to pelt, to strike at.~~ <‡>
The grecian phalanx moveless as a tower
On all sides batter'd yet resists his power
Pope[1]

{To BA'TTER. *v.n.*}
<**a** ‡>
If your work be too cold it will not feel the
weight of the hammer, as smiths say,
when it will not batter under it Mox.[2]

{BA'VAROY. *n.s.*}
**<^[probably bavarois from bavaria, as a certain kind of coach is called a landau]>**

{BA'TTLE. *n.s.* 4.}
~~A body of men in gen~~[l] <**b** ‡>
From camp to camp
Fire ans$^{rs}$. fire & through their paly flames
Each battle sees the others umber'd face
Shak.[3]

Battled adj. /from Battle/
Famous in battle
High battled Cæsar will
Unstate his happiness be stagd to the Shew
Against a sworder. Shak. A. & C.[4]

1 Pope, *Iliad* (*Poems* VII), bk XV, ll. 744-45. S-G. *1755* MOVELESS *adj.*, PHALANX *n.s.*
2 Joseph Moxon, *Mechanick Exercises*, 'Of Smithing in General', p. 8. S-G. *1755* REDSEAR *v.n.*(different)
3 Shakespeare, *Henry V* (**Works* IV), 4.1, p. 380 [4. Prologue. 4-9]. S-G. *1755* PALY *adj.*, UMBERED *adj.*, To ANSWER *v.n.* 16 (shorter, with differences)
4 Shakespeare, *Antony and Cleopatra* (**Works* VII), 3.9, p. 172 [3.13.29-31]. S-G (with smudged comma or other sign after 'happiness'; aman. cannot decipher, leaving gap on IL after 'happiness'). *1755* SWORDER *n.s.* (shorter), To UNSTATE *v.a.* (shorter)

{IL facing 2S$^{v}$}

{BAY. *n.s.* 1, new.} <**a** ‡>
The hunt is up, the Morn is bright & gray
The fields are fragrant & the Woods are green
Uncouple here and let us make a bay   Shak.[1]

[1] Shakespeare, *Titus Andronicus* (**Works* VI), 2.3, p. 266 [2.2.1-3]. S-G (with '~~2~~ abboi' at top; see etymological note to second entry for BAY *n.s. 1755*). *1755* To UNCOUPLE *v.a.*, HUNT *n.s.* (shorter)

{IL facing 2S2$^{r}$}

BAWD. *n.s.* {…} A procurer, or procuress; one that introduces men and women to each to each other, for the promotion of debauchery. <**This now only used of women**>

To BAWD. *v.n.* {…}

~~And i~~<I>n four months a batter'd harridan;
Now nothing's left, but wither'd, pale, and shrunk,
To *bawd* for others, and go shares with punk. *Swift.*

To BAWL. *v.n.* {…}

1. To hoot; to cry with great vehemence, whether for joy <^ **eagerness**> or pain. A word always used in contempt.

{…}

Loud menaces were heard, and foul disgrace,
And *bawling* infamy, in language base,
Till sense was lost in sound, and silence fled the place.
*Dryden~~'s Fables~~.*

So on the tuneful Margarita's tongue
The list'ning nymphs, and ravish'd heroes hung;
But citts and fops the heav'n born musick blame,
And *bawl*, and hiss, and damn her into fame.
*Smith ~~on J. Philips~~.*

2. {…}

A ~~little~~ child was *bawling*, and a~~n old~~ woman chiding it. *L'Estrange's Fables.*

If ~~they~~ <^ **children**> were never suffered to have what they cried for, they would never, with *bawling* and peevishness, contend for mastery. *Locke.*



BAY. *adj.* {…}

~~I remember,~~ my lord, you gave good words the other day of a *bay* courser I rode on. 'Tis yours because you liked it. *Shakesp. Timon.*

{…}

<**Be h**>~~H~~is colour grey,
For beauty dappled, or the brightest *bay*. *Dryden's Virgil.*

BAY. *n.s.* {…}

1. {…}

We have ~~also some~~ works in the midst of the sea, and some *bays* upon the shore for some works, wherein is required the air and vapour of the sea. *Bacon.*

BAY. *n.s.* [*abboi*, Fr. signifies the last extremity; {…} It is taken from *abboi*, the barking of a dog at hand, and thence signified the condition of a stag when the hounds were almost upon him.] <^ **1 The cry of a pack of hounds a ‡**> The state of any thing sourrounded by enemies, <**4**> and obliged to face them by an impossibility of escape.

This ship, for fifteen hours, sate like a stag among hounds at the *bay*, and was sieged and fought with, in turn, by fifteen great ships. *Bacon's War with Spain.*

{…} *Denham.*

{…} *Dryden's Æneid.*

{…} *Dryden's Virgil.*

<**2 It ~~use~~ is used of those that press another**>

{…} *Swift.*

He stands at bay,
And puts his last weak refuge in despair. ~~*Thomson.*~~

<~~**3 The c**~~>

{J. inserts new def. 1 and keys in new Shakespeare q. from IL; other changes not completely clear: 'The state of any thing surrounded by enemies …' possibly designated def. 4 (or 2), with Denham q. and two Dryden qs. as illustrations; 'It is used of those that press another' perhaps intended as def. 2 or 3 (marked '2'), with Swift (and possibly Bacon?) qs. as illustrations; J. originally thought to insert 'The cry of a pack of hounds' as new def. 3, probably with Bacon q. as illustration.}◆

BAY *Tree*. {…} <^ **1**> This tree hath a flower of one leaf, {…} The first and second sorts are old inhabitants of the English gardens~~; and as there are varieties obtained from the same seeds, they are promiscously cultivated, and are not to be distinguished asunder until they have produced flowers. These plants are propagated either from seeds, or by laying down the tender branches, which will take root in one year's time.~~ *Mill.*

<**2**> ~~BAY. *n.s.*~~ A poetical name for an honorary crown or garland, {…}

{To BAY *v.n.*}

2. [from *bay*, an inclosed place.] To encompass about; to shut in.

<2> We are at the stake,
And *bay'd* about with many enemies. *Shakesp. Julius Caesar.*

<1> To BAY. *v.a.* <^ ^1> To follow with barking; to bark at. {...}
{...} *Shakesp. Midsum. Night's Dream.*
{...} *Shak. Henry* IV.

{J. moves sense 2 with Shakespeare q. from To BAY. *v.n.* to second sense under To BAY. *v.a.;* vertical strokes inking from facing IL.}

BAY *Salt.* Salt made of sea water, ~~which receives its consistence from~~ <**by**> the heat of the sun, ~~as is~~ so called from its brown colour. The greatest quantities of this salt are made in France, on the coast of Bretagne, ~~Saintonge, *&c.* from the middle of May to the end of August,~~ by letting the sea water into square pits ~~or basons;~~ where its surface being struck ~~and agitated~~ by the rays of the sun, it ~~thickens at first imperceptibly, and~~ becomes covered over with a slight crust, which ~~hardening~~ by the continuance of the heat, is ~~wholly~~ converted into salt. The water in this condition is scalding hot, and the crystallization is perfected in eight, ten, or at most fifteen days. *Chamb.*

All eruptions of air, though small and slight, give sound, which we call crackling, puffing, spitting, ~~*&c.*~~ as in *bay salt* and bay leaves cast into the fire. *Bacon's Nat. History,* N° 123.

BAY *Window.* {...}

It hath *bay windows* transparent as barricadoes.
*Shakesp.*/~~*Twelfth Night*~~.

To BE. *v.n.* {...}

1. {...}

Be but about
To say, she\ <**is**> a goodly lady, and
The justice of your hearts will add thereto,
'Tis pity she'*s* not honest, honourable. *Shak. Winter's Tale.*

{...}

Is it not easy to discern what such men would *be* at. *Stillingfl.*

{J. ital. 'is'.}



BE'ACON. *n.s.* {...}

1. {...}

The king seemed to account of the designs of Perkin as a may-game; yet had given order for the watching of *beacons* ~~upon the coasts~~, and erecting more where they stood too thin.
*Bacon*/*s* ~~*Henry* VII~~.

BEAD. *n.s.* {...}

2. {...}

With scarfs and fans, and double change of brav'ry,
With amber bracelets, *beads*, and all such knav'ry.
*Shakesp.*/~~*Taming of a Shrew*~~.

BEAD *Tree.* {...} <**A tree**>

~~It hath pennated leaves, like those of the ash, the flowers~~ consist of five leaves, which expand in form of a rose; in the centre of the flower is a long fimbriated tube, containing the style; the fruit is roundish and fleshy, containing a hard furrowd nut, di~~vided into five cells, each containing one oblong broadish seed~~. The outside pulp of the fruit in some countries is eaten; but the nut is, by religious persons, bored through, and strung as beads; whence it takes its name. It produces ripe fruits in Italy and Spain. *Millar.*

{To BAY. *v.n.*}
With Showers of Stones he drives them far away
The scattring dogs around at distance bay[1]

{To BE. *v.n.*}
To be out. at a loss. to be puzzled.
This youth was such a mercurial as could make
his own part if at anytime he chancd to be out
Bac.[2]

{To BE. *v.n.*}
To be in with To side with. to espouse
any cause
Those who pretended to be in with the prin:
ciples upon which her Majesty proceeded, either
absent themselves where the whole cause depend
ed, or side directly with the enemy. Swift[3]

{Colon in 'prin:/ciples' written off edge of page.}

{BEAD. *n.s.*}
Mine eyes
Seeing those beads of sorrow stand in thine
Began to water. Shak.[4]

[1] Pope, *Odyssey* (*Poems* X), bk XIV, ll. 39-40. S-G. *1755* SHOWER *n.s.*
[2] Bacon, *History of King Henry VII* (**Works* III), p. 448 [VI, p. 132]. S-G. *1755* OUT *adv.* 15, MERCURIAL *adj.*
[3] Swift, 'Some Free Thoughts Upon the Present State of Affairs' (*Prose* VIII), pp. 82-3. S-G. *1755* To SIDE *v.n.* (slightly different)
[4] Shakespeare, *Julius Caesar* (**Works* VII), 3.4, p. 54 [3.1. 283-285]. S-G. *1755* To WATER *v.n.*

{IL facing 2S2$^v$}

{BEAK. *n.s.* 2.}
<‡>
No <u>beaks</u> of ships in naval triumph borne
Prior.[1]

{BEAN. *n.s.*}
Names have been taken of civil honours, as king, knight, partly for their ancestors were such, or were kings of the <u>bean</u>, Christmass lords. Cambden[3]

{To BEAR. *v.a.*}
To contain as a cargo in a ship
The mind of Man is too light & narrow a bottom to bear much certainty among the ruffling winds and tumultuary waves of passion humour & opinion and if the luggage be prized equally with the Jewels none will be cast out till all be lost and Shipwreck'd Glanv. to Alb.[4]

{BEAM. *n.s.* 4.}
<**a** ‡> ~~the scent~~
~~Was of a~~ <**A w**>~~w~~ell grown Stag whose antlers rise
High on his front, his <u>beams</u> invade the skies
Dryd. Virg. Æ. 7.667[2]

1 Matthew Prior, 'Carmen Seculare, 1700' (*Works* I), canto XXV, l. 327. S-G (slip misbound opposite 3M2$^{r}$ near BORNE; '2 Bear' written at top).
2 Dryden, *Virgil's Aeneis* (*Works* VI), bk VII, ll. 669-70. S-G ('4' superimposed on '2' in top left corner). *1755* ANTLER *n.s.* (slightly shorter)
3 William Camden, *Remains Concerning Britain*, p. 107. S-G (with 'for y$^{t}$ y$^{ir}$ ancestors' and 'christmas').
4 Joseph Glanvill, 'To the Learned Tho. Albius' (*Scepsis Scientifica*), sig. a3$^{v}$. *1755* LUGGAGE *n.s.* (slightly shorter)

{IL facing 2T$^{r}$}

## BEA

BE´AGLE. *n.s.* {...}

~~The rest were various huntings.~~
The graceful goddess was array'd in green;
About her feet were little *beagles* seen,
That watch'd with upward eyes the motions of their queen.
*Dryden's Fables.*

BEAK. *n.s.* {...}
2. A piece of brass like a beak,{...}
{...} *Dryden.*
<‡————————>
{J. keyes in Prior q. from IL.}

BEAM. *n.s.* {...}
4. The horn of a stag.
{...} *Denham.*
<**a** ‡ ————————>
{J. keys in Dryden q. from IL.}

## BEA

7. {...}
~~Let them present me death upon the wheel,~~
~~Or~~ pile ten hills on the Tarpeian rock,
That the precipitation might downstretch
Below the *beam* of sight. *Shakesp. Coriolanus.*
<**8**> BEAM *of an anchor.* {...}
<**9**> BEAM *Compasses.* {...}
{J. consolidates entries under BEAM *n.s.*}

BEAM *Tree.* <**The**> ~~See~~ WILDSERVICE, ~~of which it is a species.~~

BEAN. *n.s.* {...}
It hath a papilionaceous flower, {...}
There are several varieties of the garden *beans*, ~~differing either in colour or size. The principal sorts which are cultivated in England, are the Mazagan, the small Lisbon, the Spanish, the Tokay, the Sandwich, and Windsor *beans*.~~ The Mazagan *bean* is brought from a settlement ~~of the Portuguese on the coast of~~ <**in**> Africa, ~~of the same name~~; and is by far the best sort to plant for an early crop, ~~a great bearer, and also an excellent tasted *bean*.~~ The broad Spanish, Tokay, Sandwich, and Windsor *beans* are for the latter crops. *Millar.*

BEAN *Caper.* {...} <**an herb**>
~~The leaves of this plant are produced by pairs upon the same~~ footstalk, and the footstalks grow opposite at the joints of the stalks; the cup of the flower consists of five leaves; and the flowers have also five leaves, expanded like a rose, with stamina surrounding the style, in the center of the flower cup. This style becomes a cylindrical fruit, five cornered, divided ~~into five cells, each containing many flat seeds.~~ *Millar.*

To BEAR. *v.a.* {...}♦
2. {...}
{...} *Decay of Piety.*
<————> {Slip with new quotation glued to page (see below).}
3. {...}
<————> {Slip with new quotation glued to page (see below).}
4. {...}
I do commit into your hand
Th' unstained sword that you have us'd to *bear*.
*Shakesp.* ~~*Henry* IV. *p.* ii~~.
5. {...}
~~So we say, to *bear* arms in a coat.~~

{sig. 2T[r]}

---

{attached slip}
{To BEAR. *v.a.* 2.}♦
Each sacred accent <u>bears</u> eternal weight
And each irrevocable word is fate.
Pope[1]

{attached slip}
{To BEAR. *v.a.* 3.}♦
The lad may prove well enough, if he oversoon
think not too well of himself, and will bear away
that he heareth of his Elders Sidney[2]

[1] Pope, 'The First Book of Statius His Thebais' (*Poems* I), ll. 298-99. S-G (with 'To bear To carry along with' at top of slip; this and following slip clipped from IL facing 2T2[r], whose printed text contains other entries for To BEAR *v.a.*; J. draws lines from page onto slips, indicating slips were glued in place before his revision). *1755* IRREVOCABLE *adj.*
[2] Sidney, *Arcadia*, bk II, p. 141. S-G (with 'To bear away To retain in memory' at top; see note 1, above). *1755* OVERSOON *adv.*

{slips attached to sig. 2T[r]}

{To BEAR. *v.a.*}♦

**<6 to carry in coat armour r ‡>** {J. keys in Dryden q. from IL for new def. 6; J. fails to renumber remaining defs.}

6. To carry as in show. {...}

8. {...}

Under colour of rooting out popery, the most effectual means to *bear* up the state of religion may be removed, ~~and~~ so a way be made either for paganism, or for extreme barbarism to enter. *Hooker, b.* iv. §1.

11. {...}

How did the open multitude reveal
The wond'rous love they *bear* him under hand!
*Daniel~~'s Civil War.~~*

13. {...}

I have *born* chastisements, I will not offend any more.
*Job,* ~~xxxiv. 31.~~

That which was torn of beasts, I brought not unto thee, I I *bare* the loss of it; of my hand didst thou require it.
*Genesis,* ~~xxxi. 39.~~

14. To permit;<~~to allow;~~> to suffer without resentment.

15. {...}

~~Being~~**<He was>** the son of one earl of Pembroke, and younger brother to another, who liberally supplied his expence, beyond what his annuity from his father would *bear*. *Clarendon.*

20. {...}



As ~~it~~ **<Cyprus>** more concerns the Turk than Rhodes,
So may he with more facile question *bear* it;
For that it stands not in such warlike brace. *Shakesp. Othello.*

22. {...}

I was carried on to observe, how they did *bear* their fortunes, and ~~principally~~, how they did employ their times.
*Bacon~~'s Holy War.~~*

23. To exhibit.

<——————— **s ‡**> {J. keys in Shakespeare q. from IL.}

26. {...}

I'll be your father and your brother too;
Let me but *bear* your love, I'll bear your cares.
*Shakesp.* ~~*Henry* IV. *p.* ii.~~

27. To behave; to act in character. **<with the reciprocal pronoun. Now out of use.>**

{...}

Hath he *born* himself penitent in prison?
*Shakesp.* ~~*Measure for Measure.*~~

29. To impel; to urge; to push.

<———————>

{J. keys in Spenser q. on slip originally glued to page (come loose, now on IL facing 2T[v]); slip clipped from IL facing 2T2[r], whose printed text contains other entries for To BEAR *v.a.*}

{...}

Their broken oars, and floating planks, withstand
Their passage, while they labour to the land;
And ebbing tides *bear* back upon th' uncertain sand.
*Dryden's Æneid.*

Now with a noiseless gentle course
It keeps within the middle bed;
Anon it lifts aloft the head,
And *bears* down all before it with impetuous force. *Dryden.*

Truth is *born* down, attestations neglected, the testimony of sober persons despised. *Swift.*

The hopes of enjoying the abbey lands would soon *bear* down all considerations, and be an effectual incitement to their perversion. *Swift.* <2>

{J. ital. 'down' in both Swift qs. Inking from facing IL.}

<1>

35. ~~*To bear a price.* To have a certain value.~~ **<To bear down. To overpower>**

{J. apparently intends to move second Dryden and two Swift qs. to new sense 35 'To bear down', then smears line out around Dryden q., leaving that q. under sense 29. J.'s intentions for *Dryden's Æneid* q. unclear.}

To bear out
Be it thy course to busy giddy minds
With foreign quarrels that faction hence borne
May waste the memory of former days[1] out

{To BEAR. *v.a.* 6.}♦
~~In heraldry to bear any thing in a Coat.~~
<**r**‡> Their Ensigns belgic lions bear.
Dryd.[2]

{To BEAR. *v.a.* 23.}♦
~~To contain to register, to record.~~
<‡> <**s** ‡> If I could find examples
Of thousands that had struck anointed kings
And flourish'd after, I'd not do't; But since
Nor brass nor stone nor parchment bears not one
Let villany itself forswear Shak.[3]

{To BEAR. *v.a.* 29.} {slip formerly pasted on to sig. 2T$^{v}$} ♦
Yet so great was the puissance of his push
That from his saddle quite he did him bear.
F.Q. 1. 335[4]

{To BEAR. *v.a.*} ♦
To come up to, to advance
When the but is out, we will drink water,
not a drop before, therefore bear up & board him
Shak.[5]

1 Shakespeare, *2 Henry IV* (**Works* IV), 4.11, p. 294 [4.5.213-215]. S-G (with 'action' instead of 'faction'). *1755* To BUSY *v.a.* (shorter)
2 Dryden, 'Annus Mirabilis' (*Works* I), l. 288. S-G.
3 Shakespeare, *Winter's Tale* (**Works* III), 1.3, p. 292 [1.2.357-361]. S-G (with 'forswear't' instead of 'forswear'). *1755* To FLOURISH *v.n.* 2
4 Spenser, *Faerie Queene* (*Works* I), bk I, canto III, st. xxxv, ll. 6-7. *1755* PUSH *n.s.* 1
5 Shakespeare, *Tempest* (**Works* I), 3.1, p. 51 [3.2.1-3]. S-G. *1755* OUT *adv.* 9

{IL facing 2T$^{v}$}

{To BEAR.}◆

v.a.

That proud Painim forward came so fierce
And full of wrath, that with his sharphead spear
Through vainly crossed shield he quite did pierce
And had his staggering steed not shrunk for fear
Through shield & body eke he should him bear[1]

[1] Spenser, *Faerie Queene* (*Works* I), bk I, canto III, st. xxxv, ll. 1-5. S-G. Just beneath this q., large rectangular portion of IL cut out, and annotations divided into slips and distributed to other locations in the text for the entry To BEAR *v.a.* Repair made to page contemporary with the ms.; countermark 'iv' on patch.

{IL facing 2T2r}

{36. *To bear in hand.*}

{He repaired to Bruges, desiring of the states of Bruges, to} enter peaceably into their town, with a retinue fit for his estate; and *bearing* them *in hand*, that he was to communicate with **<*d*>** them of divers matters ~~of great importance,~~ for their good. *Bacon's Henry* VII./

37. *To bear off.* To carry away ~~by force~~.

{...} *Creech.*

**<38. To bear off. To carry away by force.** ——— >

Give but the word, we'll snatch this damsel up,
And *bear* her *off.* *Addison's Cato.*
My soul grows desperate.
I'll *bear* her *off.* *A Philips's Distrest Mother.*

{J. intends Addison and Philips qs., formerly under def. 37, to illustrate new def. 38.}

~~38~~<9>. *To bear out.* {...}

To BEAR. *v.n.* {...}◆

1. {...}

Stranger, cease thy care;
Wise is th~~e~~<y> soul; but man is born to *bear:*
Jove weighs affairs of earth in dubious scales,
And the good suffers while the bad prevails. *Pope's Odyssey.*

3. {...}

A fruit tree hath been blown up almost by the roots, and set up again, and the next year <^ **did**> *bear* exceedingly. *Bacon.*

**<*d*>** ~~Betwixt two season comes th' auspicious air,~~
This age to blossom, and the next to *bear.* *Dryden.*

4. {...}

~~Having~~<I> pawned a full suit of cloaths for a sum of money, which, my operator assured me, was the last he should want to bring all our matters to *bear.* *Guardian,* Nº 166.

5. To act in character. **<Not in use.>**

6. {...}

~~Whose~~**<Their>** navy like a stiff-stretch'd cord did shew,
Till he *bore* in, and bent them into flight. *Dryden.*
On this the hero fix'd an oak in sight,
The mark to guide the mariners aright:
To *bear* with this, the seamen stretch their oars,
**<*d*>** Then round the rock they steer, ~~and seek the former shores.~~ *Dryden's Æneid.*

7. {...}

~~As a~~<A>lion bounding in his way,
With force augmented *bears against* his prey,
Sideling to seize. *Dryden's Fables.*

{...}

The waves of the sea *bear* violently and rapidly *upon* some shores, the waters being pent up by the land. *Broome on ~~the~~/Odyssey.*

BEA

10. *To bear up.* To stand firm without falling.<;^ **to endure without terrour, ~~or~~ or dejection; ~~or fa~~**>

So long as nature
**<2>** Will *bear up* with this exercise, so long
I daily vow to use it. *Shakesp. Winter's Tale.*

{...} *Broome's Notes on the Odyssey.*

**<1>** {...} *Atterbury.*

**<11. To bear up. ~~To~~ Not to faint; not to sink>** < ——— >

{J. moves Shakespeare q. to first place under new def. 11.}

**<12 To bear up To advance**
**Bear up and board her Shakesp.>**

{Shakespeare, *Tempest* [3.2.1-2]; also under BUTT *n.s.* on IL facing 3Tv (longer); *1755* under OUT *adv.* 9}

1~~+~~<3>. *To bear with.* {...}

BEAR. *n.s.* {...}

1. {...}

Every part of the body of these animals is covered with thick shaggy hair, {...} They abound in Poland, Muscovy, Lithuania, and the great forests in Germany; and also in the ~~remote~~ northern countries, where the species is white. **<*d*>** *Calmet.*/

Call hither to the stake my two brave *bears,*
Bid Salisbury and Warwick come to me. —
— Are these thy *bears?* we'll bait thy *bears* to death,
~~And manacle the bearward in their chains.~~ *Shak. Henry* VI.**<*d*>**

BEAR-GARDEN. *n.s.* {...}

1. {...}

~~H~~**<He h>urrying**<es> me from the playhouse, and the scenes there, to the *bear-garden,* to the apes, and asses, and tygers. *Stillingfl.*

BEAR'S-BREECH. *n.s.* [*acanthus.*] The name of a plant.

The leaves are like those of the thistle; the flowers labiated; the under lip of the flower is divided into three segments, which, in the beginning, is curled up in the form of a tube; in the place of the under lip are produced the stamina, which support the pointals; the cup of the flowers is composed of prickly leaves, the upper part of which is bent over, like an arch, and supplies the defect of the upper lip of the flower; the fruit is of ~~an oval form, divided in the middle into two cells, each containing one smooth seed.~~ The species are {...}

~~They are easily propagated by paring the roots in February or March, or by the seeds sown at the same time.~~ *Millar.*

{Cursive 'l' apparently written by J., purpose uncertain; see identical letter at top of 3L2$^{v}$ and 3M$^{r}$.}

BEAR'S-EAR, or *Auricula*. {…}
It hath a perennial root {…} ~~every year it produces vast quantities of new flowers, differing in shape, size, or colour; and there is likewise a great variety in the leaves of these plants. They flower in April, and ripen their seeds in June.~~ *Millar.*

BEAR'S-EAR, or *Sanicle*. {…}
This plant ~~hath a perennial root; the leaves are roundish, rough, and crenated on the edges, like those of ground ivy; the cup of the flower is small, and divided into six parts; the flowers are shaped, like a funnel, cut at the top into many segments, and disposed in an umbel; the fruit is roundish, terminating in a point, and is closely fixt in the cup, in which are contained many small angular seeds. We have but one species of this plant, which~~ is nearly allied to the *auricula ursi*; but the flowers are not quite so large and fair. ~~It loses its leaves in winter, but puts out new ones early in the spring; and, in April, it produces flowers, which are sometimes succeeded by seed pods; but it is very rare that they perfect their seeds with us.~~ *Millar.*

BEAR'S-FOOT. *n.s.* ~~See~~ HELLEBORE <3> of <2> ~~which it is~~ a species. <1>

{J. reorders to read 'A species of HELLEBORE'.}

BEARD. *n.s.* {…}
3. {…}
Would it not be ~~an~~ insufferable ~~thing~~, for a professor to have his authority, of forty years standing, confirmed by general tradition, and a reverend *beard*, overturned by an upstart novelist? *Locke.*
4. {…}
The ploughman lost his sweat, and the green corn
Hath rotted ere its youth attain'd a *beard*.
*Shakesp.* ~~*Midsummer Night's Dream.*~~

To BEARD. *v.a.* {…}
1. To take or pluck by the beard, in contempt or anger.
<2> No man so potent breathes upon the ground,
But I will *beard* him. *Shakesp. Henry* IV. *p.* i.
<1> 2. To oppose to the face; to set at open defiance.
He, whensoever he should swerve from duty, may be able to *beard* him. *Spenser's State of Ireland.*

{J. moves Shakespeare q. to second place under def. 2.}

BE'ARDLESS. *adj.* {…}
1. W~~ithout~~**<anting>** a beard.

BE'ARER. *n.s.* {…}
1. A carrier ~~of any thing,~~ who conveys any thing from one place or person to another.

~~7. In heraldry. See SUPPORTER.~~

BE'ARHERD. *n.s.* [from *bear* and ~~*herd*~~ <hyрƀ **a keeper.**>; as *shepherd*, from *sheep*.]

BE'ARING. *n.s.* {…}
2. {…}
That is Claudio; I know him by his *bearing*.
*Shakesp.* ~~*Much ado about Nothing.*~~
3. In architecture. *Bearing* of a piece of timber, ~~with carpenters,~~ is the space either between the two fixt extremes thereof, or between one extreme and a post~~, brick-wall, &c. trimmed up~~ between the ends, to shorten its *bearing*. *Builder's Dict.*

BEAST. *n.s.* {…}
2. An<y> irrational animal, opposed to man; as man and *beast*.

3. A brutal savage man, a man acting in any manner unworthy of a reasonable creature. <†> <——— **a** ‡>

{J. keys in Swift q. from IL.}

BE'ASTINGS. See BEESTINGS. <——— **b**>

{J. keys in entry for BEASTLIHEAD from IL.}

BE'ASTLY. *adj.* {…}
1. Brutal; <$_{\wedge}$**odiously mean**> contrary to the nature and dignity of man. It is used commonly as a term of reproach.
{…}
<2> Vain idols,
<1> It is commonly charged upon the gentlemen of the army, that the *beastly* vice of drinking to excess, hath been lately, from their example, restored among us. *Swift.*
2. Having the nature or form of beasts.
*Beastly* divinities, and droves of gods. *Prior.*

{J. moves misplaced 'Vain idols' to its proper place at the beginning of the Prior q. under def. 2.}

{BEAST. *n.s.* 3.}

**<a** ‡> You should try your graving Tools
On the odious groupe of Fools
Draw the beasts as I describe them
From their features while I give them
Swift[1]

<b> Beastlihead. **<ns [from beast]>**
**<The quality of beast, as manhood of Man>**
~~A greeting or compellation to a beast.~~
Sick, sick, alas, a little lack of dead,
But, I be relieved by your beastlihead
Spenser Kal.[2]

[1] Swift, 'The Legion Club' (*Poems* III), ll. 223-26, p. 839. S-G (with '3' at top; with 'gibe' instead of 'give'). *1755* GROUP *n.s.* (much shorter), GIBE *v.a.* (much shorter)

[2] Spenser, *Shepheardes Calendar* (*Works* VII), 'May', ll. 264-265. S-G (with '[Beastly ~~& head~~]').

{IL facing sig. 2T2[v]}

{To BEAT. *v.a.* 8.}

**<a ‡>**

The walls of Bulloigne sore beaten and shaken and scarce maintainable he defended ~~the place against the Dauphin~~

Sr. J. Haywd.[1]

[1] John Hayward, *Life of King Edward the Sixth*, p. 45. S-G (with '8 To beat. v.a.' at top). *1755* MAINTAINABLE *adj.*

{IL facing 2Ur}

To BEAT. *v.a.* preter. *beat*, <^ **anciently bet**> part. pass. *beat*, or *beaten*. {…}

4. To break ~~to powder,~~ or comminute by blows.

{…}

Nestor, ~~we see,~~ furnished the gold, and he *beat* it into leaves, so that he had occasion ~~to make~~ use ~~of~~ his anvil and hammer. *Broome's ~~Notes on the~~ Odyssey.*

6. {…}

She gleaned ~~in the field,~~ and *beat* out that she had gleaned. *Ruth,* ii. 17.

7. {…}

By long *beating* the white of an egg **<with alum>**, you may bring it into white curds. *Boyle.*

8. To batter with engines of war.

{…} *Judges*, viii. 17.

**<a‡**———————— >

{J. keys in Hayward q. from IL.}

10. {…}

While I this unexampled task essay,
Pass awful gulfs, and *beat* my painful way,
Celestial ~~d~~<D>ove, divine assistance bring. *Blackmore.*

BEA

15. ~~To~~<**To beat down**> depress; to crush by repeated opposition; usually with the particle *down*. <2>

{…}

16. To drive by violence.

{…}

17. To move with fluttering agitation. <1>

{…} *Dryden's State of Innocence.*

18. *To beat down.* To endeavour by treaty to lessen the price demanded.

{…}

19. *To beat down.* To sink or lessen the value.

{…}

{J. moves sense 15 beneath current sense 17; in this way, three senses with phrasal combination 'To beat down' are grouped together. J. fails to renumber newly-arranged senses.}

~~21. *To beat the hoof.* To walk, to go on foot.~~ <*d*>

To BEAT. *v.n.*

~~1. To move in a pulsatory manner.~~

<2> I would gladly understand the formation of a soul, and see it beat the first conscious pulse. *Collier on Thought.*

<1>~~2~~. To dash, as a flood or storm.

~~This~~ publick envy seemeth to *beat* chiefly upon ministers. *Bacon's ~~Essays, Nº 9~~.*

{…}

<1> 4. To move with frequent repetitions of the same act or stroke. **<to move in a pulsa tory manner.>**

No pulse shall keep
His nat'ral progress, but surcease to *beat*. *Sh. Rom. and Jul.*

My temp'rate pulse does regularly beat;
Feel, and be satisfy'd. *Dryden's Persius, Sat.* iii.

{J. crosses out def. 1, adding it to def. 4, and moves Collier q. to third place under def. 4.}

BEAT. *n.s.* {...}
2. {...}

<**He**> With a careless *beat*,
Struck out the mute creation at a heat. *Dryd. Hind and P.*

3. Manner of being struck; as, the *beat* of ~~the pulse, or~~ a drum.

To BEA'TIFY. *v.a.* {...}
1. {...}

We shall know him to be the fullest good, the nearest to us, and the most certain; and, consequently, the most *beatifying* of all others. <**Grews**> ~~*Brown's*~~ *Cosmologia Sacra, b.* iii. *c.* 4.

2. {...}

~~Over-against this church~~ <**There**> stands a large hospital, erected by a shoemaker, who has been *beatified*, though never sainted. *Addison~~/on Italy~~.*

BEA'TITUDE. *n.s.* {...}♦
1. {...}

~~He~~ <**Mahomet**> set out the felicity of his heaven, by the delights of sense; slightly passing over the accomplishment of the soul, and the *beatitude* of that part which earth and visibilities too weakly affect. *Brown's Vulgar Errours, b.* i. *c.* 2.

BEAU. *n.s.* [*beau*, Fr. It is sounded like *bo*, and has often the French plural *beaux*.<^ ^**sounded** **boes**>] {...}

BEA

BE'AVERED. *adj.* {...}

His *beaver'd* brow a birchen garland bears,
Dropping with infant's blood, and mother's tears:
~~All flesh is humbled.~~ *Pope's Dunciad.*

BEAU'TIFUL. *adj.* {...} Fair; <^**pleasing to the eye; pleasing to the imagina-tion.**> having the qualities that constitute beauty~~/~~<^ ~~or give high~~>
<——— **b ‡**>

{J. keys in Sidney q. ('He might hear...', mis-keyed 'a ‡') from IL.}

BEAU'TIFULNESS. *n.s.* {...}
{J. keys in Sidney q. ('Can I ...') from IL.} <——— **c ‡**>

To BEAU'TIFY. *v.a.* {...} To adorn; to embellish; to deck; to grace; to ~~add beauty to~~. <**improve in beauty**>
<—— **a ‡**>

{J. keys in Hooker q. from IL.]

~~Beavoir n.s. [beau & voir] fr. face visage. not in use~~◆
She then her beavoir did veil
But first she thankd him & then 'gan her tale
Spens.[1]

{BEAU'TIFUL. *adj.*}
Pleasing. harmonious. delightful to the ear
In Sidney we find a transition of the common attributes of the Eyes & Ears.

<a ‡> He might hear her sing this song with a Voice no less beautiful to his Ears, than her goodliness was full of harmony to his Eyes
Sidney[2]

{BEAU'TIFULNESS. *n.s.*}
<c ‡> Can I without the detestable stain of ungrateful: ness abstain from loving him, who far exceeds the beautifulness of his shape with the beautiful ness of his mind, is content so to abase himself as to become Dametas servant for my sake
Sidney[3]

{To BEAU'TIFY. *v.a.*}
<a ‡> Then are the public duties of religion best d{?}oder: ed, when the militant church doth resemble by sensible means that hidden dignity and glory wherewith the church triumphant in heaven is beautified
Hooker 5.5[4]
{aman. smears out letter, writes 'oder:' instead of 'order:'}

Nor is't too hard to beautify each month
With files of party colour'd fruits that please
The tongue & view at once
Philips[5]

[1] Edward Fairfax, tr., *Recovery of Jerusalem*, bk II, st. xlviii, p. 48 (misattributed to Spenser). S-G (aman. queries text, writes 'Q?' next to 'visage'). *1755* To VAIL *v.a.* 1 (different, signed 'Fairfax')
[2] Sidney, *Arcadia*, bk I, p. 69. S-G (def., note, and q. on same slip; 'Beautiful 2' at top). *1755* GOODLINESS *n.s.* (slightly shorter)
[3] Sidney, *Arcadia*, bk II, p. 152. S-G. *1755* UNGRATEFULNESS *n.s.*
[4] Richard Hooker, *Ecclesiastical Polity*, vol. II, bk V, ch. v, p. 34. S-G (with 'ordered' instead of 'odered'). *1755* MILITANT *adj.*
[5] John Philips, 'Cyder', bk I, ll. 312-14. S-G. *1755* PARTY-COLOURED *adj.* (shorter)

{IL facing 2Uv}

<a ‡ **Be is an inseparable particle placed before verbs of which it seldom augments or changes the signification as to ~~bedeck~~ bedeck, and some nouns which it changes into verbs. as dew, to bedew.**>[1] ♦

[1] IL entirely in J.'s hand.

{IL facing 2U2[r]}

## BEC　　BEC

{BEAU'TY. *n.s.*}♦

2. A particular grace, feature, or ornament. <^ ^**it is used of whatever delights the ~~si~~ eye or mind ~~as of~~**>

{With addition of note, J. proposes new readings of usage in *Dryden's Dufresnoy* and Addison qs. below.}

The ancient pieces are beautiful, because they resemble the *beauties* of nature; and nature will ever be beautiful, which resembles those *beauties* of antiquity. *Dryden's Dufresnoy.*

Wherever you place a patch, you destroy a *beauty.* *Addison.*

To BEAU'TY. *v.a.* {...} To adorn; to beautify; to embellish. <**not in use.**>

BECAFI'CO. *n.s.* {...}

{...} *Pope.*

<—————————>

{J. keys in note marked **a ‡** from IL.}

BECA'USE. *conjunct.* {...}♦

1. For this reason that; on this account that; for this cause that.

<☞> How great soever the sins of any person are, Christ died for him, *because* he died for all; and he died for those sins, *because* he died for all sins; only he must reform. *Hammond's Fundam.*

{J. draws hand pointing to Hammond q.; not intended for compositor.}

To BECHA'NCE. *v.n.* {...}

My sons, God knows what has *bechanced* them. *Shakesp. ~~Henry VI. p. ii~~.*

All happiness *bechance* to thee at Milan. *Shakesp. ~~Two Gentlemen of Verona~~.*

To BECK. *v.a.* [beacn, Sax. <^ **a sign;**> *bec*, Fr. head.] {...}

To BECO'ME. *v.a.* {...}

3. In the following passage, the phrase, *where is he become*, is used for *what is become of him.* <**this is not used**>

{sig. 2U2[r]}

## BED

BECO'MING. *particip. adj.* {…}

Of thee, kind boy, I ask no red and white
To make up my delight,
No odd *becoming* graces,
Black eyes, or little <‸**I**> know not what, in faces. *Suckling.*

BECO'MINGLY. *adv.* {…}

**<a ‡**―――――― > {J. keys in More q. from IL.}

BECO'MINGNESS. *n.s.* [from *becoming*. See To BECOME.] Decency; elegant congruity; propriety. **<not elegant.>**

BED. *n.s.* {…}

2. {…}

On my knees I beg,
That you'll vouchsafe me, raiment, *bed*, and food.
*Shakesp.* ~~*King Lear*~~.

3. {…}

George, the eldest son of this second *bed*, was, ~~after the death of his father, by the singular care and affection of his mother,~~ well brought up. *Clarendon.*

4. Bank of earth raised in a garden.

{…} *Bacon's Nat. Hist.* N° 459.

**<c ‡**―――――― > {J. keys in Dryden q. from IL.}

5. {…}

The great magazine for all kinds of treasure is supposed to be the *bed* of the Tiber. ~~We may be sure,~~ when the Romans lay under the apprehensions of seeing their city sacked ~~by a barbarous enemy~~, ~~that~~ they would ~~take care to~~ bestow such ~~of their~~ riches that way, as could best bear the water. *Addison.*

**<10>** BED *of a Mortar*. {…}

**<11>** BED *of a great gun*. {…}

## BED

To BED. *v.n.* {…}

If he be married, and *bed* with his wife, and ~~afterwards~~ relapse, he may ~~possibly~~ fancy that she infected him.
*Wiseman*~~'s Surgery~~.

To BEDA'BBLE. *v.a.* {…}

Never so weary, never so in woe,
*Bedabbled* with the dew, and torn with briars,
I can no further crawl, no further go.
*Shakesp.* ~~*Midsummer Night's Dream*~~.

To BEDA'ZZLE. *v.a.* {…}

My mistaken eyes,
That have been so *bedazzled* by the sun,
That every thing I look on seemeth green.
*Shakesp.* ~~*Taming of the Shrew*~~.

BEDCLO'ATHS. *n.s.* {…}

~~For~~ he will be swine drunk, and, in his sleep, he does little harm, save to his *bedcloaths* about him.
*Shakesp.* ~~*All's well that ends well*~~.

BE'DDER. ~~BEDE'TTER.~~ } <‸**or Bedetter**> *n.s.* {…}

To BEDE'CK. *v.a.* {…}

Thou sham'st thy shape, thy love, thy wit,
And usest none in that true use indeed,
Which should *bedeck* thy shape, thy love, thy wit.
*Shakesp.* ~~*Romeo and Juliet.*~~

{sig. 2U2v}

---

{To BECO'ME. *v.a.*}

for what is ~~become~~ of him, or where is he
I cannot Joy untill I be resolv'd
Where our right valiant father is become
Shak. H. 6 p. 3d.[1]

{BECO'MINGLY. *adv.*}

**<a ‡>**

How becomingly does Philopolis exercise
his office, like a long practisd moderator
More. D. D.[2]

{BED. *n.s.* 4.}

**<c ‡>**

Fearing to be seen within a bed
Of Coleworts he conceald his wily head
There sculk'd Dryd.[3]

1 Shakespeare, *3 Henry VI* (**Works* V), 2.1, p. 130-31 [2.1.9-10]. S-G (with 'where he is'). *1755* To BECOME *v.n.* 3 (shorter), To JOY *v.n.* (shorter)

2 Henry More, *Divine Dialogues*, 'Second Dialogue', p. 88. S-G. *1755* RESPONDENT *n.s.* 2, OPPONENT *n.s.*, MODERATOR *n.s.* (different)

3 Dryden, 'The Cock and the Fox' (*Works* VII), ll. 495-97. S-G. *1755* To SCULK *v.n.*

{IL facing 2U2v}

{To BEDE'W. *v.a.*}
Gladsome they quaff yet not exceed the bounds
Of healthy temp'rance, nor encroach on night
Season of rest, but well bedew'd repair
Each to his home with unsupplanted feet
Philips[1]

{To BEDI'M. *v.a.*}
<**o** ‡>
His venerable Age bedim'd with tears
Pope Odyss.[2]

{BE'DLAM. *n.s.*}
Upstarts the bedlam
And reverence made accosted thus the Queen
Dryd.[3]

{BE'DLAM. *n.s.* 2.} <**p** ‡>
The venom was insinuated into the whole mass, and the world was little better than a com :mon fold of phrentics and bedlams
Woodw^d^.[4]

[1] John Philips, 'Cyder', bk II, ll. 380-83. S-G. *1755* UNSUPPLANTED *adj.* (shorter)
[2] Pope, *Odyssey* (*Poems* X), bk XXIV, l. 325. S-G (with 'eyes' instead of 'Age').
3 Dryden, 'The Wife of Bath Her Tale' (*Works* VII), ll. 291-92. S-G (with '2 n.s.' at top; contains this q. and Woodward q. below). *1755* REVERENCE *n.s.*
[4] John Woodward, *Natural History of the Earth,* pt II, p. 88. S-G (on same slip with Dryden q. above).

{IL facing 2X^r^}

BE´DFELLOW. *n.s.* {...} <‸1> One that lies in the same bed.

{...}

Misery acquaints a man with strange *bedfellows*.
*Shakesp.* ~~*Tempest*~~.

<2> And how doth my cousin, your *bedfellow?*
~~And your fairest daughter, and mine?~~ *Shakesp. Henry* IV.
Why doth the crown lie there upon his pillow,
Being so troublesom a *bedfellow?* *Shakesp. Henry* IV.

<1> A man would as soon choose him for his *bedfellow* as his play-fellow. *L'Estrange.*

**<2. A husband or wife. Familiarly >**

{J. numbers existing def. '1', adds new def. 2 and inserts initial line of first *Shakesp. Henry* IV q. in first place under def. 2.}

To BEDI´M. *v.a.* {...}
{...} *Shakesp. Tempest.*
**<o** ‡——————> {J. keys in Pope q. from IL.}
To BEDI´ZEN. *v.a.* {...} To dress out. **<a low word>**
BE´DLAM. *n.s.* {...}
2. A madman; a lunatick.
{...} *Shakesp. King Lear.*
**<p** ‡——————> {J. keys in Woodward q. from IL.}

BE´DMOULDING. } *n.s.* {...} A term
BE´DDING MOULDING. } used by workmen, to signify ~~those~~ members in the cornice, ~~which are~~ placed below the coronet.
*Builder's Dict.*/

To BEDRE´NCH. *v.a.* {...}
Far off from the mind of Bolingbroke
It is, such crimson tempest should *bedrench*
The fresh green lap of fair king Richard's land.
*Shakesp.*/~~*King Richard* III~~.

BE´DRID. *adj.* {...}



Lies he not *bedrid?* and, again, does nothing,
But what he did being childish? *Shakesp. Winter's Tale.*
Now, as a myriad **<Stet>**
Of ants durst th'emperor's lov'd snake invade:
The crawling galleys, seagulls, finny chips,
Might brave our pinnaces, our *bedrid* ships. *Donne.*

{J. writes 'stet' indicating that the lines resulting from inking from the facing IL should be ignored.}

BE´DRITE. *n.s.* {...}
~~Whose~~ **<The>** vows are, that no *bedrite* shall be paid
Till Hymen's torch be lighted. *Shakesp. Tempest.*

BEDSWE´RVER. *n.s.* {...} One that is false to the bed; one that ranges or swerves from one bed to another. **<Not now in use.>**

BE´DWORK. *n.s.* {...} Work done in bed; work performed without toil of the hands. **<Speculation; idle theory. Not in use.>**

{...}
Why this hath not a finger's dignity,
They call this *bedwork*, mapp'ry, closet war.
*Shakesp.*/~~*Troilus and Cressida*~~.

BEE. *n.s.* {...}
1. {...}
~~A company~~ of poor insects, ~~whereof~~ some are *bees*, delighted with flowers, and their sweetness; others beetles, delighted with other viands. *Locke.*

BEE-FLOWER. *n.s.* {...} A species of foolstones; ~~which see~~. {...}
BEE-GARDEN. *n.s.* {...} A place to set hives of bees in. <~~{??}~~> **<an Apiary.>**

BEECH. *n.s.* {...}

This tree hath leaves {...} divided into four parts. ~~There is but one species of this tree at present known, except two varieties, with striped leaves.~~ It will grow to a considerable stature {...} The shade of this tree is ~~very~~ injurious to most sorts of plants, ~~which grow near it;~~ but is ~~generally~~ believed to be ~~very~~ salubrious to human bodies. The timber is of great use to turners and joiners. The mast is ~~very~~ good to fatten swine {...}. *Millar.*

{...}

Nor is that sprightly wildness in their notes,
Which, clear and vigorous, warbles from the *beech.*
*Thomson*/~~*'s Spring*~~.

BEEF. *n.s.* {...}

1. {...}

What say you to a piece of *beef* and mustard?
*Shakesp.*/~~*Taming of the Shrew*~~.

{Vertical lines inking from facing IL.}

BEEN. {...} The *participle preterite* of To BE; ~~which see.~~

BEET. *n.s.* {...}

It hath a thick, fleshy root; {...} ~~The species are; 1. The common white~~ *beet.* 2. The common green *beet.* 3. The common red *beet.* 4. The turnep-rooted red *beet.* 5. The great red *beet.* 6. The yellow *beet.* 7. The Swiss or Chard *beet.* The two first mentioned are preserved in gardens for the use of their leaves in pot herbs. The other sorts are propagated for their roots, which are boiled as parsneps. The red *beet* is most commonly cultivated and used in garnishing dishes. The Swiss ~~*beet* is by some much esteemed.~~ *Millar.*

BE'ETLE. *n.s.* {...}♦

1. {...}

Others c<a>me in place, sharp of sight, and too provident for that which concerned their own interest; but as blind as *beetles* in foreseeing this great and common danger.
*Knolles's History of the Turks.*

2. A heavy mallet, or wooden hammer, with which wedges are driven. **<This is probable corrupted from beatle of beat.>**♦

To BE'ETLE. *v.n.* ~~[from the noun.]~~ To jut out; to hang over. **<I know not the ground of this signification.>**♦

To BEFA'LL. *v.n.* {...}

5. *To befall of.* {...}

{...} *Shakespeare's Comedy of Errours.*

<——————————————‡>

{J. keys in new def. 6 and Bacon q. from IL.}

To BEFI'T. *v.a.* {...}

Blind is his love, and best *befits* the dark.
*Shakesp.* ~~*Romeo and Juliet*~~.

{sig. 2X^v}

{BE´ETLE. *n.s.*}
A Dover-court Beetle I suppose signifies
a very large Beetle, alluding to the rood of ~
Dover, which was very large & remarkable in
our Authors time; or from the proverb yet in
use, a Dover-Court, all speakers & no hearers,
signifying a great noise, which a great Beetle
may be supposed to make Tuss. no[1]

A Dover court bet[2]

{To BEFA´LL. *v.n.*}
**<‡ 6 To come by descent, ~~not~~ or accidence>**
The empire of Almaigne were not unlike
to befal to Spain, if it should break
Bacon.[3]

[1] Thomas Tusser, *Husbandry*, 'September', p. 118 (q. from editor's notes to Tusser).
[2] Letter 't' smeared out after 'be'.
[3] Bacon, *Essays Civil and Moral* (**Works* III), 'LIX: Of Vicissitude of Things', p. 382 [VI, LVIII, p. 515]. S-G. *1755* UNLIKE *adj.* 2, LIKEWISE *adv.*

{IL facing 2X^v}

{To BEG. *v.a.* 1.}

**<a ‡>**

The palm tree alone giveth unto man what:
:soever his Life beggeth at natures hand.
Ral.[1]

[1] Sir Walter Raleigh, *History of the World*, vol. I, bk I, ch. iii, § 15, p. 39. S-G. *1755* PALM *n.s.*

{IL facing 2X2r}

## BEF

To BEFO'OL. *v.a.* {…}

Men *befool* themselves infinitely, when, by venting a few sighs, they ~~will needs~~ persuade themselves ~~that~~ they have repented. South./

BEFO'RE. *prep.* {…}

2. {…}

Who shall go
*Before* them in a cloud, and pillar of fire:
By day a cloud, by night a pillar of fire,
To guide them in their journey~~, and remove~~
~~Behind them, while th' obdurate king pursues.~~ *Par. Lost.*

BEFORE. *adv.* {…}

2. In <^**any**> time past.

BEFO'REHAND. *adv.* {…}

## BEG

4. {…}

What is a man's contending with insuperable difficulties, but the rolling of Sisyphus's stone up the hill, which is ~~soon~~ **<~~sur~~ sure>** *beforehand* to return upon him again? *L'Estrange's Fables.*

To BE'FORTUNE. *v.n.* {…}♦ To happen to; to betide. **<elegant but not in use.>**

To BEG. *v.a.* {…}

1. To ask; to seek by petition. **<to solicite>**
{…} *Matth.* xxvii. 58.

<———————————— **a ‡>**

{J. keys in Raleigh q. from IL.}

2. {…}

We have not *begged* any principles or suppositions, for the proof of this; but tak~~ing~~**<en>** that common ground, which both Moses and all antiquity present. *Burnet's Theory of the Earth.*

To BEGE'T. *v.a.* {…} . [{…} to obtain. ~~See To GET.~~]

{sig. 2X2r}

## BEG

{BEGE´TTER. *n.s.*}

For what their prowess gain'd, the law declares
Is to themselves alone, and to their heirs:
No share of that goes back to the *begetter*,
~~But if the son fights well, and plunders better,~~ ——— *Dryden.*

BE´GGAR. *n.s.* {...}
1. {...}

He raiseth up the poor out of the dust, and lifteth up the *beggar* from the dunghill, to set them among princes.
+ Sam~~uel, ii. 8.~~

To BE´GGAR. *v.a.* {...}
1. {...}

~~Whose~~ **<His>** heavy hand hath bow'd you to the grave,
And *beggar'd* your's forever. *Shakesp. Macbeth.*

{Inking from facing IL.}

## BEG

BEGI´NNER. *n.s.* {...}
1. He that gives the first cause, or original, to any thing.
{...} *Hook.*
< ——————————— ╫> {J. keys in def. and More q. from IL.}
~~2.~~ <3> An unexperienced attempter; {...}

To BEGI´RD. *v.a.* {...}
3. {...}

It was so closely *begirt* before the king's march ~~into the west,~~ that the council ~~humbly~~ desired his majesty, that he would relieve it. *Clarendon, b.* viii.

{sig. 2X2v}

---

Beg~~g~~ing n.s. [beg~~u~~in Fr.~~]~~ an in~~f~~ants ~~f~~irst cloat~~h~~s[1]

{BEGI´NNER. *n.s.* 2.}
<╫>
**<He that does the first part of any thing>**
~~He who leads the way, he who first treats of a thing~~
You full little think that you must be the beginner of the Discourse yourself.
More[2]

[1] S-G.
[2] Henry More, *Divine Dialogues*, 'First Dialogue', p. 7. S-G. *1755* FULL *adv.* 5.

{IL facing 2X2v}

{BEGO'NE.}
Begone in composition, as woe begone, depressd with woe

A man so spiritless
So dull, so dead in look, so woe begone
Drew Priams curtain in the dead of night
And would have told him all his Troy was burn'd
But Priam found the fire, 'ere he his Tongue
Shak. H. 4. 2.[1]

Begone Oppresst
Tancred be sure his life's Joy set at nought
So woe begone was he with pains of love
Fairf. 1.9[2]

{To BEGUI'LE. *v.a.*}
Of before the thing beguiled of
Other mens insatiable desire of revenge, wholly beguiled church & state of the benefit of all my retractions & concessions
K. Charles.[3]

[1] Shakespeare, *2 Henry IV* (*Works IV), 1.3, p. 208 [1.1.70-74]. S-G. *1755* WOBEGONE *n.s.* (slightly different), SPIRITLESS *adj.* (much shorter)
[2] Edward Fairfax, tr., *Recovery of Jerusalem*, bk I, st. ix, p. 4. S-G. *1755* WOBEGONE *n.s.*
[3] Charles I, *Eikon Basilike*, ch. xv, p. 90. S-G (with '4 With of …' at beginning of text). *1755* RETRACTION *n.s.* (slightly different)

{IL facing 2Y$^r$}

To BEGI'RT. *v.a.* {...}

And, Lentulus, *begirt* you Pompey's house,
To seize his sons alive; ~~for they are they~~
~~Must make our peace with him.~~ *Ben. Johnson's Catiline.*

To BEGNA'W. *v.a.* {...}

His horse is stark spoiled with the staggers, *begnawn* with the bots, waid in the back, and shoulder shotten. *Shakesp.* ~~*Taming of the Shrew*~~.

The worm of conscience still *begnaw* thy soul. *Shakesp.* ~~*Richard* III~~.

To BEGRI'ME. *v.a.* [from *be* and *grime.* ~~See GRIME and GRIM.~~]

To BEGUI'LE. *v.a.* {...}♦

1. {...}

The serpent me *beguil'd*, and I did eat! *Milton's* ~~*Paradise Lost, b.* x~~.

Whosoever sees a man, who would have *beguiled*, and imposed upon him, by making him believe a lie, ~~he~~ may truly say, that is the man who would have ruined me. *South.*

3. {...}

{...} *Sir J. Davies.* <2>

Sweet leave me here a while;
My spirits grow dull, and fain I would *beguile* <1>
The tedious day with sleep. ~~*Hamlet*~~. <**Shakesp.**>

{J. moves *Sir J. Davies* q. beneath *Shakesp.* q. for chronological reasons, though mistakenly (Davies's *Nosce teipsum* published in 1599, *Hamlet* in 1603).}

To BEHA'VE. *v.a.* {...}

1. {...}

We *behaved* not *ourselves* disorderly among you. ~~2~~ *Thessal.* ~~iii. 7.~~

{...}

We so live, and so act, as if we were secure of the final issue ~~and event~~ of things, however we may *behave ourselves.* *Atterbury.*



BEHA'VIOUR. *n.s.* {...}

4. {...}

The beautiful prove accomplished, but not of great spirit; and study, for the most part, rather *behaviour* than virtue. *Bacon's* ~~*Ornam. Rational.* N° 63~~.

He who advise~~th~~<**d**> the philosopher, altogether devoted to the Muses, sometimes to offer sacrifice to the altars of the Graces, thought knowledge imperfect without *behaviour.* *Wotton.*

To BEHE'AD. *v.a.* {...}♦

His *beheading* ~~he~~ <**Laud**> underwent with all christian magnanimity. *Clarendon, b.* vii.

BEHE'ST. *n.s.* {...} Command; precept; mandate. <**a word now not used except in poetry**>

## BEH

{To BEHI'GHT. *v.a.* 1.}

Sir Guyon, mindful of his vow yplight,
Up rose from drowsy couch, and him addrest,
Unto the journey which he had *behight.*

*Fairy Queen,* ~~*b. ii. cant. ii*~~.

3. Perhaps to call; to name; *hight* being often put, in old authors, for *named,* or *was named.* **<it is in all senses quite obsolete>**

<**c** ‡> {J. keys in Spenser q. from IL.}

BEHI'ND. *prep.* {...}

1. {...}

Acomates hasted with ~~two hundred~~ harquebusiers, which he had caused his horsemen to take *behind* them upon their horses.

*Knolles*~~*'s History of the Turks*~~.

3. Towards the back.**<of>**

5. Remaining after the departure of something else.

<2> He left *behind* him, myself, and sister, both born in one hour. *Shakesp. Twelfth Night.*

<1> {...} *Tillotson*

6. Remaining after the death of those to whom it belonged.

{J. moves Shakespeare q. correctly to first place under def. 6.}

BEHI'NDHAND. *adv.* {...}

2. {...}

Consider, whether it is not better to be half a year *behindhand with* the fashionable part of the world, than to strain beyond ~~his~~ **<your>** circumstances. *Spectator,* Nº 488.

To BEHO'LD. *v.a.* {...}

When some young Thessalians, on horseback, were *beheld* afar off, while their horses watered, while their heads were depressed, they were conceived ~~by the spectators~~ to be one animal.

*Brown*~~*'s Vulgar Errours, b. i. c. 4*~~.

BEHO'LDEN. *particip. adj.* {...} Obliged; bound in gratitude; with the particle *to* <^ ^ **before the person or cause befriending, and for before the advantage granted. as I am beholden to you for this money.>**

{...}

## BEI

I think myself mightily *beholden to* you for the reprehension you then gave us. *Addison. Guardian,* Nº 109.

{J. underlines 'for' in conjunction with usage note added above.}

BEHO'LDER. *n.s.* {...}.

**<Thou hidst>** These beasts among
*Beholders* rude, and shallow to discern
Half what in thee is fair, one man except,
Who sees thee? *Milton's Paradise Lost, b.* ix. *l.* 543.

{J. crosses out 'among', then smears out stroke, as he rereads Milton's syntax.}

BEHO'OF. *n.s.* {...}

Her majesty may alter ~~any thing of~~ those laws, that may be more both for her own *behoof,* and for the good of the people.

*Spenser*~~*on Ireland*~~.

To BEHO'OVE. *v.n.* {...} To be fit; to be meet; either with respect to duty, necessity, or convenience. It is used only impersonally with *it.* **<and is somewhat antiquated.>**

BEHO'OVEFUL. *adj.* {...}

It may be most *behooveful* for princes, in matters of grace, to transact the same publickly: so it is as requisite, in matters of ~~judgment,~~ punishment, ~~and censure~~, that the same be transacted privately. *Clarendon.*

BEHO'OVEFULLY. *adv.* {...}

{...} *Spenser on Ireland.*

<———— **o** ‡>

{J. keys in Hooker q. from IL.}

{sig. 2Yv}

---

{To BEHI'GHT. *v.a.*}

~~3. To call; to give out~~ <**c** ‡>

Aread old father, why of late
Didst thou behight me born of English blood
Whom all a fairys son doen nominate
F. Q. 1. 10. 64[1]

{BEHO'OVEFULLY. *adv.*}

<**o** ‡>

No untruth can prossibly avail the patron and
defender long, for things most truly are like:
:wise most behoovefully spoken
Hooker[2]

[1] Spenser, *Faerie Queene* (*Works* I), bk I, canto X, st. lxiv, ll. 5-7. S-G. *1755* To NOMINATE *v.a.* 2

[2] Richard Hooker, *Ecclesiastical Polity*, vol. I, bk III, ch. x, p. 246. S-G. *1755* UNTRUTH *n.s.*, TRULY *adv.* 1 (shorter)

{IL facing 2Yv}

{To BELE´AGUER. *v.a.*}

<o ~~}~~ >

~~To surround, to encompass, to set round~~

He wears no limbs about him sound
With sores and sicknesses beleaguer'd round

Dryd.[1]

[1] Dryden, 'The Tenth Satyr of Juvenal' (*Works* IV), ll. 346-7. S-G. *1755* FINE *n.s.* 4

{IL facing 2Y2r}

## BEL

To BELA´Y. *v.a.* {...}

<3> *To* BELAY *a rope.* {...} ~~To splice; to mend a rope, by laying one end over another.~~ **<To fasten a running rope.>**

To BELCH. *v.n.* {...}

1. To eject the wind from the stomach; to eruct.

<2> The waters boil, and, *belching* from below,
Black sands as from a forceful engine throw. *Dryden's Virg.*

{...} *Arbuthnot on Aliments.*

<1> 2. To issue out < **as**> by eructation.

A triple pile of plumes his crest adorn'd,
On which with *belching* flames Chimæra burn'd. *Dryden.*

{J. moves *Dryden's Virg.* q. correctly to first place under def. 2.}

To BELCH. *v.a.* {...}

## BEL

The gates that now
Stood open wide, *belching* outrageous flame
Far into chaos, ~~since the fiend pass'd through.~~ *Parad. Lost.*

{...}

~~There~~ **<He>** *belcht* the mingl'd streams of wine and blood,
And human flesh, his indigested food. *Pope's Odyssey, b.* ix.

{J. changes Pope q. so that it illustrates transitive (*v.a.*) use of verb.}

To BELE´AGUER. *v.a.* {...} To besiege; to block up a place; to lie before a town. **<To surround as enemies.>**

{J. adds def. in order to gloss new Dryden q. from IL.}

{...} *Dryden. Ovid.*

< ———————— o ~~}~~ >

{J. keys in Dryden q. from IL.}

BELFLO´WER. *n.s.* {...}

The flower consists of one leaf. {...} There is a vast number of the species of this plant. ~~1. The tallest pyramidal *belflower*. 2. The blue peach-leaved *belflower*. 3. The white peach-leaved *belflower*. 4. Garden *belflower*, with oblong leaves and flowers; commonly called *Canterbury bells*. 5. Canary *belflower*, with orrach leaves and a tuberose root. 6. Blue *belfower*, with edible roots, commonly called *rampions*. 7. Venus looking-glass *belflower*, &c. The first sort is commonly cultivated to adorn chimnies, halls, &c. in summer. It produces sometimes twelve branches, four or five feet high, with large beautiful flowers, almost the whole length of the stalks. The peach-leaved *belflowers* are very hardy, and may be planted in open beds or borders, where they will flower very strong. The *Canterbury bells* are biennial. The *Canary belflower* is one of the most beautiful plants of the greenhouse, yielding its flowers in December, January, and February. The *rampion* is propagated for its root, which was formerly in greater esteem in England than at present. The sorts of *Venus looking-glass* are annual plants.~~ *Millar.*

BE´LFRY. *n.s.* {...}

Fetch the leathern bucket that hangs in the *belfry*; that is curiously painted before, and will make a figure.

Gay~~'s What d' ye call it.~~

To BELI´E. *v.a.* {...}

1. {...}

~~The~~**<He,>** shape of man, and imitated beast
The walk, the words, the gesture could supply,
The habit mimick, and the mien *belie.* *Dryden's Fables.*

{sig. 2Y2r}

{To BELI'E *v.a.*}♦
3. To calumniate; to raise false reports of any man.

'Tis slander, whose breath
<2> Rides on the posting winds, and doth *belie*
All corners of the world. *Shakesp. Cymbeline.*
{...} *Shakesp. Henry* IV.
<1> 4. To give a false representation of any thing.
{...}
{...} *Prior.*
**<5 To fill with lies.**
**Not in use.** ——— >

{J. moves *Shakesp. Cymbeline* q. under new def. 5.}

BELI'EF. *n.s.* {...}♦
3. Religion; the body of tenets held by the professors of **<the true>** faith.
{...} *Hooker, b.*v.
**<o ‡** ——— > {J. keys in Blackmore q. from IL.}

To BELI'EVE. *v.a.* {...}
1. {...}
**<To hold>** A proposition, which they are persuaded, but do not know to be true, ~~it~~ is not seeing, but *believing*. *Locke.*

To BELIEVE. *v.n.* {...}
**<5 To have an**
**opinion or esteem** ——— >
**<q ‡>** {J. keys in Raleigh q. from IL.}
~~5~~<6>. *I believe*, {...}
{Inking from facing IL.}

BELI'KE. *adv.* {...}
1. {...}
Josephus affirmeth, that one of them remained even in his time; meaning, *belike*, some ruin ~~or foundation~~ thereof.
*Raleigh's ~~History of the World~~.*
2. {...}
God appointed the sea to ~~one of them~~ **<the whale>**, and the land to the ~~other~~ **<Elephant>**, because they were so great, that the sea could not hold them both; for else, *belike*, if the sea had been large enough, we might have gone a fishing for elephants. *Brerew. on Languages.*

BELL. *n.s.* {...}
1. A vessel, or hollow body of cast metal, formed to make a noise by the act of a clapper, hammer, or some other instrument striking against it. *Bells* are ~~always~~ in the towers of churches, **<*d*>** to call the congregation together.

BELL-FASHIONED. *adj.* {...} Having the form of a bell. **<; campaniform.>**

{Inking from facing IL.}

{sig. 2Y2v}

{BELIEF. *n.s.* 3.}
**<o ‡>**
~~Vanenius next, a hardy modern chief~~
A bold opposer of divine belief
Attempts religious fences to subvert
Strong in his rage, but destitute of art
Blackm. Crea.[1]

{To BELIEVE. *v.n.*}♦
Now stub up the bushes, the grass to be fine,
Least neighbour do dailie so hack them believe
That neither thy bushes nor pasture can thrive
Tusser. Husb. for Jan$^{ry}$.[2]
Tussers annotator takes believe to signify in the night, which, adds he, is more put in for rhymes sake that the neighbour should be sup posed to work in the night [This is contra: :dictory for the Original says daily hack[3]
In Scotland it signifies soon, immediately, as when will you come, belive, from believen Germ

{To BELI'EVE. *v.a.* 5.}
**<q ‡>**
As he had an inventive brain so there never lived any man that believed better of it and of himself Raleigh[4]

Bellgarde [belle & garde Fr]♦
pretty bower or retreat
Upon her Eyelids many graces sat
Under the shadow of her even brows
Working bellguards and amorous retrait
And every one her with a grace endows
F.Q. 2.3.25[5]

1 Richard Blackmore, *Creation*, bk III, p. 98. S-G. *1755* OPPOSER *n.s.* (much shorter)
2 Thomas Tusser, *Husbandry*, 'January', pp. 6-7.
3 Thomas Tusser, *Husbandry*, 'January', p. 7.
4 Sir Walter Raleigh, *History of the World*, vol. I, bk I, ch. iv, § 2, p. 40. S-G. *1755* INVENTIVE *adj.*
5 Spenser, *Faerie Queene* (*Works* II), bk II, canto III, st. xxv, ll. 1-4. S-G. *1755* RETRAICT *n.s.*, BELGARD *n.s.* (shorter)

{IL facing 2Y2v}

To bellow. v.a. To utter a thing with loud noise
A Numidian Priest bellowing out certain super
:stitious charms, cast divers scrowls of paper on
each side the way, wherin he cursd & ban'd the
Christians Knolles[1]

{BE´LLUINE. *adj.*} <z ‡>
~~Not any fowl, but~~ my folk and people are grown
half wild in many places; they would not worry
one another so in that wolvish belluine manner
else; ~~they would not precipitate themselves into
such a mixt mongrel war~~ Howel Eng. tea[2]

[1] Richard Knolles, 'Solyman the Magnificent, Fourth Emperor of the Turks' (*Turkish History* I), p. 446. S-G. *1755* SCROLL *n.s.*, To BAN *v.a.* (different)
[2] James Howell, 'England's Teares for the present Warres', p. 166. *1755* WOLVISH *adj.* (shorter)

{IL facing 2Z$^{r}$}



BE´LLUINE. *adj.* {...}
<z ‡ ———— >
{J. keys in Howell q. from IL.}

BE´LLY. *n.s.* {...}
3. {...}
I shall answer that better, than you can the getting up of the negro's *belly:* the Moor is with child by you.
*Shakesp. ~~Merchant of Venice~~.*

To BE´LLY. *v.n.* {...}

Thus by degrees day wastes, signs cease to rise,
For *bellying* earth, still rising up, denies
Their light a passage, and confines our eyes.
*Creech's ~~Manilius~~.*

BE´LLYGOD. *n.s.* {...} A glutton; one who makes a god of his belly. **<a low term.>**
What infinite waste they made this way, the only story of Apic<^ i>us, a famous *bellygod*, may suffice to shew.
*Hakewell/~~on Providence~~.*

BE´LLY-TIMBER. *n.s.* {...} Food; materials to support the belly. **<a low word.>**

BE´LOMANCY. *n.s.* {...}
*Belomancy*, or divination by arrows, hath been in request with Scythians, Alans, Germans, with the Africans and Turks of Algier. *Brown's Vulgar Errours, b.* v. *c.* 22.
{J. ital. 'divination by arrows'.}

To BELO´NG. *v.n.* {...}
5. To be the quality or attribute~~s~~ of.

{sig. 2Z$^{r}$}

BELO′W. *prep.* {…}
1. {…}
He'll beat Ausidius' head *below* his knee,
And tread upon his neck. *Shakesp.* ~~*Macbeth*~~.
2. {…}
The noble Venetians think themselves equal ~~at least~~ to the electors of the empire, and but one degree *below* kings.
*Addison*/~~*on Italy*~~.

BELO′W. *adv.* {…}
2. {…}
And let no tears from erring pity flow,
For one that's bless'd above, immortaliz'd *below*.
*Smith,* ~~*To the Memory of J. Philips*~~.
~~T~~<**Then t**>he fairest child of Jove,
*Below* for ever sought, and bless'd above. *Prior.*
3. In hell; {…}
{…} *Tickell.*
**<4 Below is used ——— by Swift as a noun for** **<u>the places below</u>**
**p ‡** > {J. keys in Swift q. from IL.}

BEL<′>WE\THER. *n.s.* [from *bell* and *wether*. <^ **it was anciently accented on the second syllable.**>] {…}
{J.'s note prompted by Spenser q. following.}
The fox will serve my sheep to gather,
And drive to follow after their belwether. *Spens. Hub. Tale.*
{…}
The flock of sheep, and *belwether*, thinking to break into another's pasture, and being to pass over ~~another~~ bridge, justled till both fell into the ditch. *Howel's England's Tears.*

To BEMA′D. *v.a.* {…}
~~Making just report~~
Of how unnatural and *bemadding* sorrow,
The king hath cause to plain. *Shakesp. King Lear.*
To BEMI′RE. *v.a.* {…}
**<o ‡**——— > {J. keys in Sidney q. from IL.}
To BEMO′AN. *v.a.* {…}



The gods themselves the ruin'd seats *bemoan*,
And blame the mischiefs that themselves have done.
*Addison's* ~~*Remarks on Italy*~~.
BEMO′ANER. *n.s.* {…}
<——— **z ‡**>
{J. keys in new entry for BEMOCK with Shakespeare q. from IL.}

BENCH. *n.s.* {…}
2. {…}
A son <^ ^ **shall try to**> set your decrees at naught:
To pluck down justice from your awful *bench*;
To trip the course of law, and blunt the sword
That guards the peace and safety of your person.
*Shakesp.* ~~*Henry* IV. *p.* ii~~.
{Further inking accidental.}

To BENCH. *v.a.* {…}
1. {…}
'Twas *bench'd* with turf, and, goodly to be seen,
The thick young grass arose ~~in fresher green~~. *Dryden's Fab.*

To BEND. *v.a.* {…}◆
1. {…}
They *bend* their bows, they whirl their slings around:
Heaps of spent arrows fall, and strew the ground;
~~And helms, and shields, and rattling arms resound.~~
{J. crosses out third line and triplet bracket.} *Dryden's* ~~*Aeneid*~~.
**<2 To set awry; to pervert from certitude** ——— >
{Slip with Raleigh q. glued to printed page. J. inserts Raleigh q.; J.'s line drawn from page onto slip indicates slip was attached before J. made annotation.}
~~2~~<**3**>. To direct to a certain point.
{…}
Then, with a rushing sound, th' assembly *bend*
Diverse their steps: ~~the rival rout ascend~~
~~The royal dome~~. *Pope's Odyssey, b.* ii. *l.* 295.
3. To apply. **<to intend; to use with close attention.>**

{BELO'W. *adv.* 4.}

**<p ‡>**

~~Subst. the place below in opposition to above~~
But with the upside down to show
Its inclination for below. Swift[1]

{To BEND. *v.a.* 2.} {Slip pasted onto 2Z$^{v}$.}♦
Never any man whose mind the Act of education hath not <u>bended</u>; whose eyes a foolish superstition hath not afterwards blinded whose apprehensions are sober, but hath found by irresistible necessity One true God

Sir W. Ral.[2]

{To BEMI'RE. *v.*a.}

**<o ‡>**

~~2 To soil or to debase mentally~~
Base minded wretches are your thoughts so deeply <u>bemired</u> in the trade of Ordinary Worldlings, as for respect of ~~gain~~ some paultry wool ~~may yield you~~, to let ~~so much~~ time pass without knowing perfectly her estate

Sidney.[3]

**<z ‡>**

<[**from ~~to~~<u>mock</u>**]> {J. writes 'to', then superimposes 'm' on 'o'.}
Bemock v.a to mock at; to scorn **<to deride.>**
~~The elements~~
~~Of whom~~ your swords ~~are temper'd~~ may as well
Wound the loud winds, or with <u>bemockt</u> at stabs
Kill the still closing waters  Shak[4]

1 Swift, 'The Story of Baucis and Philemon' (*Poems* I), ll. 99-100, p. 92. S-G (slip reads 'The kettle to the top' before 'But with …'). *1755* FOR *prep.* 29 (with 'The kettle to the top')
2 Sir Walter Raleigh, *History of the World*, vol. I, bk I, ch. vi, § 7, p. 56. Clipped from IL facing 2Z2$^{r}$. S-G (with 'art' instead of 'Act'). *1755* NECESSITY *n.s.* 5 (very different)
3 Sidney, *Arcadia*, bk I, p. 3. S-G. *1755* WRETCH *n.s.*, WORLDLING *n.s.* (much shorter)
4 Shakespeare, *Tempest* (**Works* I), 3.4, p. 59 [3.3. 61-64]. S-G. *1755* STAB *n.s.*

{IL facing 2Z$^{v}$}

To pervert[1]

{BEND. *n.s.* 1.}

The posture of flattery <**p** ‡>
Thinkst thou the fiery fever will go out
With titles blown from adulation?
Will it give place to flexure & low bends?
Shak.[2]

{To BEND. *v.n.* 3.}

To yield to submit <**o** ‡>
So when a lion shakes his dreadful mane
And angry grows: If he that first took pain
To tame his Youth, approach the haughty beast
He bends to him but frights away the rest
Waller[3]

{BENEFA´CTION. *n.s.* 2.}

<‡ **q**>
~~In all the~~ light and influence ~~that~~ the heavens bestow upon this lower world, tho the lower world cannot equal the benefaction yet with grateful return, it reflects those rays that it cannot recompense
South.[4]

{BE´NEFICED. *adj.*}

I will engage to find him above an hundred beneficed clergymen who have not so much among them all to maintain themselves and their families Swift[5]

1 Sir Walter Raleigh q. illustrating To BEND. *v.a.* 2, excised as slip and pasted onto 2Z$^{v}$. IL subsequently patched.
2 Shakespeare, *Henry V* (**Works* IV), 4.5, p. 390 (marked book: 'bending' instead of 'bends') [4.1.253-255]. S-G. *1755* FLEXURE *n.s.* 4, FEVER *n.s.* (with 'bending' instead of 'bends'), ADULATION *n.s.* (shorter), To GO *v.n.* 65 (shorter), OUT *adv.* 8 (shorter)
3 Edmund Waller, 'Panegyric to my Lord Protector', p. 120. S-G. *1755* PAIN *n.s.* 5, MANE *n.s.* (much shorter)
4 Robert South, 'Sermon XI' (*Twelve Sermons* 1692), p. 559. S-G. *1755* REQUITAL *n.s.* 2 (slightly different)
5 Swift, 'Preface to *the Bishop of Sarum's Introduction'* (*Prose* VI), p. 65. S-G.

{IL facing 2Z2$^{r}$}

## BEN

{To BEND. *v.a.*}
{...}
4. To put any thing in order for use; a metaphor taken from bending the bow.
{...}
5. To incline. **<to apply.>**
{...}
6. To subdue; to make submissive; as, war and famine will *bend* our enemies.
7. *To bend the brow.* To knit the brow; to frown.
{...}
To BEND. *v.n.* {...}
1. To be incurvated.
2. To lean ~~or jut~~ over.
{...} *Thomson.*
3. To ~~resolve; to~~ determine/<; **to fix. This is scarcely used but in the participle passive**>
{...} *Addison's Essay on the Georgicks.*

{J. moves sense 3 of To BEND *v.n.* to become the new sense 4 under To BEND *v.a.*; J. fails to renumber defs.}
~~4~~<**3**>. To be submissive; to bow.
{...} *Isaiah,* lx. 14.
<**o** ‡——— > {J. keys in new def. and Waller q. from IL.}
BEND. *n.s.* {...}
1. Flexure; incurvation.
{...} *Shakesp. Julius Cæsar.*
<**p** ‡——— > {J. keys in new def. and Shakespeare q. from IL.}
2. The crooked timber~~s~~ which make<**s**> the ribs or sides of a ship.
*Skinner.*

BE'NDER. *n.s.* {...}
2. {...}
These bows, being ~~somewhat~~ like the long bows in use amongst us, were bent ~~only~~ by a man's immediate strength, without the help of any *bender*, or rack, ~~that are~~ used to others.
*Wilkins*~~'s Mathematical Magick.~~

## BEN

BENEDI'CTION. *n.s.* {...}
1. {...}
~~A sov'reign shame so bows him,~~ his unkindness,
That stript her from his *benediction,* turn'd her
To foreign casualties, gave her dear rights
To his doghearted daughters. *Shakesp. King Lear.*
~~F~~<**He f**>rom him will raise
A mighty nation; and upon him show'r
His *benediction* so, that, in his seed,
All nations shall be blest. *Milton's Par. Lost. b.* xii. *l.* 125.

BENEFA'CTION. *n.s.* {...}
2. The benefit conferred; {...}
< ——— **q** ‡>
{J. keys in South q. from IL.}

BENE'FICENCE. *n.s.* {...}
You could not extend your *beneficence* to so many persons; yet you have lost as few days as ~~that excellent emperour~~ <^~~Mr~~{?}**Titus.**>.
*Dryden*~~'s Juvenal, Dedicat.~~

BENE'FICENT. *adj.* {...}
~~Such a creature~~ <**Man**> could not have his origination from any less than the most wise and *beneficent* being, the great God.
*Hale's Origin of Mankind.*
~~But~~ Phoebus, thou, to man *beneficent,*
Delight'st in building cities. *Prior.*
BENEFI'CIAL. *adj.*
1. {...}
Not that any thing is made to be *beneficial to* him, but all things for him, to shew beneficence and grace in them.
*Hooker,*~~/b. i. § 8~~.
This supposition grants the opinion to conduce to order ~~in the world,~~ and consequently to be very *beneficial* to mankind.
*Tillotson,*~~/sermon~~ i.

{sig. 2Z2r}

## BEN

To BE´NEFIT. *v.a.* {...}
{...} *Shakesp. Wint. Tale.*

<——— o┼> {J. keys in Bacon q. from IL.}

To BE<´>NEFIT. *v.n.* {...} {J. inserts missing stress mark on first syllable.}

BENE´MPT. ~~*adj.*~~ ~~[See NEMPT.]~~ **<preterite of an obsolete verb.>** {...}

To BENE´T. *v.a.* {...} To ensnare; to surround as with toils. **<to hamper>**

BE´NJAMIN. *n.s.* {...} The name of a tree.
~~From a calyx, which consists of four leaves, are produced~~ three small flowers, which have an oblong tube; the upper part, which is expanded, is divided into eight segments; between which are several short threads, and, in the middle of the tube, is the ~~ovarium, which becomes a fruit.~~ It was brought from Virginia into England, ~~and is propagated by laying down the tender branches in the spring of the year~~. *Millar.*
{Smear unintentional.}

## BEN

To BENI´GHT. *v.a.* {...}
2. {...}
~~Or~~ **<Were there>** some *benighted* angel, in his way,
Might ease his wings; and, seeing heav'n appear
In its best work of mercy, think it there. *Dryden.*

BENI´GN. *adj.* {...}
1. {...}
What heaven bestows upon the earth, in kind influences and *benign* aspects, is paid it back again in ~~sacrifice and~~ adoration. *South.*
2. Wholesome; not malignant. {...}
{Inking from facing IL.}
**<3>** BENIGN *Disease* {...}
{J. consolidates two separate entries under BENIGN. *adj.* with three senses.}

BE´NNET. *n.s.* An herb; the same with *avens*, ~~which see.~~
BENT. *n.s.* {...}
2. {...}
There are divers subtle inquiries concerning the strength required to the bending of ~~them~~**<bows>** <^ ^bows>; {...}.
{J. appears to write 'bows' above 'them'; because word is smudged, he adds 'bows' in the margin.}

{sig. 2Z2v}

{To BE´NEFIT. *v.a.*}

<o+>

The benefited subject should render some
small portion of his gain as well towards the
maintenance of his own commodity as for
the supporting of the Kings expence
Bacon[1]

{To BENI´GHT. *v.a.*}
made duskish or black
If virtue no benighted beauty lack
Your son in law is far more fair than black
Shak.[2]

{BENI´GNLY. *adv.*}
Your grace and those your nobles here
present, be pleased benignly to bow your
ears to hear the tragedy of a Young Man
Bacon[3]

1 Bacon, 'An Historical Account of the Office of Alienations' (*Works* III), p. 552 [now attributed to William Lombarde, in *Some few notes of the orders, proceedings, punishments, and priveleges of the Lower House of Parliament* (c. 1584)]. J. first crosses out 'as well', then smears out stroke to maintain coherence of passage. S-G. *1755* SUPPORTATION *n.s.* (without 'as well')

2 Shakespeare, *Othello* (*Works* VIII), 1.9, p. 299 [1.3.289-290]. Warburton reads 'belighted'; J. specifically questions this reading in his edn of Shakespeare, proposing 'delight or'; doubtful reading may have prompted rejection of this new def. and q. S-G. *1755* SON-IN-LAW *n.s.*

3 Bacon, *History of King Henry VII* (*Works* III), p. 464 [VI, p.163]. S-G. *1755* BALL *n.s.* 5 (different)

{IL facing 2Z2v}

{To BEQUE'ATH. *v.a.*}
Improperly used by Denham for left as a token.

Viewing the Trojan reliques she unsheathd
Æneas' sword, not for that use bequeath'd
Denh.[1]

{To BERE'AVE. *v.n.* 3.} <‡ l >

Came he to sing a ravens note
Whose dismal tune bereft my Vital powers
Shak[2]

The rights for which I love are bereft me
Shak. Othello[3]

{BE'RGAMOT. *n.s.* 1.}

Alcinous Orchard various apples bears <‡ k>
Unlike are bergamots & pounder pears
Dryd. V. Geo.[4]

[1] John Denham,'The Passion of Dido for Æneas', ll. 213-4. S-G.
[2] Shakespeare, *2 Henry VI* (*Works V), 3.4, p. 56 [3.2.40-41]. S-G. *1755* TUNE *n.s.* 1
[3] Shakespeare, *Othello* (**Works* VIII), 1.9, p. 298 [1.3.257]. S-G (with 'love him are bereft me').
[4] Dryden,*Virgil's Georgics* (*Works* V), bk II, ll. 126-7. S-G. *1755* POUNDER *n.s.*

{IL facing 3A[r]}

{BENT. *n.s.* 6.}

O who does know the *bent* of womens fantasy!

*Fairy Queen~~, b. i. cant. iv. stanz. 24~~.*

{...}

Let there be the same propensity and *bent* of will to religion, and there will be the same sedulity and ~~indefatigable~~ industry. South./

7. {...}

~~Yet~~ we saw them forced to give way to the *bent*, and current humour of the people, in favour of their ancient and lawful government. *Temple.*

8. {...}

Two of them hath the very *bent* of honour.

*Shakesp.* ~~*Much ado about Nothing*~~.

9. {...}

The exercising the understanding, in the several ways of reasoning, teacheth the mind suppleness, to apply itself ~~more~~ dexterously to *bents* and turns of the matter, in ~~all~~ its researches. *Locke.*/

10. {...}

~~Then the flowers of the vines;~~ it is a little dust, like the dust of a *bent*, which grows upon the cluster, ~~in the first coming forth~~. *Bacon's Essays.*

June is drawn in a mantle of dark grass-green, upon his head a garland of *bents*, kingcups, and maidenhair. *Peacham*/~~*on Drawing*~~.

To BENU'M. *v.a.* {...}♦

1. To make torpid; to take away the sensation and any use of any part by cold, or by some obstruction.

So stings a snake that to the fire is brought,
Which harmless lay with cold *benumm'd* before.

*Fairfax,* ~~*b. ii. stanz. 85.*~~

{Diagonal lines result of inking from facing IL.}

{...}

<2> It seizes upon the vitals, and *benums* the senses; and where there is no sense, there can be no pain. *South.*

<1> {...} *L'Estrange, fab.* ix.

2. To stupify.

{J. moves South q. to first place under def. 2.}



To BEPA'INT. *v.a.* {...}

Thou know'st, the mask of night is on my face,
Else would a maiden blush *bepaint* my cheek.

*Shakesp.* ~~*Romeo and Juliet.*~~

To BEPI'NCH. *v.a.* {...}

In their sides, arms, shoulders, all *bepincht*,
Ran thick the weals, ~~red~~ with blood, ready to start ~~out~~.

*Chapman's Iliad.*

To BEQUE'ATH. *v.a.* {...}

My father *bequeath'd* me by will ~~but~~ a ~~poor~~ thousand crowns.

*Shakesp.* ~~*As you like it.*~~

BEQUE'ST. *n.s.* {...}

He claimed the crown ~~to himself,~~ pretending an adoption, or *bequest*, of the kingdom unto him by the Confessor.

*Hale's* ~~*Common Law of England.*~~

To BERE'AVE. *v.n.* {...}

1. {...}

That when thou com'st to kneel at Henry's feet,
Thou may'st *bereave* him *of* his wits with wonder.

*Shakesp.* ~~*Henry IV. p. i.*~~

3. To take away from. **<not used>**

{J. keys in Shakespeare q. from IL.} <———— ‡ **l**>

BE'RGAMOT. *n.s.*

1. A sort of pear, {...}

{J. keys in Dryden q. from IL.} <———— **k** ‡>

3. A sort of snuff, which is only ~~clean~~ tobacco, with a little of the essence rubbed into it.

{J. crosses out 'clean'; smear is unintentional.}

*BERME. n.s.* {...} A space of ground three, four, or five feet wide, left without between the foot of the rampart and the side of the mote, to prevent the earth from falling down into the mote; ~~and~~ sometimes ~~it is~~ palisadoed.

*Harris.*

BE´RRY-BEARING *Cedar.* {...}

The leaves are squamose, somewhat like those of the cypress. The katkins, or male flowers, are produced at remote distances from the fruit on the same tree. The fruit is a berry, inclosing three hard seeds in each. The species are, 1. The yellow *berry-bearing cedar.* 2. The Phœnician *cedar.* These trees are propagated by sowing their berries, which are brought from the Streights, in boxes of light sandy earth; but they are at pre~~sent very rare, and only to be found in some curious old collections.~~ The wood ~~is of great use in the Levant, is~~ large timber, and may be thought the shittim-wood mentioned in the Scripture, of which many of the ornaments to the famous temple of Solomon were made. It is accounted excellent for carving, and esteemed equal almost to any sort of timber for its durableness.

*Millar.*

BE´RYL. *n.s.* {...}

The *beryl* of our lapidaries is only a fine sort of cornelian, of a more deep bright red, sometimes with a cast of yellow, and more transparent than the common cornelian.

*Woodward's ~~Method of Fossils~~.*

To BESE´ECH. *v.a.* {...}

1. To entreat; to supplicate; to implore/ ~~sometimes before~~ a person.

2. To beg; to ask/ ~~before~~ a thing.

To BESE´EM. *v.n.* {...}



This oversight
*Beseems* thee not, in whom such virtues spring.

*Fairfax ~~b. i. stanz. 78.~~*

Verona's ancient citizens
Cast by their brave *beseeming* ornaments.

*Shakesp. ~~Romeo and Juliet~~.*

To BESE´T. *v.a.* {...}

1. To besiege; to hem in; to inclose, as with a siege.

{...}

I know thou look'st on me, as on a wretch
*Beset* with ills, and cover'd with misfortunes. *Addis. Cato.* <2>

2. To embarrass; to perplex; to entangle without any means of escape. <1>

{...}

{...} *Locke.*

{J. moves Addison q. to last place under def. 2.}

To BESHRE´W. *v.a.*

2. To happen ill to. **<it is used impersonally>**

BESI´DE.
BESI´DES. } *prep.* {...}

2. Over and above.

Doubtless, in man there is a nature found,
*Beside* the senses, and above them far. *Sir J. Davies.* <2>

{...}

We may be sure there were great numbers of wise and learned men, *beside* those whose names are in the christian records, who ~~took care to~~ examine<d> our Saviour's history.

*Addison ~~on the Christian Religion.~~* <1>

Precepts of morality, *besides* the natural corruption of our tempers, are abstracted from ideas of sense.

*Addison's ~~Essay on the Georgicks.~~*

3. Not according to, though not contrary; as we say, some things are *beside* nature, some are *contrary* to nature.

{J. moves Davies q. to first place under def. 3.}

{sig. 3A$^{v}$}

{blank page}

{IL facing 3A$^{v}$}

{To BESI'EGE. *v.a.*}♦
~~To attend, to crowd~~
Frequent hearses shall besiege your gates **<l ‡>**
Pop.[1]
~~To invest. To block up with a fleet~~
Your much lov'd fleet shall with a wide command
Besiege the petty Monarchs of the Land **<k ‡>**
Dryd.[2]

{To BESPE'AK. *v.a.*}♦
Here too the Thresher brandishing his flail
Bespeaks a Master.
Dodslys Agricult.[3]

[1] Pope, 'Elegy to the Memory of an Unfortunate Lady' (*Poems* II), l. 38. S-G. *1755* FREQUENT *adj.*, HERSE *n.s.* 2
[2] Dryden, 'Astræa Redux' (*Works* I), ll. 300-01. S-G. *1755* MUCH *adv.* 3 (different)
[3] Robert Dodsley, 'Agriculture', canto I, ll. 118-119. S-G (slip written in an unfamiliar hand; appears to have been clipped out from ms. list of qs. from Dodsley's 'Agriculture', with q. illustrating To TWIRL *v.a.* (*1755*) written underneath, and crossed out; 'Thresher' underlined, then underlining crossed out). *1755* THRESHER *n.s.*

{IL facing 3A2ʳ}

## BES

BESI'DE. } *adv.*
BESI'DES. }
1. {...}

If Cassio ~~do~~ remain,
He hath a daily beauty in his life,
That makes me ugly; and, *besides*, the Moor
May unfold me to him; there stand I in peril. *Othello.*

{...}

That man that doth not know ~~those~~ things, which are of necessity for him to know, is but an ignorant man, whatever he may know *besides*. *Tillotson, serm.* i.

Some wondered, that the Turk never attacks this treasury. But, *besides*, that he has attempted it formerly with no success, it is certain the Venetians keep too watchful an eye. *Addison's ~~Remarks on Italy~~.*

2. {...}

~~And~~ the men said unto Lot, hast thou here any *besides?* *Genesis*, ~~xix. 12~~.

{...}

All that we feel of ~~it,~~ **<fame>** begins and ends
In the small circle of our foes or friends;
To all *beside* as much an empty shade,
An Eugene living, as a Cæsar dead. *Pope's Essay on Man.*

To BESI'EGE. *v.a.* {...}
{...} *Shakesp. Henry* VI.
**<k‡ l‡ ——— >**
{J. keys in Dryden and Pope qs. from IL.}

## BES

To BESO'T. *v.a.* {...}
1. To infatuate; to stupify; to dull; to ~~take away the~~ **<deprive of>** senses.

{...}

~~Or~~ fools *besotted* with their crimes,
That know not how to shift betimes. *Hudibras, p.* iii. *c.* ii.

{...}

2. To make to doat. **<with on before the object.>**

Paris, you speak
Like one *besotted* on your sweet delights. *Shakesp. ~~Troilus and Cressida~~.*

BESO'UGHT. {...}

Hasten to appease
Th' incensed Father, and th' incensed Son,
While pardon may be found, in time *besought*. *Milt. Paradise Lost*, ~~b. v. l. 848~~.

To BESPA'TTER. *v.a.* {...}

His weapons are the same which women and children use; a pin to scratch, and a squirt to *bespatter*. ~~Swift~~<^ ^ **Pope**>, *lett.* lxix.

To BESPE'AK. *v.a.* {...}
1. {...}

Here is the cap your worship did *bespeak*. *Shakesp. ~~Taming of the Shrew~~.*

4. {...}

~~Then staring on her with a ghastly look,~~
~~And~~ **<With>** hollow voice, he thus the queen *bespoke*. *Dryden.*

{sig. 3A2ʳ}

BESPO´KE. [*irreg.* ~~*particip.*~~ **<preterite>** from *bespeak*; which see.]
<^——————
**Bespoken part.**
**passive from <u>bespeak</u>>** {J. inserts new head-word.}

To BESPRI´NKLE. *v.a.* {...}

He ~~indeed,~~ imitating the father poet, whose life he had ~~also~~ written, hath *besprinkled* his work with many fabulosities.
*Brown's* ~~*Vulgar Errours, b.* i. *c.* 8.~~

BEST is sometimes used in composition.

These latter *best-be-trust-spies* had some of them further instructions, to draw off the best friends ~~and servants~~ of Perkin, ~~by making remonstrances to them, how weakly his enterprize and hopes were built.~~ *Bacon's Henry* VII.



BESTIA´LITY. *n.s.* {...}

What can be a greater absurdity, than to affirm *bestiality* to be the essence of humanity, ~~and darkness the center of light?~~
*Arbuthnot and Pope's* ~~*Mart. Scriblerus.*~~

To BESTO´W. *v.a.* {...}

1. To give; to confer upon. **<with <u>on</u> rarely with <u>to</u> before the receiver.>**

All men would ~~willingly~~ have yielded him praise; but his nature was ~~such as~~ to *bestow* it <u>upon</u> himself, before any could give it. *<u>Sidney.</u>*/
{J. ital. 'upon'.}

All the de\dicate things of the house of the Lord\ did\ they *bestow* upon Baalim. 2 *Chron.* xxiv. 7.

Sir Julius Cæsar had, in his office, the disposition of the six clarks places; which he had *bestowed* <u>to</u> such persons as he thought fit. *Clarendon.*
{J. ital. 'to'.}

2. {...}

You always exceed expectations: as if yours was not your own, but to *bestow* <u>on</u> wanting merit. *Dryden's Fables, Ded.*
{J. ital. 'on'.}

3. {...}

I could have *bestowed* her <u>upon</u> a fine gentleman, who extremely admired her. *Tatler,* N° 75.
{J. ital. 'upon'.}

7. To lay up; to stow; to place.
**<—————— ‡ a.b.c>**
{J. keys in Spenser, Shakespeare and Fairfax qs. from IL.}

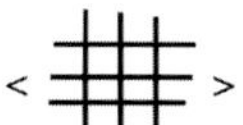

{J.'s sign, apparently not intended for compositor.}

{BEST. *adj.*}

You with the rest,
Causeless have laid disgraces on my head
And with your best endeavours have stirrd up
My lifefest liege to be mine enemy[1]

Bestadde for bestaid [stay]
the pret of bestay
To hinder, to prevent, to indispose,
to disorder, not as Spens. Glos. would
have it Ordered, disposed.
Whate foul evil hath thee so bestad?
Whilom thou wast peregal to the best,
And wont to make the shepherds glad
With piping & dancing did pass the rest
Mischief mought to that mischance befall
That so hath reft us of our merriment
But reds me with pain doth thee apall[2]

{To BESTO'W. *v.a.*}
To apply ones thoughts or mind to any thing
That other on his friends his thoughts bestows
The Covetous Worldling in his anxious mind
Thinks only on the wealth he left behind
To dispose; to arrange in order \ Dryd.[3]

{To BESTO'W. *v.a.* 7.}
<a ‡> ~~Through the Hall there walk'd~~
A jolly yeoman, ~~Marshal of the same~~
Whose name was Appetite, he did bestow
Both guests & meats, whenever in they came
~~And know them how to order without blame~~
Spens[4]

Having with before the thing bestowed
Sowr eyed disdain & discord shall bestow
The union of their bed with weed so loathly
That you shall hate it Shak.[5]
We hear our bloody Cousins are bestowd
<b> In England & in Ireland not confessing
Their cruel parricide filling their hearers
With strange invention Shak[6]
<c> 7 In fenced towrs bestowed is their grain
Before thou camst this kingdom to invade
Fairf.[7]
If I had had time to have made new liverys
I would have bestowed the thousand I borrowed.
But it is no matter. Shak.[8]

{To BESTRE'W. *v.a.*}
This arm had aided yours this hand bestrown
Our floors with blood, and pushd the slaughter on
~~Nor had the sire been seprate from the son.~~
Pop. Odyss.[9]

1 Shakespeare, *2 Henry VI* (**Works* V), 3.3, p. 48 [3.1.161-164]. Aman. begins writing 'lif', then smears out 'f' and corrects to 'liefest'. *1755* LIEF *adj.*
2 Spenser, *Shepheardes Calendar* (*Works* VII), 'August', ll. 6-10, 13-15.
3 Dryden, 'Ceyx and Alcyone' (*Works* VII), ll. 184-87. Dividing line indicates attribution 'Dryd.' refers to previous four lines, while def. 'To dispose; to arrange in order' pertains to following Spenser q. S-G. *1755* WORLDLING *n.s.*
4 Spenser, *Faerie Queene* (*Works* II), bk II, canto IX, st. xxviii, ll. 2-5. Q. also transcribed on IL for BLAME *n.s.* 2. S-G. *1755* MARSHAL *n.s.* 3, YEOMAN *n.s.* (much shorter)
5 Shakespeare, *The Tempest* (**Works* I), 4.1, p. 61 (with 'bestrew' instead of 'bestow') [4.1.20-22]. S-G. *1755* LOATHLY *adj.*
6 Shakespeare, *Macbeth* (**Works* VI), 3.1, p. 373 [3.1.29-32]. S-G. *1755* INVENTION *n.s.* 4 (shorter)
7 Edward Fairfax, tr., *Recovery of Jerusalem*, bk II, st. lxxv, p. 57. S-G. *1755* To FENCE *v.a.*1
8 Shakespeare, *2 Henry IV* (**Works* IV), 5.7, p. 309 [5.5.10-13]. S-G ('livries' for 'liverys'). *1755* MATTER *n.s.* 8, ZEAL *n.s.*
9 Pope, *Odyssey* (*Poems* X), bk XXIV, ll. 441-443. Probably intended to be keyed in to printed text. S-G.

{IL facing 3A2v}

{BET. The old *preterite* of *beat.*}

**<b ‡>**

They on his shield like Iron Sledges bet
F. Q. 2. 2. 22[1]

{To BETI'DE. *v.n.* 3.}

**<a ‡ >**

To fall out; to happen
Whatever fortune good or bad betide
No time shall find me wanting to my truth
Dryd.[2]

Betight pret pass fr betyde
Say it out Diggon whatever it hight
For nought but well mought him betight
He is so meek wise merciable
And with his Word his work is convenable
Spens. Pa.[3]

{To BETO'KEN. *v.a.*}◆
To indicate
All Æthiops are fleshy & plumb & have great lips, all which betoken moisture retaind and not drawn out Bacon[4]
Betoken n.s.
is retaind in Scotland the Same with token[5]

1 Spenser, *Faerie Queene* (*Works* II), bk II, canto II, st. xxii, l. 4. S-G ('old pret. of beat' at top). *1755* SLEDGE *n.s.* 7

2 Dryden, *Virgil's Æneis* (*Works* VI), bk IX, ll. 373-75. S-G. *1755* To WANT *v.n.* 2

3 Spenser, *Shepheardes Calendar* (*Works* VII), 'September', ll. 172-75. Inking on 'convenable' from facing p. S-G. *1755* CONVENABLE *adj.* (much shorter), MERCIABLE *adj.* (much shorter), To SAY *v.a.* (much shorter)

4 Bacon, *Natural History* (**Works* III), cent. IV, § 399, p. 84 [II, cent. IV, § 399, p. 473]. S-G (on same slip: 'To indicate {...} with token'). *1755* FLESHY *adj.*

5 S-G (on slip with Bacon q.).

{IL facing 3B^r}

{To BESTRI´DE. *v.a.*}

3. {...}

That horse, that thou so often hast *bestrid:*
~~That horse, that I so carefully have dress'd~~. *Shakesp. R.* II.

4. {...}

He *bestrid*
An o'erpress'd Roman, and i' th' consul's view
Slew three opposers: ~~Tarquin's self he met,~~
~~And struck him on his knee.~~ *Shakesp. Coriolanus.*

{...}

He doth *bestride* a bleeding land,
Gasping for life, ~~under great Bolingbroke.~~ *Shak. Henry* IV.

BET. The old *preterite* of *beat.*

**<b ‡ ——>**

{J. keys in Spenser q. from IL; inking from facing IL.}

To BETA´KE. *v.a.*

2. To have recourse to; with the reciprocal pronoun.

~~Thou tyrant!~~
Do not repent these things; for they are heavier
Than all thy woes can stir: therefore *betake thee*
To nothing but despair. *Shakesp. Winter's Tale.*
The rest, in imitation, to like arms
*Betook them*, and the neighb'ring hills up tore.
*Milton's ~~Paradise Lost, b. vi. l. 663~~.*

3. To apply; with the reciprocal pronoun. <2>
{...} *Dryden.*

As my observations have been the light whereby I have hitherto steer'd my course, so I here *betake myself* to them again. <1>
*Woodward's Natural History.*

{J. moves Woodward q. to final position under def. 2.}

To BETE´EM. *v.a.* {...} **<~~not~~ obsolete.>**♦

BET

Belike for want of rain; which I could well
*Beteem* them from the tempest of mine eyes.
*Shakesp. ~~Midsummer Night's Dream.~~*

BE´THLEHEM. *n.s.* [See BEDLAM.] {J. changes to small caps. all but initial letter of both head-words.}

To BETHRA´L. *v.a.* {...} **<not in use>**♦

To BETI´DE. *v.n.* {...}♦

1. To happen to; to befal; to bechance; whether good or bad. **<some what antiquated>**

3. To come to pass; to fall out; to happen.
{...} *Sh. Two Gent. of Ver.*

**< —— a ‡>**

{J. keys in def., though redundant, and Dryden q. from IL.}

4. To become. **<not in use.>**

BETI´ME. }
BETI´MES. } *adv.* {...}

1. Seasonably; early.
Send succours, lords, and stop the rage *betime.* <2>
*Shakesp. ~~Henry VI. p. ii~~.*
{...} *Par. Reg.*

2. Soon; before long time has passed.
Whiles they are weak, *betimes* with them contend;
For when they once to perfect strength do grow, <1>
Strong wars they make. *Fairy Queen, b.* ii. *c.* iv. *st.* 34.

{J. moves *Fairy Queen* q. from def. 2 to first place under def. 1.}

3. {...}
They rose *betimes* in the morning, ~~and offered sacrifice.~~
1 *Macc.* iv. 52.

BE´TLE.
~~BE´TRE.~~ } <or betre> *n.s.* {...}

BE´TONY. *n.s.* {…} A plant. < —— —— —— >

~~The leaves are green, rough, and crenated on the edges: the~~ flowers are disposed in a spike; the upper crest of the flower is advanced, and divided into two segments; the beard, or lower part of the flower, is divided into three, and the middle segment is bifid; each flower is, for the most part, succeeded by four naked seeds. The species are, 1. Common or wood *betony*. ~~2. *Betony*, with a white flower. 3. Greater Danish *betony*. The first is~~ very common in woods and shady places, and is greatly esteemed as a vulnerary herb. *Millar.*

To BETRA´Y. *v.a.*

1. To give into the hands of enemies by treachery, or breach of trust.

{…}

{…} *Knolles's History of the Turks.*

**<a ‡** ———— > {J. mistakenly keys in first Bacon q. from IL under def. 1.}

4. To make liable to fall into something inconvenient. **<to insnare>**

**<c ‡** ———— > {J. keys in def. and second Bacon q. from IL; unclear if or where def. is to be inserted.}

His abilities created in him great confidence; and this was like enough to *betray* him to great errours, ~~and many enemies~~. *King Charles.*

**<b ‡** ———— > {J. keys in def. and Walton q. from IL.}

BETRA´YER. *n.s.* {…}

~~They are~~ only a few *betrayers* of their country; ~~they~~ are to purchase coin, ~~perhaps, at half price~~, and vend it ~~among us~~ to the ruin of the publick. *Swift.*

To BETRO´TH. *v.a.* {…}

2. {…}

And what man is there that hath *betrothed* a wife, and hath not taken her? let him go and return unto his house. *Deut.* ~~xx. 7.~~

BE´TTER. *adj.* {…} See GOOD. {J. changes to small caps all but initial letter.}

He has a horse *better* than the Neapolitan's; a *better* bad habit of frowning than the count Palatine. *Shakesp.* ~~*Merchant of Venice.*~~

BET

*The* BETTER.

1. {…}

Dionysius, ~~his countryman,~~ in an epistle to Pompey, after an express comparison, affords him *the better of* Thucydides. *Brown's* ~~*Vulgar Errours, b. i. c. 8*~~.

BE´TTER. *adv.* [comparative of *well.*] *Well*/ in a greater degree.

To BE´TTER. *v.a.*

1. {…}

The very cause of ~~his~~ **<Christ's>** taking upon him our nature, was to *better* the quality, and to advance the condition thereof. *Hooker,* ~~*b. viii. § 54*~~.

{…}

Heir to all his lands and goods,
Which I have *better'd*, rather than decreas'd.
*Shakesp.* ~~*Taming of the Shrew.*~~

BE´TTER. *n.s.* {…} **<One>** Superior in goodness/**<, or rank or any estimable quality.>**

{J. expands def. to reflect usage in qs.}

BE´TTOR. *n.s.* [from *to bet.* <^ **written bettor to distinguish it from better**>] One that lays betts or wagers.

{To BETRA′Y. *v.a.* 1.}
~~To lead away by any means~~

<a ‡>

The emission of the loose & Adventitious
Moisture doth betray the radical Moisture
and Carrieth it for Company Bac.[1]

{To BETRA′Y. *v.a.* 4.}
To catch with a snare or trap **<b ‡>**
With gins betray the fi~~c~~shat & the Moldinarp
Walton Ang.[2]
These ingenious exercises <u>betrayd</u> in
him an extraordinary quickness of
Wit and learning Peacham[3]

~~To seize with an infection: to taint~~

<c ‡>

Stinks which the nostrils strait abhor are
not the most pernicious but such airs as **<stet>**
have some similitude with mans body; and
So insinuate themselves & betray the spirits
Bac.[4]

{BE′TTOR. *n.s.*}
Unlucky <u>bettors</u> will lose on both sides
Sheffiel Buck.[5]

[1] Bacon, *Natural History* (**Works* III), cent. IV, § 345, p. 73 [II, cent. IV, § 345, p. 455]. J. erroneously inserts q. to illustrate def. 1. S-G *1755* RADICAL *adj.* 2, To TOLL *v.a.* (different)

[2] Izaak Walton, *Compleat Angler*, pt I, p. 183 (Walton reads 'Fichat' and 'Mouldwarp' or 'Mould-warp'). J. intends q. without def. to be inserted under To BETRAY *v.a.* 4. Aman. superimposes 's' on 'c' in 'fichat'. S-G (with 'To betray 6' at top of slip and with 'fichat' and 'moldiwarp'). *1755* MOULDWARP *n.s.*

[3] Henry Peacham, *The Compleat Gentleman*, ch. x, pp. 92-93. S-G (with '5 v.a.' at top). J. perhaps intended q. for inclusion under def. 5.

[4] Bacon, *Natural History* (**Works* III), cent. X, § 915, p. 193 [II, cent. X, § 915, p. 646]. J. apparently attempts to smear out vertical cross-out strokes on q. and writes 'stet' to indicate q. should stand. Smearing of cross-out stroke through def. probably accidental. *1755* STINK *n.s.* (shorter), STRAIGHT *adv.* (much shorter), NOSTRIL *n.s.* (much shorter)

[5] John Sheffield, 'Some Account of the Revolution' (*Works* II), p. 96. S-G.

{IL facing 3B$^{v}$}

{To BEWA´RE. *v.n.* 1.}

**<o ‡>**

~~To guard against in order to avoid a thing~~
Vapours fired do shew the mariner
From what point of his compass to beware
Impetuous winds Milt.[1]

**<p ‡>**

To bewonder v.a. <[**from wonder.**]>
To amaze, astonish.
We stood bewondered, another while
delighted with the rare bravery ~~thereof~~
~~till seeing such streams of blood as threatned~~
~~a drowning life, we galloped towards them~~
~~to part them~~ Sidney b. 2.[2]

[1] Milton, *Paradise Lost,* bk IV, ll. 557-60. S-G. *1755* POINT *n.s.* 13
[2] Sidney, *Arcadia*, bk II, p. 262. S-G. *1755* To GALLOP *v.n.* 2 (much shorter)

{IL facing 3B2$^{r}$}

**BEW**

To BEWA´IL. *v.a.* {...}

Thy ambition,
Thou scarlet sin, robb'd this *bewailing* land
Of noble Buckingham, ~~my father in law~~. *Shakesp. H.* VIII.

To BEWA´RE. *v.n.* {...}
1. To regard with caution; {...}

**BEY**

<——— **o** ‡>

{J. keys in Milton q. from IL.}

To BEWE´T. *v.a.* {...}
His napkin, with his true tears all *bewet*,
Can do no service on her sorrowful cheeks.
*Shakesp.* ~~*Titus Andronicus*~~.

To BEWI´LDER. *v.a.* {...}
It is good sometimes to lose and *bewilder* ourselves in such studies. *Watts's* ~~*Improvement of the Mind*~~.

BEWI´TCHMENT. *n.s.* {...}
{...} *Shakesp. Coriolanus.*

<————— **p** ‡>

{J. keys in new entry for To BEWONDER with Sidney q. from IL.}

{sig. 3B2$^{r}$}

{BEYO'ND. *prep.* 2.}

Now we are on land, we are but between death and life; for we are *beyond* the old world and the new.

*Bacon~~'s New Atlantis~~*.

4. {...}

Yet these declare
Thy goodness *beyond* thought, and pow'r divine.

*Milton~~'s Paradise Lost, b. v. l. 158~~*.

BE'ZOAR. *n.s.* {...}

A medicinal stone {...} growing to the size of an acorn, and sometimes to that of a pigeon's egg. ~~Were the real virtues of this stone answereable to its reputed ones, it were doubtless a panacea. Indeed~~ its rarity, and the peculiar manner of its formation {...}.

*Savary. Chambers.*

BI'AS. *n.s.* {...}



3. Propension; inclination. **<declina~~ta~~tion>**

BI'AS. *adv.* {...}

Every action that hath gone before,
Whereof we have record, trial did draw
*Bias* and thwart, not answering the aim.

*Shakesp. ~~Troilus and Cressida.~~*

To BIB. *v.n.* {...}

He playeth with *bibbing* mother Meroë, as though ~~she were~~ so named, because she would drink mere wine without water.

*Camden./*

BI'BLE. *n.s.* {...}

We must take heed how we accustom ourselves to a slight and irreverent use of the name of God, and of the phrases and expressions of the holy *bible*, which ought not be applied upon every slight occasion. *Tillotson, ~~sermon i~~*.

BICA'PSULAR. *adj.* {...} ~~A~~ <^**A word applied to a**> plant whose seed vesis divided into two parts.

To BI'CKER. *v.n.*

2. {...}

And from about him fierce effusion rowl'd
Of smoke, and *bickering* flame, and sparkles dire.

*Milton's ~~Paradise Lost, b. vi. l. 674~~*.

An icy gale, oft shifting o'er the pool,
Breathes a blue film, and, in its mid career,
Arrests the *bickering* stream. *Thomson~~'s Winter, l. 730~~*.

{sig. 3B2v}

{blank page}

{IL facing 3B2v}

{To BID. *v.a.* 2.}

**<q ‡>**

In threats the foremost, but the lag in fight
When didst thou thrust amidst the mingled press
Content to bid the war aloof in peace
Dryd. Il[1]

{To BIDE. *v.n.* 4.}

**<r~~a~~ ‡>**

He durst not <u>bide</u>
~~A rude~~ rabblement whose like he never saw
But got his ready steed & fast away
'gan ride
F. Q. 1. 65[2]

[1] Dryden, 'The First Book of Homer's *Ilias*' (*Works* VII), ll. 337-39. S-G. *1755* DASTARD *n.s.* (much shorter)

[2] Spenser, *Faerie Queene* (*Works* I), bk I, canto VI, st. viii, ll. 7-9. S-G ('v.n. r' at top of slip, perhaps related to 'r' key on IL and facing page; 'F. Q. 1. 6. 8' given as source. Passage on slip is written-over and rearranged, causing aman. to miscopy on IL. Intended wording: 'A rude rabblement,/Whose like he never saw, he durst not bide,/But got his ready steed, & fast away 'gan ride. F.Q.1.6.8'). *1755* RABBLEMENT *n.s.*

{IL facing 3C[r]}

## BID

To BID. *v.a.* {...}

2. To command; to order; {...}

{...} *Dryden's Fables.*

**<q ‡ ———— >** {J. keys in Dryden q. from IL.}

Curse on the tongue that *bids* this general joy.
— ~~Can they be friends of Antony, who revel~~
When Antony's in danger? *Dryd. All for Love.*

{...}

Acquire a government over your ideas, that they may come when they are called, and depart when they are *bidden*.
*Watts's ~~Logick~~.*

4. {...}

Our bans thrice *bid!* and for our wedding day
My kerchief bought! then press'd, then forced away.
*Gay's ~~What d'ye call it~~.*

5. {...}

Divers of them, ~~as we passed by them,~~ put their arms a little abroad; which is their gesture, when they *bid* any welcome.
*Bacon's ~~New Atlantis~~.*

6. {...}

Thyself and Oxford, with five thousand men,
Shall cross the seas, and *bid* false Edward battle.
*Shakesp. ~~Henry VI. p. iii~~.*

~~She~~ **<Spain>** *bid* war to all that durst supply
The place of those her cruelty made die. *Waller.*

**<~~q~~ —~~|~~—>**

{J. keys in Dryden q. from IL, then crosses out insertion key and line.}

## BIG

BI'DDING. *n.s.* {...}

At his second *bidding*, darkness fled,
Light shone, and order from disorder sprung.
*Milton's ~~Paradise Lost, b. iii. l. 712~~.*

To BIDE. *v.n.* {...}

2. {...}

Safe in a ditch he *bides*,
With twenty trenched gashes on his head;
~~The least a death to nature.~~ *Shakesp. ~~Macbeth~~.*

4. It has probably all the significations of the word *abide*; ~~which see:~~ but it being grown somewhat obsolete, the examples of its various meanings are not easily found.

**<———————— ~~a~~ r ‡>**

{J. keys in Spenser q. from IL.}

BIER. *n.s.* {...}

They bore him barefaced on the *bier*,
And on his grave ~~remains~~ **<rain>** many a tear. *Shakesp. Hamlet.*

{sig. 3C[r]}

## BIG

{BIG. *adj.* 1.}♦

{Both in addition and division, either of space or duration, when the idea under consideration becomes very *big*, or very} small, its precise bulk becomes ~~very~~ obscure and confused. *Locke.*/

5. {...}

Thy heart is *big*, get thee apart, and weep. *Shakesp.* ~~*Julius Cæsar.*~~

6. {...}

Of governments that once made such a noise, and looked so *big* in the eyes of mankind, as being founded upon the deepest counsels, and the strongest force; nothing remains ~~of them~~ but a name. *South.*

In his ~~most~~ prosperous season, he fell under the reproach of being a man of *big* looks, and of a mean and abject spirit. *Clarendon.*/

**<8. Loud sounding**
**not exile; not slender>**

**<c ‡>** {J. keys in Shakespeare q. from IL.}

BIGBE'LLIED. *adj.* {...}

When we have laught to see the sails conceive,
And grow *bigbellied* with the wanton wind.
*Shakesp.* ~~*Midsummer Night's Dream.*~~

{...}

So many well shaped innocent virgins are ~~blocked~~ **<bloaoated>** up, and waddling up and down like *bigbellied* women. *Addison. Spect.*

{J. writes 'oa' over blotted letters, clarifying spelling of 'bloated'.}

We pursued our march, to the terrour of the market people, and the miscarriage of half a dozen *bigbellied* women. *Addison's Freeholder.*

BI'GGIN. *n.s.* {...} A child's cap. **<It seems to mean in Shakespeare coarse cloath>**♦

## BIL

BI'GNESS. *n.s.* {...}

1. Bulk; greatness of quantity.

{...} *L'Estrange's Fables.*

**<2>** The brain of man, in respect of his body, is much larger than in any other animal's; exceeding in *bigness* three oxens brains. *Ray on the Creation.*

**<1>** 2. Size; <^**comparative**> whether greater or smaller.

{J. moves Ray q. to first place under def. 2.}

BI'LBERRY. *n.s.* {...}

Cricket, to Windsor chimneys shalt thou leap;
There pinch the maids as blue as *bilberries*.
*Shakesp.* ~~*Merry Wives of Windsor.*~~

{sig. 3C^v}

{BIG. *adj.* 8.}

~~With regard to the voice~~

**<c ‡>**

His big manly voice
Turning again towards childish treble pipes
And Whistles in his sound Shak.[1]

Bigg n.s.
In the northern counties of England it signi:
fies a species of barley.
It might save abundance of labour in our
northern parts, where they reap their barley
Oats and bigg. Tuss. Notes[2]

[1] Shakespeare, *As You Like It* (**Works* II), 2.9. p. 329 [2.7.161-163]. S-G. *1755* To PIPE *v.n.* 2, To WHISTLE *v.n.* 3

[2] Thomas Tusser, *Husbandry*, 'September', p. 120 (q. from editor's notes to Tusser). S-G.

{IL facing 3C^v}

{BILL. *n.s.*}
11 A kind of hook; an offensive weapon
That beastly rabble that came down
From all the garrets in the town
And stall & shop boards in vast swarms
with new chalkd bills & rusty arms
Hudib.[1]

**<d ‡>**
Billed Adj. fr. Bill
having a Bill or Beak
A christian boy in Constantinople had
like to have been stoned for gagging in
a waggishness a long billed fowl[2]

{To BI'LLET. *v.a.*}
The Centurions and their charges
distinctly billeted, already in the enter.
tainment to be on foot at an hours warning
Shaks. Cor.[3]

1 Samuel Butler, *Hudibras*, pt III, canto II, ll.1505-1508. S-G. *1755* SHOPBOARD *n.s.*
2 Bacon, *Essays Civil and Moral* (* *Works* III), 'XIII: Of Goodness, and Goodness of Nature', p. 316 [VI, XIII, p. 403 ]. S-G (slip has 'Bacon' as source). *1755* WAGGISHNESS *n.s.*
3 Shakespeare, *Coriolanus* (* *Works* VI), 4.3, p. 519 [4.3.43-45]. S-G. *1755* CENTURION *n.s.*, ENTERTAINMENT *n.s.* 5, FOOT *n.s.* 7, READINESS *n.s.* 2 (slightly different)

{BILE. *n.s.*}

A furunculus is a painful tubercle, with a broad basis, arising in a cone. It is ~~generally~~ called a *bile*, and, in it its state, is accompanied with inflammation, pulsation, and tension.

*Wiseman*~~*'s Surgery*~~*.*

BI'LINGSGATE. *n.s.* {…} Ribaldry; foul language. **<a low word>**

BILL. *n.s.* {…} **<ʌ ʌ1>** The beak of a fowl.

Their *bills* were thwarted crossways at the end, and, with these, they would cut an apple in two at one snap.

*Carew*~~*'s Survey of Cornwal.*~~

It may be tried, whether birds may not be made to have greater or longer *bills*, or greater and longer talons.

*Bacon*~~*'s Natural History,* N^r 757~~.

<2> ~~BILL. *n.s.*~~ {…}
~~1.~~ A kind of hatchet {…}
<3>~~2~~. A kind of weapon {…}
<4> ~~BILL. *n.s.*~~ {…}
~~1~~. A written paper {…}
<5>~~2~~. An account of money. {…}
<6>~~3~~. A law {…}

{…} *Bacon's Advice to Villiers.* **<2>**

{…} *Shakesp. Henry* V. **<1>**

{J. reverses order of Shakespeare and Bacon qs. presumably to establish chronological sequence under new def. 6.}

<7>~~4~~. An act of parliament. {…}
<8>~~5~~. A physician's prescription. {…}

The medicine was prepar'd according to the *bill*.

*L'Estrange,* ~~*fab.* 183.~~

Let them, but under ~~your~~ **<their>** superiours, kill,
When doctors first have sign'd the bloody *bill*. *Dryden.*

<9>~~6~~. An advertisement. {…}
<10>~~7~~. In law. {…}

BIL

<11>~~8~~. *A bill of mortality.* {…}
<12>~~9~~. *A bill of fare.* {…}
<13>~~10~~. *A bill of exchange.* {…}

{J. consolidates three separate entries for BILL *n.s.* under a single head-word with 13 senses.}

{…} *Locke.*

**<——————— d ‡>**

{J. keys in new entry for BILLED *adj.* with Bacon q. from IL.}

To BI'LLOW. *v.n.* {...}

The *billowing* snow, and violence of the show'r,
That from the hills disperse their dreadful store,
And o'er the vales collected ruin pour. < } >

{J. adds bracket to Prior q., identifying it as a triplet.}

BI'LLOWY. *adj.* {...}

~~And~~ whitening down the mossy-tinctur'd stream,
Descends the *billowy* foam. *Thomson's Spring, l.* 380.

To BIND. *v.a.* {...}

4. To fasten together.

{...} *Matt.* xiii. 20.

**<e ‡ ———— >** {J. keys in new senses 5 and 6 from IL.}

<7><8>~~5~~. To cover a wound with dressings and bandages. **<often with <u>up</u>>**

When he saw him, he had compassion on him, and went to him, and *bound* <u>up</u> his wounds. *Luke*, x. 34.

Having filled up the bared cranium with our dressings, we *bound* <u>up</u> the wound. *Wiseman's Surgery.*

{J. ital. 'up' in Luke and Wiseman qs.}

<8>~~6~~. To compel; to constrain. **<to be obligatory to>**

<9>~~7~~. To oblige by stipulation {...}

<10>~~8~~. To oblige by duty or law. {...}

<11>~~9~~. To oblige by kindness. {...}

<12 &c>~~10~~. To confine {...}

<13>~~11~~. To hinder the flux of the bowels {...}

<4> 1~~2~~ <4>. To ~~restrain~~ **<<u>bind up</u> to confine; to restrain.>**

<1> 1~~3~~ <5>. *To bind a book.* {...}

<~~2~~ 3> 1~~4~~ <6>. *To bind to.* {...}
1~~5~~ <7>. *To bind to.*

<~~1~~ 2> 1~~6~~ <8>. *To bind over.* {...}

{Addition of two new senses 5 and 6 causes J. to renumber senses 5-16 as 7-18. J. then draws lines to indicate that senses 14-18 are to be reorderd (necessitating smearing out of freshly inked numbers). J. combines former senses 14 and 15 for new sense 16. Final renumbering not added. J. writes '12&c', presumably indicating following defs. to be renumbered sequentially.}

BI'NDWEED. *n.s.* {...}

It hath, for the most part, trailing stalks; {...}

The species are thirty six. ~~1. The common white great *bindweed*, vulgarly called *bindweed*.~~ 2. Lesser field *bindweed*, with a rose coloured flower, vulgarly called *gravelbind*. 3. Common sea *bindweed*, with round leaves. 4. Great American *bindweed*, with spacious yellow sweet scented flowers, commonly called *Spanish arbour vine*, or *Spanish woodbine*. 5. White and yellow Spanish potatoes. 6. Red Spanish potatoes. 7. The jalap, *&c.* The first of these species is a very troublesome weed in gardens; and the second sort is still a worse weed than the former. The third sort is found upon gravelly or sandy shores, where the salt water overflows: this is a strong purge, and, as such, is often used in medicine.{...} The jalap, whose root has been long used in medicine, ~~is a native of the province of Italapa, about two days journey from La Vera Cruz.~~ *Millar.*

BINO'MIAL *Root.* {...} A root composed of only two parts ~~or members~~, connected with the signs *plus* or *minus*.
<u>*Harris.*</u>/

BI'OVAC.
~~BI'HOVAC.~~
~~BI'VOUAC.~~ } *n.s.* **<or <u>bihovac</u> or <u>bivouac</u> {?}>** [Fr. from *wey wach*, a double guard, Germ. ~~in war~~.] {...}

16. To bind over
in law to give bail for appearance
by entring into recognizances
So tho my ankle she has quitted
My heart continues still committed
And like a baild & main prizd lover
Altho at large I am bound over
Hudib.[1]

{Final 's' of 'recognizances' smeared out for erasure.}

{To BIND. *v.a.*}

<6> <e ‡> {key intended for entire text below}

<~~7~~>~~17~~ to confine, to circumscribe as in bounds
The ministry is not now bound to any
one tribe; now none is secluded from
that function of any degree
Whitgift[2]

{To BIND. *v.a.*}

<↑>

<5><~~6~~>~~18~~ To unite, to tie together as with cement
They were now {????} like sand without lime
ill bound together, and at a gaze, looking
strange one upon another, not knowing
who was faithful to their side
Bacon. H. 7 [3]

<2>

<1>

[1] Samuel Butler, *Hudibras*, pt II, canto III, ll. 71-74. S-G. *1755* To COMMIT *v.a.* 3

[2] John Whitgift, 'Defence of the Answer to the Admonition' (*Works* I), tract iii, p. 316. J. crosses out '17', renumbers '7', then crosses that out and renumbers '6'. S-G. *1755* FUNCTION *n.s.* 2, To SECLUDE *v.a.* (much shorter)

[3] Bacon, *History of King Henry VII* (*Works* III), p. 459 [VI, p. 153]. J. crosses out '18', renumbers '6', then crosses that out and renumbers '5'. J. reverses order of new senses 5 and 6. Aman. writes 'like' over illegible word smeared out. S-G. *1755* LIME *n.s.*, STRANGE *adj.* 7 (shorter)

{IL facing 3C2$^{v}$}

{blank page}

{IL facing 3Dr}

## BIR

BI'PED. *n.s.* {...}

No serpent, or fishes oviparous, have any stones at all; neither *biped* nor quadruped oviparous, have any exteriourly.

*Brown's ~~Vulgar Errours, b. iii. c. 4~~.*

BIPE'NNATED. *adj.* {...}

All *bipennated* insects have poises joined to the body.

*Derham's ~~Physico-Theology~~.*

BIPE'TALOUS. *adj.* {...} ~~A flower~~ consisting of two leaves. **<used of a ~~{????}~~ flower>** *Dict.*

BIRCH *Tree.* {...}

The leaves are like those of the poplar {...} ~~This tree is propagated by suckers, which may be transplanted either in October or February; it delights in a poor soil. The timber of this tree is used to make chairs, &c. It is also planted for hop poles, hoops, &c. and it is often used to make brooms.~~ *Millar.*

BIRD. *n.s.* {...}

~~Some squire perhaps~~ you take delight to rack,
~~Who visits with a gun,~~ presents with *birds.* *~~Pope.~~*

BI'RDBOLT. *n.s.* {...}

To be generous, guiltless, and of free disposition, is to take ~~those~~ things for *birdbolts*, that you deem cannon bullets.

*Shakesp. Twelfth Night.*

BI'RDCAGE. *n.s.* [{...} See CAGE.] <^ **A small enclosure commonly made of wire or twigs woven into lattice, to confine birds.>**

BI'RDLIME. *n.s.* {...}

## BIR

Heav'ns *birdlime* wraps me round, and glues my wings.

*Dryden's ~~King Arthur~~.*

The woodpecker, and other birds of this kind, because they prey upon flies which they catch with their tongue, have a couple of bags filled with a viscous humour, as if it were a natural *birdlime*, or liquid glue.

*Grew's Cosmo~~logia~~ Sacra~~, b. i. c. 5~~.*

BI'RDSEYE. *n.s.* {...}

~~The leaves are like fennel or chamomile; the flowers con~~sist of many leaves, which are expanded in form of a rose; the seeds are collected into oblong heads. The species are, 1. The common red *birds eye.* 2. The long leaved yellow *birds eye*, *&c.* The first sort is sown in open borders, as an annual ~~flower plant. The yellow sort is uncommon in England.~~

*~~Millar.~~*

BI'RDSFOOT. {...}

It has a papilionaceous flower {...} ~~The species are, 1.~~ The tallest hairy *birdsfoot* trefoil, with a glomerated flower. ~~2. Upright hoary *birdsfoot* trefoil, &c. The first of these plants~~ is, by some, supposed to be the *cytis~~is~~*<^us> of Virgil; ~~it dies to the ground with us every winter, and rises again~~ the succeeding spring; and, when the roots are strong, the shoots will rise to four or five feet high, and produce flowers in great plenty; if it be cut while young, the cows are very fond of it, but horses will not eat it, unless ~~they are very hungry.~~

*Millar.*

BIRTH. *n.s.* {...}

3. {...}

He doth object, I am too great of *birth.*

*Shakesp. ~~Merry Wives of Windsor.~~*

5. {...}

Who of themselves
Abhor to join: and, by imprudence mix'd,
Produce prodigious *births*, of body, or mind.

*Milton's ~~Paradise Lost, b. xi. l. 687.~~*

~~She, for~~ **<Nature>** this many thousand years,
Seems to have practis'd with much care,
To frame the race of woman fair;
Yet never could a perfect *birth*
Produce before, to grace the earth. *Waller.*

{sig. 3Dr}

BI´RTHPLACE. *n.s.* {...}

A degree of stupidity beyond even what we have been ~~ever~~ charged with, upon the score of our *birthplace* and climate.

*Swift's ~~Address to Parliament.~~*

BI´RTHRIGHT. *n.s.* {...}

And hast been found
By merit, more than *birthright*, Son of God.

*Milton's ~~Parad. Lost, b. iii. l. 308.~~*

BI´RTHWORT. *n.s.* {...}

The stalks are flexible; {...} the flower cup turns to a membraneous, oval shaped fruit, divided into five cells, and full of flat seeds. ~~The species are, 1. The round rooted *birthwort*. 2. The climbing *birthwort*. 3. Spanish *birthwort*, &c. The first and second are sometimes used in medicine, and are easily propagated by parting their roots.~~ *Millar.*

*BI´SCOTIN. n.s.* {...} A confection made of flour, sugar, marmalade, <**and**> eggs, ~~*&c.*~~ <**Dict.**>

{J. indicates def. taken from published reference work.}

BI´SCUIT. *n.s.* {...}

1. {...}

The *biscuit* ~~also~~ in the ships, ~~especially in the Spanish gallies,~~ was grown hoary, and unwholesome.

*Knolles's ~~History of the Turks~~.*

Many have been cured<^**of dropsie**>by abstinence from drink, eating dry *biscuit*, which creates no thirst, and strong frictions four or five times a day. *Arbuthnot on Diet.*

BI´SHOP. *n.s.* {...}



You shall find him well accompany'd
With reverend fathers, and well learned *bishops*.

*Shakesp.* ~~*Richard* III~~.

BI´SHOPSWEED. {...}

~~This is an umbelliferous weed,~~ with small striated seeds; the petals of the flowers are unequal, and shaped like a heart. The seeds of the greater *bishopsweed* are used in medicine, and ~~should be sown in an open situation, early in the spring.~~ *Mill.*

{J. deletes passage, leaving attribution '*Mill.*'}

BISK. *n.s.* {...}

A prince, who in a forest rides astray,
And, weary, to some cottage finds the way,
Talks of no pyramids, or fowl, or *bisks* of fish,
But hungry sups his cream serv'd up in earthen dish.

*King's ~~Art of Cookery~~.*

BI´SSEXTILE. *n.s.* {...}

The year of the sun consisteth of three hundred and sixty five days and six hours, wanting eleven minutes; which six hours omitted, will, in time, deprave the compute; and this was the occasion of *bissextile*, or leap year.

*Brown's ~~Vulgar Errours, b. iv. c. 12~~.*

BISU´LCOUS. *adj.* {...}

~~For the~~ swine, although multiparous, yet being *bisulcous*, and only clovenhoofed, are farrowed with open eyes, and other *bisulcous* animals. *Brown's Vulgar Errours, b.* iii. *c.* 26.

BIT. *n.s.* {...}<**1**> ~~Signifies~~ the whole machine of all the {iron appurtenances of a bridle....}

{sig. 3D$^{v}$}

{blank page}

{IL facing 3D$^{v}$}

{BIT. *n.s.* 5.} <**a** ‡>

<5> Bit the extremity of any thing that fastens perhaps for bite

The gimlet hath a worm at the end of its bit Mox Mech Exer.[1]

{To BIT. *v.a.*}

<**b ‡ Bit the preterite of bite**>

The sharp steel arriving forcibly
On his broad shield bit not but glancing fell
On his Horse Neck
F. Q. 2.5.4[2]

{BI'TTER. *adj.*}

Not for that silly old morality
That as these links were knit our loves should be
Mourn I that I thy sevenfold chain have lost
Nor for the lucks sake but the bitter cost.
Donne[3]

1 Joseph Moxon, *Mechanick Exercises,* 'The Art of Joinery', p. 94. S-G. *1755* GIMLET *n.s.*

2 Spenser, *Fairie Queene* (*Works* II), bk II, canto V, st. iv, ll. 3-5. S-G. *1755* To QUILT *v.a.* (very different)

3 John Donne, 'Elegy XI: The Bracelet', ll. 5-8, p. 86. S-G. *1755* SEVENFOLD *adj.*

{IL facing 3D2r}

{BIT. *n.s.*}

We have strict statutes, and most biting laws,
The needful *bits* and curbs of headstrong steeds.
*Shakesp.* ~~*Measure for Measure.*~~

<2> ~~BIT. *n.s.*~~ {...}
~~1.~~ As much meat as is put into the mouth at once.

<3>~~2~~. A small piece of any thing.

4. *A bit the better or worse.* {...}
{...} *Arbuthnot's History of J. Bull.*

**<a** ‡———— > {J. keys in new def. 5 and Moxon q. from IL; J. consolidates entry for BIT *n.s.* under one head-word with five senses.}

To BIT. *v.a.* {...}

**<b** ‡———— > {J. keys in new entry and Spenser q. from IL.}

To BITE. *v.a.* {...}

1. {...}

Such smiling rogues as these,
Like rats, oft *bite* the holy cords in twain,
Too intricate t' unloose. *Shakesp.* ~~*King Lear.*~~

{Diagonal inkmarks from facing IL.}

2. {...}

Here feel we the icy ~~ph~~<f>ang,
And churlish chiding of the winter's wind;
Which when it *bites* and blows upon my body,
Ev'n till I shrink with cold, I smile. *Shakesp. As you like it.*
Full fifty years harness'd in rugged steel,
I have endur'd the *biting* winter's blast,
And the severer heats of parching summer.
*Rowe's* ~~*Ambitious Stepmother.*~~



BITE. *n.s.* {...}
4. A sharper; one who commits frauds. **<a ~~low~~ow word>**

BI'TTER. *adj.* {...}

1. {...}

Though a man in a fever should, from sugar, have a *bitter* taste, which, at another time, produces a sweet one; yet the idea of *bitter* in that man's mind, would be as clear and distinct from the idea of sweet, as if he had tasted ~~only~~ gall.
*Locke.*/

2. Sharp; cruel; severe. **<malicious.>**

3. Calamitous; miserable.

Noble friends and fellows, whom to leave
Is only *bitter* to ~~him~~ **<me>**, only dying;
Go with me, like good angels, to my end. *Shakesp. H.* VIII.
{...} *Shakesp. Rich.* III.
{...} *Dryden's Æneis.*

4. Painful; inclement.

And shun the *bitter* consequence: for know,
The day thou eat'st thereof, my sole command
Transgrest, inevitably thou shalt die. *Paradise Lost, b.* viii. **<1>**

{J. moves *Paradise Lost* q. to third place under def. 3.}

BI'TTERGOURD. *n.s.* {...} The name of a plant.— ~~It is,~~ in all respects, like the gourd, excepting the leaves of the plant being deeply jagged, and the fruit being excessively bitter, and not eatable. ~~There are several varieties of this plant, which are very common in divers parts of the East and West Indies.~~ *Millar.*

{sig. 3D2r}

BI'TTERN. *n.s.* {...}

~~So that scarce~~

The *bittern* knows his time, with bill ingulpht,
To shake the sounding marsh. *Thomson's Spring.*

BI'TTERNESS. *n.s.* {...}

1. {...}

The idea of whiteness, or *bitterness*, is in the mind, ~~exactly~~ answering that power which is in any body to produce it there. *Locke.*

2. {...}

The *bitterness* and animosity between the chief commanders was ~~such, that~~ a great ~~part of the army was marched~~. *Clarend.*

BI'TTERVETCH. *n.s.* {...} **<A plant>**

This plant hath a papilionaceous flower, out of whose empalement rises the pointal, wrapt up in the membrane, which becomes a round pod, full of oval shaped seeds; two leaves, joined together, grow upon a rib that terminates in a point. *Millar.*

BITU'ME. *n.s.* {...} Bitumen. See BITUMEN. {J. indicates small caps. for all but 'B', yet fails to alter head-word below.}

Mix with these
**<Stet>** Idæan pitch, quick sulphur, silver's spume, **<Stet>**
Sea-onion, hellebore, and black *bitume.* *May's Virgil.*

{Apparent cross-outs are a result of inking from IL; J. indicates marks should be ignored.}

BITU'MEN. *n.s.* {...}

BITU'MINOUS. *adj.* {...}

The fruitage fair to sight, like that which grew
Near that *bituminous* lake, where Sodom flam'd.
*Milton's* ~~*Par. Lost, b. x. l. 562*~~.

BIVA'LVE. *adj.* {...}



In the cavity lies loose the shell of some sort of *bivalve*, larger than could be introduced in at either ~~of those~~ holes. *Woodward* ~~*on Fossils*~~.

To BLAB. *v.a.* {...}

1. {...}

{Nature of ink blotting unclear.}

2. To tell; in a good sense. **<not in use.>**

To BLAB. *v.n.* {...}

Your mute I'll be;
When my tongue *blabs*, then let mine eyes not see.
*Shakesp.* ~~*Twelfth Night*~~.

BLAB. *n.s.* {...}

I should have ~~certainly~~ gone about shewing my letters, under the charge of secrecy, to every *blab* of my acquaintance. *Swift's* ~~*Letters*~~.

{J. crosses out 'should', then smears out stroke.}

BLACK-BROWED. *adj.* {...}

Thus when a *black-brow'd* gust begins to rise,
White foam at first on the curl'd ocean fries,
Then roars the main, the billows mount the skies.
*Dryden,* ~~*Æneid* vii. *l.* 736~~.

{sig. 3D2v}

{BLACK. *adj.*}

What black magician conjures up this fiend
To stop devoted charitable deeds
Shak. R. 3.

[1] Shakespeare, *Richard III* (**Works* V), 1.2, p. 219 [1.2.34-35]. S-G ('4 Black' written at top of slip). *1755* To CONJURE *v.a.*, To DEVOTE *v.a.*, MAGICIAN *n.s.*

{IL facing 3D2v}

{blank page}

{IL facing 3E^r}

## BLA

BLACK-BRYONY. *n.s.* {...}

It is male and female in different plants; {...} ~~The species are, 1. The common~~ *black-bryony.* 2. *Black-bryony* of Crete, with a trifid leaf, *&c.* The first is rarely cultivated in gardens, but grows wild under hedges, and is gathered for medicinal use. It may be easily propagated by sowing the seeds, soon after they are ripe, under the shelter of bushes; where, in the spring, ~~the plants will come up, and spread their branches over the bushes.~~ *Millar.*

BLACK-CATTLE. {...}

~~The other part of~~ the grazier's business is what we call *black-cattle*, producing hides, tallow, and beef, for exportation. *Swift.*

BLACK-MAIL. *n.s.* A certain rate of money, corn, cattle, or other consideration, paid to men allied with robbers, to be by them protected from ~~the danger of~~ such as ~~usually~~ rob ~~or steal~~. *Cowel.*

BLACK. *n.s.* {...}

1. {...}

*Black* is the badge of hell,
The hue of dungeons, and the scowl of night.
*Shakesp.* ~~*Love's Labour Lost.*~~

4. {...}

It suffices that it be ~~in every part of the air, which is~~ as big as the *black* or sight of the eye. *Digby.*

To BLACK. *v.a.* {. . .}

Then in his fury *black'd* the raven o'er,
And bid him prate in his white plumes no more.
*Addison's* ~~*Ovid's Metamorph. b. ii.*~~

BLA'CKBERRIED *Heath.* {...}

It hath leaves like those of the heath {...} the female are succeeded by blackberries, ~~in each of which are contained three or four hard seeds. This little shrub grows wild upon the mountains in Staffordshire, Devonshire, and Yorkshire.~~ *Millar.*

## BLA

To BLA'CKEN. *v.n.* {...}

The hollow sound
Sung in the leaves, the forest shook around,
Air *blacken'd*, roll'd the thunder, groan'd the ground. *Dryden.*

{J. adds bracket to Dryden q. to identify it as a triplet.}

B<L> A'CKISH. *adj.* {...}

BLA'CKNESS. *n.s.* {...}

1. {...}

*Blackness* is only a disposition to absorb, or stifle, without reflection, ~~most of~~ the rays of every sort that fall on ~~the~~ bodies. *Locke's* ~~*Elements of Natural Philosophy, c. ii.*~~

BLA'CKTHORN. *n.s.* {...} The same with the sloe. ~~See PLUM, of which it is~~ a species. **<of plum>**

BLA'DDER. *n.s.* {...}

2. {...}

A *bladder* but moderately filled with air, and strongly tied, being held near the fire, grew exceeding turgid and hard; but afterwards being brought nearer to the fire, it ~~suddenly~~ broke, with so loud a noise as made us for a while after almost deaf. *Boyle.*

BLA'DDER-NUT. *n.s.* {...}

~~The flower consists of several leaves, which are placed circularly, and expand in form of a rose, out of whose many headed~~ flower cup rises the pointal, which becomes a membranaceous fruit, somewhat like the inflated bladder of fishes, and divided into two or three cells, containing seeds in form of a scull. The species are, 1. The common wild *bladder-nut.* 2. Three leaved Virginian *bladder-nut.* 3. *Bladder-nut*, with single shining leaves. 4. *Bladder-nut*, with narrow bay leaves. 5. Three leaved American *bladder-nut*, with cut leaves. The first of these trees is found wild in the woods and other shady places, in the northern parts of England. The second sort is a native of America, but is so hardy ~~as to endure~~ the severest cold of our ~~climate, in the open air. Both these kinds may be~~ propagated, by sowing the~~ir~~ seeds early in the spring. They will commonly grow in England to the height of twelve or fourteen feet. *Mill.*

{J. crosses out 'They', then smears out stroke; he may have written a word, now illegible, above 'They'.}

BLA'DDER-SENA. *n.s.* {...}

~~It hath a papilionaceous flower, succeeded by pods, resembling the inflated bladder of fishes, in which are contained several kidney shaped seeds. The species are five.~~ These shrubs {...} {*Millar.*}

{sig. 3E^r}

## BLA

BLADE. *n.s.* {...} <^ ^1> The spire of grass before it grows to seed; {...}

~~S~~<**He** s>ends ~~h~~ his feeding flocks betimes, t' invade
The rising bulk of the luxuriant *blade*. *Dryden's Georg.*

{...}

~~Hung on every spray, on every~~ *blade*
~~Of grass, the myriad dewdrops~~ twinkle round. *Thomson.*

<2>~~BLADE. *n.s.*~~ {...}

~~1.~~ The sharp or striking part of a weapon or instrument, distinct from the handle. It is usually taken for <^ **the whole**> ~~a~~ weapon, and so called probably from the likeness of a sword *blade* to a *blade* of grass.

{...} *Fairy Queen, b.* i.

<**o** ‡———— > {J. keys in Sandys q. from IL.}

<**3**>~~2.~~ A brisk man, {...}

{J. consolidates two separate entries for BLADE under a single headword with three senses.}

BLA'DED. *adj.* {...}

~~Her silver visage in the wat'ry glass;~~
<**She**> Deck~~ing~~ <**s**> with liquid pearl the *bladed* grass.
*Shakesp. Midsummer Night's Dream.*

BLA'MABLENESS. *n.s.* {...} Fault<^ **iness**>; the state of being liable to blame.

BLA'MABLY. *adv.* {...} Culpabl~~e~~<**y**>; in a manner liable to censure.

To BLAME. *v.a.* {...}

1. {...}

Porphyrius, you too far did tempt your fate;
'Tis true, your duty to me it became;
But praising that, I must your conduct *blame*.
*Dyrden~~'s Tyrannick Love~~.*

BLAME. *n.s.* {...}

1. {...}

In arms, the praise of success is shared amongst many; yet the *blame* of misadventures is charged upon one.
~~*Sir J.*~~ *Hayward.*

## BLA

2. Crime; that which produces or deserves censure.

<———— **q** ‡>

{J. keys in Spenser q. from IL.}

3. Hurt. <**out of use**>

4. {...}

You were *to blame*, I must be plain with you,
To part so slightly with your wife's first gift.
*Shakesp.* ~~*Merchant of Venice*~~.

I do not ask whether they were mistaken; but, on supposition they were not, whether they were *to blame* ~~in the manner~~.
*Stillingfleet.*

BLA'MEFUL. *adj.* {...} Criminal; guilty; meriting blame. <**not in use**>

BLAMEWO'RTHY. *adj.* {...}

{...} *Hooker, b.* v. § 12.

<———— **p** ‡>

{J. keys in definition and Sidney q. from IL.}

{sig. 3E$^{v}$}

{BLADE. *n.s.*2}

~~3 A natural instrument of defence~~

<**o** ‡>

He who made
This knowing beast hath arm'd him with a
<u>blade</u>
He feeds on lofty hills nor lives by prey
Sandys Job.[1]

{BLAME. *n.s.* 2.}

<**q** ‡>

~~5 Irregularity, confusion, cause of blame~~
~~A jolly yeoman Marshall of the hall~~
~~Whose name was Appetite~~ he did bestow
Both guests and meats whenever in they
came
And knew them how to Order without blame
Spens[2]

<**p** ‡>

~~b~~<**B**>lameworthiness ns <[>from blameworthy<]>
<**State of deserving blame**>

There is no cause to blame the Prince for sometimes hearing them, the blameworthiness is, that to hear them, he rather goes to solitary ness, than makes them come to company
Sidney[3]

[1] George Sandys, 'A Paraphrase upon Job', ch. xl, pp. 74-75. S-G.
[2] Spenser, *Fairie Queene* (*Works* II), bk II, canto IX, st. xxviii, ll. 2-5. Q. also transcribed on IL for To BESTOW *v.a.* 7. S-G. *1755* MARSHAL *n.s.*, YEOMAN *n.s.* (much shorter).
[3] Sidney, *Arcadia*, bk I, p. 25. S-G. *1755* SOLITARINESS *n.s.*

{IL facing 3E$^{v}$}

{blank page}

{IL facing 3E2$^r$}

## BLA

BLA´NDISHMENT *n.s.* {…}
{Inking from facing IL.}

BLANK. *adj.* {…}
2. ~~Without~~ <**Having no**> writing; {…}

Our substitutes at home shall have *blank* charters,
Whereto, when they know that men are rich,
They shall subscribe them for large sums of gold.
*Shakesp.~~ Richard~~* ~~II~~.

3. {…}

Adam soon as he heard
The fatal trespass done by Eve, amaz'd,
Astonied stood, and *blank*, while horrour chill
Ran through his veins, and all his joints relax'd.
*Milton~~'s Paradise Lost, b.~~* ~~ix.~~ *~~l.~~* ~~888.~~

4. {…}

Long have your ears been fill'd with tragick parts;
Blood and *blank* verse have harden'd all your hearts.
*Addison~~'s Drummer, Prologue.~~*

BLANK. *n.s.* {…}
4. {…}

For him, I think not on him; for his thoughts,
Would they were *blanks*, rather than fill'd with me.
*Shakesp.~~ Twelfth Night.~~*

## BLA

A life so spent is one great *blank*, which, though not blotted with sin, is yet without any characters of grace or virtue.
*Rogers,* ~~*serm.* xii~~.

7. {…}

See better, Lear, and let me still remain
The true *blank* of thine <**eye**>. *Shakesp. King Lear.*

BLA´SPHEMOUS. *adj.* [from *blaspheme.* It is usually spoken with the accent on the first syllable, but used by <‸**Sidney and**> *Milton* with it on the second.] {…}
{J. reads Sidney as well as Milton qs. and notes the scansion of word in line.}◆

O man, take heed how thou the gods do move,
To cause full wrath, which thou canst not resist;
*Blasphemous* words the speaker vain do prove. *Sidney, b.* ii.
And dar'st thou to the Son of God propound,
To worship thee accurst; now more accurst
For this attempt, bolder than that on Eve,
And more *blasphemous?* *Milton's Paradise Regained, b.* iii.

{sig. 3E2$^r$}

BLAST. *n.s.* {...}♦
1. A gust, or puff of wind. **<the power of the wind>**

They that stand high, have many *blasts* to shake them;
And, if they fall, they dash themselves to pieces.
*Shakesp.* ~~*Richard III*~~.

{...} *Fairfax, b.* i.

**<2 A particular wind ——————** > {...}
{J. provides new gloss for *Dryden's Æneid* q. below.}

Three ships were hurry'd by the southern *blast*,
And on the secret shelves with fury cast. *Dryden's Æneid.*

<3>~~2~~. The sound made by blowing any instrument of wind musick.
{...}

Whether there be two different goddesses called Fame, or one goddess sounding two different trumpets, it is certain, villainy has as good a title to a blast from the proper trumpet, as virtue has from the former. *Swift.*
{J. ital. 'blast'; 'a' underlined inadvertently.}

<4>~~3~~. The stroke of a malignant planet; the infection of any thing pestilential.
<‡—————— > {J. keys in Dryden q. from IL.}

To BLAST. *v.a.* {...}♦
2. To make to wither. **<to wither before the time>**
{...}

She that like lightning shin'd, while her face lasted,
The oak now resembles, which lightning had *blasted*.
*Waller.*/

<2> ~~3~~<4>. To injure; to invalidate. {...}
{...} *Stillingfleet's Defence of Discourses on Romish Idolatry.*
<1> <3>~~4~~. To cut off; to hinder from coming to maturity. {...}
{...} *Arbuthnot on Coins.*
{J. reverses order of senses 3 and 4.}
5. {...}

Trumpeters,
With brazen din, *blast* you the city's ears;
Make mingle with your ratt'ling tabourines.
*Shakesp.* ~~*Antony and Cleopatra.*~~

BLA

BLAY. *n.s.* A small white river fish; called also a *bleak*, ~~which see.~~

BLAZE. *n.s.* {...}
1. {...}

They are in ~~a most~~ warlike preparation, and hope to come upon them in the heat of their division.—The main *blaze* of it is past; but a small thing would make it flame again.
*Shakesp.* ~~*Coriolanus.*~~

{...}

What groans of men shall fill the martial field!
How fierce a *blaze* his flaming pile shall yield!
~~What fun'ral pomp shall floating Tiber see!~~ *Dryden's Æn.*

To BLAZE. *v.n.* {...}
1. {...}

Thus you may long live an happy instrument for your king and country; you shall not be a meteor, or a *blazing* star, but *stella fixa*; happy here, and more happy hereafter.
*Bacon's* ~~*Advice to Villiers.*~~

2. To be conspicuous.
<—————‡ **b**>
{J. intends mark to be a double dagger. J. keys in South q. from IL.}

To BLAZE. *v.a.* {...}
1. {...}

Thou shalt live, till we can find a time
To *blaze* your marriage, reconcile your friends,
Beg pardon of thy prince, and call thee back.
*Shakesp.* ~~*Romeo and Juliet.*~~

{...}

Such musick worthiest were to *blaze*
The peerless height of her immortal praise,
~~Whose lustre leads us.~~ *Milton.*

{...}

~~Whose~~**<His>** follies, *blaz'd* about, to all are known,
And are a secret to himself alone. *Granville.*

BLA'ZER. *n.s.* {...} One that spreads reports. **<~~obsolete~~ antiquated>**

To BLA'ZON. *v.a.* {...}
2. {...}

~~Then~~ **<She>** *blazons* in dread smiles her hideous form;
So lightning gilds the unrelenting storm. *Garth's Dispensat.*

3. {...}

O thou goddess,
Thou divine nature! how thyself thou *blazon'st*
In these two princely boys! they are as gentle
As zephyrs blowing below the violet,
~~Not wagging his sweet head.~~ *Shakesp. Cymbeline.*

4. To celebrate; to ~~set out.~~ <{?} **~~to be~~ praise praise>** {first 'praise' smudged, 'praise' rewritten}
5. To blaze about; to make publick. <**this is not now**{?}> {smeared out for deletion}

**<none of these senses except the first are now much in use.>**

{BLAST. *n.s.* 4.}

<‡>

If envious eyes their hurtful rays have cast,
More powerful verse shall free thee from
their <u>blast</u>.

Dryd.[1]

{To BLAZE. *v.n.* 2.}

<**b** ‡>

If matter of fact breaks out & <u>blazes</u> with too great an evidence to be denied; Why still there are other lenitives that friendship will apply.

South[2]

[1] Dryden, 'Cinyras and Myrrha' (*Works* VII), ll. 176-77. S-G (with '3' at top). *1755* VERSE *n.s.* 3

[2] Robert South, 'Sermon XX' (**Twelve Sermons* 1694), p. 76. S-G (with '2 v.n.' at top). *1755* SENTENCE *n.s.*1, FACT *n.s.* 1 (much shorter), DECRETORY *adj.* 1 (very different), LENITIVE *n.s.* 2 (very different)

{IL facing 3E2v}

{To BLEED. *v.a.*}

**<c ‡>**

<2>To stain with blood
His shining helmet he gan soon unlace
And left his headless body bleeding all the
place.

F.Q. 2. 8. 52[2]

{To BLEAR. *v.a.*}

2 Siker, thou's but a lazy loorde
And rekes much of thy swinke
That with fond terms & witless words
To bleer mine eyes dost think

Spenser[1]

[1] Spenser, *Shepheardes Calendar* (*Works* VII), 'July', ll. 33-36. S-G. *1755* LOORD *n.s.*, RECK *v.n.*, SWINK *n.s.* (shorter)

[2] Spenser, *Fairie Queene* (*Works* II), bk II, canto VIII, st. lii, ll. 8-9. S-G (with 'To bleed v.a.' at top). *1755* HEADLESS *adj.* 1

{IL facing 3F[r]}

To BLEACH. *v.a.* {...}

When turtles tread, and rooks and daws;
And maidens *bleach* their summer smocks.
*Shakesp.* ~~*Love's Labour Lost.*~~

{...}

~~For there are various penances enjoin'd,~~
<2> And some are hung to *bleach* upon the wind;
Some plung'd in waters. *Dryden's Æneid.*

<1> To BLEACH. *v.n.* To grow white; to grow white in the open air.
The white sheet *bleaching* in the open field. *Sh. W. Tale.*

{J. moves the last two lines of the Dryden q. correctly from To BLEACH. *v.a.* to second place under To BLEACH. *v.n.*}

BLEAK. *adj.* {...}
1. Pale. **<not in use.>**

BLEAR. *adj.* {...}
2. Dim; obscure ~~in general~~, or that which makes dimness.

To BLEAR. *v.a.* {...}
1. to make the eyes watry, or sore with rheum.
{...} *Shakesp. Coriolanus.*

**<2. To smear through rheum>**
The Dardanian wives,
<2> With *bleared* visages, come forth to view
Th' issue of th' exploit. *Shakesp. Merchant of Venice.*

When I was young, I, like a lazy fool,
<1> Would *blear* my eyes with oil, to stay from school;
Averse to pains. *Dryden's Persius, sat.* iii.

{J. moves Dryden q. to second place under def. 1, and creates new sense 2.}

<3>~~2.~~ To dim the eyes. {...}

BLE

To BLEAT. *v.n.* {...}

You may as well use question with the wolf,
Why he hath made the ewe *bleat* for the lamb.
*Shakesp.* ~~*Merchant of Venice.*~~

To BLEED. *v.n.* {...}
1. To lose blood; to run with blood.
{...}
Many, upon the seeing of others *bleed*, or strangled, or tortured, themselves are ready to faint, as if they *bled*.
*Bacon's* ~~*Nat. History,* N^r 795.~~

To BLEED. *v.a.* <^1> To let blood; to take blood from.

Th~~at~~**<ese>** from a patriot of distinguish'd note,
Have *bled*, and purg'd me to a simple vote. *Pope.*

<———— ‡ c >

{J. keys in new def. 2 and Spenser q. from IL.}

BLE'MISH. *n.s.* {...}♦
1. A mark of deformity; a scar; a diminution of beauty.
{...} *Lev.* xxiv. 20.
Open it such a distance ~~off~~ from the eyelid, that you divide not that; for, in so doing, you ~~will~~ leave a remediless *blemish*.
<✶————> *Wiseman's* ~~*Surgery.*~~ <2>

{J. keys in Addison q. from top of 3F^v.}

2. Reproach; disgrace; imputation.
{...} *Fairy Queen, b.* ii.
{...} *Hooker, Preface.*
{...} *Sprat.*
{...} *Addison. Spectator,* N° 256.

3. A soil; turpitude; taint; deformity. **<disgrace>**
{...} *Sidney, b.* i.
Is conformity with Rome a *blemish* unto the church of England, and unto churches abroad an ornament? <4>
*Hooder,* ~~*b.* iv. §. 6.~~

{Misprint for *Hooker*, not corrected.}

Not a hair perish'd:
On their sustaining garments not a *blemish*, <1>
But fresher than before. *Shakesp. Tempest.*

Evadne's husband 'tis a fault
To love, a *blemish* to my thought. *Waller's M. Trag.* <3>
That your duty may no *blemish* take,
I will myself your father's captive make. *Dryd. Indian Emp.*

{J. moves Shakespeare q. to first place under def. 1, Waller and Dryden qs. to fourth and fifth places under def. 2.}

## BLE

{BLE´MISH. *n.s.* 3.}

**<Put to ∗>** Such a mirth as this is capable of making a beauty, as well as a *blemish*, the subject of derision. *Addison. Spect.* N° 291.

{J. indicates Addison q. to be moved to last place under sense 1 on 3F^r^.}

To BLENCH. *v.a.* To hinder; to obstruct. <‸ **of this ~~noun~~ word whether active or neuter I know not the original. It is in both senses now disused>**

To BLEND. *v.a.* {…}

1. {…}

'Tis beauty truly *blent*, whose red and white
Nature's own sweet and cunning hand hath laid on.

*Shakesp.* ~~*Twelfth Night.*~~

BLE´SSED *Thistle.* ~~[*cnicus*, Lat.]~~ The name of a plant.

The characters are; It hath flosculous flowers; consisting of many florets, which are multifid, and stand upon the embryo; these florets are inclosed in a scaly cup, surrounded with leaves. ~~The species are; 1. The *blessed thistle*. 2. The yellow distaff *thistle*.~~ ~~The *blessed thistle* is~~ cultivated in gardens for the herb, which is dried and preserved for medicinal uses; but of late years it hath been less used than formerly. *Millar.*

## BLI

BLE´SSING. *n.s.* {…}

2. A declaration by which happiness is promised in a prophetick and authoritative manner.

{…} *Bacon's New Atlantis.*

3. Any of the means of happiness; a gift; an advantage; a benefit.

{…} *Denham.*
{…} *Addison.* **<2>**
{…} *Atterbury.*

4. Divine favour.

{…} *Shakesp. Macbeth.*
{…} *Shakesp. Macbeth.*

Honour thy father and mother, both in word and deed, that a *blessing* may come upon thee from them. *Ecclus,* iii, 8. **<1>**

{…} *Psalm* xxix. 5.

{J. moves *Ecclus.* q. to first place under def. 2.}

BLIGHT. *n.s.* {…}

1. {…}

~~I complained to~~ the oldest and best gardeners, ~~who~~ often fell into the same misfortune, and esteemed it some *blight* of the spring. *Temple.*

To BLIGHT. *v.a.* {…}

1. To corrupt <‸**as**> with mildew.

This vapour bears up ~~along with it any~~ noxious mineral steams; ~~it then~~ blasts vegetables, *blights* corn and fruit, and is sometimes injurious even to men. *Woodward's Natural Hist.*

BLIND. *adj.* {…}

1. W~~ithout~~**<anting>** sight; deprived of the sense of seeing; dark.

{sig. 3F^v^}

{To BLESS. *v.a.* 5.}

<5> Blesse, Cisley, good Mistress, that Bishop doth ban
For burning the Milk of her Cheese to the Pan.
Tusser husb. for Apr.[1]

When the Bishop passed by, in former times, every one ran out to partake of his blessing; and those who left their milk upon the fire might find it burnt to the pan when they came back, & perhaps ban or curse the Bishop as the Occasion of it: Hence it is likely it grew into a Custom to curse the Bishop when any such disaster happend; for which our Author would have the Mistress bless anglice ({??}rather ironice) correct her Servant both for her negligence & unmannerliness.

Tuss. Notes[2]

[1] Thomas Tusser, *Husbandry*, 'April', p. 53.
[2] Thomas Tusser, *Husbandry*, 'April', p. 53 (q. from editor's notes to Tusser).

{IL facing 3F^v^}

{blank page}



## BLI

{BLIND. *adj.*}
2. {...}

All authors *to* their own defects are *blind*;
~~Hadst thou, but Janus like, a face behind,~~
~~To see the people, what splay mouths they make;~~
~~To mark their fingers, pointed at thy back.~~ *Dryden's Pers.*

BLIND. *n.s.* {...}
1. {...}

Hardly any thing in our conversation is pure and genuine; civility casts a *blind* over ~~the~~ duty, ~~under some customary words.~~ *L'Estrange.*

BLI'NDFOLD. *adj.* {...}

The~~y~~ <^**women**> will look into the state of the nation with their own eyes, and be no longer led *blindfold* by a male legislature. *Addison. Freeholder,* N° 32.

BLI'NDLY. *adv.* {...}
2. {...}

The old king <**is**>, after ~~a~~ long debate,
By his imperious mistress *blindly* led,
~~Has given Cydaria to Orbellan's bed~~. *Dryd. Indian Emp.*

## BLI

BLI'NDNESS. *n.s.* {...}
2. {...}

Whensoever we would proceed beyond ~~these~~ simple ideas, we fall presently into darkness and difficulties, and can discover nothing farther but our own *blindness* and ignorance. *Locke.*

BLI'NDWORM. *n.s.* {...}

The greater slow worm, called also the *blindworm*, is ~~commonly~~ thought to be blind, because of the littleness of his eyes. *Grew~~'s Musæum~~.*

To BLINK. *v.n.* {...}
1. To wink, or twinkle with the eyes.

<2> {...} *Hudibras, p.* iii, *c.* ii.

<1> 2. To see obscurely.

What's here! the portrait of a *blinking* idiot. *Shakesp. Merchant of Venice.*

{J. moves Shakespeare q. to illustrate correctly def. 1.}

BLI'NKARD. *n.s.* {...}
2. Something twinkling <**with faint light**>.
{J. alters def. to gloss adequately Hakewell q. below.}

<2>

BLISS. *n.s.* {...}
1. The highest degree of happiness; blessedness; felicity; generally used of the happiness of blessed souls.
{...} *Hooker, b.* i.
{...} *Par. Lost, b.* x. *l.* 25.
{...} *Par. Lost, b.* xi.
{...} *Pope.*

<**The**{?} **blisfu**> {Smeared out for deletion.}

<1>

BLI'S~~S~~FUL. *adj.* {...}
{...} *Fairy Queen, b.* i. *c.* i. *stan.* 41.
{...} *Hammond.*
{...} *Milton's Paradise Lost, b.* iii, *l.* 89.
2. Felicity in general.
{...} *Pope.*
BLI'S~~S~~FULLY. *adv.* {...} Happily.
BLI'S~~S~~FULNESS. *n.s.* {...} Happiness; fulness of joy.

{J. changes spelling of BLISSFUL *adj.*, BLISSFULLY *adv.*, BLISSFULNESS *n.s.* and then moves these entries above BLISS *n.s.* to conform with alphabetical order. J. draws line (concluding beneath Pope q.) to indicate that BLISFUL is to be moved; after changing spelling of BLISSFULLY and BLISSFULNESS, J. extends line to include these entries.}

BLI'STER. *n.s.* {...}
1. {...}

In this state she gallops, night by night,
O'er ladies lips, who strait on kisses dream,
Which oft the angry mob with *blisters* plagues,
Because their breaths with sweetmeats tainted are. *Shakesp.* ~~*Romeo and Juliet*~~.

I found a great *blister* drawn by the garlick, but had it cut, which run a good deal of water, ~~but filled again by next night.~~ *Temple.*

## BLO

BLI´THNESS. } *n.s.* {…}
~~BLI´THSOMNESS.~~

To BLOAT. *v.a.* {…}

~~His rude essays~~
Encourage him, and *bloat* him up with praise,
That he may get more bulk before he dies. *Dryden.*

BLO´BLIPPED. } *adj.* {…}
BLO´BBERLIPPED.

A *bloblipped* shell, ~~which~~ seemeth to be a kind of mussel. *Grew's ~~Musæum.~~*

His person <**was**> deformed to the highest degree; flat nosed, and *blobberlipped.* *L'Estrange.*

BLOCK. *n.s.* {…}

## BLO

9. {…}

~~The country is a desert, where the good~~
~~Gain'd, inhabits not; born's not understood;~~
There men become beasts, and prone to all evils; <**2**>
In cities, *blocks.* *Donne.*
{…} *Shakesp. Richard* III. <**1**>

{J. re-orders Donne and Shakespeare qs. for chronological sequence.}

To BLOCK. *v.a.* {…} <**To obstruct**> To shut up; to inclose, so as to hinder egress. <**commonly with up emphatical**>♦

{Vertical lines result of inking from facing IL.}

BLO´CKHEADED. *adj.* {…}

Says a *blockheaded* boy, these are villainous ~~creatures~~. *L'Estrange's ~~Fables~~.*

BLOOD. *n.s.* {…}

2. {…}

We'll no more meet, no more see one another:
But yet thou art my flesh, my *blood*, my daughter. *Shakesp. ~~King Lear~~.*

3. {…}

According to the common law of England, ~~in administrations,~~ the whole *blood* ought to be preferred to the half *blood*. *Ayliffe's Parergon.*

{sig. 3F2v}

{BLITHE. *adj.*}
Fill out the black bole of blithe to the Song
And let them be merrie all harvest time long
Tuss. hush for Aug$^{t}$.[1]

[1] Thomas Tusser, *Husbandry*, 'August', p. 104. S-G.

{IL facing 3F2v}

{blank page}

{IL facing 3G[r]}



{BLOOD. *n.s.*}
12. Hot spark; man of fire. <**is**{?}> {Smeared out.}

The news put divers young *bloods* into such a fury, as the English ambassadors were not, without peril, to be outraged.
*Bacon's Henry* VII.

To BLOOD. *v.a.* {…}
3. ~~To blood, is sometimes~~ to let blood medically.

BLOOD-BOLTERED. *adj.* {…} {J. removes hyphen to make one word.}
<◡>

BLOOD-HOT. *adj.* {…} {J. removes hyphen to make one word.}
<◡>

To BLOOD-LET. *v.a.* {…} {J. removes hyphen to make one word.}
<◡>

BLOOD-LETTER. *n.s.* {…} {J. removes hyphen to make one word.}
<◡>

BLOOD-STONE. *n.s.* {…} {J. removes hyphen to make one word.}
<◡>

BLOOD-THIRSTY. *adj.* {…} {J. removes hyphen to make one word.}
<◡>

~~And~~<^ **He**> high advancing his *blood-thirsty* blade,
Struck^one of those deformed heads. *Fairy Queen, b.* i.

BLO'ODFLOWER. *n.s.* {…}

~~This plant was~~ originally brought from the Cape of Good Hope~~, and has been many years preserved in the curious gardens in Holland, where they now have many sorts, but in England it is still very rare.~~ *Millar.*

BLO'ODHOUND. *n.s.* {…}

A *bloodhound* will follow the tract of the person he pursues, and all hounds the particular game they have in chace.
*Arbuthnot ~~on Aliments.~~*

BLO'ODLESS. *adj.* {…}
1. ~~Without~~ <**Having no**> blood; dead.

2. ~~W~~<^**Being w**>ithout slaughter.

BLO'ODSHED. *n.s.* {…}
1. {…}

All murders past do stand excus'd in this;
And this so sole, and so unmatchable,
Shall prove a deadly *bloodshed* but a jest,
~~Exampled by this heinous spectacle.~~ *Shakesp. King John.*

BLO'ODSHOT. } *adj.* {…}
BLO<'>ODSHO\TTEN. }

BLO'ODY. *adj.* {…}
2. {…}

The *bloody* fact
Will be avenge'd; and th' other's faith approv'd,
Lose no reward; though here thou see him die,
Rolling in dust and gore. *Milton's Paradise Lost, b.* xi. *l.* 457.

BLOODY-FLUX. {…} {J. removes hyphen to make one word.}
<◡>

BLOODY-MINDED. *adj.* {…} {J. removes hyphen to make one word.}
<◡>

~~I think you'll make me mad~~: truth has been at my tongue's end this half hour, and I have not the power to bring it out, for fear of this *bloody-minded* colonel. *Dryden's Spanish Friar.*

{sig. 3G[r]}

To BLOOM. *v.n.* {...}

1. {...}

The rod of Aaron for the house of Levi was budded, and brought forth buds, and *bloomed* blossoms, ~~and yielded almonds~~. *Numb.* xvii. 8.

{...} *Bacon's Natural Hist. N° 449.*

**<To Bloom va>**

~~2~~. To produce, as blossoms.

<2> Rites and customs, now superstitious, when the strength of virtuous, devout, or charitable affection *bloomed* them, no man could justly have condemned as evil. *Hooker, b.* v. § 3.

~~3~~<2>. To be in a state of youth and improvement.

<1> {...} *Pope's Epistles.* <2>

{...} *Pope's Odyss. b.* i. <1>

{J. inserts 'To Bloom va' to create a new *v.a.* entry from former *v.n.* def. 2 and Hooker q.; J. draws lines and renumbers senses, correctly keying in former *v.n.* def. 3 and two Pope qs. as sense 2 under To Bloom *v.n.*; J. re-orders Pope qs., presumably for chronological sequence.}

BLORE. *n.s.* {...} Act of blowing; blast. **<a word not used>**

BLO'SSOM. *n.s.* {...}♦

~~Sweeter than spring,~~
Thou sole surviving *blossom* from the root,
That nourish'd up my fortune. ~~*Thomson's Autumn.*~~

To BLOT. *v.a.* {...}♦

3. {...}

Heads overfull of matter, be like pens over full of ink, which will sooner *blot*, than make ~~any~~ fair letter ~~at all~~. *Ascham's ~~Schoolmaster.~~*

{J. crosses out 'which', then smears out stroke to retain coherence.}

BLO

4. To disgrace; to disfigure. **<to soil; to sully.>**

{J. changes def. to reflect more accurately illustrations from Dryden and Rowe.}

{...} *Shakesp. Taming of the Shrew.*

<2> My guilt thy growing virtues did defame;
My blackness *blotted* thy unblemish'd name. *Dryden's Æn.*
For mercy's sake, restrain thy hand,
*Blot* not thy innocence with guiltless blood. *Rowe.*

<1> ~~5~~<4>. To darken.

{...} *Cowley.*

{J. reverses order of senses 4 and 5, neglecting to renumber previous def. 4 as '5'.}

BLOT. *n.s.* {...}

4. [At backgammon.] ~~W~~<^**A blot is w**>hen a single man lies open to be taken up; whence to hit a *blot.*

BLOTCH. *n.s.* {...}

Spots and *blotches*, of several colours and figures, straggling over the body; some ~~are~~ red, others yellow, livid, ~~or~~ black. *Harvey* ~~*on Consumptions.*~~

To BLOW. *v.n.* {...}

1. To move with a current of air~~.~~**<; to act as wind.>** {J. alters full stop to semi-colon.}

2. {...}

If *it blows* a happy gale, we must set up all our sails, ~~though~~ it sometimes happens, that our natural heat is more powerful than our care and correctness. *Dryden's Dufresnoy.*

{To BLOT. *v.a.*}

Corruption like a general flood
Shall deluge all; and av'rice creeping on
Spread like a low-born mist & blot the sun
Pope[3]

{To BLO'SSOM. *v.n.*}♦

Crashaw transfers it to the effulgence
of light
He saw heaven blossom with a new born light
On which as on a glorious stranger gaz'd
The golden eyes of night whose beams made bright
The way to bethlem and as boldly blaz'd
Nor askt leave of the sun by day as Night
Crashaw[1]

I've seen the mornings lovely ray
Hover o'er the new born day,
With rosy wings so richly bright
As if he scornd to think of night
When a ruddy storm whose scoule
Made heavens radian face look foul
Call'd for an untimely night
To blot the newly blossom'd light
Crashaw[2]

{To BLOW. *v.a.*}

~~To spread or publish with a view to betray~~

Is a man betrayd lost & blown by such agents
as he employs in his greatest & nearest concerns
The cause of it is from this that he misplaced
his confidence & took hypocrisy for fidelity
South[4]

To promulgate to publish
Th' appospostles could not be confin'd
To these or those but severally design'd
Their large commission round the world to blow
Dryd.[5]

6 To blow nails: a proverbial expression
for poor Comfort, akin to that in Scotland♦
He blows a cald coal
Our love is not so great Hortensius
But we may blow our nails together
And fast it fairly out Shak[6]
When isicles hang down from wall
And Dick the shepherd blows his nail. Idem.[7]

1 Richard Crashaw, 'Sospetto d' Herode. Libro Primo', canto XVII, p. 227. S-G ('2' at top). *1755* NEW *adv.*

2 Richard Crashaw, 'Upon the Death of the most desired Mr. Herrys', p. 468. S-G. *1755* NEW *adv.*, SCOWL *n.s.*, To SCORN *v.n.* (shorter)

3 Pope, 'Epistle III: To Lord Bathurst' (*Poems* III.II), ll. 135-138. Not keyed in, though probably intended for insertion under old def. 5, now new def. 4. S-G (with '5' written at top). *1755* LOW *adv.* 1, To DELUGE *v.a.*2 (much shorter)

4 Robert South, 'Sermon XXI' (**Twelve Sermons* 1694), pp. 474-5. S-G. Not keyed in, though prepared for insertion, possibly under To BLOW *v.a.* 7 on 3G2r. *1755* To MISPLACE *v.a.*

5 Dryden, 'The Hind and the Panther' (**Works* III), pt II, ll. 324-26. Aman. first writes 'appos' then smears out and corrects to 'apostles'. Not keyed in, though prepared for insertion, possibly under To BLOW *v.a.* 7 on 3G2r. *1755* SEVERALLY *adv.*

6 Shakespeare, *Taming of the Shrew* (**Works* II), 1.3, p. 403 [1.1.106-108]. S-G (with following *Love's Labour's Lost* q. on same slip). *1755* To FAST *v.n.*1

7 Shakespeare, *Love's Labour's Lost* (**Works* II), 5.10, p. 287 [5.2.912-13]. S-G (with above q.). *1755* To BLOW *v.a.* 6, To NIP *v.a.* 4

{IL facing 3Gv}

Blue n.s. The sky
Throw out our Eyes for brave Othello
Ev'n till we make the main & th'aerial blue
An indistinct regard Shak.[1]

[1] Shakespeare, *Othello* (**Works* VIII), 2.2, p. 305 [2.1.37-39]. *1755* INDISTINCT *adj.*, REGARD *n.s.* 7, To THROW *v.a.* 10 (shorter)

{IL facing 3G2$^r$}

{To BLOW. *v.n.* 7. *To blow over.*}

But those clouds being now happily *blown over*, and our sun clearly shining out again, I have recovered ~~the relapse~~. *Denham.*

8. *To blow up.* {…}

< ✱ ——— > {J. keys in Knolles q. from def. 10 below, as marked.}

~~On the next day, some of~~ the enemy's magazines *blew up*; and it is thought they were destroyed on purpose ~~by some of their men.~~ *Tatler,* Nº 59.

To BLOW. *v.a.*{…}

2. To inflame with wind.

< ✱ 2 ——— > {J. keys in Sidney q. from adjacent column under BLOWN, as marked.}

5. To sound an instrument of wind musick.

{…} *Milton.*

< ✱ 3 ——— > {J. keys in Pope q. from adjacent column under BLOWN, as marked.}

9. *To blow up.* To raise or swell <^as> with breath.

10. *To blow up.* {…}

< **To** ✱> The captains hoping, by a mine, to gain the city, approached ~~with soldiers~~ ready to enter upon *blowing up* of the mine. *Knolles~~'s History of the Turks.~~*

{J. moves Knolles q. to To BLOW. *v.n.* 8.}

To BLOW. *v.n.* {…} To bloom; to blossom. <^**to spread by growth.**>

We lose the prime to mark how spring
Our tended plants, how *blows* the citron grove,
What drops the myrrh, and what the balmy reed.
*Milton~~'s Paradise Lost, b. v. l. 22.~~*



BLOWN. The *participle passive* of *blow.*

{…} <——— to ✱2>

*Sidney, b.* ii.

{J. moves Sidney q. to first place under To BLOW. *v.a.* 2.}

{…} <——— to ✱3 3>

*Pope.*

{J. moves Pope q. to second place under To BLOW. *v.a.* 5; J. writes '3' in margin, smears it out for deletion, then rewrites '3'.}

BLOWTH. *n.s.* {…} Bloom, or blossom. **<a word proper but not used>**

<2> BLU'BBER. *n.s.* {…}

<1> To BLU'BBER. *v.n.* [~~from the noun.~~ **<from Blob>**] {…}

Even so lies she,
*Blubb'ring* and weeping, weeping and *blubb'ring.*
*Shakesp.* ~~*Romeo and Juliet.*~~

To BLU'BBER. *v.a.* {…}

{…} *Dryden.*

{J. moves the entry for BLUBBER. *n.s.* to follow To BLUBBER. *v.a.*}

BLU'DGEON. *n.s.* A short stick, with one end loaded/<^ ~~with~~> used as an offensive weapon. {J. draws caret and writes 'with' in the margin; J. then crosses out word and smears out both caret and word.}

BLUE. *adj.* {…}

Where fires thou find'st unrak'd, and hearths unswept,
There pinch the maids as *blue* as bilberry.
*Shakesp.* ~~*Merry Wives of Windsor.*~~

BLUEBO'TTLE. *n.s.* {…}

1. A flower of the bell shape; a species of *bottleflower*; ~~which see.~~

BLU<'>E-EYED. *adj.* {…}

{J. indicates deletion of hyphen to make one word, then smears out closing-up mark.}

BLU<'>EHA'IRED. *adj.* {…}

{J. moves stress mark.}

{sig. 3G2r}

## BLU

To BLU'NDER. *v.n.* {...}
1. {...}

The grandees and giants in knowledge, who laughed at all besides themselves, as barbarous ~~and insignificant~~, yet *blundered*, and stumbled, about their grand and principal concern.
*South.*/

To BLU'NDER. *v.a.* To mix foolishly or blindly. **<a low word.>**

BLU'NDERER. *n.s.* {...}

~~Another sort of~~ judges will decide in favour of an authour, or will pronounce him a mere *blunderer*, according to the company they have kept. *Watts's Improvement of the Mind.*

BLUNT. *adj.* {...}
2. Dull in unerstanding; not quick.

Valentine being gone, I'll quickly cross,
By some sly trick, *blunt* Thurio's dull proceeding.
*Shakesp.* ~~*Two Gentlemen of Verona.*~~

<2> Whitehead, a grave divine, was of a blunt stoical nature; one day the queen happened to say, I like thee the better, because thou livest unmarried. He answered; Madam, I like you the worse. *Bacon's Apophthegms.*

<1> 3. Rough; not delicate; not civil.

{J. moves *Bacon's Apophthegms* q. correctly to first place under def. 3.}

5. {...}

I find my heart hardened and *blunt* to new impressions; it will scarce receive or retain affections of yesterday.
*Pope,* ~~*Lett.* lxxxiii, *to Swift.*~~

## BLU

To BLURT. *v.a.* {...}

They had some belief of a Deity, which they, upon surprizal, thus *blurt* out. *Government of the Tongue,* ~~§ 5.~~

To BLUSH. *v.n.* {...}◆
1. To betray shame or confusion, by a red colour in the cheek.

I have mark'd
A thousand *blushing* apparitions
To start into her face; a thousand innocent shames,
In angel whiteness, bear away these blushes.
*Shakesp.* ~~*Much ado about Nothing.*~~ <2>

Pale and bloodless,
Being all descended to the lab'ring heart,
Which with the heart there cools, and ne'er returneth
To *blush* and beautify the cheek again. *Shakesp. Henry* VI.

{...} *Shakesp. Cymbeline.*
{...} *Bacon, Essay* 28.
{...} *Bacon's Nat. History.* <1>
{...} *Smith's Phædr. and Hippolitus.*

2. To carry a red colour, or any soft and bright colour.

{J. moves *Much ado about Nothing* q. and *Henry* VI q. to first and second place under def. 2.}

{Vertical lines inking from facing IL.}

{sig. 3G2v}

{BLUNT. *adj.*}
Brutal; roughly insolent
They say the world is warre than it wont
All for her Shepherds is beastly & bloont
Others saine but how truly I note
All for they holden shame of their Cote
Spens. past.[1]

{To BLUSH. *v.n.* ?}
To blush according to Thomson
To exhibit, show.
Her lips blush deeper sweets
Spring 690[2]

[1] Spenser, *Shepheardes Calendar* (*Works* VII), 'September', ll. 108-111. S-G. *1755* WARRE *adj.*
[2] James Thomson, *The Seasons,* 'Spring', l. 966. S-G (slip reads 'To blush v.a.' and '960'). *1755* LIP *n.s.* 1

{IL facing 3G2v}

{BLUSH. *n.s.* 4.}

<‡>

4 a cast or tinge of colour ~~particularly red~~
A loose earth of a pale flesh colour, that is
white with a blush of red
Wood$^{d}$. foss.[1]

{To BOARD. *v.a.* 4.}
4 To accost; to address
Him the prince with gentle court did <u>board</u>
Sir Knight ~~moght~~ mought I of you this courtsy read
To weet why on your Shield so goodly scor'd
Bear ye the picture of that ladys head
F. Q. 2. 9. 2.[2]

{To BOARD. *v.a.* 3.}
3 v.a. with off
Do not smile at me, that I boast her off
For thou shalt find she will outstrip all praise
Shak.[3]

[1] John Woodward, *Natural History of Fossils,* vol. I, class I, sect. II, p. 7. *1755* FLESHCOLOUR *n.s.*
[2] Spenser, *Fairie Queene* (*Works* II), bk II, canto IX, st. ii, ll. 5-8. S-G. *1755* To WEET *v.n.*
[3] Shakespeare, *Tempest* (**Works* I), 4.1, p. 61 [4.1.9-10]. S-G. *1755* OUTSTRIP *v.a.*

{IL facing 3H$^{r}$}

## BOA

{BLUSH. *n.s.*}
3. {...} *Locke.*
<‡————— > {J. keys in Woodward q. from IL.}

BLU'SHY. *adj.* {...}
Blossoms of trees, that are white, are commonly inodorate; those of apples, ~~crabs,~~ and peaches, are *blushy*, and smell sweet. *Bacon's ~~Natural Hist. N° 507.~~*
Stratonica entering, moved a *blushy* colour in his face; but, deserting him, he relapsed into the same paleness ~~and languour.~~ *Harvey ~~on Consumptions.~~*

To BLU'STER. *v.n.* {...}
2. {...}
Either he must sink to a ~~downright~~ confession, or else he must huff and *bluster*, till perhaps he raise a counter-storm. *~~Government~~ of ~~the~~ Tongue.*

BOAR. *n.s.* {...}
She sped the *boar* away;
His eyeballs glare with fire, suffus'd with blood;
His neck sh~~u~~<**oo**>ts up a thickest thorny wood;
~~His bristled back a trench impal'd appears.~~ *Dryden's Fables.*

BOARD. *n.s.* {...}
1. {...}
With the saw they ~~have~~ sundred trees in *boards* and planks. *Raleigh's ~~Essays.~~*
3. Entertainment; food. <**as he gave me my <u>board</u>.**>

## BOA

To BOARD. *v.a.* {...}
1. To enter a ship by force; the same as to storm, used of a city.
{...}
~~Yet~~<**He**> not inclin'd the English ship to *board*,
More on his guns relies than on his sword,
From whence a fatal volley we receiv'd;
It miss'd the duke; but his great heart it griev'd. *Waller.*

2. To attack, or make the first attempt upon a man; *aborder quelqu'un*, Fr.
{...}
Sure unless he knew some strain in me, that I knew not myself, he would never have *boarded* me in this fury. *Shakespeare.*
3. To lay or pave with boards.
{...} *Moxon's Mechanical Exercises.*
<2> To BOARD. *v.n.* To live in a house, where a certain rate is paid for eating.
{...} *Herbert.*
<1> {...} *Spectator*, N° 961.
<4> ~~To BOARD. *v.a.*~~ To place as a boarder in another's house. <**To entertain at**>
{J. consolidates two entries for To BOARD. *v.a.* under one head-word with 4 senses.}

BO'ARDING-SCHOOL. *n.s.*{...} A school where the scholars live with the teacher.<**, commonly used of the schools for girls.**>

To BOAST. *v.a.* {...}
2. To magnify; to exalt. <**Sometimes with <u>of</u> because the ground of boast.**>

{sig. 3H$^{r}$}

{BOAST. *n.s.* {…}
1. A cause of boasting; an occasion of pride; the thing boasted.}
<2> {…} *Pope's Odyss.*
2. An expression of ostentation; a proud speech.
<1> Thou that makest thy *boast* of the law, through breaking the law dishonourest thou God? *Rom.* ii. 23.

{J. moves Romans q. to first place under def. 1.}

BO'ASTINGLY. *adv.* {…}
We look on it as a pitch of impiety, *boastingly* to avow our sins; ~~and it deserves to be considered, whether this kind of confessing them, have not some affinity with it.~~ *Decay of Piety.*

BOA'TION. *n.s.* {…}
In Messina insurrection, the guns were heard ~~from thence~~ as far as ~~Augusta and~~ Syracuse, about an hundred Italian miles. ~~These distances being, in a short time,~~ in loud *boations.* *Derham~~'s Physico Theology.~~*

{J. crosses out 'as', then smears out stroke to retain 'as'; the smearing of the stroke through '*Physico Theology*' in the attribution is unintentional.}

BO'ATSWAIN. *n.s.* {…} An officer on board a ship, who has charge of all her rigging, ropes, cables, anchors, sails, flags, colours, pendants, ~~*&c.*~~ He also takes care of the long-boat and its furniture {…}. *Harris.*
Sometimes the meanest *boatswain* may help to preserve the ship from sinking. *Howel~~'s Pre-eminence of Parliament.~~*

To BOB. *v.a.* {…}
1. To cut. *Junius.* **<Not used>**
2. To beat; to drub; to bang. **<little used>**

Those bastard Britons, whom our fathers
Have in their own land beaten, *bobb'd*, and thump'd.
*Shakesp. ~~Richard III.~~*

3. To cheat; to gain by fraud. **<a low word>**
{…}
~~Live, Rodorigo!~~
He calls me to a restitution large,
Of gold and jewels, that I *bobb'd* from him,
As gifts to Desdemona. *Shakesp. Othello.*

BOB. *n.s.* {…}
3. A blow. **<Not used>**

B'OBWIG. *n.s.* {…}
A young fellow riding ~~towards us full gallop,~~ with a *bobwig* and a black silken bag ~~tied to it,~~ stopt ~~short at the coach,~~ to ask us how far the judges were behind. *Spectator,* N° 129.

To BODE. *v.a.* {…} <^1> To portend; to be the omen of. It is used in a sense of either good or bad.
{…}
By this design, you have opposed their false policy, with true and great wisdom; what they *boded* would be a mischief to us, ~~you are providing,~~ shall be one of our principal strengths. *Sprat's Sermons.* <2>
{…}
If firy red ~~his~~ <^**Sols**> glowing globe descends,
High winds and furious tempests he portends:
But if his cheeks are swoln with livid blue,
He *bodes* wet weather by his watry hue. *Dryden's Georg.* <1>
<——— **2.To predict ill.**>

{J. moves Sprat q. under new def. 2.}

BO'DEMENT. *n.s.* {…} Portent; omen; prognostick. **<little in use>**

BO'DICE. *n.s.* {…}
{…} *Locke on Education,* § 11.
<——— ‡>

{J. keys in new entry for BODIED *adj.* with Mayne q. from IL.}

BO'DILESS. *adj.* {…}
~~Which~~**<These>** *bodiless* and immaterial are,
And can be only lodg'd within our minds. *Davies.*

{sig. 3H^v}

---

{BO'ASTFUL. *adj.*}
Imperious with a teachers Air
Boastful he claims a right to wisdoms Chair
Blackm.[1]

{To BODE. *v.a.*}
O earth bear witness
And crown what I profess with kind event
If I speak true; if hollowly invert
What best ye boded me to Mischief
Shak Temp.[2]

{BODIED. *adj.*}
<‡>
Bodied adj. [body] Having a body ~~or outward form~~ **<corporeal>**
I wish you would assume some constant figure wherin I might say I grappled with a bodied Adversary. D^r. Maine[3]

[1] Richard Blackmore, *Creation*, bk III, p. 99. S-G. *1755* TEACHER *n.s.*
[2] Shakespeare, *Tempest* (*Works* I), 3.1, p. 50 [3.1.68-71]. S-G. *1755* HOLLOWLY *adv.* 2
[3] Jasper Mayne, *A late Printed Sermon Against False Prophets*, p. 41. S-G.

{IL facing 3H^v}

1 Bodle n.s.♦
Is a small Scotish coin of copper as big as a doit,
three of which make a babee or halfpenny
It is otherwise called twa pennies [daa pheign
Erse] This coin is now wore out to make way
for the English Copper, as the Scottish Silver and
gold Coins have before done for the Sterling
money of England.

{BO'DDLE. new}
Boddle is a weed like the may weed, but
bears a large yellow flower: It is hardy and
will grow again, unless the roots are clean pulld
up. The seed is also very spreading

Tuss. Notes

The brake & the cockle be noisome too much
Yet like unto boddle no weed there is such

Tuss. husb. for May[1]

{To BOIL. *v.n.*}
v.n.

To dilute as boiling water
Air in Ovens tho it doth boil & dilate itself
and is repercussed, yet it is without noise

Bacon[2]

1 Thomas Tusser, *Husbandry*, 'May', p. 58. Q. also on IL for BRAKE *n.s. 1755* NOISOME *adj.* 1
2 Bacon, *Natural History* (**Works* III), cent. II, § 118, p. 33. [II, cent. II, § 118, p. 392]. S-G. *1755* To REPERCUSS *v.a.*

{IL facing 3H2$^{r}$}

## BOD

BO'DY. *n.s.* {...}
1. {...}
All the valiant men arose, and ~~went all night, and~~ took the *body* of Saul, and the *bodies* of his sons, from the wall.

1 *Sam.* xxxi. 12.

{...}
By custom, ~~practice,~~ and patience, all difficulties and hardships, whether of *body* or of fortune, are made easy ~~to us~~.

*L'Estrange.*

3. {...}

'Tis a passing shame,
That I, unworthy *body* as I am,
Should censure thus one lovely gentlema<e>n.

*Sh. Two G. of Ver.*

5. {...}
When ~~these~~ pigmies pretend to form themselves into a *body*, it is time for us, ~~who are~~ men of figure, to look about us.

*Addison.* ~~*Guardian,* Nº 108.~~

{J. crosses out 'for us, who are', then smears out stroke to retain 'for us'.}

## BOI

BODY-CLOATHS. *n.s.* {...}
~~However it be, I am informed,~~ that several asses are kept in *body-cloaths*, and sweated every morning upon the heath.

*Addison.* ~~*Spectator,* Nº 173.~~

BOG. *n.s.* {...} A marish; a morass; <$_{\wedge}$**a fen; a swamp;**> a ground too soft to bear the weight of the body.

To BO'GGLE. *v.n.* {...}
3. To play fast and loose; to dissemble. **<not in use~~da~~{?} or $_{\wedge}$proper>**

BOHE'A. *n.s.* {...}
As some frail cup of China's fairest mold,
The tumults of the boiling *bohea* braves,
And holds secure the coffee's sable waves.

~~*Tickell.*~~

{sig. 3H2$^{r}$}

BO'ILER. *n.s.* {...}
1. {...}

That ~~such~~ alterations of terrestrial matter are not impossible, seems evident from that notable practice of the *boilers* of salt-petre. *Boyle.*

BO'ISTEROUS. *adj.* {...}
2. {...}

~~Spirit of peace,~~
Wherefore do you so ill translate yourself
Out of the speech of peace, that bears such grace,
Into the harsh and *boist'rous* tongue of war? *Shakesp. H.* IV.
{...}
~~Still must I beg thee not to name Sempronius:~~
Lucia; I like not that loud *boisterous* man. *Addison's Cato.*

3. Unwieldy.<; **bulky; ponderous; rude.**>
{...} *Fairy Q. b.*i.
{Inking in first line of q. accidental.}
<**b ‡**———— > {J. keys in note and Dryden q. from IL.}

BOLD. *adj.* {...}

8. *To make bold.* To take freedoms: a phrase not grammatical, though common. <∧> *To be bold* is better; as, *I was bold to speak.*
{J. keys in his note from IL.}

*Making* so *bold*,
My fears forgetting manners, ~~to unseal~~
~~Their grand commission.~~ *Shakesp. Hamlet.*

To BO'LDEN. *v.a.* {...}
{...} *Shakesp. Henry* VIII.
{J. keys in Daniel q. from IL.} <———— **a ‡**>

BO'LDFACE. *n.s.* {...}

How now, *boldface!* cries an old trot; sirrah, we eat our own hens, ~~I'd have you to know;~~ and what you eat, you steal. *L'Estrange.*
{Line through 'trot' result of bleeding through from recto of page.}

BO'LDLY. *adv.* {...}
1. In a bold manner; with courage; with spirit. **<without fear.>**

BO'LDNESS. *n.s.* {...}
5. Assurance; freedom from ~~fear~~ **<awe or bashfulness>**
{...} *Bacon's Essays,* N° 12.
**<6>~~5~~ <Freedom from terrour.>**

Sure if the guilt were theirs, they could not charge thee
With such a gallant *boldness*: if 'twere thine,
<2> Thou couldst not hear't with such a silent scorn. *Denham.*

His distance, though it does not instruct him to think wiser than other princes, yet it helps him to speak with more *boldness* what he thinks. *Temple.*

<1> *Boldness* is the power to speak or do what we intend, before others, without fear or disorder. *Locke.*

{J. creates new sense 6 with new def. and Denham and Temple qs. J. moves Locke q. to second place under sense 5.}

~~6~~<7>. Impudence.

{BOLD. *adj.* 8.}
**<‸ Perhaps borrowed from the French term faire le brave not well understood.>**[1]

{To BO'LDEN. *v.a.*}
~~v. a. with to~~ **<a ‡>**
There is that hand bolden'd to blood & war
That must the sword in wondrous actions weild
Daniel c. w.[3]

{BO'ISTEROUS. *adj.* 3.}
**<b ‡>**
5 Dryden uses it for rough, tough, unweildy
The leathern outside boist'rous as it was
Gave way and bent beneath her strict embrace
Dryd. Boc.[2]

[1] Inserted at caret under BOLD. *adj.* 8. *To make bold.*
[2] Dryden, 'Sigismonda and Guiscardo' (*Works* VII), ll. 159-160. Apparently to be inserted as new sense 4. S-G. *1755* OUTSIDE *n.s.*1 (shorter)
[3] Samuel Daniel, *Civil Wars*, bk IV, st. xlviii, p.165. S-G. To WIELD *v.a.* 1

{To BO´LSTER. *v.a.*?}♦

clean renouncing
Short bolsterd Breeches & those types of travel
Shak[1]

{BOLT. *n.s.*}
Pease bolt with thy pease he will have
His housholde to and his hog
Tuss. husb.
Pease bolt is pease in the hawm or straw
Tuss Notes[2]

4 We must bind our passions in chains & double
our guards least like mad folks they break their
locks & bolts & do all the mischief they can
Tayl. Com^t.[3]

{BO´LTED. *adj.* new}
Resembling a bolt applied to thunder
Was this a face
To stand against the deep dread bolted thunder
In the most terrible & nimble stroke
Of quick cross lightning Shak. L.[4]

{To BOLT. *v.n.*}
Forth popp'd the sprite so thin
And from the Keyhole bolted out
All upright as a pin Swift[5]

{BOLT. *n.s.* 1.}
< ^ **hence the proverb a fools bolt is soon shot.**>[6]

[1] Shakespeare, *Henry VIII* (**Works* V), 2.6, pp. 362-63 [1.3.29-31]. *1755* TYPE *n.s.* 1
[2] Thomas Tusser, *Husbandry*, 'July', p. 91. S-G. Aman. cannot read word 'feed' on slip and leaves blank.
[3] Jeremy Taylor, *The Worthy Communicant*, ch. ii, § 5, pp. 123-24. S-G. *1755* MAD *adj.* 1
[4] Shakespeare, *King Lear* (**Works* VI), 4.10, p. 124 [4.7.30-34]. S-G (with 'Bolted adj. (fm bolt)' written at top). *1755* CROSS *adj.* 2, TERRIBLE *adj.*, DREADFUL *adj.* 1 (shorter), To WAR *v.n.* (shorter)
[5] Pope, 'Sandys's Ghost' (*Poems* VI), ll. 30-32, p. 172. Poem published in the Pope-Swift *Miscellanies,* attributed to *Swift's Miscellanies* in *1755* under To POP *v.n.* S-G ('Bolt v.n.' written at top). *1755* To POP *v.n.* (much shorter)
[6] Inserted at caret under BOLT *n.s.* 1.

{IL facing 3I^r}

BOLT. *n.s.* {...}

1. An arrow; a dart shot from a crossbow.<∧>

{J. keys in his note from IL.}

2. Lightning; a thunderbolt. **<the arrows of heaven>**

**<∧>5. {...}**

{No material keyed in by caret.}

6. A spot or stain. ~~See BLOOD-BOLTERED.~~

To BOLT. *v.a.* {...}

2. To blurt out, <∧**to shoot**> or throw out precipitantly. **<from bolt an arrow>**



4. {...}

It is great
To do that thing that ends all other deeds,
Which shackles accidents, and *bolts* up change.
*Shakesp.* ~~*Antony and Cleopatra.*~~

5. {...}

~~Saying~~ **<She said>**, he now had *boulted* all the flour,
And that it was a groom of base degree,
Which of my love was partner. *Fairy Queen, b.* ii. *c.* 4.

6. {...}

The judge, ~~or~~ jury, ~~or~~ parties, ~~or the~~ council, or attornies, propounding occasional questions, beats and *bolts* out the truth much better than when the witness delivers only a formal series.
*Hale*~~*'s History of the Common Law.*~~

To BOLT. *v.n.* {...}

They erected a fort, and ~~from thence they~~ *bolted* like beasts of the forest, sometimes into the forest, sometimes into the woods and fastnesses, and sometimes back again to their den.
*Bacon*~~*'s War with Spain.*~~

BO'LTER. *n.s.* {...} <∧ ∧**1**> A sieve {...}.

These hakes, and divers others of the fore-cited, are taken with threads, and some of them with the *bolter*, which is a spiller of a bigger size. *Carew's Survey of Cornwal.* <2>

{...} *Shakesp. Henry* IV.

{...} *Bacon's Natural Hist.* N° 408.

{...} *Hudibras, p.* i. *c.* iii. <1>

<——— **2 a kind of net**>

{J. moves Carew q. under new def. 2; new def. a result of fresh reading of Carew q.}

BO'LTHEAD. *n.s.* {...}

This ~~spirit abounds in~~ salt, which may be separted, by putting the liquour into a *bolthead*, with a long and narrow neck.
*Boyle*~~*'s Sceptical Chymistry.*~~

## BON

BOMB-CHEST. *n.s.* {…} A kind of chest filled usually with bombs, and sometimes only with gunpowder, placed under ground, to tear and blow it up in the air, with those who stand on it. They are now ~~much~~ disused. <u>*Chambers.*</u>/

BO´MBAST. *n. s.* [This word ~~seems to~~ <{**mi**}> be derived from *Bombastius*, one of the names of Paracelsus; a man remarkable for sounding professions, and unintelligible language. <^ **or from <u>bombast</u> the name of some kind of stuff perhaps of dissimilar materials whence it came to be applied to style of which one part suits all with the other, as Fustian has the same use.**>] {…}.
{J. apparently begins writing the word 'might' above cross-out.}♦

BOMBILA´TION. *n.s.*
{…} *Brown's Vulgar Errours, b.* ii *c.* 5.
<**a** ‡ ——— >
{J. keys in new entry for BOMBILIOUS *adj.* from IL.}

*BONA ROBA. n.s.* {J. indicates small caps. after 'B'.}
*BONA´SUS. n.s.* {J. indicates small caps. after 'B'.}
*BONCHRE´TIEN. n.s.* {…} A species of pear {…}. ~~See PEAR.~~
{J. indicates small caps. after 'B'.}

BOND. *n.s.* {…}
1. Cord~~s~~, or chain~~s~~, with which any one is bound.
3. {…}

## BON

Observe, ~~in working up the walls,~~ that no side of the house, nor any part of the walls, be wrought up three feet above the other, before the next adjoining wall be wrought up to it, so that they may be all joined together, and made ~~a~~ good *bond.* *Mortimer's Husbandry.*

BOND. *adj.* [from *bind*, perhaps for *bound;* ~~from~~ ȝebonden, Saxon.]

BO´NDAGE. *n.s.* {…} Captivity; <^**slavery**> imprisonment; state of restraint.
{…}
The king, ~~when~~<**if**> he design'd you for my guard,
Resolv'd he would not make my *bondage* hard. *Dryden.*

BO´NDSLAVE. *n.s.* {…}
{…}
~~All her ornaments are taken away,~~ of a freewoman she is become a *bondslave.* 1 *Mac.* ii. 11.

BO´NDSMAN. *n.s.* {…}
1. {…}
Carnal greedy people, without ~~such~~ a precept, would have no mercy upon their poor *bondsmen* and beasts. *Derh. Ph. Theol.*

{sig. 3I^v}

<**a** ‡>
Bombilious adj. [Bombil~~x~~<**o**> Latin]
~~to hum like a bee or bombylis a fly~~
<**making ~~hu~~ a humming noise**>
The whame or burrel fly is vexatious to Horses is summer, not by stinging them, but only by their <u>bombilious</u> noise, or tickling in sticking their nits or eggs in the hair
Derh. Ph. Th.[1]

[1] William Derham, *Physico-Theology*, bk IV, ch. xv, § 2, p. 248, note k. S-G ('Horses in summer' instead of 'Horses is summer'). *1755* NIT *n.s.*, WHAME *n.s.* (slightly shorter)

{IL facing 3I^v}

{BONJOUR. new}

<**o ‡**>

Bonjour [French] ~~a Complimental Salutation~~

<**Good day**>

An it please your majesty
To hunt the panther & the hart with me,
With horn & hound, we'll give your grace bonjour

Shak[1]

[1] Shakespeare, *Titus Andronicus* (**Works* VI), 1.6, p. 261 [1.1.492-94]. S-G. *1755* PANTHER *n.s.* (shorter)

{IL facing 3I2r}

## BON

BONE. *n.s.* {...}

1. The solid part~~s~~ of the body of an animal<**. Bones**> are made up of hard fibres, {...}

They are all spongy, and full of little cells, or ~~are~~ of a considerable firm thickness, {...} *Quincy.*

4. *To make no bones.* To make no scruple; a metaphor taken from a <^**hungry**> dog, who ~~readily~~ swallows meat ~~that has no~~ <**without stopping at the**> bones.

5. ~~BONES.~~ A sort of bobbins, ~~made of trotter bones,~~ for weaving bonelace.

6. ~~BONES.~~ Dice.

BO'NELESS. *adj.* {...}W~~ithout~~<**anting**> bones.

BO'NESETTER. *n.s.* {...}

~~At present~~ my desire is only to have a good *bonesetter.*

*Denham~~'s Sophy.~~*

BO'NGRACE. *n.s.* {...}

{...} *Hakewell on Providence.*

<**o ‡**———> {J. keys in new entry for BONJOUR from IL.}

BO'NNET. *n.s.* {...} <^ ^**1**> A covering for the head; a hat; a cap.

Go to them with this *bonnet* in thy hand,
And thus far having stretch'd it, here be with them,
Thy knee buffing the stones; ~~for, in such business,~~
~~Action is eloquence.~~ *Shakesp. Coriolanus.*

<**2**> BO'NNET. [In fortification.] {...}

<**3**> BO'NNET *à prestre* {...}

<**4**> BO'NNETS. [In the sea language.] {...}

{J. consolidates entries for BONNET under one head-word with four senses.}

## BOO

BONNY-CLABBER. *n.s.* {...}

We scorn, for want of talk, to jabber,
Of parties o'er our *bonny-clabber*;
~~Nor are we studious to enquire,~~
~~Who votes for manours, who for hire.~~ *Swift.*

BO'NY. *adj.* {...}

1. {...}

~~At the end of this hole~~ <**In the ear**> is a membrane, fastened to a round *bony* limb, and stretched like the head of a drum; and therefore, by anatomists, called *tympanum.* *Ray on the Creation.*

BOOK. *n.s.* {...}

1. {...}

Receive the sentence of the law for sins,
Such as by God's *book* are adjudg'd to death.

*Shakesp.* ~~*Henry IV.*~~

{sig. 3I2r}

## BOO

BO'OKISH. *adj.* {...}

I'll make him yield the crown,
Whose *bookish* rule hath pull'd fair England down.

*Shakesp.* ~~*Henry VI. p. ii.*~~

I'm not *bookish*, yet I can read waiting gentlewom<a>n in the 'scape. *Shakesp. Winter's Tale.*

Xantippe follows ~~the example of~~ her namesake; being married to a *bookish* man, who has no knowledge of the world.

*Spectator,* ~~Nº 482.~~

BO'OKMAN. *n.s.* {...}

This civil war of wits were much better us'd
On Navarre and his *bookmen*; for here 'tis abus'd.

*Shakesp.* ~~*Love's Labour Lost.*~~

BO'OKMATE. *n.s.* {...}

This Armado is ~~a Spaniard that keeps here in court,~~
~~A phantasm, a monarch, and~~ one that makes sport
To the prince and his *bookmates*. *Shakesp. Love's Labour Lost.*

BO'OKSELLER. *n.s.* {...}

He went to the *bookseller*, and told him in anger, he had sold a book in which there was false divinity.

*Walton*~~*'s Life of Bishop*~~ *Saunderson.*

BO'OLY. *n.s.* {...}

All the Tartarians, and the people about the Caspian sea, which are naturally Scythians, live in h<o>rds; being the very same that the Irish *boolies* are, driving their cattle ~~continually~~ with them, and feeding only on their milk and white meats.

*Spenser*~~*'s Ireland.*~~

BOOM. *n.s.* {...}

2. A pole with bushes or baskets, set up as a mark to shew ~~the sailors~~ how to steer in the channel, when a country is overflown.

*Sea Dict.*

BOON. *n.s.* {...}

Vouchsafe me for my meed but one fair look:
A smaller *boon* than this I cannot beg,
And less than this, I'm sure, you cannot give.

*Shakesp.* ~~*Two Gentlemen of Verona.*~~

BOON. *adj.* {...}

## BOO

~~I know~~ the infirmity of our family; we are apt to play the *boon* companion, and throw our money away in our cups.

*Arbuthnot's Hist. of J. Bull.*

{J. crosses out 'I know the infirmity of', then smears out part of stroke to retain 'the infirmity of'.}

To BOOT. *v.a.* {...}

1. {...}

What *boots* the regal circle on his head,<?>
~~That long behind he trails his pompous robe!~~ *Pope.*

BOOT. *n.s.* {...}

1. {...}

That my leg is too long—
—No; that it is too little.—
—I'll wear a *boot*, to make it somewhat rounder.

*Shakesp.* ~~*Two Gentlemen of Verona.*~~

<~~Death~~ **Death**> Shew'd ~~him~~ his room, where he must lodge that night,
Pull'd off his *boots*, and took away the light. *Milton.*

Bishop Wilkins ~~says, he~~ does not question, but it will be as usual for a man to call for his wings, when he is going a journey, as it is now to call for his *boots*. *Addison. Guardian.*

2. {...}

**<3>** BOOT *of a Coach*. {...}

To BOOT. *v.*<n>. {...}

BOOT-HOSE. *n.s.* {...}

His lacquey with a linen stock on one leg, and a *boot-hose* on the other, gartered with a red and blue list.

*Shakesp.* ~~*Taming of the Shrew.*~~

{sig. 312v}

{Boot *of a Coach*}
If in a coach one side of the boot be down & the other up, and if a beggar beg on the close Side, you will think that he were on the open Side. Bac.[1]

[1] Bacon, *Natural History* (**Works* III), cent. III, § 203, p. 47 [II, cent. III, § 203, p. 414]. S-G ('Boot of a coach' at top of slip).

{IL facing 312v}

{BOORY. *n.s.* new}
The people that thus lived in those
grow thereby the more barbarous & practising
what villanies they will against private men
by stealing their goods or murdering them
Spens[1]

{To BORDER. *v.a.*}
3. v.a.
~~To confine, to keep within bounds~~
**<p ‡>**
I fear your disposition
That nature which contemns its Origin
Cannot be border'd certain in itself
~~She that herself will sliver & disbranch~~
From her material sap perforce must wither
And come to deadly use Shak.[2]

{To BORE. *v.a.*}
v.a.
2 To peirce thro' by struggling
Consider
What riots seen, what bustling crouds I bor'd
How oft I cross'd where carts & coaches roard
Gay[3]

[1] Spenser, *Ireland* (*Works* IX), ll. 1542-47. S-G ('Boory, boories plur. boorack Scottish Hut in w^ch^ y^e^ Irish & Highlanders lie in' squeezed in above q., consequently illegible to aman. copying onto IL; head-word written as 'Booty, Booties' then altered to 'Boory, Boories' throughout; word 'boories' at end of first line illegible to aman. and left blank on IL; Spenser reads 'bollies'). *1755* To MALIGN *v.a.* (different)
[2] Shakespeare, *King Lear* (**Works* VI), 4.2, p. 102-03 [4.2.31-36]. S-G. *1755* To DISBRANCH *v.a.*, ORIGINAL *n.s.* 2 (shorter)
[3] John Gay, 'Trivia' (*Poetry and Prose* I), bk III, l. 396. S-G. *1755* To ROAR *v.n.* 4

{IL facing 3K^r^}

BO'OTED. *adj.* {...} <‸**Being**> In boots; in a horseman's habit.

BO'OTLESS. *adj.* {...}

1. Useless; unprofitable; unavailing; ~~without~~ <**producing no**> advantage.

~~When those accursed messengers of hell~~
~~Came to their wicked man, and~~ <**They**> 'gan tell
Their *bootless* pains, and ill succeeding night. *Fairy Q. b.* i.

2. ~~Without~~<**Gaining no**> success; perhaps ~~without~~<**no**> booty {...}

BOPE'EP. *n.s.* {...}

~~Rivers,~~
~~That~~ <**Rivers**> serve ~~in~~<'>stead of peaceful barriers,
To part th'engagements of their warriours,
Where both from side to side may skip,
And only encounter at *bopeep*. *Hudibras, p.* iii. *c.* iii.

*BORA'CHIO. n.s.* {...}

How you stink of wine! D'ye think my niece will ever endure such a *borachio!* you're an absolute *borachio*.
*Congreve's ~~Way of the World.~~*

BO'RAGE. *n.s.* {...}

The leaves are broad and rough; the flowers consist of one leaf; are of a wheel shape, and divided into five segments, almost to the bottom, which end in sharp points, like a star; the apices, in the middle of the flower, are sharp-pointed, and adhere together; ~~the seeds are rough, and appear like a viper's head.~~ This plant is often used in the kitchen, and for a cool tankard in the summer time; and the flowers are used in medicinal cordials. *Millar.*

BO'RDEL. *n.s.* {...}

Making even his own house a stews, a *bordel*, and a school of lewdness, to instil vice into ~~the unwary years of~~ his poor children. *South.*

BOR

BO'RDER. *n.s.* {...}

1. {...}

~~They have, of Paris work,~~ looking-glasses, bordered with broad *borders* of crystal, and great counterfeit precious stones.
*Bacon's ~~Natural Hist. Nr. 960.~~*

4. {...}

~~There he~~ <**The fly**> arriving, round about doth fly
From bed to bed, from one to other *border,*
And takes survey, with curious busy eye,
Of every flower and herb there set in order. *Spenser's Muiop.*
All with a *border* of rich fruit trees crown'd,
Whose loaded branches hide the lofty mound:
~~Such various ways the spacious alleys lead,~~
~~My doubtful muse knows not what path to tread.~~ *Waller.*

To BO'RDER. *v.n.* {...}

1. {...}

It *bordereth* upon the province of Croatia, which, ~~in time past,~~ was <**in**> continual wars with the Turks garrisons.
*Knolles's ~~History of the Turks.~~*

To BO'RDER. *v.a.* {...}

2. {...}

{...} *Raleigh's History.*

<———————— **3 To bound; to restrain. p ‡**>

{J. keys in Shakespeare q. from IL. Vertical lines result of inking from facing IL.}

BO'RDERER. *n.s.* {...}

A~~n ordinary~~ horse will carry two sacks of sand; and, of such, the *borderers* on the sea ~~do~~ bestow sixty, ~~at least~~ in every acre; but most ~~husbands~~ double that number. *Carew's Survey.*

The easiest to be drawn
~~To our society, and~~ to aid the war:
The rather for their seat, being next *bord'rers*
On Italy; ~~and that they abound with horse.~~ *B. Johns. Catil.*

{J. draws line conflating first and end of second line into single line.}

The king of Scots ~~in person,~~ with Perkin ~~in his company,~~ entered with a great army, though it chiefly consisted of *borderers*, being raised ~~somewhat~~ suddenly. *Bacon's Henry* VII.

To BO'RDRAGE. *v.n.* {...} To plunder the borders. <**out of use.**>

To BORE. *v.a.* {...}

~~These~~ diminutive caterpillars are able, by degrees, to pierce or *bore* their way into a tree, with very small holes; which, after they are fully entered, grow together. *Ray.*

Consider, reader, what fatigues I've known,
What riots seen, what bustling crouds I *bor'd*,
How oft I cross'd where carts and coaches roar'd. *Gay.*

{J. crosses out 'Consider, reader,' and then smears out stroke.}

## BOR

BORE. *n.s.* {...}
1. {...}

~~Into h~~<H>ollow engines long and round,
Thick ramm'd, at th' other *bore* with touch of fire
Dilated, and infuriate. *Milton's Paradise Lost, b.* vi.

{Vertical lines across entries for BORE and BOREAL result of inking from facing IL.}

*BO'REAS. n.s.* {...}
*Boreas*, and Cærias, and Argestas loud,
And Thrascias, rend the woods, and seas up-turn.
*Milton's ~~Paradise Lost, b. x. l. 699.~~*

BO'RER. *n.s.* {...}
The ~~master~~-bricklayer must try ~~all~~ the foundations, with a *borer*, such as well-diggers use, to try what ground they have. *Moxon's ~~Mechanical Exercises.~~*

BORN. {...}
~~Upon some occasions,~~ Clodius may be ~~bold and~~ insolent, *born* away by his passion. *Swift.*

To be BORN. *v.n. pass.* {...}
1. To come into life.
{...} *Shakesp. King Lear.*
{...} *Prior.*
{...} *Locke.*
2. It is usually spoken with regard to circumstances; {...}
<2> The stranger that dwelleth with you, shall be unto you as one *born* among you, and thou shalt love him as thyself. *Levit.*/~~xix. 34.~~
~~Yet~~ man is *born* unto trouble, as the sparks fly upward. *Job.*/v. 7.
{...} *Prov.* xvii. 17.
<1> The new *born* babe by nurses overlaid. *Dryden.*

{J. moves Dryden q. correctly to second place under def. 1.}

## BOS

BO'RREL. *n.s.* {...}
Siker thou speak'st like a lewd ~~s~~<l>orrel,
Of heaven, to deemen so:
Howbe I am but rude and *borrel*,
Yet nearer ways I know. *Spenser's Past.*

To BO'RROW. *v.a.* {...}
1. {...}
He *borrowed* a box of the ear of the Englishman, and swore he would pay him again when he was able.
*Shakesp.* ~~*Merchant of Venice.*~~

BO'SCAGE. *n.s.* {...}
~~We bent our course thither, where we saw the appearance of land; and, the next day,~~ we might plainly discern that it was a land flat to our sight, and full of *boscage*, which made it shew the more dark. *Bacon's N. Atlantis.*

{sig. 3Kv}

Borrel n.s. a poor rude illiterate person, who
is of no other service to the public than to get chil
:dren. So it is used in Chaucer. Unless you would
derive it from poraille in the same author
which signifies the low or poor people Jun[1]

Siker thou speakst like a lewd lorell
Of heaven to deemen so
How be I am but rude & borrell
Yet nearer ways I know Spens.[2]◆

[1] Franciscus Junius, *Etymologicum Anglicanum,* sig. M2r and sig. 4Or.
[2] Spenser, *Shepheardes Calendar* (*Works* VII), 'July', ll. 93-96. An entry for BORREL *n.s.* with this q. already exists in *1755.* S-G (Junius and Spenser qs. on same slip). *1755* BORREL *n.s.*, HOWBE *adv.*, LOREL *n.s.*

{IL facing 3Kv}

{Boss. *n.s.* 4.}

<**4** ‡>

~~Boss n.s.~~ a small sea fish
Of round fish there are smelts
~~cudles, conger~~ <**and**> Boss. Carew[1]

Boted adj. troubled with the botts, a kind of
worm in horses
So are the horses of the enemy
In general boted & brought low
The better part of ours are full of rest
Shak.[2]♦

[1] Richard Carew, *The Survey of Cornwall,* bk I, [30]. S-G (aman. alters 'Bass' to 'Boss' in head-word and q.; Carew reads 'bass'). *1755* CHAD *n.s.* (different), SCAD *n.s.* (different), SMELT *n.s.* (different), SPRAT *n.s.* (different), all without 'bass' or 'boss'

[2] Shakespeare, *1 Henry IV* (**Works* IV), 4.4, p. 179 ('In general journey-bated' instead of 'In general boted') [4.3.25-27]. Aman. corrects 'bott' to 'bots'. S-G ('journey boted'). *1755* JOURNEY *n.s.* 2 (shorter, with 'In general journey bated')

{IL facing 3K2$^{r}$}



<‡> {Purpose uncertain.}

{BO'SOM. *n.s.*}
3. ~~The~~ inclosure. <~~**the**~~ **pale.**>

<7> Bosom, in composition, implies intimacy; {...}

Boss. *n.s.* {...}
< ‡ **4**> {J. keys in def. and Carew q. from IL.}

{sig. 3K2$^{r}$}

BO'TTLEFLOWER. *n.s.* {...}

~~It hath a squamose hairy calyx; the disk of the flower is almost plain, but the outer florets, round the borders, are large, tubulous, and deeply cut in; these outer florets are always barren; but the inner florets have a single naked seed succeeding each.~~ The species are, ~~1. The greater broad-leaved *blue-bottle*, commonly~~ called *globe-flower*. ~~2. The greater narrow-leaved *blue bottle*, or *globe-flower*. 3. The purple *sweet sultan*.~~ 4. *Corn-bottle*, with a white flower. The first and second sorts are abiding plants, which increase greatly by their creeping roots. The *sweet sultans* will begin to flower, and continue till the frost prevents them. The *corn-bottles* were also annuals, which, for the diversity of their flowers, were propagated in gardens; but ~~of late years they are almost excluded.~~ *Millar.*

{J. probably first intended to retain abbreviated version of q., beginning 'The species are', then deleted entire q.}

{sig. 3K2^v}

{To BOUGEON *v.n.* new}
The Caledonian Oak begirt with Cions of his own Stem: The lillies and the Roses red and white did bougeon round about him
Howel.[1]

[1] James Howell, *Dendrologia,* p. 35. S-G (with 'v.n.' at top).

{IL facing 3K2^v}

{BOUGH. *n.s.*}
Bough, a gibbet or gallows
Perhaps it might be on the bough of the
nearest tree they came to that was strong enough
for the purpose

Some who have not deserved {??}Judgment of
death tho otherwise perhaps offending have been
for their goods sake caught up and carried
straight to the bough a thing indeed very piti
ful & horrible Spens. Irel.[1]

He bar'd an ancient oak of all her boughs
Then on a rising ground the trunk he placd
Which with the spoils of his dead foe he grac'd
Dry. Æ.[2]

[1] Spenser, *Ireland* (*Works* IX), ll. 5017-5020. S-G (def., note, and Spenser q. all on same slip, with the following added between 'purpose' and Spenser q.: 'If it be not bought or any thing bent{?}: And may be explained by y$^{e}$ follow$^{g}$ passage in Virg. Dryd'. Suggests there was probably a S-G slip for the following Dryden q., no longer extant). *1755* INDEED *adv.* (shorter), PITIFUL *adj.* (shorter)

[2] Dryden, *Virgil's Æneis* (*Works* VI), bk XI, ll. 6-8. See note above. *1755* To RISE *v.n.* 23, To BARE *v.a.* (shorter)

{IL facing 3L$^{r}$}

**BOU**

BOUGHT. preter. of *to buy*; ~~which see.~~

BOUNCE. *n.s.* {…}
**<2. A leap; a start.>**
~~2~~<3>. <A sudden crack or noise.**<as by a quick disruption>**
~~3~~<4>. A boast; {…}

BOUND. *n.s.* {…}
1. {…}
Th~~ose~~<e> vast Scythian regions were separated by the common natural *bounds*, of rivers, ~~lakes,~~ mountains, woods, or marshes.
*Temple.*

**BOU**

{Vertical lines across entries for BOUND *n.s.*, To BOUND *v.a.* and To BOUND *v.n.* result of inking from facing IL.}

BO'UNDEN. *participle passive* of *bind.* **<bound is used in all the senses of bind**
**bounden perhaps only, for obliged; requi red by law, or duty.>**

{sig. 3L$^{r}$}

BOU

BOW

BO'USY. *adj.* {...}
{...} *King.* <2>
{...} *Dryden's Juv. sat.* x. <1>

{J. re-orders for chronological sequence.}

*BO'UTEFEU. n.s.* {...} An incendiary; one who kindles feuds and discontents. **<Not in use.>**

To BOW. *v.a.* {...}
1. To bend, or inflect.
{...} *Shakesp. Henry* VIII.
<———— **a+**>

{J. keys in Milton q. from IL facing 3L2ʳ.}

{sig. 3Lᵛ}

{To BOW. *v.a.*}
~~To turn as a ballance, to weigh down~~
the fair soul herself weighd
between lothness & obedience at which end
the beam should bow Shak.[1]

{To BOW. *v.n.*}
To incline, to dispose
She that should all parts to reunion bow
She that had all magnetic force alone
To draw and fasten sundred parts in one
Donne[2]

[1] Shakespeare, *Tempest* (**Works* I), 2.1, p. 33 [2.1.130-132]. Q. not keyed in to printed text. S-G ('To bow v.n.' written at top). *1755* LOATHNESS *n.s.*
[2] John Donne, 'An Anatomie of of the World. The First Anniversary', ll. 220-22. S-G ('5 To bow. v.a.' written at top). *1755* MAGNETICK *adj.* 3, REUNION *n.s.*, SUNDER *v.a.*, FASTEN *v.a.* 2 (much shorter)

{IL facing 3Lᵛ}

{Bow. *n.s.* 2.}
~~10~~ Bent. ~~byass~~ **<b ‡>**
Children like tender Osiers take the bow
And as they first are fashiond always grow
Dryd junr. Juv. 14[1]

{To BOW. *v.a.*}
Now my task is smoothly done **<a ‡> <~~over the leaf~~>**
I can fly, or I can run
Quickly to the green earths end
Where the <u>bow'd</u> Welkin slow doth bend
Milt[2]

[1] John Dryden, junior, 'Juvenal. The Fourteenth Satyr', p. 203. S-G. *1755* To GROW *v.n.* 3

[2] Milton, *Comus*, ll. 1012-15. S-G ('1' at top). J. writes 'over the leaf' to indicate that q. is to be inserted on 3Lv as third q. under To BOW *v.a.* 1; he crosses out note, probably because precise meaning is unclear. J. first intended q. to be inserted on facing page (3L2r) under To BOW *v.n.* 3; he wrote the original key in margin on 3L2r, then crossed it out.

{IL facing 3L2r}

## BOW

{To Bow. *v.n.*}
3. To stoop.
{...} *Judges*, vii. 6.
<~~a ‡~~ ——— >
{J. originally intended to key in Milton q. from IL.}

Bow. *n.s.* {...}**<1>** an act of reverence or submission, {...}
{...} *Swift.*
**<2>**
**<b ‡>**
{J. keys in new def. and John Dryden, junior, q. from IL.}

## BOW

Bo'wer. *n.s.* {...}
2. It seems to signify, in *Spenser*, a blow, a stroke: *bourrer*, Fr. to fall upon. **<or rather a flexure, a joint.>**

Bo'wer. *n.s.* {...} **<An>** Anchor~~s~~ so called. {...}

Bo'wery. *adj.* {...}
~~Snatch'd through the verdant maze, the hurried eye~~
~~Distracted wanders: now~~ the *bowery* walk
Of covert close, where scarce a speck of day
Falls on the lengthen'd gloom, ~~protracted sweeps~~. *Thomson.*

BO'WMAN. *n.s.* {...} An archer; he that shoots with a bow. **<a man armed with a bow>**

BOX. *n.s.* {...}

The characters are; The leaves are pennated, {...}. ~~The species are; 1. The *box-tree.* 2. The narrow-leaved *box-tree.* 3. Striped *box.* 4. The golden edged *box-tree.* 5. The dwarf *box.* 6. The dwarf striped *box.* 7. The silver edged *box.* On Boxhill, near Darking in Surrey, were formerly many large trees of this kind; but, of late years, their number is pretty much decreased; yet some remain of a considerable bigness.~~ The wood is very useful ~~for engravers and mathematical instrument-makers;~~ being so hard, close, and ponderous, as to sink in water. *Millar.*

~~*Box,* there are two sorts of it, the dwarf *box,* and a taller sort, that grows to a considerable height.~~ The dwarf *box* is very good for borders, and is easily kept in order, with one clipping in the year. It will ~~increase of slips set in March, or about Bartholomew-tide, and may be raised of layers and suckers, and will~~ prosper on the declivity of cold, dry, barren, chalky hills, where nothing else will grow. *Mortimer.*

**<The Spiry fir, and shape**
**ly Box Pope.>**

{Q. also under SPIRY *adj.* in *1755*.}♦

BOX. *n.s.* {...}

1. {...}

This head <^ **of the lion>** is to open a most wide voracious mouth, which shall take in letters and papers. There will be under it a *box,* of which the key will be kept in my custody, to receive such papers as are dropped into it. *Addison. Guard.* N° 98.

BOX. *n.s.* {...}

If one should take my hand perforce, and give another a *box* on the ear with it, the law punisheth the other. *Bramhall ~~against Hobbes.~~*

To BOX. *v.n.* {...} To fight with the fist.<{?}>

{J. makes mark, now illegible, then smears it out.}

<*ℓ*> 

{Cursive 'l' apparently written by J., purpose uncertain; see identical letter at top of 2T2v and 3Mr.}

{Vertical lines across entries for BOXEN *adj.*, BOXER *n.s.* and BOY *n.s.* result of inking from facing IL.}

BOY. *n.s.* {...}

3. {...}

The pale *boy*<->senator yet tingling stands,
~~And holds his breeches close with both his hands.~~ *Pope.*

To BOY. *v.n.* {...}To act apishly, or like a boy. **<not in use.>**

BO'YHOOD. *n.s.* {...} The state of a boy; the part of life in which we are boys. **<a word proper but perhaps innovated by Swift>**

BO'YISHNESS. *n.s.* {...} Childishness; tri~~vial~~**<fling>**ness.

<2> BRA'BBLE. *n.s.* [~~*brabbelen,* Dutch.~~ **<from the noun>**] A clamourous contest; a squabble; a broil.

Here in the streets, desperate in shame and state,
In private *brabble* did we apprehend him. *Shakesp. T. Night.*

<1> To BRABBLE. *v.n.* [~~from the noun.~~ **<brabbelen Dutch>**] To clamour; to contest noisily.

{J. reverses order of entries BRABBLE *n.s.* and To BRABBLE *v.n.* and smears out line of bracket, incorrectly drawn.}

{BOWSY. new}

The bowsy sire
Then shook from out his pipe the seeds of fire
And snapt his Box: ~~He stroakd his belly down~~
~~Rosy and reverend~~ Pope[1]

[1] Pope, *Dunciad* (*Poems* V), bk IV, ll. 493-95. J. apparently first intended to retain first part of q. through 'Box:', then deleted entire q. *1755* To SNAP *v.a.*

{IL facing 3L2$^v$}

<‡>

3 Brag n.s. a game at cards

Bragg adv. boastingly
Seest how bragg yon bullock bears
So smirk so smooth his pricked ears
His horns been as brade as rainbow bent
His dewlap as lithe as lass of Kent
See how he venteth into the wind
Ween'st of love is not his mind
Spenser[3]

{BRAGGADO'CIO. *n.s.*}
Unto the bush her eye did sudden glance
In which vain Braggadocio was mewed
And saw it stir F. Q. 2. 3. 34[4]

{BRACH. *n.s.*}
If this poor brach of Venice whom I cherish
For his quick hunting, stand the putting on
I'll have our Mich.[1] Cassio on the hip
Shak. Oth.[1]

{BRA'CKISH. *adj.*}
The salt Medway that trickling streams
Adown the dales of Kent
Till with the elder Brother Thames
His brackish waves be-meynt
Spens Pa.[2]

1 Shakespeare, *Othello* (**Works* VIII), 2.8, p. 315 [2.1.303-305]. S-G ('Masculine gender' squeezed in at top of slip). *1755* HIP *n.s.* 2
2 Spenser, *Shepheardes Calendar* (*Works* VII), 'July', ll. 81-84. S-G. *1755* MEYNT *adv.*
3 Spenser, *Shepheardes Calendar* (*Works* VII), 'February', ll. 71-76. S-G.
4 Spenser, *Fairie Queene* (*Works* II), bk II, canto III, st. xxxiv, ll. 2-4. S-G. *1755* To MEW *v.a.* 1

{IL facing 3M^r}

{Cursive 'l' apparently written by J., purpose uncertain; see identical letter at top of 2T2$^{v}$ and 3L2$^{v}$.}

{BRACE. *n.s.*}♦
6. Harness. **<traces.>**

8. Warlike preparation; from *bracing* the armour; as we say, *girded* for the battle. **<this is not now in use.>**

As ~~it~~ **<Cyprus>** more concerns the Turk than Rhodes,
So may he with more facile question bear it;
For that it stands not in such warlike *brace*,
But altogether lacks th' abilities
That Rhodes is dress'd in. *Shakesp. Othello.*

**<10>** ~~BRACE. *n.s.*~~ {...}
~~1~~. A pair; {...}
**<11>**~~2~~. It is used generally in conversation {...}
**<12>**~~3~~. It is applied to men in contempt.
{J. consolidates two separate entries for BRACE *n.s.* under one head-word with twelve senses. Inking on BRACE and BRACER from facing IL.}

BRA´CELET. *n.s.* {...}
1. {...}
A very ingenious lady used to wear, in rings and *bracelets*, store of ~~those~~ gems. *Boyle.*

BRA´CKISH. *adj.* {...}
Pits upon the sea shore turn **<^salt>** into fresh water, by percolation of the salt through the sand: but it is farther noted, after a time, the water in such pits will become *brackish* again. *Bacon.*
**<*d*>** ~~When I had gain'd the brow and top,~~
A lake of *brackish* waters on the ground,
Was all I found. *Herbert.*

<*ℓ*>



BRAD. *n.s.* **<^[from bꞃaꝺ Saxon]>** {...}

To BRAG. *v.n.* {...}♦
1. To boast; to display ostentatiously; to tell boastful stories.
{...}
In *bragging* out some of their private tenets, as if they were the received established doctrine of the church of England. **<2>**
*Sanderson's Pax Ecclesiæ.*
{...} *Clarendon.* **<1>**
{...} *Arbuthnot's Hist. of J. Bull.*
2. It has *of* before the thing boasted.
{...} *Sidney.*
{...} *Shakesp.*
{...} *Roscommon.*
3. *On* is used, but improperly.
{...} *Pope's Dunciad.*
**<4 <u>out</u> is used without propriety ~~or exami~~>**
{J. begins writing 'examination'{?}, then crosses it out.}
{J. moves *Sanderson's Pax Ecclesiæ.* q. under new def. 4.}
BRAG. *n.s.* {...}
2. The thing boasted.
{...} *Milton.*
{J. keys in new sense 3: '3 Brag n.s. a game at cards' from IL.} **<‡>**
BRAGGADO´CIO. *n.s.* {...}
The world abounds in terrible fanfarons, in the masque of men of honour; but these *braggadocios* are ~~easy to be~~ detected. <u>*L'Estrange.*</u>/

By the plot, you may guess ~~much of~~ the characters of the persons; a *braggadocio* captain, a parasite, and a lady of pleasure. <u>*Dryden.*</u>/

BRA´GGART. *n.s.* {...} A boaster. **<both the adjective and substantive are obsolete.>**♦

Who knows himself a *braggart*,
Let him fear this; for it will come to pass,
That every *braggart* shall be found an ass.
*Shakesp.* ~~*All's well that ends well.*~~

BRA´GLESS. *adj.* {...} ~~W~~**<Being w>**ithout a boast; without ostentation. **<proper but little used>**♦

BRA´GLY. *adv.* {...} Finely; so as it may be bragged. **<obsolete.>**♦

To BRAID. *v.a.* {...} To weave together. **<To form into a texture.>**

BRAIN. *n.s.* {…}

{Vertical lines across entry for BRAIN n.s. result of inking from facing IL.}



BRAKE. The *preterite* of *break.* {…}
{…} *Knolles's Hist.*

**<‸+ a>**

BRAKE. *n.s.* {…} <‸> <‸2> A thicket of brambles, or of thorns.

{J. keys in new def. 1 and q. from IL for BRAKE. *n.s.,* marked on IL with double dagger. J. smears out caret, probably by mistake.}

~~BRAKE. *n.s.*~~
<3>~~1~~ . <‸**From break**> An instrument for dressing hemp or flax.
<4>~~2~~ . The handle of a ship's pump. **<Dict>**
<5>~~3~~ . A baker's kneading trough. **<Dict>**
<6>~~4~~ . A sharp bit or snaffle for horses. *Dict.*

{J. consolidates two separate entries under one head-word, BRAKE. *n.s.* with six senses.}

BRA'MBLE. *n.s.* {…}
1. This plant hath a flower consisting of five leaves {…}. The species are; ~~1.~~ The ~~common *bramble*, or~~ blackberry bush. ~~2~~. The dewberry bush, ~~or lesser *bramble*. 3.~~ The common greater *bramble* bush, with white fruit. ~~4. The greater bramble bush, with a beautiful~~ striped leaf. ~~5~~. The raspberry bush, or hindberry. ~~6~~. The raspberry bush, with white fruit. ~~7. The raspberry bush, with late red fruit. 8. The raspberry bush, without thorns. 9. The Virginian raspberry bush, with black fruit.~~ The first and second sorts are very common in hedges, and upon dry banks, in most parts of England, and are rarely cultivated in gardens. The third sort was found by Mr. Jacob Bobart in a hedge, not far from Oxford. The fourth sort is a variety of the common *bramble*, differing therefrom only in having striped leaves. The raspberry bush is also very common in divers woods, in the northern counties of England; but is cultivated in all curious gardens for the sake of its fruit. All these plants are easily propagated by suckers, which they send from the roots in great ~~plenty. The best time to take them off, and transplant them, is in October.~~ *Millar.*

{BRAKE. *n.s.* 1.}♦

<a ‡> <1> ~~Brake or~~ fern <**This forms the original signification.**>

This is notoriously discoverable in some differencies of brake or fern Bro. V. E.[1]

The brake & the cockle be noisome too much
Yet like unto boddle no weed there is such
Tuss. Husb. for May[2]

[1] Sir Thomas Browne, *Pseudodoxia Epidemica,* vol. I, bk II, ch. vii, p. 155, ll. 2-3. *1755* NOTORIOUSLY *adv.*

[2] Thomas Tusser, *Husbandry*, 'May', p. 58. Q. also transcribed on IL facing 3H2r to illustrate BODDLE. S-G ('Brake, or fern, Brachans Scottish' written at top, with text from 'Tuss. no. for May' (from editor's notes to Tusser) crossed out). *1755* NOISOME *adj.* (shorter)

{IL facing 3Mv}

{To BRANCH v.a.?}
With the reciprocal pronoun
To distribute itself
The many pairs of nerves distributing and branching themselves to all parts of the body are wonderfull to behold[1]

Brandy-Shop n.s. Brandy & Shop.♦
A public place where brandy is drank and sold
A swinging store to the brandy shop
Shop.[2]

[1] John Ray, *Creation*, pt II, p. 233; no source noted on IL; no S-G slip extant. *1755* PAIR *n.s.* (slightly shorter)

[2] Swift, *Directions to Servants* (*Prose* XIII), p. 43 (Swift reads: 'a swinging Debt to the Ale-wife and the Brandy-shop'). Aman. mistakenly repeats word 'Shop' for 'Swift'. S-G (with 'Swift' as attribution). *1755* TOUPET *n.s.* (very different)

{IL facing 3M2$^{r}$}

**BRA** **BRA**

To BRAND. *v.a.* {...}♦
The spreader of the pardons answered ~~him an easier way,~~ **<Luther>** by *branding* him with heresy. *Atterbury.*

{sig. 3M2$^{r}$}

## BRA

BRASI'L. } *n.s.* An American wood, commonly supposed to have
BRAZI'L. } been thus denominated, because first brought from Brasil: though Huet shews it had been known by that name, many years before the discovery of that country; ~~and the best sort comes from Fernambuc.~~ The tree ordinarily grows in dry barren rocky places, {...} It is used by turners, and takes a good polish; but chiefly in dying, though it gives but a spurious red. *Chamb.*

## BRA

BRA'VERY. *n.s.* {...}
2. Splendour; magnificence.
{...} *Spenser's Hubberd's Tale.*
< ———————— **a** ‡>

{J. keys in Isaiah q. from IL.}

{sig. 3M2v}

<for>
~~Brast part of burst v.n.~~
This for burst is still retaind in Scotland
No gate so strong, no lock so firm & fast
But with that piercing noise flew open
quite or brast
F. Q. 1. 8. 4[1]

{BRA'VERY. *n.s.*}
1 Bravery
We stood bewondered another while delighted
with the rare bravery thereof till seeing streams
of blood we gallop'd towards them to part them
Sidney[2]

{BRA'VERY. *n.s.* 2.}
<**a** ‡>~~6~~The Lord will take away the bravery of ~
Your tinkling Ornaments Isaiah[3]

{BRA'VERY. *n.s.* 5.}
5 Beauty, splendour, delightful charms
How are the glories of the field spun, and
by what pencil are they limn'd in their ~
unaffected bravery. Glanv. Scep[4]

[1] Spenser, *Fairie Queene* (*Works* I), bk I, canto VIII, st. iv, ll. 8-9. J. initially intends to alter note to 'Brast for burst', then crosses out entire addition. S-G. *1755* LOCK *n.s.* 1

[2] Sidney, *Arcadia*, bk II, p. 262. Identical addition under To BEWONDER *v.a.* S-G (Sidney and Isaiah qs. on same slip).

[3] Bible (King James), Isaiah, ch. 3, verse 18. S-G (Sidney and Isaiah qs. on same slip). *1755* MUFFLER *n.s.* (slightly different)

[4] Joseph Glanvill, *Scepsis Scientifica*, ch. vii, § 2, p. 33. S-G. *1755* To LIMN *v.a.*

{IL facing 3M2v}

{BRAWN. *n.s.* 3.}

<‡>

3 This This is his hand
His foot mercurial, his martial thighs
The Brawns of Hercules Shak[1]

{'This' smeared out by amanuensis.}

~~3~~ <4> The flesh of any ~~other~~ Animal <‡>
A Mortress made with the Brawn of
Capons, stampt, strain'd and mingled with like
quantity of Almond butter is excellent to nourish
the weak Bac.[2]

{J. crosses out 'The flesh of any other', then smears out stroke, deleting only 'other'.}

{BRA'WNY. *adj.*}♦
The sharp humour fretted the skin downward
& in process of time became serpiginous and
was covered with white brawny scales.
Wisem.[3]

{To BRAY. *v.n.*}
A gentle hind, whose sides with cruel steel
Through lanced, her bleeding life does rain:
While the sad pang approaching she does feel
Brays out her latest breath & up her eyes doth
seal
F.Q. 2. 1. 39[4]

[1] Shakespeare, *Cymbeline* (**Works* VII), 4.5, p. 321 [4.2.309-11]. S-G. *1755* MERCURIAL *adj.* 1

[2] Bacon, *Natural History* (**Works* III), cent. I, § 48, p. 13 [II, cent. I, § 48, p. 360]. S-G. *1755* MORTRESS *n.s.*

[3] Richard Wiseman, *Eight Chirurgical Treatises*, vol. I, bk I, ch. xvii, p. 134 (Wiseman reads 'branny' for 'brawny'). S-G . *1755* BRANNY *adj.* (shorter), SERPIGINOUS *adj.* (shorter)

[4] Spenser, *Fairie Queene* (*Works* II), bk II, canto I, st. xxxviii, ll, 6-9. S-G. *1755* SEEL *v.a.*

{IL facing 3N^r}

BRA

BRAWL. *n.s.* {...}
Never since that middle summer's spring
Met we on hill, in dale, forest, or mead,
But with thy *brawls* thou hast disturb'd our sport.
*Shakesp.* ~~*Midsummer Night's Dream.*~~

BRAWN. *n.s.* {...}
3. Bulk; muscular strength.
<‡——— > {J. keys in Shakespeare q. from IL.}
{...} *Dryden's Fables.*
<‡——— > {J. keys in new sense 4 from IL.}
~~4~~<5>. The flesh of a boar.

~~5~~<6>. A boar.

BRE

To BRA'ZEN. *v.n.* {...}
When I used to reprimand him ~~for his tricks~~, he would talk saucily, lye, and *brazen* it out, as if he had done nothing amiss.
*Arbuthnot*~~*'s Hist. of J. Bull.*~~

{sig. 3N^r}

BREAD-CORN. *n.s.* {...}

~~When it is ripe,~~ they gather it, and, bruising it among *bread-corn*, ~~they put it up into a vessel,~~ and keep it as food for their slaves. *Broome's ~~Notes~~ on ~~the Odyssey, b. viii.~~*

To BREAK. *v.a.* {...}

13. {...}

A command or call to be liberal, ~~all~~ of a sudden impoverishes the rich, *breaks* the merchant, and shuts up every private man's exchequer. *South.*

{J. apparently crosses out 'command or', then smears out stroke.}

{sig. 3N^v}

---

{BREAD. *n.s.*}

Where mice and rats devour'd poetic bread
And with heroic verse luxuriously were fed
Dry. Juv.[1]

[1] Dryden, 'The Third Satyr of Juvenal' (*Works* IV), ll. 340-1. S-G. *1755* LUXURIOUSLY *adv.*, MOUSE *n.s.*

{IL facing 3N^v}

{To BREAK. *v.a.*}

< —— ‡>

26 break fast
A thousand men have broke their fasts today,
That ne'er shall dine, unless thou yield the Crown
Shak.[1]

34 To break up
He brake up his court and retired himself
his wife and children unto a forrest thereby,
wherein he hath built two fine lodges
Sidney[2]

To break the Ice, a proverbial expression
for to open a way.
Thus I have broke the ice to invention for
the lively representation of floods & rivers ~
necessary for painters and poets Peacham[3]

To break forth
To declare to quit allegiance
The Earl of Desmond before his breaking forth
into rebellion, conveyed secretly all his lands
to Feoffees in trust Spenser[4]

To discompose to interrupt sleep
Lull'd with the sweet nepenthe of a Court
There where no fathers brothers friendships
Once break their rest or stir them from their grace
place
Pope[5]

[1] Shakespeare, *3 Henry VI* (**Works* V), 2.4, p. 141 [2.2.127-28]. S-G. *1755* FAST *n.s.* 1

[2] Sidney, *Arcadia*, bk I, p. 17. S-G. *1755* LODGE *n.s.* 1 (shorter), To RETIRE *v.a.* (shorter)

[3] Henry Peacham, 'The Gentleman's Exercise', bk II, ch. ii, p. 408. S-G. *1755* ICE *n.s.* 3, MASK *n.s.* 5

[4] Spenser, *Ireland* (*Works* IX), ll. 830-32. S-G. *1755* FEOFEE *n.s.*

[5] Pope, 'Epilogue to the Satires. Written in 1738. Dialogue I' (*Poems* IV), ll. 98-100. S-G. *1755* NEPENTHE *n.s.*

{IL facing 3N2r}

**BRE** **BRE**

{To BREAK. *v.a.*}

26. *To break fast.* {...}

< —————— **a ‡>**

{J. keys in Shakespeare q. from IL.}

34. {...}

~~He threatened, that~~ the tradesmen would beat out his teeth, if he did not retire ~~immediately~~, and *break up* the meeting.
*Arbuthnot*~~*'s History of J. Bull.*~~

36. *To break up.* {...}

After taking ~~the strong city of~~ Belgrade, Solyman returning to Constantinople, *broke up* his army, and ~~there~~ lay still ~~the whole year following.~~ *Knolles*~~*'s History of the Turks.*~~

{sig. 3N2r}

## BRE

{To BREAK *v.n.*}

24. *To break up.* {...}

What we obtain by conversation, is oftentimes lost again, as soon as the company *breaks up*, ~~or, at least, when the day va-nishes.~~ *Watts.*

## BRE

BRE'AKFAST. *n.s.* {...}

3. {...}

I lay me down to gasp my latest breath,
The wolves will get a *breakfast* by my death,
Yet scarce enough their hunger to supply. *Dryden.*

{J. crosses out the first line, then smears out stroke.}

BREAST. *n.s.* {...}

1. The middle part of the human body, between the neck and the belly. <——— ‡>

{J. keys in Prior q. from IL.}

2. The dugs or teats of women which contain the milk.
{...} **<Stet>**

{Inking from facing IL has marked this quotation; J. writes 'Stet' to make clear that passage is not to be deleted.}

{sig. 3N2v}

{BREAST. *n.s.*}

2 the breast of Hecuba
When she did suckle Hector lookd not lovelier
Than Hectors foreheard when it spit forth blood
At Grecian swords contending
Shak.[1]

<>

Round their lovely breast & head
Fresh flowers their mingled Odours shed
Prior[2]

[1] Shakespeare, *Coriolanus* (**Works* VI), 1.6, p. 445 [1.3.40-43]. *1755* FOREHEAD *n.s.*, LOVELY *adj.*, To CONTEND *v.n.* 1 (shorter), To SUCKLE *v.a.* (shorter)

[2] Matthew Prior, 'Alma: Or, The Progress of the Mind' (*Works* I), canto II, ll. 413-14. J. mistakenly or inadvertently adds extra vertical stroke to double dagger. S-G. *1755* LOVELY *adj.*

{IL facing 3N2v}

{BREAST. *n.s.*}
2 The breast of Hecuba
When she did suckle Hector lookd not lovelier
Shak[1]

{BREASTED. *adj.* new}
Breasted [breast] **<b ‡>**
Having a breast heart or disposition of any kind
Since you to nonregardance cast my faith
And that I partly know the instrument
That screws me from my true place in your favour
Live you the marble-breasted tyrant still
Shak.[2]

{BREATH. *n.s.*}
Breath in Shakespear is transferd to Suffrage or Vote
Were he to stand for Consul, never would he
Appear in the market place, nor on him put
The hapless Vesture of humility
Nor shewing as the manner is his wounds
To th' people, beg their stinking breaths
Shak. Cor.[3]

{BREATH. *n.s.* 6.}
**<o ‡>**
~~8 Any efflux, any visible emanation~~
Holding the electrick unto the light, many particles thereof will be discharged from it, which motion is performd by the breath of the effluvium issuing with agility: ~~For as the electric cooleth the projection of the atoms ceaseth~~ Bro. V. E.[4]

{To BREATHE. *v.a.*}
3 to nightly trance or breathed spell
Inspires the pale ey'd priest from the prophetic cell Milton[5]

v.a.
4 One strange draught prescribed by Hippocrates for a short breathed man was half a gallon of hydromel with a little vinegar, to be taken at once. This seems to be prescribed as well for exercise as medicine Arbuth.[6]

{To BREATHE. *v.a.* 7.}◆
~~5 v.a.~~ **<‡ c** 7 **To utter vocally>**
The Captives as their tyrant shall require
That they should breath the song & touch the lire
Shall say e'an Jacobs servile race rejoice
Untun'd the music & disus'd the Voice
Prior[7]

Breathful adj. [breath] {new} **<d ‡>**
Odorous strong scented
~~Imbathed balm & cheerful galingale~~
Fresh Costmary & breathful Camomil
~~Dull poppy and drink-quickning~~
Spens.[8]

1 Shakespeare, *Coriolanus* (**Works* VI), 1.6., p. 445 [1.3. 40-41] (see note 1 on IL facing 3N2v). S-G.
2 Shakespeare, *Twelfth Night* (**Works* III), 5.3, p. 197 [5.1.121-124]. S-G. *1755* NON *v.a.*
3 Shakespeare, *Coriolanus* (**Works* VI), 2.6, p. 470 [2.1.232-36]. S-G.
4 Sir Thomas Browne, *Pseudodoxia Epidemica*, vol. I, bk II, ch. iv, ll. 12-17. J. deletes aman.'s def. and reads q. as illustrating existing def. 6. S-G. *1755* PROJECTION *n.s.*
5 Milton, 'On the Morning of Christ's Nativity', st. xix, ll. 179-180. S-G (with 'No' instead of 'To'). *1755* PALEEYED *adj.*
6 John Arbuthnot, 'A Dissertation Concerning the Doses of Medicines given by Ancient Physicians' (*Tables*), p. 291. S-G. *1755* SHORT *adv.* (shorter)
7 Matthew Prior, 'Solomon on the Vanity of the World' (*Works* I), bk III, ll. 810-13. J. reads Prior q. correctly and redirects under new def. 7. S-G. *1755* To UNTUNE *v.a.* 1
8 Spenser, 'Muiopotmos, or The Fate of the Butterflie' (*Works* VIII), ll. 194-96. S-G (final word 'Setuale' in passage on slip illegible and therefore not copied onto IL; slip gives source as 'Spens Muiop'). *1755* CHAMOMILE *n.s.*

BRE´ASTBONE. *n.s.* {...}
{...} *Peacham.*
<**b** ‡————>

{J. keys in new entry for BREASTED *adj.* from IL, but not in correct alphabetical order.}

BRE´ASTKNOT. *n.s.* {...}

Our ladies have still faces, and our men hearts, why may we not hope for ~~the same~~ atchievements from ~~the influence of~~ this *breastknot?* *Addison. Freeholder,* N° 11.

{Inking on entries for BREASTPLATE *n.s.* and BREASTWORK *n.s.* from facing IL.}

BREATH. *n.s.* {...}

BRE

6. Breeze; moving air.

<———— **o** ‡ >

{J. keys in Browne q. from IL.}

To BREATHE. *v.a.* {...}♦

6. To exhale; to send out as breath.
{...} *Milton's Par. Lost.*

<———— ‡ **c** >

{J. keys in new def. 7 and Prior q. from IL.}

~~7~~<8>. To utter privately.

~~8~~<9>. To give air or vent to.

BRE´ATHER. n.s. {...}

3. Inspirer; {...}
{...} *Norris.*

{BRE´ATHFUL. *adj.*}

<———— ‡ **d** >

{J. keys in new entry for BREATHFUL *adj.* with Spenser q. from IL.}

BREECH. *n.s.* {...}
2. {...}

~~Ah! that thy father had been so resolv'd !—~~
—~~That~~ you might still have worn the petticoat,
And ne'er have stoln the *breech* from Lancaster. *Shakespeare.*

{sig. 3O^v}

{blank page}

{IL facing 3O^v}

{BRENT. *adj.*}
Faint, weary, sore, embroiled,
grieved, brent
With heat, toil, wounds, arms smart & fire
F. Q. 1.11.28[1]

{BRE´VITY. *n.s.*}
2 Shortness of breath
Sure he means brevity
in breath short winded
Shak.[2]

{To BREW. *v.a.*}
2 Winds that tempests brew
When through Arabian groves they take their flight
Made wanton with rich odours, lose their spite
Dryd[3]

[1] Spenser, *Fairie Queene* (*Works* I), bk I, canto XI, st. xxviii, ll. 1-2. S-G.
[2] Shakespeare, *2 Henry IV* (**Works* IV), 2.5, p. 234 [2.2.124-125]. S-G. *1755* SHORTWINDED *adj.*
[3] Dryden, 'Astræa Redux' (*Works* I), ll. 269-01. S-G. *1755* FLIGHT *n.s.* 3

{IL facing 3O2r}

**BRE** **BRI**

BRI´BERY. *n.s.* {...}
There was a law made by the Romans, against the *bribery* and extortion of the governours of provinces: before, says Cicero, the governours did bribe ~~and extort as much as was sufficient~~ for themselves; but now they bribe ~~and extort~~ as ~~much as may be enough not~~ only for themselves, but for judges, ~~jurors, and magistrates.~~ *Bacon.*

{sig. 3O2r}

## BRI

BRI´DAL. *n.s.* {...}

{...} *Dryden.*

<‡ ———————— >

{J. keys in new entry for BRIDALTEE or BRIDALTY *n.s.* from IL.}

## BRI

BRIDGE. *n.s.* {...}

2. The upper part of the nose.

< ———————— **a** ‡>

{J. keys in Shakspeare q. from IL.}

BRIEF. *adj.* {...}

1. {...}

I must begin with rudiments of art,
To teach you gamut in a *briefer* sort,
~~More pleasant, pretty, and effectual.~~ *Shakesp. Tam. Shrew.*

{sig. 3O2v}

<‡>

Bridalte **<or Bridalty>** } n.es. ~~Bridal~~ **<Wedding>**

At Quintin he
In honour of this bridaltee
Hath challeng'd either wide Countee
B. Johns. Underw.[1]

{Aman. begins to write 'ne{?}', perhaps for 'new', then smears out 'e' and alters to 'n.s.'}

{BRIDGE. *n.s.* 2.}

**<a ‡>**

~~2~~ Down with the nose
Down with it flat, take the bridge quite away
Shak. T. A[2]

{To BRIDLE. *v.a.*}◆

v.a.

To restrain the flux of humour
Both bodies are clammy and bridle the
Deflux to the hurting without penning them
in too much Bac.[3]

[1] Ben Jonson, 'The King's Entertainment at Welbeck' (*Works* VII), ll. 164-166. S-G. *1755* CUT *n.s.* 14, QUINTIN *n.s.*

[2] Shakespeare, *Timon of Athens* (**Works* VI), 4.6, p. 213 [4.3.157-8]. S-G. *1755* To FORFEND *v.a.* 2, NOSE *n.s.* (shorter), To SMELL *v.n.* (shorter)

[3] Bacon, *Natural History* (**Works* III), cent. VII, § 677, p. 133 [II, cent.VII, § 677, p. 550]. S-G (with 'deflux of humours to the hurting'). *1755* CONGLUTINATION *n.s.* (different)

{IL facing 3O2v}

{To BRI´GHTEN. *v.a.* 6.}

<‡>

6 To excite, to rub up, in allusion to polishing.
This faith must be not only living, but lively,
it must be brightend and stirred up & put into
a posture by a particular exercise of the Several
Virtues requisite to a due performance of this
duty South[1]

[1] South, 'Sermon XX' (**Twelve Sermons* 1694), p. 378. S-G. *1755* LIVELY *adj.* (slightly shorter), SPECIFICALLY *adv.* (slightly shorter)

{IL facing 3Pr}

## BRI

To BRI´GHTEN. *v.a.* {…}

5. To make acute, or witty.

<‡——————— >

{J. keys in new def. 6 and South q. from IL.}

## BRI

BRI´MFUL. *adj.* {…}

Her *brimful* eyes, that ready stood,
~~And only wanted will to weep a flood,~~
Releas'd their watry store. *Dryden's Fables.* <**d**>

{J. makes deletion sign then smears it out, yet leaves line of print crossed out.}

{sig. 3Pr}

{Ink marks in this column result of inking from facing IL.}

To BRING. *v.a.* {...}

4. {...}

{Lines across Locke q. result of bleeding through from recto of printed leaf.}



12. *To bring about.* {...}

This turn of mind ~~threw off the oppositions of envy and competition; it~~ enabled him to gain the most vain and impracticable into his designs, and to *bring about* several great events, for the advantage of the publick. *Addison's Freeholder.*

13. *To bring forth.* {...}

~~Bellona leads thee to thy lover's hand,~~
Another queen *brings forth* another brand,
To burn with foreign fires her native land!

*Dryden, Æneid* vii. *l.* 444.

{J. crosses out the bracket that marks the q. as a triplet.}

21. *To bring out.* {...}

{Ink marks result of bleeding through from recto of printed leaf.}

{sig. 3P[v]}

To bring v.a. [from the Noun]
To season, to salt.
This custom of picking out of the sheaves all smutty corn may be saved where the seed was well brin'd; for that takes off all the poor thin corn which produces the smutty ears[1]

{To BRING. *v.a.*}
To bring acquainted
Now we being brought known unto her, the time that we spent in curing some wounds after once we were acquainted she con:tinually haunted us Sidney[2]

To bring. In the following passage the dis:tinction now a days made betwixt bringing from a place and carrying to another is not regarded. Bring is used in both.

he who brought me hither
~~w~~Will bring me hence, no other guide I seek
Parad. reg$^{d}$. 1[3]

To bring to with the reciprocal pronoun
To induce to prevail on
The real or supposed unpleasantness of the actions seems so preposterous a thing to make them:
:selves unhappy in order to happiness, that they do not easily bring themselves to it
Locke[4]

To bring low
To reduce to subject, to take from a former state into another more depressed, to degrade to dispirit.
How comes it then to pass that having been once so low brought & thoroughly subjected, they afterwards lifted up themselves so strongly again Spenser Irl$^{d}$.[5]

To bring to death, to execute publickly
The Earl of Desmond was by false sub:ornation of K. Edw. IV$^{ths}$ Queen brought to his death at most unjustly tho a good subject Spenser[6]

To bring on v.a.◆
To induce as an efficient cause
Men corrupted themselves so monstruously, that the Deity brought on a flood which destroyed the whole earth P. Forbes[7]

To import in a Mercantile sense
As for any Merchandise you have brought
You shall have your return in merchandise gold or silver Bacon[8]

Let him be testimonied in his own bringings forth, and he shall appear a scholar, a states man and a soldier Shak.[9]

To give Opinion or Verdict
He sent letters to the Council, wherin he acknowledged himself much favoured by them in that they had brought his cause fineable
Hayw$^{d}$[10]

1 Thomas Tusser, *Husbandry*, 'August', p. 106 (q. from editor's notes to Tusser). S-G ('Tuss. husb. no.' at end).
2 Sidney, *Arcadia*, bk II, p. 249. S-G ('almost haunted us'). *1755* To HAUNT *v.a.* 1 (different)
3 Milton, *Paradise Regained*, bk I, ll. 335-6. S-G. *1755* HITHER *adv.* 1
4 John Locke, *Essay*, ch. xxi, § 68, pp. 279-80. S-G ('a thing to men to make').
5 Spenser, *Ireland* (*Works* IX), ll. 403-405. S-G ('26' at top). *1755* LOW *adv.* 5 (slightly shorter)
6 Spenser, *Ireland* (*Works* IX), ll. 2034-7. S-G (aman. cannot read word 'Tredagh' on slip and leaves blank on IL). *1755* SUBORNATION *n.s.* (slightly shorter)
7 Duncan Forbes, *Thoughts Concerning Religion*, p. 27. 'P.' probably stands for 'President of the Court of Session'. S-G.
8 Bacon, *New Atlantis* (**Works* III), p. 240 [III, p.135]. S-G. *1755* MERCHANDISE *n.s.* 1, RETURN *n.s.* 5
9 Shakespeare, *Measure for Measure* (**Works* I), 3.6, p. 414 [3.2.144-46]. S-G ('13' at top; with 'be but testimonied'). To TESTIMONY *v.a.*
10 John Hayward, *The Life of King Edward the Sixth*, p. 114. S-G. *1755* FINABLE *adj.*

{IL facing 3P$^{v}$}

{blank page}

{IL facing 3P2r}

**BRI** **BRO**

BRI´STLE. *n.s.* {...}

~~He is covered with hair, and not, as the~~ boar, with *bristles*, ~~which~~ probably spend<s> more upon the same matter which, in other creatures, makes the horns; for *bristles* seem to be nothing else but a horn split into a multitude of little ones. *Grew.*

BRI´STLY. *adj.* {...}

If the eye were so acute as to rival the finest microscope, the sight of our own selves would affright us; the smoothest skin would be beset all over with rugged scales and *bristly* hairs. *Bentley.*

{J. begins to cross out 'rugged scales and', probably to save a line of type, and draws line raising 'Bentley' to line above, then smears out both strokes.}

< | >

{J. draws vertical stroke, purpose unknown, presumably not for compositor.}

{sig. 3P2r}

**BRO**

{Inking on entries BROACHER *n.s.* and BROAD *adj.* from facing IL.}

BROAD. *adj.* {...}
6. Bold; not delicate; not reserved.

**BRO**

{...} *Shakesp. Macbeth*

<———— ‡>

{J. keys in new def. 7 and Milton q. from IL.}

BROAD-LEAVED. *adj.* {...}
Narrow and *broad-leaved* cyprus-grass ~~of the same sort.~~
*Woodward ~~on Fossils.~~*

BRO'ADWISE. *adv.* {...}
If one should, with his hand, thrust a piece of iron *broadwise* against the flat cieling of his chamber, the iron would not fall as long as the ~~force of the hand~~ perseveres to press against it.
Boyle./

{sig. 3P2v}

{BROAD. *adj.*}
<‡>
7 Diffused spread every way
Fame is no plant that grows on mortal soil
Nor in the glistering foil
Set off to th' world, nor in broad rumour lies
Milt[1]

Broad Seal n.s. [broad & Seal]
Patent to which the great Seal of Britain is appended
You will wonder how such an ordinary fellow, as this Mr Wood, could have got his Majestys broad seal Swift[2]

To broaden v.a. [from broad]♦
To make any thing spacious & wide.
'Tis used in Scotland and perhaps in no other place to be found but in the following passage unless he he mistook it for browden'd which in the Scottish dialect denotes louring frightful, alluding to knitting the brows
Whence glaring oft with many a broaden'd Orb
He frights the Nations
Thoms. Aut. 780[3]

Broad fronted [broad & front]
Having a spacious large forehead
broad-fronted Cæsar
When thou wast here above the ground I was a Morsel for a monarch Shak A & Cl.[4]

[1] Milton, 'Lycidas', ll. 78-80. *1755* FOIL *n.s.* 2
[2] Swift, 'A Letter to the Shop-Keepers, Tradesmen, Farmers and Common-People of Ireland' (*Prose* X), p. 4. S-G. *1755* FELLOW *n.s.* 8, ORDINARY *adj.* 3
[3] Thomson, *The Seasons*, 'Autumn', ll. 723-24. *1755* To FRIGHT *v.a.*
[4] Shakespeare, *Antony and Cleopatra* (**Works* VII), 1.6, p. 116 [1.5.29-31]. S-G. *1755* MONARCH *n.s.* 1 (much shorter), MORSEL *n.s.* 1 (much shorter)

{IL facing 3P2v}

To broid *v.n.* [broder fr.]
To be in any winding figure as embroidery
Over the chairs a state of Ivy; which is curiously wrought with silver & silk of divers colours, broiding or binding in the Ivy; ever the work of some of the Daughters
Bac. n. atl.[1]

{BRO´NCHIAL. *adj.*}
~~Bronchial~~ <‡>
~~A scaly fish with a forked tail.~~
The head, **<and>** one of the bronchial fins, ~~& the body with the scales & tail~~, appear ~~all~~ very fair Woodw.[2]

[1] Bacon, *New Atlantis* (**Works* III), p. 248 [III, p. 148]. S-G (aman. superimposes 'i' on 'e' in 'curiously'). *1755* STATE *n.s.* 12 (much shorter)
[2] John Woodward, 'A Catalogue of the Foreign Fossils in the Collection of J. Woodward M. D.' (*Natural History of Fossils* II), pt II, p. 20. S-G.

{IL facing 3Q$^{r}$}

**BRO** **BRO**

BRO´KEN MEAT. {...}
Get ~~three or~~ four chairwomen ~~to attend you constantly~~ in the kitchen, whom you pay ~~at small charges, only~~ with the *broken meat*, a few coals, and ~~all the~~ cinders. *Swift.*

BRO´NCHIAL.
BRO´NCHICK. } *adj.* {...} Belonging to the throat.

< ——————— ‡>

{J. keys in Woodward q. from IL.}

To BROOD. *v.n.* {...}
2. {...}
~~Exalted hence, and drunk with secret joy,~~
Their young succession all their cares employ;
They breed, they *brood*, instruct and educate,
And make provision for the future state. *Dryden's Virgil.*

{sig. 3Q$^{r}$}

**BRO**

BROOM. *n.s.* {...}
2. {...}

~~Not a mouse~~
~~Shall disturb this hallow'd house;~~
I am sent with *broom* before,
To sweep the dust behind the door. *Sh. Midsum. Night's Dr.*

**BRO**

BRO'THER. *n.s.* {...}
2. Any one closely united.
{...} *Shakesp. Henry* V.

<———————— **a** ‡>

{J. keys in Dryden q. from IL.}
3. Any one resembling another in manner, form, or profession.
{...} *Prov.* xviii. 9.

<———————— **b** ‡>

{J. keys in new def. 4 and Bacon q. from IL.}
<5>~~4~~. *Brother* is used, in theological language, for man in general.
BRO'THERHOOD. *n.s.* {...}
2. {...}

There was a fraternity of men at arms, called the *brotherhood* of St. George, ~~erected by parliament, consisting of thirteen the most noble and worthy persons.~~ *Davies on Ireland.*

{sig. 3Q[v]}

{BRO'THER. *n.s.* 2.}

<**a** ‡>

~~3~~ With these I went a brother of the war
Nor idle stood with unassisting hands
When savage beasts and mens more savage bands
Their virtuous toil subdued: Yet these I sway[d] Dryd.[1]

{BRO'THER. *n.s.* 4.}

<**b** ‡>

<4>~~5~~ A member of some particular order who lives under certain rules
~~In either of these ships~~ there should be a mission of the fellows or brethren of Solomons house ~~to give us knowledge of the sciences manufactures and inventions of all the World~~
Bac. N. Atl.[2]

[1] Dryden, 'The First Book of Homer's *Ilias*' (*Works* VII), ll. 379-383. S-G (misbound for BAND). *1755* UNASSISTING *adj.*, To SWAY *v.a.* 3 (slightly different)

[2] Bacon, *New Atlantis* (**Works* III), p. 246 [III, p. 146]. S-G (misbound for 'BRETHREN'; 'fellows' underlined then underlining crossed out). *1755* MISSION *n.s.* 2 (slightly different), FELLOW *n.s.* 10 (shorter)

{IL facing 3Q[v]}

{BRUSH SCYTHE. new}
A brush scythe I take to be an old scythe
to cut up weeds as nettles hemlock &c Tuss. no
A brush sith & grass sith with rifle to stand
Tuss: Hus.[1]

[1] Thomas Tusser, *Husbandry*, 'September', p. 120. S-G.

{IL facing 3Q2ʳ}



BROWSE. *n.s.* {…}
{Vertical strokes the result of inking from facing IL.}

To BRUSH. *v.a.* {…}
2. {…}
His son Cupavo *brush'd* the briny flood,
~~Upon his stern a brawny centaur stood.~~ *Dryden's Æneid.*

{sig. 3Q2ʳ}

BRU

BRU'TAL. *adj.* {...}

1. That which belongs to a brute {...}.

**<a‡** ———————— >

{J. keys in Hale q. from IL.}

BUB

BRY'ONY. *n.s.* {...}

It has a climbing stalk, with spines; the leaves are like those of the vine; the flowers consist of one leaf, which is expanded at the top, and divided into five parts, and, in the female plants, succeeded by round berries, growing on footstalks; the flowers of the male plants have five apices in each, but are barren. ~~The species are, 1. The common white *bryony*. 2. Smooth African *bryony*, with deep cut leaves, and yellow flowers, *&c.* The first sort grows upon dry banks, under hedges, in many parts of England; but may be cultivated in a garden for use, by sowing the berries in the spring of the year, in a dry poor soil.~~ The roots of this plant have been formerly cut into a human shape, and carried about the country, and shewn as mandrakes. *Mill.*

{sig. 3Q2v}

{BRU'TAL. *adj.* 1.}

**<a ‡>**

1 The human body hath preference above
the most perfect brutal nature J. Hale[1]

The Goddess with disdain bestows
Mast & accorns brutal food
Pope[2]

[1] Matthew Hale, *Primitive Origination of Mankind, sect. I, ch. ii, p. 64. 'J.' probably stands for 'Judge' or 'Justice'. S-G. *1755* PREFERENCE *n.s.* 3

[2] Pope, *Odyssey* (*Poems* IX), bk X, ll. 282-283. S-G. *1755* CORNELIAN-TREE *n.s.*

{IL facing 3Q2v}

Bubukle n.s. for bubo or carobuncle.
A word of Shakespears making, if not a mistake for buboile.
His face is all <u>Bubukles</u> & whelks & knobs and flames of fire Shak.[1]

To buck v.n. To be washed in strong lye
Throw foul linnen upon him as if it were going to bucking Shak[2]

5. To buckle v.a
To comprize, to measure the compass of any thing alluding to a belt buckled round ones waste **<o ‡>**

Will you with counters sum
The vast proportion of his infinite
And <u>buckle</u> in a waste most fathomless
With spans & Inches so diminutive
As fears & reasons? Shak[3]

1 Shakespeare, *Henry V* (**Works* III), 3.8, p. 373 [3.6.102-103]. S-G. *1755* WHELK *n.s.* 1
2 Shakespeare, *Merry Wives of Windsor* (**Works* I), 3.9, p. 307 [3.3.130-31]. S-G. *1755* BASKET *n.s.*, LINEN *n.s.*, To BUCK *v.a.*
3 Shakespeare, *Troilus and Cressida* (**Works* VII), 2.3, p. 401 [2.2.28-32]. S-G. *1755* FATHOMLESS *adj.* 2, SPAN *n.s.* 1

{IL facing 3R$^r$}



To BU´CKLE. *v.a.* {…}◆
4. To confine. **<To enclose>**

**<——————————— o ‡>**

{J. keys in Shakespeare q. from IL.}

To BU´CKLE. *v.n.* {…}
2. {…}
~~This is to be done~~ in children, ~~by~~ try~~ing~~ them, when they are by laziness unbent, or by avocation bent another way, and endeavouring to make them *buckle to* the thing proposed. *Locke.*

{sig. 3R$^r$}

BU′CKSHORN PLANTAIN. *n.s.* {...}

It agrees in flower and fruit with the plantain; but its leaves are deeply cut in on the edges; whereas the leaves of the plantain are either entire, or but slightly indented. ~~The species are~~ four; 1. ~~Garden *buckshorn plantain*,~~ or hartshorn, *&c.* The first species, though entitled a garden plant, yet is found wild upon most commons, and barren heaths; where, from the poorness of the soil, it appears to be very different from the garden kind, as being little more than a fourth part so large. This species was formerly cultivated in gardens as a salad herb, but, ~~at present, is little regarded, and wholly disused.~~ *Miller.*

BU′CKTHORN. *n.s.* {...}

It hath a funnel-shaped flower {...} a soft roundish berry, very full of juice, inclosing four hard seeds. ~~The species are, Common purging *buckthorn*. 2. Lesser purging *buckthorn*. 3. *Buckthorn*, with long spines, and a white bark of Montpelier. The first of~~ these trees ~~is~~ **<are>** very common in hedges; {...} for these have commonly four. ~~The second sort is less c~~ommon in England. Both these sorts may be propagated, by laying down their tender branches in autumn. The first sort will grow to the height of eighteen or twenty feet; the second sort sel~~dom rises above eight fee~~t high. They may also be propagated ~~by seeds.~~ *Miller.*

BU′CKWHEAT. *n.s.* {...}

The flowers grow in a spike {...} the seeds are black, and three cornered. ~~The species are, 1. Common upright *buckwheat*. 2. Common creeping *buckwheat*. The first is~~ **<It is>** cultivated in England, and is a great improvement to dry barren lands. ~~The second grows wild, and is seldom cultivated.~~ *Miller.*

{sig. 3R$^{v}$}

{To BUD. *v.n.*}
Applied to light

let truth be
Ne'er so far distant, yet chronology
Will have a perspicil to find her out
Discern the dawn of her eternal day
As when the rosy morn buds into day
Crashaw[1]

[1] Richard Crashaw, 'On the Frontispiece of Isaacson's Chronologie explained' ('Or Thus'), p. 491. See To BLOSSOM *v.n.* in 'Notes on selected changes and annotations'. S-G (with 'eternal ray' instead of 'eternal day'). *1755* PERSPICIL *n.s.*

{IL facing 3R$^{v}$}

{BUG. *n.s.*}

<‡>

What hinder'd? Did fear of envy, distrust
of want? Alas what bugs are these to
fright men from heaven
Bp. Hall to Sutton[1]

Builded partt. pass. of build
Antony
Let not the piece of virtue which is set
As the cement of our love,
To keep it builded be the ram to batter
The fortress of it Shak[2]

{To BUILD. *v.a.*}
3 To build to compose, to frame any intellectual piece
Who would not sing for Lycidas he knew
Himself to sing & build the lofty rhyme
Milton[3]

{BUI'LDER. *n.s.* 2.}
~~2 The materials for building~~ <‡ **d** >
Oak Cedar and chesnut are the best
builders and some for piers
Bacon[4]

[1] Joseph Hall, 'Epistles upon different Subjects' ('To Mr. Thomas Sutton'), p. 544. S-G.
[2] Shakespeare, *Antony and Cleopatra* (**Works* VII), 3.2, p. 152 [3.2.27-31]. S-G. Aman. superimposes 'd' on 't' in 'build'. RAM *n.s.* 2 (slightly shorter), CEMENT *n.s.* 2 (shorter)
[3] Milton, 'Lycidas', ll. 10-11. S-G. *1755* RHYME *n.s.* 3, LOFTY *adj.* 2 (shorter)
[4] Bacon, *Natural History* (**Works* III), cent. VII, § 658, p. 129 [II, cent. VII, § 658, p. 543]. S-G. *1755* PIER *n.s.*

{IL facing 3R2ʳ}

## BUI

{Inking at top of column from facing IL.}

BUG. } *n.s.* {…}
BU'GBEAR. }
{…} *Shakesp.*
<A‡ ———— >
{J. keys in Hall q. from IL.}

BU'GLE. *n.s.* {…} A plant.
~~It hath a flower consisting of one leaf, divided into three~~ parts; out of the flower-cup arises the pointal, fixed like a nail, attended by four embryos, which become so many oblong seeds, shut up in a husk; the flowers are placed in whorles round the stalk. The species are, 1. Common *bugle*. 2. The greatest *bugle* of the Alps. 3. Hairy eastern *bugle*, with an inverted blue flower, spotted with white. 4. Eastern *bugle*, with a purplish violet coloured flower, *&c.* The first and second sorts grow wild in moist woods and meadows, and continue in flower from May to September. The *bugle* is greatly esteemed as a vulnerary herb, and is used both externally and internally. They ~~are very hardy plants, and propagate greatly~~ by their ~~trailing stalks.~~ *Miller.*
{Cross-outs unintentionally smeared; cross-out over entries BUGLE. *n.s.* ('A sort of wild ox') and BUGLOSS unintentional.}

## BUL

BUI'LDER. *n.s.* [from *build*] <‸1> He that builds; {…}
{…} *Prior.*
<———— **2 Something useful in building d** ‡>

{J. keys in Bacon q. from IL.}

{sig. 3R2ʳ}

BULL. *n.s.* {...}

1. {...}

A ~~proper~~ gentlewoman, Sir, and a kinswoman of my master's.—~~Even~~ such kin as the parish heifers are to the town *bull*.

*Shakesp.* ~~*Henry* IV. *p.* ii.~~

{...}

The trebler herds,
Where round the lordly *bull*, in rural ease,
They ruminating lie. *Thomson's Summer, l.* 920.

{Inking on entry for BULL-DOG *n.s.* from facing IL.}



BU'LLET. *n.s.* {...} <^ ^1> A round ball of metal, usually shot out of guns.

{...} *Dryden.*

<———————— ‡>

{J. keys in new def. 2 and Swift q. from IL.}

{sig. 3R2^v}

---

{BULK. *n.s.*}
6 Enormity
That they are sins of no small bulk,
none can doubt that observes Heresy is
rankd with Idolatry Witchcraft & Hatred
D. Piety[1]

{BU'LLET. *n.s.*}♦
<‡ 2> 2 A play at bowls called long bullets.
When at long bullets Paddy long did play
You sat and lous'd him all the sun shine day
Swift[2]

{To BU'LLY. *v.n.*}
v.n.
He began to leave off his roaring & bullying
about the streets, he put on a serious air.
Arb. J. Bull[3]

1 [Richard Allestree?], *Decay of Piety*, ch. xvii, p. 385. S-G. *1755* To RANK *v.a.* 2 (much shorter)
2 Swift, 'A Pastoral Dialogue' (*Poems* III), ll. 33-4. S-G. *1755* To LOUSE *v.a.* (shorter)
3 John Arbuthnot, 'Lewis Baboon Turned Honest' (*John Bull*), ch. iv, p.109. S-G. *1755* To LEAVE *off v.a.* 13

{IL facing 3R2^v}

{BUMPING *n.s.* new}
That a Bittern maketh that mugient noise,
or <u>bumping</u>, by putting its bill into a reed, or as
Aldrovandus conceives, by putting the same in
water or mud, and after a while retaining the
air, by suddenly excluding it again, is not ~
easily made out Bro. V. E. 3. 26.[1]

[1] Sir Thomas Browne, *Pseudodoxia Epidemica*, vol. I, bk III, ch. xxvii, ll. 7-11. S-G (aman. writes 'Bitter a kind', then changes to 'That a Bitter maketh that mugient noise'). *1755* MUGIENT *adj.* (slightly shorter)

{IL facing 3S$^{r}$}



BU'LWARK. *n.s.* {...}
1. {...}
Our naval strength is a general *bulwark* to the ~~British~~ nation.
*Addison's ~~Freeholder, N$^{o}$ 42.~~*

BUM. *n.s.* {...}
1. {...}
~~This said,~~ he gently rais'd the knight,
And set him on his *bum* upright. *Hudibras.*

BU'MBARD. *n.s.* {...}
1. {...}
Yond same black cloud, yond huge one looks
Like a foul *bumbard*, that would shed his liquour.
*Shakesp. ~~Tempest.~~*

BU'MBAST. *n.s.* [falsely written for *bombast*; ~~the etymology of which I am now very doubtful of~~; *bombast* and *bombasine* ~~being~~ <are> mentioned, with great probability, by *Junius*, as coming from *boom*, a tree, and *sein*, silk; the silk or cotton of a tree.]♦

To BU'NDLE. *v.a.* {...}
We ~~ought to~~ put things together, ~~as well~~ as we can, ~~*doctrinæ causâ*;~~ but, after all, several things will not be *bundled up* together, under our terms and ways of speaking. *Locke.*

{sig. 3S$^{r}$}

BU´NGLER. *n.s.* {...}

Painters, at the first, were such *bunglers*, and so rude, that, when they drew a cow or a hog, they were fain to write over the head what it was; ~~otherwise the beholder knew not what to make of it.~~ *Peacham on Drawing.*

{Vertical lines across entries for To BUNT. *v.n.*, BUNTER *n.s.*, BUNTING *n.s.* result of inking from facing IL.}

BU´RDEN. *n.s.* {...}♦

3. A birth: now obsolete.

{...} *Shakesp.*

< ——————— **b** ‡>

{J. keys in Prior q. from IL.}

To BU´RDEN. *v.a.* [from the noun.] **<1 ∧1>** To load; to incumber.♦

{...} *Cor.* viii. 13.

**<2 To freight.>** < ——————— **c** ‡>

{J. keys in Dryden q. from IL under new def. 2.}

BU´RDENOUS. *adj.* {...}

1. Grievous; oppressive; wearisome. **<antiquated>**

BU´RGAGE. *n.s.* {...}

The gross of the borough is surveyed together ~~in the beginning of the county;~~ but there are some other particular *burgages* thereof, mentioned under ~~the titles of~~ particular mens possessions. *Hale's Origin of Mankind.*

{sig. 3S$^v$}

---

{To BU´RDEN. *v.a.* 2.}

~~Burdened. Adj. [from burden]~~

<c ‡> ~~Carying a burden or fraught~~

In burden'd Vessels first with speedy care
His plenteous stores do seasond timber send

Dry. A. M.[1]

{BU´RDEN. *n.s.* 3.}♦

Ews that erst brought forth but single lambs
<**b** ‡>Now drop'd their two-fold burdens Prior.[2]
Sh[3]

{BU´RDENOUS. *adj.*}♦

3 She hath the bones broke of eternal night
Her soul unbodied of the burdenous corpse

Spens.[4]

3 Weighty, unwieldy.

To what a cumbersome unwieldiness
And burdenous Corpulence my love had ~~grow~~ grown
But what I did to make it less
Give it a Diet made it feed upon
That which love worst endures, Discretion

Donne.[5]

[1] Dryden, 'Annus Mirabilis' (*Works* I), ll. 565-6. S-G. *1755* CARPENTER *n.s.*, To SEASON *v.a.* 5 (shorter)

[2] Matthew Prior, 'The Second Hymn of Callimachus. To Apollo' (*Works* I), ll. 63-64. S-G ('3' superimposed on '4' at top of slip). *1755* TWOFOLD *adj.*

[3] Aman. begins writing Spenser q. illustrating BURDENOUS, then smears out letters, re-writing q. so as to correspond to the appropriate part of the printed text on facing page.

[4] Spenser, *Shepheardes Calendar* (*Works* VII), 'November', ll. 165-66. S-G. *1755* UNBODIED *adj.* 2

[5] John Donne, 'Loves Diet', ll. 3-6. S-G ('But that' instead of 'But what'). *1755* CORPULENCE *n.s.* (much shorter), UNWIELDINESS *n.s.* (much shorter)

{IL facing 3S$^v$}

{BU´RIAL. *n.s.*}
The <u>Burial</u> must be by the smallness of the proportion, as fifty to one, which will be but sixpence gain in fifty shillings; or it must be holpen by somewhat which may fix the silver, never to be restored or vapor'd away when incorporated into such a mass of gold
Bacon[1]

{To BURN. *v.n.*}
To kill
The maieweed doth <u>burn</u> & the thistle doth fret
The fitches pull downward both rie and the wheat
Tuss. husb. May
Mayweed is like camomile, but a filthy Stinking weed & burns, that is kills all the Corn near it. Tuss. notes[2]

{To BURN. *v.a.?*}
She spited with great courtesy that one that did nothing should be able to resist her, <u>burned</u> away with choler any notions that might grow out of her sweet Disposition Sidney.[3]
{To BURN. *v.n.*}
5. To shine as fire
The knights with their bright burning blades
Broke their rude troops & orders did confound
Hewing and slashing. F.Q. 2. 9. 15[4]

[1] Bacon, 'Physiological Remains' (**Works* III), p. 212 [III, pp. 802-3]. S-G ('a chemical incorporation' at top of slip). *1755* TO *preposition* 9 (shorter), To VAPOUR *v.a.* (much shorter)
[2] Thomas Tusser, *Husbandry*, 'May', p. 58. S-G (both qs. on same slip). *1755* MAY-WEED *n.s.*
[3] Sidney, *Arcadia*, bk II, pp. 196-97. S-G. A second S-G slip exists for this passage with text as follows: 'v.a. 3 To conform by any passion; to destroy/ Zelmane spited that one that did nothing should be able to resist her burned away with choler any motions which might grow out of her own disposition Sidney 2'. *1755* To SPITE *v.a.* 2 (slightly different)
[4] Spenser, *Fairie Queene* (*Works* II), bk II, canto IX, st. xiv, ll. 6-8. S-G ('v.n.' at top of slip). *1755* To SLASH *v.n.*

{IL facing 3S2^r}

**BUR**

BURLE´SQUE. *adj.* {…}

Homer, in his character of Vulcan and Thersites, in his story of Mars and Venus, in his behaviour of Irus, ~~and in other passages,~~ has ~~been observed to have~~ lapsed into the *burlesque* character, and ~~to have~~ departed from that serious air, which seems essential to the magnificence of an epick poem.
*Addison.* ~~*Spectator,* N° 279.~~

BU´RLY. *adj.* {…}

**BUR**

Her husband, it seems, being a very *burly* man, ~~she thought~~ it would be less trouble for her to bring away little Cupid.
*Addison.* ~~*Spectator,* N° 499.~~

{sig. 3S2^r}

BU'RR *Pump.* {...}

{...} *Harris.*

<c ‡ ———— >

{J. apparently keys in new entry for BURRANET from IL, then smears out marginal key. Unclear whether insertion is ultimately intended.}

BU'RREL *Fly.* {...}

{...} *Dict.*

<b ‡———— >

{J. keys in Derham q. from IL.}

BU'RROW, BERG, BURG, BURGH. *n.s.* {...}

2. {...}

When they shall see his crest up again, ~~and the man in blood~~, they will out of their *burrows*, like conies after rain, and revel all with him. *Shakesp. Coriolanus.*

To BU'RROW. *v.n.* {...}

Little sinuses ~~would~~ often form, and *burrow* underneath. *Sharp's ~~Surgery.~~*



BUSH. *n.s.* {...}

1. {...}

The poller, and exactor of fees, justifies the resemblance of the courts of justice to the *bush*, whereunto while the sheep flies ~~for defence~~ from the weather, he is sure to lose part of the fleece. *Bacon's ~~Essays, N°-47.~~*

{...}

~~The sacred ground~~
~~Shall weeds and pois'nous plants refuse to bear;~~
Each common *bush* shall Syrian roses wear. *Dryden's Virg.*

{sig. 3S2v}

{BURNT. [*particip. pass.* of *burn*]}
Choose skilfully Saltfish not burnt at the Stone
Byuy such as be good or else let it alone
Tuss. Husb.
By burnt to the stone I understand as is
dried on the beach in too hot weather, ~
whereby it loses its whiteness & is apt to have
a rank smell Tuss no.[1]

Burranet n.s. a sea bird
Amongst the first sort we reckon ~
Pewets, Meaws, murrs creyfers and
Burranets Carew[2]

{BURRAGE. *n.s.* new}
If in the must of wine or wort of beer,
while it worketh before it be tunn'd, the
burrage stay a small time, & be chang'd
with fresh, it is a sovereign drink for ~
Melancholy Bac.[3]

{BU'RREL *Fly. n.s.*} <———— b ‡>
The whame or burrel fly is vexatious
to horses in summer, not by stinging them,
but only by their bombylous noise or
tickling them in sticking their nits or
eggs on the hair
Derh. ph. Theo.[4]

{To BU'RY. *v.a.*}
In 1578 was that famous lammas day which
buried the reputation of Don Jhohn of
Austria Bac. Spain[5]

1 Thomas Tusser, *Husbandry*, 'August', p. 107. Smearing of J.'s cross-out lines probably unintentional. S-G (both qs. on same slip; 'I understand such fish as is dried').

2 Richard Carew, *Survey of Cornwall*, bk I, [35]. J. deletes proposed entry for BURRANET. *n.s.* and apparently smears his cross-outs as if to restore proposed entry; however, the entry is not keyed in to printed text. Marginal key 'c ‡' on 3S2v, smeared out, was probably original key for passage. J.'s final intention unclear. S-G ('creyser' instead of 'creyfer'). *1755* MURRE *n.s.* (slightly shorter), PEWET *n.s.* (slightly shorter), PUFFIN *n.s.* (slightly shorter), WIDGEON *n.s.* (slightly shorter)

3 Bacon, *Natural History* (**Works* III), cent. I, § 18, p. 4 [II, cent. I, § 18, p. 345]. S-G. *1755* MUST *n.s.* (slightly shorter), To TUN *v.a.* (slightly shorter), WORK *n.s.* (slightly shorter), WORT *n.s.* (slightly shorter)

4 William Derham, *Physico-Theology*, § 2, p. 248, note k. Same q. on IL facing 3Iv to illustrate BOMBILIOUS *adj.* S-G. *1755* WHAME *n.s.* (slightly shorter)

5 Bacon, 'Considerations Touching a War with Spain' (**Works* III), p. 522 [XIV, p. 483]. S-G. *1755* LAMMAS *n.s.*

{IL facing 3S2v}

{BU´SINESS. *n.s.*}

<—— **1 State of being busy**>

~~10 A fantastic unnecessary intermeddling,~~
~~in the same sense with busy body & is still~~
~~retaind in Scotland~~

He with no more civility, tho with much more
<u>business</u> than those under fellows had shewd
began in a captious manner to put interrogatories
unto him Sidney[1]

[1] Sidney, *Arcadia*, bk II, p.169. S-G. *1755* INTERROGATORY *n.s.*, UNDERFELLOW *n.s.*

{IL facing 3T^r}

## BUS

BU´SHMENT. *n.s.* {…}

Princes thought how they might discharge the earth of woods, briars, *bushments,* and waters, to make it ~~more~~ habitable ~~and fertile~~. *Raleigh's ~~History of the World.~~*

BU´SINESS. *n.s.* {…}

<————> {J. keys in new def. 1 and Sidney q. from IL.}

<2>~~1~~. Employment; multiplicity of affairs.

<3>~~2~~. An affair. {…}

<&c>

{J.'s 'etcetera' indicates that all following senses should be renumbered sequentially.}

To BU´SS. *v.a.* {…}

~~Yonder walls, that partly front your town,~~
Yond towers, whose wanton tops do *buss* the clouds,
Must kiss their feet. *Shakesp. Troilus and Cressida.*

{sig. 3T^r}

## BUT

BUT. *conjunct.* {...}

## BUT

14. Otherwise than. **<little in use>**

15. Even; not longer ago than. **<Not more than>**

18. But for; without; {...}
{J. ital. 'But for'.}

{Vertical stroke on this page is result of inking from facing IL.}

{sig. 3T^v}

---

{To BUTT. *v.a.*}◆
2 To push, to run against with any thing flat
If I join but with the words in construction and sense, as but I will not, a butt of wine, the ram will but, shoot at but, the meaning of it will be ready to you.
Holder Sp.[1]

{BUTT. *n.s.*}
Butt a certain measure containing Liquor
When the Butt is out we will drink water
See also Holder under But, boundary[2]

{To BU'TTER. *v.a.*}
~~Fortunes displeasure is but sluttish, if it smell so strongly as thou speakst of, I will henceforth eat no fish of~~ fortunes buttering.
Shak[3]

[1] William Holder, *Elements of Speech*, pp. 122-23. S-G ('but' underlined in 'ram will but'; this and following passage on same slip). Passage mistakenly copied here instead of on IL facing 3T2^r opposite entry To BUTT *v.a. 1755* BUT *n.s.*
[2] Shakespeare, *Tempest* (*Works I), 3.2. p. 51 [3.2.1-2]. S-G (this and previous passage on same slip). Passage mistakenly copied here instead of on IL facing 3T2^r opposite entry BUTT *n.s. 1755* OUT *adv.* 9
[3] Shakespeare, *All's Well that Ends Well* (*Works III), 5.2, p. 97 [5.2.6-8]. Passage mistakenly copied here instead of on IL facing 3T2^r opposite entry To BUTTER *v.a.*; passage recopied on IL in correct place. S-G ('1. v.a.' at top of slip). *1755* SLUTTISH *adj.*

{IL facing 3T^v}

{To BUT. *v.n.* new}
Any thing that strikes in to another abuts or is
is directed in some kind of angle into it
The fen and quamire so marish by kind
  And are to be drained
Which yearly undrained & suffered uncut
 Annoieth the Meadows that thereon do <u>but</u>
Tuss. Husb. for May.[1]

{BU′TLERAGE. *n.s.*}
Prisage now called <u>butlerage</u> is a custom <———>
whereby the Prince challenges out of every
Bark loaden with wine containing less than
forty tuns two tons of wine at his price
Cowel[2]

{To BU′TTER. *v.a.*}
Fortunes displeasure is but slutish, if it
Smell so strongly as thou speakst of: I will
henceforth eat no fish of fortunes <u>buttering</u>
Shak.[3]

[1] Thomas Tusser, *Husbandry*, 'May', p. 61 (Tusser reads 'and are to drained, now win to thy mind'). S-G ('To but. v.n.' at top). *1755* MARISH *adj.* (much shorter), QUAGMIRE *adj.* (much shorter)

[2] John Cowell, *Interpreter*, sig. Eee4$^{v}$. Smearing of cross-out stroke probably accidental, as q. is not keyed in to printed text. However, the horizontal line after 'custom' may indicate J.'s intention to include passage. S-G. PRISAGE *n.s.*

[3] Shakespeare, *All's Well that Ends Well* (*Works III), 5.2, p. 97 [5.2.6-8]. Passage recopied from IL facing 3T$^{v}$ (see n. 3 on that page).

{IL facing 3T2$^{r}$}

## BUT

BUTCHERS-BROOM, ~~or KNEEHOLLY.~~ *n.s.* {…} <∧
**Kneeholly; a plant.>**

The flower-cup consists of one leaf, cut into several divisions, out of which is produced a globular bell-shaped flower, consisting also of one leaf, in the center of which rises the pointal, which afterwards becomes a soft roundish fruit, in which are inclosed one or two hard seeds. ~~It is very common in the woods, in divers parts of England, and is rarely cultivated in gardens. The roots are sometimes used in medicine, and~~ the green shoots are cut and bound into bundles, and sold to the butchers, who use it as besoms to sweep their blocks; from whence it had the name ~~of *butchers-broom.*~~ *Millar.*

{J. crosses out 'and b' in line 8, then smears out stroke to retain coherence.}

BU′TCHERLINESS. *n.s.* {…} ~~In a butcherly manner.~~ **<Brutality; cruelty; grossness.>**

{Inking in entry for BU′TCHERY *n.s.* from facing IL.}

BU′TMENT. *n.s.* {…}

The supporters or *butments* of the ~~said~~ arch cannot suffer so much violence, as in the ~~precedent~~ flat posture. *Wotton.*

## BUT

BU′TTERBUR. *n.s.* {…}

It is a plant with a flosculous flower, consisting of many florets, {…} and the flowers appear before the leaves. ~~It is used in medicine, and grows wild in great plenty by the sides of ditches.~~ *Millar.*

BU′TTERMILK. *n.s.* {…}

A young man, ~~who was~~ fallen into an ulcerous consumption, devoted himself to *buttermilk*, by which sole diet he recovered. *Harvey on Consumptions.*

BU′TTERTOOTH. *n.s.* {…} The great broad foret~~ee~~**<oo>**th.

{sig. 3T2$^{r}$}

BUX

BU'TTON. *n.s.* {...}

1. {...}

~~I mention those ornaments~~ <**Their cloaths**>, because, of the simplicity of the shape, want of ornaments, *buttons*, loops, gold and silver lace, they must have been cheaper than ours. *Arbuthnot on Coins.*

{Vertical lines and spotting on this page result of inking from facing IL.}

To BU'TTRESS. *v.a.*

<**b** ‡———— > {J. keys in new def. and Tusser q. from IL.}

BU'XOM. *adj.* {...}

BUZ

2. Gay; lively; brisk.

{...} *Milton.*

<———— **c** ‡>

{J. keys in Dryden q. from IL.}

{Inking on this page from IL.}

{sig. 3T2v}

<**b** ‡>

<**Buttrice ns A kind of cutting in strument with which the hoofs of horses are pared**>

A buttrice & pincers, & hammer & nail

Tuss. husb.[1]

{BU' XOM. *adj.* 2.}

<**c** ‡>

When <**yet**> the world was buxome fresh & young
Her sons were undebauchd & therefore strong

Dryd. Juv.[2]

{To BUY. *v.a.*}

To procure

his possessions
Altho' by confiscation they are ours
We do instate & widow you with all
To buy you a better husband

Shak: M.M.[3]

To buy of

and I bought the field of Hanameel

Jer. 32.9[4]

[1] Thomas Tusser, *Husbandry*, 'September', p. 116. S-G. *1755* SIZERS *n.s.*

[2] Dryden, 'The Sixth Satyr of Juvenal' (*Works* IV), ll. 16-7. S-G ('brisk; fresh' at top, with spelling 'bucksome'; misbound for 'brisk'). *1755* UNDEBAUCHED *adj.* ('bucksome' for 'buxome')

[3] Shakespeare, *Measure for Measure* (**Works* I), 5.6, p. 453 [5.1.422-24]. S-G. *1755* To WIDOW *v.a.* 2, To INSTATE *v.a.* (shorter).

[4] Bible (King James), Jeremiah, ch. 32, v. 9. S-G.

{IL facing 3T2v}

{blank page}

{IL facing 3U[r]}

## BY

BY. *prep.* {...}

6. {...}

The captains were obliged to break that piece of ordnance, and so *by* pieces to carry it away, ~~that the enemy should not get so great a spoil.~~ *Knolles's History of the Turks.*

{...}

~~Others will soon take pattern and encouragement by your building; and so~~ house *by* house, street *by* street, there will at last be finished a magnificent city. *Sprat.*

8. At, or in; noting place.

{...}

Arms, and the man, I sing, who forc'd *by* fate,
Expell'd, and exil'd, left the Trojan shore;
Long labours both *by* sea and land he bore. *Dryden's Æn.*

{J. crosses out 'Arms, and the man, I sing, who', then smears out stroke; J. removes italics from '*by*' in first line.}

## BY

12. From; noting judgment or token.

Thus, *by* the musick, we may know,
When noble wits a hunting go,
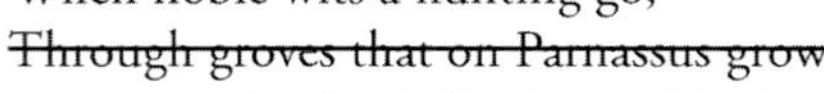
~~Through groves that on Parnassus grow.~~ *Waller.*

{J. crosses out bracket indicating a triplet.}

{...}

The punishment is not to be measured *by* the greatness or smallness of the matter, but *by* the opposition it carries, ~~and stands in,~~ to ~~that respect and submission that is due to~~ the father. *Locke*

15. For; noting continuance of time. {...}

Ferdinand and Isabella recovered ~~the kingdom of~~ Granada from the Moors; having been in possession thereof *by* the space of seven hundred years. *Bacon's Henry* VII.

16. As soon as; {...}

Hector, *by* the fifth hour of the sun,
Will, with a trumpet, 'twixt our tents and Troy,
Tomorrow morning call some knight to arms.
*Shakesp.* ~~*Troilus and Cressida.*~~

{...}

*By* the beginning of the fourth century from the building of Rome, the tribunes proceeded ~~so far, as~~ to ~~accuse and~~ fine the consuls. *Swift.*/

17. Beside; noting passage.

Many beautiful places ~~standing~~ along the sea-shore, make the town appear ~~much~~ longer ~~than it is,~~ to those that sail *by* it. *Addison on Italy.*/

18. Beside; near to; {...}

~~Here he comes himself;~~
If he be worth any man's good voice,
That good man sit down *by* him. *Ben. Johnson's Catiline.*

{sig. 3U[r]}

{BY. *prep.*}
22. {…}

Which, O! avert *by* yon etherial light,
~~Which I have lost for this eternal night;~~
Or if, by dearer ties, you may be won,
*By* your dead fire, and *by* your living son. *Dryden's Æn.*

BY. *adv.* {…}
2. {…}

I did hear
The galloping of horse. Who was't came *by?*
*Shakesp.* ~~*Macbeth.*~~

**13 JA 54**
{BL accession number in red ink.}

BY. *n.s.* {…}

In this instance, there is, upon the *by*, to be noted, the percolation of the verjuice through the wood.
*Bacon's* ~~*Natural History,* N° 79.~~

{…}

So, while my lov'd revenge is full and high,
I'll give you back your kingdom by the *by*.
*Dryden's* ~~*Conquest of Granada.*~~



BY-COFFEEHOUSE. *n.s.* {…}

I afterwards entered a *by-coffeehouse,* ~~that stood~~ at the upper end of a narrow lane, ~~where I met with a nonjuror~~.
*Addison.* ~~*Spectator,* N° 403.~~

BY-CONCERNMENT. *n.s.* {…}

Our plays, besides the main design, have under-plots, or *by-concernments*, or less considerable persons and intrigues, ~~which are~~ carried on with the motion of the main plot.
*Dryden*/~~*on Dramatick Poetry.*~~

BY-DESIGN. *n.s.* {…}

And if she miss the mouse-trap lines,
They'll serve for other *by-designs*,
And make an artist understand,
To copy out her seal or hand;
~~Or find void places in the paper,~~
~~To steal in something to entrap her~~. *Hudibras, p.* iii. *c.* iii.

BY-GONE. *adj.* {…}

As we have a conceit of motion coming, as well as *bygone*; so have we of time, which dependeth thereupon.
*Grew's* ~~*Cosmologia Sacra, b.* ii. *c.* iii.~~

BY-LAW. *n.s.* {…}

In the beginning ~~of this record~~ is inserted the ~~law or~~ institution; to which are added two *by-laws,* as a comment upon the general law. *Addison. Spectator,* N° 608.

{J. crosses out 'the', then smears out stroke.}

BY-MATTER. *n.s.* {…}

I knew one, that, when he wrote a letter, ~~he~~ would put that which was most material into the postscript, as if it had been a *by-matter.* *Bacon's Essays*, N° 23.

BY-NAME. *n.s.* {…}

Robert, eldest son to the Conquerour, used short hose, and thereupon was *by-named* Court-hose, ~~and shewed first the use of them to the English~~. *Camden's Remains.*

# Appendix

# The Sneyd-Gimbel copy

The Sneyd-Gimbel copy (so called after two of its former owners, the Sneyds of Keele Hall, and Col. Richard Gimbel of Philadelphia and New Haven) represents the previous stage in the revision of the *Dictionary* for the fourth edition, just preceding the preparation of the British Library materials; therefore it occupies a close relationship to the B materials in the British Library copy reproduced in this volume.[1] Along with the B materials, the Sneyd-Gimbel copy is part of the enormous mass of Johnson's working papers for the fourth edition, displaying the stages of composition, with the author's choice and subsequent deletion or refinement of additional material. The slips in the Sneyd-Gimbel copy were the means by which the amanuensis presented new material for the revision of the *Dictionary* to be copied on to the interleaves (as in the interleaved B material in the British Library copy), then reviewed by Johnson for inclusion in the printer's copy for the fourth edition. Bound in three volumes, the copy is made up of the first-edition text of the *Dictionary* from A through the middle of the entry PUMPION [sig. 20S2$^{v}$], lacking from ABIDE, def. 4 through the middle of ABOLISH, def. 2, H through HYGROSCOPE, MACTATION through MYTHOLOGY, and OARY through PACK, *n.s.*, def. 1. All preliminary material (title page, Preface, History of the English Language, and A Grammar of the English Tongue) is also lacking. The existing text thus consists of complete, or nearly complete, letters: all but one leaf of text for the letter A, the complete text for letters B through G, the complete text of I/J, K, L and N, and all but one page at the beginning, and twelve at the end, of the letter P. In all, 1,842 slips of paper, varying in size, but with dimensions usually somewhere near 9.7 cm by 4 cm, are mounted on stubs and bound into the copy and distributed throughout most of the three volumes; there are some places in the sections for F and G, however, with several pages in succession with no slips, and there are only two slips bound in for I/J (one or both intended for E), a handful for all of N, and two slips (both misplaced) for all of P.[2] The examples reproduced in the following pages are representative of the slips in this copy.

The pages bear marginal and interlinear annotations made principally by one hand, the same hand on the slips, probably that of the amanuensis William Macbean, though many are also in Johnson's hand. A few annotations may have been made by others, but they are too brief to provide certain evidence. On the slips are written manuscript additions (usually definitions and illustrations, nearly all in the hand most likely of William Macbean) to the adjacent printed page. Leaves and slips are bound into three volumes as follows: volume I, A through COMPUTE, *v.a.* (sigs. B-5D), lacking CI); volume II, COMPUTE, *n.s.* through EYRY (sigs. 5E-8Q); and volume III, F through the middle of PUMPION (sigs. 8R-20S, with the lacunae described above). The red morocco binding was executed in the 1840s by the London binders John Clarke and Francis Bedford.

These sheets were probably given to Johnson by the printers some time during the printing of the first edition. He may well have asked for two or three corrected proofs of each sheet, for internal use during the course of doing the edition: it would have been natural for him to have a set, or sets, of the growing number of completed leaves for reference. Ink smudges, black fingerprints, crooked printing, greying of the paper, or other defects of production mar many of the leaves in the Sneyd-Gimbel copy, suggesting either that they were corrected proof, or simply spoiled copy, or a combination of both. An arrangement may have been agreed upon between Johnson and the printer whereby Johnson would get a certain number of the first-edition printed sheets for his own use, but they would come from the pile of rejected sheets when possible. It is difficult to know whether Johnson was given sheets for the entire *Dictionary*, or only for the text of some letters. Although it would appear that some slips were lost before they could be bound, an examination of the Sneyd-Gimbel materials and the fourth-edition text suggests that the lost slips may be few in number. It was probably never a complete copy, but a collection of autonomous sections independently revised.

Leaf C2, as well as the annotations written on the recto, which are more extensive than those on any other page, appears to be of a different state from the rest of the copy. Leaf C2 possibly represents an early state (before stop-press correction) of the first-edition printing, although none of the changes are incorporated.[3] Almost all of the changes are in Johnson's hand, unlike those on the other Sneyd-Gimbel pages, and are similar in nature and quantity to those which Johnson marked on the leaves for the letter B in the British Library copy. It is possible that this leaf stems from the stage of revision represented by the B materials, and was originally a part of that set. One leaf, a singleton at the end of G in the Sneyd-Gimbel copy, is blank on its verso. This blank page prompted earlier describers to assume incorrectly that the materials constitute proof sheets for the first edition.

[1] For a description and discussion of this material, see Allen Reddick, *The Making of Johnson's Dictionary, 1746–1773* (Cambridge: Cambridge University Press, 1990; 2nd rev. edn 1996), *passim*, and Appendix A, pp. 179–89.

[2] The printed sheets are collated as follows: 2°:B$^{2}$ C2 D – 10T$^{2}$ 10U1 11R – 12N$^{2}$ 11O$^{2}$ 16P$^{2}$ 12Q–Z$^{2}$ (13B–14Z)1 15A–U$^{2}$ 18A–I$^{2}$ 19A–20S$^{2}$[$1 signed (last leaf of vol. I in first edition signed 13B–14Z as above)]. The slips are distributed in the copy under the following letters: A – 277; B – 290; C – 524; D – 352; E – 188; F – 142; G – 49; I/J – 2; N – 16; P – 2.

[3] See the discussion of evidence in Reddick, *Making*, pp. 180–81.

While the annotations on the pages of the Sneyd-Gimbel materials (with the exception of C2^r) were executed mainly by the amanuensis, Johnson also made many additions and emendations to the text. His changes include the correction of misprints and misspellings, and other small errors, the addition of etymological information or foreign language usage, and notes on usage in English; the shortening of quotations and their attributions; the addition or expansion of definitions; the rearrangement of existing material, particularly quotations; and the addition of new entries or quotations. The annotations in the amanuensis's hand are usually etymological additions or notes on usage, particularly on Scottish or Irish usage, or short new quotations. In most cases, the annotations on the printed page do not appear to have been incorporated into either the fourth edition or later printed editions, although in some instances changes in the fourth edition seem to bear some relation to the proposed change. Occasionally, the amanuensis drew a line with a caret, or made some other indication of the place where the information on a slip should be inserted. Although most pages throughout the first two-and-one-third volumes are annotated in some way, usually with one or two changes per page, for the nearly 410 pages stretching from the end of G until the end of the third volume, there are only six annotations of any kind. In almost all cases, the manuscript ink which was used is of a brown colour, occasionally so dark as to be almost black. At various intervals, primarily in a several-page stretch in the middle of the text for the letter A, Johnson used a purplish ink on the slips and the pages.

Although this material is clearly linked to the revision of the *Dictionary* carried out between 1771–73, material evidence dates the paper of the slips and some of the writing on the slips to decades before. Several contain evidence of the crowned Posthorn shield watermark, with 'LVGERREVINK' or occasionally 'LVG' as an appendage. Others contain part of the ornate JW cypher countermark, used in paper manufactured by the great English papermaker James Whatman the elder. This suggests that the paper was made probably no later than 1760. Furthermore, words and fragments of sentences and passages in the hand of Johnson's earliest and most trusted amanuensis, Francis Stewart, appear at random on several of the slips (usually on the back). Stewart did a considerable amount of copying for the *Dictionary*, but he died or left the project, probably in 1752, long before its completion.

The answer to this mystery is solved in part through the examination of fragments of writing (by Stewart and others) appearing at random on the slips, not obviously related to the principal text copied on to the slips, for they have a coherence of their own: the remnants of a pre-first-edition version of the text of the *Dictionary*. Many of the nearly two thousand slips of paper in the Sneyd-Gimbel copy are actually pieces of an early manuscript composed in notebooks in the late 1740s or 1750. This manuscript, in the hand of Stewart and others, was sketched out and partially completed, though it was eventually abandoned by Johnson when he made the decision to recast his materials. These fragments constitute the only extensive manuscript evidence yet found of the first edition of Johnson's *Dictionary*.

The manuscript was apparently composed in notebooks with the paper folded into quarto. The text was written in two vertical columns to the page, on both sides of the leaf (one of the reasons, apparently, Johnson abandoned this attempt, because copy could not be set from text written on both sides). Once he decided to abandon this attempt, much of the material was recopied into a form more congenial to the printer and to Johnson's methods of composing. Some of the material may have been clipped out and (presumably) pasted into the new printer's copy. Years later, most if not all of the manuscript material remained and was used for the recycling of illustrations for the fourth edition. The amanuensis, at Johnson's behest, found materials in the old manuscript, chiefly illustrations, that had been used under entries in the first edition and marked them for recycling under other entries in the fourth edition. Of material added to the revised 1773 *Dictionary*, the overwhelming bulk consists of recycled quotations executed in this manner. These quotations and other material were copied out on to free parts of the manuscript, then clipped out as slips, or in some cases simply clipped directly out of the manuscript without recopying. In more than 95 per cent of the cases, the chain lines run parallel to the long side of the slip; this evidence supports my argument that the format of the abandoned manuscript was quarto. In virtually all those cases in which the chain lines run parallel to the short side, the slip is either unusually long or short, implying that the passage was written vertically down a clear space on a page rather than horizontally, confined within the width of one column.

On each slip is transcribed a short text of some sort, usually by (probably) William Macbean. In isolated instances, Johnson himself wrote part of the text on the slip. The passages on the slip usually consist of some combination of the following: a word either currently in the wordlist or a new entry, often with its designation of part of speech, in the top left corner; an etymology, particularly if the word is new to the wordlist; a number indicating where the definition or illustration is to be inserted into an existing entry; a definition; a note on usage, written or oral, occasionally commenting directly on the use by the author in the quotation proposed; and a quotation, with the word it is intended to illustrate underlined. There may also be a mark of some sort on the slip, matched by an identical mark written on to the printed page, keying the new material into its place in the text. Frequently, part of the text on the slip has been crossed out or otherwise altered by Johnson or the same amanuensis. Occasionally, a slip contains only a passage with no word underlined, making it difficult to tell to which entry it applies. As previously stated, the quotation is in almost all cases recycled from the first edition through the use of the abandoned manuscript text.

In some cases, stray words or numbers, which apparently have nothing to do with the main text written on the slip, appear on the front or back. Usually in unfamiliar hands, these odd strays are generally left over from a previous use of the paper from which the slip was cut. The numbers, usually in the top right corner, can often be identified as page numbers from notebooks used by Johnson and his helpers in composing the abandoned *Dictionary* text. Others appear to be mathematical computations. In some cases, the random marks consist of fragments of notes or letters, instructions from Johnson to his workers or to himself, or merely cryptic scribblings. The various weights of the paper, the distance between chain lines, and the number of wire lines per measure within the slips, suggest that the slips were cut from a variety of papers, both printing and writing paper. Four slips contain part of the British Coat of Arms watermark (for ABUNDANTLY, CIRCLE, CONTINENT and ACCORD) and at least one reveals the 'GR' appendage to the Posthorn shield watermark (for BODE).

Many of the fragments found in the Sneyd-Gimbel copy from the original manuscript of the *Dictionary*, compiled in the late 1740s and abandoned long before it was completed, provide useful examples of the physical characteristics and the content of that early document and the way Johnson used it. The columns in the abandoned manuscript material were apparently no wider than 9.7 cm, for that is the usual maximum width of the slips. To avoid confusion and to enable as much as possible of the abandoned manuscript text to be reused, it was important that the quotations which were transcribed for use in the fourth edition be copied in a space in the manuscript where no part of the earlier text would be removed from the other column on the reverse of the leaf when the material was cut out on to a slip. When the quotations were copied into a space wider than the manuscript column in the abandoned manuscript, the text on the reverse side could be disturbed, as is occasionally the case.

A few words should be said concerning the extraordinary history of these materials in the twentieth century. In 1955 James K. Sledd and Gwin J. Kolb publicized the existence of this material, sold at Sotheby's to Col. Richard Gimbel on 27 November 1927 as 'final proofs submitted to the author' for the first edition of the *Dictionary*.[4] Gimbel had thereafter hid the materials from view (apparently buying them in the first place to spite rival A. Edward Newton, the great Johnsonian collector, who had outbid him for a valuable item associated with Dickens, Gimbel's real interest), rebuffing all appeals for access, including those of Sledd and Kolb. These authors were forced to examine, in their groundbreaking study of the *Dictionary*, the photograph of one annotated page ($C2^r$) and its adjoining slips reproduced in the Sotheby sale catalogue. Not surprisingly, their investigation remained inconclusive. Gimbel did finally agree to show the volumes at Yale University in April 1955, in an exhibition marking the $200^{th}$ anniversary of the publication of the *Dictionary*. Scholars including Sledd and Kolb eagerly awaited the revelation. But in fact, when the occasion arrived, Gimbel opened only one of the three volumes and exhibited only one page – the page previously published in the Sotheby sale catalogue – with the facing page covered. At his sudden death in 1970 (on a bibliophiles' excursion to Neuschwanstein), he had made no provision for the copy, and it remained unavailable within the Gimbel estate.

In 1973, after repeated entreaties by Herman W. Liebert, the director of the Beinecke Library and noted Johnsonian scholar and collector, Col. Gimbel's widow presented the volumes to Yale University. Liebert was able to proclaim, following his initial examination of the Sneyd-Gimbel copy after its arrrival, 'This is the largest and most important source of fresh knowledge about Samuel Johnson at the present time known to exist.'[5] The Sneyd-Gimbel copy, together with the material prepared for the revision of the letter B in the British Library materials, provides the only extensive evidence in existence of Johnson's processes of composing and revising his *Dictionary*, and makes possible the discovery, recording and analysis of the stages in the long evolution of the work. The two sets of annotated materials, the one at Yale the first in the sequence, followed by the British Library copy, together contain: fragments of the earliest known version of the *Dictionary* text, a draft manuscript for the first edition; the record of Johnson's process during the one major revision of the work; and hundreds of revisions intended for publication by the author yet never published.

[4] See James K. Sledd and Gwin J. Kolb, *Dr. Johnson's Dictionary: Essays in the Biography of a Book* (Chicago: Chicago University Press, 1955), pp. 116–21, and p. 235, n. 75; and Reddick, *Making*, pp. 3–4, and p. 195, n.9.

[5] Herman W. Liebert, 'Johnson, Samuel', *Yale University Library Gazette*, 48 (1973), p. 64.

# Examples from the Sneyd-Gimbel copy

Ban dog may be a dog of bad omen
the Scriech owl, which reckon'd so, being added.
For In Scotland the common people observe
that before a person's death
happens, some dog & generally
it is a strange dog, comes at the dead of night
howling three or four times
and then goes off quietly
at the door.

Not my fowl, but my folk & people are grown half wild in many places; they wod not worry one anor so in ye wolvish belluine manner else; they wod not precipitate yms[e]lves else into such a most mungrel war. Howel Eng. Tea.

Bellgarde | belle & garde Fr.
Pretty bower or retreat
Upon her eyelids many graces sat
Under ye shadow of her even brows
Working bellgualds & amorous retrait
And every one her wth a grace endows
F. Q. 2.3.25

1 v. a
Here too the Thresher bran-
-dishing his Flail
Bespeaks a Master.
Dodsly's Agricult.

See Kindly Maids some
[illegible]

S.9.2.2.22

—If I thought that, I tell thee, homicide,
These nails should rend that *beauty* from my cheeks.
*Shakesp. Richard* III.

*Beauty* is best in in a body that hath rather dignity of presence than *beauty* of aspect. The beautiful prove accomplished, but not of great spirit, and study for the most part rather behaviour than virtue. *Bacon.*

Beavoir n. v. [Beau & voir. Fr.] saw; visage. Not in use.
She [illegible] her beavoir did veil
But first she thank'd him & [illegible] 'gan her tale
Spens

Remember that Pellean conquerour,

Beautiful
2, pleasing; harmonious: delightful to the ear. In Sidney we find a transposition of the [illegible] of the [illegible] ears.
He might hear her sing [illegible] song, a voice no less beautiful to his ears [illegible] her goodliness was full of harm to his eyes. Sidney

Can I without [illegible] detestable stain of ungratefulness abstain from loving him, who far exceeding [illegible] beautifulness of his shape with [illegible] beautifulness of his mind, is content so to abase himself as to become Dametas' servant for my sake
Sidney

To beautify v.a.
Then are [illegible] publick duties of religion best ordered, when [illegible] militant church doth resemble by sensible means [illegible] hidden dignity & glory wherewith [illegible] church triumphant in heaven [illegible] beautified Hooker 5.5.

...h, this false soul of Egypt, this gay charm,
...se eye *beck'd* forth my wars, and called them home.
*Shakesp. Antony and Cleopatra.*

*s.* [from the verb.]

1. A sign with the head; a nod.
Haste thee, nymph, and bring with thee
Quips, and cranks, and wanton wiles,
Nods, and *becks*, and wreathed smiles. *Milton.*

Beck in Scotl[d] denotes a female curt'sey

2. A nod of command.
Neither the lusty kind shewed any roughness, nor the easier any idleness; but still like a well obeyed master, whose *beck* is enough for discipline. *Sidney, b.* ii.

Then forthwith to him takes a chosen band
Of spirits, likest to himself in guile,
To be at hand, and at his *beck* appear. *Milton's Par. Reg.*

The menial fair, that round her wait,
At Helen's *beck* prepare the room of state. *Pope's Odyss. b.* iii.

BE'CKON. *v. a.* [from *beck*, or beacn, Sax. a sign.] To make a sign to.
With her two crooked hands she signs did make,
And *beckon'd* him. *Fairy Queen, b.* ii. *cant.* iv. *stanz.* 13.

It *beckons* you to go away with it,
As if it some impartment did desire
To you alone. *Shakesp. Hamlet.*

With this his distant friends he *beckons* near,
Provokes their duty, and prevents their fear. *Dryden.*

BE'CKON. *v. n.* To make a sign.
Alexander *beckoned* with the hand, and would have made his ...efence unto the people. *Acts*, xix. 33.

When he had raised my thoughts by those transporting airs, ...e *beckoned* to me, and, by the waving of his hand, directed me to approach. *Addison. Spectator,* Nº 159.

Sudden you mount! you *beckon* from the skies,
Clouds interpose, waves roar, and winds arise. *Pope.*

...ECLI'P. *v. a.* [of be clyppan, Sax.] To embrace. *Dict.*

...ECO'ME. *v. a.* pret. *I became*; comp. pret. *I have become.* ...om *by* and *come.*]

...o enter into some state or condition, by a change from some ...

...Lord God breathed into his nostrils the breath of life, ... *became* a living soul. *Gen.* ii. 7.

...unto the Jews I *became* a Jew, that I might gain the ... *1 Cor.* ix. 20.

...aller pear, grafted upon a stock that beareth a greater ...l *become* great. *Bacon's Natural History,* Nº 453.

...voice thou oft hast heard, and hast not fear'd,
...ill rejoic'd; how is it now *become*
...adful to thee? *Milton's Paradise Lost, b.* x. *l.* 120.

...he least faults, if mix'd with fairest dead,
...ture ill *become* the fatal seed. *Prior.*

...e *of.* To be the fate of; to be the end of; to be the ...dition of. It is observable, that this word is never, or ...om, used but with the interrogative *what*.

...is then *become of* so huge a multitude, as would have ...d a great part of the continent? *Raleigh's Essays.*

Perplex'd with thoughts, *what* would *become*
*Of* me, and all mankind. *Milton's Par. Lost, b.* xii. *l.* 275.

The first hints of the circulation of the blood were taken ...rom a common person's wondering *what became of* all the ...lood which issued out of the heart. *Graunt's Bills of Mortality.*

*What* will *become of* me then? for when he is free, he will ...nfallibly accuse me. *Dryden's Spanish Friar.*

*What became of* this thoughtful busy creature, when removed ...rom this world, has amazed the vulgar, and puzzled the wise. *Rogers's Sermons.*

In the following passage, the phrase, *where is he become*, is used ...or *what is become of him*.

I cannot joy, until I be resolved
*Where* our right valiant father *is become*. *Shakesp. Hen.* VI.

...ECO'ME. *v. a.* [from *be* or *by*, and cpemen, Sax. to please.] ...plied to persons; to appear in a manner suitable to some...g.

I *become* not a cart as well as another man, a plague on ... bringing up. *Shakesp. Henry* IV. *p.* i.

Why would I be a queen? because my face
...Vould wear the title with a better grace;
...I *became* it not, yet it would be
...art of your duty, then, to flatter me. *Dryd. Conq. of Gran.*

...lied to things; to be suitable to the person; to befit; to ...uous to the appearance, or character, or circumstances, ... manner as to add grace; to be graceful.

... to her sire made humble reverence,
...owed low, that her right well *became*,
...dded grace unto her excellence. *Fairy Queen, b.* i.

...ould I had some flowers of the spring that might
... your time of day; and your's, and your's,
...wear upon your virgin branches yet
...maidenheads growing. *Shakesp. Winter's Tale.*

Yet be sad, good brothers;
...o speak truth, it very well *becomes* you. *Sh. Henry* IV.

Your

5 Irregularity, confusion, cause of blame
A jolly yeoman marshal of ye hall
Whose name was appetite, he did bestow
Both guests & meats, when ever in they came
And knew ym how to order wthout blame
Spens.

3 A natural instrumt of defence
He who made
This knowing beast hath arm'd him wth a blade.
He feeds on lofty hills, nor lives by prey
Sandys Job

644274